# Business

A Changing World

# Business

**7e**

## A Changing World

**O.C. Ferrell**
University of New Mexico

**Geoffrey A. Hirt**
DePaul University

**Linda Ferrell**
University of New Mexico

McGraw-Hill Irwin

Boston   Burr Ridge, IL   Dubuque, IA   New York   San Francisco   St. Louis
Bangkok   Bogotá   Caracas   Kuala Lumpur   Lisbon   London   Madrid   Mexico City
Milan   Montreal   New Delhi   Santiago   Seoul   Singapore   Sydney   Taipei   Toronto

# McGraw-Hill Irwin

BUSINESS: A CHANGING WORLD
Published by McGraw-Hill/Irwin, a business unit of The McGraw-Hill Companies, Inc., 1221 Avenue of the Americas, New York, NY, 10020. Copyright © 2009, 2008, 2006, 2003, 2000, 1996, 1993 by The McGraw-Hill Companies, Inc. All rights reserved. No part of this publication may be reproduced or distributed in any form or by any means, or stored in a database or retrieval system, without the prior written consent of The McGraw-Hill Companies, Inc., including, but not limited to, in any network or other electronic storage or transmission, or broadcast for distance learning.

Some ancillaries, including electronic and print components, may not be available to customers outside the United States.

This book is printed on acid-free paper.

Printed in China

3 4 5 6 7 8 9 0 CTP/CTP 14 13 12 11 10 09

ISBN 978-0-07-351172-6
MHID 0-07-351172-2

Vice president and editor-in-chief: *Brent Gordon*
Publisher: *Paul Ducham*
Executive editor: *Doug Hughes*
Senior developmental editor: *Christine Scheid*
Editorial coordinator: *Devon Raemisch*
Senior marketing manager: *Sarah Schuessler*
Senior project manager: *Susanne Riedell*
Production supervisor: *Gina Hangos*
Interior designer: *JoAnne Schopler*
Senior photo research coordinator: *Jeremy Cheshareck*
Photo researcher: *Keri Johnson*
Senior media project manager: *Greg Bates*
Cover design: *JoAnne Schopler*
Typeface: *10.5/12 Minion*
Compositor: *Laserwords Private Limited*
Printer: *CTPS*

**Library of Congress Cataloging-in-Publication Data**

Ferrell, O. C.
    Business : a changing world / O.C. Ferrell, Geoffrey Hirt, Linda Ferrell.—7th ed.
       p. cm.
    Includes index.
    ISBN-13: 978-0-07-351172-6 (alk. paper)
    ISBN-10: 0-07-351172-2 (alk. paper)
    1. Business. 2. Management—United States. I. Hirt, Geoffrey A. II. Ferrell, Linda. III. Title.
HF1008.F47 2009
   650—dc22

                                            2008038677

To George C. Ferrell

To Linda Hirt

To Newell and Aileen Henderson

# Welcome

Welcome to the seventh edition of *Business: A Changing World.* Our success is the result of your feedback and support, which has helped us develop one of the most successful introduction to business texts in the market. Our book contains all of the essentials that most students should learn in a semester. *Business: A Changing World* has, since its inception, been a concise presentation of the essential material needed to teach introduction to business. From our experience in teaching the course, we know that the most effective way to engage a student is by making business exciting, relevant, and up-to-date. Our teachable, from-the-ground-up approach involves a variety of media, application exercises, and subject matter; including up-to-date content supplements, boxed examples, video cases, PowerPoints, and testing materials that work for entry-level business students. We have worked hard to make sure that the content of this edition is as up-to-date as possible in order to best reflect today's dynamic world of business. We cover major changes in our economy related to commodity prices, the business cycle, global competition, and concerns about sustainability.

## The Seventh Edition

While the title of our book remains *Business: A Changing World,* we could have changed the title to *Business: A Green World.* Throughout the book we recognize the importance of sustainability and "green" business. Using the philosophy *reduce, reuse, and recycle,* we believe every business can be more profitable and contribute to a better world through green initiatives. The United States uses more than 100 billion plastic bags each year. Only 1 percent of these bags are recycled, while the rest end up in landfills. It takes an estimated 1,000 years for plastic bags to photo-degrade. Recycling just one aluminum can save enough energy to run a TV for three hours, or the energy equivalent of about a half-gallon of gasoline. There is no known limit to the number of times aluminum can be re-recycled. Furthermore, to produce each week's Sunday papers, 500,000 trees must be cut down.

Reducing carbon emissions has become the focal point of most reports on how to minimize global warming, and even emerging economies such as China will be forced to rethink their approaches to business. China is now the largest producer of carbon emissions in the world, a country so polluted that the air in some cities is hazardous to human life. All of these developments create business challenges and opportunities to create new products and change consumption patterns. Entrepreneurs will be the leaders in developing new solutions and will be rewarded for helping to deal with these challenges. There is a new "Going Green" box in each chapter that covers these environmental changes. Our "Entrepreneurship in Action" boxes also discuss many innovations and opportunities to use green business for success.

To make introduction to business relevant and up-to-date, the book has to reflect our current economic environment. The very visible hand of the government creates a constantly shifting business environment, and we pay special attention to how changes in policies relating to housing and banking markets have affected the economic business cycle. Due to the subprime mortgage meltdown, many consumers have lost their homes and their consumption patterns have changed. Fluctuating prices in commodities, such as oil, and agricultural products, such as corn, wheat, and soybeans, have also changed consumer behavior. In a consumer-driven industry, American automobile companies have fallen on hard times because they were not making the products that consumers want. We address all of these issues in this text through the use of examples and embedded content in order to help students better appreciate the dynamic changes in the business world. Success in business comes from anticipating these changes and being prepared to deal with the business risks associated with change.

We have been careful to continue our coverage of global business, ethics and social responsibility, and e-business as it relates to the foundations important in an introduction to business course. Our co-author team has a diversity of expertise in these important areas. O.C. Ferrell and Linda Ferrell have been recognized as leaders in business ethics education, and their insights are reflected in every chapter and in the "Consider Ethics and Social Responsibility" boxes. They have even written a supplement for instructors on teaching business ethics and introduction to business. In addition, they maintain a Web site, www.e-businessethics.com, that provides free resources such as PowerPoints and cases that can be used in the classroom. Geoff Hirt has a strong background in global business development, especially world financial markets and trade relationships.

The foundational areas of introduction to business, entrepreneurship, small business management, marketing, accounting, and finance have been completely revised. Examples have been provided to which students can easily relate. An understanding of core functional areas of business is presented so students get a holistic view of the world of business. Box examples related to "Responding to Business Challenges," "Think Globally," "Going Green," and "Consider Ethics and Social Responsibility" help provide real-world examples in these areas.

Our goal is to make sure that the content and teaching package for this book are of the highest quality possible. We wish to seize this opportunity to gain your trust, and we appreciate any feedback to help us continually improve these materials. We hope that the real beneficiary of all of our work will be well-informed students who appreciate the role of business in society and take advantage of the opportunity to play a significant role in improving our world. As students understand how our free enterprise system operates and how we fit into the global competitive environment, they will be developing the foundation for creating their own success and improving our quality of life.

# Created from the ground up,

The best-selling paperback text on the market, *Business: A Changing World* was built from the ground up—that is, developed and written expressly for faculty and students who value a brief, flexible, and affordable paperback with the most up-to-date coverage available.

Conversly, most brief Introduction to Business textbooks on the market today are simply "ground-down" versions of much longer hardcover books. None of these books is truly designed to meet the needs of students or instructors; they're after-thoughts, products chiefly designed to leverage existing content, not to help you teach your course.

With market-leading teaching support and fresh content and examples, *Business: A Changing World* offers just the right mix of currency, flexibility, and value that you need. It is the fastest-growing book—and the best value available—in the brief Introductory Business market.

What sets Ferrell/Hirt/Ferrell apart from the competition? An unrivaled mixture of current content, topical depth, and the best teaching support around:

## The Freshest Topics and Examples

Because it isn't tied to the revision cycle of a larger book, *Business: A Changing World* inherits no outdated or irrelevant examples or coverage. Everything in the seventh edition reflects the very latest developments in the business world, from the growth of outsourcing in India, to the Xbox's pricing strategy. In addition, ethics continues to be a key issue and Ferrell et al. use "Consider Ethics and Social Responsibility" boxes to instill in students the importance of ethical conduct in business.

## Just Enough of a Good Thing

It's easy for students taking their first steps into business to become overwhelmed. Longer books try to solve this problem by chopping out examples or topics to make ad hoc shorter editions. *Business: A Changing World* carefully builds just the right mix of coverage and applications to give your students a firm grounding in business principles. Where other books have you sprinting through the semester to get everything in, Ferrell et al. allows you the breathing space to explore topics and incorporate other activities that are important to you and your students.

## Teaching Assistance that Makes a Difference

The first and often most serious hurdle in teaching is engaging your students' interest, making them understand how textbook material plays a very real role in real business activities. The instructor's material for *Business: A Changing World* is full of helpful resources that enable you to do this, including detailed teaching notes and additional material in the Instructor's Manual, even for role-playing exercises found on the Web site. Furthermore, the **Active Classroom Resource Manual** is loaded with additional projects, cases, and exercises. The Instructor's Manual contains a matrix to help you decide which exercise to use with which chapter.

There's much more to **Business: A Changing World,** and much more it can do for your course. To learn about Ferrell et al.'s great pedagogical features and top-notch ancillaries, keep reading.

not ground down

# Getting a Handle on Business

*Business: A Changing World's* pedagogy helps your students get the most out of their reading, from handy outlines at the beginning of the chapter to a range of questions and exercises at the end of it.

## Chapter Outlines

These provide a useful overview of all the topics covered in the chapter, giving students a sneak preview of what they'll be learning.

**CHAPTER OUTLINE**

Introduction

Business Ethics and Social Responsibility

The Role of Ethics in Business
  Recognizing Ethical Issues in Business
  Making Decisions about Ethical Issues
  Improving Ethical Behavior in Business

The Nature of Social Responsibility
  Social Responsibility Issues

# Business Ethics and Social Responsibility

## OBJECTIVES

*After reading this chapter, you will be able to:*

• Define business ethics and social responsibility and examine their importance.

• Detect some of the ethical issues that may arise in business.

• Specify how businesses can promote ethical behavior.

• Explain the four dimensions of social responsibility.

## Chapter Objectives

These appear at the beginning of each chapter to provide goals for students to reach in their reading. The objectives are then used in the "Review Your Understanding," the summary at the end of each chapter, and help the students gauge whether they've learned and retained the material.

## OBJECTIVES

*After reading this chapter, you will be able to:*

• Define business ethics and social responsibility and examine their importance.

• Detect some of the ethical issues that may arise in business.

• Specify how businesses can promote ethical behavior.

• Explain the four dimensions of social responsibility.

• Debate an organization's social responsibilities to owners, employees, consumers, the environment, and the community.

• Evaluate the ethics of a business's decision.

## Chapter-Opening Vignette

These anecdotes neatly illustrate the real-world implications of the business issues students will encounter in their reading. At the end of the chapter, students are asked to "Revisit the World of Business" and apply what they've learned throughout the chapter.

ENTER THE WORLD OF BUSINESS

**Fresh & Easy Grocery Shopping for One & All!**

You may not have heard of Tesco—the largest retailer in the United Kingdom and the third largest retailer in the world, behind only Wal-Mart in the United States and Carrefour in France—but if the company has its way, it will soon become a household name in America! Tesco operates more than 3,000 grocery stores, varying from the Tesco superstore to the Tesco Express, in 12 countries and is now expanding into the United States. Why, you might ask, would a company, already so successful in other countries, take on the likes of Wal-Mart, Kroger, and Albertsons? Valid question, but Tesco feels it is bringing a new shopping experience to U.S. consumers—filling a gaping hole in the grocery market. And, looking at the company's plan for its U.S. stores, it sounds like they're right!

To figure out how best to approach the U.S. market, Tesco conducted years of research into the way Americans live—even living with American families, checking out their cupboards and shopping and cooking with them. As a result, Tesco has developed the Fresh & Easy Neighborhood Market, a smaller store than the typical supermarket sized at 10,000 square feet. The concept behind Fresh & Easy is fresh and wholesome food at affordable prices for everyone. The stores will provide fresh meats and produce along with a host of prepared meals. Offerings will be comprised, as much as possible, of a Fresh & Easy label along with locally sourced foods. What makes this new market unique is the proposed array of freshly prepared dishes—something busy Americans of today may just fall in love with. Industry analysts agree that the United States currently has no grocery store fitting this mold.

*continued*

## Destination CEO

### Destination CEO
#### VF Corporation—Matthew McDonald

VF Corporation is not a household name; however, its brands are extremely well known globally—and that is precisely the strategic objective of CEO matthew McDonald. VF's brands include Wrangler Jeans, Nautica, and North Face. Under McDonald's leadership, VF elected to reduce its U.S. labor force by 13,000 jobs and to outsource manufacturing to China. Locating jobs in global markets, reducing costs, and focusing on brand are the key competitive elements of McDonald's global strategy. The clothing industry is highly competitive. McDonald avoids the high-risk fashion market in favor of a commodity approach for his brands. The goal is to dominate globally in the midprice-range market segment with its lifestyle brands such as North Face. Consumer recognition of the brand across the globe, according to McDonald, is integral to the current success and to the future sustainability of VF Corporation. Brand recognition remains the strategic driver for the corporation.

**Discussion Questions**

1. What is the key global business strategy for VF Corporation?
2. What is the potential impact of relocating jobs to a country in which you want to position your brands?
3. What role could culture play in the success of the lifestyle brands for VF Corporation?

## Destination CEO

These boxes correspond to videos available directly to students on the text Web site at **www.mhhe.com/ferrell7e.** Key leaders in the industry tell of their personal journeys, how they got to the top, and what it took to get there.

## "So You Want a Job In . . ."

These end-of-chapter features offer valuable advice on a wide spectrum of business career choices.

### So You Want a Job in Business Ethics and Social Responsibility

In the words of Kermit the Frog, "It's not easy being green." Maybe it is not easy, however, green business opportunities abound. A popular catch phrase, "Green is the new black," indicating how fashionable green business is becoming. Consumers are more in tune with and concerned about green products, policies, and behaviors by companies than ever before. Companies are looking for new hires to help them see their business creatively and bring insights to all aspects of business operations. The American Solar Energy Society estimates that the number of green jobs could rise to 40 million in the United States by 2030. Green business strategies not only give a firm a commercial advantage in the marketplace, but help lead the way toward a greener world. The fight to reduce our carbon footprint in an attempt against climate change has opened up opportunities for renewable energy, recycling, conservation and increasing overall efficiency in the way resources are used. New businesses that focus on hydro, wind, and solar power are on the rise and will need talented business people to lead them. Carbon emissions' trading is gaining popularity as large corporations and individuals alike seek to lower their footprints. A job

and management. An entry-level position might be as a communication specialist or trainer for programs in a business ethics department. Eventually there's an opportunity to become an ethics officer that would have typical responsibilities of meeting with employees, the Board of Directors and top management to discuss and provide advice about ethics issues in the industry, developing and distributing a code of ethics, creating and maintaining an anonymous, confidential service to answer questions about ethical issues, taking actions on possible ethics code violations and reviewing and modifying the code of ethics of the organization.

There are also opportunities to help with initiatives to help company's relate social responsibility to stakeholder interests and needs. These jobs could involve coordinating and implementing philanthropic programs that give back to others important to the organization or developing a community volunteering program for employees. In addition to the human relations function, most companies develop programs to assist employees and their families to improve their quality of life. Companies have found that the healthier and happier employees are the more pro-

# Getting a Handle on Business

These features, scattered liberally throughout the book, use real and often familiar companies to highlight various issues of importance in business today.

## Consider Ethics and Social Responsibility

Ethics in business continues to be a major public concern, and it is vital for students to understand that unethical conduct hurts investors, customers, and indeed the entire business world. These features highlight the importance of ethical conduct and show how businesses can serve a vital, positive function in their communities.

## Think Globally

The global economy is important to more than large multinationals these days: issues of economics, culture, language and more can affect all levels of domestic business, and "Think Globally" boxes encourage students to keep their eyes on the big picture.

## Going Green

Businesses are becoming more aware of how their operations and products affect the world and environment they operate in. These boxes highlight companies taking steps to minimize their "carbon footprint"—or the measure of the impact their processes have on the environment.

NEW!

## Responding to Business Challenges

These boxes illustrate how businesses overcome tough challenges and provide an excellent vehicle for stimulating class discussions.

## Entrepreneurship in Action

Successful entrepreneurs and their endeavors are spotlighted.

# End-of-Chapter Material

Whether your students discover it on their own or you make it an integral part of your classroom and homework assignments, the end-of-chapter material provides a great opportunity to reinforce and expand upon the chapter content.

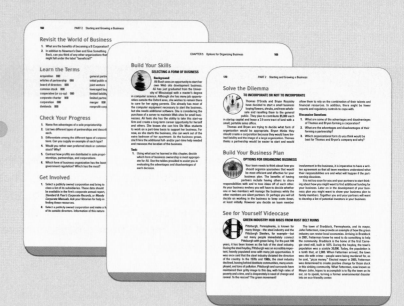

## Review Your Understanding

**Define and examine the advantages and disadvantages of the sole proprietorship form of organization.**

Sole proprietorships—businesses owned and managed by one person—are the most common form of organization. Their major advantages are the following: (1) They are easy and inexpensive to form, (2) they allow a high level of secrecy, (3) all profits belong to the owner, (4) the owner has complete control over the business, (5) government regulation is minimal, (6) taxes are paid only once, and (7) the business can be closed easily. The disadvantages include: (1) The owner may have to use personal assets to borrow money, (2) sources of external funds are difficult to find, (3) the owner must have many diverse skills, (4) the survival of the business is tied to the life of the owner and his or her ability to work, (5) qualified employees are hard to find, and (6) wealthy sole proprietors pay a higher tax than they would under the corporate form of business.

**Identify two types of partnership, and evaluate the advantages and disadvantages of the partnership form of organization.**

A partnership is a business formed by several individuals; a partnership may be general or limited. Partnerships offer the following advantages: (1) They are easy to organize,

of corporate officers or people from outside the company. Corporations, whether private or public, are owned by stockholders. Common stockholders have the right to elect the board of directors. Preferred stockholders do not have a vote but get preferential dividend treatment over common stockholders.

Advantages of the corporate form of business include: (1) The owners have limited liability, (2) ownership (stock) can be easily transferred, (3) corporations usually last forever, (4) raising money is easier than for other forms of business, and (5) expansion into new businesses is simpler because of the ability of the company to enter into contracts. Corporations also have disadvantages: (1) The company is taxed on its income, and owners pay a second tax on any profits received as dividends; (2) forming a corporation can be expensive; (3) keeping trade secrets is difficult because so much information must be made available to the public and to government agencies; and (4) owners and managers are not always the same and can have different goals.

**Define and debate the advantages and disadvantages of mergers, acquisitions, and leveraged buyouts.**

A merger occurs when two companies (usually corporations) combine to form a new company. An acquisition

## Review Your Understanding

Are your students sometimes unsure whether they've properly absorbed the chapter material? This feature resummarizes the chapter objectives, leaving students in no doubt of what they're expected to remember.

## Revisit the World of Business

These exercises refer to the chapter opening vignettes (see page xi) and ask students to answer more in-depth questions using the knowledge they gained in their reading.

### Revisit the World of Business

1. What are the benefits of becoming a B Corporation?
2. In addition to Newman's Own and Give Something Back, can you think of any other organizations that might fall under the label "beneficial?"
3. What were Hannigan and Marx's reasons for not going public?

## Build Your Skills

### SELECTING A FORM OF BUSINESS

**Background:**
Ali Bush sees an opportunity to start her own Web site development business. Ali has just graduated from the University of Mississippi with a master's degree in computer science. Although she has many job opportunities outside the Oxford area, she wishes to remain there to care for her aging parents. She already has most of the computer equipment necessary to start the business, but she needs additional software. She is considering the purchase of a server to maintain Web sites for small businesses. Ali feels she has the ability to take this start-up firm and create a long-term career opportunity for herself and others. She knows she can hire Ole Miss students to work on a part-time basis to support her business. For now, as she starts the business, she can work out of the extra bedroom of her apartment. As the business grows, she'll hire the additional full- and/or part-time help needed and reassess the location of the business.

**Task:**
1. Using what you've learned in this chapter, decide which form of business ownership is most appropriate for Ali. Use the tables provided to assist you in evaluating the advantages and disadvantages of each decision.

| Sole Proprietorships | |
|---|---|
| Advantages | Disadvantages |
| • | • |
| • | • |
| • | • |
| • | • |
| • | • |
| • | • |

| Corporation | |
|---|---|
| Advantages | Disadvantages |
| • | • |
| • | • |
| • | • |
| • | • |
| • | • |
| • | • |

## Build Your Skills

These activities are designed to be carried out in teams, giving you a launching pad for a lively in-class discussion.

## Solve the Dilemma

These boxes give students an opportunity to think creatively in solving a realistic business situation.

## Solve the Dilemma

### TO INCORPORATE OR NOT TO INCORPORATE

Thomas O'Grady and Bryan Rossisky have decided to start a small business buying flowers, shrubs, and trees wholesale and reselling them to the general public. They plan to contribute $5,000 each in startup capital and lease a 2.5-acre tract of land with a small, portable sales office.

Thomas and Bryan are trying to decide what form of organization would be appropriate. Bryan thinks they should create a corporation because they would have limited liability and the image of a large organization. Thomas thinks a partnership would be easier to start and would allow them to rely on the combination of their talents and financial resources. In addition, there might be fewer reports and regulatory controls to cope with.

**Discussion Questions**
1. What are some of the advantages and disadvantages of Thomas and Bryan forming a corporation?
2. What are the advantages and disadvantages of their forming a partnership?
3. Which organizational form do you think would be best for Thomas and Bryan's company and why?

## Build Your Business Plan

### OPTIONS FOR ORGANIZING BUSINESS

Your team needs to think about how you should organize yourselves that would be most efficient and effective for your business plan. The benefits of having partners include having others to share responsibilities with and to toss ideas off of each other. As your business evolves you will have to decide whether one or two members will manage the business while the other members are silent partners. Or perhaps you will all decide on working in the business to keep costs down, at least initially. However you decide on team member involvement in the business, it is imperative to have a written agreement so that all team members understand what their responsibilities are and what will happen if the partnership dissolves.

It is not too soon for you and your partners to start thinking about how you might want to find additional funding for your business. Later on in the development of your business plan you might want to show your business plan to family members. Together you and your partners will want to develop a list of potential investors in your business.

## Build Your Business Plan

Written by Therese Maskulka of Walsh University, and used in her own classroom, the end-of-chapter feature "Build Your Business Plan" and Appendix A, "Guidelines for the Development of the Business Plan," help students through the steps of the business plan relating to each chapter. Additional information and resources can be found in the Instructor's Manual.

## See For Yourself Videocase

Stimulate your students with these engaging case videos, all of which are new to this edition.

## See for Yourself Videocase

### GREEN INDUSTRY HUB RISES FROM RUST BELT RUINS

Pittsburgh, Pennsylvania, is known for many things—the steel industry and the Pittsburgh Steelers, for example—but not many people immediately connect Pittsburgh with green living. For the past 100 years, it has been known as the hub of the steel industry. During the steel heyday, Pittsburgh was an incredibly important, heavily populated area with many job opportunities. It was once said that the steel industry dictated the direction of the country. In the 1970s and 1980s, the steel industry declined, leaving behind destitute communities, many unemployed, and tons of pollution. Pittsburgh and surrounds have maintained their gritty image to this day, with high rates of poverty and crime, and is desperately in need of change and revival. To the rescue? The green movement!

The town of Braddock, Pennsylvania, and its mayor, John Fetterman, now provide an example of how the green industry can revive local economies. Arriving in Braddock in 2001, Fetterman knew he need to do something to help the community. Braddock is the home of the first Carnegie steel mill, built in 1875. During the heyday, the town's population was a sizable 20,000. Today, the population is a tenth that, at 2,800. When Fetterman arrived, the town was rife with crime—people were being murdered for, as he said, "pizza money." Elected mayor in 2005, Fetterman was determined to create positive change for those stuck in this sinking community. What Fetterman, now known as Mayor John, hopes to accomplish is to flip the town on its ear, so to speak, turning a former environmental disaster into an eco-friendly center.

# Instructor Supplements

**Instructor's Resource CD-ROM** MHID 007-724638-1 ISBN: 9780077246389
Everything you need to get the most from your textbook, including:

**Instructor's Manual** Includes learning objectives; lecture outlines; PowerPoint notes; supplemental lecture; answers to discussion questions and end-of-chapter exercises; notes for video cases; term paper and project topics; suggestions for guest speakers; and roles and options for implementing role playing exercises.

## Test Bank

**Assurance of Learning Ready**: Educational institutions are often focused on the notion of assurance of learning, an important element of many accreditation standards. *Business: A Changing World* is designed specifically to support your assurance of learning initiatives with a simple, yet powerful, solution. We've aligned our Test Bank questions with Bloom's Taxonomy and AACSB guidelines, tagging each question according to its knowledge and skills areas.

Each test bank question for *Business: A Changing World* also maps to a specific chapter learning objective listed in the text. You can use our test bank software, EZ Test, to easily query for learning objectives that directly relate to the learning objectives for your course. You can use the reporting features of EZ Test to aggregate student results in a similar fashion, making the collection and presentation of assurance of learning data quick and easy.

**AACSB Statement:** McGraw-Hill Companies is a proud corporate member of AACSB International. Understanding the importance and value of AACSB accreditation, the authors of *Business: A Changing World* have sought to recognize the curricula guidelines detailed in the AACSB standards for business accreditation by connecting selected questions in the Test Bank to the general knowledge and skill guidelines found in the AACSB standards.

The statements contained in *Business: A Changing World* are provided only as a guide for the users of this text. The AACSB leaves content coverage and assessment clearly within the realm and control of individual schools, the mission of the school, and the faculty. The AACSB does also charge schools with the obligation of doing assessment against their own content and learning goals. While *Business: A Changing World* and the teaching package make no claim of any specific AACSB qualification or evaluation, we have, within *Business: A Changing World,* labeled selected questions according to the six general knowledge and skills areas. The labels or tags within *Business: A Changing World* are as indicated. There are, of course, many more within the Test Bank, the text, and the teaching package which may be used as a standard for your course.

**EZ Test Online:** McGraw-Hill's EZ Test Online is a flexible and easy-to-use electronic testing program. The program allows instructors to create tests from book specific items, accommodates a wide range of question types, and enables instructors to even add their own questions. Multiple versions of the test can be created, and any test can be exported for use with course management systems such as WebCT, BlackBoard, or any course management system. EZ Test Online is accessible to busy instructors virtually anywhere via the Web, and the program eliminates the need for them to install test software. Utilizing EZ Test Online also allows instructors to create and deliver multiple-choice or true/false quiz questions using iQuiz for iPod. For more information about EZ Test Online, please see the Web site at: **www.eztestonline.com.**

## PowerPoint Presentations

Developed by Tony Chelte, Midwestern State University, the PowerPoints consist of two formats: a detailed presentation (with additional infromation, figures, and links) and an outline presentation (an outline of the chapter). Each chapter contains 20–30 slides. Additional figures and tables from the text may be found on the CD-ROM in the "Digital Image Library."

## Online Learning Center (OLC) with Premium Content

**www.mhhe.com/ferrell7e**

Access everything you need to teach a great course through our convenient online resource. A secured Instructor Resource Center stores your essential course materials to save you prep time before class. The Instructor's Manual, PowerPoint™, and additional resources are now just a couple of clicks away.

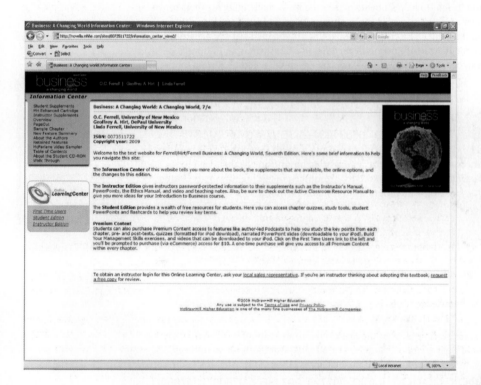

## Instructor Video DVD    MHID: 007-724634-9 ISBN: 9780077246341

**Destination CEO**    Each chapter contains 2 possible video teaching opportunities. The first, the "Destination CEO" feature, is located *within* the chapter. This feature contains a summary and discussion questions that pertain to a video found on the Instructor DVD for viewing inside the classroom and also for the student on the Online Learning Center for viewing outside the classroom. Each video centers around a real-world company's CEO and his/her path to success. Accompanying quizzes can be found online as well.

**End of Chapter Video**    The second opportunity offers a stimulating mix of topical reinforcement and real-world insight to help students master the most challenging business topics with segments such as "Disney's Global Appeal" or "Organic and Recycled Clothing" or "Ritz Carlton—Customer Service Commitment." The videos can be found on the Instructor DVD-Rom and as downloadable files within the Instructor portion of the Web site. Summaries and discussion questions for the students can be found at the end of each chapter of the text and quizzes found online.

## A Guide for Introducing and Teaching Ethics in Introduction to Business    MHID 007331634-2 ISBN: 9780073316345

Written by O.C. Ferrell and Linda Ferrell, this is your one-stop guide for integrating this important issue into all aspects of your course. It helps you to demonstrate how business ethics lead to business success and offers a wide range of business ethics resources, including university centers, government resources, and corporate ethics programs. It can also be found with the Instructor Resources on the Web Site.

## Active Classroom Resource Guide    MHID 0073342130 ISBN: 9780073342139

An additional collection of team projects, cases, and exercises that instructors can choose from to be used in class or out, which can also be found electronically with the Instructor Resources on the Web Site.

## eBooks

eBooks, or digital textbooks, are exact replicas of the print version, and can offer substantial savings to your students off the cost of their textbook. *Business: A Changing World* offers two options:

## CourseSmart eBook option    (MHID: 0077297997 ISBN: 9780077297992):

With the CourseSmart eTextbook version of this title, students can save up to 50 percent off the cost of a print book, reduce their impact on the environment, and access powerful Web tools for learning. Faculty can also review and compare the full text online without having to wait for a print desk copy. CourseSmart is an online eTextbook, which means users need to be connected to the Internet in order to access. Students can also print sections of the book for maximum portability.

## VitalSource eBook option    (MHID: 0077241606 ISBN: 9780077241605):

Students who choose the VitalSource version of this title have access to powerful digital learning tools. Students that share notes with others, customize the appearance and layout of the content, and organize all their digital course materials from a single program. VitalSource is a downloadable eBook. Students can install their eBook on up to two machines. Students can also print sections of the book for maximum portability.

# Student Supplements

## Online Learning Center (OLC) with Premium Content
**www.mhhe.com/ferrell7e**

More and more students are studying online. That's why we offer an Online Learning Center (OLC) that follows *Business: A Changing World* chapter by chapter. It doesn't require any building or maintenance on your part, and is ready to go the moment you and your students type in the URL.

As your students study, they can refer to the OLC Web site for such benefits as:

- Internet-based activities
- Self-grading quizzes
- Learning objectives
- Additional video and related video exercises

The site includes an **online running video case** highlighting entrepreneur Todd McFarlane, who parlayed his artistic ability (and a passion for sports) into a multimillion dollar business that straddles film and television production, toys, comic books, sports licensing and games. Students watch and learn as McFarlane explains how he leads his company across all functional areas of business, illustrating how firms deal with the problems and opportunities of today's business world. With one video case for each part of the textbook highlighting this fun and unique company, students and instructors are provided a complete context for discussing every aspect of introductory business.

# Acknowledgments

The seventh edition of *Business: A Changing World* would not have been possible without the commitment, dedication, and patience of Jennifer Jackson, Michelle Watkins, Alexi Sherrill, and Melanie Drever. Jennifer Jackson provided oversight for editing and developing text content, cases, boxes, and the supplements. Michelle Watkins assisted in the development of chapter content, cases, boxes, and ancillary materials. Melanie Drever assisted in revising and updating most of the tables and figures in this edition. Alexi Sherrill assisted in developing most of the boxes in this edition. Doug Hughes, Executive Editor, provided leadership and creativity in planning and implementing all aspects of the seventh edition. Christine Scheid, Senior Developmental Editor, did an outstanding job of coordinating all aspects of the development and production process. Susanne Riedell was the Project Manager. Greg Bates managed the technical aspects of the Online Learning Center. Others important in this edition include Sarah Schuessler (Marketing Manager) and JoAnne Schopler (Design).

Michael Hartline developed the Personal Career Plan in Appendix C. Vickie Bajtelsmit developed Appendix D on personal financial planning. Eric Sandberg of Interactive Learning assisted in developing the interactive exercises found on the OLC.

Many others have assisted us with their helpful comments, recommendations, and support throughout this and previous editions. We'd like to express our thanks to the reviewers who helped us shape the seventh edition:

Brenda Anthony
*Tallahassee Community College*

Vondra Armstrong
*Pulaski Tech College*

Lia Barone
*Norwalk Community College*

Ellen Benowitz
*Mercer County Community College*

Dennis Brode
*Sinclair Community College*

Margaret Clark
*Cincinnati State Tech & Community College*

Peter Dawson
*Collin County Community College—Plano*

Mike Drafke
*College of DuPage*

Gil Feiertag
*Columbus State Community College*

Jackie Flom
*University of Toledo*

Kris Gossett
*Ivy Tech Community College of Indiana*

Peggy Hager
*Winthrop University*

Daniel Montez
*South Texas College*

Mark Nygren
*Brigham Young University—Idaho*

Delores Reha
*Fullerton College*

Morgan Shepherd
*University of Colorado*

Kurt Stanberry
*University of Houston Downtown*

Scott Taylor
*Moberly Area Community College*

Evelyn Thrasher
*University of Mass—Dartmouth*

# We extend special appreciation to the following people who reviewed previous editions:

Linda Anglin, Mankato State University
Phyllis Alderdice, Jefferson Community College
John Bajkowski, American Association of Individual Investors
James Bartlett, University of Illinois
Stephanie Bibb, Chicago State University
Barbara Boyington, Brookdale County College of Monmouth
Suzanne Bradford, Angelina College
Alka Bramhandkar, Ithaca College
Eric Brooks, Orange County Community College
Nicky Buenger, Texas A&M University
Anthony Buono, Bentley College
Tricia Burns, Boise State University
William Chittenden, Texas Tech University
Michael Cicero, Highline Community College
M. Lou Cisneros, Austin Community College
Debbie Collins, Anne Arundel Community College—Arnold
Karen Collins, Lehigh University
Katherine Conway, Borough of Manhattan Community College
Rex Cutshall, Vincennes University
Dana D'Angelo, Drexel University
Laurie Dahlin, Worcester State College
John DeNisco, Buffalo State College
Tom Diamante, Adelphi University
Joyce Domke, DePaul University
Michael Drafke, College of DuPage
John Eagan, Erie Community College/City Campus SUNY
Glenda Eckert, Oklahoma State University
Thomas Enerva, Lakeland Community College
Robert Ericksen, Craven Community College
Joe Farinella, DePaul University
James Ferrell, R. G. Taylor, P.C.
Art Fischer, Pittsburg State University
Toni Forcino, Montgomery College—Germantown
Jennifer Friestad, Anoka—Ramsey Community College
Chris Gilbert, Tacoma Community College/University of Washington
Ross Gittell, University of New Hampshire
Frank Godfrey, St. Augustine's College
Bob Grau, Cuyahoga Community College—Western Campus

Gary Grau, Northeast State Tech Community College
Jack K. Gray, Attorney-at-Law, Houston, Texas
Catherine Green, University of Memphis
Claudia Green, Pace University
Phil Greenwood, University of St. Thomas
David Gribbin, East Georgia College
Peggy Hager, Winthrop University
Michael Hartline, Florida State University
Neil Herndon, University of Missouri
James Hoffman, Borough of Manhattan Community College
Joseph Hrebenak, Community College of Allegheny County—Allegheny Campus
Stephen Huntley, Florida Community College
Rebecca Hurtz, State Farm Insurance Co.
Roger Hutt, Arizona State University—West
Verne Ingram, Red Rocks Community College
Scott Inks, Ball State University
Steven Jennings, Highland Community College
Carol Jones, Cuyahoga Community College—Eastern Campus
Gilbert "Joe" Joseph, University of Tampa
Norm Karl, Johnson County Community College
Janice Karlan, LaGuardia Community College
Eileen Kearney, Montgomery County Community College
Craig Kelley, California State University—Sacramento
Ina Midkiff Kennedy, Austin Community College
Arbrie King, Baton Rouge Community College
John Knappenberger, Mesa State College
Gail Knell, Cape Cod Community College
Anthony Koh, University of Toledo
Daniel LeClair, AACSB
Frank Lembo, North Virginia Community College
Richard Lewis, East Texas Baptist College
Corinn Linton, Valencia Community College
Corrine Livesay, Mississippi College
Thomas Lloyd, Westmoreland Community College
Terry Loe, Kennerow University
Scott Lyman, Winthrop University
Dorinda Lynn, Pensacola Junior College
Isabelle Maignan, ING
Larry Martin, Community College of Southern Nevada—West Charles

Therese Maskulka, Youngstown State University
Kristina Mazurak, Albertson College of Idaho
Debbie Thorne McAlister, Texas State University—San Marcos
John McDonough, Menlo College
Tom McInish, University of Memphis
Noel McDeon, Florida Community College
Mary Meredith, University of Louisiana at Lafayette
Michelle Meyer, Joliet Junior College
George Milne, University of Massachusetts—Amherst
Glynna Morse, Augusta College
Stephanie Narvell, Wilmington College—New Castle
Fred Nerone, International College of Naples
Laura Nicholson, Northern Oklahoma College
Stef Nicovich, University of New Hampshire
Michael Nugent, SUNY—Stony Brook University New York
Wes Payne, Southwest Tennessee Community College
Dyan Pease, Sacramento City College
Constantine G. Petrides, Borough of Manhattan Community College
John Pharr, Cedar Valley College
Shirley Polejewski, University of St. Thomas
Daniel Powroznik, Chesapeake College
Krista Price, Heald College
Larry Prober, Rider University
Stephen Pruitt, University of Missouri—Kansas City
Kathy Pullins, Columbus State Community College
Charles Quinn, Austin Community College
Victoria Rabb, College of the Desert
Tom Reading, Ivy Tech State College
Susan Roach, Georgia Southern University
Dave Robinson, University of California—Berkely
Marsha Rule, Florida Public Utilities Commission
Carol A. Rustad, Sylvan Learning

Martin St. John, Westmoreland Community College
Don Sandlin, East Los Angeles College
Nick Sarantakes, Austin Community College
Andy Saucedo, Dona Ana Community College—Las Cruces
Elise "Pookie" Sautter, New Mexico State University
Dana Schubert, Colorado Springs Zoo
Marianne Sebok, Community College of Southern Nevada—West Charles
Jeffery L. Seglin, Seglin Associates
Daniel Sherrell, University of Memphis
Nicholas Siropolis, Cuyahoga Community College
Robyn Smith, Pouder Valley Hospital
Cheryl Stansfield, North Hennepin Community College
Ron Stolle, Kent State University—Kent
Jeff Strom, Virginia Western Community College
Wayne Taylor, Trinity Valley Community College
Ray Tewell, American River College
Steve Tilley, Gainesville College
Jay Todes, Northlake College
Amy Thomas, Roger Williams University
Ted Valvoda, Lakeland Community College
Sue Vondram, Loyola University
Elizabeth Wark, Springfield College
Emma Watson, Arizona State University—West
Jerry E. Wheat, Indiana University Southeast
Frederik Williams, North Texas State University
Pat Wright, Texas A&M University
Timothy Wright, Lakeland Community College
Lawrence Yax, Pensacola Junior College—Warrington

**O.C. Ferrell**
**Geoffrey Hirt**
**Linda Ferrell**
**— August 2008**

# Authors

## O.C. Ferrell

O.C. Ferrell is Professor of Management and Creative Enterprise Scholar in the Anderson Schools of Management, University of New Mexico. He recently served as the Bill Daniels Distinguished Professor of Business Ethics at the University of Wyoming, and the Chair of the Department of Marketing and the Ehrhardt, Keefe, Steiner, and Hottman P. C. Professor of Business Administration at Colorado State University. He also has held faculty positions at the University of Memphis, University of Tampa, Texas A&M University, Illinois State University, and Southern Illinois University, as well as visiting positions at Queen's University (Ontario, Canada), University of Michigan (Ann Arbor), University of Wisconsin (Madison), and University of Hannover (Germany). He has served as a faculty member for the Master's Degree Program in Marketing at Thammasat University (Bangkok, Thailand). Dr. Ferrell received his B.A. and M.B.A. from Florida State University and his Ph.D. from Louisiana State University. His teaching and research interests include business ethics, corporate citizenship, and marketing.

Dr. Ferrell is widely recognized as a leading teacher and scholar in business. His articles have appeared in leading journals and trade publications. In addition to *Business: A Changing World,* he has two other textbooks, *Marketing: Concepts and Strategies* and *Business Ethics: Ethical Decision Making and Cases,* that are market leaders in their respective areas. He also has co-authored other textbooks for marketing, management, business and society, and other business courses, as well as a trade book on business ethics. He chaired the American Marketing Association (AMA) ethics committee that developed its current code of ethics. He was the vice president of marketing education and president of the Academic Council for the AMA. Currently he is vice president of publications for the Academy of Marketing Science.

Dr. Ferrell's major focus is teaching and preparing learning material for students. He has taught the introduction to business course using this textbook. This gives him the opportunity to develop, improve, and test the book and ancillary materials on a first-hand basis. He has traveled extensively to work with students and understands the needs of instructors of introductory business courses. He lives in Albuquerque, New Mexico, and enjoys skiing, golf, and international travel.

## Geoffrey A. Hirt

Geoffrey A. Hirt is currently Professor of Finance at DePaul University and a Mesirow Financial Fellow. From 1987 to 1997 he was Chairman of the Finance Department at DePaul University. He teaches investments, corporate finance, and strategic planning. He developed and was director of DePaul's M.B.A. program in Hong Kong and has taught in Poland, Germany, Thailand, and Hong Kong. He received his Ph.D. in Finance from the University of Illinois at Champaign–Urbana, his M.B.A. from Miami University of Ohio, and his B.A. from Ohio-Wesleyan University. Dr. Hirt has directed the Chartered Financial Analysts Study program for the Investment Analysts Society of Chicago since 1987.

Dr. Hirt has published several books, including *Foundations of Financial Management* published by McGraw-Hill/Irwin. Now in its thirteenth edition, this book is used at more than 600 colleges and universities worldwide. It has been used in more than 31 countries and has been translated into more than 10 different languages. Additionally, Dr. Hirt is well known for his text, *Fundamentals of Investment Management,* also published by McGraw-Hill/Irwin, and now in its ninth edition. He plays tennis and golf, is a music lover, and enjoys traveling with his wife, Linda.

## Linda Ferrell

Dr. Linda Ferrell is Associate Professor and Creative Enterprise Scholar in the Anderson Schools of Management at the University of New Mexico. She completed her Ph.D. in Business Administration, with a concentration in management, at the University of Memphis. She has taught at the University of Tampa, Colorado State University, University of Northern Colorado, University of Memphis, and the University of Wyoming. She also team teaches a class at Thammasat University in Bangkok, Thailand, as well as an online Business Ethics Certificate course through the University of New Mexico.

Her work experience as an account executive for McDonald's and Pizza Hut's advertising agencies supports her teaching of advertising, marketing management, marketing ethics and marketing principles. She has published in the *Journal of Public Policy and Marketing, Journal of Business Research, Journal of Business Ethics, Journal of Marketing Education, Marketing Education Review, Journal of Teaching Business Ethics, Case Research Journal,* and is co-author of *Business Ethics: Ethical Decision Making and Cases* (7th edition) and *Business and Society* (3rd edition). She is the ethics content expert for the AACSB Ethics Education Resource Center (**www.aacsb.edu/eerc**) and was co-chair of the 2005 AACSB Teaching Business Ethics Conference in Boulder, CO.

Dr. Ferrell is the Vice President of Programs for the Academy of Marketing Science, Vice President of Development for the Society for Marketing Advances, and the immediate past president for the Marketing Management Association. She is a member of the college advisory board for Petco Vector. She frequently speaks to organizations on "Teaching Business Ethics," including the Direct Selling Education Foundation's training programs and AACSB International Conferences. She has served as an expert witness in cases related to advertising, business ethics, and consumer protection.

# Brief Contents

**PART 1   Business in a Changing World   1**

1   The Dynamics of Business and Economics   2

Appendix A   Guidelines for the Development of the Business Plan   33

2   Business Ethics and Social Responsibility   36

Appendix B   The Legal and Regulatory Environment   70

3   Business in a Borderless World   84

4   Managing Information Technology and E-Business   114

**PART 2   Starting and Growing a Business   141**

5   Options for Organizing Business   142

6   Small Business, Entrepreneurship, and Franchising   172

**PART 3   Managing for Quality and Competitiveness   199**

7   The Nature of Management   200

8   Organization, Teamwork, and Communication   232

9   Managing Service and Manufacturing Operations   262

**PART 4   Creating the Human Resource Advantage   293**

10   Motivating the Workforce   294

11   Managing Human Resources   320

Appendix C   Personal Career Plan   353

**PART 5   Marketing: Developing Relationships   359**

12   Customer-Driven Marketing   360

13   Dimensions of Marketing Strategy   386

**PART 6   Financing the Enterprise   421**

14   Accounting and Financial Statements   422

15   Money and the Financial System   458

16   Financial Management and Securities Markets   486

Appendix D   Personal Financial Planning   515

Notes   532
Glossary   552
Photo Credits   565
Indexes   567

# Contents

## PART I
## Business in a Changing World    1

### CHAPTER I
### The Dynamics of Business and Economics    2

Enter the World of Business:
Crocs Attack    3

Introduction    4

The Nature of Business    4

   *The Goal of Business    5*

   *The People and Activities of Business    6*

   *Why Study Business?    9*

The Economic Foundations of Business    9

   *Economic Systems    10*

   *The Free-Enterprise System    12*

   *The Forces of Supply and Demand    13*

   *The Nature of Competition    14*

Destination CEO: New Balance: Can America compete?    15

   *Economic Cycles and Productivity    16*

Responding to Business Challenges: Lowe's vs. The Home Depot: Location, Location, Location    16

Going Green: The Electric Sports Can—Reality or Fantasy?    20

The American Economy    20

   *A Brief History of the American Economy    20*

   *The Role of the Entrepreneur    22*

Entrepreneurship in Action: Wikipedia Provides Accessible Collaborative Knowledge    24

   *The Role of Government in the American Economy    24*

   *The Role of Ethics and Social Responsibility in Business    24*

Can You Learn Business in a Classroom?    25

**So You Want a Job in the Business World    27**

**Review Your Understanding    27**

**Revisit the World of Business    28**

**Learn the Terms    28**

**Check Your Progress    29**

**Get Involved    29**

**Build Your Skills: The Forces of Supply and Demand    29**

**Solve the Dilemma: Mrs. Acres Homemade Pies    30**

**Build Your Business Plan: The Dynamics of Business and Economics    30**

**See for Yourself Videocase: Environmental Responsibility: New Belgium Brewery    31**

**Appendix A**

   *Guidelines for the Development of the Business Plan    33*

### CHAPTER 2
### Business Ethics and Social Responsibility    36

Enter the World of Business:
*Ethisphere* Links Ethics to Profits    37

Introduction    38

Business Ethics and Social Responsibility    38

The Role of Ethics in Business    40

   *Recognizing Ethical Issues in Business    41*

Consider Ethics and Social Responsibility: Repainting Mattel's Image    47

   *Making Decisions about Ethical Issues    48*

   *Improving Ethical Behavior in Business    49*

The Nature of Social Responsibility    51

   *Social Responsibility Issues    54*

Destination CEO: Bakery with a Conscience    55

Entrepreneurship in Action: Capturing the Wind to Power the Future    56

Going Green: EarthCraft Houses: Crafted for Earth    60

**So You Want a Job in Business Ethics and Social Responsibility    64**

**Review Your Understanding    64**

**Revisit the World of Business    65**

**Learn the Terms    65**

**Check Your Progress    65**

**Get Involved    66**

**Build Your Skills: Making Decisions about Ethical Issues  66**

**Solve the Dilemma: Customer Privacy  67**

**Build Your Business Plan: Business Ethics and Social Responsibility  68**

**See for Yourself Videocase: Is Your Shirt Organic? The Clothing Industry Goes Green  68**

**Appendix B**

*The Legal and Regulatory Environment  70*

## CHAPTER 3
## Business in a Borderless World  84

**Enter the World of Business:**
**Fresh & Easy Grocery Shopping for One & All!  85**

Introduction  86

The Role of International Business  86

*Why Nations Trade  87*

*Trade between Countries  88*

*Balance of Trade  88*

International Trade Barriers  90

*Economic Barriers  90*

*Ethical, Legal, and Political Barriers  91*

Think Globally: Japanese and Americans Swap Food  92

*Social and Cultural Barriers  95*

Entrepreneurship on Action: Wildnet makes Wi-Fi Available to Everyone  95

*Technological Barriers  97*

Trade Agreements, Alliances, and Organizations  97

*General Agreement on Tariffs and Trade  97*

*The North American Free Trade Agreement  98*

*The European Union  100*

*Asia-Pacific Economic Cooperation  100*

*World Bank  101*

*International Monetary Fund  101*

Getting Involved in International Business  102

*Exporting and Importing  102*

*Trading Companies  103*

*Licensing and Franchising  106*

*Contract Manufacturing  104*

*Outsourcing  104*

*Joint Ventures and Alliances  105*

*Direct Investment  105*

International Business Strategies  106

*Developing Strategies  106*

Destination CEO: VF Corporation—Matthew McDonald  107

*Managing the Challenges of Global Business  107*

Going Green: Entrepreneurs Defeat Hunger with Plumpy'nut  108

**So You Want a Job in Global Business  109**

**Review Your Understanding  109**

**Revisit the World of Business  110**

**Learn the Terms  110**

**Check Your Progress  110**

**Get Involved  111**

**Build Your Skills: Global Awareness  111**

**Solve the Dilemma: Global Expansion or Business as Usual?  112**

**Build Your Business Plan: Business in a Borderless World  112**

**See for Yourself Videocase: Walt Disney Around the Globe  113**

## CHAPTER 4
## Managing Information Technology and E-Business  114

**Enter the World of Business:**
**Online Bargaining for the Lowest Price  115**

Introduction  116

The Impact of Technology on Our Lives  116

Entrepreneurship in Action: Business.com  117

Managing Information  118

*Management Information Systems  119*

*Collecting Data  120*

Destination CEO: Adobe Corporation—Bruce Chizen, CEO  120

The Internet  121

*Wireless Technologies  123*

Going Green: Virtually Protesting to Save the Environment  123

E-Business  125

*The Nature of E-Business  125*

*E-Business Models  127*

*Customer Relationship Management  129*

Legal and Social Issues   130

    *Privacy   131*

    *Spam   131*

Responding to Business Challenges: The Internet Provides the Opportunity for a Real Second Life   134

    *Identity Theft   134*

    *Intellectual Property and Copyrights   135*

    *Taxing the Internet?   135*

    *The Dynamic Nature of Information Technology and E-Business   135*

**So You Want a Job in Information Technology   136**

**Review Your Understanding   137**

**Revisit the World of Business   137**

**Learn the Terms   137**

**Check Your Progress   138**

**Get Involved   138**

**Build Your Skills: Planning a Web Site   138**

**Solve the Dilemma: Developing Successful Freeware   139**

**Build Your Business Plan: Managing Information Technology and E-Business   139**

**See for Yourself Videocase: Viacom and YouTube Fight Over Copyrighted Material   140**

## PART 2
## Starting and Growing a Business   141

### CHAPTER 5
**Options for Organizing Business   142**

**Enter the World of Business:**
**"B" Is for Beneficial: A New Model for a Changing Business Community   143**

Introduction   144

Sole Proprietorships   145

    *Advantages of Sole Proprietorships   145*

    *Disadvantages of Sole Proprietorships   147*

Entrepreneurship in Action: Carpinteros: Focusing on Quality and Tradition   148

Partnerships   149

    *Types of Partnership   149*

    *Articles of Partnership   149*

    *Advantages of Partnerships   150*

Destination CEO: My StudentBiz: Student Entrepreneurs and Snacks   150

    *Disadvantages of Partnerships   152*

Going Green: CSAs for Everyone

    *Taxation of Partnerships   153*

Corporations   154

    *Creating a Corporation   155*

    *Types of Corporations   155*

    *Elements of a Corporation   158*

    *Advantages of Corporations   159*

    *Disadvantages of Corporations   161*

Other Types of Ownership   161

    *Joint Ventures   162*

    *S Corporations   162*

    *Limited Liability Companies   162*

    *Cooperatives   162*

Trends in Business Ownership: Mergers and Acquisitions   163

Consider Ethics and Social Responsibility: Kids Kick Their Way to Stronger Self-Esteem   163

**So You'd Like to Start a Business   166**

**Review Your Understanding   167**

**Revisit the World of Business   168**

**Learn the Terms   168**

**Check Your Progress   168**

**Get Involved   168**

**Build Your Skills: Selecting a Form of Business   169**

**Solve the Dilemma: To Incorporate or Not to Incorporate   170**

**Build Your Business Plan: Options for Organizing Business   170**

**See for Yourself Videocase: Green Industry Hub Rises from Rest Belt Reins   170**

### CHAPTER 6
**Small Business, Entrepreneurship, and Franchising   172**

**Enter the World of Business:**
**Cheese Goes from Smelly to Hip   173**

Introduction   174

The Nature of Entrepreneurship and Small Business   174

    *What Is a Small Business?   175*

*The Role of Small Business in the American Economy* 175

Destination CEO: Robert Johnson 177

*Industries That Attract Small Business* 178

Advantages of Small-Business Ownership 180

*Independence* 180

Entrepreneurship in Action: Cultivating Success: The Growth of Albaugh Inc. 181

*Costs* 181

*Flexibility* 181

*Focus* 181

*Reputation* 182

Disadvantages of Small-Business Ownership 182

*High Stress Level* 182

*High Failure Rate* 182

Consider Ethics and Social Responsibility: Dinosaur Fossils Incite Controversy and Enterprise 184

Starting a Small Business 185

*The Business Plan* 185

*Forms of Business Ownership* 185

*Financial Resources* 186

*Approaches to Starting a Small Business* 187

*Help for Small-Business Managers* 188

Going Green: Would you By a Recycled Toothbrush? 189

The Future for Small Business 190

*Demographic Trends* 190

*Technological and Economic Trends* 191

Making Big Businesses Act "Small" 192

**So You Want to be an Entrepreneur or Small Business Owner 193**

**Review Your Understanding 194**

**Revisit the World of Business 194**

**Learn the Terms 195**

**Check Your Progress 195**

**Get Involved 195**

**Build Your Skills: Creativity 195**

**Solve the Dilemma: The Small-Business Challenge 196**

**Build Your Business Plan: Small Business, Entrepreneurship, and Franchising 197**

**See for Yourself Videocase: Not Just Tupperware or Avon Anymore 197**

# PART 3
## Managing for Quality and Competitiveness 199

CHAPTER 7

**The Nature of Management 200**

**Enter the World of Business:**
**The Best Buzz: High-End Coffee 201**

Introduction 202

The Importance of Management 202

Management Functions 203

*Planning* 203

Entrepreneurship in Action: Finding Beauty in Blight: Dennie Ibbotson's Carved Wood Designs 204

*Organizing* 207

*Staffing* 207

*Directing* 208

*Controlling* 208

Types of Management 209

*Levels of Management* 209

*Areas of Management* 213

Destination CEO: Universal Music 215

Skills Needed by Managers 216

*Leadership* 216

Going Green: Compact Fluorescent Light Bulbs: A Bright Idea 218

*Technical Expertise* 219

*Conceptual Skills* 219

*Analytical Skills* 219

*Human Relations Skills* 219

Where Do Managers Come From? 220

Decision Making 221

*Recognizing and Defining the Decision Situation* 221

Responding to Business Challenges: At 100, GM Tries for a Turnaround 222

*Developing Options* 223

*Analyzing Options* 223

*Selecting the Best Option* 223

*Implementing the Decision* 224

*Monitoring the Consequences* 224

The Reality of Management 224

**So You Want to be a Manager 225**

Review Your Understanding    226

Revisit the World of Business    226

Learn the Terms    227

Check Your Progress    227

Get Involved    227

Build Your Skills: Functions of Management    228

Solve the Dilemma: Making Infinity Computers
Competitive    229

Build Your Business Plan: The Nature of
Management    229

See for Yourself Videocase: Panera Bread: More Than
Just a Good Place to Eat    229

## CHAPTER 8
Organization, Teamwork,
and Communication    232

Enter the World of Business:
PetConnection.Com Has a Simple Organizational
Structure    233

Introduction    234

Organizational Culture    234

Business in a Changing World: Dell Changes Its
Organizational Culture    235

Developing Organizational Structure    236

Assigning Tasks    238
  Specialization    238
  Departmentalization    239

Assigning Responsibility    242
  Delegation of Authority    242
  Degree of Centralization    243

Entrepreneurship in Action: Hydroponics Helps Green
Garlic Harvest Profits    244
  Span of Management    244
  Organizational Layers    245

Forms of Organizational Structure    246
  Line Structure    246
  Line-and-Staff Structure    246
  Multidivisional Structure    247
  Matrix Structure    248

The Role of Groups and Teams in Organizations    249
  Committees    250
  Task Forces    250
  Teams    250

Destination CEO: Spectrum Brands CEO    251

Communicating in Organizations    253
  Formal Communication    253

Going Green: Communicating to Save Trees and
Sidewalks    254
  Informal Communication Channels    255
  Monitoring Communications    255

So You Want a Job in Managing Organizational
Culture, Teamwork, and Communication    256

Review Your Understanding    256

Revisit the World of Business    257

Learn the Terms    257

Check Your Progress    258

Get Involved    258

Build Your Skills: Teamwork    258

Solve the Dilemma: Quest Star in Transition    259

Build Your Business Plan: Organization, Teamwork,
and Communication    260

See for Yourself Videocase: Brewing up Fun in the
Workplace    260

## CHAPTER 9
Managing Service and Manufacturing
Operations    262

Enter the World of Business:
Goya Foods: Quality operations and Products    263

Introduction    264

The Nature of Operations Management    264
  The Transformation Process    265

Responding to Business Challenges: JetBlue Recovers
and Excels in Service    266
  Operations Management in Service Businesses    267

Destination CEO: Robert Lane, CEO, John Deere
& Company    269

Planning and Designing Operations Systems    270
  Planning the Product    270
  Designing the Operations Processes    271
  Planning Capacity    272

Entrepreneurship in Action: MINK Shoes Are Friendly
and Fashionable    273
  Planning Facilities    273

Green Operations and Manufacturing    276

Managing the Supply Chain    277
  Purchasing    278

*Managing Inventory  278*

*Outsourcing  280*

*Routing and Scheduling  281*

Going Green: Concerned about Gas Mileage or the Environment? Get Smart!  282

Managing Quality  283

*International Organization for Standardization (ISO)  286*

*Inspection  286*

*Sampling  287*

**So You Want a Job in Operations Management  288**

**Review Your Understanding  288**

**Revisit the World of Business  289**

**Learn the Terms  289**

**Check Your Progress  290**

**Get Involved  290**

**Build Your Skills: Reducing Cycle Time  290**

**Solve the Dilemma: Planning for Pizza  291**

**Build Your Business Plan: Managing Service and Manufacturing Operations  291**

**See for Yourself Videocase: McDonald's 24/7 Turnaround Based on Service and Quality  292**

# PART 4
## Creating the Human Resource Advantage  293

### CHAPTER 10
### Motivating the Workforce  294

**Enter the World of Business:**
**Amadeus Consulting: Where Employees Are the Company  295**

Introduction  296

Nature of Human Relations  296

Historical Perspectives on Employee Motivation  299

*Classical Theory of Motivation  299*

Going Green: Motivating Employees by Being Green  300

*The Hawthorne Studies  300*

Theories of Employee Motivation  301

*Maslow's Hierarchy of Needs  301*

*Herzberg's Two-Factor Theory  303*

*McGregor's Theory X and Theory Y  304*

Consider Ethics and Social Responsibility: Best Buy Brongs Diversity to the Greek Squad  305

*Theory Z  306*

*Variations on Theory Z  306*

*Equity Theory  307*

*Expectancy Theory  308*

Strategies for Motivating Employees  309

*Behavior Modification  309*

*Job Design  309*

Destination CEO: Corporate Health  308

Entrepreneurship in Action:  Matching Workers with Employers  313

*Importance of Motivational Strategies  313*

**So You Think You May Be Good at Motivating a Workforce  314**

**Review Your Understanding  315**

**Revisit the World of Business  315**

**Learn the Terms  316**

**Check Your Progress  316**

**Get Involved  316**

**Build Your Skills: Motivating  316**

**Solve the Dilemma: Motivating to Win  317**

**Build Your Business Plan: Motivating the Workforce  318**

**See for Yourself Videocase: Taking Vacations Can Improve Your Career  318**

### CHAPTER 11
### Managing Human Resources  320

**Enter the World of Business:**
**Managing the Workforce during Slow Times  321**

Introduction  322

The Nature of Human Resources Management  322

Planning for Human Resources Needs  323

Recruiting and Selecting New Employees  323

*Recruiting  324*

*Selection  324*

Entrepreneurship in Action: Terry Gou Finds the Right Employees in China  325

*Legal Issues in Recruiting and Selecting  328*

Developing the Workforce  329

*Training and Development  329*

*Assessing Performance* 330

*Turnover* 331

Destination CEO: Anne Mulcahy, Xerox 332

Compensating the Workforce 334

Going Green: Green Coffee? 335

*Financial Compensation* 335

*Benefits* 337

Managing Unionized Employees 340

*Collective Bargaining* 340

*Resolving Disputes* 341

The Importance of Workforce Diversity 343

*The Characteristics of Diversity* 343

*Why Is Diversity Important?* 344

Consider Ethics and Social Responsibility: AT&T Achieves Supplier Diversity 344

*The Benefits of Workforce Diversity* 345

*Affirmative Action* 346

**So You Want to Work in Human Resources** 347

**Review Your Understanding** 347

**Revisit the World of Business** 348

**Learn the Terms** 348

**Check Your Progress** 349

**Get Involved** 349

**Build Your Skills: Appreciating and Valuing Diversity** 349

**Solve the Dilemma: Morale among the Survivors** 351

**Build Your Business Plan: Managing Human Resources** 351

**See for Yourself Videocase: Patagonia Focuses on Employees and the Environment** 352

**Appendix C**

*Personal Career Plan* 353

**PART 5**
Marketing: Developing Relationships 359

CHAPTER 12

**Customer-Driven Marketing** 360

**Enter the World of Business:**
**Bargain Shopping for Bridel Gowns** 361

Introduction 362

Nature of Marketing 362

*The Exchange Relationship* 363

*Functions of Marketing* 364

Entrepreneurship in Action: Samatha's Table Sparks High-End Romances 366

*The Marketing Concept* 367

*Evolution of the Marketing Concept* 367

Developing a Marketing Strategy 369

*Selecting a Target Market* 369

Destination CEO: Tom Ryan, CVS 369

Responding to Business Challenges: Apple and Phinnaeus or Julie and David: What's in a Name? 372

*Developing a Marketing Mix* 373

Marketing Research and Information Systems 375

Buying Behavior 377

*Psychological Variables of Buying Behavior* 377

Going Green: Making Reusable Cool 378

*Social Variables of Buying Behavior* 378

*Understanding Buying Behavior* 379

The Marketing Environment 379

**So You Want a Job in Marketing** 381

**Review Your Understanding** 382

**Revisit the World of Business** 382

**Learn the Terms** 382

**Check Your Progress** 383

**Get Involved** 383

**Build Your Skills: The Marketing Mix** 383

**Solve the Dilemma: Will It Go?** 384

**Build Your Business Plan: Customer-Driven Marketing** 384

**See for Yourself Videocase: Will Luxury Hotels Fell the Pinch of a Slow Economy?** 385

CHAPTER 13

**Dimensions of Marketing Strategy** 386

**Enter the World of Business:**
**Concord Music Has a Flair for Marketing** 387

Introduction 388

The Marketing Mix 388

Product Strategy 389

*Developing New Products* 389

*Classifying Products* 391

*Product Line and Product Mix* 392

*Product Life Cycle* 392

*Identifying Products* 395

Pricing Strategy 399

*Pricing Objectives* 400

*Specific Pricing Strategies  400*

Going Green: Levi's Blue Jeans Go Green  401

Destination CEO: Nordstrom  402

Distribution Strategy  402

*Marketing Channels  402*

*Intensity of Market Coverage  406*

*Physical Distribution  407*

Entrepreneurship in Action: Kombucha Tea Tastes Different!  408

*Importance of Distribution in a Marketing Strategy  408*

Promotion Strategy  408

*The Promotion Mix  409*

*Promotion Strategies: To Push or To Pull  412*

*Objectives of Promotion  413*

*Promotional Positioning  414*

**So You Want to Be a Marketing Manager  415**

**Review Your Understanding  416**

**Revisit the World of Business  416**

**Learn the Terms  417**

**Check Your Progress  417**

**Get Involved  417**

**Build Your Skills: Analyzing Motel 6's Marketing Strategy  417**

**Solve the Dilemma: Better Health with Snacks  418**

**Build Your Business Plan: Dimensions of Marketing Strategy  419**

**See for Yourself Videocase: Wal-Mart Revises Its Marketing Strategy  419**

# PART 6
## Financing the Enterprise  421

### CHAPTER 14
**Accounting and Financial Statements  422**

Enter the World of Business:
**The Richest Man in the World  423**

Introduction  425

The Nature of Accounting  425

*Accountants  426*

*Accounting or Bookkeeping?  427*

*The Uses of Accounting Information  427*

Going Green: Hertz Goes Green: Generating Cost versus Benefit Decisions  430

The Accounting Process  430

*The Accounting Equation  430*

*Double-Entry Bookkeeping  431*

*The Accounting Cycle  431*

Financial Statements  431

*The Income Statement  435*

Entrepreneurship in Action: Pursuing a Life-Long Dream, a Social Worker and Teacher Gets an A+ for His Goat's Milk Cheeses  438

*The Balance Sheet  439*

*The Statement of Cash Flow  442*

Ratio Analysis: Analyzing Financial Statements  444

*Profitability Ratios  445*

Consider Ethics and Social Responsibility: Holding Companies Responsible: The Public Company Accounting Oversight Board  446

*Asset Utilization Ratios  447*

*Liquidity Ratios  448*

*Debt Utilization Ratios  448*

*Per Share Data  449*

*Industry Analysis  450*

**So You Want to Be an Accountant  451**

**Review Your Understanding  452**

**Revisit the World of Business  452**

**Learn the Terms  452**

**Check Your Progress  453**

**Get Involved  453**

**Build Your Skills: Financial Analysis  453**

**Solve the Dilemma: Exploring the Secrets of Accounting  454**

**Build Your Business Plan: Accounting and Financial Statements  454**

**See for Yourself Videocase: Enron: Questionable Accounting Practices Bring New Regulation to the United States  454**

### CHAPTER 15
**Money and the Financial System  458**

Enter the World of Business:
**Peer-to-Peer Lending: Seeking New Ways to Prosper  458**

Introduction  460

Money in the Financial System  460

*Functions of Money  461*

*Characteristics of Money   462*

*Types of Money   463*

The American Financial System   467

*The Federal Reserve System   467*

Destination CEO: Clarence Otis—Darden Restaurants   471

*Banking Institutions   471*

Responding to Business Challenges: Wells Fargo Uses Family Histories to Gain New Clients   473

*Nonbanking Institutions   474*

Going Green: Metabolix: A Small Film with Big Plans to Reduce Waste   476

*Electronic Banking   478*

*Challenge and Change in the Commercial Banking Industry   479*

Entrepreneurship in Action: Independent Bank Hits Gold by Staying True to Its Roots   480

**So You're Interested in Financial Systems or Banking   481**

**Review Your Understanding   482**

**Revisit the World of Business   482**

**Learn the Terms   483**

**Check Your Progress   483**

**Get Involved   483**

**Build Your Skills: Managing Money   483**

**Solve the Dilemma: Seeing the Financial Side of Business   484**

**Build Your Business Plan: Money and the Financial System   484**

**See for Yourself Videocase: Strategic Planning: State Farm Bank   484**

CHAPTER 16

**Financial Management and Securities Markets   486**

Enter the World of Business:
**Sears Holdings Corporation: Using Brand Names to Create Bonds   487**

Introduction   488

Destination CEO: Charles Schwab   489

Managing Current Assets and Liabilities   489

*Managing Current Assets   489*

Going Green: Going Green, or Greenwashing?   490

*Managing Current Liabilities   493*

Managing Fixed Assets   495

*Capital Budgeting and Project Selection   496*

*Assessing Risk   496*

*Pricing Long-Term Money   497*

Financing with Long-Term Liabilities   498

*Bonds: Corporate IOUs   499*

*Types of Bonds   500*

Entrepreneurship in Action: Ready for Takeoff: RealKidz Clothing   501

Financing with Owners' Equity   501

Investment Banking   504

The Securities Markets   504

*Stock Markets   505*

*The Over-the-Counter Market   505*

*Measuring Market Performance   506*

Consider Ethics and Social Responsibility: Subprime Lending: What Is It, and Why Has It Caused So Much Trouble?   506

**So You Want to Work in Financial Management or Securities   509**

**Review Your Understanding   510**

**Revisit the World of Business   511**

**Learn the Terms   511**

**Check Your Progress   511**

**Get Involved   511**

**Build Your Skills: Choosing among Projects   512**

**Solve the Dilemma: Surviving Rapid Growth   513**

**Build Your Business Plan: Financial Management and Securities Market   513**

**See for Yourself Videocase: Leadership: The McFarlane Companies   513**

**Appendix D**

*Personal Financial Planning   515*

Notes   532

Glossary   552

Photo Credits   565

Indexes   567

Name Index

Company Index

Subject Index

part

# Business in a Changing World

CHAPTER 1    The Dynamics of Business and Economics

APPENDIX A   Guidelines for the Development of the Business Plan

CHAPTER 2    Business Ethics and Social Responsibility

APPENDIX B   The Legal and Regulatory Environment

CHAPTER 3    Business in a Borderless World

CHAPTER 4    Managing Information Technology and E-Business

## CHAPTER OUTLINE

Introduction

The Nature of Business
*The Goal of Business*
*The People and Activities of Business*
*Why Study Business?*

The Economic Foundations of Business
*Economic Systems*
*The Free-Enterprise System*
*The Forces of Supply and Demand*
*The Nature of Competition*
*Economy Cycles and Productivity*

The American Economy
*A Brief History of the American Economy*
*The Role of the Entrepreneur*
*The Role of Government in the American Economy*
*The Role of Ethics and Social Responsibility in Business*

Can You Learn Business in a Classroom?

# The Dynamics of Business and Economics

## OBJECTIVES

*After reading this chapter, you will be able to:*

- Define basic concepts such as business, product, and profit.

- Identify the main participants and activities of business and explain why studying business is important.

- Define economics and compare the four types of economic systems.

- Describe the role of supply, demand, and competition in a free enterprise system.

- Specify why and how the health of the economy is measured.

- Trace the evolution of the American economy and discuss the role of the entrepreneur in the economy.

- Evaluate a small-business owner's situation and propose a course of action.

## Crocs Attack

You have probably heard of Crocs and more than likely own a pair of the strange-looking plastic shoes. But have you ever thought about their history and why they became so popular? The company started when three friends from Boulder, Colorado, went sailing in the Caribbean, where a foam clog one of them had bought in Canada inspired them to build a business. Despite a lack of venture capital funding and the derision of many, the multicolored Crocs—with their vent holes, light weight, skid-resistant, nonmarking soles, quick drying speed, and built-in antibacterial material to ward off smell—became a global phenomenon. The three friends bought the Canadian company, Foam Creations, that created the shoes and began marketing and distributing the products in the United States under the Crocs brand in 2002. Initially they targeted their product at water sports enthusiasts, but the comfort and functionality, combined with word-of-mouth advertising, meant the shoes appealed to a much larger and more diverse group of consumers.

Restaurant workers, doctors, nurses, and others who spend lots of time on their feet were early adopters. By focusing on their core competencies, things a firm does extremely well, Crocs was able to make a name for itself. By focusing on the market opportunity, or combination of circumstances and timing that permits an organization to take action to reach a particular target market, Crocs was able to find a niche market for its products. Crocs slowly started to develop different types of shoes such as closed Crocs for hospital staff and a Croc version of flip-flops.

The Crocs line now includes more than 25 models in a wide variety of colors, color combinations, and patterns. Crocs is also diversifying into other

*continued*

products such as Crocs-branded apparel and accessory items, which are intended to increase awareness of the brand and the product. Crocs is also pursuing an acquisition strategy. Crocs acquired Jibbitz, a company that specializes in accessories for Crocs footwear. The company now features more than 1,100 different products being sold through 4,000 retail outlets in the United States, Canada, Asia, and Europe. That same year, Crocs bought Fury, a producer and distributor of hockey and lacrosse equipment for adults and children. Fury now produces products using the patented Crosslite™ material from Crocs. Crosslite™ is a proprietary closed-cell resin that is used in the Crocs shoes to make them anti-microbial, lightweight, and odor-resistant while providing flexibility and support. Exo Italia was the next company Crocs purchased. Exo is an Italian design house that has been instrumental in the development of cutting edge EVA (ethylene vinyl acetate)-based footwear. Exo has been collaborating with Crocs to design a new line of footwear for the company. The new *YOU by Crocs*™ line combines Crocs' legendary comfort with Italian design. Crocs also bought Ocean Minded, a designer and manufacturer of high-quality leather and EVA-based sandals primarily for the beach, adventure and action sports market. Crocs' newest acquisition is Bite Inc., a leader in comfortable and supportive performance shoes and sports sandals. This acquisition will help expand and complement Crocs' RX™ medical line. By diversifying its product line and adding new companies to its existing portfolio, Crocs should be able to improve its overall image and build on its successful Crocs brand.[1]

# Introduction

We begin our study of business in this chapter by examining the fundamentals of business and economics. First, we introduce the nature of business, including its goals, activities, and participants. Next, we describe the basics of economics and apply them to the United States's economy. Finally, we establish a framework for studying business in this text.

## The Nature of Business

**business**
individuals or organizations who try to earn a profit by providing products that satisfy people's needs

A **business** tries to earn a profit by providing products that satisfy people's needs. The outcome of its efforts are **products** that have both tangible and intangible characteristics that provide satisfaction and benefits. When you purchase a product, you are buying the benefits and satisfaction you think the product will provide. A Subway sandwich, for example, may be purchased to satisfy hunger; a Porsche Cayenne sport utility vehicle, to satisfy the need for transportation and the desire to present a certain image.

**product**
a good or service with tangible and intangible characteristics that provide satisfaction and benefits

Most people associate the word *product* with tangible goods—an automobile, computer, loaf of bread, coat, or some other tangible item. However, a product can also be a service, which results when people or machines provide or process something of value to customers. Dry cleaning, photo processing, a checkup by a doctor, a performance by a movie star or basketball player—these are examples of services. A product can also be an idea. Consultants and attorneys, for example, generate ideas for solving problems.

## The Goal of Business

The primary goal of all businesses is to earn a **profit,** the difference between what it costs to make and sell a product and what a customer pays for it. If a company spends $2.00 to manufacture, finance, promote, and distribute a product that it sells for $2.75, the business earns a profit of 75 cents on each product sold. Businesses have the right to keep and use their profits as they choose—within legal limits—because profit is the reward for the risks they take in providing products. Not all organizations are businesses. **Nonprofit organizations,** such as Greenpeace, Special Olympics, and other charities and social causes, do not have the fundamental purpose of earning profits, although they may provide goods or services.

To earn a profit, a person or organization needs management skills to plan, organize, and control the activities of the business and to find and develop employees so that it can make products consumers will buy. A business also needs marketing expertise to learn what products consumers need and want and to develop, manufacture, price, promote, and distribute those products. Additionally, a business needs financial resources and skills to fund, maintain, and expand its operations. Other challenges for businesspeople include abiding by laws and government regulations; acting in an ethical and socially responsible manner; and adapting to economic, technological, and social changes. Even nonprofit organizations engage in management, marketing, and finance activities to help reach their goals.

To achieve and maintain profitability, businesses have found that they must produce quality products, operate efficiently, and be socially responsible and ethical in dealing with customers, employees, investors, government regulators, the community, and society. Because these groups have a stake in the success and outcomes of a business, they are sometimes called **stakeholders.** Many businesses, for example, are concerned about how the production and distribution of their products affect the environment. Hewlett-Packard Company recycled nearly 250 million pounds of hardware and print cartridges globally in 2007, an increase of almost 50 percent over the previous year and the equivalent of more than double the weight of the Titanic. It

*Terra Cycle, founded by two former Princeton students, is a U.S. firm that's helping to preserve the environment. The company's flagship product, TerraCycle Plant Food™, is an all-natural, all-organic, liquid plant food made from waste (worm excrement ) and packaged in waste —reused soda bottles.*

**profit**
the difference between what it costs to make and sell a product and what a customer pays for it

**nonprofit organizations**
organizations that may provide goods or services but do not have the fundamental purpose of earning profits

**stakeholders**
groups that have a stake in the success and outcomes of a business

also reused 65 million pounds of hardware to be refurbished for resale or donation.[2] Concerns about landfills becoming high-tech graveyards plague many electronics firms. As consumers adjust to the switch to digital television transmissions, millions will be discarding their old TVs and creating a landfill crisis. Televisions containing lead, mercury, and cadmium have been piling into landfills with the advent of plasma and high-definition technology. According to the Environmental Protection Agency, in recent years only 2.5 million of more than 20 million replaced televisions were recycled. Some states now require manufacturers to ensure recycling of televisions.[3] Other businesses are concerned about the quality of life in the communities in which they operate. Cummins Inc., an Indiana-based manufacturing firm with operations around the world has helped to develop a technical school in Soweto, South Africa, to aid with education and skill development in a previously disadvantaged community.[4] Others are concerned with promoting business careers among African American, Hispanic, and Native American students. The Diversity Pipeline Alliance is a network of national organizations that work toward preparing students and professionals of color for leadership and management in the 21st-century workforce. The Pipeline assists individuals in getting into the appropriate college, pursuing a career in business, or earning an advanced degree in business.[5] Still other companies such as The Home Depot have a long history of supporting natural disaster victims from Hurricanes Andrew to Katrina. Other companies, such as U-Haul, are finding ways to provide services to assist storm victims. In Arkansas, U-Haul offered 30 days of free storage to victims of tornados and floods in early 2008.[6]

## The People and Activities of Business

Figure 1.1 shows the people and activities involved in business. At the center of the figure are owners, employees, and customers; the outer circle includes the primary

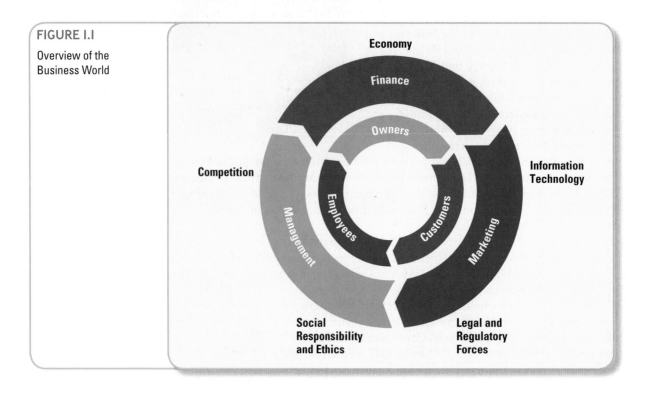

**FIGURE 1.1**

Overview of the Business World

business activities—management, marketing, and finance. Owners have to put up resources—money or credit—to start a business. Employees are responsible for the work that goes on within a business. Owners can manage the business themselves or hire employees to accomplish this task. The president of Procter & Gamble, Alow Latley does not own P.G., but is an employee who is responsible for managing all the other employees in a way that earns a profit for investors, who are the real owners. Finally, and most importantly, a business's major role is to satisfy the customers who buy its goods or services. Note also that people and forces beyond an organization's control—such as legal and regulatory forces, the economy, competition, technology, and ethical and social concerns—all have an impact on the daily operations of businesses. You will learn more about these participants in business activities throughout this book. Next, we will examine the major activities of business.

**Management.**   Notice that in Figure 1.1 management and employees are in the same segment of the circle. This is because management involves coordinating employees' actions to achieve the firm's goals, organizing people to work efficiently, and motivating them to achieve the business's goals. NASCAR has been a family-run business since its inception. Brian France, current chairman and chief executive officer (CEO), is following in the footsteps of his father and grandfather in providing leadership for the sport. NASCAR is now the second most popular spectator sport in the country, outperforming fan numbers and viewership for the IRL (Indianapolis Racing League). NASCAR is also the second biggest television draw in sports, behind the NFL.[7] Management is also concerned with acquiring, developing, and using resources (including people) effectively and efficiently. Under CEO Eric Schmidt's leadership, Google will continue to advance broadband adoption in all forms, knowing that broadband users visit Google sites more often.

Production and manufacturing is another element of management. In essence, managers plan, organize, staff, and control the tasks required to carry out the work of the company or nonprofit organization. We take a closer look at management activities in Parts 3 and 4 of this text.

To illustrate the importance of management, consider a rug and furniture retailer in Bozeman, Montana. Mark DeFalco, who started his career in Colorado in the jewelry business cutting and polishing turquoise, found himself trading jewelry for rugs on Navajo reservations. As he realized the value of the rugs, DeFalco started selling the rugs. Eventually he was the owner/operator of Montana Rugs and Furniture. He was responsible for finding the retail location and managing the inventory, which ultimately consisted of 60 percent Turkish tribal and Orientals, 20 percent Navajo replicas and Western-style rugs 20 percent, with fine antiques and home furnishings making up the remaining inventory. In buying and managing the inventory, DeFalco had to be aware of the market for rugs with an average sales price of $7,500, with some rugs selling for $30,000. With an annual growth rate of 30 percent since its opening in 2003, DeFalco had to hire a larger staff and move into a larger location in 2005. In 2008, DeFalco decided to sell the business, using the guidelines for valuing a rug retailer: 20 percent of revenue plus the value of the inventory. The selling price for Montana Rugs is $1.64 million. DeFalco's decision to sell was based on a desire to retire and a belief that someone "younger and smarter" could maximize the potential of the business.[8] Consequently, making decisions to ensure the business achieves its short- and long-term goals is a vital part of management.

*Did the "Got Milk?" campaign with famous celebrities and their milk mustaches get you to drink more milk?*

**Marketing.**   Marketing and consumers are in the same segment of Figure 1.1 because the focus of all marketing activities is satisfying customers. Marketing includes all the activities designed to provide goods and services that satisfy consumers' needs and wants. Marketers gather information and conduct research to determine what customers want. Using information gathered from marketing research, marketers plan and develop products and make decisions about how much to charge for their products and when and where to make them available. In response to growing concerns over childhood obesity, Kellogg's has agreed to phase out advertising to children under the age of 12, unless those cereals are healthy (low calorie, low sugar and salt). In addition, Kellogg's will stop using cartoon and licensed characters such as Shrek to promote its products to children.[9] Other food producers have responded to consumer health concerns by modifying their products to make them healthier. PepsiCo, for example, has eliminated all transfats from its line of snack chips through a full conversion to nonhydrogenated oils. Such a move reduces consumers' risk of coronary disease.[10] Marketers use promotion—advertising, personal selling, sales promotion (coupons, games, sweepstakes, movie tie-ins), and publicity—to communicate the benefits and advantages of their products to consumers and increase sales. Nonprofit organizations also use promotion. For example, the National Fluid Milk Processor Promotion Board's "milk mustache" advertising campaign has featured Brooke Shields, Beyonce Knowles, Sheryl Crow, Elizabeth Hurley, Serena Williams, and even Bill Germanakos, winner of NBC's Biggest Loser, as well as animated "celebrities" such as Garfield.[11] We will examine marketing activities in Part 5 of this text.

**Finance.**   Owners and finance are in the same part of Figure 1.1 because, although management and marketing have to deal with financial considerations, it is the primary responsibility of the owners to provide financial resources for the operation of the business. Moreover, the owners have the most to lose if the business fails to make a profit. Finance refers to all activities concerned with obtaining money and using it effectively. People who work as accountants, stockbrokers, investment advisors, or bankers are all part of the financial world. Owners sometimes have to borrow money to get started or attract additional owners who become partners or stockholders. A mentoring group called 8 Wings helps women entrepreneurs obtain funding by assisting them in perfecting their business plan, preparing their presentation to potential funding sources, and introducing them to potential investors and other business contacts. The 8 Wings partners typically take stock or options in the companies they help.[12] Owners of small businesses in particular often rely on bank loans for funding. Part 6 of this text discusses financial management.

## Why Study Business?

Studying business can help you develop skills and acquire knowledge to prepare for your future career, regardless of whether you plan to work for a multinational *Fortune* 500 firm, start your own business, work for a government agency, or manage or volunteer at a nonprofit organization. The field of business offers a variety of interesting and challenging career opportunities throughout the world, such as human resources management, information technology, finance, production and operations, wholesaling and retailing, and many more.

Studying business can also help you better understand the many business activities that are necessary to provide satisfying goods and services—and that these activities carry a price tag. For example, if you buy a new compact disk, about half of the price goes toward activities related to distribution and the retailer's expenses and profit margins. The production (pressing) of the CD represents about $1, or a small percentage of its price. Most businesses charge a reasonable price for their products to ensure that they cover their production costs, pay their employees, provide their owners with a return on their investment, and perhaps give something back to their local communities. Bill Daniels founded Cablevision, building his first cable TV system in Casper, Wyoming, in 1953, and is now considered "the father of cable television." Upon Daniels' passing in 2000, he had established a foundation that currently has funding of $1.4 billion and supports a diversity of causes from education to business ethics. During his career, Daniels created the Young American Bank, where children could create bank accounts and learn about financial responsibility, and this remains the world's only charter bank for young people. He created the Daniels College of Business through a donation of $20 million to the University of Denver. During his life, he affected many individuals and organizations, and his business success has allowed his legacy to be one of giving and impacting communities throughout the United States.[13] Thus, learning about business can help you become a well-informed consumer and member of society.

Business activities help generate the profits that are essential not only to individual businesses and local economies but also to the health of the global economy. Without profits, businesses find it difficult, if not impossible, to buy more raw materials, hire more employees, attract more capital, and create additional products that in turn make more profits and fuel the world economy. Understanding how our free-enterprise economic system allocates resources and provides incentives for industry and the workplace is important to everyone.

# The Economic Foundations of Business

To continue our introduction to business, it is useful to explore the economic environment in which business is conducted. In this section, we examine economic systems, the free-enterprise system, the concepts of supply and demand, and the role of competition. These concepts play important roles in determining how businesses operate in a particular society.

**Economics** is the study of how resources are distributed for the production of goods and services within a social system. You are already familiar with the types of resources available. Land, forests, minerals, water, and other things that are not made by people are **natural resources. Human resources,** or labor, refers to the physical and mental abilities that people use to produce goods and services. **Financial resources,** or capital, are the funds used to acquire the natural and

**economics**
the study of how resources are distributed for the production of goods and services within a social system

**natural resources**
land, forests, minerals, water, and other things that are not made by people

**human resources**
the physical and mental abilities that people use to produce goods and services; also called labor

**financial resources**
the funds used to acquire the natural and human resources needed to provide products; also called capital

human resources needed to provide products. Because natural, human, and financial resources are used to produce goods and services, they are sometimes called *factors of production.*

## Economic Systems

**economic system**
a description of how a particular society distributes its resources to produce goods and services

An **economic system** describes how a particular society distributes its resources to produce goods and services. A central issue of economics is how to fulfill an unlimited demand for goods and services in a world with a limited supply of resources. Different economic systems attempt to resolve this central issue in numerous ways, as we shall see.

Although economic systems handle the distribution of resources in different ways, all economic systems must address three important issues:

1. What goods and services, and how much of each, will satisfy consumers' needs?
2. How will goods and services be produced, who will produce them, and with what resources will they be produced?
3. How are the goods and services to be distributed to consumers?

Communism, socialism, and capitalism, the basic economic systems found in the world today (Table 1.1), have fundamental differences in the way they address these issues.

| TABLE 1.1 | | Communism | Socialism | Capitalism |
|---|---|---|---|---|
| Comparison of Communism, Socialism, and Capitalism | Business ownership | Most businesses are owned and operated by the government. | The government owns and operates major industries; individuals own small businesses. | Individuals own and operate all businesses. |
| | Competition | None. The government owns and operates everything. | Restricted in major industries; encouraged in small business. | Encouraged by market forces and government regulations. |
| | Profits | Excess income goes to the government. | Profits earned by small businesses may be reinvested in the business; profits from government-owned industries go to the government. | Individuals are free to keep profits and use them as they wish. |
| | Product availability and price | Consumers have a limited choice of goods and services; prices are usually high. | Consumers have some choice of goods and services; prices are determined by supply and demand. | Consumers have a wide choice of goods and services; prices are determined by supply and demand. |
| | Employment options | Little choice in choosing a career; most people work for government-owned industries or farms. | Some choice of careers; many people work in government jobs. | Unlimited choice of careers. |

Source: "Gross Domestic Product or Expenditure, 1930–2002," *InfoPlease* (n.d.), www.infoplease.com/ipa/A0104575.html (accessed February 16, 2004).

**Communism.**   Karl Marx (1818–1883) first described **communism** as a society in which the people, without regard to class, own all the nation's resources. In his ideal political-economic system, everyone contributes according to ability and receives benefits according to need. In a communist economy, the people (through the government) own and operate all businesses and factors of production. Central government planning determines what goods and services satisfy citizens' needs, how the goods and services are produced, and how they are distributed. However, no true communist economy exists today that satisfies Marx's ideal.

On paper, communism appears to be efficient and equitable, producing less of a gap between rich and poor. In practice, however, communist economies have been marked by low standards of living, critical shortages of consumer goods, high prices, and little freedom. Russia, Poland, Hungary, and other Eastern European nations have turned away from communism and toward economic systems governed by supply and demand rather than by central planning. However, their experiments with alternative economic systems have been fraught with difficulty and hardship. China, North Korea, and Cuba continue to apply communist principles to their economies, but these countries are also enduring economic and political change. China has become the first communist country to make strong economic gains by adopting capitalist approaches to business. Chinese investors saw its stock market rise sixfold, only to drop 50 percent in 2008 before again rebounding. Economic prosperity has advanced in China with the government claiming to ensure market openness, equality, and fairness.[14] Consequently, communism is declining and its future as an economic system is uncertain. When Fidel Castro stepped down as president of Cuba, his younger brother Raul formally assumed the role and eliminated many of the bans, including allowing the purchase of electric appliances, microwaves, computers, and cell phones. The communist country appears more open to free enterprise now.[15]

**Socialism.**   Closely related to communism is **socialism,** an economic system in which the government owns and operates basic industries—postal service, telephone, utilities, transportation, health care, banking, and some manufacturing—but individuals own most businesses. Central planning determines what basic goods and services are produced, how they are produced, and how they are distributed. Individuals and small businesses provide other goods and services based on consumer demand and the availability of resources. As with communism, citizens are dependent on the government for many goods and services.

Most socialist nations, such as Sweden, India, and Israel, are democratic and recognize basic individual freedoms. Citizens can vote for political offices, but central government planners usually make decisions about what is best for the nation. People are free to go into the occupation of their choice, but they often work in government-operated organizations. Socialists believe their system permits a higher standard of living than other economic systems, but the difference often applies to the nation as a whole rather than to its individual citizens. Socialist economies profess egalitarianism—equal distribution of income and social services. They believe their economies are more stable than those of other nations. Although this may be true, taxes and unemployment are generally higher in socialist countries. Perhaps as a result, many socialist countries are also experiencing economic turmoil.

**Capitalism.**   **Capitalism,** or **free enterprise,** is an economic system in which individuals own and operate the majority of businesses that provide goods and services. Competition, supply, and demand determine which goods and services

**communism**
first described by Karl Marx as a society in which the people, without regard to class, own all the nation's resources

**socialism**
an economic system in which the government owns and operates basic industries but individuals own most businesses

**capitalism, or free enterprise**
an economic system in which individuals own and operate the majority of businesses that provide goods and services

are produced, how they are produced, and how they are distributed. The United States, Canada, Japan, and Australia are examples of economic systems based on capitalism.

There are two forms of capitalism: pure capitalism and modified capitalism. In pure capitalism, also called a **free-market system,** all economic decisions are made without government intervention. This economic system was first described by Adam Smith in *The Wealth of Nations* (1776). Smith, often called the father of capitalism, believed that the "invisible hand of competition" best regulates the economy. He argued that competition should determine what goods and services people need. Smith's system is also called *laissez-faire* ("to leave alone") *capitalism* because the government does not interfere in business.

Modified capitalism differs from pure capitalism in that the government intervenes and regulates business to some extent. One of the ways in which the United States and Canadian governments regulate business is through laws. Laws such as the Federal Trade Commission Act, which created the Federal Trade Commission to enforce antitrust laws, illustrate the importance of the government's role in the economy.

**Mixed Economies.**   No country practices a pure form of communism, socialism, or capitalism, although most tend to favor one system over the others. Most nations operate as **mixed economies,** which have elements from more than one economic system. In socialist Sweden, most businesses are owned and operated by private individuals. In capitalist United States, the federal government owns and operates the postal service and the Tennessee Valley Authority, an electric utility. In Great Britain and Mexico, the governments are attempting to sell many state-run businesses to private individuals and companies. In once-communist Russia, Hungary, Poland, and other Eastern European nations, capitalist ideas have been implemented, including private ownership of businesses. Communist China allows citizens to invest in stocks and permits some private and foreign ownership of businesses.

## The Free-Enterprise System

Many economies—including those of the United States, Canada, and Japan—are based on free enterprise, and many communist and socialist countries, such as China and Russia, are applying more principles of free enterprise to their own economic systems. Free enterprise provides an opportunity for a business to succeed or fail on the basis of market demand. In a free-enterprise system, companies that can efficiently manufacture and sell products that consumers desire will probably succeed. Inefficient businesses and those that sell products that do not offer needed benefits will likely fail as consumers take their business to firms that have more competitive products.

A number of basic individual and business rights must exist for free enterprise to work. These rights are the goals of many countries that have recently embraced free enterprise.

1. Individuals must have the right to own property and to pass this property on to their heirs. This right motivates people to work hard and save to buy property.

2. Individuals and businesses must have the right to earn profits and to use the profits as they wish, within the constraints of their society's laws and values.

---

**free-market system**
pure capitalism, in which all economic decisions are made without government intervention

**mixed economies**
economies made up of elements from more than one economic system

3. Individuals and businesses must have the right to make decisions that determine the way the business operates. Although there is government regulation, the philosophy in countries like the United States and Australia is to permit maximum freedom within a set of rules of fairness.

4. Individuals must have the right to choose what career to pursue, where to live, what goods and services to purchase, and more. Businesses must have the right to choose where to locate, what goods and services to produce, what resources to use in the production process, and so on.

Without these rights, businesses cannot function effectively because they are not motivated to succeed. Thus, these rights make possible the open exchange of goods and services.

### The Forces of Supply and Demand

In the United States and in other free-enterprise systems, the distribution of resources and products is determined by supply and demand. **Demand** is the number of goods and services that consumers are willing to buy at different prices at a specific time. From your own experience, you probably recognize that consumers are usually willing to buy more of an item as its price falls because they want to save money. Consider handmade rugs, for example. Consumers may be willing to buy six rugs at $350 each, four at $500 each, but only two at $650 each. The relationship between the price and the number of rugs consumers are willing to buy can be shown graphically, with a *demand curve* (see Figure 1.2).

**Supply** is the number of products that businesses are willing to sell at different prices at a specific time. In general, because the potential for profits is higher, businesses are willing to supply more of a good or service at higher prices. For example, a company that sells rugs may be willing to sell six at $650 each, four at $500 each, but just two at $350 each. The relationship between the price of rugs and the quantity the company is willing to supply can be shown graphically with a *supply curve* (see Figure 1.2).

**demand**
the number of goods and services that consumers are willing to buy at different prices at a specific time

**supply**
the number of products—goods and services—that businesses are willing to sell at different prices at a specific time

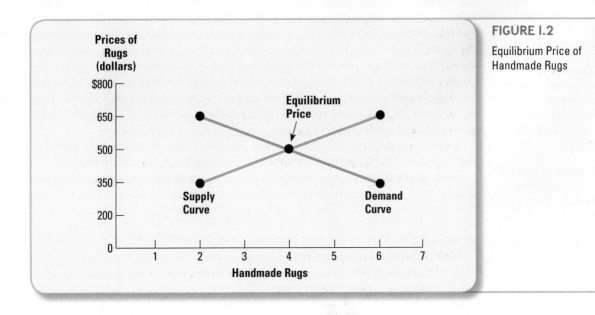

**FIGURE I.2**

Equilibrium Price of Handmade Rugs

In Figure 1.2, the supply and demand curves intersect at the point where supply and demand are equal. The price at which the number of products that businesses are willing to supply equals the amount of products that consumers are willing to buy at a specific point in time is the **equilibrium price.** In our rug example, the company is willing to supply four rugs at $500 each, and consumers are willing to buy four rugs at $500 each. Therefore, $500 is the equilibrium price for a rug at that point in time, and most rug companies will price their rugs at $500. As you might imagine, a business that charges more than $500 (or whatever the current equilibrium price is) for its rugs will not sell many and might not earn a profit. On the other hand, a business that charges less than $500 accepts a lower profit per rug than could be made at the equilibrium price.

**equilibrium price**
the price at which the number of products that businesses are willing to supply equals the amount of products that consumers are willing to buy at a specific point in time

If the cost of making rugs goes up, businesses will not offer as many at the old price. Changing the price alters the supply curve, and a new equilibrium price results. This is an ongoing process, with supply and demand constantly changing in response to changes in economic conditions, availability of resources, and degree of competition. For example, gasoline prices rose sharply in 2008 in response to a shrinking supply of gasoline and crude oil and rising demand.[16] In contrast to the oil boom, in 2008 there were nearly 1 million homes in foreclosure and more than 3 million homeowners were behind in their mortgage payments. The inventory of homes for sale grew rapidly and prices fell because of the large supply of houses on the market.[17] Prices for goods and services vary according to these changes in supply and demand. This concept is the force that drives the distribution of resources (goods and services, labor, and money) in a free-enterprise economy.

Critics of supply and demand say the system does not distribute resources equally. The forces of supply and demand prevent sellers who have to sell at higher prices (because their costs are high) and buyers who cannot afford to buy goods at the equilibrium price from participating in the market. According to critics, the wealthy can afford to buy more than they need, but the poor are unable to buy enough of what they need to survive.

## The Nature of Competition

**Competition,** the rivalry among businesses for consumers' dollars, is another vital element in free enterprise. According to Adam Smith, competition fosters efficiency and low prices by forcing producers to offer the best products at the most reasonable price; those who fail to do so are not able to stay in business. Thus, competition should improve the quality of the goods and services available or reduce prices. For example, thanks to smart design and excellent timing, Apple dominates the market for downloadable music with its iTunes online service and iPod MP3 player. However, many companies have set their sights on capturing some of the firm's market share with new products of their own.

**competition**
the rivalry among businesses for consumers' dollars

**pure competition**
the market structure that exists when there are many small businesses selling one standardized product

Within a free-enterprise system, there are four types of competitive environments: pure competition, monopolistic competition, oligopoly, and monopoly.

**Pure competition** exists when there are many small businesses selling one standardized product, such as agricultural commodities like wheat, corn, and cotton. No one business sells enough of the product to influence the product's price. And, because there is no difference in the products, prices are determined solely by the forces of supply and demand.

**monopolistic competition**
the market structure that exists when there are fewer businesses than in a pure-competition environment and the differences among the goods they sell are small

**Monopolistic competition** exists when there are fewer businesses than in a pure-competition environment and the differences among the goods they sell is small. Aspirin, soft drinks, and vacuum cleaners are examples of such goods. These

# Destination CEO
## NBC News: New Balance: Can America Compete?

Many manufacturing firms have outsourced their production to achieve labor costs savings. As competition increases, labor cost considerations have become very significant factors in determining the competitiveness and sustainability of firms. The athletic shoe industry is no exception. In fact, there is only one company in this industry sector that has manufacturing operations in the United States. New Balance keeps 25 percent of its labor force in the United States. Its major competitors, Nike and Reebok, have no manufacturing facilities domestically. New Balance's production costs are significantly higher than either of their chief rivals. However, they are able to remain competitive in terms of their market responsiveness. Manufacturing a case of shoes, for example, traditionally took eight days from point of order to completion. Today, it takes three hours. This is the key to New Balance's success. The company feels strongly that the quality dynamics in the United States cannot be matched by other countries' labor forces. Not only does New Balance intend to remain in the United States, they are planning to expand their operations here. Other companies (e.g., North Fork Bank and Pioneer Airlines) have also achieved competitive advantages by keeping labor in the United States rather than outsourcing to other countries.

### Discussion Questions

1. Explain how New Balance can remain competitive yet have a quarter of its manufacturing labor force based in the United States with significantly higher labor costs.
2. Using the fundamentals of economics, what would occur if New Balance overproduced a shoe line? In other words, what if its sales forecast was overly optimistic and missed the mark by say, 100,000 units that remain unsold?
3. New Balance, Nike, and Reebok are competitors in the athletic shoe industry. These companies operate in a free-enterprise system. Which competitive environment most likely characterizes this competition?

products differ slightly in packaging, warranty, name, and other characteristics, but all satisfy the same consumer need. Businesses have some power over the price they charge in monopolistic competition because they can make consumers aware of product differences through advertising. Consumers value some features more than others and are often willing to pay higher prices for a product with the features they want. For example, Advil, a nonprescription pain reliever, contains ibuprofen instead of aspirin. Consumers who cannot take aspirin or who believe ibuprofen is a more effective pain reliever may not mind paying a little extra for the ibuprofen in Advil.

An **oligopoly** exists when there are very few businesses selling a product. In an oligopoly, individual businesses have control over their products' price because each business supplies a large portion of the products sold in the marketplace. Nonetheless, the prices charged by different firms stay fairly close because a price cut or increase by one company will trigger a similar response from another company. In the airline industry, for example, when one airline cuts fares to boost sales, other airlines quickly follow with rate decreases to remain competitive. Oligopolies exist when it is expensive for new firms to enter the marketplace. Not just anyone can acquire enough financial capital to build an automobile production facility or purchase enough airplanes and related resources to build an airline.

When there is one business providing a product in a given market, a **monopoly** exists. Utility companies that supply electricity, natural gas, and water are monopolies. The government permits such monopolies because the cost of creating the good or supplying the service is so great that new producers cannot compete for sales. Government-granted monopolies are subject to government-regulated prices. Some monopolies exist because of technological developments that are protected by patent laws. Patent laws grant the developer of new technology a period of time (usually 17 years) during which no other producer can use the same technology without the agreement of the original developer. The United States granted the first patent in

**oligopoly**
the market structure that exists when there are very few businesses selling a product

**monopoly**
the market structure that exists when there is only one business providing a product in a given market

15

# Responding to Business Challenges
## Lowe's vs. The Home Depot: Location, Location, Location

Here's a question: which do you prefer, Lowe's or The Home Depot? It may not be that important to you, but to both companies your answer is critical. Competition for consumer dollars is always going to be prevalent in free enterprise. It serves many functions, such as driving down prices on quality merchandise. There are four forms of competition within the free-enterprise system: pure competition, monopolistic competition, oligopoly, and monopoly. Lowe's and The Home Depot fall into the monopolistic competition category because, among other things, they supply a large proportion of home-improvement products and the goods sold by both chains are similar. In a recent survey, 53 percent of those surveyed preferred Lowe's, versus 47 percent preferring The Home Depot. Those preferring Lowe's cited better product selection and customer service (however, other surveys reveal just the opposite regarding customer service). Prices are quite comparable at both stores. So, what accounts for the fact that in 2006 The Home Depot netted $5.8 billion while Lowe's netted $3.1 billion? In a word . . . location!

Throughout the United States, Lowe's boasts 1,400 stores, while The Home Depot boasts 2,206. Although consumers regularly shop in both stores, those preferring Lowe's still spent an average of $454 at The Home Depot in a six-month period. Those preferring The Home Depot spent well over $100 less at Lowe's in the same time frame. After reading many articles and blogs regarding the competition between The Home Depot and Lowe's, it is clear that, on average, The Home Depot caters more toward men, contractors, and serious do-it-yourselfers, while Lowe's caters more toward women and those looking to put finishing touches on decorating projects.

However, this is merely a generalization based on research; there are always exceptions.

Although The Home Depot does get more traffic, consumers visit both stores regularly. This is important in the competitive process because it forces each store to fight for sales. For example, Lowe's might want to add more locations, while The Home Depot might want to focus on improving its product line. In fact, according to The Home Depot annual report, the company has been placing its focus on improving its in-stock product options and creating a better shopping environment (take note—these are the very factors that caused Lowe's to score a bit higher in the survey cited earlier). The company recently replaced its CEO and sold its wholesale distribution business. Company representative Paula Drake has indicated that The Home Depot aimed to spend $2.2 billion in 2007 on creating a better shopping experience for consumers. On the flip side, Lowe's annual report indicated that Lowe's planned major expansion of store locations. In other words, no one is more aware of what is on the line than these two companies. Each is trying to improve upon the other, which, one would think, can only lead to better shopping experiences for consumers all around.[18]

**Discussion Questions**

1. Why is there so much competition between Lowe's and The Home Depot in the home improvement market?
2. How have Lowe's and The Home Depot differentiated their stores in the minds of consumers?
3. Which home improvement company do you feel has the best competitive image? Lowe's or The Home Depot?

---

1790, and the patent office received more than 452,000 patent applications in 2006.[19] This monopoly allows the developer to recover research, development, and production expenses and to earn a reasonable profit. Examples of this type of monopoly are the dry-copier process developed by Xerox and the self-developing photographic technology created by Polaroid. Both companies operated for years without competition and could charge premium prices because no alternative products existed to compete with their products. Through continuous development, Polaroid maintains market dominance. Xerox's patents have expired, however, and many imitators have forced market prices to decline.

## Economic Cycles and Productivity

**Expansion and Contraction.** Economies are not stagnant; they expand and contract. **Economic expansion** occurs when an economy is growing and people are spending more money. Their purchases stimulate the production of goods and services, which in turn stimulates employment. The standard of living rises because more people are employed and have money to spend. Rapid expansions of

**economic expansion** the situation that occurs when an economy is growing and people are spending more money; their purchases stimulate the production of goods and services, which in turn stimulates employment

the economy, however, may result in **inflation,** a continuing rise in prices. Inflation can be harmful if individuals' incomes do not increase at the same pace as rising prices, reducing their buying power. Zimbabwe has the highest inflation rate at 100,000 percent.[20]

**Economic contraction** occurs when spending declines. Businesses cut back on production and lay off workers, and the economy as a whole slows down. Contractions of the economy lead to **recession**—a decline in production, employment, and income. Recessions are often characterized by rising levels of **unemployment,** which is measured as the percentage of the population that wants to work but is unable to find jobs. Figure 1.3 shows the overall unemployment rate in the civilian labor force over the past 80 years. Rising unemployment levels tend to stifle demand for goods and services, which can have the effect of forcing prices downward, a condition known as *deflation.* The United States has experienced numerous recessions, the most recent ones occurring in 1990–1991, 2001, and 2008. The 2008 recession (or economic slowdown) was caused by the collapse in housing prices and consumers' inability to stay current on their mortgage and credit card payments. This in turn caused a slowdown in spending on consumer goods and a reduction in employment. Don't forget that personal consumption makes up almost 70 percent of gross domestic product, so consumer behavior is extremely important for economic activity. A severe recession may turn into a **depression,** in which unemployment is very high, consumer spending is low, and business output is sharply reduced, such as occurred in the United States in the early 1930s.

Economies expand and contract in response to changes in consumer, business, and government spending. War also can affect an economy, sometimes stimulating it (as in the United States during World Wars I and II) and sometimes stifling it (as during the Vietnam, Persian Gulf, and Iraq wars). Although fluctuations in the

**inflation**
a condition characterized by a continuing rise in prices

**economic contraction**
a slowdown of the economy characterized by a decline in spending and during which businesses cut back on production and lay off workers

**recession**
a decline in production, employment, and income

**unemployment**
the condition in which a percentage of the population wants to work but is unable to find jobs

**depression**
a condition of the economy in which unemployment is very high, consumer spending is low, and business output is sharply reduced

---

**FIGURE 1.3**   Overall Unemployment Rate in the U.S. Civilian Labor Force

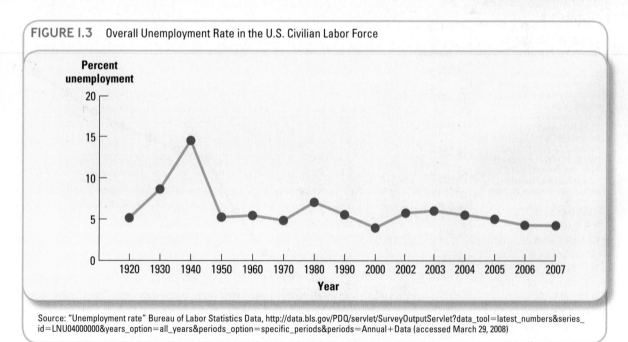

Source: "Unemployment rate" Bureau of Labor Statistics Data, http://data.bls.gov/PDQ/servlet/SurveyOutputServlet?data_tool=latest_numbers&series_id=LNU04000000&years_option=all_years&periods_option=specific_periods&periods=Annual+Data (accessed March 29, 2008)

economy are inevitable and to a certain extent predictable, their effects—inflation and unemployment—disrupt lives and thus governments try to minimize them.

**Measuring the Economy.**    Countries measure the state of their economies to determine whether they are expanding or contracting and whether corrective action is necessary to minimize the fluctuations. One commonly used measure is **gross domestic product (GDP)**—the sum of all goods and services produced in a country during a year. GDP measures only those goods and services made within a country and therefore does not include profits from companies' overseas operations; it does include profits earned by foreign companies within the country being measured. However, it does not take into account the concept of GDP in relation to population (GDP per capita). Figure 1.4 shows the increase in GDP over several years, while Table 1.2 compares a number of economic statistics for a sampling of countries.

Another important indicator of a nation's economic health is the relationship between its spending and income (from taxes). When a nation spends more than it takes in from taxes, it has a **budget deficit.** In the 1990s, the U.S. government eliminated its long-standing budget deficit by balancing the money spent for social, defense, and other programs with the amount of money taken in from taxes.

In recent years, however, the budget deficit has reemerged and grown to record levels, partly due to defense spending in the aftermath of the terrorist attacks of September 11, 2001. Because Americans do not want their taxes increased, it is difficult for the federal government to bring in more revenue and reduce the deficit. Like consumers and businesses, when the government needs money, it borrows from the public, banks, and other institutions. The national debt (the amount of money the nation owes its lenders) exceeded $9.4 trillion in 2008, due largely to increased spending by the government.[21] This figure is especially worrisome because, to reduce

**gross domestic product (GDP)**
the sum of all goods and services produced in a country during a year

**budget deficit**
the condition in which a nation spends more than it takes in from taxes

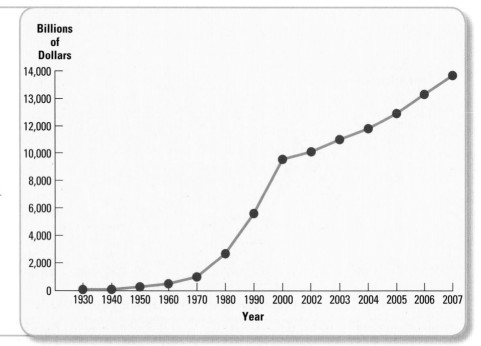

**FIGURE 1.4**

Growth in U.S. Gross Domestic Product

Source: "Gross Domestic Product or Expenditure, 1930–2004," *InfoPlease* (n.d.), www.infoplease.com/ipa/A0104575.html (accessed February 22, 2008); "Table 1.1.5, Gross Domestic Product," Bureau of Economic Analysis National Income and Product Accounts Table, http://www.bea.gov/national/nipaweb/TablePrint.asp (accessed March 29, 2008).

| Country | GDP (in billions of U.S. dollars) | GDP per capita (in U.S. dollars) | Unemployment Rate (%) | Inflation Rate (%) |
|---|---|---|---|---|
| Argentina | 523.7 | 13,000 | 8.9 | 8.5 |
| Australia | 766.8 | 37,500 | 4.4 | 3 |
| Brazil | 1.838 (trillion) | 9,700 | 9.8 | 4.1 |
| Canada | 1.274 (t) | 38,200 | 5.9 | 2.4 |
| China | 7.043 (t) | 5,300 | 4* | 4.7 |
| France | 2.067 (t) | 33,800 | 8 | 1.5 |
| Germany | 2.833 (t) | 34,400 | 9.1 | 2 |
| India | 2.965 (t) | 2,700 | 7.2 | 5.9 |
| Israel | 184.9 | 28,800 | 7.6 | 0.4 |
| Japan | 4.346 (t) | 33,800 | 4 | 0 |
| Mexico | 1.353 (t) | 12,500 | 3.7 | 3.8 |
| Russia | 2.076 (t) | 14,600 | 5.9 | 11.9 |
| South Africa | 467.6 | 10,600 | 24.2 | 6.5 |
| United Kingdom | 2.147 (t) | 35,300 | 5.4 | 2.4 |
| United States | 13.86 (t) | 46,000 | 4.6 | 2.7 |

**TABLE I.2**

A Comparative Analysis of a Sampling of Countries

*Estimated for urban areas; unemployment rates in rural areas may be higher.
Source: CIA, "Country Listing," *The World Fact Book 2008*. https://www.cia.gov/library/publications/the-world-factbook/ (accessed April 4, 2008).

the debt to a manageable level, the government either has to increase its revenues (raise taxes) or reduce spending on social, defense, and legal programs, neither of which is politically popular. The national debt figure changes daily and can be seen at the Department of the Treasury, Bureau of the Public Debt, Web site. Table 1.3 describes some of the other ways we evaluate our nation's economy.

| Unit of Measure | Description |
|---|---|
| Trade balance | The difference between our exports and our imports. If the balance is negative, as it has been since the mid-1980s, it is called a trade deficit and is generally viewed as unhealthy for our economy. |
| Consumer Price Index | Measures changes in prices of goods and services purchased for consumption by typical urban households. |
| Per capita income | Indicates the income level of "average" Americans. Useful in determing how much "average" consumers spend and how much money Americans are earning. |
| Unemployment rate | Indicates how many working age Americans are not working who otherwise want to work.* |
| Inflation | Monitors price increases in consumer goods and services over specified periods of time. Used to determine if costs of goods and services are exceeding worker compensation over time. |
| Worker productivity | The amount of goods and services produced for each hour worked. |

**TABLE I.3**

How Do We Evaluate Our Nation's Economy?

*Americans who do not work in a traditional sense, such as househusbands/housewives, are not counted as unemployed.

## Going Green
### The Electric Sports Car—Reality or Fantasy?

Rumors abound regarding the electric car . . . failing batteries, fire risks, and, yes, conspiracies used to pull them off the market! Therefore, is it any great surprise that the introduction of not only an electric car but an elite electric sports car might be met with skepticism? Well, Tesla Motors aims to change all that with its new Tesla Roadster.

Although many of us may only know about electric cars as science fiction, they have in fact been in production for more than a century—that is correct, a century. So what has been keeping them out of the mainstream? Above all else, battery technology (and, who knows, maybe a conspiracy or two?). If the Tesla roadster is a reality, are things looking up? After trying lead-acid batteries and nickel-metal hydride batteries in recent years, companies are now looking to the same type of lithium-ion batteries used to power our computers, cell phones, and more. Tesla's new roadster is powered in just this fashion, and it's on its way to consumers.

Having heard this exciting news, you may be wondering where and when you can purchase one. Hold your horses— it's going to be some time before us average Joe types can get our hands on this beauty. In 2008, Tesla is producing 600 Roadsters. To put this in perspective, Toyota can manufacture this many cars in less than one day. And, people in line for the $98,950 Roadster are those with names like George Clooney and Matt Damon.

So, is Tesla's roadster a dream car to be used by the rich and famous once in a while when they're feeling particularly green? No. According to automotive experts, the Tesla is, in fact, an eco-friendly car that actually looks like it may lead to more mainstream electric cars sooner rather than later. Unlike most hybrid cars, which accelerate slowly, the roadster surges to 60 mph in 4.7 seconds and can run up to an estimated 220 miles on one battery charge, which makes it a car that can actually perform. The Tesla electric car also produces only a tenth of the pollution emitted by a gas-powered vehicle. Over time, electric cars may actually begin to free us from dependence on oil, because electric power may be generated from natural gas, solar, wind, hydro, and so on. The Roadster is just the beginning.

Founded in 2003 by Martin Eberhard and Marc Tarpenning and financially supported in part by multimillionaire Elon Musk, Tesla is new to the electric car arena, and, although the company has made some amazing progress, it could be facing a steep uphill fight to remain on top. Both BMW and Mercedes-Benz are coming out as rivals, and, although Tesla is working on a sedan to complete with BMW's 5-series and Mercedes' E-class, it's going to be tough to stay in the game.[22]

### Discussion Questions

1. How does the development of the Tesla Roadster contribute to developing green initiatives in the auto industry?
2. Why do you think that major auto companies such as General Motors, Ford and Chrysler have been so slow in developing electric cars?
3. If Tesla is successful with its electric sports car, will it be a role model and influence the future of the electric car in our society?

# The American Economy

As we said previously, the United States is a mixed economy based on capitalism. The answers to the three basic economic issues are determined primarily by competition and the forces of supply and demand, although the federal government does intervene in economic decisions to a certain extent. To understand the current state of the American economy and its effect on business practices, it is helpful to examine its history and the roles of the entrepreneur and the government.

## A Brief History of the American Economy

**The Early Economy.**   Before the colonization of North America, Native Americans lived as hunter/gatherers and farmers, with some trade among tribes. The colonists who came later operated primarily as an *agricultural economy*. People were self-sufficient and produced everything they needed at home, including food, clothing, and furniture. Abundant natural resources and a moderate climate nourished industries such as farming, fishing, shipping, and fur trading. A few manufactured goods and money for the colonies' burgeoning industries came from England and other countries.

As the nation expanded slowly toward the West, people found natural resources such as coal, copper, and iron ore and used them to produce goods such as horseshoes, farm implements, and kitchen utensils. Farm families who produced surplus goods sold or traded them for things they could not produce themselves, such as fine furniture and window glass. Some families also spent time turning raw materials into clothes and household goods. Because these goods were produced at home, this system was called the domestic system.

**The Industrial Revolution.**    The 19th century and the Industrial Revolution brought the development of new technology and factories. The factory brought together all the resources needed to make a product—materials, machines, and workers. Work in factories became specialized as workers focused on one or two tasks. As work became more efficient, productivity increased, making more goods available at lower prices. Railroads brought major changes, allowing farmers to send their surplus crops and goods all over the nation for barter or for sale.

Factories began to spring up along the railways to manufacture farm equipment and a variety of other goods to be shipped by rail. Samuel Slater set up the first American textile factory after he memorized the plans for an English factory and emigrated to the United States. Eli Whitney revolutionized the cotton industry with his cotton gin. Francis Cabot Lowell's factory organized all the steps in manufacturing cotton cloth for maximum efficiency and productivity. John Deere's farm equipment increased farm production and reduced the number of farmers required to feed the young nation. Farmers began to move to cities to find jobs in factories and a higher standard of living. Henry Ford developed the assembly-line system to produce automobiles. Workers focused on one part of an automobile and then pushed it to the next stage until it rolled off the assembly line as a finished automobile. Ford's assembly line could manufacture many automobiles efficiently, and the price of his cars was $200, making them affordable to many Americans.

**The Manufacturing and Marketing Economies.**    Industrialization brought increased prosperity, and the United States gradually became a *manufacturing economy*—one devoted to manufacturing goods and providing services rather than producing agricultural products. The assembly line was applied to more industries, increasing the variety of goods available to the consumer. Businesses became more concerned with the needs of the consumer and entered the *marketing economy*. Expensive goods

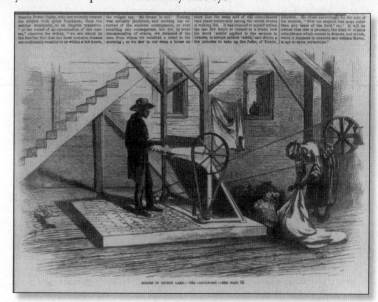

American Eli Whitney is credited with creating the cotton gin in 1793. The device removed the seeds from cotton, which was much more efficient than removing them by hand. But the machine was so easy to copy that Whitney's cotton-gin-producing company was driven out of business by competitors just four years after he had invented the device.

such as cars and appliances could be purchased on a time-payment plan. Companies conducted research to find out what products consumers needed and wanted. Advertising made consumers aware of differences in products and prices.

Because these developments occurred in a free-enterprise system, consumers determined what goods and services were produced. They did this by purchasing the products they liked at prices they were willing to pay. The United States prospered, and American citizens had one of the highest standards of living in the world.

**The Service and Internet-based Economy.**   After World War II, with the increased standard of living, Americans had more money and more time. They began to pay others to perform services that made their lives easier. Beginning in the 1960s, more and more women entered the workforce. The profile of the family changed: Today there are more single-parent families and individuals living alone, and in two-parent families, both parents often work. One result of this trend is that time-pressed Americans are increasingly paying others to do tasks they used to do at home, like cooking, laundry, landscaping, and child care. These trends have gradually changed the United States to a *service economy*—one devoted to the production of services that make life easier for busy consumers. Service industries such as restaurants, banking, medicine, child care, auto repair, leisure-related industries, and even education are growing rapidly and may account for as much as 80 percent of the U.S. economy. These trends continue with advanced technology contributing to new service products such as overnight mail, electronic banking, and shopping through cable television networks and the Internet. Table 1.4 provides an overview of e-commerce in the United States. More about the Internet and e-commerce can be found in Chapter 4.

> **Did You Know?**   60 percent of adult women work.[23]

**entrepreneur**
an individual who risks his or her wealth, time, and effort to develop for profit an innovative product or way of doing something

## The Role of the Entrepreneur

An **entrepreneur** is an individual who risks his or her wealth, time, and effort to develop for profit an innovative product or way of doing something. Emeterio Ortiz was making homemade salsa in 1918 during the Mexican Revolution. Nearly

| TABLE 1.4 | | |
|---|---|---|
| U.S. e-Commerce Overview | Total retail sales of all types | $4,495 billion |
| | Total e-commerce sales (excluding travel) | $131 billion |
| | Total travel sales online | $91.3 billion |
| | Internet advertising | $25.5 billion |
| | Number of VOIP subscribers, U.S. | $13.7 million |
| | Active home Internet users in the U.S. | 215.1 million |
| | Number of high-speed Internet connections | 90 million |
| | Number of Web logs (blogs) | 112.8 million |
| | Percent of U.S. adults online | 71 |

Source: http://www.plunkettresearch.com/Industries/ECommerceInternet/ECommerceInternetStatistics/tabid/167/Default.aspx (accessed April 19, 2008).

a century later Juanita Carmack, her great granddaughter, started sharing the recipe with friends. When her children left home, she started her own business, Taco Chic Salsa. The salsa, still made from the secret family recipe, has been enormously successful—it is available in over 60 stores, and plans to seek a distributor are under way. The successful entrepreneur started her business in Rathdrum, Idaho.[24]

*Beck Hickey, an avid skateboarder, found a way to turn used skateboards into a business opportunity by transforming them into Sk8bags—a line of handbag-related products. Her products are sold at sports shops across the United States as well as in Australia, Brazil, Europe, Canada, and Japan.*

The free-enterprise system provides the conditions necessary for entrepreneurs to succeed. In the past, entrepreneurs were often inventors who brought all the factors of production together to produce a new product. Thomas Edison, whose inventions include the record player and lightbulb, was an early American entrepreneur. Henry Ford was one of the first persons to develop mass assembly methods in the automobile industry. Other entrepreneurs, so-called captains of industry, invested in the country's growth. John D. Rockefeller built Standard Oil out of the fledgling oil industry, and Andrew Carnegie invested in railroads and founded the United States Steel Corporation. Andrew Mellon built the Aluminum Company of America and Gulf Oil. J. P. Morgan started financial institutions to fund the business activities of other entrepreneurs. Although these entrepreneurs were born in another century, their legacy to the American economy lives on in the companies they started, many of which still operate today. Milton Hershey began producing chocolate in 1894 in Lancaster, Pennsylvania. In 1900, the company was mass producing chocolate in many forms, lowering the cost of chocolate and making it more affordable to the masses, where it had once been a high-priced, luxury good. Early advertising touted chocolate as "a palatable confection and most nourishing food." Today, the Hershey Company employs more than 13,000 employees and sells almost $5 billion in chocolates and candies throughout the world.[25]

Entrepreneurs are constantly changing American business practices with new technology and innovative management techniques. Bill Gates, for example, built Microsoft, a software company whose products include MS-DOS (a disk operating system), Word, and Windows, into a multibillion-dollar enterprise. Frederick Smith had an idea to deliver packages overnight, and now his FedEx Company plays an important role in getting documents and packages delivered all over the world for businesses and individuals. Entrepreneurs have been associated with such uniquely American concepts as Dell Computers, Ben & Jerry's, Levi's, Holiday Inns, McDonald's, Dr Pepper, and Wal-Mart. Wal-Mart, founded by entrepreneur Sam Walton, was the first retailer to reach $100 billion in sales in one year and now routinely passes that mark. Wal-Mart has more than 1.9 million employees and operates more than 6,700 stores in the United States, Canada, Mexico, Asia, Europe, and South America. San Walton's heirs own about 40 percent of the company.[27] We will examine the importance of entrepreneurship further in Chapter 6.

## The Role of Government in the American Economy

The American economic system is best described as modified capitalism because the government regulates business to preserve competition and protect consumers and employees. Federal, state, and local governments intervene in the economy with laws and regulations designed to promote competition and to protect consumers, employees, and the environment. Many of these laws are discussed in Appendix A.

Additionally, government agencies such as the U.S. Department of Commerce measure the health of the economy (GDP, productivity, etc.) and, when necessary, take steps to minimize the disruptive effects of economic fluctuations and reduce unemployment. When the economy is contracting and unemployment is rising, the federal government through the Federal Reserve Board (see Chapter 14) tries to spur growth so that consumers will spend more money and businesses will hire more employees. To accomplish this, it may reduce interest rates or increase its own spending for goods and services. When the economy expands so fast that inflation results, the government may intervene to reduce inflation by slowing down economic growth. This can be accomplished by raising interest rates to discourage spending by businesses and consumers. Techniques used to control the economy are discussed in Chapter 14.

## The Role of Ethics and Social Responsibility in Business

In the past few years, you may have read about a number of scandals at a number of well-known corporations, including Enron, WorldCom, Tyco, and Arthur Andersen. In many cases, misconduct by individuals within these firms had an adverse effect on current and retired employees, investors, and others associated with these firms. In some cases, individuals went to jail for their actions. Top executives at General Re, an insurance division of Berkshire Hathaway, were convicted of fraud stemming from transactions between AIG and General Re Corporation.

The convicted former employees faced prison sentences up to 230 years and fines up to $46 million for the fraudulent misrepresentation of assets.[28] These scandals undermined public confidence in Corporate America and sparked a new debate about ethics in business. Business ethics generally refers to the standards and principles used by society to define appropriate and inappropriate conduct in the workplace. In many cases, these standards have been codified as laws prohibiting actions deemed unacceptable.

Society is increasingly demanding that businesspeople behave ethically and socially responsibly toward not only their customers but also their employees, investors, government regulators, communities, and the natural environment. "Intel helped establish a goal for PFCs (perfluorocompounds) that the entire industry could support," Intel President and CEO Paul Otellini told *CRO*. "It came together before Kyoto and was the first worldwide, industry-wide goal to address climate change. We view our environmental strategies as integral to the way we do business. We strive to lead by example, and to be trusted stakeholders to governments worldwide."[29] Green business strategies create long-run relationships with all stakeholders by maintaining, supporting, and enhancing the natural environment.

One of the primary lessons of the scandals of the early 2000s has been that the reputation of business organizations depends not just on bottom-line profits but also on ethical conduct and concern for the welfare of others. Consider that in the aftermath of these scandals, the reputations of every U.S. company suffered regardless of their association with the scandals. However, there are signs that business ethics is improving. One respected survey reported well-implemented formal ethics and compliance programs dramatically increase reporting of observed misconduct and also help to decrease the rate of misconduct.[30] Although these results suggest that ethics is improving, the fact that employees continue to report observing misconduct and experiencing pressure to engage in unethical or illegal acts remains troubling and suggests that companies need to continue their efforts to raise ethical standards. In fact, during 2007 and 2008, ethical questions surfaced about lending practices in the mortgage industry. It seems that mortgage lenders had been making adjustable rate mortgage loans in previous years to people who were not necessarily good credit risks. The brokers earned fees for making the loans, and the fees were not contingent on the ability of the borrower to pay. As interest rates rose and the monthly cost of the mortgage was adjusted upward, many borrowers were unable to make their monthly payments and so ended up defaulting on their loans and losing their homes. Many faulted the lenders for a lack of ethical behavior. We take a closer look at ethics and social responsibility in business in Chapter 2.

## Can You Learn Business in a Classroom?

Obviously, the answer is yes, or there would be no purpose for this textbook! To be successful in business, you need knowledge, skills, experience, and good judgment. The topics covered in this chapter and throughout this book provide some of the knowledge you need to understand the world of business. The opening vignette at the beginning of each chapter, boxes, examples within each chapter, and the case at the end of each chapter describe experiences to help you develop good business judgment. The "Build Your Skills" exercise at the end of each chapter and the "Solve the Dilemma" box will help you develop skills that may be useful in your future

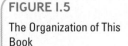

**FIGURE I.5**

The Organization of This Book

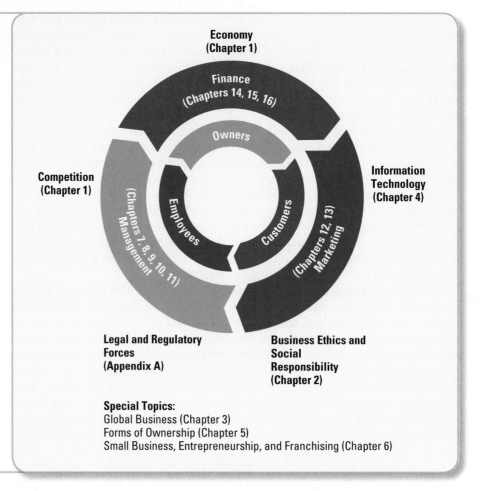

career. However, good judgment is based on knowledge and experience plus personal insight and understanding. Therefore, you need more courses in business, along with some practical experience in the business world, to help you develop the special insight necessary to put your personal stamp on knowledge as you apply it. The challenge in business is in the area of judgment, and judgment does not develop from memorizing an introductory business textbook. If you are observant in your daily experiences as an employee, as a student, and as a consumer, you will improve your ability to make good business judgments.

Figure 1.5 is an overview of how the chapters in this book are linked together and how the chapters relate to the participants, the activities, and the environmental factors found in the business world. The topics presented in the chapters that follow are those that will give you the best opportunity to begin the process of understanding the world of business.

# So You Want a Job in the Business World

When most people think of a career in business, they see entering the door to large companies and multinationals that they read about in the news and discussed in class. In a national survey, students indicated they would like to work for Google, Walt Disney, Apple, and Ernst & Young. In fact, most jobs are not with large corporations, but are in small companies, nonprofit organizations, government and even self-employed individuals. There are 20 million individuals the Small Business Administration says own their businesses and have no employees. In addition, there are nearly 5 million small businesses which employ 10 or fewer workers. With over 75% of the economy based on services, there are jobs available in industries such as healthcare, finance, education, hospitality, entertainment and transportation. The world is changing quickly and large corporations replace the equivalent of their entire workforce every four years.

The fast pace of technology today means that you have to be prepared to take advantage of emerging job opportunities and markets. You must also become adaptive and recognize that business is becoming more global, with job opportunities around the world. If you may want to obtain such a job, you shouldn't miss a chance to spend some time overseas. As get you started on the path to thinking about job opportunities, consider all of the changes in business today that might affect your possible long-term track and that could bring you lots of success. You may want to stay completely out of large organizations and corporations and put yourself in a position for an entrepreneurial role as a self-employed contractor or small-business owner. However, there are many that feel that experience in larger businesses is helpful to your success later as an entrepreneur.

You're on the road to learning the key knowledge, skills and trends that you can use to be a star in business. Businesses impact on our society, especially in the area of sustainability and improvement of the environment is a growing challenge and opportunity. Green businesses and green jobs in the business world are provided to give you a glimpse at the possibilities. Along the way, we will introduce you to some specific careers and offer advice on developing your own job opportunities. Research indicates that you won't be that happy with your job unless you enjoy your work and feel that it has a purpose. Since you spend most of your waking hours every day at work, you need to seriously think about what is important to you in a job.[31]

# Review Your Understanding

### *Define basic concepts such as business, product, and profit.*

A business is an organization or individual that seeks a profit by providing products that satisfy people's needs. A product is a good, service, or idea that has both tangible and intangible characteristics that provide satisfaction and benefits. Profit, the basic goal of business, is the difference between what it costs to make and sell a product and what a customer pays for it.

### *Identify the main participants and activities of business and explain why studying business is important.*

The three main participants in business are owners, employees, and customers, but others—government regulators, suppliers, social groups, etc.—are also important. Management involves planning, organizing, and controlling the tasks required to carry out the work of the company.

Marketing refers to those activities—research, product development, promotion, pricing, and distribution—designed to provide goods and services that satisfy customers. Finance refers to activities concerned with funding a business and using its funds effectively. Studying business can help you prepare for a career and become a better consumer.

### *Define economics and compare the four types of economic systems.*

Economics is the study of how resources are distributed for the production of goods and services within a social system; an economic system describes how a particular society distributes its resources. Communism is an economic system in which the people, without regard to class, own all the nation's resources. In a socialist system, the government owns and operates basic industries, but individuals own most businesses. Under capitalism, individuals own and operate the majority of businesses that provide goods and services. Mixed economies have elements from more than one economic system; most countries have mixed economies.

### Describe the role of supply, demand, and competition in a free-enterprise system.

In a free-enterprise system, individuals own and operate the majority of businesses, and the distribution of resources is determined by competition, supply, and demand. Demand is the number of goods and services that consumers are willing to buy at different prices at a specific time. Supply is the number of goods or services that businesses are willing to sell at different prices at a specific time. The price at which the supply of a product equals demand at a specific point in time is the equilibrium price. Competition is the rivalry among businesses to convince consumers to buy goods or services. Four types of competitive environments are pure competition, monopolistic competition, oligopoly, and monopoly. These economic concepts determine how businesses may operate in a particular society and, often, how much they can charge for their products.

### Specify why and how the health of the economy is measured.

A country measures the state of its economy to determine whether it is expanding or contracting and whether the country needs to take steps to minimize fluctuations. One commonly used measure is gross domestic product (GDP), the sum of all goods and services produced in a country during a year. A budget deficit occurs when a nation spends more than it takes in from taxes.

### Trace the evolution of the American economy and discuss the role of the entrepreneur in the economy.

The American economy has evolved through several stages: the early economy, the Industrial Revolution, the manufacturing economy, the marketing economy, and the service and Internet-based economy of today. Entrepreneurs play an important role because they risk their time, wealth, and efforts to develop new goods, services, and ideas that fuel the growth of the American economy.

### Evaluate a small-business owner's situation and propose a course of action.

"Solve the Dilemma" on page 30 presents a problem for the owner of the firm. Should you, as the owner, raise prices, expand operations, or form a venture with a larger company to deal with demand? You should be able to apply your newfound understanding of the relationship between supply and demand to assess the situation and reach a decision about how to proceed.

## Revisit the World of Business

1. Why do you think Crocs shoes are so successful in the marketplace?
2. Do Crocs appeal to consumers because of their unique technology or because they appeal to the fashion conscious?
3. What will be the global opportunities for selling Crocs in countries such as China, India or Brazil?

## Learn the Terms

| | | |
|---|---|---|
| budget deficit   18 | entrepreneur   22 | nonprofit organizations   5 |
| business   4 | equilibrium price   14 | oligopoly   15 |
| capitalism, or free enterprise   11 | financial resources   9 | product   4 |
| communism   11 | free-market system   12 | profit   5 |
| competition   14 | gross domestic product (GDP)   18 | pure competition   14 |
| demand   13 | human resources   9 | recession   17 |
| depression   17 | inflation   17 | socialism   11 |
| economic contraction   17 | mixed economies   12 | stakeholders   5 |
| economic expansion   16 | monopolistic competition   14 | supply   13 |
| economic system   10 | monopoly   15 | unemployment   17 |
| economics   9 | natural resources   9 | |

# Check Your Progress

1. What is the fundamental goal of business? Do all organizations share this goal?

2. Name the forms a product may take and give some examples of each.

3. Who are the main participants of business? What are the main activities? What other factors have an impact on the conduct of business in the United States?

4. What are four types of economic systems? Can you provide an example of a country using each type?

5. Explain the terms *supply, demand, equilibrium price,* and *competition.* How do these forces interact in the American economy?

6. List the four types of competitive environments and provide an example of a product of each environment.

7. List and define the various measures governments may use to gauge the state of their economies. If unemployment is high, will the growth of GDP be great or small?

8. Why are fluctuations in the economy harmful?

9. How did the Industrial Revolution influence the growth of the American economy? Why do we apply the term *service economy* to the United States today?

10. Explain the federal government's role in the American economy.

# Get Involved

1. Discuss the economic changes occurring in Russia and Eastern European countries, which once operated as communist economic systems. Why are these changes occurring? What do you think the result will be?

2. Why is it important for the government to measure the economy? What kinds of actions might it take to control the economy's growth?

3. Is the American economy currently expanding or contracting? Defend your answer with the latest statistics on GDP, inflation, unemployment, and so on. How is the federal government responding?

# Build Your Skills

### THE FORCES OF SUPPLY AND DEMAND

**Background**
WagWumps are a new children's toy with the potential to be a highly successful product. WagWumps are cute, furry, and their eyes glow in the dark. Each family set consists of a mother, a father, and two children. Wee-Toys' manufacturing costs are about $6 per set, with $3 representing marketing and distribution costs. The wholesale price of a WagWump family for a retailer is $15.75, and the toy carries a suggested retail price of $26.99.

**Task**
Assume you are a decision maker at a retailer, such as Target or Wal-Mart, that must determine the price the stores in your district should charge customers for the WagWump family set. From the information provided, you know that the SRP (suggested retail price) is $26.99 per set and that your company can purchase the toy set from your wholesaler for $15.75 each. Based on the following assumptions, plot your company's supply curve on the graph provided in Figure 1.6 and label it "supply curve."

| Quantity | Price |
|----------|-------|
| 3,000 | $16.99 |
| 5,000 | 21.99 |
| 7,000 | 26.99 |

Using the following assumptions, plot your customers' demand curve on Figure 1.6, and label it "demand curve."

| Quantity | Price |
|----------|-------|
| 10,000 | $16.99 |
| 6,000 | 21.99 |
| 2,000 | 26.99 |

For this specific time, determine the point at which the quantity of toys your company is willing to supply equals the quantity of toys the customers in your sales district are willing to buy, and label that point "equilibrium price."

**FIGURE I.6**

Equilibrium Price of
WagWumps

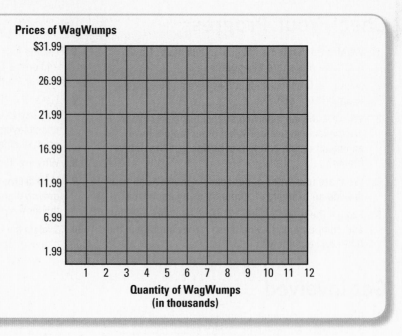

**Prices of WagWumps**

Graph with y-axis values: $31.99, 26.99, 21.99, 16.99, 11.99, 6.99, 1.99

**Quantity of WagWumps
(in thousands)**

x-axis values: 1 2 3 4 5 6 7 8 9 10 11 12

## Solve the Dilemma

### MRS. ACRES HOMEMADE PIES

Shelly Acres, whose grandmother gave her a family recipe for making pies, loved to cook so she decided to start a business she called Mrs. Acres Home-made Pies. The company produces specialty pies and sells them in local supermarkets and select family restaurants. In each of the first six months, Shelly and three part-time employees sold 2,000 pies for $4.50 each, netting $1.50 profit per pie. The pies were quite successful and Shelly could not keep up with demand. The company's success results from a quality product and productive employees who are motivated by incentives and who enjoy being part of a successful new business.

To meet demand, Shelly expanded operations, borrowing money and increasing staff to four full-time employees. Production and sales increased to 8,000 pies per month,

and profits soared to $12,000 per month. However, demand for Mrs. Acres Homemade Pies continues to accelerate beyond what Shelly can supply. She has several options: (1) maintain current production levels and raise prices; (2) expand the facility and staff while maintaining the current price; or (3) contract the production of the pies to a national restaurant chain, giving Shelly a percentage of profits with minimal involvement.

**Discussion Questions**

1. Explain and demonstrate the relationship between supply and demand for Mrs. Acres Homemade Pies.

2. What challenges does Shelly face as she considers the three options?

3. What would you do in Shelly's position?

## Build Your Business Plan

### THE DYNAMICS OF BUSINESS AND ECONOMICS

Have you ever thought about owning your business? If you have, how did your idea come about? Is it your experience with this particular field? Or might it be an idea that evolved from your desires

for a particular product or service not being offered in your community? For example, perhaps you and your friends have yearned for a place to go have coffee, relax, and talk. Now is an opportunity to create the café bar you have been thinking of!

Whether you consider yourself a visionary or a practical thinker, think about your community. What needs are not being met? While it is tempting to suggest a new restaurant (maybe even one near campus), easier-to-implement business plans can range from a lawn care business or a designated driver business, to a placement service agency for teenagers.

Once you have an idea for a business plan, think about how profitable this idea might be. Is there sufficient demand for this business? How large is the market for this particular business? What about competitors? How many are there?

To learn about your industry you should do a thorough search of your initial ideas of a product/service on the Internet.

# See for Yourself Videocase

### ENVIRONMENTAL RESPONSIBILITY: NEW BELGIUM BREWERY

While not everyone may recognize the name New Belgium Brewery, many people are familiar with Fat Tire beer, New Belgium's flagship brand. The brewery was founded by Jeff Lebesch, who first began brewing beer with a roommate in his basement. Although the first few attempts failed disastrously, he persevered. Later, Lebesch and his wife, Kim Jordon, continued to brew beer in their basement, eventually creating the now famous Fat Tire, named after the tires he used to mountain bike through villages in Europe famous for beer.

When Lebesch and Jordon first looked into brewing beer commercially, they were uninterested in taking on business partners and were turned down for business loans. Out of necessity, Lebesch embarked on a path of innovation and efficiency. Using old dairy equipment, he created a homebrewing kit and set about launching a business. The basement brewery officially went commercial in 1991, selling first to friends, family, and neighbors. A quality product, concern for employees and good environmental stewardship has led to fast sales growth, now making New Belgium the third largest craft brewer in the United States. The total craft brew industry makes up about 7% of the total beer market in the U.S. and is the fastest-growing segment of the U.S. alcoholic-beverage market.

For Lebesch and Jordon, the basement brewery turned out to be a blessing. Jordon became the brewery's first bottler, sales representative, distributor, marketer, and financial planner. (Today, she is CEO.) This, combined with the low overhead, allowed Lebesch the freedom to experiment with creative beer formulas and innovative techniques without panicking over bank payments and the expectations of investors.

From the beginning, Lebesch and Jordon have been concerned with the brewery's impact on the environment and have made every effort to minimize that impact. When they grew beyond the basement and created what is today's New Belgium brewery, they continued to put this concern at the forefront of all business operations. Today, the company is dedicated to balancing profitability with social and environmental responsibility. The brewery, continuing on that initial path of innovation and efficiency, has implemented a number of environmentally friendly practices. Some label it the green brewery. The company has used 100% wind-powered electricity since 1999, using sun-tubes, light shelves and evaporative coolers to reduce energy consumption. New Belgium is now using aluminum cans for some of its Fat Tire beer. Not only are aluminum cans more convenient for customers because they can be taken to places glass cannot, like baseball parks and other outdoor venues, but they are environmentally friendly as well.

Aluminum cans are 100 percent recyclable into new cans, and recycling just 1 can saves enough energy to power a 100-watt lightbulb for 4 hours or run your television for 3 hours.

Although many in the business world believe that to aid the environment is to destroy a business and to profit is to destroy the environment, New Belgium is an example of how a business can truly succeed financially while maintaining a dedication to the environment. Supporting this balance is the company's structure. New Belgium has what is called a horizontal hierarchy. After one year of employment, each employee becomes an owner in the brewery. All major decisions, such as the decision to use more expensive wind power, must be voted upon by employee-owners. And all owners work together to support the goals of the company. *Outside Magazine* named New Belgium the "Best Place to Work in America." The magazine took into account benefits, compensation, job satisfaction, and environmental initiatives and looks at companies with 250 or more employees. New Belgium's employee-owners have access to a volleyball court, a climbing wall, yoga, an indoor slide, a foosball table, and a ping-pong table. Each employee receives a signature Fat Tire bicycle after their first year, encouraging them to bike to work. At the five year mark, each employee receives a trip to Belgium to soak up the beer culture that started it all. It goes without saying that happy employees are bound to put their best into their company.

New Belgium began with innovation and a dedication to the environment and has stayed true to these elements throughout. As the company continues to grow, it focuses on the balance between profit and environmental steward-ship. Ever dedicated to bringing great, unique, and creative beer to its customers, today New Belgium is also striving to reduce its carbon footprint by 50 percent, reduce water usage by 10 percent, and increase waste stream diversion rate from 70–80 percent.[32]

**Discussion Questions**

1. What type(s) of business model(s) did Lebesch and Jordan develop with their brewery?

2. What are some of New Belgium's goals beyond sim-ply making a profit?

3. What does New Belgium do to make the workplace better for its employees?

**Remember to check out our Online Learning Center at www.mhhe.com/ferrell7e.**

# Appendix A

# Guidelines for the Development of the Business Plan

These guidelines are for students to create a hypothetical business plan for a product/service/business of their choice. Students should assume to have $25,000 to start this new business in their community.

At the end of every chapter there will be a section entitled "Build Your Business Plan" to assist you in the development of the business plan.

## Phase I: Development of the Business Proposal

You are encouraged to submit your idea for approval to your instructor as soon as possible. This will eliminate wasted effort on an idea that is not feasible in the instructor's view. Business plan proposals will be evaluated based on their thoroughness and your ability to provide support for the idea.

The business proposal consists of:

**Business Description.** This consists of an overview of the existing product/service or the product/service/business you will be starting (manufacturer, merchandiser, or service provider). This includes developing a mission (reason for existence; overall purpose of the firm) and a rationale for why you believe this business will be a success. What is your vision for this proposed product/business?

**Brief Marketing Plan.** (The marketing plan will be further developed as the plan evolves.) A description of your business/product/service is required. Identify the target market and develop a strategy for appealing to it. Justify your proposed location for this business. Describe how you will promote the new business and provide a rationale for your pricing strategy. Select a name for this business. The name should be catchy yet relate to the competencies of the business.

**Competitive Analysis.** Identify the competition as broadly as possible. Indicate why this business will be successful given the market.

## Phase 2: Final Written Business Plan

**Executive Summary.** The executive summary appears first, but should be written last.

**Business Description.** This section requires fleshing out the body of the business plan including material from your revised preliminary proposal with more data, charts, appendices. Include a description of the proposed form of organization, either a partnership or corporation, and the rationalization of the form chosen.

**Industry and Market Analysis.** An analysis of the industry including the growth rate of the industry and number of new entrants into this field is necessary. Identify uncontrollable variables within the industry. Determine an estimate of the proposed realistic size of the potential market. This will require interpretation of statistics from U.S. Census, as well as local sources such as the Chamber of Commerce.

**Competitive Analysis.** Include an exhaustive list of the primary and secondary competition, along with the competitive advantage of each.

**Marketing Strategy.** Target market specifics need to be developed.
Decisions on the marketing mix variables need to be made:

- Price (at the market, below market, above market).
- Promotion (sales associates, advertising budget, use of sales promotions, and publicity/goodwill).
- Distribution—Rationale of choice and level of distribution.
- Product/Service—A detailed rationale of the perceived differential advantage of your product/service offering.

**Operational Issues.**    How will you make or provide your product/service? Location rationale, facility type, leasing considerations and sources of suppliers need to be detailed. Software/hardware requirements necessary to maintain operations determined.

**Human Resource Requirement.**    Number and description of personnel needed including realistic required education and skills.

**Financial Projections.**    Statement of cash flows must be prepared for the first twelve months of the business. This must include start-up costs, opening expenses, estimation of cash inflows and outflows. A breakeven analysis should be included and an explanation of all financial assumptions.

**Appendices**

# Phase 3: Oral Presentation

Specific separate guidelines on the oral presentation will be provided.

chapter 2

## CHAPTER OUTLINE

Introduction

Business Ethics and
Social Responsibility

The Role of Ethics in
Business
*Recognizing Ethical Issues
in Business*
*Making Decisions about
Ethical Issues*
*Improving Ethical Behavior
in Business*

The Nature of Social
Responsibility
*Social Responsibility
Issues*

# Business Ethics and Social Responsibility

## OBJECTIVES

*After reading this chapter, you will be able to:*

- Define business ethics and social responsibility and examine their importance.

- Detect some of the ethical issues that may arise in business.

- Specify how businesses can promote ethical behavior.

- Explain the four dimensions of social responsibility.

- Debate an organization's social responsibilities to owners, employees, consumers, the environment, and the community.

- Evaluate the ethics of a business's decision.

## *Ethisphere* Links Ethics to Profits

*Ethisphere* magazine (www.ethisphere.com) is published by the Ethisphere Institute to illuminate the correlation between ethics and profits. Their mission is to "help corporate executives guide their enterprises toward gaining market share and creating sustainable competitive advantage through better business practices and corporate citizenship." Business has found that good ethics doesn't happen automatically. Employees need a shared vision that results in all employees abiding by the company's code of ethics and policies on business conduct. The editors and writers for the magazine attempt to determine absolute behaviors that can be utilized to differentiate one organization from another. For example, *Ethisphere* has developed a methodology to examine companies' codes of ethics and provide a grade for how the business compares with others. Issues relate to how the code itself is written, what it contains, what it omits, and how it is communicated. All play instrumental underlying roles in whether the code has the power to influence not only perceptions, but actions as well. For example, Centex Corp. received an A because of a terrific layout and thoughtful learning guide that speaks directly to employee conduct. An employee reporting mechanism called the "Speak Up" line was made very visible so that employees could easily discuss issues of concern. Other companies highly ranked in the study included Alcoa, Eaton Corporation, Kiplingers, GE, Kellogg's, and John Deere.

A recent ranking of government contractors found that Verizon Wireless had the best code of business ethics and the best overall ethics program. Other companies that were found to have high-ranking codes of ethics included General Electric, Procter & Gamble, Lockheed Martin, and

Honeywell. Companies use benchmarking, that is, comparing themselves with others in their industry, to gain insights about how to improve their code of ethics programs. Providing the criteria for evaluating codes of ethics also assists companies in developing and revising their codes. Organizations are expected to establish ethical standards and provide compliance systems to maintain appropriate conduct within all levels of the organization. Many companies are starting to recognize that providing jobs and profits are not sufficient criteria to be a responsible member of society. It is important to be socially responsible—that is, to work with stakeholders such as employees, customers, communities, and governments to make sure that the company does its part to minimize negative impacts on society and maximize contributions to important issues that are being addressed worldwide. Global warming, recycling, and sustainability are social responsibility issues; employee misconduct in performing business activities is a significant concern of business ethics. Both business ethics and social responsibility are essential parts of being a good corporate citizen.[1]

# Introduction

As the opening vignette illustrates, the Ethisphere Institute has taken on the challenge of contributing to society by linking ethics and profits. At the other extreme, wrongdoing by some businesses has focused public attention and government involvement on encouraging more acceptable business conduct. Any business decision may be judged as right or wrong, ethical or unethical, legal or illegal.

In this chapter, we take a look at the role of ethics and social responsibility in business decision making. First we define business ethics and examine why it is important to understand ethics' role in business. Next we explore a number of business ethics issues to help you learn to recognize such issues when they arise. Finally, we consider steps businesses can take to improve ethical behavior in their organizations. The second half of the chapter focuses on social responsibility. We survey some important responsibility issues and detail how companies have responded to them.

# Business Ethics and Social Responsibility

**business ethics**
principles and standards that determine acceptable conduct in business

In this chapter, we define **business ethics** as the principles and standards that determine acceptable conduct in business organizations. The acceptability of behavior in business is determined by customers, competitors, government regulators, interest groups, and the public, as well as each individual's personal moral principles and values. Enron, one of the largest ethical disasters in the 21st century, is an example. Two former Enron CEOs, Ken Lay and Jeff Skilling, were found guilty on all counts of conspiring to hide the company's financial condition. The judge in the case said the defendants could be found guilty of consciously avoiding knowing about wrongdoing at the company. Many other top executives including Andy Fastow, the chief financial officer, were found guilty of misconduct and are serving time in prison. The fall of Enron took many layers of management pushing the envelope

TABLE 2.I   A Timeline of Ethical and Socially Responsible Concerns

| 1960s | 1970s | 1980s | 1990s | 2000s |
|-------|-------|-------|-------|-------|
| • Environmental issues<br>• Civil rights issues<br>• Increased employee-employer tension<br>• Honesty<br>• Changing work ethic<br>• Rising drug use | • Employee militancy<br>• Human rights issues<br>• Covering up rather than correcting issues<br>• Discrimination<br>• Harassment | • Bribes and illegal contracting practices<br>• Influence peddling<br>• Deceptive advertising<br>• Financial fraud (e.g., savings and loan scandal)<br>• Transparency issues | • Sweatshops and unsafe working conditions in third-world countries<br>• Rising corporate liability for personal damages (e.g., cigarette companies)<br>• Financial mismanagement and fraud | • Employee benefits<br>• Privacy issues<br>• Financial mismanagement<br>• Intellectual property theft<br>• Responsible consumption<br>• The role of business in promoting sustainable development |

Source: Adapted from "Business Ethics Timeline," Copyright © 2003, *Ethics Resource Center* (n.d.), www.ethics.org, updated 2008. Used with permission.

and a great deal of complacency on the part of employees who saw wrongdoing and ignored it. Enron is not alone. Most unethical activities within organizations are supported by an organizational culture that encourages employees to bend the rules.[2]

Many consumers and social advocates believe that businesses should not only make a profit but also consider the social implications of their activities. We define **social responsibility** as a business's obligation to maximize its positive impact and minimize its negative impact on society. Although many people use the terms *social responsibility* and *ethics* interchangeably, they do not mean the same thing. Business ethics relates to an *individual's* or a *work group's* decisions that society evaluates as right or wrong, whereas social responsibility is a broader concept that concerns the impact of the *entire business's* activities on society. From an ethical perspective, for example, we may be concerned about a health care organization overcharging the government for Medicare services. From a social responsibility perspective, we might be concerned about the impact that this overcharging will have on the ability of the health care system to provide adequate services for all citizens. A more specific issue is the concern that mobile phone companies are acting irresponsibly by targeting children as young as 6 with brightly colored kiddie phones. Some worry that such phones addict the very young, and proper research has not yet been conducted on the health risks to young brains and tissue.[3]

The most basic ethical and social responsibility concerns have been codified by laws and regulations that encourage businesses to conform to society's standards, values, and attitudes. For example, after accounting scandals at a number of well-known firms in the early 2000s shook public confidence in the integrity of Corporate America, the reputations of every U.S. company suffered regardless of their association with the scandals.[4] To help restore confidence in corporations and markets, Congress passed the Sarbanes-Oxley Act, which criminalized securities fraud and stiffened penalties for corporate fraud. At a minimum, managers are expected to obey all laws and regulations. Most legal issues arise as choices that society deems unethical, irresponsible, or otherwise unacceptable. However, all actions deemed unethical by society are not necessarily illegal, and both legal and ethical concerns change over time (see Table 2.1). Business law refers to the laws and regulations that

**social responsibility** a business's obligation to maximize its positive impact and minimize its negative impact on society govern the conduct of business. Many problems and conflicts in business can be avoided if owners, managers, and employees know more about business law and the legal system. Business ethics, social responsibility, and laws together act as a compliance system, requiring that businesses and employees act responsibly in society. In this chapter, we explore ethics and social responsibility; Appendix A addresses business law, including the Sarbanes-Oxley Act.

# The Role of Ethics in Business

You have only to pick up *The Wall Street Journal* or *USA Today* to see examples of the growing concern about legal and ethical issues in business. HealthSouth, for example, has joined the growing list of companies tarnished by accounting improprieties and securities fraud. Former CEO Richard Scrushy was indicted for allegedly conspiring to inflate the health care firm's reported revenues by $2.7 billion to meet shareholder expectations. Although Scrushy pleaded "not guilty" to the 85 criminal charges, 15 former HealthSouth executives have admitted to participating in the deception. Scrushy was ultimately acquitted by a jury trial in the first attempt to hold a chief executive accountable under the Sarbanes-Oxley Act. The defense called the star witness, former HealthSouth finance chief William T. Owens, a big rat.[5] Scrushy was found guilty on six counts of bribery and mail fraud by an Alabama court for paying an Alabama governor to be on the state hospital regulatory board. He plans to appeal the conviction. Regardless of what an individual believes about a particular action, if society judges it to be unethical or wrong, whether correctly or not, that judgment directly affects the organization's ability to achieve its business goals.[6]

Well-publicized incidents of unethical and illegal activity—ranging from accounting fraud to using the Internet to steal another person's credit-card number, from deceptive advertising of food and diet products to unfair competitive practices in the computer software industry—strengthen the public's perceptions that ethical standards and the level of trust in business need to be raised. Author David Callahan has commented, "Americans who wouldn't so much as shoplift a pack of chewing gum are committing felonies at tax time, betraying the trust of their patients, misleading investors, ripping off their insurance companies, lying to their clients, and much more."[7] Often, such charges start as ethical conflicts but evolve into legal disputes when cooperative conflict resolution cannot be accomplished. Headline-grabbing scandals like Enron are not limited to the United States. For example, in Germany the president of Deutsche Post AG, parent of DHL, had to resign after being accused of tax evasion.[8] In the United States, Charles O. Prince III, former CEO of Citigroup; Stanley O'Neal, former CEO of Merrill Lynch; and Angela Mozilo, founder and CEO of Countrywide Financial, rejected suggestions that they reaped lavish compensation packages while engaging in highly risky subprime lending associated with an international financial crisis. While O'Neal was fired for Merrill Lynch's poor performance, he was given a $161 million severance package on top of the $70 million he earned during four years as CEO.[9]

However, it is important to understand that business ethics goes beyond legal issues. Ethical conduct builds trust among individuals and in business relationships, which validates and promotes confidence in business relationships. Establishing trust and confidence is much more difficult in organizations that have reputations for acting unethically. If you were to discover, for example, that a manager had misled you about company benefits when you were hired, your trust and confidence in that company would probably diminish. And if you learned that a colleague had lied to you about something, you probably would not trust or rely on that person in the future.

Ethical issues are not limited to for-profit organizations either. In government, several politicians and some high-ranking officials have been forced to resign in disgrace over ethical indiscretions. Irv Lewis "Scooter" Libby, a White House advisor, was indicted on five counts of criminal charges: one count of obstruction of justice, two counts of perjury, and two counts of making false statements. Libby was convicted on four of those counts in 2007. Although President Bush commuted the sentence, Libby was still ordered to pay a $250,000 fine.[10] While serving as attorney general of New York, Eliot Spitzer had a reputation for fighting crime. He too has stumbled into an ethical mess of his own making. The New York governor appeared in a federal complaint charging others with managing an international prostitution ring. Spitzer was named as a client of the crime ring, having hired a prostitute in Washington, D.C., for $4,300.[11] During his race for governor of New York, Spitzer spoke of his duties as attorney general, saying: "I had a simple rule. I never asked if a case was popular or unpopular. I never asked if it was big or small, hard or easy. I simply asked if it was right or wrong." Spitzer resigned as governor of New York, his career destroyed by his misconduct. Even sports can be subject to ethical lapses. At many universities, for example, coaches and athletic administrators have been put on administrative leave after allegations of improper recruiting practices came to light.[12] Jimmy Johnson's crew chief, Chad Knaus, was thrown out of the Daytona 500 for illegal modifications made to Johnson's car during NASCAR pole qualifying. Although Johnson finished fifth in qualifying, he was required to start from the rear of the field. He then went on to win the Daytona 500.[13] Thus, whether made in science, politics, sports, or business, most decisions are judged as right or wrong, ethical or unethical. Negative judgments can affect an organization's ability to build relationships with customers and suppliers, attract investors, and retain employees.[14]

Although we will not tell you in this chapter what you ought to do, others—your superiors, co-workers, and family—will make judgments about the ethics of your actions and decisions. Learning how to recognize and resolve ethical issues is an important step in evaluating ethical decisions in business.

## Recognizing Ethical Issues in Business

Learning to recognize ethical issues is the most important step in understanding business ethics. An **ethical issue** is an identifiable problem, situation, or opportunity that requires a person to choose from among several actions that may be evaluated as right or wrong, ethical or unethical. In business, such a choice often involves weighing monetary profit against what a person considers appropriate conduct. The best way to judge the ethics of a decision is to look at a situation from a customer's or competitor's viewpoint: Should liquid-diet manufacturers make unsubstantiated claims about their products? Should an engineer agree to divulge her former employer's trade secrets to ensure that she gets a better job with a competitor? Should a salesperson omit facts about a product's poor safety record in his presentation to a customer? Such questions require the decision maker to evaluate the ethics of his or her choice.

Many business issues may seem straightforward and easy to resolve or the surface, but are in reality very complex. A person often needs several years of experience in business to understand what is acceptable or ethical. For example, if you

**ethical issue** an identifiable problem, situation, or opportunity that requires a person to choose from among several actions that may be evaluated as right or wrong, ethical or unethical

**TABLE 2.2**    Types and Incidences of Observed Misconduct

| Type of Conduct Observed | Employees Observing It |
|---|---|
| Putting own interests ahead of organization | 22% |
| Abusive behavior | 21 |
| Lying to employees | 20 |
| Misreporting hours worked | 17 |
| Internet abuse | 16 |
| Safety violations | 15 |
| Lying to stakeholders | 14 |
| Discrimination | 13 |
| Stealing | 11 |

Source: "National Business Ethics Survey 2007: An Inside View of Private Sector Ethics," *Ethics Resource Center,* http://www.ethics.org/ (accessed April 4, 2008).

are a salesperson, when does offering a gift—such as season basketball tickets—to a customer become a bribe rather than just a sales practice? Clearly, there are no easy answers to such a question. But the size of the transaction, the history of personal relationships within the particular company, as well as many other factors may determine whether an action will be judged as right or wrong by others. Companies across the United States are starting to prevent access to Internet-video services at work. At issue is the theft of time by employees, who use YouTube and MySpace for an hour on average each workday.[15] Another issue is the use of company resources to provide personal internet access.

Ethics is also related to the culture in which a business operates. In the United States, for example, it would be inappropriate for a businessperson to bring an elaborately wrapped gift to a prospective client on their first meeting—the gift could be viewed as a bribe. In Japan, however, it is considered impolite *not* to bring a gift. Experience with the culture in which a business operates is critical to understanding what is ethical or unethical.

To help you understand ethical issues that perplex businesspeople today, we will take a brief look at some of them in this section. Ethical issues can be more complex now than in the past. The vast number of news-format investigative programs has increased consumer and employee awareness of organizational misconduct. In addition, the multitude of cable channels and Internet resources has improved the awareness of ethical problems among the general public. The National Business Ethics Survey of more than 3,400 U.S. employees found that workers witness many instances of ethical misconduct in their organizations (see Table 2.2). The most common types of observed misconduct in the private sector were putting one's own interests ahead of the organization, abusive behavior, and lying to employees.[16]

One of the principal causes of unethical behavior in organizations is overly aggressive financial or business objectives. Many of these issues relate to decisions and concerns that managers have to deal with daily. It is not possible to discuss every issue, of course. However, a discussion of a few issues can help you begin to recognize the ethical problems with which businesspersons must deal. Many ethical issues in business can be categorized in the context of their relation with abusive and intimidating behavior, conflicts of interest, fairness and honesty, communications, and business associations.

**Abusive and Intimidating Behavior.**   Abusive or intimidating behavior is the second most common ethical problem for employees. These concepts can mean anything from physical threats, false accusations, being annoying, profanity, insults, yelling, harshness, ignoring someone, to unreasonableness; and the meaning of these words can differ by person—you probably have some ideas of your own. Abusive behavior can be placed on a continuum from a minor distraction to a disruption of the workplace. For example, what one person may define as yelling might be another's definition of normal speech. Civility in our society is a concern, and the workplace is no exception. The productivity level of many organizations has been diminished by the time spent unraveling abusive relationships.

Abusive behavior is difficult to assess and manage because of diversity in culture and lifestyle. What does it mean to speak profanely? Is profanity only related to specific words or other such terms that are common in today's business world? If you are using words that are normal in your language but others consider profanity, have you just insulted, abused, or disrespected them?

Within the concept of abusive behavior, intent should be a consideration. If the employee was trying to convey a compliment but the comment was considered abusive, then it was probably a mistake. The way a word is said (voice inflection) can be important. Add to this the fact that we now live in a multicultural environment—doing business and working with many different cultural groups—and the businessperson soon realizes the depth of the ethical and legal issues that may arise. There are problems of word meanings by age and within cultures. For example an expression such as "Did you guys hook up last night?" can have various meanings, including some that could be considered offensive in a work environment.

Bullying is associated with a hostile workplace when a person or group is targeted and is threatened, harassed, belittled, verbally abused, or overly criticized. Bullying may create what some consider a hostile environment, a term generally associated with sexual harassment. Although sexual harassment has legal recourse, bullying has little legal recourse at this time. Bullying is a widespread problem in the United States, and can cause psychological damage that can result in health endangering consequences to the target. The Workplace Bullying Institute's latest survey found that "37% of U.S. workers have been bullied, that is 54 million Americans."[17] Another 12 percent of workers have witnessed bullying. As Table 2.3 indicates, bullying can use a mix of verbal, nonverbal, and manipulative threatening expressions to damage workplace productivity. One may wonder why workers tolerate such activities,

| | |
|---|---|
| 1. Spreading rumors to damage others | **TABLE 2.3** |
| 2. Blocking others' communication in the workplace | Actions Associated with Bullies |
| 3. Flaunting status or authority to take advantage of others | |
| 4. Discrediting others ideas and opinions | |
| 5. Use of e-mails to demean others | |
| 6. Failing to communicate or return communication | |
| 7. Insults, yelling, and shouting | |
| 8. Using terminology to discriminate by gender, race, or age | |
| 9. Using eye or body language to hurt others or their reputation | |
| 10. Taking credit for others' work or ideas | |

Source: © O. C. Ferrell, 2008.

the problem is that 81 percent of workplace bullies are supervisors. A top officer at Boeing cited an employee survey indicating 26 percent had observed abusive or intimidating behavior by management.[18]

**Conflict of Interest.**   A conflict of interest, the most common ethical issue identified by employees, exists when a person must choose whether to advance his or her own personal interests or those of others. For example, a manager in a corporation is supposed to ensure that the company is profitable so that its stockholder-owners receive a return on their investment. In other words, the manager has a responsibility to investors. If she instead makes decisions that give her more power or money but do not help the company, then she has a conflict of interest—she is acting to benefit herself at the expense of her company and is not fulfilling her responsibilities as an employee. To avoid conflicts of interest, employees must be able to separate their personal financial interests from their business dealings. For example, a $1 million donation by Citigroup to the 92nd Street Y nursery school represents a possible conflict of interest. Jack Grubman, an analyst for Salomon Smith Barney, upgraded his rating for AT&T stock after Sanford Weill, the CEO of Citigroup (the parent company of Salomon Smith Barney), agreed to use his influence to help Grubman's twins gain admission to the elite Manhattan nursery school. During the late 1990s, Weill, an AT&T board member, had been upset that Citigroup wasn't getting any of AT&T's business. Grubman changed AT&T's rating to buy, and a year later bragged in an e-mail that he had made the switch to placate Weill in exchange for Weill's help in getting Grubman's children into the 92nd Street Y nursery school. Grubman has denied elevating his rating for AT&T's stock to gain his children admission to the school, but they were enrolled. Industry leaders still avoid him, publicly anyway, but on the fringes of telecom, Grubman has had no trouble finding people who are willing to overlook his past or are simply unaware of it. According to a *Fortune* article, although Grubman was "banned from Wall Street, the former Telecom King wants to prove that he wasn't a huckster."[19]

**bribes**
payments, gifts, or special favors intended to influence the outcome of a decision

As mentioned earlier, it is considered improper to give or accept **bribes**—payments, gifts, or special favors intended to influence the outcome of a decision. A bribe is a conflict of interest because it benefits an individual at the expense of an organization or society. Companies that do business overseas should be aware that bribes are a significant ethical issue and are, in fact, illegal in many countries. For example, three former executives of IBM Korea went to jail in Seoul after being convicted of using bribes to win orders for computer parts.[20] While bribery is an increasing issue in many countries, it is more prevalent in some countries than in others. Transparency International has developed a Corruption Perceptions Index (Table 2.4). Note there are 19 countries perceived as less corrupt than the United States.[21]

**Fairness and Honesty.**   Fairness and honesty are at the heart of business ethics and relate to the general values of decision makers. At a minimum, business persons are expected to follow all applicable laws and regulations. But beyond obeying the law, they are expected not to harm customers, employees, clients, or competitors knowingly through deception, misrepresentation, coercion, or discrimination. Honesty and fairness can relate to how the employees use the resources of the organization. More than two-thirds of employees have taken office supplies from work to use for matters unrelated to their job. Most employees do not view taking office supplies as stealing or dishonest, with 97 percent saying they have never gotten caught and it would not matter if they were. In addition, only 3.7 percent say they

| Rank | Country | CPI Score[*] |
|---|---|---|
| 1 | Finland/Denmark/New Zealand | 9.4 |
| 4 | Singapore/Sweden | 9.3 |
| 6 | Iceland | 9.2 |
| 7 | Netherlands/Switzerland | 9.0 |
| 9 | Canada/Norway | 8.7 |
| 11 | Australia | 8.6 |
| 12 | Luxembourg/United Kingdom | 8.4 |
| 14 | Hong Kong | 8.3 |
| 15 | Austria | 8.1 |
| 16 | Germany | 7.8 |
| 17 | Ireland/Japan | 7.5 |
| 19 | France | 7.3 |
| 20 | United States | 7.2 |

**TABLE 2.4**

Corruption Perceptions Index

[*]CPI score relates to perceptions of the degree of corruption as seen by businesspeople and country analysts, and ranges between 10 (highly clean) and 0 (highly corrupt).

Source: "Transparency International 2007 Corruption Perception Index," Transparency International, http://www.transparency.org/policy_research/surveys_indices/cpi/2007 (accessed April 4, 2008).

have taken items like keyboards, software, and memory sticks. Still, an employee should be aware of policies on taking items and recognize how these decisions relate to ethical behavior.[22] Figure 2.1 on page 46 provides an overview of the most pilfered office supplies.

One aspect of fairness relates to competition. Although numerous laws have been passed to foster competition and make monopolistic practices illegal, companies sometimes gain control over markets by using questionable practices that harm competition. Bullying can also occur between companies that are intense competitors. Even respected companies such as Intel have been accused of monopolistic bullying. A competitor, Advanced Micro Devices (AMD), claimed in a lawsuit that 38 companies, including Dell and Sony, were strong-arming customers (such as Apple) into buying Intel chips rather than those marketed by AMD. The AMD lawsuit seeks billions of dollars and will take years to litigate. In many cases, the alleged misconduct can have not only monetary and legal implications but can threaten reputation, investor confidence, and customer loyalty. A front-cover *Forbes* headline stated "Intel to ADM: Drop Dead." The intensely competitive atmosphere and Intel's ability to use its large size won it the high-profile Apple account, displacing IBM and Freescale. ADM claims it had no opportunity to bid because Intel had offered to deploy 600 Indian engineers to help Apple software run more smoothly on Intel chips.[23]

Another aspect of fairness and honesty relates to disclosure of potential harm caused by product use. Mitsubishi Motors, Japan's number-four automaker, faced criminal charges and negative publicity after executives admitted that the company had systematically covered up customer complaints about tens of thousands of defective automobiles over a 20-year period. They allegedly made the cover-up in order to avoid expensive and embarrassing product recalls.[24]

Dishonesty has become a significant problem in the United States. As reported earlier in this chapter, lying was the second most observed form of misconduct

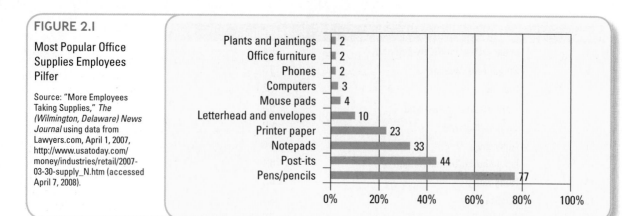

**FIGURE 2.1**

Most Popular Office Supplies Employees Pilfer

Source: "More Employees Taking Supplies," *The (Wilmington, Delaware) News Journal* using data from Lawyers.com, April 1, 2007, http://www.usatoday.com/money/industries/retail/2007-03-30-supply_N.htm (accessed April 7, 2008).

in the National Business Ethics Survey. Dishonesty is not found only in business, however.

A survey of nearly 25,000 high school students revealed that 62 percent of the students admitted to cheating on an exam at least once, 35 percent confessed to copying documents from the Internet, 27 percent admitted to shoplifting, and 23 percent owned up to cheating in order to win in sports.[25] If today's students are tomorrow's leaders, there is likely to be a correlation between acceptable behavior today and tomorrow. This adds to the argument that the leaders of today must be prepared for the ethical risks associated with this downward trend. According to a poll by Deloitte and Touche of teenagers aged 13 to 18, when asked if people who practice good business ethics are more successful than those who don't, 69 percent of teenagers agreed.[26] The same poll found only 12 percent of teens think business leaders today are ethical. On the other hand, another survey indicated that many students do not define copying answers from another students' paper or download-ing music or content for classroom work as cheating.[27]

**Communications.**   Communications is another area in which ethical concerns may arise. False and misleading advertising, as well as deceptive personal-selling tac-tics, anger consumers and can lead to the failure of a business. Truthfulness about product safety and quality are also important to consumers. Claims about dietary supplements and weight-loss products can be particularly problematic. For exam-ple, the Fountain of Youth Group LLC and its founder, Edita Kaye, settled charges brought by the Federal Trade Commission that the company made unsubstantiated claims about its weight-loss products. Under the settlement, the firm agreed to stop making specific weight-loss and health claims without competent scientific proof. It was also fined $6 million, but that fine was suspended because the firm lacked the resources to pay it.[28]

Some companies fail to provide enough information for consumers about dif-ferences or similarities between products. For example, driven by high prices for medicines, many consumers are turning to Canadian, Mexican, and overseas Inter-net sources for drugs to treat a variety of illnesses and conditions. However, research suggests that a significant percentage of these imported pharmaceuticals may not actually contain the labeled drug, and the counterfeit drugs could even be harmful to those who take them.[29]

Another important aspect of communications that may raise ethical concerns relates to product labeling. The U.S. Surgeon General currently requires cigarette

# Consider Ethics and Social Responsibility
## Repainting Mattel's Image

What comes to mind when you think "Mattel"? Do you remember the Mattel toys that you loved as a kid; that you've purchased for your children, nieces, or nephews? Or do you think of recalls and danger? During 2007 alone, Mattel was required to recall millions of toys, creating negative press and horrified parents. As Christmas 2007 loomed, Mattel was struggling to revive its image, as the company seemed in danger of consumer abandonment. Parents interviewed throughout the United States were vowing to steer clear of toys sold by Mattel. So what caused the recalls and the uproar? Although responsibility ultimately rests with Mattel, the issue brought to light was Mattel's relationship with and reliance on Chinese toy manufacturers—companies that proved not to adhere to U.S. safety standards.

A recent estimate indicates that China produces 70 to 80 percent of all toys sold in the United States. It is a challenge for any shopper to avoid purchasing toys made in China. So what about China's manufacturing process caused Mattel to recall so many children's products? The answer might shock us in the United States—lead paint! You might ask hasn't this been outlawed? Yes, paint containing more than 0.06 percent lead has been banned for residential use since 1978. So, how could this toxic substance possibly end up on children's toys? It turns out that the rules set for residential paint do not translate to paint used on toys. It is no secret that companies such as Mattel produce their toys in China in order to cut costs, even though China has different health and safety standards than the United States. Does this create a problem? It certainly looks like it does.

As Mattel struggles to convince consumers that these mistakes will never be repeated, many are wondering how well the company will survive this scandal. As much as the company might like to place the blame on China, it is Mattel's ultimate responsibility to ensure the production of safe toys. The U.S. Consumer Product Safety Commission is now working with China to eliminate the use of lead paint in production, but what is Mattel doing? According to the company, production processes and testing procedures have been strengthened. It claims to have implemented a "3-stage safety check" designed to make sure that all paint is tested prior to use, testing and unannounced inspections are also being increased, and every production run will be tested before toys are released. The company, which has also been saddled with issues resulting from recalls of toys containing small magnets that were found to be choking hazards, continues to scramble to put a fresh veneer on its tainted image. However, some analysts suggest that the best move would be to break off relations with China altogether. Others suggest that Mattel ought to become more actively involved in helping China work toward stricter rules and the use of safer products. Therefore, as Mattel works to correct its mistakes and China starts to strengthen its regulations, consumers will be watching and thinking twice before purchasing toys labeled "Mattel" and "Made in China."[30]

### Discussion Questions

1. Lead paint in toys may not technically be illegal, so what did Mattel do wrong in this situation? Could the company have prevented this crisis? How?

2. Now that the damage has been done, what can Mattel do to restore its image?

3. Lead paint on toys is not the only health hazard scare coming out of China (there have also been problems with tainted medicines, fish with high levels of mercury, and other products containing high levels of lead). Should U.S. companies stop sourcing goods from China? Why or why not?

manufacturers to indicate clearly on cigarette packaging that smoking cigarettes is harmful to the smoker's health. In Europe, at least 30 percent of the front side of product packaging and 40 percent of the back needs to be taken up by the warning. The use of descriptors such as "light" or "mild" has been banned.[31] However, labeling of other products raises ethical questions when it threatens basic rights, such as freedom of speech and expression. This is the heart of the controversy surrounding the movement to require warning labels on movies and videogames, rating their content, language, and appropriate audience age. Although people in the entertainment industry claim that such labeling violates their First Amendment right to freedom of expression, other consumers—particularly parents—believe that labeling is needed to protect children from harmful influences. Similarly, alcoholic beverage and cigarette manufacturers have argued that a total ban on cigarette and alcohol advertisements violates the First Amendment. Internet regulation, particularly that designed to protect children and the elderly, is on the forefront in consumer protection legislation. Because of the debate surrounding the acceptability of these business activities, they remain major ethical issues.

**Business Relationships.**   The behavior of businesspersons toward customers, suppliers, and others in their workplace may also generate ethical concerns. Ethical behavior within a business involves keeping company secrets, meeting obligations and responsibilities, and avoiding undue pressure that may force others to act unethically.

Managers, in particular, because of the authority of their position, have the opportunity to influence employees' actions. For example, a manager might influence employees to use pirated computer software to save costs. The use of illegal software puts the employee and the company at legal risk, but employees may feel pressured to do so by their superior's authority. The National Business Ethics Survey found that employees who feel pressure to compromise ethical standards view top and middle managers as the greatest source of such pressure.[32]

It is the responsibility of managers to create a work environment that helps the organization achieve its objectives and fulfill its responsibilities. However, the methods that managers use to enforce these responsibilities should not compromise employee rights. Organizational pressures may encourage a person to engage in activities that he or she might otherwise view as unethical, such as invading others' privacy or stealing a competitor's secrets. For example, Betty Vinson, an accounting executive at WorldCom, protested when her superiors asked her to make improper accounting entries in order to cover up the company's deteriorating financial condition. She acquiesced only after being told that it was the only way to save the troubled company. She, along with several other WorldCom accountants, pleaded guilty to conspiracy and fraud charges related to WorldCom's bankruptcy after the accounting improprieties came to light.[33] The firm may provide only vague or lax supervision on ethical issues, creating the opportunity for misconduct. Managers who offer no ethical direction to employees create many opportunities for manipulation, dishonesty, and conflicts of interest.

**plagiarism**
the act of taking someone else's work and presenting it as your own without mentioning the source

**Plagiarism**—taking someone else's work and presenting it as your own without mentioning the source—is another ethical issue. As a student, you may be familiar with plagiarism in school; for example, copying someone else's term paper or quoting from a published work or Internet source without acknowledging it. In business, an ethical issue arises when an employee copies reports or takes the work or ideas of others and presents it as his or her own. At *USA Today,* for example, an internal investigation into the work of veteran reporter Jack Kelley identified dozens of stories in which Kelley appeared to have plagiarized material from competing newspapers. The investigation also uncovered evidence Kelley fabricated significant portions of at least eight major stories and conspired to cover up his lapses in judgment. The newspaper later apologized to its readers, and Kelley resigned.[34] A manager attempting to take credit for a subordinate's ideas is engaging in another type of plagiarism.

## Making Decisions about Ethical Issues

Although we've presented a variety of ethical issues that may arise in business, it can be difficult to recognize specific ethical issues in practice. Whether a decision maker recognizes an issue as an ethical one often depends on the issue itself. Managers, for example, tend to be more concerned about issues that affect those close to them, as well as issues that have immediate rather than long-term consequences. Thus, the

| TABLE 2.5 |
|---|
| Are there any potential legal restrictions or violations that could result from the action? |
| Does your company have a specific code of ethics or policy on the action? |
| Is this activity customary in your industry? Are there any industry trade groups that provide guidelines or codes of conduct that address this issue? |
| Would this activity be accepted by your co-workers? Will your decision or action withstand open discussion with co-workers and managers and survive untarnished? |
| How does this activity fit with your own beliefs and values? |

**TABLE 2.5**

Questions to Consider in Determining Whether an Action Is Ethical

perceived importance of an ethical issue substantially affects choices. However, only a few issues receive scrutiny, and most receive no attention at all.[35]

Table 2.5 lists some questions you may want to ask yourself and others when trying to determine whether an action is ethical. Open discussion of ethical issues does not eliminate ethical problems, but it does promote both trust and learning in an organization.[36] When people feel that they cannot discuss what they are doing with their co-workers or superiors, there is a good chance that an ethical issue exists. Once a person has recognized an ethical issue and can openly discuss it with others, he or she has begun the process of resolving that issue.

## Improving Ethical Behavior in Business

Understanding how people make ethical choices and what prompts a person to act unethically may reverse the current trend toward unethical behavior in business. Ethical decisions in an organization are influenced by three key factors: individual moral standards, the influence of managers and co-workers, and the opportunity to engage in misconduct (Figure 2.2). While you have great control over your personal ethics outside the workplace, your co-workers and superiors exert significant control over your choices at work through authority and example. In fact, the activities and examples set by co-workers, along with rules and policies established by the firm, are critical in gaining consistent ethical compliance in an organization. If the company fails to provide good examples and direction for appropriate conduct, confusion and conflict will develop and result in the opportunity for misconduct. If your boss or co-workers leave work early, you may be tempted to do so as well. If you see co-workers engaged in personal activities such as shopping online or watching YouTube, then you may be more likely to do so also. In addition, having sound personal values contributes to an ethical workplace.

Because ethical issues often emerge from conflict, it is useful to examine the causes of ethical conflict. Business managers and employees often experience some tension between their own ethical beliefs and their obligations to the organizations in which they work. Many employees utilize different ethical standards at work than

**FIGURE 2.2**

Three Factors That Influence Business Ethics

Individual Standards and Values + Managers' and Co-workers' Influence + Opportunity: Codes and Compliance Requirements = Ethical/Unethical Choices in Business

**TABLE 2.6**

Key Things to Consider in Developing a Code of Ethics

- Create a team to assist with the process of developing the code (include management and nonmanagement employees from across departments and functions).
- Solicit input from employees from different departments, functions, and regions to compile a list of common questions and answers to include in the code document.
- Make certain that the headings of the code sections can be easily understood by all employees.
- Avoid referencing specific U.S. laws and regulations or those of specific countries, particularly for codes that will be distributed to employees in multiple regions.
- Hold employee group meetings on a complete draft version (including graphics and pictures) of the text using language that everyone can understand.
- Inform employees that they will receive a copy of the code during an introduction session.
- Let all employees know that they will receive future ethics training which will, in part, cover the important information contained in the code document.

Source: Adapted from William Miller, "Implementing an Organizational Code of Ethics," *International Business Ethics Review* 7 (Winter 2004), pp. 1, 6–10.

**codes of ethics**
formalized rules and standards that describe what a company expects of its employees

they do at home. This conflict increases when employees feel that their company is encouraging unethical conduct or exerting pressure on them to engage in it.

It is difficult for employees to determine what conduct is acceptable within a company if the firm does not have established ethics policies and standards. And without such policies and standards, employees may base decisions on how their peers and superiors behave. Professional **codes of ethics** are formalized rules and standards that describe what the company expects of its employees. Codes of ethics do not have to be so detailed that they take into account every situation, but they should provide guidelines and principles that can help employees achieve organizational objectives and address risks in an acceptable and ethical way. The development of a code of ethics should include not only a firm's executives and board of directors, but also legal staff and employees from all areas of a firm.[37] Table 2.6 lists some key things to consider when developing a code of ethics.

Codes of ethics, policies on ethics, and ethics training programs advance ethical behavior because they prescribe which activities are acceptable and which are not, and they limit the opportunity for misconduct by providing punishments for violations of the rules and standards. According to the National Business Ethics Survey (NBES), employees in organizations that have written standards of conduct, ethics training, ethics offices or hotlines, and systems for anonymous reporting of misconduct are more likely to report misconduct when they observe it. The survey also found that such programs are associated with higher employee perceptions that they will be held accountable for ethical infractions.[38] The enforcement of such codes and policies through rewards and punishments increases the acceptance of ethical standards by employees.

One of the most important components of an ethics program is a means through which employees can report observed misconduct anonymously. The NBES found that although employees are increasingly reporting illegal and unethical activities they observe in the workplace, 54 percent of surveyed employees indicated they are unwilling to report misconduct because they fear that no corrective action will be taken, or that their report will not remain confidential.[39] The lack of anonymous reporting mechanisms may encourage **whistleblowing,** which occurs when an employee exposes an employer's wrongdoing to outsiders, such as the media or government regulatory agencies. However, more companies are establishing programs

**whistleblowing**
the act of an employee exposing an employer's wrongdoing to outsiders, such as the media or government regulatory agencies

to encourage employees to report illegal or unethical practices internally so that they can take steps to remedy problems before they result in legal action or generate negative publicity. In recent years, whistle-blowers have provided crucial evidence documenting illegal actions at a number of companies. At Enron, for example, Sherron Watkins, a vice president, warned the firm's CEO, Ken Lay, that the energy company was using improper accounting procedures. Lay forwarded Watkins's concerns to Vinson and Elkins, Enron's outside lawyers, and they provided opinion letters approving the questionable transactions. Watkins also took her concerns to senior accountants at Arthur Andersen, and it is unclear if any action was taken. Watkins sold some of her Enron stock based on her knowledge, but was not indicted for insider trading. Soon after, Watkins testified before Congress that Enron had con-cealed billions of dollars in debt through a complex scheme of off-balance sheet partnerships.[40] Enron ultimately went bankrupt when its improprieties and high levels of debt were exposed. Unfortunately, whistleblowers are often treated nega-tively in organizations. The government seeks to discourage this practice by reward-ing firms that encourage employees to report misconduct—with reduced fines and penalties when violations occur.

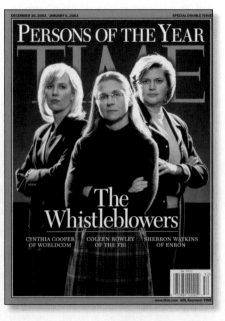

Sherron Watkins, Colleen Rowley, and Cynthia Cooper (left to right) jeopardized their careers by blowing the whistle at Enron, the FBI, and WorldCom, respectively. The three women later ended up on the cover of Time after being named the magazine's 2002 "Persons of the Year."

The current trend is to move away from legally based ethical initiatives in orga-nizations to cultural- or integrity-based initiatives that make ethics a part of core organizational values. Organizations recognize that effective business ethics pro-grams are good for business performance. Firms that develop higher levels of trust function more efficiently and effectively and avoid damaged company reputations and product images. Organizational ethics initiatives have been supportive of many positive and diverse organizational objectives, such as profitability, hiring, employee satisfaction, and customer loyalty.[41] Conversely, lack of organizational ethics ini-tiatives and the absence of workplace values such as honesty, trust, and integrity can have a negative impact on organizational objectives and employee retention. According to one report on employee loyalty and work practices, 79 percent of employees who questioned their bosses' integrity indicated that they felt uncom-mitted or were likely to quit soon.[42]

# The Nature of Social Responsibility

There are four dimensions of social responsibility: economic, legal, ethical, and voluntary (including philanthropic) (Figure 2.3).[43] Earning profits is the economic foundation of the pyramid in Figure 2.3, and complying with the law is the next step. However a business whose *sole* objective is to maximize profits is not likely to consider its social responsibility, although its activities will probably be legal. (We looked at ethical responsibilities in the first half of this chapter.) Finally, voluntary responsibilities are additional activities that may not be required but which promote

**FIGURE 2.3**

The Pyramid of Social
Responsibility

Source: Reprinted with
permission from A. B. Carroll,
"The Pyramid of Corporate
Social Responsibility: Toward
the Moral Management of
Organizational Stakeholders,"
*Business Horizons,* July/August
1991. Copyright © 1991 by the
Board of Trustees at Indiana
University, Kelley School of
Business.

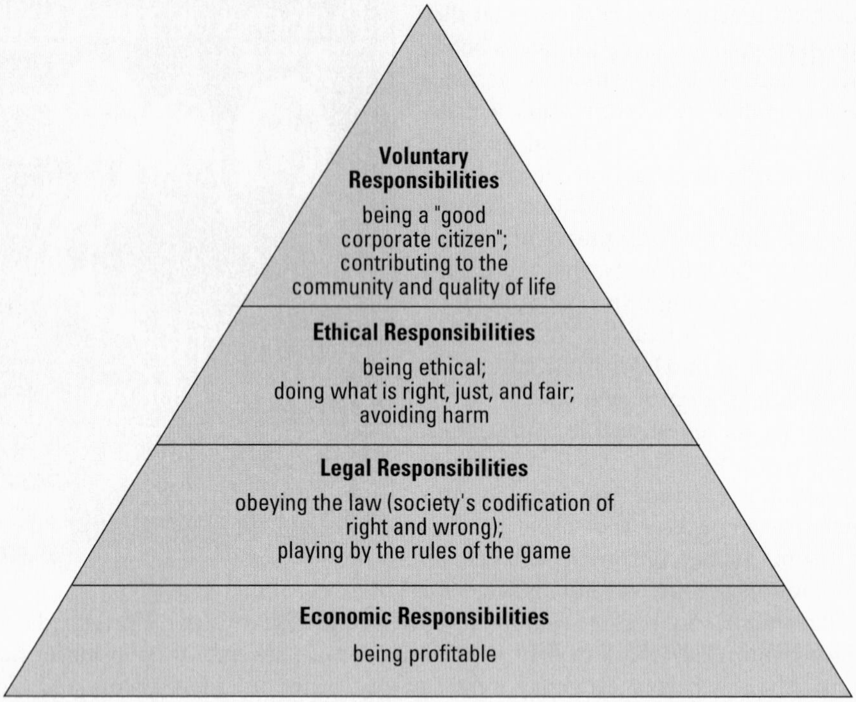

**Voluntary
Responsibilities**
being a "good
corporate citizen";
contributing to the
community and quality of life

**Ethical Responsibilities**
being ethical;
doing what is right, just, and fair;
avoiding harm

**Legal Responsibilities**
obeying the law (society's codification of
right and wrong);
playing by the rules of the game

**Economic Responsibilities**
being profitable

**corporate citizenship**
the extent to which
businesses meet the
legal, ethical, eco-
nomic, and voluntary
responsibilities placed
on them by their stake-
holders

human welfare or goodwill. Legal and economic concerns have long been acknowledged in business, but voluntary and ethical issues are more recent concerns.

**Corporate citizenship** is the extent to which businesses meet the legal,
ethical, economic, and voluntary responsibilities placed on them by their various stakeholders. It involves the activities and organizational processes adopted
by businesses to meet their social responsibilities. A commitment to corporate
citizenship by a firm indicates a strategic focus on fulfilling the social responsibilities expected of it by its stakeholders. Corporate citizenship involves action
and measurement of the extent to which a firm embraces the corporate citizenship philosophy and then follows through by implementing citizenship and social
responsibility initiatives. One of the major corporate citizenship issues is the focus
on preserving the environment. Consumers, governments, and special interest
groups such as The Nature Conservancy are concerned about greenhouse gases
and $CO_2$ carbon emissions that are contributing to global warming. The United
States was the number-one $CO_2$ producer, at nearly a quarter of the world's greenhouse gas emissions, until China's emissions surpassed the country sometime in
2006 or 2007. The majority of people agree that climate change is a global emergency, but there is not agreement on how to solve the problem.[44] One study done
at Princeton University calls for a reduction of 25 billion tons of carbon emissions
over the next 50 years—the equivalent of erasing nearly four years of global emissions at today's rates.[45]

Part of the answer to this crisis is alternative energy such as solar, wind, biofuels,
and hydro applications. The American Solar Energy Society estimates that the

| 1 | Intel Corp. | **TABLE 2.7** |
| 2 | Eaton Corp. | Best Corporate Citizens |
| 3 | Nike Inc. | |
| 4 | Deere and Co. | |
| 5 | Genentech Inc. | |
| 6 | Corning Inc. | |
| 7 | Humana Inc. | |
| 8 | Bank of America Corp. | |
| 9 | ITT Corp. | |
| 10 | PG&E Corp. | |
| 11 | Dominion Resources Inc. | |
| 12 | State Street Corp. | |
| 13 | Dow Chemical Co. | |
| 14 | Cisco Systems Inc. | |
| 15 | Wisconsin Energy Corp. | |
| 16 | Progress Energy Inc. | |
| 17 | Entergy Corp. | |
| 18 | Norfolk Southern Corp. | |
| 19 | Sun Microsystems Inc. | |
| 20 | Public Service Enterprise Group Inc. | |

Source: Dennis Schaal, "100 Best Corporate Citizens 2008," *Corporate Responsibility Officer,* http://www.thecro.com/files/100best-JanFeb08-Listing.pdf (accessed April 4, 2008).

number of "green" jobs could rise to 40 million by 2030.[46] The drive for alternative fuels such as ethanol from corn has added new issues such as food price increases and food shortages. More than 2 billion consumers earn less than $2 a day in wages. Sharply increased food costs has led to riots and government policies to restrict trade in basic commodities such as rice, corn, and soybeans.[47]

To respond to these developments, most companies are introducing eco-friendly products and marketing efforts. Americans as consumers are generally concerned about the environment, but only 47 percent trust companies to tell them the truth in environmental marketing.[48] This is because most businesses are promoting themselves as green-conscious and concerned about the environment without actually making the necessary commitments to environmental health. Even employees feel their employers aren't doing enough to protect the environment, with nearly 60 percent feeling that more needs to be to done to reduce, recycle, and support green policies.[49]

*Corporate Responsibility Officer (CRO)* magazine publishes an annual list of the 100 best American corporate citizens based on service to seven stakeholder groups: stockholders, local communities, minorities, employees, global stakeholders, customers, and the environment. Table 2.7 shows the top 20 from that list.

Although the concept of social responsibility is receiving more and more attention, it is still not universally accepted. Table 2.8 lists some of the arguments for and against social responsibility.

| TABLE 2.8 | **For:** |
|---|---|
| The Arguments For and Against Social Responsibility | 1. Business helped to create many of the social problems that exist today, so it should play a significant role in solving them, especially in the areas of pollution reduction and cleanup. |
| | 2. Businesses should be more responsible because they have the financial and technical resources to help solve social problems. |
| | 3. As members of society, businesses should do their fair share to help others. |
| | 4. Socially responsible decision making by businesses can prevent increased government regulation. |
| | 5. Social responsibility is necessary to ensure economic survival: If businesses want educated and healthy employees, customers with money to spend, and suppliers with quality goods and services in years to come, they must take steps to help solve the social and environmental problems that exist today. |
| | **Against:** |
| | 1. It sidetracks managers from the primary goal of business—earning profits. Every dollar donated to social causes or otherwise spent on society's problems is a dollar less for owners and investors. |
| | 2. Participation in social programs gives businesses greater power, perhaps at the expense of particular segments of society. |
| | 3. Some people question whether business has the expertise needed to assess and make decisions about social problems. |
| | 4. Many people believe that social problems are the responsibility of government agencies and officials, who can be held accountable by voters. |

## Social Responsibility Issues

As with ethics, managers consider social responsibility on a daily basis. Among the many social issues that managers must consider are their firms' relations with owners and stockholders, employees, consumers, the environment, and the community. For example, Indra Nooyi, CEO of PepsiCo, believes that companies must embrace "purpose," not just for financial results, but also for the imprint they leave on society. She goes on to say that stakeholders, including employees, consumers, and regulators, "will leave no doubt that performance without purpose is not a long-term sustainable formula."[50]

Social responsibility is a dynamic area with issues changing constantly in response to society's demands. There is much evidence that social responsibility is associated with improved business performance. Consumers are refusing to buy from businesses that receive publicity about misconduct. A number of studies have found a direct relationship between social responsibility and profitability, as well as a link that exists between employee commitment and customer loyalty—two major concerns of any firm trying to increase profits.[51] This section highlights a few of the many social responsibility issues that managers face; as managers become aware of and work toward the solution of current social problems, new ones will certainly emerge.

**Relations with Owners and Stockholders.**   Businesses must first be responsible to their owners, who are primarily concerned with earning a profit or a return on their investment in a company. In a small business, this responsibility is fairly easy to fulfill because the owner(s) personally manages the business or knows the managers well. In larger businesses, particularly corporations owned by thousands of stockholders, ensuring responsibility becomes a more difficult task.

# Destination CEO
## Bakery with a Conscience

The Dancing Deer Baking Company, located in Boston, Massachusetts, is one of a growing number of small companies that takes social responsibility seriously. They bake all of their products from all-natural ingredients and mix them all with a liberal helping of social conscientiousness. Social responsibility is clearly a core value for Dancing Deer. Social responsibility is practiced both internally with its employees, and externally, with the community. All employees have a direct stake in the company with ownership interests, a practice introduced when the company was only two years old and hadn't yet posted a profit. Employee ownership is only one of a number of progressive employee benefits provided by the company. In addition to strong employee relations, Trish Karter, the company's CEO, is committed to the social cause of ensuring that people are educated and can play productive roles in society. To support this core value, she has emphasized social programs sponsored by the company.

The company was founded in 1994, its core values of social responsibility driving its mission. That remains true today. The company contributes 35 percent of proceeds from one of its product lines to the Sweet Home Project that provides education and a fresh start for those who have had unfortunate lives: drug addictions, poverty, single parents, and other challenges. While Dancing Deer may be a small business, it bakes up a large number of cookies and brownies each day: 43,000 cookies and 12,000 brownies, daily! The company has experienced growth each year, with $10.5 million in sales—up 30 percent from 2006. CEO Trish Karter is not satisfied, however. The company has a goal of $50 million in sales within the next few years.

### Discussion Questions

1. Do you think that Dancing Deer Bakery's social responsibility can positively affect sales? Why or why not?
2. What is the difference between business ethics and social responsibility? In which does Dancing Deer Bakery's programs fit best?
3. Dancing Deer Bakery prides itself on its employee relations. Why are employee relations important?

A business's obligations to its owners and investors, as well as to the financial community at large, include maintaining proper accounting procedures, providing all relevant information to investors about the current and projected performance of the firm, and protecting the owners' rights and investments. In short, the business must maximize the owners' investment in the firm.

**Employee Relations.** Another issue of importance to a business is its responsibilities to employees. Without employees, a business cannot carry out its goals. Employees expect businesses to provide a safe workplace, pay them adequately for their work, and keep them informed of what is happening in their company. They want employers to listen to their grievances and treat them fairly. When employees at Ramtech Building Systems Inc. approached management with their concerns about cursing used in the company's manufacturing facilities, a Language Code of Ethics was instituted. Many employees indicate that obscene language is common in the workplace, particularly in high-stress jobs. For example, 43 percent of the 12,000 U.S. Postal Service employees surveyed recently reported being cursed at in the workplace.[52] Companies are adjusting their policies and offering training to clean up employee language.

*BNSF Railways offers its workers a whole host of employee health-related services, including weight management help and smoking cessation programs.*

# Entrepreneurship in Action
## Capturing Wind to Power the Future

David Calley and Andy Kruse

**Business:** Southwest Windpower

**Founded:** 1987

**Success:** Skystream 3.7 named a Top 10 Green Building Project by *Sustainable Industries* magazine

Companies globally and nationally are jumping on the renewable energy bandwagon, as consumers demand more environmentally friendly alternatives to traditional coal-fired electricity. Consumers are seeking to minimize their carbon footprint and their global greenhouse gas emissions, while at the same time circumnavigating higher energy costs. This being the case, the idea that consumers might generate their own electricity via wind turbines has never been more viable. Southwest Windpower, based in Flagstaff, Arizona, has recognized this tremendous market niche. The Skystream 3.7 is the newest creation from Southwest to hit the markets. At between 34 and 70 feet tall, with 12-foot rotors, the Skystream 3.7 is capable of producing power with breezes of 8 mph and achieves full output in 23 mph winds. The Skystream can be installed in lots as small as one acre, and is exceptionally quiet. (Its range of 40 to 50 decibels is quieter than the average background noise level in an office.) The target market is not yet the average consumer, as costs per turbine range from $12,000 to $15,000. However, depending on installation costs, wind-speed average, rebates, and local electricity costs, the Skystream 3.7 can pay for itself in as little as five years. With energy use at an all-time high and increasing, consumers are demanding more environmentally friendly alternatives. The wind turbines produced by Southwest Windpower hold a lot of potential and may soon be a viable energy alternative for a much broader range of consumers.[53]

Congress has passed several laws regulating safety in the workplace, many of which are enforced by OSHA. Labor unions have also made significant contributions to achieving safety in the workplace and improving wages and benefits. Most organizations now recognize that the safety and satisfaction of their employees are critical ingredients in their success, and many strive to go beyond what is legally expected of them. Healthy, satisfied employees also supply more than just labor to their employers. Employers are beginning to realize the importance of obtaining input from even the lowest-level employees to help the company reach its objectives.

A major social responsibility for business is providing equal opportunities for all employees regardless of their sex, age, race, religion, or nationality. Women and minorities have been slighted in the past in terms of education, employment, and advancement opportunities; additionally, many of their needs have not been addressed by business. For example, as many as 1.6 million current and former female Wal-Mart employees filed a class-action discrimination lawsuit accusing the giant retailer of paying them lower wages and salaries than it does men in comparable positions. Pretrial proceedings not only uncovered discrepancies between the pay of men and women but also the fact that men dominate higher-paying store manager positions while women occupy more than 90 percent of cashier jobs, most of which pay about $14,000 a year. Wal-Mart faces fines and penalties in the millions of dollars if found guilty of sexual discrimination.[54] Women, who continue to bear most child-rearing responsibilities, often experience conflict between those responsibilities and their duties as employees. Consequently, day care has become a major employment issue for women, and more companies are providing day care facilities as part of their effort to recruit and advance women in the workforce. In addition, companies are considering alternative scheduling such as flex-time and job sharing to accommodate employee concerns. Telecommuting has grown significantly over the past 5 to 10 years as well. Many Americans today believe business has a social obligation to provide special opportunities for women and minorities to improve their standing in society.

**Consumer Relations.**   A critical issue in business today is business's responsibility to customers, who look to business to provide them with satisfying, safe products and to respect their rights as consumers. The activities that independent individuals, groups, and organizations undertake to protect their rights as consumers are known as **consumerism.** To achieve their objectives, consumers and their advocates write letters to companies, lobby government agencies, make public service announcements, and boycott companies whose activities they deem irresponsible.

**consumerism**
the activities that independent individuals, groups, and organizations undertake to protect their rights as consumers

Many of the desires of those involved in the consumer movement have a foundation in John F. Kennedy's 1962 consumer bill of rights, which highlighted four rights. The *right to safety* means that a business must not knowingly sell anything that could result in personal injury or harm to consumers. Defective or dangerous products erode public confidence in the ability of business to serve society. They also result in expensive litigation that ultimately increases the cost of products for all consumers. The right to safety also means businesses must provide a safe place for consumers to shop. In recent years, many large retailers have been under increasing pressure to improve safety in their large warehouse-type stores. At The Home Depot, for example, three consumer deaths and numerous serious injuries have been caused by falling merchandise. One lawsuit brought against the company over injuries received in one of its stores resulted in a $1.5 million judgment. To help prevent further deaths, injuries, and litigation, The Home Depot now has a corporate safety officer and has hired 130 safety managers to monitor store compliance with new safety measures.[55]

The *right to be informed* gives consumers the freedom to review complete information about a product before they buy it. This means that detailed information about ingredients, risks, and instructions for use are to be printed on labels and packages. The *right to choose* ensures that consumers have access to a variety of products and services at competitive prices. The assurance of both satisfactory quality and service at a fair price is also a part of the consumer's right to choose. Some consumers are not being given this right. Many are being billed for products and services they never ordered. According to the Federal Trade Commission, complaints about unordered merchandise and services recently jumped 169 percent over a two-year period. The *right to be heard* assures consumers that their interests will receive full and sympathetic consideration when the government formulates policy. It also assures the fair treatment of consumers who voice complaints about a purchased product.

The role of the Federal Trade Commission's Bureau of Consumer Protection exists to protect consumers against unfair, deceptive, or fraudulent practices. The bureau, which enforces a variety of consumer protection laws, is divided into five divisions. The Division of Enforcement monitors legal compliance and investigates violations of laws, including unfulfilled holiday delivery promises by online shopping sites, employment opportunities fraud, scholarship scams, misleading advertising for health care products, and more.

*The Home Depot acknowledges the importance of all stakeholders in operating its business.*

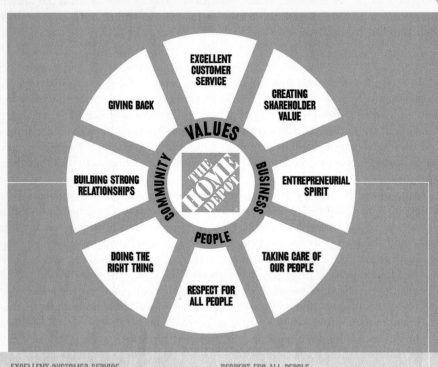

**EXCELLENT CUSTOMER SERVICE**

Along with our quality products, service, price and selection, we must go the extra mile to give customers knowledgeable advice about merchandise and to help them use those products to their maximum benefit.

**CREATING SHAREHOLDER VALUE**

The investors who provide the capital necessary to allow our Company to grow need and expect a return on their investment. We are committed to providing it.

**ENTREPRENEURIAL SPIRIT**

The Home Depot associates are encouraged to initiate creative and innovative ways of serving our customers and improving the business, as well as to adopt good ideas from others.

**TAKING CARE OF OUR PEOPLE**

The key to our success is treating people well. We do this by encouraging associates to speak up and take risks, by recognizing and rewarding good performance and by leading and developing people so they may grow.

**RESPECT FOR ALL PEOPLE**

In order to remain successful, our associates must work in an environment of mutual respect where each associate is regarded as part of The Home Depot team.

**DOING THE RIGHT THING**

We exercise good judgment by "doing the right thing" instead of just "doing things right." We strive to understand the impact of our decisions, and we accept responsibility for our actions.

**BUILDING STRONG RELATIONSHIPS**

Strong relationships are built on trust, honesty and integrity. We listen and respond to the needs of customers, associates, communities and vendors, treating them as partners.

**GIVING BACK**

An important part of the fabric of The Home Depot is in giving our time, talents, energy and resources to worthwhile causes in our communities and society.

**Environmental Issues.** Environmental responsibility has become a leading issue as both business and the public acknowledge the damage done to the environment in the past. Today's consumers are increasingly demanding that businesses take a greater responsibility for their actions and how they impact the environment.

*Animal Rights.* One area of environmental concern in society today is animal rights. Probably the most controversial business practice in this area is testing of cosmetics and drugs on animals, that may be injured or killed as a result. Animal-rights activists, such as People for the Ethical Treatment of Animals (PETA), say such research is morally wrong because it harms living creatures. Consumers who share this sentiment may boycott companies that test products on animals and take their business instead to companies, such as The Body Shop and John Paul Mitchell Systems, that do not use animal testing. However, researchers in the cosmetics and pharmaceutical industries argue that animal testing is necessary to prevent harm to human beings who will eventually use the products. Business practices that harm endangered wildlife and their habitats are another environmental issue.

*MooShoes, Inc., is a vegan-owned business that sells an assortment of cruelty-free footwear, bags, t-shirts, wallets, books, and other accessories. MooShoes offers its services through an online store as well as in its retail store in New York City, the first cruelty-free store of its kind in New York City.*

**Pollution.**   Another major issue in the area of environmental responsibility is pollution. Water pollution results from dumping toxic chemicals and raw sewage into rivers and oceans, oil spills, and the burial of industrial waste in the ground where it may filter into underground water supplies. Fertilizers and insecticides used in farming and grounds maintenance also run off into water supplies with each rainfall. Water pollution problems are especially notable in heavily industrialized areas. Medical waste—such as used syringes, vials of blood, and HIV-contaminated materials—has turned up on beaches in New York, New Jersey, and Massachusetts, as well as other places. Society is demanding that water supplies be clean and healthful to reduce the potential danger from these substances.

Air pollution is usually the result of smoke and other pollutants emitted by manufacturing facilities, as well as carbon monoxide and hydrocarbons emitted by motor vehicles. In addition to the health risks posed by air pollution, when some chemical compounds emitted by manufacturing facilities react with air and rain, acid rain results. Acid rain has contributed to the deaths of many forests and lakes in North America as well as in Europe. Air pollution may also contribute to global warming;

| | |
|---|---|
| • 50 percent of National Association of Home Builders members incorporate "green" into their building practices. | Facts Related to Reducing Energy Consumption |
| • 2 percent of homes built in 2006 were considered "green." By 2010, that number will rise to an estimated 10 percent of homes built. | |
| • You can make 20 cans out of recycled material with the same amount of energy it takes to make one new one. | |
| • About 2,700 pounds of $CO_2$ per person annually (18 percent of total emissions) come from operating our homes, and most of that is from the energy used to power electrical appliances. | |
| • ENERGY STAR appliances incorporate advanced technologies that use between 10 and 15 percent less energy and water than standard models. | |
| • Preventing one ton of paper waste saves between 15 and 17 medium-sized trees. | |

Source: The National Association of Home Builders; http://www.epa.gov; NAHB House Keys, March 2007.

# Going Green

## EarthCraft Houses: Crafted for Earth

These days, almost everyone seems to be going green. However, most people seek easy solutions, such as purchasing local organic produce, buying chemical-free household products, or driving a hybrid car. Most of us probably believe that not many people live in homes that are entirely "green." Although it may not be page-one news, the green trend is growing in today's housing market. Among those companies promoting green living is EarthCraft House. Founded in 1999 by the Atlanta Home Builders Association and Southface Home, EarthCraft aims to build comfortable homes that reduce utility costs while at the same time benefiting the environment.

As of 2007, EarthCraft House had certified more than 4,000 single-family homes and 1,500 multifamily dwelling units within the Atlanta metro area. Atlanta also boasts six EarthCraft communities. EarthCraft House has expanded beyond Georgia to South Carolina, Alabama, Tennessee, and Virginia. All are supported by local state agencies and home-builder's associations. Similar organizations exist in Florida (Green Building Coalition) and North Carolina (Healthy Built Homes).

So, what is an EarthCraft house? The house can be newly constructed or renovated, and can be tailored to fit price point. To be certified by EarthCraft, a house must meet certain guidelines in energy efficiency, durability, indoor air quality, resource efficiency, waste management, and water conservation. All new homes must meet ENERGY STAR certification criteria and must score at least 150 points on an EarthCraft scoring sheet. Those homes that score 200 or 230 points are awarded *select* or *premium* status, respectively.

So, how does an EarthCraft house benefit the environment, and how does it benefit the homeowner? To answer these questions, a little background information is required. Construction and maintenance of homes and offices are major sources of $CO_2$ emissions. EarthCraft houses, on the other hand, can reduce emissions by more than 1,100 pounds of greenhouse gases per home each year. EarthCraft homes also use many recycled and renewable materials as possible, as well as conserving water and reducing storm water pollution.

Homeowner benefits are twofold. One of the aims of EarthCraft is to create a healthier home. For example, an EarthCraft home can reduce levels of mold, mildew, and dust. Therefore EarthCraft homes can benefit our bodies in addition to reducing our carbon footprint. An EarthCraft home can also benefit our wallets. EarthCraft home buyers can take advantage of two different kinds of mortgage incentives. The Energy Efficient Mortgage increases the buyer's purchasing power due to the lower operating costs of an energy-efficient home. The Energy Improvement Mortgage can be used to finance energy-efficient upgrades on an existing home. All in all, EarthCraft and similar companies predict that by 2010, 10 percent of all homes will be green.[56]

### Discussion Questions

1. In addition to reducing carbon dioxide emissions, what are other reasons to build an energy-efficient, "green" house?
2. What type of incentive would cause you to pay extra for an energy-efficient house?
3. What additional incentives might convince people to go green when building or remodeling their homes?

as carbon dioxide collects in the earth's atmosphere, it traps the sun's heat and prevents the earth's surface from cooling. It is indisputable that the global surface temperature has been increasing over the past 35 years. Worldwide passenger vehicle ownership has been growing due to rapid industrialization and consumer purchasing power in China, India, and other developing countries with large populations. The most important way to contain climate change is to control carbon emissions. The move to green buildings, higher-mileage cars, and other emissions reductions resulting from better efficiency have the potential to generate up to 50 percent of the reductions needed to keep warming at no more than 2° C above present temperatures—considered the "safe" level.[57] The 2007 U.S. Federal Energy bill raised average fuel economy (CAFE) standards to 35 mpg for cars by 2020, while Europe has the goal of a 40 mpg standard by the same deadline. Because buildings create half of U.S. greenhouse emissions, there is tremendous opportunity to develop conservation measures. For example, some utilities charge more for electricity in peak demand periods, which encourages behavioral changes that reduce consumption. On the positive side, there are more than 100 million bicycles produced annually worldwide, more than double the passenger vehicles produced.[58]

Land pollution is tied directly to water pollution because many of the chemicals and toxic wastes that are dumped on the land eventually work their way into the water supply. A 2008 study conducted by the Environmental Protection Agency found residues of prescription drugs, soaps, and other contaminants in virtually every waterway in the United States. Effects of these pollutants on humans and wildlife are uncertain, but there is some evidence to suggest that fish and other water-dwellers are starting to suffer serious effects.[59] Land pollution results from the dumping of residential and industrial waste, strip mining, forest fires, and poor forest conservation. In Brazil and other South American countries, rain forests are being destroyed—to make way for farms and ranches, at a cost of the extinction of the many animals and plants (some endangered species) that call the rain forest home. In the second half of 2007 alone, an area the size of Rhode Island was lost in the Brazilian Amazon—a rate that is speeding up as agriculture becomes a more attractive industry.[60] Large-scale deforestation also depletes the oxygen supply available to humans and other animals.

Related to the problem of land pollution is the larger issue of how to dispose of waste in an environmentally responsible manner. Americans are producing more trash, with the average person producing about 5 pounds of trash every day, up from about 3.3 pounds in 1970. At the same time, more than 30 percent of Americans recycle, up from 8 percent in 1970.[61] Americans use 100 billion plastic bags each year, which is between 10 and 20 percent of the total global usage (estimated at 500 billion to 1 trillion bags).[62] It takes 1,000 years for the bags to decompose. San Francisco has banned plastic bags; Ireland is now charging a nationwide tax of 15 cents on all supermarket shopping bags; and Australia and China are planning a similar program.[63] Whole Foods, the nation's leading natural and organic supermarket, ended its use of plastic bags on Earth Day 2008.[64] Whole Foods estimates that this move will keep 150 million new plastic grocery bags out of the environment each year.

*Response to Environmental Issues.*   Partly in response to federal legislation such as the National Environmental Policy Act of 1969 and partly due to consumer concerns, businesses are responding to environmental issues. Many small and large companies, including Walt Disney Company, Chevron, and Scott Paper, have created a new executive position—a vice president of environmental affairs—to help them achieve their business goals in an environmentally responsible manner. A survey indicated that 83.5 percent of *Fortune* 500 companies have a written environmental policy, 74.7 percent engage in recycling efforts, and 69.7 percent have made investments in waste-reduction efforts.[65] In early 2008, the EPA announced that 53 *Fortune* 500 companies had exceeded their goals for purchasing green energy credits.[66] Many companies, including Alcoa, Dow Chemical, Phillips Petroleum, and Raytheon, now link executive pay to environmental performance.[67] Some companies are finding that environmental consciousness can save them money. DuPont saved more than $3 billion through energy conservation by replacing natural gas with methane in its industrial boilers in many of its plants.[68]

Many firms are trying to eliminate wasteful practices, the emission of pollutants, and/or the use of harmful chemicals from their manufacturing processes. Other companies are seeking ways to improve their products. Utility providers, for example, are increasingly supplementing their services with

**Did You Know?**   In one year, Americans generated 230 million tons of trash and recycled 23.5 percent of it.[69]

alternative energy sources, including solar, wind, and geothermal power. Duke Power is the third largest corporate emitter of carbon dioxide (after American Electric Power and Southern Companies) in the United States. Duke is proactively going green with 500,000 solar panels on rooftops over a five-state territory. The utility is also installing a $1 billion communication network to optimize the flow of electricity through the grid. The firm is looking to nuclear power plants and a Save-A-Watt program to encourage consumers to use less energy. Environmentalists are concerned that the company is merely *greenwashing,* or "creating a positive association with environmental issues for an unsuitable product, service, or practice." Even while preaching conservation as a solution, Duke plans to invest $23 billion in the next five years to build new coal and gas plants.[70] In many places, local utility customers can even elect to purchase electricity from green sources—primarily wind power—for a few extra dollars a month. Austin Energy of Austin, Texas, has an award-winning GreenChoice program that includes many small and large businesses among its customers.[71] Indeed, a growing number of businesses and consumers are choosing green power sources where available. New Belgium Brewing, the third largest craft brewer in the United States, is the first all-wind-powered brewery in the country. Many businesses have turned to *recycling,* the reprocessing of materials—aluminum, paper, glass, and some plastic—for reuse. Such efforts to make products, packaging, and processes more environmentally friendly have been labeled "green" business or marketing by the public and media. Lumber products at The Home Depot may carry a seal from the Forest Stewardship Council to indicate that they were harvested from sustainable forests using environmentally friendly methods.[72] Likewise, most Chiquita bananas are certified through the Better Banana Project as having been grown with more environmentally and labor-friendly practices.[73]

It is important to recognize that, with current technology, environmental responsibility requires trade-offs. Society must weigh the huge costs of limiting or eliminating pollution against the health threat posed by the pollution. Environmental responsibility imposes costs on both business and the public. Although people certainly do not want oil fouling beautiful waterways and killing wildlife, they insist on low-cost, readily available gasoline and heating oil. People do not want to contribute to the growing garbage-disposal problem, but they often refuse to pay more for "green" products packaged in an environmentally friendly manner, to recycle as much of their own waste as possible, or to permit the building of additional waste-disposal facilities (the "not in my backyard," or NIMBY, syndrome). Managers must coordinate environmental goals with other social and economic ones.

**Community Relations.**   A final, yet very significant, issue for businesses concerns their responsibilities to the general welfare of the communities and societies in which they operate. Many businesses simply want to make their communities better places for everyone to live and work. The most common way that businesses exercise their community responsibility is through donations to local and national charitable organizations. Corporations contribute more than $12 billion each year to environmental and social causes.[74] For example, Safeway, the nation's fourth-largest grocer, has donated millions of dollars to organizations involved in medical research, such as Easter Seals and the Juvenile Diabetes Research Foundation International. The company's employees have also raised funds to support social causes of interest.[75] Avon's Breast Cancer Awareness Crusade has helped raise $300 million to fund community-based breast cancer education and early detection services. Avon, a marketer of women's cosmetics, is also known for employing a large number of women and promoting them to top management; the firm has more female top managers (86 percent) than any other *Fortune* 500 company.[76] Even small companies participate in philanthropy through donations and volunteer support of local causes and national charities, such as the Red Cross and the United Way.

After realizing that the current pool of prospective employees lacks many basic skills necessary to work, many companies have become concerned about the quality of education in the United States. Recognizing that today's students are tomorrow's employees and customers, firms such as Kroger, Campbell's Soup, Kodak, American Express, Apple Computer, Xerox, and Coca-Cola are donating money, equipment, and employee time to help improve schools in their communities and around the nation. They provide scholarship money, support for teachers, and computers for students, and they send employees out to tutor and motivate young students to stay in school and succeed. Target, for example, contributes significant resources to education, including direct donations of $100 million to schools as well as fund-raising and scholarship programs that assist teachers and students. Through the retailer's Take Charge of Education program, customers using a Target Guest Card can designate a specific school to which Target donates 1 percent of their total purchase price. This program is designed to make customers feel that their purchases are benefiting their community while increasing the use of Target Guest Cards.[77]

*Many companies encourage their employees to volunteer for charitable organizations such as Habitat for Humanity.*

Another tactic taken by some companies is to let consumers decide whether they want to contribute to socially responsible activities. What if Dell sold one notebook computer for $1,000 and the same computer for $1,150, with the understanding that the purchase of *this* computer would support the fight against AIDS around the world? Dell and Microsoft recently created products for the Product(Red) campaign, joining other large corporations such as The Gap, Apple, and Motorola in support of The Global Fund, an international organization fighting AIDS, tuberculosis, and malaria. The Product(Red) computer sold by Dell is significant to consumers and communicates their support to others.[79]

Business is also beginning to take more responsibility for the hard-core unemployed. These are people who have never had a job or who have been unemployed for a long period of time. Some are mentally or physically handicapped; some are homeless. Organizations such as the National Alliance of Businessmen fund programs to train the hard-core unemployed so that they can find jobs and support themselves. In addition to fostering self-support, such opportunities enhance self-esteem and help people become productive members of society.

# So You Want a Job in Business Ethics and Social Responsibility

In the words of Kermit the Frog, "It's not easy being green." Maybe it is not easy, however, green business opportunities abound. A popular catch phrase, "Green is the new black," indicates how fashionable green business is becoming. Consumers are more in tune with and concerned about green products, policies, and behaviors by companies than ever before. Companies are looking for new hires to help them see their business creatively and bring insights to all aspects of business operations. The American Solar Energy Society estimates that the number of green jobs could rise to 40 million in the United States by 2030. Green business strategies not only give a firm a commercial advantage in the marketplace, but help lead the way toward a greener world. The fight to reduce our carbon footprint in an attempt against climate change has opened up opportunities for renewable energy, recycling, conservation and increasing overall efficiency in the way resources are used. New businesses that focus on hydro, wind, and solar power are on the rise and will need talented business people to lead them. Carbon emissions' trading is gaining popularity as large corporations and individuals alike seek to lower their footprints. A job in this growing field could be similar to that of a stock trader or you could lead the search for carbon efficient companies in which to invest.

In the ethics arena, current trends in business governance strongly support the development of ethics and compliance departments to help guide organizational integrity. This alone is a billion-dollar business, and there are jobs in developing organizational ethics programs, developing company policies and training employees and management. An entry-level position might be as a communication specialist or trainer for programs in a business ethics department. Eventually there's an opportunity to become an ethics officer that would have typical responsibilities of meeting with employees, the Board of Directors, and top management to discuss and provide advice about ethics issues in the industry, developing and distributing a code of ethics, creating and maintaining an anonymous, confidential service to answer questions about ethical issues, taking actions on possible ethics code violations, and reviewing and modifying the code of ethics of the organization.

There are also opportunities to help with initiatives to help companies relate social responsibility to stakeholder interests and needs. These jobs could involve coordinating and implementing philanthropic programs that give back to others important to the organization or developing a community volunteering program for employees. In addition to the human relations function, most companies develop programs to assist employees and their families to improve their quality of life. Companies have found that the healthier and happier employees are the more productive they will be in the workforce.

Social responsibility, ethics, and sustainable business practices are not a trend, they are good for business and the bottom line. Just ask Toyota who sold well over a 1 million hybrid cars worldwide in ten years. New industries are being created and old ones are adapting to the new market demands, opening up many varied job opportunities that will lead to more than a paycheck, but to the satisfaction of making the world a better place.[78]

# Review Your Understanding

***Define business ethics and social responsibility and examine their importance.***

Business ethics refers to principles and standards that define acceptable business conduct. Acceptable business behavior is defined by customers, competitors, government regulators, interest groups, the public, and each individual's personal moral principles and values. Social responsibility is the obligation an organization assumes to maximize its positive impact and minimize its negative impact on society. Socially responsible businesses win the trust and respect of their employees, customers, and society and, in the long run, increase profits. Ethics is important in business because it builds trust and confidence in business relationships. Unethical actions may result in negative publicity, declining sales, and even legal action.

**Detect some of the ethical issues that may arise in business.**

An ethical issue is an identifiable problem, situation, or opportunity requiring a person or organization to choose from among several actions that must be evaluated as right or wrong. Ethical issues can be categorized in the context of their relation with conflicts of interest, fairness and honesty, communications, and business associations.

**Specify how businesses can promote ethical behavior by employees.**

Businesses can promote ethical behavior by employees by limiting their opportunity to engage in misconduct. Formal codes of ethics, ethical policies, and ethics training programs reduce the incidence of unethical behavior by informing employees what is expected of them and providing punishments for those who fail to comply.

**Explain the four dimensions of social responsibility.**

The four dimensions of social responsibility are economic (being profitable), legal (obeying the law), ethical (doing what is right, just, and fair), and voluntary (being a good corporate citizen).

**Debate an organization's social responsibilities to owners, employees, consumers, the environment, and the community.**

Businesses must maintain proper accounting procedures, provide all relevant information about the performance of the firm to investors, and protect the owners' rights and investments. In relations with employees, businesses are expected to provide a safe workplace, pay employees adequately for their work, and treat them fairly. Consumerism refers to the activities undertaken by independent individuals, groups, and organizations to protect their rights as consumers. Increasingly, society expects businesses to take greater responsibility for the environment, especially with regard to animal rights, as well as water, air, land, and noise pollution. Many businesses engage in activities to make the communities in which they operate better places for everyone to live and work.

**Evaluate the ethics of a business's decision.**

"Solve the Dilemma" on page 67 presents an ethical dilemma at Checkers Pizza. Using the material presented in this chapter, you should be able to analyze the ethical issues present in the dilemma, evaluate Barnard's plan, and develop a course of action for the firm.

# Revisit the World of Business

1. What are some of the advantages of having a corporate code of ethics? Is it important?

2. Who is the reading audience for *Ethisphere* magazine? How might such a publication help these readers?

3. Think of some methods of benchmarking. How would these tools help a company seeking to improve its code of ethics and compliance systems?

# Learn the Terms

| | | |
|---|---|---|
| bribes   44 | consumerism   57 | plagiarism   48 |
| business ethics   38 | corporate citizenship   52 | social responsibility   39 |
| codes of ethics   50 | ethical issue   41 | whistleblowing   50 |

# Check Your Progress

1. Define business ethics. Who determines whether a business activity is ethical? Is unethical conduct always illegal?

2. Distinguish between ethics and social responsibility.

3. Why has ethics become so important in business?

4. What is an ethical issue? What are some of the ethical issues named in your text? Why are they ethical issues?

5. What is a code of ethics? How can one reduce unethical behavior in business?

6. List and discuss the arguments for and against social responsibility by business (Table 2.8). Can you think of any additional arguments (for or against)?

7. What responsibilities does a business have toward its employees?

8. What responsibilities does business have with regard to the environment? What steps have been taken by some responsible businesses to minimize the negative impact of their activities on the environment?

9. What are a business's responsibilities toward the community in which it operates?

# Get Involved

1. Discuss some recent examples of businesses engaging in unethical practices. Classify these practices as issues of conflict of interest, fairness and honesty, communications, or business relationships. Why do you think the businesses chose to behave unethically? What actions might the businesses have taken?

2. Discuss with your class some possible methods of improving ethical standards in business. Do you think that business should regulate its own activities or that the federal government should establish and enforce ethical standards? How do you think businesspeople feel?

3 . Find some examples of socially responsible businesses in newspapers or business journals. Explain why you believe their actions are socially responsible. Why do you think the companies chose to act as they did?

# Build Your Skills

## MAKING DECISIONS ABOUT ETHICAL ISSUES

### Background
The merger of Lockheed and Martin Marietta created Lockheed Martin, the number-one company in the defense industry—an industry that includes such companies as McDonnell Douglas and Northrop Grumman.

You and the rest of the class are managers at Lockheed Martin Corporation, Orlando, Florida. You are getting ready to do the group exercise in an ethics training session. The training instructor announces you will be playing *Gray Matters: The Ethics Game.* You are told that *Gray Matters,* which was prepared for your company's employees, is also played at 41 universities, including Harvard University, and at 65 other companies. Although there are 55 scenarios in *Gray Matters,* you will have time during this session to complete only the four scenarios that your group draws from the stack of cards.[80]

### Task
Form into groups of four to six managers and appoint a group leader who will lead a discussion of the case, obtain a consensus answer to the case, and be the one to report the group's answers to the instructor. You will have five minutes to reach each decision, after which time, the instructor will give the point values and rationale for each choice. Then you will have five minutes for the next case, etc., until all four cases have been completed. Keep track of your group's score for each case; the winning team will be the group scoring the most points.

Since this game is designed to reflect life, you may believe that some cases lack clarity or that some of your choices are not as precise as you would have liked. Also, some cases have only one solution, while others have more than one solution. Each choice is assessed points to reflect which answer is the most correct. **Your group's task is to select only one option in each case.**

---

**4**

**Mini-Case**

For several months now, one of your colleagues has been slacking off, and you are getting stuck doing the work. You think it is unfair. What do you do?

**Potential Answers**

A. Recognize this as an opportunity for you to demonstrate how capable you are.
B. Go to your supervisor and complain about this unfair workload.
C. Discuss the problem with your colleague in an attempt to solve the problem without involving others.
D. Discuss the problem with the human resources department.

---

**7**

**Mini-Case**

You are aware that a fellow employee uses drugs on the job. Another friend encourages you to confront the person instead of informing the supervisor. What do you do?

**Potential Answers**

A. You speak to the alleged user and encourage him to get help.
B. You elect to tell your supervisor that you suspect an employee is using drugs on the job.
C. You confront the alleged user and tell him either to quit using drugs or you will "turn him in."
D. Report the matter to employee assistance.

---

**36**

**Mini-Case**

You work for a company that has implemented a policy of a smoke-free environment. You discover employees smoking in the restrooms of the building. You also smoke and don't like having to go outside to do it. What do you do?

**Potential Answers**

A. You ignore the situation.
B. You confront the employees and ask them to stop.
C. You join them, but only occasionally.
D. You contact your ethics or human resources representative and ask him or her to handle the situation.

---

**40**

**Mini-Case**

Your co-worker is copying company-purchased software and taking it home. You know a certain program costs $400, and you have been saving for a while to buy it. What do you do?

**Potential Answers**

A. You figure you can copy it too since nothing has ever happened to your co-worker.
B. You tell your co-worker he can't legally do this.
C. You report the matter to the ethics office.
D. You mention this to your supervisor.

---

## Solve the Dilemma

### CUSTOMER PRIVACY

Checkers Pizza was one of the first to offer home delivery service, with overwhelming success. However, the major pizza chains soon followed suit, taking away Checkers's competitive edge. Jon Barnard, Checkers's founder and co-owner, needed a new gimmick to beat the competition. He decided to develop a computerized information database that would make Checkers the most efficient competitor and provide insight into consumer buying behavior at the same time. Under the system, telephone customers were asked their phone number; if they had ordered from Checkers before, their address and previous order information came up on the computer screen.

After successfully testing the new system, Barnard put the computerized order network in place in all Checkers outlets. After three months of success, he decided to give an award to the family that ate the most Checkers pizza.

Through the tracking system, the company identified the biggest customer, who had ordered a pizza every weekday for the past three months (63 pizzas). The company put together a program to surprise the family with an award, free-food certificates, and a news story announcing the award. As Barnard began to plan for the event, however, he began to think that maybe the family might not want all the attention and publicity.

**Discussion Questions**

1. What are some of the ethical issues in giving customers an award for consumption behavior without notifying them first?

2. Do you see this as a potential violation of privacy? Explain.

3. How would you handle the situation if you were Barnard?

# Build Your Business Plan

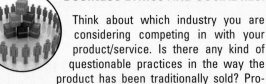

### BUSINESS ETHICS AND SOCIAL RESPONSIBILITY

Think about which industry you are considering competing in with your product/service. Is there any kind of questionable practices in the way the product has been traditionally sold? Produced? Advertised? Have there been any recent accusations regarding safety within the industry? What about any environmental concerns?

For example, if you are thinking of opening a lawn care business, you need to be thinking about what possible effects the chemicals you are using will have on the client and the environment. You have a responsibility to keep your customers safe and healthy. You also have the social responsibility to let the community know of any damaging effect you may be directly or indirectly responsible for.

# See for Yourself Videocase

### IS YOUR SHIRT ORGANIC? THE CLOTHING INDUSTRY GOES GREEN

Social responsibility is defined as a business's obligation to maximize its positive impact and minimize its negative impact on society; therefore it stands to reason that environmental responsibility may be defined as a business's obligation to maximize its positive impact and minimize its negative impact on the environment. As global warming concerns escalate and threats to wildlife, plants, and humans increase, it is becoming necessary for individuals and businesses to admit the problem and address their environmental responsibility. The clothing industry has long been a large polluter responsible for hefty negative impact on the environment. Environmental groups such as Earth Pledge, a non-profit that encourages sustainable development, have been urging the clothing industry to clean up its act. Finally, it appears as if these pleas may finally be heard, as consumers across the board have begun to lend their support to environmentally responsible companies.

Switching to more eco-friendly clothing materials can do much to benefit the environment. For example, according to Organic Exchange, a nonprofit supporting the use of organic cotton, a single cotton t-shirt produced with conventional cotton requires the application of 1/3 of a pound of chemicals. According to the environmentally responsible outdoor clothier Patagonia, conventional cotton crops

in California alone are treated with 6.9 million pounds of chemicals annually. These chemicals can easily seep into the ground, creating a host of environmental and health dangers. Research indicates that synthetic fertilizers, soil additives, defoliants, and other substances do untold damage to soil, water, air, and living organisms.

Even though consumers are beginning to demand environmentally and socially responsible goods, they are also the group inhibiting the clothing industry's transition to greener practices. Regardless of heightened eco-friendly awareness, clothing consumers, on average, still tend to base their purchases primarily on price and style. There is also the green "granola" image to overcome. Many people still do not think that eco-friendly clothing can be fashionable, although a number of top designers and fashion brands like Stella McCartney, Donna Karan, H&M, and Rogan for Target have all released organic lines. Barneys New York, the high end department store, now stocks organic fashions; and popular celebrities such as Bono from U2 and actress Natalie Portman are lending their star power to promoting the cause as well.

Outdoor clothing retailers have less of a challenge, being that their target market spends more time out in nature and may, therefore, care more about environmental responsibility. For example, many of us are familiar with Teva sandals and shoes. Teva's parent company, Deckers

Outdoor, was founded by a river guide who wanted to run a green company from the start. Even so, Teva is just now beginning to become heavily involved in using recycled materials in its shoes. In 2007, the company introduced a new collection of shoes, dubbed the Curbside collection that is composed of recycled materials such as car tires, factory scrap rubber, and plastic bottles.

A longtime pioneer in eco-friendly practices, Patagonia goes all out to make its clothing as green as possible. The company began creating clothing from recycled soda bottles in 1993. Today it has expanded the materials it uses to include second hand garments and other fabrics. In 1996, the company transitioned to using organic cotton exclusively. This one small change has lessened Patagonia's dependence on oil, reduced toxic emissions, lessened its contribution to landfills, and reduced levels of soil, air, and water contamination. In 2005, the company also implemented its Common Threads Garment Recycling program so that customers may return old garments to Patagonia stores for reuse in new clothing.

Although the progress toward eco-friendly clothing and sustainable clothing practices has been slow, fashion is moving in the right direction. Marshall Cohen of the market research firm NDP Group states that the number of consumers interested in eco-friendly products (excluding cars and food) grew 15 percent in 2007. Leslie Hoffman of Earth Pledge, a group supporting sustainable practices in corporations and government, notes that in 2004 clothing designers could make use of only about 50 or 60 renewable, non-polluting materials. Today, she says designers have access to around 700 different eco-friendly materials. Hopefully, consumers will support the environmentally responsible steps taken in the fashion industry in order to further the cause.[81]

### Discussion Questions

1. What is driving the transition to more eco-friendly clothing?
2. What are the advantages of switching to environmentally friendly clothing production practices?
3. What are the challenges faced by the fashion industry when making this switch?

**Remember to check out our Online Learning Center at www.mhhe.com/ferrell7e.**

# Appendix B

# The Legal and Regulatory Environment

**Business law** refers to the rules and regulations that govern the conduct of business. Problems in this area come from the failure to keep promises, misunderstandings, disagreements about expectations, or, in some cases, attempts to take advantage of others. The regulatory environment offers a framework and enforcement system in order to provide a fair playing field for all businesses. The regulatory environment is created based on inputs from competitors, customers, employees, special interest groups, and the public's elected representatives. Lobbying by pressure groups who try to influence legislation often shapes the legal and regulatory environment.

## Sources of Law

Laws are classified as either criminal or civil. *Criminal law* not only prohibits a specific kind of action, such as unfair competition or mail fraud, but also imposes a fine or imprisonment as punishment for violating the law. A violation of a criminal law is thus called a crime. *Civil law* defines all the laws not classified as criminal, and it specifies the rights and duties of individuals and organizations (including businesses). Violations of civil law may result in fines but not imprisonment. The primary difference between criminal and civil law is that criminal laws are enforced by the state or nation, whereas civil laws are enforced through the court system by individuals or organizations.

Criminal and civil laws are derived from four sources: the Constitution (constitutional law), precedents established by judges (common law), federal and state statutes (statutory law), and federal and state administrative agencies (administrative law). Federal administrative agencies established by Congress control and influence business by enforcing laws and regulations to encourage competition and protect consumers, workers, and the environment. The Supreme Court is the ultimate authority on legal and regulatory decisions for appropriate conduct in business.

## Courts and the Resolution of Disputes

The primary method of resolving conflicts and business disputes is through **lawsuits,** where one individual or organization takes another to court using civil laws. The legal system, therefore, provides a forum for businesspeople to resolve disputes based on our legal foundations. The courts may decide when harm or damage results from the actions of others.

Because lawsuits are so frequent in the world of business, it is important to understand more about the court system where such disputes are resolved. Both financial restitution and specific actions to undo wrongdoing can result from going before a court to resolve a conflict. All decisions made in the

*Marcia & Bill Baker found Heinz was underfilling their 20-oz. ketchup bottles by 1.5 oz. Heinz paid civil penalties and costs of $180,000 and had to overfill all ketchup bottles in California by 1/8 oz. for a year.*

courts are based on criminal and civil laws derived from the legal and regulatory system.

A businessperson may win a lawsuit in court and receive a judgment, or court order, requiring the loser of the suit to pay monetary damages. However, this does not guarantee the victor will be able to collect those damages. If the loser of the suit lacks the financial resources to pay the judgment—for example, if the loser is a bankrupt business—the winner of the suit may not be able to collect the award. Most business lawsuits involve a request for a sum of money, but some lawsuits request that a court specifically order a person or organization to do or to refrain from doing a certain act, such as slamming telephone customers.

## The Court System

**Jurisdiction** is the legal power of a court, through a judge, to interpret and apply the law and make a binding decision in a particular case. In some instances, other courts will not enforce the decision of a prior court because it lacked jurisdiction. Federal courts are granted jurisdiction by the Constitution or by Congress. State legislatures and constitutions determine which state courts hear certain types of cases. Courts of general jurisdiction hear all types of cases; those of limited jurisdiction hear only specific types of cases. The Federal Bankruptcy Court, for example, hears only cases involving bankruptcy. There is some combination of limited and general jurisdiction courts in every state.

In a **trial court** (whether in a court of general or limited jurisdiction and whether in the state or the federal system), two tasks must be completed. First, the court (acting through the judge or a jury) must determine the facts of the case. In other words, if there is conflicting evidence, the judge or jury must decide who to believe. Second, the judge must decide which law or set of laws is pertinent to the case and must then apply those laws to resolve the dispute.

An **appellate court,** on the other hand, deals solely with appeals relating to the interpretation of law. Thus, when you hear about a case being appealed, it is not retried, but rather reevaluated. Appellate judges do not hear witnesses but instead base their decisions on a written transcript of the original trial. Moreover, appellate courts do not draw factual conclusions; the appellate judge is limited to deciding whether the trial judge made a mistake in interpreting the law that probably affected the outcome of the

trial. If the trial judge made no mistake (or if mistakes would not have changed the result of the trial), the appellate court will let the trial court's decision stand. If the appellate court finds a mistake, it usually sends the case back to the trial court so that the mistake can be corrected. Correction may involve the granting of a new trial. On occasion, appellate courts modify the verdict of the trial court without sending the case back to the trial court.

### Alternative Dispute Resolution Methods

Although the main remedy for business disputes is a lawsuit, other dispute resolution methods are becoming popular. The schedules of state and federal trial courts are often crowded; long delays between the filing of a case and the trial date are common. Further, complex cases can become quite expensive to pursue. As a result, many businesspeople are turning to alternative methods of resolving business arguments: mediation and arbitration, the mini-trial, and litigation in a private court.

**Mediation** is a form of negotiation to resolve a dispute by bringing in one or more third-party mediators, usually chosen by the disputing parties, to help reach a settlement. The mediator suggests different ways to resolve a dispute between the parties. The mediator's resolution is nonbinding—that is, the parties do not have to accept the mediator's suggestions; they are strictly voluntary.

**Arbitration** involves submission of a dispute to one or more third-party arbitrators, usually chosen by the disputing parties, whose decision usually is final. Arbitration differs from mediation in that an arbitrator's decision must be followed, whereas a mediator merely offers suggestions and facilitates negotiations. Cases may be submitted to arbitration because a contract—such as a labor contract—requires it or because the parties agree to do so. Some consumers are barred from taking claims to court by agreements drafted by banks, brokers, health plans, and others. Instead, they are required to take complaints to mandatory arbitration. Arbitration can be an attractive alternative to a lawsuit because it is often cheaper and quicker, and the parties frequently can choose arbitrators who are knowledgeable about the particular area of business at issue.

A method of dispute resolution that may become increasingly important in settling complex disputes is the **mini-trial,** in which both parties agree to present a summarized version of their case to an independent third party. That person then advises them of his or her impression of the probable outcome if the case were to be tried. Representatives of both sides then attempt to negotiate a settlement based on the advisor's recommendations. For example, employees in a large corporation who believe they have muscular or skeletal stress injuries caused by the strain of repetitive motion in using a computer could agree to a mini-trial to address a dispute related to damages. Although the mini-trial itself does not resolve the dispute, it can help the parties resolve the case before going to court. Because the mini-trial is not subject to formal court rules, it can save companies a great deal of money, allowing them to recognize the weaknesses in a particular case.

In some areas of the country, disputes can be submitted to a private nongovernmental court for resolution. In a sense, a **private court system** is similar to arbitration in that an independent third party resolves the case after hearing both sides of the story. Trials in private courts may be either informal or highly formal, depending on the people involved. Businesses typically agree to have their disputes decided in private courts to save time and money.

| TABLE B.I | The Major Regulatory Agencies |
|---|---|
| **Agency** | **Major Areas of Responsibility** |
| Federal Trade Commission (FTC) | Enforces laws and guidelines regarding business practices; takes action to stop false and deceptive advertising and labeling. |
| Food and Drug Administration (FDA) | Enforces laws and regulations to prevent distribution of adulterated or misbranded foods, drugs, medical devices, cosmetics, veterinary products, and particularly hazardous consumer products. |
| Consumer Product Safety Commission (CPSC) | Ensures compliance with the Consumer Product Safety Act; protects the public from unreasonable risk of injury from any consumer product not covered by other regulatory agencies. |
| Interstate Commerce Commission (ICC) | Regulates franchises, rates, and finances of interstate rail, bus, truck, and water carriers. |
| Federal Communications Commission (FCC) | Regulates communication by wire, radio, and television in interstate and foreign commerce. |
| Environmental Protection Agency (EPA) | Develops and enforces environmental protection standards and conducts research into the adverse effects of pollution. |
| Federal Energy Regulatory Commission (FERC) | Regulates rates and sales of natural gas products, thereby affecting the supply and price of gas available to consumers; also regulates wholesale rates for electricity and gas, pipeline construction, and U.S. imports and exports of natural gas and electricity. |
| Equal Employment Opportunity Commission (EEOC) | Investigates and resolves discrimination in employment practices. |
| Federal Aviation Administration (FAA) | Oversees the policies and regulations of the airline industry. |
| Federal Highway Administration (FHA) | Regulates vehicle safety requirements. |
| Occupational Safety and Health Administration (OSHA) | Develops policy to promote worker safety and health and investigates infractions. |
| Securities and Exchange Commission (SEC) | Regulates corporate securities trading and develops protection from fraud and other abuses; provides an accounting oversight board. |

# Regulatory Administrative Agencies

Federal and state administrative agencies (listed in Table B.1) also have some judicial powers. Many administrative agencies, such as the Federal Trade Commission, decide disputes that involve their regulations. In such disputes, the resolution process is usually called a "hearing" rather than a trial. In these cases, an administrative law judge decides all issues.

Federal regulatory agencies influence many business activities and cover product liability, safety, and the regulation or deregulation of public utilities. Usually, these bodies have the power to enforce specific laws, such as the Federal Trade Commission Act, and have some discretion in establishing operating rules and regulations to guide certain types of industry practices. Because of this discretion and overlapping areas of responsibility, confusion or conflict regarding which agencies have jurisdiction over which activities is common.

Of all the federal regulatory units, the **Federal Trade Commission (FTC)** most influences business activities related to questionable practices that create disputes between businesses and their customers. Although the FTC regulates a variety of business practices, it allocates a large portion of resources to curbing false advertising, misleading pricing, and deceptive packaging and labeling. When it receives a complaint or otherwise has reason to believe that a firm is violating a law, the FTC issues a complaint stating that the business is in violation.

If a company continues the questionable practice, the FTC can issue a cease-and-desist order, which is an order for the business to stop doing whatever has caused the complaint. In such cases, the charged firm can appeal to the federal courts to have the order rescinded. However, the FTC can seek civil penalties in court—up to a maximum penalty of $10,000 a day for each infraction—if a cease-and-desist order is violated. In its battle against unfair pricing, the FTC has issued consent decrees alleging that corporate attempts to engage in price fixing or invitations to competitors to collude are violations even when the competitors in question refuse the invitations. The commission can also require companies to run corrective advertising in response to previous ads considered misleading.

The FTC also assists businesses in complying with laws. New marketing methods are evaluated every year. When general sets of guidelines are needed to improve business practices in a particular industry, the FTC sometimes encourages firms within that industry to establish a set of trade practices voluntarily. The FTC may even sponsor a conference bringing together industry leaders and consumers for the purpose of establishing acceptable trade practices.

Unlike the FTC, other regulatory units are limited to dealing with specific products, services, or business activities. The Food and Drug Administration (FDA) enforces regulations prohibiting the sale and distribution of adulterated, misbranded, or hazardous food and drug products. For example, the FDA outlawed the sale and distribution of most over-the-counter hair-loss remedies after research indicated that few of the products were effective in restoring hair growth.

The Environmental Protection Agency (EPA) develops and enforces environmental protection standards and conducts research into the adverse effects of pollution. The Consumer Product Safety Commission recalls about 300 products a year, ranging from small, inexpensive toys to major appliances. The Consumer Product Safety Commission's Web site provides details regarding current recalls.

The Consumer Product Safety commission has fallen under increasing scrutiny in the wake of a number of product safety scandals involving children's toys. The most notable of these issues was lead paint discovered in toys produced in China. Other problems have included the manufacture of toys that include small magnets that pose a choking hazard, and lead-tainted costume jewelry.[82]

# Important Elements of Business Law

To avoid violating criminal and civil laws, as well as discouraging lawsuits from consumers, employees, suppliers, and others, businesspeople need to be familiar with laws that address business practices.

## The Uniform Commercial Code
At one time, states had their own specific laws governing various business practices, and transacting business across state lines was difficult because of

# Consider Ethics and Social Responsibility
## Pfizer: Puffery or Deception?

Pfizer Inc. is a well-known drug company that produces a number of popular medications. Its blockbuster cholesterol-reducing product, Lipitor, has been proven to lower cholesterol. However, increased competition brought on by the introduction of a generic version of Merck & Co.'s Zocor cholesterol medication prompted Pfizer to rethink its advertising strategy. In order to promote this product, the company hired Robert Jarvik, inventor of a kind of artificial heart, to star in new ads for the drug. Although a doctor, Jarvik is not a practicing physician and this has called into question the validity and morality of the endorsement. The ads had been running since 2006 when the company abruptly pulled them in January 2008, in the wake of a federal investigation into the matter.

The accusations do not call into question the importance of Jarvik's accomplishments or the effectiveness of the medication. They do, however, question Jarvik's credentials, as he is not a practicing physician. They also question whether or not the ads sought to mislead consumers in a fraudulent way. One of the television advertisements shows Jarvik at a lake discussing the benefits of Lipitor. In the ad he states, "just because I'm a doctor doesn't mean I don't worry about my cholesterol," thereby potentially leading the audience to believe that he is a physician.

Exaggerated marketing claims are known as *puffery*, which is defined by the FTC as "exaggerations reasonably to be expected of a seller" where "truth or falsity cannot be precisely determined." Advertising moves beyond puffery into the realm of deceptive, or false, advertising if it gives consumers untrue or unrealistic ideas about the product being promoted. False advertising can range from straight out misrepresenting the product, advertising the maximum or best features rather than the basic or standards ones, or using fillers or oversized packaging to make the consumer think that he or she is buying more. Deceptive advertising can be considered fraud, which is illegal. The House Committee on Energy and Commerce probe has called into question the validity of the claims asserted by Jarvik in the ad, and is considering whether the ads should be considered deceptive, or merely puffery. This distinction can be difficult to determine. According to the Better Business Bureau's Code of Advertising, "subjective claims are not subject to test of their truth or accuracy," meaning there is no objective test of such claims. Some believe that the best approach for Pfizer would be to move towards advertising that utilizes scientific data over emotional appeals.[83]

### Discussion Questions

1. If the information conveyed in the ads is truthful, should it matter that Dr. Jarvik is associated with development of an artificial heart but is not a practicing physician?
2. What advertising approaches do you think that Pfizer should take in the future in order to avoid the same kind of scrutiny and criticism engendered by the Jarvik Lipitor ads?
3. How might one determine when a company has crossed the line between puffery and outright deception?

---

the variation in the laws from state to state. To simplify commerce, every state—except Louisiana—has enacted the Uniform Commercial Code (Louisiana has enacted portions of the code). The **Uniform Commercial Code (UCC)** is a set of statutory laws covering several business law topics. Article II of the Uniform Commercial Code, which is discussed in the following paragraphs, has significant impact on business.

**Sales Agreements.** Article II of the Uniform Commercial Code covers sales agreements for goods and services such as installation but does not cover the sale of stocks and bonds, personal services, or real estate. Among its many provisions, Article II stipulates that a sales agreement can be enforced even though it does not specify the selling price or the time or place of delivery. It also requires that a buyer pay a reasonable price for goods at the time of delivery if the buyer and seller have not reached an agreement on price. Specifically, Article II addresses the rights of buyers and sellers, transfers of ownership, warranties, and the legal placement of risk during manufacture and delivery.

Article II also deals with express and implied warranties. An **express warranty** stipulates the specific terms the seller will honor. Many automobile manufacturers, for example, provide three-year or 36,000-mile warranties on their vehicles, during which period they will fix any and all defects specified in the warranty. An **implied warranty** is imposed on the producer or seller by law, although it may not be a written document provided at the time of sale. Under Article II, a consumer may assume that the product for sale has a clear title (in other words, that it is not stolen) and that the product will both serve the purpose for which it was made and sold as well as function as advertised.

## The Law of Torts and Fraud

A **tort** is a private or civil wrong other than breach of contract. For example, a tort can result if the driver of a Domino's Pizza delivery car loses control of the vehicle and damages property or injures a person. In the case of the delivery car accident, the injured persons might sue the driver and the owner of the company—Domino's in this case—for damages resulting from the accident.

**Fraud** is a purposeful unlawful act to deceive or manipulate in order to damage others. Thus, in some cases, a tort may also represent a violation of criminal law. Health care fraud has become a major issue in the courts.

An important aspect of tort law involves **product liability**—businesses' legal responsibility for any negligence in the design, production, sale, and consumption of products. Product liability laws have evolved from both common and statutory law. Some states have expanded the concept of product liability to include injuries by products whether or not the producer is proven negligent. Under this strict product liability, a consumer who files suit because of an injury has to prove only that the product was defective, that the defect caused the injury, and that the defect made the product unreasonably dangerous. For example, a carving knife is expected to be sharp and is not considered defective if you cut your finger using it. But an electric knife could be considered defective and unreasonably dangerous if it continued to operate after being switched off.

Reforming tort law, particularly in regard to product liability, has become a hot political issue as businesses look for relief from huge judgments in lawsuits. Although many lawsuits are warranted—few would disagree that a wrong has occurred when a patient dies because of negligence during a medical procedure or when a child is seriously injured by a defective toy, and that the families deserve some compensation—many suits are not. Because of multimillion-dollar judgments, companies are trying to minimize their liability, and sometimes they pass on the costs of the damage awards to their customers in the form of higher prices. Some states have passed laws limiting damage awards and some tort reform is occurring at the federal level. Table B.2 lists the state courts systems the U.S. Chamber of Commerce's Institute for Legal Reform has identified as being "friendliest" and "least friendly" to business in terms of juries' fairness, judges' competence and impartiality, and other factors.

## The Law of Contracts

Virtually every business transaction is carried out by means of a **contract,** a mutual agreement between two or more parties that can be enforced in a court if one party chooses not to comply with the terms of the contract. If you rent an apartment or house, for example, your lease is a contract. If you have borrowed money under a student loan program, you have a contractual agreement to repay the money. Many aspects of contract law are covered under the Uniform Commercial Code.

*New car buyers receive express warranties stating what is covered for repair or replacement over a specific period of time.*

**TABLE B.2**   State Court Systems' Reputations for Supporting Business

| Most Friendly to Business | Least Friendly to Business |
|---|---|
| Delaware | Mississippi |
| Nebraska | West Virginia |
| Virginia | Alabama |
| Iowa | Louisiana |
| Idaho | California |
| Utah | Texas |
| New Hampshire | Illinois |
| Minnesota | Montana |
| Kansas | Arkansas |
| Wisconsin | Missouri |

Source: U.S. Chamber of Commerce Institute for Legal Reform, in Martin Kasindorf, "Robin Hood Is Alive in Court, Say Those Seeking Lawsuit Limits," *USA Today,* March 8, 2004, p. 4A.

A "handshake deal" is in most cases as fully and completely binding as a written, signed contract agreement. Indeed, many oil-drilling and construction contractors have for years agreed to take on projects on the basis of such handshake deals. However, individual states require that some contracts be in writing to be enforceable. Most states require that at least some of the following contracts be in writing:

- Contracts involving the sale of land or an interest in land.
- Contracts to pay somebody else's debt.
- Contracts that cannot be fulfilled within one year.
- Contracts for the sale of goods that cost more than $500 (required by the Uniform Commercial Code).

Only those contracts that meet certain requirements—called *elements*—are enforceable by the courts. A person or business seeking to enforce a contract must show that it contains the following elements: voluntary agreement, consideration, contractual capacity of the parties, and legality.

For any agreement to be considered a legal contract, all persons involved must agree to be bound by the terms of the contract. *Voluntary agreement* typically comes about when one party makes an offer and the other accepts. If both the offer and the acceptance are freely, voluntarily, and knowingly made, the acceptance forms the basis for the contract. If, however, either the offer or the acceptance are the result of fraud or force, the individual or organization subject to the fraud or force can void, or invalidate, the resulting agreement or receive compensation for damages.

The second requirement for enforcement of a contract is that it must be supported by *consideration*— that is, money or something of value must be given in return for fulfilling a contract. As a general rule, a person cannot be forced to abide by the terms of a promise unless that person receives a consideration. The something-of-value could be money, goods, services, or even a promise to do or not to do something.

*Contractual capacity* is the legal ability to enter into a contract. As a general rule, a court cannot enforce a contract if either party to the agreement lacks contractual capacity. A person's contractual capacity may be limited or nonexistent if he or she is a minor (under the age of 18), mentally unstable, retarded, insane, or intoxicated.

*Legality* is the state or condition of being lawful. For an otherwise binding contract to be enforceable, both the purpose of and the consideration for the contract must be legal. A contract in which a bank loans money at a rate of interest prohibited by law, a practice known as usury, would be an illegal contract, for example. The fact that one of the parties may commit an illegal act while performing a contract does not render the contract itself illegal, however.

**Breach of contract** is the failure or refusal of a party to a contract to live up to his or her promises. In the case of an apartment lease, failure to pay rent would be considered breach of contract. The breaching party—the one who fails to comply—may be liable for monetary damages that he or she causes the other person.

## The Law of Agency

An **agency** is a common business relationship created when one person acts on behalf of another and under that person's control. Two parties are involved in an agency relationship: The **principal** is the one who wishes to have a specific task accomplished; the **agent** is the one who acts on behalf of the principal to accomplish the task. Authors, movie stars, and athletes often employ agents to help them obtain the best contract terms.

An agency relationship is created by the mutual agreement of the principal and the agent. It is usually not necessary that such an agreement be in writing, although putting it in writing is certainly advisable. An agency relationship continues as long as both the principal and the agent so desire. It can be terminated by mutual agreement, by fulfillment of the purpose of the agency, by the refusal of either party to continue in the relationship, or by the death of either the principal or the agent. In most cases, a principal grants authority to the agent through a formal *power of attorney,* which is a legal document authorizing a person to act as someone else's agent. The power of attorney can be used for any agency relationship, and its use is not limited to lawyers. For instance, in real estate transactions, often a lawyer or real estate agent is given power of attorney with the authority to purchase real estate for the buyer. Accounting firms often give employees agency relationships in making financial transactions.

Both officers and directors of corporations are fiduciaries, or people of trust, who use due care and loyalty as an agent in making decisions on behalf of the organization. This relationship creates a duty of care, also called duty of diligence, to make informed decisions. These agents of the corporation are not held responsible for negative outcomes if they are informed and diligent in their decisions. The duty of loyalty means that all decisions should be in the interests of the corporation and its stakeholders. Scandals at Enron, Tyco, and WorldCom are associated with officers and directors who failed to carry out their fiduciary duties. Lawsuits from shareholders called for the officers and directors to pay large sums of money from their own pockets.

## The Law of Property

Property law is extremely broad in scope because it covers the ownership and transfer of all kinds of real, personal, and intellectual property. **Real property** consists of real estate and everything permanently attached to it; **personal property** basically is everything else. Personal property can be further subdivided into tangible and intangible property. *Tangible property* refers to items that have a physical existence, such as automobiles, business inventory, and clothing. *Intangible property* consists of rights and duties; its existence may be represented by a document or by some other tangible item. For example, accounts receivable, stock in a corporation, goodwill, and trademarks are all examples of intangible personal property. **Intellectual property** refers to property, such as musical works, artwork, books, and computer software, that is generated by a person's creative activities.

Copyrights, patents, and trademarks provide protection to the owners of property by giving them the exclusive right to use it. *Copyrights* protect the ownership rights on material (often intellectual property) such as books, music, videos, photos, and computer software. The creators of such works, or their heirs, generally have exclusive rights to the published or unpublished works for the creator's lifetime, plus 50 years. *Patents* give inventors exclusive rights to their invention for 17 years. The most intense competition for patents is in the pharmaceutical industry. Most patents take a minimum of 18 months to secure.

A *trademark* is a brand (name, mark, or symbol) that is registered with the U.S. Patent and Trademark Office and is thus legally protected from use by any other firm. Among the symbols that have been so protected are McDonald's golden arches and Coca-Cola's distinctive bottle shape. It is estimated that large multinational firms may have as many as 15,000 conflicts related to trademarks. Companies are diligent about protecting their trademarks both to avoid confusion in consumers' minds and because a term that becomes part of everyday language can no longer be trademarked. The names *aspirin* and *nylon,* for example, were once the exclusive property of their creators but became so widely used as product names (rather than brand names) that now anyone can use them.

As the trend toward globalization of trade continues, and more and more businesses trade across national boundaries, protecting property rights, particularly intellectual property such as computer software, has become an increasing challenge. While a company may be able to register as a trademark a brand name or symbol in its home country, it may not be able to secure that protection abroad. Some countries have copyright and patent laws that are less strict than those of the United States; some countries will not enforce U.S. laws. China, for example, has often been criticized for permitting U.S. goods to be counterfeited there. Such counterfeiting harms not only the sales of U.S. companies but also their reputations if the knockoffs are of poor quality. Thus, businesses engaging in foreign trade may have to take extra steps to protect their property because local laws may be insufficient to protect them.

## The Law of Bankruptcy

Although few businesses and individuals intentionally fail to repay (or default on) their debts, sometimes they cannot fulfill their financial obligations. Individuals may charge goods and services beyond their ability to pay for them. Businesses may take on too much debt in order to finance growth or business events such as an increase in the cost of commodities can bankrupt a company. An option of last resort in these cases is bankruptcy, or legal insolvency. For example, a number of prominent airlines have recently filed for bankruptcy as a result of a weakening economy and problems inherent to the industry. Frontier Airlines is among those experiencing trouble. In order to attempt a recovery, the airline filed for Chapter 11 bankruptcy in April 2008. The airline blames its recent financial troubles on its credit card processing company, which has begun to claim a larger proportion of Frontier's revenues. This problem combined with fuel prices that rose 74 percent between 2007 and 2008, high-profile safety issues on a number of planes, and falling demand have created an environment difficult for even the strongest of carriers. In March 2008, Aloha Airlines took a more drastic step, filing for Chapter 7 bankruptcy. After filing, the carrier quickly closed for business—while United Airlines and Hawaiian Airlines stepped in to honor Aloha's tickets and reservations. Prior to bankruptcy, the carrier was the island state's 10th-largest employer, with 3,400 employees.[84]

Individuals or companies may ask a bankruptcy court to declare them unable to pay their debts and thus release them from the obligation of repaying those debts. The debtor's assets may then be sold to pay off as much of the debt as possible. In the case of a personal bankruptcy, although the individual is released from repaying debts and can start over with a clean slate, obtaining credit after bankruptcy proceedings is very difficult. About 2 million households in the United States filed for bankruptcy in 2005, the most ever. However, a new, more restrictive law went into effect in late 2005, and fewer consumers are using bankruptcy to eliminate their debts. The law makes it harder for consumers to prove that they should be allowed to clear their debts for what is called a "fresh start" or Chapter 7 bankruptcy. Although the person or company in debt usually initiates bankruptcy proceedings, creditors may also initiate them. The subprime mortgage crisis of early 2008 caused a string of bankruptcies among individuals; and chapter 7 and 11 bankruptcies among banks, and other businesses as well. Tougher bankruptcy laws and a slowing economy converged on the subprime crisis to create a situation where bankruptcy filings skyrocketed.

Table B.3 describes the various levels of bankruptcy protection a business or individual may seek.

# Laws Affecting Business Practices

One of the government's many roles is to act as a watchdog to ensure that businesses behave in accordance with the wishes of society. Congress has enacted a number of laws that affect business practices; some of the most important of these are summarized in Table A.4. Many state legislatures have enacted similar laws governing business within specific states.

The **Sherman Antitrust Act,** passed in 1890 to prevent businesses from restraining trade and monopolizing markets, condemns "every contract, combination, or conspiracy in restraint of trade." For example, a request that a competitor agree to fix prices or divide markets would, if accepted, result in a violation of the Sherman Act. Recently antitrust authorities have investigated the chocolate industry for evidence of price fixing. Over 50 civil suits have been filed against Hershey and other chocolate makers accusing the companies of collusion in order to boost profits.[85] Proof of intent plays an important role in attempted monopolization cases under the Sherman Act. Enforced by the Antitrust Division of the Department of Justice, the Sherman Antitrust Act applies to firms operating in interstate commerce and to U.S. firms operating in foreign commerce. For example, in early 2008 the American company, Intel Corp., found its German offices raided by European

| TABLE B.3 | Types of Bankruptcy |
|---|---|
| Chapter 7 | Requires that the business be dissolved and its assets liquidated, or sold, to pay off the debts. Individuals declaring Chapter 7 retain a limited amount of exempt assets, the amount of which may be determined by state or federal law, at the debtor's option. Although the type and value of exempt assets varies from state to state, most states' laws allow a bankrupt individual to keep an automobile, some household goods, clothing, furnishings, and at least some of the value of the debtor's residence. All nonexempt assets must be sold to pay debts. |
| Chapter 11 | Temporarily frees a business from its financial obligations while it reorganizes and works out a payment plan with its creditors. The indebted company continues to operate its business during bankruptcy proceedings. Often, the business sells off assets and less-profitable subsidiaries to raise cash to pay off its immediate obligations. |
| Chapter 13 | Similar to Chapter 11 but limited to individuals. This proceeding allows an individual to establish a three- to five-year plan for repaying his or her debt. Under this plan, an individual ultimately may repay as little as 10 percent of his or her debt. |

**TABLE B.4**   Major Federal Laws Affecting Business Practices

| Act (Date Enacted) | Purpose |
|---|---|
| Sherman Antitrust Act (1890) | Prohibits contracts, combinations, or conspiracies to restrain trade; establishes as a misdemeanor monopolizing or attempting to monopolize. |
| Clayton Act (1914) | Prohibits specific practices such as price discrimination, exclusive dealer arrangements, and stock acquisitions in which the effect may notably lessen competition or tend to create a monopoly. |
| Federal Trade Commission Act (1914) | Created the Federal Trade Commission; also gives the FTC investigatory powers to be used in preventing unfair methods of competition. |
| Robinson-Patman Act (1936) | Prohibits price discrimination that lessens competition among wholesalers or retailers; prohibits producers from giving disproportionate services of facilities to large buyers. |
| Wheeler-Lea Act (1938) | Prohibits unfair and deceptive acts and practices regardless of whether competition is injured; places advertising of foods and drugs under the jurisdiction of the FTC. |
| Lanham Act (1946) | Provides protections and regulation of brand names, brand marks, trade names, and trademarks. |
| Celler-Kefauver Act (1950) | Prohibits any corporation engaged in commerce from acquiring the whole or any part of the stock or other share of the capital assets of another corporation when the effect substantially lessens competition or tends to create a monopoly. |
| Fair Packaging and Labeling Act (1966) | Makes illegal the unfair or deceptive packaging or labeling of consumer products. |
| Magnuson-Moss Warranty (FTC) Act (1975) | Provides for minimum disclosure standards for written consumer product warranties; defines minimum consent standards for written warranties; allows the FTC to prescribe interpretive rules in policy statements regarding unfair or deceptive practices. |
| Consumer Goods Pricing Act (1975) | Prohibits the use of price maintenance agreements among manufacturers and resellers in interstate commerce. |
| Antitrust Improvements Act (1976) | Requires large corporations to inform federal regulators of prospective mergers or acquisitions so that they can be studied for any possible violations of the law. |
| Trademark Counterfeiting Act (1980) | Provides civil and criminal penalties against those who deal in counterfeit consumer goods or any counterfeit goods that can threaten health or safety. |
| Trademark Law Revision Act (1988) | Amends the Lanham Act to allow brands not yet introduced to be protected through registration with the Patent and Trademark Office. |
| Nutrition Labeling and Education Act (1990) | Prohibits exaggerated health claims and requires all processed foods to contain labels with nutritional information. |
| Telephone Consumer Protection Act (1991) | Establishes procedures to avoid unwanted telephone solicitations; prohibits marketers from using automated telephone dialing system or an artificial or prerecorded voice to certain telephone lines. |
| Federal Trademark Dilution Act (1995) | Provides trademark owners the right to protect trademarks and requires relinquishment of names that match or parallel existing trademarks. |

*continued*

**TABLE B.4**   *continued*

| Act (Date Enacted) | Purpose |
|---|---|
| Digital Millennium Copyright Act (1998) | Refined copyright laws to protect digital versions of copyrighted materials, including music and movies. |
| Children's Online Privacy Protection Act (2000) | Regulates the collection of personally identifiable information (name, address, e-mail address, hobbies, interests, or information collected through cookies) online from children under age 13. |
| Sarbanes-Oxley Act (2002) | Made securities fraud a criminal offense; stiffened penalties for corporate fraud; created an accounting oversight board; and instituted numerous other provisions designed to increase corporate transparency and compliance. |
| Do Not Call Implementation Act (2003) | Directs FCC and FTC to coordinate so their rules are consistent regarding telemarketing call practices, including the Do Not Call Registry. |

Union Anti-Trust regulators. The firm had been suspected of running a cartel, and attempting to squeeze out smaller competitors through its position as market leader. The 2008 raids were part of an ongoing series of international anti-trust allegations aimed at Intel.[86] The Sherman Antitrust Act, still highly relevant 100 years after its passage, is being copied throughout the world as the basis for regulating fair competition.

Because the provisions of the Sherman Antitrust Act are rather vague, courts have not always interpreted it as its creators intended. The Clayton Act was passed in 1914 to limit specific activities that can reduce competition. The **Clayton Act** prohibits price discrimination, tying and exclusive agreements, and the acquisition of stock in another corporation where the effect may be to substantially lessen competition or tend to create a monopoly. In addition, the Clayton Act prohibits members of one company's board of directors from holding seats on the boards of competing corporations. The act also exempts farm cooperatives and labor organizations from antitrust laws.

In spite of these laws regulating business practices, there are still many questions about the regulation of business. For instance, it is difficult to determine what constitutes an acceptable degree of competition and whether a monopoly is harmful to a particular market. Many mergers were permitted that resulted in less competition in the banking, publishing, and automobile industries. In some industries, such as utilities, it is not cost effective to have too many competitors. For this reason, the government permits utility monopolies, although recently, the telephone, electricity, and communications industries have been deregulated. Furthermore, the antitrust laws are often rather vague and require interpretation, which may vary from judge to judge and court to court. Thus, what one judge defines as a monopoly or trust today may be permitted by another judge a few years from now. Businesspeople need to understand what the law says on these issues and try to conduct their affairs within the bounds of these laws.

# The Internet: Legal and Regulatory Issues

Our use and dependence on the Internet is increasingly creating a potential legal problem for businesses. With this growing use come questions of maintaining an acceptable level of privacy for consumers and proper competitive use of the medium. Some might consider that tracking individuals who visit or "hit" their Web site by attaching a "cookie" (identifying you as a Web site visitor for potential recontact and tracking your movement throughout the site) is an improper use of the Internet for business purposes. Others may find such practices acceptable and similar to the practices of non-Internet retailers who copy information from checks or ask customers for their name, address, or phone number before they will process a transaction. There are few specific laws that regulate business on the Internet, but the standards for acceptable behavior that are reflected in the basic laws and regulations designed for traditional businesses can be applied to business on the Internet

*Lawyer Robert Ellis Smith, the publisher of the* Privacy Journal, *has made a business out of protecting people's privacy, including their credit and medical records, and Internet use. In addition to the journal, he is the author of several books on privacy.*

as well. On law aimed specifically at advertising on the internet is the CAN-SPAM Act of 2004. The law restricts unsolicited email advertisements by requiring the consent of the recipient. Furthermore, the CAN-SPAM Act follows the "opt-out" model wherein recipients can elect to not receive further emails from a sender simply by clicking on a link.[87]

The central focus for future legislation of business conducted on the Internet is the protection of personal privacy. The present basis of personal privacy protection is the U.S. Constitution, various Supreme Court rulings, and laws such as the 1971 Fair Credit Reporting Act, the 1978 Right to Financial Privacy Act, and the 1974 Privacy Act, which deals with the release of government records. With few regulations on the use of information by businesses, companies legally buy and sell information on customers to gain competitive advantage. Sometimes existing laws are not enough to protect people, and the ease with which information on customers can be obtained becomes a problem. For example, identity theft has increased due to the proliferation of the use of the internet. In March 2008, two grocery-store chains, Hannaford Bros and Sweetbay, both experienced a security breach that potentially exposed 4.2 million customers' cards. By mid March, the companies were aware of 1,800 fraudulent charges stemming from the security incident. Without proper legislation to protect information on the internet, issues like this will continue to plague businesses.[88] It has been suggested that the treatment of personal data as property will

ensure privacy rights by recognizing that customers have a right to control the use of their personal data.

Internet use is different from traditional interaction with businesses in that it is readily accessible, and most online businesses are able to develop databases of information on customers. Congress has restricted the development of databases on children using the Internet. The Children's Online Privacy Protection Act of 2000 prohibits Web sites and Internet providers from seeking personal information from children under age 13 without parental consent.

The Internet has also created a copyright dilemma for some organizations that have found that the Web addresses of other online firms either match or are very similar to their company trademark. "Cybersquatters" attempt to sell back the registration of these matching sites to the trademark owner. Companies such as Taco Bell, MTC, and KFC have paid thousands of dollars to gain control of domain names that match or parallel company trademarks. The Federal Trademark Dilution Act of 1995 helps companies address this conflict. The act provides trademark owners the right to protect trademarks, prevents the use of trademark-protected entities, and requires the relinquishment of names that match or closely parallel company trademarks. The reduction of geographic barriers, speed of response, and memory capability of the Internet will continue to create new challenges for the legal and regulatory environment in the future.

# Legal Pressure for Responsible Business Conduct

To ensure greater compliance with society's desires, both federal and state governments are moving toward increased organizational accountability for misconduct. Before 1991, laws mainly punished those employees directly responsible for an offense. Under new guidelines established by the Federal Sentencing Guidelines for Organizations (FSGO), however, both the responsible employees and the firms that employ them are held accountable for violations of federal law. Thus, the government now places responsibility for controlling and preventing misconduct squarely on the shoulders of top management. The main objectives of the federal guidelines are to train employees, self-monitor and supervise employee conduct, deter unethical acts, and punish those organizational members who engage in illegal acts.

A 2004 amendment to the FSGO requires that a business's governing authority be well informed about its ethics program with respect to content, implementation, and effectiveness. This places the responsibility squarely on the shoulders of the firm's leadership, usually the board of directors. The board must ensure that there is a high-ranking manager accountable for the day-to-day operational oversight of the ethics program. The board must provide for adequate authority, resources, and access to the board or an appropriate subcommittee of the board. The board must ensure that there are confidential mechanisms available so that the organization's employees and agents may report or seek guidance about potential or actual misconduct without fear of retaliation. Finally, the board is required to oversee the discovery of risks and to design, implement, and modify approaches to deal with those risks.

If an organization's culture and policies reward or provide opportunities to engage in misconduct through lack of managerial concern or failure to comply with the seven minimum requirements of the FSGO (provided in Table B.5), then the organization may incur not only penalties but also the loss of customer trust, public confidence, and other intangible assets. For this reason, organizations cannot succeed solely through a legalistic approach to compliance with the sentencing guidelines; top management must cultivate high ethical standards that will serve as barriers to illegal conduct. The organization must want to be a good citizen and recognize the importance of compliance to successful workplace activities and relationships.

The federal guidelines also require businesses to develop programs that can detect—and that will deter employees from engaging in—misconduct. To be considered effective, such compliance programs must include disclosure of any wrongdoing, cooperation with the government, and acceptance of responsibility for the misconduct. Codes of ethics, employee ethics training, hotlines (direct 800 phone numbers), compliance directors, newsletters, brochures, and other communication methods are typical components of a compliance program. The ethics component, discussed in Chapter 2, acts as a buffer, keeping firms away from the thin line that separates unethical and illegal conduct.

Despite the existing legislation, a number of ethics scandals in the early 2000s led Congress to pass—almost unanimously—the **Sarbanes-Oxley Act,** which criminalized securities fraud and strengthened penalties for corporate fraud. It also created an accounting oversight board that requires corporations to establish codes of ethics for financial reporting and to develop greater transparency in financial reports to investors and other interested parties. Additionally, the law requires top corporate executives to sign off on their firms' financial reports, and they risk fines and jail sentences if they misrepresent their companies' financial position. Table B.6 summarizes the major provisions of the Sarbanes-Oxley Act.

The Sarbanes Oxley Act has created a number of concerns and is considered burdensome and expensive to corporations. Large corporations report spending more than $4 million each year to comply with the Act according to Financial Executives International. The Act has caused more than 500 public companies a year to report problems in their accounting systems.

---

**TABLE B.5    Seven Steps to Compliance**

1. Develop standards and procedures to reduce the propensity for criminal conduct.

2. Designate a high-level compliance manager or ethics officer to oversee the compliance program.

3. Avoid delegating authority to people known to have a propensity to engage in misconduct.

4. Communicate standards and procedures to employees, other agents, and independent contractors through training programs and publications.

5. Establish systems to monitor and audit misconduct and to allow employees and agents to report criminal activity.

6. Enforce standards and punishments consistently across all employees in the organization.

7. Respond immediately to misconduct and take reasonable steps to prevent further criminal conduct.

Source: United States Sentencing Commission, *Federal Sentencing Guidelines for Organizations,* 1991.

More than 1,000 businesspersons have been convicted of corporate crimes since the law was passed in 2002. This means that the overwhelming majority of businesses are in compliance with the law.

On the other hand, there are many benefits, including greater accountability of top managers and boards of directors, that improve investor confidence and protect employees, especially their retirement plans. It is believed that the law has more benefits than drawbacks—with the greatest benefit being that boards of directors and top managers are better informed. Some companies such as Cisco and Pitney Bowes report improved efficiency and cost savings from better financial information.

TABLE B.6   Major Provisions of the Sarbanes-Oxley Act

1. Requires the establishment of a Public Company Accounting Oversight Board in charge of regulations administered by the Securities and Exchange Commission.

2. Requires CEOs and CFOs to certify that their companies' financial statements are true and without misleading statements.

3. Requires that corporate boards of directors' audit committees consist of independent members who have no material interests in the company.

4. Prohibits corporations from making or offering loans to officers and board members.

5. Requires codes of ethics for senior financial officers; code must be registered with the SEC.

6. Prohibits accounting firms from providing both auditing and consulting services to the same client without the approval of the client firm's audit committee.

7. Requires company attorneys to report wrongdoing to top managers and, if necessary, to the board of directors; if managers and directors fail to respond to reports of wrongdoing, the attorney should stop representing the company.

8. Mandates "whistleblower protection" for persons who disclose wrongdoing to authorities.

9. Requires financial securities analysts to certify that their recommendations are based on objective reports.

10. Requires mutual fund managers to disclose how they vote shareholder proxies, giving investors information about how their shares influence decisions.

11. Establishes a 10-year penalty for mail/wire fraud.

12. Prohibits the two senior auditors from working on a corporation's account for more than five years; other auditors are prohibited from working on an account for more than seven years. In other words, accounting firms must rotate individual auditors from one account to another from time to time.

Source: O. C. Ferrell, John Fraedrich, and Linda Ferrell, *Business Ethics: Ethical Decision Making and Cases,* 6th ed. (Boston: Houghton Mifflin, 2005), p. 63.

# chapter 3

## CHAPTER OUTLINE

Introduction

The Role of International Business
- Why Nations Trade
- Trade between Countries
- Balance of Trade

International Trade Barriers
- Economic Barriers
- Ethical, Legal, and Political Barriers
- Social and Cultural Barriers
- Technological Barriers

Trade Agreements, Alliances, and Organizations
- General Agreement on Tariffs and Trade
- The North American Free Trade Agreement
- The European Union
- Asia-Pacific Economic Cooperation
- World Bank
- International Monetary Fund

Getting Involved in International Business
- Exporting and Importing
- Trading Companies
- Licensing and Franchising
- Contract Manufacturing
- Outsourcing
- Joint Ventures and Alliances
- Direct Investment

International Business Strategies
- Developing Strategies
- Managing the Challenges of Global Business

# Business in a Borderless World

## OBJECTIVES

*After reading this chapter, you will be able to:*

- Explore some of the factors within the international trade environment that influence business.

- Investigate some of the economic, legal-political, social, cultural, and technological barriers to international business.

- Specify some of the agreements, alliances, and organizations that may encourage trade across international boundaries.

- Summarize the different levels of organizational involvement in international trade.

- Contrast two basic strategies used in international business.

- Assess the opportunities and problems facing a small business considering expanding into international markets.

## Fresh & Easy Grocery Shopping for One & All!

You may not have heard of Tesco—the largest retailer in the United Kingdom and the third largest retailer in the world, behind only Wal-Mart in the United States and Carrefour in France—but if the company has its way, it will soon become a household name in America. Tesco operates more than 3,000 grocery stores, varying from the Tesco supercenter to the Tesco Express, in 12 countries and is now expanding into the United States. Why, you might ask, would a company, already so successful in other countries, take on the likes of Wal-Mart, Kroger, and Albertsons? Valid question, but Tesco feels it is bringing a new shopping experience to U.S. consumers—filling a gaping hole in the grocery market. And, looking at the company's plan for its U.S. stores, it sounds like they're right.

To figure out how best to approach the U.S. market, Tesco conducted years of research into the way Americans live—even living with American families, checking out their cupboards and shopping and cooking with them. As a result, Tesco has developed the Fresh & Easy Neighborhood Market, a smaller store than the typical supermarket sized at 10,000 square feet. The concept behind Fresh & Easy is fresh and wholesome food at affordable prices for everyone. The stores will provide fresh meats and produce along with a host of prepared meals. Offerings will be comprised, as much as possible, of a Fresh & Easy label along with locally sourced foods. What makes this new market unique is the proposed array of freshly prepared dishes—something busy Americans of today may just fall in love with. Industry analysts agree that the United States currently has no grocery store fitting this mold.

*continued*

**ENTER THE WORLD OF BUSINESS**

If the Fresh & Easy Neighborhood Market sounds good to you, you might be thinking, "Where are they? Will there be one near me?" Well, Tesco is beginning by opening stores in southern California (one of the few areas in which Wal-Mart does not have firm footing), Arizona, and Nevada. The company announced 122 planned store locations, with the first 30 open by the end of 2007. Some will be located in poverty-stricken areas desperately in need of grocery stores. If Tesco can succeed in maintaining its Fresh & Easy markets in impoverished areas where other chains have failed, it will truly be filling a void that *needs* filling.

Tesco's U.S. foray is nothing short of ambitious. However, the company, which was once a low-ranked British chain, has faced its share of challenges in the past and come out ahead. The success or failure of the Fresh & Easy Neighborhood Market depends both on whether Tesco can live up to its promises and on the sometimes loyal, sometimes fickle American consumer. Still, if you happen to be on the West Coast, it sounds like it's worth checking out the latest import from the United Kingdom.[1]

# Introduction

Consumers around the world can drink Coca-Cola and Pepsi; eat at McDonald's and Pizza Hut; see movies from Mexico, England, France, Australia, and China; and watch CNN and MTV on Toshiba and Sony televisions. It may surprise you that the Japanese firm Komatsu sells earth-moving equipment to China that is manufactured in Peoria, Illinois.[2] The products you consume today are just as likely to have been made in China, Korea, or Germany as in the United States. Likewise, consumers in other countries buy Western electrical equipment, clothing, rock music, cosmetics, and toiletries, as well as computers, robots, and earth-moving equipment.

Many U.S. firms are finding that international markets provide tremendous opportunities for growth. Accessing these markets can promote innovation, while intensifying global competition spurs companies to market better and less expensive products. Today, the 6.7 billion people that inhabit the earth create one tremendous marketplace.

> **Did You Know?** McDonald's serves 52 million customers a day at more than 30,000 restaurants in more than 100 countries.[3]

In this chapter, we explore business in this exciting global marketplace. First, we'll look at the nature of international business, including barriers and promoters of trade across international boundaries. Next, we consider the levels of organizational involvement in international business. Finally, we briefly discuss strategies for trading across national borders.

## The Role of International Business

**international business**
the buying, selling, and trading of goods and services across national boundaries

**International business** refers to the buying, selling, and trading of goods and services across national boundaries. Falling political barriers and new technology are making it possible for more and more companies to sell their products overseas as well as at home. And, as differences among nations continue to narrow, the trend toward the globalization of business is becoming increasingly important. Starbucks, for example, serves 20 million customers a week at almost 16,000 coffee shops in 44 countries.[4] The Internet provides many companies easier entry to access global markets than opening bricks-and-mortar stores.[5] Amazon.com, an online retailer, has distribution centers from Nevada to Germany that fill millions of orders a day and ship them to customers in every corner of the world. In China, Procter & Gamble has developed bargain-priced versions of Tide, Crest, and Oil of Olay, and it regularly relies on groups that live in the countryside for consumer information.[6] Indeed, most of the world's population and two-thirds of its total purchasing power are outside the United States.

When McDonald's sells a Big Mac in Moscow, Sony sells a stereo in Detroit, or a small Swiss medical supply company sells a shipment of orthopedic devices to a hospital in Monterrey, Mexico, the sale affects the economies of the countries involved. The U.S. market, with 300 million consumers, makes up only a small part of the 6.7 billion people elsewhere in the world to whom global companies must consider marketing. Global marketing requires balancing your global brand with the needs of local consumers.[7] To begin our study of international business, we must first consider some economic issues: why nations trade, exporting and importing, and the balance of trade.

## Why Nations Trade

Nations and businesses engage in international trade to obtain raw materials and goods that are otherwise unavailable to them or are available elsewhere at a lower price than that at which they themselves can produce. A nation, or individuals and organizations from a nation, sell surplus materials and goods to acquire funds to buy the goods, services, and ideas its people need. Poland and Hungary, for example, want to trade with Western nations so that they can acquire new technology and techniques to revitalize their formerly communist economies. Which goods and services a nation sells depends on what resources it has available.

Some nations have a monopoly on the production of a particular resource or product. Such a monopoly, or **absolute advantage,** exists when a country is the only source of an item, the only producer of an item, or the most efficient producer of an item. Because South Africa has the largest deposits of diamonds in the world, one company, De Beers Consolidated Mines Ltd. controls a major portion of the world's diamond trade and uses its control to maintain high prices for gem-quality diamonds. The United States, until recently, held an absolute advantage in oil-drilling equipment. But an absolute advantage not based on the availability of natural resources rarely lasts, and Japan and Russia are now challenging the United States in the production of oil-drilling equipment.

Most international trade is based on **comparative advantage,** which occurs when a country specializes in products that it can supply more efficiently or at a lower cost than it can produce other items. The United States has a comparative advantage in producing agricultural commodities such as corn and wheat. Until recently, the United States had a comparative advantage in manufacturing automobiles, heavy machinery, airplanes, and weapons; other countries now hold the comparative advantage for many of these products. While Colombia has fewer oil reserves than Venezuela, its oil and gas industry is growing rapidly. Colombia may have greater reserves than leading oil producers such as Mexico and Algeria and has a comparative advantage in that its significant resources are accessible to global companies and markets.[8] Other countries, particularly India and Ireland, are also

**absolute advantage**
a monopoly that exists when a country is the only source of an item, the only producer of an item, or the most efficient producer of an item

**comparative advantage**
the basis of most international trade, when a country specializes in products that it can supply more efficiently or at a lower cost than it can produce other items

**outsourcing**
the transferring of manufacturing or other tasks—such as data processing—to countries where labor and supplies are less expensive

gaining a comparative advantage over the United States in the provision of some services, such as call-center operations, engineering, and software programming. As a result, U.S. companies are increasingly **outsourcing,** or transferring manufacturing and other tasks to countries where labor and supplies are less expensive. Outsourcing has become a controversial practice in the United States because many jobs have moved overseas where those tasks can be accomplished for lower costs. For example, India is a popular choice for call centers for U.S. firms. As call centers are the first job choice for millions of young Indians, employers are getting choosier about the people they hire, and it is difficult to train Indians to speak the kind of colloquial English, French, Spanish, German, or Dutch that customers want, although there are estimates that by 2010 more than 160,000 workers with excellent English and foreign-language skills will be needed.

## Trade between Countries

**exporting**
the sale of goods and services to foreign markets

To obtain needed goods and services and the funds to pay for them, nations trade by exporting and importing. **Exporting** is the sale of goods and services to foreign markets. The United States exported more than *$1.6 trillion in goods* and services last year.[9] In China, General Motors is targeting wealthier customers with the Cadillac, middle management with the Buick Excelle, office workers with the Chevrolet Spark, and rural consumers with the Wuling minivan.[10] U.S. companies such as General Motors that view China as both a growth market for exports and a market for lower cost labor for imports and can strategically integrate these into their operations enjoy significantly higher profits than companies who only focus on one of these opportunities.[11] U.S. businesses export many goods and services, particularly agricultural, entertainment (movies, television shows, etc.), and technological products. **Importing** is the purchase of goods and services from foreign sources. Many of the goods you buy in the United States are likely to be imports or to have some imported components. Sometimes, you may not even realize they are imports. The United States imported more than *$2.3 trillion* in goods and services last year.[12]

**importing**
the purchase of goods and services from foreign sources

**balance of trade**
the difference in value between a nation's exports and its imports

## Balance of Trade

You have probably read or heard about the fact that the United States has a trade deficit, but what is a trade deficit? A nation's **balance of trade** is the difference in value between its exports and imports. Because the United States (and some other nations as well) imports more products than it exports, it has a negative balance of trade, or **trade deficit.** In 2007 the United States had a $711 billion trade deficit, a 6.5 percent decrease from 2006. This is the first decrease since 2000 to 2001. China accounted for most of this deficit increase. Total U.S. imports reached $2.3 trillion in 2007, 44 percent more than the $1.6 trillion in exports (see Table 3.1).[13] The trade

**trade deficit**
a nation's negative balance of trade, which exists when that country imports more products than it exports

| TABLE 3.I | | 1980 | 1990 | 2000 | 2005 | 2006 | 2007 |
|---|---|---|---|---|---|---|---|
| U.S. Trade Deficit, 1980–2006 (in billions of dollars) | Exports | $ 333 | $ 576 | $ 1,133 | $ 1,300 | $ 1,455.7 | $ 1,621.8 |
| | Imports | 326 | 632 | 1,532 | 2,026 | 2,204.2 | 2,333.4 |
| | Trade Surplus/Deficit | 7 | 57 | 399 | 726 | 758.5 | 711.6 |

Source: Department of Commerce and Robert E. Scott and David Ratner, "Trade Picture," The Economic Policy Institute, February 10, 2006, http://www.epinet.org/content.cfm/webfeatures_econindicators_tradepich20060210 (accessed June 5, 2006); "2006 Annual Trade Highlights, Dollar Change from Prior Year," *U.S. Census Bureau, Foreign Trade Statistics,* http://www.census.gov/foreign-trade/statistics/highlights/annual.html (accessed April 4, 2008).

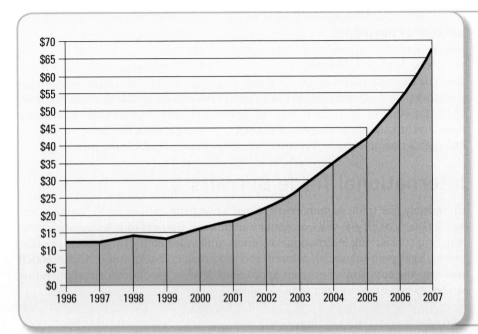

FIGURE 3.1

U.S. Exports to China
Increase ($ billions)

Source: David J. Lynch,
"Building Explosion in China
Pumps Up Exports from USA,"
*USA Today,* April 20, 2006.
p. B1.s; "U.S. Domestic Exports
for Selected World Areas and
the Top Ten Countries- 2006,"
*U.S. Census Bureau, Foreign
Trade Statistics,* http://www.
census.gov/foreign-trade/
Press-Release/2006pr/aip/
related_party/ (accessed April
4, 2008).

deficit fluctuates according to such factors as the health of the United States and other economies, productivity, perceived quality, and exchange rates. In 2007 the U.S. had a $232.5 billion deficit with China. As Figure 3.1 indicates, U.S. exports to China have been rapidly increasing but not fast enough to offset the imports from China. Trade deficits are harmful because they can mean the failure of businesses, the loss of jobs, and a lowered standard of living.

Of course, when a nation exports more goods than it imports, it has a favorable balance of trade, or trade surplus. Until about 1970, the United States had a trade surplus due to an abundance of natural resources and the relative efficiency of its manufacturing systems. Table 3.2 shows the top 10 countries with which the United States has a trade deficit and a trade surplus.

| Trade Deficit | Trade Surplus |
|---|---|
| 1. China | Netherlands |
| 2. Japan | United Arab Emirates |
| 3. Canada | Hong Kong |
| 4. Mexico | Belgium |
| 5. Venezuela | Australia |
| 6. Nigeria | Singapore |
| 7. Saudi Arabia | Panama |
| 8. Germany | Egypt |
| 9. Italy | Dominican Republic |
| 10. Malaysia | United Kingdom |

TABLE 3.2

Top 10 Countries Maintaining Trade Deficits/Surpluses with the United States

Source: "Top Ten Countries with which the U.S. Has a Trade Deficit," http://www.census.gov/foreign-trade/top/dst/current/deficit.html (accessed April 4, 2008), "Top Ten Countries with which the U.S. Has a Trade Surplus," http://www.census.gov/foreign-trade/top/dst/current/surplus.html (accessed April 4, 2008).

**balance of payments**
the difference between
the flow of money into
and out of a country

The difference between the flow of money into and out of a country is called its **balance of payments.** A country's balance of trade, foreign investments, foreign aid, loans, military expenditures, and money spent by tourists comprise its balance of payments. As you might expect, a country with a trade surplus generally has a favorable balance of payments because it is receiving more money from trade with foreign countries than it is paying out. When a country has a trade deficit, more money flows out of the country than into it. If more money flows out of the country than into it from tourism and other sources, the country may experience declining production and higher unemployment, because there is less money available for spending.

# International Trade Barriers

Completely free trade seldom exists. When a company decides to do business outside its own country, it will encounter a number of barriers to international trade. Any firm considering international business must research the other country's economic, legal, political, social, cultural, and technological background. Such research will help the company choose an appropriate level of involvement and operating strategies, as we will see later in this chapter.

### Economic Barriers

When looking at doing business in another country, managers must consider a number of basic economic factors, such as economic development, infrastructure, and exchange rates.

**Economic Development.**   When considering doing business abroad, U.S. business people need to recognize that they cannot take for granted that other countries offer the same things as are found in *industrialized nations*—economically advanced countries such as the United States, Japan, Great Britain, and Canada. Many countries in Africa, Asia, and South America, for example, are in general poorer and less economically advanced than those in North America and Europe; they are often called *less-developed countries* (LDCs). LDCs are characterized by low per-capita income (income generated by the nation's production of goods and services divided by the population), which means that consumers are less likely to purchase nonessential products. Nonetheless, LDCs represent a potentially huge and profitable market for many businesses because they may be buying technology to improve their infrastructures, and much of the population may desire consumer products. For example, cellular and wireless phone technology is reaching many countries at less expense than traditional hard-wired telephone systems. Consequently, opportunities for growth in the cell phone market remain strong in Southeast Asia, Africa, and the Middle East. Haier, China's top appliance maker, makes larger washing machines for Chinese cities, but has also developed a smaller model costing just $37 for poorer areas.[14]

**infrastructure**
the physical facilities
that support a country's
economic activities, such
as railroads, highways,
ports, airfields, utilities
and power plants,
schools, hospitals,
communication systems,
and commercial
distribution systems

A country's level of development is determined in part by its **infrastructure,** the physical facilities that support its economic activities, such as railroads, highways, ports, airfields, utilities and power plants, schools, hospitals, communication systems, and commercial distribution systems. When doing business in LDCs, for example, a business may need to compensate for rudimentary distribution and communication systems, or even a lack of technology.

**exchange rate**
the ratio at which one
nation's currency can be
exchanged for another
nation's currency

**Exchange Rates.**   The ratio at which one nation's currency can be exchanged for another nation's currency is the **exchange rate.** Exchange rates vary daily and can be found in newspapers and through many sites on the Internet. Familiarity with exchange rates is important because they affect the cost of imports and exports. The weak value of the U.S. dollar has made export of U.S.-made vehicles more attractive around the world. General Motors is exporting the Buick Enclave sport-utility vehicle to China, and Chrysler is exporting its Voyager as well as Dodge and Jeep models to European countries. Ford is exporting the Ranger pickup truck and the Focus compact car to Mexico and Brazil.[15]

Occasionally, a government may alter the value of its national currency. Devaluation decreases the value of currency in relation to other currencies. If the U.S. government were to devalue the dollar, it would lower the cost of American goods abroad and make trips to the United States less expensive for foreign tourists. Thus, devaluation encourages the sale of domestic goods and tourism. Mexico has repeatedly devalued the peso for this reason. Revaluation, which increases the value of a currency in relation to other currencies, occurs rarely.

## Ethical, Legal, and Political Barriers

A company that decides to enter the international marketplace must contend with potentially complex relationships among the different laws of its own nation, international laws, and the laws of the nation with which it will be trading; various trade restrictions imposed on international trade; changing political climates; and different ethical values. Legal and ethical requirements for successful business are increasing globally. Samsung Group Chairman Lee Kum-hee was forced to resign under a possible criminal indictment for tax evasion and breach of trust. Samsung accounts for 15 percent of South Korea's economy and 20 percent of its exports. The departure of Lee triggered a broad restructuring within Samsung to yield improved ethics with greater accountability and transparency.[16]

### Laws and Regulations.
The United States has a number of laws and regulations that govern the activities of U.S. firms engaged in international trade. For example, the Webb-Pomerene Export Trade Act of 1918 exempts American firms from anti-trust laws if those firms are acting together to enter international trade. This law allows selected U.S. firms to form monopolies to compete with foreign monopolistic organizations, although they are not allowed to limit free trade and competition within the United States or to use unfair methods of competition in international trade. The United States also has a variety of friendship, commerce, and navigation treaties with other nations. These treaties allow business to be transacted between citizens of the specified countries. For example, Belgium is a gateway to European markets and has lowered its taxes to give U.S. companies greater reason to locate their European operations there. For example, Belgium has the lowest patent income tax and has 0 percent withholding tax on corporate dividends and interest from a U.S. company. This prevents a company from paying both U.S. and Belgian tax, or double taxation.[17]

The salt-and-pepper shaker on the right, manufactured by Shantou Lian Plastic Products of Guangdong, China, was one of 13 winners of a "2008 Plagiarius Award." The dubious honor is given to the "best" product knockoffs by the organization Aktion Plagiarius in an effort to shame their makers by singling them out. (The salt-and-pepper set on the left, made by WMF, a German company, is the original product.)

## Think Globally
### Japanese and Americans Swap Food

The Japanese have long been known for their longevity and slender physiques, thanks to a healthy diet consisting of foods such as rice, fish, and vegetables. Although this is true, things have begun to change as the Japanese, particularly younger generations, have become interested in all things American—including American foods. Creeping into the Japanese diet is a taste for all things sweet, and who better to capitalize on this than the ever-fabulous, ever-fattening American fast-food chain?

Among the American fast-food chains doing a booming business in Japan are Krispy Kreme and McDonald's. The ice cream giant Cold Stone Creamery has also been embraced by the Japanese. Krispy Kreme opened its doors to Japan in December 2006, and people have been going crazy for it. In the first three days, more than 10,000 people flocked to one location. There have been numerous reports of people waiting in lines for more than two hours just to purchase a Krispy Kreme doughnut. Why is Krispy Kreme doing so well? According to think-tank researcher Hikaru Hakuhodo, people in Japan are interested in what is considered new and cool. Right now, all things American seem to have this status. Doughnuts have been featured in American films for years, and, to those in Japan, to taste a Krispy Kreme doughnut may just be a way to taste a little bit of what it's like to be American. However,

things don't stay cool forever. Doughnut Planet and Dunkin' Donuts had their day in the Japanese market and are long gone. Will Krispy Kreme and others riding the current wave be able to stay on?

And how will the Japanese fare if they continue to indulge like Americans? In 20 years, Japanese obesity rates have grown by more than 10 percent and illnesses such as diabetes (often related to weight and diet) have increased by almost 50 percent. The average Japanese woman is now 26.5 pounds heavier than the average Japanese woman of the 1950s. Meanwhile, Americans are loving sushi restaurants and embracing Japanese-style food in an effort to counteract their own struggles with diet. Will this one day swing back around to the Japanese as the epitome of cool? Will Krispy Kreme and the like be able to survive, or will the Japanese realize that they have been the cool ones all along?[18]

### Discussion Questions
1. What is going to happen to Japanese consumers if they start consuming much more American fast food?
2. Why is Krispy Kreme doing so well in Japan?
3. What is the possibility that the Japanese will recognize that their increasingly Western diet is not as healthy as their previous diet?

Once outside U.S. borders, businesspeople are likely to find that the laws of other nations differ from those of the United States. Many of the legal rights that Americans take for granted do not exist in other countries, and a firm doing business abroad must understand and obey the laws of the host country. Many countries forbid foreigners from owning real property outright; others have strict laws limiting the amount of local currency that can be taken out of the country and the amount of foreign currency that can be brought in.

Some countries have copyright and patent laws that are less strict than those of the United States, and some countries fail to honor U.S. laws. Because copying is a tradition in China and Vietnam and laws protecting copyrights and intellectual property are weak and minimally enforced, those countries are flooded with counterfeit videos, movies, CDs, computer software, furniture, and clothing. Companies are angry because the counterfeits harm not only their sales, but also their reputations if the knockoffs are of poor quality. Such counterfeiting is not limited to China or Vietnam. Thirty-five percent of the packaged software installed on personal computers worldwide in 2006 was illegal, amounting to $40 billion in global losses due to software piracy. However, some improvements in a number of markets indicate education, enforcement, and policy efforts are beginning to pay off in emerging economies such as China, Russia, and India and in Central/Eastern Europe and in the Middle East and Africa.[19] In countries where these activities occur, laws against them may not be sufficiently enforced, if counterfeiting is in fact deemed illegal. Thus, businesses engaging in foreign trade may have to take extra steps to protect their products because local laws may be insufficient to do so.

Tariffs and Trade Restrictions.    Tariffs and other trade restrictions are part of a country's legal structure but may be established or removed for political reasons. An **import tariff** is a tax levied by a nation on goods imported into the country. A *fixed tariff* is a specific amount of money levied on each unit of a product brought into the country, while an *ad valorem tariff* is based on the value of the item. Most countries allow citizens traveling abroad to bring home a certain amount of merchandise without paying an import tariff. A U.S. citizen may bring $200 worth of merchandise into the United States duty free. After that, U.S. citizens must pay an ad valorem tariff based on the cost of the item and the country of origin. Thus, identical items purchased in different countries might have different tariffs.

Countries sometimes levy tariffs for political reasons, as when they impose sanctions against other countries to protest their actions. However, import tariffs are more commonly imposed to protect domestic products by raising the price of imported ones. Such protective tariffs have become controversial, as Americans become increasingly concerned over the U.S. trade deficit. Protective tariffs allow more expensive domestic goods to compete with foreign ones. In early 2008, food shortages required that countries in the developing world cut import taxes and restrict exports to keep more affordable food in country. Saudi Arabia, for example, cut wheat tariffs from 25 percent to zero and reduced tariffs on poultry, dairy, and vegetable oils to forestall rising food prices.[20]

Critics of protective tariffs argue that their use inhibits free trade and competition. Supporters of protective tariffs say they insulate domestic industries, particularly new ones, against well-established foreign competitors. Once an industry matures, however, its advocates may be reluctant to let go of the tariff that protected it. Tariffs also help when, because of low labor costs and other advantages, foreign competitors can afford to sell their products at prices lower than those charged by domestic companies. Some Americans argue that tariffs should be used to keep domestic wages high and unemployment low.

**Exchange controls** restrict the amount of currency that can be bought or sold. Some countries control their foreign trade by forcing businesspeople to buy and sell foreign products through a central bank. If John Deere, for example, receives payments for its tractors in a foreign currency, it may be required to sell the currency to that nation's central bank. When foreign currency is in short supply, as it is in many Third World and Eastern European countries, the government uses foreign currency to purchase necessities and capital goods and produces other products locally, thus limiting its need for foreign imports.

A **quota** limits the number of units of a particular product that can be imported into a country. A quota may be established by voluntary agreement or by government decree. After U.S. yarn suppliers complained that cotton yarn (used in underwear, socks, and T-shits) from Pakistan was flooding the market, a quota was imposed. Pakistan complained, and a textile-monitoring panel recommended that the United States lift the restrictions. The United States refused. However, in 2001, the quota was ruled a violation of global trade rules, and the United States was ordered to remove it.[21]

An **embargo** prohibits trade in a particular product. Embargoes are generally directed at specific goods or countries and may be established for political, economic, health, or religious reasons. While the U.S. maintains a trade embargo with Cuba, European hotel chains are engaged in a building boom on the Caribbean island, where tourism is the number-one industry. U.S. hotel chains are eager to build in Cuba but have no opportunity until the embargo is lifted. Even U.S.

**import tariff**
a tax levied by a nation on goods imported into the country

**exchange controls**
regulations that restrict the amount of currency that can be bought or sold

**quota**
a restriction on the number of units of a particular product that can be imported into a country

**embargo**
a prohibition on trade in a particular product

tourists are forbidden by the U.S. government to vacation in Cuba. If permitted, cruise ships would likely be the first type of U.S. tourism to reach the island since the early 1960s. It may be surprising to know that U.S. farmers export hundreds of millions of dollars worth of commodities to Cuba each year, based on a 2000 law that provided permission for some trade to the embargoed country.[22] Health embargoes prevent the importing of various pharmaceuticals, animals, plants, and agricultural products. Muslim nations forbid the importation of alcoholic beverages on religious grounds.

**dumping**
the act of a country or business selling products at less than what it costs to produce them

One common reason for setting quotas or tariffs is to prohibit **dumping,** which occurs when a country or business sells products at less than what it costs to produce them. The United States, for example, levied extra import duties against some types of Canadian lumber after the U.S. International Trade Commission found evidence that lower prices on the partially subsidized Canadian lumber threatened to harm the domestic lumber industry. However, some of the antidumping tariffs were later found to be in violation of global trade rules, and the United States was ordered to rescind them.[23] A company may dump its products for several reasons. Dumping permits quick entry into a market. Sometimes dumping occurs when the domestic market for a firm's product is too small to support an efficient level of production. In other cases, technologically obsolete products that are no longer salable in the country of origin are dumped overseas. Dumping is relatively difficult to prove, but even the suspicion of dumping can lead to the imposition of quotas or tariffs.

*Sometimes companies face political backlash not of their own making. In 2008, angry Chinese citizens threatened to boycott France's Carrefour, the world's No. 2 retailer. The boycott was meant to protest France's efforts to use the Beijing Olympics to pressure China to provide Tibetans with human rights.*

**Political Barriers.**    Unlike legal issues, political considerations are seldom written down and often change rapidly. Nations that have been subject to economic sanctions for political reasons in recent years include Cuba, Iran, Syria, and North Korea. While these were dramatic events, political considerations affect international business daily as governments enact tariffs, embargoes, or other types of trade restrictions in response to political events.

Businesses engaged in international trade must consider the relative instability of countries such as Iraq, Haiti, and Venezuela. Political unrest in countries such as Pakistan, Somalia, and Russia may create a hostile or even dangerous environment for foreign businesses. And, a sudden change in power can result in a regime that is hostile to foreign investment. Some businesses have been forced out of a country altogether, as when Hugo Chávez conducted a socialist revolution in Venezuela to force out or take over American oil companies. Whether they like it or not, companies are often involved directly or indirectly in international politics.

**cartel**
a group of firms or nations that agrees to act as a monopoly and not compete with each other, in order to generate a competitive advantage in world markets

Political concerns may lead a group of nations to form a **cartel,** a group of firms or nations that agrees to act as a monopoly and not compete with each other, to generate a competitive advantage in world markets. Probably the most famous cartel is OPEC, the Organization of Petroleum Exporting Countries, founded in the 1960s to increase the price of petroleum throughout the world and to maintain high prices. By working to ensure stable oil prices, OPEC hopes to enhance the economies of its member nations.

# Entrepreneurship in Action
## Wildnet Makes Wi-Fi Available to Everyone

Eric Brewer

**Business:** Wildnet (Wi-Fi over long distance)

**Founded:** Began to work on Wildnet in 2003, after selling Inktomi to Yahoo!

**Success:** Brewer and his team are providing some of the poorest areas in the world with Wi-Fi.

Eric Brewer is no stranger to working with the Internet. In 1996, he co-founded Inktomi Corporation—an Internet search company sold to Yahoo! in 2003 for $235 million. In 2000, he worked with the Clinton administration to help make it possible to search federal documents. He is widely respected in his field, becoming a tenured professor of computer science at the age of 32. However, after achieving notable accomplishments nationally, Brewer began looking at ways that he could use his knowledge to make a global impact and truly help people. These days, Brewer, now 40, and his graduate students are deep into the creation and implementation of an affordable and effective way to provide poor villages throughout the world with wireless Internet access. Their creation, Wildnet, uses publicly available radio spectrum and Linux (a free operating system) along with Intel computer boards and store-bought Wi-Fi radio chips to create affordable transmitters that work as quickly as a typical cable modem, transmitting data up to 60 miles. So far, Wildnets have been constructed in Philippines, Ghana, Guinea-Bissau, and India. Wildnet has made an important impact in these areas, particularly in India, where poor villagers are actually receiving improved eye care thanks to Wildnet. The development of Wildnet technology now takes up the bulk of Brewer's time as director of the Intel Research Berkeley Lab.[24]

## Social and Cultural Barriers

Most businesspeople engaged in international trade underestimate the importance of social and cultural differences; but these differences can derail an important transaction. For example, when Big Boy opened a restaurant in Bangkok, it quickly became popular with European and American tourists, but the local Thais refused to eat there. Instead, they placed gifts of rice and incense at the feet of the Big Boy statue (a chubby boy holding a hamburger) because it reminded them of Buddha. In Japan, customers were forced to tiptoe around a logo painted on the floor at the entrance to an Athlete's Foot store because in Japan, it is considered taboo to step on a crest.[25] And in Russia, consumers found the American-style energetic happiness of McDonald's employees insincere and offensive when the company opened its first stores there.[26] Unfortunately, cultural norms are rarely written down, and what is written down may well be inaccurate.

Cultural differences include differences in spoken and written language. Although it is certainly possible to translate words from one language to another, the true meaning is sometimes misinterpreted or lost. Consider some translations that went awry in foreign markets:

- A Scandinavian vacuum manufacturer Electrolux used the following in an American campaign: "Nothing sucks like an Electrolux."
- The Coca-Cola name in China was first read as "Ke-kou-ke-la," meaning "bite the wax tadpole."
- In Italy, a campaign for Schweppes Tonic Water translated the name into Schweppes Toilet Water.[27]

Translators cannot just translate slogans, advertising campaigns, and Web site language; they must know the cultural differences that could affect a company's success.

Differences in body language and personal space also affect international trade. Body language is nonverbal, usually unconscious communication through gestures,

**TABLE 3.3**

Cultural Behavioral Differences

| Region | Gestures Viewed as Rude or Unacceptable |
|---|---|
| Japan, Hong Kong, Middle East | Summoning with the index finger |
| Middle and Far East | Pointing with index finger |
| Thailand, Japan, France | Sitting with soles of shoes showing |
| Brazil, Germany | Forming a circle with fingers (e.g., the "O.K." sign in the United States) |
| Japan | Winking means "I love you" |
| Buddhist countries | Patting someone on the head |

Source: Adapted from Judie Haynes, "Communicating with Gestures," *EverythingESL* (n.d.), www.everythingesl.net/inservice/body_language.php (accessed March 2, 2004).

posture, and facial expression. Personal space is the distance at which one person feels comfortable talking to another. Americans tend to stand a moderate distance away from the person with whom they are speaking. Arab businessmen tend to stand face-to-face with the object of their conversation. Additionally, gestures vary from culture to culture, and gestures considered acceptable in American society—pointing, for example—may be considered rude in others. Table 3.3 shows some of the behaviors considered rude or unacceptable in other countries. Such cultural differences may generate uncomfortable feelings or misunderstandings when business people of different countries negotiate with each other.

Family roles also influence marketing activities. Many countries do not allow children to be used in advertising, for example. Advertising that features people in nontraditional social roles may or may not be successful either. The California Milk Processor Board aired a commercial in which a father and his young daughter shop at a supermarket for sugar, flour, cinnamon, and milk for a cake to be baked when they get home. The ad does not seem unusual except that when it was aired on Spanish-language television, the concept was striking. It is rare for Latino men to appear along with their daughters in Spanish-language ads and even rarer for the commercials to be set outside the home. The Hispanic culture typically reinforces how little boys need their fathers, not how little girls do.[28]

The people of other nations quite often have a different perception of time as well. Americans value promptness; a business meeting scheduled for a specific time seldom starts more than a few minutes late. In Mexico and Spain, however, it is not unusual for a meeting to be delayed half an hour or more. Such a late start might produce resentment in an American negotiating in Spain for the first time.

Companies engaged in foreign trade must observe the national and religious holidays and local customs of the host country. In many Islamic countries, for example, workers expect to take a break at certain times of the day to observe religious rites. Companies also must monitor their advertising to guard against offending customers. In Thailand and many other countries, public displays of affection between the sexes are unacceptable in advertising messages; in many Middle Eastern nations, it is unacceptable to show the soles of one's feet. In the Muslim world, exposure of a woman's skin, even her arms, is considered offensive.[29]

With the exception of the United States, most nations use the metric system. This lack of uniformity creates problems for both buyers and sellers in the international marketplace. American sellers, for instance, must package goods destined for foreign markets in liters or meters, and Japanese sellers must convert to the English system if they plan to sell a product in the United States. Tools also must be calibrated in the correct system if they are to function correctly. Hyundai and Honda service technicians need metric tools to make repairs on those cars.

The literature dealing with international business is filled with accounts of sometimes humorous but often costly mistakes that occurred because of a lack of understanding of the social and cultural differences between buyers and sellers. Such problems cannot always be avoided, but they can be minimized through research on the cultural and social differences of the host country.

### Technological Barriers

Many countries lack the technological infrastructure found in the United States, and some marketers are viewing such barriers as opportunities. For instance, marketers are targeting many countries such as India and China and some African countries where there are few private phone lines. Citizens of these countries are turning instead to wireless communication through cell phones. Technological advances are creating additional global marketing opportunities. The U.S. share of the global personal computer market has dropped from 35 percent in 2003 to 26 percent in 2007. PC sales are growing in the United States, but not as quickly as sales in the rest of the world. The average family in the United States has three PCs. In China, there is one PC for every 10 families. Dell Computer is trying to increase sales by expanding into these international markets.[30] In some countries, broadband access to the Internet is spreading much faster than in the United States. In fact, 10 nations, including South Korea, Hong Kong, and Canada, outrank the United States in terms of subscribers to broadband Internet access. The growth of high-speed Internet access should facilitate online commerce.[31]

# Trade Agreements, Alliances, and Organizations

Although these economic, political, legal, and sociocultural issues may seem like daunting barriers to international trade, there are also organizations and agreements—such as the General Agreement on Tariffs and Trade, the World Bank, and the International Monetary Fund—that foster international trade and can help companies get involved in and succeed in global markets. Various regional trade agreements, such as the North American Free Trade Agreement and the European Union, also promote trade among member nations by eliminating tariffs and trade restrictions. In this section, we'll look briefly at these agreements and organizations.

### General Agreement on Tariffs and Trade

During the Great Depression of the 1930s, nations established so many protective tariffs covering so many products that international trade became virtually impossible. By the end of World War II, there was considerable international momentum to liberalize trade and minimize the effects of tariffs. The **General Agreement on Tariffs and Trade (GATT),** originally signed by 23 nations in 1947, provided a forum for tariff negotiations and a place where international trade problems could be discussed and resolved. More than 100 nations abided by its rules. GATT sponsored rounds of negotiations aimed at reducing trade restrictions. The most recent round, the Uruguay Round (1988–1994), further reduced trade barriers for most products and provided new rules to prevent dumping.

**General Agreement on Tariffs and Trade (GATT)** a trade agreement, originally signed by 23 nations in 1947, that provided a forum for tariff negotiations and a place where international trade problems could be discussed and resolved

**World Trade Organization (WTO)** international organization dealing with the rules of trade between nations

The **World Trade Organization (WTO),** an international organization dealing with the rules of trade between nations, was created in 1995 by the Uruguay Round. Key to the World Trade Organization are the WTO agreements, which are the legal ground rules for international commerce. The agreements were negotiated and signed by most of the world's trading nations and ratified by their parliaments. The goal is to help producers of goods and services and exporters and importers conduct their business. In addition to administering the WTO trade agreements, the WTO presents a forum for trade negotiations, monitors national trade policies, provides technical assistance and training for developing countries, and cooperates with other international organizations. Based in Geneva, Switzerland, the WTO has also adopted a leadership role in negotiating trade disputes among nations.[32] For example, the WTO investigated complaints from the European Union and seven countries about a U.S. tariff on imported steel and ultimately ruled the U.S. duties illegal under international trade rules. The United States had imposed the tariffs to protect domestic steel producers from less expensive imported steel, but the WTO found that the United States had failed to prove that its steel industry had been harmed by dumping.[33] Facing the prospect of retaliatory sanctions against American goods, the U.S. dropped the tariffs 16 months early after the ruling.[34]

## The North American Free Trade Agreement

**North American Free Trade Agreement (NAFTA)** agreement that eliminates most tariffs and trade restrictions on agricultural and manufactured products to encourage trade among Canada, the United States, and Mexico

The **North American Free Trade Agreement (NAFTA),** which went into effect on January 1, 1994, effectively merged Canada, the United States, and Mexico into one market of nearly 440 million consumers. NAFTA will have eliminated virtually all tariffs on goods produced and traded among Canada, Mexico, and the United States to create a free trade area by 2009. The estimated annual output for this trade alliance is more than $14 trillion. NAFTA makes it easier for U.S. businesses to invest in Mexico and Canada; provides protection for intellectual property (of special interest to high-technology and entertainment industries); expands trade by requiring equal treatment of U.S. firms in both countries; and simplifies country-of-origin rules, hindering Japan's use of Mexico as a staging ground for further penetration into U.S. markets. Although most tariffs on products coming to the United States are being lifted, duties on more sensitive products, such as household glassware, footware, and some fruits and vegetables, are being phased out over a 15-year period.

Canada's 33.4 million consumers are relatively affluent, with a per capita GDP of $38,200.[35] Trade between the United States and Canada totals approximately $532 billion. Currently, exports to Canada support approximately 1.5 million U.S. jobs. Canadian investments in U.S. companies are also increasing, and various markets, including air travel, are opening as regulatory barriers dissolve.[36] In fact, Canada is the single largest trading partner of the United States.[37]

With a per capita GDP of $12,500, Mexico's 108.7 million consumers are less affluent than Canadian consumers. However, they bought more than $134 billion worth of U.S. products last year.[38] In addition, there are 28.3 million Mexican Americans in the United States, with an average household income of $38,661. These individuals often have close ties to relatives in Mexico and assist in Mexican-U.S. economic development and trade. Mexico is on a course of a market economy, rule of law, respect for human rights, and responsible public policies. There is also a commitment to the environment and sustainable human development.[39] Many U.S. companies have taken advantage of Mexico's low labor costs and proximity to the United States to set up production facilities, sometimes called *maquiladoras.*

Aerospace companies are moving to Mexico, drawn by lower wages and government promotions. Mexico's aerospace industry has tripled in the last few years, based on wages as low as US$3.50 per hour for jobs such as building rudders and wiring systems.[40] With the *maquiladoras* accounting for roughly half of Mexico's exports, Mexico has risen to become the world's ninth-largest economy.[41]

However, there is great disparity within Mexico. The country's southern states cannot seem to catch up with the more affluent northern states on almost any socioeconomic indicator. For example, 47 percent of rural Mexicans in the south are considered extremely poor, compared with just 12 percent in the north. The disparities are growing, as can be seen comparing the south to the northern industrial capital of Monterrey, which is beginning to seem like south Texas.[42]

Mexico's membership in NAFTA links the United States and Canada with other Latin American countries, providing additional opportunities to integrate trade among all the nations in the Western Hemisphere. Indeed, efforts to create a free trade agreement among the 34 nations of North and South America was expected to be completed by 2005. Like NAFTA, the *Free Trade Area of the Americas (FTAA)* will progressively eliminate trade barriers and create the world's largest free trade zone with 800 million people.[43] However, opposition and demonstrations have hampered efforts to move forward with the proposed plan. Although the deadline was missed and it is not in place yet, there is still a chance for the FTAA to become a reality. A trade dispute between the United States and Brazil over investment, intellectual property rights, antidumping tariffs, and agriculture subsidies may also delay the final agreement.[44]

Despite its benefits, NAFTA has been controversial, and disputes continue to arise over the implementation of the trade agreement. Archer Daniels Midland, for example, filed a claim against the Mexican government for losses resulting from a tax on soft drinks containing high-fructose corn syrup, which the company believes violates the provisions of NAFTA.[45] While many Americans feared the agreement would erase jobs in the United States, Mexicans have been disappointed that the agreement failed to create more jobs. Moreover, Mexico's rising standard of living has increased the cost of doing business there; some 850 *maquiladoras* have closed their doors and transferred work to China and other nations where labor costs are cheaper. Indeed, China has become the United States's second largest importer.[46]

Although NAFTA has been controversial, it has become a positive factor for U.S. firms wishing to engage in international marketing. Because licensing requirements have been relaxed under the pact, smaller businesses that previously could not afford to invest in Mexico and Canada will be able to do business in those markets without having to locate there. NAFTA's long phase-in period provides ample time for adjustment by those firms affected by reduced tariffs on imports. Furthermore, increased competition should lead to a more efficient market, and the long-term prospects of including most countries in the Western Hemisphere in the alliance promise additional opportunities for U.S. marketers.

*Although both the United States and most Central American countries have passed the Central America Free Trade Agreement (CAFTA), there is still a great deal of opposition to CAFTA's full implementation. Those critical of the agreement claim it will harm small farmers in Central America, will erode workers' rights, and protect pharmaceutical companies at the expense of the poor. Proponents argue that on balance, participating countries will be made better off.*

## The European Union

The **European Union (EU),** also called the *European Community* or *Common Market,* was established in 1958 to promote trade among its members, which initially included Belgium, France, Italy, West Germany, Luxembourg, and the Netherlands. East and West Germany united in 1991, and by 1995 the United Kingdom, Spain, Denmark, Greece, Portugal, Ireland, Austria, Finland, and Sweden had joined as well. The Czech Republic, Estonia, Hungary, Latvia, Lithuania, Poland, Slovakia, and Slovenia joined in 2004. In 2007, Bulgaria and Romania also became members, and Cyprus and Malta joined in 2008, which brought total membership to 27. Croatia, the Former Yugoslav Republic of Macedonia, and Turkey are candidate countries that hope to join the European Union in the near future.[47] Until 1993 each nation functioned as a separate market, but at that time the members officially unified into one of the largest single world markets, which today has 395 million consumers with a GDP of $16.8 trillion. The European Union continues to grow above potential, with job creation between 1998 and 2008 outpacing that in the United States.[48]

To facilitate free trade among members, the EU is working toward standardization of business regulations and requirements, import duties, and value-added taxes; the elimination of customs checks; and the creation of a standardized currency for use by all members. Many European nations (Austria, Belgium, Finland, France, Germany, Greece, Ireland, Italy, Luxembourg, the Netherlands, Portugal, Spain, and Slovenia) link their exchange rates together to a common currency, the *euro;* however, several EU members have rejected use of the euro in their countries. Although the common currency requires many marketers to modify their pricing strategies and will subject them to increased competition, the use of a single currency frees companies that sell goods among European countries from the nuisance of dealing with complex exchange rates.[49] The long-term goals are to eliminate all trade barriers within the EU, improve the economic efficiency of the EU nations, and stimulate economic growth, thus making the union's economy more competitive in global markets, particularly against Japan and other Pacific Rim nations, and North America. However, several disputes and debates still divide the member nations, and many barriers to completely free trade remain. Consequently, it may take many years before the EU is truly one deregulated market.

The EU has enacted some of the world's strictest laws concerning antitrust issues, which have had unexpected consequences for some non-European firms. For example, after a five-year investigation, the union fined U.S.-based Microsoft a record 497 million euros ($750 million U.S.) for exploiting its "near-monopoly" in computer operating systems in Europe by including a free media player with Windows to the detriment of software offered by European makers. In addition to the fine, the European Commission insisted that Microsoft release its programming codes to European rivals to allow them to make their competing products compatible with computers relying on Microsoft's Windows operating system.[50]

## Asia-Pacific Economic Cooperation

The **Asia-Pacific Economic Cooperation (APEC),** established in 1989, promotes open trade and economic and technical cooperation among member nations, which initially included Australia, Brunei Darussalam, Canada, Indonesia, Japan, Korea, Malaysia, New Zealand, the Philippines, Singapore, Thailand, and the United States. Since then the alliance has grown to include China, Hong Kong, Chinese Taipei, Mexico, Papua New Guinea, Chile, Peru, Russia, and Vietnam. The 21-member alliance represents approximately 41 percent of the world's population, 49 percent of world trade, and 55 percent of world GDP. APEC differs from other international trade alliances in its commitment to facilitating business and its practice of allowing the business/private sector to participate in a wide range of APEC activities.[51]

Companies of the APEC have become increasingly competitive and sophisticated in global business in the last three decades. The Japanese and South Koreans in particular have made tremendous inroads on world markets for automobiles, motorcycles, watches, cameras, and audio and video equipment. Products from Samsung, Sony, Sanyo, Toyota, Daewoo, Mitsubishi, Suzuki, and Toshiba are sold all over the world and have set standards of quality by which other products are often judged. The People's Republic of China, a country of 1.3 billion people, has launched a program of economic reform to stimulate its economy by privatizing many industries, restructuring its banking system, and increasing public spending on infrastructure (including railways and telecommunications).[52] As a result, China has become a manufacturing powerhouse with an economy growing at a rate of more than 10 percent a year.[53] China's manufacturing advances can be seen in Shengzhou, a city that claims to make 40 percent of the world's neckties. One company in Shengzhou sells 70 percent of its ties to Wal-Mart Stores Inc. China's export market has consistently outpaced its import growth in recent years. China ranks behind the United States as the world's largest importer and exporter, and China's GDP is the world's third biggest economy, behind the United States and Japan. As it becomes a major driver of economic growth, China overtook the United States as the country with the largest number of Internet users in 2008. On the negative side, China became the world's largest emitter of greenhouse gases in 2008. China mainly uses coal-fired power plants; in fact, it builds a new one every 10 days, so it has become the world's largest emitter of carbon dioxide. As companies transfer their manufacturing to China, they increase their $CO_2$ emissions because China emits 22 percent more than the global average of carbon per kilowatt-hour.[54] Less visible Pacific Rim regions, such as Thailand, Singapore, Taiwan, Vietnam, and Hong Kong, have also become major manufacturing and financial centers. Vietnam, with one of the world's most open economies, has bypassed its communist government with private firms moving ahead despite bureaucracy, corruption, and poor infrastructure. In a country of 85 million barely able to feed themselves, Vietnamese firms now compete internationally with an agricultural miracle, making the country one of the world's main providers of farm produce. Intel recently opened a $1 billion factory near Hanoi.[55]

## World Bank

The **World Bank,** more formally known as the International Bank for Reconstruction and Development, was established by the industrialized nations, including the United States, in 1946 to loan money to underdeveloped and developing countries.

It loans its own funds or borrows funds from member countries to finance projects ranging from road and factory construction to the building of medical and educational facilities. The World Bank and other multilateral development banks (banks with international support that provide loans to developing countries) are the largest source of advice and assistance for developing nations. The International Development Association and the International Finance Corporation are associated with the World Bank and provide loans to private businesses and member countries.

## International Monetary Fund

The **International Monetary Fund (IMF)** was established in 1947 to promote trade among member nations by eliminating trade barriers and fostering

**World Bank**
an organization established by the industrialized nations in 1946 to loan money to underdeveloped and developing countries; formally known as the International Bank for Reconstruction and Development

**International Monetary Fund (IMF)**
organization established in 1947 to promote trade among member nations by eliminating trade barriers and fostering financial cooperation

financial cooperation. It also makes short-term loans to member countries that have balance-of-payment deficits and provides foreign currencies to member nations. The International Monetary Fund tries to avoid financial crises and panics by alerting the international community about countries that will not be able to repay their debts. The IMF's Internet site provides additional information about the organization, including news releases, frequently asked questions, and members.

The IMF is the closest thing the world has to an international central bank. If countries get into financial trouble, they can borrow from the World Bank. The IMF has bailed out Thailand, Russia, and Argentina and, in recent years, has focused on loans to developing countries. The usefulness of the IMF for developed countries is limited because these countries use private markets as a major source of capital.[56]

# Getting Involved in International Business

Businesses may get involved in international trade at many levels—from a small Kenyan firm that occasionally exports African crafts to a huge multinational corporation such as Shell Oil that sells products around the globe. The degree of commitment of resources and effort required increases according to the level at which a business involves itself in international trade. This section examines exporting and importing, trading companies, licensing and franchising, contract manufacturing, joint ventures, direct investment, and multinational corporations.

## Exporting and Importing

Many companies first get involved in international trade when they import goods from other countries for resale in their own businesses. For example, a grocery store chain may import bananas from Honduras and coffee from Colombia. A business may get involved in exporting when it is called upon to supply a foreign company with a particular product. Such exporting enables enterprises of all sizes to participate in international business. For example, Tesla, a U.S. electric car start-up firm, is targeting Europe, with its shorter average driving distance than in the United States and generous tax incentives for low-emission vehicles.[57] Table 3.4 shows the number of U.S. exporters and the export value by company size, while Figure 3.2 shows the major export markets for U.S. companies.

**countertrade agreements** foreign trade agreements that involve bartering products for other products instead of for currency

Exporting sometimes takes place through **countertrade agreements,** which involve bartering products for other products instead of for currency. Such arrangements are fairly common in international trade, especially between Western companies and Eastern European nations. An estimated 40 percent or more of all international trade agreements contain countertrade provisions.

Although a company may export its wares overseas directly or import goods directly from their manufacturer, many choose to deal with an intermediary, commonly

**TABLE 3.4**

U.S. Exporters and Value by Company Size

| | Number of Exporters | % | Value (billions of dollars) | % |
|---|---|---|---|---|
| Small (<100 employees) | 215,991 | 90.3 | 151.3 | 19.3 |
| Medium (100–499 employees) | 16,621 | 7 | 77.1 | 9.9 |
| Large (500 + employees) | 6,482 | 2.7 | 556 | 70.9 |

Source: "Profile of U.S. Exporting Companies, 2004–2005," U.S. Census Bureau, press release, January 10, 2007, http://www.census.gov/foreign-trade/Press-Release/edb/2005/ (accessed April 4, 2008).

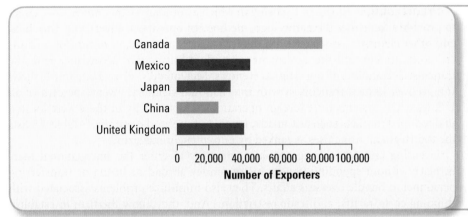

**FIGURE 3.2**

U.S. Exporting Companies for Selected Countries

Source: "Profile of U.S. Exporting Companies, 2004–2005," U.S. Census Bureau, press release, January 10, 2007, http://www.census.gov/foreign-trade/Press-Release/edb/2005/ (accessed April 4, 2008).

called an *export agent.* Export agents seldom produce goods themselves; instead, they usually handle international transactions for other firms. Export agents either purchase products outright or take them on consignment. If they purchase them outright, they generally mark up the price they have paid and attempt to sell the product in the international marketplace. They are also responsible for storage and transportation.

An advantage of trading through an agent instead of directly is that the company does not have to deal with foreign currencies or the red tape (paying tariffs and handling paperwork) of international business. A major disadvantage is that, because the export agent must make a profit, either the price of the product must be increased or the domestic company must provide a larger discount than it would in a domestic transaction.

## Trading Companies

A **trading company** buys goods in one country and sells them to buyers in another country. Trading companies handle all activities required to move products from one country to another, including consulting, marketing research, advertising, insurance, product research and design, warehousing, and foreign exchange services to companies interested in selling their products in foreign markets. Trading companies are similar to export agents, but their role in international trade is larger. By linking sellers and buyers of goods in different countries, trading companies promote international trade. The best known U.S. trading company is Sears World Trade, which specializes in consumer goods, light industrial items, and processed foods.

**trading company**
a firm that buys goods in one country and sells them to buyers in another country

## Licensing and Franchising

**Licensing** is a trade arrangement in which one company—the *licensor*—allows another company—the *licensee*—to use its company name, products, patents, brands, trademarks, raw materials, and/or production processes in exchange for a fee or royalty. The Coca-Cola Company and PepsiCo frequently use licensing as a means to market their soft drinks, apparel, and other merchandise in other countries. Licensing is an attractive alternative to direct investment when the political stability of a foreign country is in doubt or when resources are unavailable for direct investment. Licensing is especially advantageous for small manufacturers wanting to launch a well-known brand internationally. Yoplait is a French yogurt that is licensed for production in the United States.

**licensing**
a trade agreement in which one company—the licensor—allows another company—the licensee—to use its company name, products, patents, brands, trademarks, raw materials, and/or production processes in exchange for a fee or royalty

**franchising**
a form of licensing in which a company—the franchiser—agrees to provide a franchisee a name, logo, methods of operation, advertising, products, and other elements associated with a franchiser's business, in return for a financial commitment and the agreement to conduct business in accordance with the franchiser's standard of operations

**Franchising** is a form of licensing in which a company—the *franchiser*—agrees to provide a *franchisee* the name, logo, methods of operation, advertising, products, and other elements associated with the franchiser's business, in return for a financial commitment and the agreement to conduct business in accordance with the franchiser's standard of operations. Wendy's, McDonald's, Pizza Hut, and Holiday Inn are well-known franchisers with international visibility. Twenty percent of all U.S. franchise systems have foreign operations. The majority of these were located in developed markets such as Canada, Japan, Europe, and Australia.[58] Table 3.5 lists the top 10 global franchises as ranked by *Entrepreneur* magazine.

Licensing and franchising enable a company to enter the international marketplace without spending large sums of money abroad or hiring or transferring personnel to handle overseas affairs. They also minimize problems associated with shipping costs, tariffs, and trade restrictions. And, they allow the firm to establish goodwill for its products in a foreign market, which will help the company if it decides to produce or market its products directly in the foreign country at some future date. However, if the licensee (or franchisee) does not maintain high standards of quality, the product's image may be hurt; therefore, it is important for the licensor to monitor its products overseas and to enforce its quality standards.

## Contract Manufacturing

**contract manufacturing**
the hiring of a foreign company to produce a specified volume of the initiating company's product to specification; the final product carries the domestic firm's name

**Contract manufacturing** occurs when a company hires a foreign company to produce a specified volume of the firm's product to specification; the final product carries the domestic firm's name. Spalding, for example, relies on contract manufacturing for its sports equipment; Reebok uses Korean contract manufacturers to manufacture many of its athletic shoes.

## Outsourcing

Earlier, we defined outsourcing as transferring manufacturing or other tasks (such as information technology operations) to companies in countries where labor and supplies are less expensive. Many U.S. firms have outsourced tasks to India, Ireland, Mexico, and the Philippines, where there are many well-educated workers and significantly lower labor costs. Experts estimate that 80 percent of *Fortune* 500 companies have some relationship with an offshore company.[59] Bank of America, for example, set up a subsidiary in India to outsource 1,000 back-office support jobs. The bank also contracts with several Indian firms to provide software services.

**TABLE 3.5**

Top 10 Global Franchise Operations

1. Subway
2. KFC Corp.
3. McDonald's
4. Dunkin' Donuts
5. Domino's Pizza LLC
6. Curves
7. RE/MAX Int'l. Inc.
8. Sonic Drive In Restaurants
9. Pizza Hut
10. The UPS Store/Mail Boxes Etc.

Source: "Top 10 Global Franchises for 2008," *Entrepreneur,* http://www.entrepreneur.com/topglobal/index.html (accessed April 4, 2008).

Experts believe that two-thirds of U.S. banks outsource services to China, India, and Russia.[60] Even small firms can outsource. For example, Avalon, an Irish manufacturer of high-end guitars played by musicians like Eric Clapton, contracted with Cort Musical Instruments Company in South Korea to augment the firm's production and help it build a global brand. The outsourcing arrangement helped the small business boost output from 1,500 guitars a year to 8,000 annually, helping it become more competitive with larger manufacturers.[61]

Although outsourcing has become politically controversial in recent years amid concerns over jobs lost to overseas workers, foreign companies transfer tasks and jobs to U.S. companies—sometimes called *insourcing*—far more often than U.S. companies outsource tasks and jobs abroad.[62] For example, Indian-based Bharti TeleVentures, a cell-phone operator, signed a 10-year contract to insource its software, hardware, and other information-technology tasks to IBM in the United States.[63] March 29, 2004, http://online.wsj.com. However, some firms are bringing their outsourced jobs back after concerns that foreign workers were not adding enough value.

Domino's Pizza has expanded its operations into more than 60 international markets via franchising. In Asia, the chain's stores serve up pizzas with toppings such as squid, sweet mayonnaise, and duck gizzards.

## Joint Ventures and Alliances

Many countries, particularly LDCs, do not permit direct investment by foreign companies or individuals. Or, a company may lack sufficient resources or expertise to operate in another country. In such cases, a company that wants to do business in another country may set up a **joint venture** by finding a local partner (occasionally, the host nation itself) to share the costs and operation of the business. General Motors, for example, has a joint venture with Russian automaker Avtovaz in Togliatti, which manufactures four-wheel-drive Chevrolet Nivas and Opel Astras for the Russian market. Demand for the relatively pricey Astra has grown along with Russian household incomes.[64]

In some industries, such as automobiles and computers, strategic alliances are becoming the predominant means of competing. A **strategic alliance** is a partnership formed to create competitive advantage on a worldwide basis. In such industries, international competition is so fierce and the costs of competing on a global basis are so high that few firms have the resources to go it alone, so they collaborate with other companies. An example of such an alliance is New United Motor Manufacturing Inc. (NUMMI), formed by Toyota and General Motors in 1984 to make automobiles for both firms. This alliance joined the quality engineering of Japanese cars with the marketing expertise and market access of General Motors. Today, NUMMI manufactures the popular Toyota Tacoma compact pick-up truck as well as the Toyota Corolla, Pontiac Vibe, and a right-hand drive Toyota Voltz for sale in Japan.[65]

## Direct Investment

Companies that want more control and are willing to invest considerable resources in international business may consider **direct investment,** the ownership of overseas facilities. Direct investment may involve the development and operation of new facilities—such as when Starbucks opens a new coffee shop in Japan—or the purchase of all or part of an existing operation in a foreign country. India's

**joint venture**
the sharing of the costs and operation of a business between a foreign company and a local partner

**strategic alliance**
a partnership formed to create competitive advantage on a worldwide basis

**direct investment**
the ownership of overseas facilities

**TABLE 3.6**

The 10 Largest Global Corporations

| Rank | Company | Revenues (in millions) |
|---|---|---|
| 1. | Wal-Mart Stores | $351,139 |
| 2. | ExxonMobil | 347,254 |
| 3. | Royal Dutch Shell | 318,845 |
| 4. | BP | 274,316 |
| 5. | General Motors | 207,349 |
| 6. | Toyota Motor | 294,746 |
| 7. | Chevron | 200,567 |
| 8. | DaimlerChrysler | 190,191 |
| 9. | ConocoPhillips | 172,451 |
| 10. | Total | 168,357 |

Source: "Global 500: Fortune's Annual Ranking of the World's Largest Corporations," *Fortune*, http://money.cnn.com/magazines/fortune/global500 (accessed April 4, 2008).

Tata Motors purchased Jaguar and Land Rover from Ford Motor Company. Tata, a maker of cars and trucks, is attempting to broaden its global presence, including manufacturing these vehicles in the United Kingdom.[66]

**multinational corporation (MNC)**
a corporation that operates on a worldwide scale, without significant ties to any one nation or region

The highest level of international business involvement is the **multinational corporation (MNC),** a corporation, such as IBM or ExxonMobil, that operates on a worldwide scale, without significant ties to any one nation or region. Table 3.6 lists the 10 largest multinational corporations. MNCs are more than simple corporations. They often have greater assets than some of the countries in which they do business. General Motors, ExxonMobil, Ford Motors, and General Electric, for example, have sales higher than the GDP of many of the countries in which they operate. Nestlé, with headquarters in Switzerland, operates more than 300 plants around the world and receives revenues from Europe; North, Central, and South America; Africa; and Asia. The Royal Dutch/Shell Group, one of the world's major oil producers, is another MNC. Its main offices are located in The Hague and London. Other MNCs include BASF, British Petroleum, Cadbury Schweppes, Matsushita, Mitsubishi, Siemens, Texaco, Toyota, and Unilever. Many MNCs have been targeted by antiglobalization activists at global business forums, and some protests have turned violent. The activists contend that MNCs increase the gap between rich and poor nations, misuse and misallocate scarce resources, exploit the labor markets in LDCs, and harm their natural environments.[67]

# International Business Strategies

Planning in a global economy requires businesspeople to understand the economic, legal, political, and sociocultural realities of the countries in which they will operate. These factors will affect the strategy a business chooses to use outside its own borders.

## Developing Strategies

**multinational strategy**
a plan, used by international companies, that involves customizing products, promotion, and distribution according to cultural, technological, regional, and national differences

Companies doing business internationally have traditionally used a **multinational strategy,** customizing their products, promotion, and distribution according to cultural, technological, regional, and national differences. In France, for example,

# Destination CEO
## VF Corporation—Matthew McDonald

VF Corporation is not a household name; however, its brands are extremely well known globally—and that is precisely the strategic objective of CEO Matthew McDonald. VF's brands include Wrangler Jeans, Nautica, and North Face. Under McDonald's leadership, VF elected to reduce its U.S. labor force by 13,000 jobs and to outsource manufacturing to China. Locating jobs in global markets, reducing costs, and focusing on brand are the key competitive elements of McDonald's global strategy. The clothing industry is highly competitive. McDonald avoids the high-risk fashion market in favor of a commodity approach for his brands. The goal is to dominate globally in the midprice-range market segment with its lifestyle brands such as North Face. Consumer recognition of the brand across the globe, according to McDonald, is integral to the current success and to the future sustainability of VF Corporation. Brand recognition remains the strategic driver for the corporation.

### Discussion Questions

1. What is the key global business strategy for VF Corporation?
2. What is the potential impact of relocating jobs to a country in which you want to position your brands?
3. What role could culture play in the success of the lifestyle brands for VF Corporation?

---

South Korean–owned AmorePacific Corporation marketed its Lolita Lempicka perfume, with a decidedly French accent. Named for a French fashion designer, the fifth best-selling fragrance in France was formulated by French experts and marketed in a bottle designed by a French artist. Indeed, few French consumers realize the popular perfume is owned by a Korean firm.[68] Many soap and detergent manufacturers have adapted their products to local water conditions, washing equipment, and washing habits. For customers in some less-developed countries, Colgate-Palmolive Co. has developed an inexpensive, plastic, hand-powered washing machine for use in households that have no electricity. Even when products are standardized, advertising often has to be modified to adapt to language and cultural differences. Also, celebrities used in advertising in the United States may be unfamiliar to foreign consumers and thus would not be effective in advertising products in other countries.

More and more companies are moving from this customization strategy to a **global strategy (globalization),** which involves standardizing products (and, as much as possible, their promotion and distribution) for the whole world, as if it were a single entity. Examples of globalized products are American clothing, movies, music, and cosmetics. ExxonMobil launched a $150 million marketing effort to promote its brands: Exxon, Esso, Mobil, and General. The ads have the same look and feel regardless of the country in which they appear. The ad's message was the same for all countries except the story was told in one of 25 languages.[69]

Before moving outside their own borders, companies must conduct environmental analyses to evaluate the potential of and problems associated with various markets and to determine what strategy is best for doing business in those markets. Failure to do so may result in losses and even negative publicity. Some companies rely on local managers to gain greater insights and faster response to changes within a country. Astute businesspeople today "think globally, act locally." That is, while constantly being aware of the total picture, they adjust their firms' strategies to conform to local needs and tastes.

**global strategy (globalization)** a strategy that involves standardizing products (and, as much as possible, their promotion and distribution) for the whole world, as if it were a single entity

### Managing the Challenges of Global Business

As we've pointed out in this chapter, many past political barriers to trade have fallen or been minimized, expanding and opening new market opportunities. Managers

## Going Green
### Entrepreneurs Defeat Hunger with Plumpy'nut

Nutriset, a private company in France founded by former African aid worker Michel Lescanne, has been selling food products to combat hunger and malnutrition since 1986. Nutriset's mandate is to facilitate the access and the availability of products designed for the enhancement of the nutritional status of children and other vulnerable people. In 1998 the company invented a product called "Plumpy'nut," a true revolution in the management of severe malnutrition. One three-ounce packet delivers 500 calories, and severely malnourished children can thrive on three or four a day. The product is similar to Nutella, the chocolate-hazelnut spread popular in Europe. It is a thick brown paste made from ground peanuts, sugar, and powdered milk, and it is fortified with vitamins. It does not require clean water for dilution and can easily be eaten by a child on his or her own without help from a mother or trained aid workers. Plumpy'nut isn't perishable and does not require refrigeration, and its small size and weight means that it is easy to transport.

More than 850 million people live in a state of hunger. Malnutrition kills more people annually than AIDS, malaria, and tuberculosis combined. The majority of malnourished people live in the developing world, especially India, and sub-Saharan Africa. Niger has become Plumpy'nut's proving grounds. A daily dose costs about $1, and Nutriset has partnered with local entrepreneurs to produce the product locally, even using local ingredients when possible. Doctors Without Borders help distribute Plumpy'nut to the children who need it. They can distribute a week's supply of Plumpy'nut to mothers who can then treat their children at home. Every week they come in to get another week's supply, and the children are given a weight check. The success rate is astonishing, with hospitals that had more patients than beds now having empty beds. But Plumpy'nut can only help if children get it early enough. Unfortunately, some parents still wait too long before bringing their children into the hospitals, so children are still dying from malnutrition. According to Dr. Tectonidis of Doctors Without Borders, if the United States and the European Union were willing to spend part of their food aid on Plumpy'nut, more companies will start making it. By taking a miniscule portion of the global food aid budget, they will have a huge impact, says Tectonidis.

Nutriset reinvests 80 percent of its profit, or about $2.5 million last year, into developing new products. Nutriset is partnering with entrepreneurs in the Democratic Republic of Congo, Ethiopia, Malawi, and Niger to produce Plumpy'nut locally. These African franchisees will be nonprofit entities that will use less expensive local ingredients for their Plumpy'nut recipe. Nutriset has found a way to combine entrepreneurship, social responsibility, and the opportunity to be profitable.[70]

**Discussion Questions**

1. Why is Plumpy'nut considered a socially responsible food product for Africa?
2. How can this company contribute to environmental causes?
3. Can you think of other uses for Plumpy'nut to help feed hungry people around the world?

who can meet the challenges of creating and implementing effective and sensitive business strategies for the global marketplace can help lead their companies to success. For example, the Commercial Service is the global business solutions unit of the U.S. Department of Commerce that offers U.S. firms wide and deep practical knowledge of international markets and industries, a unique global network, inventive use of information technology, and a focus on small and mid-sized businesses. Another example is the benchmarking of best international practices that benefits U.S. firms, which is conducted by the network of CIBERs (Centers for International Business Education and Research) at leading business schools in the United States. These 30 CIBERs are funded by the U.S. government to help U.S. firms become more competitive globally. A major element of the assistance that these governmental organizations can provide firms (especially for small and medium-sized firms) is knowledge of the internationalization process.[71] Small businesses, too, can succeed in foreign markets when their managers have carefully studied those markets and prepared and implemented appropriate strategies. Being globally aware is therefore an important quality for today's managers and will become a critical attribute for managers of the 21st century.

# So You Want a Job in Global Business

Have you always dreamt of traveling the world? Whether backpacking your way through Central America or sipping espressos at five-star European restaurants is your style, the increasing globalization of business might just give you your chance to see what the world has to offer. Most new jobs will have at least some global component, even if located within the United States, so being globally aware and keeping an open mind to different cultures is vital in today's business world. Think about the 1.3 billion consumers in China that have already purchased 500 million mobile phones. In the future, some of the largest markets will be in Asia.

Many jobs discussed in chapters throughout this book tend to have strong international components. For example, product management and distribution management are discussed as marketing careers in Chapter 13. As more and more companies sell products around the globe, their function, design, packaging, and promotions need to be culturally relevant to many different people in many different places. Products very often cross multiple borders before reaching the final consumer, both in their distribution and through the supply chain to produce the products.

Jobs exist in export and import management, product and pricing management, distribution and transportation, and advertising. Many "born global" companies such as Google operate virtually and consider all countries their market. Many companies sell their products through eBay and other internet sites and never leave the U.S. Today communication and transportation facilitates selling and buying products worldwide with delivery in a few days. You may have sold or purchased a product on eBay outside the U.S. without thinking about how easy and accessible international markets are to business. If you have, welcome to the world of global business.

To be successful you must have an idea not only of differing regulations from country to country, but of different language, ethics, and communication styles and varying needs and wants of international markets. From a regulatory side, you may need to be aware of laws related to intellectual property, copyrights, antitrust, advertising, and pricing in every country. Translating is never only about translating the language. Perhaps even more important is ensuring that your message gets through. Whether on a product label or in advertising or promotional materials, the use of images and words varies widely across the globe.

# Review Your Understanding

**Explore some of the factors within the international trade environment that influence business.**

International business is the buying, selling, and trading of goods and services across national boundaries. Importing is the purchase of products and raw materials from another nation; exporting is the sale of domestic goods and materials to another nation. A nation's balance of trade is the difference in value between its exports and imports; a negative balance of trade is a trade deficit. The difference between the flow of money into a country and the flow of money out of it is called the balance of payments. An absolute or comparative advantage in trade may determine what products a company from a particular nation will export.

**Investigate some of the economic, legal-political, social, cultural, and technological barriers to international business.**

Companies engaged in international trade must consider the effects of economic, legal, political, social, and cultural differences between nations. Economic barriers are a country's level of development (infrastructure) and exchange rates. Wide-ranging legal and political barriers

include differing laws (and enforcement), tariffs, exchange controls, quotas, embargoes, political instability, and war. Ambiguous cultural and social barriers involve differences in spoken and body language, time, holidays and other observances, and customs.

**Specify some of the agreements, alliances, and organizations that may encourage trade across international boundaries.**

Among the most important promoters of international business are the General Agreement on Tariffs and Trade, the World Trade Organization, the North American Free Trade Agreement, the European Union, the Asia-Pacific Economic Cooperation, the World Bank, and the International Monetary Fund.

**Summarize the different levels of organizational involvement in international trade.**

A company may be involved in international trade at several levels, each requiring a greater commitment of resources and effort, ranging from importing/exporting to multinational corporations. Countertrade agreements occur at the import/export level and involve bartering products for other products instead of currency. At the next level, a trading company links buyers and sellers in different countries to foster trade. In licensing and franchising, one company agrees to allow a foreign company the use of its company name, products, patents, brands, trademarks, raw materials, and production processes, in exchange for a flat fee or royalty. Contract manufacturing occurs when a company hires a foreign company to produce a specified volume of the firm's product to specification; the final product carries the domestic firm's name. A joint venture is a partnership in which companies from different countries agree to share the costs and operation of the business. The purchase of overseas production and marketing facilities is direct investment. Outsourcing, a form of direct investment, involves transferring manufacturing to countries where labor and supplies are cheap. A multinational corporation is one that operates on a worldwide scale, without significant ties to any one nation or region.

### Contrast two basic strategies used in international business.

Companies typically use one of two basic strategies in international business. A multinational strategy customizes products, promotion, and distribution according to cultural, technological, regional, and national differences. A global strategy (globalization) standardizes products (and, as much as possible, their promotion and distribution) for the whole world, as if it were a single entity.

### Assess the opportunities and problems facing a small business considering expanding into international markets.

"Solve the Dilemma" on page 112 presents a small business considering expansion into international markets. Based on the material provided in the chapter, analyze the business's position, evaluating specific markets, anticipating problems, and exploring methods of international involvement.

## Revisit the World of Business

1. Do you think a British grocery retailer can be successful in the United States?
2. Is the Fresh & Easy grocery concept a good retailing concept for the United States?

3. How can American retailers such as Wal-Mart, Safeway, or Whole Foods compete against Tesco?

## Learn the Terms

absolute advantage  87
Asia-Pacific Economic Cooperation (APEC)  100
balance of payments  90
balance of trade  88
cartel  94
comparative advantage  87
contract manufacturing  104
countertrade agreements  102
direct investment  105
dumping  94
embargo  93
European Union (EU)  100
exchange controls  93

exchange rate  90
exporting  88
franchising  104
General Agreement on Tariffs and Trade (GATT)  97
global strategy (globalization)  107
import tariff  93
importing  88
infrastructure  90
international business  86
International Monetary Fund (IMF)  101
joint venture  105
licensing  103

multinational corporation (MNC)  106
multinational strategy  106
North American Free Trade Agreement (NAFTA)  98
outsourcing  88
quota  93
strategic alliance  105
trade deficit  88
trading company  103
World Bank  101
World Trade Organization (WTO)  98

## Check Your Progress

1. Distinguish between an absolute advantage and a comparative advantage. Cite an example of a country that has an absolute advantage and one with a comparative advantage.

2. What effect does devaluation have on a nation's currency? Can you think of a country that has devaluated or revaluated its currency? What have been the results?

3. What effect does a country's economic development have on international business?

4. How do political issues affect international business?

5. What is an import tariff? A quota? Dumping? How might a country use import tariffs and quotas to control its balance of trade and payments? Why can dumping result in the imposition of tariffs and quotas?

6. How do social and cultural differences create barriers to international trade? Can you think of any additional social or cultural barriers (other than those mentioned in this chapter) that might inhibit international business?

7. Explain how a countertrade agreement can be considered a trade promoter. How does the World Trade Organization encourage trade?

8. At what levels might a firm get involved in international business? What level requires the least commitment of resources? What level requires the most?

9. Compare and contrast licensing, franchising, contract manufacturing, and outsourcing.

10. Compare multinational and global strategies. Which is best? Under what circumstances might each be used?

# Get Involved

1. If the United States were to impose additional tariffs on cars imported from Japan, what would happen to the price of Japanese cars sold in the United States? What would happen to the price of American cars? What action might Japan take to continue to compete in the U.S. automobile market?

2. Although NAFTA has been controversial, it has been a positive factor for U.S. firms desiring to engage in international business. What industries and specific companies have the greatest potential for opening stores in Canada and Mexico? What opportunities exist for small businesses that cannot afford direct investment in Mexico and Canada?

3. Identify a local company that is active in international trade. What is its level of international business involvement and why? Analyze the threats and opportunities it faces in foreign markets, as well as its strengths and weaknesses in meeting those challenges. Based on your analysis, make some recommendations for the business's future involvement in international trade. (Your instructor may ask you to share your report with the class.)

# Build Your Skills

### GLOBAL AWARENESS

**Background**
As American businesspeople travel the globe, they encounter and must quickly adapt to a variety of cultural norms quite different from the United States. When encountering individuals from other parts of the world, the best attitude to adopt is "Here is my way. Now what is yours?" The more you see that you are part of a complex world and that your culture is different from, not better than, others, the better you will communicate and the more effective you will be in a variety of situations. It takes time, energy, understanding, and tolerance to learn about and appreciate other cultures. Naturally you're more comfortable doing things the way you've always done them. Remember, however, that this fact will also be true of the people from other cultures with whom you are doing business.

**Task**
You will "travel the globe" by answering questions related to some of the cultural norms that are found in other countries. Form groups of four to six class members and determine the answers to the following questions. Your instructor has the answer key, which will allow you to determine your group's Global Awareness IQ, which is based on a maximum score of 100 points (10 points per question).

Match the country with the cultural descriptor provided.

A. Saudi Arabia
B. Japan
C. Great Britain
D. Germany
E. Venezuela

_____ 1. When people in this country table a motion, they want to discuss it. In America, "to table a motion" means to put off discussion.

_____ 2. In this country, special forms of speech called *keigo* convey status among speakers. When talking with a person in this country, one should know the person's rank. People from this country will not initiate a conversation without a formal introduction.

_____ **3.** People from this country pride themselves on enhancing their image by keeping others waiting.

_____ **4.** When writing a business letter, people in this country like to provide a great deal of background information and detail before presenting their main points.

_____ **5.** For a man to inquire about another man's wife (even a general question about how she is doing) is considered very offensive in this country.

Match the country with the cultural descriptor provided.

    **F.** China
    **G.** Greece
    **H.** Korea
    **I.** India
    **J.** Mexico

_____ **6.** When in this country, you are expected to negotiate the price on goods you wish to purchase.

_____ **7.** While North Americans want to decide the main points at a business meeting and leave the details for later, people in this country need to have all details decided before the meeting ends, to avoid suspicion and distrust.

_____ **8.** Children in this country learn from a very early age to look down respectfully when talking to those of higher status.

_____ **9.** In this country the husband is the ruler of the household, and the custom is to keep the women hidden.

_____ **10.** Many businesspeople from the United States experience frustration because yes does not always mean the same thing in other cultures. For example, the word *yes* in this country means, "OK, I want to respect you and not offend you." It does not necessarily show agreement.

# Solve the Dilemma

### GLOBAL EXPANSION OR BUSINESS AS USUAL?

Audiotech Electronics, founded in 1959 by a father and son, currently operates a 35,000-square-foot factory with 75 employees. The company produces control consoles for television and radio stations and recording studios. It is involved in every facet of production—designing the systems, installing the circuits in its computer boards, and even manufacturing and painting the metal cases housing the consoles. The company's products are used by all the major broadcast and cable networks. The firm's newest products allow television correspondents to simultaneously hear and communicate with their counterparts in different geographic locations. Audiotech has been very successful meeting its customers' needs efficiently.

Audiotech sales have historically been strong in the United States, but recently growth is stagnating. Even though Audiotech is a small, family-owned firm, it believes it should evaluate and consider global expansion.

### Discussion Questions

1. What are the key issues that need to be considered in determining global expansion?
2. What are some of the unique problems that a small business might face in global expansion that larger firms would not?
3. Should Audiotech consider a joint venture? Should it hire a sales force of people native to the countries it enters?

# Build Your Business Plan

### BUSINESS IN A BORDERLESS WORLD

Think about the product/service you are contemplating for your business plan. If it is an already established product or service, try to find out if the product is currently being sold internationally. If not, can you identify opportunities to do so in the future? What countries do you think would respond most favorably to your product? What problems would you encounter if you attempted to export your product to those countries?

If you are thinking of creating a new product or service for your business plan, think about the possibility of eventually marketing that product in another country. What countries or areas of the world do you think would be most responsive to your product?

Are there countries that the U.S. has trade agreements or alliances with which would make your entry into the market easier? What would be the economic, social, cultural, and technological barriers you would have to recognize before entering the prospective country (ies)? Think about the specific cultural differences that would have to be taken into consideration before entering the prospective country.

# See for Yourself Videocase

## WALT DISNEY AROUND THE GLOBE

Mickey Mouse has been a cherished American icon since the 1930s. He has become a beloved character to children everywhere as his image has spread around the globe. Mickey's first "home," the Disneyland theme park, opened in Anaheim, California, in 1955, with a second, larger park opening in Florida 16 years later. Americans and tourists from around the globe have traveled in droves to California or Florida to experience the "happiest place on earth." What could be a more natural growth for the popular Disney theme parks than to follow Mickey around the globe with international parks? Disneyland first opened on the international front in Tokyo, Japan, in 1983. Ten years later The Walt Disney Company brought the magic to Paris, France. Finally, in 2005, Disneyland opened its gates in Hong Kong, China.

Global expansion is tricky for any business. There are many challenges to overcome, such as economic, legal, political, social, and cultural barriers. Disney may have been an American icon, but that did not mean that simply duplicating the American parks and placing these replicas overseas would work. Among the many challenges faced by Disney when entering a global market, perhaps the most challenging has been handling cultural differences.

The second international theme park, Euro Disney, opened outside of Paris in 1992 with much fanfare and many well-publicized problems. During construction, many well-known French citizens openly opposed the park. French labor unions also organized protests. The main theme of these objections was an aversion to allowing an American icon and symbol of American culture to become a focal point in France. Attendance for the first three years remained well below expectations, causing Euro Disney S.C.A. grave financial difficulties. Finally, in 1995, the park experienced a turn around. Financial restructuring helped the park began to be profitable. New attractions, lower admissions prices, and a massive marketing campaign, including a name change to Disneyland Paris, led to increased attendance. Now the park is the number one tourist attraction in Europe.

Having learned from its experience in France, The Walt Disney Company entered its venture in Hong Kong with an eye to embracing and honoring local culture. The company had learned that while its stories and themes appear universal, events, trends, cuisine, and more must vary country by country. Theme parks, in particular, must embrace local culture while expressing the Disney message. To this end, Disney hired a feng shui consultant to assist with the layout of the entire Hong Kong park. The fourth floor has been passed over at all hotels because of a cultural belief that the number four is bad luck. One of the Hong Kong Disneyland ballrooms measures 888 square meters, since eight signifies wealth in Chinese culture. Even with this attention to detail, Hong Kong Disneyland's first years have been rough. As in France, attendance has hovered consistently below projections. Protesters have again brought up various cultural or social objections to the park, including that Disney serves shark fin soup in some restaurants. A major complaint among guests is that the park is small and offers little. In truth, the park is the smallest of the Disney theme parks located throughout the world. Disney is taking steps to address this and other complaints, and expansion has already begun.

While some locals continue to protest Disney's presence, there are many benefits to allowing a global company like Disney to enter foreign markets. Disney theme parks attract both local and global tourists, which can be a major stimulus to the local economy. For example, Hong Kong expects that Hong Kong Disneyland will bring over 50,000 jobs to the city between 2005 and 2025. It has been predicted that the park will bring $19 billion (U.S.) to the local economy during the park's first 40 years. It is likely that with expansion and further refinement, Hong Kong Disneyland will succeed with a turnaround as seen in France, which now boasts over 12 million visitors annually. These initial stumbles have not deterred The Walt Disney Company from further global expansion. Though no official announcements have been confirmed, the company has long been in talks with China about opening another park there, most likely in Shanghai. After its experiences in Paris and Hong Kong, Disney might be better positioned to navigate the rocky terrain of expansion into another global market. Hopefully the company has learned that it cannot rely only on Mickey, but that it must pay close attention to cultural and social variances in different global markets.[72]

### Discussion Questions

1. Why would the Walt Disney Company want to venture into global markets with its theme parks?

2. What troubles has the company had to overcome in opening theme parks outside of its U.S. home base?

3. What steps might Disney take to ensure better success with a future Chinese theme park location?

**Remember to check out our Online Learning Center at www.mhhe.com/ferrell7e.**

## CHAPTER OUTLINE

Introduction

The Impact of Technology on Our Lives

Managing Information
  *Management Information Systems*
  *Collecting Data*

The Internet
  *Wireless Technologies*

E-Business
  *The Nature of E-Business*
  *E-Business Models*
  *Customer Relationship Management*

Legal and Social Issues
  *Privacy*
  *Spam*
  *Identity Theft*
  *Intellectual Property and Copyrights*
  *Taxing the Internet?*
  *The Dynamic Nature of Information Technology and E-Business*

# Managing Information Technology and E-Business

## OBJECTIVES

*After reading this chapter, you will be able to:*

- Summarize the role and impact of technology in the global economy.
- Specify how information is managed and explain a management information system.
- Describe the Internet and explore its main uses.
- Define e-business and discuss the e-business models.
- Identify the legal and social issues of information technology and e-business.
- Assess the opportunities and problems faced by an individual in an e-business and suggest a course of action.

orite#1

**Falcon Bomber**
by Ulla Johnson
> $770 retail
> Active Endeavors

JANESCLOSET.
coupon code:
20 % OFF

BAREFOOT T

line codes

w to use this page:
Sort by clicking on the "Added" column title to see newly added codes.
To add a code, use the Add form located at the bottom of this page. Do not abuse this privilege, or it
be removed. Please refrain from posting affiliate codes or codes for private or secret sales.
lease contact us if we have listed a code in error. Thank you.

laimer: Codes listed on this page are shared and posted by users. Codes may be
ed or entered incorrectly. Neither Reesycakes.com nor the retailers guarantee the
ty of the codes. Always check your cart before checkout to ensure that the deal has
applied to your order.

| | Deal | Code | Added | Start | End |
|---|---|---|---|---|---|
| ors | 20% off | toutie | 11/5/2005 | | |
| | 20% off | hive20 | 3/11/2007 | 3/1/2007 | |
| | 20% off | Grechen | 3/11/2007 | 3/1/2007 | |
| | 20% off for MUA members | MUA20 | 10/28/2005 | 9/12/2005 | |
| | off non-sale | reesy | 3/27/2007 | | |
| | | Celebstyle | 11/24/2007 | | |
| | | ON27 | 2/25/2007 | | |

## Online Bargaining for the Lowest Price

Has anyone in your family ever related a story about bargaining for a lower price at the local flea market or on a trip overseas? When you envision the scene, do you picture something old fashioned and picturesque? If you think haggling is passé, you haven't attempted it in today's world—on the Internet. It turns out that bargaining on the Internet not only happens regularly, but is something some individuals have refined to a science. Entire sites are devoted to comparison shopping, giving the savvy shopper the ammunition he or she needs to do battle for the lowest price.

Thanks to the Internet, haggling has never been easier, especially in the area of online apparel sales. While some brick-and-mortar stores such as Nordstrom have had price-matching policies in place for years, many consumers only engage in this process online. The reason for this may lie in the fact that search engines have given consumers the freedom to quickly and easily find the items they want for the lowest prices—all while sitting in the comfort of their own homes. It is no longer a matter of going to the only store in town and being forced to pay whatever price is asked.

Internet sites such as Reesycakes.com post large numbers of apparel discount codes, the codes consumers need in order to receive price cuts. The knowledgeable shopper can also visit a site such as Shopstyle.com, which allows the consumer to locate all sites carrying a specific item. With that information in hand, the shopper can then visit Reesycakes.com to match retailers from Shopstyle.com with discount codes. Once this information has been gathered, the shopper can contact his or her online retailer of choice to request a price match or discount. Why go through all of this, you might

*continued*

ENTER THE WORLD OF BUSINESS

ask? It turns out that many people prefer to shop on sites with which they are familiar. If you're willing to take the time, you'll discover that many retailers, with online competition running high, are willing whatever it takes to retain loyal customers.

While online haggling sounds terrific for the consumer, how does it affect businesses? In general, a business loses money when it agrees to a price match or a discount. In addition to agreeing to lower its price, it costs a company more money to deal with a customer via phone than it does to simply process an order via the Internet ($2 to $5 for phone-based customer service, versus 20 cents for a straightforward Internet order, according to Forrester Research). However, if a company is able to retain a customer over the long term by offering a discount now and then, it may pay off. It's all part of the risk of business.[1]

# Introduction

**information technology (IT)**
processes and applications that create new methods to solve problems, perform tasks, and manage communication

The technology behind computers, the Internet, and their applications has changed the face of business over the past few decades. **Information technology (IT)** relates to processes and applications that create new methods to solve problems, perform tasks, and manage communication. Information technology has been associated with using computers and Internet appliances to obtain and process information as well as using application software to organize and communicate information. Information technology's impact on the economy is very powerful, especially with regard to productivity, employment, and working environments. Technology has resulted in social issues related to privacy, intellectual property, quality of life, and the ability of the legal system to respond to this environment. Most businesses are using information technology to develop new strategies, enhance employee productivity, and improve services to customers.

In this chapter we first examine the role and impact of technology in our information-driven economy. Next, we discuss the need to manage information. We then analyze management information systems and take a look at information technology applications. Then we provide an overview of the Internet and examine e-business as a strategy to improve business performance and create competitive advantage. Finally, we examine the legal and social issues associated with information technology and e-business.

## The Impact of Technology on Our Lives

**technology**
the application of knowledge, including the processes and procedures to solve problems, perform tasks, and create new methods to obtain desired outcomes

**Technology** relates to the application of knowledge, including the processes and procedures to solve problems, perform tasks, and create new methods to obtain desired outcomes. IT includes intellectual knowledge as well as the computer systems devised to achieve business objectives. Technology has been a driving force in the advancement of economic systems and the quality of life. Today, our economic productivity is based more on technology than on any other advance. Information technology is important because our economy is service based. Technology has changed the way consumers take vacations, make purchases, drive cars, and

# Entrepreneurship in Action
## Business.com

Jake Winebaum and Sky Dayton

**Business:** Business.com

**Founded:** 1999

**Success:** Business.com was sold to R.H. Donnelley Corporation for $350 million and deferred purchase consideration in 2007.

In 1999, Jake Winebaum and Sky Dayton spent $7.5 million to buy the Internet domain name "Business.com." This is the third largest price tag ever for a domain name. Although Winebaum and Dayton were widely ridiculed at the time, their "wild" purchase turns out to have been a wise one. Why buy the domain name in the first place? It seems that a site such as Business.com can generate a good deal of its traffic due not to people who are searching for the site specifically, but to people typing in a generic name as part of a search. Therefore, people looking for information on business in general would be likely to end up at Business.com. What is Business.com? It is a business-to-business search engine, directory, and pay-per-click advertising network. Advertisers include companies such as *The Wall Street Journal, Entrepreneur.com,* and Hoover. The site currently generates about 6 million unique visitors per month, and, in its wake, the company has launched Business.com Network (distribution partnerships with top-tier online business properties including *BusinessWeek.com* and *Forbes.com*) and Work.com (a business-oriented community site). Eight years after their original purchase, Winebaum and Dayton decided to put the company up for auction. It was snatched up by R.H. Donnelly Corporation, a yellow pages and online local commercial search company, for a reported $350 million and deferred purchase consideration—about 24 times Business.com's 2007 cash flow.[2]

obtain entertainment. At Apple's iTunes Music Store, for example, legal downloads of music (at 99 cents per song) have exceeded 4 billion songs since the program launched five years ago.[3] Consider the encyclopedia. Thanks to the ever-growing amount of information available on the Internet, sales of traditional hard-bound encyclopedias have plummeted as more people turn to Internet search engines to help them with research for school, work, or fun. Sales of *Encyclopedia Britannica,* first published in 1768, have declined rapidly over the last decade, while other publishers went out of business. The firms that survived did so by adapting and providing computerized encyclopedia or online access to encyclopedia content. Even such savvy companies cannot rest. The website Wikipedia.org was created in 2001 as a free online encyclopedia that anyone can use. Users across the globe may access and edit the contents of the more than 10,000,000 articles in more than 250 languages.[4] In the workplace, technology has improved productivity and efficiency, reduced costs, and enhanced customer service. The economy of the 21st century is based on these dynamic changes in our society.

Information technology also is changing many traditional products. AFE Cosmetics and Skincare operates www.cosmetics.com, which provides customized cosmetics and skin care products. Lip gloss can be customized to match a specific outfit. Foundation can be matched to skin tone. From the time an order is received, there is a flow of information to achieve this one-to-one fulfillment strategy. A similar company, Reflect.com, was launched by Procter & Gamble to provide customized beauty products. The company is no longer in business.[5] Keeping pace with new information technology is a challenge for businesses adjusting to new competitive environments. Even the British government has launched a YouTube site. The Royal Channel serves as a way for Queen Elizabeth to connect to the younger generation in Britain. Similarly, all 2008 U.S. presidential hopefuls maintained YouTube channels. Barack Obama's channel was highly popular and included more than 1,000 video clips promoting his campaign.[6]

Information technology has improved global access by linking people in businesses through telecommunications. Satellites permit instant visual and electronic

*Handheld computers are improving the productivity of workers by letting them access their e-mail and other information on the Web in real time.*

voice connections almost anywhere in the world. The self-sustaining nature of technology acts as a catalyst to spur even faster development. As new innovations are introduced, they stimulate the need for more technology to facilitate further development. Technologies begin a process that creates new opportunities in every industry segment or customer area that is affected. Crossing global borders can be tricky for Internet companies, as Google Inc. has found with its popular YouTube site. Foreign governments in Asia and the Middle East have repeatedly banned the video Web site. China, which tightly controls the flow of information, has blocked YouTube several times, for politically sensitive content relating to Tibet, for example. Google and YouTube must walk a fine line between censorship and doing business under such regimes.[7]

Productivity, the amount of output per hour of work, is a key ingredient in determining the standard of living. For the past eight years, the United States has enjoyed significantly faster productivity growth than it did over the preceding two decades. Some analysts believe that the potential gains in productivity from technological advances associated with the computer revolution are far from over.[8] In recent years, economic and productivity growth has resulted in the annual addition of 2 million jobs.[9] For example, the ability to access information in "real time" through the electronic data interface between retailers, wholesalers, and manufacturers has reduced delivery lead times, as well as the hours required to produce and deliver products. The process of releasing an album with a major record label is arduous, with the input and consent of lawyers, marketers, promoters, CD manufacturers, and retail conglomerates. In 2003, the five-member band Radiohead decided to use the expiration of their contract with record label EMI to reinvent the launch of an album. Their next album, *In Rainbows,* was released electronically on Radiohead.com, with no set price. Downloaders were free to choose their own fee for the 10-song album.[10]

## Managing Information

**data**
numerical or verbal descriptions related to statistics or other items that have not been analyzed or summarized

**knowledge**
an understanding of data gained through study or experience

**information**
meaningful and useful interpretation of data and knowledge that can be used in making decisions

**Data** refers to numerical or verbal descriptions related to statistics or other items that have not been analyzed or summarized. Data can exist in a variety of forms—as patterns of numbers or letters printed on paper, stored in electronic memory, or accumulated as facts in a person's mind.[11] **Knowledge** is usually referred to as an understanding of data gained through study or experience. **Information** then includes meaningful and useful interpretation of data and knowledge that can be used in making decisions. The less information available, the more risk associated with a decision. For example, when a manager purchases a new computer without conducting any research, the risk of a poor decision is great. A more informed decision could be made after determining existing, and likely, computing needs and the price, capability, and quality of available computers from a number of sources. Information is necessary for good decision making. When information is properly understood, guidelines can be developed that help simplify and improve decisions in future similar circumstances. Therefore, effective information management is crucial.

Businesses often engage in data processing efforts to improve data flow and the usefulness of information. Often, computers are communicating this data without the direct interface or help of an individual. Goods can be ordered when inventories drop or a previous customer can be notified automatically when new product information is available. All of this depends on software and equipment that has been put in place to make data more useful based on established decision criteria.

## Management Information Systems

Because information is a major business resource, it should be viewed as an asset that must be developed and distributed to managers. Technology has been used to develop systems that provide managers with the information needed to make decisions. A **management information system (MIS)** is used for organizing and transmitting data into information that can be used for decision making. The purpose of the MIS is to obtain data from both internal and external sources to create information that is easily accessible and structured for user-friendly communication to managers. The MIS can range from a simple system in which information is delivered through e-mail to a complex system of records and data that is delivered through sophisticated communications software. At Anheuser-Busch, for example, a system called BudNet compiles information about past sales at individual stores, inventory, competitors' displays and prices, and a host of other information collected by distributors' sales representatives on handheld computers. The system allows company executives to respond quickly to changes in demographic or social

**management information system (MIS)**
used for organizing and transmitting data into information that can be used for decision making

Scheid Vineyards produces premium wine grapes and operates approximately 5,700 acres of vineyards, primarily in Monterey County, California. The company sells most of its grapes to wineries that produce high-quality table wines. Scheid's clients can get real-time information about the specific grape blocks they're purchasing via the company's "Vit Watch" information system, accessible on the Web. Vit Watch allows both Scheid and its client to keep abreast of what is happening "in the field"—literally.

# Destination CEO
## Adobe Corporation—Bruce Chizen, CEO

Adobe is synonymous with innovation. Adobe has revolutionized the way we use our computers. Adobe technology is responsible for the software that is responsible for the fabric design of a chair to the label on a soft-drink bottle. Twenty-five years ago, Adobe pioneered the concept of desktop publishing and is now employed throughout the world in all aspects of digital communications from magazine publishing to television graphics. Bruce Chizen, CEO, attributes the profound success of Adobe to listening to the customer, watching future technological trends, and anticipating what customers will want from technology in the future. Adobe's Flash is installed on more than 700 million computers across the globe. YouTube, for example, makes use of Flash in order to stream media. The amount of information continues to explode and much of it is in digital form. Adobe is committed to finding innovative and interactive ways of delivering and using that information.

### Discussion Questions

1. Why is Adobe's Flash technology considered to be ubiquitous?
2. Adobe has had a tremendous impact across all industries. Provide some examples of how Adobe has had improved magazine publishing, television broadcasts, and upholstery design.
3. Explain why Adobe is considered an IT company.

---

trends or competitors' strategies with an appropriate promotional message, package, display, or discount. The system also helps the company pinpoint demographic consumption trends, craft promotional messages, and even develop new products.[12]

The MIS breaks down time and location barriers, making information available when and where it is needed to solve problems. An effective MIS can make information available around the globe in seconds, and with wireless communications, it is possible for users to carry the system in a briefcase or pocket. Wireless devices in use today include computers, personal data assistants, cell phones, pagers, and GPS positioning devices found in cars. For example, General Motors provides OnStar Telematics that provide advanced satellite-based communication to pinpoint a car's location. The system can put the car's driver in touch with an advisor for emergency assistance or requests for directions, or connect with an online concierge for entertainment, restaurant, and shopping information. When an airbag deploys in a vehicle equipped with OnStar, the system automatically alerts an adviser, who calls immediately to discern the nature of the emergency.[13]

## Collecting Data

To be effective, an MIS must be able to collect, store and update data, and process and present information. Much of the data that are useful for managers typically come from sources inside the organization. Such internal data can be obtained from company records, reports, and operations. The data may relate to customers, suppliers, expenses, and sales. Information about employees such as salaries, benefits, and turnover can be of great value and is usually incorporated into the system. External sources of data include customers, suppliers, industry publications, the mass media, and firms that gather data for sale.

**database**
a collection of data stored in one place and accessible throughout the network

A **database** is a collection of data stored in one place and accessible throughout the network. A database management program permits participants to electronically store information and organize the data into usable categories that are arranged by decision requirements. For example, if management needs to know the 20 top customers by sales volume, then the system can access the database and print a list of the customers in a matter of moments. This same type of information retrieval can occur throughout the functional areas of the business with the appropriate database management software.

Database marketing provides a method to identify different types of customers and the data to develop strategies for interacting with each customer. Databases developed by Information Resources Inc. (IRI) allow businesses to tap into an abundance of information on sales, pricing, and promotion for hundreds of consumer product categories using data from scanners at the checkouts in stores. IRI can track new products to assess their performance and gauge competitors' reactions. Once new products are on store shelves, IRI monitors related information, including the prices and market share of competing products. IRI can also help companies assess customers' reactions to changes in a product's price, packaging, and display. By tracking a product's sales in relation to promotional efforts, the effect of a company's advertising as well as that of competitors can be known.[14] Nearly all of the consumer package goods firms in the *Fortune* Global 500 use Information Resources Inc.'s services.[15]

# The Internet

The **Internet,** the global information system that links many computer networks together, has profoundly altered the way people communicate, learn, do business, and find entertainment. Although many people believe the Internet began in the early 1990s, its origins can actually be traced to the late 1950s (see Table. 4.1). Over the past four decades, the network evolved from a system for government and university researchers into a tool used by millions around the globe for communication, information, entertainment, and e-business.

> **Internet**
> global information system that links many computer networks together

With the development of the **World Wide Web,** a collection of interconnected Web sites or "pages" of text, graphics, audio, and video within the Internet, use of the Internet has exploded globally.

Internet use has expanded worldwide, providing the communication infrastructure for global business and personal advancement. Globally, about 6 million new Internet users are added each month. China has passed the United States in Internet use, with 228.5 million Internet users compared with 217.1 million in the United States.

> **World Wide Web**
> a collection of interconnected Web sites or pages of text, graphics, audio, and video within the Internet

China is the largest Internet user, but companies that desire to sell to China have a limited opportunity. The United States is much more advanced with online advertising and e-business. According to the Organization for Economic Cooperation and Development, the United States has the largest total number of broadband subscribers, with 66.2 million utilizing the faster Internet service. China's online advertising stands at $1.3 billion compared with $21.4 billion for the United States. Looking to the future, China only has about a 16 percent Internet penetration rate, compared with a global average of 19 percent and a U.S. rate of 70 percent. Japan, Canada, Germany, Australia, and the United Kingdom are approaching an Internet penetration rate of 70 percent. Even developing countries such as Chile and Argentina have 40 percent Internet usage, with Mexico and Russia at 20 percent.[16]

An **intranet** is a network of computers similar to the Internet that is available only to people inside an organization. Businesses establish intranets to make the MIS available for employees and to create interactive communication about data. The intranet allows employees to participate in creating information useful throughout the organization. The development of an intranet saves money and time because paper is eliminated and data becomes available on an almost instantaneous basis. Over half of all businesses are running some type of intranet. Even universities are capturing the benefits of intranets. Duke University has introduced an intranet system to help students manage their on-campus recruiting work. With this system,

> **intranet**
> a network of computers similar to the Internet that is available only to people inside an organization

**TABLE 4.1**    History of Information Technology

| Year | Event | Significance |
|------|-------|--------------|
| 1836 | Telegraph | The telegraph revolutionized human (tele)communications with Morse code, a series of dots and dashes used to communicate between humans. |
| 1858–1866 | Transatlantic cable | Transatlantic cable allowed direct instantaneous communication across the Atlantic Ocean. |
| 1876 | Telephone | The telephone created voice communication, and telephone exchanges provide the backbone of Internet connections today. |
| 1957 | USSR launches Sputnik | Sputnik was the first artificial earth satellite and the start of global communications. |
| 1962–1968 | Packet switching networks developed | The Internet relies on packet switching networks, which split data into tiny packets that may take different routes to a destination. |
| 1971 | Beginning of the Internet | People communicate over the Internet with a program to send messages across a distributed network. |
| 1973 | Global networking becomes a reality | Ethernet outlined—this is how local networks are basically connected today, and gateways define how large networks (maybe of different architecture) can be connected together. |
| 1991 | World Wide Web established | User-friendly interface to World Wide Web established with text-based, menu-driven interface to access Internet resources. |
| 1992 | Multimedia changes the face of the Internet | The term "surfing the Internet" is coined. |
| 1993 | World Wide Web revolution begins | Mosaic, user-friendly Graphical Front End to the World Wide Web, makes the Internet more accessible and evolves into Netscape. |
| 1995 | Internet service providers advance | Online dial-up systems (CompuServe, America Online, Prodigy) begin to provide Internet access. |
| 2000 | Broadband connections to the Internet emerge | Provides fast access to multimedia and large text files. |
| 2002 | Advances in wireless | Mobile phones, handheld computers, and personal data assistants provide wireless access to the Internet. |
| 2004 | Wireless technology expands | Use of radio waves to send e-mail, Web pages, and other information through the air (Wi-Fi). |
| 2009 | WiMax Network | Faster and covers North America, creating one big hot spot. Internet appliance options are advanced. |

**extranet**
a network of computers that permits selected companies and other organizations to access the same information and may allow collaboration and communication about the information

Duke MBA students can apply for jobs, sign up for career counseling, bid on interview slots, post job leads, and network with other students.[17]

Some businesses open up their intranets to other selected individuals or companies through an **extranet,** a network of computers that permits selected companies and other organizations to access the same information and may allow different managers in various organizations to collaborate and communicate about the information. For example, one of the most common uses of an extranet is for a company such as Wal-Mart to permit suppliers such as Procter & Gamble or Kraft to access the Wal-Mart MIS to determine inventory levels and product

# Going Green
## Virtually Protesting to Save the Environment

The Internet has changed our lives in numerous ways, but did you ever think that we'd be staging protests online? Well, the day has arrived. In countries throughout the world, workers, students, organizations, and individuals are taking to the Internet to stage protests and fight for what they believe is right. Although businesses or individuals on the receiving end of these protests may not agree, there are a number of positive reasons to stage virtual protests beyond the obvious goal of achieving change.

For workers looking to stage protests, using the Internet provides them a way to protest without losing work time or pay. These protests actually benefit companies by creating little or no disruption in productivity. Among many examples is that of 2,000 employees of Italy's IBM branch staging a virtual protest in Second Life. Logging in from their home computers (in order to avoid legal issues), these employees protested a pay settlement. As a result, the union gave them a new pay deal. In addition, the head of IBM's Italian offices resigned.

Again using Second Life, fashion designer Stella McCartney staged an anti-fur protest along with People for the Ethical Treatment of Animals (PETA). As part of the protest, people in Second Life were able to dress their avatars in T-shirts stating, "I'd Rather be Pixelated Than Wear Fur." PETA also staged a competition looking for a slogan to replace its famous "I'd Rather Go Naked Than Wear Fur." Because millions of users frequent Second Life, this was a clever way to reach a large number of individuals.

Moving from Europe to Asia, the virtual protest trend continues. In Hong Kong, students staged a virtual protest on Facebook when their bank, HSBC, threatened to axe free overdraft protection on its checking accounts. As a result, the bank did away with interest fees and maintained the program.

The virtual protest is widely used in the United States. For example, visit the Web site **stopglobalwarming.org** and you can join an online protest that boasts members such as the Nobel Peace Prize Laureate Wangari Maathal. The protest currently claims 1,044,030 supporters. **MoveOn.org** is well known for its virtual protests, some of which are environmentally or politically based.

When you stop to think about it, the virtual protest is beneficial for many reasons. It is easier to organize, potentially safer for protesters, can reach a much wider audience, and can be more efficient. And, believe it or not, it can be environmentally beneficial—virtual protests can save energy and paper and have a smaller carbon footprint than traditional protests.[18]

**Discussion Questions**

1. What are the advantages for groups that use the Internet as a method to stage protests about their concerns?
2. How may a virtual protest have limitations compared with a personal, onsite protest?
3. Because virtual protests are environmentally friendly, is it possible that this green method of communication may become much more popular?

availability. An extranet allows users to share data, process orders, and manage information.

In the next few pages, we will take a brief look at wireless technologies that are making the Internet easier to use.

> **"Did You Know?"** Every day, 600,000 illegal copies of movies are downloaded from the Internet.[19]

## Wireless Technologies

Future wireless technologies are driving us beyond personal computers (PC) toward an array of Internet appliances such as personal digital assistants (PDAs), smart phones, and other digital devices. The BlackBerry and Palm Pilot are established PDAs with millions of users. Livescribe's new Pulse is a smart pen that can store audio along with written notes to be downloaded to a Windows PC, which can in turn be sent or accessed by other wireless devices. When it was launched in 2007, the Apple iPhone was named *Time* magazine's Invention of the Year for its integrated wireless multimedia features, including e-mail, web browsing, iPod-like media player, and a camera.[20]

Internet browsing by a mobile phone is growing throughout the world as cell phone penetration increases. In South Korea, Japan, and urban China, at least 90 percent of the households have at least one mobile phone, and the total number of Chinese mobile phones is approaching 500,000. In the United States, 75 percent of households own a mobile phone. Globally, around one-fourth of cell phone owners have used their phone to browse the Web.[21] Additionally, the number of digital photos taken by cell phones has outstripped the number taken by digital cameras. Camera phones are so popular in Japan that funeral attendees are now using the phones to take pictures of deceased friends and relatives. A funeral director in Tokyo stated, "I get the sense that people no longer respect the dead. It's disturbing."[22]

Wireless fidelity (Wi-Fi) networks are changing the way individuals and businesses use the Internet. Wi-Fi sends Web pages and other information to your laptop computer or other electronic device using radio waves. In the not-too-distant future, experts expect Wi-Fi to link all sorts of devices—not just computers, but lamps, stereos, appliances, and more—and to fully integrate the Internet into our lives. Cooks using wireless notebook computers can take advantage of Epicuriuos's Web site, which allows access to "how to" videos that can be watched while cooking in the kitchen.[23] Wi-Fi is also transforming how companies use the Internet. Some firms use Wi-Fi to replace expensive wired networks or to maintain communications even in hard-to-reach places like warehouses. As such, investments in Wi-Fi can boost productivity and improve the ease and connectivity of multiple devices. Bluetooth technology allows mobile phones, computers, and personal digital assistants, as well as other devices, to be interconnected using a short-range wireless connection. Using this technology, users can have all mobile and fixed computer devices in sync with one another. Bluetooth wireless technology is installed on more than 5 million units every week as well as some automobiles, such as select BMWs.[24]

WiMax is a new technology trying to move beyond Wi-Fi by covering a much larger area. In fact, this new technology is trying to turn North America into one big hot spot. Leading information technology companies such as Sprint, Google, Comcast, and Time Warner are creating a new company to utilize this technology, Clearwire, which has the potential to give the United States an opportunity to be the leader in wireless broadband. WiMax offers download speeds three times faster than the current average mobile download speed. The technology works through WiMax transmitters on cell phone towers.[25]

*RFID chips aren't just for tracking products anymore. They're for people, too. Verichip Corporation, a Florida-based firm, has begun making tiny implantable radio frequency identification chips to protect infants, to identify unconscious people, or to prevent people with dementia from wandering off and never being found. The roots of VeriChip trace back to the events of September 11, 2001, when New York firemen were writing their badge ID numbers on their chests in case they were found injured or unconscious.*

Internet Voice, also known as Voice over Internet Protocol (VOIP), allows you to make telephone calls using broadband Internet connections instead of traditional hard-wired, land lines. While some services only work through your computer, others allow you to use your traditional phone line with an adapter. Companies operating in this market include Vonage, Skype, Sunrocket, Time Warner Cable, and Net Zero, to name a few.[26]

Another emerging technology of great importance to business is radio frequency identification (RFID) systems, which use radio waves to identify and track resources and products within the distribution channel. Goods tagged with an RFID tag can be tracked electronically from supplier to factory floor, from warehouse to retail store. Companies are also increasingly employing global positioning systems (GPS) to facilitate shipping and inventory management tasks. Wal-Mart is a leader in the use of RFID technology, getting its suppliers to use RFID chips in the pallets and cases shipped to stores. This helps minimize one of the most costly problems in retailing—empty shelves with replacement product hiding in the store room. In a study by the University of Arkansas, stores using this technology and process saw a 16 percent reduction in product missing from shelves.[27]

The growth of wireless voice communications and their increasing integration with Internet technologies generates opportunities for further innovations and applications. For example, location-based wireless technologies already aid police and parents in protecting children from kidnapping and other crimes. Multimedia messaging services (MMS) and streaming mobile video raise exciting possibilities for more person-to-person services and even personalized entertainment.[28] However, these possibilities also raise privacy questions, as we shall see later in this chapter.

# E-Business

Because the phenomenal growth of the Internet and the World Wide Web have provided the opportunity for e-business to grow faster than any other innovation in recent years, we have devoted an entire section to this subject. E-business growth has not been without some setbacks as businesses experimented with new approaches to utilizing information technology and the Internet. Since e-business is based on an interactive model to conduct business, it has expanded the methods for maintaining business relationships. The nature of the Internet has created tremendous opportunities for businesses to forge relationships with consumers and business customers, target markets more precisely, and even reach previously inaccessible markets. The Internet also facilitates business transactions, allowing companies to network with manufacturers, wholesalers, retailers, suppliers, and outsource firms to serve customers more efficiently. Traditional methods included conducting business personally, through the mail (package document delivery service), and via telephone. The telecommunication opportunities created by the Internet have set the stage for e-business development and growth.

## The Nature of E-Business

In general, e-business has the same goal as traditional business. All businesses try to earn a profit by providing products that satisfy people's needs. **E-business** can be distinguished from traditional business as carrying out the goals of business through utilization of the Internet. There are many different areas of e-business that use familiar terms. For example, e-commerce uses the Internet to carry out marketing activities, including buying and selling activities conducted online. These activities include communicating and fostering exchanges and relationships with customers, suppliers, and the public. Amazon.com is the most successful e-business, with $14.8 billion in revenue, and is ranked as the 171st largest U.S. company on the 2008 *Fortune* 500 list ranked by revenue. Amazon now accounts for 6 percent of the $136 billion online retail market in the United States Retail sales are Amazon's biggest business, but now one-third of the company's sales are between businesses, including small stores and retailers as large as Target. Amazon takes a commission, or charges a fee, to fill such orders. Amazon is a true global e-business, with 50 percent of its revenue from international sales. The United Kingdom, Japan, and Germany each account for 10 percent of Amazon sales.[29]

E-commerce includes activities such as conducting marketing research, providing and obtaining price and product information, and advertising, as well as online

**e-business**
carrying out the goals of business through utilization of the Internet

selling. Even the U.S. government engages in e-commerce activities—marketing everything from bonds and other financial instruments to oil-drilling leases and wild horses. Procter & Gamble uses the Internet as a fast, cost-effective means for marketing research, judging consumer demand for potential new products by inviting online consumers to sample new prototype products and provide feedback. If a product gets rave reviews from the samplers, the company might decide to introduce it. Procter & Gamble already conducts nearly 100 percent of its concept testing and 40 percent of its 6,000 product tests and other studies online, saving the company significant time and money in getting new products to market.[30]

E-business has changed our economy with companies that could not exist without the technology available through the Internet. The top independent U.S. video Web site, Veoh, for example, is trying to give consumers the broadest collection of video available anywhere on the Internet. Veoh allows users easy access to full-length TV shows and other video, often hosted elsewhere on the Web. A key feature differentiating the site from others such as YouTube and Yahoo! is the ability to download shows for later viewing.[31]

Many companies that attempted to transact business on the Internet, often called dot-coms, had problems making a profit. Most of the early dot-coms, such as eToys.com, Pets.com, Garden.com, Hardware.com, and BigWords.com, found that no single technology could completely change the nature of business, and many failed. Some dot-coms failed because they thought the only thing that mattered was brand awareness they created through advertising. The reality, however, is that Internet markets are more similar to traditional markets than they are different. Thus, successful e-business strategies, like traditional business strategies, depend on creating products that customers need or want, not merely developing a brand name or reducing the costs associated with online transactions.

Instead of e-business changing all industries, it has had much more impact in certain industries where the cost of business and customer transactions is very high. For example, investment trading is less expensive online because customers can buy and sell investments, such as stocks and mutual funds, on their own. Firms such as Charles Schwab Corp, the biggest online brokerage firm, have been innovators in online trading. Traditional brokers such as Merrill Lynch have had to follow these companies and provide online trading for their customers. ING is the largest online bank in the United States and the world.

E-business can use many benefits of the Internet to reduce the cost of both customer and business transactions. Since the Internet lowers the cost of communication, it can contribute significantly in any industry or activity that depends on the flow of information. Opportunities exist for information-intensive industries such as entertainment, health care, government services, education, and computer services such as software.[32] For example, some insurance companies now pay for doctor–patient e-visits. Computer-literate patients can now consult their doctors through many Web sites, including Superior Health Medical Group. Patients of Superior Health can access e-Visit to obtain diagnoses, advice, and prescriptions without ever leaving their homes. Visitors can expect a response within 24 hours, and the approximate cost is $35.00 versus $63.00 for an office visit. During the first four months the service was offered, there was no charge for using e-Visit to familiarize consumers with the service and to encourage use.[33]

Also, online courses are now available from most universities for complete degree programs. There is also open university courseware, free to anyone who wants to access the course materials. Yale University has launched 30 open courses involving complete videotaped lectures. Apple iTunes U Web site enables free access to audio and video of lectures supplied by dozens of universities.[34]

A recent trend to help companies control the rising labor costs associated with providing customer service and support is the practice of outsourcing service jobs. The federal government does not keep track of how many U.S. jobs have moved to companies overseas, but there are estimates that 300,000 to 400,000 jobs have gone to places like China, Russia, and India in the last three years. Whether U.S. citizens are aware or not, they may be talking to an employee in India whenever they call the technical support number for Delta Airlines, American Express, Sprint, Citibank, IBM, or Hewlett-Packard. Even McDonald's is outsourcing drive-through orders.

In the future, most benefits and significant gains will come from restructuring the way work is done within businesses. While e-business can reduce the cost of both customer and business transactions, it can also improve coordination within and across businesses. E-business systems can become the communications backbone linking traditional relationships and storing employee knowledge in management information systems so that co-workers can access this knowledge instead of starting from the ground up. Leading experts suggest that most e-business benefits will come from changes in business practices and the way organizations function. With the crucial role of communication and information in business, the long-term impact of e-business on economic growth could be substantial.[35]

One area where e-business may have promised too much is in the area of manufacturing. Intranets can be important in reducing inventories and in eliminating costs in purchasing and other supply chain activities, as well as in eliminating unnecessary transactions. The Internet can be useful in determining the cost of components and other supplies and detailed information on customers to help customize products. Still the Internet mainly helps in moving information, while most manufacturing involves making things and motivating employees to maintain quality. Manufacturers still need to move truckloads of materials through congested highways and maintain a labor force that can get the job done. E-business can help manage manufacturing operations but is only one component that can provide quality and productivity.

Productive consequences of a firm's electronic communication systems can also be a challenge. For example, companies across the United States have employees who are accessing online video sources such as Google and YouTube for as much as an hour during the workday. Many are trying to curb this lost productivity by preventing employees' access to such sites, following previous steps to shut down employees' access to instant messaging services, streaming music, and Web sites with adult content.[36]

## E-Business Models

There are three major e-business models or markets with unique challenges and opportunities that represent areas with shared characteristics and decisions related to organizational structure, job requirements, and financial needs. The models are based on e-business customer profiles and how the Internet is used to maintain relationships.

**Busines-to-Business.** **Business-to-business (B2B)** e-business, sometimes called collaborative commerce, is the use of the Internet for transactions and communications between organizations. B2B activities are the largest and fastest growing area of e-business, with one-fourth of all B2B transactions taking place on the Internet. Typical ways that a company might join the B2B world range from the

**business-to-business (B2B)**
use of the Internet for transactions and communications between organizations

easiest—going online with an electronic catalog—to the more complex—creating a private trading network, using collaborative design, engaging in supply chain management, and creating a public exchange.[37]

Many B2B companies combine these to be successful. For example, Internet infrastructure maker Cisco Systems receives 68 percent of its orders online, and 70 percent of its service calls are resolved online. Cisco is in the process of linking all of its contract manufacturers and key suppliers into an advanced Web supply-chain management system called the e-HUB. This advanced Internet communication system speeds up the information about demand and is distributed to suppliers.[38] Ford Motor Company links 30,000 auto parts suppliers and its 6,900-member dealer network for transactions. Ford expects to save $8.9 billion a year on costs and earn approximately $3 million a year from fees it charges for the use of its supplier network.[39]

The forces unleashed by the Internet are particularly important in B2B relationships, where uncertainties are being reduced by improving the quantity, reliability, and timeliness of information. General Motors, IBM, and Procter & Gamble are learning to consolidate and rationalize their supply chains using the Internet. Covisint is a leading provider of services that provide linkages between partners, customers, and suppliers. One Web site seeks to give small businesses and inventors a place on the Internet. Eureka ranch Technology Ltd.'s USA National Innovations Marketplace is an online registry for inventors and researchers to post their ideas. Small and large businesses can search the ideas and develop partnerships. This allows big business access to outside help and small businesses and inventors get a chance to land a big partner.[40]

**business-to-consumer (B2C)**
delivery of products and services directly to individual consumers through the Internet

Business-to-Consumer.    **Business-to-consumer (B2C)** e-business means delivering products and services directly to individual consumers through the Internet. The Internet provides an opportunity for mass customization, meaning that individuals can communicate electronically over the Internet and receive responses that satisfy their individual needs. If products and communication can be customized to fit the individual, then long-term relationships can be nurtured. For example, after a consumer makes a purchase at Amazon.com, the site provides recommendations for books, music, DVD, and toys, as well as electronics and software on future site visits by that consumer. Dell Computer is a leading B2C e-business that not only custom-builds computers for consumers but also provides customer service online.

U.S. e-tailers generated more than $136 billion in sales in 2007. Experts believe the escalation of online retail sales will come primarily from first-time Internet buyers and that the online buying population will continue to grow to include one-half the adult population.[41] Figure 4.1 indicates the growth on online advertising revenues from the top four portals.

Services provided in e-business relationships are often referred to as e-services. E-services are efforts to enhance the value of products through an experience that is created for the consumer. While traditional retailers provide many services, e-business companies have discovered that the unique characteristics of the Internet provide additional opportunities for enhancing the value to the consumer. Some examples of e-services include MapQuest's driving direction service and travel services provided by Travelocity.com and Expedia. A majority of travelers use the Internet for booking travel. Nearly 80 percent use the Internet for travel information or planning.[42] Web sites such as RetailMeNot.com and CouponCabin.com provide e-services by allowing online shoppers to access coupon codes and locate the

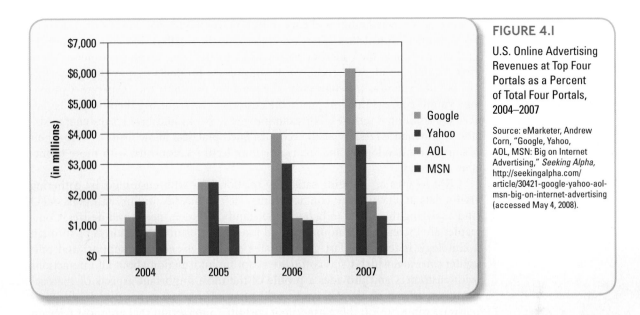

FIGURE 4.1

U.S. Online Advertising Revenues at Top Four Portals as a Percent of Total Four Portals, 2004–2007

Source: eMarketer, Andrew Corn, "Google, Yahoo, AOL, MSN: Big on Internet Advertising," *Seeking Alpha,* http://seekingalpha.com/article/30421-google-yahoo-aol-msn-big-on-internet-advertising (accessed May 4, 2008).

best deals on the Internet.[43] The key to the success of e-service sites is creating and nurturing one-to-one relationships with consumers. For example, some e-service travel sites also sell books/maps, apparel, insurance, and bags/luggage.[44]

**Consumer-to-Consumer.**   One market that is sometimes overlooked is the **consumer-to-consumer (C2C)** market, where consumers market goods and services to each other through the Internet. C2C e-business has become very popular thanks to eBay and other online auctions through which consumers can sell goods, often for higher prices than they might receive through newspaper classified ads or garage sales. Some consumers have even turned their passion for trading online into successful businesses. For example, a collector of vintage guitars might find items in local markets, such as pawnshops or flea markets, and then sell them for a higher price on eBay. Others use Zshops at Amazon.com for selling used items. The growing C2C market may threaten some traditional businesses if consumers find it more efficient to sell their books, CDs, and other used items through online auctions or other C2C venues.[45]

**consumer-to-consumer (C2C)**
market in which consumers market goods and services to each other through the Internet

### Customer Relationship Management[46]
One characteristic of companies engaged in e-business is a renewed focus on building customer loyalty and retaining customers. **Customer relationship management (CRM)** focuses on using information about customers to create strategies that develop and sustain desirable long-term customer relationships. This focus is possible because today's technology helps companies target customers more precisely and accurately than ever before. CRM technology allows businesses to identify specific customers, establish interactive dialogs with them to learn about their needs, and combine this information with their purchase histories to customize products to meet those needs. Procter & Gamble, for example, encourages Oil of Olay customers to join their Club Olay. Members receive special offers, free samples, and skin type/product pairings. In addition, Proctor & Gamble is able to collect information on products registrants use as well as reactions to P&G products.[47]

**customer relationship management (CRM)**
focuses on using information about customers to create strategies that develop and sustain desirable long-term customer relationships

Advances in technology and data collection techniques now permit firms to profile customers in real time. The goal is to assess the worth of individual customers and thus estimate their lifetime value (LTV) to the firm. Some customers—those that require considerable coddling or who return products frequently—may simply be too expensive to retain given the low level of profits they generate. Companies can discourage these unprofitable customers by requiring them to pay higher fees for additional services. For example, many banks and brokerages charge sizable maintenance fees on small accounts. Such practices allow firms to focus their resources on developing and managing long-term relationships with more profitable customers.[48]

CRM focuses on building satisfying relationships with customers by gathering useful data at all customer-contact points—telephone, fax, online, and personal—and analyzing those data to better understand customers' needs and desires. Companies are increasingly automating and managing customer relationships through technology. Indeed, one fast-growing area of CRM is customer-support and call-center software, which helps companies capture information about all interactions with customers and provides a profile of the most important aspects of the customer experience on the Web and on the phone. Customer-support and call-center software can focus on those aspects of customer interaction that are most relevant to performance, such as how long customers have to wait on the phone to ask a question of a service representative or how long they must wait to receive a response from an online request. This technology can also help marketers determine whether call-center personnel are missing opportunities to promote additional products or to provide better service. For example, after buying a new Saab automobile, the customer is supposed to meet a service mechanic who can answer any technical questions about the new car during the first service visit. Saab follows up this visit with a telephone survey to determine whether the new car buyer met the Saab mechanic and to learn about the buyer's experience with the first service call.

Sales automation software can link a firm's sales force to applications that facilitate selling and providing service to customers. Often these applications enable customers to assist themselves instead of using traditional sales and service organizations. Salesforce.com provides salesforce automation for clients such as Accenture, Cisco, Deloitte, and Intel. Systems such as Salesforce make tracking and forecasting sales more efficient and effective.[49] In addition, CRM systems can provide sales managers with information that helps provide the best product solution for customers and thus maximize service. Dell Computer, for example, employs CRM data to identify those customers with the greatest needs for computer hardware and then provides these select customers with additional value in the form of free, secure, customized Web sites. These "premier pages" allow customers—typically large companies—to check their order status, arrange deliveries, and troubleshoot problems. Although Dell collects considerable data about its customers from its online sales transactions, the company avoids selling customer lists to outside vendors.[50]

# Legal and Social Issues

The extraordinary growth of information technology, the Internet, and e-business has generated many legal and social issues for consumers and businesses. These issues include privacy concerns, identity theft, and protection of intellectual property and copyrights. Each of these is discussed below, as well as steps taken by individuals, companies, and the government to address the issues.

## Privacy

Businesses have long tracked consumers' shopping habits with little controversy. However, observing the contents of a consumer's shopping cart or the process a consumer goes through when choosing a box of cereal generally does not result in specific, personally identifying data. Although consumers' use of credit cards, shopping cards, and coupons involves giving up a certain degree of anonymity in the traditional shopping process, consumers can still choose to remain anonymous by paying cash. Shopping on the Internet, however, allows businesses to track consumers on a far more personal level, from their online purchases to the Web sites they favor.[51] Current technology has made it possible to amass vast quantities of personal information, often without consumers' knowledge, and allows for the collection, sharing, and selling of this information to interested third parties. Privacy has, therefore, become one of Web users' biggest concerns.

How is personal information collected on the Web? Many sites follow users' online "tracks" by storing a "cookie," or identifying string of text, on their computers. Cookies permit Web site operators to track how often a user visits the site, what he or she looks at while there, and in what sequence. Cookies allow Web site visitors to customize services, such as virtual shopping carts, as well as the particular content they see when they log onto a Web page, but the potential for misuse has left many consumers uncomfortable with this technology.

Some measure of protection of personal privacy is provided by the U.S. Constitution, as well as Supreme Court rulings and federal laws (see Table 4.2). Some of these laws relate specifically to Internet privacy while others protect privacy both on and off the Internet. The U.S. Federal Trade Commission (FTC) also regulates and enforces privacy standards and monitors Web sites to ensure compliance. The corporate world has also had to deal with identity theft as hackers get into their systems to steal the personal data of millions of people. One of the most serious such problems occurred with TJX Cos, the large discount retailer. Millions of customers' credit card numbers were compromised.[52]

Businesses are beginning to recognize that the only way to circumvent further government regulation with respect to privacy is to develop systems and policies to protect consumers' interests. Several nonprofit organizations have also stepped in to help companies develop privacy policies. Among the best known of these are TRUSTe and the Better Business Bureau Online. TRUSTe is a nonprofit organization devoted to promoting global trust in Internet technology. Companies that agree to abide by TRUSTe's privacy standards may display a "trustmark" on their Web sites. More than 2,200 Web sites display the trustmark seal of approval from TRUSTe.[53] The BBBOnLine program provides verification, monitoring and review, consumer dispute resolution, a compliance seal, enforcement mechanisms, and an educational component. It is managed by the Council of Better Business Bureaus, an organization with considerable experience in conducting self-regulation and dispute- resolution programs, and it employs guidelines and requirements outlined by the Federal Trade Commission and the U.S. Department of Commerce.[54]

## Spam

**Spam,** or unsolicited commercial e-mail (UCE), has become a major source of discontent with the Internet. Many Internet users believe spam violates their privacy and steals their resources. Many companies despise spam because it costs them $50 billion a year in lost productivity, new equipment, antispam filters, and

**spam**
unsolicited commercial e-mail

**TABLE 4.2**     Privacy Laws

| Act (Date Enacted) | Purpose |
| --- | --- |
| Privacy Act (1974) | Requires federal agencies to adopt minimum standards for collecting and processing personal information; limits the disclosure of such records to other public or private parties; requires agencies to make records on individuals available to them on request, subject to certain conditions. |
| Right to Financial Privacy Act (1978) | Protects the rights of financial-institution customers to keep their financial records private and free from unjust government investigation. |
| Computer Security Act (1987) | Brought greater confidentiality and integrity to the regulation of information in the public realm by assigning responsibility for standardization of communication protocols, data structures, and interfaces in telecommunications and computer systems to the National Institute of Standards and Technology (NIST), which also announces security and privacy guidelines for federal computer systems. |
| Computer Matching and Privacy Protection Act (1988) | Amended the Privacy Act by adding provisions regulating the use of computer matching, the computerized comparison of individual information for purposes of determining eligibility for federal benefits programs. |
| Video Privacy Protection Act (1988) | Specifies the circumstances under which a business that rents or sells videos can disclose personally identifiable information about a consumer or reveal an individual's video rental or sales records. |
| Telephone Consumer Protection Act (1991) | Regulates the activities of telemarketers by limiting the hours during which they can solicit residential subscribers, outlawing the use of artificial or prerecorded voice messages to residences without prior consent, prohibiting unsolicited advertisements by telephone facsimile machines, and requiring telemarketers to maintain a "do not call list" of any consumers who request not to receive further solicitation. |
| Driver Privacy Protection Act (1993) | Restricts the circumstances under which state departments of motor vehicles may disclose personal information about any individual obtained by the department in connection with a motor vehicle record. |
| Fair Credit Reporting Act (amended in 1997) | Promotes accuracy, fairness, and privacy of information in the files of consumer reporting agencies (e.g., credit bureaus); grants consumers the right to see their personal credit reports, to find out who has requested access to their reports, to dispute any inaccurate information with the consumer reporting agency, and to have inaccurate information corrected or deleted. |
| Children's Online Privacy Protection Act (2000) | Regulates the online collection of personally identifiable information (name, address, e-mail address, hobbies, interests, or information collected through cookies) from children under age 13 by specifying what a Web site operator must include in a privacy policy, when and how to seek consent from a parent, and what responsibilities an operator has to protect children's privacy and safety online. |
| Do Not Call Implementation Act (2003) | Directs the FCC and FTC to coordinate so that their rules are consistent regarding telemarketing call practices, including the Do Not Call Registry and other lists, as well as call abandonment. |
| CAN-SPAM Act (2004) | Bans unsolicited commercial e-mail and requires special labeling and procedures to opt-out to prevent future e-mails. |

manpower. Spam has been likened to receiving a direct mail promotional piece with postage due. Some angry recipients of spam have even organized boycotts against companies that advertise in this manner. Other recipients, however, appreciate the opportunity to learn about new products. By some estimates, spam accounts for 95 percent of all e-mail. However, it is not just the rising volume of spam that is a problem, but also the size of the spam messages. To defeat content filters, spammers are increasingly using images, which means that unsolicited

| | Users (%) |
|---|---|
| Getting more spam in personal e-mail account | 37 |
| Getting less spam in personal e-mail account | 10 |
| Have not noticed a change | 51 |
| Getting more spam in work e-mail account | 29 |
| Getting less spam in work e-mail account | 8 |
| Have not noticed a change | 55 |

**TABLE 4.3**

How Spam Volume Has Changed

Source: Enid Burnes, "Computer Users More Savvy About E-mail Spam," *ClickZ Stats,* May 25, 2007, http://www.clickz.com/showPage.html?page=3625976 (accessed April 8, 2008).

bulk e-mail is getting bulkier.[55] Table 4.3 shows how spam volume has changed in personal and corporate e-mail accounts.

Most commercial online services (e.g., AmericaOnline) and Internet service providers offer their subscribers the option to filter out e-mail from certain Internet addresses that generate a large volume of spam. Businesses are installing software to filter out spam from outside their networks. Some companies have filed suit against spammers under the Controlling the Assault of Non-Solicited Pornography and Marketing (CAN-SPAM) Law, which went into effect in 2004 and bans fraudulent or deceptive unsolicited commercial e-mail and requires senders to provide information on how recipients can opt out of receiving additional messages. However, spammers appear to be ignoring the law and finding creative ways to get around spam filters.[56] Although North America is believed to be the source of 80 percent of spam, the European Union ordered eight member nations to enact antispam and privacy-protection legislation. The EU already has strict regulations concerning electronic communications and bans all unsolicited commercial e-mail, but not all member nations have ratified the regulations.[57] Figure 4.2 shows the volume of spam by country.

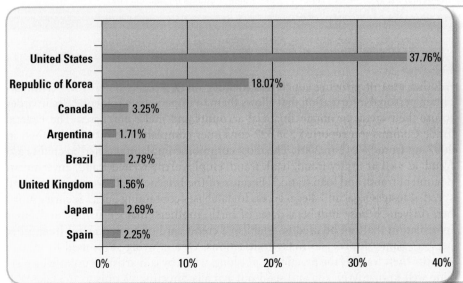

**FIGURE 4.2**

Spam Volume by Country

Source: "Messaging Security Resources: Percentage of Total Spam Volumes by Country," *Secure Computing,* http://www.ciphertrust.com/resources/statistics/spam_sources.php (accessed April 8, 2008).

# Responding to Business Challenges
## The Internet Provides the Opportunity for a Real Second Life

While many of us tire of the day-to-day "business" of life and day dream of how our ideal day, week, month, year, or life might be, some people out there are doing more than day dreaming. These people actually live an alternate life in a virtual world called Second Life. If you've never heard of Second Life, it's a three-dimensional world completely constructed and owned by those who "live" there. Second Life is full of people, opportunities, entertainment, and much more. The people inhabiting Second Life interact with each other, purchase land, build houses, and run businesses. They can buy, sell, and trade products with others and even have their own currency, the Linden dollar. Second Life, owned by Linden Labs, went public in 2003 and is now populated by almost 11 million people, although just over a million log on during in the course of a month.

Second Life is not a game. It is what some have deemed a parallel universe of sorts. Residents of Second Life create avatars to represent themselves in the virtual world. These avatars do much of what we do in real life, with a few twists—residents of Second Life can fly, walk underwater, and make their avatars look like humans, animals, or pretty much anything they desire. Second Life also has its own economy. Residents can purchase Linden dollars at an exchange rate of about $1 to 270 Linden dollars. The site keeps track of how much money comes in and out of Second Life each day, and a recent record showed that as much as $500,000 was changing hands on a given day.

While originally created and inhabited by people enjoying the opportunity to live in an alternate reality, Second Life has become attractive to businesses as well. Corporate marketers are beginning to use Second Life as a way to test products and entice customers. This has caused some concern among Second Life residents, many of whom run the profitable businesses that are already part of the world. But Linden Labs is not concerned. It claims that businesses must learn to play under different rules in Second Life. In this virtual world, there is no such thing as economies of scale and the residents can easily avoid patronizing any company they choose.

Despite the objections of some Second Life residents, corporations are eager to wet their feet in Second Life. Some companies, such as American Apparel, spent time promoting products in Second Life only to pull out, but others, such as Toyota have found their time in the alternate reality productive. IBM uses Second Life to conduct "in-world" meetings and trainings and to maintain a 24-hour business center populated by avatars. Recently, another type of business made its foray into Second Life. CNN has established a news-gathering center in Second Life. The company will allow Second Life residents to gather information and report on what is happening in Second Life. It will also offer journalistic trainings from the likes of Larry King.

Although it has recently been reported that Second Life is experiencing financial trouble and that user numbers are falling, there are those who argue that the entire Web is headed the direction of Second Life. Whether Second Life's population continues to grow, as does its influx of corporate participation, remains to be seen.[58]

### Discussion Questions

1. Why do you think that Second Life has become so popular?
2. Why do some people view Second Life as not a game, but a real-life experience?
3. What are some of the opportunities for companies to promote their products on Second Life?

## Identity Theft

Another area of growing concern is identity theft, which occurs when criminals obtain personal information that allows them to impersonate someone else in order to use their credit to obtain financial accounts and make purchases. The Federal Trade Commission reported 258,427 consumer complaints about identity theft in 2007, up from 86,212 in 2001. The most common complaints related to credit card fraud, as well as utility fraud, bank fraud, employment-related fraud, government document fraud, and loan fraud.[59] Because of the Internet's relative anonymity and speed, it fosters legal and illegal access to databases containing Social Security numbers, drivers' license numbers, dates of birth, mothers' maiden names, and other information that can be used to establish a credit card or bank account in another person's name in order to make transactions. One growing scam used to initiate identity theft fraud is the practice of *phishing*, whereby con artists counterfeit a genuine well-known Web site and send out e-mails directing victims to the fake Web site where they find instructions to reveal sensitive information such as credit card numbers. Phishing scams have faked Web sites for PayPal, AOL, and the Federal Deposit Insurance Corporation.[60]

Typically, it takes 14 months before a victim discovers identity theft, and in 45 percent of the cases, it took nearly two years to resolve the theft.[61] The Javelin Strategy and Research 2007 Identity Fraud Survey Report indicated that 8.4 million U.S. adults were a victim of identity theft in 2007, totaling $49.3 billion in fraud.[62] To deter identity theft, the National Fraud Center wants financial institutions to implement new technologies, such as digital certificates, digital signatures, and biometrics—the use of fingerprinting or retina scanning.[63]

## Intellectual Property and Copyrights

In addition to protecting personal privacy, Internet users and others are concerned about protecting their rights to property they may create, including songs, movies, books, and software. Such intellectual property consists of the ideas and creative materials developed to solve problems, carry out applications, and educate and entertain others. Intellectual property is generally protected via patents and copyrights. The American Society for Industrial Security estimates that intellectual property and proprietary information losses in the United States total tens of billions of dollars per year.[64] This issue has become a global concern because of disparities in enforcement of laws throughout the world. In fact, the Business Software Alliance estimates that global losses from software piracy amount to $48 billion a year, including movies, music, and software downloaded from the Internet.[65]

U.S. copyright laws protect original works in text form, pictures, movies, computer software, musical multimedia, and audiovisual work. Owners of copyrights have the right to reproduce, derive from, distribute and publicly display, and perform the copyrighted works. Copyright infringement is the unauthorized execution of the rights reserved by a copyright holder. Congress passed the Digital Millennium Copyright Act (DMCA) in 1998 to protect copyrighted materials on the Internet and limit the liability of online service providers.

## Taxing the Internet?

An increasingly controversial issue in e-business is whether states should be able to levy a sales tax on Internet sales. The issue of collecting taxes on online purchases had been subject to a moratorium that went into effect in 2001. However, many states—facing huge budget deficits—have been lobbying for the right to charge a sales tax on Internet sales originating within their states. In 2005, the Sales Tax Simplification Agreement passed with the support of 18 states. The purpose of the agreement is to simplify the nation's varying state tax laws. Under this system, it is expected that companies who are not required by law to remit sales tax on Internet sales may voluntarily collect taxes.[66]

## The Dynamic Nature of Information Technology and E-Business

As we have pointed out in this chapter, information technology and e-business are having a major effect on the business world and thus your future career. Future leaders of businesses will need more than just a technical understanding of information technology; they will need a strategic understanding of how information technology and e-business can help make business more efficient and productive. Companies that depend on information technology as their core focus provide

# So You Want a Job in Information Technology

The business world is increasingly dependent on information technologies to conduct daily business activities. It is becoming more and more important to pair your IT skills with appropriate business knowledge. A wide variety of jobs in information technology (IT) are available, from technical support specialists and network administrators to internet-technology strategists and chief information officers. Many types of firms employ IT professionals, including large corporations and technology service providers as well as smaller businesses and even nonprofit organizations.

Employers have a higher demand for certain skills, such as network security, software development, and programming in Java and XML. Certain industries present a more dynamic market for IT professionals, including entertainment, health care, biotechnology, food and beverage industries, and pharmaceuticals.

Offshoring remains an issue in searching for many types of IT jobs. Jobs such as technical or customer support specialists are frequently outsourced. Even so, hiring managers in IT expect jobs to be difficult to fill due to a lack of skilled workers. With the right combination of IT skills and business understanding, this field is still a vibrant source of jobs. IT job titles in growing demand include project manager, business analyst, program manager, and security analyst. Executive-level titles such as chief technology officer or chief information officer are becoming more common in corporate America. Salaries for IT jobs range widely, depending on the type and level of job. Technical support specialists earn around $44,000, information security officers make about $80,000, while chief information officers often reach salaries around $125,000; even a help desk support specialist makes about $45,000.

E-business requires not only IT skills but also knowledge about all the functional areas of business. E-business uses the internet to carry out marketing, finance, management, and operations activities. These activities include communicating and creating relationships with customers, suppliers, and the public. Amazon.com is the world's number one retailer, but most retailers have an online element to their business. Customer relationship management is based on information systems but also requires marketing knowledge to determine how to target and satisfy customers.

If you are interested in an IT job, you need to be flexible—adapt and keep yourself up-to-date on current and expected changes in information technology. Preparing yourself to create and manage databases, make and distribute Podcasts, set up Web sites, and manage information systems can position you for a job in almost any size organization. Businesses, nonprofits, and government need IT assistance, and once you have developed the right skill set and knowledge, there are many different types of positions available.

examples of how savvy managers can adapt to using our knowledge in this area. Companies such as UPS have found that information systems make their "bricks, mortar, and trucks" world come alive to provide service to customers. Charles Schwab has made stock trading and obtaining securities information more efficient while providing significant savings to customers. Dell Computer and Cisco have found it possible to sell over half their products online. Many medium- and large-sized companies are changing the way they do business in response to the availability of new technologies that facilitate business in a changing world. Small businesses, too, can succeed by using information technology as leverage to implement appropriate strategies. In the future, manufacturing, retailing, health care, and even government will continue to adapt and use information technologies that will improve business operations. Today, technology presents a tremendous range of potential applications that can improve the efficiency of employees and companies while providing better service to customers. With technology changing on an almost daily basis, it is impossible to predict the long-term effect on the global world of business.

# Review Your Understanding

### Summarize the role and impact of technology in the global economy.

Technology relates to the application of knowledge, including the processes and procedures to solve problems, perform tasks, and create new methods to obtain desired outcomes. It has been a driving force in the advancement of economic systems and improvement in quality of life. Economic productivity is based more on technology than any other advance. Technology has changed the way consumers take vacations, make purchases, drive cars, and obtain entertainment. It has changed many traditional products and has improved global access by linking people through telecommunications.

### Specify how information is managed and explain a management information system.

Information includes data and knowledge that can be used in making decisions. Businesses often engage in data processing efforts to improve data flow and the usefulness of information. A management information system (MIS) is used for organizing and transmitting data into information that can be used for decision making. The purpose of the MIS is to obtain data from both internal and external sources to create information that is easily accessible and structured for user-friendly communication to managers. The MIS breaks down time and location barriers, making information available when and where it is needed to solve problems.

### Describe the Internet and explore its main uses.

The Internet is a global information system that links many computer networks together. It is used mainly for communication, information, entertainment, and e-business.

### Define e-business and discuss the e-business models.

E-business can be distinguished from traditional business as carrying out the goals of business through utilization of the Internet. The three major e-business models are business-to-business (use of the Internet for transactions and communications between organizations), business-to-consumer (delivering products and services directly to individual consumers through utilization of the Internet), and consumer-to-consumer (markets in which consumers market goods and services to each other through utilization of the Internet).

### Identify the legal and social issues of information technology and e-business.

The extraordinary growth of information technology, the Internet, and e-business has generated many legal and social issues for consumers and businesses, including concerns about privacy, identity theft, and protection of intellectual property and copyrights.

### Assess the opportunities and problems faced by an individual in an e-business and suggest a course of action.

"Solve the Dilemma" on page 139 introduces an individual trying to survive in an e-business in today's rapidly changing business environment. Based on the material presented in the chapter, you should be able to evaluate the individual's efforts and suggest an appropriate course of action.

# Revisit the World of Business

1. Why is the Internet so useful in locating where to find the lowest price on comparable products?
2. Why do many online retailers provide codes that give discounts on their sometimes already low-priced merchandise?
3. Do you think that online discount codes and coupons develop customer retail loyalty?

# Learn the Terms

business-to-business (B2B)  127
business-to-consumer (B2C)   128
consumer-to-consumer (C2C)   129
customer relationship management (CRM)   129
data   118
database   120

e-business   125
extranet   122
information   118
information technology (IT)   116
Internet   121
intranet   121
knowledge   118

management information system (MIS)   119
spam   131
technology   116
World Wide Web   121

# Check Your Progress

1. What is information technology? How has technology influenced the economy?

2. Define *data, knowledge,* and *information.* Why is information important in business?

3. What is the purpose of a management information system and how is it used?

4. How has the evolution of the Internet affected the world?

5. What is an intranet? An extranet? How are they used?

6. What are the four main uses of the Internet? Provide examples of each.

7. What is e-business? Describe the e-business models.

8. What are some of the privacy concerns associated with the Internet and e-business? How are these concerns being addressed in the United States?

9. What is identity theft?

10. Why is protection of intellectual property a concern? Provide an example on the Internet where intellectual property may not be protected or where a copyright has been infringed.

# Get Involved

1. Amazon.com is one of the most recognized e-businesses. Visit the site (www.amazon.com) and identify the types of products the company sells and explain its privacy policy.

2. Art.com (www.art.com) displays and sells art prints via its online store. GE (www.geappliances.com) displays its appliances but does not sell them online. Visit the two sites and compare how each company uses the Internet.

3. It has been stated that information technology is to business today what manufacturing was to business during the Industrial Revolution. The information technology revolution requires a strategic understanding greater than learning the latest software or determining which computer is the fastest. Leaders in business can no longer delegate information technology to computer information systems specialists and must be the connectors and the strategists of how information technology will be used in the company. Outline a plan for how you will prepare yourself to function in a business world where information technology knowledge will be important to your success.

# Build Your Skills

### PLANNING A WEB SITE

**Background**

Most companies design a Web site that reflects the company's image and goals and strives to ensure consistency in customer service, loyalty, and satisfaction. Many enlist virtual partners, linking their Web site to others where like-minded individuals (i.e., potential customers) might browse. Companies also use various graphics, animation, games, or other interesting information to improve Web site "stickiness" (prolonging the amount of time a user stays at the site).

The U.S. economy surged through the late 1990s as a result of e-commerce. With the coming of the 21st century, however, many dot-coms collapsed. Others, such as E*Trade.com and Amazon.com, survived and continue to compete in the marketplace. Many of the companies that have survived, such as eBay, have done so as a result of catering to a very specific market need that would not be feasible in a "brick-and-mortar" business (a physical marketplace). This is referred to as being a "niche" player.

As a manager of Biodegradable Packaging Products, Inc., a small business that produces packaging foam from recycled agricultural waste (mostly corn), you want to expand into e-business. It will be important to develop a Web site or to obtain links on existing Web sites to reach potential customers. Your major potential customers are in the business-to-business arena and could include environmentally friendly companies like Tom's of Maine (natural toothpaste) and Celestial Seasonings.

**Task**

Plan a Web site that is compatible with your company's current operations by using the form below.

Web site objective _____

URL (Web site name) _____

Overall image and graphic design of your Web site

_____

_____

_____

Images you will use to increase Web site stickiness

_____

_____

Potential virtual partners where your customers may be browsing _____

_____

# Solve the Dilemma

## DEVELOPING SUCCESSFUL FREEWARE

Paul Easterwood, a recent graduate of Colorado State University in computer science, entered the job market during a slow point in the economy. Tech sector positions were hard to come by, and Paul felt he wouldn't be making anywhere near what he was worth. The only offer he had received was from an entrepreneurial firm, Pentaverate Inc., that produced freeware. Freeware, or public domain software, is software that is offered to consumers free of charge in exchange for revenues generated later. Makers of freeware (such as Adobe and Netscape) can bring in high profit margins through advertisements, purchases made on the freeware site, or for more specialized software, through tutorials and workshops offered to help end users. Paul did some research and found an article in *Worth* magazine documenting the enormous success of freeware.

Pentaverate Inc. offered compensation mainly in the form of stock options, which had the potential to be highly compensatory if the company did well. Paul's job would be to develop freeware that people could download from the Internet and that would generate significant income for Pentaverate. With this in mind, he decided to accept the position, but he quickly realized he knew very little about business. With no real experience in marketing, Paul was at a loss as to what software he should produce that would make the company money. His first project, IOWatch, was designed to take users on virtual tours of outer space, especially the moons of Jupiter (Paul's favorite subject), by continually searching the Internet for images and video clips associated with the cosmos and downloading them directly to a PC. The images would then appear as soon as the person logged on. Advertisements would accompany each download, generating income for Pentaverate. However, IOWatch experienced low end-user interest and drew little advertising income as a result. Historically at Pentaverate, employees were fired after two failed projects.

Desperate to save his job, Paul decides to hire a consultant. He needs to figure out what people might want so that he can design some useful freeware for his second project. He also needs to figure out what went wrong with IOWatch, as he loved the software and can't figure out why it failed. The job market has not improved, so Paul realizes how important it is to be successful in this project.

### Discussion Questions

1. As a consultant, what would you do to help Paul figure out what went wrong with IOWatch?

2. What ideas for new freeware can you give Paul? What potential uses will the new software have?

3. How will it make money?

# Build Your Business Plan

## MANAGING INFORMATION TECHNOLOGY AND E-BUSINESS

If you are considering developing a business plan for an **established** product or service, explore whether or not the product is currently sold on the Internet. If it is currently not being sold on the Internet, think about why that is the case. Can you think of how you might be able to overcome any obstacles and market this product over the Internet?

If you are thinking about introducing a **new** product or service, now is the time to think about whether you might want to market this product on the Internet. Remember you do not have to have a brick-and-mortar store to open your own business anymore. Perhaps you might want to consider click instead of brick!

# See for Yourself Videocase

## VIACOM AND YOUTUBE FIGHT OVER COPYRIGHTED MATERIAL

In 2007, entertainment giant Viacom sued Internet superstar Google. The ongoing law suit involves YouTube, which Google purchased in October 2007 for $1.65 billion. Viacom is asking for $1 billion in damages, claiming that YouTube has failed to prevent its users from sharing copyrighted material. Viacom, which owns media outlets such as MTV, Comedy Central, and Paramount Pictures, alleges that 160,000 copyrighted video clips, including TV shows such as South Park, The Colbert Report, and the documentary "An Inconvenient Truth," have been posted on YouTube, and that these clips have received more than 1.5 billion views.

Google claims that YouTube has safe harbor under the Digital Millennium Copyright Act (DCMA). Under the DMCA, a company is not liable for copyright infringement when the material has been posted by a third party user as long as the company removes the material when notified of its existence by the copyright holder. The DMCA does not force site operators to actively survey content looking for copyright infringement, even though Viacom believes Google should be made to do exactly this. Google claims it is complying with the DMCA and is actually going above and beyond by creating a content fingerprinting system to better prevent the posting of copyrighted material. It has said that it will not settle with Viacom out of court and will, if necessary, defend its actions all the way to the Supreme Court.

In addition to the DMCA defense, Google has publicly stated its concern that Viacom's suit threatens the overall freedom of Internet users. Viacom claims that YouTube does not qualify for safe harbor under the DMCA since, as Viacom sees it, Google and YouTube are well aware of posts infringing on copyright and earn a profit thanks to this content. In fact, Viacom actually altered its accusation, claiming that YouTube has been engaging in "public performance" of copyrighted material. Viacom cites the embedding and sharing elements of YouTube as aiding infringement, therefore making YouTube, rather than its users, the infringer.

Viacom and traditional entertainment companies like it are now being dubbed "old media," while YouTube and other Web 2.0 outlets are considered "new media." As the trend toward new media continues, old media is vying for a piece of the popularity. Traditional media companies such as CBS and the BBC have been attempting, with varying success, to broker deals with digital media companies such as YouTube in order to receive compensation for videos posted on the Internet. Others have been beefing up their own Web sites in an attempt to draw traffic directly from Internet users while maintaining control of content and corresponding advertisements. In fact, many in the media world label Viacom's suit as a fight to gain advertising dollars, saying Viacom would be willing to allow YouTube to post its material if the price was right. Those at Viacom deny this claim.

Many claim that YouTube would never have amounted to much had the company not allowed users to upload copyrighted material. TV shows like South Park and The Colbert Report, for example, have audiences closely overlapping YouTube's younger users. Viacom and others claim that their copyrighted material draws audiences to YouTube, who then gains advertising revenue for those visits. A fear that strictly patrolling the site for copyrighted material threatens YouTube core users may be at the heart of Google's claim that Viacom's suit threatens the use and freedom of the Internet as a whole.

While the technologies involved in sharing entertainment are ever changing, the fight for advertising dollars remains a huge component in the struggle between old and new media. As ever newer technologies emerge, more traditional companies must fight to keep a foothold while responding to consumers' demands. Laws must be developed that respond to the rapidly changing business models inherent in such technology-dependent industries. Someday, even YouTube and Google might be part of the old guard fighting to complete with an even newer media.

### Discussion Questions

1. Why do new media outlets like YouTube threaten traditional media entertainment companies such as Viacom?

2. Which side do you think will prevail in this lawsuit—Google or Viacom?

3. What can traditional media companies do to keep up in the Web 2.0 digital age?

Remember to check out our Online Learning Center at www.mhhe.com/ferrell7e.

part

# 2

# Starting and Growing a Business

**CHAPTER 5**    **Options for Organizing Business**

**CHAPTER 6**    **Small Business, Entrepreneurship, and Franchising**

# Options for Organizing Business

**CHAPTER OUTLINE**

**Introduction**

**Sole Proprietorships**
*Advantages of Sole Proprietorships*
*Disadvantages of Sole Proprietorships*

**Partnerships**
*Types of Partnership*
*Articles of Partnership*
*Advantages of Partnerships*
*Disadvantages of Partnerships*
*Taxation of Partnerships*

**Corporations**
*Creating a Corporation*
*Types of Corporations*
*Elements of a Corporation*
*Advantages of Corporations*
*Disadvantages of Corporations*

**Other Types of Ownership**
*Joint Ventures*
*S Corporations*
*Limited Liability Companies*
*Cooperatives*

**Trends in Business Ownership: Mergers and Acquisitions**

## OBJECTIVES

*After reading this chapter, you will be able to:*

- Define and examine the advantages and disadvantages of the sole proprietorship form of organization.

- Identify two types of partnership, and evaluate the advantages and disadvantages of the partnership form of organization.

- Describe the corporate form of organization, and cite the advantages and disadvantages of corporations.

- Define and debate the advantages and disadvantages of mergers, acquisitions, and leveraged buyouts.

- Propose an appropriate organizational form for a startup business.

## "B" Is for Beneficial: A New Model for a Changing Business Community

Even if you're new to the business world, you've probably heard talk of private and public corporations, franchises, and distributors, but have you heard of "B Corporations"? The *B* stands for *beneficial,* and this designation signals that member companies conform to a set of transparent and comprehensive social and environmental performance standards. The goal is not only to benefit shareholders, but stakeholders as well. These businesses are purpose driven, and are designed to give back to communities, the environment, and employees.

In 1991, San Francisco Area–based Mike Hannigan and Sean Marx founded Give Something Back, a company that sells office supplies with the aim of following in the footsteps of Paul Newman's Newman's Own foods line. Give Something Back is the largest privately owned office supplier in California, yet the company remains locally focused. It donates most of its profits to community-level causes throughout the United States. Give Something Back is one of the more prominent examples of a B Corporation. Founders Hannigan and Marx started the company with only $40,000, and in 2006 achieved $25 million in sales. In their first 15 years, the company donated more than $3 million dollars back to communities around the nation.

Give Something Back has never privatized, and although there is no denying that the company has been successful, some argue that it could have been even *more* successful had it taken on outside investors. However, Hannigan and Marx were afraid that, in going public they would no longer be able to protect their social commitments. Hannigan and Marx are not alone. Many

*continued*

companies share this concern; this is where B Labs and the B Corporation certification come in. Once a company can prove that it is dedicated to its stakeholders, it is eligible to be certified as a B Corporation via B Labs. The B Corporation designation signifies to consumers and businesses alike that this business is truly dedicated to its purported mission and that it stands out as a market leader. There are already thousands of B Corporations, representing billions of dollars of market presence.

Upon certification with B Labs, a company must give 1/10 of 1 percent of its annual revenue to B Labs. It must also continue to maintain certain standards, such as scoring 40 or more out of 100 on a B Labs survey. In exchange, that company distinguishes itself as having high ethical standards and it benefits from the marketing boost generated through association with B Labs.

Some criticize the B Corporation certification process, questioning the way in which the survey is designed and whether or not such criteria as the amendments to company articles of incorporation are necessary. While not a perfect system, the popularity of B Labs signals a need in the market for guidelines and the benefits derived from association with such a group. In fact, B Labs is not the only organization currently utilizing such an arrangement. The founders of B Labs fully admit their business's shortcomings, but they are certain that they are on the right track to creating a system that will benefit the business community.[1]

## Introduction

The legal form of ownership taken by a business is seldom of great concern to you as a customer. When you eat at a restaurant, you probably don't care whether the restaurant is owned by one person (a sole proprietorship), has two or more owners who share the business (a partnership), or is an entity owned by many stockholders (a corporation); all you want is good food. If you buy a foreign car, you probably don't care whether the company that made it has laws governing its form of organization that are different from those for businesses in the United States. You are buying the car because it is well made, fits your price range, or appeals to your sense of style. Nonetheless, a business's legal form of ownership affects how it operates, how much tax it pays, and how much control its owners have.

This chapter examines three primary forms of business ownership—sole proprietorship, partnership, and corporation—and weighs the advantages and disadvantages of each. These forms are the most often used whether the business is a traditional bricks and mortar company, an online-only one, or a combination of both. We also take a look at S corporations, limited liability companies, and cooperatives and discuss some trends in business ownership. You may wish to refer to Table 5.1 to compare the various forms of business ownership mentioned in the chapter.

TABLE 5.I   Various Forms of Business Ownership

| Structure | Ownership | Taxation | Liability | Use |
|---|---|---|---|---|
| Sole Proprietorship | 1 owner | Individual income taxed | Unlimited | Individual starting a business and easiest way to conduct business |
| Partnership | 2 or more owners | Individual owners' income taxed | Somewhat limited | Easy way for two individuals to conduct business |
| Corporation | Any number of shareholders | Corporate and shareholder taxed | Limited | A legal entity with shareholders or stockholders |
| S Corporation | Up to 75 shareholders | Taxed as a partnership | Limited | A legal entity with tax advantages for restricted number of shareholders |
| Limited Liability Company | Unlimited number of shareholders | Taxed as a partnership | Limited | Avoid personal lawsuits |

# Sole Proprietorships

**Sole proprietorships,** businesses owned and operated by one individual, are the most common form of business organization in the United States. Common examples include many restaurants, hair salons, flower shops, dog kennels, and independent grocery stores. In 1962, Gordon Segal and his wife Carole opened a flatware and china store in Chicago with a $17,000 loan. They never could have guessed that the store would become Crate & Barrel and would eventually operate in more than 165 locations. Segal ran the company until 2008, when he stepped down as CEO at the age of 69. Crate & Barrel is an unusual example of a proprietorship growing very large. Many sole proprietors focus on services—small retail stores, financial counseling, appliance repair, child care, and the like—rather than on the manufacture of goods, which often requires large sums of money not available to most small businesses. (see Figure 5.1)[2]

Sole proprietorships are typically small businesses employing fewer than 50 people. (We'll look at small businesses in greater detail in Chapter 6.) There are 15 to 20 million sole proprietorships in the United States, constituting more than 80 percent of all businesses in the United States. It is interesting to note that men are twice as likely as women to start their own business.[3]

**sole proprietorships** businesses owned and operated by one individual; the most common form of business organization in the United States

## Advantages of Sole Proprietorships

Sole proprietorships are generally managed by their owners. Because of this simple management structure, the owner/manager can make decisions quickly. This is just one of many advantages of the sole proprietorship form of business.

**Ease and Cost of Formation.**   Forming a sole proprietorship is relatively easy and inexpensive. In some states, creating a sole proprietorship involves merely announcing the new business in the local newspaper. Other proprietorships, such as barber shops and restaurants, may require state and local licenses and permits because of the nature of the business. The cost of these permits may run from $25 to

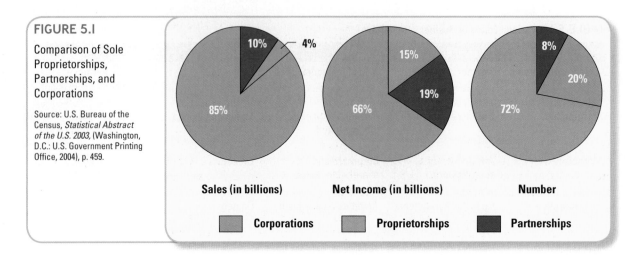

**FIGURE 5.1**

Comparison of Sole Proprietorships, Partnerships, and Corporations

Source: U.S. Bureau of the Census, *Statistical Abstract of the U.S. 2003,* (Washington, D.C.: U.S. Government Printing Office, 2004), p. 459.

**Sales (in billions)**     **Net Income (in billions)**     **Number**

■ **Corporations**     ■ **Proprietorships**     ■ **Partnerships**

$100. No lawyer is needed to create such enterprises, and the owner can usually take care of the required paperwork without outside assistance.

Of course, an entrepreneur starting a new sole proprietorship must find a suitable site from which to operate the business. Some sole proprietors look no farther than their garage or a spare bedroom when seeking a workshop or office. Among the more famous businesses that sprang to life in their founders' homes are Google, Walt Disney, Dell, eBay, Hewlett-Packard, Apple Computer, and Mattel.[4] Computers, personal copiers, fax machines, scanners, and other high-tech gadgets have been a boon for home-based businesses, permitting them to interact quickly with customers, suppliers, and others. Many independent salespersons and contractors can perform their work using a notebook computer as they travel. E-mail and cell phones have made it possible for many proprietorships to develop in the services area. Internet connections also allow small businesses to establish Web sites to promote their products and even to make low-cost long-distance phone calls with voice-over Internet protocol (VOIP) technology. One of the most famous services using VOIP is Skype, which allows people to make free calls over the Internet.

**Secrecy.**     Sole proprietorships make possible the greatest degree of secrecy. The proprietor, unlike the owners of a partnership or corporation, does not have to discuss publicly his or her operating plans, minimizing the possibility that competitors can obtain trade secrets. Financial reports need not be disclosed, as do the financial reports of publicly owned corporations.

**Distribution and Use of Profits.**     All profits from a sole proprietorship belong exclusively to the owner. He or she does not have to share them with any partners or stockholders. The owner decides how to use the funds—for expansion of the business, or salary increases, for travel to purchase additional inventory, or to find new customers.

**Flexibility and Control of the Business.**     The sole proprietor has complete control over the business and can make decisions on the spot without anyone else's approval. This control allows the owner to respond quickly to competitive business conditions or to changes in the economy.

**Government Regulation.**   Sole proprietorships have the most freedom from government regulation. Many government regulations—federal, state, and local—apply only to businesses that have a certain number of employees, and securities laws apply only to corporations that issue stock. Nonetheless, sole proprietors must ensure that they follow all laws that do apply to their business.

**Taxation.**   Profits from sole proprietorships are considered personal income and are taxed at individual tax rates. The owner, therefore, pays one income tax that includes the business and individual income. Another tax benefit is that a sole proprietor is allowed to establish a tax-exempt retirement account or a tax-exempt profit-sharing account. Such accounts are exempt from current income tax, but payments taken after retirement are taxed when they are received.

**Closing the Business.**   A sole proprietorship can be dissolved easily. No approval of co-owners or partners is necessary. The only legal condition is that all loans must be paid off.

## Disadvantages of Sole Proprietorships

What may be seen as an advantage by one person may turn out to be a disadvantage to another. For profitable businesses managed by capable owners, many of the following factors do not cause problems. On the other hand, proprietors starting out with little management experience and little money are likely to encounter many of the disadvantages.

**Unlimited Liability.**   The sole proprietor has unlimited liability in meeting the debts of the business. In other words, if the business cannot pay its creditors, the owner may be forced to use personal, nonbusiness holdings such as a car or a home to pay off the debts. There are only a few states in which houses and homesteads cannot be taken by creditors, even if the proprietor declares bankruptcy. The more wealth an individual has, the greater is the disadvantage of unlimited liability.

**Limited Sources of Funds.**   Among the relatively few sources of money available to the sole proprietorship are banks, friends, family, the Small Business Administration, or his or her own funds. The owner's personal financial condition determines his or her credit standing. Additionally, sole proprietorships may have to pay higher interest rates on funds borrowed from banks than do large corporations because they are considered greater risks. Often, the only way a sole proprietor can borrow for business purposes is to pledge a car, a house, other real estate, or other personal assets to guarantee the loan. If the business fails, the owner may lose the personal assets as well as the business. Publicly owned corporations, in contrast, can not only obtain funds from commercial banks but can sell stocks and bonds to the public to raise money. If a public company goes out of business, the owners do not lose personal assets.

**Limited Skills.**   The sole proprietor must be able to perform many functions and possess skills in diverse fields such as management, marketing, finance, accounting, bookkeeping, and personnel management. Business owners can rely on specialized professionals for advice and services, such as accountants and attorneys. Musicians, for example, can turn to agents for assistance in navigating through the complex maze of the recording business. One startup firm specializing in this type of assistance for online musicians and bands is the Digital Artists Agency, whose

# Entrepreneurship in Action
## Carpinteros: Focusing on Quality and Tradition

Keith Gorges and Kurt Faust

**Business:** Taos Furniture of Santa Fe

**Founded:** 2000

**Success:** Have kept a 500-year-old woodworking tradition alive through their traditional carving methods and attention to quality.

Keith Gorges and Kurt and Eric Faust were already running a business, Tierra Concepts Inc., when they decided to take a chance and purchase another in 2000. Taos Furniture of Santa Fe was in danger of going out of business when the partners bought it for $60,000, giving the investors the company name and the machinery; many of the company's craftsmen remained as well. To distinguish the company from other Southwestern furniture companies, and to recover from a business slowdown after 9/11, the partners rebranded the company *Carpinteros,* which means carpenters in Spanish. The name is meant to evoke a long tradition of woodworking, stretching back to the early 17th century, carried on in the company. In 2005, the company expanded into a larger showroom. Then, in 2006, sales topped $1 million for the first time.

The company has been successful because it was able to set itself apart from the competition through the high quality of its products and the attention to detail that goes into every piece. Customers love the high quality of the furniture, and the long tradition, unique to New Mexico, associated with it. No sandpaper ever touches the wood as the woodworkers at Carpinteros use a hand planer to smooth every surface. Gorges and the Fausts have sought to hire local artisans as much as possible to further accent the quality and regional style of the pieces.

Because of the time and care that goes into their products, it would be impossible for Gorges and the Fausts to compete with manufactured furniture companies, and therefore they do not. They market to the high-end customer; the fact that the business is a partnership and that craftsmen are local adds to the small-business, boutique feel of the company. The founders are not completely tied up in the business, however. To protect their personal assets, Gorges and the Fausts created a separate identity for the business through establishing it as a limited liability company (LLC). They are not above seeking to lower fixed costs either. Gorges and the Fausts also saved money by purchasing, rather than renting, their production workshop. Through differentiating their product, and fostering an intimate feel for their companies, the partners have been successful in both of their endeavors. In so doing they have also forged a name for themselves that is recognized far beyond the companies' home base of northern New Mexico.[5]

clients include Dream Works Animation, Sony Pictures Imageworks, Pixel Magic, and Chris LeDoux. The DAA researches, markets, and cultivates online music talent in exchange for a commission on online sales of music, tickets, and merchandise.[6] In the end, however, it is up to the business owner to make the final decision in all areas of the business.

**Lack of Continuity.** The life expectancy of a sole proprietorship is directly linked to that of the owner and his or her ability to work. The serious illness of the owner could result in failure of the business if competent help cannot be found.

It is difficult to arrange for the sale of a proprietorship and at the same time assure customers that the business will continue to meet their needs. For instance, how does one sell a veterinary practice? A veterinarian's major asset is patients. If the vet dies suddenly, the equipment can be sold, but the patients will not necessarily remain loyal to the office. On the other hand, a veterinarian who wants to retire could take in a younger partner and sell the practice to the partner over time. One advantage to the partnership is that some of the customers are likely to stay with the business, even if ownership changes.

**Lack of Qualified Employees.** It is usually difficult for a small sole proprietorship to match the wages and benefits offered by a large competing corporation because the proprietorship's profits may not be as high. In addition, there is little room for advancement within a sole proprietorship, so the owner may have difficulty attracting and retaining qualified employees. On the other hand, the trend of large corporations downsizing and outsourcing tasks has created renewed opportunities for small business to acquire well-trained employees.

Taxation.    Although we listed taxation as an advantage for sole proprietorships, it can also be a disadvantage, depending on the proprietor's income. Under current tax rates, sole proprietors pay a higher marginal tax rate than do small corporations on income of less than $75,000. The tax effect often determines whether a sole proprietor chooses to incorporate his or her business.

# Partnerships

One way to minimize the disadvantages of a sole proprietorship and maximize its advantages is to have more than one owner. Most states have a model law governing partnerships based on the Uniform Partnership Act. This law defines a **partnership** as "an association of two or more persons who carry on as co-owners of a business for profit." Partnerships are the least used form of business. (see Figure 5.1). They are typically larger than sole proprietorships but smaller than corporations.

## Types of Partnership

There are two basic types of partnership: general partnership and limited partnership. A **general partnership** involves a complete sharing in the management of a business. In a general partnership, each partner has unlimited liability for the debts of the business. For example, Cirque du Soleil grew from a group of Quebec street performers, who acted as partners, into a half-billion-dollar global company. Cirque du Soleil, however, ended its 16-year run as a partnership in the year 2000. Guy Laliberte bought out the other principle partner, Daniel Gauthier. Laliberte now has 95 percent controlling share of the company.[7] Professionals such as lawyers, accountants, and architects often join together in general partnerships.

A **limited partnership** has at least one general partner, who assumes unlimited liability, and at least one limited partner, whose liability is limited to his or her investment in the business. Limited partnerships exist for risky investment projects where the chance of loss is great. The general partners accept the risk of loss; the limited partners' losses are limited to their initial investment. Limited partners do not participate in the management of the business but share in the profits in accordance with the terms of a partnership agreement. Usually the general partner receives a larger share of the profits after the limited partners have received their initial investment back. Popular examples are oil-drilling partnerships and real-estate partnerships.

## Articles of Partnership

**Articles of partnership** are legal documents that set forth the basic agreement between partners. Most states require articles of partnership, but even if they are not required, it makes good sense for partners to draw them up. Articles of partnership usually list the money or assets that each partner has contributed (called *partnership capital*), state each partner's individual management role or duty, specify how the profits and losses of the partnership will be divided among the partners, and describe how a partner may leave the partnership as well as any other restrictions that might apply to the agreement. Table 5.2 lists some of the issues and provisions that should be included in articles of partnership.

**partnership**
a form of business organization defined by the Uniform Partnership Act as "an association of two or more persons who carry on as co-owners of a business for profit"

**general partnership**
a partnership that involves a complete sharing in both the management and the liability of the business

**limited partnership**
a business organization that has at least one general partner, who assumes unlimited liability, and at least one limited partner, whose liability is limited to his or her investment in the business

**articles of partnership**
legal documents that set forth the basic agreement between partners

# Destination CEO
## My StudentBiz: Student Entrepreneurs and Snacks

My StudentBiz introduces young people to the world of business. The mission of the company, according to founder and CEO, Richard LaMotta, is to teach young students about entrepreneurship. Students buy snack foods wholesale from My StudentBiz and resell to convenience store operators and other small-market venues such as the corner store. Students learn a wide range of business concepts such as profit and loss, negotiations, sales, marketing and branding.

Catherine Herman, a 16-year-old entrepreneur, is very positive about the concept and the impact that it has had on her development. She enthusiastically says that the program has enhanced her self-esteem, her confidence, and her ability to interact with a wide range of individuals.

My StudentBiz CEO LaMotta, is attempting to involve the student entrepreneurs in a product branding and distribution effort for the new ice cream sandwich called Chipwich.

Once the brand has been developed and the concept sold to a large snack-food manufacturer, CEO LaMotta is offering to share the profits from the sale equally with his student entrepreneurs. If successful, the student share could be as much as $25 million.

**Discussion Questions**
1. What type of business ownership model do the student entrepreneurs and My StudentBiz demonstrate?
2. If My StudentBiz and the student entrepreneurs are organized as a partnership, which type of partnership would it most likely be?
3. If you were one of the student entrepreneurs acting as a sole proprietorship, what would be your major advantages associated with this type of business ownership?

## Advantages of Partnerships

Law firms, accounting firms, and investment firms with several hundred partners have partnership agreements that are quite complicated in comparison with the partnership agreement among two or three people owning a computer repair shop. The advantages must be compared with those offered by other forms of business organization, and not all apply to every partnership.

**TABLE 5.2**

Issues and Provisions in Articles of Partnership

1. Name, purpose, location
2. Duration of the agreement
3. Authority and responsibility of each partner
4. Character of partners (i.e., general or limited, active or silent)
5. Amount of contribution from each partner
6. Division of profits or losses
7. Salaries of each partner
8. How much each partner is allowed to withdraw
9. Death of partner
10. Sale of partnership interest
11. Arbitration of disputes
12. Required and prohibited actions
13. Absence and disability
14. Restrictive covenants
15. Buying and selling agreements

Source: Adapted from "Partnership Agreement Sample," State of New Jersey, http://www.state.nj.us/njbusiness/starting/basics/partnership_agreement_sample.shtml (accessed May 4, 2008).

**Ease of Organization.**   Starting a partnership requires little more than drawing up articles of partnership. No legal charters have to be granted, but the name of the business should be registered with the state.

**Availability of Capital and Credit.**   When a business has several partners, it has the benefit of a combination of talents and skills and pooled financial resources. Partnerships tend to be larger than sole proprietorships and therefore have greater earning power and better credit ratings. Because many limited partnerships have been formed for tax purposes rather than for economic profits, the combined income of all U.S. partnerships is quite low, as shown in Figure 5.1. Nevertheless, the professional partnerships of many lawyers, accountants, and investment banking firms make quite large profits. Goldman Sachs, a large New York investment banking partnership, earns several hundred million dollars in an average year.

**Combined Knowledge and Skills.**   Partners in the most successful partnerships acknowledge each other's talents and avoid confusion and conflict by specializing in a particular area of expertise such as marketing, production, accounting, or service. The diversity of skills in a partnership makes it possible for the business to be run by a management team of specialists instead of by a generalist sole proprietor. Service-oriented partnerships in fields such as law, financial planning, and accounting may attract customers because clients may think that the service offered by a diverse team is of higher quality than that provided by one person. Larger law firms, for example, often have individual partners who specialize in certain areas of the law—such as family, bankruptcy, corporate, entertainment, and criminal law.

*Friends since junior high, Ben Cohen and Jerry Greenfield initially began Ben & Jerry's Homemade Ice Cream as a partnership in 1978. The pair took a correspondence course in ice-cream making before founding the company in a renovated Vermont gas station.*

**Decision Making.**   Small partnerships can react more quickly to changes in the business environment than can large partnerships and corporations. Such fast reactions are possible because the partners are involved in day-to-day operations and can make decisions quickly after consultation. Large partnerships with hundreds of partners in many states are not common. In those that do exist, decision making is likely to be slow.

**Regulatory Controls.**   Like a sole proprietorship, a partnership has fewer regulatory controls affecting its activities than does a corporation. A partnership does not have to file public financial statements with government agencies or send out quarterly financial statements to several thousand owners, as do corporations such as Apple and Ford Motor Co. A partnership does, however, have to abide by all laws relevant to the industry or profession in which it operates as well as state and federal laws relating to hiring and firing, food handling, and so on, just as the sole proprietorship does.

| TABLE 5.3 | 1. Keep profit sharing and ownership at 50/50, or you have an employer/employee relationship. |
|---|---|
| Keys to Success in Business Partnerships | 2. Partners should have different skill sets to complement one another. |
| | 3. Honesty is critical. |
| | 4. Must maintain face-to-face communication in addition to phone and e-mail. |
| | 5. Maintain transparency, sharing more information over time. |
| | 6. Be aware of funding constraints, and do not put yourself in a situation where neither you nor your partner can secure additional financial support. |
| | 7. To be successful, you need experience. |
| | 8. Whereas family should be a priority, be careful to minimize the number of associated problems. |
| | 9. Do not become too infatuated with "the idea" as opposed to implementation. |
| | 10. Couple optimism with realism in sales and growth expectations and planning. |

Source: Abstracted from J. Watananbe, "14 Reasons Why 80% of New Business Partnerships Would Fail Within Their First 5 Years of Existence," May 1, 2007, http://ezinearticles.com/?14-Reasons-Why-80-Percent-Of-New-Business-Partnerships-Would-Fail-Within-Their-First-5-Years-Of-Exis&id=472498, (accessed May 9, 2008).

## Disadvantages of Partnerships

Partnerships have many advantages compared to sole proprietorships and corporations, but they also have some disadvantages. Limited partners have no voice in the management of the partnership, and they may bear most of the risk of the business while the general partner reaps a larger share of the benefits. There may be a change in the goals and objectives of one partner but not the other, particularly when the partners are multinational organizations. This can cause friction, giving rise to an enterprise that fails to satisfy both parties or even forcing an end to the partnership. Many partnership disputes wind up in court or require outside mediation. For example in early 2008, Russian partners of the 50/50 oil partnership THK-BP began demanding the ouster of some of BP's upper-level management. The Russians expressed concern over potentially unethical behavior, with accusations ranging from spying to tax evasion, committed by BP's employees. The partners also accused BP's CEO, Robert Dudley, of acting in BP's interest and not taking into account Russian shareholders' concerns. Because of this dispute, the company is considering selling the Russian-owned THK half of the business to the Russian government–run oil company Gazprom.[8] In such cases, the ultimate solution may be dissolving the partnership. Major disadvantages of partnerships include the following.

**Unlimited Liability.**  In general partnerships, the general partners have unlimited liability for the debts incurred by the business, just as the sole proprietor has unlimited liability for his or her business. Such unlimited liability can be a distinct disadvantage to one partner if his or her personal financial resources are greater than those of the others. A potential partner should check to make sure that all partners have comparable resources to help the business in time of trouble. This disadvantage is eliminated for limited partners, who can lose only their initial investment.

**Business Responsibility.**  All partners are responsible for the business actions of all others. Partners may have the ability to commit the partnership to a contract without approval of the other partners. A bad decision by one partner may put the other partners' personal resources in jeopardy. Personal problems such as a divorce

# Going Green
## CSAs for Everyone

As people become more and more concerned about the state of the environment, *sustainable, local,* and *green* are just some of the words being tossed around with increasing frequency. Individuals are looking for ways to reduce their carbon footprint, protect the land, and take better care of their own health. To this end, community-supported agriculture (CSA) is becoming a popular alternative to large-chain grocery stores. The CSA is not a new idea. It originated in Japan around 30 years ago and was adopted in the United States in the 1980s.

A CSA is a way for local farmers to bypass the bureaucracy of traditional corporate grocery stores and to conduct business directly with consumers. Under this model, a farmer first creates a budget for his or her growing season that includes all costs (such as land payments, seeds, salaries, equipment, and so on). The farmer then divides this budget into the number of shares of crops available for purchase. Usually a CSA share is designed to feed a family of four for a week. People become members of a farm's CSA by purchasing shares. They will then receive a portion of local, often organic, produce each week during the growing season. Items vary depending on what is in season. The CSA creates a sustainable relationship in which members receive quality produce and farmers have a reliable method for distributing their crops.

How does the CSA benefit the environment and contribute to health? The farms offering CSAs are usually small and dedicated to ecologically sound farming practices, such as permaculture and avoiding chemical pesticides. Because the cost of distribution is lower for these farmers, members often receive produce at prices competitive with conventional produce sold in grocery stores. Farmers, knowing that their basic costs are covered, can focus their full attention on growing high-quality produce rather than searching for distributors. In addition, because deliveries are made locally, produce is fresher. The local aspect of delivery also cuts down on pollution because the products do not need to travel great distances.

One of the first CSAs in the United States was Indian Line Farm, founded in 1985 in Egremont, Massachusetts. Today there are said to be close to 2,000 CSAs nationwide. In a world where people are looking to take better care of themselves and the environment, as well as to understand where their food came from, the CSA is becoming a popular alternative to traditional stores.[9]

### Discussion Questions
1. What are some of the benefits gained by farmers by switching to the CSA model?
2. Why are people opting to use CSAs over traditional grocery stores?
3. Can you think of any drawbacks to the CSA model?

---

can eliminate a significant portion of one partner's financial resources and weaken the financial structure of the whole partnership.

**Life of the Partnership.** A partnership is terminated when a partner dies or withdraws. In a two-person partnership, if one partner withdraws, the firm's liabilities would be paid off and the assets divided between the partners. Obviously, the partner who wishes to continue in the business would be at a serious disadvantage. The business could be disrupted, financing would be reduced, and the management skills of the departing partner would be lost. The remaining partner would have to find another or reorganize the business as a sole proprietorship. In very large partnerships such as those found in law firms and investment banks, the continuation of the partnership may be provided for in the articles of partnership. The provision may simply state the terms for a new partnership agreement among the remaining partners. In such cases, the disadvantage to the other partners is minimal.

Selling a partnership interest has the same effect as the death or withdrawal of a partner. It is difficult to place a value on a partner's share of the partnership. No public value is placed on the partnership, as there is on publicly owned corporations. What is a law firm worth? What is the local hardware store worth? Coming up with a fair value that all partners can agree to is not easy. Selling a partnership interest is easier if the articles of partnership specify a method of valuation. Even if there is not a procedure for selling one partner's interest, the old partnership must still be dissolved and a new one created. In contrast, in the corporate form of business, the departure of owners has little effect on the financial resources of the business, and the loss of managers does not cause long-term changes in the structure of the organization.

**Distribution of Profits.**    Profits earned by the partnership are distributed to the partners in the proportions specified in the articles of partnership. This may be a disadvantage if the division of the profits does not reflect the work each partner puts into the business. You may have encountered this disadvantage while working on a student group project: You may have felt that you did most of the work and that the other students in the group received grades based on your efforts. Even the perception of an unfair profit-sharing agreement may cause tension between the partners, and unhappy partners can have a negative effect on the profitability of the business.

**Limited Sources of Funds.**    As with a sole proprietorship, the sources of funds available to a partnership are limited. Because no public value is placed on the business (such as the current trading price of a corporation's stock), potential partners do not know what one partnership share is worth. Moreover, because partnership shares cannot be bought and sold easily in public markets, potential owners may not want to tie up their money in assets that cannot be readily sold on short notice. Accumulating enough funds to operate a national business, especially a business requiring intensive investments in facilities and equipment, can be difficult. Partnerships also may have to pay higher interest rates on funds borrowed from banks than do large corporations because partnerships may be considered greater risks.

### Taxation of Partnerships

Partnerships are quasi-taxable organizations. This means that partnerships do not pay taxes when submitting the partnership tax return to the Internal Revenue Service. The tax return simply provides information about the profitability of the organization and the distribution of profits among the partners. Partners must report their share of profits on their individual tax returns and pay taxes at the income tax rate for individuals.

# Corporations

**corporation**
a legal entity, created by the state, whose assets and liabilities are separate from its owners

When you think of a business, you probably think of a huge corporation such as General Electric, Procter & Gamble, or Sony because a large portion of your consumer dollars go to such corporations. A **corporation** is a legal entity, created by the state, whose assets and liabilities are separate from its owners. As a legal entity, a corporation has many of the rights, duties, and powers of a person, such as the right to receive, own, and transfer property. Corporations can enter into contracts with individuals or with other legal entities, and they can sue and be sued in court.

Corporations account for the majority of all U.S. sales and income. Thus, most of the dollars you spend as a consumer probably go to incorporated businesses (see Figure 5.1). Most corporations are not mega-companies like General Mills or Ford Motor; even small businesses can incorporate. As we shall see later in the chapter, many smaller firms elect to incorporate as "S Corporations," which operate under slightly different rules and have greater flexibility than do traditional "C Corporations" like General Mills.

**stock**
shares of a corporation that may be bought or sold

Corporations are typically owned by many individuals and organizations who own shares of the business, called **stock** (thus, corporate owners are often called *shareholders* or *stockholders*). Stockholders can buy, sell, give or receive as gifts, or inherit their shares of stock. As owners, the stockholders are entitled to all profits that are left after all the corporation's other obligations have been paid. These profits may be distributed in the form of cash payments called **dividends.** For example, if a corporation earns $100 million after expenses and taxes and decides to pay the owners $40 million in dividends, the stockholders receive 40 percent of the profits in cash dividends. However, not all after-tax profits are paid to stockholders in dividends. In this example, the corporation retained $60 million of profits to finance expansion.

**dividends**
profits of a corporation that are distributed in the form of cash payments to stockholders

## Creating a Corporation

A corporation is created, or incorporated, under the laws of the state in which it incorporates. The individuals creating the corporation are known as *incorporators.* Each state has a specific procedure, sometimes called *chartering the corporation,* for incorporating a business. Most states require a minimum of three incorporators; thus, many small businesses can be and are incorporated. Another requirement is that the new corporation's name cannot be similar to that of another business. In most states, a corporation's name must end in "company," "corporation," "incorporated," or "limited" to show that the owners have limited liability. (In this text, however, the word *company* means any organization engaged in a commercial enterprise and can refer to a sole proprietorship, a partnership, or a corporation.)

The incorporators must file legal documents generally referred to as *articles of incorporation* with the appropriate state office (often the secretary of state). The articles of incorporation contain basic information about the business. The following 10 items are found in the Model Business Corporation Act, issued by the American Bar Association, which is followed by most states:

1. Name and address of the corporation.
2. Objectives of the corporation.
3. Classes of stock (common, preferred, voting, nonvoting) and the number of shares for each class of stock to be issued.
4. Expected life of the corporation (corporations are usually created to last forever).
5. Financial capital required at the time of incorporation.
6. Provisions for transferring shares of stock between owners.
7. Provisions for the regulation of internal corporate affairs.
8. Address of the business office registered with the state of incorporation.
9. Names and addresses of the initial board of directors.
10. Names and addresses of the incorporators.

Based on the information in the articles of incorporation, the state issues a **corporate charter** to the company. After securing this charter, the owners hold an organizational meeting at which they establish the corporation's bylaws and elect a board of directors. The bylaws might set up committees of the board of directors and describe the rules and procedures for their operation.

**corporate charter**
a legal document that the state issues to a company based on information the company provides in the articles of incorporation

## Types of Corporations

If the corporation does business in the state in which it is chartered, it is known as a *domestic corporation.* In other states where the corporation does business, it is known as a *foreign corporation.* If a corporation does business outside the nation in which

*Not all large corporations are publicly traded. The snack and food company, Mars Inc., is entirely owned by the Mars family. As such, it is one of the largest privately owned corporations in the United States.*

**private corporation**
a corporation owned by just one or a few people who are closely involved in managing the business

**public corporation**
a corporation whose stock anyone may buy, sell, or trade

**initial public offering (IPO)**
selling a corporation's stock on public markets for the first time

it incorporated, it is called an *alien corporation.* A corporation may be privately or publicly owned.

A **private corporation** is owned by just one or a few people who are closely involved in managing the business. These people, often a family, own all the corporation's stock, and no stock is sold to the public. Many corporations are quite large, yet remain private, including Koch, an energy and natural resource business. It is the nation's largest private corporation. By acquiring Georgia-Pacific, Charles Koch turned his family business into the world's largest private corporation. The fifth largest privately held company in the United States is Mars, founded by Forrest Mars Sr. who spent time in Switzerland learning to create chocolate confectionaries. Mars recently grew significantly through the acquisition of the Wm. Wrigley Jr. Company. Mars was founded in Tacoma, Washington, in 1911. The business was successful early on because it paid employees three times the normal wage for the time. The company remains successful to this day, largely because of its established brands, such as M&Ms, and healthy snack lines for kids, like Generation Max.[10] Other well-known privately held companies include Chrysler, Cargill, Publix Supermarkets, Dollar General, and MGM Entertainment.[11] Privately owned corporations are not required to disclose financial information publicly, but they must, of course, pay taxes.

A **public corporation** is one whose stock anyone may buy, sell, or trade. Table 5.4 lists the largest U.S. corporations by revenues. Thousands of smaller public corporations in the United States have sales under $10 million. In large public corporations such as AT&T, the stockholders are often far removed from the management of the company. In other public corporations, the managers are often the founders and the major shareholders. Ford Motor Company, for example, was founded by Henry Ford; his great grandson William Clay Ford Jr. is executive chairman of the company today.[12] *Forbes* Global 2000 companies generate around $30 trillion in revenues, $2.4 trillion in profits, $119 trillion in assets; are worth $39 trillion in market value; and provide work for 72 million people.[13] Publicly owned corporations must disclose financial information to the public under specific laws that regulate the trade of stocks and other securities.

A private corporation that needs more money to expand or to take advantage of opportunities may have to obtain financing by "going public" through an **initial public offering (IPO),** that is, becoming a public corporation by selling stock so that it can be traded in public markets. For example, Intrepid Potash, a mining company headquartered in Denver with mines in New Mexico and Utah, is this country's largest producer of potash, serving nearly 10 percent of the market. Potash is a substance that serves as a fertilizer in crop and plant production. The stock initially sold for $32.00 per share when the company went public in 2008. The value immediately skyrocketed, with stocks soon selling for more than $51.00 per share. Although this type of price jump is not common for IPOs, it does occur.[14]

| Rank | Company | Revenues (in millions of dollars) |
|---|---|---|
| 1. | Wal-Mart | $378,799.0 |
| 2. | ExxonMobil | 372,824.0 |
| 3. | Chevron | 210,783.0 |
| 4. | General Motors | 182,347.0 |
| 5. | Conoco Phillips | 178,558.0 |
| 6. | General Electric | 176,656.0 |
| 7. | Ford Motor | 172,468.0 |
| 8. | Citigroup | 159,229.0 |
| 9. | Bank of America Corp. | 119,190.0 |
| 10. | AT&T | 118,928.0 |
| 11. | Berkshire Hathaway | 118,245.0 |
| 12. | JPMorgan Chase & Co. | 116,353.0 |
| 13. | American International Group | 110,064.0 |
| 14. | Hewlett-Packard | 104,286.0 |
| 15. | International Business Machines (IBM) | 98,786.0 |
| 16. | Valero Energy | 96,758.0 |
| 17. | Verizon Communications | 93,775.0 |
| 18. | McKeeson | 93,574.0 |
| 19. | Cardinal Health | 88,363.9 |
| 20. | Goldman Sachs Group | 87,968.0 |

**TABLE 5.4**

The Largest U.S. Corporations, Arranged by Revenues

Source: "Fortune 500: *Fortune*'s Annual Ranking of America's Largest Corporations," *Fortune*, http://money.cnn.com/magazines/fortune/fortune500/2008/full_list/ (accessed May 4, 2008).

*Google founders Larry Page and Sergey Brin were able to raise a whopping $1.66 billion via an initial public offering of the company's stock in 2004. The Google IPO was one of the largest in stock market history.*

Also, privately owned firms are occasionally forced to go public with stock offerings when a major owner dies and the heirs have large estate taxes to pay. The tax payment may only be possible with the proceeds of the sale of stock. This happened to the brewer Adolph Coors Inc. After Adolph Coors died, the business went public and his family sold shares of stock to the public in order to pay the estate taxes.

On the other hand, public corporations can be "taken private" when one or a few individuals (perhaps the management of the firm) purchase all the firm's stock so that it can no longer be sold publicly. Taking a corporation private may be desirable when new owners want to exert more control over the firm or they want to avoid the necessity of public disclosure of future activities for competitive reasons. For example,

Chrysler was split from Daimler when Cerebus, a private equity investment firm assumed controlling interest of Chrysler from DaimlerChrysler. Chrysler has been attempting to grow its profitability through the sale of plants, closing of production facilities for a period in the summer, mandatory vacations for employees, and consolidation of its dealer network. The company's goal is to be the "best little car company in America," according to Vice Chairman Jim Press.[15] Taking a corporation private is also one technique for avoiding a takeover by another corporation.

Quasi-public corporations and nonprofit, are two types of public corporations. **Quasi-public corporations** are owned and operated by the federal, state, or local government. The focus of these entities is to provide a service to citizens, such as mail delivery, rather than earning a profit. Indeed, many quasi-public corporations operate at a loss. Examples of quasi-public corporations include the National Aeronautics and Space Administration (NASA) and the U.S. Postal Service.

Like quasi-public corporations, **nonprofit corporations** focus on providing a service rather than earning a profit, but they are not owned by a government entity. Organizations such as the Children's Television Workshop, the Elks Clubs, the American Lung Association, the American Red Cross, museums, and private schools provide services without a profit motive. To fund their operations and services, nonprofit organizations solicit donations from individuals and companies and grants from the government and other charitable foundations.

## Elements of a Corporation

**The Board of Directors.** A **board of directors,** elected by the stockholders to oversee the general operation of the corporation, sets the long-range objectives of the corporation. It is the board's responsibility to ensure that the objectives are achieved on schedule. Board members are legally liable for the mismanagement of the firm or for any misuse of funds. An important duty of the board of directors is to hire corporate officers, such as the president and the chief executive officer (CEO), who are responsible to the directors for the management and daily operations of the firm. The role and expectations of the board of directors took on greater significance after the accounting scandals of the early 2000s and the passage of the Sarbanes-Oxley Act.[16] As a result, most corporations have restructured how they compensate board directors for their time and expertise.

Directors can be employees of the company (*inside directors*) or people unaffiliated with the company (*outside directors*). Inside directors are usually the officers responsible for running the company. Outside directors are often top executives from other companies, lawyers, bankers, even professors. Directors today are increasingly chosen for their expertise, competence, and ability to bring diverse perspectives to strategic discussions. Outside directors are also thought to bring more independence to the monitoring function because they are not bound by past allegiances, friendships, a current role in the company, or some other issue that may create a conflict of interest. Many of the corporate scandals uncovered in recent years might have been prevented if each of the companies' boards of directors had been better qualified, more knowledgeable, and more independent. There is a growing shortage of available and qualified board members. Boards are increasingly telling their own CEOs that they should be focused on serving their company, not serving on outside boards. Because of this, the average CEO sits on less than one outside board. This represents a decline from a decade ago when the average was two. As many CEOs are turning down outside positions, many companies have taken steps to ensure that boards have experienced directors. They have increased the mandatory retirement

**quasi-public corporations** corporations owned and operated by the federal, state, or local government

**nonprofit corporations** corporations that focus on providing a service rather than earning a profit but are not owned by a government entity

**board of directors** a group of individuals, elected by the stockholders to oversee the general operation of the corporation, who set the corporation's long-range objectives

age to 72 or older, and 11 percent have raised it to 75 or even older. Minimizing the amount of overlap between directors sitting on different boards helps to limit conflicts of interest and provides for independence in decision making.[17]

Stock Ownership.    Corporations issue two types of stock: preferred and common. Owners of **preferred stock** are a special class of owners because, although they generally do not have any say in running the company, they have a claim to profits before any other stockholders do. Other stockholders do not receive any dividends unless the preferred stockholders have already been paid. Dividend payments on preferred stock are usually a fixed percentage of the initial issuing price (set by the board of directors). For example, if a share of preferred stock originally cost $100 and the dividend rate was stated at 7.5 percent, the dividend payment will be $7.50 per share per year. Dividends are usually paid quarterly. Most preferred stock carries a cumulative claim to dividends. This means that if the company does not pay preferred-stock dividends in one year because of losses, the dividends accumulate to the next year. Such dividends unpaid from previous years must also be paid to preferred stockholders before other stockholders can receive any dividends.

> **preferred stock**
> a special type of stock whose owners, though not generally having a say in running the company, have a claim to profits before other stockholders do

Although owners of **common stock** do not get such preferential treatment with regard to dividends, they do get some say in the operation of the corporation. Their ownership gives them the right to vote for members of the board of directors and on other important issues. Common stock dividends may vary according to the profitability of the business, and some corporations do not issue dividends at all, but instead plow their profits back into the company to fund expansion.

> **common stock**
> stock whose owners have voting rights in the corporation, yet do not receive preferential treatment regarding dividends

Common stockholders are the voting owners of a corporation. They are usually entitled to one vote per share of common stock. During an annual stockholders' meeting, common stockholders elect a board of directors. Some boards find it easier than others to attract high profile individuals. For example, the board of Procter & Gamble consists of Ernesto Zedillo, former president of Mexico; John F. Smith, former chairman and CEO of General Motors; Rajat Gupta, former managing director at McKinsey; as well as the former CEOs of Archer Daniels Midland, Boeing, Verizon, and eBay.[18] Because they can choose the board of directors, common stockholders have some say in how the company will operate. Common stockholders may vote by *proxy,* which is a written authorization by which stockholders assign their voting privilege to someone else, who then votes for his or her choice at the stockholders' meeting. It is a normal practice for management to request proxy statements from shareholders who are not planning to attend the annual meeting. Most owners do not attend annual meetings of the very large companies, such as Westinghouse or Boeing, unless they live in the city where the meeting is held.

Common stockholders have another advantage over preferred shareholders. In most states, when the corporation decides to sell new shares of common stock in the marketplace, common stockholders have the first right, called a *preemptive right,* to purchase new shares of the stock from the corporation. A preemptive right is often included in the articles of incorporation. This right is important because it allows stockholders to purchase new shares to maintain their original positions. For example, if a stockholder owns 10 percent of a corporation that decides to issue new shares, that stockholder has the right to buy enough of the new shares to retain the 10 percent ownership.

## Advantages of Corporations

Because a corporation is a separate legal entity, it has some very specific advantages over other forms of ownership. The biggest advantage may be the limited liability of the owners.

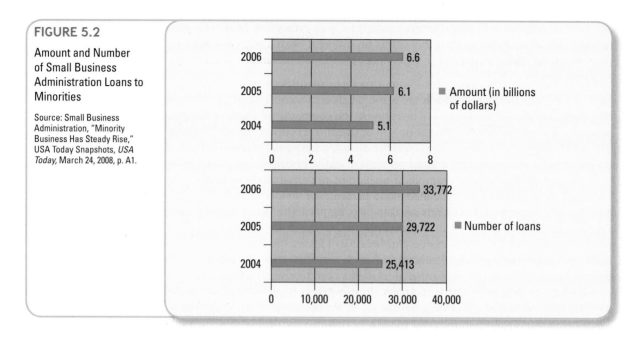

**FIGURE 5.2**

Amount and Number of Small Business Administration Loans to Minorities

Source: Small Business Administration, "Minority Business Has Steady Rise," USA Today Snapshots, *USA Today,* March 24, 2008, p. A1.

**Limited Liability.**    Because the corporation's assets (money and resources) and liabilities (debts and other obligations) are separate from its owners', in most cases the stockholders are not held responsible for the firm's debts if it fails. Their liability or potential loss is limited to the amount of their original investment. Although a creditor can sue a corporation for not paying its debts, even forcing the corporation into bankruptcy, it cannot make the stockholders pay the corporation's debts out of their personal assets. Occasionally, the owners of a private corporation may pledge personal assets to secure a loan for the corporation; this would be most unusual for a public corporation.

**Ease of Transfer of Ownership.**    Stockholders can sell or trade shares of stock to other people without causing the termination of the corporation, and they can do this without the prior approval of other shareholders. The transfer of ownership (unless it is a majority position) does not affect the daily or long-term operations of the corporation.

**Perpetual Life.**    A corporation usually is chartered to last forever unless its articles of incorporation stipulate otherwise. The existence of the corporation is unaffected by the death or withdrawal of any of its stockholders. It survives until the owners sell it or liquidate its assets. However, in some cases, bankruptcy ends a corporation's life. Bankruptcies occur when companies are unable to compete and earn profits. Eventually, uncompetitive businesses must close or seek protection from creditors in bankruptcy court while the business tries to reorganize.

**External Sources of Funds.**    Of all the forms of business organization, the public corporation finds it easiest to raise money. When a corporation needs to raise more money, it can sell more stock shares or issue bonds (corporate "IOUs," which pledge to repay debt), attracting funds from anywhere in the United States and even overseas. The larger a corporation becomes, the more sources of financing are available to it. We take a closer look at some of these in Chapter 16.

Expansion Potential.   Because large public corporations can find long-term financing readily, they can easily expand into national and international markets. And, as a legal entity, a corporation can enter into contracts without as much difficulty as a partnership.

## Disadvantages of Corporations

Corporations have some distinct disadvantages resulting from tax laws and government regulation.

Double Taxation.   As a legal entity, the corporation must pay taxes on its income just like you do. When after-tax corporate profits are paid out as dividends to the stockholders, the dividends are taxed a second time as part of the individual owner's income. This process creates double taxation for the stockholders of dividend paying corporations. Double taxation does not occur with the other forms of business organization.

Forming a Corporation.   The formation of a corporation can be costly. A charter must be obtained, and this usually requires the services of an attorney and payment of legal fees. Filing fees ranging from $25 to $150 must be paid to the state that awards the corporate charter, and certain states require that an annual fee be paid to maintain the charter.

Disclosure of Information.   Corporations must make information available to their owners, usually through an annual report to shareholders. The annual report contains financial information about the firm's profits, sales, facilities and equipment, and debts, as well as descriptions of the company's operations, products, and plans for the future. Public corporations must also file reports with the Securities and Exchange Commission (SEC), the government regulatory agency that regulates securities such as stocks and bonds. The larger the firm, the more data the SEC requires. Because all reports filed with the SEC are available to the public, competitors can access them. Additionally, complying with securities laws takes time.

> **Did You Know?**   The first corporation with a net income of more than $1 billion in one year was General Motors, with a net income in 1955 of $1,189,477,082.[19]

Employee–Owner Separation.   Many employees are not stockholders of the company for which they work. This separation of owners and employees may cause employees to feel that their work benefits only the owners. Employees without an ownership stake do not always see how they fit into the corporate picture and may not understand the importance of profits to the health of the organization. If managers are part owners but other employees are not, management–labor relations take on a different, sometimes difficult, aspect from those in partnerships and sole proprietorships. However, this situation is changing as more corporations establish employee stock ownership plans (ESOPs), which give shares of the company's stock to its employees. Such plans build a partnership between employee and employer and can boost productivity because they motivate employees to work harder so that they can earn dividends from their hard work as well as from their regular wages.

# Other Types of Ownership

In this section we take a brief look at joint ventures, S corporations, limited liability companies, and cooperatives—businesses formed for special purposes.

## Joint Ventures

**joint venture**
a partnership established for a specific project or for a limited time

A **joint venture** is a partnership established for a specific project or for a limited time. The partners in a joint venture may be individuals or organizations, as in the case of the international joint ventures discussed in Chapter 3. Control of a joint venture may be shared equally, or one partner may control decision making. Joint ventures are especially popular in situations that call for large investments, such as extraction of natural resources and the development of new products. Audi and Volkswagen entered into a joint venture to share a manufacturing plant in the United States. Through this arrangement, Audi hopes to eliminate some of the risk associated with U.S. dollar fluctuations. Audi's hope is that this arrangement will allow the company to sell 200,000 vehicles annually in the United States.[20]

## S Corporations

**S corporation**
corporation taxed as though it were a partnership with restrictions on shareholders

An **S corporation** is a form of business ownership that is taxed as though it were a partnership. Net profits or losses of the corporation pass to the owners, thus eliminating double taxation. The benefit of limited liability is retained. Formally known as Subchapter S Corporations, they have become a popular form of business ownership for entrepreneurs and represent almost half of all corporate filings.[21] Accounting Systems, a Fort Collins, Colorado, accounting software firm, elected to incorporate as an S corporation to gain credibility, tax advantages, and limited liability. Advantages of S corporations include the simple method of taxation, the limited liability of shareholders, perpetual life, and the ability to shift income and appreciation to others. Disadvantages include restrictions on the number (75) and types (individuals, estates, and certain trusts) of shareholders and the difficulty of formation and operation.

## Limited Liability Companies

**limited liability company (LLC)**
form of ownership that provides limited liability and taxation like a partnership but places fewer restrictions on members

A **limited liability company (LLC)** is a form of business ownership that provides limited liability, as in a corporation, but is taxed like a partnership. Although relatively new in the United States, LLCs have existed for many years abroad. Professionals such as lawyers, doctors, and engineers often use the LLC form of ownership. Many consider the LLC a blend of the best characteristics of corporations, partnerships, and sole proprietorships. One of the major reasons for the LLC form of ownership is to protect the members' personal assets in case of lawsuits. LLCs are flexible, simple to run, and do not require the members to hold meetings, keep minutes, or make resolutions, all of which are necessary in corporations. For example, Segway, which markets the Segway Human Transporter, is a limited liability company.

## Cooperatives

**cooperative or co-op**
an organization composed of individuals or small businesses that have banded together to reap the benefits of belonging to a larger organization

Another form of organization in business is the **cooperative or co-op,** an organization composed of individuals or small businesses that have banded together to reap the benefits of belonging to a larger organization. Blue Diamond Growers, for example, is a cooperative of California almond growers; Ocean Spray is a cooperative of cranberry farmers. A co-op is set up not to make money as an entity but so that its members can become more profitable or save money. Co-ops are generally expected to operate without profit or to create only enough profit to maintain the co-op organization.

Many cooperatives exist in small farming communities. The co-op stores and markets grain; orders large quantities of fertilizer, seed, and other supplies at discounted prices; and reduces costs and increases efficiency with good management.

A former ballerina and stuntwoman, Dawn Barnes discovered karate in 1984 through the encouragement of her two sons. Thanks to her background and three-hour-long daily training sessions, she earned her first-level black belt within four years. Barnes then decided to become a karate instructor herself and began teaching in elementary schools. After teaching as a freelance instructor for five years, Barnes borrowed $15,000 and opened her own studio in Santa Monica, California, in 1995 as a sole proprietorship.

Because of her history teaching in schools, Barnes's studio had 60 students before the doors even opened for business. She also performed demonstrations at schools and distributed flyers to parents to attract new kids. Student enrollment doubled within a short time, and after a year and a half, the studio became quite profitable. Barnes then expanded the business, hiring a receptionist and an instructor. Dawn Barnes Karate Kids LLC has since expanded to six more studios throughout the Los Angeles metro area.

Due to high competition, opening a karate school in California is no small feat. Part of what differentiated Barnes's studio from others was her more sensitive approach to teaching martial arts. As a mother and an educator, she suspected that the reason many children leave the discipline is because of the traditional, fear-based approach. Barnes takes a different tack and seeks to instill self-esteem in her students through positive reinforcement. The Dawn Barnes Karate Kids studios are committed to teaching patience, focus, kindness, and honesty—not fear—as they promote physical fitness.

Barnes's mission struck the right chord among parents and children, and she has been able to expand this concept into a children's book series as well as her seven successful studios. Dawn Barnes Karate Kids now attains annual revenues in excess of $3 million. In addition, Dawn Barnes was inducted into the Black Belt Hall of Fame as "Woman of the Year 2006." In spite of all of her additional successes, Barnes still loves helping children first and foremost. She hopes that through her school and her books that she is making a positive difference in the world.[22]

### Discussion Questions

1. What are the advantages and disadvantages of choosing the limited liability corporation form of business organization?
2. Would remaining a sole proprietorship have changed Dawn Barnes's business
3. What is the sustainable competitive advantage of Dawn Barnes Karate Kids?

---

A co-op can purchase supplies in large quantities and pass the savings on to its members. It also can help distribute the products of its members more efficiently than each could on an individual basis. A cooperative can advertise its members' products and thus generate demand. Ace Hardware, a cooperative of independent hardware store owners, allows its members to share in the savings that result from buying supplies in large quantities; it also provides advertising, which individual members might not be able to afford on their own.

## Trends in Business Ownership: Mergers and Acquisitions

Companies large and small achieve growth and improve profitability by expanding their operations, often by developing and selling new products or selling current products to new groups of customers in different geographic areas. Such growth, when carefully planned and controlled, is usually beneficial to the firm and ultimately helps it reach its goal of enhanced profitability. But companies also grow by merging with or purchasing other companies.

A **merger** occurs when two companies (usually corporations) combine to form a new company. An **acquisition** occurs when one company purchases another, generally by buying most of its stock. The acquired company may become a subsidiary of the buyer, or its operations and assets may be merged with those of the buyer. The government sometimes scrutinizes mergers and acquisitions in an attempt to protect

**merger**
the combination of two companies (usually corporations) to form a new company

**acquisition**
the purchase of one company by another, usually by buying its stock

customers from monopolistic practices. For example, the decision to authorize Whole Foods' acquisition of Wild Oats was carefully analyzed, as was the merger of Sirius and XM Satellite Radio. One of the largest acquisitions of 2008 was the Mars candy company buyout of the Wrigley confectionary company. Mars acquired the popular chewing gum and mints company for $23 billion, creating one of the world's largest confectionary companies and putting pressure on smaller competitors like Cadbury and Hershey.[23] Acquisitions sometimes involve the purchase of a division or some other part of a company rather than the entire company. The late 1990s saw a merger and acquisition frenzy, which is slowing in the 21st century (see Table 5.5).

When firms that make and sell similar products to the same customers merge, it is known as a *horizontal merger,* as when Martin Marietta and Lockheed, both defense contractors, merged to form Lockheed Martin. Horizontal mergers, however, reduce the number of corporations competing within an industry, and for this reason they are usually reviewed carefully by federal regulators before the merger is allowed to proceed.

When companies operating at different but related levels of an industry merge, it is known as a *vertical merger.* In many instances, a vertical merger results when one corporation merges with one of its customers or suppliers. For example, if Burger King were to purchase a large Idaho potato farm—to ensure a ready supply of potatoes for its french fries—a vertical merger would result.

A *conglomerate merger* results when two firms in unrelated industries merge. For example, the purchase of Sterling Drug, a pharmaceutical firm, by Eastman Kodak, best-known for its films and cameras, represents a conglomerate merger because the two companies are of different industries.

When a company (or an individual), sometimes called a *corporate raider,* wants to acquire or take over another company, it first offers to buy some or all of the other company's stock at a premium over its current price in a *tender offer.* Most such

| TABLE 5.5 | | | | | |
|---|---|---|---|---|---|
| Major Mergers and Acquisitions Worldwide 2000–2006 | **Rank** | **Year** | **Acquirer\*** | **Target** | **Transaction Value (in millions of US dollars)** |
| | 1. | 2000 | America Online Inc. (AOL) *(Merger)* | Time Warner | $164,747 |
| | 2. | 2000 | Glaxo Wellcome Plc. | SmithKline Beecham Plc. | 75,961 |
| | 3. | 2004 | Royal Dutch Petroleum Co. | Shell Transport & Trading Co. | 74,559 |
| | 4. | 2006 | AT&T Inc. | BellSouth Corporation | 72,671 |
| | 5. | 2001 | Comcast Corporation | AT&T Broadband & Internet Svcs. | 72,041 |
| | 6. | 2004 | Sanofi-Synthelabo SA | Aventis SA | 60,243 |
| | 7. | 2000 | Nortel Networks Corporation *(spinoff)* | | 59,974 |
| | 8. | 2002 | Pfizer Inc. | Pharmacia Corporation | 59,515 |
| | 9. | 2004 | JPMorgan Chase & Co. | Bank One Corporation | 58,761 |
| | 10. | 2006 | E.on AG *(pending)* | Endesa SA | 56,266 |

\*Unless noted, deal was an acquisition.

Source: Institute of Mergers, Acquisitions and Alliances Research, *Thomson Financial,* http://www.manda-institute. org/en/statistics-top-m&a-deals-transactions.htm (accessed May 4, 2008).

offers are "friendly," with both groups agreeing to the proposed deal, but some are "hostile," when the second company does not want to be taken over. Belgian brewing giant InBev recently sought to acquire Anheuser Busch—an offer that was not welcomed by Anheuser. InBev offered Anheuser $46.3 billion in cash to acquire the American lager company, a move that would help the European brewer shore up business in a region where it does not have a strong presence. Anheuser expressed strong opposition to the proposal, going so far as to team up with Mexico's Grupo Modelo and seeking the aid of Warren Buffet to keep it from happening. August Busch IV, CEO of Anheuser, has expressed strong public opposition to the buyout.[24] InBev was

*Delta Airlines and Northwest Airlines are among the many airlines that have merged in recent years. The two companies saw the merger as a way to cut costs by combining their fleets and retiring their oldest aircraft.*

successful in acquiring Anheuser Busch for $52 billion. The deal was criticized for losing another American business icon.

To head off a hostile takeover attempt, a threatened company's managers may use one or more of several techniques. They may ask stockholders not to sell to the raider; file a lawsuit in an effort to abort the takeover; institute a *poison pill* (in which the firm allows stockholders to buy more shares of stock at prices lower than the current market value) or *shark repellant* (in which management requires a large majority of stockholders to approve the takeover); or seek a *white knight* (a more acceptable firm that is willing to acquire the threatened company). In some cases, management may take the company private or even take on more debt so that the heavy debt obligation will "scare off" the raider.

In a **leveraged buyout (LBO),** a group of investors borrows money from banks and other institutions to acquire a company (or a division of one), using the assets of the purchased company to guarantee repayment of the loan. In some LBOs, as much as 95 percent of the buyout price is paid with borrowed money, which eventually must be repaid.

Because of the explosion of mergers, acquisitions, and leveraged buyouts in the 1980s and 1990s, financial journalists coined the term *merger mania.* Many companies joined the merger mania simply to enhance their own operations by consolidating them with the operations of other firms. Mergers and acquisitions enabled these companies to gain a larger market share in their industries, acquire valuable assets, such as new products or plants and equipment, and lower their costs. Mergers also represent a means of making profits quickly, as was the case during the 1980s when many companies' stock was undervalued. Quite simply, such companies represent a bargain to other companies that can afford to buy them. Additionally, deregulation of some industries has permitted consolidation of firms within those industries for the first time, as is the case in the banking and airline industries.

Some people view mergers and acquisitions favorably, pointing out that they boost corporations' stock prices and market value, to the benefit of their stockholders. In many instances, mergers enhance a company's ability to meet foreign competition in an increasingly global marketplace. And, companies that are victims of hostile takeovers generally streamline their operations, reduce unnecessary staff, cut

**leveraged buyout (LBO)** a purchase in which a group of investors borrows money from banks and other institutions to acquire a company (or a division of one), using the assets of the purchased company to guarantee repayment of the loan

costs, and otherwise become more efficient with their operations, which benefits their stockholders whether or not the takeover succeeds.

Critics, however, argue that mergers hurt companies because they force managers to focus their efforts on avoiding takeovers rather than managing effectively and profitably. Some companies have taken on a heavy debt burden to stave off a takeover, later to be forced into bankruptcy when economic downturns left them unable to handle the debt. Mergers and acquisitions also can damage employee morale and productivity, as well as the quality of the companies' products.

Many mergers have been beneficial for all involved; others have had damaging effects for the companies, their employees, and customers. No one can say if mergers will continue to slow, but many experts say the utilities, telecommunications, financial services, natural resources, computer hardware and software, gaming, managed health care, and technology industries are likely targets.

# So You'd Like to Start a Business

If you have a good idea and want to turn it into a business, you are not alone. Small businesses are popping up all over the United States and the concept of entrepreneurship is hot. Entrepreneurs seek opportunities and creative ways to make profits. Business emerges in a number of different organizational forms, each with its own advantages and disadvantages. Sole proprietorships are the most common form of business organization in the U.S. They tend to be small businesses and can take pretty much any form— anything from a hair salon to a scuba shop, from an organic produce provider to a financial advisor. Proprietorships are everywhere serving consumers' wants and needs. Proprietorships have a big advantage in that they tend to be simple to manage—decisions get made quickly when the owner and the manager are the same person and they are fairly simple and inexpensive to set up. Rules vary by state, but at most all you will need is a license from the state.

Many people have been part of a partnership at some point in their life. Group work in school is an example of a partnership. If you ever worked as a DJ on the weekend with your friend and split the profits then you have experienced a partnership. General and limited are the two main types of partnerships. General partners have unlimited liability and share completely in the management, debts and profits of the business. Limited partners, on the other hand, consist of at least one general partner and one or more limited partners who do not participate in the management of the company but share in the profits. This form of partnership is used more often in risky investments where the limited partner stands only to lose his or her initial investment. Real estate limited partnerships are an example of how investors can minimize their financial exposure, given the poor performance of the real estate market in recent years. Although it has its advantages, partnership is the least utilized form of business. Part of the reason is that all partners are responsible for the actions and decisions of all other partners, whether or not all of the partners were involved. Usually, partners will have to write up an Articles of Partnership that outlines respective responsibilities in the business. Even in states where it is not required, it is a good idea to draw up this document as a way to cement each partner's role and hopefully minimize conflict. Unlike a corporation, proprietorships and partnerships both expire upon the death of one or more of those involved.

Corporations tend to be larger businesses, but do not need to be. A corporation can consist of nothing more than a small group of family members. In order to become a corporation you will have to file in the state under which you wish to incorporate. Each state has its own procedure for incorporation, meaning there are no general guidelines to follow. You can make your corporation private or public, meaning the company issues stocks and shareholders are the owners. While incorporating is a popular form of organization because it gives the company an unlimited lifespan and limited liability (meaning that if your business fails you cannot lose personal funds to make up for losses), there is a downside. You will be taxed as a corporation and as an individual resulting in double taxation. No matter what form of organization suits your business idea best, there is a world of options out there for you if you want to be or experiment with being an entrepreneur.

# Review Your Understanding

### Define and examine the advantages and disadvantages of the sole proprietorship form of organization.

Sole proprietorships—businesses owned and managed by one person—are the most common form of organization. Their major advantages are the following: (1) They are easy and inexpensive to form, (2) they allow a high level of secrecy, (3) all profits belong to the owner, (4) the owner has complete control over the business, (5) government regulation is minimal, (6) taxes are paid only once, and (7) the business can be closed easily. The disadvantages include: (1) The owner may have to use personal assets to borrow money, (2) sources of external funds are difficult to find, (3) the owner must have many diverse skills, (4) the survival of the business is tied to the life of the owner and his or her ability to work, (5) qualified employees are hard to find, and (6) wealthy sole proprietors pay a higher tax than they would under the corporate form of business.

### Identify two types of partnership, and evaluate the advantages and disadvantages of the partnership form of organization.

A partnership is a business formed by several individuals; a partnership may be general or limited. Partnerships offer the following advantages: (1) They are easy to organize, (2) they may have higher credit ratings because the partners possibly have more combined wealth, (3) partners can specialize, (4) partnerships can make decisions faster than larger businesses, and (5) government regulations are few. Partnerships also have several disadvantages: (1) General partners have unlimited liability for the debts of the partnership, (2) partners are responsible for each others' decisions, (3) the death or termination of one partner requires a new partnership agreement to be drawn up, (4) it is difficult to sell a partnership interest at a fair price, (5) the distribution of profits may not correctly reflect the amount of work done by each partner, and (6) partnerships cannot find external sources of funds as easily as can large corporations.

### Describe the corporate form of organization, and cite the advantages and disadvantages of corporations.

A corporation is a legal entity created by the state, whose assets and liabilities are separate from those of its owners. Corporations are chartered by a state through articles of incorporation. They have a board of directors made up of corporate officers or people from outside the company. Corporations, whether private or public, are owned by stockholders. Common stockholders have the right to elect the board of directors. Preferred stockholders do not have a vote but get preferential dividend treatment over common stockholders.

Advantages of the corporate form of business include: (1) The owners have limited liability, (2) ownership (stock) can be easily transferred, (3) corporations usually last forever, (4) raising money is easier than for other forms of business, and (5) expansion into new businesses is simpler because of the ability of the company to enter into contracts. Corporations also have disadvantages: (1) The company is taxed on its income, and owners pay a second tax on any profits received as dividends; (2) forming a corporation can be expensive; (3) keeping trade secrets is difficult because so much information must be made available to the public and to government agencies; and (4) owners and managers are not always the same and can have different goals.

### Define and debate the advantages and disadvantages of mergers, acquisitions, and leveraged buyouts.

A merger occurs when two companies (usually corporations) combine to form a new company. An acquisition occurs when one company buys most of another company's stock. In a leveraged buyout, a group of investors borrows money to acquire a company, using the assets of the purchased company to guarantee the loan. They can help merging firms to gain a larger market share in their industries, acquire valuable assets such as new products or plants and equipment, and lower their costs. Consequently, they can benefit stockholders by improving the companies' market value and stock prices. However, they also can hurt companies if they force managers to focus on avoiding takeovers at the expense of productivity and profits. They may lead a company to take on too much debt and can harm employee morale and productivity.

### Propose an appropriate organizational form for a startup business.

After reading the facts in "Solve the Dilemma" on page 170 and considering the advantages and disadvantages of the various forms of business organization described in this chapter, you should be able to suggest an appropriate form for the start-up nursery.

# Revisit the World of Business

1. What are the benefits of becoming a B Corporation?
2. In addition to Newman's Own and Give Something Back, can you think of any other organizations that might fall under the label "beneficial?"
3. What were Hannigan and Marx's reasons for not going public?

# Learn the Terms

acquisition   163
articles of partnership   149
board of directors   158
common stock   159
cooperative (or co-op)   162
corporate charter   155
corporation   154
dividends   155

general partnership   149
initial public offering (IPO)   156
joint venture   162
leveraged buyout (LBO)   165
limited liability company (LLC)   162
limited partnership   149
merger   163
nonprofit corporations   158

partnership   149
preferred stock   159
private corporation   156
public corporation   156
quasi-public corporations   158
S corporation   162
sole proprietorships   145
stock   154

# Check Your Progress

1. Name five advantages of a sole proprietorship.
2. List two different types of partnerships and describe each.
3. Differentiate among the different types of corporations. Can you supply an example of each type?
4. Would you rather own preferred stock or common stock? Why?
5. Contrast how profits are distributed in sole proprietorships, partnerships, and corporations.
6. Which form of business organization has the least government regulation? Which has the most?
7. Compare the liability of the owners of partnerships, sole proprietorships, and corporations.
8. Why would secrecy in operating a business be important to an owner? What form of organization would be most appropriate for a business requiring great secrecy?
9. Which form of business requires the most specialization of skills? Which requires the least? Why?
10. The most common example of a cooperative is a farm co-op. Explain the reasons for this and the benefits that result for members of cooperatives.

# Get Involved

1. Select a publicly owned corporation and bring to class a list of its subsidiaries. These data should be available in the firm's corporate annual report, *Standard & Poor's Corporate Records,* or *Moody Corporate Manuals.* Ask your librarian for help in finding these resources.
2. Select a publicly owned corporation and make a list of its outside directors. Information of this nature can be found in several places in your library: the company's annual report, its list of corporate directors, and various financial sources. If possible, include each director's title and the name of the company that employs him or her on a full-time basis.

# Build Your Skills

### SELECTING A FORM OF BUSINESS

**Background:**
Ali Bush sees an opportunity to start her own Web site development business. Ali has just graduated from the University of Mississippi with a master's degree in computer science. Although she has many job opportunities outside the Oxford area, she wishes to remain there to care for her aging parents. She already has most of the computer equipment necessary to start the business, but she needs additional software. She is considering the purchase of a server to maintain Web sites for small businesses. Ali feels she has the ability to take this start-up firm and create a long-term career opportunity for herself and others. She knows she can hire Ole Miss students to work on a part-time basis to support her business. For now, as she starts the business, she can work out of the extra bedroom of her apartment. As the business grows, she'll hire the additional full- and/or part-time help needed and reassess the location of the business.

**Task:**
1. Using what you've learned in this chapter, decide which form of business ownership is most appropriate for Ali. Use the tables provided to assist you in evaluating the advantages and disadvantages of each decision.

| Sole Proprietorships | |
|---|---|
| Advantages | Disadvantages |
| • | • |
| • | • |
| • | • |
| • | • |
| • | • |
| • | • |
| • | • |

| Corporation | |
|---|---|
| Advantages | Disadvantages |
| • | • |
| • | • |
| • | • |
| • | • |
| • | • |
| • | • |
| • | • |

| Limited Liability Company | |
|---|---|
| Advantages | Disadvantages |
| • | • |
| • | • |
| • | • |
| • | • |
| • | • |
| • | • |

# Solve the Dilemma

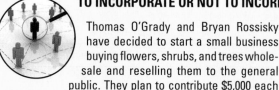

### TO INCORPORATE OR NOT TO INCORPORATE

Thomas O'Grady and Bryan Rossisky have decided to start a small business buying flowers, shrubs, and trees wholesale and reselling them to the general public. They plan to contribute $5,000 each in startup capital and lease a 2.5-acre tract of land with a small, portable sales office.

Thomas and Bryan are trying to decide what form of organization would be appropriate. Bryan thinks they should create a corporation because they would have limited liability and the image of a large organization. Thomas thinks a partnership would be easier to start and would allow them to rely on the combination of their talents and financial resources. In addition, there might be fewer reports and regulatory controls to cope with.

### Discussion Questions

1.  What are some of the advantages and disadvantages of Thomas and Bryan forming a corporation?

2.  What are the advantages and disadvantages of their forming a partnership?

3.  Which organizational form do you think would be best for Thomas and Bryan's company and why?

# Build Your Business Plan

### OPTIONS FOR ORGANIZING BUSINESS

Your team needs to think about how you should organize yourselves that would be most efficient and effective for your business plan. The benefits of having partners include having others to share responsibilities with and to toss ideas off of each other. As your business evolves you will have to decide whether one or two members will manage the business while the other members are silent partners. Or perhaps you will all decide on working in the business to keep costs down, at least initially. However you decide on team member involvement in the business, it is imperative to have a written agreement so that all team members understand what their responsibilities are and what will happen if the partnership dissolves.

It is not too soon for you and your partners to start thinking about how you might want to find additional funding for your business. Later on in the development of your business plan you might want to show your business plan to family members. Together you and your partners will want to develop a list of potential investors in your business.

# See for Yourself Videocase

### GREEN INDUSTRY HUB RISES FROM RUST BELT RUINS

Pittsburgh, Pennsylvania, is known for many things—the steel industry and the Pittsburgh Steelers, for example—but not many people immediately connect Pittsburgh with green living. For the past 100 years, it has been known as the hub of the steel industry. During the steel heyday, Pittsburgh was an incredibly important, heavily populated area with many job opportunities. It was once said that the steel industry dictated the direction of the country. In the 1970s and 1980s, the steel industry declined, leaving behind destitute communities, many unemployed, and tons of pollution. Pittsburgh and surrounds have maintained their gritty image to this day, with high rates of poverty and crime, and is desperately in need of change and revival. To the rescue? The green movement!

The town of Braddock, Pennsylvania, and its mayor, John Fetterman, now provide an example of how the green industry can revive local economies. Arriving in Braddock in 2001, Fetterman knew he need to do something to help the community. Braddock is the home of the first Carnegie steel mill, built in 1875. During its heyday, the town's population was a sizable 20,000. Today, the population is a tenth that, at 2,800. When Fetterman arrived, the town was rife with crime—people were being murdered for, as he said, "pizza money." Elected mayor in 2005, Fetterman was determined to create positive change for those stuck in this sinking community. What Fetterman, now known as Mayor John, hopes to accomplish is to flip the town on its ear, so to speak, turning a former environmental disaster into an eco-friendly center.

To this end, green recruiting has begun. One of the first businesses to take root, literally, is an urban farm. The farm, known as Braddock Farm, is part of Grow Pittsburgh—an organization dedicated to promoting local farming and education on urban farming. Organic, local growing prevents pollution—organic through avoiding the use of chemicals and pesticides, and local growth by reducing the pollution associated with shipping produce long distances. The ultimate goal for Braddock Farm is to create an urban farming infrastructure that includes spinoff farms and a farm cooperative. In the works is Fossil Free Fuel, a business that arrived in 2007 and converts diesel cars and trucks to run on vegetable oil. Fossil Free Fuel began life as a sole proprietorship and later became an LLC partnership.

The question to be asked is this: Is Braddock, once home to a blue-collar industry, effectively becoming a "green-collar" town? In other words, will those accustomed to blue-collar work be driven out or made obsolete? The answer is no. Although Fetterman is encouraging green growth and green businesses are eager to take part, this green revolution is creating blue-collar jobs as well. For example, if a business arrives ready to build windmills to create wind energy, it will need welders and electricians to accomplish its goal. Therefore, Braddock shows that going green can benefit everyone, creating an all-around more profitable community.

To see the green industry at work on a larger scale, one can look to Pittsburgh itself. Once a city bursting with more than a million residents, Pittsburgh now tallies a third of that at only around 300,000. Here, too, people are looking toward a green revival. Businesses such as GTECH (a not-for-profit organization that reclaims vacant lots and uses them to plant biofuel crops) and Steel City Biofuels (a nonprofit that encourages oil companies to convert to biofuel production) are thriving in Pittsburgh and creating both jobs and a sense of purpose among residents.

Both wind and nuclear power are becoming popular energy alternatives in Pittsburgh. And the city can use all the help it can get—it stands behind only Los Angeles, California, as the smoggiest city in the United States. PPG Industries, formerly Pittsburgh Plate Glass, is a wind power company that is also at work developing new glass that lets in light but deflects heat. In spite of the controversy surrounding it, nuclear power generates some of the cleanest electricity. While it only accounts for roughly 20 percent of U.S. electricity, other countries, such as France, get up to 80 percent of their power from nuclear.

As concerns over global warming and climate change continue to grow, it is clear that each town, city, and country needs to make drastic changes in order to positively affect the environment. It is quite a feat for such an environmentally harmful sector of the United States to make a turn around, but Pittsburgh is certainly showing its greener side.[25]

### Discussion Questions

1. What are some of the advantages for towns like Braddock and Pittsburgh of encouraging the growth of the green industry?

2. What other industries benefit from increasing the number of green businesses?

3. What might be some of the downsides of encouraging the growth of the wind and nuclear energy industries?

**Remember to check out our Online Learning Center at www.mhhe.com/ferrell7e**

## chapter 6

# Small Business, Entrepreneurship, and Franchising

## CHAPTER OUTLINE

**Introduction**

**The Nature of Entrepreneurship and Small Business**
*What Is a Small Business?*
*The Role of Small Business in the American Economy*
*Industries That Attract Small Business*

**Advantages of Small-Business Ownership**
*Independence*
*Costs*
*Flexibility*
*Focus*
*Reputation*

**Disadvantages of Small-Business Ownership**
*High Stress Level*
*High Failure Rate*

**Starting a Small Business**
*The Business Plan*
*Forms of Business Ownership*
*Financial Resources*
*Approaches to Starting a Small Business*
*Help for Small-Business Managers*

**The Future for Small Business**
*Demographic Trends*
*Technological and Economic Trends*

**Making Big Businesses Act "Small"**

## OBJECTIVES

*After reading this chapter, you will be able to:*

- Define *entrepreneurship* and *small business.*

- Investigate the importance of small business in the U.S. economy and why certain fields attract small business.

- Specify the advantages of small-business ownership.

- Summarize the disadvantages of small-business ownership, and analyze why many small businesses fail.

- Describe how you go about starting a small business and what resources are needed.

- Evaluate the demographic, technological, and economic trends that are affecting the future of small business.

- Explain why many large businesses are trying to "think small."

- Assess two entrepreneurs' plans for starting a small business.

## Cheese Goes from Smelly to Hip

These days, people all over the country and all over the world are searching for new, unique artisan cheeses to sample. One of the businesses serving the demand is a mother-son operation, Cato Corner Farm, in Colchester, Connecticut. Mark Gillman, the son, is in charge of the cheese, and his mother, Elizabeth MacAlister, runs the farm. When MacAlister first began exploring cheese production in the 1990s she was simply looking for a way to branch out and to run her farm in a more sustainable fashion. MacAlister had been raising sheep and goats for meat since the late 1970s and was searching for new ways to grow her business. Cheese-making looked like a viable avenue, so MacAlister traded in her livestock for cows and took some classes. MacAlister took technical cheese-making courses at California Polytechnic, as well as with a Belgian cheese master. After thoroughly studying the craft, MacAlister started production of raw milk cheeses in 1997. In 1999, her son Mark, a former seventh-grade teacher, joined her and gradually took over the cheese-making operations. With time, their hard work has been rewarded with success. Aided by the rise of the whole foods movement and the increasing popularity of farmers' markets and local food, Cato Corner has built a name for itself based on quality. Cato Corner Farm currently produces about 40,000 pounds of cheese annually and has a herd of 40 free-range Jersey cows. Because MacAlister and Gillman believe that good gourmet cheese starts with healthy, hormone-free cows, none of their cows are given growth hormones, antibiotics, or animal-based feeds.

The farm sells most of its cheese through Greenmarket, a New York–based farmer's market organization. The cheeses are also popular in upscale

*continued*

restaurants and wine and cheese shops. To serve individuals, Cato Corner takes on-farm orders on Saturdays and will ship orders to anywhere in the country. Many of Cato Corner's cheeses are award winning, and the dairy has received two Gallo Family Vineyards awards for Outstanding Family-Owned Artisanal Food Production and Outstanding Dairy Product. Cato Corner's cheeses do not fit any traditional cheese-making mold, and it takes time to learn about all the unique varieties. However, with names like Hooligan, Desperado, Drunken Hooligan, Drunk Monk, and Vivace, who wouldn't want to bring one of these treats out at their next wine and cheese party?[1]

# Introduction

Although many business students go to work for large corporations upon graduation, others may choose to start their own business or to find employment opportunities in small organizations with 500 or fewer employees. There are nearly 24 million small businesses operating in the United States, providing 75 percent of the net new jobs in the workforce.[2] Each small business represents the vision of its owners to succeed through providing new or better products. Small businesses are the heart of the U.S. economic and social system because they offer opportunities and demonstratic the freedom of people to make their own destinies. Today, the entrepreneurial spirit is growing around the world, from Russia and China to Germany, Brazil, and Mexico.

This chapter surveys the world of entrepreneurship and small business. First we define entrepreneurship and small business and examine the role of small business in the American economy. Then we explore the advantages and disadvantages of small-business ownership and analyze why small businesses succeed or fail. Next, we discuss how an entrepreneur goes about starting a business and the challenges facing small businesses today. Finally, we look at entrepreneurship in larger organizations.

# The Nature of Entrepreneurship and Small Business

**enterpreneurship**
the process of creating and managing a business to achieve desired objectives

In Chapter 1, we defined an entrepreneur as a person who risks his or her wealth, time, and effort to develop for profit an innovative product or way of doing something. **Entrepreneurship** is the process of creating and managing a business to achieve desired objectives. Many large businesses you may recognize (Levi Strauss and Co., Procter & Gamble, McDonald's, Dell Computers, Microsoft, and Federal Express) all began as small businesses based on the visions of their founders. Some entrepreneurs who start small businesses have the ability to see emerging trends; in response, they create a company to provide a product that serves customer needs. For example, rather than inventing a major new technology, an innovative company may take advantage of technology to create new markets, such as Amazon.com. Or they may offer a familiar product that has been improved or repackaged, such as Starbucks and its coffee shops. A company may innovate by focusing on a particular market segment and delivering a combination of features that consumers in that segment could not find anywhere else (e.g., Patagonia, a company that uses many organic materials in its clothing, has pledged 1 percent of sales to the preservation and restoration of the natural environment. Customers can return their worn-out Capilene® Performance Baselayers for recycling.)[3]

Of course, smaller businesses do not have to evolve into such highly visible companies to be successful, but those entrepreneurial efforts that result in rapidly growing businesses gain visibility along with success. Entrepreneurs who have achieved success, like Michael Dell, Bill Gates (Microsoft), and Larry Page and Sergey Brin (Google), are some of the most well known.

The entrepreneurship movement is accelerating, and many new, smaller businesses are emerging. Technology once available only to the largest firms can now be obtained by a small business. Printers, fax machines, copiers, voice-mail, computer bulletin boards and networks, cellular phones, and even overnight delivery services enable small businesses to be more competitive with today's giant corporations. Small businesses can also form alliances with other companies to produce and sell products in domestic and global markets.

## What Is a Small Business?

This question is difficult to answer because smallness is relative. In this book, we will define a **small business** as any independently owned and operated business that is not dominant in its competitive area and does not employ more than 500 people. A local Mexican restaurant may be the most patronized Mexican restaurant in your community, but because it does not dominate the restaurant industry as a whole, the restaurant can be considered a small business. This definition is similar to the one used by the **Small Business Administration (SBA),** an independent agency of the federal government that offers managerial and financial assistance to small businesses. On its Web site, the SBA outlines the first steps in starting a small business and offers a wealth of information to current and potential small business owners.

## The Role of Small Business in the American Economy

No matter how you define a small business, one fact is clear: They are vital to the American economy. As you can see in Table 6.1, more than 99 percent of all U.S. firms are classified as small businesses, and they employ 50 percent of private workers. Small firms are also important as exporters, representing 97 percent of U.S. exporters of goods and contributing 29 percent of the value of exported goods.[4] In addition, small businesses are largely responsible for fueling job creation and innovation. Small businesses also provide opportunities for minorities and women to succeed in business. Women-owned businesses total nearly 10.5 million—with more than 50 percent employing more than 12.8 million people—and they generate $1.9 trillion in sales. Over the past 20 years, the number of women-owned businesses has grown at a rate twice that of the average rate of 10 percent for firms overall. In addition, women owned firms account for 41 percent of all privately held firms.[5] Minority-owned businesses have been growing faster than other classifiable firms as well, representing 17.6 percent of all small businesses. The number of minority-owned businesses is increasing at a rate of 30 percent, even higher than for women-owned firms. Hispanics own the most small businesses (7 percent) followed by African Americans (5.3 percent) Asian (4.9 percent), American Indian and Native Alaskan (0.9 percent), and Native Hawaiian and other Pacific Islander (0.1 percent).[6] For example, Cuban-born Jose M. Ledon decided it was time to start his own business after running various trenching and excavating companies in and around Las Vegas. Starting out with only $30,000, he hired 17 employees and was able to secure credit to purchase some equipment. By the business's second year, sales were $46 million,

**small business**
any independently owned and operated business that is not dominant in its competitive area and does not employ more than 500 people

**Small Business Administration (SBA)**
an independent agency of the federal government that offers managerial and financial assistance to small businesses

| TABLE 6.1 Facts About Small Businesses | • Represent 99.7% of all employer firms. |
|---|---|
| | • Employ half of all private-sector employees. |
| | • About 6 to 7% of the U.S. population is in the process of starting a business at any given time. |
| | • 53% of new small businesses begin in the home with less than $10,000. |
| | • Responsible for 39% of gross national product (GNP). |
| | • Account for 44% of all sales in the country. |
| | • Twice as innovative per employee as larger firms (producing 13 times more patents per employee). |
| | • Provide the first job for most U.S. workers. |
| | • Contribute roughly $40 billion to their communities and generally believe in public participation. |

Sources: "Small Business Facts," National Federation of Independent Business, http://www.nfib.com/object/smallBusinessFacts (accessed May 4, 2008); "Small Business Facts," National Telecommunications and Information Administration, http://www.ntia.doc.gov/opadhome/mtdpweb/sbfacts.htm (accessed May 4, 2008); and Mike Diegel, "Fast Facts: Why Small Business is Good for America," *NFIB*, April 18, 2008, http://www.nfib.com/object/ID363931.html (accessed May 13, 2008).)

a dramatic increase over his first year, which was $3.8 million. Jose now has 212 employees and has added a division installing curbs, gutters, and sidewalks.[7]

**Job Creation.**    The energy, creativity, and innovative abilities of small-business owners have resulted in jobs for many people. In fact, in the last decade, between 60 to 80 percent of net new jobs annually were created by small businesses.[8] Table 6.2 indicates that 99.7 percent of all businesses employ fewer than 500 people, and businesses employing 19 or fewer people account for 89 percent of all businesses.[9]

Many small businesses today are being started because of encouragement from larger ones. Many new jobs are also created by big-company/small-company alliances. Whether through formal joint ventures, supplier relationships, or product or marketing cooperative projects, the rewards of collaborative relationships are creating many jobs for small-business owners and their employees. Some publishing companies, for example, contract out almost all their editing and production to small businesses. Elm Street Publishing Services Inc. is a small editing house in Hinsdale, Illinois, which offers complete project management and production support to publishers of books and journals.

**Innovation.**    Perhaps one of the most significant strengths of small businesses is their ability to innovate and to bring significant benefits to customers. Small firms produce 55 percent of all innovations. Among the important 20th-century innovations by U.S. small firms are the airplane, the audio tape recorder, double-knit fabric, fiber-optic examining equipment, the heart valve, the optical scanner, the

*The overwhelming majority of U.S. firms are small businessess. Like this drycleaning business, many of them are family owned and operated.*

# Destination CEO
## Robert Johnson

Robert Johnson may not be a household name, but his accomplishments are widely known. He is the first African American billionaire, and the first black majority owner of a professional sports team; actually two teams. Who is Robert Johnson and how did he become so successful?

He was born in rural Mississippi to a very poor family. So poor in fact, that there are no photographs of his childhood. Not surprisingly, he was the first in his family to attend and graduate from college and the first to achieve outstanding financial success.

Johnson began his business career by using his modest savings and some financial backing to create the first cable television channel for the African American community, Black Entertainment Television (BET). Johnson founded the company, fostered its growth, and assured its long-term success. He then sold the channel to Viacom for $3.3 billion in 2001. He remained BET's CEO until recently.

After leaving BET, Johnson embarked on a new mission to achieve his primary goal: create wealth. His entrepreneurial spirit motivates him to pursue new challenges using, in his words, the same business model that led to BET's success. Today, Johnson is the majority owner of the third new NBA team, the Charlotte Bobcats, as well as the WNBA's Charlotte Sting. In addition, he has acquired a large block of Marriott and Hilton hotels under his minority holding company and has established equity and hedge funds primarily focused on underserved markets. That, in essence, is the foundation of his entrepreneurial business model: to fulfill needs in traditionally underserved minority markets, establish strategic partnerships, and work with financial institutions that are willing to invest in minority communities.

Most of Johnson's entrepreneurial ventures have common threads running through them: big money, big stars, and agents. While his goal is wealth creation, his ventures have uplifted the black community and demonstrates the progress that African American business owners have realized. For Johnson, successful entrepreneurship means doing well and doing good.

### Discussion Questions

1. How does Johnson's BET Channel exemplify innovation as an important entrepreneurial factor?
2. Potentially, what may be the most important disadvantage for an entrepreneur like Johnson?
3. What are the essential elements of Johnson's business plan or business model?

---

pacemaker, the personal computer, soft contact lenses, and the zipper. Paul Moller, an entrepreneur and inventor, is working on what may be one of the most important 21st-century innovations: a flying car. Although currently still in the testing phase, Moller's SkyCar may one day help commuters avoid congested freeways. The car is currently being tested at Stanford University, tethered to a large crane.[10]

The innovation of successful firms take many forms. Small businessman Ray Kroc found a new way to sell hamburgers and turned his ideas into one of the most successful fast-food franchises in the world—McDonald's. Small businesses have become an integral part of our lives. James Dyson's name is synonymous with high-quality vacuum cleaners. Today, his $1 billion company produces a bag-less vacuum cleaner that commands 25 percent of the U.S. market. However, it took a lot of work to achieve such success. Dyson developed 5,127 prototypes before he got the design and function

| Firm Size | Number of Firms | Percentage of All Firms |
|---|---|---|
| 0–19 employees | 5,150,316 | 89.3 |
| 20–99 employees | 515,056 | 8.9 |
| 100–499 employees | 84,829 | 1.5 |
| 500 or more employees | 16,926 | 0.3 |

**TABLE 6.2**

Number of Firms by Employment Size

Source: U.S. Census Bureau, "Statistics about Business Size (including small businesses) from the U.S. Census Bureau," www.census.gov/epcd/www/smallbus.html (accessed May 4, 2008).

right. He recently created a successful hand dryer and is working to develop other innovative appliances. Similarly, Bikram Choudhury's name is associated with yoga. Bikram Yoga uses a sequence of 26 signature poses, and the business has expanded to training courses, books, CDs, clothing, and numerous franchises. Choudhury is credited with popularizing yoga in the United States and with turning "his particular brand of yoga into the McDonald's of a $3 billion industry."[11] Entrepreneurs provide fresh ideas and usually have greater flexibility to change than do large companies.

## Industries That Attract Small Business

Small businesses are found in nearly every industry, but retailing and wholesaling, services, manufacturing, and high technology are especially attractive to entrepreneurs. These fields are relatively easy to enter and require low initial financing. Small-business owners in these industries also find it easier to focus on specific groups of consumers; new firms in these industries, initially suffer less from heavy competition, than do established firms.

Susan Brown, the inventor of the Boppy® pillow, has sold millions of this product online and in retail stores.

**Retailing and Wholesaling.**  Retailers acquire goods from producers or wholesalers and sell them to consumers. Main streets and shopping strips and malls are generally lined with independent music stores, sporting-goods shops, dry cleaners, boutiques, drugstores, restaurants, caterers, service stations, and hardware stores that sell directly to consumers. Retailing attracts entrepreneurs because gaining experience and exposure in retailing is relatively easy. Additionally, an entrepreneur opening a new retail store does not have to spend the large sums of money for the equipment and distribution systems that a manufacturing business requires. All that a new retailer needs is a lease on store space, merchandise, money to sustain the business, knowledge about prospective customers' needs and desires, and basic management and marketing skills. Some small retailers are also taking their businesses online. For example, Susan Brown invented a donut-shaped pillow with an opening in one side called the "Boppy." The product is sold online at **www. boppy.com,** and in Babies R Us and Pottery Barn Kids stores. Although approached by Wal-Mart, Brown declined the offer in a desire to keep a more upscale feel. The Boppy has annual sales around $50 million and was provided startup capital through a microloan of $25,000 from the Colorado Enterprise Fund (a nonprofit, community-development institution).[12] In 2007 it was the number-one baby product in the nation, according to *American Baby Magazine.*

Wholesalers supply products to industrial, retail, and institutional users for resale or for use in making other products. Wholesaling activities range from planning and negotiating for supplies, promoting, and distributing (warehousing and transporting) to providing management and merchandising assistance to clients. Wholesalers are extremely important for many products, especially consumer goods, because of the marketing activities they perform. Although it is true that wholesalers themselves can be eliminated, their functions must be passed on to some other organization such as the producer, or another intermediary, often a small business. Frequently, small businesses are closer to the final customers and know what it takes to keep them satisfied. Some smaller businesses start out manufacturing, but find their real niche as a supplier or distributor of larger firms' products.

**Services.**    The service sector includes businesses that do not actually produce tangible goods. It represents one of the fastest growing sectors in the United States, accounting for 66 percent of the economy and employing roughly 70 percent of the workforce.[13] Real-estate, insurance and personnel agencies, barbershops, banks, television and computer repair shops, copy centers, dry cleaners, and accounting firms are all service businesses. Services also attract individuals—such as beauticians, morticians, jewelers, doctors, and veterinarians—whose skills are not usually required by large firms. Many of these service providers are also retailers because they provide their services to ultimate consumers.

*Geek Squad employees vow to "fix any PC problem anytime, anywhere." The Geek Squad began as a one-man service firm in Minnesota in 1994. Founder Robert Stephens initially traveled by bicycle to and from service calls. Best Buy owns the firm today.*

**Manufacturing.**    Manufacturing goods can provide unique opportunities for small businesses. Started in 1988, the Malcolm Baldrige Award recognizes achievements in quality and performance in businesses of all sizes. It is designed to spur competitive business practices in American industry, but it has been rare for small businesses (with 500 or fewer employees) to win the award. However, the winner in the Small Business category in 2007 was Pro-Tec Coating Company in Leipsic, Ohio. Pro-Tec provides coated sheet metal to the automotive industry. Pro-Tec's product helps to improve vehicle crash worthiness and fuel economy through innovations in weight reduction.[14] Small businesses sometimes have an advantage over large firms because they can customize products to meet specific customer needs and wants. Such products include custom artwork, jewelry, clothing, and furniture.

**High Technology.**    *High technology* is a broad term used to describe businesses that depend heavily on advanced scientific and engineering knowledge. People who were able to innovate or identify new markets in the fields of computers, biotechnology, genetic engineering, robotics, and other markets have become today's high-tech giants. Mark Zuckerberg, the 24-year-old CEO of Facebook (a social networking Web site), for instance, has created a company that is one of the fastest growing dot-coms in history. With international expansion in 2007, the number of Web site visitors tripled. In early 2008, users spent 20 billion total minutes on the site versus 6.4 billion minutes the previous year. In 2007, Microsoft paid $240 million for 1.6 percent of Facebook, bringing its valuation to roughly $15 billion. The company continues to grow, and Zuckerberg has hired Google's Sheryl Sandberg as chief operating officer (COO) in order to "impose some corporate discipline on an undergraduate flip-flops-and-Red-Bull vibe." Other successful young entrepreneurs in high-tech companies include the founders of Google, MySpace, and Yahoo!.[15] In general, high-technology businesses require greater capital and have higher initial startup costs than do other small businesses. Many of the biggest, nonetheless, started out in garages, basements, kitchens, and dorm rooms.

> **Did You know?**  39 percent of high-tech jobs are in small businesses.[16]

## Advantages of Small-Business Ownership

There are many advantages to establishing and running a small business. These can be categorized into personal advantages and business advantages. Table 6.3 lists some of the traits that can help entrepreneurs succeed.

### Independence

Independence is probably one of the leading reasons that entrepreneurs choose to go into business for themselves. Being a small-business owner means being your own boss. Many people start their own businesses because they believe they will do better for themselves than they could do by remaining with their current employer or by changing jobs. They may feel stuck on the corporate ladder and that no business would take them seriously enough to fund their ideas. Sometimes people who venture forth to start their own small business are those who simply cannot work for someone else. Such people may say that they just do not fit the "corporate mold."

More often, small-business owners just want the freedom to choose whom they work with, the flexibility to pick where and when to work, and the option of working in a family setting. The availability of the computer, copy machine, business telephone, and fax machine has permitted many people to work at home. Only a few years ago, most of them would have needed the support that an office provides.

| TABLE 6.3 | |
| --- | --- |
| Traits Needed to Succeed in Entrepreneurship | Neuroticism—helps entrepreneurs focus on details |
| | Extroversion—facilitates network building |
| | Conscientiousness—facilitates planning |
| | Agreeableness—facilitates networking |
| | Openness to new ideas |

Source: Alex de Noble in Joshua Kurlantzick, "About Face," *Entrepreneur,* January 2004, www.entrepreneur.com/article/0,4621,312260,00.html (accessed May 19, 2008).

# Entrepreneurship in Action
## Cultivating Success: The Growth of Albaugh Inc.

Dennis Albaugh

**Business:** Albaugh, Inc.

**Founded:** 1979

**Success:** The largest wholly owned formulator/packager of pesticides in the country.

When Dennis Albaugh first entered the realm of entrepreneurial capitalism, he hit came up against many roadblocks. However, a willingness to take risks allowed him to persevere. Albaugh started out selling fertilizer and other chemicals for a cooperative. He then advanced to sales rep at Thompson Hayward, a crop chemical company. In 1979, after refusing to relocate for the company, Albaugh decided to start his own company at home in Joseph, Missouri. He invested $2,000 savings in the weed killer 2-4-D, manufactured by Helena Chemical. At the outset he had only a single customer, but his company grew with time. After selling 2-4-D for a number of years, Albaugh took out a $100,000 loan and purchased mixing tanks and pumps in order to manufacture the formula himself. Throughout the 1980s Albaugh continued to sell 2-4-D, even as new companies and products intensified the competitive atmosphere. In 1990, Albaugh jumped on the opportunity to purchase the factory of a competitor, Agrolinz, for $750,000. He did not have sufficient capital, but was able to raise the money through liquidation of inventory. Within a year, his sales more than doubled. In 1995, Albaugh began a battle to purchase Atanor, one of his major suppliers. Finally, in 1999, he achieved his goal of vertical integration through the purchase of a glyphosate factory. Glyphosate is the active ingredient found in Monsanto's pesticide Roundup, exclusive rights to which the company was scheduled to lose in 2000, after the patent expired. Today, glyphosate is a $3 billion market, and Albaugh Inc. is the second largest producer.[17]

## Costs

As already mentioned, small businesses often require less money to start and maintain than do large ones. Obviously, a firm with just 25 people in a small factory spends less money on wages and salaries, rent, utilities, and other expenses than does a firm employing tens of thousands of people in several large facilities. Rather than maintain the expense and staff of keeping separate departments for accounting, advertising, and legal counseling, small businesses often hire other firms (sometimes small businesses themselves) to supply these services as they are needed. Additionally, small-business owners can sometimes rely on friends and family members to help them save money by volunteering to work on a difficult project.

## Flexibility

With small size comes the flexibility to adapt to changing market demands. Small businesses usually have only one layer of management—the owners. Decisions therefore can be made and executed quickly. In larger firms, decisions about even routine matters can take weeks because they must pass through multiple levels of management before action is authorized. When McDonald's introduces a new product, for example, it must first research what consumers want, then develop the product and test it before introducing it nationwide—a process that sometimes takes years. An independent snack shop, however, can develop and introduce a new product (perhaps to meet a customer's request) in a much shorter time.

## Focus

Small firms can focus their efforts on a precisely defined market niche—that is, a specific group of customers. Many large corporations must compete in the mass market or for large market segments. Smaller firms can develop products for particular groups of customers or to satisfy a need that other companies have not addressed. For example, Fatheadz, based in Indianapolis, Indiana focuses on

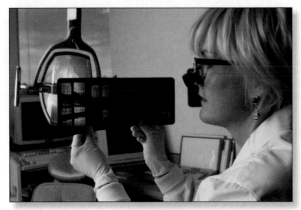

*Small-business owners, such as dentists, know that maintaining a high-quality reputation is essential to their success. Courtesy of localnewsonly.com.*

producing sunglasses for people with big heads. To be an official "fathead" you need a ball cap size of at least $7\frac{5}{8}$ and a head circumference above the ear of at least 23.5 inches. The idea arose when Rico Elmore was walking down the Las Vegas strip with his brother and realized that he had lost his sunglasses. He went to a nearby sunglass shop, and out of 300 pairs of glasses, he could not find one that fit. He decided to start a company addressing this need, and Fatheadz now distributes three of its designs in select Wal-Mart optical stores throughout the country.[18] By targeting small niches or product needs, small businesses can sometimes avoid competition from larger firms, helping them to grow into stronger companies.

### Reputation

Small firms, because of their capacity to focus on narrow niches, can develop enviable reputations for quality and service. A good example of a small business with a formidable reputation is W. Atlee Burpee and Co., which has the country's premier bulb and seed catalog. Burpee has an unqualified returns policy (complete satisfaction or your money back) that demonstrates a strong commitment to customer satisfaction.

## Disadvantages of Small-Business Ownership

The rewards associated with running a small business are so enticing that it's no wonder many people dream of it. However, as with any undertaking, small-business ownership has its disadvantages.

### High Stress Level

A small business is likely to provide a living for its owner, but not much more (although there are exceptions as some examples in this chapter have shown). There are ongoing worries about competition, employee problems, new equipment, expanding inventory, rent increases, or changing market demand. In addition to other stresses, small-business owners tend to be victims of physical and psychological stress. The small-business person is often the owner, manager, sales force, shipping and receiving clerk, bookkeeper, and custodian. Having to multitask can result in long hours for most small-business owners. Figure 6.1 demonstrates the major problems small businesses face. Many creative persons fail, not because of their business concepts, but rather because of difficulties in managing their business.

### High Failure Rate

Despite the importance of small businesses to our economy, there is no guarantee of success. Roughly 90 percent of all new businesses fail within the first five years.[19] Restaurants are a case in point. Look around your own neighborhood, and you can probably spot the locations of several restaurants that are no longer in business.

Small businesses fail for many reasons (see Table 6.4). A poor business concept—such as insecticides for garbage cans (research found that consumers are not concerned with insects in their garbage)—will produce disaster nearly every time. Expanding a hobby into a business may work if a genuine market niche exists, but

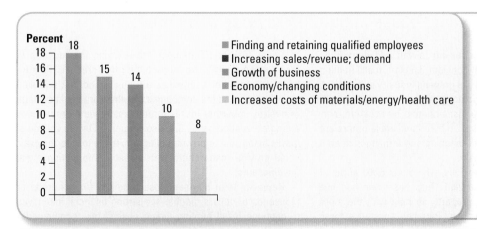

**FIGURE 6.1**

Top Five Biggest Challenges, Concerns, and Goals of Small and Medium Businesses

Source: "Entrepreneurial Challenges Survey Results," *Entrepreneur,* http://www.entrepreneur.com/encyclopedia/businessstatistics/article81812.html (accessed May 4, 2008).

all too often people start such a business without identifying a real need for the goods or services. Other notable causes of small-business failure include the burdens imposed by government regulation, insufficient funds to withstand slow sales, and vulnerability to competition from larger companies. However, three major causes of small-business failure deserve a close look: undercapitalization, managerial inexperience or incompetence, and inability to cope with growth; roughly 90 percent of small business failures can be attributed to these faults.[20]

**Undercapitalization.**   The shortest path to failure in business is **undercapitalization,** the lack of funds to operate a business normally. Too many entrepreneurs think that all they need is enough money to get started, that the business can survive

**undercapitalization**
the lack of funds to operate a business normally

- Failing to spend enough time researching the business idea to see if it's viable.
- Miscalculating market size, timing, ease of entry, and potential market share.
- Underestimating financial requirements and timing.
- Overprojecting sales volume and timing.
- Making cost projections that are too low.
- Hiring too many people and spending too much on offices and facilities.
- Lacking a contingency plan for a shortfall in expectations.
- Bringing in unnecessary partners.
- Hiring for convenience rather than skill requirements.
- Neglecting to manage the entire company as a whole.
- Accepting that it's "not possible" too easily rather than finding a way.
- Focusing too much on sales volume and company size rather than profit.
- Seeking confirmation of your actions rather than seeking the truth.
- Lacking simplicity in your vision.
- Lacking clarity of your long-term aim and business purpose.
- Lacking focus and identity.
- Lacking an exit strategy.

Source: John Osher, in Mark Henricks, "What Not to Do," *Entrepreneur,* February 2004, www.entrepreneur.com/article/0,4621,312661,00.html.

**TABLE 6.4**

Most Common Mistakes Made by Startup Businesses

# Consider Ethics and Social Responsibility
## Dinosaur Fossils Incite Controversy and Enterprise

Entrepreneurs are known for coming up with wild ideas. Even so, most probably would not consider dinosaur fossil hunting to be a viable venture. Yet it is a growing industry in the West, with ranchers and farmers, among others, entering the business. Some have fallen into fossil hunting by accident, perhaps stumbling across a fossil on their land, while others are purposely turning away from ranching and farming in search of a more lucrative career path.

One such farmer is Larry Tuss, who owns 6,000 acres of farmland in Montana. Since 2001, Tuss has unearthed five dinosaur skeletons on this property. To help with the more technical aspects of excavation, Tuss has enlisted a fossil company to help him clean and prepare the fossils for sale and has all but given up farming. With a Triceratops skull going for $250,000 and a T. rex skeleton selling for something in the range of $1 to 8 million, Tuss's land could yield him a lot of cash.

Another fossil hunter is rancher and rodeo rider Bucky Derflinger. In 1998, Derflinger discovered the skeleton of a juvenile Tyrannosaurus rex on his father's ranch. The skeleton is now part of an exhibit at the Children's Museum of Indianapolis. Derflinger made enough profit on the sale to finance a down payment on a 4,000-acre ranch. In the intervening years since that first discovery, Derflinger has located a number of other dinosaur fossils on the family's land. Although the fossils bring in a good income for Bucky and his father, they do not have plans to give up ranching.

While Tuss and Derflinger are enjoying the rewards of fossil hunting, some are infuriated by this practice. Paleontologists and other academics are concerned that unskilled fossil hunters and the companies that they hire could damage or destroy important fossils through inadequate precautions during excavations; they are also concerned by the volume of fossils being sold to private collectors; those fossils, they say, could provide researchers with valuable information about the dinosaurs.

However, with dinosaur fossils selling for hundreds or thousands of dollars, people see strong financial incentives to continue fossil hunting, going against the recommendations of researchers. Many are doubtful that scientists and profit-seeking fossil hunters will ever reach an agreement on what is best.[21]

### Discussion Questions
1. Why might ranchers continue their businesses as fossil hunters even after they have heard the reasons scientists have for being concerned about fossil hunting?
2. How could the fossil hunters gain more control over their businesses and more market share?
3. Could incentives ever be aligned enough so that fossil hunters and scientists both get what they want?

on cash generated from sales soon thereafter. But almost all businesses suffer from seasonal variations in sales, which make cash tight, and few businesses make money from the start. Many small rural operations cannot obtain financing within their own communities because small rural banks often lack the necessary financing expertise or assets sizable enough to counter the risks involved with small-business loans. Without sufficient funds, the best small-business idea in the world will fail.

**Managerial Inexperience or Incompetence.**  Poor management is the cause of many business failures. Just because an entrepreneur has a brilliant vision for a small business does not mean he or she has the knowledge or experience to manage a growing business effectively. A person who is good at creating great product ideas and marketing them may lack the skills and experience to make good management decisions in hiring, negotiating, finance, and control. Moreover, entrepreneurs may neglect those areas of management they know little about or find tedious, at the expense of the business's success.

**Inability to Cope with Growth.**  Sometimes, the very factors that are advantages for a small business turn into serious disadvantages when the time comes to grow. Growth often requires the owner to give up a certain amount of direct authority, and it is frequently hard for someone who has called all the shots to give up control. It has often been said that the greatest impediment to the success of a business is the entrepreneur. Similarly, growth requires specialized management skills in areas such as credit analysis and promotion—skills that the founder may lack or not have time to apply. The founders of many small businesses, including those of Gateway and Dell Computers, found that they needed to bring in more experienced managers to help manage their companies through growing pains.

Poorly managed growth probably affects a company's reputation more than anything else, at least initially. And products that do not arrive on time or goods that are poorly made can quickly reverse a success. The principle immediate threats to small and mid-sized businesses include rising inflation, collapse of the dollar's value, energy and other supply shortages, excessive household and/or corporate debt, and the growing federal deficit.[22]

# Starting a Small Business

We've told you how important small businesses are, and why they succeed and fail, but *how do you go about* starting your own business in the first place? To start any business, large or small, you must have some kind of general idea. Sam Walton, founder of Wal-Mart stores, had a vision of a discount retailing enterprise that spawned the world's largest retailing empire and changed the way companies look at business. Next, you need to devise a strategy to guide planning and development in the business. Finally, you must make decisions about form of ownership, the financial resources needed, and whether to acquire an existing business, start a new one, or buy a franchise.

### The Business Plan

A key element of business success is a **business plan**—a precise statement of the rationale for the business and a step-by-step explanation of how it will achieve its goals. The business plan should include an explanation of the business, an analysis of the competition, estimates of income and expenses, and other information. It should also establish a strategy for acquiring sufficient funds to keep the business going. Many financial institutions decide whether to loan a small business money based on its business plan. A good business plan should act as a guide and reference document—not a shackle that limits the business's flexibility and decision making ability. The business plan must be revised periodically to ensure that the firm's goals and strategies adapt to changes in the environment. Ben and Matthew Freund, who grew up on their father's dairy farm in Connecticut, developed an innovative way to deal with their abundance of cow manure. They created a digestion and dehydration process to eliminate the odor and to form the product into CowPots, which can be buried in the ground to fertilize plants. CowPots will last for months above ground but begin to degrade when planted. Business plans allow for companies such as Ben and Matthew's to assess market potential, determine price, manufacturing possibilities and requirements, identify optimal distribution channels, and brand the products. The U.S. Department of Agriculture's Cooperative State Research, Education, and Extension Service funded this project.[23] The Small Business Administration Web site provides an overview of a plan for small businesses to use to gain financing. Appendix B presents a comprehensive business plan.

**business plan**
a precise statement of the rationale for a business and a step-by-step explanation of how it will achieve its goals

### Forms of Business Ownership

After developing a business plan, the entrepreneur has to decide on an appropriate legal form of business ownership—whether it is best to operate as a sole proprietorship, partnership, or corporation—and to examine the many factors that affect that decision, which we explored in Chapter 5.

## Financial Resources

The old adage "it takes money to make money" holds especially true in developing a business enterprise. To make money from a small business, the owner must first provide or obtain money (capital) to get started and to keep it running smoothly. Even a small retail store will probably need at least $50,000 in initial financing to rent space, purchase or lease necessary equipment and furnishings, buy the initial inventory, and provide working capital. Often, the small-business owner has to put up a significant percentage of the necessary capital. Few new business owners have a large amount of their own capital and must look to other sources for additional financing.

**Equity Financing.**   The most important source of funds for any new business is the owner. Many owners include among their personal resources ownership of a home, the accumulated value in a life-insurance policy, or a savings account. A new business owner may sell or borrow against the value of such assets to obtain funds to operate a business. Additionally, the owner may bring useful personal assets—such as a computer, desks and other furniture, a car or truck—as part of his or her ownership interest in the firm. Such financing is referred to as *equity financing* because the owner uses real personal assets rather than borrowing funds from outside sources to get started in a new business. The owner can also provide working capital by reinvesting profits into the business or simply by not drawing a full salary.

Small businesses can also obtain equity financing by finding investors for their operations. They may sell stock in the business to family members, friends, employees, or other investors. When Tony Volk developed the pop-up turkey timer, he probably had no idea that he would one day sell around $100 million and be the only maker of the small, plastic gadget that pops out of the turkey at 180 degrees. The Volk pop-ups are embedded in 30 million of the 46 million turkeys consumed for Thanksgiving. To support the company's early growth, Tony had to convince his brother Henry to quit his job as an auditor and join the company. For more than 40 years, this family-run business has been a leader in innovative packaging and products.[24] **Venture capitalists** are persons or organizations that agree to provide some funds for a new business in exchange for an ownership interest or stock. Venture capitalists hope to purchase the stock of a small business at a low price and then sell the stock for a profit after the business has grown successful. The renewable energy industry has recently become a popular investment option among venture capitalists, whose funding for "cleantech," or renewable energy technology, increased 70 percent in 2007. Cleantech represented almost 10 percent of all venture capital funding, with most of the money going to solar companies.[25] Although these forms of equity financing have helped many small businesses, they require that the small-business owner share the profits of the business—and sometimes control, as well—with the investors.

**venture capitalists** persons or organizations that agree to provide some funds for a new business in exchange for an ownership interest or stock

**Debt Financing.**   New businesses sometimes borrow more than half of their financial resources. Banks are the main suppliers of external financing to small businesses. On the federal level, the Small Business Administration offers financial assistance to qualifying businesses. More detail on the SBA's loan programs can be found at the SBA Web site. They can also look to family and friends as sources for long-term loans or other assets, such as computers or an automobile, that are exchanged for an ownership interest in a business. In such cases, the business owner can usually structure a favorable repayment schedule and sometimes negotiate an interest rate below current bank rates. If the business goes bad, however, the emotional losses for all concerned may greatly exceed the money involved. Anyone lending a friend or family member money for a venture should state the agreement clearly in writing before any money changes hands.

The amount a bank or other institution is willing to loan depends on its assessment of the venture's likelihood of success and of the entrepreneur's ability to repay the loan. The bank will often require the entrepreneur to put up *collateral,* a financial interest in the property or fixtures of the business, to guarantee payment of the debt. Additionally, the small-business owner may have to provide personal property as collateral, such as his or her home, in which case the loan is called a *mortgage.* If the small business fails to repay the loan, the lending institution may eventually claim and sell the collateral or mortgage to recover its loss.

Banks and other financial institutions can also grant a small business a *line of credit*—an agreement by which a financial institution promises to lend a business a predetermined sum on demand. A line of credit permits an entrepreneur to take quick advantage of opportunities that require a bank loan. Small businesses may obtain funding from their suppliers in the form of a *trade credit*—that is, suppliers allow the business to take possession of the needed goods and services and pay for them at a later date or in installments. Occasionally, small businesses engage in *bartering*—trading their own products for the goods and services offered by other businesses. For example, an accountant may offer accounting services to an office supply firm in exchange for computer paper and disks.

Additionally, some community groups sponsor loan funds to encourage the development of particular types of businesses. State and local agencies may guarantee loans, especially to minority business people or for development in certain areas.

## Approaches to Starting a Small Business

**Starting from Scratch versus Buying an Existing Business.**   Although entrepreneurs often start new small businesses from scratch much the way we have discussed in this section, they may elect instead to buy an existing business. This has the advantage of providing a built-in network of customers, suppliers, and distributors and reducing some of the guesswork inherent in starting a new business from scratch. However, an entrepreneur who buys an existing business also takes on any problems the business already has.

**Franchising.**   Many small-business owners find entry into the business world through franchising. A license to sell another's products or to use another's name in business, or both, is a **franchise.** The company that sells a franchise is the **franchiser.** Dunkin' Donuts, McDonald's, and Jiffy Lube are well-known franchisers with national visibility. The purchaser of a franchise is called a **franchisee.**

The franchisee acquires the rights to a name, logo, methods of operation, national advertising, products, and other elements associated with the franchiser's business in return for a financial commitment and the agreement to conduct business in accordance with the franchiser's standard of operations. The initial fee to join a franchise varies greatly. In addition, franchisees buy equipment, pay for training, and obtain a mortgage or lease. The franchisee also pays the franchiser a monthly or annual fee based on a percentage of sales or profits. In return, the franchisee often receives building specifications and designs, site recommendations, management and accounting support, and perhaps most importantly, immediate name recognition. Visit the Web site of the International Franchise Association to learn more on this topic.

The practice of franchising first began in the United States in the 19th century when Singer used it to sell sewing machines. The method of goods distribution soon became commonplace in the automobile, gasoline, soft drink, and hotel industries. The concept of franchising grew especially rapidly during the 1960s, when it

**franchise**
a license to sell another's products or to use another's name in business, or both

**franchiser**
the company that sells a franchise

**franchisee**
the purchaser of a franchise

expanded to diverse industries. Table 6.5 shows the 10 fastest growing franchises and the top 10 new franchises.

The entrepreneur will find that franchising has both advantages and disadvantages. Franchising allows a franchisee the opportunity to set up a small business relatively quickly, and because of its association with an established brand, a franchise outlet often reaches the breakeven point faster than an independent business would. Franchisees commonly report the following advantages:

- Management training and support.
- Brand-name appeal.
- Standardized quality of goods and services.
- National advertising programs.
- Financial assistance.
- Proven products and business formats.
- Centralized buying power.
- Site selection and territorial protection.
- Greater chance for success.[26]

However, the franchisee must sacrifice some freedom to the franchiser. Some shortcomings experienced by franchisees include:

- Franchise fees and profit sharing with the franchiser.
- Strict adherence to standardized operations.
- Restrictions on purchasing.
- Limited product line.
- Possible market saturation.
- Less freedom in business decisions.[27]

Strict uniformity is the rule rather than the exception. Entrepreneurs who want to be their own bosses are often frustrated with a franchise.

## Help for Small-Business Managers

Because of the crucial role that small business and entrepreneurs play in the U.S. economy, a number of organizations offer programs to improve the small-business

**TABLE 6.5**

Fastest Growing and Hottest New Franchises

| Top 10 Fastest-Growing Franchises | Top 10 New Franchises |
|---|---|
| 1. Jan-Pro Franchising International Inc. | Instant Tax Service |
| 2. 7-Eleven Inc. | Message Envy |
| 3. Subway | Snap Fitness Inc. |
| 4. Jani-King | System4 |
| 5. Dunkin' Donuts | One Hour Air Conditioning & Heating |
| 6. Jackson Hewitt Tax Service | Super Suppers |
| 7. Bonus Building Care | Mathnasium Learning Centers |
| 8. Instant Tax Service | The Growth Coach |
| 9. Liberty Tax Service | Play N Trade Franchise Inc. |
| 10. RE/Max International Inc. | N-Hance |

Sources: "Fastest-Growing Franchises, 2008 Rankings," *Entrepreneur,* http://www.entrepreneur.com/franzone/fastestgrowing/ (accessed May 4, 2008); "Top New Franchises, 2008 Rankings," *Entrepreneur,* http://www.entrepreneur.com/franchises/topnew/ (accessed May 4, 2008).

## Going Green
### Would You Buy a Recycled Toothbrush?

Many eco-responsible entrepreneurial companies are investigating the viability of new products that utilize recycling in some way. Eric Hudson, founder of Recycline, has even developed a toothbrush made out of recycled materials. The company makes a line of toothbrushes, tongue cleaners, and razors called "Preserve." In 2006, *Inc.* magazine recognized the company in its list of the top 50 sustainable businesses. Recycline already has sales deals with Target, Whole Foods, and Stop & Shop; and increased publicity helped sales jump 45 percent between 2005–2006.

Hudson also sends samples of his products to movie companies in hopes of enhancing the profile of the Preserve line. In 2006, he had the pleasure of discovering that Will Ferrell's character in the movie *Stranger Than Fiction* would be using a Recycline toothbrush. The company was able to leverage its increased visibility with promotional efforts at Target stores. Articles in newspapers, trade publications, and the movie itself helped promote the product. The company even offered free toothbrushes and movie tickets to volunteers who passed out postcards that read: "Meet Harold Crick's toothbrush."

The cards directed moviegoers to visit a Target store in order to buy the product.

To make its toothbrushes and the handles of its razors, Recycline has developed a sustainable partnership with Stonyfield Farm. Recycline creates the plastic components of its products out of Stonyfield's waste yogurt containers. Many believe that this type of system, wherein one company's waste is another's raw materials is the way of the future. Recycline has also launched a line of kitchen products, which it has introduced in Whole Foods Markets. The company hopes that it will become the brand that environmentally conscious consumers turn to for high-quality, innovative, and stylish personal care products.[28]

### Discussion Questions
1. What are the advantages for Recycline in partnering with Stonyfield Farm?
2. List some additional ways that Hudson could market his recycled-plastic toothbrushes and shavers.
3. How will the company have to change as it grows larger?

owner's ability to compete. These include entrepreneurial training programs and programs sponsored by the Small Business Administration. Such programs provide small-business owners with invaluable assistance in managing their businesses, often at little or no cost to the owner.

Entrepreneurs can learn critical marketing, management, and finance skills in seminars and college courses. In addition, knowledge, experience, and judgment are necessary for success in a new business. While knowledge can be communicated and some experiences can be simulated in the classroom, good judgment must be developed by the entrepreneur. Local chambers of commerce and the U.S. Department of Commerce offer information and assistance helpful in operating a small business. National publications such as *Inc.* and *Entrepreneur* share statistics, advice, tips, and success/failure stories. Additionally, many urban areas—including Chicago, Illinois; Jacksonville, Florida; Portland, Oregon; St. Louis, Missouri, and Nashville, Tennessee—have weekly business journal/newspapers that provide stories on local businesses as well as on business techniques that a manager or small business can use.

The Small Business Administration offers many types of management assistance to small businesses, including counseling for firms in difficulty, consulting on improving operations, and training for owner/managers and their employees. Among its many programs, the SBA funds Small Business Development Centers (SBDCs). These are business clinics, usually located on college campuses, that provide counseling at no charge and training at only a nominal charge. SBDCs are often the SBA's principal means of providing direct management assistance.

The Service Corps of Retired Executives (SCORE) and the Active Corps of Executives (ACE) are volunteer agencies funded by the SBA to provide advice for owners of small firms. Both are staffed by experienced managers whose talents and experience the small firms could not ordinarily afford. SCORE has 10,500 volunteers at nearly 400 locations in the United States and has served 7.9 million small businesses since 1964.[29] The SBA also has organized Small Business Institutes (SBIs) on almost 500 university and college campuses in the United States. Seniors, graduate students, and faculty at each SBI provide on-site management counseling.

Finally, the small-business owner can obtain advice from other small-business owners, suppliers, and even customers. A customer may approach a small business it frequents with a request for a new product, for example, or a supplier may offer suggestions for improving a manufacturing process. Networking—building relationships and sharing information with colleagues—is vital for any businessperson, whether you work for a huge corporation or run your own small business. Communicating with other business owners is a great way to find ideas for dealing with employees and government regulation, improving processes, or solving problems. New technology is making it easier to network. For example, some states are establishing computer bulletin boards for the use of their businesses to network and share ideas.

# The Future for Small Business[30]

Although small businesses are crucial to the economy, their size and limited resources can make them more vulnerable to turbulence and change in the marketplace than large businesses. Next, we take a brief look at the demographic, technological, and economic trends that will have the most impact on small business in the future.

## Demographic Trends

America's baby boom started in 1946 and ended in 1964. The earliest boomers are already past 50, and in the next few years, millions more will pass that mark. The boomer generation numbers about 76 million, or 28 percent of U.S. citizens.[31] Table 6.6 shows some prominent baby boomers. This segment of the population is wealthy, but many small businesses do not actively pursue it. Some exceptions, however, include Gold Violin, which sells designer canes and other products online and through a catalog, and LifeSpring, which delivers nutritional meals and snacks directly to the customer. Industries such as travel, financial planning, and health care will continue to grow as boomers age. Many experts believe that the boomer demographic is the market of the future.

Another market with huge potential for small business is the echo boomers, also called millennials or Generation Y. Millennials number around 75 million and possess a number of unique characteristics. Born between 1977 and 1994, this cohort is not solely concerned about money. Those that fall into this group are also concerned with advancement, recognition, and improved capabilities. They need direct, timely feedback and frequent encouragement and recognition. Millennials do well when training sessions combine entertainment with learning. Working remotely is more acceptable to this group than previous generations, and virtual communication may become as important as face-to-face meetings.[32]

Yet another trend is the growing number of immigrants living in the United States, who now represent about one-eighth, or 12 percent of the population. If this trend continues, by 2050 nearly one in five Americans will be classified as immigrants. The Latino population, the nation's largest minority group, is expected to triple in size by 2050.[33]

This vast group provides still another greatly untapped market for small businesses. Retailers who specialize in ethnic products, and service providers who offer bi- or multilingual employees, will find a large amount of business potential in this market. Table 6.7 ranks top cities in the United States for entrepreneurs.

| | TABLE 6.6 |
|---|---|
| Cher | Entertainers |
| Sylvester Stallone | Who Are Baby Boomers |
| Oliver Stone | |
| Steven Spielburg | |
| Jimmy Buffet | |
| Suzanne Somers | |
| Howard Stern | |
| Ron Howard | |
| Katie Couric | |
| Bono | |
| Val Kilmer | |
| Kevin Spacey | |
| Rob Lowe | |
| Heather Locklear | |
| David Bowie | |
| David Letterman | |
| O.J. Simpson | |
| Michael Jackson | |

## Technological and Economic Trends

Advances in technology have opened up many new markets to small businesses. Although thousands of small dot-coms have failed, experts predict that Internet usage will continue to increase. One of the hot areas will be Internet infrastructure, which enables companies to improve communications with employees, suppliers, and customers.

Technological advances and an increase in service exports have created new opportunities for small companies to expand their operations abroad. Changes in communications and technology can allow small companies to customize their services quickly for international customers. Also, free trade agreements and trade alliances are helping to create an environment in which small businesses have fewer regulatory and legal barriers.

In recent years, economic turbulence has provided both opportunities and threats for small businesses. As large information technology companies such as Cisco, Oracle, and Sun Microsystems had to recover from an economic slowdown and an oversupply of Internet infrastructure products, some smaller firms found new niche markets. Smaller companies can react quickly to change and can stay close to their customers. While well-funded dot-coms were failing, many small businesses were learning how to use the Internet to promote themselves and sell products online. For example, arts and crafts dealers and makers of specialty products found they could sell their wares on existing Web sites, such as eBay. Service providers related to tourism, real estate, and construction also found they could reach customers through their own or existing Web sites.

Deregulation of the energy market and interest in alternative fuels and in fuel conservation have spawned many small businesses. Earth First Technologies Inc. produces clean-burning fuel from contaminated water or sewage. Southwest Wind-power Inc. manufactures and markets small wind turbines for producing electric

| TABLE 6.7 | | |
|---|---|---|
| Top U.S. Cities for Entrepreneurs (Large Cities) | 1 | Phoenix–Mesa, AZ |
| | 2 | Charlotte–Gastonia–Rock Hill, NC/SC |
| | 3 | Raleigh–Durham–Chapel Hill, NC |
| | 4 | Las Vegas, NV/AZ |
| | 5 | Austin–San Marcos, TX |
| | 6 | Washington–Baltimore, DC/MD/VA/WV |
| | 7 | Memphis, TN–AR–MS |
| | 8 | Nashville, TN |
| | 9 | Norfolk–Virginia Beach-Newport News, VA/NC |
| | 10 | San Antonio, TX |

Source: "Hot Cities for Entrepreneurs," *Entrepreneur.com,* http://www.entrepreneur.com/bestcities (accessed May 4, 2008).

power for homes, sailboats, and telecommunications. Solar Attic Inc. has developed a process to recover heat from home attics to use in heating water or swimming pools. As entrepreneurs begin to realize that worldwide energy markets are valued in the hundreds of billions of dollars, the number of innovative companies entering this market will increase. In addition, many small businesses have the desire and employee commitment to purchase such environmentally friendly products. New Belgium Brewing Company received the U.S. Environmental Protection Agency and Department of Energy Award for leadership in conservation for making a 10-year commitment to purchase wind energy. The company's employees unanimously agreed to cover the increased costs of wind-generated electricity from the employee profit-sharing program.

The future for small business remains promising. The opportunities to apply creativity and entrepreneurship to serve customers are unlimited. While large organizations such as Wal-Mart, which has more than 1.8 million employees, typically must adapt to change slowly, a small business can adapt immediately to customer and community needs and changing trends. This flexibility provides small businesses with a definite advantage over large companies.

## Making Big Businesses Act "Small"

The continuing success and competitiveness of small businesses through rapidly changing conditions in the business world have led many large corporations to take a closer look at what makes their smaller rivals tick. More and more firms are emulating small businesses in an effort to improve their own bottom line. Beginning in the 1980s and continuing through the present, the buzzword in business has been to *downsize,* or *right-size* to reduce management layers, corporate staff, and work tasks in order to make the firm more flexible, resourceful, and innovative. Many well-known U.S. companies, including IBM, Ford, Apple Computer, General Electric, Xerox, and 3M, have downsized to improve their competitiveness, as have German, British, and Japanese firms. Other firms have sought to make their businesses "smaller" by making their operating units function more like independent small businesses, each responsible for its profits, losses, and resources. Of course, some large corporations, such as Southwest Airlines, have acted like small businesses from their inception, with great success.

Trying to capitalize on small-business success in introducing innovative new products, more and more companies are attempting to instill a spirit of entrepreneurship into even the largest firms. In major corporations, **intrapreneurs,** like entrepreneurs, take responsibility for, or "champion," the development of innovations of any kind *within* the larger organization.[34] Often, they use company resources and time to develop a new product for the company.

**intrapreneurs** individuals in large firms who take responsibility for the development of innovations within the organizations

# So You Want to be an Entrepreneur or Small Business Owner

In times when jobs are scarce many people turn to entrepreneurship as a way to find employment. As long as there continue to be new niches and unfulfilled needs from consumers there will be a demand for entrepreneurs and small businesses. Entrepreneurs and small business owners have, and will continue to be, a vital part of the U.S. economy; whether in retailing, wholesaling, manufacturing, technology, or even services. There are a lot of advantages to forming a business around your idea. Independence is perhaps the biggest one for a lot of people—especially those who do not work well in a corporate setting and like to call their own shots. Smaller businesses are also clearly cheaper to start up than large ones—in terms of salaries that must be paid, infrastructure, and equipment. Smallness also gives you a lot of flexibility to change with the times. If consumers suddenly start demanding new and different products or services, a small business is more likely to deliver quickly.

Starting your own business is not easy, however—especially in slow economic times. Even in good times, taking an idea and turning it into a business has a very high failure rate. This can be even worse when money is tight. Reduced revenues and expensive materials can hurt a small business more than a large one because it has fewer resources to begin with. When people are feeling the pinch from rising food and fuel prices they tend to cut back on other expenditures—potentially harming your small business or entrepreneurship. Increased costs of materials will also cut into your bottom line. There are a number of things you can do to help keep your company afloat, however.

- First of all, set clear payment schedules for all clients. Small businesses tend to be worse about collecting payments than large ones, especially if the clients are acquaintances. However, you need to keep cash flowing into the company in order to keep business going.

- Take the time to learn about tax breaks. A lot of people do not realize all of the deductions they can claim on items such as equipment and health insurance, among others.

- Focus on the customers you have, not spending a lot of time looking for new ones—this idea plays into relationship management. It is far less expensive for a company to keep their existing customers happy than it is attract new ones.

- Although entrepreneurs and small business owners are more likely to be friends with their customers, do not let this be a temptation to give things away for free. Make it clear to your customers what the basic price is for what you are selling, charge for extra features, extra service, etc.

- Make sure the office has the conveniences employees need—like a good coffee maker and other drinks and snacks. This will help keep employees happy, but it will also help keep productivity up by keeping employees closer to their desks.

- A really important consideration is how a manager/owner's actions set an example. If money is tight, show your commitment to cutting costs and making the business work by doing simple things like taking the bus to work or bringing a sack lunch (in a cheap, reusable bag) every day.

- Don't be so focused on cost cutting that you don't try to increase sales while keeping costs the same. Do not forget to increase productivity—do not only look at cutting costs.

In unsure economic times, these measures should help new entrepreneurs and small business owners sustain their businesses. Learning how to run a business on a shoestring is a great way to cut the fat and to establish lean, efficient operations.[35]

# Review Your Understanding

### *Define* entrepreneurship *and* small business.

An entrepreneur is a person who creates a business or product and manages his or her resources and takes risks to gain a profit; entrepreneurship is the process of creating and managing a business to achieve desired objectives. A small business is one that is not dominant in its competitive area and does not employ more than 500 people.

### *Investigate the importance of small business in the U.S. economy and why certain fields attract small business.*

Small businesses are vital to the American economy because they provide products, jobs, innovation, and opportunities. Retailing, wholesaling, services, manufacturing, and high technology attract small businesses because these industries are relatively easy to enter, require relatively low initial financing, and may experience less heavy competition.

### *Specify the advantages of small-business ownership.*

Small-business ownership offers some personal advantages, including independence, freedom of choice, and the option of working at home. Business advantages include flexibility, the ability to focus on a few key customers, and the chance to develop a reputation for quality and service.

### *Summarize the disadvantages of small-business ownership, and analyze why many small businesses fail.*

Small businesses have many disadvantages for their owners such as expense, physical and psychological stress, and a high failure rate. Small businesses fail for many reasons: undercapitalization, management inexperience or incompetence, neglect, disproportionate burdens imposed by government regulation, and vulnerability to competition from larger companies.

### *Describe how you go about starting a small business and what resources are needed.*

First, you must have an idea for developing a small business. Next, you need to devise a business plan to guide planning and development of the business. Then you must decide what form of business ownership to use: sole proprietorship, partnership, or corporation. Small-business owners are expected to provide some of the funds required to start their businesses, but funds also can be obtained from friends and family, financial institutions, other businesses in the form of trade credit, investors (venture capitalists), state and local organizations, and the Small Business Administration. In addition to loans, the Small Business Administration and other organizations offer counseling, consulting, and training services. Finally, you must decide whether to start a new business from scratch, buy an existing one, or buy a franchise operation.

### *Evaluate the demographic, technological, and economic trends that are affecting the future of small business.*

Changing demographic trends that represent areas of opportunity for small businesses include more elderly people as baby boomers age, a large group in the 11 to 28 age range known as echo boomers, millennials, or Generation Y, and an increasing number of immigrants to the United States. Technological advances and an increase in service exports have created new opportunities for small companies to expand their operations abroad, while trade agreements and alliances have created an environment in which small business has fewer regulatory and legal barriers. Economic turbulence presents both opportunities and threats to the survival of small businesses.

### *Explain why many large businesses are trying to "think small."*

More large companies are copying small businesses in an effort to make their firms more flexible, resourceful, and innovative, and generally to improve their bottom line. This effort often involves downsizing (reducing management layers, laying off employees, and reducing work tasks) and intrapreneurship, where an employee takes responsibility for (champions) developing innovations of any kind within the larger organization.

### *Assess two entrepreneurs' plans for starting a small business.*

Based on the facts given in "Solve the Dilemma" on page 196 and the material presented in this chapter, you should be able to assess the feasibility and potential success of Gray and McVay's idea for starting a small business.

# Revisit the World of Business

1. Based on the information given, what type of business organization do you think Cato Corner Farm uses?

2. Do you think Cato Corner competes with big cheese companies like Kraft or Sargento?

3. What is Cato Corner's target market?

## Learn the Terms

business plan   185

entrepreneurship   174

franchise   187

franchisee   187

franchiser   187

intrapreneurs   193

small business   175

Small Business Administration
    (SBA)   175

undercapitalization   183

venture capitalists   186

## Check Your Progress

1. Why are small businesses so important to the U.S. economy?

2. Which fields tend to attract entrepreneurs the most? Why?

3. What are the advantages of starting a small business? The disadvantages?

4. What are the principal reasons for the high failure rate among small businesses?

5. What decisions must an entrepreneur make when starting a small business?

6. What types of financing do small entrepreneurs typically use? What are some of the pros and cons of each?

7. List the types of management and financial assistance that the Small Business Administration offers.

8. Describe the franchising relationship.

9. What demographic, technological, and economic trends are influencing the future of small business?

10. Why do large corporations want to become more like small businesses?

## Get Involved

1. Interview a local small-business owner. Why did he or she start the business? What factors have led to the business's success? What problems has the owner experienced? What advice would he or she offer a potential entrepreneur?

2. Using business journals, find an example of a company that is trying to emulate the factors that make small businesses flexible and more responsive.

Describe and evaluate the company's activities. Have they been successful? Why or why not?

3. Using the business plan outline in Appendix B, create a business plan for a business idea that you have. (A man named Fred Smith once did a similar project for a business class at Yale. His paper became the basis for the business he later founded: Federal Express!)

## Build Your Skills

**CREATIVITY**

**Background:**
The entrepreneurial success stories in this chapter are about people who used their creative abilities to develop innovative products or ways of doing something that became the basis of a new business. Of course, being creative is not just for entrepreneurs or inventors; creativity is an important tool to help you find the optimal solutions to the problems you face on a daily basis. Employees rely heavily on their creativity skills to help them solve daily workplace problems.

According to brain experts, the right-brain hemisphere is the source of creative thinking; and the creative part of the brain can "atrophy" from lack of use. Let's see how much "exercise" you're giving your right-brain hemisphere.

**Task:**

1. Take the following self-test to check your Creativity Quotient.[36]

2. Write the appropriate number in the box next to each statement according to whether the statement describes your behavior always (3), sometimes (2), once in a while (1), or never (0).

| | Always 3 | Sometimes 2 | Once in a While 1 | Never 0 |
|---|---|---|---|---|
| 1. I am a curious person who is interested in other people's opinions. | | | | |
| 2. I look for opportunities to solve problems. | | | | |
| 3. I respond to changes in my life creatively by using them to redefine my goals and revising plans to reach them. | | | | |
| 4. I am willing to develop and experiment with ideas of my own. | | | | |
| 5. I rely on my hunches and insights. | | | | |
| 6. I can reduce complex decisions to a few simple questions by seeing the "big picture." | | | | |
| 7. I am good at promoting and gathering support for my ideas. | | | | |
| 8. I think further ahead than most people I associate with by thinking long term and sharing my vision with others. | | | | |
| 9. I dig out research and information to support my ideas. | | | | |
| 10. I am supportive of the creative ideas from my peers and subordinates and welcome "better ideas" from others. | | | | |
| 11. I read books and magazine articles to stay on the "cutting edge" in my areas of interest. I am fascinated by the future. | | | | |
| 12. I believe I am creative and have faith in my good ideas. | | | | |
| Subtotal for each column | | | | |
| Grand Total | | | | |

3. Check your score using the following scale:

30–36   High creativity. You are giving your right-brain hemisphere a regular workout.

20–29   Average creativity. You could use your creativity capacity more regularly to ensure against "creativity atrophy."

10–19   Low creativity. You could benefit by reviewing the questions you answered "never" in the above assessment and selecting one or two of the behaviors that you could start practicing.

0–9     Undiscovered creativity. You have yet to uncover your creative potential.

# Solve the Dilemma

**The Small-Business Challenge**

Jack Gray and his best friend, Bruce McVay, decided to start their own small business. Jack had developed recipes for fat-free and low-fat cookies and muffins in an effort to satisfy his personal health needs. Bruce had extensive experience in managing food-service establishments. They knew that a startup company needs a quality product, adequate funds, a written business plan, some outside financial support, and a good promotion program. Jack and Bruce felt they had all of this and more and were ready to embark on their new low-fat cookie/muffin store. Each had $35,000 to invest and with their homes and other resources they had borrowing power of an additional $125,000.

However, they still have many decisions to make, including what form or organization to use, how to market their product, and how to determine exactly what products to sell—whether just cookies and muffins or additional products.

**Discussion Questions**

1. Evaluate the idea of a low-fat cookie and muffin retail store.

2. Are there any concerns in connection with starting a small business that Jack and Bruce have not considered?

3. What advice would you give Jack and Bruce as they start up their business?

# Build Your Business Plan

## SMALL BUSINESS, ENTREPRENEURSHIP, AND FRANCHISING

Now you can get started writing your business plan! Refer to Guidelines for the Development of the Business Plan following Chapter 1, which provides you with an outline for your business plan. As you are developing your business plan keep in mind that potential investors might be reviewing it. Or you might have plans to go to your local Small Business Development Center for an SBA loan.

At this point in the process you should think about collecting information from a variety of (free) resources. For example, if you are developing a business plan for a local business, product or service you might want to check out any of the following sources for demographic information: your local Chamber of Commerce, Economic Development Office, Census Bureau, or City Planning Office.

Go on the Internet and see if there have been any recent studies done or articles on your specific type of business, especially in your area. Remember, you always want to explore any secondary data before trying to conduct your own research.

# See for Yourself Videocase

## NOT JUST TUPPERWARE OR AVON ANYMORE

The Direct Selling Association (DSA) defines *direct selling* as "the sale of a consumer product or service person-to-person, away from a fixed retail location." Independent distributors (also known as representatives, consultants, and other terms) generally sell products and services via home shows, parties, and one-on-one meetings. In 2007, direct selling sales reached $30.8 billion—up almost $8 billion from 1997. The same year, the DSA states, there were 15 million individuals working through direct sales.

Direct selling appeals to individuals for a number of reasons. Many are looking for part-time income, flexible hours, and the ability to be one's own boss. Recent statistics state that 75 percent of those involved in direct selling are women and that 74 percent of Americans have made at least one purchase through direct selling. The DSA breaks down the direct selling market into the following categories: clothing and jewelry, 33.7 percent; home/family care and home durables, 26.7 percent; wellness, 20.3 percent; services and other, 15.1 percent; and leisure or educational, 4.2 percent.

Doncaster falls into the first category of clothing and jewelry. Originally founded in 1931 as Doncaster Collar and Shirt Company, today it retails high-end women's clothing via direct selling. In 1935, the Junior League of Charlotte, North Carolina, suggested selling shirtwaist dresses (a popular style at the time) from Doncaster as a way to raise Junior League funds. The idea was successful and inspired the founders of Doncaster; they soon launched their own direct selling program. The first saleswomen were members of the Junior League. They were part of a large social network, and word spread quickly. In the 1950s, the personal service offered through in-home shopping jumped in popularity. Doncaster began focusing on selling high-quality women's fashions through "Wardrobe Consultants."

Although the fashion world has changed a good deal over the years, Doncaster has continued to flourish through a dedication to elegance and style. Today, Doncaster offers three lines of clothing—the luxury Doncaster Collection, the professional Doncaster line, and the casual Doncaster Sport. A design team in New York puts together four seasonal collections annually with a focus on timeless styles. Doncaster Wardrobe Consultants earn money via commission and a bonus plan. They also receive incentives such as discounts on Doncaster clothing, gift certificates, and trips.

Two other popular direct selling businesses falling into the home/family care/home durables category are Longaberger and Pampered Chef. Longaberger consultants sell baskets, wrought iron furniture, and numerous accessories by hosting or recruiting their friends to host basket home shows. The Longaberger consultant earns 25 percent commission on sales, plus hostess dollars and discounts on Longaberger products. The company currently boasts around 45,000 consultants. Pampered Chef consultants generally utilize cooking demonstrations to show the wide variety of cooking utensils and to demonstrate them. In addition to commissions, salespeople can earn rewards such as vacations, jewelry, free products, and more. As of 2008, there were 60,000 Pampered Chef consultants worldwide, serving 12 million customers.

Direct selling businesses cover a wide variety of areas. Shoppers can purchase home products, cosmetics, body care products, candles, lingerie, and much more. While the products and services can vary greatly, the basic opportunity appears to follow a specific formula. For little upfront investment (Pampered Chef, for example, sells a $155 starter kit to its new consultants), any individual can begin his or her own business. The hours one works and the income one earns are based entirely on the desires and effort of the individual. As more stay-at-home mothers are looking for employment with a flexible schedule, and as more people becoming dissatisfied with traditional work environments, direct selling is expanding and gaining popularity.[37]

## Discussion Questions

1. Why are more people turning to direct selling as a means of making a living, and as a means of purchasing the goods they need?

2. Are any goods or services not suited for the direct selling method, or could it be adapted to all products and services?

3. What personal characteristics would help a person to become a good direct salesperson?

**Remember to check out our Online Learning Center at www.mhhe.com/ferrell7e.**

# Managing for Quality and Competitiveness

**CHAPTER 7**   **The Nature of Management**

**CHAPTER 8**   **Organization, Teamwork, and Communication**

**CHAPTER 9**   **Managing Service and Manufacturing Operations**

# The Nature of Management

## CHAPTER OUTLINE

**Introduction**

**The Importance of Management**

**Management Functions**
- *Planning*
- *Organizing*
- *Staffing*
- *Directing*
- *Controlling*

**Types of Management**
- *Levels of Management*
- *Areas of Management*

**Skills Needed by Managers**
- *Leadership*
- *Technical Expertise*
- *Conceptual Skills*
- *Analytical Skills*
- *Human Relations Skills*

**Where Do Managers Come From?**

**Decision Making**
- *Recognizing and Defining the Decision Situation*
- *Developing Options*
- *Analyzing Options*
- *Selecting the Best Option*
- *Implementing the Decision*
- *Monitoring the Consequences*

**The Reality of Management**

## OBJECTIVES

*After reading this chapter, you will be able to:*

- Define *management,* and explain its role in the achievement of organizational objectives.

- Describe the major functions of management.

- Distinguish among three levels of management and the concerns of managers at each level.

- Specify the skills managers need in order to be successful.

- Summarize the systematic approach to decision making used by many business managers.

- Recommend a new strategy to revive a struggling business.

## The Best Buzz: High-End Coffee

Seattle-based Espresso Vivace storeowner David Schomer is a man dedicated to all things coffee. The former Boeing engineer and classical musician
first joined the gourmet coffee scene in 1988 when he and his wife purchased
a coffee cart. By that time, Starbucks' mission to transform the city into the
epicenter of the coffee scene was well under way, making Seattle a logical
place for a fledgling coffee business. Schomer and his wife set up shop in the
posh Capital Hill neighborhood, but they almost immediately ran into trouble
with the Broadway Avenue Chamber of Commerce. The Chamber was concerned about allowing a street vendor to conduct business in the prestigious
area. Schomer finally convinced the group to allow his business to stay by
promising that he would employ classical musicians to play for customers as
a way of signaling the high-end nature of this particular cart.

Within four years Schomer was ready to expand. After borrowing $120,000,
he was able to purchase a storefront on Broadway Avenue. The extra space
allowed them to experiment more and laid the groundwork for success to
come. Interested in creating a unique experience for the true coffee lover,
Schomer carefully roasted beans in small batches, thereby preserving the
essential oils and creating a richer, better tasting product. Schomer also pioneered the now ubiquitous gourmet coffee shop technique of drawing intricate designs in the crema that tops all good espresso. Finally, Schomer turned
his attention to the espresso machine itself, a technology that was advanced
in Europe but shoddy and unreliable in the United States. By 2001, Schomer
succeeded in creating a precision device that maintained temperatures
within two degrees of the ideal. This breakthrough made Schomer famous

*continued*

in coffee circles, and he could have taken strides to patent the machine and thereby protect his technology. Instead, Schomer has been surprisingly open. He has published his research and created instructional videos.

Today, Espresso Vivace remains a local Seattle establishment and continues to enjoy a strong reputation as the "espresso roasting and preparation specialists." Although decades have passed since the opening of the first coffee cart, Schomer maintains the attention to detail and high standards that make Vivace a standout in an espresso-soaked city. All employees must attend six months of training before becoming official baristas, and baristas require a total of two years of training and supervision before they can work alone. It is because of all of the training that Vivace can live up to its motto "una bella tazza de caffe" (a beautiful cup of coffee), from the beans all the way down to the designs drawn in the crema. To repay his workers for living up to these exacting standards, Schomer provides generous compensation and benefits packages to all employees.[1]

# Introduction

For any organization—small or large, for profit or nonprofit—to achieve its objectives, it must have equipment and raw materials to turn into products to market, employees to make and sell the products, and financial resources to purchase additional goods and services, pay employees, and generally operate the business. To accomplish this, it must also have one or more managers to plan, organize, staff, direct, and control the work that goes on.

This chapter introduces the field of management. It examines and surveys the various functions, levels, and areas of management in business. The skills that managers need for success and the steps that lead to effective decision making are also discussed.

## The Importance of Management

**management**
a process designed to achieve an organization's objectives by using its resources effectively and efficiently in a changing environment

**managers**
those individuals in organizations who make decisions about the use of resources and who are concerned with planning, organizing, staffing, directing, and controlling the organization's activities to reach its objectives

**Management** is a process designed to achieve an organization's objectives by using its resources effectively and efficiently in a changing environment. *Effectively* means having the intended result; *efficiently* means accomplishing the objectives with a minimum of resources. **Managers** make decisions about the use of the organization's resources and are concerned with planning, organizing, staffing, directing, and controlling the organization's activities so as to reach its objectives. The decision to introduce new products in order to reach objectives is often a key management duty. For example, in an effort to reclaim its title as overall sales leader among commercial jet companies, Boeing launched the 787 Dreamliner in 2007. At the time of writing, Boeing had sold 892 of the $162 million jets to 57 customers worldwide. This amounts to total sales of $145 billion. The decision to launch the Dreamliner, and its subsequent success, emphasizes the importance of management decisions in determining the success of a company.[2] Management is universal. It takes place not only in business, but also in government, the military, labor unions, hospitals, schools, and religious groups—any organization requiring the coordination of resources.

Every organization must acquire resources (people, raw materials and equipment, money, and information) to effectively pursue its objectives and coordinate their use to turn out a final good or service. Employees are one of the most important resources in helping a business attain its objectives. Successful companies such as Starbucks recruit, train, compensate, and provide benefits (such as shares of stock and health insurance) to foster employee loyalty. Acquiring suppliers is another important part of managing resources and in ensuring that products are made available to customers. As firms reach global markets, companies such as General Motors, Union Pacific, and Cargill enlist hundreds of diverse suppliers that provide goods and services to support operations. A good supplier maximizes efficiencies and provides creative solutions to help the company reduce expenses and reach its objectives.[3] Finally, the manager needs adequate financial resources to pay for essential activities: Primary funding comes from owners and shareholders, as well as banks and other financial institutions. All these resources and activities must be coordinated and controlled if the company is to earn a profit. Organizations must also have adequate supplies of resources of all types, and managers must carefully coordinate their use if they are to achieve the organization's objectives.

## Management Functions

To harmonize the use of resources so that the business can develop, produce, and sell products, managers engage in a series of activities: planning, organizing, staffing, directing, and controlling (Figure 7.1). Although this book discusses each of the five functions separately, they are interrelated; managers may perform two or more of them at the same time.

### Planning

**Planning,** the process of determining the organization's objectives and deciding how to accomplish them, is the first function of management. Planning is a crucial activity, for it designs the map that lays the groundwork for the other functions. It involves forecasting events and determining the best course of action from a set of options or choices. The plan itself specifies what should be done, by whom, where, when, and how. Ford is struggling to find the right strategy in an atmosphere of

**planning**
the process of determining the organization's objectives and deciding how to accomplish them; the first function of management

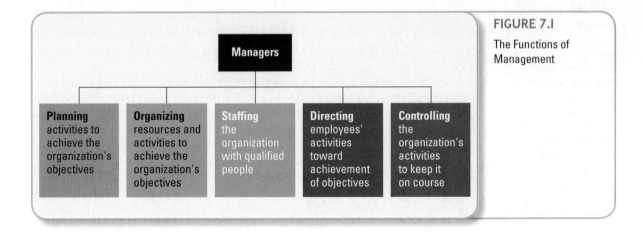

**FIGURE 7.1**

The Functions of Management

# Entrepreneurship in Action

## Finding Beauty in Blight: Dennie Ibbotson's Carved Wood Designs

Dennie Ibbotson

**Business:** Laughing Sun Custom Handcarved Signs and Doors

**Founded:** 1977

**Success:** Has received 33 awards from the Evergreen Chamber of Commerce. Counts Coors, Anheuser-Busch, Merrill Lynch, and Willie Nelson among his clients.

The mountain pine beetle plagues pine trees in forests throughout the United States, particularly in western states like Colorado. While dying forests is not something anyone wants, Dennie Ibbotson has managed to find a silver lining to this scourge. An Evergreen, Colorado–based Ohioan, Ibbotson noticed artistic potential in the dead trees found throughout the Colorado Rockies. The beetle leaves a blue stain, caused by a fungus, on wood that it attacks. It is this pigment that helps give Ibbotson's works uniqueness. He uses the pine beetle–felled trees to fashion signs, doors, and other decorative and functional objects. He often personalizes his pieces with scenes inspired by his surroundings—images of Colorado wildlife and Native American motifs. Using a mallet and chisel to carve the images into the wood can sometimes take hundreds of hours. His original pieces often sell for nearly $20,000. While Ibbotson's art provides him with a good living, it has a secondary benefit as well. As mountain pine beetle–induced tree mortality increases (up 500 percent from 2004), more trees litter the forest floor, increasing the risk of fire. By clearing out wood to use in art, Ibbotson indirectly helps prevent forest fires. Ibbotson's art, therefore, is not only an homage to the forest and to the Colorado lifestyle, but it also helps to preserve these things for the future.[4]

---

global competition and high fuel prices. The company lost its focus over the past decade or so, and now it is seeking to sharpen its image. Ford is attempting to associate itself with smaller cars in order to appeal to an international market. The Fiesta is the model Ford hopes will catch on abroad. It is rolling out in Europe first; it enters North American markets in 2010. If the global market accepts the new Fiesta, all the management and planning that went into it will have paid off.[5] All businesses—from the smallest restaurant to the largest multinational corporation—need to develop plans for achieving success. But before an organization can plan a course of action, it must first determine what it wants to achieve.

**Objectives.**    Objectives, the ends or results desired by an organization, derive from the organization's **mission**. A mission statement describes an organization's fundamental purpose and basic philosophy. A photo lab, for example, might say that its mission is to provide customers with memories. To carry out its mission, the photo lab sets specific objectives, such as reducing development defects to less than 2 percent, introducing a selection of photo albums and frames for customers' use in displaying their photos, providing customers' proofs over the Internet, providing technical assistance, and so on. Herbal tea marketer Celestial Seasonings says that its mission is "To create and sell healthful, naturally oriented products that nurture people's bodies and uplift their souls.[6]

A business's objectives may be elaborate or simple. Common objectives relate to profit, competitive advantage, efficiency, and growth. Organizations with profit as a goal want to have money and assets left over after paying off business expenses. Objectives regarding competitive advantage are generally stated in terms of percentage of sales increase and market share, with the goal of increasing those figures. Efficiency objectives involve making the best use of the organization's resources. The photo lab's objective of holding defects to less than 2 percent is an example of an efficiency objective. Growth objectives relate to an organization's ability to adapt and to get new products to the marketplace in a timely fashion. The mission

**mission**
the statement of an organization's fundamental purpose and basic philosophy

of Procter & Gamble is to continue to improve customers' quality of life through meaningful product research, development, and innovation. It took more than eight years and 180 researchers to develop the polymer that helps prevent diaper rash, resulting in happier and healthier babies. P&G spends nearly $2 billion annually on product research and development.[7] Other organizational objectives include service, ethical, and community goals. Cisco Systems was honored by the Points of Light "Awards for Excellence in Workplace Volunteer Programs" for their long-term commitment to volunteerism. Cisco's volunteerism program has a $1.2 million operating budget and more than $2 million in matching grants. Cisco operates the "Volunteer Connection" online tool that matches employees' skills with the needs of nonprofit organizations.[8] Objectives provide direction for all managerial decisions; additionally, they establish criteria by which performance can be evaluated.

**Plans.**   There are three general types of plans for meeting objectives—strategic, tactical, and operational. A firm's highest managers develop its **strategic plans,** which establish the long-range objectives and overall strategy or course of action by which the firm fulfills its mission. Strategic plans generally cover periods ranging from 2 to 10 years or even longer. They include plans to add products, purchase companies, sell unprofitable segments of the business, issue stock, and move into international markets. Faced with stiff competition, rising costs, and slowing sales, some companies are closing U.S. plants and moving production to factories abroad. For example, Converse Inc. (sneaker maker), Lionel LLC (producer of model trains), and Zebco (fishing reel manufacturer) all stopped U.S. production in favor of Asian factories.[9] Strategic plans must take into account the organization's capabilities and resources, the changing business environment, and organizational objectives. Plans should be market-driven, matching customers' desire for value with operational capabilities, processes, and human resources.[10]

**strategic plans**
those plans that establish the long-range objectives and overall strategy or course of action by which a firm fulfills its mission

**Tactical plans** are short range and designed to implement the activities and objectives specified in the strategic plan. These plans, which usually cover a period of one year or less, help keep the organization on the course established in the strategic plan. Because tactical plans allow the organization to react to changes in the environment while continuing to focus on the company's overall strategy, management must periodically review and update them. Declining performance or failure to meet objectives set out in tactical plans may be one reason for revising them. For example, when fuel prices rose rapidly in 2008, airlines and other transportation firms such as FedEx and UPS had to add extra surcharges to maintain control over expenses. Another example is the recent helicopter shortage. In 2008, demand surged because of increases in military spending and disaster relief, an oil boom, and crowded airports. Manufacturers tried to quickly increase production, and the cost of used helicopters went up 40 percent, causing firms requiring the use of helicopters to make tactical changes.[11] When public concern emerged over Americans' high level of plastic bag consumption, which stands at more than 110 billion bags a year, the grocery chain Whole Foods stopped offering plastic bags altogether. Wal-Mart and Kroger also began to offer reusable canvas and nylon bags in response to this problem.[12] These situations both required companies to develop short-run or tactical plans to deal with stakeholder concerns.

**tactical plans**
short-range plans designed to implement the activities and objectives specified in the strategic plan

A retailing organization with a five-year strategic plan to invest $5 billion in 500 new retail stores may develop five tactical plans (each covering one year) specifying how much to spend to set up each new store, where to locate, and when to open each new store. Tactical plans are designed to execute the overall strategic plan.

**operational plans**
very short-term plans that specify what actions individuals, work groups, or departments need to accomplish in order to achieve the tactical plan and ultimately the strategic plan

Because of their short-term nature, they are easier to adjust or abandon if changes in the environment or the company's performance so warrant.

**Operational plans** are very short term and specify what actions specific individuals, work groups, or departments need to accomplish in order to achieve the tactical plan and ultimately the strategic plan. They may apply to just one month, week, or even day. For example, a work group may be assigned a weekly production quota to ensure there are sufficient products available to elevate market share (tactical goal) and ultimately help the firm be number one in its product category (strategic goal). Returning to our retail store example, operational plans may specify the schedule for opening one new store, hiring and training new employees, obtaining merchandise, and opening for actual business.

Another element of planning is **crisis management or contingency planning,** which deals with potential disasters such as product tampering, oil spills, fire, earthquake, computer viruses, or even a reputation crisis due to unethical or illegal conduct by one or more employees. Investment bank Bear Stearns found itself on the brink of collapse in 2008. Its problems were largely due to the credit crisis and subprime lending disasters. Within minutes, Bear Stearns lost half of its market value. The bank's financial condition deteriorated to the point of failure within 24 hours, which could have brought down the U.S. stock market. To save the company and to prevent widespread financial panic, another bank, JPMorgan Chase, joined with the U.S. Federal Reserve to provide loans and to create a merger between Bear Stearns and JPMorgan Chase. Businesses that have contingency plans tend to respond more effectively when problems occur than do businesses who lack such planning, hopefully avoiding a Bear Stearns–level disaster.

Many companies, including Ashland Oil, H. J. Heinz, and Johnson & Johnson, have crisis management teams to deal specifically with problems, permitting other managers to continue to focus on their regular duties. Some companies even hold periodic disaster drills to ensure that their employees know how to respond when a crisis does occur. Crisis management plans generally cover maintaining business operations throughout a crisis and

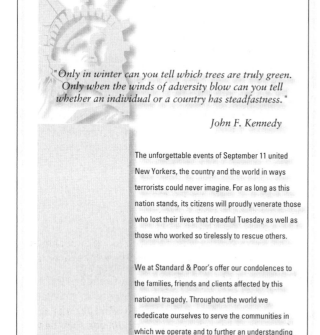

*"Only in winter can you tell which trees are truly green. Only when the winds of adversity blow can you tell whether an individual or a country has steadfastness."*

*John F. Kennedy*

The unforgettable events of September 11 united New Yorkers, the country and the world in ways terrorists could never imagine. For as long as this nation stands, its citizens will proudly venerate those who lost their lives that dreadful Tuesday as well as those who worked so tirelessly to rescue others.

We at Standard & Poor's offer our condolences to the families, friends and clients affected by this national tragedy. Throughout the world we rededicate ourselves to serve the communities in which we operate and to further an understanding and an appreciation for the democratic institutions that came under attack.

**STANDARD &POOR'S**

*A Division of The McGraw-Hill Companies*

*Companies that housed operations in and around the World Trade Center, many of them key players in the financial markets, had to rely on contingency plans after 9/11. Those that could, reassured clients and the world that operations would continue. Many took out patriotic, inspirational ads such as this one from Standard & Poor's.*

**crisis management or contingency planning**
an element in planning that deals with potential disasters such as product tampering, oil spills, fire, earthquake, computer virus, or airplane crash

communicating with the public, employees, and officials about the nature of and the company's response to the problem. Communication is especially important to minimize panic and damaging rumors; it also demonstrates that the company is aware of the problem and plans to respond. In 2005, major hurricanes hitting the Gulf Coast region disrupted many business activities. Airlines are damaged when many Americans are reluctant to travel. Incidents such as this highlight the importance of tactical planning for crises and the need to respond publicly and quickly when a disaster occurs.

## Organizing

Rarely are individuals in an organization able to achieve common goals without some form of structure. **Organizing** is the structuring of resources and activities to accomplish objectives in an efficient and effective manner. Managers organize by reviewing plans and determining what activities are necessary to implement them; then, they divide the work into small units and assign it to specific individuals, groups, or departments. As companies reorganize for greater efficiency, more often than not, they are organizing work into teams to handle core processes such as new product development instead of organizing around traditional departments such as marketing and production.

Organizing is important for several reasons. It helps create synergy, whereby the effect of a whole system equals more than that of its parts. It also establishes lines of authority, improves communication, helps avoid duplication of resources, and can improve competitiveness by speeding up decision making. When media company Thompson, a business information giant, purchased Reuters Group, a news agency and financial data group, a new organizational structure was needed in order to merge core services for customers. The new organization resulted in four customer divisions: financial data and trading, legal and tax, scientific and health care, and media.[13] Because organizing is so important, we'll take a closer look at it in Chapter 8.

**organizing**
the structuring of resources and activities to accomplish objectives in an efficient and effective manner

## Staffing

Once managers have determined what work is to be done and how it is to be organized, they must ensure that the organization has enough employees with appropriate skills to do the work. Hiring people to carry out the work of the organization is known as **staffing.** Beyond recruiting people for positions within the firm, managers must determine what skills are needed for specific jobs, how to motivate and train employees, how much to pay, what benefits to provide, and how to prepare employees for higher-level jobs in the firm at a later date. These elements of staffing will be explored in detail in Chapters 10 and 11.

**staffing**
the hiring of people to carry out the work of the organization

Another aspect of staffing is **downsizing,** the elimination of significant numbers of employees from an organization, which has been a pervasive and much-talked-about trend. Whether it is called downsizing, rightsizing, trimming the fat, or the new reality in business, the implications of downsizing have been dramatic. Ford Motor Company is in the process of implementing a major North American restructuring. The company is closing at least 10 assembly and component plants and eliminating 25,000 to 30,000 hourly jobs by 2010. Ford also eliminated top executive positions. The goal is to reverse a prolonged market share slide.[14] Staffing can be outsourced to companies that focus on hiring and managing employees. The Bartech Group bills and manages $1 billion for customers such as General Motors and Verizon.[15] Many firms downsize by outsourcing production, sales, and technical positions to companies in other countries with lower labor costs. Downsizing has helped numerous firms reduce costs quickly and become more profitable (or become profitable after lengthy losses) in a short period of time.

**downsizing**
the elimination of a significant number of employees from an organization

*Planning, especially long term planning, can be tricky for managers. For example, after spending the better part of the past decade frantically trying to downsize their firms due to a recession, Japanese executives are now finding it hard to find workers since the economy has improved.*

Downsizing and outsourcing, however, have painful consequences. Obviously, the biggest casualty is those who lose their jobs, along with their incomes, insurance, and pensions. Some find new jobs quickly; others do not. Another victim is the morale of the remaining employees at downsized firms. Those left behind often feel insecure, angry, and sad, and their productivity may decline as a result, the opposite of the effect sought. Managers can expect that 70 to 80 percent of those surviving a downsize will take a "wait-and-see" attitude and will require active leadership. Ten to 15 percent will be openly hostile or try to sabotage change in order to return to the way things were before. The remaining 10 to 15 percent will be the leaders who will try proactively to help make the situation work.[16] A survey of workers who remained after a downsizing found that many felt their jobs demanded more time and energy.[17]

After a downsizing situation, an effective manager will promote optimism and positive thinking and minimize criticism and fault-finding. Management should also build teamwork and encourage positive group discussions. Honest communication is important during a time of change and will lead to trust. Truthfulness about what has happened and also about future expectations is essential.

## Directing

**directing**
motivating and leading employees to achieve organizational objectives

Once the organization has been staffed, management must direct the employees. **Directing** is motivating and leading employees to achieve organizational objectives. Good directing involves telling employees what to do and when to do it through the implementation of deadlines, and then encouraging them to do their work. For example, as a sales manager you would need to learn how to motivate salespersons; provide leadership; teach sales teams to be responsive to customer needs; manage organizational issues; as well as evaluate sales results. Finally, directing also involves determining and administering appropriate rewards and recognition.[18] All managers are involved in directing, but it is especially important for lower-level managers who interact daily with the employees operating the organization. For example, an assembly-line supervisor for Frito-Lay must ensure that her workers know how to use their equipment properly and have the resources needed to carry out their jobs, and she must motivate her workers to achieve their expected output of packaged snacks.

Managers may motivate employees by providing incentives—such as the promise of a raise or promotion—for them to do a good job. But most workers want more than money from their jobs: They need to know that their employer values their ideas and input. Smart managers, therefore, ask workers to contribute ideas for reducing costs, making equipment more efficient, improving customer service, or even developing new products. This participation makes workers feel important, and the company benefits. Recognition and appreciation are often the best motivators. Employees who understand more about their effect on the financial success of the company may be induced to work harder for that success, and managers who understand the needs and desires of workers can encourage their employees to work harder and more productively. The motivation of employees is discussed in detail in Chapter 10.

## Controlling

Planning, organizing, staffing, and directing are all important to the success of an organization, whether its objective is earning a profit or something else. But what happens when a firm fails to reach its goals despite a strong planning effort?

**Controlling** is the process of evaluating and correcting activities to keep the organization on course. Control involves five activities: (1) measuring performance, (2) comparing present performance with standards or objectives, (3) identifying deviations from the standards, (4) investigating the causes of deviations, and (5) taking corrective action when necessary.

Controlling and planning are closely linked. Planning establishes goals and standards. By monitoring performance and comparing it with standards, managers can determine whether performance is on target. When performance is substandard, management must determine why and take appropriate actions to get the firm back on course. In short, the control function helps managers assess the success of their plans. When the outcomes of plans do not meet expectations, the control process facilitates revision of the plans. ExxonMobil has run ads indicating that peak oil is decades away. This message conflicts with ads that Chevron is running, indicating that world consumes two barrels of oil for every one that it finds. A strategy for dealing with concerns about depleting energy resources is for oil companies to invest in finding and developing new supplies of petroleum.[19]

The control process also helps managers deal with problems arising outside the firm. For example, if a firm is the subject of negative publicity, management should use the control process to determine why and to guide the firm's response.

# Types of Management

All managers—whether the sole proprietor of a small video store or the hundreds of managers of a large company such as Paramount Pictures—perform the five functions just discussed. In the case of the video store, the owner handles all the functions, but in a large company with more than one manager, responsibilities must be divided and delegated. This division of responsibility is generally achieved by establishing levels of management and areas of specialization—finance, marketing, and so on.

## Levels of Management

As we have hinted, many organizations have multiple levels of management—top management, middle management, and first-line, or supervisory management. These levels form a pyramid, as shown in Figure 7.2. As the pyramid shape implies, there are generally more middle managers than top managers, and still more first-line managers. Very small organizations may have only one manager (typically, the owner), who assumes the responsibilities of all three levels. Large businesses have many managers at each level to coordinate the use of the organization's resources. Managers at all three levels perform all five management functions, but the amount of time they spend on each function varies, as we shall see (Figure 7.3).

Top Management.   In businesses, **top managers** include the president and other top executives, such as the chief executive officer (CEO), chief financial officer (CFO), and chief operations officer (COO), who have overall responsibility for the organization. For example, Carlos Ghosn, CEO of both Renault and Nissan, utilizes quick decision making to adapt to changing tastes in global markets. His joint ventures for Nissan and Renault include electric car projects in Denmark; creating a $3,000 car for India; and orchestrating the exit strategy for the full-size Nissan Titan in the United States. The Titan plant in Mississippi is being converted to light commercial truck production. In addition, Ghosn agreed to supply small cars to Chrysler. In emerging markets, he is focused on local tastes and export designs in order

**controlling**
the process of evaluating and correcting activities to keep the organization on course

**top managers**
the president and other top executives of a business, such as the chief executive officer (CEO), chief financial officer (CFO), and chief operations officer (COO), who have overall responsibility for the organization

**FIGURE 7.2**

Levels of Management

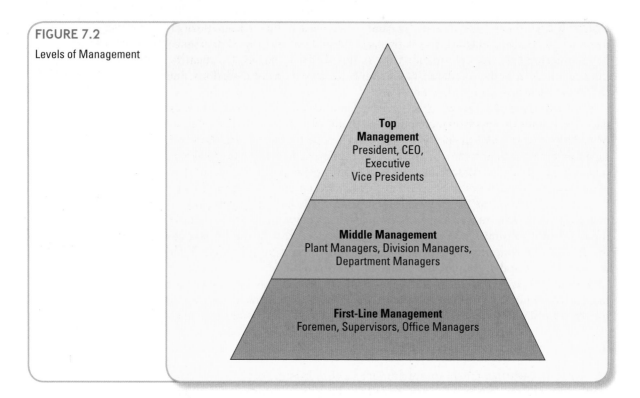

**FIGURE 7.3**

Importance of
Management Functions
to Managers in Each
Level

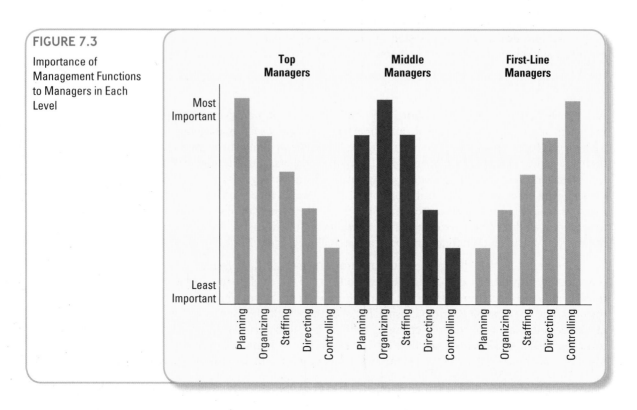

to ride global trends.[20] In public corporations, even chief executive officers have a boss—the firm's board of directors. With technological advances accelerating and privacy concerns increasing, some companies are adding a new top management position—chief privacy officer (CPO). There are currently an estimated 2,000 CPOs in U.S. corporations, and that number is expected to rise over the next few years in response to growing concerns as well as new legislation such as the Sarbanes-Oxley Act. Among the companies that have appointed CPOs are American Express, Citigroup, Hewlett-Packard, Microsoft, and the U.S. Postal Service.[21] In government, top management refers to the president, a governor, or a mayor or city manager; in education, a chancellor of a university or a county superintendent of education.

> **Did You Know?**   Women represent only 15.7 percent of corporate officers and just 5.2 percent of all top earners.[22]

Top-level managers spend most of their time planning. They make the organization's strategic decisions, decisions that focus on an overall scheme or key idea for using resources to take advantage of opportunities. They decide whether to add products, acquire companies, sell unprofitable business segments, and move into foreign markets. Top managers also represent their company to the public and to government regulators.

Given the importance and range of top management's decisions, top managers generally have many years of varied experience and command top salaries. In addition to salaries, top managers' compensation packages typically include bonuses, long-term incentive awards, stock, and stock options. Table 7.1 lists the 10 highest paid CEOs including bonuses, stock options and other compensation. Top management may also get perks and special treatment that is criticized by stakeholders. Consider the case of Mark Fields, the North America chief for Ford Motor Company. The company was recently censured when it was revealed that it had paid out more than $500,000 in 2006 to fly Fields between Detroit and his home in Florida

**TABLE 7.I**   The 10 Highest Paid CEOs

| Rank | CEO | Company | Total Compensation[a] ($ in millions) |
|---|---|---|---|
| 1. | Lawrence J. Ellison | Oracle | $192.92 |
| 2. | Frederic M. Poses | Trane | 127.10 |
| 3. | Aubrey K. McClendon | Chesapeake Energy | 116.89[b] |
| 4. | Angelo R. Mozilo | Countrywide Financial | 102.84[b] |
| 5. | Howard D. Schultz | Starbucks | 98.60[c] |
| 6. | Nabeel Gareeb | MEMC Electronic Mats | 79.56 |
| 7. | Daniel P. Amos | Aflac | 75.16 |
| 8. | Lloyd C. Blankfein | Goldman Sachs Group | 73.72 |
| 9. | Richard D. Fairbank | Capital One Financial | 73.17 |
| 10. | Bob R. Simpson | XTO Energy | 72.27[b] |

[a]2007 compensation includes salary, bonuses, other compensation, and stock gains.
[b]Prior-year data.
[c]New chief executive; compensation may be for another executive office.

Source: Scott DeCarlo, "Top Paid CEOs," *Forbes,* April 30, 2008, http://www.forbes.com/2008/04/30/ceo-pay-compensation-lead-bestbosses08-cx-sd_0430ceo_intro.html?boxes=custom (accessed May 14, 2008).

on a company jet—almost three times Ford CEO Alan Mulally's travel expenses during the same period.[23]

Compensation committees are increasingly working with boards of directors and CEOs to attempt to keep pay in line with performance in order to benefit stockholders and key stakeholders. The majority of major companies cite their concern about attracting capable leadership for the CEO and other top executive positions in their organizations. Sixty-seven percent are concerned about their ability to attract and retain the most competent leadership. A new trend in shareholder activism supports shareholders voting on executives' compensation packages. Aflac chairman and CEO Dan Amos accepted this process and, in early 2008, stockholders voted on his 2009 compensation package. Aflac stock had soared 38 percent the previous year. More than 93 percent of shareholders approved Amos's compensation of $14.8 million. Amos is the eighth-longest tenured CEO in the United States, having served 18 years on the job, and the return to shareholders had been a compound growth of 22 percent. Successful management translates into happy stockholders who are willing to compensate their top executives fairly and in line with performance.[24]

Workforce diversity is an important issue in today's corporations. Effective managers at enlightened corporations have found that diversity is good for workers and for the bottom line. Putting together different kinds of people to solve problems often results in better solutions. Betsy Holden, CEO of Kraft Foods, said, "When we look at the composition of teams within our company, we have found that those with a variety of perspectives are simply the most creative."[25] A diverse workforce is better at making decisions regarding issues related to consumer diversity. W. Garrison Jackson runs a multicultural public relations and advertising agency that helps corporate America reach black, Hispanic, Asian, and other minority consumers. These fastgrowing demographic groups are key target markets for many companies including Colgate-Palmolive, General Mills, and IBM.[26] Managers from companies devoted to workforce diversity devised five rules that make diversity recruiting work (see Table 7.2). Diversity is explored in greater detail in Chapter 11.

**TABLE 7.2**

Five Rules of Successful Diversity Recruiting

| Rule | Action |
|---|---|
| 1. Get everyone involved. | Educate all employees on the tangible benefits of diversity recruiting to garner support and enthusiasm for those initiatives. |
| 2. Showcase your diversity. | Prospective employees are not likely to become excited about joining your company just because you say that your company is diversity-friendly; they need to see it. |
| 3. Work with diversity groups within your community. | By supporting community-based diversity organizations, your company will generate the priceless word-of-mouth publicity that will lead qualified diversity candidates to your company. |
| 4. Spend money. | If you are serious about diversity recruiting, you will need to spend some money getting your message out to the right places. |
| 5. Sell, sell, sell—and measure your return on investment. | Employers need to sell their company to prospective diversity employees and present them with a convincing case as to why their company is a good fit for the diversity candidate. |

Source: Adapted from Juan Rodriguez, "The Five Rules of Successful Diversity Recruiting," *Diversityjobs.com*, http://www.diversityjobs.com/Rules-of-Successful-Diversity-Recruiting (accessed May 14, 2008).

**Middle Management.**   Rather than making strategic decisions about the whole organization, **middle managers** are responsible for tactical planning that will implement the general guidelines established by top management. Thus, their responsibility is more narrowly focused than that of top managers. Middle managers are involved in the specific operations of the organization and spend more time organizing than other managers. In business, plant managers, division managers, and department managers make up middle management. The product manager for laundry detergent at a consumer products manufacturer, the department chairperson in a university, and the head of a state public health department are all middle managers. The ranks of middle managers have been shrinking as more and more companies downsize to be more productive.

**middle managers**
those members of an organization responsible for the tactical planning that implements the general guidelines established by top management

**First-Line Management.**   Most people get their first managerial experience as **first-line managers,** those who supervise workers and the daily operations of the organization. They are responsible for implementing the plans established by middle management and directing workers' daily performance on the job. They spend most of their time directing and controlling. Common titles for first-line managers are foreman, supervisor, and office manager.

**first-line managers**
those who supervise both workers and the daily operations of an organization

## Areas of Management

At each level, there are managers who specialize in the basic functional areas of business: finance, production and operations, human resources (personnel), marketing, and administration.

**financial managers**
those who focus on obtaining needed funds for the successful operation of an organization and using those funds to further organizational goals

**Financial Management.**   **Financial managers** focus on obtaining the money needed for the successful operation of the organization and using that money in

*Top managers use online resources such as ceoexpress.com to gather economic, competitive, and other business information.*

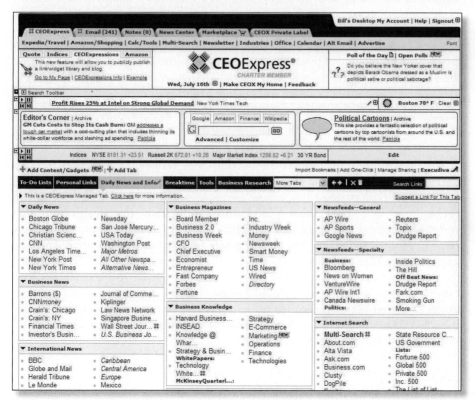

accordance with organizational goals. Among the responsibilities of financial managers are projecting income and expenses over a specified period, determining short- and long-term financing needs and finding sources of financing to fill those needs, identifying and selecting appropriate ways to invest extra funds, monitoring the flow of financial resources, and protecting the financial resources of the organization. A financial manager at General Motors, for example, may be asked to analyze the costs and revenues of a car model to determine its contribution to GM's profitability. All organizations must have adequate financial resources to acquire the physical and human resources that are necessary to create goods and services. Consequently, financial resource management is of the utmost importance.

**Production and Operations Management.** **Production and operations managers** develop and administer the activities involved in transforming resources into goods, services, and ideas ready for the marketplace. Production and operations managers are typically involved in planning and designing production facilities, purchasing raw materials and supplies, managing inventory, scheduling processes to meet demand, and ensuring that products meet quality standards. Because no business can exist without the production of goods and services, production and operations managers are vital to an organization's success. At Pfizer Global Research, for example, Robert Swanson works as an associate director of logistics and supply chain management, which makes him responsible for transporting and caring for lab equipment, protective gear, chemicals, and maintenance and office supplies and shipping scientific documents, materials, and other equipment to other Pfizer facilities around the world.[27]

**Human Resources Management.** **Human resources managers** handle the staffing function and deal with employees in a formalized manner. Once known as personnel managers, they determine an organization's human resource needs; recruit and hire new employees; develop and administer employee benefits, training, and performance appraisal programs; and deal with government regulations concerning employment practices. For example, some companies recognize that their employees' health affects their costs. Therefore, more progressive companies provide health care facilities and outside health club memberships, encourage proper nutrition, and discourage smoking in an effort to improve employee health and lower the costs of providing health care benefits.

**Marketing Management.** **Marketing managers** are responsible for planning, pricing, and promoting products and making them available to customers through distribution. The marketing manager who oversees Sony televisions, for example, must make decisions regarding a new television's size, features, name, price, and packaging, as well as plan what type of stores to distribute the television through and the advertising campaign that will introduce the new television to consumers. General Motors' leadership has to find a way to be profitable in North America, where oil prices are pushing drivers into smaller vehicles, which yield low profits for the company. General Motors must determine a way to make the vehicles that consumers want to buy while still turning a profit.[28] This will require top management to get rank-and-file employees to understand and support a fleet of green, eco-friendly cars, including the Volt, a plug-in hybrid scheduled for launch in 2010.[29] Within the realm of marketing, there are several areas of specialization: product development and management, pricing, promotion, and distribution. Specific jobs are found in areas such as marketing research, advertising, personal selling, retailing, telemarketing, and Internet marketing.

**production and operations managers** those who develop and administer the activities involved in transforming resources into goods, services, and ideas ready for the marketplace

**human resources managers** those who handle the staffing function and deal with employees in a formalized manner

**marketing managers** those who are responsible for planning, pricing, and promoting products and making them available to customers

Universal Music is considered the premier leading and global company in the music industry today. That was not always the case, however. Universal was in a state of decline. The company was poorly managed by any set of standards. Recognizing the importance that effective management and leadership play in corporate performance, Doug Morris was brought on board as Universal's CEO. Acquisitions of smaller labels and hiring talented executives represent two of the strategic management tactics that Morris implemented. These strategic actions, according to Morris, are largely responsible for the company's turnaround.

Morris now recognizes that management at Universal was very slow to recognize the importance of technology, specifically the Internet. Part of Universal's fundamental management challenge is that the company was slow to adopt practices that leverage the digital technology and the Internet for profitability in the music and entertainment business. To demonstrate how far behind the digital curve management at Universal was, Morris tells the story of how his grandson was downloading music from the Internet, which provided the realization that streaming media for digital downloads could be a tremendous source of new revenue.

Ten years ago, Doug Morris was fired from Warner Music. Warner's loss became Universal's management coup. Universal is widely known for its strong talent base including recording artists Sting, U2, and Mariah Carey.

Morris began his career as a songwriter and music producer. He argues that to be a successful manager in the music industry, you must have a passion for music itself; you must understand music and artists, not just sound management practices. Universal still faces serious challenges that include music piracy and illegal downloads. However, Morris now understands the significance of the digital world for the future of the music industry. Understanding the potential of digital technology and adopting effective management practices will be the key to continued success at Universal.

### Discussion Questions

1. Doug Morris has apparently had a significant impact on Universal Music's success. Which of the managerial skills would be most important for Morris as CEO?
2. Which type of manager, according to the text, would Doug Morris most likely be classified?

**Information Technology (IT) Management.** **Information technology (IT) managers** are responsible for implementing, maintaining, and controlling technology applications in business, such as computer networks. Google, the online search engine, is one of the five most popular sites on the Internet and employs more than 18,000 employees, many of whom are IT managers. CEO Eric Schmidt thinks that Google IT managers are best suited to change the game in their industry through innovation. Therefore, IT managers are allowed to spend 20 percent of their time on projects outside their main job. The Google culture is the key to its innovativeness.[30] Other ways that Google maintains its creative and productive culture are through providing access to workout rooms, and roller hockey is played in the parking lot twice a week. The Google Café provides healthy lunches and dinners for all staff.[31] One major task in IT management is securing computer systems from unauthorized users while making the system easy to use for employees, suppliers, and others who have legitimate reason to access the system. Another crucial task is protecting the systems' data, even during a disaster such as a fire. IT managers are also responsible for teaching and helping employees use technology resources efficiently through training and support. At many companies, some aspects of IT management are outsourced to third-party firms that can perform this function expertly and efficiently.

**Administrative Management.** **Administrative managers** are not specialists; rather they manage an entire business or a major segment of a business, such as the Cadillac Division of General Motors. Such managers coordinate the activities of specialized managers, which in the GM Cadillac Division would include marketing managers, production managers, and financial managers. Because of the broad

**information technology (IT) managers** those who are responsible for implementing, maintaining, and controlling technology applications in business, such as computer networks

**administrative managers** those who manage an entire business or a major segment of a business; they are not specialists but coordinate the activities of specialized managers

nature of their responsibilities, administrative managers are often called general managers. However, this does not mean that administrative managers lack expertise in any particular area. Many top executives have risen through the ranks of financial management, production and operations management, or marketing management; but most top managers are actually administrative managers, employing skills in all areas of management.

# Skills Needed by Managers

Managers are typically evaluated using the metrics of how effective and efficient they are. Managing effectively and efficiently requires certain skills—leadership, technical expertise, conceptual skills, analytical skills, and human relations skills. Table 7.3 describes some of the roles managers may fulfill.

## Leadership

**leadership**
the ability to influence employees to work toward organizational goals

**Leadership** is the ability to influence employees to work toward organizational goals. Strong leaders manage and pay attention to the culture of their organizations

**TABLE 7.3**    Managerial Roles

| Type of Role | Specific Role | Examples of Role Activities |
|---|---|---|
| Decisional | Entrepreneur | Commit organizational resources to develop innovative goods and services; decide to expand internationally to obtain new customers for the organization's products. |
| | Disturbance handler | Move quickly to take corrective action to deal with unexpected problems facing the organization from the external environment, such as a crisis like an oil spill, or from the internal environment, such as producing faulty goods or services. |
| | Resource allocator | Allocate organizational resources among different functions and departments of the organization; set budgets and salaries of middle and first-level managers. |
| | Negotiator | Work with suppliers, distributors, and labor unions to reach agreements about the quality and price of input, technical, and human resources; work with other organizations to establish agreements to pool resources to work on joint projects. |
| Informational | Monitor | Evaluate the performance of managers in different functions and take corrective action to improve their performance; watch for changes occurring in the external and internal environment that may affect the organization in the future. |
| | Disseminator | Inform employees about changes taking place in the external and internal environment that will affect them and the organization; communicate to employees the organization's vision and purpose. |
| | Spokesperson | Launch a national advertising campaign to promote new goods and services; give a speech to inform the local community about the organization's future intentions. |
| Interpersonal | Figurehead | Outline future organizational goals to employees at company meetings; open a new corporate headquarters building; state the organization's ethical guidelines and the principles of behavior employees are to follow in their dealings with customers and suppliers. |
| | Leader | Provide an example for employees to follow; give direct commands and orders to subordinates; make decisions concerning the use of human and technical resources; mobilize employee support for specific organizational goals. |
| | Liaison | Coordinate the work of managers in different departments; establish alliances between different organizations to share resources to produce new goods and services. |

Source: Gareth R. Jones and Jennifer M. George, *Essentials of Contemporary Management* (Burr Ridge, IL: McGraw-Hill/Irwin, 2004), p. 14.

Source: Susan M. Heathfield, "Seven Tips About Successful Management," *About.com,* http://humanresources. about.com/cs/managementissues/qt/mgmtsuccess.htm (accessed May 14, 2008)

**TABLE 7.4**

Seven Tips for Successful Leadership

- Build effective and responsive interpersonal relationships.
- Communicate effectively—in person, print, e-mail, etc.
- Build the team and enable employees to collaborate effectively.
- Understand the financial aspects of the business.
- Know how to create an environment in which people experience positive morale and recognition.
- Lead by example.
- Help people grow and develop.

and the needs of their customers. Table 7.4 offers some tips for successful leadership while Table 7.5 lists the world's 10 most admired companies and their CEOs. The list is compiled annually for *Fortune* magazine by executives and analysts who grade companies according to nine attributes, including quality of management. A survey of 150 senior executives indicated that 89 percent believe it is more challenging today to be a leader compared with five years ago.[32]

Managers often can be classified into three types based on their leadership style. *Autocratic leaders* make all the decisions and then tell employees what must be done and how to do it. They generally use their authority and economic rewards to get employees to comply with their directions. *Democratic leaders* involve their employees in decisions. The manager presents a situation and encourages his or her subordinates to express opinions and contribute ideas. The manager then considers the employees' points of view and makes the decision. *Free-rein leaders* let their employees work without much interference. The manager sets performance standards and allows employees to find their own ways to meet them. For this style to be effective, employees must know what the standards are, and they must be motivated to attain them. The free-rein style of leadership can be a powerful motivator because it demonstrates a great deal of trust and confidence in the employee.

**TABLE 7.5**

America's Most Admired Companies and Their CEOs

| Company | Chief Executive Officer |
|---|---|
| Apple | Steve Jobs |
| Berkshire Hathaway | Warren Buffett |
| General Electric | Jeffrey Immelt |
| Google | Eric Schmidt |
| Toyota Motor | Katsuaki Watanabe |
| Starbucks | Howard D. Schultz |
| FedEx | Fred Smith |
| Procter & Gamble | A. G. Lafley |
| Johnson & Johnson | William C. Weldon |
| Goldman Sachs Group | Lloyd C. Blankfein |

Source: Adapted from "America's Most Admired Companies 2008," *Fortune,* http://money.cnn.com/magazines/fortune/mostadmired/2008/ (accessed May 14, 2008).

# Going Green
## Compact Fluorescent Light Bulbs: A Bright Idea

Compact fluorescent lights, or CFLs, are more popular than ever, thanks to concerns about climate change and the use of electricity. The CFL bulb's appeal is that it uses 75 percent less energy than traditional incandescent bulbs. In 2006, Americans purchased around 200 million CFLs, a number that is growing every year. Technical Consumer Products, Inc. (TCP) is currently the largest provider of CFLs in the United States, accounting for about 70 percent of all CFLs sold. The man behind TCP is Ellis Yan. Yan owns four factories in Shanghai that currently produce more than 1 million CFLs daily. TCP supplies such large chains as Home Depot and Wal-Mart, among many others.

Although CFLs initially cost more money than standard incandescent bulbs, over time the reduced energy requirements add up to substantial savings. For example, if a CFL bulb gives 10,000 hours of life, a user saves 550 kilowatt-hours (kWh) over the lifetime of the bulb. At 10 cents per kWh, a user would save $55 in energy costs per bulb, substantially more than the light bulb cost in the first place. This is the amount of savings before one factors in the longer lifespan of CFLs. One would need to replace an incandescent bulb 10 to 13 times during the life of a single CFL bulb. According to the TCP Web site, if every home in the United States replaced one light bulb with a CFL bulb, the United States would save enough energy to light more than 3 million homes for one year, would save more than $600 million in annual energy costs, and would reduce greenhouse gas emissions by an amount equivalent to that emitted annually by 800,000 cars.

Ellis Yan, who has been working with CFLs since the early 1990s, is a man dedicated to his business. He has often been known to create customized products for customers based on their stipulations. Yan is also passionate about the opportunity to make a positive impact in the world through working on a product that reduces energy consumption.

In 2007, a bill was passed requiring all newly manufactured bulbs use 25 to 30 percent less energy than they did before, while producing the same light as traditional incandescent bulbs. Because of this and other legislation, there is no doubt that CFLs will be important long into the future. TCP is certain to be a part of this future as well. However, there soon may be more competition. Large lighting companies such as GE and Sylvania are becoming more involved in the CFL market. However, TCP should manage to stay on top for a while. The company has first-mover advantage and a good reputation because of its strong leader, Yan, to maintain its position at the head of the CFL pack.[33]

**Discussion Questions**
1. What kind of leader do you think Yan is?
2. What reasons does TCP have for being confident of the continued success of the company?
3. What are the advantages of switching to CFLs, and how should this help boost business for TCP?

The effectiveness of the autocratic, democratic, and free-rein styles depends on several factors. One consideration is the type of employees. An autocratic style of leadership is generally best for stimulating unskilled, unmotivated employees; highly skilled, trained, and motivated employees may respond better to democratic or free-rein leadership styles. Employees who have been involved in decision making generally require less supervision than those not similarly involved. Other considerations are the manager's abilities and the situation itself. When a situation requires quick decisions, an autocratic style of leadership may be best because the manager does not have to consider input from a lot of people. If a special task force must be set up to solve a quality-control problem, a normally democratic manager may give free rein to the task force. Many managers, however, are unable to use more than one style of leadership. Some are incapable allowing their subordinates to participate in decision making, let alone make any decisions. Thus, what leadership style is "best" depends on specific circumstances, and effective managers will strive to adapt their leadership style as circumstances warrant. Many organizations offer programs to develop goal leadership skills. When plans fail, very often leaders are held responsible for what goes wrong. For example, banking giant Citigroup's CFO Charles Prince resigned after the subprime credit meltdown forced Citigroup to write down billions of dollars. While at Citigroup, Prince had focused on improving ethics. He also supported a corporate creed that leaders should "accept account-ability for our failures."[34]

## Technical Expertise

Managers need **technical expertise,** the specialized knowledge and training required to perform jobs related to their area of management. Accounting managers need to be able to perform accounting jobs, and production managers need to be able to perform production jobs. Although a production manager may not actually perform a job, he or she needs technical expertise to train employees, answer questions, provide guidance, and solve problems. Technical skills are most needed by first-line managers and least critical to top-level managers.

Today, most organizations rely on computers to perform routine data processing, simplify complex calculations, organize and maintain vast amounts of information to communicate, and help managers make sound decisions. For this reason, most managers have found computer expertise to be an essential skill in doing their jobs well.

> **technical expertise** the specialized knowledge and training needed to perform jobs that are related to particular areas of management

## Conceptual Skills

**Conceptual skills,** the ability to think in abstract terms, and to see how parts fit together to form the whole, are needed by all managers, but particularly top-level managers. Top management must be able to evaluate continually where the company will be in the future. Conceptual skills also involve the ability to think creatively. Recent scientific research has revealed that creative thinking, which is behind the development of many innovative products and ideas, including fiber optics and compact disks, can be learned. As a result, IBM, AT&T, GE, Hewlett-Packard, Intel, and other top U.S. firms hire creative consultants to teach their managers how to think creatively.

> **conceptual skills** the ability to think in abstract terms and to see how parts fit together to form the whole

## Analytical Skills

**Analytical skills** refer to the ability to identify relevant issues and recognize their importance, understand the relationships between them, and perceive the under-lying causes of a situation. When managers have identified critical factors and causes, they can take appropriate action. All managers need to think logically, but this skill is probably most important to the success of top-level managers. For example, Volvo is the world's largest producer of heavy, diesel-engine trucks, and the second largest heavy-duty truck maker behind Daimler AG. A major challenge is compliance with U.S. Environmental Protection Agency (EPA) pollution regulations. Companies such as Waste Management and UPS purchased large numbers of trucks in years leading up to a tightening of emission standards, resulting in dips in sales of up to 60 percent in the proceeding year. Management at Volvo's U.S. Mack truck unit is trying to get the EPA to provide an easier way to ease into the new pollution standards and to get buyers to desire cleaner vehicles. This challenge requires analytical skills to understand why major buyers are not willing to pay approximately $7,000 for a move to a greener truck design that would reduce pollution. Skills are also needed to figure out a way to gain the support of the EPA to help deal with demand issues.[35]

> **analytical skills** the ability to identify relevant issues, recognize their importance, understand the relationships between them, and perceive the underlying causes of a situation

## Human Relations Skills

People skills, or **human relations skills,** are the ability to deal with people, both inside and outside the organization. Those who can relate to others, communicate

> **human relations skills** the ability to deal with people, both inside and outside the organization

well with others, understand the needs of others, and show a true appreciation for others are generally more successful than managers who lack such skills. People skills are especially important in hospitals, airline companies, banks, and other organizations that provide services. For example, at Southwest Airlines, every new employee attends "You, Southwest and Success," a day-long class designed to teach employees about the airline and its reputation for impeccable customer service. All employees in management positions at Southwest take mandatory leadership classes that address skills related to listening, staying in touch with employees, and handling change without compromising values.

*Anne Mulcahy, the CEO of Xerox, knows that her firm's success lies more than just in the machines it produces. Mulcahy understands that managers with good human relations skills are critical to attracting and retaining top talent.*

## Where Do Managers Come From?

Good managers are not born; they are made. An organization acquires managers in three ways: promoting employees from within, hiring managers from other organizations, and hiring managers straight out of universities.

Promoting people within the organization into management positions tends to increase motivation by showing employees that those who work hard and are competent can advance in the company. Internal promotion also provides managers who are already familiar with the company's goals and problems. Procter & Gamble prefers to promote managers from within, which creates managers who are familiar with the company's products and policies and builds company loyalty. Promoting from within, however, can lead to problems: It may limit innovation. The new manager may continue the practices and policies of previous managers. Thus it is vital for companies—even companies committed to promotion from within—to hire outside people from time to time to bring fresh ideas to the table.

Finding managers with the skills, knowledge, and experience required to run an organization or department can be difficult. Specialized executive employment agencies—sometimes called headhunters, recruiting managers, or executive search firms—can help locate candidates from other companies. The downside is that even though outside people can bring fresh ideas to a company, hiring them may cause resentment among existing employees as well as involve greater expense in relocating an individual to another city or state.

Schools and universities provide a large pool of potential managers, and entry-level applicants can be screened for their developmental potential. People with specialized management skills, such as those with an MBA (Master's of Business Administration) degree, may be good candidates.

Some companies offer special training programs for future potential managers. For example, Lehman Brothers Holdings Inc. financed a one-day run-through at the Marine Corps base at Quantico, Virginia, for MBA candidates from the University of Pennsylvania's Wharton School of Business. In an effort to teach them leadership skills, student volunteers faced physically daunting tasks, including climbing an 18-foot wall with an 18-degree incline, crossing a rope 20 feet above the ground, crawling facedown under barbed wire through mud, and wading through a four-foot-deep stretch of 50-degree swampy water. The course challenged the students to stay composed in stressful situations, such as rescuing an "injured hostage" in an allotted time and carrying a 20-pound can of "ammunition" across a stream before advancing enemy troops arrived. According to the commanding officer, "The course is designed to take you beyond your self-imposed limits." Top business schools compete to produce the most sought-after graduates. The course at Quantico is designed to develop leadership skills, decisiveness, and teamwork, and Wharton hopes the "taste of life in the trenches" was a valuable experience for the students who participated.[36]

# Decision Making

Managers make many different kinds of decisions, such as the hours in a workday, which employees to hire, what products to introduce, and what price to charge for a product. Decision making is important in all management functions and at all levels, whether the decisions are on a strategic, tactical, or operational level. A systematic approach using the following six steps usually leads to more effective decision making: (1) recognizing and defining the decision situation, (2) developing options to resolve the situation, (3) analyzing the options, (4) selecting the best option, (5) implementing the decision, and (6) monitoring the consequences of the decision (Figure 7.4).

## Recognizing and Defining the Decision Situation

The first step in decision making is recognizing and defining the situation. The situation may be negative—for example, huge losses on a particular product—or positive—for example, an opportunity to increase sales.

Situations calling for small-scale decisions often occur without warning. Situations requiring large-scale decisions, however, generally occur after some warning signs. Effective managers pay attention to such signals. Declining profits, small-scale losses in previous years, inventory buildup, and retailers' unwillingness to stock a product are signals that may foreshadow huge losses to come. If managers pay attention to such signals, problems can be contained.

Once a situation has been recognized, management must define it. Losses reveal a problem—for example, a failing product. One manager may define the situation as a product quality problem; another may define it as a change in consumer preference.

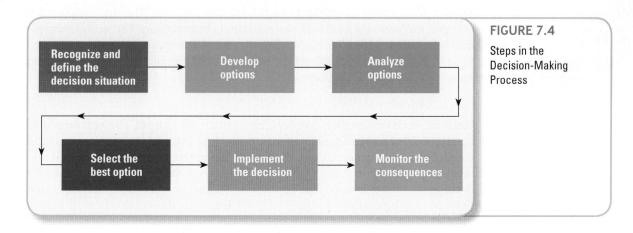

**FIGURE 7.4**

Steps in the Decision-Making Process

# Responding to Business Challenges
## At 100, GM Tries for a Turnaround

General Motors' CEO Rick Wagoner predicted early on that 2008 would be a challenging year for the troubled automaker. However, he also predicted that 2008 would mark the beginning of GM's turnaround. He went so far as to compare the company's future to the boom years of the mid-1950s to the early 1970s. Wagoner, CEO since 2000, has a reputation for embracing change. In 2005, he officially took personal control over product development, manufacturing, and marketing for North America. There is no denying that GM, under Wagoner's direction, started to produce a number of new products and has initiated talks about ambitious plans for future vehicles. However, not all of Wagoner's changes have been pleasant.

The threat of bankruptcy has loomed over GM for some time. To make the system leaner, Wagoner has aimed to cut factory costs considerably. To this end, he has reduced the number of hourly and salaried employees and cut down on health care costs. He has also managed to increase productivity. The two moves together have reduced GM's fixed operating costs by $9 billion. Wagoner also orchestrated an agreement of historic proportion with the United Auto Workers (UAW) union. As of 2010, GM will no longer be responsible for retiree health care—saving the company an estimated $4 billion annually. GM and the UAW have agreed to establish a voluntary employees' beneficiary association (VEBA) instead. GM's contribution to this fund will be $29.5 billion, and after that GM will bear no more financial responsibility.

As Wagoner has worked to improve GM's financial position, he has also been lobbying to improve the company's image. For years, consumers have considered GM vehicles to be somewhat boring, but change is in the air. GM's Cadillac was named *Motor Trend*'s 2008 Car of the Year. The company, known for its gas-guzzlers, is also entering both the hybrid and electric vehicle markets. Wagoner aims to release the Chevrolet Volt, a plug-in electric vehicle, in late 2010.

As much as Wagoner and GM have been striving toward positive transformation, the dire predictions for the 2008 economy may put a damper on future momentum. Rising oil prices, commodity and steel price inflation, a looming economic crisis, the decline in the housing market, and the subprime debacle compounded GM's own problems. Delphi, a supplier of parts for GM declared bankruptcy, and reorganization plans have yet to prove successful. GM originally pledged $2 billion toward assistance, but it may have to give even more. American Axle is another of GM's suppliers, and the company has suffered blows brought on by a prolonged strike. American Axle's problems are sure to have a ripple effect on GM's production as well. Lastly, Saturn has not been popular among consumers. In March 2008, Saturn sales were down 28.8 percent. Although Wagoner claims he is not going to discontinue any GM brands, some analysts suggest that dropping the model would be wise.

Although GM is struggling more than expected, Wagoner remains convinced that resuscitation is on the horizon. With a drop in share price from $43 to $21 between the end of 2007 and April 2008, it is difficult to predict what the future will hold for the automaker.[37]

**Discussion Questions**
1. What are the management and leadership issues facing Rick Wagoner?
2. Do you think GM's challenges are surmountable, or is this the beginning of a long decline for the company?
3. What do you think Wagoner should do to try to get his company back on track?

These two viewpoints may lead to vastly different solutions. The first manager, for example, may seek new sources of raw materials of better quality. The second manager may believe that the product has reached the end of its lifespan and decide to discontinue it. This example emphasizes the importance of carefully defining the problem rather than jumping to conclusions.

## Developing Options
Once the decision situation has been recognized and defined, the next step is to develop a list of possible courses of action. The best lists include both standard and creative plans. As a general rule, more time and expertise are devoted to the development stage of decision making when the decision is of major importance. When the decision is of lesser importance, less time and expertise will be spent on this stage. Options may be developed individually, by teams, or through analysis of similar

situations in comparable organizations. Creativity is a very important part of selecting the most viable option. Creativity depends on new and useful ideas, regardless of where they originate or the method used to create them. The best option can range from a required solution to an identified problem a to a volunteered solution, to an observed problem by an outside work group member.[38]

## Analyzing Options

After developing a list of possible courses of action, management should analyze the practicality and appropriateness of each option. An option may be deemed impractical because of a lack of financial resources, legal restrictions, ethical and social responsibility considerations, authority constraints, technological constraints, economic limitations, or simply a lack of information and expertise. For example, a small computer manufacturer may recognize an opportunity to introduce a new type of computer but lack the financial resources to do so. Other options may be more practical for the computer company: It may consider selling its technology to another computer company that has adequate resources, or it may allow itself to be purchased by a larger company that can introduce the new technology.

When assessing appropriateness, the decision maker should consider whether the proposed option adequately addresses the situation. When analyzing the consequences of an option, managers should consider its impact on the situation and on the organization as a whole. For example, when considering a price cut to boost sales, management must think about the consequences of the action on the organization's cash flow and consumers' reaction to the price change.

## Selecting the Best Option

When all courses of action have been analyzed, management must select the best one. Selection is often a subjective procedure because many situations do not lend themselves to quantitative analysis. Of course, it is not always necessary to select only one option and reject all others; it may be possible to select and use a combination of several options. William Wrigley Jr. made a decision to sell his firm to Mars for $23 billion. The firm was founded by his great-grandfather in 1891, but hard times forced Wrigley to take what was considered to be the best option. This option was to create the Mars-Wrigley firm, currently the world's largest confectionary company with a distribution network in 180 countries.[39] A different set of choices would have been available to the company had it been able to purchase Hershey for $12 billion a few years ago.

## Implementing the Decision

To deal with the situation at hand, the selected option or options must be put into action. Implementation can be fairly simple or very complex, depending on the nature of the decision. Effective implementation of a decision to abandon a product, close a plant, purchase a new business, or something similar requires planning. For example, when a product is dropped, managers must decide how to handle distributors and customers and what to do with the idle production facility. Additionally, they should anticipate resistance from people within the organization (people tend to resist change because they fear the unknown). Finally, management should be ready to deal with the unexpected consequences. No matter how well planned implementation is, unforseen problems will arise. Management must be ready to address these situations when they occur.

## Monitoring the Consequences

After managers have implemented the decision, they must determine whether it has accomplished the desired result. Without proper monitoring, the consequences of decisions may not be known quickly enough to make efficient changes. If the desired result is achieved, management can reasonably conclude that it made a good choice. If the desired result is not achieved, further analysis is warranted. Was the decision simply wrong, or did the situation change? Should some other option have been implemented?

If the desired result is not achieved, management may discover that the situation was incorrectly defined from the beginning. That may require starting the decisionmaking process all over again. Finally, management may determine that the decision was good even though the desired results have not yet shown up, or it may determine a flaw in the decision's implementation. In the latter case, management would not change the decision but would change the way in which it is implemented.

# The Reality of Management

Management is not a cut-and-dried process. There is no mathematical formula for managing an organization and achieving organizational goals, although many managers passionately wish for one! Managers plan, organize, staff, direct, and control, but management expert John P. Kotter says even these functions can be boiled down to two basic activities:

1. Figuring out what to do despite uncertainty, great diversity, and an enormous amount of potentially relevant information, and
2. Getting things done through a large and diverse set of people despite having little direct control over most of them.[40]

Managers spend as much as 75 percent of their time working with others—not only with subordinates but with bosses, people outside their hierarchy at work, and people outside the organization itself. In these interactions they discuss anything and everything remotely connected with their business.

**agenda**
a calender, containing both specific and vague items, that covers short-term goals and long-term objectives

Managers spend a lot of time establishing and updating an agenda of goals and plans for carrying out their responsibilities. An **agenda** contains both specific and vague items, covering short-term goals and long-term objectives. Like a calendar, an agenda helps the manager figure out what must be done and how to get it done to meet the objectives set by the organization. Technology tools, such as personal digital assistants (PDAs) can help managers manage their agendas, contacts, and time.

**networking**
the building of relationships and sharing of information with colleagues who can help managers achieve the items on their agendas

Managers also spend a lot of time **networking**—building relationships and sharing information with colleagues who can help them achieve the items on their agendas. Managers spend much of their time communicating with a variety of people and participating in activities that on the surface do not seem to have much to do with the goals of their organization. Nevertheless, these activities are crucial to getting the job done. Networks are not limited to immediate subordinates and bosses; they include other people in the company as well as customers, suppliers, and friends. These contacts provide managers with information and advice on diverse topics. Managers ask, persuade, and even intimidate members of their network in order to get information and to get things done. Networking helps managers carry out their responsibilities. Andrea Nierenberg, independent business consultant and founder of Nierenberg Group Inc., has been called a "networking success story" by

*The Wall Street Journal.* She writes three notes a day: one to a client, one to a friend, and one to a prospective client. She maintains a database of 3,000 contacts. However, she believes that it isn't how many people you know, but how many you have helped and who know you well enough to recommend you that really count. Opportunity can knock almost anywhere with such extensive networking. Grateful for numerous referrals to her friends, Nierenberg's dentist introduced her to a Wall Street executive who happened to be in the dentist's office at the same time as Nierenberg. She followed up on the meeting and later landed four consulting projects at the executive's firm.[42] Her clients include Citigroup, Time Inc., TIAA-CREF, Food Network, Coach, and Tiffany.[43]

Finally, managers spend a great deal of time confronting the complex and difficult challenges of the business world today. Some of these challenges relate to rapidly changing technology (especially in production and information processing), increased scrutiny of individual and corporate ethics and social responsibility, the changing nature of the workforce, new laws and regulations, increased global competition and more challenging foreign markets, declining educational standards (which may limit the skills and knowledge of the future labor and customer pool), and time itself—that is, making the best use of it. But such diverse issues cannot simply be plugged into a computer program that supplies correct, easy-to-apply solutions. It is only through creativity and imagination that managers can make effective decisions that benefit their organizations.

# So You Want to be a Manager
## What Kind of Manager Do You Want to be?

Managers are needed in a wide variety of organizations. Experts suggest that employment will increase by millions of jobs by 2016. But the requirements for the jobs become more demanding with every passing year— with the speed of technology and communication increasing by the day, and the stress of global commerce increasing pressures to perform. However, if you like a challenge and if you have the right kind of personality, management remains a viable field. Even as companies are forced to restructure, management remains a vital role in business. In fact, the Bureau of Labor Statistics predicts that management positions in public relations, marketing and advertising are set to increase around 12% overall between 2006 and 2016. Financial managers will be in even more demand, with jobs increasing 13% in the same time period. Computer and IT managers will continue to be in strong demand, with the number of jobs increasing 16% between 2006 and 2016.

Salaries for managerial positions remain strong overall. While pay can vary significantly depending on your level of experience, the firm where you work, and the region of the country where you live, below is a list of the nationwide average incomes for a variety of different managers in 2007:

Chief Executives: $151,370
Computer and Information Systems Managers: $113, 880
Financial Managers: $106,200
Marketing Managers: $113,400
Human Resource Managers: $99,810
Operations Managers: $103,780
Medical/ Health Services Managers: $84,980
Administrative Managers: $76,370
Sales Managers: $106,790

In short, if you want to be a manager, there are opportunities in almost every field. There may be fewer middle management positions available in firms, but managers remain a vital part of most industries and will continue to be long into the future—especially as navigating global business becomes ever more complex.

# Review Your Understanding

### Define management, and explain its role in the achievement of organizational objectives.

Management is a process designed to achieve an organization's objectives by using its resources effectively and efficiently in a changing environment. Managers make decisions about the use of the organization's resources and are concerned with planning, organizing, staffing, directing, and controlling the organization's activities so as to reach its objectives.

### Describe the major functions of management.

Planning is the process of determining the organization's objectives and deciding how to accomplish them. Organizing is the structuring of resources and activities to accomplish those objectives efficiently and effectively. Staffing obtains people with the necessary skills to carry out the work of the company. Directing is motivating and leading employees to achieve organizational objectives. Controlling is the process of evaluating and correcting activities to keep the organization on course.

### Distinguish among three levels of management and the concerns of managers at each level.

Top management is responsible for the whole organization and focuses primarily on strategic planning. Middle management develops plans for specific operating areas and carries out the general guidelines set by top management. First-line, or supervisory, management supervises the workers and day-to-day operations. Managers can also be categorized as to their area of responsibility: finance, production and operations, human resources, marketing, or administration.

### Specify the skills managers need in order to be successful.

To be successful, managers need leadership skills (the ability to influence employees to work toward organizational goals), technical expertise (the specialized knowledge and training needed to perform a job), conceptual skills (the ability to think in abstract terms and see how parts fit together to form the whole), analytical skills (the ability to identify relevant issues and recognize their importance, understand the relationships between issues, and perceive the underlying causes of a situation), and human relations (people) skills.

### Summarize the systematic approach to decision making used by many business managers.

A systematic approach to decision making follows these steps: recognizing and defining the situation, developing options, analyzing options, selecting the best option, implementing the decision, and monitoring the consequences.

### Recommend a new strategy to revive a struggling business.

Using the decision-making process described in this chapter, analyze the struggling company's problems described in "Solve the Dilemma" on page 229 and formulate a strategy to turn the company around and aim it toward future success.

# Revisit the World of Business

1. As a manager, what kinds of decisions did Schomer make about his company's image and its consumer base?
2. Is it a high-end market or a mass-market that Vivace serves? Does the target market affect how a manager runs her or his business?
3. Shomer could have made his espresso machine technology proprietary but he did not. What does this say about his business philosophy and management style?

## Learn the Terms

administrative managers   215

agenda   224

analytical skills   219

conceptual skills   219

controlling   209

crisis management or contingency
   planning   206

directing   208

downsizing   207

financial managers   213

first-line managers   213

human relations skills   219

human resources managers   214

information technology (IT)
   managers   215

leadership   216

management   202

managers   202

marketing managers   214

middle managers   213

mission   204

networking   224

operational plans   206

organizing   207

planning   203

production and operations
   managers   214

staffing   207

strategic plans   205

tactical plans   205

technical expertise   219

top managers   209

## Check Your Progress

1. Why is management so important, and what is its purpose?

2. Explain why the American Heart Association would need management, even though its goal is not profit related.

3. Why must a company have financial resources before it can use human and physical resources?

4. Name the five functions of management, and briefly describe each function.

5. Identify the three levels of management. What is the focus of managers at each level?

6. In what areas can managers specialize? From what area do top managers typically come?

7. What skills do managers need? Give examples of how managers use these skills to do their jobs.

8. What are three styles of leadership? Describe situations in which each style would be appropriate.

9. Explain the steps in the decision-making process.

10. What is the mathematical formula for perfect management? What do managers spend most of their time doing?

## Get Involved

1. Give examples of the activities that each of the following managers might be involved in if he or she worked for the Coca-Cola Company:

   Financial manager
   Production and operations manager
   Personnel manager
   Marketing manager
   Administrative manager
   Information technology manager
   Foreman

2. Interview a small sample of managers, attempting to include representatives from all three levels and all areas of management. Discuss their daily activities and relate these activities to the management functions of planning, organizing, staffing, directing, and controlling. What skills do the managers say they need to carry out their tasks?

3. You are a manager of a firm that manufactures conventional ovens. Over the past several years, sales of many of your products have declined; this year, your losses may be quite large. Using the steps of the decision-making process, briefly describe how you arrive at a strategy for correcting the situation.

# Build Your Skills

### FUNCTIONS OF MANAGEMENT

**Background:**
Although the text describes each of the five management functions separately, you learned that these five functions are interrelated, and managers sometimes perform two or more of them at the same time. Here you will broaden your perspective of how these functions occur simultaneously in management activities.

**Task:**

1. Imagine that you are the manager in each scenario described in the table below and you have to decide which management function(s) to use in each.

2. Mark your answers using the following codes:

| Codes | Management Functions |
|---|---|
| P | Planning |
| O | Organizing |
| S | Staffing |
| D | Directing |
| C | Controlling |

| No. | Scenario | Answer(s) |
|---|---|---|
| 1 | Your group's work is centered around a project that is due in two months. Although everyone is working on the project, you have observed your employees involved in what you believe is excessive socializing and other time-filling behaviors. You decide to meet with the group to have them help you break down the project into smaller subprojects with mini-deadlines. You believe this will help keep the group members focused on the project and that the quality of the finished project will then reflect the true capabilities of your group. | |
| 2 | Your first impression of the new group you'll be managing is not too great. You tell your friend at dinner after your first day on the job: "Looks like I got a baby sitting job instead of a management job." | |
| 3 | You call a meeting of your work group and begin it by letting them know that a major procedure used by the work group for the past two years is being significantly revamped, and your department will have to phase in the change during the next six weeks. You proceed by explaining to them the reasoning your boss gave you for this change. You then say, "Let's take the next 5 to 10 minutes to let you voice your reactions to this change." After 10 minutes elapse with the majority of comments being critical of the change, you say: "I appreciate each of you sharing your reactions; and I, too, recognize that *all* change creates problems. The way I see it, however, is that we can spend the remaining 45 minutes of our meeting focusing on why we don't want the change and why we don't think it's necessary; or we can work together to come up with viable solutions to solve the problems that implementing this change will most likely create." After about five more minutes of comments being exchanged, the consensus of the group is that the remainder of the meeting needs to be focused on how to deal with the potential problems the group anticipates having to deal with as the new procedure is implemented. | |
| 4 | You are preparing for the annual budget allocation meetings to be held in the plant manager's office next week. You are determined to present a strong case to support your department getting money for some high-tech equipment that will help your employees do their jobs better. You will stand firm against any suggestions of budget cuts in your area. | |
| 5 | Early in your career you learned an important lesson about employee selection. One of the nurses on your floor unexpectedly quit. The other nurses were putting pressure on you to fill the position quickly because they were overworked even before the nurse left, and then things were really bad. After a hasty recruitment effort, you made a decision based on insufficient information. You ended up regretting your quick decision during the three months of problems that followed until you finally had to discharge the new hire. Since then, you have never let anybody pressure you into making a quick hiring decision. | |

# Solve the Dilemma

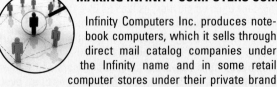

### MAKING INFINITY COMPUTERS COMPETITIVE

Infinity Computers Inc. produces notebook computers, which it sells through direct mail catalog companies under the Infinity name and in some retail computer stores under their private brand names. Infinity's products are not significantly different from competitors', nor do they have extra product-enhancing features, although they are very price competitive. The strength of the company has been its CEO and president, George Anderson, and a highly motivated, loyal workforce. The firm's weakness is having too many employees and too great a reliance on one product. The firm switched from the Intel 486 chip to the Pentium chip only after it saw a significant decline in 486 notebook computer sales.

Recognizing that the strategies that initially made the firm successful are no longer working effectively, Anderson wants to reorganize the company to make it more responsive and competitive and to cut costs. The threat of new technological developments and current competitive conditions could eliminate Infinity.

**Discussion Questions**

1. Evaluate Infinity's current situation and analyze its strengths and weaknesses.

2. Evaluate the opportunities for Infinity, including using its current strategy, and propose alternative strategies.

3. Suggest a plan for Infinity to compete successfully over the next 10 years.

# Build Your Business Plan

### THE NATURE OF MANAGEMENT

The first thing you need to be thinking about is "What is the mission of your business? What is the shared vision your team members have for this business? How do you know if there is demand for this particular business? Remember, you need to think about the customer's *ability and willingness* to try this particular product.

Think about the various processes or stages of your business in the creation and selling of your product, or service.

What functions need to be performed for these processes to be completed? These functions might include buying, receiving, selling, customer service and/or merchandising.

Operationally, if you are opening up a retail establishment, how do you plan to provide your customers with superior customer service? What hours will your customers expect you to be open? At this point in time, how many employees are you thinking you will need to run your business? Do you (or one of your partners) need to be there all the time to supervise?

# See for Yourself Videocase

### PANERA BREAD: MORE THAN JUST A GOOD PLACE TO EAT

Today, Panera Bread is a popular choice for people of all ages looking for tasty, and speedy, restaurant food. Established in 1981 as Au Bon Pain Co. Inc. by current chairman and CEO Ronald M. Shaich and Louis Kane, the restaurant quickly became a leader within the bakery/café category. In 1993, the company purchased the Saint Louis Bread Company, a small company with cafés in the St. Louis area, and renamed the stores Panera. A few years later, in 1997, Shaich and others realized that they were spread too thin. In 1999, they sold all Au Bon Pain units so as to focus all of their energy on Panera. At that point, they officially renamed the company Panera Bread. As of March 25, 2008, Panera Bread consisted of 1,185 stores in 40 states. Five hundred and ten of these stores are company owned; 675 are franchised.

There is no denying Panera's popularity. TNS Intersearch, a market research firm, has reported that Panera has the highest level of customer loyalty among quick-casual restaurants. In 2007, Panera had been at the top of the Sandelman and Associates Quick-Track "Awards of Excellence" for six consecutive years. The esteemed *Zagat* restaurant guide rated Panera number one in four different categories in 2007: overall, food, facilities, and popularity.

How has Panera achieved such success? It all comes back to the way the company is run. When Ron Shaich first established his bakery/café concept, his primary goal was to provide nourishing food to his customers. This sounds simple, but keeping it simple is part of what makes Panera successful. Over time, Panera has made changes, but none of them have complicated the initial concept of offering healthy, delicious food quickly. For example, in 1996, the company added bagels to its line of products, an item that increased the company's volume by 25 percent. In 1997, the company created its gathering-place concept, which increased volume by another 30 percent. These small changes have followed in line with consumer demand, and are part of what have continued to make Panera a success.

Perhaps even more important to success than the food the company serves is the fact that Shaich and others at Panera remain focused on the importance of people, both customers and employees, to the business. As chairman and CEO, it would not be unusual for Ron Shaich to spend most of his time in corporate headquarters, away from the day-to-day dealings of the stores. However, many people are often surprised to discover that he spends a good portion of his time getting touch with the people by visiting Panera stores. Thanks to his personal, hands-on management style, Schaich has helped Panera to become known as a model of business management.

Panera has consistently been labeled one of the best places to work by the *St. Louis Business Journal.* The company places a lot of emphasis on respecting and taking care of its employees, as well as its customers. To this end, Panera makes every effort to promote from within the company. By offering frequent training and support, Panera makes it easier for employees to rise within the company. Employees have noted that both supervisors and Panera executives are easily accessible to employees of all levels throughout the organization. By treating every member of the team with respect, employees are motivated to perform well and are given the freedom to express their ideas and concerns. From Shaich down, many employees say that Panera feels like family.[44]

### Discussion Questions

1. Why did Shaich decide to sell his first business, Au Bon Pain?

2. What kind of manager is Ronald Shaich, and how has his management style helped Panera become a successful company?

3. In a company like Panera, why is it important to encourage internal promotion over external hiring?

**Remember to check out our Online Learning Center at www.mhhe.com/ferrell7e.**

# Organization, Teamwork, and Communication

## CHAPTER OUTLINE

**Introduction**

**Organizational Culture**

**Developing Organizational Structure**

**Assigning Tasks**
*Specialization*
*Departmentalization*

**Assigning Responsibility**
*Delegation of Authority*
*Degree of Centralization*
*Span of Management*
*Organizational Layers*

**Forms of Organizational Structure**
*Line Structure*
*Line-and-Staff Structure*
*Multidivisional Structure*
*Matrix Structure*

**The Role of Groups and Teams in Organizations**
*Committees*
*Task Forces*
*Teams*

**Communicating in Organizations**
*Formal Communication*
*Informal Communication Channels*
*Monitoring Communications*

## OBJECTIVES

*After reading this chapter, you will be able to:*

- Define *organizational structure,* and relate how organizational structures develop.

- Describe how specialization and departmentalization help an organization achieve its goals.

- Distinguish between groups and teams, and identify the types of groups that exist in organizations.

- Determine how organizations assign responsibility for tasks and delegate authority.

- Compare and contrast some common forms of organizational structure.

- Describe how communication occurs in organizations.

- Analyze a business's use of teams.

## PetConnection.com Has a Simple Organizational Structure

PetConnection.com has developed an organization based on blogging that provides a unique competitive advantage. Although many people feel that blogs, and more and more Internet sites in general, are either dumping grounds for individual thought or for fluff reporting, there are situations in which this viewpoint is proven 100 percent wrong. One such situation is the recent recalling of contaminated pet food and the deaths of thousands of pets. In the midst of scandal and sadness, sites previously dedicated to locating doggie parks or products for animal hygiene, and to providing humorous pet photos and anecdotes, have become the only reliable sources of information for millions of pet owners.

PetConnection.com, founded by writer Gina Spadafori and veterinarian Marty Becker, runs a weekly pet care feature that is syndicated to newspapers, magazines, and Internet sites throughout the United States and Canada. The site also sells pet care books and provides numerous links and answers to common pet-related questions. In the wake of the pet food recalls, PetConnection.com has also become a major source of information for pet owners. In the beginning, PetConnection.com posted information on what owners needed to know about recalled food. Then the site created an online database to record symptoms of affected pets, outcomes, and veterinarian information. Although the Centers for Disease Control and Prevention would handle statistics in human cases, no system was in place for recording what was happening to these animals as a result of the tainted food. Therefore,

*continued*

PetConnection.com's database remains the only real source of statistical information. PetConnection.com also began publishing "live blogs" of the Food and Drug Administration (FDA) phone news conferences regarding the topic. According to Spadafori, thousands of people logged in for each press conference.

The development of PetConnection.com illustrates an organizational structure based on specialization. This blog focuses on a target market of consumers interested in their pets' welfare and provides a service around the needs of these customers. Since Gina and Marty are the only employees providing this service, they do not require a complex organizational structure, and they take care of all of the responsibilities related to the blog. While some organizations have a centralized organizational structure, small organizations like PetConnection.com avoid decisions about forms of organizational structure and delegation of authority. The advantage of a small organization is limited bureaucracy and efficient decision making.[1]

# Introduction

An organization's structure determines how well it makes decisions and responds to problems, and it influences employees' attitudes toward their work. A suitable structure can minimize a business's costs and maximize its efficiency. For these reasons, many businesses, such as Motorola, Apple Computer, and Hewlett-Packard, have changed their organizational structures in recent years in an effort to enhance their profits and competitive edge.

Because a business's structure can so profoundly affect its success, this chapter will examine organizational structure in detail. First, we discuss how an organization's culture affects its operations. Then we consider the development of structure, including how tasks and responsibilities are organized through specialization and departmentalization. Next, we explore some of the forms organizational structure may take. Finally, we consider communications within business.

## Organizational Culture

**organizational culture**
a firm's shared values, beliefs, traditions, philosophies, rules, and role models for behavior

One of the most important aspects of organizing a business is determining its **organizational culture,** a firm's shared values, beliefs, traditions, philosophies, rules, and role models for behavior. Also called corporate culture, an organizational culture exists in every organization, regardless of size, organizational type, product, or profit objective. For example, the organizational culture of the Marine Corps focuses on teamwork, often splitting into buddy teams. The Marines drill recruits to do the right thing whether it's good for you or not, whether it is easy or difficult.[2] A firm's culture may be expressed formally through its mission statement, codes of ethics, memos, manuals, and ceremonies, but it is more commonly expressed informally. Examples of informal expressions of culture include dress codes (or the lack thereof), work habits, extracurricular activities, and stories. Employees often learn the accepted standards through discussions with co-workers.

# Business in a Changing World
## Dell Changes Its Organizational Culture

After spending years as the leader in the personal computer (PC) market, Dell has been overtaken by rival Hewlett-Packard. In an effort to regain the top spot, Dell is delving into the retail market and changing its organizational culture. Since its beginning in the 1980s, Dell has succeeded by selling PCs and computer-related products via direct sales (over the phone or Internet). At the same time that Dell was having such success, many other computer companies sold their products through retail outlets. Dell's direct sales technique allowed it to retain a cost advantage over competitors and pushed it into the number-one slot. However, almost two decades later, companies that sell their products via a combination of retail and direct sales are gaining ground. Hewlett-Packard now holds the number-one slot, and Acer, Toshiba, Apple, and others are picking up the pace. With Dell's market share dropping to 15 percent, things need to change.

To alter the organizational culture to be more responsive to changes in the market, Dell's founder, Michael Dell, came back to lead the company during this cultural transformation, replacing former CEO Kevin Rollins. Michael Dell was responsible for creating the company's model of building computers to order at a time when the concept was innovative. Analysts feel that he is just the person to lead the company in a new organizational culture focused on innovation. Dell had become complacent focusing on production, efficiency, and online one-to-one customer contacts.

Perhaps the most notable change is Dell's new affiliation with Wal-Mart stores. Although Dell has forayed into the retail sector before, selling in both Costco and CompUSA, its partnership with Wal-Mart takes a very different approach. Wal-Mart is considered by many to be the largest and most popular retail chain around. It is estimated that some 90 percent of Americans shop at Wal-Mart. Because of Wal-Mart's popularity, Dell will now be approaching retail on a huge scale and with more fanfare than its previous forays warranted. This will change the marketing, organization, and to some extent overall production and operations.

If, in fact, Dell plans to continue its expansion into retail, the marriage of Dell and Wal-Mart should provide Dell with much needed experience. To sell retail, the company must make changes in areas such as supply chain and advertising. The overall culture of the organization will change to become more mass marketing focused, depending on retailers such as Wal-Mart to be a vital link in its marketing organization. These changes will also provide Dell with valuable information as it continues to expand to other retailers and change its culture to become more competitive.[3]

### Discussion Questions
1. Why was Michael Dell the ideal person to change the corporate culture to become more competitive?
2. Why does changing the marketing and operations of a company require a new organizational culture?
3. How will the information gained from retail partners such as Wal-Mart and Costco change the corporate culture at Dell?

Google keeps its culture of innovation alive by allowing engineers to spend around 20 percent of their time working on projects that are not related to their main job. Mixing up responsibilities keeps the organization fresh and productive. The chief operating officer is also a licensed neurosurgeon, the international webmaster creates the Google holiday logos and translates Web sites into different languages, and everyone contributes to the company's success. The overall "Google Culture" is reflected through "hallway décor" consisting of bicycles and large rubber balls as well as press clippings from around the world. Offices are "clusters" with three or four employees sharing space with couches and maybe pets.[4] Disneyland/Disney World and McDonald's have organizational cultures focused on cleanliness, value, and service. At Matsushita, employees sing a company song every morning that translates, "As individuals we will work to improve life and contribute to human progress." The company's president, Kunio Nakamura, also believes the highest paid employee should earn no more than 10 times the lowest paid employee. The effort to hire younger employees and more women is also affecting the Japanese firm's culture.[5] When such values and philosophies are shared by all members of an organization, they will be expressed in its relationships with stakeholders. However, organizational cultures that lack such positive values may result in employees who are unproductive and indifferent and have poor attitudes, which will be reflected

*Bill Gore and his wife Vieve Gore are the founders of W. L. Gore & Associates, which makes Gore-Tex fabrics, and a myriad of other products. Because the couple wanted to instill a culture of innovation at the company, there are no bosses. Employees are hired as "associates" and are assigned to "sponsors" in the functional groups in which they work.*

**structure**
the arrangement or relationship of positions within an organization

externally to customers. Unethical cultures may have contributed to the misconduct at a number of well-known companies, such as Enron and WorldCom, at the turn of the century. Merck & Company agreed to pay $58 million to settle Vioxx advertising claims in 2008 with 29 states and the District of Columbia. Many agree that Merck operated with an aggressive and very competitive organizational culture in the late '90s. Pennsylvania Attorney General Tom Corbett said that in 1999, Merck ran "an aggressive and deceptive advertising campaign which misrepresented the safety and improperly concealed the increased risks associated with Vioxx." These ads continued to run until 2004. In addition, Merck has agreed to stop ghost writing articles in medical journals promoting its interests.[6]

Organizational culture helps ensure that all members of a company share values and suggests rules for how to behave and deal with problems within the organization. Figure 8.1 indicates that corporate culture is the most important driver of innovation. The key to success in any organization is satisfying stakeholders, especially customers. Establishing a positive organizational culture sets the tone for all other decisions, including building an efficient organizational structure.

## Developing Organizational Structure

**Structure** is the arrangement or relationship of positions within an organization. Rarely is an organization, or any group of individuals working together, able to achieve common objectives without some form of structure, whether that structure is explicitly defined or only implied. A professional baseball team such as the Colorado Rockies is a business organization with an explicit formal structure that guides the team's activities so that it can increase game attendance, win games, and sell souvenirs such as T-shirts. But even an informal group playing softball for fun has an organization that specifies who will pitch, catch, bat, coach, and so on. Governments and nonprofit organizations also have formal organizational structures to facilitate the achievement of their objectives. Getting people to work together efficiently and coordinating the skills of diverse individuals require careful planning. Developing appropriate organizational structures is therefore a major challenge for managers in both large and small organizations.

An organization's structure develops when managers assign work tasks and activities to specific individuals or work groups and coordinate the diverse activities required to reach the firm's objectives. When Macy's, for example, has a sale, the store manager must work with the advertising department to make the public aware of the sale, with department managers to ensure that extra salespeople are

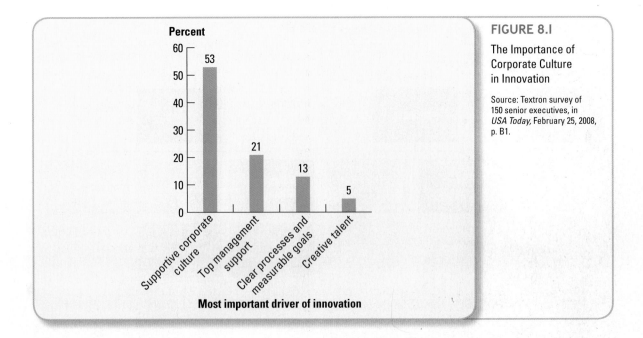

**FIGURE 8.1**

The Importance of
Corporate Culture
in Innovation

Source: Textron survey of
150 senior executives, in
*USA Today,* February 25, 2008,
p. B1.

scheduled to handle the increased customer traffic, and with merchandise buyers to ensure that enough sale merchandise is available to meet expected consumer demand. All the people occupying these positions must work together to achieve the store's objectives.

The best way to begin to understand how organizational structure develops is to consider the evolution of a new business such as a clothing store. At first, the business is a sole proprietorship in which the owner does everything—buys, prices, and displays the merchandise; does the accounting and tax records; and assists customers. As the business grows, the owner hires a salesperson and perhaps a merchandise buyer to help run the store. As the business continues to grow, the owner hires more salespeople. The growth and success of the business now require the owner to be away from the store frequently, meeting with suppliers, engaging in public relations, and attending trade shows. Thus, the owner must designate someone to manage the salespeople and maintain the accounting, payroll, and tax functions. If the owner decides to expand by opening more stores, still more managers will be needed. Figure 8.2 shows these stages of growth with three **organizational charts** (visual displays of organizational structure, chain of command, and other relationships).

Growth requires organizing—the structuring of human, physical, and financial resources to achieve objectives in an effective and efficient manner. Growth necessitates hiring people who have specialized skills. With more people and greater specialization, the organization needs to develop a formal structure to function efficiently. Endangered Species Chocolate moved from Oregon to Indianapolis and has seen its sales explode in three years from $3 million to $17 million, with a goal of reaching $30 million by 2013. The company's success can be attributed to a major reorganization and focus on the triple bottom line (financial, environmental, and the social side of the business). The company has grown its workforce from 18 employees to nearly 50 and gives 10 percent of profits to support "species, habitat, and humanity."[7] As we shall see, structuring an organization requires that management assign

**organizational chart**
a visual display
of the organizational
structure, lines of
authority (chain of
command), staff
relationships,
permanent committee
arrangements, and lines
of communication

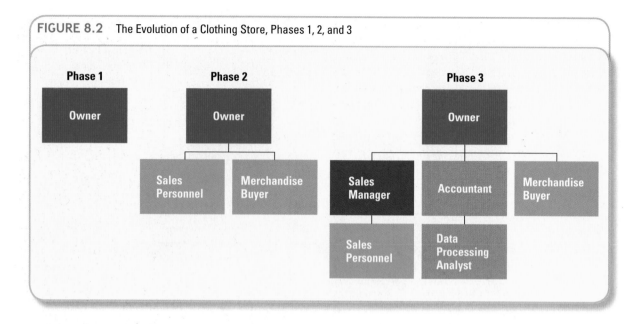

**FIGURE 8.2**    The Evolution of a Clothing Store, Phases 1, 2, and 3

work tasks to specific individuals and departments and assign responsibility for the achievement of specific organizational objectives.

# Assigning Tasks

For a business to earn profits from the sale of its products, its managers must first determine what activities are required to achieve its objectives. At Celestial Seasonings, for example, employees must purchase herbs from suppliers, dry the herbs and place them in tea bags, package and label the tea, and then ship the packages to grocery stores around the country. Other necessary activities include negotiating with supermarkets and other retailers for display space, developing new products, planning advertising, managing finances, and managing employees. All these activities must be coordinated, assigned to work groups, and controlled. Two important aspects of assigning these work activities are specialization and departmentalization.

## Specialization

After identifying all activities that must be accomplished, managers then break these activities down into specific tasks that can be handled by individual employees. This division of labor into small, specific tasks and the assignment of employees to do a single task is called **specialization**.

The rationale for specialization is efficiency. People can perform more efficiently if they master just one task rather than all tasks. In *The Wealth of Nations*, 18th-century economist Adam Smith discussed specialization, using the manufacture of straight pins as an example. Individually, workers could produce 20 pins a day when each employee produced complete pins. Thus, 10 employees working independently of each other could produce 200 pins a day. However, when one worker drew the wire, another straightened it, a third cut it, and a fourth ground the point, 10 workers could produce 48,000 pins per day.[8] To save money and achieve the benefits of specialization, some companies outsource and hire temporary workers to provide key skills. Many highly skilled, diverse, experienced workers are available through temp agencies.

**specialization**
the division of labor into small, specific tasks and the assignment of employees to do a single task

Specialization means workers do not waste time shifting from one job to another, and training is easier. However, efficiency is not the only motivation for specialization. Specialization also occurs when the activities that must be performed within an organization are too numerous for one person to handle. Recall the example of the clothing store. When the business was young and small, the owner could do everything; but when the business grew, the owner needed help waiting on customers, keeping the books, and managing other business activities.

Overspecialization can have negative consequences. Employees may become bored and dissatisfied with their jobs, and the result of their unhappiness is likely to be poor quality work, more injuries, and high employee turnover. This is why some manufacturing firms allow job rotation so that employees do not become dissatisfied and leave. Although some degree of specialization is necessary for efficiency, because of differences in skills, abilities, and interests, all people are not equally suited for all jobs. We examine some strategies to overcome these issues in Chapter 10.

*Henry Ford, the founder of Ford Motor Company revolutionized the transportation industry by creating assembly lines like this one so as to specialize the tasks his workers performed.*

### Departmentalization

After assigning specialized tasks to individuals, managers next organize workers doing similar jobs into groups to make them easier to manage. **Departmentalization** is the grouping of jobs into working units usually called departments, units, groups, or divisions. As we shall see, departments are commonly organized by function, product, geographic region, or customer (Figure 8.3). Most companies use more than one departmentalization plan to enhance productivity. For instance, many consumer goods manufacturers have departments for specific product lines (beverages, frozen dinners, canned goods, and so on) as well as departments dealing with legal, purchasing, finance, human resources, and other business functions. For smaller companies, accounting can be set up online, almost as an automated department. Accounting software can handle electronic transfers so you never have to worry about a late bill.[9] Many city governments also have departments for specific services (e.g., police, fire, waste disposal) as well as departments for legal, human resources, and other business functions. Figure 8.4 depicts the organizational chart for the city of Corpus Christi, Texas, showing these departments.

**departmentalization** the grouping of jobs into working units usually called departments, units, groups, or divisions

**Functional Departmentalization.** **Functional departmentalization** groups jobs that perform similar functional activities, such as finance, manufacturing, marketing, and human resources. Each of these functions is managed by an expert in the work done by the department—an engineer supervises the production department; a financial executive supervises the finance department. This approach is common in small organizations. A weakness of functional departmentalization is that, because it tends to emphasize departmental units rather than the organization as a whole, decision making that involves more than one department may be slow, and

**functional departmentalization** the grouping of jobs that perform similar functional activities, such as finance, manufacturing, marketing, and human resources

FIGURE 8.3   Departmentalization

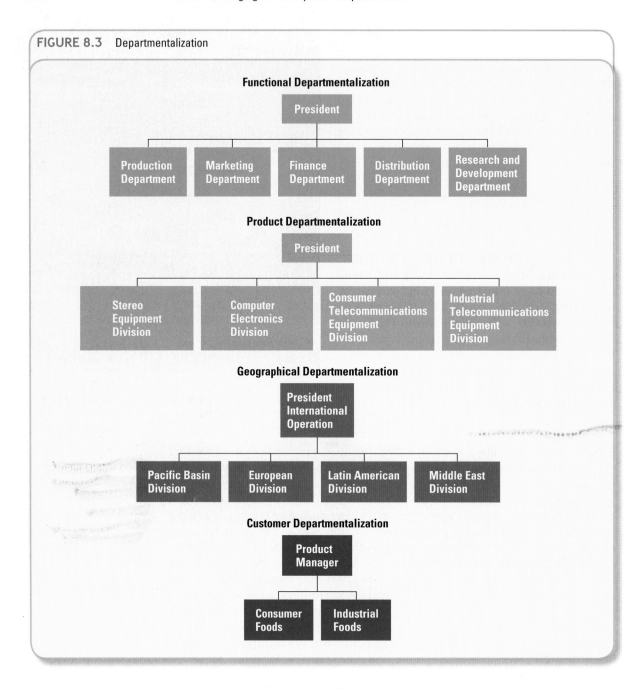

it requires greater coordination. Thus, as business grow, they tend to adopt other approaches to organizing jobs.

**product departmentalization**
the organization of jobs in relation to the products of the firm

Product Departmentalization.   **Product departmentalization,** as you might guess, organizes jobs around the products of the firm. Procter & Gamble has global units, such as laundry and cleaning products, paper products, and health care products. Each division develops and implements its own product plans, monitors the results, and takes corrective action as necessary. Functional activities— production, finance, marketing, and others—are located within each product

FIGURE 8.4    An Organizational Chart for the City of Corpus Christi

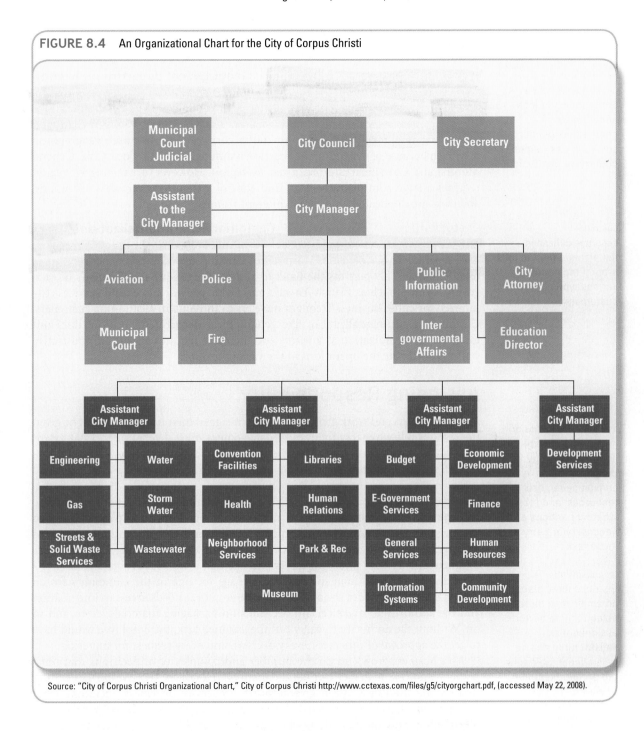

Source: "City of Corpus Christi Organizational Chart," City of Corpus Christi http://www.cctexas.com/files/g5/cityorgchart.pdf, (accessed May 22, 2008).

division. Consequently, organizing by products duplicates functions and resources and emphasizes the product rather than achievement of the organization's overall objectives. However, it simplifies decision making and helps coordinate all activities related to a product or product group. Kodak, for example, reorganized into special product groups devoted to digital business (Consumer Digital Imaging Group and the Graphic Communications Group) and the Film Producers Group. President and

COO Philip J. Faraci hopes this structure will support continued profitable growth in digital markets.[10]

Geographical Departmentalization. **Geographical departmentalization** groups jobs according to geographic location, such as a state, region, country, or continent. FritoLay, for example, is organized into four regional divisions, allowing the company to get closer to its customers and respond more quickly and efficiently to regional competitors. Multinational corporations often use a geographical approach because of vast differences between different regions. Coca-Cola, General Motors, and Caterpillar are organized by region. However, organizing by region requires a large administrative staff and control system to coordinate operations, and tasks are duplicated among the different regions.

Customer Departmentalization. **Customer departmentalization** arranges jobs around the needs of various types of customers. Banks, for example, typically have separate departments for commercial banking activities and for consumer or retail banking. This permits the bank to address the unique requirements of each group. Airlines, such as British Airways and Delta, provide prices and services customized for either business/frequent travelers or infrequent/vacationing customers. Customer departmentalization, like geographical departmentalization, does not focus on the organization as a whole and therefore requires a large administrative staff to coordinate the operations of the various groups.

# Assigning Responsibility

After all workers and work groups have been assigned their tasks, they must be given the responsibility to carry them out. Management must determine to what extent it will delegate responsibility throughout the organization and how many employees will report to each manager.

## Delegation of Authority

**Delegation of authority** means not only giving tasks to employees but also empowering them to make commitments, use resources, and take whatever actions are necessary to carry out those tasks. Let's say a marketing manager at Nestlé has assigned an employee to design a new package that is less wasteful (more environmentally responsible) than the current package for one of the company's frozen dinner lines. To carry out the assignment, the employee needs access to information and the authority to make certain decisions on packaging materials, costs, and so on. Without the authority to carry out the assigned task, the employee would have to get the approval of others for every decision and every request for materials.

As a business grows, so do the number and complexity of decisions that must be made; no one manager can handle them all. Hotels such as Westin Hotels and Resorts and the Ritz-Carlton give authority to service providers, including front desk personnel, to make service decisions such as moving a guest to another room or providing a discount to guests who experience a problem at the hotel. Delegation of authority frees a manager to concentrate on larger issues, such as planning or dealing with problems and opportunities.

Delegation also gives a **responsibility,** or obligation, to employees to carry out assigned tasks satisfactorily and holds them accountable for the proper execution of their assigned work. The principle of **accountability** means that employees who accept an assignment and the authority to carry it out are answerable to a

---

**geographical departmentalization** the grouping of jobs according to geographic location, such as state, region, country, or continent

**customer departmentalization** the arrangement of jobs around the needs of various types of customers

**delegation of authority** giving employees not only tasks, but also the power to make commitments, use resources, and take whatever actions are necessary to carry out those tasks

**responsibility** the obligation, placed on employees through delegation, to perform assigned tasks satisfactorily and be held accountable for the proper execution of work

**accountability** the principle that employees who accept an assignment and the authority to carry it out are answerable to a superior for the outcome

superior for the outcome. Returning to the Nestlé example, if the packaging design prepared by the employee is unacceptable or late, the employee must accept the blame. If the new design is innovative, attractive, and cost-efficient, as well as environmentally responsible, or is completed ahead of schedule, the employee will accept the credit.

The process of delegating authority establishes a pattern of relationships and accountability between a superior and his or her subordinates. The president of a firm delegates responsibility for all marketing activities to the vice president of marketing. The vice president accepts this responsibility and has the authority to obtain all relevant information, make certain decisions, and delegate any or all activities to his or her subordinates. The vice president, in turn, delegates all advertising activities to the advertising manager, all sales activities to the sales manager, and so on. These managers then delegate specific tasks to their subordinates. However, the act of delegating authority to a subordinate does not relieve the superior of accountability for the delegated job. Even though the vice president of marketing delegates work to subordinates, he or she is still ultimately accountable to the president for all marketing activities.

**centralized organization**
a structure in which authority is concentrated at the top, and very little decision-making authority is delegated to lower levels

## Degree of Centralization
The extent to which authority is delegated throughout an organization determines its degree of centralization.

Centralized Organizations. In a **centralized organization,** authority is concentrated at the top, and very little decision-making authority is delegated to lower levels. Although decision-making authority in centralized organizations rests with top levels of management, a vast amount of responsibility for carrying out daily and routine procedures is delegated to even the lowest levels of the organization. Many government organizations, including the U.S. Army, the Postal Service, and the IRS, are centralized.

Businesses tend to be more centralized when the decisions to be made are risky and when low-level managers are not highly skilled in decision making. In the banking industry, for example, authority to make routine car loans is given to all loan managers, while the authority to make high-risk loans, such as for a large residential development, may be restricted to upper-level loan officers.

Overcentralization can cause serious problems for a company, in part because it may take longer for the organization as a whole to implement decisions and to respond to changes and problems on a regional scale. McDonald's, for example, was one of the last chains to introduce a chicken sandwich because of the amount of research, development, test marketing, and layers of approval the product had to go through.

*Bed, Bath & Beyond empowers its store managers who know their customers better than anyone else. Each manager selects about 70 percent of his or her store's merchandise, including linens, appliances, picture frames, and imported olive oil, to ensure they match that store's customers.*

# Entrepreneurship in Action
## Hydroponics Helps Green Garlic Harvest Profits

Dilip Naik

**Business:** Gourmet Country Farm

**Founded:** 1999

**Success:** Dilip Naik now sells green garlic to large chains such as Whole Foods.

Green garlic, like the kind used by Dilip Naik's grandmother in their native India, wasn't available in the United States year round. When grown outdoors, the mild garlic can be harvested only from March to May. Even during these months, the garlic is difficult to come by—only available in certain specialty stores and at some farmer's markets. As a result, Naik resolved to grow it for himself. However, he still had to combat the short growing season. A breakthrough occurred when he attempted hydroponics, a method of growing plants in water. After perfecting this method, he, through his company Gourmet Country Farm, began to sell fresh green garlic

and other green garlic products to Whole Foods, Central Market, and other specialty stores. His secret to success was developing the technology to harvest the product year round. To do so, he had to create special growing beds and a water system that would hydrate the plants without oversaturating them. He also needed to design a method of harvesting that did not crush the cloves. As his business began to grow, Naik recognized the need to assign tasks and hire employees to carry out specialized functions. Labor is a big issue in agriculture, so he made his daughter-in-law the business development manager and hired three employees to harvest the product. He contracted with a local food distributor to deliver to area stores. His son also works in the operation. As further expansion occurs, more employees will be required to engage in specialized functions. Naik is building a business culture focused on execution, family involvement, and the delivery of a high-quality unique product.[11]

**decentralized organization**

an organization in which decision-making authority is delegated as far down the chain of command as possible

**Decentralized Organizations.** A **decentralized organization** is one in which decision-making authority is delegated as far down the chain of command as possible. Decentralization is characteristic of organizations that operate in complex, unpredictable environments. Businesses that face intense competition often decentralize to improve responsiveness and enhance creativity. Lower-level managers who interact with the external environment often develop a good understanding of it and thus are able to react quickly to changes.

Delegating authority to lower levels of managers may increase the organization's productivity. Decentralization requires that lower-level managers have strong decision-making skills. In recent years the trend has been toward more decentralized organizations, and some of the largest and most successful companies, including GE, IBM, Google, Nike, and JCPenney, have decentralized decision-making authority. McDonald's, realizing most of its growth outside the United States, is becoming increasingly decentralized and "glo-cal," varying products in specific markets to better meet consumer demands. This change in organizational structure for McDonald's is fostering greater innovation and local market success. In Brazil, Italy, or Portugal, you can order a Big Tasty. The Big Tasty is a giant burger (5.5 oz.) smothered in barbecue sauce, topped with square cut lettuce, tomatoes, three slices of cheese, and weighing in at 840 calories. Try to find this sandwich in the United States, and you will not. The sandwich was concocted in a test kitchen in Germany, tested and launched in Sweden; and has been a success in other parts of Europe, Latin American, and Australia. Diversity and decentralization seem to be McDonald's keys to being better, not just bigger.[12] Nonprofit organizations benefit from decentralization as well.

## Span of Management

How many subordinates should a manager manage? There is no simple answer. Experts generally agree, however, that top managers should not directly supervise more than four to eight people, while lower-level managers who supervise routine tasks are capable of managing a much larger number of subordinates. For example, the manager of the finance department may supervise 25 employees, whereas the vice president of finance may supervise only five managers. **Span of management** refers to the number of subordinates who report to a particular manager. A *wide span of management* exists when a manager directly supervises a very large number of employees. A *narrow span of management* exists when a manager directly supervises only a few subordinates (Figure 8.5). At Whole Foods, each store consists of eight teams that oversee departments (seafood, produce, checkout, etc). After training, teams vote as to whether a new hire will be a productive member and a two-thirds vote is required to win a full-time position. These teams are responsible for all key operational decisions from pricing, ordering, and staffing to in-store promotions. Compared with centralized department stores, this combination of a small span of control with decentralization allows Whole Foods to uniquely appeal to local markets' needs.[13]

> **span of management**
> the number of subordinates who report to a particular manager

Should the span of management be wide or narrow? To answer this question, several factors need to be considered. A narrow span of management is appropriate when superiors and subordinates are not in close proximity, the manager has many responsibilities in addition to the supervision, the interaction between superiors and subordinates is frequent, and problems are common. However, when superiors and subordinates are located close to one another, the manager has few responsibilities other than supervision, the level of interaction between superiors and subordinates is low, few problems arise, subordinates are highly competent, and a set of specific operating procedures governs the activities of managers and their subordinates, a wide span of management will be more appropriate. Narrow spans of management are typical in centralized organizations, while wide spans of management are more common in decentralized firms.

## Organizational Layers

Complementing the concept of span of management is **organizational layers,** the levels of management in an organization.

> **organizational layers**
> the levels of management in an organization

A company with many layers of managers is considered tall; in a tall organization, the span of management is narrow (see Figure 8.5). Because each manager supervises only a few subordinates, many layers of management are necessary to carry out the operations of the business. McDonald's, for example, has a tall organization with many layers, including store managers, district managers, regional managers, and functional managers (finance, marketing, and so on), as well as a chief executive officer and many vice presidents. Because there are more managers in tall organizations

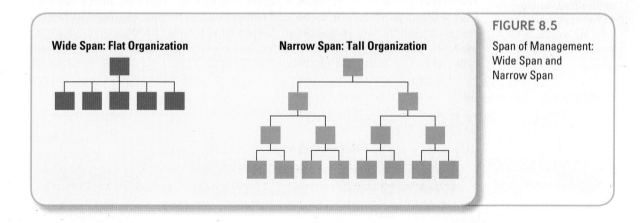

**FIGURE 8.5**

Span of Management: Wide Span and Narrow Span

than in flat organizations, administrative costs are usually higher. Communication is slower because information must pass through many layers.

Organizations with few layers are flat and have wide spans of management. When managers supervise a large number of employees, fewer management layers are needed to conduct the organization's activities. Managers in flat organizations typically perform more administrative duties than managers in tall organizations because there are fewer of them. They also spend more time supervising and working with subordinates.

Many of the companies that have decentralized also flattened their structures and widened their spans of management, often by eliminating layers of middle management. Many corporations, including Avon, AT&T, and Ford Motor Company, did so to reduce costs, speed decision making, and boost overall productivity.

## Forms of Organizational Structure

Along with assigning tasks and the responsibility for carrying them out, managers must consider how to structure their authority relationships—that is, what structure the organization itself will have and how it will appear on the organizational chart. Common forms of organization include line structure, line-and-staff structure, multidivisional structure, and matrix structure.

### Line Structure

**line structure**
the simplest organizational structure in which direct lines of authority extend from the top manager to the lowest level of the organization

The simplest organizational structure, **line structure,** has direct lines of authority that extend from the top manager to employees at the lowest level of the organization. For example, a convenience store employee may report to an assistant manager, who reports to the store manager, who reports to a regional manager, or, in an independent store, directly to the owner (Figure 8.6). This structure has a clear chain of command, which enables managers to make decisions quickly. A mid-level manager facing a decision must consult only one person, his or her immediate supervisor. However, this structure requires that managers possess a wide range of knowledge and skills. They are responsible for a variety of activities and must be knowledgeable about them all. Line structures are most common in small businesses.

### Line-and-Staff Structure

**line-and-staff structure**
a structure having a traditional line relationship between superiors and subordinates and also specialized managers—called staff managers—who are available to assist line managers

The **line-and-staff structure** has a traditional line relationship between superiors and subordinates, and specialized managers—called staff managers—are available to assist line managers (Figure 8.7). Line managers can focus on their area of expertise in the operation of the business, while staff managers provide advice and support to line departments on specialized matters such as finance, engineering, human resources, and the law. In the city of Corpus Christi (refer back for Figure 8.4), for example, assistant city managers are line managers who oversee groups of related

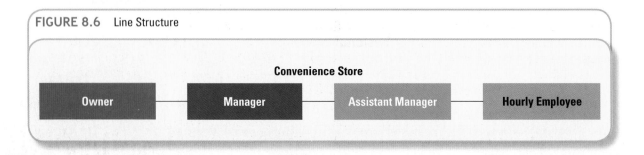

**FIGURE 8.6**　Line Structure

**Convenience Store**

Owner — Manager — Assistant Manager — Hourly Employee

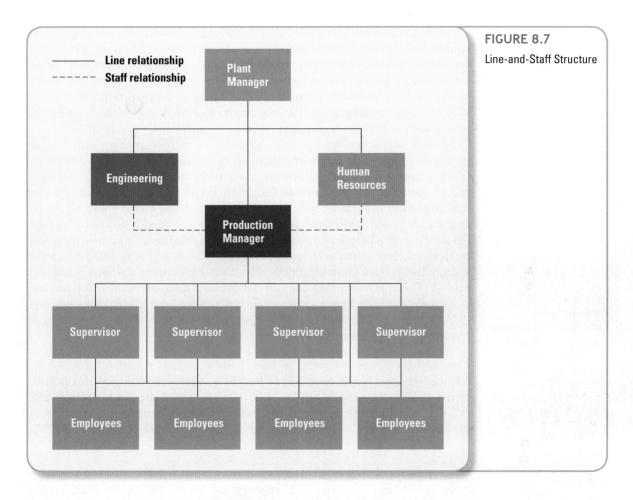

FIGURE 8.7
Line-and-Staff Structure

departments. However, the city attorney, police chief, and fire chief are effectively staff managers who report directly to the city manager (the city equivalent of a business chief executive officer). Staff managers do not have direct authority over line managers or over the line manager's subordinates, but they do have direct authority over subordinates in their own departments. However, line-and-staff organizations may experience problems with overstaffing and ambiguous lines of communication. Additionally, employees may become frustrated because they lack the authority to carry out certain decisions.

## Multidivisional Structure

As companies grow and diversify, traditional line structures become difficult to coordinate, making communication difficult and decision making slow. When the weaknesses of the structure—the "turf wars," miscommunication, and working at cross-purposes—exceed the benefits, growing firms tend to restructure, often into the divisionalized form. A **multidivisional structure** organizes departments into larger groups called divisions. Just as departments might be formed on the basis of geography, customer, product, or a combination of these, so too divisions can be formed based on any of these methods of organizing. Within each of these divisions, departments may be organized by product, geographic region, function, or some combination of all three. General Motors, for example, operates with divisions structured around its well-known automotive brands (for example,

**multidivisional structure**
a structure that organizes departments into larger groups called divisions

Chevrolet, Pontiac, and Buick). Within that structure, production and engineering tend to be centralized, while marketing is decentralized under each automotive division. To get away from some of the problems with aged organizational structures, General Motors tried an experiment in the 1980s known as Saturn. Saturn was to be a completely different type of company—an organizational structure with no-haggle pricing and nonunion, empowered employees. Unfortunately, the only artifact of the Saturn dream is the Saturn nameplate.[14]

Multidivisional structures permit delegation of decision-making authority, allowing divisional and department managers to specialize. They allow those closest to the action to make the decisions that will affect them. Delegation of authority and divisionalized work also mean that better decisions are made faster, and they tend to be more innovative. Most importantly, by focusing each division on a common region, product, or customer, each is more likely to provide products that meet the needs of its particular customers. However, the divisional structure inevitably creates work duplication, which makes it more difficult to realize the economies of scale that result from grouping functions together. For example, Cadbury Schweppes made its Dr Pepper Snapple Group an independent company because this division was mainly in the declining nonalcoholic U.S. market, where soft-drink sales were sharply down. This allowed Cadbury Schweppes to focus on the profitability of its candy and chewing gum business.[15]

## Matrix Structure

**matrix structure**
a structure that sets up teams from different departments, thereby creating two or more intersecting lines of authority; also called a project-management structure

Another structure that attempts to address issues that arise with growth, diversification, productivity, and competitiveness, is the matrix. A **matrix structure,** also called a project management structure, sets up teams from different departments, thereby creating two or more intersecting lines of authority (Figure 8.8). The

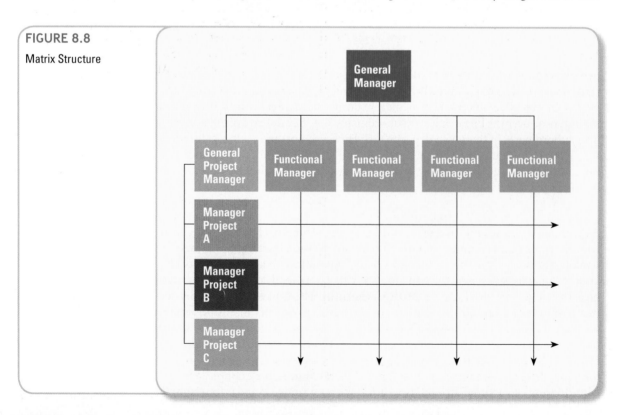

**FIGURE 8.8**

Matrix Structure

matrix structure superimposes project-based departments on the more traditional, function-based departments. Project teams bring together specialists from a variety of areas to work together on a single project, such as developing a new fighter jet. In this arrangement, employees are responsible to two managers—functional managers and project managers. Matrix structures are usually temporary: Team members typically go back to their functional or line department after a project is finished. However, more firms are becoming permanent matrix structures, creating and dissolving project teams as needed to meet customer needs. The aerospace industry was one of the first to apply the matrix structure, but today it is used by universities and schools, accounting firms, banks, and organizations in other industries.

Matrix structures provide flexibility, enhanced cooperation, and creativity, and they enable the company to respond quickly to changes in the environment by giving special attention to specific projects or problems. However, they are generally expensive and quite complex, and employees may be confused as to whose authority has priority—the project manager's or the immediate supervisor's.

## The Role of Groups and Teams in Organizations

Regardless of how they are organized, most of the essential work of business occurs in individual work groups and teams, so we'll take a closer look at them now. Although some experts do not make a distinction between groups and teams, in recent years there has been a gradual shift toward an emphasis on teams and managing them to enhance individual and organizational success. Some experts now believe that highest productivity results only when groups become teams.[16]

Traditionally, a **group** has been defined as two or more individuals who communicate with one another, share a common identity, and have a common goal. A **team** is a small group whose members have complementary skills; have a common purpose, goals, and approach; and hold themselves mutually accountable.[17] All teams are groups, but not all groups are teams. Table 8.1 points out some important

**group**
two or more individuals who communicate with one another, share a common identity, and have a common goal

**team**
a small group whose members have complementary skills; have a common purpose, goals, and approach; and hold themselves mutually accountable

| Working Group | Team |
|---|---|
| Has strong, clearly focused leader | Has shared leadership roles |
| Has individual accountability | Has individual and group accountability |
| Has the same purpose as the broader organizational mission | Has a specific purpose that the team itself delivers |
| Creates individual work products | Creates collective work products |
| Runs efficient meetings | Encourages open-ended discussion and active problem-solving meetings |
| Measures its effectiveness indirectly by its effects on others (e.g., financial performance of the business) | Measures performance directly by assessing collective work products |
| Discusses, decides, and delegates | Discusses, decides, and does real work together |

**TABLE 8.1**

Differences between Groups and Teams

Source: Robert Gatewood, Robert Taylor, and O. C. Ferrell, *Management: Comprehension Analysis and Application,* 1995, p. 427. Copyright © 1995 Richard D. Irwin, a Times Mirror Higher Education Group, Inc., company. Reproduced with permission of the McGraw-Hill Companies.

differences between them. Work groups emphasize individual work products, individual accountability, and even individual leadership. Salespeople working independently for the same company could be a work group. In contrast, work teams share leadership roles, have both individual and mutual accountability, and create collective work products. In other words, a work group's performance depends on what its members do as individuals, while a team's performance is based on creating a knowledge center and a competency to work together to accomplish a goal. When CEO Joe Albanese had to leave his CEO position at Commodore Builders for active duty in the Army, his team rebalanced his workload and continued its projects. Albanese had established teams that focused on collaboration. A core team was prepared to lead the company in his absence. Albanese simply unplugged himself, leaving the team to perform his duties, including day-to-day leadership.[18]

The type of groups an organization establishes depends on the tasks it needs to accomplish and the situation it faces. Some specific kinds of groups and teams include committees, task forces, project teams, product-development teams, quality-assurance teams, and self-directed work teams. All of these can be *virtual teams*—employees in different locations who rely on e-mail, audio conferencing, fax, Internet, videoconferencing, or other technological tools to accomplish their goals. One survey found that almost 48 percent of workers have participated in virtual teams.[19]

## Committees

**committee**
a permanent, formal group that performs a specific task

A **committee** is usually a permanent, formal group that does some specific task. For example, many firms have a compensation or finance committee to examine the effectiveness of these areas of operation as well as the need for possible changes. Ethics committees are formed to develop and revise codes of ethics, suggest methods for implementing ethical standards, and review specific issues and concerns.

## Task Forces

**task force**
a temporary group of employees responsible for bringing about a particular change

A **task force** is a temporary group of employees responsible for bringing about a particular change. They typically come from across all departments and levels of an organization. Task force membership is usually based on expertise rather than organizational position. Occasionally, a task force may be formed from individuals outside a company. Such was the case in the task force selected by the Coca-Cola Company and the class representatives in a discrimination lawsuit filed against the company. Creation of the seven-member independent task force was one of the key elements in the settlement between the two parties. The task force will ensure the company's compliance with the settlement agreement and provide oversight of its diversity efforts.[20]

## Teams

Teams are becoming far more common in the U.S. workplace as businesses strive to enhance productivity and global competitiveness. In general, teams have the benefit of being able to pool members' knowledge and skills and make greater use of them than can individuals working alone. Team building is becoming increasingly popular in organizations, with 48 percent of executives indicating their companies had team-building training.[21] Teams require harmony, cooperation, synchronized effort, and flexibility to maximize their contribution.[22] Teams can also create more solutions to problems than can individuals. Furthermore, team participation enhances employee acceptance of, understanding of, and commitment to team goals. Teams

# Destination CEO
## Spectrum Brands CEO

Born in Barberville, Kentucky, David Jones began as first-line supervisor at General Electric, where he spent the first 13 years of his successful career before moving on and moving up. Jones has held chief executive positions with Electrolux, direct selling of vacuum cleaners, Regina Corporation, an appliances company, and Thermal Scan, a medical products company. This varied industry background and his enthusiasm for sports as a young man, helped shape Jones's management style. He emphasizes the importance of commitment, enthusiasm, and teamwork as important elements for success. Jones is convinced that pride in one's company, its employees, and its management team are keys to a successful operation.

Jones joined Rayovac in 1996. At that time, the company almost exclusively produced batteries. In his first year, Rayovac generated sales of $400 million. Since that time, Jones has changed the strategic direction of the company, introducing a diversified product line and competing in several different markets. Jones's strategy has ultimately led to a name change for the corporation. Today, the former Rayovac Corporation is known as Spectrum Brands Corporation. While still producing batteries, the company's products are diversified into the markets of pet products, personal grooming, and lawn and garden care. There is no doubt that Jones's team-oriented style and diversification strategy have had a positive impact on Spectrum Brands. Today's gross sales are $2.8 billion.

### Discussion Questions

1. How did David Jones's early involvement with sports influence his management style?
2. The organizational structure of Electrolux differs significantly from that of Spectrum Brands. What would David Jones see as a common thread running across different companies that he has been involved with?
3. Spectrum Brands was formerly Rayovac, which produced only batteries. Today, Spectrum Brands produces a diversified product mix. Explain how departmentalization would play an important role to ensure the success of this new corporate strategy.

---

motivate workers by providing internal rewards in the form of an enhanced sense of accomplishment for employees as they achieve more, and external rewards in the form of praise and certain perks. Consequently, they can help get workers more involved. They can help companies be more innovative, and they can boost productivity and cut costs.

According to psychologist Ivan Steiner, team productivity peaks at about five team members. People become less motivated and group coordination becomes more difficult after this size. Jeff Bezos, Amazon.com CEO, says that he has a "two-pizza rule": If a team cannot be fed by two pizzas, it is too large. Keep teams small enough where everyone gets a piece of the action.[23]

**Project Teams.** **Project teams** are similar to task forces, but normally they run their operation and have total control of a specific work project. Like task forces, their membership is likely to cut across the firm's hierarchy and be composed of people from different functional areas. They are almost always temporary, although a large project, such as designing and building a new airplane at Boeing Corporation, may last for years.

**Product-development teams** are a special type of project team formed to devise, design, and implement a new product. Sometimes product-development teams exist within a functional area—research and development—but now they more frequently include people from numerous functional areas and may even include customers to help ensure that the end product meets the customers' needs. Students at the University of Wisconsin–Madison formed a product development team to compete in the Institute of Food Technologists' annual competition, creating new food products with high potential for grocery store sales. The team is diverse, made up of undergraduates, graduate students, food chemists, food engineers and

**project teams**
groups similar to task forces which normally run their operation and have total control of a specific work project

**product-development teams**
a specific type of project team formed to devise, design, and implement a new product

bacteriologists. Some are research oriented, while others focus on business. Additionally, members hail from all corners of the globe. This has proved successful, with the team winning multiple awards for such food items as Handicotti, a hand-held snack featuring cheese, pasta sauce and vegetables enclosed by a large pasta shell, and Healthy sTarts, a breakfast item featuring a yogurt-filled granola cup, topped with blueberries and strawberries.[24]

**quality-assurance teams (or quality circles)** small groups of workers brought together from throughout the organization to solve specific quality, productivity, or service problems

**Quality-Assurance Teams.** **Quality-assurance teams,** sometimes called **quality circles,** are fairly small groups of workers brought together from throughout the organization to solve specific quality, productivity, or service problems. Although the *quality circle* term is not as popular as it once was, the concern about quality is stronger than ever. The use of teams to address quality issues will no doubt continue to increase throughout the business world.

**self-directed work team (SDWT)** a group of employees responsible for an entire work process or segment that delivers a product to an internal or external customer

**Self-directed Work Teams.** A **self-directed work team (SDWT)** is a group of employees responsible for an entire work process or segment that delivers a product to an internal or external customer.[25] Sometimes called self-managed teams or autonomous work groups, SDWTs reduce the need for extra layers of management and thus can help control costs. For example, MySQL, a $40 million software maker,

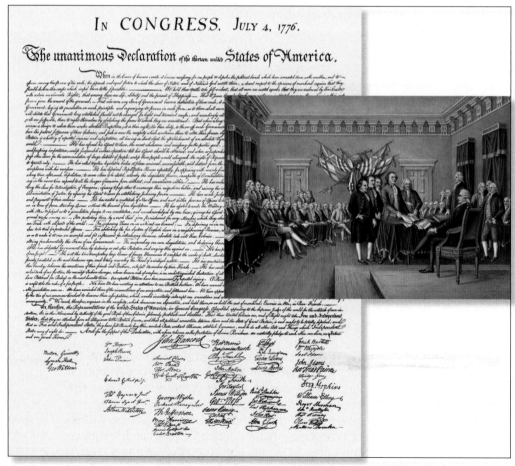

Our country's forefathers, who were charged with the task of coming together to write the Constitution—were they a group or a team? Use the criteria in Table 8.1 to decide.

operates a worldwide workforce with no office. At MySQL people are matched with the technology task. The company relies on phone contact via Skype Internet voice communication. Voice communication is considered better than e-mail and helpful in building real contacts and understanding of tasks. One problem, though, is that a self-directed team does not end at the end of the day. It is always 8 a.m. somewhere for MySQL employees.[26]

SDWTs permit the flexibility to change rapidly to meet the competition or respond to customer needs. The defining characteristic of an SDWT is the extent to which it is empowered or given authority to make and implement work decisions. Thus, SDWTs are designed to give employees a feeling of "ownership" of a whole job. With shared team responsibility for work outcomes, team members often have broader job assignments and cross-train to master other jobs, thus permitting greater team flexibility.

# Communicating in Organizations

Communication within an organization can flow in a variety of directions and from a number of sources, each using both oral and written forms of communication. The success of communication systems within the organization has a tremendous effect on the overall success of the firm. Communication mistakes can lower productivity and morale.

> **Did You Know?**   Managers spend an average of one to one-and-a-half days per week in meetings.[27]

Alternatives to face-to-face communications—such as meetings—are growing thanks to technology such as voice-mail, e-mail, and online newsletters. At Matsushita, for example, company executives are required to file reports to president Kunio Nakamura by mobile e-mail and are provided an Internet-equipped mobile phone for that purpose.[28] Companies use intranets or internal computer networks to share information and to increase collaboration. Intranets help employees quickly find or view information, any time, subject to security provisions.[29] Capital One, IBM, Merrill Lynch, and Staples have been recognized as having some of the best intranets in corporate America.[30] At many companies, however, such communications technology has contributed to a state of information overload for employees, who spend more and more time managing e-mail. A growing problem is employees abusing e-mail. In some companies, up to 75 percent of e-mail messages are not business related.[31]

Experts say that managers must (1) plan how they will share important news, (2) repeat important information, and (3) rehearse key presentations. According to one study, 62 percent of executives think employees and companies benefit from fun and humor in communications and management style.[32]

## Formal Communication

Formal channels of communication are intentionally defined and designed by the organization. They represent the flow of communication within the formal organizational structure, as shown on organizational charts. Traditionally, formal communication patterns were classified as vertical and horizontal, but with the increased use of teams and matrix structures, formal communication may occur in a number of patterns (Figure 8.9).

*Upward communication* flows from lower to higher levels of the organization and includes information such as progress reports, suggestions for improvement, inquiries, and grievances. *Downward communication* refers to the traditional flow

# Going Green
## Communicating to Save Trees and Sidewalks

Lindsay Smith, a communications expert, a screenwriter at the time, discovered that 26 perfectly healthy trees in her neighborhood were about to be uprooted and destroyed thanks to the damage their roots had caused to the surrounding sidewalks. Driven to save the trees, Smith was granted 48 hours to use her communication skills to come up with an alternate solution. During that 48-hour period, Smith persuaded Richard Valeriano who helped her develop a prototype of a sidewalk paver made out of old recycled tires. She also had to convince county officials who were ready to tear down the trees in Smith's neighborhood to agree to leave them for the time being and to consider the green alternative. Smith then had to convince others to help her with the prototype and her company, Rubbersidewalks, was born.

Once again her communication skills were needed to obtain a $250,000 matching grant from California Integrated Waste Management Board. She was then able to match that sum using her own credit. Although the prototype was a good one, Smith worked to improve both the look and the durability of the material. Next, she used informal communication channels to reach an investor, who heard about the rubber sidewalks from a news story on television. This investment allowed Smith to launch the sales portion of her business.

If you are interested in how her product works, the rubber sidewalk paving blocks have spaces in between them, which allows water to permeate to the tree roots. As a result, roots don't press up through the sidewalks in search of moisture. It is also possible to remove each paver if repairs are necessary, making it a much easier product to maintain. Although the pavers can initially cost a city more than the concrete variety, a city can save a substantial amount on root pruning and easements.

Through excellent communications with suppliers, government officials, and the mass media her company has installed sidewalks composed of recycled tires in 60 cites throughout the United States and Canada. Other countries are requesting information. The Rubbersidewalks product both recycles tires and saves trees, which makes it doubly beneficial environmentally.[33]

### Discussion Questions

1. Why was communication so important to Lindsay Smith in developing her company Rubbersidewalks?
2. How was communication used to not only save trees, but to get various business partners to participate in the new company?
3. Do you think that companies focused on the importance of green business have an advantage in reaching out to community stakeholders for support?

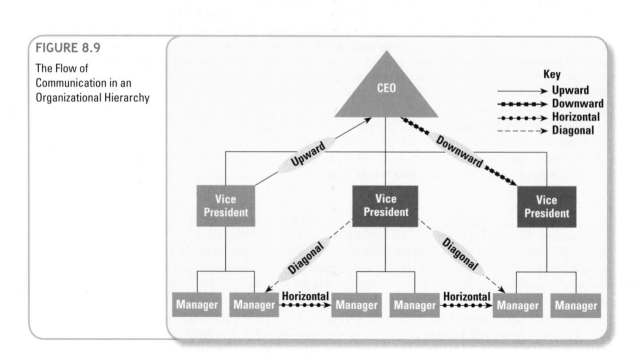

### FIGURE 8.9

The Flow of Communication in an Organizational Hierarchy

of information from upper organizational levels to lower levels. This type of communication typically involves directions, the assignment of tasks and responsibilities, performance feedback, and certain details about the organization's strategies and goals. Speeches, policy and procedures manuals, employee handbooks, company leaflets, telecommunications, and job descriptions are examples of downward communication.

*Horizontal communication* involves the exchange of information among colleagues and peers on the same organizational level, such as across or within departments. Horizontal information informs, supports, and coordinates activities both within the department and with other departments. At times, the business will formally require horizontal communication among particular organizational members, as is the case with task forces or project teams.

With more and more companies downsizing and increasing the use of selfmanaged work teams, many workers are being required to communicate with others in different departments and on different levels to solve problems and coordinate work. When these individuals from different units and organizational levels communicate, it is *diagonal communication.* At OpenAir.com Inc., all staff members meet every day at 9:30 a.m. to share information and anecdotes about customer calls from the previous day. No chairs are allowed, and everyone is encouraged to participate. COO Morris Panner says that the communication style "reemphasizes the fact that our company is based on collaboration."[34]

## Informal Communication Channels

Along with the formal channels of communication shown on an organizational chart, all firms communicate informally as well. Communication between friends, for instance, cuts across department, division, and even management-subordinate boundaries. Such friendships and other nonwork social relationships comprise the *informal organization* of a firm, and their impact can be great.

The most significant informal communication occurs through the **grapevine,** an informal channel of communication, separate from management's formal, official communication channels. Grapevines exist in all organizations. Information passed along the grapevine may relate to the job or organization, or it may be gossip and rumors unrelated to either. The accuracy of grapevine information has been of great concern to managers.

**grapevine**
an informal channel of communication, separate from management's formal, official communication channels

Additionally, managers can turn the grapevine to their advantage. Using it as a "sounding device" for possible new policies is one example. Managers can obtain valuable information from the grapevine that could improve decision making. Some organizations use the grapevine to their advantage by floating ideas, soliciting feedback, and reacting accordingly. People love to gossip, and managers need to be aware that grapevines exist in every organization. Managers who understand how the grapevine works also can use it to their advantage by feeding it facts to squelch rumors and incorrect information.

## Monitoring Communications

Technological advances and the increased use of electronic communication in the workplace have made monitoring its use necessary for most companies. Failing to monitor employee's use of e-mail and the Internet can be costly. Chevron Corp. agreed to pay $2 million to employees who claimed that unmonitored, sexually harassing e-mail created a threatening environment for them.[35] Instituting practices that show respect for employee privacy but do not abdicate employer responsibility are increasingly necessary in today's workplace. Several Web sites provide model policies and detailed guidelines for conducting electronic monitoring, including the Model Electronic Privacy Act on the American Civil Liberties Union site.

# So You Want a Job in Managing Organizational Culture, Teamwork and Communication

Jobs dealing with organizational culture and structure are usually at the top of the organization. If you want to be a CEO or high level manager you will help shape these areas of business. On the other hand, if you are an entrepreneur or small business person you will need to make decisions about assigning tasks, departmentalization and assigning responsibility. Even managers in small organizations have to make decisions about decentralization, span of management and forms of organizational structure. While these decisions may be part of your job, there are usually no job titles dealing with these specific areas. Specific jobs that attempt to improve organizational culture could include ethics and compliance positions as well as those who are in charge of communicating memos, manuals and policies that help establish the culture. These positions will be in communications, human resources and positions that assist top organizational managers.

Teams are becoming more common in the workplace and it is possible to become a member of a product development group or quality assurance team. There are also human resource positions that encourage teamwork through training activities. The area of corporate communications provides lots of opportunities for specific jobs that facilitate communication systems. Thanks to technology, there are job positions to help disseminate information through online newsletters, intranets or internal computer networks to share information to increase collaboration. In addition to the many advances using electronic communications, there are technology concerns that create new job opportunities. Monitoring workplace communications such as the use of e-mail and the Internet have created new industries. There have to be internal controls in the organization to make sure that the organization does not engage in any copyright infringement. If this is an area of interest, there are specific jobs that provide an opportunity to use your technological skills to assist in maintaining appropriate standards in communicating and using technology.

If you go to work for a large company with many divisions, you can expect a number of positions dealing with the tasks discussed here. If you go to work for a small company you will probably engage in most of these tasks as a part of your position. Organizational flexibility requires individual flexibility and those employees willing to take on new domains and challenges will be the employees who survive and prosper in the future.

# Review Your Understanding

**Define organizational structure, and relate how organizational structures develop.**

Structure is the arrangement or relationship of positions within an organization; it develops when managers assign work activities to work groups and specific individuals and coordinate the diverse activities required to attain organizational objectives. Organizational structure evolves to accommodate growth, which requires people with specialized skills.

**Describe how specialization and departmentalization help an organization achieve its goals.**

Structuring an organization requires that management assign work tasks to specific individuals and groups. Under specialization, managers break labor into small, specialized tasks and assign employees to do a single task, fostering efficiency. Departmentalization is the grouping of jobs into working units (departments, units, groups, or divisions). Businesses may departmentalize by function, product, geographic region, or customer, or they may combine two or more of these.

### Distinguish between groups and teams, and identify the types of groups that exist in organizations.

A group is two or more persons who communicate, share a common identity, and have a common goal. A team is a small group whose members have complementary skills, a common purpose, goals, and approach; and who hold themselves mutually accountable. The major distinction is that individual performance is most important in groups, while collective work group performance counts most in teams. Special kinds of groups include task forces, committees, project teams, product-development teams, quality-assurance teams, and self-directed work teams.

### Determine how organizations assign responsibility for tasks and delegate authority.

Delegation of authority means assigning tasks to employees and giving them the power to make commitments, use resources, and take whatever actions are necessary to accomplish the tasks. It lays responsibility on employees to carry out assigned tasks satisfactorily and holds them accountable to a superior for the proper execution of their assigned work. The extent to which authority is delegated throughout an organization determines its degree of centralization. Span of management refers to the number of subordinates who report to a particular manager. A wide

span of management occurs in flat organizations; a narrow one exists in tall organizations.

### Compare and contrast some common forms of organizational structure.

Line structures have direct lines of authority that extend from the top manager to employees at the lowest level of the organization. The line-and-staff structure has a traditional line relationship between superiors and subordinates, and specialized staff managers are available to assist line managers. A multidivisional structure gathers departments into larger groups called divisions. A matrix, or project-management, structure sets up teams from different departments, thereby creating two or more intersecting lines of authority.

### Describe how communication occurs in organizations.

Communication occurs both formally and informally in organizations. Formal communication may be downward, upward, horizontal, and even diagonal. Informal communication takes place through friendships and the grapevine.

### Analyze a business's use of teams.

"Solve the Dilemma" on page 259 introduces a firm attempting to restructure to a team environment. Based on the material presented in this chapter, you should be able to evaluate the firm's efforts and make recommendations for resolving the problems that have developed.

## Revisit the World of Business

1. Why do you think small organizations with limited organizational structure have the potential to be more specialized and efficient in their operations?
2. If PetConnection.com started growing quickly and hired more employees what tasks would have to be assigned?

3. How do you think Gina Spadafori and veterinarian Marty Becker divide their responsibilities for managing the PetConnection.com blog?

## Learn the Terms

accountability   242
centralized organization   243
committee   250
customer departmentalization   242
decentralized organization   244
delegation of authority   242
departmentalization   239
functional departmentalization   239
geographical departmentalization   242
grapevine   255

group   249
line-and-staff structure   246
line structure   246
matrix structure   248
multidivisional structure   247
organizational chart   237
organizational culture   234
organizational layers   245
product departmentalization   240
product-development teams   251
project teams   251

quality-assurance teams (or quality circles)   252
responsibility   242
self-directed work team (SDWT)   252
span of management   245
specialization   238
structure   236
task force   250
team   249

# Check Your Progress

1. Identify four types of departmentalization and give an example of each type.

2. Explain the difference between groups and teams.

3. What are self-managed work teams and what tasks might they perform that traditionally are performed by managers?

4. Explain how delegating authority, responsibility, and accountability are related.

5. Distinguish between centralization and decentralization. Under what circumstances is each appropriate?

6. Define span of management. Why do some organizations have narrow spans and others wide spans?

7. Discuss the different forms of organizational structure. What are the primary advantages and disadvantages of each form?

8. Discuss the role of the grapevine within organizations. How can managers use it to further the goals of the firm?

9. How have technological advances made electronic oversight a necessity in many companies?

10. Discuss how an organization's culture might influence its ability to achieve its objectives. Do you think that managers can "manage" the organization's culture?

# Get Involved

1. Explain, using a specific example (perhaps your own future business), how an organizational structure might evolve. How would you handle the issues of specialization, delegation of authority, and centralization? Which structure would you use? Explain your answers.

2. Interview the department chairperson in charge of one of the academic departments in your college or university. Using Table 8.1 as a guideline, explore whether the professors function more like a group or a team. Contrast what you find here with what you see on your school's basketball, football, or baseball team.

# Build Your Skills

### TEAMWORK

**Background:**
Think about all the different kinds of groups and teams you have been a member of or been involved with. Here's a checklist to help you remember them—with "Other" spaces to fill in ones not listed. Check all that apply.

**School Groups/Teams**
- ☐ Sports teams
- ☐ Cheerleading squads
- ☐ Musical groups
- ☐ Hobby clubs
- ☐ Foreign language clubs
- ☐ Study groups
- ☐ Other _____

**Community Groups/Teams**
- ☐ Fund-raising groups
- ☐ Religious groups
- ☐ Sports teams
- ☐ Political groups
- ☐ Boy/Girl Scout Troops
- ☐ Volunteer organizations
- ☐ Other _____

**Employment Groups/Teams**
- ☐ Problem-solving teams
- ☐ Work committees
- ☐ Project teams
- ☐ Labor union groups
- ☐ Work crews
- ☐ Other _____

**Task**

1.  Of those you checked, circle those that you would categorize as a "really great team."

2.  Examine the following table[36] and circle those characteristics from columns two and three that were represented in your "really great" team experiences.

| Indicator | Good Team Experience | Not-So-Good Team Experience |
|---|---|---|
| Members arrive on time? | Members are prompt because they know others will be. | Members drift in sporadically, and some leave early. |
| Members prepared? | Members are prepared and know what to expect. | Members are unclear what the agenda is. |
| Meeting organized? | Members follow a planned agenda. | The agenda is tossed aside, and freewheeling discussion ensues. |
| Members contribute equally? | Members give each other a chance to speak; quiet members are encouraged. | Some members always dominate the discussion; some are reluctant to speak their minds. |
| Discussions help members make decisions? | Members learn from others' points of view, new facts are discussed, creative ideas evolve, and alternatives emerge. | Members reinforce their belief in their own points of view, or their decisions were made long before the meeting. |

| Indicator | Good Team Experience | Not-So-Good Team Experience |
|---|---|---|
| Any disagreement? | Members follow a conflict-resolution process established as part of the team's policies. | Conflict turns to argument, angry words, emotion, blaming. |
| More cooperation or more conflict? | Cooperation is clearly an important ingredient. | Conflict flares openly, as well as simmering below the surface. |
| Commitment to decisions? | Members reach consensus before leaving. | Compromise is the best outcome possible; some members don't care about the result. |
| Member feelings after team decision? | Members are satisfied and are valued for their ideas. | Members are glad it's over, not sure of results or outcome. |
| Members support decision afterward? | Members are committed to implementation. | Some members second-guess or undermine the team's decision. |

3.  What can you take with you from your positive team experiences and apply to a work-related group or team situation in which you might be involved?

_____
_____
_____

# Solve the Dilemma

### QUEST STAR IN TRANSITION

Quest Star (QS), which manufactures quality stereo loudspeakers, wants to improve its ability to compete against Japanese firms. Accordingly, the company has launched a comprehensive quality-improvement program for its Iowa plant. The QS Intracommunication Leadership Initiative (ILI) has flattened the layers of management. The program uses teams and peer pressure to accomplish the plant's goals instead of multiple management layers with their limited opportunities for communication. Under the initiative, employees make all decisions within the boundaries of their responsibilities, and they elect team representatives to coordinate with other teams. Teams are also assigned tasks ranging from establishing policies to evaluating on-the-job safety.

However, employees who are not self-motivated team players are having difficulty getting used to their peers' authority within this system. Upper-level managers face stress and frustration because they must train workers to supervise themselves.

### Discussion Questions

1. What techniques or skills should an employee have to assume a leadership role within a work group?

2. If each work group has a team representative, what problems will be faced in supervising these representatives?

3. Evaluate the pros and cons of the system developed by QS.

# Build Your Business Plan

## ORGANIZATION, TEAMWORK, AND COMMUNICATION

Developing a business plan as a team is a deliberate move of your instructor to encourage you to familiarize yourself with the concept of teamwork. You need to realize that you are going to spend a large part of your professional life working with others. At this point in time you are working on the business plan for a grade, but after graduation you will be "teaming" with co-workers and the successfulness of your endeavor may determine whether or not you get a raise or a bonus. It is important that you be comfortable as soon as possible with working with others and holding them accountable for their contributions.

Some people are natural "leaders" and leaders often feel that if team members are not doing their work, they take it upon themselves to "do it all." This is not leadership, but rather micro-managing.

Leadership means holding members accountable for their responsibilities. Your instructor may provide ideas on how this could be implemented, possibly by utilizing peer reviews. Remember you are not doing a team member a favor by doing their work for them.

If you are a "follower" (someone who takes directions well) rather than a leader, try to get into a team where others are hard workers and you will rise to their level. There is nothing wrong with being a follower; not everyone can be a leader!

# See For Yourself Videocase

## BREWING UP FUN IN THE WORKPLACE

New Belgium Brewing emerged out of a biking trip in Belgium on a fat-tired bike. When founder Jeff Lebesch returned to Fort Collins, Colorado, he wanted to produce similar high quality ales to those that he had tasted on his trip. New Belgium's dedication to quality, the environment, and its employees and customers is expressed in its mission statement: "To operate a profitable brewery which makes our love and talent manifest." The company's stated core values and beliefs about its role as an environmentally concerned and socially responsible brewer include:

- Producing world-class beers

- Promoting beer culture and the responsible enjoyment of beer

- Continuous, innovative quality and efficiency improvements

- Transcending customers' expectations

- Environmental stewardship: minimizing resource consumption, maximizing energy efficiency, and recycling

- Kindling social, environmental, and cultural change as a business role model

- Cultivating potential: through learning, participative management, and the pursuit of opportunities

- Balancing the myriad needs of the company, staff, and their families

- Committing ourselves to authentic relationships, communications, and promises

- Having Fun.

At New Belgium, a synergy of brand and values occurred naturally as the firm's ethical culture in the form of core values and beliefs and was in place long before the company had a marketing department. Back in early 1991, before they signed any business paperwork, Jeff Lebesch and Kim Jordan took a hike into Rocky Mountain National Park. Armed with a pen and a notebook, they took their first stab at what the fledgling company's core purpose would be. If they were going forward with this venture, what were their aspirations beyond profitability? What was the real root cause of their dream? What they wrote down that spring day, give or take a little wordsmithing, were the core values and beliefs you can read on the New Belgium Web site today. More importantly, ask just about any New Belgium worker, and she or he can list for you many, if not all, of these shared values and can inform you which are the most personally poignant. For New Belgium Brewing, branding strategies are as rooted in their company values as in other business practices.

Jeff and Kim decided early on what their values and goals were. Having fun and allowing their employees to have fun was important to them. They decided that after a year of working for the company employees would receive "cruiser bikes"— like the one pictured on its Fat Tire Amber Ale label— and encourage them to ride to work. Recognizing employees' role in the company's success, New Belgium provides many generous benefits. In addition to the usual paid health and dental insurance and retirement plans, employees get a free lunch every other week as well as a free massage once a year, and they can bring their children and dogs to work. Employees who stay with the company for five years earn an all-expenses paid trip to Belgium to "study beer culture." Perhaps most importantly, employees can also earn stock in the privately-held corporation, which grants them a vote in company decisions once they have worked there for a year. An open book policy reinforces this mentality and ensures that all employees feel more involved in day-to-day operations of running the business. Employees can access all the company's financial information. New Belgium even provides education to employees on how to read the financials to ensure that they understand what they read.

By empowering employees, New Belgium allows everyone to think about the benefits of investing in the future as well as the risks involved. The decentralized structure of the company also allows decisions to be made as far down the company hierarchy as possible. Empowerment allows employees to make decisions without having to seek approval. The environment of employee/owners creates a desire for success by all involved. Team members are all held mutually accountable for decisions and the success of the company. According to Kim Jordan, "the vibe here is amazing . . . you can tell people really like being here."

Even the philanthropy committee is a group of people from all parts of the company. The group collectively decides where the company's philanthropy money should be spent. By allowing employees to help make such decisions, everyone is involved in all aspects of the business

and the ownership and empowerment ensures the company's continued success. The open communication creates real relationships with people, which according to Kim "creates magical vibes."

From the very beginning, New Belgium was a green business. While the company tries to continue to decrease its carbon footprint, it also encourages employees to help improve our natural environment. To do this, employees are encouraged to bring personal items that are sometimes difficult to recycle, such as batteries, to recycling bins at New Belgium. Employees took an active role In the company's green efforts by voting to run the brewery on wind power. They also enjoy related social activities, often riding their New Belgium bikes to local events and outdoor activities.

Every six-pack of New Belgium Beer displays the phrase, "In this box is our labor of love, we feel incredibly lucky to be creating something fine that enhances people's lives." The founders of New Belgium hope this statement captures the spirit of the company. According to employee Dave Kemp, New Belgium's commitment to its employees, along with its concern for the environment and social responsibility, give it a competitive advantage because consumers want to believe in and feel good about the products they purchase. New Belgium's most important asset is its image—a corporate brand that stands for quality, responsibility, and concern for society. Defining itself as more than just a beer company, the brewer also sees itself as a caring organization that is concerned with all stakeholders, including employees, the community, and the environment.[37]

## Discussion Questions

1. How does New Belgium foster a corporate culture that promotes clear communication among all employees?

2. How does New Belgium communicate its core values and beliefs in its everyday business actions?

3. What role do employees play in decision making at New Belgium that is different than in many other companies?

Remember to check out our Online Learning Center at www.mhhe.com/ferrell7e.

chapter 9

## CHAPTER OUTLINE

**Introduction**

**The Nature of Operations Management**
*The Transformation Process*
*Operations Management in Service Businesses*

**Planning and Designing Operations Systems**
*Planning the Product*
*Designing the Operations Processes*
*Planning Capacity*
*Planning Facilities*
*Green Operations and Manufacturing*

**Managing the Supply Chain**
*Purchasing*
*Managing Inventory*
*Outsourcing*
*Routing and Scheduling*

**Managing Quality**
*International Organization for Standardization (ISO)*
*Inspection*
*Sampling*

# Managing Service and Manufacturing Operations

## OBJECTIVES

*After reading this chapter, you will be able to:*

- Define operations management, and differentiate between operations and manufacturing.

- Explain how operations management differs in manufacturing and service firms.

- Describe the elements involved in planning and designing an operations system.

- Specify some techniques managers may use to manage the logistics of transforming inputs into finished products.

- Assess the importance of quality in operations management.

- Evaluate a business's dilemma and propose a solution.

## Goya Foods: Quality Operations and Products

Founded in 1936, Goya Foods has always revolved around family and the desire to provide authentic, high-quality Hispanic foods. Don Prudencio Unanue, the company's founder, came to America from Spain and saw a need for authentic Hispanic food. With his wife, he opened a small storefront in Lower Manhattan, New York. It provided Hispanic foods such as olives, olive oil, and sardines. As the demand for such foods expanded, so did Goya Foods. Today, Goya Foods offers a wide range of products such as condiments, pantry items, beverages, and frozen foods. Although it originally focused on foods of Spanish origin, the company now offers Spanish, Puerto Rican, Cuban, Mexican, and South and Central American foods as well.

Since 2004, the company has been run by CEO Bob Unanue and other family members. They are part of the third generation of Unanues running the 72-year-old company, and they hope the fourth generation takes an interest as well. Only 10 percent of family-owned businesses remain in the family through the third generation. Bob Unanue, his two brothers and four cousins all continue in active roles with the company and are dedicated to its continued success.

As Goya's product lines have expanded, the company has had to pay intense attention to detail. For example, many Hispanic meals begin with rice and beans. Sounds simple enough. However, the preference for beans—red, black, or pink, for example—can vary between Mexican, Cuban, Peruvian, or people of other origins. This attention to detail and dedication to meeting a wide variety of needs means that Goya must also focus on the delivery of its products. Which products are delivered to which stores is dictated

*continued*

by the heritage of those living in each area. To provide such origin-specific products, Goya delivers products to stores on a daily basis. In this way, the company differs from many companies that drop off large weekly shipments, forcing stores to warehouse goods.

Although they could easily sell such an enticing company (Goya Foods is debt free and growing), Bob Unanue and his family enjoy and believe strongly in their business. With a growing Hispanic population eager and grateful for authentic foods, Goya has the opportunity to prosper for years to come, and the Unanues hope family members remain at the helm.[1]

# Introduction

All organizations create products—goods, services, or ideas—for customers. Thus, organizations as diverse as Dell Computer, Campbell Soup, UPS, and a public hospital share a number of similarities relating to how they transform resources into the products we consume. Most hospitals use similar admission procedures, while Burger King and Dairy Queen use similar food preparation methods to make hamburgers. Such similarities are to be expected. But even organizations in unrelated industries take similar steps in creating goods or services. The check-in procedures of hotels and commercial airlines are comparable, for example. The way Subway assembles a sandwich and the way GMC assembles a truck are similar (both use automation and an assembly line). These similarities are the result of operations management, the focus of this chapter.

Here, we discuss the role of production or operations management in acquiring and managing the resources necessary to create goods and services. Production and operations management involves planning and designing the processes that will transform those resources into finished products, managing the movement of those resources through the transformation process, and ensuring that the products are of the quality expected by customers.

# The Nature of Operations Management

**operations management (OM)**
the development and administration of the activities involved in transforming resources into goods and services

**Operations management (OM),** the development and administration of the activities involved in transforming resources into goods and services, is of critical importance. Operations managers oversee the transformation process and the planning and designing of operations systems, managing logistics, quality, and productivity. Quality and productivity have become fundamental aspects of operations management because a company that cannot make products of the quality desired by consumers, using resources efficiently and effectively, will not be able to remain in business. OM is the "core" of most organizations because it is responsible for the creation of the organization's goods or services.

Historically, operations management has been called "production" or "manufacturing" primarily because of the view that it was limited to the manufacture of physical goods. Its focus was on methods and techniques required to operate a factory efficiently. The change from "production" to "operations" recognizes the increasing importance of organizations that provide services and ideas. Additionally, the term *operations* represents an interest in viewing the operations function as a whole rather than simply as an analysis of inputs and outputs.

Today, OM includes a wide range of organizational activities and situations outside of manufacturing, such as health care, food service, banking, entertainment, education, transportation, and charity. Thus, we use the terms **manufacturing** and **production** interchangeably to represent the activities and processes used in making *tangible* products, whereas we use the broader term **operations** to describe those processes used in the making of *both tangible and intangible products*. Manufacturing provides tangible products such as Hewlett-Packard's latest printer, and operations provides intangibles such as a stay at Wyndham Hotels and Resorts.

## The Transformation Process

At the heart of operations management is the transformation process through which **inputs** (resources such as labor, money, materials, and energy) are converted into **outputs** (goods, services, and ideas). The transformation process combines inputs in predetermined ways using different equipment, administrative procedures, and technology to create a product (Figure 9.1). To ensure that this process generates quality products efficiently, operations managers control the process by taking measurements (feedback) at various points in the transformation process and comparing them to previously established standards. If there is any deviation between the actual and desired outputs, the manager may take some sort of corrective action. All adjustments made to create a satisfying product are a part of the transformation process.

Transformation may take place through one or more processes. In a business that manufactures oak furniture, for example, inputs pass through several processes before being turned into the final outputs—furniture that has been designed to meet the desires of customers (Figure 9.2). The furniture maker must first strip the oak trees of their bark and saw them into appropriate sizes—one step in the transformation process. Next, the firm dries the strips of oak lumber, a second form of transformation. Third, the dried wood is routed into its appropriate shape and made smooth. Fourth, workers assemble and treat the wood pieces, then stain or

**manufacturing**
the activities and processes used in making tangible products; also called production

**production**
the activities and processes used in making tangible products; also called manufacturing

**operations**
the activities and processes used in making both tangible and intangible products

**inputs**
the resources—such as labor, money, materials, and energy—that are converted into outputs

**outputs**
the goods, services, and ideas that result from the conversion of inputs

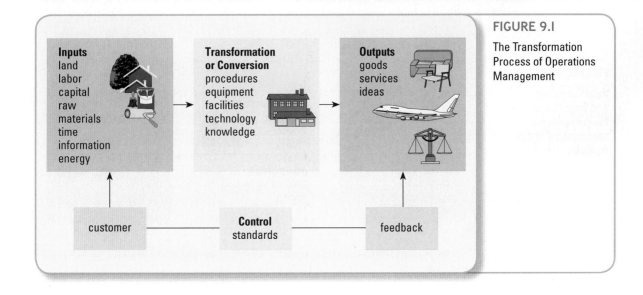

**FIGURE 9.1**

The Transformation Process of Operations Management

# Responding to Business Challenges
## JetBlue Recovers and Excels in Service

Founded in 2000, JetBlue quickly gathered a loyal cult following thanks to its emphasis on customer service and its unique offerings (such as individual televisions—LiveTV—and special in-flight snacks). In 2003, the company was flying high with a profit of $103 million. In addition to its offerings, part of JetBlue's success rested on its policy for delaying rather than canceling flights. The company believed that customers would prefer arriving at their destinations late as opposed to not at all. Although travelers appreciated the idea, it placed JetBlue at the bottom of the list of airlines able to meet their flight schedules. The company began to falter after hitting its high in 2003. In 2004, the company profited $46 million. A year later, the company lost $20 million. If this wasn't enough, in February 2007, on Valentine's Day to be exact, everything not already crumbling seemed to fall apart.

JetBlue's Valentine's Day debacle has been widely publicized in the media: on February 14, 2007, a huge storm revealed JetBlue's flaws to those within and outside the company. Hit with severe weather, JetBlue lacked sufficient response time due to a lack of manpower and poor decision making. As a result, more than 1,000 travelers were stranded in their planes for more than six hours. Thousands of travelers were also stuck inside JetBlue terminals for up to four days. By the time JetBlue was able to tackle the issue, the company had canceled 1,200 flights. It also lost $41 million, in a combination of lost revenue and reimbursements for delayed and canceled flights.

The media painted an extremely negative picture of Jet-Blue's prospects after the debacle, but the company honored those elements that originally made it a customer favorite. The company, already aware that change was necessary, set about revamping its entire structure immediately. It also issued an immediate apology and acknowledged its faults, such as not having enough staff available to handle such a crisis. Refunds and the ability to rebook without fees were offered to travelers affected by the storm. The company also improved its ability to forecast weather. As a result, when another ice storm hit the company's hub, New York's JFK airport, on March 16, 2007, the company completed 98 percent of its flights by the next day—a vast improvement in just over one month.

Going even further, JetBlue created a "Flier's Bill of Rights"—the first of its kind in the airline industry. Thanks to this bill, customers who are delayed either on the ground or on their planes will receive vouchers ranging from $25 to the full ticket price, depending on the amount of time they are delayed. Many other airlines issue vouchers only with the approval of supervisors or managers on a case-by-case basis.

Thanks to its Bill of Rights and its dedication to customers, analysts believe JetBlue will survive. In fact, in one survey of airline quality, JetBlue ranked second behind AirTran for 2007. However, in the midst of both change and growth, the company is going to have to continue to provide the unique experience that customers have loved from the beginning.[2]

**Discussion Questions**

1. How did JetBlue implement service recovery to restore the confidence of consumers?
2. How can a company such as JetBlue plan in advance to prevent major failures in customer service?
3. Why do you think JetBlue is now one of the most highly ranked airlines in terms of quality service?

---

**FIGURE 9.2**

Inputs, Outputs, and Transformation Processes in the Manufacture of Oak Furniture

**Inputs**
oak trees
labor
information/knowledge
stain or varnish
router/saw
warehouse space/time

**Transformation**
cutting or sawing
routing
measuring
assembling
staining/varnishing
storing

**Outputs**
oak furniture

varnish the piece of assembled furniture. Finally, the completed piece of furniture is stored until it can be shipped to customers at the appropriate time. Of course, many businesses choose to eliminate some of these stages by purchasing already processed materials—lumber, for example—or outsourcing some tasks to third-party firms with greater expertise.

## Operations Management in Service Businesses

Different types of transformation processes take place in organizations that provide services, such as airlines, colleges, and most nonprofit organizations. An airline transforms inputs such as employees, time, money, and equipment through processes such as booking flights, flying airplanes, maintaining equipment, and training crews. The output of these processes is flying passengers and/or packages to their destinations. In a nonprofit organization like Habitat for Humanity, inputs such as money, materials, information, and volunteer time and labor are used to transform raw materials into homes for needy families. In this setting, transformation processes include fund-raising and promoting the cause in order to gain new volunteers and donations of supplies, as well as pouring concrete, raising walls, and setting roofs. Transformation processes occur in all organizations, regardless of what they produce or their objectives. For most organizations, the ultimate objective is for the produced outputs to be worth more than the combined costs of the inputs.

Unlike tangible goods, services are effectively actions or performances that must be directed toward the consumers who use them. The service sector represents approximately 70 percent of all employment in the United States, and the fastest growth of jobs is in service industries.[3] Consider Whole Foods, the all-natural grocery chain that is growing rapidly. By creating a fun shopping experience, Whole Foods turns the drudgery of grocery shopping into entertainment and pleasure (see Table 9.1).[4] Thus, there is a significant customer-contact component to most services. Examples of high-contact services include health care, real estate, tax preparation, and food service. At the world-renowned Inn at Little

The staff at the world-renowned Inn at Little Washington in the Shenandoah Valley take operations management to new heights in terms of how well they attend to patrons. Eating at the restaurant has been likened to "a performance in which the guest is always the star."

| TABLE 9.1 | How Whole Foods Makes Grocery Shopping Fun |
|---|---|
| Candy Island | Dip a fresh strawberry in a flowing, chocolate fountain for $1.59 each. |
| Lamar Street Greens | Sit among the organic produce and have a salad handmade for you to enjoy with a glass of chardonnay. |
| Fifth Street Seafood | A version of Seattle's Pike Place Market; have any of 150 fresh seafood items cooked, sliced, smoked, or fried for instant eating. |
| Whole Body | A massage therapist works the kinks out with a 25-minute, deep-tissue massage for $50. |

Sources: Bruce Horovitz, "A Whole New Ballgame in Grocery Shopping," *USA Today,* March 9, 2005, p. B1; http://www.usatoday.com/money/industries/food/2005-03-08-wholefoods-cover-usat_x.htm (accessed May 15, 2008).

Washington, for example, food servers are critical to delivering the perfect dining experience expected by the most discriminating diners. Wait staff are expected not only to be courteous, but also to demonstrate a detailed knowledge of the restaurant's offerings, and even to assess the mood of guests in order to respond to diners appropriately.[5] Low-contact services, such as online auction services like eBay, often have a strong high-tech component.

Regardless of the level of customer contact, service businesses strive to provide a standardized process, and technology offers an interface that creates an automatic and structured response. The ideal service provider will be high-tech and high-touch. JetBlue, for example, strives to maintain an excellent Web site; friendly, helpful customer contact; and satellite TV service at every seat on each plane. Thus, service organizations must build their operations around good execution, which comes from hiring and training excellent employees, developing flexible systems, customizing services, and maintaining adjustable capacity to deal with fluctuating demand.[6]

Another challenge related to service operations is that the output is generally intangible and even perishable. Few services can be saved, stored, resold, or returned.[7] A seat on an airline or a table in a restaurant, for example, cannot be sold or used at a later date. Because of the perishability of services, it is can be extremely difficult for service providers to accurately estimate the demand in order to match the right supply of a service. If an airline overestimates demand, for example, it will still have to fly each plane even with empty seats. The flight costs the same regardless of whether it is 50 percent full or 100 percent full, but the former will result in much higher costs per passenger. If the airline underestimates demand, the result can be long lines of annoyed customers or even the necessity of bumping some customers off of an overbooked flight.

Businesses that manufacture tangible goods and those that provide services or ideas are similar yet different. For example, both types of organizations must make design and operating decisions. Most goods are manufactured prior to purchase, but most services are performed after purchase. Flight attendants at Southwest Airlines, hotel service personnel, and even the Tennessee Titans football team engage in performances that are a part of the total product. Though manufacturers and service providers often perform similar activities, they also differ in several respects. We can classify these differences in five basic ways.

**Nature and Consumption of Output.**   First, manufacturers and service providers differ in the nature and consumption of their output. For example, the term *manufacturer* implies a firm that makes tangible products. A service provider, on the other hand, produces more intangible outputs such as U.S. Postal Service delivery of priority mail or a business stay in a Hyatt hotel. As mentioned earlier, the very nature of the service provider's product requires a higher degree of customer contact. Moreover, the actual performance of the service typically occurs at the point of consumption. At the Hyatt, the business traveler may evaluate in-room communications and the restaurant. Toyota and other automakers, on the other hand, can separate the production of a car from its actual use. Manufacturing, then, can occur in an isolated environment, away from the customer. On the other hand, service providers, because of their need for customer contact, are often more limited than manufacturers in selecting work methods, assigning jobs, scheduling work, and exercising control over operations. At Toyota, for example, any employee who observes a problem can pull a cord and bring the assembly line to a stop to address the issue.[8] The quality of the service experience is often controlled by a service contact employee. However, some hospitals are studying the manufacturing processes

# Destination CEO
## Robert Lane, CEO, John Deere & Company

The John Deere Company is widely known for its tractors with the distinctive John Deere green color. The 170-year-old company is the world's largest manufacturer of agricultural and forestry harvesting products. Recently, the company has successfully integrated high technology such as GPS into its product lines enhancing the productivity of farmers everywhere. The company has even branched out into robotic machinery for military use.

Robert Lane, CEO of Deere and Company, is only the third outsider to assume the leadership of the company. Like other U.S. manufacturers, Deere has had its challenges and has had to reduce costs through eliminating jobs. Reduction in costs and increasing sales, worldwide, has had a positive effect on its shareholders as the stock is trading at the highest that it has been in history. Despite the layoffs, Lane maintains effective relations with the unionized labor force of Deere. This is reflected in the comments of one manufacturing employee who observes that "ten years ago this was a factory, today it is a business" under Lane's leadership. Lane's strategic goal for the company is global growth through exports and acquisitions. Fifty percent of Deere's sales are generated from overseas, primarily Brazil and China.

### Discussion Questions

1. Deere & Company is focused on agricultural machinery. Where will the company most likely see its most significant growth in sales?
2. What role does quality play in ensuring Deere & Company's success?
3. Does outsourcing play an important role in Lane's strategy for growth of John Deere globally?

and quality control mechanisms applied in the automotive industry in an effort to improve their service quality. By analyzing work processes to find unnecessary steps to eliminate and using teams to identify and address problems as soon as they occur, these hospitals are slashing patient waiting times, decreasing inventories of wheelchairs, readying operating rooms sooner, and generally moving patients through their hospital visit more quickly, with fewer errors, and at a lower cost.[9]

**Uniformity of Inputs.** A second way to classify differences between manufacturers and service providers has to do with the uniformity of inputs. Manufacturers typically have more control over the amount of variability of the resources they use than do service providers. For example, each customer calling Fidelity Investments is likely to require different services due to differing needs, whereas many of the tasks required to manufacture a Lincoln Navigator sport utility vehicle are the same across each unit of output. Consequently, the products of service organizations tend to be more "customized" than those of their manufacturing counterparts. Consider, for example, a haircut versus a bottle of shampoo. The haircut is much more likely to incorporate your specific desires (customization) than is the bottle of shampoo.

**Uniformity of Output.** Manufacturers and service providers also differ in the uniformity of their output, the final product. Because of the human element inherent in providing services, each service tends to be performed differently. Not all grocery checkers, for example, wait on customers in the same way. If a barber or stylist performs 15 haircuts in a day, it is unlikely that any two of them will be exactly the same. Consequently, human and technological elements associated with a service can result in a different day-to-day or even hour-to-hour performance of that service. The service experience can even vary at McDonald's or Burger King despite the fact that the two chains employ very similar procedures and processes. Moreover, no two customers are exactly alike in their perception of the service experience. Health care offers another excellent example of this challenge. Every diagnosis, treatment, and surgery varies because every individual is different. In manufacturing, the high degree of automation available allows manufacturers to generate uniform outputs

269

and, thus, the operations are more effective and efficient. For example, we would expect every Movado or Rolex watch to maintain very high standards of quality and performance.

**Labor Required.**   A fourth point of difference is the amount of labor required to produce an output. Service providers are generally more labor-intensive (require more labor) because of the high level of customer contact, perishability of the output (must be consumed immediately), and high degree of variation of inputs and outputs (customization). For example, Adecco provides temporary support personnel. Each temporary worker's performance determines Adecco's product quality. A manufacturer, on the other hand, is likely to be more capital-intensive because of the machinery and technology used in the mass production of highly similar goods. For instance, it would take a considerable investment for Nokia to make a digital phone that has a battery with longer life.

**Measurement of Productivity.**   The final distinction between service providers and manufacturers involves the measurement of productivity for each output produced. For manufacturers, measuring productivity is fairly straightforward because of the tangibility of the output and its high degree of uniformity. For the service provider, variations in demand (for example, higher demand for air travel in some seasons than in others), variations in service requirements from job to job, and the intangibility of the product make productivity measurement more difficult. Consider, for example, how much easier it is to measure the productivity of employees involved in the production of Intel computer processors as opposed to serving the needs of Prudential Securities' clients.

It is convenient and simple to think of organizations as being either manufacturers or service providers as in the preceding discussion. In reality, however, most organizations are a combination of the two, with both tangible and intangible qualities embodied in what they produce. For example, Porsche provides customer services such as toll-free hotlines and warranty protection, while banks may sell checks and other tangible products that complement their primarily intangible product offering. Thus, we consider "products" to include both tangible physical goods as well as intangible service offerings. It is the level of tangibility of its principal product that tends to classify a company as either a manufacturer or a service provider. From an OM standpoint, this level of tangibility greatly influences the nature of the company's operational processes and procedures.

# Planning and Designing Operations Systems

Before a company can produce any product, it must first decide what it will produce and for what group of customers. It must then determine what processes it will use to make these products as well as the facilities it needs to produce them. These decisions comprise operations planning. Although planning was once the sole realm of the production and operations department, today's successful companies involve all departments within an organization, particularly marketing and research and development, in these decisions.

## Planning the Product

Before making any product, a company first must determine what consumers want and then design a product to satisfy that want. Most companies use marketing research (discussed in Chapter 12) to determine the kinds of goods and services to provide and the features they must possess. Nissan, for example, conducted intensive market research before launching its first full-size pick-up truck, the Titan. The company interviewed truck buyers about their likes and dislikes and sent researchers to drive competing trucks for a month to learn firsthand about how the large vehicles handle in a variety of situations.[10] Even with good marketing research about consumer driving habits and other opinions, a sudden spike in oil prices pushed consumers to lighter, more fuel efficient trucks. Nissan sold only 60,000 Titans in 2008, compared to 165,000 Tundras. Toyota decided to convert the Titan factory in Mississippi to light commercial trucks.[11] Marketing research can also help gauge the demand for a product and how much consumers are willing to pay for it. But when a market's environment changes, firms such as Nisson have to be flexible.

Developing a product can be a lengthy, expensive process. For example, in the automobile industry, developing the new technology for night vision, bumper-mounted sonar systems that make parking easier, and a satellite service that locates and analyzes car problems has been a lengthy, expensive process. Most companies work to reduce development time and costs. For example, through Web collaboration, faucet manufacturer Moen has reduced the time required to take an idea to a finished product in stores to just 16 months, a drop of 33 percent.[12] Once management has developed an idea for a product that customers will buy, it must then plan how to produce the product.

Within a company, the engineering or research and development department is charged with turning a product idea into a workable design that can be produced economically. In smaller companies, a single individual (perhaps the owner) may be solely responsible for this crucial activity. Regardless of who is responsible for product design, planning does not stop with a blueprint for a product or a description of a service; it must also work out efficient production of the product to ensure that enough is available to satisfy consumer demand. How does a lawn mower company transform steel, aluminum, and other materials into a mower design that satisfies consumer and environmental requirements? Operations managers must plan for the types and quantities of materials needed to produce the product, the skills and quantity of people needed to make the product, and the actual processes through which the inputs must pass in their transformation to outputs.

## Designing the Operations Processes

Before a firm can begin production, it must first determine the appropriate method of transforming resources into the desired product. Often, consumers' specific needs and desires dictate a process. Customer needs, for example, require that all 3/4-inch bolts have the same basic thread size, function, and quality; if they did not, engineers and builders could not rely on 3/4-inch bolts in their construction projects. A bolt manufacturer, then, will likely use a standardized process so that every 3/4-inch bolt produced is like every other one. On the other hand, a bridge often must be customized so that it is appropriate for the site and expected load; furthermore, the bridge must be constructed on site rather than in a factory. Typically, products are designed to be manufactured by one of three processes: standardization, modular design, or customization.

**Standardization.**   Most firms that manufacture products in large quantities for many customers have found that they can make them cheaper and faster by standardizing designs. **Standardization** is making identical, interchangeable components or even complete products. With standardization, a customer may not get

**standardization**
the making of identical interchangeable components or products

exactly what he or she wants, but the product generally costs less than a custom-designed product. Television sets, ballpoint pens, and tortilla chips are standardized products; most are manufactured on an assembly line. Standardization speeds up production and quality control and reduces production costs. And, as in the example of the 3/4-inch bolts, standardization provides consistency so that customers who need certain products to function uniformly all the time will get a product that meets their expectations. As a result of its entry into the World Trade Organization, China promoted the standardization of agricultural production across the country, resulting in increased agricultural production.

**modular design**
the creation of an item in self-contained units, or modules, that can be combined or interchanged to create different products

**Modular Design.**   **Modular design** involves building an item in self-contained units, or modules, that can be combined or interchanged to create different products. Personal computers, for example, are generally composed of a number of components—CPU case, motherboard, chips, hard drives, graphics card, etc.—that can be installed in different configurations to meet the customer's needs. Because many modular components are produced as integrated units, the failure of any portion of a modular component usually means replacing the entire component. Modular design allows products to be repaired quickly, thus reducing the cost of labor, but the component itself is expensive, raising the cost of repair materials. Many automobile manufacturers use modular design in the production process. Manufactured homes are built on a modular design and often cost about one-fourth the cost of a conventionally built house.

**customization**
making products to meet a particular customer's needs or wants

**Customization.**   **Customization** is making products to meet a particular customer's needs or wants. Products produced in this way are generally unique. Such products include repair services, photocopy services, custom artwork, jewelry, and furniture, as well as large-scale products such as bridges, ships, and computer software. Custom designs are used in communications and service products. A Web-based design service, myemma.com, creates a custom template using a company's logo and colors to create a unique page for a Web site. It also provides tools for interacting with customers and tracking deliveries.[13] Although there may be similarities among ships, for example, builders generally design and build each ship to meet the needs of the customer who will use it. Delta Marine Industries custom-builds each luxury yacht to the customer's exact specifications and preferences for things like helicopter garages, golf courses, and swimming pools. Mass customization relates to making products that meet the needs or wants of a large number of individual customers. The customer can select the model, size, color, style, or design of the product. Dell can customize a computer with the exact configuration that fits a customer's needs. Services such as fitness programs and travel packages can also be custom designed for a large number of individual customers. For both goods and services, customers get to make choices and have options to determine the final product.

## Planning Capacity

**capacity**
the maximum load that an organizational unit can carry or operate

Planning the operational processes for the organization involves two important areas: capacity planning and facilities planning. The term **capacity** basically refers to the maximum load that an organizational unit can carry or operate. The unit of measurement may be a worker or machine, a department, a branch, or even an entire plant. Maximum capacity can be stated in terms of the inputs or outputs provided. For example, an electric plant might state plant capacity in terms of the maximum number of kilowatt-hours that can be produced without causing a power outage, while a restaurant might state capacity in terms of the maximum number

# Entrepreneurship in Action
## MINK Shoes Are Friendly and Fashionable

Rebecca Brough
**Business:** MINK Shoes
**Founded:** 2003

**Success:** Brough has managed to blend style and an environmental consciousness to create a product that people truly want.

In 2000, Rebecca Brough began looking into creating a line of animal- and environmentally-friendly shoes that would stand up to the traditional competition. Brough, a fashion stylist and vegan herself, took a chance, packed up her designs, and headed to the Lineapelle Fair shoe convention held in Italy. Once there, she began making the rounds to cobblers. She was turned down 16 times before meeting Marco Gambassi, who agreed to collaborate on MINK Shoes. Because Brough's designs must be constructed by hand and with specific materials, forcing the maker to produce small, time-consuming batches, not many cobblers felt the project to be worthwhile. Gambassi, a third-generation cobbler, was interested in the process and actually created a resin from a Para rubber tree plant to replace the traditional non-vegan glue that binds a sole to the top of a shoe. Once Brough and Gambassi had teamed up, Brough still had to locate stores willing to sell her shoes. Many high-end retailers were skeptical that environmentally friendly shoes could also be fashionable. After visiting 287 stores, Brough still had no takers. Using contacts she had made during her fashion stylist days, Brough convinced celebrities such as Paris Hilton and Natalie Portman to sport her designs. The exposure brought on set things in motion. Four stores bought 90 pairs of shoes and sold them all in a little over one month. Since then, Brough has also begun selling shoes on her Web site. Now, Brough is selling thousands of pairs of shoes and making a profit.[14]

of customers who can be effectively—comfortably and courteously—served at any one particular time. Honda Motor Company's Marysville, Ohio, plant, which produces the Accord sedan, Accord coupe, and Acura TL, has an annual production capacity of 440,000 vehicles.[15]

Efficiently planning the organization's capacity needs is an important process for the operations manager. Capacity levels that fall short can result in unmet demand, and consequently, lost customers. On the other hand, when there is more capacity available than needed, operating costs are driven up needlessly due to unused and often expensive resources. To avoid such situations, organizations must accurately forecast demand and then plan capacity based on these forecasts. Another reason for the importance of efficient capacity planning has to do with long-term commitment of resources. Often, once a capacity decision—such as factory size—has been implemented, it is very difficult to change the decision without incurring substantial costs. For example, with support from the 2007 Energy Independence and Security Act, biofuels are advancing as a renewable replacement for petroleum-based gasoline. The goal is for 23 percent of fuels to be renewable by 2022. This requires planning for flex-fuel, hybrid, and electric vehicles in automobile manufacturers' fleets as well as the infrastructure of ethanol and flex-fuel gas pumps. Already, most cars in Brazil can use sugar cane ethanol, and nearly all drivers in Sweden can buy E85 (85 percent ethanol) fuel. Saab and Volvo have developed cars to optimize running on these E85 flex fuels.[17] To meet the goals for alternative fuels there must be enough alternative fuel distribution sites and automobiles capable of using the fuels.

> **Did you know?** Hershey's has the production capacity to make 33 million Hershey's kisses per day or more than 12 billion per year.[16]

## Planning Facilities

Once a company knows what process it will use to create its products, it then can design and build an appropriate facility in which to make them. Many products

*IBM learned an important lesson in terms of capacity planning the hard way. When its Thinkpads first came out, the laptops were a smash success. Unfortunately, IBM didn't plan for the high demand and couldn't produce all of the machines consumers wanted.*

are manufactured in factories, but others are produced in stores, at home, or where the product ultimately will be used. Companies must decide where to locate their operations facilities, what layout is best for producing their particular product, and even what technology to apply to the transformation process.

Many firms are developing both a traditional organization for customer contact as well as a virtual organization. Charles Schwab Corporation, a securities brokerage and investment company, maintains traditional offices and has developed complete telephone and Internet services for customers. Through its Web site, investors can obtain personal investment information and trade securities over the Internet without leaving their home or office.

**Facility Location.**   Where to locate a firm's facilities is a significant question because, once the decision has been made and implemented, the firm must live with it due to the high costs involved. When a company decides to relocate or open a facility at a new location, it must pay careful attention to factors such as proximity to market, availability of raw materials, availability of transportation, availability of power, climatic influences, availability of labor, community characteristics (quality of life), and taxes and inducements. Inducements and tax reductions have become an increasingly important criterion in recent years. Tesla Motors received tax reductions and other financial support, such as infrastructure investments, to open its production facility to manufacture electric cars in Albuquerque, New Mexico, rather than near the company's home in California.[18] According to the Institute for Local Self-Reliance, Wal-Mart often receives millions of dollars in free roads, land, sewers, and tax abatements from local governments as incentives to locate new stores or distribution centers in certain areas.[19] The facility-location decision is complex because it involves the evaluation of many factors, some of which cannot be measured with precision. Because of the long-term impact of the decision, however, it is one that cannot be taken lightly.

**fixed-position layout**
a layout that brings all resources required to create the product to a central location

**project organization**
a company using a fixed-position layout because it is typically involved in large, complex projects such as construction or exploration

**Facility Layout.**   Arranging the physical layout of a facility is a complex, highly technical task. Some industrial architects specialize in the design and layout of certain types of businesses. There are three basic layouts: fixed-position, process, and product.

A company using a **fixed-position layout** brings all resources required to create the product to a central location. The product—perhaps an office building, house, hydroelectric plant, or bridge—does not move. A company using a fixed-position layout may be called a **project organization** because it is typically involved in large, complex projects such as construction or exploration. Project organizations generally make a unique product, rely on highly skilled labor, produce very few units, and have high production costs per unit.

Firms that use a **process layout** organize the transformation process into departments that group related processes. A metal fabrication plant, for example, may have a cutting department, a drilling department, and a polishing department. A hospital may have an X-ray unit, an obstetrics unit, and so on. These types of organizations are sometimes called **intermittent organizations,** which deal with products of a lesser magnitude than do project organizations, and their products are not necessarily unique but possess a significant number of differences. Doctors, makers of custom-made cabinets, commercial printers, and advertising agencies are intermittent organizations because they tend to create products to customers' specifications and produce relatively few units of each product. Because of the low level of output, the cost per unit of product is generally high.

The **product layout** requires that production be broken down into relatively simple tasks assigned to workers, who are usually positioned along an assembly line. Workers remain in one location, and the product moves from one worker to another. Each person in turn performs his or her required tasks or activities. Companies that use assembly lines are usually known as **continuous manufacturing organizations,** so named because once they are set up, they run continuously, creating products with many similar characteristics. Examples of products produced on assembly lines are automobiles, television sets, vacuum cleaners, toothpaste, and meals from a cafeteria. Continuous manufacturing organizations using a product layout are characterized by the standardized product they produce, the large number of units produced, and the relatively low unit cost of production.

Many companies actually use a combination of layout designs. For example, an automobile manufacturer may rely on an assembly line (product layout) but may also use a process layout to manufacture parts.

*Technology.*   Every industry has a basic, underlying technology that dictates the nature of its transformation process. The steel industry continually tries to improve steelmaking techniques. The health care industry performs research into medical technologies and pharmaceuticals to improve the quality of health care service. Two developments that have strongly influenced the operations of many businesses are computers and robotics.

Computers have been used for decades and on a relatively large scale since IBM introduced its 650 series in the late 1950s. The operations function makes great use of computers in all phases of the transformation process. **Computer-assisted design (CAD),** for example, helps engineers design components, products, and processes on the computer instead of on paper. **Computer-assisted manufacturing (CAM)** goes a step further, employing specialized computer systems to actually guide and control the transformation processes. Such systems can monitor the transformation process, gathering information about the equipment used to produce the products and about the product itself as it goes from one stage of the transformation process to the next. The computer provides information to an operator who may, if necessary, take corrective action. In some highly automated systems, the computer itself can take corrective action. At Dell's OptiPlex Plant, electronic instructions are sent to double-decker conveyor belts that speed computer components to assembly stations. Two-member teams are told by computers which PC or server to build, with initial assembly taking only three to four minutes. Then more electronic commands move the products (more than 20,000 machines on a typical day) to a finishing area to be customized, boxed, and sent to waiting delivery trucks.

---

**process layout**
a layout that organizes the transformation process into departments that group related processes

**intermittent organizations**
organizations that deal with products of a lesser magnitude than do project organizations; their products are not necessarily unique but possess a significant number of differences

**product layout**
a layout requiring that production be broken down into relatively simple tasks assigned to workers, who are usually positioned along an assembly line

**continuous manufacturing organizations**
companies that use continuously running assembly lines, creating products with many similar characteristics

**computer-assisted design (CAD)**
the design of components, products, and processes on computers instead of on paper

**computer-assisted manufacturing (CAM)**
manufacturing that employs specialized computer systems to actually guide and control the transformation processes

Although the plant covers 200,000 square feet, enough to enclose 23 football fields, it is managed almost entirely by a network of computers.[20]

Using **flexible manufacturing,** computers can direct machinery to adapt to different versions of similar operations. For example, with instructions from a computer, one machine can be programmed to carry out its function for several different versions of an engine without shutting down the production line for refitting.

Robots are also becoming increasingly useful in the transformation process. These "steel-collar" workers have become particularly important in industries such as nuclear power, hazardous-waste disposal, ocean research, and space construction and maintenance, in which human lives would otherwise be at risk. Robots are used in numerous applications by companies around the world. Many assembly operations—cars, television sets, telephones, stereo equipment, and numerous other products—depend on industrial robots. The Robotic Industries Association estimates that about 160,000 robots are now at work in U.S. factories, making the United States one of the two largest the users of robotics, second only to Japan.[21] Researchers continue to make more sophisticated robots, and some speculate that in the future robots will not be limited to space programs and production and operations, but will also be able to engage in farming, laboratory research, and even household activities. Moreover, robotics are increasingly being used in the medical field. Voice-activated robotic arms operate video cameras for surgeons. Similar technology assists with biopsies, as well as heart, spine, and nervous system procedures. A heart surgeon at London Health Science Centre in Ontario uses a surgical robot to perform bypass operations on patients without opening their chests, except for five tiny incisions, while their hearts continue beating. More than 400 surgeons around the world currently use surgical robots with far fewer post-operative complications than encountered in conventional operations.[22] It is estimated that over 150 hospitals in the U.S. use minimally invasive surgical robots for heart surgery.[23]

When all these technologies—CAD/CAM, flexible manufacturing, robotics, computer systems, and more—are integrated, the result is **computer-integrated manufacturing (CIM),** a complete system that designs products, manages machines and materials, and controls the operations function. Companies adopt CIM to boost productivity and quality and reduce costs. Such technology, and computers in particular, will continue to make strong inroads into operations on two fronts—one dealing with the technology involved in manufacturing and one dealing with the administrative functions and processes used by operations managers. The operations manager must be willing to work with computers and other forms of technology and to develop a high degree of computer literacy.

## Green Operations and Manufacturing

Manufacturing and operations systems are moving quickly to establish environmental sustainability and minimize negative impact on the natural environment. Many efforts, such as conservation, recycling, alternative energy usage, and reduction of pollution, especially greenhouse gas pollution, are also consistent with increasing productivity and satisfying customers.

For example, Wal-Mart works with suppliers to reduce the amount of cardboard and plastic packaging used. To cut carbon emissions, Wal-Mart has set a goal to have zero waste and use 100 percent renewable energy.[24] Wal-Mart also desires to sell products that sustain our resources and the environment. Wal-Mart is on track to reduce its truck fleet's fuel consumption by 25 percent with aerodynamic trailers, and Peterbuilt is building hybrid trucks for Wal-Mart.[25] Wal-Mart is also changing its lighting and other electrical use for maximum efficiency. All of these initiatives relate to making operations greener, contributing to environmental sustainability, providing savings, and being a role model for other businesses.

While Wal-Mart illustrates green initiatives in operations, New Belgium Brewing illustrates green initiatives in operations and manufacturing. New Belgium was the first brewery to adopt 100 percent wind-powered electricity, reducing carbon emissions by 1,800 metric tons a year. They use a steam condenser to capture hot water to be reused for boiling the next batch of barley and hops, then the steam is redirected to heat the floor tiles and de-ice the loading docks in cold Colorado weather. Used barley and hops are given to local farmers to feed cattle. New Belgium gives employees a bicycle after one year of employment to ride to work, further reducing carbon emissions. The company is moving to aluminum cans because they can be recycled an infinite number of times and recycling one can saves enough electricity to run a television for three hours or save a half gallon of gasoline. The company has won an award from the Environmental Protection Agency and is a role model for other businesses.

Wal-Mart and New Belgium Brewing demonstrate that reducing waste, recycling, conserving, and using renewable energy not only protect the environment, but can also gain the support of stakeholders. Green operations and manufacturing can improve a firm's reputation and customer and employee loyalty that leads to improved profits.

Much of the movement to green manufacturing and operations is the belief that global warming and climate change must decline. The McKinsey Global Institute (MGI) says that just by taking opportunities to cut waste, the world's energy use could be reduced by 50 percent by the year 2020. Just creating green buildings and higher mileage cars could yield $900 billion savings per year by 2020.[26] General Motors killed its experimental EV1 electric car, but now the Chevrolet Volt will be launched in 2010. The sedan plug-in hybrid will charge in six hours and run 40 miles before a small gasoline engine kicks in to provide 100 miles per gallon.[27] Green products produced through green operations and manufacturing is our future. A report authored by the Center for American Progress cites ways that cities and local governments can play a role. For example, Los Angeles plans to save the city utility costs by retrofitting hundreds of city buildings while creating a green careers training program for low-income residents. Newark, New Jersey, and Richmond, California, also have green jobs training programs. Albuquerque, New Mexico, was the first city to sign on to a pledge to build a green economy as part of its efforts to create green jobs to stimulate the city's economy.[28] Government initiatives provide space for businesses to innovate their green operations and manufacturing.

## Managing the Supply Chain

A major function of operations is **supply chain management,** which refers to connecting and integrating all parties or members of the distribution system in order to satisfy customers.[29] Also called logistics, supply chain management includes all the activities involved in obtaining and managing raw materials and component parts, managing finished products, packaging them, and getting them to customers. Sunny Delight had to quickly recreate its supply chain after spinning off from Procter & Gamble. This means it had to develop ordering, shipping, and billing, as

**supply chain management** connecting and integrating all parties or members of the distribution system in order to satisfy customers

When you think about UPS, you usually think of the nice drivers in brown uniforms and brown trucks that deliver packages around the world. In this ad, UPS promotes its "Supply Chain Solutions," its ability to solve logistics and distribution issues for companies, synchronizing "the movement of goods, information, and funds."

well as warehouse management systems and transportation, so it could focus on growing and managing the Sunny Delight brand.[30] The supply chain integrates firms such as raw material suppliers, manufacturers, retailers, and ultimate consumers into a seamless flow of information and products.[31] Some aspects of logistics (warehousing, packaging, distributing) are so closely linked with marketing that we will discuss them in Chapter 13. In this section, we look at purchasing, managing inventory, outsourcing, and scheduling, which are vital tasks in the transformation of raw materials into finished goods. To illustrate logistics, consider a hypothetical small business—we'll call it Rushing Water Canoes Inc.—that manufactures aluminum canoes, which it sells primarily to sporting goods stores and river-rafting expeditions. Our company also makes paddles and helmets, but the focus of the following discussion is the manufacture of the company's quality canoes as they proceed through the logistics process.

## Purchasing

**Purchasing,** also known as procurement, is the buying of all the materials needed by the organization. The purchasing department aims to obtain items of the desired quality in the right quantities at the lowest possible cost. Rushing Water Canoes, for example, must procure not only aluminum and other raw materials, and various canoe parts and components, but also machines and equipment, manufacturing supplies (oil, electricity, and so on), and office supplies in order to make its canoes.

**purchasing**
the buying of all the materials needed by the organization; also called procurement

People in the purchasing department locate and evaluate suppliers of these items. They must constantly be on the lookout for new materials or parts that will do a better job or cost less than those currently being used. The purchasing function can be quite complex and is one area made much easier and more efficient by technological advances.

Not all companies purchase all the materials needed to create their products. Oftentimes, they can make some components more economically and efficiently than can an outside supplier. Coors, for example, manufactures its own cans at a subsidiary plant. On the other hand, firms sometimes find that it is uneconomical to make or purchase an item, and instead arrange to lease it from another organization. Some airlines, for example, lease airplanes rather than buy them. Whether to purchase, make, or lease a needed item generally depends on cost, as well as on product availability and supplier reliability.

## Managing Inventory

Once the items needed to create a product have been procured, some provision has to be made for storing them until they are needed. Every raw material, component, completed or partially completed product, and piece of equipment a firm uses—its **inventory**—must be accounted for, or controlled. There are three basic types of inventory. *Finished-goods inventory* includes those products that are ready for sale, such as a fully assembled automobile ready to ship to a dealer. *Work-in-process inventory* consists of those products that are partly completed or are in some stage of the transformation process. At McDonald's, a cooking hamburger represents work-in-process inventory because it must go through several more stages before it can be sold to a customer. *Raw materials inventory* includes all the materials that have been purchased to be used as inputs for making other products. Nuts and bolts are raw materials for an automobile manufacturer, while hamburger patties, vegetables, and buns are raw materials for the fast-food restaurant. Our fictional Rushing Water Canoes has an inventory of materials for making canoes, paddles, and helmets, as well as its inventory of finished products for sale to consumers. **Inventory control** is the process of determining how many supplies and goods are needed and keeping track of quantities on hand, where each item is, and who is responsible for it.

Operations management must be closely coordinated with inventory control. The production of televisions, for example, cannot be planned without some knowledge of the availability of all the necessary materials—the chassis, picture tubes, color guns, and so forth. Also, each item held in inventory—any type of inventory—carries with it a cost. For example, storing fully assembled televisions in a warehouse to sell to a dealer at a future date requires not only the use of space, but also the purchase of insurance to cover any losses that might occur due to fire or other unforeseen events.

Inventory managers spend a great deal of time trying to determine the proper inventory level for each item. The answer to the question of how many units to hold in inventory depends on variables such as the usage rate of the item, the cost of maintaining the item in inventory, future costs of inventory and other procedures associated with ordering or making the item, and the cost of the item itself. In 2008, fast-rising steel prices caused some projects such as bridges and other construction to be placed on hold due to material cost overruns. Globally, steel prices increased 50 percent and iron ore went up 71 percent, with global demand for the commodities soaring. Steelmaking materials such as coal and scrap steel doubled in price.[32] Steel purchased in advance of these price increases would have helped control prices by maintaining a larger inventory for construction use during this time period. Several approaches may be used to determine how many units of a given item should be procured at one time and when that procurement should take place.

**inventory**
all raw materials, components, completed or partially completed products, and pieces of equipment a firm uses

**inventory control**
the process of determining how many supplies and goods are needed and keeping track of quantities on hand, where each item is, and who is responsible for it

*By tracking its sales in real time, 7-Eleven Japan manages its inventory on a minute-by-minute basis at each of its thousands of stores. Four times each day the stores receive fresh inventory, and at least three times a day employees rearrange the shelves, depending on what's selling well.*

### The Economic Order Quantity Model.

**economic order quantity (EOQ) model**
a model that identifies the optimum number of items to order to minimize the costs of managing (ordering, storing, and using) them

To control the number of items maintained in inventory, managers need to determine how much of any given item they should order. One popular approach is the **economic order quantity (EOQ) model,** which identifies the optimum number of items to order to minimize the costs of managing (ordering, storing, and using) them.

### Just-in-Time Inventory Management.

**just-in-time (JIT) inventory management**
a technique using smaller quantities of materials that arrive "just in time" for use in the transformation process and therefore require less storage space and other inventory management expense

An increasingly popular technique is **just-in-time (JIT) inventory management,** which eliminates waste by using smaller quantities of materials that arrive "just in time" for use in the transformation process and therefore require less storage space and other inventory management expense. JIT minimizes inventory by providing an almost continuous flow of items from suppliers to the production facility. Many U.S. companies, including General Motors, Hewlett-Packard, IBM, and Harley Davidson, have adopted JIT to reduce costs and boost efficiency.

Let's say that Rushing Water Canoes uses 20 units of aluminum from a supplier per day. Traditionally, its inventory manager might order enough for one month at a time: 440 units per order (20 units per day times 22 workdays per month). The expense of such a large inventory could be considerable because of the cost of insurance coverage, recordkeeping, rented storage space, and so on. The just-in-time approach would reduce these costs because aluminum would be purchased in smaller quantities, perhaps in lot sizes of 20, which the supplier would deliver once a day. Of course, for such an approach to be effective, the supplier must be extremely reliable and relatively close to the production facility.

### Material-requirements Planning.

**material-requirements planning (MRP)**
a planning system that schedules the precise quantity of materials needed to make the product

Another inventory management technique is **material-requirements planning (MRP),** a planning system that schedules the precise quantity of materials needed to make the product. The basic components of MRP are a master production schedule, a bill of materials, and an inventory status file. At Rushing Water Canoes, for example, the inventory-control manager will look at the production schedule to determine how many canoes the company plans to make. He or she will then prepare a bill of materials—a list of all the materials needed to make that quantity of canoes. Next, the manager will determine the quantity of these items that RWC already holds in inventory (to avoid ordering excess materials) and then develop a schedule for ordering and accepting delivery of the right quantity of materials to satisfy the firm's needs. Because of the large number of parts and materials that go into a typical production process, MRP must be done on a computer. It can be, and often is, used in conjunction with just-in-time inventory management.

## Outsourcing

Increasingly, outsourcing has become a component of supply chain management in operations. As we mentioned in Chapter 3, outsourcing refers to the contracting of manufacturing or other tasks to independent companies, often overseas. Many companies elect to outsource some aspects of their operations to companies that can provide these products more efficiently, at a lower cost, and with greater customer satisfaction. Globalization has put pressure on supply chain managers to improve speed and balance resources against competitive pressures. Companies outsourcing to China, in particular, face heavy regulation, high transportation costs, inadequate facilities, and unpredictable supply chain execution. Therefore, suppliers need to provide useful, timely, and accurate information about every aspect of the quality requirements, schedules, and solutions to dealing with problems. For example,

> **TABLE 9.2**   The World's Top Five Outsourcing Providers
>
> | Company | Services* |
> |---|---|
> | Accenture | Human resource management; information and communication technology management; financial management |
> | IBM | Customer relationship management; human resource management; information and communication technology management |
> | Infosys Technologies | Information and communication technology management; transaction processes, information technology, and strategic consulting |
> | Sodexo | Real estate and asset management; facility services; service vouchers and cards |
> | Capgemini | Customer relationship management; information and communication technology management; financial management |
>
> Source: "The 2008 Global Outsourcing 100™," International Association of Outsourcing Professionals™, http://www.outsourcingprofessional.org/content/23/152/1197/ (accessed May 15, 2008).
> *The services section was provided by the authors.

Chinese suppliers took responsibility for the lead paint on children's toys crisis in the United States, but it was an overall management and supply chain system failure that permitted these toxic toys to be sold in U.S. stores.[33]

Many high-tech firms have outsourced the production of chips, computers, and telecom equipment to Asian companies.[34] The hourly labor costs in countries such as China, India, and Vietnam are far less than in the United States, Europe, or even Mexico. These developing countries have improved their manufacturing capabilities, infrastructure, and technical and business skills, making them more attractive regions for global sourcing. On the other hand, the cost of outsourcing halfway around the world must be considered in decisions.[35] While information technology is often outsourced today, transportation, human resources, services, and even marketing functions can be outsourced. Our hypothetical Rushing Water Canoes might contract with a local janitorial service to clean its offices and with a local accountant to handle routine bookkeeping and tax-preparation functions.

Outsourcing, once used primarily as a cost-cutting tactic, has increasingly been linked with the development of competitive advantage through improved product quality, speeding up the time it takes products to get to the customer, and overall supply-chain efficiencies. Table 9.2 provides the world's top five outsourcing providers that assist mainly in information technology. Outsourcing allows companies to free up time and resources to focus on what they do best and to create better opportunities to focus on customer satisfaction. Many executives view outsourcing as an innovative way to boost productivity and remain competitive against low-wage offshore factories. However, outsourcing may create conflict with labor and negative public opinion when it results in U.S. workers being replaced by lower-cost workers in other countries. According to a survey by Opinion Research Corporation, 69 percent of respondents believed that boycotting products and services from companies that actively send jobs overseas would influence companies.[36]

## Routing and Scheduling

After all materials have been procured and their use determined, managers must then consider the **routing,** or sequence of operations through which the product must

**routing**
the sequence of operations through which the product must pass

# Going Green
## Concerned about Gas Mileage or the Environment? Get Smart!

With gas prices on the rise and environmental concerns growing daily, people are looking for smarter solutions to transportation. Those at Smart Car of America hope individuals will look no further than the car dubbed "smart." The brainchild of Nicholas Hayek, known for Swatch watches, and built by Mercedes-Benz, the Smart car is like no other car on the American market. If you remember seeing the MiniCooper arrive on the scene and thinking, "boy, that car is tiny," the Smart car will shock you! Futuristic in design, the Smart car measures just over 106 inches long, making it three feet shorter than the MiniCooper. The car, called the fortwo (although there are other designs, such as the forfour, slated to be released in the future), seats two people, has no back seat, and has minimal storage space at the rear. Despite its small size, test drivers have found the interior to be roomier than expected. More than 770,000 of the original fortwo have been sold in 36 countries since 2001, but is America ready to get Smart? Roger Penske certainly thinks so.

Penske, at the helm of Penske Automotive Group, has signed on as the only U.S. distributor of the Smart car. Taking an extremely unconventional approach, Penske and his group have targeted customers via the Internet. In one year, about a million people have perused the Smart USA Web site. Thanks to the site, 52,000 people signed up to receive the company's newsletter. When the company opened up its $99 reservation service, it received more than 30,000 reservations in record time. Americans are interested in this smart little vehicle.

So what made Penske think that a country full of individuals interested in the fastest or sometimes the biggest cars would consider the Smart? The car appeals to American buyers for a number of reasons. For one thing, gas prices in the United States continue to rise. The Smart fortwo receives 33 miles per gallon (mpg) in the city and 40 mpg on the highway. Under the old 2007 EPA standards, which were revised for 2008, Smart would have received 40 mpg in the city and 45 mpg on the highway. Just about everyone is looking to save money on gasoline these days. For those looking to go green, the fortwo has earned the Ultra Low Emission Vehicle designation due to its low exhaust emissions. At some point in the future, Mercedes-Benz does plan to come out with two variations on the hybrid. In addition, as U.S. cities become more and more crowded, parking becomes a challenge. The Smart car is ideal for city driving and even more for city parking because it is small enough to back into parallel parking spaces. It's true that the Smart car does not get the best gas mileage among all cars on the market, is not quite as environmentally friendly as the Tesla Roadster featured in Chapter 1, and may not speed down the highway (although it can accelerate to a maximum speed of 84 mph—over any U.S. speed limit). However, when you combine all that the Smart car does offer with its price tag—from $11,590 to $16,590—it becomes a car consider.[37]

**Discussion Questions:**

1. Mercedes-Benz is known for quality cars. Should the Smart car maintain that same quality as other Mercedes?
2. Will American consumers be able to accept and pay the appropriate price for a small car that is also very high quality?
3. How is the Smart car contributing to the reduction of greenhouse gases and educating consumers to go green?

---

pass. For example, before employees at Rushing Water Canoes can form aluminum sheets into a canoe, the aluminum must be cut to size. Likewise, the canoe's flotation material must be installed before workers can secure the wood seats. The sequence depends on the product specifications developed by the engineering department of the company.

Once management knows the routing, the actual work can be scheduled. **Scheduling** assigns the tasks to be done to departments or even specific machines, workers, or teams. At Rushing Water, cutting aluminum for the company's canoes might be scheduled to be done by the "cutting and finishing" department on machines designed especially for that purpose.

Many approaches to scheduling have been developed, ranging from simple trial and error to highly sophisticated computer programs. One popular method is the *Program Evaluation and Review Technique (PERT)*, which identifies all the major activities or events required to complete a project, arranges them in a sequence or path, determines the critical path, and estimates the time required for each event. Producing a McDonald's Big Mac, for example, involves removing meat,

**scheduling**
the assignment of required tasks to departments or even specific machines, workers, or teams

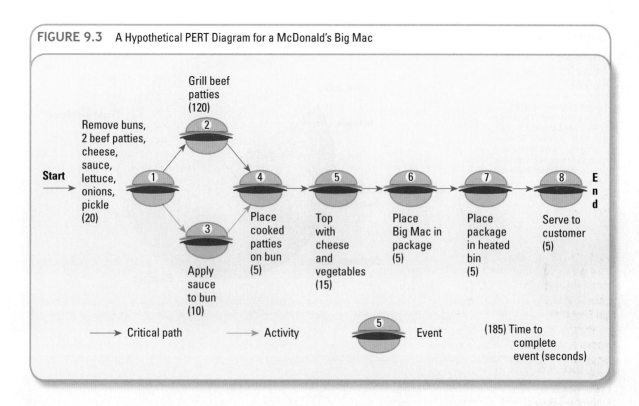

**FIGURE 9.3**    A Hypothetical PERT Diagram for a McDonald's Big Mac

cheese, sauce, and vegetables from the refrigerator; grilling the hamburger pat-ties; assembling the ingredients; placing the completed Big Mac in its package; and serving it to the customer (Figure 9.3). The cheese, pickles, onions, and sauce can-not be put on before the hamburger patty is completely grilled and placed on the bun. The path that requires the longest time from start to finish is called the *critical path* because it determines the minimum amount of time in which the process can be completed. If any of the activities on the critical path for production of the Big Mac fall behind schedule, the sandwich will not be completed on time, causing cus-tomers to wait longer than they usually would.

# Managing Quality

Quality, like cost and efficiency, is a critical element of operations management, for defective products can quickly ruin a firm. Quality reflects the degree to which a good or service meets the demands and requirements of customers. Customers are increasingly dissatisfied with the quality of service provided by many airlines. Figure 9.4 provides an overview of the types of complaints reported to the Avia-tion Consumer Protection Division. Determining quality can be difficult because it depends on customers' perceptions of how well the product meets or exceeds their expectations. University researchers, using U.S. Department of Transporta-tion data, scored 16 airlines for overall service quality and found three smaller dis-count carriers, AirTran, then JetBlue, followed by Southwest, the highest ranked for overall service. Northwest was ranked fourth and had the highest quality rating among large carriers. Of the 16 airlines ranked, more than a quarter of their flights arrived late.[38]

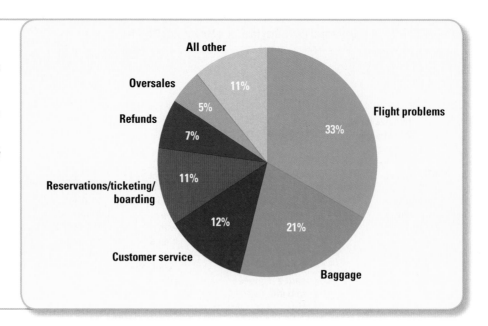

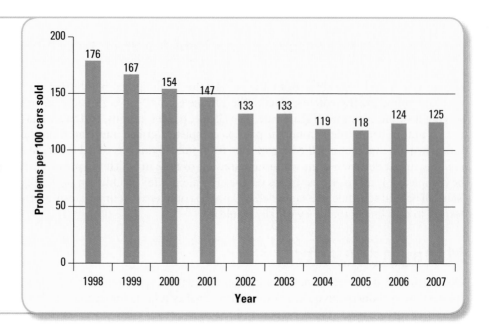

The fuel economy of an automobile or its reliability (defined in terms of frequency of repairs) can be measured with some degree of precision. Although automakers rely on their own measures of vehicle quality, they also look to independent sources such as the J. D. Power & Associates annual initial quality survey for confirmation of their quality assessment as well as consumer perceptions of quality for the industry, as indicated in Figure 9.5.

It is especially difficult to measure quality characteristics when the product is a service. A company has to decide exactly which quality characteristics it considers important and then define those characteristics in terms that can be measured. The inseparability of production and consumption and the level of customer contact influence the selection of characteristics of the service that are most important. Employees in high-contact services such as hairstyling, education, legal services, and even the barista at Starbucks are an important part of the product.

The Malcolm Baldrige National Quality Award is given each year to companies that meet rigorous standards of quality. The Baldrige criteria are (1) leadership, (2) information and analysis, (3) strategic planning, (4) human resource development and management, (5) process management, (6) business results, and (7) customer focus and satisfaction. The criteria have become a worldwide framework for driving business improvement. Five companies received the award last year, representing three different categories, including two nonprofit organizations, in the first year of that category: PRO-TEC Coating Co. (small business); Mercy Health System (health care); Sharp HealthCare (health care); City of Coral Springs (nonprofit); and the U.S. Army Armament Research, Development and Engineering Center (nonprofit).[39]

Quality is so important that we need to examine it in the context of operations management. **Quality control** refers to the processes an organization uses to maintain its established quality standards. Consumers bring back 11 to 20 percent of all the electronic products they purchase, with wireless phones, GPS units, MP3 players, and wireless networking gear having the highest return rates. When the returned products are analyzed, 68 percent had no problems ("consumer operating error"), 27 percent were returned because of buyers' remorse ("spouse didn't like it"), and only 5 percent were defective.[40] Best Buy's Geek Squad helps reduce returns of PCs by 40 percent when they deliver and set up a computer. This demonstrates that measuring perceived quality relates to more than just technical defects of a product, but also to other characteristics.[41]

**quality control**
the processes an organization uses to maintain its established quality standards

Quality has become a major concern in many organizations, particularly in light of intense foreign competition and increasingly demanding customers. To regain a competitive edge, a number of firms have adopted a total quality management approach. **Total quality management (TQM)** is a philosophy that uniform commitment to quality in all areas of the organization will promote a culture that meets customers' perceptions of quality. It involves coordinating efforts to improve customer satisfaction, increase employee participation and empowerment, form and strengthen supplier partnerships, and foster an organizational culture of continuous quality improvement. TQM requires continuous quality improvement and employee empowerment.

**total quality management (TQM)**
a philosophy that uniform commitment to quality in all areas of an organization will promote a culture that meets customers' perceptions of quality

Continuous improvement of an organization's goods and services is built around the notion that quality is free; by contrast, *not* having high-quality goods and services can be very expensive, especially in terms of dissatisfied customers.[42] A primary tool of the continuous improvement process is *benchmarking,* the measuring and evaluating of the quality of the organization's goods, services, or processes as compared with the quality produced by the best-performing companies in the industry.[43] Benchmarking lets the organization know where it stands competitively in its industry, thus giving it a goal to aim for over time.

Companies employing total quality management (TQM) programs know that quality control should be incorporated throughout the transformation process, from the initial plans to develop a specific product through the product and production-facility design processes to the actual manufacture of the product. In other words, they view quality control as an element of the product itself, rather than as simply a function of the operations process. When a company makes the product correctly from the outset, it eliminates the need to rework defective products, expedites the transformation process itself, and allows employees to make better use of their time and materials. One method through which many companies have tried to improve quality is **statistical process control,** a system in which management collects and analyzes information about the production process to pinpoint quality problems in the production system.

**statistical process control** a system in which management collects and analyzes information about the production process to pinpoint quality problems in the production system

## International Organization for Standardization (ISO)

Regardless whether a company has a TQM program for quality control, it must first determine what standard of quality it desires and then assess whether its products meet that standard. Product specifications and quality standards must be set so the company can create a product that will compete in the marketplace. Rushing Water Canoes, for example, may specify that each of its canoes has aluminum walls of a specified uniform thickness, that the front and back be reinforced with a specified level of steel, and that each contain a specified amount of flotation material for safety. Production facilities must be designed that can produce products with the desired specifications.

Quality standards can be incorporated into service businesses as well. A hamburger chain, for example, may establish standards relating to how long it takes to cook an order and serve it to customers, how many fries are in each order, how thick the burgers are, or how many customer complaints might be acceptable. Once the desired quality characteristics, specifications, and standards have been stated in measurable terms, the next step is inspection.

**ISO 9000** a series of quality assurance standards designed by the International Organization for Standardization (ISO) to ensure consistent product quality under many conditions

The International Organization for Standardization (ISO) has created a series of quality management standards—**ISO 9000**—designed to ensure the customer's quality standards are met. The standards provide a framework for documenting how a certified business keeps records, trains employees, tests products, and fixes defects. To obtain ISO 9000 certification, an independent auditor must verify that a business's factory, laboratory, or office meets the quality standards spelled out by the International Organization for Standardization. The certification process can require significant investment, but for many companies, the process is essential to being able to compete. Thousands of U.S. firms have been certified, and many more are working to meet the standards. Certification has become a virtual necessity for doing business in Europe in some high-technology businesses. ISO 9002 certification was established for service providers. Global Investment Recovery takes e-scrap (monitors, televisions, cell phones, etc). The company recycles 65 million pounds a year, with ISO 14001 certification, an environmental credential that ensures safe pollution liability.[44]

## Inspection

Inspection reveals whether a product meets quality standards. Some product characteristics may be discerned by fairly simple inspection techniques—weighing the contents of cereal boxes or measuring the time it takes for a customer to receive his or her hamburger. As part of the ongoing quality assurance program at Hershey Foods, all wrapped Hershey Kisses are checked, and all imperfectly wrapped kisses are rejected.[45] Other inspection techniques are more elaborate. Automobile manufacturers use automated machines to open and close car doors to test the durability of latches and hinges. The food-processing and pharmaceutical industries use various chemical tests to determine the quality of their output. Rushing Water Canoes might use a special device that can precisely measure the thickness of each canoe wall to ensure that it meets the company's specifications.

Organizations normally inspect purchased items, work-in-process, and finished items. The inspection of purchased items and finished items takes place after the fact; the inspection of work-in-process is preventive. In other words, the purpose of inspection of purchased items and finished items is to determine what the quality level is. For items that are being worked on—an automobile moving down the assembly line or a canoe being assembled—the purpose of the inspection is to find defects before the product is completed so that necessary corrections can be made.

## Sampling

An important question relating to inspection is how many items should be inspected. Should all canoes produced by Rushing Water be inspected or just some of them? Whether to inspect 100 percent of the output or only part of it is related to the cost of the inspection process, the destructiveness of the inspection process (some tests last until the product fails), and the potential cost of product flaws in terms of human lives and safety.

Some inspection procedures are quite expensive, use elaborate testing equipment, destroy products, and/or require a significant number of hours to complete. In such cases, it is usually desirable to test only a sample of the output. If the sample passes inspection, the inspector may assume that all the items in the lot from which the sample was drawn would also pass inspection. By using principles of statistical inference, management can employ sampling techniques that assure a relatively high probability of reaching the right conclusion—that is, rejecting a lot that does not meet standards and accepting a lot that does. Nevertheless, there will always be a risk of making an incorrect conclusion—accepting a population that *does not* meet standards (because the sample was satisfactory) or rejecting a population that *does* meet standards (because the sample contained too many defective items).

Sampling is likely to be used when inspection tests are destructive. Determining the life expectancy of lightbulbs by turning them on and recording how long they last would be foolish: There is no market for burned-out lightbulbs. Instead, a generalization based on the quality of a sample would be applied to the entire population of lightbulbs from which the sample was drawn. However, human life and safety often depend on the proper functioning of specific items, such as the navigational systems installed in commercial airliners. For such items, even though the inspection process is costly, the potential cost of flawed systems—in human lives and safety—is too great not to inspect 100 percent of the output.

# So You Want a Job in Operations Management

While you might not have been familiar with terms such as *supply chain* or *logistics* or *total quality management* before taking this course, careers abound in the operations management field. You will find these careers in a wide variety of organizations—manufacturers, retailers, transportation companies, third-party logistics firms, government agencies, and service firms. Approximately $1.3 trillion is spent on transportation, inventory, and related logistics activities, and logistics alone accounts for more than 9.5 percent of U.S. gross domestic product.[46] Closely managing how a company's inputs and outputs flow from raw materials to the end consumer is vital to a firm's success. Successful companies also need to ensure that quality is measured and actively managed at each step.

Supply chain managers have a tremendous impact on the success of an organization. These managers are engaged in every facet of the business process, including planning, purchasing, production, transportation, storage and distribution, customer service, and more. Their performance helps organizations control expenses, boost sales, and maximize profits.

Warehouse managers are a vital part of manufacturing operations. A typical warehouse manager's duties include overseeing and recording deliveries and pickups, maintaining inventory records and the product tracking system, and adjusting inventory levels to reflect receipts and disbursements. Warehouse managers also have to keep in mind customer service and employee issues. Warehouse managers can earn up to $60,000 in some cases.

Operations management is also required in service businesses. With more than 80 percent of the U.S. economy in services, jobs exist for services operations. Many service contact operations require standardized processes that often use technology to provide an interface that provides an automatic quality performance. Consider jobs in health care, the travel industry, fast food, and entertainment. Think of any job or task that is a part of the final product in these industries. Even an online retailer such as Amazon.com has a transformation process that includes information technology and human activities that facilitate a transaction. These services have a standardized process and can be evaluated based on their level of achieved service quality.

Total quality management is becoming a key attribute for companies to ensure that quality pervades all aspects of the organization. Quality assurance managers may make salaries in the $55,000 to $65,000 range. These managers monitor and advise on how a company's quality management system is performing and publish data and reports regarding company performance in both manufacturing and service industries.

# Review Your Understanding

### Define operations management, and differentiate between operations and manufacturing.

Operations management (OM) is the development and administration of the activities involved in transforming resources into goods and services. Operations managers oversee the transformation process and the planning and designing of operations systems, managing logistics, quality, and productivity. The terms *manufacturing* and *production* are used interchangeably to describe the activities and processes used in making tangible products, whereas *operations* is a broader term used to describe the process of making both tangible and intangible products.

### Explain how operations management differs in manufacturing and service firms.

Manufacturers and service firms both transform inputs into outputs, but service providers differ from manufacturers in several ways: They have greater customer contact because the service typically occurs at the point of consumption; their inputs and outputs are more variable than manufacturers', largely because of the human element; service providers are generally more labor intensive; and their productivity measurement is more complex.

### Describe the elements involved in planning and designing an operations system.

Operations planning relates to decisions about what product(s) to make, for whom, and what processes and facilities are needed to produce them. OM is often joined by marketing and research and development in these decisions. Common facility layouts include fixed-position layouts, process layouts, or product layouts. Where to locate operations facilities is a crucial decision that depends on proximity to the market, availability of raw materials, availability of transportation, availability of power, climatic influences, availability of labor, and community characteristics.

Technology is also vital to operations, particularly computer-assisted design, computer-assisted manufacturing, flexible manufacturing, robotics, and computer-integrated manufacturing.

***Specify some techniques managers may use to manage the logistics of transforming inputs into finished products.***

Logistics, or supply chain management, includes all the activities involved in obtaining and managing raw materials and component parts, managing finished products, packaging them, and getting them to customers. The organization must first make or purchase (procure) all the materials it needs. Next, it must control its inventory by determining how many supplies and goods it needs and keeping track of every raw material, component, completed or partially completed product, and piece of equipment, how many of each are on hand, where they are, and who has responsibility for them. Common approaches to inventory control include the economic order quantity (EOQ) model, the just-in-time

(JIT) inventory concept, and material-requirements planning (MRP). Logistics also includes routing and scheduling processes and activities to complete products.

***Assess the importance of quality in operations management.***

Quality is a critical element of OM because low-quality products can hurt people and harm the business. Quality control refers to the processes an organization uses to maintain its established quality standards. To control quality, a company must establish what standard of quality it desires and then determine whether its products meet that standard through inspection.

***Evaluate a business's dilemma and propose a solution.***

Based on this chapter and the facts presented in "Solve the Dilemma" on page 291, you should be able to evaluate the business's problem and propose one or more solutions for resolving it.

## Revisit the World of Business

1. What role did the need for high-quality, authentic Hispanic food play in the success of Goya?
2. Goya potentially was selling commodities, so how did the company customize its operations for the Hispanic market?
3. What is the importance of distribution and the delivery of its products to stores serving Hispanic customers in Goya's success?

## Learn the Terms

capacity   272
computer-assisted design (CAD)   275
computer-assisted manufacturing (CAM)   275
computer-integrated manufacturing (CIM)   276
continuous manufacturing organizations   275
customization   272
economic order quantity (EOQ) model   280
fixed-position layout   274
flexible manufacturing   276
inputs   265

intermittent organizations   275
inventory   279
inventory control   279
ISO 9000   286
just-in-time (JIT) inventory management   280
manufacturing   265
material-requirements planning (MRP)   280
modular design   272
operations   265
operations management (OM)   264
outputs   265

process layout   275
product layout   275
production   265
project organization   274
purchasing   278
quality control   285
routing   281
scheduling   282
standardization   271
statistical process control   286
supply chain management   277
total quality management (TQM)   285

# Check Your Progress

1. What is operations management?
2. Differentiate among the terms *operations, production,* and *manufacturing.*
3. Compare and contrast a manufacturer versus a service provider in terms of operations management.
4. Who is involved in planning products?
5. In what industry would the fixed-position layout be most efficient? The process layout? The product layout? Use real examples.
6. What criteria do businesses use when deciding where to locate a plant?
7. What is flexible manufacturing? How can it help firms improve quality?
8. Define supply chain management and summarize the activities it involves.
9. Describe some of the methods a firm may use to control inventory.
10. When might a firm decide to inspect a sample of its products rather than test every product for quality?

# Get Involved

1. Compare and contrast OM at McDonald's with that of Honda of America. Compare and contrast OM at McDonald's with that of a bank in your neighborhood.
2. Find a real company that uses JIT, either in your local community or in a business journal. Why did the company decide to use JIT? What have been the advantages and disadvantages of using JIT for that particular company? What has been the overall effect on the quality of the company's products or services? What has been the overall effect on the company's bottom line?
3. Interview someone from your local Chamber of Commerce and ask him or her what incentives the community offers to encourage organizations to locate there. (See if these incentives relate to the criteria firms use to make location decisions.)

# Build Your Skills

### REDUCING CYCLE TIME

**Background:**
An important goal of production and operations management is reducing cycle time—the time it takes to complete a task or process. The goal in cycle time reduction is to reduce costs and/or increase customer service.[47] Many experts believe that the rate of change in our society is so fast that a firm must master speed and connectivity.[48] Connectivity refers to a seamless integration of customers, suppliers, employees, and organizational, production, and operations management. The use of the Internet and other telecommunications systems helps many organizations connect and reduce cycle time.

**Task:**
Break up into pairs throughout the class. Select two businesses (local restaurants, retail stores, etc.) that both of you frequent, are employed by, and/or are fairly well acquainted with. For the first business, one of you will role-play the "manager" and the other will role-play the "customer." Reverse roles for the second business you have selected. As managers at your respective businesses, you are to prepare a list of five questions you will ask the customer during the role-play. The questions you prepare should be designed to get the customer's viewpoint on how good the cycle time is at your business. If one of the responses leads to a problem area, you may need to ask a follow-up question to determine the nature of the dissatisfaction. Prepare one main question and a follow-up, if necessary, for each of the five dimensions of cycle time:

1. **Speed**—the delivery of goods and services in the minimum time; efficient communications; the elimination of wasted time.
2. **Connectivity**—all operations and systems in the business appear connected with the customer.
3. **Interactive relationships**—a continual dialog exists between operations units, service providers, and customers that permits the exchange of feedback on concerns or needs.
4. **Customization**—each product is tailored to the needs of the customer.
5. **Responsiveness**—the willingness to make adjustments and be flexible to help customers and to provide prompt service when a problem develops.

Begin the two role-plays. When it is your turn to be the manager, listen carefully when your partner answers your prepared questions. You need to elicit information on how to improve the cycle time at your business. You will achieve this by identifying the problem areas (weaknesses) that need attention.

After completing both role-play situations, fill out the form below for the role-play where you were the manager. You may not have gathered enough information to fill in all the boxes. For example, for some categories, the customer may have had only good things to say; for others, the comments may all be negative. Be prepared to share the information you gain with the rest of the class.

I role-played the manager at _____ (business). After listening carefully to the customer's responses to my five questions, I determined the following strengths and weaknesses as they relate to the cycle time at my business.

| Dimension | Strength | Weakness |
| --- | --- | --- |
| Speed | | |
| Connectivity | | |
| Interactive relationships | | |
| Customization | | |
| Responsiveness | | |

## Solve the Dilemma

### PLANNING FOR PIZZA

McKing Corporation operates fast-food restaurants in 50 states, selling hamburgers, roast beef and chicken sandwiches, french fries, and salads. The company wants to diversify into the growing pizza business. Six months of tests revealed that the ideal pizza to sell was a 16-inch pie in three varieties: cheese, pepperoni, and deluxe (multiple toppings). Research found the size and toppings acceptable to families as well as to individuals (single buyers could freeze the leftovers), and the price was acceptable for a fast-food restaurant ($7.99 for cheese, $8.49 for pepperoni, and $9.99 for deluxe).

Marketing and human resources personnel prepared training manuals for employees, advertising materials, and the rationale to present to the restaurant managers (many stores are franchised). Store managers, franchisees, and employees are excited about the new plan. There is just one problem: The drive-through windows in current restaurants are too small for a 16-inch pizza to pass through. The largest size the present windows can accommodate is a 12-inch pie. The managers and franchisees are concerned that if this aspect of operations has been overlooked perhaps the product is not ready to be launched. Maybe there are other problems yet to be uncovered.

#### Discussion Question

1. What mistake did McKing make in approaching the introduction of pizza?

2. How could this product introduction have been coordinated to avoid the problems that were encountered?

3. If you were an executive at McKing, how would you proceed with the introduction of pizza into the restaurants?

## Build Your Business Plan

### MANAGING SERVICE AND MANUFACTURING OPERATIONS

For your business you need to determine if you are providing raw materials that will be used in further production, or you are a reseller of goods and services, known as a retailer. If you are the former, you need to determine what processes you go through in making your product.

The text provides ideas of breaking the process into inputs, transformation processes and outputs. If you are a provider of a service or a link in the supply chain, you need to know exactly what your customer expectations are. Services are intangible so it is all the more important to better understand what exactly the customer is looking for in resolving a problem or filling a need.

# See for Yourself Videocase

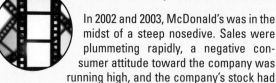

## McDONALD'S 24/7 TURNAROUND BASED ON SERVICE AND QUALITY

In 2002 and 2003, McDonald's was in the midst of a steep nosedive. Sales were plummeting rapidly, a negative consumer attitude toward the company was running high, and the company's stock had fallen to $12 to $13 per share. The McDonald's crisis was the company's own fault. During the previous 10 years, the corporation had gone expansion crazy—building 2,000 units each year. The insanity of such expansion hit existing stores hard and left customers in the dust. To make matters worse, the company was also being accused of heavily contributing to America's obesity epidemic.

At this time, former McDonald's vice chairman and president Jim Cantalupo returned with a vision to revive the company. His return, however, was treated with pessimism and skepticism, in part because his ideas for saving the company were hardly revolutionary. Critics viewed his ideas with a "been there, done that" attitude. But, Cantalupo's lack of innovation proved to be just what McDonald's needed.

Just as McDonald's was about to crash and burn, Cantalupo pushed gently on the throttle and, over time, McDonald's has begun to climb again. How did Cantalupo create what some deem one of the greatest corporate turnarounds of all time? He did it by going back to the basics: service, quality, and cleanliness. Cantalupo first pointed out that offering clean restrooms and food appearing fresh and warm would be a welcome change for consumers. While many might greet such a statement with, "duh," what Cantalupo was really saying was that McDonald's had forgotten to cater to the customer in even the simplest of ways. By taking small, basic steps to improve the dining experience, Cantalupo believed the company could return to favor.

Cantalupo also saw that it was necessary to alter the McDonald's menu, but, rather than coming up with fancy, new-fangled concepts, the company launched "Premium Salads." By doing this, McDonald's could claim that it was offering more nutritious, low-fat menu options. Since then, the chain has also launched more white meat chicken products and snack wraps.

In 2005, the McDonald's corporation began encouraging stores to remain open 24 hours a day, seven days a week in order to increase profits. By remaining open, stores could take advantage of two new sets of consumers, early birds and night owls. Being open continuously also eliminated the costs of opening and closing stores. As of 2007, about 40 percent of McDonald's stores were open 24/7. Thanks in part to this movement, breakfast now leads McDonald's sales.

Also in order to serve a wider variety of consumers, some McDonald's stores are receiving face lifts. For example, the Garner, North Carolina, store now sports what is known as the McCafé, an area of the store offering desserts and wraps. The McCafé is filled with music, flat-panel televisions, plants, cushy chairs, and more.

Thanks to numerous changes, none of them innovative and all of them simple, by 2008, McDonald's was soaring once again. According to *BusinessWeek,* McDonald's was serving 27 million people per day, and shares were trading near $60, an eight-year record. McDonald's proved that efficient operations that provide consumers what they want is the key to success.[49]

### Discussion Questions:

1. Why do you think McDonald's lost its customer focus in the early 2000s?

2. How did service, improved quality and cleanliness turn McDonald's profits and stock price in a positive direction?

3. Discuss some of the operational challenges of keeping so many restaurants open 24/7.

**Remember to check out our Online Learning Center at www.mhhe.com/ferrell7e.**

part

4

# Creating the Human Resource Advantage

CHAPTER 10    Motivating the Workforce

CHAPTER 11    Managing Human Resources

APPENDIX C    Personal Career Plan

# Motivating the Workforce

## CHAPTER OUTLINE

**Introduction**

**Nature of Human Relations**

**Historical Perspectives on Employee Motivation**
*Classical Theory of Motivation*
*The Hawthorne Studies*

**Theories of Employee Motivation**
*Maslow's Hierarchy of Needs*
*Herzberg's Two-Factor Theory*
*McGregor's Theory X and Theory Y*
*Theory Z*
*Variations on Theory Z*
*Equity Theory*
*Expectancy Theory*

**Strategies for Motivating Employees**
*Behavior Modification*
*Job Design*
*Importance of Motivational Strategies*

## OBJECTIVES

*After reading this chapter, you will be able to:*

- Define human relations, and determine why its study is important.

- Summarize early studies that laid the groundwork for understanding employee motivation.

- Compare and contrast the human-relations theories of Abraham Maslow and Frederick Herzberg.

- Investigate various theories of motivation, including theories X, Y, and Z; equity theory; and expectancy theory.

- Describe some of the strategies that managers use to motivate employees.

- Critique a business's program for motivating its sales force.

## Amadeus Consulting: Where Employees Are the Company

At a time when Americans are among those working the longest hours of individuals in any developed country, many employees are tired, stressed, and pining for jobs in which they receive even the smallest amount of respect and attention. Therefore, when a company actually goes above and beyond the rare pat on the back, we should stand up and take notice. Founded in 1994, Amadeus Consulting is one such company. The company develops custom software from its headquarters in Boulder, Colorado. Founders Lisa Calkins and John Basso intended, from the beginning, to create a company for which people would be motivated to work long term.

To retain employees, Calkins and Basso believe that it is important to acknowledge the fact that employees have lives outside their jobs and to encourage a balance between life and work. To achieve this mind-set, they strive to help their employees blend work, family, community involvement, and the meeting of customer needs. It helps that Calkins and Basso are not interested in building a business only to sell it to the highest bidder; rather, they are dedicated to creating lifelong customers and employees.

Amadeus's attention to employee well-being begins with the headquarters itself. The 11,000-square-foot building is completely free from cubicles and full of windows letting in tons of light. Employees may make use of a bistro-like lounge, a living room–like meeting place, and a library. Going beyond the setting is the way employees approach their jobs. Life at Amadeus includes team lunches, at which employees are likely to discuss personal as well as work-related topics. Like many companies, Amadeus takes its employees on

*continued*

retreats, but here families come along. Employees are also encouraged to champion causes, which Amadeus then supports.

Amadeus sounds like an ideal place to work, but does the performance match up? According to *Inc.* magazine it does. In 2007, the magazine placed Amadeus number 1,155 on its list of the 5,000 Fastest Growing Private Companies in America. Also in 2007, the company doubled its employee count and brought its revenue up to $2.6 million. Amadeus has been named a Microsoft Gold Certified Partner, and it has won awards such as the Microsoft XP Solution Challenge for Ascriptus. The company was also named 2004 Colorado Woman-Owned Business of the Year by Business & Professional Women. Amadeus is proof that it is possible to succeed in business without leaving life behind.[1]

# Introduction

Successful businesses like Amadeus teach some important lessons about how to interact with and motivate employees to do their best. Because employees do the actual work of the business and influence whether the firm achieves its objectives, most top managers agree that employees are an organization's most valuable resource. To achieve organizational objectives, employees must have the motivation, ability (appropriate knowledge and skills), and tools (proper training and equipment) to perform their jobs. These topics are the subject of Chapter 11; this chapter focuses on employee motivation.

We examine employees' needs and motivation, managers' views of workers, and several strategies for motivating employees. Managers who understand the needs of their employees can help them reach higher levels of productivity and thus contribute to the achievement of organizational goals.

# Nature of Human Relations

**human relations**
the study of the behavior of individuals and groups in organizational settings

What motivates employees to perform on the job is the focus of **human relations,** the study of the behavior of individuals and groups in organizational settings. In business, human relations involves motivating employees to achieve organizational objectives efficiently and effectively. The field of human relations has become increasingly important over the years as businesses strive to understand how to boost workplace morale, maximize employees' productivity and creativity, and motivate their ever more diverse employees to be more effective.

**motivation**
an inner drive that directs a person's behavior toward goals

**Motivation** is an inner drive that directs a person's behavior toward goals. A goal is the satisfaction of some need, and a need is the difference between a desired state and an actual state. Both needs and goals can be motivating. Motivation explains why people behave as they do; similarly, a lack of motivation explains, at times, why people avoid doing what they should do. A person who recognizes or feels a need is motivated to take action to satisfy the need and achieve a goal (Figure 10.1). Consider a person who feels cold. Because of the difference between the actual temperature and the desired temperature, the person recognizes a need. To satisfy the need

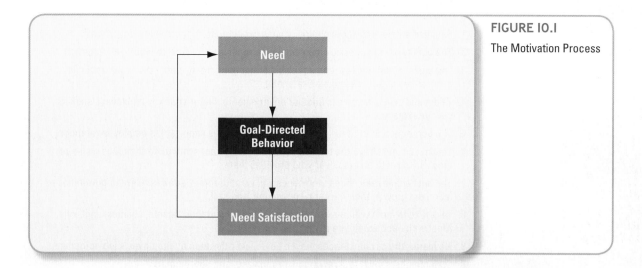

and achieve the goal of being warm, the person may adjust the thermostat, put on a sweater, reach for a blanket, start a fire, or hug a friend. Human relations is concerned with the needs of employees, their goals and how they try to achieve them, and the impact of those needs and goals on job performance.

One prominent aspect of human relations is **morale**—an employee's attitude toward his or her job, employer, and colleagues. High morale contributes to high levels of productivity, high returns to stakeholders, and employee loyalty. Conversely, low morale may cause high rates of absenteeism and turnover (when employees quit or are fired and must be replaced by new employees). Google recognizes the value of happy, committed employees and strives to engage in practices that will minimize turnover. Employees have the opportunity to have a massage every other week; onsite laundry service; free all-you-can-eat gourmet meals and snacks; and the "20% a week" rule, which allows engineers to work on whatever project they want for one day each week. However, Google has recently faced turnover of employees wanting to start their own businesses and going to other companies such as Facebook. Although morale is high, employees see opportunities and are solicited heavily by other firms.[2]

Employees are motivated by their perceptions of extrinsic and intrinsic rewards. An **intrinsic reward** is the personal satisfaction and enjoyment that you feel from attaining a goal. For example, in this class you may feel personal enjoyment in learning how business works and aspire to have a career in business or to operate your own business one day. **Extrinsic rewards** are benefits and/or recognition that you receive from someone else. In this class, your grade is extrinsic recognition of your efforts and success in the class. In business, praise and recognition, pay increases, and bonuses are extrinsic rewards. If you believe that your job provides an opportunity to contribute to society or the environment, then that aspect would represent an intrinsic reward. Both intrinsic and extrinsic rewards contribute to motivation that stimulates employees to do their best in contributing to business goals.

Respect, involvement, appreciation, adequate compensation, promotions, a pleasant work environment, and a positive organizational culture are all morale boosters. Nike seeks to provide a comprehensive compensation and benefits package, which includes traditional elements such as medical, dental, vision, life and disability insurance, paid holidays and time off as well as sabbaticals, and team

**morale**
an employee's attitude toward his or her job, employer, and colleagues

**intrinsic rewards**
the personal satisfaction and enjoyment feel after attaining a goal

**extrinsic rewards**
benefits and/or recognition received from someone else

**TABLE IO.I**

Top 10 Ways to Retain Great Employees

| | |
|---|---|
| 1. | Satisfied employees know clearly what is expected from them every day at work. |
| 2. | The quality of the supervision an employee receives is critical to employee retention. |
| 3. | The ability of the employee to speak his or her mind freely within the organization is another key factor in employee retention. |
| 4. | Talent and skill utilization is another environmental factor your key employees seek in your workplace. |
| 5. | The perception of fairness and equitable treatment is important in employee retention. |
| 6. | Employees must have the tools, time, and training necessary to do their jobs well—or they will move to an employer who provides them. |
| 7. | The best employees, those employees you want to retain, seek frequent opportunities to learn and grow in their careers, knowledge, and skill. |
| 8. | Take time to meet with new employees to learn about their talents, abilities, and skills. Meet with each employee periodically. |
| 9. | No matter the circumstances, never, never, ever threaten an employee's job or income. |
| 10. | Staff members must feel rewarded, recognized, and appreciated. |

Source: Susan M. Heathfield, "Top Ten Ways to Retain Your Great Employees," About.com, http://humanresources.about.com/od/retention/a/more_retention.htm (accessed May 15, 2008).

as well as individual compensation plans. More comprehensive benefits include employee discounts on Nike products, health care and family care reimbursement accounts, scholarships for children of employees, employee assistance plans, work/life balance resources and referrals, adoption assistance, tuition assistance, group legal plan, group long-term care plan, and matching gift programs. At the Beaverton, Oregon, world headquarters, employees may take advantage of onsite day care; onsite fitness centers, cafés and restaurants; a convenience store; an onsite hair and nail salon, annual TriMet transit pass ($20 annual fee versus $600); chances to test products under development; and an opportunity to become a headquarters tour guide.[4] Many companies offer a diverse array of benefits designed to improve the quality of employees' lives and increase their morale and satisfaction. As mentioned earlier, many companies offer reward programs to improve morale, lower turnover, and motivate employees. Some of the "best companies to work for" offer onsite day care,

**Did You Know?**    Absenteeism costs a typical large company more than $3 million a year[3]

**TABLE IO.2**

You Can Make Their Day: Tips for the Leader about Employee Motivation

| | |
|---|---|
| 1. | Use simple, powerful words. |
| 2. | Make sure people know what you expect. |
| 3. | Provide regular feedback. |
| 4. | People need positive and not so positive consequences. |
| 5. | It ain't magic. It's discipline. |
| 6. | Continue learning and trying out new ideas for employee motivation. |
| 7. | Make time for people. |
| 8. | Focus on the development of people. |
| 9. | Share the goals and the context: communicate. |

Source: Susan M. Heathfield, "You Can Make Their Day: Ten Tips for the Leader About Employee Motivation," About.com, http://humanresources.about.com/od/motivationsucces3/a/lead_motivation.htm (accessed May 15, 2008).

concierge services (e.g., dry cleaning, shoe repair, prescription renewal), domestic partner benefits to same-sex couples, and fully paid sabbaticals. Table 10.2 offers suggestions as to how leaders can motivate employees on a daily basis.

# Historical Perspectives on Employee Motivation

Throughout the 20th century, researchers have conducted numerous studies to try to identify ways to motivate workers and increase productivity. From these studies have come theories that have been applied to workers with varying degrees of success. A brief discussion of two of these theories—the classical theory of motivation and the Hawthorne studies—provides a background for understanding the present state of human relations.

## Classical Theory of Motivation

The birth of the study of human relations can be traced to time and motion studies conducted at the turn of the century by Frederick W. Taylor and Frank and Lillian Gilbreth. Their studies analyzed how workers perform specific work tasks in an effort to improve the employees' productivity. These efforts led to the application of scientific principles to management.

According to the **classical theory of motivation,** money is the sole motivator for workers. Taylor suggested that workers who were paid more would produce more, an idea that would benefit both companies and workers. To improve productivity, Taylor thought that managers should break down each job into its component tasks (specialization), determine the best way to perform each task, and specify the output to be achieved by a worker performing the task. Taylor also believed that incentives would motivate employees to be more productive. Thus, he suggested that managers link workers' pay directly to their output. He developed the piece-rate system, under which employees were paid a certain amount for each unit they produced; those who exceeded their quota were paid a higher rate per unit for all the units they produced.

We can still see Taylor's ideas in practice today in the use of mathematical models, statistics, and incentives. Moreover, companies are increasingly striving to relate pay to performance at both the hourly and managerial level. According to Marriott Hotels, roughly 40 percent of incentive planners choose an individual incentive to motivate and reward their employees. In contrast, team incentives are used to generate partnership and working together to accomplish organizational goals. The state of Washington offers teams 25 percent of the revenue generated (not to exceed $10,000) as the result of a continuous improvement or total quality process.[5]

More and more corporations are tying pay to performance in order to motivate—even up to the CEO level. The topic of executive pay has become controversial in recent years, and many corporate boards of directors have taken steps to link executive compensation more closely to corporate performance. CEO compensation, although increasing, is not rising at the level of previous years. Compensation rose 5 percent, which is down from 13 percent in the previous year. Larry Elllison, CEO of Oracle, topped the list with total compensation of $192.92 million and is considered by many to be a valuable CEO.[6]

Like most managers of the early 20th century, Taylor believed that satisfactory pay and job security would motivate employees to work hard. However, later studies showed that other factors are also important in motivating workers.

**classical theory of motivation** theory suggesting that money is the sole motivator for workers

# Going Green
## Motivating Employees by Being Green

Interface Inc., the largest modular tile carpet maker in the United States, was founded in 1973. At the time, it was simply another company. Today, thanks to its founder Ray Anderson, Interface is a leader in sustainable and environmentally sound practices. Anderson has been featured in two environmental documentaries and received numerous awards such as the Purpose Prize from Civic Ventures and the International Quality of Life award from Auburn University.

So, what makes this company so unique and so green? Simply put, it's the company's Mission Zero, involving all employees. While team efforts to reduce the company's environmental footprint to zero by 2020 is a target, they don't plan to stop there. Once they've achieved carbon neutrality, Interface employees plan to begin working toward restoring portions of the earth in need of care. In the move toward Mission Zero, Interface recycles old carpet to avoid filling up landfills; created Cool Carpet to offset emissions; uses 100 percent recycled carpet tile backing on its Cool Blue line; and is partially powering the Cool Blue line with landfill gas captured by a method invented, in part, by Interface. Interface has also reduced its greenhouse gas emissions by 60 percent in absolute tonnage and runs many of its operations on wind and solar power. And this is just the tip of the iceberg! Interface has achieved about 50 percent of Mission Zero.

Anderson and Interface's other executives know full well that they could not achieve their goals without their dedicated employees. In fact, Anderson recently stepped down as CEO in order to educate companies and individuals around the world about sustainability and environmentally sound practices. When the push toward Mission Zero began, Anderson asked his employees to work with him to achieve this goal. Initially, employees reacted to Mission Zero with skepticism, but today this goal gives Interface employees something to be passionate about at work—it makes their jobs meaningful, and some note that they feel great about giving their children and children around the world a better future. To motivate employees, Interface has invented the Fast Forward training program to establish every employee as a Mission Zero ambassador. Interface believes that by encouraging employees at work, they then become better spouses, parents, friends, and community members. Employees have also been encouraged to take their own steps toward helping the environment. For example, a night shift factory worker helped suggest what has become the Cool $Co_2$mmute program for offsetting employee commuting emissions.

There is no arguing that Mission Zero is an important step and that businesses and individuals would do well to take note of Ray Anderson and Interface and to follow this example.[7]

### Discussion Questions

1. How does Ray Anderson set an example as CEO to motivate employees toward green business practices?
2. How does being green motivate employees in their everyday jobs?
3. What does Interface do to involve employees in its decisions for running a green business?

### The Hawthorne Studies

Elton Mayo and a team of researchers from Harvard University wanted to determine what physical conditions in the workplace—such as light and noise levels—would stimulate employees to be most productive. From 1924 to 1932, they studied a group of workers at the Hawthorne Works Plant of the Western Electric Company and measured their productivity under various physical conditions.

What the researchers discovered was quite unexpected and very puzzling: Productivity increased regardless of the physical conditions. This phenomenon has been labeled the Hawthorne effect. When questioned about their behavior, the employees expressed satisfaction because their co-workers in the experiments were friendly and, more importantly, because their supervisors had asked for their help and cooperation in the study. In other words, they were responding to the attention they received, not the changing physical work conditions. The researchers concluded that social and psychological factors could significantly affect productivity and morale. Medtronic, often called the "Microsoft of the medical-device industry," has a built-in psychological factor that influences employee morale. The company makes life-saving medical devices, such as pacemakers, neurostimulators, and stents. New hires at Medtronic receive medallions inscribed with a portion of the firm's mission statement, "alleviate pain, restore health, and extend life." There is

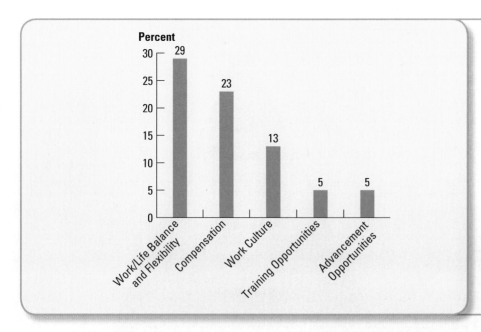

**FIGURE 10.2**

Work/Life Balance Is
More Important than Pay

*What is the primary reason
you accepted your current
position?*

Source: "Work-life Balance
Tops Pay," *USA Today
Snapshots,* March 13, 2008,
p. B1.

an annual party where people whose bodies function thanks to Medtronic devices give testimonials. Obviously, Medtronic employees feel a sense of satisfaction in their jobs. Figure 10.2 indicates that work/life balance is important to many employees.

The Hawthorne experiments marked the beginning of a concern for human relations in the workplace. They revealed that human factors do influence workers' behavior and that managers who understand the needs, beliefs, and expectations of people have the greatest success in motivating their workers.

# Theories of Employee Motivation

The research of Taylor, Mayo, and many others has led to the development of a number of theories that attempt to describe what motivates employees to perform. In this section, we will discuss some of the most important of these theories. The successful

The employees who participated in the Hawthorne studies responded to the attention they received during the study and thereby improved their performance, not the changing of the physical characteristics of their workplace. Do you think the workers in this photo improved their pace or level of quality as this photo was taken?

implementation of ideas based on these theories will vary, of course, depending on the company, its management, and its employees. It should be noted, too, that what worked in the past may no longer work today. Good managers must have the ability to adapt their ideas to an ever-changing, diverse group of employees.

## Maslow's Hierarchy of Needs

Psychologist Abraham Maslow theorized that people have five basic needs: physiological, security, social, esteem, and self-actualization. **Maslow's hierarchy** arranges these needs into the order in which people strive to satisfy them (Figure 10.3).[8]

**Maslow's hierarchy**
a theory that arranges the five basic needs of people—physiological, security, social, esteem, and self-actualization—into the order in which people strive to satisfy them

**FIGURE 10.3**

Maslow's Hierarchy
of Needs

Source: Adapted from Abraham
H. Maslow, "A Theory of Human
Motivation," *Psychology
Review* 50 (1943), pp. 370–396.
American Psychology
Association.

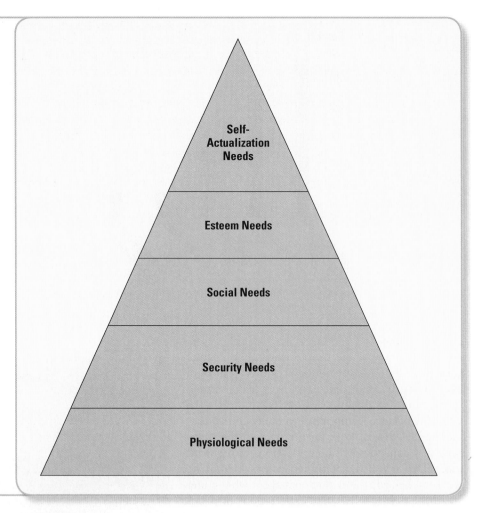

*New parents who work for
Colgate-Palmolive get three
additional weeks of paid
leave in addition to the leave
mandated by the Family
Leave Act. Employees can
also take advantage of onsite
banking, a travel agency, and
film processing at work.*

**physiological needs**
the most basic human
needs to be satisfied—
water, food, shelter, and
clothing

**security needs**
the need to protect
oneself from physical
and economic harm

**Physiological needs,** the most basic
and first needs to be satisfied, are the
essentials for living—water, food, shelter, and clothing. According to Maslow,
humans devote all their efforts to satisfying physiological needs until they are
met. Only when these needs are met can
people focus their attention on satisfying
the next level of needs—security.

**Security needs** relate to protecting yourself from physical and economic
harm. Actions that may be taken to
achieve security include reporting a dangerous workplace condition to management, maintaining safety equipment, and
purchasing insurance with income protection in the event you become unable to
work. Once security needs have been satisfied, people may strive for social goals.

**Social needs** are the need for love, companionship, and friendship—the desire for acceptance by others. To fulfill social needs, a person may try many things: making friends with a co-worker, joining a group, volunteering at a hospital, throwing a party. Once their social needs have been satisfied, people attempt to satisfy their need for esteem.

**Esteem needs** relate to respect—both self-respect and respect from others. One aspect of esteem needs is competition—the need to feel that you can do something better than anyone else. Competition often motivates people to increase their productivity. Esteem needs are not as easily satisfied as the needs at lower levels in Maslow's hierarchy because they do not always provide tangible evidence of success. However, these needs can be realized through rewards and increased involvement in organizational activities. Until esteem needs are met, people focus their attention on achieving respect. When they feel they have achieved some measure of respect, self-actualization becomes the major goal of life.

**Self-actualization needs,** at the top of Maslow's hierarchy, mean being the best you can be. Self-actualization involves maximizing your potential. A self-actualized person feels that she or he is living life to its fullest in every way. For Stephen King, self-actualization might mean being praised as the best fiction writer in the world; for actress Halle Berry, it might mean winning an Oscar.

Maslow's theory maintains that the more basic needs at the bottom of the hierarchy must be satisfied before higher-level goals can be pursued. Thus, people who are hungry and homeless are not concerned with obtaining respect from their colleagues. Only when physiological, security, and social needs have been more or less satisfied do people seek esteem. Maslow's theory also suggests that if a low-level need is suddenly reactivated, the individual will try to satisfy that need rather than higher-level needs. Many laid off workers probably shift their focus from high-level esteem needs to the need for security. Almost 10,000 employees in 32 countries in business, government, and nonprofit organizations were surveyed for the Global Employee Relationship Report. Fifty percent of the respondents said they believe their organization cares about developing people for the long term, not just for their current job. Just over half of the employees believed their employers show them genuine care and concern.[9] Managers should learn from Maslow's hierarchy that employees will be motivated to contribute to organizational goals only if they are able to first satisfy their physiological, security, and social needs through their work.

## Herzberg's Two-Factor Theory

In the 1950s psychologist Frederick Herzberg proposed a theory of motivation that focuses on the job and on the environment where work is done. Herzberg studied various factors relating to the job and their relation to employee motivation and concluded that they can be divided into hygiene factors and motivational factors (Table 10.3).

**Hygiene factors,** which relate to the work setting and not to the content of the work, include adequate wages, comfortable and safe working conditions, fair company policies, and job security. These factors do not necessarily motivate employees to excel, but their absence may be a potential source of dissatisfaction and high turnover. Employee safety and comfort are clearly hygiene factors.

Many people feel that a good salary is one of the most important job factors, even more important than job security and the chance to use one's mind and abilities. Salary and security, two of the hygiene factors identified by Herzberg, make it possible for employees to satisfy the physiological and security needs identified by

**social needs**
the need for love, companionship, and friendship—the desire for acceptance by others

**esteem needs**
the need for respect—both self-respect and respect from others

**self-actualization needs**
the need to be the best one can be; at the top of Maslow's hierarchy

**hygiene factors**
aspects of Herzberg's theory of motivation that focus on the work setting and not the content of the work; these aspects include adequate wages, comfortable and safe working conditions, fair company policies, and job security

| | TABLE I0.3 | Hygiene Factors | Motivational Factors |
|---|---|---|---|
| | Herzberg's Hygiene and Motivational Factors | Company policies | Achievement |
| | | Supervision | Recognition |
| | | Working conditions | Work itself |
| | | Relationships with peers, supervisors, and subordinates | Responsibility |
| | | Salary | Advancement |
| | | Security | Personal growth |

Maslow. However, the presence of hygiene factors is unlikely to motivate employees to work harder.

**motivational factors**
aspects of Herzberg's theory of motivation that focus on the content of the work itself; these aspects include achievement, recognition, involvement, responsibility, and advancement

**Motivational factors,** which relate to the content of the work itself, include achievement, recognition, involvement, responsibility, and advancement. The absence of motivational factors may not result in dissatisfaction, but their presence is likely to motivate employees to excel. Many companies are beginning to employ methods to give employees more responsibility and control and to involve them more in their work, which serves to motivate them to higher levels of productivity and quality. L.L. Bean employees have tremendous latitude to satisfy customer's needs. One employee drove 500 miles from Maine to New York to deliver a canoe to a customer who was leaving on a trip. L.L. Bean was number two on *BusinessWeek's* list of "Customer Service Champs" behind USAA Insurance. Besides empowering employees, the company has strict service training, answering every call within 20 seconds.[10] Disney has a similar commitment to empowering employees and making customers happy.[11]

Herzberg's motivational factors and Maslow's esteem and self-actualization needs are similar. Workers' low-level needs (physiological and security) have largely been satisfied by minimum-wage laws and occupational-safety standards set by various government agencies and are therefore not motivators. Consequently, to improve productivity, management should focus on satisfying workers' higher-level needs (motivational factors) by providing opportunities for achievement, involvement, and advancement and by recognizing good performance.

## McGregor's Theory X and Theory Y

In *The Human Side of Enterprise,* Douglas McGregor related Maslow's ideas about personal needs to management. McGregor contrasted two views of management— the traditional view, which he called Theory X, and a humanistic view, which he called Theory Y.

**Theory X**
McGregor's traditional view of management whereby it is assumed that workers generally dislike work and must be forced to do their jobs

According to McGregor, managers adopting **Theory X** assume that workers generally dislike work and must be forced to do their jobs. They believe that the following statements are true of workers:

1. The average person naturally dislikes work and will avoid it when possible.
2. Most workers must be coerced, controlled, directed, or threatened with punishment to get them to work toward the achievement of organizational objectives.
3. The average worker prefers to be directed and to avoid responsibility, has relatively little ambition, and wants security.[12]

Managers who subscribe to the Theory X view maintain tight control over workers, provide almost constant supervision, try to motivate through fear, and make decisions in an autocratic fashion, eliciting little or no input from their subordinates. The Theory X style of management focuses on physiological and security needs and virtually ignores the higher needs discussed by Maslow.

The Theory X view of management does not take into account people's needs for companionship, esteem, and personal growth, whereas Theory Y, the contrasting view of management, does. Managers subscribing to the **Theory Y** view assume that workers like to work and that under proper conditions employees will seek out responsibility in an attempt to satisfy their social, esteem, and self-actualization needs. McGregor describes the assumptions behind Theory Y in the following way:

1. The expenditure of physical and mental effort in work is as natural as play or rest.
2. People will exercise self-direction and self-control to achieve objectives to which they are committed.
3. People will commit to objectives when they realize that the achievement of those goals will bring them personal reward.
4. The average person will accept and seek responsibility.
5. Imagination, ingenuity, and creativity can help solve organizational problems, but most organizations do not make adequate use of these characteristics in their employees.
6. Organizations today do not make full use of workers' intellectual potential.[14]

Obviously, managers subscribing to the Theory Y philosophy have a management style very different from managers subscribing to the Theory X philosophy.

**Theory Y**
McGregor's humanistic view of management whereby it is assumed that workers like to work and that under proper conditions employees will seek out responsibility in an attempt to satisfy their social, esteem, and self-actualization needs

Theory Y managers maintain less control and supervision, do not use fear as the primary motivator, and are more democratic in decision making, allowing subordinates to participate in the process. Theory Y managers address the high-level needs in Maslow's hierarchy as well as physiological and security needs. Today, Theory Y enjoys widespread support and may have displaced Theory X.

## Theory Z

**Theory Z** is a management philosophy that stresses employee participation in all aspects of company decision making. It was first described by William Ouchi in his book *Theory Z—How American Business Can Meet the Japanese Challenge.* Theory Z incorporates many elements associated with the Japanese approach to management, such as trust and intimacy, but Japanese ideas have been adapted for use in the United States. In a Theory Z organization, managers and workers share responsibilities; the management style is participative; and employment is long term and often lifelong. Theory Z results in employees feeling organizational ownership. Research has found that such feelings of ownership may produce positive attitudinal and behavioral effects for employees.[15] In a Theory Y organization, managers focus on assumptions about the nature of the worker. The two theories can be seen as complementary. Table 10.4 compares the traditional American management style, the Japanese management style, and Theory Z (the modified Japanese management style).

**Theory Z**
a management philosophy that stresses employee participation in all aspects of company decision making

## Variations on Theory Z

Theory Z has been adapted and modified for use in a number of U.S. companies. One adaptation involves workers in decisions through quality circles. Quality circles (also called quality-assurance teams) are small, usually having five to eight members who discuss ways to reduce waste, eliminate problems, and improve quality, communication, and work satisfaction. Such quality teams are a common technique for harnessing the knowledge and creativity of hourly employees to solve problems in companies.

**TABLE 10.4**   Comparison of American, Japanese, and Theory Z Management Styles

|  | American | Japanese | Theory Z |
|---|---|---|---|
| **Duration of employment** | Relatively short term; workers subject to layoffs when business slows | Lifelong; no layoffs | Long term; layoffs rare |
| **Rate of promotion** | Rapid | Slow | Slow |
| **Amount of specialization** | Considerable; worker develops expertise in one area only | Minimal; worker develops expertise in all aspects of the organization | Moderate; worker learns all aspects of the organization |
| **Decision making** | Individual | Consensual; input from all concerned parties is considered | Consensual; emphasis on quality |
| **Responsibility** | Assigned to the individual | Shared by the group | Assigned to the individual |
| **Control** | Explicit and formal | Less explicit and less formal | Informal but with explicit performance measures |
| **Concern for workers** | Focus is on work only | Focus extends to worker's whole life | Focus includes worker's life and family |

Source: Adapted from William Ouchi, *Theory Z—How American Business Can Meet the Japanese Challenge*, p. 58. © 1981 by Addison-Wesley Publishing Company, Inc. Reprinted by permission of Perseus Books Publishers, a member of Perseus Books, L.L.C.

Even more involved than quality circles are programs that operate under names such as *participative management, employee involvement,* or *self-directed work teams.* Regardless of the term used to describe such programs, they strive to give employees more control over their jobs while making them more responsible for the outcome of their efforts. Such programs often organize employees into work teams of 5 to 15 members who are responsible for producing an entire product item. Team members are cross-trained and can therefore move from job to job within the team. Each team essentially manages itself and is responsible for its quality, scheduling, ordering and use of materials, and problem solving. Many firms have successfully employed work teams to boost morale, productivity, quality, and competitiveness.

## Equity Theory

According to **equity theory,** how much people are willing to contribute to an organization depends on their assessment of the fairness, or equity, of the rewards they will receive in exchange. In a fair situation, a person receives rewards proportional to the contribution he or she makes to the organization. However, in practice, equity is a subjective notion. Each worker regularly develops a personal input-output ratio by taking stock of his or her contribution (inputs) to the organization in time, effort, skills, and experience and assessing the rewards (outputs) offered by the organization in pay, benefits, recognition, and promotions. The worker compares his or her ratio to the input-output ratio of some other person—a "comparison other," who may be a co-worker, a friend working in another organization, or an "average"of several people working in the organization. If the two ratios are close, the individual will feel that he or she is being treated equitably.

> **equity theory**
> an assumption that how much people are willing to contribute to an organization depends on their assessment of the fairness, or equity, of the rewards they will receive in exchange

Let's say you have a high-school education and earn $25,000 a year. When you compare your input-output ratio with that of a co-worker who has a college degree and makes $35,000 a year, you will probably feel that you are being paid fairly. However, if you perceive that your personal input-output ratio is lower than that of your college-educated co-worker, you may feel that you are being treated unfairly and be motivated to seek change. But, if you learn that co-worker who makes $35,000 has only a high-school diploma, you may feel cheated by your employer. To achieve equity, you could try to increase your outputs by asking for a raise or promotion. You could also try to have your co-worker's inputs increased or his or her outputs decreased. Failing to achieve equity, you may be motivated to look for a job at a different company.

Because almost all the issues involved in equity theory are subjective, they can be problematic. Author David Callahan has argued that feelings of inequity may underlie some unethical or illegal behavior in business. Due to employee theft and shoplifting, Wal-Mart is experiencing increased inventory losses to nearly $3 billion on sales of more than $348 billion. The growth is possibly tied to the company's decision to not prosecute minor cases of shoplifting. Declines in economic condition may also contribute to this growth.[16] Callahan believes that employees who do not feel they are being treated equitably may be motivated to equalize the situation by lying, cheating, or otherwise "improving" their pay, perhaps by stealing.[17] Managers should try to avoid equity problems by ensuring that rewards are distributed on the basis of performance and that all employees clearly understand the basis for their pay and benefits.

# Destination CEO
## Corporate Health

U.S. corporations are confronting a crisis of epic proportions. Health care and insurance costs are exorbitant. Companies have come to realize and embrace the fact that investment in proactive programs designed to promote health and healthy lifestyles is an important business decision. In fact, an investment of $1 in proactive healthy choice programs such as exercise clinics, nutritional education, or even onsite health care clinics, saves an average of $2 to $3 on lost productivity.

Pitney Bowes is a leader among businesses in programs designed to promote and develop healthy lifestyles among their employees. In their corporate facilities, there is a fully staffed health care clinic, an exercise facility, and a cafeteria that emphasizes nutritionally healthy food choices including fresh fruits and vegetables. In addition, there are numerous educational programs designed to promote healthy lifestyles.

According to Pitney Bowes and to its employees, healthy employees are happier and more productive than those who are not focused on promoting healthy lifestyles. For the corporation, promoting health is a sound business decision that positively affects the bottom line, and that is great for shareholders.

These types of programs must be driven from the top down, and this is true at Pitney Bowes. The CEO walks the talk, literally. He wears a pedometer on his waist throughout the working day to ensure that he is walking a sufficient amount. If he finds that he is not meeting his goals, he will have those in his meetings walk around with him and hold the meeting in that fashion. The key to successfully promoting this proactive approach is education. More companies will be willing to make an investment in improving the health of their employees given the outstanding financial results from the Pitney Bowes experience.

**Discussion Questions**
1. What is the primary motivation of companies such as Pitney Bowes in investing in health care programs?
2. Which theory of motivation would Pitney Bowes's emphasis on health care programs be most aligned with?
3. Would a health care onsite facility be a motivator or hygiene factor according to Herzberg's theory of motivation?

---

## FIGURE 10.4

Workers' Worth

*Percentage of employers attributing certain traits to workers by career stage*

Source: "Workers' Worth," *USA Today Snapshots,* April 21, 2008, p. A1.

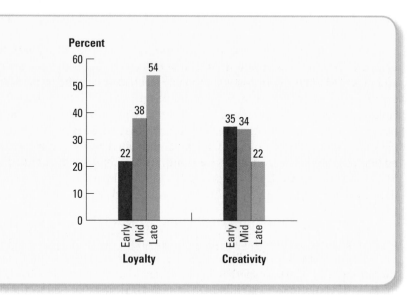

**expectancy theory**
the assumption that motivation depends not only on how much a person wants something but also on how likely he or she is to get it

## Expectancy Theory

Psychologist Victor Vroom described **expectancy theory,** which states that motivation depends not only on how much a person wants something but also on the person's perception of how likely he or she is to get it. A person who wants something and has reason to be optimistic will be strongly motivated. For example, say you really want a promotion. And, let's say because you have taken some night classes to improve your skills, and moreover, have just made a large, significant sale, you feel confident that you are qualified and able to handle the new position. Therefore, you are motivated to try to get the promotion. In contrast, if you do not believe you are likely to get what you want, you may not be motivated to try to get it, even though you really want it.

# Strategies for Motivating Employees

Based on the various theories that attempt to explain what motivates employees, businesses have developed several strategies for motivating their employees and boosting morale and productivity. Some of these techniques include behavior modification and job design, as well as the already described employee involvement programs and work teams.

## Behavior Modification

**Behavior modification** involves changing behavior and encouraging appropriate actions by relating the consequences of behavior to the behavior itself. The concept of behavior modification was developed by psychologist B. F. Skinner, who showed that there are two types of consequences that can modify behavior—reward and punishment. Skinner found that behavior that is rewarded will tend to be repeated, while behavior that is punished will tend to be eliminated. For example, employees who know that they will receive a bonus such as an expensive restaurant meal for making a sale over $2,000 may be more motivated to make sales. Workers who know they will be punished for being tardy are likely to make a greater effort to get to work on time.

> **behavior modification** changing behavior and encouraging appropriate actions by relating the consequences of behavior to the behavior itself

However, the two strategies may not be equally effective. Punishing unacceptable behavior may provide quick results but may lead to undesirable long-term side effects, such as employee dissatisfaction and increased turnover. In general, rewarding appropriate behavior is a more effective way to modify behavior.

## Job Design

Herzberg identified the job itself as a motivational factor. Managers have several strategies that they can use to design jobs to help improve employee motivation. These include job rotation, job enlargement, job enrichment, and flexible scheduling strategies.

### Job Rotation.   **Job rotation** allows employees to move from one job to another in an effort to relieve the boredom that is often associated with job specialization. Businesses often turn to specialization in hopes of increasing productivity, but there is a negative side effect to this type of job design: Employees become bored and dissatisfied, and productivity declines. Job rotation reduces this boredom by allowing workers to undertake a greater variety of tasks and by giving them the opportunity to learn new skills. With job rotation, an employee spends a specified amount of time performing one job and then moves on to another, different job. The worker eventually returns to the initial job and begins the cycle again.

> **job rotation** movement of employees from one job to another in an effort to relieve the boredom often associated with job specialization

Job rotation is a good idea, but it has one major drawback. Because employees may eventually become bored with all the jobs in the cycle, job rotation does not totally eliminate the problem of boredom. Job rotation is extremely useful, however,

*Nucor Corporation's 11,000-plus nonunion employees in Charlotte, North Carolina, don't see themselves as ordinary workers. There are no special benefits or compensation plans for executives, and the company's flat organizational structure encourages employees to adopt the mind-set of owner-operators.*

in situations where a person is being trained for a position that requires an understanding of various units in an organization. Eli Lilly is a strong believer in the benefits of job rotation. The company leaves employees in their current jobs and asks them to take on additional assignments outside their field of expertise or interest. The results of the process have been positive, and Nokia is trying the same process with similar outcomes.[18] Many executive training programs require trainees to spend time learning a variety of specialized jobs. Job rotation is also used to cross-train today's self-directed work teams.

**Job Enlargement.**   **Job enlargement** adds more tasks to a job instead of treating each task as separate. Like job rotation, job enlargement was developed to overcome the boredom associated with specialization. The rationale behind this strategy is that jobs are more satisfying as the number of tasks performed by an individual increases. Employees sometimes enlarge, or craft, their jobs by noticing what needs to be done and then changing tasks and relationship boundaries to adjust. Individual orientation and motivation shape opportunities to craft new jobs and job relationships. Job enlargement strategies have been more successful in increasing job satisfaction than have job rotation strategies. IBM, AT&T, and Maytag are among the many companies that have used job enlargement to motivate employees.

**Job Enrichment.**   **Job enrichment** incorporates motivational factors such as opportunity for achievement, recognition, responsibility, and advancement into a job. It gives workers not only more tasks within the job, but more control and authority over the job. Job enrichment programs enhance a worker's feeling of responsibility and provide opportunities for growth and advancement when the worker is able to take on the more challenging tasks. Hyatt Hotels Corporation and General Foods use job enrichment to improve the quality of work life for their employees. The potential benefits of job enrichment are great, but it requires careful planning and execution.

**Flexible Scheduling Strategies.**   Many U.S. workers work a traditional 40-hour workweek consisting of five 8-hour days with fixed starting and ending times. Facing problems of poor morale and high absenteeism as well as a diverse workforce with changing needs, many managers have turned to flexible scheduling strategies such as flextime, compressed workweeks, job sharing, part-time work, and telecommuting. A survey by CareerBuilder.com showed that 40 percent of working fathers were offered flexible work schedules versus 53 percent of working mothers.[19]

**job enlargement** the addition of more tasks to a job instead of treating each task as separate

**job enrichment** the incorporation of motivational factors, such as opportunity for achievement, recognition, responsibility, and advancement, into a job

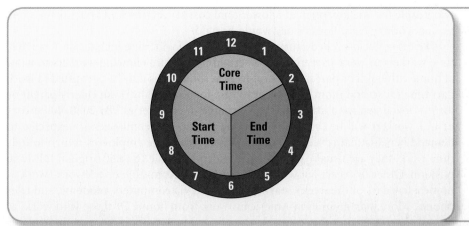

**FIGURE I0.5**

Flextime, Showing Core and Flexible Hours

**Flextime** is a program that allows employees to choose their starting and ending times, as long as they are at work during a specified core period (Figure 10.5). It does not reduce the total number of hours that employees work; instead, it gives employees more flexibility in choosing which hours they work. A firm may specify that employees must be present from 10:00 a.m. to 3:00 p.m. One employee may choose to come in at 7:00 a.m. and leave at the end of the core time, perhaps to attend classes at a nearby college after work. Another employee, a mother who lives in the suburbs, may come in at 9:00 a.m. in order to have time to drop off her children at a day-care center and commute by public transportation to her job. Flextime provides many benefits, including improved ability to recruit and retain workers who wish to balance work and home life. Customers can be better served by allowing more coverage of customers over longer hours, workstations and facilities can be better utilized by staggering employee use, and rush hour traffic may be reduced. In addition, flexible schedules have been associated with an increase in healthy behaviors on the part of employees. More flexible schedules are associated with healthier lifestyle choices such as increased physical activity and healthier sleep habits.[20]

Related to flextime are the scheduling strategies of the compressed workweek and job sharing. The **compressed workweek** is a four-day (or shorter) period in which an employee works 40 hours. Under such a plan, employees typically work 10 hours per day for four days and have a three-day weekend. The compressed workweek reduces the company's operating expenses because its actual hours of operation are reduced. It is also sometimes used by parents who want to have more days off to spend with their families. The U.S. Bureau of Labor Statistics notes that the following career options provide greater flexibility in scheduling: medical transcriptionist, financial manager, nurse, database administrator, accountant, software developer, physical therapist assistant, paralegal, graphic designer, and private investigator.[21]

**Job sharing** occurs when two people do one job. One person may work from 8:00 a.m. to 12:30 p.m.; the second person comes in at 12:30 p.m. and works until 5:00 p.m. Job sharing gives both people the opportunity to work as well as time to fulfill other obligations, such as parenting or school. Thirty percent of companies allow job sharing.[22] With job sharing, the company has the benefit of the skills of

**flextime**
a program that allows employees to choose their starting and ending times, provided that they are at work during a specified core period

**compressed workweek**
a four-day (or shorter) period during which an employee works 40 hours

**job sharing**
performance of one full-time job by two people on part-time hours

two people for one job, often at a lower total cost for salaries and benefits than one person working eight hours a day would be paid.

Two other flexible scheduling strategies attaining wider use include allowing full-time workers to work part time for a certain period and allowing workers to work at home either full or part time. Employees at some firms may be permitted to work part time for several months in order to care for a new baby or an elderly parent or just to slow down for a little while to "recharge their batteries." By 2020, 40 percent of U.S. workers will be caring for an aging parent, and employees are expected to demand benefits that reflect this major shift.[23] When the employees return to full-time work, they are usually given a position comparable to their original full-time position. Other firms are allowing employees to telecommute or telework (work at home a few days of the week), staying connected via computers, modems, and telephones. More than 45 million Americans work from home. Of those who work "at home," the average number of places these individuals work is 3.4, and these places can include home, car, and restaurant or coffee shop.[24] Table 10.6 shows the companies in the *Fortune* 100 Best Companies to Work For with the highest percentage of telecommuters. Although many employees ask for the option of working at home to ease the responsibilities of caring for family members, some have discovered that they are more productive at home without the distractions of the workplace. An assessment of 12 company telecommuting programs, including Apple, AT&T, and the state of California, found that positive productivity changes occurred. Traveler's Insurance Company reports its telecommuters to be 20 percent more productive than its traditional employees.[25] Other employees, however, have discovered that they are not suited for working at home. Human resource management executives are split as to whether telecommuting helps or hurts employees' careers. Thirty percent feel telecommuting helps their careers, 25 percent feel that it hurts, while 39 percent feel it does neither.[26] Still, work-at-home programs do help reduce overhead costs for businesses. For example, some companies used to maintain a surplus of office space but have reduced the surplus through employee telecommuting, "hoteling" (being assigned to a desk through a reservation system), and "hot-desking" (several people using the same desk but at different times).

Companies are turning to flexible work schedules to provide more options to employees who are trying to juggle their work duties with other responsibilities and

**TABLE 10.6**

Best Companies to Work For

Companies with Most Opportunities for Telecommuters in the *Fortune* "100 Best Companies to Work For"

| Company | Best Companies Rank |
|---|---|
| Cisco Systems | 6 |
| eBay | 69 |
| Booz Allen Hamilton | 81 |
| S.C. Johnson & Son | 27 |
| American Fidelity Assurance | 24 |
| Shared Technologies | 25 |
| Principal Financial Group | 21 |
| Goldman Sachs | 9 |
| Yahoo | 87 |
| Qualcomm | 8 |

Source: http://money.cnn.com/magazines/fortune/bestcompanies/2008/benefits/telecommuting.html, (accessed June 2, 2008).

# Entrepreneurship in Action
## Matching Workers with Employers

Eli Portnoy

**Business:** HireWorkers.com

**Founded:** 2005

**Success:** Eli Portnoy founded HireWorkers.com in 2005 with $20,000 startup money. The company has done almost $2 million in sales.

A large number of low-wage jobs in the United States are filled by Latin American immigrants. Both finding and filling these jobs can be difficult. Jobseekers looking for low-wage jobs such as janitor, housekeeper, dishwasher, and so on often lack access to the Internet. As a result, those looking to hire these workers have three options: posting a "help wanted" sign, advertising in print classifieds, or hiring a staffing agency. The last two commonly used options can be expensive for employers. As a Mexican immigrant himself, Portnoy understood the problems immigrant jobseekers face and saw an opportunity to fill a void and help both low-wage

jobseekers and their employers. Portnoy designed HireWorkers.com. Jobseekers are able to fill out HireWorkers.com postcards with their job experience and background information. Portnoy's company distributes these postcards to a large number of retail locations (a form is also available online for those who do have Internet access). The HireWorkers.com service is free for jobseekers. Employers may use HireWorkers.com to post jobs and to search the company's database. Fees begin at $69 to post a job for a month and go up to $99 to search the database. Once jobseekers and employers have entered information with HireWorkers.com, the company's system goes to work. Via patent-pending technology, the company is able to match employers' requests with appropriate jobseekers in as little as two hours. Once matches have been made, the system automatically sends phone calls to the jobseekers. Portnoy says there are currently around 1 million low-wage jobs available per month in the United States. HireWorkers.com makes filling and finding these jobs easier.[27]

---

needs. Preliminary results indicate that flexible scheduling plans increase job satisfaction, which, in turn, leads to increases in productivity. Some recent research, however, has indicated there are potential problems with telecommuting. Some managers are reluctant to adopt the practice because the pace of change in today's workplace is faster than ever, and telecommuters may be left behind or actually cause managers more work in helping them stay abreast of changes. Some employers also worry that telecommuting workers create a security risk by creating more opportunities for computer hackers or equipment thieves. Some employees have found that working outside the office may hurt career advancement opportunities, and some report that instead of helping them balance work and family responsibilities, telecommuting increases the strain by

After implementing its Initiative for the Retention and Advancement of Women, the accounting firm Deloitte can now boast that it has the highest percentage of women partners among America's Big Four public accounting firms. The program has been successful because many of the initiatives are aimed at both women and men. For example, Deloitte is now testing a "mass career customization" program that allows employees to increase or decrease their work responsibilities as their personal needs change over the course of their careers.

blurring the barriers between the office and home. Co-workers call at all hours, and telecommuters are apt to continue to work when they are not supposed to (after regular business hours or during vacation time).[28]

## Importance of Motivational Strategies

Motivation is more than a tool that managers can use to foster employee loyalty and boost productivity. It is a process that affects all the relationships within an organization and influences many areas such as pay, promotion, job design, training opportunities, and reporting relationships. Employees are motivated by the nature of the relationships they have with their supervisors, by the nature of their jobs, and by characteristics of the organization. Even the economic environment can change an employee's motivation. In a slow growth or recession economy, sales can flatten or decrease and morale can drop because of the need to cut jobs. The firm may have to work harder to keep good employees and to motivate all employees to work to overcome obstacles.[29] New rewards or incentives may help motivate workers in such economies. Motivation tools, then, must be varied as well. Managers can further nurture motivation by being honest, supportive, empathetic, accessible, fair, and open. Motivating employees to increase satisfaction and productivity is an important concern for organizations seeking to remain competitive in the global marketplace.

# So You Think You May Be Good at Motivating a Workforce

If you are good at mediation, smoothing conflict, and have a good understanding of motivation and human relations theories, then you might be a good leader, human resource manager, or training expert. Most organizations, especially as they grow, will need to implement human relations programs. These are necessary to teach employees about sensitivity to other cultures, religions, and beliefs, as well as for teaching the workforce about the organization so that they understand how they fit in the larger picture. Employees need to appreciate the benefits of working together to make the firm run smoothly, and they also need to understand how their contributions help the firm. To stay motivated, most employees need to feel like what they do each day contributes something of value to the firm. Disclosing information and including employees in decision-making processes will also help employees feel valuable and wanted within the firm.

There are many different ways employers can reward and encourage employees. However, employers must be careful when considering what kinds of incentives to use. Different cultures value different kinds of incentives more highly than others. For example, a Japanese worker would probably not like it if she were singled out from the group and given a large cash bonus as reward for her work. Japanese workers tend to be more group oriented, and therefore anything that singles out individuals would not be an effective way of rewarding and motivating. American workers, on the other hand, are very individualistic, and a raise and public praise might be more effective. However, what might motivate a younger employee (bonuses, raises, and perks) may not be the same as what motivates a more seasoned, experienced, and financially successful employee (recognition, opportunity for greater influence, and increased training). Motivation is not an easy thing to understand, especially as firms become more global and more diverse.

Another important part of motivation is enjoying where you work and your career opportunities. Here is a list of the best places to do business and start careers in the United States, according to *Forbes* magazine. Chances are, workers who live in these places have encountered fewer frustrations than those places at the bottom of the list and, therefore, would probably be more content with where they work.[30]

**Best Places for Business and Careers**

| Rank | Metro Area | Job Growth Rank | Metro Area Population (in thousands) |
|------|------------|-----------------|--------------------------------------|
| 1. | Raleigh, NC | 21 | 1,034 |
| 2. | Boise, ID | 13 | 585 |
| 3. | Fort Collins, CO | 80 | 281 |
| 4. | Des Moines, IA | 60 | 543 |
| 5. | Lexington, KY | 110 | 443 |
| 6. | Atlanta, GA | 69 | 5,266 |
| 7. | Richmond, VA | 75 | 1,211 |
| 8. | Olympia, WA | 22 | 240 |
| 9. | Spokane, WA | 36 | 452 |
| 10. | Knoxville, TN | 84 | 673 |

# Review Your Understanding

### Define human relations, and determine why its study is important.

Human relations is the study of the behavior of individuals and groups in organizational settings. Its focus is what motivates employees to perform on the job. Human relations is important because businesses need to understand how to motivate their increasingly diverse employees to be more effective, boost workplace morale, and maximize employees' productivity and creativity.

### Summarize early studies that laid the groundwork for understanding employee motivation.

Time and motion studies by Frederick Taylor and others helped them analyze how employees perform specific work tasks in an effort to improve their productivity. Taylor and the early practitioners of the classical theory of motivation felt that money and job security were the primary motivators of employees. However, the Hawthorne studies revealed that human factors also influence workers' behavior.

### Compare and contrast the human-relations theories of Abraham Maslow and Frederick Herzberg.

Abraham Maslow defined five basic needs of all people and arranged them in the order in which they must be satisfied: physiological, security, social, esteem, and self-actualization. Frederick Herzberg divided characteristics of the job into hygiene factors and motivational factors. Hygiene factors relate to the work environment and must be present for employees to remain in a job. Motivational factors—recognition, responsibility, and advancement—relate to the work itself. They encourage employees to be productive. Herzberg's hygiene factors can be compared to Maslow's physiological and security needs; motivational factors may include Maslow's social, esteem, and self-actualization needs.

### Investigate various theories of motivation, including Theories X, Y, and Z; equity theory; and expectancy theory.

Douglas McGregor contrasted two views of management: Theory X (traditional) suggests workers dislike work, while theory Y (humanistic) suggests that workers not only like

work but seek out responsibility to satisfy their higher-order needs. Theory Z stresses employee participation in all aspects of company decision making, often through participative management programs and self-directed work teams. According to equity theory, how much people are willing to contribute to an organization depends on their assessment of the fairness, or equity, of the rewards they will receive in exchange. Expectancy theory states that motivation depends not only on how much a person wants something but also on the person's perception of how likely he or she is to get it.

### Describe some of the strategies that managers use to motivate employees.

Strategies for motivating workers include behavior modification (changing behavior and encouraging appropriate actions by relating the consequences of behavior to the behavior itself) and job design. Among the job design strategies businesses use are job rotation (allowing employees to move from one job to another to try to relieve the boredom associated with job specialization), job enlargement (adding tasks to a job instead of treating each task as a separate job), job enrichment (incorporating motivational factors into a job situation), and flexible scheduling strategies (flextime, compressed work weeks, job sharing, part-time work, and telecommuting).

### Critique a business's program for motivating its sales force.

Using the information presented in the chapter, you should be able to analyze and defend Eagle Pharmaceutical's motivation program in "Solve the Dilemma" on page 317 including the motivation theories the firm is applying to boost morale and productivity.

# Revisit the World of Business

1. In what ways do founders Lisa Calkins and John Basso motivate employees for the long term?
2. How does Amadeus's office building help motivate employees?
3. What could other companies learn from Amadeus's performance in relation to its treatment of employees?

# Learn the Terms

behavior modification   309

classical theory of motivation   299

compressed workweek   311

equity theory   307

esteem needs   303

expectancy theory   308

extrinsic rewards   297

flextime   311

human relations   296

hygiene factors   303

intrinsic rewards   297

job enlargement   310

job enrichment   310

job rotation   309

job sharing   311

Maslow's hierarchy   301

morale   297

motivation   296

motivational factors   304

physiological needs   302

security needs   302

self-actualization needs   303

social needs   303

Theory X   304

Theory Y   305

Theory Z   306

# Check Your Progress

1. Why do managers need to understand the needs of their employees?

2. Describe the motivation process.

3. What was the goal of the Hawthorne studies? What was the outcome of those studies?

4. Explain Maslow's hierarchy of needs. What does it tell us about employee motivation?

5. What are Herzberg's hygiene and motivational factors? How can managers use them to motivate workers?

6. Contrast the assumptions of Theory X and Theory Y. Why has Theory Y replaced Theory X in management today?

7. What is Theory Z? How can businesses apply Theory Z to the workplace?

8. Identify and describe four job-design strategies.

9. Name and describe some flexible scheduling strategies. How can flexible schedules help motivate workers?

10. Why are motivational strategies important to both employees and employers?

# Get Involved

1. Consider a person who is homeless: How would he or she be motivated and what actions would that person take? Use the motivation process to explain. Which of the needs in Maslow's hierarchy are likely to be most important? Least important?

2. View the video *Cheaper by the Dozen* (1950) and report on how the Gilbreths tried to incorporate their passion for efficiency into their family life.

3. What events and trends in society, technology, and economics do you think will shape human relations management theory in the future?

# Build Your Skills

**MOTIVATING**

**Background:**
Do you think that, if employers could make work more like play, employees would be as enthusiastic about their jobs as they are about what they do in their leisure time? Let's see where this idea might take us.

**Task:**
After reading the "Characteristics of PLAY," place a √ in column one for those characteristics you have experienced in your leisure time activities. Likewise, check column three for those "Characteristics of WORK" you have experienced in any of the jobs you've held.

| All That Apply | Characteristics of PLAY | All That Apply | Characteristics of WORK |
|---|---|---|---|
| | 1. New games can be played on different days. | | 1. Job enrichment, job enlargement, or job rotation. |
| | 2. Flexible duration of play. | | 2. Job sharing. |
| | 3. Flexible time of when to play. | | 3. Flextime, telecommuting. |
| | 4. Opportunity to express oneself. | | 4. Encourage and implement employee suggestions. |
| | 5. Opportunity to use one's talents. | | 5. Assignment of challenging projects. |
| | 6. Skillful play brings applause, praise, and recognition from spectators. | | 6. Employee-of-the-month awards, press releases, employee newsletter announcements. |
| | 7. Healthy competition, rivalry, and challenge exist. | | 7. Production goals with competition to see which team does best. |
| | 8. Opportunity for social interaction. | | 8. Employee softball or bowling teams. |
| | 9. Mechanisms for scoring one's performance are available (feedback). | | 9. Profit sharing; peer performance appraisals. |
| | 10. Rules ensure basic fairness and justice. | | 10. Use tactful and consistent discipline. |

## Discussion Questions

1. What prevents managers from making work more like play?

2. Are these forces real, or imagined?

3. What would be the likely (positive and negative) results of making work more like play?

4. Could others in the organization accept such creative behaviors?

# Solve the Dilemma

### MOTIVATING TO WIN

Eagle Pharmaceutical has long been recognized for its innovative techniques for motivating its salesforce. It features the salesperson who has been the most successful during the previous quarter in the company newsletter, "Touchdown." The salesperson also receives a football jersey, a plaque, and $1,000 worth of Eagle stock. Eagle's "Superbowl Club" is for employees who reach or exceed their sales goal, and a "Heisman Award," which includes a trip to the Caribbean, is given annually to the top 20 salespeople in terms of goal achievement.

Eagle employs a video conference hook-up between the honored salesperson and four regional sales managers to capture some of the successful tactics and strategies the winning salesperson uses to succeed. The managers summarize these ideas and pass them along to the salespeople they manage. Sales managers feel strongly that programs such as this are important and that, by sharing strategies and tactics with one another, they can be a successful team.

### Discussion Questions

1. Which motivational theories are in use at Eagle?

2. What is the value of getting employees to compete against a goal instead of against one another?

3. Put yourself in the shoes of one of the four regional sales managers and argue against potential cutbacks to the motivational program.

# Build Your Business Plan

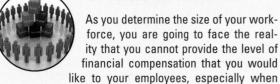

## MOTIVATING THE WORKFORCE

As you determine the size of your workforce, you are going to face the reality that you cannot provide the level of financial compensation that you would like to your employees, especially when you are starting your business.

Many employees are motivated by other things than money. Knowing that they are appreciated and doing a good job can bring great satisfaction to employees. Known as "stroking," it can provide employees with internal gratification that can be valued even more that financial incentives. Listening to your employees' suggestions, involving them in discussions about future growth and valuing their input, can go a long way toward building loyal employees and reducing employee turnover.

Think about what you could do in your business to motivate your employees without spending much money. Maybe you will have lunch brought in once a week or offer tickets to a local sporting event to the employee with the most sales. Whatever you elect to do, you must be consistent and fair with all your employees.

# See for Yourself Videocase

## TAKING VACATIONS CAN IMPROVE YOUR CAREER

It might surprise you to learn that about 36 percent of workers use little or none of their paid vacation time. Much about the workplace contributes to this issue. Many companies, in America at least, maintain a work, work, work, 24/7 mind-set, causing employees to fear that taking time off will indicate that they lack the dedication needed to maintain or move up in their positions. Another major deterrent for the employee wary of taking a vacation is the amount of work that will be waiting upon his or her return. Some employees rack up so many e-mails and voice-mail messages that they are unable to get their main work done for days as they play catch-up.

Not taking vacation time can be dangerous for both employers and employees. On the employer side, employees who lack energy and motivation can use up valuable work time puttering around. Tired employees can also make costly mistakes. On the employee side, not taking vacations can lead to burnout and serious mental and physical illness. If an employee gets ill due to the increased stress, this also has a negative impact on the employer.

Vacation and down time have long been valued in other parts of the world such as Europe, Canada, and Australia, and now a small number of American companies are beginning to realize the benefits of employees taking their allotted vacation time, thanks to research to support these benefits. The Families and Work Institute states that employees should always take their vacations and that vacations lasting more than a few days create greater benefit. The Institute claims that employees who take vacations are more productive and more creative at work. A recent Expedia.com survey reported that 80 percent of those surveyed claimed that after taking a true vacation they felt more enthusiastic about their jobs. There are also the health benefits to consider of the reduced stress and extra rest time gained during a vacation.

However, another problem presents itself. Even when one takes a vacation, in the age of the Internet and remote access it's challenging to truly get away. Rosemary Haefner of CareerBuilder.com suggests that advanced planning may be the ticket to a true vacation, and Deb Perelman of eWeek.com offers the following advice:

- Let the office know about your vacation well in advance.
- Schedule vacations at times when you're less likely to be needed and when crises (if these are ever possible to predict) are less likely to occur, such as between major projects.
- Schedule one specific time to check in with the office and stick to it. Make sure everyone else sticks to it as well.
- Make use of your "Out of the Office" auto reply on both e-mail and voice-mail. This may cut down a bit on the number of messages waiting upon your return.

For those who compulsively check in with the office, certain hotels offer to lock up cell phones and PDAs!

A number of companies are beginning to encourage employees to take advantage of vacation time. Here are a few examples:

- Electronics giant Sanyo gives employees who volunteer for social causes during certain workdays the chance to earn up to six extra paid days off annually.
- Software company Hyperion allows its employees to earn Extended Paid Time Off if they remain employed

with the company continuously from one year to the next.

- The wireless provider T-Mobile allows employees to begin earning paid vacation time as soon as they start working for the company. In many companies, vacation time is earned only after one or more years with the company.

Although there is often an imbalance between the work and personal lives of many employees throughout the United States, research clearly states that both employers and employees would benefit by each person taking his or her allotted vacation time. Health, productivity, and creativity are all given a boost when employees take time to relax and recuperate.[31]

**Discussion Questions**

1. What are some reasons employees do not take all of the vacation time allotted to them?
2. What can employers do to actively encourage employees to take their vacation time?
3. What are the benefits of employee vacations, both to the employer and to the employee?

**Remember to check out our Online Learning Center at www.mhhe.com/ferrell7e.**

# chapter 11

## CHAPTER OUTLINE

**Introduction**

**The Nature of Human Resources Management**

**Planning for Human Resources Needs**

**Recruiting and Selecting New Employees**
*Recruiting*
*Selection*
*Legal Issues in Recruiting and Selecting*

**Developing the Workforce**
*Training and Development*
*Assessing Performance*
*Turnover*

**Compensating the Workforce**
*Financial Compensation*
*Benefits*

**Managing Unionized Employees**
*Collective Bargaining*
*Resolving Disputes*

**The Importance of Workforce Diversity**
*The Characteristics of Diversity*
*Why Is Diversity Important?*
*The Benefits of Workforce Diversity*
*Affirmative Action*

# Managing Human Resources

## OBJECTIVES

*After reading this chapter, you will be able to:*

- Define human resources management, and explain its significance.
- Summarize the processes of recruiting and selecting human resources for a company.
- Discuss how workers are trained and their performance appraised.
- Identify the types of turnover companies may experience, and explain why turnover is an important issue.
- Specify the various ways a worker may be compensated.
- Discuss some of the issues associated with unionized employees, including collective bargaining and dispute resolution.
- Describe the importance of diversity in the workforce.
- Assess an organization's efforts to reduce its workforce size and manage the resulting effects.

## Managing the Workforce during Slow Times

Developing and compensating the workforce is challenging in good economic times but even more difficult during an economic slowdown. During the most recent downturn in the economy, many workers are faced with a squeeze on their pay and benefits. The downturn, combined with rapidly increasing energy prices and declining home values, placed many employees' standard of living in jeopardy. Millions of people have managed to keep their jobs, yet they have seen their pay slashed, or they have lost important benefits.

While mergers and layoffs reduce the payroll for many companies, nearly all employees who receive at least part of their compensation in the form of commissions suffer a snowball pay decline, affecting a number of industries. If a saleswoman receives a smaller commission, for example, she is likely to tip less at her next restaurant meal, in turn lowering the wait staff's salary. It is estimated that 25 million employees at just the 1,500 largest companies receive some type of variable pay. This means at least part of their pay is based on performance, commissions, or other nonguaranteed compensation. For example, there are 1.25 million real estate agents and 229,100 new car salespersons whose income depends on sales. In the recent economic downturn, these two industries saw a significant sales drop. Not included in these numbers are the 20 million individuals who the Small Business Administration says own their own businesses but have no employees. In addition, there are nearly 5 million small businesses that employ 10 or fewer workers, often using variable pay. With a downturn in the economy, everything slows down, including the time it takes to execute a business plan or gain partners

*continued*

to help financially as everyone becomes more cautious. In these situations, it is important to reassure good workers about their performance and how the organization plans to compensate them in the long run. While some workers may choose to keep their position in spite of pay cuts, the very best employees may always have other options.

Fair treatment of employees includes honoring compensation contracts and not violating labor law. For example, the Fair Labor Standards Act in 2004 established guidelines that employees must make more than $455 a week to be ineligible for overtime pay, a sharp increase over the previous benchmark of $250 a week. As a result, 1.3 million workers suddenly qualified for extra pay. The number of overtime lawsuits has exploded over the last few years. This means employers can get caught off guard during slow times by pushing employees to work overtime without pay.

With escalating gas prices, some companies try to help employees save money by allowing them to work four 10-hour days instead of five 8-hour days. A flexible schedule that helps to eliminate one day of commuting improves the environment and improves morale. Some employers try to help workers cope with higher gas prices by telecommuting (working from their home). Anything that an organization can do to appreciate and help employees during a slow time in the economy can pay results in the long run.[1]

# Introduction

Of course, most firms do not recruit such loyal and motivated employees, but these are vital tasks in any organization. If a business is to achieve success, it must have sufficient numbers of employees who are qualified and motivated to perform the required duties. Thus, managing the quantity (from hiring to firing) and quality (through training, compensating, and so on) of employees is an important business function. Meeting the challenge of managing increasingly diverse human resources effectively can give a company a competitive edge in a global marketplace.

This chapter focuses on the quantity and quality of human resources. First we look at how human resources managers plan for, recruit, and select qualified employees. Next we look at training, appraising, and compensating employees, aspects of human resources management designed to retain valued employees. Along the way, we'll also consider the challenges of managing unionized and diverse employees.

## The Nature of Human Resources Management

**human resources management (HRM)** all the activities involved in determining an organization's human resources needs, as well as acquiring, training, and compensating people to fill those needs

Chapter 1 defined human resources as labor, the physical and mental abilities that people use to produce goods and services. **Human resources management (HRM)** refers to all the activities involved in determining an organization's human resources needs, as well as acquiring, training, and compensating people to fill those needs. Human resources managers are concerned with maximizing the satisfaction of employees and motivating them to meet organizational objectives productively. In some companies, this function is called personnel management.

HRM has increased in importance over the last few decades, in part because managers have developed a better understanding of human relations through the work of Maslow, Herzberg, and others. Moreover, the human resources themselves are changing. Employees today are concerned not only about how much a job pays; they are concerned also with job satisfaction, personal performance, leisure, the environment, and their opportunities for advancement. Once dominated by white men, today's workforce includes significantly more women, African Americans, Hispanics, and other minorities, as well as disabled and older workers. Human resources managers must be aware of these changes and leverage them to increase the productivity of their employees. Every manager practices some of the functions of human resources management at all times.

## Planning for Human Resources Needs

When planning and developing strategies for reaching the organization's overall objectives, a company must consider whether it will have the human resources necessary to carry out its plans. After determining how many employees and what skills are needed to satisfy the overall plans, the human resources department (which may range from the owner in a small business to hundreds of people in a large corporation) ascertains how many employees the company currently has and how many will be retiring or otherwise leaving the organization during the planning period. With this information, the human resources manager can then forecast how many more employees the company will need to hire and what qualifications they must have, or determine if layoffs are required to meet demand more efficiently. HRM planning also requires forecasting the availability of people in the workforce who will have the necessary qualifications to meet the organization's future needs. The human resources manager then develops a strategy for satisfying the organization's human resources needs.

Next, managers analyze the jobs within the organization so that they can match the human resources to the available assignments. **Job analysis** determines, through observation and study, pertinent information about a job—the specific tasks that comprise it; the knowledge, skills, and abilities necessary to perform if; and the environment in which it will be performed. Managers use the information obtained through a job analysis to develop job descriptions and job specifications.

A **job description** is a formal, written explanation of a specific job that usually includes job title, tasks to be performed (for instance, waiting on customers), relationship with other jobs, physical and mental skills required (such as lifting heavy boxes or calculating data), duties, responsibilities, and working conditions. A **job specification** describes the qualifications necessary for a specific job, in terms of education (some jobs require a college degree), experience, personal characteristics (ads frequently request outgoing, hardworking persons), and physical characteristics. Both the job description and job specification are used to develop recruiting materials such as newspaper, trade publications, and online advertisements.

## Recruiting and Selecting New Employees

After forecasting the firm's human resources needs and comparing them to existing human resources, the human resources manager should have a general idea of how many new employees the firm needs to hire. With the aid of job analyses,

**job analysis**
the determination, through observation and study, of pertinent information about a job—including specific tasks and necessary abilities, knowledge, and skills

**job description**
a formal, written explanation of a specific job, usually including job title, tasks, relationship with other jobs, physical and mental skills required, duties, responsibilities, and working conditions

**job specification**
a description of the qualifications necessary for a specific job, in terms of education, experience, and personal and physical characteristics

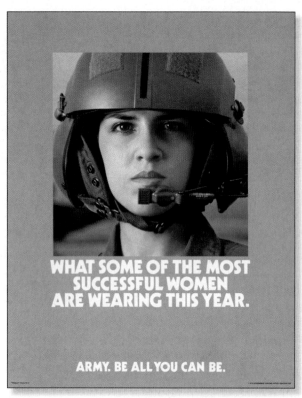

**WHAT SOME OF THE MOST SUCCESSFUL WOMEN ARE WEARING THIS YEAR.**

**ARMY. BE ALL YOU CAN BE.**

*For more than 50 years, the U.S. Army has recruited soldiers from American colleges around the country. In fact, the Army generates more officers through its Reserve Officers Training Corps (ROTC) college program than the U.S. Military Academy.*

**recruiting**
forming a pool of qualified applicants from which management can select employees

**selection**
the process of collecting information about applicants and using that information to make hiring decisions

management can then recruit and select employees who are qualified to fill specific job openings.

## Recruiting

**Recruiting** means forming a pool of qualified applicants from which management can select employees. There are two sources from which to develop this pool of applicants—internal and external.

Internal sources of applicants include the organization's current employees. Many firms have a policy of giving first consideration to their own employees—or promoting from within. The cost of hiring current employees to fill job openings is inexpensive when compared with the cost of hiring from external sources, and it is good for employee morale. However, hiring from within creates another job vacancy to be filled.

External sources consist of advertisements in newspapers and professional journals, employment agencies, colleges, vocational schools, recommendations from current employees, competing firms, unsolicited applications, and online. There are hundreds of Web sites where employers can post job openings and job seekers can post their résumés, including Monster.com, Hotjobs.com, CareerBuilder.com., and Theladders.com. Employers looking for employees for specialized jobs can use more focused sites such as computerwork.com. Increasingly, companies can turn to their own Web sites for potential candidates: Nearly all of the *Fortune* 500 firms provide career Web sites where they recruit, provide employment information, and take applications. Using these sources of applicants is generally more expensive than hiring from within, but it may be necessary if there are no current employees who meet the job specifications or there are better-qualified people outside of the organization. Recruiting for entry-level managerial and professional positions is often carried out on college and university campuses. For managerial or professional positions above the entry level, companies sometimes depend on employment agencies or executive search firms, sometimes called *headhunters,* which specialize in luring qualified people away from other companies.

## Selection

**Selection** is the process of collecting information about applicants and using that information to decide which ones to hire. It includes the application itself, as well as interviewing, testing, and reference checking. This process can be quite lengthy and expensive. Procter & Gamble, for example, offers a recruiting process that gives a realistic picture of skills, as well as strengths and interests. The process often starts with completing an online application tied to a matching process with open jobs. If your application does match an open position, then you are invited to complete an online questionnaire and a problem-solving test. If the results are positive, you then have an interview. P&G provides practice tests online for applicants.[2] Such rigorous scrutiny is necessary to find those applicants who can do the work expected and fit

# Entrepreneurship In Action
## Terry Gou Finds the Right Employees in China

Terry Gou

**Business:** Hon Hai Precision Industry Co.

**Founded:** 1974

**Success:** Terry Gou was No. 160 on *Forbes* magazine's 2008 "The World's Billionaires" list, with a net worth of $6.1 billion.

Terry Gou is a self-made billionaire thanks to his company Hon Hai Precision Industry Co. The company was founded by Gou in Taiwan in 1974. In the early days, Gou's company manufactured plastic parts for black-and-white televisions. During the first part of the next decade, Gou ventured into the PC industry. In 1988, Gou moved his factory to China and began to expand. Today, creating many of a PC's inside components is only a small part of what Gou's company does. Hon Hai also produces Apple's iPod and iPhone products, HP computers, Motorola phones, and Wii consoles. Gou's factory in Shenzhen, China, boasts about 270,000 employees. Hon Hai is now the largest exporter in China, and Gou is credited with keeping electronic production in China despite it being the age of outsourcing. Gou has watched Hon Hai's revenue increase 50 percent annually for the last decade, reaching $55 billion in 2007. Both Gou and his company have solid reputations. Gou is a leader inspiring immense loyalty. Analysts and industry insiders confirm that Hon Hai has a reputation for good quality control and competitive pricing. Although Gou shuns publicity, he cannot deny that Hon Hai is worth noticing and talking about.[3]

into the firm's structure and culture. If an organization finds the "right" employees through its recruiting and selection process, it will not have to spend as much money later in recruiting, selecting, and training replacement employees.

**The Application.**   In the first stage of the selection process, the individual fills out an application form and perhaps has a brief interview. The application form asks for the applicant's name, address, telephone number, education, and previous work experience. The goal of this stage of the selection process is to get acquainted with the applicants and to weed out those who are obviously not qualified for the job. Most companies ask for the following information before contacting a potential candidate: current salary, reason for seeking a new job, years of experience, availability, and level of interest in the position. In addition to identifying obvious qualifications, the application can provide subtle clues about whether a person is appropriate for a particular job. For instance, an applicant who gives unusually creative answers may be perfect for a position at an advertising agency; a person who turns in a sloppy, hurriedly scrawled application probably would not be appropriate for a technical job requiring precise adjustments. Many companies now accept online applications. The online application at Procter & Gamble is designed not only to collect biographical data but to create a picture of the applicant and how the person might contribute within the company. The Web site states that there are no right or wrong answers and indicates that completion takes about 30 to 45 minutes. Applicants also must submit an electronic copy of their résumé.[4]

**The Interview.**   The next phase of the selection process involves interviewing applicants. Interviews allow management to obtain detailed information about the applicant's experience and skills, reasons for changing jobs, attitudes toward the job, and an idea of whether the person would fit in with the company. Furthermore, the interviewer can answer the applicant's questions about the requirements for the job, compensation, working conditions, company policies, organizational culture, and so on. A potential employee's questions may be just as revealing as his or her answers. Table 11.1 provides some insights on finding the right work environment. Table 11.2 lists some of the most common questions asked by interviewers while Table 11.3 reveals mistakes candidates make in interviewing.

**TABLE II.I**

Interviewing Tips

1. Evaluate the work environment. Do employees seem to get along and work well in teams?
2. Evaluate the attitude of employees. Are employees happy, tense, or overworked?
3. Are employees enthusiastic and excited about their work?
4. What is the organizational culture, and would you feel comfortable working there?

Source: Adapted from "What to Look for During Office Visits," http://careercenter.tamu.edu/guides/interviews/lookforinoffice.html (accessed May 16, 2008).

**Testing.**    Another step in the selection process is testing. Ability and performance tests are used to determine whether an applicant has the skills necessary for the job. Aptitude, IQ, or personality tests may be used to assess an applicant's potential for a certain kind of work and his or her ability to fit into the organization's culture. One of the most commonly used tests is the Myers-Briggs Type Indicator. Myers-Briggs Type Indicator Test is used worldwide by more than 2 million people each year.[5] Figure 11.1 shows a few alternative tests, what they attempt to measure and an estimate of the expense per employee. Although polygraph ("lie detector") tests were once a common technique for evaluating the honesty of applicants, in 1988 their use was restricted to specific government jobs and those involving security or access to drugs. Applicants may also undergo physical examinations to determine their suitability for some jobs, and many companies require applicants to be screened for illegal drug use. There are more than 11 million heavy drinkers and 16 million illegal drug users in the United States. Of this group, 75 percent are employed full time and around half work for small businesses. On average in small businesses, 1 out of 10 employees are either alcohol or drug abusers. Small businesses may have a higher percentage of these employees because they do not engage in systematic drug testing. If you employ a drug or alcohol abuser, you can expect a 33 percent loss in productivity from this employee, which costs employers roughly $7,000 annually. Overall, substance abuse costs American employers $160 billion each year through high employee turnover and absenteeism, workplace accidents, higher workers' compensation costs, higher medical costs, and workplace theft and violence.[6] Like the application form and the interview, testing serves to eliminate those who do not meet the job specifications.

**TABLE II.2**

Top 10 Interview Questions

1. What are your weaknesses?
2. Why should we hire you?
3. Why do you want to work here?
4. What are your goals?
5. Why did you leave (or why are you leaving) your job?
6. When were you most satisfied with your job?
7. What can you do for us that the other candidate can't?
8. What are three positive things your last boss would say about you?
9. What salary are you seeking?
10. If you were an animal, which one would you want to be?

Source: Carole Martin, "Prep for the Top 10 Interview Questions," http://career-advice.monster.com/job-interview-practice/Prep-for-the-Top-10-Interview-Quest/home.aspx (accessed May 16, 2008).

| | |
|---|---|
| 1.  Not taking the interview seriously. | **TABLE 11.3** |
| 2.  Not dressing appropriately (dressing down). | Mistakes Made in |
| 3.  Not appropriately discussing experience, abilities, and education. | Interviewing |
| 4.  Being too modest about your accomplishments. | |
| 5.  Talking too much. | |
| 6.  Too much concern about compensation. | |
| 7.  Speaking negatively of a former employer. | |
| 8.  Not asking enough or appropriate questions. | |
| 9.  Not showing the proper enthusiasm level. | |
| 10.  Not engaging in appropriate follow-up to the interview. | |

Source: "Avoid the Top 10 Job Interview Mistakes," All Business, http://www.allbusiness.com/human-resources/careers-job-interview/1611-2.html (accessed June 4, 2008).

**Reference Checking.**   Before making a job offer, the company should always check an applicant's references. Reference checking usually involves verifying educational background and previous work experience. Background checking is important because applicants may misrepresent themselves on their applications or résumés. The star of *Dinner Impossible* on the Food Network fabricated portions of his résumé, including the claim that he cooked for Britain's Royal Family. The Food Network, upon learning of these errors, did not renew Robert Irvine's contract, indicating that viewers place trust in the network and the accuracy of information that it provides and that Irvine "challenged that trust."[7] Reference checking is a vital, albeit often overlooked, stage in the selection process. Managers charged with hiring should be aware, however, that many organizations will confirm only that an

| Test/Provider | Purpose | Cost/Person | |
|---|---|---|---|
| **HCG Cultural Assessment Tool** **Hagberg Consulting Group** **Foster City, CA** | **Determines workplace morale and dysfunction** | **$15.00–20.00** | **FIGURE 11.1** |
| **The Hogan Personality Inventory** **Hogan Assessment Systems** **Tulsa, OK** | **Measures potential employee fit with the company and job** | **$20.00–125.00** | Sampling of Psychological Tests |
| **The Call Center Solution** **ePredix** **Minneapolis, MN** | **Predicts success in call center jobs and potential for success in upselling** | **$25.00 and up (selection phase)** | Source: Paul Kaihla "Getting Inside the Boss's Head," *Business 2.0,* November 2003, Copyright © 2003 *Time* Inc. All rights reserved. |
| **Sigmaradius 360** **Degree Feedback** **Sigma Assessment Systems** **Port Huron, MI** | **Measures managerial effectiveness by evaluating superior's and subordinate's assessment** | **$139.00–199.00** | |

applicant is a former employee, perhaps with beginning and ending work dates, and will not release details about the quality of the employee's work.

## Legal Issues in Recruiting and Selecting

Legal constraints and regulations are present in almost every phase of the recruitment and selection process, and a violation of these regulations can result in lawsuits and fines. Therefore, managers should be aware of these restrictions to avoid legal problems. Some of the laws affecting human resources management are discussed below.

Because one law pervades all areas of human resources management, we'll take a quick look at it now. **Title VII of the Civil Rights Act** of 1964 prohibits discrimination in employment. It also created the Equal Employment Opportunity Commission (EEOC), a federal agency dedicated to increasing job opportunities for women and minorities and eliminating job discrimination based on race, religion, color, sex, national origin, or handicap. As a result of Title VII, employers must not impose sex distinctions in job specifications, job descriptions, or newspaper advertisements. Between 75,000 and 90,000 charges of discrimination are filed each year with the EEOC.[8] Sexual harassment cases make up the largest number of claims the EEOC sees each day. The Civil Rights Act of 1964 also outlaws the use of discriminatory tests for applicants. Aptitude tests and other indirect tests must be validated; in other words, employers must be able to demonstrate that scores on such tests are related to job performance, so that no one race has an advantage in taking the tests. Although many hope for improvements in organizational diversity, in a survey of 357 global senior executives, 76 percent have one or no minorities among their top executives. Minorities make up 17 percent of the U.S. workforce, and that number should hit 20 percent by 2016. In spite of a lack of diversity, many of these companies indicate an initiative to support workplace diversity.[9]

Other laws affecting HRM include the Americans with Disabilities Act (ADA), which prevents discrimination against disabled persons. It also classifies people with AIDS as handicapped and, consequently, prohibits using a positive AIDS test as reason to deny an applicant employment. The Age Discrimination in Employment Act specifically outlaws discrimination based on age. Its focus is banning hiring practices that discriminate against people between the ages of 49 and 69, but it also outlaws policies that require employees to retire before the age of 70. Generally, when companies need employees, recruiters head to college campuses, and when downsizing is necessary, many older workers are offered early retirement. However, there are many benefits that companies are realizing in hiring older workers. Some of these benefits include that they are more dedicated, punctual, honest, and detail-oriented; are good listeners; take pride in their work; exhibit good organizational skills; are efficient and confident; are mature; can be seen as role models; have good communication

**Title VII of the Civil Rights Act**
prohibits discrimination in employment and created the Equal Employment Opportunity Commission

*Merrill Lynch promotes diversity within its organization.*

skills; and offer an opportunity for a reduced labor cost because of already having insurance plans.[10] The Equal Pay Act mandates that men and women who do equal work must receive the same wage. Wage differences are acceptable only if they are attributed to seniority, performance, or qualifications. Despite these laws, one year out of college, women earn 80 percent of what men earn. A decade later, women earn only 69 percent as much as men. There is significant variation based on the job: for example, in education generally, women earn 95 percent as much as males; however, in the area of math, women earn 76 percent as much as men.[11] Figure 11.2 illustrates how women feel about this "glass ceiling" effect.

# Developing the Workforce

Once the most qualified applicants have been selected, have been offered positions, and have accepted their offers, they must be formally introduced to the organization and trained so they can begin to be productive members of the workforce. **Orientation** familiarizes the newly hired employees with fellow workers, company procedures, and the physical properties of the company. It generally includes a tour of the building; introductions to supervisors, co-workers, and subordinates; and the distribution of organizational manuals describing the organization's policy on vacations, absenteeism, lunch breaks, company benefits, and so on. Orientation also involves socializing the new employee into the ethics and culture of the new company. Many larger companies now show videotapes of procedures, facilities, and key personnel in the organization to help speed the adjustment process.

**orientation**
familiarizing newly hired employees with fellow workers, company procedures, and the physical properties of the company

## Training and Development

Although recruiting and selection are designed to find employees who have the knowledge, skills, and abilities the company needs, new employees still must undergo **training** to learn how to do their specific job tasks. *On-the-job training* allows workers to learn by actually performing the tasks of the job, while *classroom training* teaches employees with lectures, conferences, videotapes, case studies,

**training**
teaching employees to do specific job tasks through either classroom development or on-the-job experience

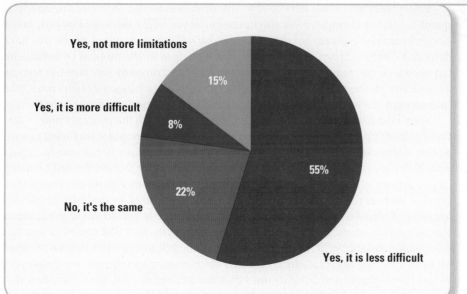

**Yes, not more limitations**

**Yes, it is more difficult**

15%

8%

55%

22%

**No, it's the same**

**Yes, it is less difficult**

**FIGURE II.2**

Glass Ceiling

*Has the "glass ceiling"\* for women in the workplace shifted in the past 10 years?*

\* Defined as limitations that prevent qualified women from being promoted to leadership positions.

Source: "Glass Ceiling," *USA Today Snapshots.* Adecco USA Workplace survey, April 22, 2008.

**development**
training that augments the skills and knowledge of managers and professionals

and Web-based training. The Cheesecake Factory spends an average $2,000 per employee on training each year. Servers benefit from 2 weeks of on-the-job training, and management candidates receive 12-week development courses. The company defends the investment in training by providing extremely high customer satisfaction rates and loyalty. In addition, turnover at the Cheesecake Factory is around 15 percent below the industry average.[12] **Development** is training that augments the skills and knowledge of managers and professionals. Training and development are also used to improve the skills of employees in their present positions and to prepare them for increased responsibility and job promotions. Training is therefore a vital function of human resources management. Training and development plans are tailored to meet each employee's needs at Procter & Gamble. In addition to on-the-job training, the company offers one-on-one coaching from managers, peer mentoring, individualized work plans that outline key projects and highlight skills to sharpen, and formal classroom training conducted at the company's "Learning Center" in Cincinnati.[13]

After creating Chinese versions of the virtual-reality world "Second Life," the Chinese software firms HiPiHi, Novo King, and UOneNet found themselves approached by businesses to work on ideas they hadn't thought of. For example, disappointed by traditional training results, Xiong Ying—a human resources manager at China's largest copper company, Jiangxi Copper—got the idea to train factory workers virtually. Xiong subsequently contracted with NovoKing to set up a training module in the software company's version of "Second Life."

## Assessing Performance

Assessing an employee's performance—his or her strengths and weaknesses on the job—is one of the most difficult tasks for managers. However, performance appraisal is crucial because it gives employees feedback on how they are doing and what they need to do to improve. It also provides a basis for determining how to compensate and reward employees, and it generates information about the quality of the firm's selection, training, and development activities. Table 11.4 identifies 16 characteristics that may be assessed in a performance review.

Performance appraisals may be objective or subjective. An objective assessment is quantifiable. For example, a Westinghouse employee might be judged by how many circuit boards he typically produces in one day or by how many of his boards have defects. A Century 21 real estate agent might be judged by the number of houses she has shown or the number of sales she has closed. A company can also use tests as an objective method of assessment. Whatever method they use, managers must take into account the work environment when they appraise performance objectively.

When jobs do not lend themselves to objective appraisal, the manager must relate the employee's performance to some other standard. One popular tool used in subjective assessment is the ranking system, which lists various performance factors on which the manager ranks employees against each other. Although used by many large companies, ranking systems are unpopular with many employees. Qualitative criteria, such as teamwork and communication skills, used to evaluate employees are generally hard to gauge. Such grading systems have triggered employee lawsuits that allege discrimination in grade/ranking assignments. Best Buy settled an age discrimination lawsuit with 44 former information technology (IT) employees aged 40 to 71 (average age 51), which required the company to reinstate the employees or pay them salaries and benefits until they reached retirement age. When Best Buy outsourced much of its IT function, they allegedly told the 820 employees that only

---

**TABLE 11.4   Performance Characteristics**

- **Productivity**—rate at which work is regularly produced
- **Quality**—accuracy, professionalism, and deliverability of produced work
- **Job knowledge**—understanding of the objectives, practices, and standards of work
- **Problem solving**—ability to identify and correct problems effectively
- **Communication**—effectiveness in written and verbal exchanges
- **Initiative**—willingness to identify and address opportunities for improvement
- **Adaptability**—ability to become comfortable with change
- **Planning and organization skills**—reflected through the ability to schedule projects, set goals, and maintain organizational systems
- **Teamwork and cooperation**—effectiveness of collaborations with co-workers
- **Judgment**—ability to determine appropriate actions in a timely manner
- **Dependability**—responsiveness, reliability, and conscientiousness demonstrated on the job
- **Creativity**—extent to which resourceful ideas, solutions, and methods for task completion are proposed
- **Sales**—demonstrated through success in selling products, services, yourself, and your company
- **Customer service**—ability to communicate effectively with customers, address problems, and offer solutions that meet or exceed their expectations
- **Leadership**—tendency and ability to serve as a doer, guide, decision maker, and role model
- **Financial management**—appropriateness of cost controls and financial planning within the scope defined by the position

Source: "Performance Characteristics," Performance Review from http://www.salary.com/Careerresources/docs/related_performance_review_part2_popup .html (accessed June 12, 2001). Used with permission.

---

40 would remain with the retailer and 650 would work for the outsource company, Accenture. Best Buy officials denied the allegation of these former employees.[14]

Another performance appraisal method used by many companies is the 360-degree feedback system, which provides feedback from a panel that typically includes superiors, peers, and subordinates. Because of the tensions it may cause, peer appraisal appears to be difficult for many. However, companies that have success with 360-degree feedback tend to be open to learning and willing to experiment and are led by executives who are direct about the expected benefits as well as the challenges.[15] Managers and leaders with a high emotional intelligence (sensitivity to their own as well as others' emotions) assess and reflect upon their interactions with colleagues on a daily basis. In addition, they conduct follow-up analysis on their projects, asking the right questions and listening carefully to responses without getting defensive of their actions.[16]

Whether the assessment is objective or subjective, it is vital that the manager discuss the results with the employee, so that the employee knows how well he or she is doing the job. The results of a performance appraisal become useful only when they are communicated, tactfully, to the employee and presented as a tool to allow the employee to grow and improve in his or her position and beyond. Performance appraisals are also used to determine whether an employee should be promoted, transferred, or terminated from the organization.

## Turnover

**Turnover,** which occurs when employees quit or are fired and must be replaced by new employees, results in lost productivity from the vacancy, fees to recruit replacement

**turnover**
occurs when employees quit or are fired and must be replaced by new employees

# Destination CEO
## Anne Mulcahy, Xerox

Anne Mulcahy is one of America's most powerful women. She is one of a handful of women occupying the CEO office of a major corporation. In this case, Xerox. Mulcahy joined the company 30 years ago following in her brother's footsteps. Starting in sales, Mulcahy rose through the ranks and served in various capacities in human resources and the printer division, served as president, and then was promoted to CEO. Her promotion came during a highly volatile period in Xerox's history. In 2000, Xerox was flirting with bankruptcy, sales were dismal, costs were out of control, and the company was not competitive. These weren't Xerox's only troubles, however. The SEC was investigating Xerox for its questionable accounting practices leading to a fine of $10 million.

Against this troubling backdrop, enter Anne Mulcahy, who many say, has Xerox running through her veins. Xerox is one of the few companies that is still considered family-friendly. It is not at all uncommon for several members of a family to be employed with the firm. Mulcahy's task was to slash costs and to revive the company's competitiveness. In her first year as CEO, she cut a billion dollars in costs, reduced the labor force substantially, and discontinued product lines that were no longer competitive. Under her leadership, Xerox moved quickly away from consumer-imaging products to the more lucrative, high-end commercial color printing and processing technologies, where profit margins are five times that of black-and-white imaging technologies.

Despite the major reductions in labor and the restructuring of the firm's divisions, Mulcahy remains highly regarded by employees at Xerox. Her eternal optimism and her unswerving commitment to Xerox seem to have had a motivating impact on the company's employees. Mulcahy has ensured that the corporate culture remains intact in spite of the company's transformation. While the company's position has improved dramatically under Mulcahy's leadership, competition remains fierce—and pressure to cut costs even further present formidable challenges.

### Discussion Questions

1. Xerox CEO Mulcahy is responsible for managing a great deal of turnover as the company seeks to remain competitive. Discuss the HR issues involved
2. Generally speaking, what role does human resources management play at Xerox?
3. Anne Mulcahy clearly demonstrates that Xerox values diversity in the workplace. What other factors would be important in addressing diversity?

employees, management time devoted to interviewing, and training costs for new employees. Clarkston Consulting in Durham, North Carolina, was going through a phase where employees were dissatisfied, working more than the industry norm of 56 hours per week (not including travel), and turnover was increasing. The company engaged in intense training to improve skills and understand competitive and best practices, and it introduced a truncated travel schedule. The travel program allowed employees to leave home on Monday, stay in a hotel and work at the client's site for four days, and return to work at home on Friday. Removing large amounts of travel from evenings and weekends significantly improved morale, productivity, and satisfaction.[17] Part of the reason for turnover may be overworked employees as a result of downsizing and a lack of training and advancement opportunities.[18] Of course, turnover is not always an unhappy occasion when its takes the form of a promotion or transfer.

A **promotion** is an advancement to a higher-level job with increased authority, responsibility, and pay. In some companies and most labor unions, seniority—the length of time a person has been with the company or at a particular job classification—is the key issue in determining who should be promoted. Most managers base promotions on seniority only when they have candidates with equal qualifications: Managers prefer to base promotions on merit.

A **transfer** is a move to another job within the company at essentially the same level and wage. Transfers allow workers to obtain new skills or to find a new position within an organization when their old position has been eliminated because of automation or downsizing.

**promotion**
an advancement to a higher-level job with increased authority, responsibility, and pay

**transfer**
a move to another job within the company at essentially the same level and wage

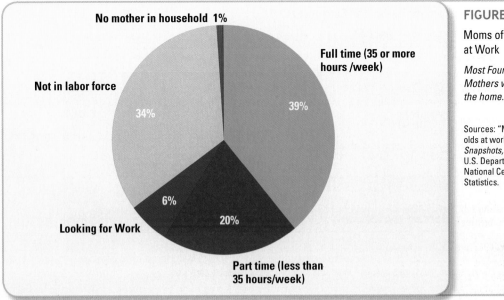

**FIGURE 11.3**

Moms of Four-Year-Olds at Work

*Most Four-Year-Olds Have Mothers who work outside the home.*

Sources: "Moms of 4-year-olds at work," *USA Today Snapshots,* April 3, 2008, p. B1; U.S. Department of Education, National Center for Education Statistics.

**Separations** occur when employees resign, retire, are terminated, or are laid off. Table 11.5 lists rules for peaceful separations from companies. Employees may be terminated, or fired, for poor performance, violation of work rules, absenteeism, and so on. Businesses have traditionally been able to fire employees *at will,* that is, for any reason other than for race, religion, sex, or age, or because an employee is a union organizer. However, recent legislation and court decisions now require that companies fire employees fairly, for just cause only. Managers must take care, then, to warn employees when their performance is unacceptable and may lead to dismissal. They should also document all problems and warnings in employees' work records. To avoid the possibility of lawsuits from individuals who may feel they have been fired unfairly, employers should provide clear, business-related reasons for any firing, supported by written documentation if possible. Employee

**separations**
employment changes involving resignation, retirement, termination, or layoff

**TABLE 11.5**   Rules for Peaceful Separations

- Leave as soon as practicable after making the decision.
- Prior to leaving, discuss your decision only with those who need to know.
- If asked, be candid about your new job; avoid the appearance of hiding something.
- Prior to leaving, do not disrupt your current employer's business.
- Be careful about any paper or electronic trails concerning the process that resulted in your resignation.
- Sign an employment agreement with a new employer only after you have resigned from your current position.
- Do not work for the new employer until after the last day of work at your current job.
- Have the recruiting employer indemnify you regarding judgments, settlements, and attorneys' fees incurred in connection with any litigation initiated by your former employer.
- Specify in a written agreement with your new employer that you will not use or disclose any trade secrets of former employers.

Source: Robert Lenzner and Carrie Shook, "Want to Go Peacefully? Some Rules," *Forbes,* February 23, 1998. Reprinted by permission of *Forbes Magazine.* Copyright 2004 Forbes Inc.

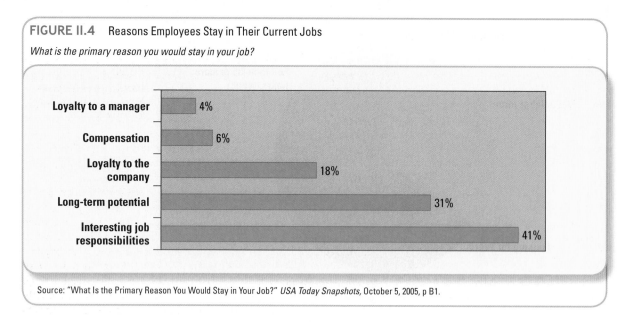

FIGURE II.4    Reasons Employees Stay in Their Current Jobs

*What is the primary reason you would stay in your job?*

- Loyalty to a manager — 4%
- Compensation — 6%
- Loyalty to the company — 18%
- Long-term potential — 31%
- Interesting job responsibilities — 41%

Source: "What Is the Primary Reason You Would Stay in Your Job?" *USA Today Snapshots,* October 5, 2005, p B1.

disciplinary procedures should be carefully explained to all employees and should be set forth in employee handbooks.

Many companies have downsized in recent years, laying off tens of thousands of employees in their effort to become more productive and competitive. General Motors, in light of declining demand for large, fuel-inefficient vehicles, launched plans to close four truck and SUV plants in the United States, Canada and Mexico, which will affect 8,350 workers. Since 2005, Ford, Chrysler, and GM have shut down 35 plants and eliminated 149,000 hourly and salaried jobs.[19] Layoffs are sometimes temporary; employees may be brought back when business conditions improve. When layoffs are to be permanent, employers often help employees find other jobs and may extend benefits while the employees search for new employment. Such actions help lessen the trauma of the layoffs.

A well-organized human resources department strives to minimize losses due to separations and transfers because recruiting and training new employees is very expensive. Note that a high turnover rate in a company may signal problems either with the selection and training process, the compensation program, or even the type of company. To help reduce turnover, companies have tried a number of strategies. Figure 11.4 shows some of the retention methods used by some businesses to retain frontline employees.

## Compensating the Workforce

People don't work for free, and how much they are paid for their work is a complicated issue. Also, designing a fair compensation plan is an important task because pay and benefits represent a substantial portion of an organization's expenses. Wages that are too high may result in the company's products being priced too high, making them uncompetitive in the market. Wages that are too low may damage employee morale and result in costly turnover. Remember that compensation is one of the hygiene factors identified by Herzberg.

Designing a fair compensation plan is a difficult task because it involves evaluating the relative worth of all jobs within the business while allowing for individual efforts.

## Going Green
### Green Coffee?

These days, unless you're traveling to remote locations, it's virtually impossible not to see a Starbucks—they seem to be everywhere. This makes sense when you consider that there are 7,087 company-operated stores and 4,081 licensed stores in the United States and 1,796 company-operated stores and 2,792 joint venture and licensed stores on the international scene. Of course, thousands of stores means thousands of employees. So how do these employees, known as "partners," fare at Starbucks? Pretty well, all things considered. In fact, the company was ranked number seven on *Fortune* magazine's list of 100 Best Companies to Work For in 2008.

Starbucks vows, as part of its Guiding Principles, to treat all of its partners with respect and dignity. To this end, all eligible full-time and part-time Starbucks partners are offered comprehensive health care. Starbucks frequently updates its pay packages, striving to maintain a competitive position at all times. In addition, all eligible global partners are offered *Bean Stock* options.

In 2002, Starbucks launched the Make Your Mark volunteer program. Through this program, partners are able to contribute to their communities with the help of the company. Starbucks donates $10 for every hour of volunteer work completed, with a limit of $1,000 per project. The company also matches the hours of any volunteer community members enlisted by Starbucks partners. Starbucks partners in the United States and Canada volunteer about 383,000 hours a year.

Like most companies, Starbucks is taking part in the green trend. For example, the company purchases Fair Trade–certified coffee, although it makes up less than 4 percent of the coffee the company purchases. In the past few years, Starbucks has also been looking to lessen its carbon emissions footprint. Although the company is currently unwilling to disclose its actual footprint, it is working toward being more carbon neutral—for example, by teaming up with the World Research Institute's Green Power Market Development Group, which assists companies in purchasing renewable energy at better prices. The company has also been increasing its use of wind power to offset the production of carbon dioxide.

Starbucks is encouraging its partners and customers to go green. It has run a few prominent campaigns, such as planetgreengame.com, and is working to track how much energy is used by specific equipment throughout its stores. Partners may take advantage of the Make Your Mark program to champion environmental causes. Although there are those that argue that such a large company is not doing enough toward going green, others feel that any step in the right direction is a positive one. We can certainly hope, thanks to the security and support that Starbucks offers its partners, that partners feel motivated to go out and do their part to help both their communities and the environment.[20]

### Discussion Questions
1. How does Starbucks compensate its employees in ways that encourage lower turnover and a more productive workforce?
2. How do Starbucks' green initiatives affect employees?
3. What might encouraging volunteerism do for employee morale and company loyalty?

Compensation for a specific job is typically determined through a **wage/salary survey,** which tells the company how much compensation comparable firms are paying for specific jobs that the firms have in common. Compensation for individuals within a specific job category depends on both the compensation for that job and the individual's productivity. Therefore, two employees with identical jobs may not receive exactly the same pay because of individual differences in performance.

**wage/salary survey** a study that tells a company how much compensation comparable firms are paying for specific jobs that the firms have in common

### Financial Compensation

Financial compensation falls into two general categories—wages and salaries. **Wages** are financial rewards based on the number of hours the employee works or the level of output achieved. Wages based on the number of hours worked are called time wages. The federal minimum wage increased to $6.55 per hour in 2008. Many states also mandate minimum wages; in the case where the two wages are in conflict, the higher of the two wages prevails. There may even be differences between city and state minimum wages. In New Mexico, the minimum wage is $7.50, whereas in the state capital of Santa Fe, the minimum wage is $10.50, due to a higher cost of living.[21] Table 11.6 compares wage and other information for Costco and Wal-Mart, two well-known discount chains. Time wages are appropriate when employees are continually interrupted

**wages** financial rewards based on the number of hours the employee works or the level of output achieved

**TABLE II.6**   Managing the workforce: Costco Versus Wal-Mart

|  | Costco | Wal-Mart |
|---|---|---|
| Number of employees | 100,000—U.S.<br>137,000—international | 1,420,000—U.S.<br>635,000—international |
| Sales | $64.4 billion | $378.79 billion |
| Average hourly wage | $17.25 | $10.11 |
| Percent of employees covered by health plans | 82% | 80% |
| Turnover (per year) | 17% | 40% |
| Profits per employee | $13,647 | $11,039 |

Sources: Costco Company Profile, http://phx.corporate-ir.net/phoenix.zhtml?c=83830&p=irol-homeprofile (accessed May 16, 2008); Consumer Reports Warehouse Clubs, http://www.consumerreports.org/cro/money/shopping/where-to-buy/warehouse-clubs-5-07/overview/0507_ware_ov.htm (accessed May 16, 2008); Esther Cervantes, "The Costco Alternative?" http://www.dollarsandsense.org/archives/2006/0106cervantes.html (accessed May 16, 2008).

and when quality is more important than quantity. Assembly-line workers, clerks, and maintenance personnel are commonly paid on a time-wage basis. The advantage of time wages is the ease of computation. The disadvantage is that time wages provide no incentive to increase productivity. In fact, time wages may encourage employees to be less productive.

To overcome these disadvantages, many companies pay on an incentive system, using piece wages or commissions. Piece wages are based on the level of output achieved. A major advantage of piece wages is that they motivate employees to supervise their own activities and to increase output. Skilled craftworkers are often paid on a piece-wage basis. At Longaberger, the world's largest maker of handmade baskets, weavers are paid per piece. The 2,500 workers produced 40,000 baskets a day, but productivity varied by as much as 400 percent among the weavers. A team of basket makers was assembled to try to improve productivity and reduce weaver downtime and the amount of leftover materials. After studying the basket makers for 19 days, the team's suggestions were implemented. The changes resulted in $3 million in annual savings for the company.[22]

**commission**
an incentive system that pays a fixed amount or a percentage of the employee's sales

The other incentive system, **commission,** pays a fixed amount or a percentage of the employee's sales. Kele & Co Jewelers in Plainfield, Illinois, make sterling silver jewelry and offer semi-precious and gemstones at affordable prices. Their handcrafted jewelry is sold through the Internet (www.keleonline.com) and through independent sales representatives (ISRs) all over the country. The unique aspect of Kele's sales process is their innovative sales and commission structure. ISRs have no minimum sales quotas, sales are shared among team members during training and after being promoted, and there is no requirement to purchase inventory as jewelry is shipped from Kele headquarters. ISRs receive a 30 percent commission on sales. Kele also pays for the design, development, and maintenance of a Web site to support ISRs. The goal is to increase the profit margin and earning potential of the salespeople. The company's goal is to become the largest direct sales company in the industry.[23] This method motivates employees to sell as much as they can. Some companies also combine payment based on commission with time wages or salaries.

**salary**
a financial reward calculated on a weekly, monthly, or annual basis

A **salary** is a financial reward calculated on a weekly, monthly, or annual basis. Salaries are associated with white-collar workers such as office personnel, executives, and professional employees. Although a salary provides a stable stream of income, salaried workers may be required to work beyond usual hours without additional financial compensation.

In addition to the basic wages or salaries paid to employees, a company may offer **bonuses** for exceptional performance as an incentive to increase productivity further. Many workers receive a bonus as a "thank you" for good work and an incentive to continue working hard. Many owners and managers are recognizing that simple bonuses and perks foster happier employees and reduce turnover. For example, the owner of Ticketcity.com, a small business in Austin, Texas, offers employees tickets to major events like the Super Bowl, Master's golf tournament, and even management retreats. The owner of a DreamMaker remodeling franchise in Peoria, Illinois, provides employees money to use toward new vehicles, takes them on staff outings to sporting games, and funds their retirement plans.[24]

Another form of compensation is **profit sharing,** which distributes a percentage of company profits to the employees whose work helped to generate those profits. Some profit-sharing plans involve distributing shares of company stock to employees. Usually referred to as *ESOPs*—employee stock ownership plans—they have been gaining popularity in recent years. One reason for the popularity of ESOPs is the sense of partnership that they create between the organization and employees. Profit sharing can also motivate employees to work hard, because increased productivity and sales mean that the profits or the stock dividends will increase. Many organizations offer employees a stake in the company through stock purchase plans, ESOPs, or stock investments through 401(k) plans. Employees below senior management levels rarely received stock options, until recently. Companies are adopting broad-based stock option plans to build a stronger link between employees' interests and the organization's interests. A study by professors at the Wharton School of the University of Pennsylvania found that companies that paid middle managers 20 percent more in options than comparable companies saw increased performance and stock prices that rose an average 5 percent faster a year. Similar results were seen in companies that paid technical specialists at least 20 percent more in options.[25]

## Benefits

**Benefits** are nonfinancial forms of compensation provided to employees, such as pension plans for retirement; health, disability, and life insurance; holidays and paid days off for vacation or illness; credit union membership; health programs; child care; elder care; assistance with adoption; and more. According to the Bureau of Labor Statistics, employer costs for employee compensation for civilian workers in the United States average $28.11 per hour worked. Wages and salaries account for approximately 69.8 percent of those costs, while benefits account for 30.2 percent of the cost. Legally required benefits (Social Security, Medicare, federal and state employment insurance, and workers' compensation) account for 7.9 percent of total compensation.[26]

**bonuses**
monetary rewards offered by companies for exceptional performance as incentives to further increase productivity

**profit sharing**
a form of compensation whereby a percentage of company profits is distributed to the employees whose work helped to generate them

*The Principal Financial Group promotes the advantages of its group benefits plan.*

**benefits**
nonfinancial forms of compensation provided to employees, such as pension plans, health insurance, paid vacation and holidays, and the like

**TABLE II.7**

Best Entry-Level
Salaries

| Major | Salary |
|-------|--------|
| Computer science | $56,921 |
| Electrical engineering | 56,429 |
| Engineering | 56,336 |
| Economics | 52,926 |
| Nursing | 52,129 |
| Chemistry | 52,125 |
| Civil engineering | 49,427 |
| Finance | 48,795 |
| Accounting | 47,413 |
| Business administration and management | 43,823 |
| Political science/government | 43,594 |
| Marketing | 43,459 |
| Human resources | 40,250 |
| History | 35,956 |
| Communications | 35,196 |
| English language and literature | 34,757 |
| Journalism | 32,250 |
| Psychology | 30,877 |
| Public relations/organizational communications | 30,667 |

Source: Rachel Zupek, "Best Entry-Level Salaries for New Grads," *CNN.com,* April 28, 2008, http://www.cnn.com/2008/
LIVING/worklife/04/28/cb.salaries.grads/ (accessed May 16, 2008).

Such benefits increase employee security and, to a certain extent, their morale and motivation.

Table 11.8 lists some of the benefits Internet search engine Google offers its employees. Although health insurance is a common benefit for full-time employees, rising health care costs have forced a growing number of employers to trim this benefit. Microsoft, for example, recently reduced its prescription drug benefit, which had cost the company 16 percent of its overall benefit budget, and now requires employees to pay $40 for brand-name prescription drugs for which a generic version is available. The company still provides many generous benefits, including free gym memberships and free drinks on the job.[27]

A benefit increasingly offered is the employee assistance program (EAP). Each company's EAP is different, but most offer counseling for and assistance with those employees'personal problems that might hurt their job performance if not addressed. The most common counseling services offered include drug- and alcohol-abuse treatment programs, fitness programs, smoking cessation clinics, stress-management clinics, financial counseling, family counseling, and career counseling. EAPs help reduce costs associated with poor productivity, absenteeism, and other workplace issues by helping employees deal with personal problems that contribute to these issues. For example, exercise and fitness programs reduce health insurance costs by helping employees stay healthy. Family counseling may help workers trying to cope with a divorce or other personal problems better focus on their jobs.

- Health insurance:
  - Employee medical insurance (spouse and domestic-partner insurance also available)
  - Dental insurance
  - Vision insurance
- Vacation (15 days per year for one–three years' employment; 20 days off for four–five years' employment; 25 days for more than six years' employment)
- Twelve paid holidays/year
- Savings plans
  - 401(k) retirement plan, matched by Google up to $2,500/year
  - Flexible spending accounts
- Disability and life insurance
- Employee Assistance Program
- Free lunches, breakfast foods, and snacks
- Massages, gym membership, hair stylist, fitness class, and bike repair
- Weekly activities
- Maternity and parental leave
- Adoption assistance
- Tuition reimbursement
- Employee referral plan
- On-site doctor
- Google child care center and backup child care
- Ski trip, company movie day, summar picnic, health fair, credit union, sauna, roller hockey, discounts for local attractions

**TABLE II.8**

Google's Employees' Benefits

Source: "Google Benefits" http://www.google.com/support/jobs/bin/static.py?page=benefits.html (accessed May 16, 2008).

Companies try to provide the benefits they believe their employees want, but diverse people may want different things. In recent years, some single workers have felt that co-workers with spouses and children seem to get "special breaks" and extra time off to deal with family issues. Some companies use flexible benefit programs to allow employees to choose the benefits they would like, up to a specified amount.

Fringe benefits include sick leave, vacation pay, pension plans, health plans, as well as any other extra compensation. Soft benefits include perks that help balance life and work. They include onsite child care, spas, food service, and even laundry services and hair salons. These soft benefits motivate employees and give them more time to focus on their job.

Cafeteria benefit plans provide a financial amount to employees so that they can select the specific benefits that fit their needs. The key is making benefits flexible, rather than giving employees identical benefits. As firms go global, the need for cafeteria or flexible benefit plans becomes even more important. For some employees, benefits are a greater motivator and differentiator in jobs than wages. For many Starbucks employees who receive health insurance when working part time, this benefit could be the most important compensation.

Over the last two decades, the list of fringe benefits has grown dramatically, and new benefits are being added every year.

# Managing Unionized Employees

Employees who are dissatisfied with their working conditions or compensation have to negotiate with management to bring about change. Dealing with management on an individual basis is not always effective, however, so employees may organize themselves into **labor unions** to deal with employers and to achieve better pay, hours, and working conditions. Organized employees are backed by the power of a large group that can hire specialists to represent the entire union in its dealings with management. Union workers make significantly more than nonunion employees. Roughly 12 percent of the workforce is unionized. The national weekly median average income for a nonunion service worker is $404, or $10 per hour, versus a union workers wages of $629 per week, or $15 per hour. One of the more dramatic differences can be found in the construction industry, where unionized workers make nearly $10 per hour more.[28]

However, union growth has slowed in recent years, and prospects for growth do not look good. One reason is that most blue-collar workers, the traditional members of unions, have already been organized. Factories have become more automated and need fewer blue-collar workers. The United States has shifted from a manufacturing to a service economy, further reducing the demand for blue-collar workers. Moreover, in response to foreign competition, U.S. companies are scrambling to find ways to become more productive and cost efficient. Job enrichment programs and participative management have blurred the line between management and workers. Because workers' say in the way plants are run is increasing, their need for union protection is decreasing.

Nonetheless, labor unions have been successful in organizing blue-collar manufacturing, government, and health care workers, as well as smaller percentages of employees in other industries. Consequently, significant aspects of HRM, particularly compensation, are dictated to a large degree by union contracts at many companies. Therefore, we'll take a brief look at collective bargaining and dispute resolution in this section.

## Collective Bargaining

**Collective bargaining** is the negotiation process through which management and unions reach an agreement about compensation, working hours, and working conditions for the bargaining unit (Figure 11.5). The objective of negotiations is to reach agreement about a **labor contract,** the formal, written document that spells out the relationship between the union and management for a specified period of time, usually two or three years.

In collective bargaining, each side tries to negotiate an agreement that meets its demands; compromise is frequently necessary. Management tries to negotiate a labor contract that permits the company to retain control over things like work schedules; the hiring and firing of workers; production standards; promotions, transfers, and separations; the span of management in each department; and discipline. Unions tend to focus on contract issues such as magnitude of wages; better pay rates for overtime, holidays, and undesirable shifts; scheduling of pay increases; and benefits. These issues will be spelled out in the labor contract, which union members will vote to either accept (and abide by) or reject.

Many labor contracts contain a *cost-of-living escalator* (or *adjustment*) *(COLA) clause,* which calls for automatic wage increases during periods of inflation to protect the "real" income of the employees. During tough economic times, unions may be forced to accept *givebacks*—wage and benefit concessions made to employers to

**labor unions**
employee organizations formed to deal with employers for achieving better pay, hours, and working conditions

**collective bargaining**
the negotiation process through which management and unions reach an agreement about compensation, working hours, and working conditions for the bargaining unit

**labor contract**
the formal, written document that spells out the relationship between the union and management for a specified period of time—usually two or three years

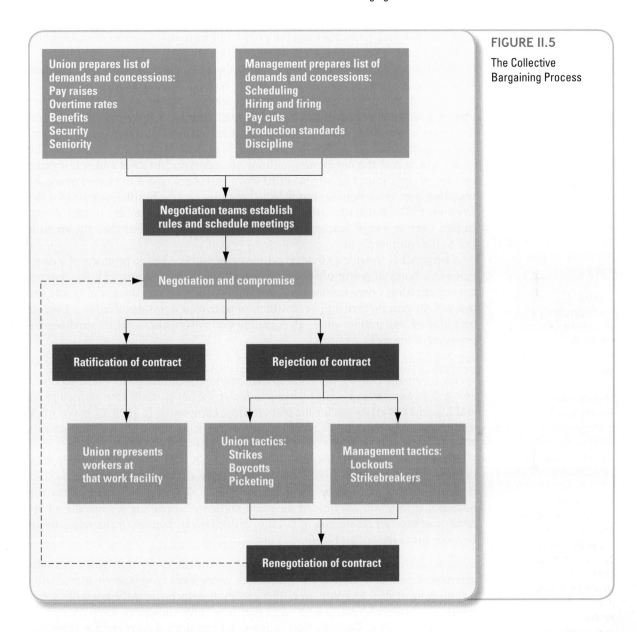

FIGURE II.5

The Collective
Bargaining Process

allow them to remain competitive or, in some cases, to survive and continue to provide jobs for union workers.

## Resolving Disputes

Sometimes, management and labor simply cannot agree on a contract. Most labor disputes are handled through collective bargaining or through grievance procedures. When these processes break down, however, either side may resort to more drastic measures to achieve its objectives.

Labor Tactics.   **Picketing** is a public protest against management practices and involves union members marching (often waving antimanagement signs and placards) at the employer's plant. Picketing workers hope that their signs will arouse

**picketing**
a public protest
against management
practices that involves
union members
marching and carrying
antimanagement signs
at the employer's plant

sympathy for their demands from the public and from other unions. Picketing may occur as a protest or in conjunction with a strike.

**strikes**
employee walkouts; one of the most effective weapons labor has

**Strikes** (employee walkouts) are one of the most effective weapons labor has. By striking, a union makes carrying out the normal operations of a business difficult at best and impossible at worst. Strikes receive widespread publicity, but they remain a weapon of last resort. In California, members of the United Food and Commercial Workers (UFCW) went on strike against Albertson's, Ralph's, and Von's supermarkets after they failed to reach agreement on a new contract. The strike, which cost the companies millions of dollars in lost sales and the striking employees significant lost wages, ended when members agreed to ratify a new contract that gave them bonuses but required them to pay for health insurance for the first time.[29] The threat of a strike is often enough to get management to back down. In fact, the number of worker-days actually lost to strikes is less than the amount lost to the common cold.

**boycott**
an attempt to keep people from purchasing the products of a company

A **boycott** is an attempt to keep people from purchasing the products of a company. In a boycott, union members are asked not to do business with the boycotted organization. Some unions may even impose fines on members who ignore the boycott. To gain further support for their objectives, a union involved in a boycott may also ask the public—through picketing and advertising—not to purchase the products of the picketed firm.

**lockout**
management's version of a strike, wherein a work site is closed so that employees cannot go to work

**Management Tactics.**   Management's version of a strike is the **lockout;** management actually closes a work site so that employees cannot go to work. Lockouts are used, as a general rule, only when a union strike has partially shut down a plant and it seems less expensive for the plant to close completely. In 2007, 21 major work stoppages involving 1,000 or more employees participating in strikes and lockouts idled 189,000 workers with 1.27 million lost workdays.[30]

**strikebreakers**
people hired by management to replace striking employees; called "scabs" by striking union members

**Strikebreakers,** called "scabs" by striking union members, are people hired by management to replace striking employees. Managers hire strikebreakers to continue operations and reduce the losses associated with strikes—and to show the unions that they will not bow to their demands. Strikebreaking is generally a last-resort measure for management because it does great damage to the relationship between management and labor.

**conciliation**
a method of outside resolution of labor and management differences in which a third party is brought in to keep the two sides talking

**Outside Resolution.**   Management and union members normally reach mutually agreeable decisions without outside assistance. Sometimes though, even after lengthy negotiations, strikes, lockouts, and other tactics, management and labor still cannot resolve a contract dispute. In such cases, they have three choices: conciliation, mediation, and arbitration. **Conciliation** brings in a neutral third party to keep labor and management talking. The conciliator has no formal power over union representatives or over management. The conciliator's goal is to get both parties to focus on the issues and to prevent negotiations from breaking down. Like conciliation, **mediation** involves bringing in a neutral third party, but the mediator's role is to suggest or propose a solution to the problem. Mediators have no formal power over either labor or management. With **arbitration,** a neutral third party is brought in to settle the dispute, but the arbitrator's solution is legally binding and enforceable. Generally, arbitration takes place on a voluntary basis—management and labor must agree to it, and they usually split the cost (the arbitrator's fee and expenses) between them. Occasionally, management and labor submit to *compulsory arbitration,* in which an outside party (usually the federal government) requests arbitration as a means of eliminating a prolonged strike that threatens to disrupt the economy.

**mediation**
a method of outside resolution of labor and management differences in which the third party's role is to suggest or propose a solution to the problem

**arbitration**
settlement of a labor/ management dispute by a third party whose solution is legally binding and enforceable

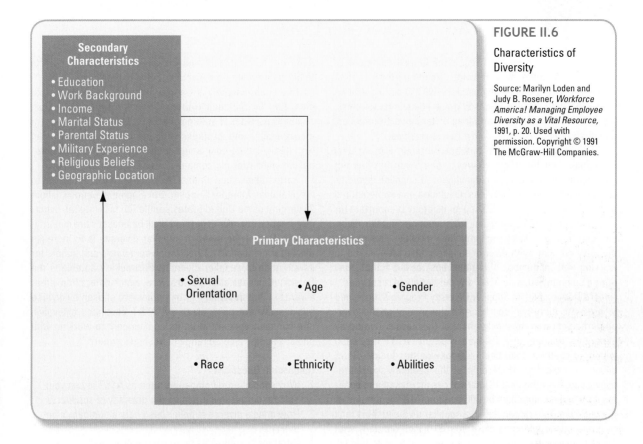

**FIGURE II.6**

Characteristics of Diversity

Source: Marilyn Loden and Judy B. Rosener, *Workforce America! Managing Employee Diversity as a Vital Resource*, 1991, p. 20. Used with permission. Copyright © 1991 The McGraw-Hill Companies.

# The Importance of Workforce Diversity

Customers, employees, suppliers—all the participants in the world of business—come in different ages, genders, races, ethnicities, nationalities, and abilities, a truth that business has come to label **diversity.** Understanding this diversity means recognizing and accepting differences as well as valuing the unique perspectives such differences can bring to the workplace.

**diversity**
the participation of different ages, genders, races, ethnicities, nationalities, and abilities in the workplace

## The Characteristics of Diversity

When managers speak of diverse workforces, they typically mean differences in gender and race. While gender and race are important characteristics of diversity, others are also important. We can divide these differences into primary and secondary characteristics of diversity. In the lower segment of Figure 11.6, age, gender, race, ethnicity, abilities, and sexual orientation represent *primary characteristics* of diversity which are inborn and cannot be changed. In the upper section of Figure 11.6 are eight *secondary characteristics* of diversity—work background, income, marital status, military experience, religious beliefs, geographic location, parental status, and education—which *can* be changed. We acquire, change, and discard them as we progress through our lives.

Defining characteristics of diversity as either primary or secondary enhances our understanding, but we must remember that each person is defined by the interrelation of all characteristics. In dealing with diversity in the workforce, managers must consider the complete person—not one or a few of a person's differences.

# Consider Ethics and Social Responsibility
## AT&T Achieves Supplier Diversity

According to revenue, AT&T Inc. is the largest communications holding company worldwide. Headquartered in San Antonio, Texas, the company employs 309,050 people around the globe and provides IP-based communications; wireless, high-speed Internet; local and long distance voice services; and directory publishing and advertising services.

AT&T is a company that has been through a great deal of change over the years. However, one thing that has not changed is the company's commitment to supplier diversity. For the past 39 years, AT&T has developed and implemented supplier diversity practices. Supplier diversity is important for a number of reasons; for example, promoting supplier diversity can help to improve communities in which businesses operate. Working with diverse suppliers also often leads to working with a number of smaller businesses, which may offer a company such as AT&T a wider variety of resources.

AT&T developed its Supplier Diversity Programs, designed to promote, increase, and improve the quality of the overall participation in its supply chain of businesses owned by minorities, women, and disabled veterans. AT&T has been willing to spend a good deal of money on this focus—$5.15 billion, representing 13 percent of the company's procurement base. Over the past 10 years, it has increased its spending with diverse suppliers by 300 percent. AT&T is a member of the Billion Dollar Roundtable, a supplier diversity think tank of corporations spending more than $1 billion annually with diverse companies. Only 12 companies qualify at this level.

AT&T has also set itself a goal of acquiring 21.5 percent of its total procurement from diversity-owned enterprises.

One such company is Georgia-based Metasys Technologies. Run by Sandeep Gauba, the Asian Indian–American company provides IT staffing solutions, services procurement management, and business process outsourcing. Working with heavy-hitting companies such as AT&T has helped propel the eight-year-old company to sales above $10 million.

Partnerships such as this are critical. Today, according to the National Minority Supplier Development Council, about 28 percent of the United States population falls into the minority category, but only 15 percent of all businesses are minority-owned. One of the goals of supplier diversity is to increase this latter number. AT&T has received awards and honors for its attention to supplier diversity. Particularly notable is the DiversityBusiness.com Top 50 award, which differs from other awards in that the winning companies are chosen by diverse businessowners themselves. As AT&T continues to evolve, one constant appears to be its commitment to working with and assisting a diverse range of businessowners.[31]

**Discussion Questions**

1. Why should large companies such as AT&T invest valuable resources in increasing the diversity of suppliers?
2. How does a diverse supplier base help a company's bottom line?
3. What else could AT&T do to ensure diversity?

---

**TABLE II.9**

Population by Race (in thousands)

| Ethnic Group | Total | Increase from 2000 to 2004 |
|---|---|---|
| Total population | 293,655.4 (100%) | 4.3% |
| White | 239,880.1 (81.7%) | 3.6 |
| Hispanic or Latino | 41,322.1 (14.1%) | 17.0 |
| Black or African American | 39,232.5 (13.4%) | 5.7 |
| American Indian and Alaska Native | 4,409.4 (1.5%) | 7.7 |
| Asian | 13,956.6 (4.8%) | 16.2 |
| Native Hawaiian and Other Pacific Islander | 976.4 (0.3%) | 7.7 |

Source: "Population by Race and Hispanic Origin: 2000 and 2004," U.S. Census Bureau, Population Estimates Program, April 1, 2000, and July 1, 2004, www.census.gov/population/pop-profile/dynamic/RACEHO.pdf (updated February 2007, accessed June 6, 2008).

## Why Is Diversity Important?

The U.S. workforce is becoming increasingly diverse. Once dominated by white men, today's workforce includes significantly more women, African Americans, Hispanics, and other minorities, as well as disabled and older workers. By 2010,

| | | |
|---|---|---|
| 1. Verizon Communications | 26. Wells Fargo & Co. | **TABLE 11.10** |
| 2. The Coca-Cola Co. | 27. Ford Motor Co. | The *Diversity Inc.* |
| 3. Bank of America | 28. PepsiCo | Top 50 Companies for |
| 4. PricewaterhouseCoopers | 29. Pepsi Bottling Group | Diversity® |
| 5. Procter & Gamble | 30. Xerox Corp. | |
| 6. Cox Communications | 31. Novartis Pharmaceuticals Corp. | |
| 7. Merrill Lynch & Co. | 32. General Mills | |
| 8. Johnson & Johnson | 33. KeyBank | |
| 9. IBM | 34. Health Care Service Corp. | |
| 10. American Express | 35. Sprint | |
| 11. Marriott International | 36. The Walt Disney Co. | |
| 12. Sodexo | 37. Abbott | |
| 13. JPMorgan Chase | 38. Accenture | |
| 14. Wachovia | 39. Macy's | |
| 15. Blue Cross and Blue Shield of Florida | 40. Henry Ford Health System | |
| 16. Deloitte LLP | 41. Bright Horizons Family Solutions | |
| 17. Ernst & Young | 42. WellPoint | |
| 18. HSBC Bank USA, NA | 43. Kaiser Permanente | |
| 19. Starwood Hotels & Resorts Worldwide | 44. General Motors | |
| 20. Cummins | 45. Citigroup | |
| 21. Merck & Co. | 46. Capital One Financial Corp. | |
| 22. AT&T | 47. CSX | |
| 23. Turner Broadcasting System | 48. Toyota Motor North America | |
| 24. Prudential | 49. KPMG | |
| 25. Monsanto Co. | 50. Hilton Hotels Corp. | |

Source: From http://www.diversityinc.com/public/3272.cfm (accessed May 16, 2008). Reprinted with permission of DiversityInc®.

women's share of the labor force will increase to 47.9 percent.[32] Table 11.9 presents some of the population data from the Census Bureau. It is estimated that within the next 50 years, Hispanics will represent 24 percent of the population, while African Americans and Asians/Pacific Islanders will comprise 15 percent and 9 percent, respectively.[33] These groups have traditionally faced discrimination and higher unemployment rates and have been denied opportunities to assume leadership roles in corporate America. Consequently, more and more companies are trying to improve HRM programs to recruit, develop, and retain more diverse employees to better serve their diverse customers. Some firms are providing special programs such as sponsored affinity groups, mentoring programs, and special career development opportunities. At US West, each manager's contributions to the company's diversity efforts are measured by a 16-point scorecard called the Diversity Accountability Tool. Managers use the scorecard to rate their own efforts to foster diversity and then explain their score in a meeting with the company's CEO. The manager receives an official diversity score that is one factor in determining the manager's annual bonus. Since the program was instituted, scores have jumped 60 percent.[34] Table 11.10 shows the top 20 companies for minorities according to a study by *Diversity, Inc.* Effectively managing diversity in the workforce involves cultivating and valuing its benefits and minimizing its problems.

## The Benefits of Workforce Diversity

There are a number of benefits to fostering and valuing workforce diversity, including the following:

1. More productive use of a company's human resources.
2. Reduced conflict among employees of different ethnicities, races, religions, and sexual orientations as they learn to respect each other's differences.
3. More productive working relationships among diverse employees as they learn more about and accept each other.
4. Increased commitment to and sharing of organizational goals among diverse employees at all organizational levels.
5. Increased innovation and creativity as diverse employees bring new, unique perspectives to decision-making and problem-solving tasks.
6. Increased ability to serve the needs of an increasingly diverse customer base.[35]

Companies that do not value their diverse employees are likely to experience greater conflict, as well as prejudice and discrimination. Among individual employees, for example, racial slurs and gestures, sexist comments, and other behaviors by co-workers harm the individuals at whom such behavior is directed. The victims of such behavior may feel hurt, depressed, or even threatened and suffer from lowered self-esteem, all of which harm their productivity and morale. In such cases, women and minority employees may simply leave the firm, wasting the time, money, and other resources spent on hiring and training them. When discrimination comes from a supervisor, employees may also fear for their jobs. A discriminatory atmosphere not only can harm productivity and increase turnover, but it may also subject a firm to costly lawsuits and negative publicity.

Astute businesses recognize that they need to modify their human resources management programs to target the needs of *all* their diverse employees as well as the needs of the firm itself. They realize that the benefits of diversity are long term in nature and come only to those organizations willing to make the commitment. Most importantly, as workforce diversity becomes a valued organizational asset, companies spend less time managing conflict and more time accomplishing tasks and satisfying customers, which is, after all, the purpose of business.

## Affirmative Action

**affirmative action programs**
legally mandated plans that try to increase job opportunities for minority groups by analyzing the current pool of workers, identifying areas where women and minorities are underrepresented, and establishing specific hiring and promotion goals, with target dates, for addressing the discrepancy

Many companies strive to improve their working environment through **affirmative action programs,** legally mandated plans that try to increase job opportunities for minority groups by analyzing the current pool of workers, identifying areas where women and minorities are underrepresented, and establishing specific hiring and promotion goals along with target dates for meeting those goals to resolve the discrepancy. Affirmative action began in 1965 as Lyndon B. Johnson issued the first of a series of presidential directives. It was designed to make up for past hiring and promotion prejudices, to overcome workplace discrimination, and to provide equal employment opportunities for blacks and whites. Since then, minorities have made solid gains.

Legislation passed in 1991 reinforces affirmative action but prohibits organizations from setting hiring quotas that might result in reverse discrimination. Reverse discrimination occurs when a company's policies force it to consider only minorities or women instead of concentrating on hiring the person who is best qualified. More companies are arguing that affirmative action stifles their ability to hire the best employees, regardless of their minority status. Because of these problems, affirmative action became politically questionable in the mid-1990s.

# So You Want to Work in Human Resources

Managing human resources is a challenging and creative facet of a business. It is the department that handles the recruiting, hiring, training, and firing of employees. Because of the diligence and detail required in hiring and the sensitivity required in firing, human resource managers have a broad skill set. Human resources, therefore, is vital to the overall functioning of the business because without the right staff a firm will not be able to effectively carry out its plans. Like in basketball, a team is only as strong as its individual players, and those players must be able to work together and to enhance strengths and downplay weaknesses. In addition, a good human resource manager can anticipate upcoming needs and changes in the business, hiring in line with the dynamics of the market and organization.

Once a good workforce is in place, human resource managers must ensure that employees are properly trained and oriented and that they clearly understand some elements of what the organization expects. Hiring new people is expensive, time consuming, and turbulent; thus, it is imperative that all employees are carefully selected, trained, and motivated so that they will remain committed and loyal to the company. This is not an easy task, but it is one of the responsibilities of the human resources manager. Because even with references, a résumé, background checks, and an interview, it can be hard to tell how a person will fit in the organization—the HR manager needs to have skills to be able to anticipate how every individual will "fit in." Human resource jobs include compensation, labor relations, benefits, training,

ethics, and compliance managers. All of the tasks associated with the interface with hiring, developing, and maintaining employee motivation come into play in human resource management. Jobs are diverse and salaries will depend on responsibilities, education, and experience.

One of the major considerations for an HR manager is workforce diversity. A multicultural, multiethnic workforce consisting of men and women will help to bring a variety of viewpoints and improve the quality and creativity of organizational decision making. Diversity is an asset and can help a company from having blindspots or harmony in thought, background, and perspective, which stifles good team decisions. However, a diverse workforce can present some management challenges. Human resource management is often responsible for managing diversity training and compliance to make sure employees do not violate the ethical culture of the organization or break the law. Different people have different goals, motivations, and ways of thinking about issues that are informed by their culture, religion, and the people closest to them. No one way of thinking is more right or more wrong and than others, and they are all valuable. A human resource manager's job can become very complicated, however, because of diversity. To be good at human resources, you should be aware the value of differences, strive to be culturally sensitive, and ideally should have a strong understanding and appreciation of different cultures and religions. Human resource managers' ability to manage diversity and those differences will affect their overall career success.

# Review Your Understanding

### Define human resources management, and explain its significance.

Human resources, or personnel, management refers to all the activities involved in determining an organization's human resources needs and acquiring, training, and compensating people to fill those needs. It is concerned with maximizing the satisfaction of employees and improving their efficiency to meet organizational objectives.

### Summarize the processes of recruiting and selecting human resources for a company.

First, the human resources manager must determine the firm's future human resources needs and develop a strategy to meet them. Recruiting is the formation of a pool of qualified applicants from which management will select

employees; it takes place both internally and externally. Selection is the process of collecting information about applicants and using that information to decide which ones to hire; it includes the application, interviewing, testing, and reference checking.

### Discuss how workers are trained and their performance appraised.

Training teaches employees how to do their specific job tasks; development is training that augments the skills and knowledge of managers and professionals, as well as current employees. Appraising performance involves identifying an employee's strengths and weaknesses on the job. Performance appraisals may be subjective or objective.

*Identify the types of turnover companies may experience, and explain why turnover is an important issue.*

A promotion is an advancement to a higher-level job with increased authority, responsibility, and pay. A transfer is a move to another job within the company at essentially the same level and wage. Separations occur when employees resign, retire, are terminated, or are laid off. Turnovers due to separation are expensive because of the time, money, and effort required to select, train, and manage new employees.

*Specify the various ways a worker may be compensated.*

Wages are financial compensation based on the number of hours worked (time wages) or the number of units produced (piece wages). Commissions are a fixed amount or a percentage of a sale paid as compensation. Salaries are compensation calculated on a weekly, monthly, or annual basis, regardless of the number of hours worked or the number of items produced. Bonuses and profit sharing are types of financial incentives. Benefits are nonfinancial forms of compensation, such as vacation, insurance, and sick leave.

*Discuss some of the issues associated with unionized employees, including collective bargaining and dispute resolution.*

Collective bargaining is the negotiation process through which management and unions reach an agreement on a labor contract—the formal, written document that spells out the relationship written between the union and management. If labor and management cannot agree on a contract, labor union members may picket, strike, or boycott the firm, while management may lock out striking employees, hire strikebreakers, or form employers' associations. In a deadlock, labor disputes may be resolved by a third party—a conciliator, mediator, or arbitrator.

*Describe the importance of diversity in the workforce.*

When companies value and effectively manage their diverse workforces, they experience more productive use of human resources, reduced conflict, better work relationships among workers, increased commitment to and sharing of organizational goals, increased innovation and creativity, and enhanced ability to serve diverse customers.

*Assess an organization's efforts to reduce its workforce size and manage the resulting effects.*

Based on the material in this chapter, you should be able to answer the questions posed in "Solve the Dilemma" on page 351 and evaluate the company's efforts to manage the human consequences of its downsizing.

# Revisit the World of Business

1.  How do you think employees' opinions about fair compensation change during an economic slowdown?

2.  How can employees who receive commissions maintain their pay if their industry has declining sales?

3.  Do you think that allowing employees more flexible scheduling of work hours can be an important contribution to a satisfying work experience?

# Learn the Terms

affirmative action programs   346
arbitration   342
benefits   337
bonuses   377
boycott   342
collective bargaining   340
commission   336
conciliation   342
development   330
diversity   343
human resources
  management (HRM)   322

job analysis   323
job description   323
job specification   323
labor contract   340
labor unions   340
lockout   342
mediation   342
orientation   329
picketing   341
profit sharing   337
promotion   332
recruiting   324

salary   336
selection   324
separations   333
strikebreakers   342
strikes   342
Title VII of the Civil Rights Act   328
training   329
transfer   332
turnover   331
wage/salary survey   335
wages   335

# Check Your Progress

1. Distinguish among job analysis, job descriptions, and job specifications. How do they relate to planning in human resources management?

2. What activities are involved in acquiring and maintaining the appropriate level of qualified human resources? Name the stages of the selection process.

3. What are the two types of training programs? Relate training to kinds of jobs.

4. What is the significance of performance appraisal? How do managers appraise employees?

5. Why does turnover occur? List the types of turnover. Why do businesses want to reduce turnover due to separations?

6. Relate wages, salaries, bonuses, and benefits to Herzberg's distinction between hygiene and motivation factors. How does the form of compensation relate to the type of job?

7. What is the role of benefits? Name some examples of benefits.

8. Describe the negotiation process through which management and unions reach an agreement on a contract.

9. Besides collective bargaining and the grievance procedures, what other alternatives are available to labor and management to handle labor disputes?

10. What are the benefits associated with a diverse workforce?

# Get Involved

1. Although many companies screen applicants and test employees for illegal drug use, such testing is somewhat controversial. Find some companies in your community that test applicants and/or employees for drugs. Why do they have such a policy? How do the employees feel about it? Using this information, debate the pros and cons of drug testing in the workplace.

2. If collective bargaining and the grievance procedures have not been able to settle a current labor dispute, what tactics would you and other employees adopt? Which tactics would be best for which situations? Give examples.

3. Find some examples of companies that value their diverse workforces, perhaps some of the companies mentioned in the chapter. In what ways have these firms derived benefits from promoting cultural diversity? How have they dealt with the problems associated with cultural diversity?

# Build Your Skills

## APPRECIATING AND VALUING DIVERSITY

**Background:**
Here's a quick self-assessment to get you to think about diversity issues and evaluate the behaviors you exhibit that reflect your level of appreciation of other cultures:

| Do you . . . | Regularly | Sometimes | Never |
|---|---|---|---|
| 1.  Make a conscious effort not to think stereotypically? | | | |
| 2.  Listen with interest to the ideas of people who don't think like you do? | | | |
| 3.  Respect other people's opinions, even when you disagree? | | | |
| 4.  Spend time with friends who are not your age, race, gender, or the same economic status and education? | | | |
| 5.  Believe your way is *not* the only way? | | | |
| 6.  Adapt well to change and new situations? | | | |
| 7.  Enjoy traveling, seeing new places, eating different foods, and experiencing other cultures? | | | |
| 8.  Try not to offend or hurt others? | | | |
| 9.  Allow extra time to communicate with someone whose first language is not yours? | | | |
| 10.  Consider the effect of cultural differences on the messages you send and adjust them accordingly? | | | |

Scoring

Number of **Regularly** checks  _____  multiplied by 5 = _____
Number of **Sometimes** checks  _____  multiplied by 3 = _____
Number of **Never** checks  _____  multiplied by 0 = _____
                                                  TOTAL _____

Indications from score

40–50     You appear to understand the importance of valuing diversity and exhibit behaviors that support your appreciation of diversity.

26–39     You appear to have a basic understanding of the importance of valuing diversity and exhibit some behaviors that support that understanding.

13–25     You appear to lack a thorough understanding of the importance of valuing diversity and exhibit only some behaviors related to valuing diversity.

0–12      You appear to lack an understanding of valuing diversity and exhibit few, if any, behaviors of an individual who appreciates and values diversity.

**Task:**

In a small group or class discussion, share the results of your assessment. After reading the following list of ways you can increase your knowledge and understanding of other cultures, select one of the items that you have done and share how it helped you learn more about another culture. Finish your discussion by generating your own ideas on other ways you can learn about and understand other cultures and fill in those ideas on the blank lines on page 351.

- Be alert to and take advantage of opportunities to talk to and get to know people from other races and ethnic groups. You can find them in your neighborhood, in your classes, at your fitness center, at a concert or sporting event—just about anywhere you go. Take the initiative to strike up a conversation and show a genuine interest in getting to know the other person.

- Select a culture you're interested in and immerse yourself in that culture. Read novels, look at art, take courses, see plays.

- College students often have unique opportunities to travel inexpensively to other countries—for example, as a member of a performing arts group, with a humanitarian mission group, or as part of a college course studying abroad. Actively seek out travel opportunities that will expose you to as many cultures as possible during your college education.

- Study a foreign language.

- Expand your taste buds. The next time you're going to go to a restaurant, instead of choosing that old familiar favorite, use the Yellow Pages to find a restaurant that serves ethnic food you've never tried before.

- Many large metropolitan cities sponsor ethnic festivals, particularly in the summertime, where you can go and take in the sights and sounds of other cultures. Take advantage of these opportunities to have a fun time learning about cultures that are different from yours.

- _____

  _____

- _____

  _____

# Solve the Dilemma

## Morale Among the Survivors

Medallion Corporation manufactures quality carpeting and linoleum for homes throughout the United States. A recession and subsequent downturn in home sales has sharply cut the company's sales. Medallion found itself in the unenviable position of having to lay off hundreds of employees in the home office (the manufacturing facilities) as well as many salespeople. Employees were called in on Friday afternoon and told about their status in individual meetings with their supervisors. The laid-off employees were given one additional month of work and a month of severance pay, along with the opportunity to sign up for classes to help with the transition, including job search tactics and résumé writing.

Several months after the cutbacks, morale was at an all-time low for the company, although productivity had improved. Medallion brought in consultants, who suggested that the leaner, flatter organizational structure would be suitable for more team activities. Medallion therefore set up task forces and teams to deal with employee concerns, but the diversity of the workforce led to conflict and misunderstandings among team members. Medallion is evaluating how to proceed with this new team approach.

### Discussion Questions

1. What did Medallion's HRM department do right in dealing with the employees who were laid off?

2. What are some of the potential problems that must be dealt with after an organization experiences a major trauma such as massive layoffs?

3. What can Medallion do to make the team approach work more smoothly? What role do you think diversity training should play?

# Build Your Business Plan

## MANAGING HUMAN RESOURCES

Now is the time to start thinking about the employees you will need to hire to implement your business plan. What kinds of background/skills are you going to look for in potential employees? Are you going to require a certain amount of work experience?

When you are starting a business you are often only able to hire part-time employees because you cannot afford to pay the benefits for a full time employee. Remember at the end of the last chapter we discussed how important it is to think of ways to motivate your employees when you cannot afford to pay them what you would like.

You need to consider how you are going to recruit your employees. When you are first starting your business, it is often a good idea to ask people you respect (and not necessarily members of your family) for any recommendations of potential employees they might have. You probably won't be able to afford to advertise in the classifieds, so announcements in sources such as church bulletins or community bulletin boards should be considered as an excellent way to attract potential candidates with little, if any, investment.

Finally, you need to think about hiring employees from diverse backgrounds. Especially if you are considering targeting diverse segments. The more diverse your employees, the greater the chance you will be able to draw in diverse customers.

# See for Yourself Videocase

## PATAGONIA FOCUSES ON EMPLOYEES AND THE ENVIRONMENT

Combine "there is no business on a dead planet" (a quote from the executive director of the Sierra Club, posted in Patagonia's front office next to daily surf reports) with "let my people surf" (the title of Yvon Chouinard's recent book), and you sum up much of what Patagonia and its founder, Yvon Chouinard, are all about. Patagonia, maker of outdoor equipment, clothing, and more, is truly a unique company. The company was founded more than 35 years ago and now boasts 1,300 employees and $275 million per year in sales. From the beginning, Chouinard and his wife and business partner, Malinda, declared that they would establish a business only on their own terms of environmental preservation above all else. The company's values are minimalistic, are in harmony with nature, and reflect those of a business founded by climbers and surfers. However, the company is not only dedicated to the environment; it's also dedicated to its people. Chouinard and those at Patagonia believe strongly that employees are to be treated as human beings whose lives outside of work are honored and attended to.

Chouinard has built Patagonia's culture based on a commitment to his ideals. To this end, Patagonia encourages all employees to balance work, play, and family and maintains a highly casual atmosphere. Unlike in many businesses where employees often leave their true personalities at the door to conform to business policies, at Patagonia Chouinard wants employees to retain who they are at all times. Chouinard, himself, is a passionate and dedicated mountain climber, surfer, and skier. He spends at least half the year in the field doing what he loves: testing Patagonia's many products and spreading Patagonia's message of environmental preservation. Much of the workforce the company attracts shares the same passions. During Patagonia's early days, the entire office (located in Ventura, California, near the beach) closed when the surf was good. Today, employees are expected to use their lunch "hours" to surf, cycle, or take company-offered yoga and Pilates classes. Patagonia employees work on flextime. When the surf is up or the snow is good, they are encouraged to go out and take advantage, and the company trusts them to make up the work time.

Benefits at Patagonia don't stop there. The company has run a child care facility at its headquarters since 1985. Here, children remain close to their parents and are considered to be as much a part of the company as its employees. The company also offers paid maternity and paternity leave and believes that if children are ever ill, the parents should be with them rather than at work. One hundred percent of insurance premiums are paid for both full- and part-time employees. Because many Patagonia employees share Chouinard's dedication to the environment, after one year of employment Patagonia covers up to 60 days worth of an employee's salary, enabling employees to take time to volunteer with grassroots organizations. Employees are simply asked to report back about their experiences upon their return. In 1985, Patagonia created the Patagonia Earth Tax. The company gives back 1 percent of sales to environmental grassroots organizations. Employees from all parts of the company serve on a council where they work together to determine which organizations the company will support.

Patagonia has received criticism from the business community for its unorthodox business practices, but employees are loyal. In fact, there are about 900 applicants for every job opening at Patagonia's headquarters. Because competition is so fierce, those who make it through are entirely committed to Chouinard, the company, and Patagonia's values. For all that Patagonia appears laidback, Chouinard and his team are striving for perfection—the highest quality with the least impact—every day. Annual turnover at Patagonia is only 4 percent. Chouinard has been quoted saying that to grow his business the way he could—to become a huge, massively profitable corporation—would be to destroy everything he believes in and has strived for from the beginning. Critics have been harsh about his inclination toward hiring the most cause-oriented rather than the most skilled employees (a point hotly contested by employees, to be sure), but there is much to be said for passionate people. Chouinard's employees value what they have at Patagonia and protect it with thorough dedication, and no one can deny that the company is a success.[36]

**Discussion Questions:**

1. How do Chouinard's personal and work values affect the daily lives of Patagonia employees?

2. What does Patagonia do for its employees to inspire such loyalty and fierce competition for jobs?

3. What can other businesses learn from Chouinard and Patagonia?

**Remember to check out our Online Learning Center at www.mhhe.com/ferrell7e.**

# Appendix C

# Personal Career Plan

The tools and techniques used in creating a business plan are just as useful in designing a plan to help sell yourself to potential employers. The outline in this appendix is designed to assist you in writing a personalized plan that will help you achieve your career goals. While this outline follows the same general format found in Appendix A, it has been adapted to be more relevant to career planning. Answering the questions presented in this outline will enable you to:

1. Organize and structure the data and information you collect about job prospects, the overall job market, and your competition.
2. Use this information to better understand your own personal strengths and weaknesses, as well as recognize the opportunities and threats that exist in your career development.
3. Develop goals and objectives that will capitalize on your strengths.
4. Develop a personalized strategy that will give you a competitive advantage.
5. Outline a plan for implementing your personalized strategy.

As you work through the following outline, it is very important that you be honest with yourself. If you do not possess a strength in a given area, it is important to recognize that fact. Similarly, do not overlook your weaknesses. The viability of your SWOT analysis and your strategy depend on how well you have identified all of the relevant issues in an honest manner.

## I. Summary
If you choose to write a summary, do so after you have written the entire plan. It should provide a brief overview of the strategy for your career. State your career objectives and what means you will use to achieve those objectives.

## II. Situation Analysis
### A. The External Environment
#### 1. Competition
   a) Who are your major competitors? What are their characteristics (number and growth in the number of graduates, skills, target employers)? Competitors to consider include peers at the same college or in the same degree field, peers at different colleges or in different degree fields, and graduates of trade, technical, or community colleges.
   b) What are the key strengths and weaknesses of the total pool of potential employees (or recent college graduates)?
   c) What are other college graduates doing in terms of developing skills, networking, showing a willingness to relocate, and promoting themselves to potential employers?
   d) What are the current trends in terms of work experience versus getting an advanced degree?
   e) Is your competitive set likely to change in the future? If so, how? Who are these new competitors likely to be?

#### 2. Economic conditions
   a) What are the general economic conditions of the country, region, state, and local area in which you live or in which you want to relocate?
   b) Overall, are potential employers optimistic or pessimistic about the economy?
   c) What is the overall outlook for major job/career categories? Where do potential employers seem to be placing their recruitment and hiring emphasis?
   d) What is the trend in terms of starting salaries for major job/career categories?

3. **Political trends**
    a) Have recent elections changed the political landscape so that certain industries or companies are now more or less attractive as potential employers?

4. **Legal and regulatory factors**
    a) What changes in international, federal, state, or local laws and regulations are being proposed that would affect your job/career prospects?
    b) Have recent court decisions made it easier or harder for you to find employment?
    c) Have global trade agreements changed in any way that makes certain industries or companies more or less attractive as potential employers?

5. **Changes in technology**
    a) What impact has changing technology had on potential employers in terms of their need for employees?
    b) What technological changes will affect the way you will have to work and compete for employment in the future?
    c) What technological changes will affect the way you market your skills and abilities to potential employers?
    d) How do technological advances threaten to make your skills and abilities obsolete?

6. **Cultural trends**
    a) How are society's demographics and values changing? What effect will these changes have on your:
        (1) Skills and abilities:
        (2) Career/lifestyle choices:
        (3) Ability to market yourself:
        (4) Willingness to relocate:
        (5) Required minimum salary:
    b) What problems or opportunities are being created by changes in the cultural diversity of the labor pool and the requirements of potential employers?

    c) What is the general attitude of society regarding the particular skills, abilities, and talents that you possess and the career/lifestyle choices that you have made?

B. **The Employer Environment**
1. **Who are your potential employers?**
    a) Identifying characteristics: industry, products, size, growth, profitability, hiring practices, union/nonunion, employee needs, etc.
    b) Geographic characteristics: home office, local offices, global sites, expansion, etc.
    c) Organizational culture: mission statement, values, priorities, employee training, etc.
    d) In each organization, who is responsible for recruiting and selecting new employees?

2. **What do your potential employers look for in new employees?**
    a) What are the basic or specific skills and abilities that employers are looking for in new employees?
    b) What are the basic or specific needs that are fulfilled by the skills and abilities that you *currently* possess and that other potential employees currently possess?
    c) How well do your skills and abilities (and those of your competitors) currently meet the needs of potential employers?
    d) How are the needs of potential employers expected to change in the future?

3. **What are the recent hiring practices of your potential employers?**
    a) How many employees are being hired? What combination of skills and abilities do these new hires possess?
    b) Is the growth or decline in hiring related to the recent expansion or downsizing of markets and/or territories? Changes in technology?
    c) Are there major hiring differences between large and small companies? If so, why?

4.  **Where and how do your potential employers recruit new employees?**
    a)  Where do employers make contact with potential employees?
        (1) College placement offices:
        (2) Job/career fairs:
        (3) Internship programs:
        (4) Headhunting firms:
        (5) Unsolicited applications:
        (6) The Internet:
    b)  Do potential employers place a premium on experience or are they willing to hire new graduates without experience?
5.  **When do your potential employers recruit new employees?**
    a)  Does recruiting follow a seasonal pattern or do employers recruit new employees on an ongoing basis?

C.  **Personal Assessment**
1.  **Review of personal goals, objectives, and performance**
    a)  What are your personal goals and objectives in terms of employment, career, lifestyle, geographic preferences, etc.?
    b)  Are your personal goals and objectives consistent with the realities of the labor market? Why or why not?
    c)  Are your personal goals and objectives consistent with recent changes in the external or employer environments? Why or why not?
    d)  How are your current strategies for success working in areas such as course performance, internships, networking, job leads, career development, interviewing skills, etc.?
    e)  How does your current performance compare to that of your peers (competitors)? Are they performing well in terms of course performance, internships, networking, job leads, career development, interviewing skills, etc.?
    f)  If your performance is declining, what is the most likely cause?

g)  If your performance is improving, what actions can you take to ensure that your performance continues in this direction?
2.  **Inventory of personal skills and resources**
    a)  What do you consider to be your marketable skills? This list should be as comprehensive as possible and include areas such as interpersonal skills, organizational skills, technological skills, communication skills (oral and written), networking/teambuilding skills, etc.
    b)  Considering the current and future needs of your potential employers, what important skills are you lacking?
    c)  Other than personal skills, what do you consider to be your other career enhancing resources? This list should be as comprehensive as possible and include areas such as financial resources (to pay for additional training, if necessary), personal contacts or "connections" with individuals who can assist your career development, specific degrees or certificates you hold, and intangible resources (family name, prestige of your educational institution, etc.).
    d)  Considering the current and future needs of your potential employers, what important resources are you lacking?

III.  **SWOT Analysis (your personal strengths and weaknesses and the opportunities and threats that may impact your career)**
A.  **Personal Strengths**
1.  Three key strengths
    a)  Strength 1:
    b)  Strength 2:
    c)  Strength 3:
2.  How do these strengths allow you to meet the needs of your potential employers?
3.  How do these strengths compare to those of your peers/competitors? Do

these strengths give you an advantage
relative to your peers/competitors?
- **B. Personal Weaknesses**
  1. Three key weaknesses
     - **a)** Weakness 1:
     - **b)** Weakness 2:
     - **c)** Weakness 3:
  2. How do these weaknesses cause you to
     fall short of meeting the needs of your
     potential employers?
  3. How do these weaknesses compare
     to those of your peers/competitors?
     Do these weaknesses put you at a
     disadvantage relative to your peers/
     competitors?
- **C. Career Opportunities**
  1. Three key career opportunities
     - **a)** Opportunity 1:
     - **b)** Opportunity 2:
     - **c)** Opportunity 3:
  2. How are these opportunities related
     to serving the needs of your potential
     employers?
  3. What actions must be taken to capitalize
     on these opportunities in the short-
     term? In the long-term?
- **D. Career Threats**
  1. Three key career threats
     - **a)** Threat 1:
     - **b)** Threat 2:
     - **c)** Threat 3:
  2. How are these threats related to serving
     the needs of your potential employers?
  3. What actions must be taken to prevent
     these threats from limiting your
     capabilities in the short-term? In the
     long-term?
- **E. The SWOT Matrix**
- **F. Matching, Converting, Minimizing, and
  Avoiding Strategies**
  1. How can you match your strengths to
     your opportunities to better serve the
     needs of your potential employers?
  2. How can you convert your weaknesses
     into strengths?
  3. How can you convert your threats into
     opportunities?
  4. How can you minimize or avoid those
     weaknesses and threats that cannot be
     converted successfully?

- **IV. Resources**
  - **A. Financial**
    1. Do you have the financial resources
       necessary to undertake and successfully
       complete this plan (that is, preparation/
       duplication/mailing of a résumé;
       interviewing costs, including proper
       attire; etc.)?
  - **B. Human**
    1. Is the industry in which you are
       interested currently hiring? Are
       companies in your area currently hiring?
  - **C. Experience and Expertise**
    1. Do you have experience from either
       part-time or summer employment that
       could prove useful in your current plan?
    2. Do you have the required expertise or
       skills to qualify for a job in your desired
       field? If not, do you have the resources
       to obtain them?

- **V. Strategies**
  - **A. Objective(s)**
    1. Potential employer A:
       - **a)** Descriptive characteristics:
       - **b)** Geographic locations:
       - **c)** Culture/values/mission:
       - **d)** Basic employee needs:
       - **e)** Recruiting/hiring practices:
       - **f)** Employee training/compensation
         practices:
       - **g)** Justification for selection:
    2. Potential employer B:
       - **a)** Descriptive characteristics:
       - **b)** Geographic locations:
       - **c)** Culture/values/mission:
       - **d)** Basic employee needs:
       - **e)** Recruiting/hiring practices:
       - **f)** Employee training/compensation
         practices:
       - **g)** Justification for selection:
  - **B. Strategy(ies) for Using Capabilities and
    Resources**
    1. Strategy A (to meet the needs of
       potential employer A)
       - **a)** Personal skills, abilities, and
         resources
         - (1) Description of your skills and
           abilities:

(2) Specific employer needs that your skills/abilities can fulfill:

(3) Differentiation relative to peers/competitors (why should *you* be hired?):

(4) Additional resources that you have to offer:

(5) Needed or expected starting salary:

(6) Expected employee benefits:

(7) Additional employer-paid training that you require:

(8) Willingness to relocate:

(9) Geographic areas to target:

(10) Corporate divisions or offices to target:

(11) Summary of overall strategy:

(12) Tactics for standing out among the crowd of potential employees:

(13) Point of contact with potential employer:

(14) Specific elements
  (*a*) Résumé:
  (*b*) Internships:
  (*c*) Placement offices:
  (*d*) Job fairs:
  (*e*) Personal contacts:
  (*f*) Unsolicited:

(15) Specific objectives and budget:

2. Strategy B (to meet the needs of potential employer B)

  a) Personal skills, abilities, and resources

    (1) Description of your skills and abilities:

    (2) Specific employer needs that your skills/abilities can fulfill:

    (3) Differentiation relative to peers/competitors (why should *you* be hired?):

    (4) Additional resources that you have to offer:

    (5) Needed or expected starting salary:

    (6) Expected employee benefits:

    (7) Additional employer-paid training that you require:

    (8) Willingness to relocate:

    (9) Geographic areas to target:

(10) Corporate divisions or offices to target:

(11) Summary of overall strategy:

(12) Tactics for standing out among the crowd of potential employees:

(13) Point of contact with potential employer:

(14) Specific elements
  (*a*) Résumé:
  (*b*) Internships:
  (*c*) Placement offices:
  (*d*) Job fairs:
  (*e*) Personal contacts:
  (*f*) Unsolicited:

(15) Specific objectives and budget:

C. **Strategy Summary**

1. How does strategy A (B) give you a competitive advantage in serving the needs of potential employer A (B)?

2. Is this competitive advantage sustainable? Why or why not?

VI. **Financial Projections and Budgets**

  A. Do you have a clear idea of your budgetary requirements (for example, housing, furnishings, clothing, transportation, food, other living expenses)?

  B. Will the expected salaries/benefits from potential employers meet these requirements? If not, do you have an alternative plan (that is, a different job choice, a second job, requesting a higher salary)?

VII. **Controls and Evaluation**

  A. **Performance Standards**

    1. What do you have to offer? Corrective actions that can be taken if your skills, abilities, and resources do not match the needs of potential employers:

    2. Are you worth it? Corrective actions that can be taken if potential employers do not think your skills/abilities are worth your asking price:

    3. Where do you want to go? Corrective actions that can be taken if potential employers do not offer you a position in a preferred geographic location:

4. How will you stand out among the
crowd?
Corrective actions that can be taken
if your message is not being heard by
potential employers or is not reaching
the right people:

B. **Monitoring Procedures**
1. What types and levels of formal control
mechanisms are in place to ensure the
proper implementation of your plan?
   a) Are your potential employers hiring?
   b) Do you need additional training/
   education?
   c) Have you allocated sufficient time to
   your career development?
   d) Are your investments in career
   development adequate?
      (1) Training/education:
      (2) Networking/making contacts:
      (3) Wardrobe/clothing:
      (4) Development of interviewing
      skills:

   e) Have you done your homework on
   potential employers?
   f) Have you been involved in an
   internship program?
   g) Have you attended job/career fairs?
   h) Are you using the resources of your
   placement center?
   i) Are you committed to your career
   development?

C. **Performance Analysis**
1. Number/quality/potential of all job
contacts made:
2. Number of job/career fairs attended and
quality of the job leads generated:
3. Number of résumés distributed:
   a) Number of potential employers who
   responded:
   b) Number of negative responses:
4. Number of personal interviews:
5. Number/quality of job offers:

# Marketing: Developing Relationships

CHAPTER 12    Customer-Driven Marketing

CHAPTER 13    Dimensions of Marketing Strategy

# Customer-Driven Marketing

## CHAPTER OUTLINE

**Introduction**

**Nature of Marketing**
*The Exchange Relationship*
*Functions of Marketing*
*The Marketing Concept*
*Evolution of the Marketing Concept*

**Developing a Marketing Strategy**
*Selecting a Target Market*
*Developing a Marketing Mix*

**Marketing Research and Information Systems**

**Buying Behavior**
*Psychological Variables of Buying Behavior*
*Social Variables of Buying Behavior*
*Understanding Buying Behavior*

**The Marketing Environment**

## OBJECTIVES

*After reading this chapter, you will be able to:*

- Define marketing, and describe the exchange process.
- Specify the functions of marketing.
- Explain the marketing concept and its implications for developing marketing strategies.
- Examine the development of a marketing strategy, including market segmentation and marketing mix.
- Investigate how marketers conduct marketing research and study buying behavior.
- Summarize the environmental forces that influence marketing decisions.
- Assess a company's marketing plans, and propose a solution for resolving its problem.

## Bargain Shopping for Bridal Gowns

Most women have been planning their wedding day for their whole lives, with a lot of their thoughts going to the wedding dress. Even into adulthood, many women are still searching for that fairytale gown. Consumed by that vision of the magical, designer-made dress, many women are willing to spend thousands of dollars to purchase it. However, such an expense is not a reality for most women. Increasingly, however, alternatives do exist. As the cost of the average wedding ceremony balloons—up to nearly $28,000 in 2007—more companies are seeking to take advantage of the large segment of the market that cannot afford this level of extravagance by offering lower-cost, yet stylish gowns.

In the past 60 years, the bridal industry has reinvented itself numerous times. In the 1950s, most women purchased their wedding dresses in department stores. Then, in the 1960s, small, exclusive, boutique-style wedding shops offering more expensive selections began popping up. Finally, in the 1990s, David's Bridal entered the market, offering affordable gowns ranging from $99 to $1,000. Today, David's Bridal maintains about 30 percent of the wedding dress market. Recognizing this company's success, a number of well-known apparel retailers also now produce low-cost wedding dresses. JC Penney offers a popular wedding gown style for $179.99, J.Crew sells gowns for $225 to $2,950, Ann Taylor has gowns for $600 to $1,200, and Target features an entire line of Isaac Mizrahi gowns all for under $160. Brides will always dream of their perfect wedding, and designers have been able to play off of that by advertising stylish, yet affordable, offerings.

To maintain the appearance of high style at a lower price, David's Bridal and other companies typically use synthetic materials and send production

*continued*

overseas. A typical designer dress makes use of expensive materials such as silk, pearls, crystals, and fine lace. Fabric alone may cost $60 to $125 per yard. Wedding dresses can require many yards of fabric. High-end dresses usually have a lot of detailing, making their design very labor intensive, and therefore even more costly. A basic designer dress usually sells for $4,000 to $6,000, with more detailed custom gowns going for much higher. If one has a limited budget and is willing to sacrifice hand-tooled buttons in favor of a zipper, David's Bridal offers acceptable alternatives.

Catering to the brides who cannot let the dream of a designer dress die, Filene's Basement's "Running of the Brides" is an occasion so famous that it hardly requires promotion. An annual event, this sale offers designer gowns originally priced up to $5,000 that are discounted all the way to $249 to $699. To secure their positions at the front of the line, brides and their friends often begin to line up the night before the sale. Complete mayhem ensues once the doors open, and racks are stripped bare within minutes. There is no time for a second look-around. A bride grabs as many dresses as she can, and tries them on. If she can find the right dress, the experience can be worth the insanity.

The wedding industry has grown by leaps and bounds, and these examples are but a few of the wedding dress shopping choices available to women. Regardless of a woman's tastes and budget, high competition, strong demand, and market segmentation have ensured that these days, there is the perfect dress at the right price for every bride.[1]

## Introduction

Marketing involves planning and executing the development, pricing, promotion, and distribution of ideas, goods, and services to create exchanges that satisfy individual and organizational goals. These activities ensure that the products consumers want to buy are available at a price they are willing to pay and that consumers are provided with information about product features and availability. Organizations of all sizes and objectives engage in these activities.

In this chapter, we focus on the basic principles of marketing. First we define and examine the nature of marketing. Then we look at how marketers develop marketing strategies to satisfy the needs and wants of their customers. Next we discuss buying behavior and how marketers use research to determine what consumers want to buy and why. Finally we explore the impact of the environment on marketing activities.

## Nature of Marketing

**marketing**
a group of activities designed to expedite transactions by creating, distributing, pricing, and promoting goods, services, and ideas

A vital part of any business undertaking, **marketing** is a group of activities designed to expedite transactions by creating, distributing, pricing, and promoting goods, services, and ideas. These activities create value by allowing individuals and organizations to obtain what they need and want. A business cannot achieve its objectives unless it provides something that customers value. Nike, for example, has created the Nike Plus system, which combines Nike's popular footwear with Apple's extremely successful iPod. For $29, users can buy the Nike Plus iPod kit, which includes a sensor that can be inserted in the bottom of a Nike Plus–equipped shoe, along with a receiver that is attached to an iPod Nano. When installed, the kit measures a runner's speed, calories burned, and distance run. The data stored in the Nano can be uploaded to the Web, where people can monitor their own progress or see how they stack up against others using the system. Researchers at Nike came up with the idea after seeing how popular the iPod had become with runners.[2] But just creating an innovative product that meets many users' needs isn't sufficient in today's volatile global marketplace. Products must be conveniently available, competitively priced, and uniquely promoted.

Of all the business concepts covered in this text, marketing may be the hardest for organizations to master. Businesses try to respond to consumer wants and needs and to anticipate changes in the environment. Unfortunately, it is difficult to understand and predict what consumers want: Motives are often unclear; few principles can be applied consistently; and markets tend to fragment, each desiring customized products, new value, or better service.

It is important to note what marketing is not: It is not manipulating consumers to get them to buy products they do not want. It is not just selling and advertising; it is a systematic approach to satisfying consumers. Marketing focuses on the many activities—planning, pricing, promoting, and distributing products—that foster exchanges. As gas prices increased in 2008, General Motors recognized that it would not be able to sell as many trucks because consumer preference was moving toward smaller cars. GM, therefore, had to shift its strategy in order to be successful in a time of high gas prices and poor U.S. economic performance. The company closed some of its truck plants, began to consider selling the Hummer brand, and increased production of more fuel-efficient vehicles.[3]

## The Exchange Relationship

At the heart of all business is the **exchange,** the act of giving up one thing (money, credit, labor, goods) in return for something else (goods, services, or ideas). Businesses exchange their goods, services, or ideas for money or credit supplied by customers in a voluntary *exchange relationship*, illustrated in Figure 12.1. The buyer must feel good about the purchase, or the exchange will not continue. If your local dry cleaner cleans your nice suit properly, on time, and without damage, you will probably feel good about using its services. But if your suit is damaged or isn't ready on time, you will probably use another dry cleaner next time.

For an exchange to occur, certain conditions are required. As indicated by the arrows in Figure 12.1, buyers and sellers must be able to communicate about the "something of value" available to each. An exchange does not necessarily take place just because buyers and sellers have something of value to exchange. Each participant must be willing to give up his or her respective "something of value" to receive the "something" held by the other. You are willing to exchange your "something of value"—your money or credit—for compact discs, soft drinks, football tickets, or new shoes because you consider those products more valuable or more important than holding on to your cash or credit potential.

When you think of marketing products, you may think of tangible things—cars, stereo systems, or books, for example. What most consumers want, however, is a

**exchange**
the act of giving up one thing (money, credit, labor, goods) in return for something else (goods, services, or ideas)

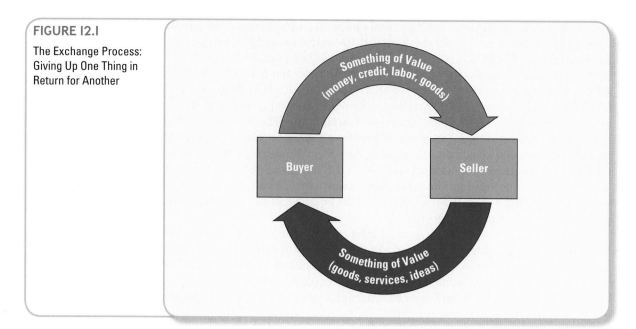

Something of Value
(money, credit, labor, goods)

Buyer

Seller

Something of Value
(goods, services, ideas)

way to get a job done, solve a problem, or gain some enjoyment. You may purchase a Hoover vacuum cleaner not because you want a vacuum cleaner but because you want clean carpets. Starbucks serves coffee drinks at a premium price, providing convenience, quality, and an inviting environment. Therefore, the tangible product itself may not be as important as the image or the benefits associated with the product. This intangible "something of value" may be capability gained from using a product or the image evoked by it, or even the bond name. Recently, wines named after animals have become popular. Names such as Dancing Bull, Smoking Loon, or The Little Penguin are fun, unpretentious, and easy to remember. They are also far less intimidating than a multisyllabic foreign name. The label or brand name may also offer the added bonus of being a conversation piece in a social environment.

## Functions of Marketing

Marketing focuses on a complex set of activities that must be performed to accomplish objectives and generate exchanges. These activities include buying, selling, transporting, storing, grading, financing, marketing research, and risk taking.

**Buying.**    Everyone who shops for products (consumers, stores, businesses, governments) decides whether and what to buy. A marketer must understand buyers' needs and desires to determine what products to make available.

*Marketing can be used by industry groups to increase demand for their industry's product—like The Beef Checkoff Program.*

Selling.   The exchange process is expedited through selling. Marketers usually view selling as a persuasive activity that is accomplished through promotion (advertising, personal selling, sales promotion, publicity, and packaging).

Transporting.   Transporting is the process of moving products from the seller to the buyer. Marketers focus on transportation costs and services.

Storing.   Like transporting, storing is part of the physical distribution of products and includes warehousing goods. Warehouses hold some products for lengthy periods in order to create time utility. Time utility has to do with being able to satisfy demand in a timely manner. This especially pertains to a seasonal good such as orange juice. Fresh oranges are only available for a few months annually, but consumers demand juice throughout the entire year. Sellers must arrange for cold storage of orange juice concentrate so that they can maintain a steady supply all of the time.

Grading.   Grading refers to standardizing products by dividing them into subgroups and displaying and labeling them so that consumers clearly understand their nature and quality. Many products, such as meat, steel, and fruit, are graded according to a set of standards that often are established by the state or federal government.

Financing.   For many products, especially large items such as automobiles, refrigerators, and new homes, the marketer arranges credit to expedite the purchase.

Marketing Research.   Through research, marketers ascertain the need for new goods and services. By gathering information regularly, marketers can detect new trends and changes in consumer tastes.

Risk Taking.   Risk is the chance of loss associated with marketing decisions. Developing a new product creates a chance of loss if consumers do not like it enough to buy it. Spending money to hire a sales force or to conduct marketing research also involves risk. The implication of risk is that most marketing decisions result in either success or failure.

## The Marketing Concept

A basic philosophy that guides all marketing activities is the **marketing concept,** the idea that an organization should try to satisfy customers' needs through coordinated activities that also allow it to achieve its own goals. According to the marketing concept, a business must find out what consumers desire and then develop the good, service, or idea that fulfills their needs or wants. The business must then get the product to the customer. In addition, the business must continually alter, adapt, and develop products to keep pace with changing consumer needs and wants. McDonald's faces increasing pressure to provide more healthful fast-food choices. The company has eliminated supersized fries and soft drinks from its menu to address these concerns.[4] McDonald's was also the first fast-food chain to put nutritional information on its food packaging.[5] In 2008, the company took a further step to address its health commitment by switching to trans-fat-free cooking oils. Now all of McDonald's french fries, pies, and cookies distributed in the United States and Canada are trans-fat free.[6] Over the years, the fast-food giant has experimented with healthier fare, but consumers often have rejected these items. To remain competitive, the company must be prepared to add to or adapt its menu to satisfy customers' desires for new fads or changes in eating habits. Each business must determine how best to implement the marketing concept, given its own goals and resources.

**marketing concept** the idea that an organization should try to satisfy customers' needs through coordinated activities that also allow it to achieve its own goals

# Entrepreneurship in Action
## Samantha's Table Sparks High-End Romance

Samantha Daniels

**Business:** Samantha's Table

**Founded:** 2001

**Success:** Daniels earns between $25,000 and $50,000 per client, plus a hefty bonus if the client marries as the result of her matching skills.

Originally a divorce attorney hailing from Pennsylvania, Samantha Daniels changed course to become a high-end matchmaker for Los Angeles's and New York's wealthy singles. If this scenario sounds at all familiar, that is because Daniels's life and business spawned a television show. The NBC comedy *Miss Match,* which starred Alicia Silverstone, was based on her life as a Hollywood matchmaker. While Daniels remains single, she has found great success finding love for some of the country's richest and most influential individuals. To differentiate herself from online dating services, Daniels takes a much more hands-on approach. She also does not limit her search to paying clients, but rather considers everyone she knows in her vast network of singles.

Daniels says that her number-one concern is finding the right match for her clients, regardless of whether the other party has paid for her services or not. She strategically matches individuals based on what she knows of them and brings together potential matches over drinks, at exclusive events, or trendy venues. Daniels does not reveal names of clients but has disclosed that she has been employed by famous actors, athletes, and those involved in high-profile professional companies. In case you're wondering how this setup works, a potential client pays around $500 for a two-hour initial consultation. She likes to conduct initial meetings in public to better observe clients' behavioral patterns in social situations. Each client is asked to supply information about ex-spouses, homes, and finances and to fill out a prepared questionnaire. Should the deal go further, Daniels charges anywhere from $25,000 to $50,000 to provide dates, coaching, personal shopping, and styling advice. If a match ends in marriage, Daniels usually gets a sizable bonus as well. While this might sound like a strange way to find love, Daniels says that business is booming, with around 200 requests for help daily.[7]

Trying to determine customers' true needs is increasingly difficult because no one fully understands what motivates people to buy things. However, Estée Lauder, founder of her namesake cosmetics company, had a pretty good idea. When a prestigious store in Paris rejected her perfume in the 1960s, she "accidentally" dropped a bottle on the floor where nearby customers could get a whiff of it. So many asked about the scent that Galeries Lafayette was obliged to place an order. Lauder ultimately built an empire using then-unheard-of tactics like free samples and gifts with purchases to market her "jars of hope."[8]

Although customer satisfaction is the goal of the marketing concept, a business must also achieve its own objectives, such as boosting productivity, reducing costs, or achieving a percentage of a specific market. If it does not, it will not survive. For example, Dell could sell computers for $50 and give customers a lifetime guarantee, which would be great for customers but not so great for Dell. Obviously, the company must strike a balance between achieving organizational objectives and satisfying customers.

To implement the marketing concept, a firm must have good information about what consumers want, adopt a consumer orientation, and coordinate its efforts throughout the entire organization; otherwise, it may be awash with goods, services, and ideas that consumers do not want or need. Successfully implementing the marketing concept requires that a business view the customer's perception of value as the ultimate measure of work performance and improving value, and the rate at which this is done, as the measure of success.[9] Everyone in the organization who interacts with customers—*all* customer-contact employees—must know what customers want. They are selling ideas, benefits, philosophies, and experiences—not just goods and services.

Someone once said that if you build a better mousetrap, the world will beat a path to your door. Suppose you do build a better mousetrap. What will happen? Actually, consumers are not likely to beat a path to your door because the market is so competitive. A coordinated effort by everyone involved with the mousetrap is needed to sell the product. Your company must reach out to customers and tell them about your mousetrap, especially how your mousetrap works better than those offered by competitors. If you do not make the benefits of your product widely known, in most cases, it will not be successful. Consider Apple's 208 national and international retail stores, which market computers and electronics in a way unlike any other computer manufacturer or retail establishments. The upscale stores, located in high-rent shopping districts, show off Apple's products in airy, stylish settings to encourage consumers to try new things—like making a movie on a computer. The stores also offer special events like concerts and classes to give customers ideas on how to maximize their use of Apple's products.[10] You must also find—or create—stores willing to sell your mousetrap to consumers. You must implement the marketing concept by making a product with satisfying benefits and making it available and visible.

Orville Wright said that an airplane is "a group of separate parts flying in close formation." This is what most companies are trying to accomplish: They are striving for a team effort to deliver the right good or service to customers. A breakdown at any point in the organization—whether it be in production, purchasing, sales, distribution, or advertising—can result in lost sales, lost revenue, and dissatisfied customers.

## Evolution of the Marketing Concept

The marketing concept may seem like the obvious approach to running a business and building relationships with customers. However, businesspeople are not always focused on customers when they create and operate businesses. Many companies fail to grasp the importance of customer relationships and fail to implement customer strategies. A recent survey indicated that only 46 percent of executives believe that their firm is committed to customers, but 67 percent of executives frequently meet with customers.[11] Our society and economic system have changed over time, and marketing has become more important as markets have become more competitive.

**The Production Orientation.**   During the second half of the 19th century, the Industrial Revolution was well under way in the United States. New technologies, such as electricity, railroads, internal combustion engines, and mass-production techniques, made it possible to manufacture goods with ever increasing efficiency. Together with new management ideas and ways of using labor, products poured into the marketplace, where demand for manufactured goods was strong.

**The Sales Orientation.**   By the early part of the 20th century, supply caught up with and then exceeded demand, and businesspeople began to realize they would have to "sell" products to buyers. During the first half of the 20th century, businesspeople viewed sales as the primary means of increasing profits, and this period came to have a sales orientation. They believed the most important marketing activities were personal selling and advertising. Today some people still inaccurately equate marketing with a sales orientation.

**The Marketing Orientation.**   By the 1950s, some businesspeople began to recognize that even efficient production and extensive promotion did not guarantee sales. These businesses, and many others since, found that they must first determine what

**marketing orientation**
an approach requiring organizations to gather information about customer needs, share that information throughout the firm, and use that information to help build long-term relationships with customers

customers want and then produce it, rather than making the products first and then trying to persuade customers that they need them. Managers at General Electric first suggested that the marketing concept was a companywide philosophy of doing business. As more organizations realized the importance of satisfying customers' needs, U.S. businesses entered the marketing era, one of marketing orientation.

A **marketing orientation** requires organizations to gather information about customer needs, share that information throughout the entire firm, and use it to help build long-term relationships with customers. Top executives, marketing managers, nonmarketing managers (those in production, finance, human resources, and so on), and customers all become mutually dependent and cooperate in developing and carrying out a marketing orientation. Nonmarketing managers must communicate with marketing managers to share information important to understanding the customer. Consider the 117-year history of Wrigley's gum. In 1891 it was given away to promote sales of baking powder. The gum was launched as a product in 1893, and after four generations of Wrigley family CEOs, the company continues to reinvent itself and focus on consumers. In 2008, the family made the decision to sell the company to Mars. Wrigley now functions as a stand-alone subsidiary of Mars. The deal combined such popular brands as Wrigley's gums and Life Savers with Mars' M&Ms, Snickers, and Skittles to form the world's largest confectionary company.

Trying to assess what customers want, difficult to begin with, is further complicated by the rate at which trends, fashions, and tastes can change. Businesses today want to satisfy customers and build meaningful long-term relationships with them. It is more efficient and less expensive for the company to retain existing customers and even increase the amount of business each customer provides the organization than to find new customers. Most companies' success depends on increasing the amount of repeat business; therefore, relationship building between company and customer is key. As we saw in Chapter 4, many companies are turning to technologies associated with customer relationship management to help build relationships and boost business with existing customers.

Communication remains a major element of any strategy to develop and manage long-term customer relationships. By providing multiple points of interactions with customers—that is, Web sites, telephone, fax, e-mail, and personal contact—companies can personalize customer relationships.[12] Like many online retailers, Amazon.com stores and analyzes purchase data in an attempt to understand each customer's interests. This information helps the retailer improve its ability to satisfy individual customers and thereby increase sales of books, music, movies, and other products to each customer. The ability to identify individual customers allows marketers to shift their focus from targeting groups of similar customers to increasing their share of an individual customer's purchases.[13] Regardless of the medium through which communication occurs, customers should ultimately be the drivers of marketing strategy because they understand what they want. Customer relationship management systems should ensure that marketers listen to customers in order to respond to their needs and concerns and build long-term relationships.

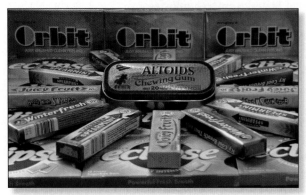

*Wrigley's originally gave gum away to promote its baking powder. The company, which sells its products in more than 180 countries, continues to reorient and reinvent itself. In 2008, it announced it would merge with the candy maker Mars.*

# Destination CEO
## Tom Ryan, CVS

Today, CVS is the largest retail pharmacy chain in the United States. The company began as a small New England chain and rapidly grew through acquisitions of other leading chains such as Eckerd Drugs. In 10 years, CVS quadrupled in size.

Tom Ryan is the CEO of CVS. He has been with the company his entire professional career, beginning as a pharmacist directly out of pharmacy school. At the age of 29, he was promoted to head the company, making him one of the youngest CEOs in the country at the time. CVS has not always had an excellent track record, however. In 2001 sales stalled for the retail chain, forcing Ryan to close more than 200 stores. This slowdown, however, was short lived, and according to industry experts, CVS, under Ryan's leadership, is not likely to slow down anytime soon.

The exceptional success of the company is attributed to Ryan's keen focus on marketing research. The company remodeled all of its retail stores based on market research that identified three prototypes. More than 80 percent of CVS's customers are women. Based on the market research, women wanted lower shelves, wider aisles, and a selection of higher-end personal care products. Using this market research data, CVS has responded directly to its customer needs. Another key differentiator for CVS is customer service. For example, robotics have been introduced in the pharmacies to count out pills to free up pharmacists to consult directly with customers.

The future of the business is constantly on the mind of Ryan. Walgreens, CVS's major rival, even though having fewer stores, generates more annual revenue. The primary reason is that Walgreens' sales are driven by products other than pharmaceutical and health-related products. CVS, on the other hand, attributes 70 percent of its revenue to prescriptions and other pharmaceutical products.

### Discussion Questions
1. In your opinion, does CVS use a marketing orientation?
2. How does CVS use market segmentation?
3. When CVS contracts for market research, what type of information is most useful to Ryan and the management team in terms of decision making?

# Developing a Marketing Strategy

To implement the marketing concept and customer relationship management, a business needs to develop and maintain a **marketing strategy,** a plan of action for developing, pricing, distributing, and promoting products that meet the needs of specific customers. This definition has two major components: selecting a target market and developing an appropriate marketing mix to satisfy that target market.

## Selecting a Target Market

A **market** is a group of people who have a need, purchasing power, and the desire and authority to spend money on goods, services, and ideas. A **target market** is a more specific group of consumers on whose needs and wants a company focuses its marketing efforts. Nike, for example, introduced a new line of golf clubs targeted at recreational golfers.[14]

Marketing managers may define a target market as a relatively small number of people within a larger market, or they may define it as the total market (Figure 12.2). Rolls Royce, for example, targets its products at a very exclusive, high-income market—people who want the ultimate in prestige in an automobile. General Motors, on the other hand, manufactures vehicles ranging from the Saturn to Cadillac to GMC trucks in an attempt to appeal to varied tastes, needs, and desires.

Some firms use a **total-market approach,** in which they try to appeal to everyone and assume that all buyers have similar needs and wants. Sellers of salt, sugar, and many agricultural products use a total-market approach because everyone

**marketing strategy**
a plan of action for developing, pricing, distributing, and promoting products that meet the needs of specific customers

**market**
a group of people who have a need, purchasing power, and the desire and authority to spend money on goods, services, and ideas

**target market**
a specific group of consumers on whose needs and wants a company focuses its marketing efforts

**total-market approach**
an approach whereby a firm tries to appeal to everyone and assumes that all buyers have similar needs

369

**FIGURE 12.2**

Target Market Strategies

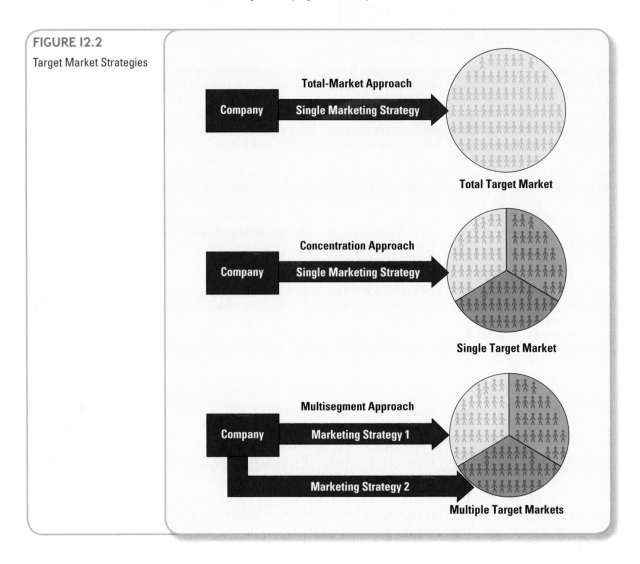

**market segmentation**
a strategy whereby a firm divides the total market into groups of people who have relatively similar product needs

**market segment**
a collection of individuals, groups, or organizations who share one or more characteristics and thus have relatively similar product needs and desires

is a potential consumer of these products. Most firms, though, use **market segmentation** and divide the total market into groups of people. A **market segment** is a collection of individuals, groups, or organizations who share one or more characteristics and thus have relatively similar product needs and desires. Women are the largest market segment, with 51 percent of the U.S. population. In addition, 11 million privately held companies are majority owned (50 percent or more) by women.[15] At the household level, segmentation can unlock each woman's social, cultural, and stage in life to determine preferences and needs.[16] One market segment on which many marketers are focusing is the growing Hispanic population. Wal-Mart has recently made a move to acknowledge the demographic shift toward more Latino shoppers. The mega-chain has long featured McDonald's and Subway restaurants within its stores, but in a move to cater to the Hispanic market some stores will feature Pollo Campero and Taco Maker as well. This agreement represent the first time an ethnic restaurant has managed to land franchise agreements with Wal-Mart.[17] Marketers are also trying to figure out ways to best reach African American consumers, without making them feel singled out or targeted.[18] One of the challenges for marketers in the future will be to effectively address an increasingly racially diverse United States. Staples gained a footing in the Hispanic market with a program called Exito Empressarial (Business Success) for small business owners. It is a seminar program to learn about accounting, taxes, and running a small business.[19] Table 12.1 shows the buying power and market share percentages of four market segments. In future decades, the purchasing power of minority market segments is set to grow by leaps and bounds. It is estimated that by 2050, African Americans will represent around 15 percent of the U.S. population, while Latinos and Hispanics will make up 24 percent.[20] Companies will have to learn how to most effectively reach these growing segments—which already outmeasure all but nine of the world's economies in terms of purchasing power.[21] Companies use market segmentation to focus their efforts and resources on specific target markets so that they can develop a productive marketing strategy. Two common approaches to segmenting markets are the concentration approach and the multisegment approach.

Market Segmentation Approaches.   In the **concentration approach,** a company develops one marketing strategy for a single market segment. The concentration approach allows a firm to specialize, focusing all its efforts on the one market segment. Porsche, for example, directs all its marketing efforts toward high-income individuals who want to own high-performance vehicles. A firm can generate a large sales volume by penetrating a single market segment deeply. The concentration approach may be especially effective when a firm can identify and develop products for a segment ignored by other companies in the industry.

In the **multisegment approach,** the marketer aims its marketing efforts at two or more segments, developing a marketing strategy for each. Many firms use a multisegment approach that includes different advertising messages for different segments. Companies also develop product variations to appeal to different market segments. The U.S. Post Office, for example, offers personalized stamps; clothing company J.Crew sells jeans customization kits; various on-demand television services ensure that consumers only watch what they want to watch; and LEGO toy company offers a service through its Web site wherein children can design their own sets.[22] Many other firms also attempt to use a multisegment approach to market segmentation, such as the manufacturer of Raleigh bicycles, which has designed separate marketing strategies for racers, tourers, commuters, and children.

*Niche marketing* is a narrow market segment focus when efforts are on one small, well-defined group that has a unique, specific set of needs. Catering to ice cream "addicts" and people who crave new, exotic flavors, several companies are selling ice cream on the Internet. This niche represents only a fraction of the $20.3 billion a year ice cream business, but online sales at some of the biggest makers

**concentration approach** a market segmentation approach whereby a company develops one marketing strategy for a single market segment

**multisegment approach** a market segmentation approach whereby the marketer aims its efforts at two or more segments, developing a marketing strategy for each

| Category | Buying Power (billions) | | | % Market Share | | |
|---|---|---|---|---|---|---|
| | 1990 | 2003 | 2005 | 1990 | 2003 | 2005 |
| Asian | 112.9 | 344.2 | 396.5 | 2.7 | 4.2 | 4.4 |
| American Indian | 19.2 | 45.2 | 51.1 | 0.5 | 0.5 | 1.0 |
| Black | 307.8 | 687.7 | 760.7 | 7.4 | 8.4 | 12.8 |
| Hispanic | 207.5 | 652.6 | 735.6 | 5.0 | 7.9 | 8.1 |

**TABLE 12.1**
Minority Buying Power by Race, 1990 versus 2003 and 2005

Source: Jeffrey M. Humphreys, "The Multicultural Economy 2005," *GBEC* 63 (3rd Quarter, 2005), pp. 10, 12, available at www.selig.uga.edu/forecast/GBEC/GBEC053Q.pdf.

# Responding to Business Challenges
## Apple and Phinnaeus or Julie and David: What's in a Name?

With celebrities setting the standard by naming their children Tallulah Belle, Apple, Moses, and Phinnaeus, many expectant parents feel pressure to come up with interesting, original names for their kids. Maryanna Korwitts has developed a business around the national concern for picking the right name. She believes that a name can even endow people with certain personality traits and is therefore a task not to be taken lightly. Korwitts is a self-designated nameologist and intuitive, meaning she studies names and how they may affect an individual's life. She believes in what she teaches so much that she changed her own name from Mary Ann, which she thought caused her to be a procrastinator overly concerned with others' opinions of her; to Maryanna, a name which she says she has helped her to become a more balanced person.

Korwitts started off working as a schoolteacher. Over the years, she and her co-workers began to notice similarities among students sharing the same name. For example, Julies tended to lose things and Davids tended to be studious. Intrigued, Korwitts began studying naming practices in ancient and traditional cultures. She found that many cultures gave great thought to naming individuals and even changed names to bring about improvements in health or in other aspects of a person's life. She soon determined that nameology was for her, and started Name Structures. Today, she writes books, lectures, makes regular appearances on the media circuit, and provides one-on-one consultations.

Some parents feel that the stress to find the perfect name is so great that they will pay hundreds of dollars to receive guidance. This is where Korwitts comes in. For $399, an expectant parent receives a copy of Korwitts' book *Name Power 101,* five online *BABYtalk* profiles of top name choices, three 30-minute phone consultations, and a personalized *Name Owner's Manual* for the baby. During the consultations, Korwitts discusses possible first and middle name choices based on the positive or negative influences they may have on the child's personality, relationships, career, finances, and health. She also considers the name as it relates to the rest of the family dynamic. Whether you believe in nameology or not, it is certain that some people do, and Maryanna Korwitts is there to help fill that need.[23]

### Discussion Questions

1. What business opportunity has Maryanna Korwitts identified and taken advantage of, and was the founding of her business customer driven?
2. What is Korwitts's target market?
3. What kinds of companies or products would represent competitive threats to Korwitts's business?

increased 30 percent in just one year. Some of the firms focusing on this market are IceCreamSource.com, Nuts About Ice Cream, and Graeter's.[24]

For a firm to successfully use a concentration or multisegment approach to market segmentation, several requirements must be met:

1. Consumers' needs for the product must be heterogeneous.
2. The segments must be identifiable and divisible.
3. The total market must be divided in a way that allows estimated sales potential, cost, and profits of the segments to be compared.
4. At least one segment must have enough profit potential to justify developing and maintaining a special marketing strategy.
5. The firm must be able to reach the chosen market segment with a particular market strategy.

**Bases for Segmenting Markets.** Companies segment markets on the basis of several variables:

1. *Demographic*—age, sex, race, ethnicity, income, education, occupation, family size, religion, social class. These characteristics are often closely related to customers' product needs and purchasing behavior, and they can be readily measured. For example, deodorants are often segmented by sex: Secret and Soft n' Dry for women; Old Spice and Mennen for men.
2. *Geographic*—climate, terrain, natural resources, population density, subcultural values. These influence consumers' needs and product usage. Climate,

for example, influences consumers' purchases of clothing, automobiles, heating and air conditioning equipment, and leisure activity equipment.

3. *Psychographic*—personality characteristics, motives, lifestyles. Soft-drink marketers provide their products in several types of packaging, including two-liter bottles and cases of cans, to satisfy different lifestyles and motives.

4. *Behavioristic*—some characteristic of the consumer's behavior toward the product. These characteristics commonly involve some aspect of product use.

## Developing a Marketing Mix

The second step in developing a marketing strategy is to create and maintain a satisfying marketing mix. The **marketing mix** refers to four marketing activities— product, price, distribution, and promotion—that the firm can control to achieve specific goals within a dynamic marketing environment (Figure 12.3). The buyer or the target market is the central focus of all marketing activities.

**marketing mix**
the four marketing activites—product, price, promotion, and distribution—that the firm can control to achieve specific goals within a dynamic marketing environment

**Product.**   A product—whether a good, a service, an idea, or some combination— is a complex mix of tangible and intangible attributes that provide satisfaction and benefits. A *good* is a physical entity you can touch. A Porsche Cayenne, an Outkast compact disc, a Hewlett-Packard printer, and a kitten available for adoption at an animal shelter are examples of goods. A *service* is the application of human and mechanical efforts to people or objects to provide intangible benefits to customers. Air travel, dry cleaning, haircuts, banking, insurance, medical care, and day care are examples of services. *Ideas* include concepts, philosophies, images, and issues. For instance, an attorney, for a fee, may advise you about what rights you have in the event that the IRS decides to audit your tax return. Other marketers of ideas include political parties, churches, and schools.

A product has emotional and psychological, as well as physical characteristics, that include everything that the buyer receives from an exchange. This definition includes supporting services such as installation, guarantees, product information, and promises of repair. Products usually have both favorable and unfavorable attributes; therefore, almost every purchase or exchange involves trade-offs as consumers try to maximize their benefits and satisfaction and minimize unfavorable attributes.

Products are among a firm's most visible contacts with consumers. If they do not meet consumer needs and expectations, sales will be difficult, and product life spans

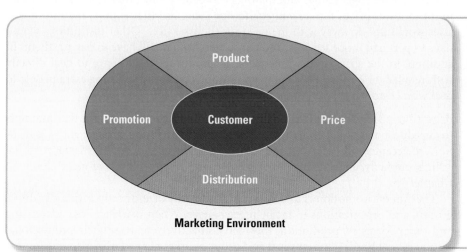

**FIGURE 12.3**

The Marketing Mix: Product, Price, Promotion, and Distribution will be brief. The product is an important variable—often the central focus—of the marketing mix; the other variables (price, promotion, and distribution) must be coordinated with product decisions.

**price**
a value placed on an object exchanged between a buyer and a seller

**Price.**   Almost anything can be assessed by a **price,** a value placed on an object exchanged between a buyer and a seller. Although the seller usually establishes the price, it may be negotiated between buyer and seller. The buyer usually exchanges purchasing power—income, credit, wealth—for the satisfaction or utility associated with a product. Because financial price is the measure of value commonly used in an exchange, it quantifies value and is the basis of most market exchanges.

Marketers view price as much more than a way of assessing value, however. It is a key element of the marketing mix because it relates directly to the generation of revenue and profits. Prices can also be changed quickly to stimulate demand or respond to competitors' actions. The sudden increase in the cost of commodities such as oil can create price increases or a drop in consumer demand for a product. The increase in the cost of oil caused price tags for even the cheapest airline tickets to double on average in 2008.[26] The demand for gas-guzzling trucks and SUVs has dropped, while small cars such as the Chevy Aveo and Ford Focus continue to see strong sales.[27]

> **Did You Know?**   During its first year of operation, sales of Coca-Cola averaged just nine drinks per day for total first-year sales of $50. Today, Coca-Cola products are consumed at the rate of 1 billion drinks per day.[25]

**distribution**
making products available to customers in the quantities desired

**Distribution.**   **Distribution** (sometimes referred to as "place" because it helps to remember the marketing mix as the "4 Ps") is making products available to customers in the quantities desired. Blockbuster realizes that its distribution network has to change in order to stay competitive. People are less likely to drive to pick up a DVD when they now have the option to receive them in the mail or watch them online. Because of this, the company has altered the way it distributes movies and video-games.[28] To better compete with companies like Netflix and cable's on-demand services, Blockbuster has gone online. It now battles Netflix on its own territory by offering a combination mail order and online video and game rental business. Intermediaries, usually wholesalers and retailers, perform many of the activities required to move products efficiently from producers to consumers or industrial buyers. These activities involve transporting, warehousing, materials handling, and inventory control, as well as packaging and communication.

Critics who suggest that eliminating wholesalers and other middlemen would result in lower prices for consumers do not recognize that eliminating intermediaries would not do away with the need for their services. Other institutions would have to perform those services, and consumers would still have to pay for them. In addition, in the absence of wholesalers, all producers would have to deal directly with retailers or customers, keeping voluminous records and hiring extra people to deal with customers.

**promotion**
a persuasive form of communication that attempts to expedite a marketing exchange by influencing individuals, groups, and organizations to accept goods, services, and ideas

**Promotion.**   **Promotion** is a persuasive form of communication that attempts to expedite a marketing exchange by influencing individuals, groups, and organizations to accept goods, services, and ideas. Promotion includes advertising, personal selling, publicity, and sales promotion, all of which we will look at more closely in Chapter 13.

The aim of promotion is to communicate directly or indirectly with individuals, groups, and organizations to facilitate exchanges. When marketers use advertising and other forms of promotion, they must effectively manage their promotional resources and understand product and target-market characteristics to ensure that these promotional activities contribute to the firm's objectives. The spike in gas prices has provided some companies with promotional opportunities. For example, Callaway Golf offered an "Increase Your Driving Distance" giveaway wherein customers are eligible to win a $100 gas card with the purchase of certain golf clubs. Chrysler also developed a "Let's Refuel America" promotion. With the purchase of certain models, customers receive a gas card that entitles them to $2.99 fixed-price gasoline for up to 12,000 miles or three years.[29]

Most major companies have set up Web sites on the Internet to promote themselves and their products. The home page for Betty Crocker, for example, offers recipes, meal planning, the company's history, descriptions for its 200 products, online shopping for complementary items such as dinnerware, linens, and gifts, and the ability to print a shopping list based on recipes chosen or ingredients on hand in the consumer's kitchen. The Web sites for The Gap and Old Navy provide consumers with the opportunity to purchase clothing and other items from the convenience of their homes or offices. Some sites, however, simply promote a company's products but do not offer them for sale online.

*Jones Soda's original distribution methods were as offbeat as the company's products. The beverages were initially placed in coolers in places like tattoo parlors, skate parks and ski shops. Only later were the drinks available in more conventional outlets, like convenience stores.*

# Marketing Research and Information Systems

Before marketers can develop a marketing mix, they must collect in-depth, up-to-date information about customer needs. **Marketing research** is a systematic, objective process of getting information about potential customers to guide marketing decisions. Such information might include data about the age, income, ethnicity, gender, and educational level of people in the target market, their preferences for product features, their attitudes toward competitors' products, and the frequency with which they use the product. For example, Toyota's marketing research about Generation Y drivers (born between 1977 and 1994) found that they practically live in their cars, and many even keep a change of clothes handy in their vehicles. As a result of this research, Toyota designed its Scion as a "home on wheels" with a 15-volt outlet for plugging in a computer, reclining front seats for napping, and a powerful audio system for listening to MP3 music files.[30] Marketing research is vital because the marketing concept cannot be implemented without information about customers.

A marketing information system is a framework for accessing information about customers from sources both inside and outside the organization. Inside the organization, there is a continuous flow of information about prices, sales, and expenses. Outside the organization, data are readily available through private or public reports and census statistics, as well as from many other sources. Computer networking technology provides a framework for companies to connect to useful databases and customers with instantaneous information about product acceptance, sales performance, and buying behavior. This information is important to planning and marketing strategy development.

**marketing research** a systematic, objective process of getting information about potential customers to guide marketing decisions

**primary data**
marketing information that is observed, recorded, or collected directly from respondents

Two types of data are usually available to decision makers. **Primary data** are observed, recorded, or collected directly from respondents. If you've ever participated in a telephone survey about a product, recorded your TV viewing habits for A. C. Nielsen or Arbitron, or even responded to a political opinion poll, you provided the researcher with primary data. Primary data must be gathered by researchers who develop a method to observe phenomena or research respondents. Many companies use "mystery shoppers" to visit their retail establishments and report on whether the stores were adhering to the companies' standards of service. Some use digital cameras and computer equipment to document their observations of store appearance, employee effectiveness and customer treatment. These mystery shoppers provide valuable information that helps companies improve their organizations and refine their marketing strategies.[31] The state of Nebraska used focus groups as part of its effort to develop a formal marketing campaign. Among other things, focus groups suggested the state promote its history and natural beauty.[32] A weakness of surveys is that respondents are sometimes untruthful in order to avoid seeming foolish or ignorant.

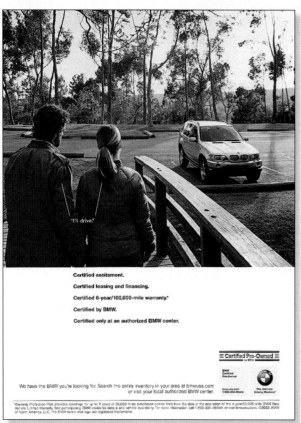

Market research can lead to a whole new market for your product. BMW targets a lower income consumer than its typical high-end one by selling "certified" used BMWs at a lower cost, but still with the BMW brand recognition and expectation.

Some methods for marketing research use passive observation of consumer behavior and open-ended questioning techniques. Called ethnographic or observational research, the approach can help marketers determine what consumers really think about their products and how different ethnic or demographic groups react to them.

**Secondary data** are compiled inside or outside the organization for some purpose other than changing the current situation. Marketers typically use information compiled by the U.S. Census Bureau and other government agencies, databases created by marketing research firms, as well as sales and other internal reports, to gain information about customers.

**secondary data**
information that is compiled inside or outside an organization for some purpose other than changing the current situation

The marketing of products and collecting of data about buying behavior—information on what people actually buy and how they buy it—represents marketing research of the future. New information technologies are changing the way businesses learn about their customers and market their products. Interactive multimedia research, or *virtual testing*, combines sight, sound, and animation to facilitate the testing of concepts as well as packaging and design features for consumer products. Computerization offers a greater degree of flexibility, shortens the staff time involved in data gathering, and cuts marketing research costs. The evolving development of telecommunications and computer technologies is allowing marketing researchers quick and easy access to a growing number of online services and a vast database of potential respondents. Online research is set to grow to $4 billion in the next few years, according to a report by Cambiar and GMI.[33] Many companies have created private online communities and research panels that bring consumer feedback into the companies 24 hours a day.

Look-Look.com is an online, real-time service that provides accurate and reliable information research and news about trendsetting youths ages 14 to 30. With this age group spending an estimated $140 billion a year, many companies are willing to shell out an annual subscription fee of about $20,000 for access to these valuable data. Look-Look pays more than 35,000 handpicked, prescreened young people from all over the world to e-mail the company information about their styles, trends, opinions, and ideas.[34]

Other companies are finding that quicker, less expensive online market research is helping them develop products faster and with greater assurance that the products will be successful. Scheduled to coincide with the presidential primaries and election, Mountain Dew opened an online survey in order to decide on a new soda flavor (strawberry, raspberry, or wild berry). The "Dewmocracy" campaign allowed consumers to vote online for their favorite flavor.[35]

# Buying Behavior

Carrying out the marketing concept is impossible unless marketers know what, where, when, and how consumers buy; marketing research into the factors that influence buying behavior helps marketers develop effective marketing strategies. **Buying behavior** refers to the decision processes and actions of people who purchase and use products. It includes the behavior of both consumers purchasing products for personal or household use as well as organizations buying products for business use. Marketers analyze buying behavior because a firm's marketing strategy should be guided by an understanding of buyers. People view pets as part of their families, and they want their pets to have the best of everything. Iams, which markets the Iams and Eukanuba pet food brands, recognized this trend and shifted its focus. Today, it markets high-quality pet food, fancy pet treats, sauces, and other items that allow pet lovers to spoil their pets.[36]

Both psychological and social variables are important to an understanding of buying behavior.

## Psychological Variables of Buying Behavior

Psychological factors include the following:

- **Perception** is the process by which a person selects, organizes, and interprets information received from his or her senses, as when hearing an advertisement on the radio or touching a product to better understand it.
- **Motivation,** as we said in Chapter 10, is an inner drive that directs a person's behavior toward goals. A customer's behavior is influenced by a set of motives rather than by a single motive. A buyer of a home computer, for example, may be motivated by ease of use, ability to communicate with the office, and price.
- **Learning** brings about changes in a person's behavior based on information and experience. If a person's actions result in a reward, he or she is likely to behave the same way in similar situations. If a person's actions bring about a negative result, however—such as feeling ill after eating at a certain restaurant—he or she will probably not repeat that action.
- **Attitude** is knowledge and positive or negative feelings about something. For example, a person who feels strongly about protecting the environment may refuse to buy products that harm the earth and its inhabitants.
- **Personality** refers to the organization of an individual's distinguishing character traits, attitudes, or habits. Although market research on the

**buying behavior** the decision processes and actions of people who purchase and use products

**perception** the process by which a person selects, organizes, and interprets information received from his or her senses

**motivation** inner drive that directs a person's behavior toward goals

**learning** changes in a person's behavior based on information and experience

**attitude** knowledge and positive or negative feelings about something

**personality** the organization of an individual's distinguishing character traits, attitudes, or habits

# Going Green
## Making Reusable Cool

Every year an estimated 500 billion to 1 trillion plastic bags are consumed globally. In the United States alone, 88.5 billion plastic bags were consumed in 2007, and less than 1 percent were recycled. The average American family of four consumes about 1,460 plastic bags every year, the production of which requires 12 million barrels of oil annually. Plastic bags take more than 1,000 years to fully photo-degrade and are a toxic threat for all of that time, representing a pollution crisis of global magnitude.

Responding to this problem, a number of environmentally conscious designers have been promoting high-fashion reusable totes. In 2007, Anya Hindmarch developed a stylish canvas tote embroidered with the phrase "I'm not a plastic bag." The limited edition $15 shoulder bag was in such high demand that people lined up in front of the department stores where they were offered in hopes of obtaining one before they ran out. Anita Ahuja, also known as the "bag lady," is the head of the profit/not-for-profit Conserve, an organization that takes used plastic grocery bags and other trash and recycles them into new, stylish, and low-priced handbags. Based in Delhi, India, Ahuja provides gainful employment to garbage pickers, who not only give her material for her bags but also provide a service by cleaning up the streets of Delhi. Ahuja's products are sold in stores in the United Kingdom, France, and the United States in chains such as Whole Foods. Anita donates some of her profits to charities, such as starting a school for the children of the ragpickers she employs, and she is trying to get her footing in the world of Parisian fashion.

Haute couture designers are also concerned with running eco-responsible businesses. Stella McCartney, the British designer and daughter of Paul McCartney, is a vegetarian and has been involved in promoting organics for years. Recently, she created a canvas shopping bag, retail $495, as a part of an organic clothing line sold in her shops. Celebrities such as Reese Witherspoon and Alicia Silverstone have been photographed carrying the Stella McCartney tote, spurring sales. Hermès, the brand famous for its silk scarves, has joined the high-fashion totes scene by adding a $960 tote to its line. A Louis Vuitton canvas tote retails for an astounding $1,740. These high-end, fashionable bags are providing the inspiration and driving the sales of lower priced versions by making canvas grocery bags fashionable, while contributing to the effort to reduce global plastic bag consumption. Designers like Anya Hindmarch and Louis Vuitton are doing their part to lend an air of exclusivity and desirability to being eco-friendly—making it cool for everyone to carry reusable shopping bags.[37]

**Discussion Questions**

1. What kinds of consumers are the designers discussed targeting?
2. What might be some good marketing strategies to further encourage the use of reusable bags?
3. What other green fashion movements could benefit from the promotional efforts of these canvas bag designers?

relationship between personality and buying behavior has been inconclusive, some marketers believe that the type of car or clothing a person buys reflects his or her personality.

## Social Variables of Buying Behavior

**social roles**
a set of expectations for individuals based on some position they occupy

Social factors include **social roles,** which are a set of expectations for individuals based on some position they occupy. A person may have many roles: mother, wife, student, executive. Each of these roles can influence buying behavior. Consider a woman choosing an automobile. Her father advises her to buy a safe, gasoline-efficient car, such as a Volvo. Her teenaged daughter wants her to buy a cool car, such as a Pontiac GTO; her young son wants her to buy a Ford Explorer to take on camping trips. Some of her colleagues at work say she should buy a hybrid Prius to help the environment. Thus, in choosing which car to buy, the woman's buying behavior may be affected by the opinions and experiences of her family and friends and by her roles as mother, daughter, and employee.

Other social factors include reference groups, social classes, and culture.

**reference groups**
groups with whom buyers identify and whose values or attitudes they adopt

- **Reference groups** include families, professional groups, civic organizations, and other groups with whom buyers identify and whose values or attitudes they adopt. A person may use a reference group as a point of comparison or a source of information. A person new to a community may ask other group members to recommend a family doctor, for example.

- **Social classes** are determined by ranking people into higher or lower positions of respect. Criteria vary from one society to another. People within a particular social class may develop common patterns of behavior. People in the upper-middle class, for example, might buy a Lexus or a Cadillac as a symbol of their social class.

- **Culture** is the integrated, accepted pattern of human behavior, including thought, speech, beliefs, actions, and artifacts. Culture determines what people wear and eat and where they live and travel. Many Hispanic Texans and New Mexicans, for example, buy *masa trigo*, the dough used to prepare flour tortillas, which are basic to Southwestern and Mexican cuisine.

**social classes**
a ranking of people into higher or lower positions of respect

**culture**
the integrated, accepted pattern of human behavior, including thought, speech, beliefs, actions, and artifacts

### Understanding Buying Behavior

Although marketers try to understand buying behavior, it is extremely difficult to explain exactly why a buyer purchases a particular product. The tools and techniques for analyzing consumers are not exact. Marketers may not be able to determine accurately what is highly satisfying to buyers, but they know that trying to understand consumer wants and needs is the best way to satisfy them. In an attempt to better understand consumer behavior, Procter & Gamble sent video crews into about 80 households around the world. The company, maker of Tide, Crest, Pampers, and many other consumer products, hoped to gain insights into the lifestyles and habits of young couples, families with children, and empty nesters. Participants were taped over a four-day period and were paid about $200–$250 a day. The behaviors caught on tape may lead the company to develop new products or change existing ones to better meet consumers' needs and give the company a competitive advantage over its rivals.[38]

# The Marketing Environment

A number of external forces directly or indirectly influence the development of marketing strategies; the following political, legal, regulatory, social, competitive, economic, and technological forces comprise the marketing environment.

- *Political, legal, and regulatory forces*—laws and regulators' interpretation of laws; law enforcement and regulatory activities; regulatory bodies, legislators and legislation, and political actions of interest groups. Specific laws, for example, require that advertisements be truthful and that all health claims be documented.

- *Social forces*—the public's opinions and attitudes toward issues such as living standards, ethics, the environment, lifestyles, and quality of life. For example, social concerns have led marketers to design and market safer toys for children.

- *Competitive and economic forces*—competitive relationships, unemployment, purchasing power, and general economic conditions (prosperity, recession, depression, recovery, product shortages, and inflation).

- *Technological forces*—computers and other technological advances that improve distribution, promotion, and new-product development.

Marketing requires creativity and consumer focus because environmental forces can change quickly and dramatically. Changes can arise from social concerns and economic forces such as price increases, product shortages, and altering levels of demand for commodities. Recently, the concern about climate change, global warming, and the impact of carbon emissions on our environment has developed social concerns leading businesses to rethink marketing strategies. Possibly the most important concern is to make businesses, consumers, and governments consider carbon emissions and the effect their purchases have. Escalating fossil fuel use in economies such as China and India has placed strong upward pressure on oil prices. China's fast development has made it the planet's largest contributor to greenhouse gases. As Figure 12.4 indicates, the public believes the government, individuals, and businesses are all responsible for leading the way in green practices. The result has been government initiatives such as tax credits for hybrid cars and increased usage of reusable bags over plastic ones, and more products are available that are easy to recycle and that consume less energy. The average American generates about five tons of greenhouse gases annually. Many people are disturbed by this statistic and have resolved to take actions that reduce their energy usage and their impact on the environment through the use of carpooling, driving hybrid cars, using Energy Star products, and even washing their clothes in cold water instead of hot. In addition to fueling the demand for low-energy products, these developments are also accelerating the development of renewable energy such as solar and wind.[39]

Because such environmental forces are interconnected, changes in one may cause changes in others. Consider that because of evidence linking children's consumption of soft drinks and fast foods to health issues such as obesity, diabetes, and osteoporosis, marketers of such products have experienced negative publicity and calls for legislation regulating the sale of soft drinks in public schools.

Although the forces in the marketing environment are sometimes called uncontrollables, they are not totally so. A marketing manager can influence some environmental variables. For example, businesses can lobby legislators to dissuade them from passing unfavorable legislation. Figure 12.5 shows the variables in the marketing environment that affect the marketing mix and the buyer.

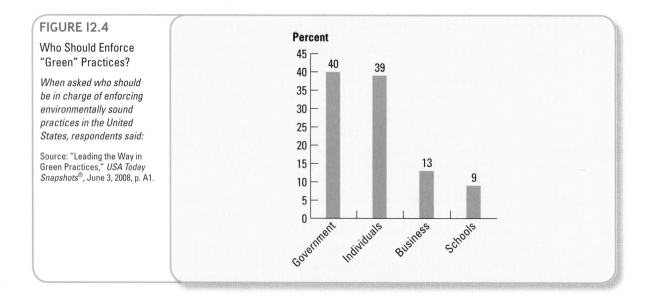

**FIGURE 12.4**

Who Should Enforce "Green" Practices?

*When asked who should be in charge of enforcing environmentally sound practices in the United States, respondents said:*

Source: "Leading the Way in Green Practices," *USA Today Snapshots*®, June 3, 2008, p. A1.

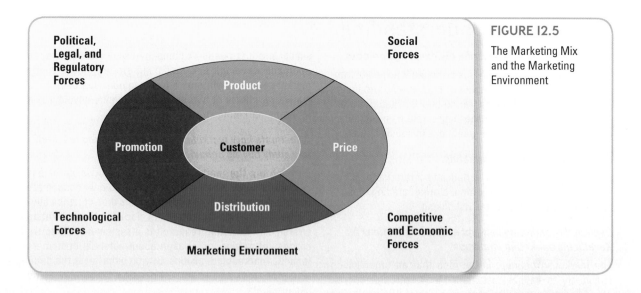

**FIGURE I2.5**

The Marketing Mix and the Marketing Environment

# So You Want a Job in Marketing

You probably did not think as a child how great it would be to grow up and become a marketer. That's because often marketing is associated with sales jobs, but opportunities in marketing, public relations, product management, advertising, e-marketing, and customer relationship management and beyond represent almost one-third of all jobs in today's business world. To enter any job in the marketing field, you must balance an awareness of customer needs with business knowledge while mixing in creativity and the ability to obtain useful information to make smart business decisions.

Marketing starts with understanding the customer. Marketing research is a vital aspect in marketing decision making and presents many job opportunities. Market researchers survey customers to determine their habits, preferences, and aspirations. Activities include concept testing, product testing, package testing, test-market research, and new-product research. Salaries vary, depending on the nature and level of the position as well as the type, size, and location of the firm. An entry-level market analyst may make between $24,000 and $50,000, while a market research director may earn from $75,000 to $200,000 or more.

One of the most dynamic areas in marketing is direct marketing, where a seller solicits a response from a consumer using direct communications methods such as telephone, online communication, direct mail, or catalogs. Jobs in direct marketing include buyers, catalog managers, research/mail-list managers, or order fulfillment managers. Most positions in direct marketing involve planning and market analysis. Some require the use of databases to sort and analyze customer information and sales history.

Use of the Internet for retail sales is growing, and the Internet continues to be very useful for business-to-business sales, so e-marketing offers many career opportunities, including customer relationship management (CRM). CRM helps companies market to customers through relationships, maintaining customer loyalty. Information technology plays a huge role in such marketing jobs, as you need to combine technical skills and marketing knowledge to effectively communicate with customers. Job titles include e-marketing manager, customer relationship manager, and e-services manager. A CRM customer service manager may receive a salary in the $40,000 to $45,000, and experienced individuals in charge of online product offerings may earn up to $100,000.

A job in any of these marketing fields will require a strong sense of the current trends in business and marketing. Customer service is vital to many aspects of marketing, so the ability to work with customers and to communicate their needs and wants is important. Marketing is everywhere, from the corner grocery or local nonprofit organization to the largest multinational corporations, making it a shrewd choice for an ambitious and creative person. We will provide additional job opportunities in marketing in Chapter 13.

# Review Your Understanding

### Define marketing, and describe the exchange process.

Marketing is a group of activities designed to expedite transactions by creating, distributing, pricing, and promoting goods, services, and ideas. Marketing facilitates the exchange, the act of giving up one thing in return for something else. The central focus of marketing is to satisfy needs.

### Specify the functions of marketing.

Marketing includes many varied and interrelated activities: buying, selling, transporting, storing, grading, financing, marketing research, and risk taking.

### Explain the marketing concept and its implications for developing marketing strategies.

The marketing concept is the idea that an organization should try to satisfy customers' needs through coordinated activities that also allow it to achieve its goals. If a company does not implement the marketing concept by providing products that consumers need and want while achieving its own objectives, it will not survive.

### Examine the development of a marketing strategy, including market segmentation and marketing mix.

A marketing strategy is a plan of action for creating a marketing mix (product, price, distribution, promotion) for a specific target market (a specific group of consumers on whose needs and wants a company focuses its marketing efforts). Some firms use a total-market approach, designating everyone as the target market. Most firms divide the total market into segments of people who have relatively similar product needs. A company using a concentration approach develops one marketing strategy for a single market segment, whereas a multisegment approach aims marketing efforts at two or more segments, developing a different marketing strategy for each.

### Investigate how marketers conduct marketing research and study buying behavior.

Carrying out the marketing concept is impossible unless marketers know what, where, when, and how consumers buy; marketing research into the factors that influence buying behavior helps marketers develop effective marketing strategies. Marketing research is a systematic, objective process of getting information about potential customers to guide marketing decisions. Buying behavior is the decision processes and actions of people who purchase and use products.

### Summarize the environmental forces that influence marketing decisions.

There are several forces that influence marketing activities: political, legal, regulatory, social, competitive, economic, and technological.

### Assess a company's marketing plans, and propose a solution for resolving its problem.

Based on the material in this chapter, you should be able to answer the questions posed in "Solve the Dilemma" on page 384 and help the business understand what went wrong and how to correct it.

# Revisit the World of Business

1.  Why can the bridal dress industry support such a broad range of different market segments?
2.  How have low-end bridal gown brands marketed themselves?

3.  If low-cost gowns are stylish, why are many brides still interested in buying the high-end gowns? What type of consumer are they?

# Learn the Terms

attitude   377
buying behavior   377
concentration approach   371
culture   379
distribution   374
exchange   363
learning   377
market   369
market segment   370
market segmentation   370

marketing   362
marketing concept   365
marketing mix   373
marketing orientation   368
marketing research   375
marketing strategy   369
motivation   377
multisegment approach   371
perception   377
personality   377

price   374
primary data   376
promotion   374
reference groups   378
secondary data   376
social classes   379
social roles   378
target market   369
total-market approach   369

# Check Your Progress

1.  What is marketing? How does it facilitate exchanges?
2.  Name the functions of marketing. How does an organization use marketing activities to achieve its objectives?
3.  What is the marketing concept? Why is it so important?
4.  What is a marketing strategy?
5.  What is market segmentation? Describe three target market strategies.
6.  List the variables in the marketing mix. How is each used in a marketing strategy?
7.  Why are marketing research and information systems important to an organization's planning and development of strategy?
8.  Briefly describe the factors that influence buying behavior. How does understanding buying behavior help marketers?
9.  Discuss the impact of technological forces and political and legal forces on the market.

# Get Involved

1.  With some or all of your classmates, watch several hours of television, paying close attention to the commercials. Pick three commercials for products with which you are somewhat familiar. Based on the commercials, determine who the target market is. Can you surmise the marketing strategy for each of the three?
2.  Discuss the decision process and influences involved in purchasing a personal computer.

# Build Your Skills

### THE MARKETING MIX

**Background:**
You've learned the four variables—product, promotion, price, and distribution—that the marketer can select to achieve specific goals within a dynamic marketing environment. This exercise will give you an opportunity to analyze the marketing strategies of some well-known companies to determine which of the variables received the most emphasis to help the company achieve its goals.

**Task:**
In groups of three to five students, discuss the examples below and decide which variable received the most emphasis.

A.   Product
B.   Distribution
C.   Promotion
D.   Price

_____ 1.   Starbucks Coffee began selling bagged premium specialty coffee through an agreement with Kraft Foods to gain access to more than 30,000 supermarkets.

_____ 2.   America Online (AOL) offers 24-hour, 9-cents-per-minute long-distance telephone service for AOL Internet customers who will provide their credit card number and receive bills and information about their account online.

_____ 3.   With 150,000 advance orders, Apple Computer launched the iMac computer with a $100 million advertising budget to obtain first-time computer buyers who could get Internet access by just plugging in the computer.

_____ 4.   After more than 35 years on the market, WD-40 is in about 80 percent of U.S. households—more than any other branded product. Although WD-40 is promoted as a product that can stop squeaks, protect metal, loosen rusted parts, and free sticky mechanisms, the WD-40 Company has received letters from customers who have sprayed the product on bait to attract fish, on pets to cure mange, and even on people to cure arthritis. Despite more than 200 proposals to expand the WD-40 product line and ideas to change the packaging and labeling, the company stands firmly behind its one highly successful and respected original product.

_____ 5.   Southwest Airlines makes flying fun. Flight attendants try to entertain passengers, and the airline has an impeccable customer service record. Employees play a key role and take classes that emphasize that having fun translates into great customer service.

____ 6. Hewlett Packard offered a $100 rebate on a $799 HP LaserJet printer when purchased with an HP LaserJet toner cartridge. To receive the rebate, the buyer had to return a mail-in certificate to certify the purchase. A one-page ad with a coupon was used in *USA Today* stating, "We're taking $100 off the top."

____ 7. Denny's, the largest full-service family restaurant chain in the United States, serves more than 1 million customers a day. The restaurants offer the Grand Slam Breakfast for about $3, lunch basket specials for $4–$6, and a dinner of prime rib for about $7.

## Solve the Dilemma

### WILL IT GO?

Ventura Motors makes midsized and luxury automobiles in the United States. Best selling models include its basic four-door sedans (priced from $20,000 to $25,000) and two-door and four-door luxury automobiles (priced from $40,000 to $55,000). The success of two-seat sports cars like the Mazda RX-8 started the company evaluating the market for a two-seat sports car priced midway between the moderate and luxury market. Research found that there was indeed significant demand and that Ventura needed to act quickly to take advantage of this market opportunity.

Ventura took the platform of the car from a popular model in its moderate line, borrowing the internal design from its luxury line. The car was designed, engineered, and produced in just over two years, but the coordination needed to bring the design together resulted in higher than anticipated costs. The price for this two-seat car, the Olympus, was set at $32,000. Dealers were anxious to take delivery on the car, and salespeople were well trained on techniques to sell this new model.

However, initial sales have been slow, and company executives are surprised and concerned. The Olympus was introduced relatively quickly, made available at all Ventura dealers, priced midway between luxury and moderate models, and advertised heavily since its introduction.

### Discussion Questions

1. What do you think were the main concerns with the Olympus two-door sports coupe? Is there a market for a two-seat, $32,000 sports car when the RX-8 sells for significantly less?

2. Evaluate the role of the marketing mix in the Olympus introduction.

3. What are some of the marketing strategies auto manufacturers use to stimulate sales of certain makes of automobiles?

## Build Your Business Plan

### CUSTOMER-DRIVEN MARKETING

The first step is to develop a marketing strategy for your product or service. Who will be the target market you will specifically try to reach? What group(s) of people has the need, ability and willingness to purchase this product? How will you segment customers within your target market? Segmenting by demographic and geographic variables are often the easiest segmentation strategies to attempt. Remember that you would like to have the customers in your segment be as homogeneous and accessible as possible. You might target several segments if you feel your product or service has broad appeal.

The second step in your marketing strategy is to develop the marketing mix for your product or service.

Whether you are dealing with an established product or you are creating your own product or service, you need to think about what is the differential advantage your product offers. What makes it unique? How should it be priced? Should the product be priced below, above, or at the market? How will you distribute the product? And last but certainly not least, you need to think about the promotional strategy for your product.

What about the uncontrollable variables you need to be aware of? Is your product something that can constantly be technologically advanced? Is your product a luxury that will not be considered by consumers when the economy is in a downturn?

# See for Yourself Videocase

## WILL LUXURY HOTELS FEEL THE PINCH OF A SLOW ECONOMY?

In times of economic uncertainty, many businesses are forced to make unpleasant changes, accept losses, or even close their doors. The year 2007 marked the beginning of an economic downturn that, by 2008, had many talking about a recession. Many companies struggled with the new economic realities, but the luxury hotel sector continued to flourish.

There are many luxury hotel chains located throughout the United States, but the Ritz-Carlton and the Four Seasons are two of the most well known. The Ritz-Carlton first opened in Boston in 1927. At the time, it revolutionized the luxury hotel market through offerings such as a private bath in each room, fresh flowers in public areas, à la carte dining, waiters in white ties and aprons, and hotel staff in morning suits. Today, the Ritz boasts locations around the world in the United States, Canada, Mexico, the Caribbean, South America, Asia-Pacific, Europe, and the Middle East. The Ritz-Carlton's motto, and the image it seeks to project, has always been "We are Ladies and Gentlemen serving Ladies and Gentlemen." The Four Seasons is a younger luxury chain. Founded in 1960, the chain also has a global presence with hotels throughout the Americas, Asia-Pacific, Europe, the Middle East, and Africa. The company describes the luxury of a Four Seasons hotel as "a true home away from home for those who know and appreciate the best." Prices at these hotels range from around $300 per night to thousands per night.

As the U.S. economy has slowed, many sectors of the hotel industry have seen occupancies plateau or decline due to increasingly price-sensitive consumers. However, as mentioned previously, the luxury hotel sector has enjoyed continued success. Part of the reason for this phenomenon has to do with target markets. Luxury goods and services companies market to a select group of people with sufficient wealth so as to be relatively immune to economic recessions. Simply put, customers of the Ritz and the Four Seasons have enough money that they do not feel recessions as much as the average person.

The continued strength of the luxury hotel sector may also be partially due to its small size. There are fewer than 80,000 luxury hotel rooms throughout the United States, a small number when you consider that the city of Chicago alone has 102,000 hotel rooms. The equation all comes down to the basic economics of supply and demand. Demand for luxury hotel rooms has far outstripped supply as more Americans enter higher income brackets. Because, at least in the short term, the number of luxury rooms is fixed and more people are requesting them, the hotel industry can name its price. The only conceivable way the luxury hotel business could lose out is if it expands too rapidly or if demand suddenly and without warning bottoms out. Helping to ensure that demand will not taper off are international customers. As the U.S. economy weakens, luxury offerings in this country have started to look like a comparatively good deal to many Europeans, for example, who then choose to travel in the United States more frequently.

Market Metrix, a data compilation and analysis company for the hospitality industry, warns of raising prices too high or too fast, lest the move inadvertently drive off some customers. They suggest that hotels should throw their energy instead into service recovery and loyalty programs. In spite of these words of warning, the luxury hotel market shows no sign of slowing down, even as individual hotels begin to raise their rates.[40]

### Discussion Questions

1. Why are luxury hotels doing better than the hotel industry as a whole?

2. What could be some potential threats to future revenue growth for the Ritz-Carlton or the Four Seasons?

3. What is the target market for luxury hotels, and what would be some effective marketing strategies for this group?

**Remember to check out our Online learning Center at www.mhhe.com/ferrell7e.**

chapter 13

# Dimensions of Marketing Strategy

## CHAPTER OUTLINE

**Introduction**

**The Marketing Mix**

**Product Strategy**
*Developing New Products*
*Classifying Products*
*Product Line and Product Mix*
*Product Life Cycle*
*Identifying Products*

**Pricing Strategy**
*Pricing Objectives*
*Specific Pricing Strategies*

**Distribution Strategy**
*Marketing Channels*
*Intensity of Marketing Coverage*
*Physical Distribution*
*Importance of Distribution in a Marketing Strategy*

**Promotion Strategy**
*The Promotion Mix*
*Promotion Strategies: To Push or To Pull*
*Objectives of Promotion*
*Promotional Positioning*

## OBJECTIVES

*After reading this chapter, you will be able to:*

- Describe the role of product in the marketing mix, including how products are developed, classified, and identified.

- Define price, and discuss its importance in the marketing mix, including various pricing strategies a firm might employ.

- Identify factors affecting distribution decisions, such as marketing channels and intensity of market coverage.

- Specify the activities involved in promotion, as well as promotional strategies and promotional positioning.

- Evaluate an organization's marketing strategy plans.

# C|O|N|C|O|R|D
## MUSIC GROUP

## Concord Music Has a Flair for Marketing

Thanks to the ability to download music from the Internet onto your iPod, CD sales are in a sharp decline, and many record labels are suffering as a result. However, one record label surviving in spite of the current environment is Concord Music Group (CMG). The company was formed in 2004 as the result of a merger between Concord Records and Fantasy Records. In 2005, Telarc Records was added to the roster. Each of these companies could boast major music milestones and critical acclaim on its own. Together, they have become one of the largest and fastest growing independent music companies worldwide.

A savvy flair for marketing has propelled Concord toward success. Television great Norman Lear (producer of such famous classics as *All in the Family* and *One Day at a Time*) and business partner Hal Gaba purchased Concord Records in 1999 and continue to guide Concord Music Group in innovative marketing plans. In 2007, for example, the company quietly supported a PBS documentary featuring the Stax record label known for showcasing Otis Redding, Isaac Hayes, and other soul music greats. Although few people made the connection between the documentary and CMG, the company had a good reason for supporting the film: it owns the Stax recordings. The popular documentary increased Concord's sales while reviving interest in some classic tunes.

In 2004, Gaba suggested that Concord team up with Starbucks to release a Ray Charles album that then became a major hit. Following this success, Lear and Gaba helped Concord become part of a joint venture with Starbucks: the Hear Music label partnership. Through Hear Music, the partners release albums from both little known and established artists. Paul McCartney signed

*continued*

to the Hear Music label to release his latest album to great success, selling 75 percent more copies in the first week than his previous release for a major record label. While 45 percent of McCartney's album sales occurred inside Starbucks locations, the rest were marketed and promoted by Concord at various locations outside the coffee chain. Joni Mitchell, who hadn't released an album of new compositions since 1998, signed on with Hear Music, and her album débuted at number 14 on the Billboard 200.

Contributing to Concord's success in turbulent times is its partnership with Starbucks, which offers the benefits of shared risk and low-cost marketing. However, the company also benefits by finding niche markets for most of its products. Unlike major labels, which must sell at least one hundred thousand copies of a given CD in order to profit, Concord makes money as products continue to sell in small increments over time. Whatever your musical tastes, Concord may just have a hand in producing the music that you love, which is just the way they like it, since they love the music too.[1]

## Introduction

Getting just the right mix of product, price, promotion, and distribution is critical if a business is to satisfy its target customers and achieve its own objectives (implement the marketing concept).

In Chapter 12, we introduced the concept of marketing and the various activities important in developing a marketing strategy. In this chapter, we'll take a closer look at the four dimensions of the marketing mix—product, price, distribution, and promotion—used to develop the marketing strategy. The focus of these marketing mix elements is a marketing strategy that builds customer relationships and satisfaction.

## The Marketing Mix

The key to developing a marketing strategy is maintaining the right marketing mix that satisfies the target market and creates long-term relationships with customers.

**Did You Know?** Domino's Pizza delivery drivers cover 9 million miles a week delivering 400 million pizzas a year.[2]

To develop meaningful customer relationships, marketers have to develop and manage the dimensions of the marketing mix to give their firm an advantage over competitors. Successful companies offer at least one dimension of value that surpasses all competitors in the marketplace in meeting customer expectations. However, this does not mean that a company can ignore the other dimensions of the marketing mix; it must maintain acceptable, and if possible distinguishable, differences in the other dimensions as well.

Wal-Mart, for example, emphasizes price ("Save money, live better"). Procter & Gamble is well known for its promotion of top consumer brands such as Tide, Cheer, Crest, Ivory, Head & Shoulders, and Folgers. Domino's Pizza is recognized for its superiority in distribution after developing the largest home delivery pizza company in the world and its innovative new product introductions.

## Product Strategy

As mentioned previously, the term *product* refers to goods, services, and ideas. Because the product is often the most visible of the marketing mix dimensions, managing product decisions is crucial. In this section, we'll consider product development, classification, mix, life cycle, and identification.

*While he was attending Yale in 1966, Fred Smith, the founder of Federal Express, wrote a paper about his idea for the business. However, his professor said the concept would never fly. After watching how the U.S. military's logistics worked while serving in Vietnam, Smith later got FedEx off the ground.*

### Developing New Products

Each year thousands of products are introduced, but few of them succeed. In early 2008, drug company Pfizer's Animal Health Group released Slentrol, a weight-loss drug for dogs. The drug controls a dog's appetite and blocks fat. The drug is meant as a weight-loss tool for dogs with a medical condition or an owner who cannot resist feeding too much or cannot give the dog more exercise.[3] Before introducing a new product, a business must follow a multistep process: idea development, the screening of new ideas, business analysis, product development, test marketing, and commercialization. A firm can take considerable time to get a product ready for the market: It took more than 20 years for the first photocopier, for example. First announced as a concept car in January 2007, the General Motors Volt will be radically different from any car on the road today when it is launched in 2010. It is an extended-range electric vehicle with a 161-horsepower engine and power to go from 0 to 60 miles per hour in 8.5 seconds.[4]

**Idea Development.**   New ideas can come from marketing research, engineers, and outside sources such as advertising agencies and management consultants. Microsoft has a separate division—Microsoft Research—where scientists devise technology of the future. The division has more than 700 full-time employees who work in a universitylike research atmosphere. Research teams then present their ideas to Microsoft engineers who are developing specific products. As we said in Chapter 12, ideas sometimes come from customers, too. Other sources are brainstorming and intracompany incentives or rewards for good ideas. New ideas can even create a company. Las Vegas–based Shuffle Master, for example, grew out of entrepreneur Mark Breeding's idea for a card-shuffling machine. The Shuffle Master has more than 26,000 shuffling units in casinos around the world.[5]

**New Idea Screening.**   The next step in developing a new product is idea screening. In this phase, a marketing manager should look at the organization's resources and objectives and assess the firm's ability to produce and market the product. Important aspects to be considered at this stage are consumer desires, the competition, technological changes, social trends, and political, economic, and environmental

**business products**
products that are used directly or indirectly in the operation or manufacturing processes of businesses

**Business products** are used directly or indirectly in the operation or manufacturing processes of businesses. They are usually purchased for the operation of an organization or the production of other products; thus, their purchase is tied to specific goals and objectives. They too can be further classified:

- *Raw materials* are natural products taken from the earth, oceans, and recycled solid waste. Iron ore, bauxite, lumber, cotton, and fruits and vegetables are examples.
- *Major equipment* covers large, expensive items used in production. Examples include earth-moving equipment, stamping machines, and robotic equipment used on auto assembly lines.
- *Accessory equipment* includes items used for production, office, or management purposes, which usually do not become part of the final product. Computers, fax machines, calculators, and hand tools are examples.
- *Component parts* are finished items, ready to be assembled into the company's final products. Tires, window glass, batteries, and spark plugs are component parts of automobiles.
- *Processed materials* are things used directly in production or management operations but not readily identifiable as component parts. Varnish, for example, is a processed material for a furniture manufacturer.
- *Supplies* include materials that make production, management, and other operations possible, such as paper, pencils, paint, cleaning supplies, and so on.
- *Industrial services* include financial, legal, marketing research, security, janitorial, and exterminating services. Purchasers decide whether to provide these services internally or to acquire them from an outside supplier.

## Product Line and Product Mix

**product line**
a group of closely related products that are treated as a unit because of similar marketing strategy, production, or end-use considerations

Product relationships within an organization are of key importance. A **product line** is a group of closely related products that are treated as a unit because of similar marketing strategy. At Colgate-Palmolive, for example, the oral-care product line includes Colgate toothpaste, toothbrushes, and dental floss. A **product mix** is all the products offered by an organization. Figure 13.2 displays a sampling of the product mix and product lines of the Colgate-Palmolive Company.

## Product Life Cycle

**product mix**
all the products offered by an organization

Like people, products are born, grow, mature, and eventually die. Some products have very long lives. Ivory Soap was introduced in 1879 and is still popular. In contrast, a new computer chip is usually outdated within a year because of technological breakthroughs and rapid changes in the computer industry. There are four stages in the life cycle of a product: introduction, growth, maturity, and decline (Figure 13.3). The stage a product is in helps determine marketing strategy. While pickup trucks have historically sold very well in the United States, sales have reached the maturity stage, declining after a peak in 2004. The percentage of new vehicles sold reveals more car sales than truck sales. As oil prices increase, consumers are looking for better gas mileage and the demand for fuel-efficient cars is on the rise. Figure 13.4 shows sales numbers of hybrid vehicles. Hybrid vehicles have been in the introductory stage, filling only around 3 percent of market share, but with continued demand are now passing into a strong growth stage.[11]

**FIGURE 13.2**   Colgate-Palmolive's Product Mix and Product Lines

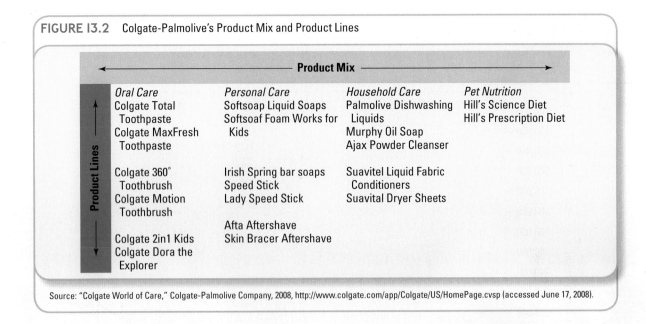

Source: "Colgate World of Care," Colgate-Palmolive Company, 2008, http://www.colgate.com/app/Colgate/US/HomePage.cvsp (accessed June 17, 2008).

In the *introductory stage,* consumer awareness and acceptance of the product are limited, sales are zero, and profits are negative. Profits are negative because the firm has spent money on research, development, and marketing to launch the product. During the introductory stage, marketers focus on making consumers aware of the product and its benefits. When Procter & Gamble introduced the Tide Stainbrush to reach the 70 percent of consumers who pretreat stains when doing laundry, it

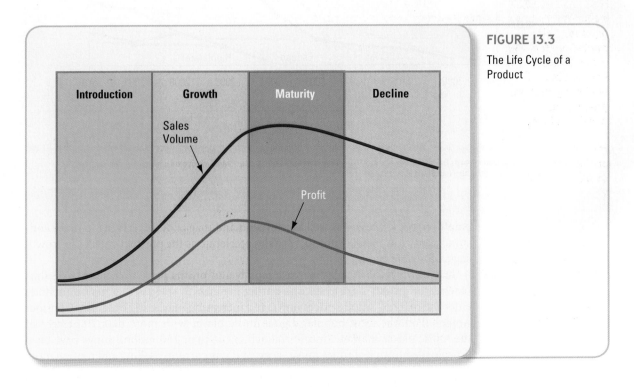

**FIGURE 13.3**

The Life Cycle of a Product

**FIGURE 13.4**    U.S. Hybrid Vehicle Sales, 1999–2008

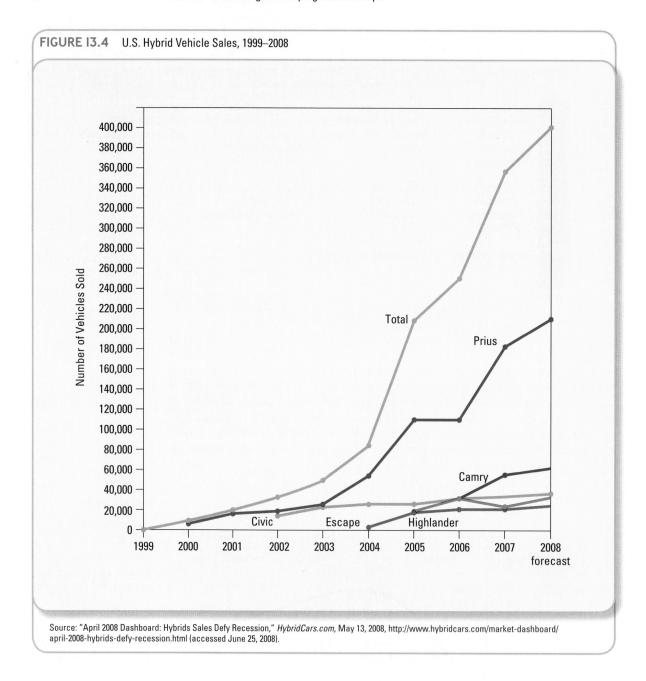

Source: "April 2008 Dashboard: Hybrids Sales Defy Recession," *HybridCars.com,* May 13, 2008, http://www.hybridcars.com/market-dashboard/april-2008-hybrids-defy-recession.html (accessed June 25, 2008).

employed press releases as well as television and magazine advertising to make consumers aware of the new product.[12] Sales accelerate as the product enters the growth stage of the life cycle.

In the *growth stage,* sales increase rapidly and profits peak, then start to decline. One reason profits start to decline during the growth stage is that new companies enter the market, driving prices down and increasing marketing expenses. Consider Apple's iPod, the most popular digital music player with more than 70 percent of the music player market. Since its launch, more than 150 million songs have been downloaded from its iTunes music store, and it is currently selling and renting more than 50,000 movies per day. Its iTunes music store surpassed Best Buy and Wal-Mart to become the biggest music retailer in the United States. iTunes has more than 20 million unique visitors a month.[13] During the growth stage, the firm tries to strengthen its position in the market by emphasizing the product's benefits and identifying market segments that want these benefits.

Sales continue to increase at the beginning of the *maturity stage,* but then the sales curve peaks and starts to decline while profits continue to decline. This stage is characterized by severe competition and heavy expenditures. In the highly competitive snack food industry, Quaker is converting mature products to single serve lower-calorie treats. Its 100-calorie packs were a smash success for Quaker and competitor Kraft, so now rivals across the industry

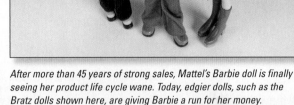

After more than 45 years of strong sales, Mattel's Barbie doll is finally seeing her product life cycle wane. Today, edgier dolls, such as the Bratz dolls shown here, are giving Barbie a run for her money.

are introducing 90-, 80-, even 60-calorie versions of mature products in hopes of maintaining sales.[14]

During the *decline stage,* sales continue to fall rapidly. Profits also decline and may even become losses as prices are cut and necessary marketing expenditures are made. As profits drop, firms may eliminate certain models or items. To reduce expenses and squeeze out any remaining profits, marketing expenditures may be cut back, even though such cutbacks accelerate the sales decline. Finally, plans must be made for phasing out the product and introducing new ones to take its place. Unfortunately for Mattel, the 50-year-old Barbie Doll has seen her status and sales slide as she has been replaced on retail shelves with edgier products such as Bratz. Barbie became vulnerable from competition not only from Bratz but American Girl and the growth of toy sales in stores such as Wal-Mart and Target when they choose to allocate shelf space to products they considered more profitable.[15]

## Identifying Products

Branding, packaging, and labeling can be used to identify or distinguish one product from others. As a result, they are key marketing activities that help position a product appropriately for its target market.

**Branding.** **Branding** is the process of naming and identifying products. A *brand* is a name, term, symbol, design, or combination that identifies a product and distinguishes it from other products. Consider that Google, iPod, and TiVo are brand names that are used to identify entire product categories, much like Xerox has become synonymous with photocopying and Kleenex with tissues. Protecting a brand name is important in maintaining a brand identity. The world's 10 most valuable brands are shown in Table 13.1. The brand name is the part of the brand that can be spoken and consists of letters, words, and numbers—such as WD-40 lubricant. A *brand mark* is the part of the brand that is a distinctive design, such as the silver star on the hood of a Mercedes or McDonald's golden arches logo. A **trademark** is a brand that is registered with the U.S. Patent and Trademark Office and is thus legally protected from use by any other firm.

Two major categories of brands are manufacturer brands and private distributor brands. **Manufacturer brands** are brands initiated and owned by the

**branding**
the process of naming and identifying products

**trademark**
a brand that is registered with the U.S. Patent and Trademark Office and is thus legally protected from use by any other firm

**manufacturer brands**
brands initiated and owned by the manufacturer to identify products from the point of production to the point of purchase

TABLE 13.1

The 10 Most Valuable Brands in the World

| Rank | Brand | Brand Value ($ Billions) | Brand Value Change |
|------|-------|--------------------------|--------------------|
| 1. | Google | 86.1 | 30% |
| 2. | GR (General Electric) | 71.4 | 15 |
| 3. | Microsoft | 70.9 | 29 |
| 4. | Coca-Cola | 58.2 | 17 |
| 5. | China Mobile | 57.2 | 39 |
| 6. | IBM | 55.3 | 65 |
| 7. | Apple | 55.2 | 123 |
| 8. | McDonald's | 49.5 | 49 |
| 9. | Nokia | 43.9 | 39 |
| 10. | Marlboro | 37.3 | −5 |

Source: "100 Most Powerful Brands," Millward Brown Optimor, http://www.millwardbrown.com/Sites/optimor/Media/Pdfs/en/BrandZ/BrandZ-2008-Report.pdf (accessed June 25, 2008).

**private distributor brands** brands, which may cost less than manufacturer brands, that are owned and controlled by a wholesaler or retailer

**generic products** products with no brand name that often come in simple packages and carry only their generic name

**packaging** the external container that holds and describes the product

manufacturer to identify products from the point of production to the point of purchase. Kellogg's, Sony, and Texaco are examples. **Private distributor brands,** which may be less expensive than manufacturer brands, are owned and controlled by a wholesaler or retailer, such as Kenmore appliances (Sears) and Sam's grocery products (Wal-Mart and Sam's Wholesale Club). The names of private brands do not usually identify their manufacturer. While private-label brands were once considered cheaper and poor quality, such as Wal-Marts Ol'Roy dog food, many private-label brands are increasing quality and image and competing with national brands. Target hired architect Michael Graves to design its private-label products including kitchen appliances such as blenders and coffee pots. Martha Stewart designed a line of home fashions for K-Mart. Other firms such as JCPenney and Wal-Mart are also following the trend.[16] Manufacturer brands are fighting hard against private distributor brands.

Another type of brand that has developed is **generic products**—products with no brand name at all. They often come in plain simple packages that carry only the generic name of the product—peanut butter, tomato juice, aspirin, dog food, and so on. They appeal to consumers who may be willing to sacrifice quality or product consistency to get a lower price.

Companies use two basic approaches to branding multiple products. In one, a company gives each product within its complete product mix its own brand name. Warner-Lambert, for example, sells many well-known consumer products—Dentyne, Chiclets, Listerine, Halls, Rolaids, and Trident—each individually branded. This branding policy ensures that the name of one product does not affect the names of others, and different brands can be targeted at different segments of the same market, increasing the company's market share (its percentage of the sales for the total market for a product). Another approach to branding is to develop a family of brands with each of the firm's products carrying the same name or at least part of the name. Gillette, Sara Lee, and IBM use this approach. Finally, consumers may react differently to domestic versus foreign brands. Figure 13.5 provides a snapshot of foreign versus domestic automobile ownership.

Packaging.    The **packaging,** or external container that holds and describes the product, influences consumers' attitudes and their buying decisions. A survey of

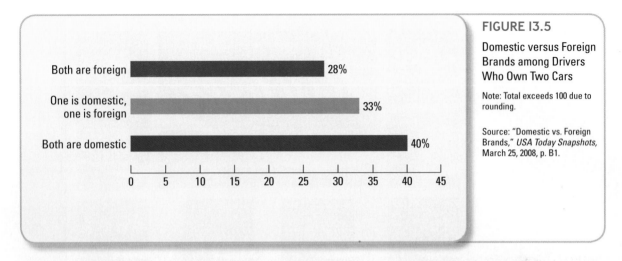

**FIGURE I3.5**

Domestic versus Foreign Brands among Drivers Who Own Two Cars

Note: Total exceeds 100 due to rounding.

Source: "Domestic vs. Foreign Brands," *USA Today Snapshots*, March 25, 2008, p. B1.

over 1,200 consumers found that 40 percent are willing to try a new product based on its packaging.[17] It is estimated that consumers' eyes linger only 2.5 seconds on each product on an average shopping trip; therefore, product packaging should be designed to attract and hold consumers' attention.

A package can perform several functions including protection, economy, convenience, and promotion. Beverage manufacturers have been redesigning their bottles to make them more convenient for consumers and to promote them to certain markets. Scientists videotaped people drinking from different types of bottles and made plaster casts of their hands. They found that the average gulp is 6.44 ounces and that half the population would rather suck liquid through a pop-up top than drink it. Since the early 1990s, soft drinks in 20-ounce plastic bottles revitalized U.S. sales for Coca-Cola and PepsiCo by getting Americans to drink larger servings. Recent concerns about health and the desire for lower-priced options have led both companies to test a variety of smaller bottle sizes to win back lost customers.[18]

**Labeling.**    **Labeling,** the presentation of important information on the package, is closely associated with packaging. The content of labeling, often required by law, may include ingredients or content, nutrition facts (calories, fat, etc.), care instructions, suggestions for use (such as recipes), the manufacturer's address and toll-free number, Web site, and other useful information. This information can have a strong impact on sales. The labels of many products, particularly food and drugs, must carry warnings, instructions, certifications, or manufacturers' identifications.

**labeling**
the presentation of important information on a package

**Product Quality.**    **Quality** reflects the degree to which a good, service, or idea meets the demands and requirements of customers. Quality products are often referred to as reliable, durable, easily maintained, easily used, a good value, or a trusted brand name. The level of quality is the amount of quality that a product possesses, and the consistency of quality depends on the product maintaining the same level of quality over time.

Quality of service is difficult to gauge because it depends on customers' perceptions of how well the service meets or exceeds their expectations. In other words, service quality is judged by consumers, not the service providers. A bank may define service quality as employing friendly and knowledgeable employees, but the bank's customers may be more concerned with waiting time, ATM access, security, and statement accuracy. Similarly, an airline traveler considers on-time arrival,

**quality**
the degree to which a good, service, or idea meets the demands and requirements of customers

*Coca-Cola is the most valuable brand in the world.*

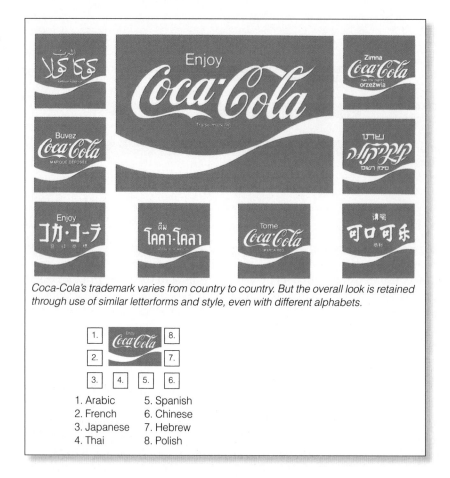

*Coca-Cola's trademark varies from country to country. But the overall look is retained through use of similar letterforms and style, even with different alphabets.*

1. Arabic      5. Spanish
2. French      6. Chinese
3. Japanese    7. Hebrew
4. Thai        8. Polish

on-board food service, and satisfaction with the ticketing and boarding process. The University of Michigan Business School's National Quality Research Center annually surveys customers of more than 200 companies and provides quarterly results for selected industries. The latest results showed that overall customer satisfaction rose to 75.2 (out of a possible 100), with increases in some industries balancing drops in others. Customer satisfaction with the airline industry dropped to its lowest point since 2001, while wireless telephone service stayed at an all-time high for the second year in a row. Table 13.2 shows the top 10 airlines in the Airline Quality Rankings. AirTran took the top ranking while U.S. Airways had the largest decline in performance and fell to number 11.[19]

The quality of services provided by businesses on the Internet can be gauged by consumers on such sites as ConsumerReports.org and BBBOnline. The subscription service offered by ConsumerReports.org provides consumers with a view of e-commerce sites' business, security, and privacy policies. BBBOnline is dedicated to promoting responsibility online. The Web Credibility Project focuses on how health, travel, advocacy, news, and shopping sites disclose business relationships with the companies and products they cover or sell, especially when such relationships pose a potential conflict of interest.[20] Quality can be associated with where the product is made. For example, "Made in U.S.A." labeling can be perceived as a different value and quality. As Table 13.3 indicates, there are differences in the perception of quality

| Top 10 Largest Airlines' Quality Ratings | |
|---|---|
| 1. | AirTran |
| 2. | JetBlue |
| 3. | Southwest |
| 4. | Northwest |
| 5. | Frontier |
| 6. | Continental |
| 7. | Alaska |
| 8. | United |
| 9. | American |
| 10. | Delta |

Source: Joe Kleinsasser, "AirTran Takes Top AQR Spot; Industry Score Falls To New Low," *This Is Wichita State,* April 16, 2008, http://www.wichita.edu/thisis/wsunews/news/?nid=182 (accessed June 26, 2008).

**TABLE 13.2**

Customer Satisfaction with Airlines

and value between the U.S. consumers and Europeans when comparing products made in the United States, Japan, Korea and China.[21]

# Pricing Strategy

Previously, we defined price as the value placed on an object exchanged between a buyer and a seller. Buyers' interest in price stems from their expectations about the usefulness of a product or the satisfaction they may derive from it. Because buyers have limited resources, they must allocate those resources to obtain the products they most desire. They must decide whether the benefits gained in an exchange are worth the buying power sacrificed. Almost anything of value can be assessed by a price. Many factors may influence the evaluation of value, including time constraints, price levels, perceived quality, and motivations to use available information about prices.[22] Indeed, consumers vary in their response to price: Some focus solely on the lowest price, while others consider quality or the prestige associated with a product and its price. Some types of consumers are increasingly "trading up" to more status-conscious products, such as automobiles, home appliances, restaurants, and even pet food, yet remain price-conscious for other products such as cleaning and grocery goods. In setting prices, marketers must consider not just a company's cost to produce a product or service, but the perceived value of that item in the marketplace.[23] This trend has benefited marketers such as Starbucks, Sub-Zero, BMW, and Petco—which can charge premium prices for high-quality,

**TABLE 13.3**   Perceived Quality and Value of Products Based on Country of Origin[*]

| | Made in U.S.A | | Made in Japan | | Made in Korea | | Made in China | |
|---|---|---|---|---|---|---|---|---|
| | Value | Quality | Value | Quality | Value | Quality | Value | Quality |
| U.S. adults | 4.0 | 4.2 | 3.2 | 3.2 | 2.6 | 2.4 | 2.8 | 2.4 |
| Western Europeans | 3.3 | 3.4 | 3.5 | 3.5 | 2.8 | 2.4 | 2.9 | 2.4 |

*On a scale of 1 (low) to 5 (high).

Source: "American Demographics 2006 Consumer Perception Survey," *Advertising Age,* January 2, 2006, p. 9. Data by Synovate.

prestige products—as well as Sam's Clubs and Costco—which offer basic household products at everyday low prices.[24]

Price is a key element in the marketing mix because it relates directly to the generation of revenue and profits. In large part, the ability to set a price depends on the supply of and demand for a product. For most products, the quantity demanded goes up as the price goes down, and as the price goes up, the quantity demanded goes down. Changes in buyers' needs, variations in the effectiveness of other marketing mix variables, the presence of substitutes, and dynamic environmental factors can influence demand. New demand has greatly increased prices for industrial-grade diamonds as jewelers have turned to the impure gems, typically used for drill bits and saws, as a fashion statement. Even diamond giant De Beers has turned to the fashion, with its Talisman collection of flawed-diamond jewelry priced up to $675,000 and making up a quarter of all De Beers jewelry sales in the United States.[25]

Price is probably the most flexible variable in the marketing mix. Although it may take years to develop a product, establish channels of distribution, and design and implement promotion, a product's price may be set and changed in a few minutes. Under certain circumstances, of course, the price may not be so flexible, especially if government regulations prevent dealers from controlling prices. Of course, price also depends on the cost to manufacture a good or provide a service or idea. A firm may temporarily sell products below cost to match competition, to generate cash flow, or even to increase market share, but in the long run it cannot survive by selling its products below cost.

## Pricing Objectives

Pricing objectives specify the role of price in an organization's marketing mix and strategy. They usually are influenced not only by marketing mix decisions but also by finance, accounting, and production factors. Maximizing profits and sales, boosting market share, maintaining the status quo, and survival are four common pricing objectives.

## Specific Pricing Strategies

Pricing strategies provide guidelines for achieving the company's pricing objectives and overall marketing strategy. They specify how price will be used as a variable in the marketing mix. Significant pricing strategies relate to the pricing of new products, psychological pricing, and price discounting.

**Pricing New Products.**    Setting the price for a new product is critical: The right price leads to profitability; the wrong price may kill the product. In general, there are two basic strategies to setting the base price for a new product. **Price skimming** is charging the highest possible price that buyers who want the product will pay. The Porsche Cayenne S V8, for example, has a starting price of $57,900, considerably higher than other sport utility vehicles.[26] This strategy allows the company to generate much-needed revenue to help offset the costs of research and development. Conversely, a **penetration price** is a low price designed to help a product enter the market and gain market share rapidly. For example, when Industrias Añaños introduced Kola Real to capitalize on limited supplies of Coca-Cola and Pepsi Cola in Peru, it set an ultralow penetration price to appeal to the poor who predominate in the region. Kola Real quickly secured one-fifth of the Peruvian market and has since made significant gains in Ecuador, Venezuela, and Mexico, forcing larger soft-drink

**price skimming**
charging the highest possible price that buyers who want the product will pay

**penetration price**
a low price designed to help a product enter the market and gain market share rapidly

# Going Green
## Levi's Blue Jeans Go Green

Levi Strauss & Co. has long been known for its 501s and affordable prices. Recently, the company delved into the premium denim market, dominated by brands such as Earl Jeans, Seven for All Mankind, Citizens for Humanity, and True Religion, by launching its Premium collection. Now, in an attempt to break into yet another hot market, Levi's is going green.

According to the research group Mintel, about 35 million people in the United States regularly purchase "green" products. Consumers are increasingly willing to pay more for earth-friendly products and services. As a result, companies are going to great lengths to prove that they are part of the green movement. Many are switching to earth-friendly packaging or new production methods that conserve energy. Levi's is producing 100 percent organic cotton jeans.

These new jeans, priced at $250 a pop, are made with 100 percent organic cotton, natural dyes, tags composed of recycled paper and soy ink, and recycled rivets. The company is also releasing less expensive lines composed partly of organic and recycled materials.

Although many of us might be willing to switch to green jeans, we may wonder at the price and find it prohibitive. Why is going green sometimes so expensive? In the case of Levi's jeans, it's the organic cotton. The demand for organic cotton is currently much greater than the supply, making it expensive. For cotton to be certified organic, it cannot be genetically modified and must be pesticide and fungicide free. In 2005, more than 50 percent of cotton in the United States was genetically modified. Many companies are turning to farmers overseas, but certification for these farmers can be a challenge. As of 2007, certified organic cotton composed less

than 1 percent of the world's cotton supply. For now, Levi's can only produce a limited number of green jeans, hence the high price.

However, the very issue that drives up prices can be used as a marketing strategy to gain customers. Many people are willing to pay more to support farmers committed to harvesting through organic methods. In fact, at the 2007 Cannes Lions International Advertising Festival, "eco-marketing" was an extremely popular topic. Consumers are excited about green products and services and companies are spending big bucks to promote their stances on going green. According to TNS Media Intelligence, marketers spent $18 million on green-focused television advertising in a three-month time span.

While going green may seem to some like a current fad, indicators point to a prolonged increase in demand for such products. According to the Organic Trade Association, U.S. organic retail sales have grown between 20 to 24 percent annually since 1990. It seems that companies can only benefit from a continued investment in eco-friendly items, and Levi's appears committed to incorporating organic cotton and other eco-friendly materials into its product lines.[27]

**Discussion Questions:**
1. Why can companies charge a premium price for green products?
2. What else might Levi's do to increase its offering of moderately priced green products?
3. How much more would you be willing to pay for environmentally friendly clothing such as Levi's new green jeans?

---

marketers to cut prices.[28] Penetration pricing is less flexible than price skimming; it is more difficult to raise a penetration price than to lower a skimming price. Penetration pricing is used most often when marketers suspect that competitors will enter the market shortly after the product has been introduced.

**Psychological Pricing.** **Psychological pricing** encourages purchases based on emotional rather than rational responses to the price. For example, the assumption behind *even/odd pricing* is that people will buy more of a product for $9.99 than $10 because it seems to be a bargain at the odd price. The assumption behind *symbolic/prestige pricing* is that high prices connote high quality. Thus the prices of certain fragrances are set artificially high to give the impression of superior quality. Some over-the-counter drugs are priced high because consumers associate a drug's price with potency.

**psychological pricing**
encouraging purchases based on emotional rather than rational responses to the price

**Price Discounting.** Temporary price reductions, or **discounts,** are often employed to boost sales. Although there are many types, quantity, seasonal, and promotional discounts are among the most widely used. Quantity discounts reflect the economies of purchasing in large volume. Seasonal discounts to buyers who

**discounts**
temporary price reductions, often employed to boost sales

purchase goods or services out of season help even out production capacity. Promotional discounts attempt to improve sales by advertising price reductions on selected products to increase customer interest. Often promotional pricing is geared to increased profits. Taco Bell, with its reputation for value, has been labeled the "best-positioned U.S. brand" to do well in a recession economy as consumers look for cheaper fast-food options. Taco Bell plans to capitalize on this by adding a "Why pay more?" menu of 11 items priced below $1.[29] McDonald's, however, is having trouble balancing its own "dollar menu" with profits. Franchisees cite rising commodity costs and an increase in minimum wage with sharply cutting their profit margins on dollar menu items. As consumers increasingly turn to these lower-priced options, McDonald's owner/operators are finding it difficult to keep up.[30]

# Distribution Strategy

The best products in the world will not be successful unless companies make them available where and when customers want to buy them. In this section, we will explore dimensions of distribution strategy, including the channels through which products are distributed, the intensity of market coverage, and the physical handling of products during distribution.

## Marketing Channels

**marketing channel**
a group of organizations that moves products from their producer to customers; also called a channel of distribution

A **marketing channel,** or channel of distribution, is a group of organizations that moves products from their producer to customers. Marketing channels make products available to buyers when and where they desire to purchase

**TABLE 13.4**   General Merchandise Retailers

| Type of Retailer | Description | Examples |
|---|---|---|
| Department store | Large organization offering wide product mix and organized into separate departments | Macy's, JCPenney, Sears |
| Discount store | Self-service, general merchandise store offering brand name and private brand products at low prices | Wal-Mart, Target |
| Supermarket | Self-service store offering complete line of food products and some nonfood products | Kroger, Albertson's, Winn-Dixie |
| Superstore | Giant outlet offering all food and nonfood products found in supermarkets, as well as most routinely purchased products | Wal-Mart Supercenters |
| Hypermarket | Combination supermarket and discount store, larger than a superstore | Carrefour |
| Warehouse club | Large-scale, members-only establishments combining cash-and-carry wholesaling with discount retailing | Sam's Club, Costco |
| Warehouse showroom | Facility in a large, low-cost building with large on-premises inventories and minimum service | Ikea |
| Catalog showroom | Type of warehouse showroom where consumers shop from a catalog and products are stored out of buyers' reach and provided in manufacturer's carton | Service Merchandise |

Source: William M. Pride and O. C. Ferrell, *Marketing: Concepts and Strategies,* 2008, p. 428. Copyright 2008 by Houghton Mifflin Company. Reprinted with permission.

them. Organizations that bridge the gap between a product's manufacturer and the ultimate consumer are called *middlemen,* or intermediaries. They create time, place, and ownership utility. Two intermediary organizations are retailers and wholesalers.

**Retailers** buy products from manufacturers (or other intermediaries) and sell them to consumers for home and household use rather than for resale or for use in producing other products. Toys 'Я' Us, for example, buys products from Mattel and other manufacturers and resells them to consumers. Retailing usually occurs in a store, but the Internet, vending machines, mail-order catalogs, and entertainment, such as going to a Chicago Bulls basketball game, also provide opportunities for retailing. With more than 215 million Americans accessing the Internet, online sales were more than $174.5 billion in 2007. By bringing together an assortment of products from competing producers, retailers create utility. Retailers arrange for products to be moved from producers to a convenient retail establishment (place utility). They maintain hours of operation for their retail stores to make merchandise available when consumers want it (time utility). They also assume the risk of ownership of inventories (ownership utility). Table 13.4 describes various types of general merchandise retailers.

Today, there are too many stores competing for too few customers, and, as a result, competition between similar retailers has never been more intense. In addition, retailers face challenges such as shoplifting, as indicated in Table 13.5. Further, competition between different types of stores is changing the nature of retailing. Supermarkets compete with specialty food stores, wholesale clubs, and discount stores. Department stores compete with nearly every other type of store

**retailers**
intermediaries who buy products from manufacturers (or other intermediaries) and sell them to consumers for home and household use rather than for resale or for use in producing other products

| TABLE 13.5 | Shoplifters in the United States | 27 million (1 in 11 people) |
|---|---|---|
| Statistics on Shoplifting in the U.S. | Amount retailers lose per year | More than $13 billion (more than $35 million per day) |
| | Percent of shoplifters who are adults | 75% |
| | Percent of adult shoplifters that started in their teens | 55% |
| | Habitual shoplifters steal on average | About 1.6 times per week |

Source: "Shoplifting Statistics," National Association for Shoplifting Prevention, http://www.shopliftingprevention.org/WhatNASPOffers/NRC/PublicEducStats.htm (accessed June 19, 2008).

including specialty stores, off-price chains, category killers, discount stores, and online retailers. Many traditional retailers, such as Wal-Mart and Macy's, have created online shopping sites to retain customers and compete with online-only retailers. One of the best-known online-only, or cyber, merchants is Amazon.com. Amazon offers millions of products from which to choose, all from the privacy and convenience of the purchaser's home. In some cases, Web merchants offer wide selections, ultra-convenience, superior service, knowledge, and the best products. More detail on the Internet's effect on marketing was presented in Chapter 4.

**wholesalers**
intermediaries who buy from producers or from other wholesalers and sell to retailers

**Wholesalers** are intermediaries who buy from producers or from other wholesalers and sell to retailers. They usually do not sell in significant quantities to ultimate consumers. Wholesalers perform the functions listed in Table 13.6.

Wholesalers are extremely important because of the marketing activities they perform, particularly for consumer products. Although it is true that wholesalers can be eliminated, their functions must be passed on to some other entity, such as the

| TABLE 13.6 | Major Wholesaling Functions |
|---|---|
| Supply chain management | Creating long-term partnerships among channel members |
| Promotion | Providing a sales force, advertising, sales promotion, and publicity |
| Warehousing, shipping, and product handling | Receiving, storing, and stockkeeping<br>Packaging<br>Shipping outgoing orders<br>Materials handling<br>Arranging and making local and long distance shipments |
| Inventory control and data processing | Processing orders<br>Controlling physical inventory<br>Recording transactions<br>Tracking sales data for financial analysis |
| Risk taking | Assuming responsibility for theft, product obsolescence, and excess inventories |
| Financing and budgeting | Extending credit<br>Making capital investments<br>Forecasting cash flow |
| Marketing research and information systems | Providing information about market<br>Conducting research studies<br>Managing computer networks to facilitate exchanges and relationships |

Source: William M. Pride and O. C. Ferrell, *Marketing: Concepts and Strategies,* 2008, p. 389. Copyright 2008 by Houghton Mifflin Company. Reprinted with permission.

producer, another intermediary, or even the customer. Wholesalers help consumers and retailers by buying in large quantities, then selling to retailers in smaller quantities. By stocking an assortment of products, wholesalers match products to demand.

**Supply Chain Management.**    In an effort to improve distribution channel relationships among manufacturers and other channel intermediaries, supply chain management creates alliances between channel members. In Chapter 9, we defined supply chain management as connecting and integrating all parties or members of the distribution system in order to satisfy customers. It involves long-term partnerships among marketing channel members working together to reduce costs, waste, and unnecessary movement in the entire marketing channel in order to satisfy customers.[31] It goes beyond traditional channel members (producers, wholesalers, retailers, customers) to include *all* organizations involved in moving products from the producer to the ultimate customer. In a survey of business managers, a disruption in the supply chain was viewed as the number-one crisis that could decrease revenue.[32]

The focus shifts from one of selling to the next level in the channel to one of selling products *through* the channel to a satisfied ultimate customer. Information, once provided on a guarded,"as needed" basis, is now open, honest, and ongoing. Perhaps most importantly, the points of contact in the relationship expand from one-on-one at the salesperson–buyer level to multiple interfaces at all levels and in all functional areas of the various organizations.

**Channels for Consumer Products.**    Typical marketing channels for consumer products are shown in Figure 13.6. In Channel A, the product moves from the

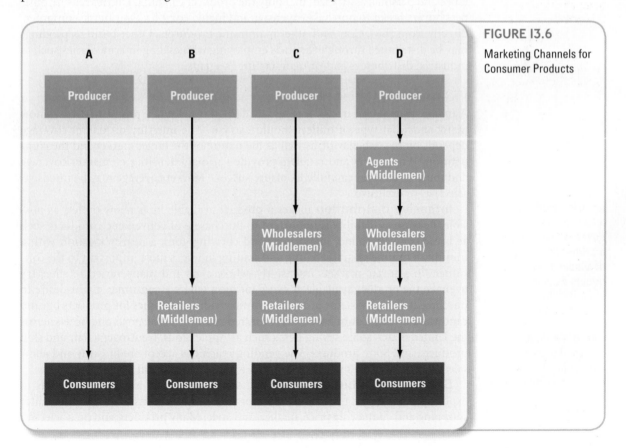

**FIGURE 13.6**

Marketing Channels for Consumer Products

producer directly to the consumer. Farmers who sell their fruit and vegetables to consumers at roadside stands use a direct-from-producer-to-consumer marketing channel.

In Channel B, the product goes from producer to retailer to consumer. This type of channel is used for products such as college textbooks, automobiles, and appliances. In Channel C, the product is handled by a wholesaler and a retailer before it reaches the consumer. Producer-to-wholesaler-to-retailer-to-consumer marketing channels distribute a wide range of products including refrigerators, televisions, soft drinks, cigarettes, clocks, watches, and office products. In Channel D, the product goes to an agent, a wholesaler, and a retailer before going to the consumer. This long channel of distribution is especially useful for convenience products. Candy and some produce are often sold by agents who bring buyers and sellers together.

Services are usually distributed through direct marketing channels because they are generally produced *and* consumed simultaneously. For example, you cannot take a haircut home for later use. Many services require the customer's presence and participation: The sick patient must visit the physician to receive treatment; the child must be at the day care center to receive care; the tourist must be present to sightsee and consume tourism services.

**Channels for Business Products.** In contrast to consumer goods, more than half of all business products, especially expensive equipment or technically complex products, are sold through direct marketing channels. Business customers like to communicate directly with producers of such products to gain the technical assistance and personal assurances that only the producer can offer. For this reason, business buyers prefer to purchase expensive and highly complex mainframe computers directly from IBM, Cray, and other mainframe producers. Other business products may be distributed through channels employing wholesaling intermediaries such as industrial distributors and/or manufacturer's agents.

## Intensity of Market Coverage

A major distribution decision is how widely to distribute a product—that is, how many and what type of outlets should carry it. The intensity of market coverage depends on buyer behavior, as well as the nature of the target market and the competition. Wholesalers and retailers provide various intensities of market coverage and must be selected carefully to ensure success. Market coverage may be intensive, selective, or exclusive.

**intensive distribution** a form of market coverage whereby a product is made available in as many outlets as possible

**Intensive distribution** makes a product available in as many outlets as possible. Because availability is important to purchasers of convenience products such as bread, milk, gasoline, soft drinks, and chewing gum, a nearby location with a minimum of time spent searching and waiting in line is most important to the consumer. To saturate markets intensively, wholesalers and many varied retailers try to make the product available at every location where a consumer might desire to purchase it. Zoom Systems provides robotic vending machines for products beyond candy and drinks. Zoom has several hundred machines in airports and hotels across the United States, some selling items such as Apple iPods, Neutrogena hair and skin products, and Sony products. The vending machines accept credit cards and allow sales to occur in places where storefronts would be impossible.[33]

**selective distribution** a form of market coverage whereby only a small number of all available outlets are used to expose products

**Selective distribution** uses only a small number of all available outlets to expose products. It is used most often for products that consumers buy only after shopping and comparing price, quality, and style. Many products sold on a selective basis require salesperson assistance, technical advice, warranties, or repair service to maintain consumer satisfaction. Typical products include automobiles, major appliances, clothes, and furniture.

**Exclusive distribution** exists when a manufacturer gives an intermediary the sole right to sell a product in a defined geographic territory. Such exclusivity provides an incentive for a dealer to handle a product that has a limited market. Exclusive distribution is the opposite of intensive distribution in that products are purchased and consumed over a long period of time, and service or information is required to develop a satisfactory sales relationship. Products distributed on an exclusive basis include high-quality musical instruments, yachts, airplanes, and high-fashion leather goods.

**exclusive distribution** the awarding by a manufacturer to an intermediary of the sole right to sell a product in a defined geographic territory

## Physical Distribution

**Physical distribution** includes all the activities necessary to move products from producers to customers—inventory control, transportation, warehousing, and materials handling. Physical distribution creates time and place utility by making products available when they are wanted, with adequate service and at minimum cost. Both goods and services require physical distribution. Many physical distribution activities are part of supply chain management, which we discussed in Chapter 9; we'll take a brief look at a few more now.

**physical distribution** all the activities necessary to move products from producers to customers—inventory control, transportation, warehousing, and materials handling

Transportation.   **Transportation,** the shipment of products to buyers, creates time and place utility for products, and thus is a key element in the flow of goods and services from producer to consumer. The five major modes of transportation used to move products between cities in the United States are railways, motor vehicles, inland waterways, pipelines, and airways.

**transportation** the shipment of products to buyers

Railroads offer the least expensive transportation for many products. Heavy commodities, foodstuffs, raw materials, and coal are examples of products carried by railroads. Trucks have greater flexibility than railroads because they can reach more locations. Trucks handle freight quickly and economically, offer door-to-door service, and are more flexible in their packaging requirements than are ships or airplanes. Air transport offers speed and a high degree of dependability but is the most expensive means of transportation; shipping is the least expensive and slowest form. Pipelines are used to transport petroleum, natural gas, semiliquid coal, wood chips, and certain chemicals. Many products can be moved most efficiently by using more than one mode of transportation.

Factors affecting the selection of a mode of transportation include cost, capability to handle the product, reliability, and availability, and, as suggested, selecting transportation modes requires trade-offs. Unique characteristics of the product and consumer desires often determine the mode selected.

Warehousing.   **Warehousing** is the design and operation of facilities to receive, store, and ship products. A warehouse facility receives, identifies, sorts, and dispatches goods to storage; stores them; recalls, selects, or picks goods; assembles the shipment; and finally, dispatches the shipment.

**warehousing** the design and operation of facilities to receive, store, and ship products

Companies often own and operate their own private warehouses that store, handle, and move their own products. They can also rent storage and related physical distribution services from public warehouses. Regardless of whether a private or a public warehouse is used, warehousing is important because it makes products available for shipment to match demand at different geographic locations.

# Entrepreneurship in Action
## Kombucha Tea Tastes Different!

G. T. Dave

**Business:** Millennium Products

**Founded:** 1995

**Success:** Dave has gone from selling Kombucha door to door from his mom's van to selling it to stores nationwide.

In 1995, when G. T. Dave was still a teenager, Dave's mother was diagnosed with breast cancer. While searching for alternatives to help combat the cancer, she discovered Kombucha tea—a substance that she and her son credit to some degree with her recovery. Although Dave was young, he was determined to share Kombucha with others. He began by brewing Kombucha at home. Kombucha is an ancient Chinese beverage, named by the Chinese as the Tea of Immortality and the elixir of life, which has been used for thousands of years. It is a living culture of beneficial microorganisms. Kombucha is cultured (similar to the fermentation process) for 30 days. During this time, nutrients such as active enzymes, viable probiotics, amino acids, antioxidants, and polyphenols grow in the culture. The end result resembles (and is often referred to as) a mushroom—a light brown, tough, gelatinous disk. It is actually a living thing that regenerates. Therefore, the new cultures produced in each batch can be used to create future batches. Dave's Kombucha still originates from the cultures he first made. People drink Kombucha for many health-related reasons such as to aid the liver, the blood, and the digestive system. Dave began distributing his Kombucha locally door to door, but he now sells his products to stores nationwide. Although his business has grown, he continues to create Kombucha in small batches that are 100 percent organic. Kombucha can be brewed at home, but, for many, the home-brewing process can be a turn-off. The taste is also a problem—it varies based on the batch and is something between apple cider and vinegar. This is where Dave comes in. He brews the tea and adds different fruit juices to create more palatable tastes. People throughout the United States and worldwide swear by this unique beverage.[34]

**materials handling**
the physical handling and movement of products in warehousing and transportation

Materials Handling. **Materials handling** is the physical handling and movement of products in warehousing and transportation. Handling processes may vary significantly due to product characteristics. Efficient materials-handling procedures increase a warehouse's useful capacity and improve customer service. Well-coordinated loading and movement systems increase efficiency and reduce costs.

### Importance of Distribution in a Marketing Strategy

Distribution decisions are among the least flexible marketing mix decisions. Products can be changed over time; prices can be changed quickly; and promotion is usually changed regularly. But distribution decisions often commit resources and establish contractual relationships that are difficult if not impossible to change. As a company attempts to expand into new markets, it may require a complete change in distribution. Moreover, if a firm does not manage its marketing channel in the most efficient manner and provide the best service, then a new competitor will evolve to create a more effective distribution system.

# Promotion Strategy

The role of promotion is to communicate with individuals, groups, and organizations to facilitate an exchange directly or indirectly. It encourages marketing exchanges by attempting to persuade individuals, groups, and organizations to accept goods, services, and ideas. Promotion is used not only to sell products but also to influence opinions and attitudes toward an organization, person, or cause. The state of Texas, for example, has successfully used promotion to educate people about the costs of highway litter and thereby reduce littering. Most people probably equate promotion with advertising, but it also includes personal selling, publicity, and sales promotion. The role that these elements play in a marketing strategy is extremely important.

## The Promotion Mix

Advertising, personal selling, publicity, and sales promotion are collectively known as the promotion mix because a strong promotion program results from the careful selection and blending of these elements. The process of coordinating the promotion mix elements and synchronizing promotion as a unified effort is called **integrated marketing communications.** When planning promotional activities, an integrated marketing communications approach results in the desired message for customers. Different elements of the promotion mix are coordinated to play their appropriate roles in delivery of the message on a consistent basis.

**Advertising.**   Perhaps the best-known form of promotion, **advertising** is a paid form of nonpersonal communication transmitted through a mass medium, such as television commercials, magazine advertisements or online ads. Even Google, one of the most powerful brands in the world, has begun advertising. Google has turned to outdoor advertising on buses, trains, and ballparks in San Francisco and Chicago to promote its Google Maps feature.[35] Commercials featuring celebrities, customers, or unique creations (the Energizer Bunny, for example) serve to grab viewers' attention and pique their interest in a product. Table 13.7 shows companies that spent more than $1 billion on ads in the United States in one year.

An **advertising campaign** involves designing a series of advertisements and placing them in various media to reach a particular target audience. The basic content and form of an advertising campaign are a function of several factors. A product's features, uses, and benefits affect the content of the campaign message and individual ads. Characteristics of the people in the target audience—gender, age, education, race, income, occupation, lifestyle, and other attributes—influence both content and form. When Procter & Gamble promotes Crest toothpaste to children, the company emphasizes daily brushing and cavity control, whereas it promotes tartar control and whiter teeth when marketing to adults. To communicate effectively, advertisers use words, symbols, and illustrations that are meaningful, familiar, and attractive to people in the target audience.

An advertising campaign's objectives and platform also affect the content and form of its messages. If a firm's advertising objectives involve large sales increases, the message may include hard-hitting, high-impact language and symbols. When

**integrated marketing communications** coordinating the promotion mix elements and synchronizing promotion as a unified effort

**advertising** a paid form of nonpersonal communication transmitted through a mass medium, such as television commercials or magazine advertisements

**advertising campaign** designing a series of advertisements and placing them in various media to reach a particular target market

| Organization | Advertising Expenditure ($ Millions) |
|---|---|
| 1.  Procter & Gamble Co. | $ 4,898.0 |
| 2.  AT&T | 3,344.7 |
| 3.  General Motors Corp. | 3,296.1 |
| 4.  Time Warner | 3,088.8 |
| 5.  Verizon Communications | 2,821.8 |
| 6.  Ford Motor Co. | 2,576.8 |
| 7.  GlaxoSmithKline | 2,444.2 |
| 8.  Walt Disney Co. | 2,320.0 |
| 9.  Johnson & Johnson | 2,290.5 |
| 10.  Unilever | 2,098.3 |

**TABLE 13.7**

Top 10 Leading National Advertisers

Source: "Datacenter: Marketer Profiles Yearbook, 50 Leading National Advertisers" *Advertising Age,* December 31, 2007, http://adage.com/images/random/datacenter/2007/annual08yearbook.pdf (accessed June 19, 2008).

campaign objectives aim at increasing brand awareness, the message may use much repetition of the brand name and words and illustrations associated with it. Thus, the advertising platform is the foundation on which campaign messages are built.

Advertising media are the vehicles or forms of communication used to reach a desired audience. Print media include newspapers, magazines, direct mail, and billboards, and electronic media include television, radio, and cyber ads. Newspapers, television, and direct mail are the most widely used advertising media.

Choice of media obviously influences the content and form of the message. Effective outdoor displays and short broadcast spot announcements require concise, simple messages. Magazine and newspaper advertisements can include considerable detail and long explanations. Because several kinds of media offer geographic selectivity, a precise message can be tailored to a particular geographic section of the target audience. For example, a company advertising in *Time* might decide to use one message in the New England region and another in the rest of the nation. A company may also choose to advertise in only one region. Such geographic selectivity lets a firm use the same message in different regions at different times.

The use of online advertising is increasing. However, advertisers are demanding more for their ad dollars and proof that they are working. Certain types of ads are more popular than pop-up ads and banner ads that consumers find annoying. One technique is to blur the lines between television and online advertising. TV commercials may point viewers to a Web site for more information, where short "advertainment" films continue the marketing message. When godaddy.com's 2008 Super Bowl commercial was rejected by Fox for being too racy, it left the racy version on its Web site. The TV commercial that aired showed people watching the original commercial featuring racecar driver Danica Patrick online.[36] To reach a younger demographic, BMW created a 30-minute online mockumentary film featuring a fictional town in Bavaria attempting to catapult a BMW car across the Atlantic using a giant ramp. The humorous take created strong buzz on the Web and led to articles in The Wall Street Journal and on CNN.com.[37]

Infomercials—typically 30-minute blocks of radio or television air time featuring a celebrity or upbeat host talking about and demonstrating a product—have evolved as an advertising method. Toll-free numbers and Web site addresses are usually provided so consumers can conveniently purchase the product or obtain additional information. Although many consumers and companies have negative feelings about infomercials, apparently they get results.

**personal selling**
direct, two-way communication with buyers and potential buyers

Personal Selling.   **Personal selling** is direct, two-way communication with buyers and potential buyers. For many products—especially large, expensive ones with specialized uses, such as cars, appliances, and houses—interaction between a salesperson and the customer is probably the most important promotional tool.

Personal selling is the most flexible of the promotional methods because it gives marketers the greatest opportunity to communicate specific information that might trigger a purchase. Only personal selling can zero in on a prospect and attempt to persuade that person to make a purchase. Although personal selling has a lot of advantages, it is one of the most costly forms of promotion. A sales call on an industrial customer can cost as much as $200 or $300.

There are three distinct categories of salespersons: order takers (for example, retail sales clerks and route salespeople), creative salespersons (for example, automobile,

*The Louisville Zoo advertises on this billboard to increase attendance.*

furniture, and insurance salespeople), and support salespersons (for example, customer educators and goodwill builders who usually do not take orders). For most of these salespeople, personal selling is a six-step process:

1. *Prospecting:* Identifying potential buyers of the product.
2. *Approaching:* Using a referral or calling on a customer without prior notice to determine interest in the product.
3. *Presenting:* Getting the prospect's attention with a product demonstration.
4. *Handling objections:* Countering reasons for not buying the product.
5. *Closing:* Asking the prospect to buy the product.
6. *Following up:* Checking customer satisfaction with the purchased product.

Publicity.   **Publicity** is nonpersonal communication transmitted through the mass media but not paid for directly by the firm. A firm does not pay the media cost for publicity and is not identified as the originator of the message; instead, the message is presented in news story form. Obviously, a company can benefit from publicity by releasing to news sources newsworthy messages about the firm and its involvement with the public. Many companies have *public relations* departments to try to gain favorable publicity and minimize negative publicity for the firm.

**publicity**
nonpersonal communication transmitted through the mass media but not paid for directly by the firm

Although advertising and publicity are both carried by the mass media, they differ in several major ways. Advertising messages tend to be informative, persuasive, or both; publicity is mainly informative. Advertising is often designed to have an immediate impact or to provide specific information to persuade a person to act; publicity describes what a firm is doing, what products it is launching, or other newsworthy information, but seldom calls for action. When advertising is used, the organization must pay for media time and select the media that will best reach target audiences. The mass media willingly carry publicity because they believe it has general public interest. Advertising can be repeated a number of times; most publicity appears in the mass media once and is not repeated.

Advertising, personal selling, and sales promotion are especially useful for influencing an exchange directly. Publicity is extremely important when communication focuses on a company's activities and products and is directed at interest groups, current and potential investors, regulatory agencies, and society in general.

A variation of traditional advertising is buzz marketing, in which marketers attempt to create a trend or acceptance of a product. Companies seek out trend-setters in communities and get them to "talk up" a brand to their friends, family, co-workers, and others. Toyota, for example, parked its new Scions outside of raves and coffee shops, and offered hip-hop magazine writers the chance for tests drives in order to get the "buzz" going about the new car.[38] Other market-ers using the buzz technique include Hebrew National ("mom squads" grilled the company's hot dogs), and Chrysler (its retro PT Cruiser was planted in rental fleets). The idea behind buzz marketing is that an accepted member of a particular social group will be more credible than any form of paid communication.[39] The concept works best as part of an integrated marketing communication program that also includes traditional advertising, personal selling, sales promotion, and publicity.

A related concept is viral marketing, which describes the concept of getting Inter-net users to pass on ads and promotions to others. For example, Ebrick offered spe-cial discounts to its shoppers and encouraged them to forward the deals to their friends and family.[40]

**sales promotion**
direct inducements offering added value or some other incentive for buyers to enter into an exchange

Sales Promotion.   **Sales promotion** involves direct inducements offering added value or some other incentive for buyers to enter into an exchange. Sales promotions are generally easier to measure and less expensive than advertising. The major tools of sales promotion are store displays, premiums, samples and dem-onstrations, coupons, contests and sweepstakes, refunds, and trade shows. More than $331 billion dollars in potential consumer savings were distributed through coupons, with more than 2.6 billion coupons redeemed. Coupon inserts in news-papers made up about 89 percent of the distribution, with 92.5 percent of all cou-pons distributed via methods sent directly to the home (direct mail, newspaper, magazine, etc).[41] While coupons can be a valuable tool in sales promotion, they cannot be relied upon to stand, but should be part of an overall promotion mix. Sales promotion stimulates customer purchasing and increases dealer effectiveness in selling products. It is used to enhance and supplement other forms of promotion. Test drives allow salespersons to demonstrate vehicles, which can help purchase decisions. Sampling a product may also encourage consumers to buy. PepsiCo, for example, used sampling to promote its Sierra Mist soft drink to reach more than 5 million potential consumers at well-traveled sites such as Times Square and Penn Station.[42] In a given year, almost three-fourths of consumer product companies may use sampling.

### Promotion Strategies: To Push or To Pull

**push strategy**
an attempt to motivate intermediaries to push the product down to their customers

**pull strategy**
the use of promotion to create consumer demand for a product so that consumers exert pressure on marketing channel members to make it available

In developing a promotion mix, organizations must decide whether to fashion a mix that pushes or pulls the product (Figure 13.7). A **push strategy** attempts to motivate intermediaries to push the product down to their customers. When a push strategy is used, the company attempts to motivate wholesalers and retailers to make the product available to their customers. Sales personnel may be used to persuade intermediaries to offer the product, distribute promotional materials, and offer special promotional incentives for those who agree to carry the product. Chrysler manufacturing plants operate on a push system. They assemble cars according to forecasts of sales demand. Dealers then sell to buyers with the help of incentives and other promotions.[43] A **pull strategy** uses promotion to create consumer demand for a product so that consumers exert pressure on marketing channel members to

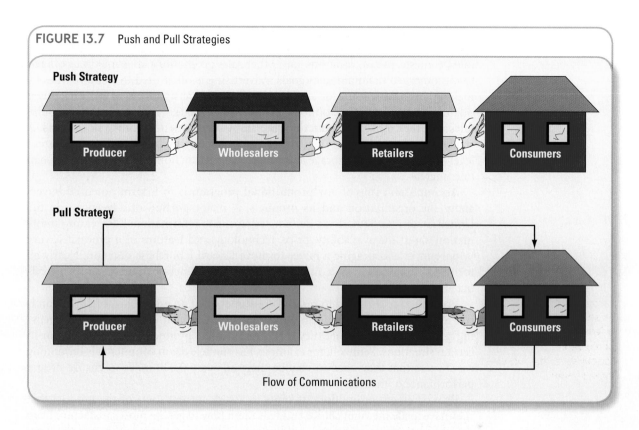

**FIGURE 13.7**   Push and Pull Strategies

Push Strategy

Producer → Wholesalers → Retailers → Consumers

Pull Strategy

Producer — Wholesalers — Retailers — Consumers

Flow of Communications

make it available. For example, when the Coca-Cola Company launched its new hybrid energy soda VAULT, the company gave away samples throughout the United States via sampling teams in VAULT-branded International CXTs, the world's largest production pickup trucks. They distributed ice-cold VAULT at concerts and targeted retail outlets, sporting events, and other locations.[44] Such sampling prior to a product rollout encourages consumers to request the product from their favorite retailer.

A company can use either strategy, or it can use a variation or combination of the two. The exclusive use of advertising indicates a pull strategy. Personal selling to marketing channel members indicates a push strategy. The allocation of promotional resources to various marketing mix elements probably determines which strategy a marketer uses.

## Objectives of Promotion

The marketing mix a company uses depends on its objectives. It is important to recognize that promotion is only one element of the marketing strategy and must be tied carefully to the goals of the firm, its overall marketing objectives, and the other elements of the marketing strategy. Firms use promotion for many reasons, but typical objectives are to stimulate demand, to stabilize sales, and to inform, remind, and reinforce customers.

Increasing demand for a product is probably the most typical promotional objective. Stimulating demand, often through advertising and sales promotion, is particularly important when a firm is using a pull strategy.

Another goal of promotion is to stabilize sales by maintaining the status quo—that is, the current sales level of the product. During periods of slack or decreasing sales, contests, prizes, vacations, and other sales promotions are sometimes offered to customers to maintain sales goals. Advertising is often used to stabilize sales by making customers aware of slack use periods. For example, auto manufacturers often provide rebates, free options, or lower-than-market interest rates to stabilize sales and thereby keep production lines moving during temporary slowdowns. A stable sales pattern allows the firm to run efficiently by maintaining a consistent level of production and storage and utilizing all its functions so that it is ready when sales increase.

An important role of any promotional program is to inform potential buyers about the organization and its products. A major portion of advertising in the United States, particularly in daily newspapers, is informational. Providing information about the availability, price, technology, and features of a product is very important in encouraging a buyer to move toward a purchase decision. Nearly all forms of promotion involve an attempt to help consumers learn more about a product and a company.

Promotion is also used to remind consumers that an established organization is still around and sells certain products that have uses and benefits. Often advertising reminds customers that they may need to use a product more frequently or in certain situations. Pennzoil, for example, has run television commercials reminding car owners that they need to change their oil every 3,000 miles to ensure proper performance of their cars.

Reinforcement promotion attempts to assure current users of the product that they have made the right choice and tells them how to get the most satisfaction from the product. Also, a company could release publicity statements through the news media about a new use for a product. Additionally, firms can have salespeople communicate with current and potential customers about the proper use and maintenance of a product—all in the hope of developing a repeat customer.

## Promotional Positioning

**promotional positioning**
the use of promotion to create and maintain an image of a product in buyers' minds

**Promotional positioning** uses promotion to create and maintain an image of a product in buyers' minds. It is a natural result of market segmentation. In both promotional positioning and market segmentation, the firm targets a given product or brand at a portion of the total market. A promotional strategy helps differentiate the product and make it appeal to a particular market segment. For example, to appeal to safety-conscious consumers, Volvo heavily promotes the safety and crashworthiness of Volvo automobiles in its advertising. Volkswagen has done the same thing with its edgy ads showing car crashes. Promotion can be used to change or reinforce an image. Effective promotion influences customers and persuades them to buy.

# So You Want to Be a Marketing Manager

Many jobs in marketing are closely tied to the marketing mix functions: distribution, product, promotion, and price. Often the job titles could be sales manager, distribution or supply chain manager, advertising account executive, or store manager.

A distribution manager arranges for transportation of goods within firms and through marketing channels. Transportation can be costly, and time is always an important factor, so minimizing their effects is vital to the success of a firm. Distribution managers must choose one or a combination of transportation modes from a vast array of options, taking into account local, federal, and international regulations for different freight classifications; the weight, size, and fragility of products to be shipped; time schedules; and loss and damage ratios. Manufacturing firms are the largest employers of distribution managers.

A product manager is responsible for the success or failure of a product line. This requires a general knowledge of advertising, transportation modes, inventory control, selling and sales management, promotion, marketing research, packaging, and pricing. Frequently, several years of selling and sales management experience are prerequisites for such a position as well as college training in business administration. Being a product manager can be rewarding both financially and psychologically.

Some of the most creative roles in the business world are in the area of advertising. Advertising pervades our daily lives, as businesses and other organizations try to grab our attention and tell us about what they have to offer. Copywriters, artists, and account executives in advertising must have creativity, imagination, artistic talent, and expertise in expression and persuasion. Advertising is an area of business in which a wide variety of educational backgrounds may be useful, from degrees in advertising itself, to journalism or liberal arts degrees. Common entry-level positions in an advertising agency are found in the traffic department, account service (account coordinator), or the media department (media assistant). Advertising jobs are also available in many manufacturing or retail firms, nonprofit organizations, banks, professional associations, utility companies, and other arenas outside of an advertising agency.

Although a career in retailing may begin in sales, there is much more to retailing than simply selling. Many retail personnel occupy management positions, focusing on selecting and ordering merchandise, promotional activities, inventory control, customer credit operations, accounting, personnel, and store security. Many specific examples of retailing jobs can be found in large department stores. A section manager coordinates inventory and promotions and interacts with buyers, salespeople, and consumers. The buyer's job is fast-paced, often involving much travel and pressure. Buyers must be open-minded and foresighted in their hunt for new, potentially successful items. Regional managers coordinate the activities of several retail stores within a specific geographic area, usually monitoring and supporting sales, promotions, and general procedures. Retail management can be exciting and challenging. Growth in retailing is expected to accompany the growth in population and is likely to create substantial opportunities in the coming years.

While a career in marketing can be very rewarding, marketers today agree that the job is getting tougher. Many advertising and marketing executives say the job has gotten much more demanding in the past 10 years, viewing their number-one challenge as balancing work and personal obligations. Other challenges include staying current on industry trends or technologies, keeping motivated/inspired on the job, and measuring success. If you are up to the challenge, you may find that a career in marketing is just right for you to utilize your business knowledge while exercising your creative side as well.

# Review Your Understanding

***Describe the role of product in the marketing mix, including how products are developed, classified, and identified.***

Products (goods, services, ideas) are among a firm's most visible contacts with consumers and must meet consumers' needs and expectations to ensure success. New-product development is a multistep process: idea development, the screening of new ideas, business analysis, product development, test marketing, and commercialization. Products are usually classified as either consumer or business products. Consumer products can be further classified as convenience, shopping, or specialty products. The business product classifications are raw materials, major equipment, accessory equipment, component parts, processed materials, supplies, and industrial services. Products also can be classified by the stage of the product life cycle (introduction, growth, maturity, and decline). Identifying products includes branding (the process of naming and identifying products); packaging (the product's container); and labeling (information, such as content and warnings, on the package).

***Define price, and discuss its importance in the marketing mix, including various pricing strategies a firm might employ.***

Price is the value placed on an object exchanged between a buyer and a seller. It is probably the most flexible variable of the marketing mix. Pricing objectives include survival, maximization of profits and sales volume, and maintaining the status quo. When a firm introduces a new product, it may use price skimming or penetration pricing. Psychological pricing and price discounting are other strategies.

***Identify factors affecting distribution decisions, such as marketing channels and intensity of market coverage.***

Making products available to customers is facilitated by middlemen, or intermediaries, who bridge the gap between the producer of the product and its ultimate user. A marketing channel is a group of marketing organizations that directs the flow of products from producers to consumers. Market coverage relates to the number and variety of outlets that make products available to customers; it may be intensive, selective, or exclusive. Physical distribution is all the activities necessary to move products from producers to consumers, including inventory planning and control, transportation, warehousing, and materials handling.

***Specify the activities involved in promotion, as well as promotional strategies and promotional positioning.***

Promotion encourages marketing exchanges by persuading individuals, groups, and organizations to accept goods, services, and ideas. The promotion mix includes advertising (a paid form of nonpersonal communication transmitted through a mass medium), personal selling (direct, two-way communication with buyers and potential buyers), publicity (nonpersonal communication transmitted through the mass media but not paid for directly by the firm), and sales promotion (direct inducements offering added value or some other incentive for buyers to enter into an exchange). A push strategy attempts to motivate intermediaries to push the product down to their customers, whereas a pull strategy tries to create consumer demand for a product so that consumers exert pressure on marketing channel members to make the product available. Typical promotion objectives are to stimulate demand, stabilize sales, and inform, remind, and reinforce customers. Promotional positioning is the use of promotion to create and maintain in the buyer's mind an image of a product.

***Evaluate an organization's marketing strategy plans.***

Based on the material in this chapter, you should be able to answer the questions posed in "Solve the Dilemma" on page 418 and evaluate the company's marketing strategy plans, including its target market and marketing mix.

# Revisit the World of Business

1. How has Concord used marketing to achieve success?
2. Why do you think Paul McCartney released his album through Concord's joint venture label Hear Music at Starbucks?
3. Why would Concord permit free downloads of songs?

# Learn the Terms

advertising   409
advertising campaign   409
branding   395
business products   392
commercialization   390
consumer products   391
discounts   401
exclusive distribution   407
generic products   396
integrated marketing
   communications   409
intensive distribution   406
labeling   397

manufacturer brands   395
marketing channel   402
materials handling   408
packaging   396
penetration price   400
personal selling   410
physical distribution   407
price skimming   400
private distributor brands   396
product line   392
product mix   392
promotional positioning   414
psychological pricing   401

publicity   411
pull strategy   412
push strategy   412
quality   397
retailers   403
sales promotion   412
selective distribution   406
test marketing   390
trademark   395
transportation   407
warehousing   407
wholesalers   404

# Check Your Progress

1. What steps do companies generally take to develop and introduce a new product?

2. What is the product life cycle? How does a product's life cycle stage affect its marketing strategy?

3. Which marketing mix variable is probably the most flexible? Why?

4. Distinguish between the two ways to set the base price for a new product.

5. What is probably the least flexible marketing mix variable? Why?

6. Describe the typical marketing channels for consumer products.

7. What activities are involved in physical distribution? What functions does a warehouse perform?

8. How do publicity and advertising differ? How are they related?

9. What does the personal selling process involve? Briefly discuss the process.

10. List the circumstances in which the push and pull promotional strategies are used.

# Get Involved

1. Pick three products you use every day (either in school, at work, or for pleasure—perhaps one of each). Determine what phase of the product life cycle each is in. Evaluate the marketer's strategy (product, price, promotion, and distribution) for the product and whether it is appropriate for the life-cycle stage.

2. Design a distribution channel for a manufacturer of stuffed toys.

3. Pick a nearby store, and briefly describe the kinds of sales promotion used and their effectiveness.

# Build Your Skills

**ANALYZING MOTEL 6'S MARKETING STRATEGY**

**Background:**
Made famous through the well-known radio and TV commercials spoken in the distinctive "down-home" voice of Tom Bodett, the Dallas-based Motel 6 chain of budget motels is probably familiar to you. Based on the information provided here and any personal knowledge you may have about the company, you will analyze the marketing strategy of Motel 6.

**Task:**

Read the following paragraphs, then complete the questions that follow.

Motel 6 was established in 1962 with the original name emphasizing its low-cost, no-frills approach. Rooms at that time were $6 per night. Today, Motel 6 has more than 760 units, and the average nightly cost is $34. Motel 6 is the largest company-owned and operated lodging chain in the United States. Customers receive HBO, ESPN, free morning coffee, and free local phone calls, and most units have pools and some business services. Motel 6 has made a name for itself by offering clean, comfortable rooms at the lowest prices of any national motel chain and by standardizing both its product offering and its operating policies and procedures. The company's national spokesperson, Tom Bodett, is featured in radio and television commercials that use humorous stories to show why it makes sense to stay at Motel 6 rather than a pricey hotel.

In appealing to pleasure travelers on a budget as well as business travelers looking to get the most for their dollar, one commercial makes the point that all hotel and motel rooms look the same at night when the lights are out—when customers are getting what they came for, a good night's sleep. Motel 6 location sites are selected based on whether they provide convenient access to the highway system and whether they are close to areas such as shopping centers, tourist attractions, or business districts.

1.  In SELECTING A TARGET MARKET, which approach is Motel 6 using to segment markets?

    a.  concentration approach

    b.  multisegment approach

2.  In DEVELOPING A MARKETING MIX, identify in the second column of the table what the current strategy is and then identify any changes you think Motel 6 should consider for carrying it successfully through the next five years.

| Marketing Mix Variable | Current Strategy | 5-Year Strategy |
|---|---|---|
| a. Product | | |
| b. Price | | |
| c. Distribution | | |
| d. Promotion | | |
| | | |

# Solve the Dilemma

### BETTER HEALTH WITH SNACKS

Deluxe Chips is one of the leading companies in the salty-snack industry, with almost one-fourth of the $10 billion market. Its Deluxos tortilla chips are the number-one selling brand in North America, and its Ridgerunner potato chip is also a market share leader. Deluxe Chips wants to stay on top of the market by changing marketing strategies to match changing consumer needs and preferences. Promoting specific brands to market segments with the appropriate price and distribution channel is helping Deluxe Chips succeed.

As many middle-aged consumers modify their snacking habits, Deluxe Chips is considering a new product line of light snack foods with less fat and cholesterol and targeted at the 35- to 50-year-old consumer who enjoys snacking but wants to be more health conscious. Marketing research suggests that the product will succeed as long as it tastes good and that consumers may be willing to pay more for it. Large expenditures on advertising may be necessary to overcome the competition. However, it may be possible to analyze customer profiles and retail store characteristics and then match the right product with the right neighborhood. Store-specific micromarketing would allow Deluxe Chips to spend its promotional dollars more efficiently.

**Discussion Questions**

1.  Design a marketing strategy for the new product line.
2.  Critique your marketing strategy in terms of its strengths and weaknesses.
3.  What are your suggestions for implementation of the marketing strategy?

# Build Your Business Plan

## DIMENSIONS OF MARKETING STRATEGY

If you think your product/business is truly new to or unique to the market, you need to substantiate your claim. After a thorough exploration on the Web, you want to make sure there has not been a similar business/service recently launched in your community. Check with your Chamber of Commerce or Economic Development Office that might be able to provide you with a history of recent business failures. If you are not confident about the ability or willingness of customers to try your new product or service, collecting your own primary data to ascertain demand is highly advisable.

The decision of where to initially set your prices is a critical one. If there are currently similar products in the market, you need to be aware of the competitors' prices before you determine yours. If your product/service is new

to the market, you can price it high (market skimming strategy) as long as you realize that the high price will probably attract competitors to the market more quickly (they will think they can make the same product for less), which will force you to drop your prices sooner than you would like. Another strategy to consider is market penetration pricing, a strategy that sets price lower and discourages competition from entering the market as quickly. Whatever strategy you decide to use, don't forget to examine your product/service's elasticity.

At this time you need to start thinking about how to promote your product. Why do you feel your product/service is different or new to the market? How do you want to position your product/service so customers view it favorably? Remember this is all occurring *within the consumer's mind.*

# See for Yourself Videocase

## WAL-MART REVISES ITS MARKETING STRATEGY

In 2006, Wal-Mart had its most dismal performance of all time. Long known for its low price motto, the company began to falter as competitors closed the price gap by actively restructuring. Wal-Mart faced competition on many fronts, including grocery competitors Kroger and Safeway and clothing and housewares competition from the likes of Target and Costco. Its primary source of competition seemed to be Target, who figured out how to draw middle-income consumers in droves by creating a flourishing fashionable reputation. Further complicating the competitive landscape for Wal-Mart, a *BusinessWeek* price comparison between Wal-Mart and Target concluded that overall differences in price came down to mere pennies. Wal-Mart was now forced to compete against stores with better aesthetics and savvier marketing favored by affluent and middle-income consumers while, at the same time, retaining its loyal, low price–dedicated customers.

Target has become a master at "cheap-chic." Consumers, especially those in the middle-income bracket, flock to Target for fashionable clothing, home accessories, and furniture. Wal-Mart decided to compete by offering its own line of cheap-chic clothing, even going so far as to run ads in *Vogue* and produce a fashion show in Times Square. The company's attempt ultimately crashed and burned. Wal-Mart underestimated demand for its "George" line of fashion basics and, with long production lead times, was unable to maintain stock of the most popular sizes.

At the same time, the company appeared to have demographic amnesia. For example, Wal-Mart's typical female shopper wears a size 14, yet the company was pushing trendy "skinny jeans" unlikely to be favored by this loyal consumer base. Analysts question whether moves aimed to gain the attention of Target's retail base might actually be turning off Wal-Mart's traditional price-conscious consumers.

As Wal-Mart stocks dropped from $60 a share to the mid-$40s, Wall Street analysts suggested that Wal-Mart, long known for rapid growth, should halt its speedy expansion in order to focus on improving the look and quality of its current stores. In response, H. Lee Scott, Wal-Mart's CEO, said that slowing down expansion would not lead to improved stores and remained unclear as to why Wal-Mart appeared unable to improve the quality of its existing stores. This is unfortunate, given that many affluent and middle-income consumers value store aesthetics as much as price. The question became: Is low price enough to keep Wal-Mart going? Scott claimed that the company planned to continue its current growth rate of about one store opening per day. Wall Street analysts saw this as a mistake, citing that Wal-Mart's prized Supercenters were not even bringing in enough money to make up for the costs of constructing them in the first place and that same-store sales were repeatedly low in many markets. Supercenters also end up, at times, located near traditional Wal-Mart stores, forcing the two to compete. Was Wal-Mart hurting itself by bullishly growing and focusing on middle-income consumers unlikely to convert to its shabby existing stores?

Wal-Mart and Target, on many levels, cater to entirely different demographics. Target excels at household goods, fashionable clothing, and electronics, while Wal-Mart excels at low-cost groceries, pharmacy, and entertainment. In fact, grocery items make up 40 percent of Wal-Mart's business, an area in which most Target stores do not compete. To enhance this competitive advantage, Wal-Mart also added low-priced organic groceries to its repertoire. This puts it in competition with high-end supermarkets and specialty stores such as Whole Foods, but with a strong price advantage over these competitors.

As the United States entered an economic downturn, Wal-Mart's focus on price again reaped rewards for the company. Consumers previously supporting higher-margin grocery stores such as Kroger and Safeway began turning back to Wal-Mart for its lower prices. Target was negatively affected as people began saving money by buying less clothing, electronics, and furniture and focusing more on the basic necessities like food and medicines that are Wal-Mart's strong points. Wal-Mart began strong marketing campaigns over low-priced prescription medicines and its new green initiatives. Partially in response to middle-income

consumers, the company launched an aggressive green business initiative to reduce carbon emissions. Wal-Mart stock prices began to recover, and these new marketing strategies seemed to be working. However, it is impossible to truly compare Wal-Mart and Target until the economy evens out again. Will Wal-Mart continue to pursue Target's middle-income customers with fashionable clothing, organic food, and green initiatives, or will it return to its own price-conscious consumer base with rock-bottom grocery prices and low-cost prescription medicines? Will it listen to analysts or continue to expand? Only time will tell.[45]

### Discussion Questions

1. What role does marketing play in Wal-Mart's decisions to try to lure Target's middle-income customers?

2. How could better marketing have prevented such snafus as Wal-Mart selling skinny jeans and consistently running out of popular sizes of its new clothing line?

3. Why is it said that Wal-Mart and Target have different target markets?

**Remember to check out our Online Learning Center at www.mhhe.com/ferrell7e.**

part

6

# Financing the Enterprise

CHAPTER 14  Accounting and Financial Statements

CHAPTER 15  Money and the Financial System

CHAPTER 16  Financial Management and Securities Markets

APPENDIX D  Personal Financial Planning

chapter | 4

CHAPTER OUTLINE

**Introduction**

**The Nature of Accounting**
   *Accountants*
   *Accounting or Bookkeeping?*
   *The Uses of Accounting Information*

**The Accounting Process**
   *The Accounting Equation*
   *Double-Entry Bookkeeping*
   *The Accounting Cycle*

**Financial Statements**
   *The Income Statement*
   *The Balance Sheet*
   *The Statement of Cash Flows*

**Ratio Analysis: Analyzing Financial Statements**
   *Profitability Ratios*
   *Asset Utilization Ratios*
   *Liquidity Ratios*
   *Debt Utilization Ratios*
   *Per Share Data*
   *Industry Analysis*

# Accounting and Financial Statements

## OBJECTIVES

*After reading this chapter, you will be able to:*

- Define accounting, and describe the different uses of accounting information.

- Demonstrate the accounting process.

- Examine the various components of an income statement in order to evaluate a firm's "bottom line."

- Interpret a company's balance sheet to determine its current financial position.

- Analyze financial statements, using ratio analysis, to evaluate a company's performance.

- Assess a company's financial position using its accounting statements and ratio analysis.

## The Richest Man in the World

It is, after all, possible to be richer than Microsoft's Bill Gates. For a brief time in 2007, *Fortune* magazine listed the Mexican telecommunications tycoon, Carlos Slim Helú, at the top of the list. By 2008, Slim slipped back to number two, with a fortune of $60 billion, while Warren Buffet took the number-one spot with net worth of $62 billion. The son of Lebanese immigrants, Slim is a self-made man. Dabbling in soft drinks, printing, and tobacco in the 1960s and 1970s, Slim managed to profit off the 1982 fiscal crisis by purchasing a number of companies for a fraction of their worth. When the country's economy bounced back at the end of the decade, Slim began to realize considerable profits. For example, he purchased Mexico's largest insurance company for $44 million, and it is now worth around $2.5 billion. However, Slim did not make his first real fortune until 1990, when he bought the formerly nationalized telephone company Teléfonos de México (Telmex).

Today, Slim owns more than 200 companies, and his wealth comprises nearly 8 percent of Mexico's entire GDP. Slim's affluence is growing at a fast pace; it has increased by more than $20 billion since 2005. In Mexico, Slim has been dubbed "Mr. Monopoly," because of his staggering wealth and the market dominance of Telmex. Although Mexico has been privatizing industries since the 1990s, competition in the telephone industry has not increased. Telmex still controls 92 percent of Mexico's phone lines and 73 percent of cell phones.

Slim's critics complain that his stranglehold on the national phone service has actually slowed development in the country. To date, only 20 percent of Mexican residents have phone service, a number that remains low because

*continued*

of the high price of service, according to the Organization for Cooperation and Economic Development. Many believe that Slim's rates have kept Mexican businesses from profiting and paying their workers as well as they should. It has always been Slim's modus operandi to purchase companies when the price is low and then begin to force the competition out of the market. Mexico's slow economic growth and lack of good jobs has fueled illegal immigration into the United States, where jobs are perceived as plentiful and the quality of life as higher. However, increasing illegal immigration has put a financial strain on the U.S. government, while decreasing the supply of workers in Mexico—further slowing development.

Lack of competition not only halts development. It also decreases the quality of services and accountability and encourages dishonest accounting practices. Along with most of Latin America, Mexico has dealt with monopolies since Colonial times. In power for around 70 years, the political party the Partido Revolucionario Institutional (PRI) represented one of the longest-lasting hegemonic powers in the Western hemisphere. The party faced little or no opposition from 1929 to the early 1990s. During this time, most monopolies were state owned and run. Finally, in the 1990s privatization movements, coupled with the PRI's loss of power, allowed private investors to step in and buy out many state-owned companies. The monopolies did not end there, however, with Slim being the preeminent example of a private monopolistic power. Mexico's president, Felipe Calderón, has taken a public stance against such monopolies as Telmex and has held talks with Slim over the issue. However, large companies like Telmex tend to receive special treatment from the government, given the huge amount of money and resources they control. Slim himself claims that he welcomes competition and that his actions, including his accounting practices, are transparent—but his behavior says otherwise.

Whether or not Slim believes that he runs monopolies, the Federal Communications Commission (FCC) plans to investigate Slim. In 1998 the FCC found Telmex guilty of colluding with Sprint to overcharge for long distance services. It is possible that new findings could result in stiffer regulations and calls for more transparent accounting practices. More rules might also have a long-term impact on Slim's wealth. As with many of the other richest men in the world, much of Slim's financial success depends on stock prices, which depend on high performance. Increased oversight could call attention to unethical accounting and other issues, which could cause prices to drop, and his wealth would follow.[1]

# Introduction

Accounting, the financial "language" that organizations use to record, measure, and interpret all of their financial transactions and records, is very important in business. All businesses—from a small family farm to a giant corporation—use the language of accounting to make sure they use their money wisely and to plan for the future. Nonbusiness organizations such as charities and governments also use accounting to demonstrate to donors and taxpayers how well they are using their funds and meeting their stated objectives.

This chapter explores the role of accounting in business and its importance in making business decisions. First, we discuss the uses of accounting information and the accounting process. Then, we briefly look at some simple financial statements and accounting tools that are useful in analyzing organizations worldwide.

# The Nature of Accounting

Simply stated, **accounting** is the recording, measurement, and interpretation of financial information. Large numbers of people and institutions, both within and outside businesses, use accounting tools to evaluate organizational operations. The Financial Accounting Standards Board has been setting the principles standards of financial accounting and reporting in the private sector since 1973. Its mission is to establish and improve standards of financial accounting and reporting for the guidance and education of the public, including issuers, auditors, and users of financial information. However, the accounting scandals at the turn of the last century resulted when many accounting firms and businesses failed to abide by generally accepted accounting principles, or GAAP. More than 1,000 firms ultimately reported flaws in their financial statements between 1997 and 2002; in 2002 alone, a record 330 companies chose to restate their earnings to avoid further questions.[2] Consequently, the federal government has taken a greater role in making rules, requirements, and policies for accounting firms and businesses through the Securities and Exchange Commission's (SEC) Public Company Accounting Oversight Board. For example, Ernst & Young, a leading accounting firm, was barred from undertaking new audit clients for six months as penalty for abusing the agency's auditor-independence rules.[3]

To better understand the importance of accounting, we must first understand who prepares accounting information and how it is used.

**accounting**
the recording, measurement, and interpretation of financial information

## Accountants

Many of the functions of accounting are carried out by public or private accountants.

**certified public accountant (CPA)**
an individual who has been state certified to provide accounting services ranging from the preparation of financial records and the filing of tax returns to complex audits of corporate financial records

**Public Accountants.**    Individuals and businesses can hire a **certified public accountant (CPA),** an individual who has been certified by the state in which he or she practices to provide accounting services ranging from the preparation of financial records and the filing of tax returns to complex audits of corporate financial records. Certification gives a public accountant the right to express, officially, an unbiased opinion regarding the accuracy of the client's financial statements. Most public accountants are either self-employed or members of large public accounting firms such as Ernst & Young, KPMG, Deloitte & Touche, and Pricewaterhouse-Coopers, together referred to as "the Big Four." In addition, many CPAs work for one of the second-tier accounting firms that are much smaller than the Big Four firms, as illustrated in Table 14.1. The accounting scandals at the turn of the century, combined with more stringent accounting requirements legislated by the Sarbanes-Oxley Act, have increased job prospects for accountants and students with accounting degrees as companies and accounting firms hire more auditors to satisfy the law and public demand for greater transparency.[4]

With the demise of Arthur Andersen there have been concerns about one of the remaining Big Four accounting firms failing. The U.S. Chamber of Commerce published a report calling for regulators and policy makers to keep such an event from happening again to maintain competition and availability of accountants.[5]

The insurance and financial services provider AIG is among the many U.S. firms hiring more forensic accountants. Forensic accountants utilize their accounting, auditing, and investigative skills to check the books of companies.

A growing area for public accountants is *forensic accounting*, which is accounting that is fit for legal review. It involves analyzing financial documents in search of fraudulent entries or financial misconduct. Functioning as much like detectives as accountants, forensic accountants have been used since the 1930s. In the wake of the accounting scandals of the early 2000s, many auditing firms are rapidly adding or expanding forensic or fraud-detection services. Additionally, many forensic accountants root out evidence of "cooked books" for federal agencies like the Federal Bureau of Investigation or the Internal Revenue Service. The Association of Certified Fraud Examiners, which certifies accounting professionals as *certified fraud examiners (CFEs)*, has grown to more than 45,000 members.[7]

**Did You Know?**    Corporate fraud costs are estimated at $600 billion annually.[6]

| Company | 2007 Revenues ($ Millions) | 2008 VAULT Accounting Firm Prestige Rankings |
|---|---|---|
| **"Big Four"** | | |
| PricewaterhouseCoopers | $25,150 | 7.616 |
| Ernst & Young | 21,100 | 7.415 |
| Deloitte & Touche | 9,800 | 7.035 |
| KPMG | 19,800 | 6.447 |
| *Second-Tier Firms* | | |
| Grant Thornton | 1,075 | 6.009 |
| BDO Seidman | 589 | 5.720 |
| McGladrey & Pullen | 1,300 | 5.708 |

**TABLE 14.1**

Leading Accounting Firms

Source: "Accounting Firm Rankings," "Vault Top 40 Accounting Firms," www.vault.com/nr/finance_rankings/accounting_rankings.jsp?accounting2008=2 (accessed May 20, 2008).

**Private Accountants.**   Large corporations, government agencies, and other organizations may employ their own **private accountants** to prepare and analyze their financial statements. With titles such as controller, tax accountant, or internal auditor, private accountants are deeply involved in many of the most important financial decisions of the organizations for which they work. Private accountants can be CPAs and may become **certified management accountants (CMAs)** by passing a rigorous examination by the Institute of Management Accountants.

## Accounting or Bookkeeping?

The terms *accounting* and *bookkeeping* are often mistakenly used interchangeably. Much narrower and far more mechanical than accounting, bookkeeping is typically limited to the routine, day-to-day recording of business transactions. Bookkeepers are responsible for obtaining and recording the information that accountants require to analyze a firm's financial position. They generally require less training than accountants. Accountants, on the other hand, usually complete course work beyond their basic four- or five-year college accounting degrees. This additional training allows accountants not only to record financial information, but to understand, interpret, and even develop the sophisticated accounting systems necessary to classify and analyze complex financial information.

## The Uses of Accounting Information

Accountants summarize the information from a firm's business transactions in various financial statements (which we'll look at in a later section of this chapter) for a variety of stakeholders, including managers, investors, creditors, and government agencies. Many business failures may be directly linked to ignorance of the information "hidden" inside these financial statements. Likewise, most business successes can be traced to informed managers who understand the consequences of their decisions. While maintaining and even increasing short-run profits is desirable, the failure to plan sufficiently for the future can easily lead an otherwise successful company to insolvency and bankruptcy court.

Basically, managers and owners use financial statements (1) to aid in internal planning and control and (2) for external purposes such as reporting to the Internal

**private accountants** accountants employed by large corporations, government agencies, and other organizations to prepare and analyze their financial statements

**certified management accountants (CMAs)** private accountants who, after rigorous examination, are certified by the National Association of Accountants and who have some managerial responsibility

Revenue Service, stockholders, creditors, customers, employees, and other interested parties. Figure 14.1 shows some of the users of the accounting information generated by a typical corporation.

**Internal Uses.** **Managerial accounting** refers to the internal use of accounting statements by managers in planning and directing the organization's activities. Perhaps management's greatest single concern is **cash flow,** the movement of money through an organization over a daily, weekly, monthly, or yearly basis. Obviously, for any business to succeed, it needs to generate enough cash to pay its bills as they fall due. However, it is not at all unusual for highly successful and rapidly growing companies to struggle to make payments to employees, suppliers, and lenders because of an inadequate cash flow. One common reason for a so-called "cash crunch," or shortfall, is poor managerial planning.

Managerial accountants also help prepare an organization's **budget,** an internal financial plan that forecasts expenses and income over a set period of time. It is not unusual for an organization to prepare separate daily, weekly, monthly, and yearly budgets. Think of a budget as a financial map, showing how the company expects to move from Point A to Point B over a specific period of time. While most companies prepare *master budgets* for the entire firm, many also prepare budgets for smaller segments of the organization such as divisions, departments, product lines, or projects. "Top-down" master budgets begin at the upper management level and filter down to the individual department level, while "bottom-up" budgets start at the department or project level and are combined at the chief executive's office. Generally, the larger and more rapidly growing an organization, the greater will be the likelihood that it will build its master budget from the ground up.

Regardless of focus, the principal value of a budget lies in its breakdown of cash inflows and outflows. Expected operating expenses (cash outflows such as wages, materials costs, and taxes) and operating revenues (cash inflows in the form of payments from customers) over a set period of time are carefully forecast and subsequently compared with actual results. Deviations between the two serve as a "trip

---

**managerial accounting** the internal use of accounting statements by managers in planning and directing the organization's activities

**cash flow** the movement of money through an organization over a daily, weekly, monthly, or yearly basis

**budget** an internal financial plan that forecasts expenses and income over a set period of time

---

**FIGURE 14.1**

The Users of Accounting Information

Source: Belverd E. Needles, Henry R. Anderson, and James C. Caldwell, *Principles of Accounting,* 4th edition. Copyright © 1990 by Houghton Mifflin Company. Reprinted with permission.

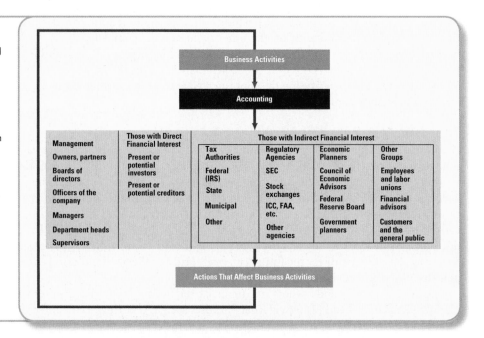

wire" or "feedback loop" to launch more detailed financial analyses in an effort to pinpoint trouble spots and opportunities.

**External Uses.**   Managers also use accounting statements to report the business's financial performance to outsiders. Such statements are used for filing income taxes, obtaining credit from lenders, and reporting results to the firm's stockholders. They become the basis for the information provided in the official corporate **annual report,** a summary of the firm's financial information, products, and growth plans for owners and potential investors. While frequently presented between slick, glossy covers prepared by major advertising firms, the single most important component of an annual report is the signature of a certified public accountant attesting that the required financial statements are an accurate reflection of the underlying financial condition of the firm. Financial statements meeting these conditions are termed *audited.* The primary external users of audited accounting information are government agencies, stockholders and potential investors, and lenders, suppliers, and employees.

Federal, state, and local governments (both domestic and overseas) require organizations to file audited financial statements concerning taxes owed and paid, payroll deductions for employees, and, for corporations, new issues of securities (stocks and bonds). Even nonprofit corporations and other nonbusiness organizations may be required to file regular financial statements. While corporations make the news most frequently for financial scandals, even governments are not immune to accounting problems. Germany's free-market party, the Freie Demokratische Partei or FDP, has been accused of falsely accounting for more than €1.66 million, or $2.5 million, in party donations between 1996 and 2000. Under the leadership of now-deceased Juergen Moelleman, the party was guilty of serious ethical and accounting infractions—including hiding large donations by recording them as small donations under false names. The federal treasury is seeking to remedy the situation and is fining the party €5 million. Because of the wrongly accounted for donations, all of the party's financial statements are also being called into question by parliamentary auditors, which could cost the FDP an additional €7.24 million.[8] Like individuals, well-managed companies generally try to minimize their taxable income by using accepted accounting practices. Usually, accounting practices that reduce taxes also reduce reported profits. By reducing taxes, the firm increases the cash available to the firm that can be used for many purposes, such as plant expansion, debt retirement, or repurchase of common stock.

A corporation's stockholders use financial statements to evaluate the return on their investment and the overall quality of the firm's management team. As a result, poor performance, as documented in the financial statements, often results in changes in top management. Potential investors study the financial statements in a firm's annual report to determine whether the company meets their investment requirements and whether the returns from a given firm are likely to compare favorably with other similar companies.

Banks and other lenders look at financial statements to determine a company's ability to meet current and future debt obligations if a loan or credit is granted. To determine this ability, a short-term lender examines a firm's cash flow to assess its ability to repay a loan quickly with cash generated from sales. A long-term lender is more interested in the company's profitability and indebtedness to other lenders.

Labor unions and employees use financial statements to establish reasonable expectations for salary and other benefit requests. Just as firms experiencing record profits are likely to face added pressure to increase employee wages, so too are

**annual report**
summary of a firm's financial information, products, and growth plans for owners and potential investors

# Going Green

## Hertz Goes Green: Generating Cost versus Benefit Decisions

As gas prices and concern for the environment grow, the demand for hybrids and fuel-efficient cars is also on the rise. Among those answering the call is the rental car company Hertz. In 2006, Hertz launched its Green Collection, which originally included four makes: Toyota Camry, Ford Fusion, Buick LaCrosse, and Hyundai Sonata. All of these cars have a fuel efficiency of 28 mpg or more, earning them a high EPA SmartWay rating. The EPA SmartWay rating system examines air pollution and greenhouse gas emissions. Cars are ranked on a scale of 0 to 10 for each criterion, with 10 being the highest and 5 being average. All Hertz Green Collection cars must score at least a 6 on both. In 2007, Hertz added the Toyota Prius to its line of Green cars. With SmartWay Elite ratings of 9.5 for air pollution and 10 for greenhouse gas emissions, the Prius holds the highest ranking in the Hertz fleet and possesses one of the highest ratings on the market today.

For consumers seeking to be eco-friendly even when away from their normal car, the Green Collection from Hertz is helping make it easier for car renters to make environmentally responsible decisions. While, Hertz's eco-friendly line is still a tiny part of its overall fleet, with offerings at only around 50 airports nationwide, the company is working to expand this number. During 2007, Hertz purchased nearly 4,500 Priuses, a move that cost the company more than $65 million. The company is also working to expand the availability of ethanol-fueled cars throughout the Midwest, where corn ethanol is plentiful.

The Green Collection costs around $5 to $10 per day more than renting a regular car, which means those not interested in environmental issues are not likely to rent from the Green collection. Business travelers might also be forbidden from renting more expensive cars by their company's accounting policies. Hertz claims that most drivers will make up the cost differential in fuel savings, although this depends on the model and how much driving a renter does. Even if this is true, for business travelers who must watch their costs, new accounting policies may need to be put in place that specify what kinds of cars employees can rent and whether they include more expensive but more fuel-efficient models. Some analysts who support this "green" movement in the rental car industry have also expressed concern that consumers will balk at paying an additional fee to drive a more efficient car.

No one is arguing, however, that moving toward a more fuel-efficient fleet is a smart step for Hertz. The company recently stated that by adding 1,000 hybrids to its fleet, it will reduce carbon dioxide emissions by about 3,000 tons annually. In addition, Hertz now donates $1 to the National Park Foundation for each Green Collection car rental. If you believe that every little step counts, then an extra $5 to $10 a day for a Prius or Camry the next time you need to rent a car is a small price to pay.[9]

### Discussion Questions

1. Aside from helping the environment, what are some of the advantages of Hertz adding a Green Collection to its fleet?
2. The up-front cost of acquiring thousands of eco-friendly cars is very high for Hertz. What is Hertz anticipating about consumer tastes and demands that would allow it to justify such a large expense?
3. How could positioning itself as the eco-friendly rental company that has low-emissions cars and donates to environmental causes help Hertz's bottom line?

---

employees unlikely to grant employers wage and benefit concessions without considerable evidence of financial distress.

# The Accounting Process

Many view accounting as a primary business language. It is of little use, however, unless you know how to "speak" it. Fortunately, the fundamentals—the accounting equation and the double-entry bookkeeping system—are not difficult to learn. These two concepts serve as the starting point for all currently accepted accounting principles.

### The Accounting Equation

**assets**
a firm's economic resources, or items of value that it owns, such as cash, inventory, land, equipment, buildings, and other tangible and intangible things

Accountants are concerned with reporting an organization's assets, liabilities, and owners' equity. To help illustrate these concepts, consider a hypothetical floral shop called Anna's Flowers, owned by Anna Rodriguez. A firm's economic resources, or items of value that it owns, represent its **assets**—cash, inventory, land, equipment, buildings, and other tangible and intangible things. The assets of Anna's Flowers include counters, refrigerated display cases, flowers, decorations, vases, cards, and other gifts, as well as something known as "goodwill," which in this case is Anna's reputation for preparing and delivering beautiful floral arrangements on a timely basis. **Liabilities,** on the other hand, are debts the firm owes to others. Among the liabilities of Anna's Flowers are a loan from the Small Business Administration and money owed to flower suppliers and other creditors for items purchased. The **owners' equity** category contains all of the money that has ever been contributed to the company that never has to be paid back. The funds can come from investors who have given money or assets to the company, or it can come from past profitable operations. In the case of Anna's Flowers, if Anna were to sell off, or liquidate, her business, any money left over after selling all the shop's assets and paying off its liabilities would comprise her owner's equity. The relationship between assets, liabilities, and owners' equity is a fundamental concept in accounting and is known as the **accounting equation:**

**liabilities**
debts that a firm owes to others

**owners' equity**
equals assets minus liabilities and reflects historical values

$$\text{Assets} = \text{Liabilities} + \text{Owner's equity}$$

**accounting equation**
assets equal liabilities plus owners' equity

## Double-Entry Bookkeeping

**Double-entry bookkeeping** is a system of recording and classifying business transactions in separate accounts in order to maintain the balance of the accounting equation. Returning to Anna's Flowers, suppose Anna buys $325 worth of roses on credit from the Antique Rose Emporium to fill a wedding order. When she records this transaction, she will list the $325 as a liability or a debt to a supplier. At the same time, however, she will also record $325 worth of roses as an asset in an account known as "inventory." Because the assets and liabilities are on different sides of the accounting equation, Anna's accounts increase in total size (by $325) but remain in balance:

**double-entry bookkeeping**
a system of recording and classifying business transactions that maintains the balance of the accounting equation

$$\text{Assets} = \text{Liabilities} + \text{Owner's equity}$$
$$\$325 = \$325$$

Thus, to keep the accounting equation in balance, each business transaction must be recorded in two separate accounts.

In the final analysis, all business transactions are classified as either assets, liabilities, or owners' equity. However, most organizations further break down these three accounts to provide more specific information about a transaction. For example, assets may be broken down into specific categories such as cash, inventory, and equipment, while liabilities may include bank loans, supplier credit, and other debts.

Figure 14.2 shows how Anna used the double-entry bookkeeping system to account for all of the transactions that took place in her first month of business. These transactions include her initial investment of $2,500, the loan from the Small Business Administration, purchases of equipment and inventory, and the purchase of roses on credit. In her first month of business, Anna generated revenues of $2,000 by selling $1,500 worth of inventory. Thus, she deducts, or (in accounting notation that is appropriate for assets) *credits,* $1,500 from inventory and adds, or *debits,* $2,000 to the cash account. The difference between Anna's $2,000 cash inflow and her $1,500 outflow is represented by a credit to owners' equity, because it is money that belongs to her as the owner of the flower shop.

**accounting cycle**
the four-step procedure of an accounting system: examining source documents, recording transactions in an accounting journal, posting recorded transactions, and preparing financial statements

## The Accounting Cycle

In any accounting system, financial data typically pass through a four-step procedure sometimes called the **accounting cycle.** The steps include examining source documents, recording transactions in an accounting journal, posting recorded transactions, and preparing financial statements. Figure 14.3 shows how Anna works

FIGURE 14.2  The Accounting Equation and Double-Entry Bookkeeping for Anna's Flowers

| | Assets | | | = Liabilities | | + Owners' Equity |
|---|---|---|---|---|---|---|
| | *Cash* | *Equipment* | *Inventory* | *Debts to suppliers* | *Loans* | *Equity* |
| *Cash invested by Anna* | $2,500.00 | | | | | $2,500.00 |
| *Loan from SBA* | $5,000.00 | | | | $5,000.00 | |
| *Purchase of furnishings* | –$3,000.00 | $3,000.00 | | | | |
| *Purchase of inventory* | –$2,000.00 | | $2,000.00 | | | |
| *Purchase of roses* | | | $325.00 | $325.00 | | |
| *First month sales* | $2,000.00 | | –$1,500.00 | | | $500.00 |
| *Totals* | $4,500.00 | $3,000.00 | $825.00 | $325.00 | $5,000.00 | $3,000.00 |

$8,325 = $5,325 + $3,000

$8,325 Assets = $8,325 (Liabilities + Owners' Equity)

through them. Traditionally, all of these steps were performed using paper, pencils, and erasers (lots of erasers!), but today the process is often fully computerized.

**Step One: Examine Source Documents.**   Like all good managers, Anna Rodriguez begins the accounting cycle by gathering and examining source documents—checks, credit-card receipts, sales slips, and other related evidence concerning specific transactions.

**Step Two: Record Transactions.**   Next, Anna records each financial transaction in a **journal,** which is basically just a time-ordered list of account transactions. While most businesses keep a general journal in which all transactions are recorded, some classify transactions into specialized journals for specific types of transaction accounts.

**Step Three: Post Transactions.**   Anna next transfers the information from her journal into a **ledger,** a book or computer program with separate files for each account. This process is known as *posting*. At the end of the accounting period (usually yearly, but occasionally quarterly or monthly), Anna prepares a *trial balance*, a summary of the balances of all the accounts in the general ledger. If, upon totalling, the trial balance doesn't (that is, the accounting equation is not in balance), Anna or her accountant must look for mistakes (typically an error in one or more of the ledger entries) and correct them. If the trial balance is correct, the accountant can then begin to prepare the financial statements.

**Step Four: Prepare Financial Statements.**   The information from the trial balance is also used to prepare the company's financial statements. In the case of public corporations and certain other organizations, a CPA must *attest,* or certify, that the organization followed generally accepted accounting principles

**journal**
a time-ordered list of account transactions

**ledger**
a book or computer file with separate sections for each account

**FIGURE 14.3** The Accounting Process for Anna's Flowers

**Step 1:**
Source documents show that a transaction took place.

**Receipt**
**Anna's Flowers**

| July 7 Wedding floral arrangements | $500.00 |
| Consultation services | 250.00 |

**Step 2:**
The transaction is recorded in the journal.

**Assets**

**Cash**

| July 7 Brown wedding | $750.00 |

**Step 3:**
The transaction is posted to the general ledger under the appropriate account (asset, liability, or some further breakdown of these main accounts).

| | | | | | | Balance | |
|---|---|---|---|---|---|---|---|
| Date | | Explanation | PR | Debit | Credit | Debit | Credit |
| 2007 | | | | | | | |
| July | 1 | | 1 | 2,000 | | 2,000 | |
| | 3 | | 1 | | 1,250 | | 1,250 |
| | 4 | | 1 | | | | |
| | 7 | Brown wedding | 1 | | 750 | | 750 |
| | 14 | | 1 | | | | |

**Step 4:** At the end of the accounting period, the ledger is used to prepare the firm's financial statements.

**Anna's Flowers**
**Income Statement**
**December 31, 2007**

| | | |
|---|---|---|
| Revenues: | | |
| Net sales | | $123,850 |
| Consulting | | 73,850 |
| Total revenues | | $197,700 |
| Expenses: | | |
| Cost of goods sold | $72,600 | |
| Selling expenses | 37,700 | |
| General and admin. | 18,400 | |
| Other expenses | 5,600 | |
| Total expenses | | 134,300 |
| Net income | | $ 63,400 |

**Anna's Flowers**
**Balance Sheet**
**December 31, 2007**

| | | |
|---|---|---|
| Assets | | |
| Current assets: | | |
| **Cash** | **$17,850** | |
| Accounts receivable | 10,200 | |
| Merch. Inventory | 8,750 | |
| Tot. assets | | $36,800 |
| Property and Equipment | | |
| Equipment | 11,050 | |
| Office building | 73,850 | |
| Tot. prop. & equip. | | 84,900 |
| Total assets | | $121,700 |
| | | |
| Liabilities and Owner's Equity | | |
| Current liabilities | | |
| Accounts payable | $12,600 | |
| Tot. cur. liabilities | | 12,600 |
| Long-term liabilities | | |
| Mortgage payable | | 23,600 |
| Total liabilities | | 36,200 |
| Owner's equity: | | |
| **Anna Rodriguez, capital** | | **$ 85,500** |
| Tot. liabilities and owners' equity | | $ 121,700 |

**Anna's Flowers**
**Annual Budget**
**for 2007**

| | Sales | Consulting | Total |
|---|---|---|---|
| January | 10,500 | 4,500 | 15,000 |
| February | 10,000 | 5,500 | 15,500 |
| March | 10,800 | 5,700 | 16,500 |
| April | 10,100 | 6,050 | 16,150 |
| May | 12,000 | 6,000 | 18,000 |
| June | 12,100 | 6,250 | 18,350 |
| July | 13,000 | 6,600 | 19,600 |
| August | 9,950 | 6,000 | 15,950 |
| September | 9,700 | 6,200 | 15,900 |
| October | 9,900 | 7,000 | 16,900 |
| November | 8,500 | 7,150 | 15,650 |
| December | 7,300 | 6,900 | 14,200 |
| Annual | $123,850 | $73,850 | $197,700 |

*Grant Thorton LLP provides comprehensive accounting services such as auditing of financial statements to its clients.*

in preparing the financial statements. When these statements have been completed, the organization's books are "closed," and the accounting cycle begins anew for the next accounting period.

# Financial Statements

The end result of the accounting process is a series of financial statements. The income statement, the balance sheet, and the statement of cash flows are the best-known examples of financial statements. They are provided to stockholders and potential investors in a firm's annual report as well as to other relevant outsiders such as creditors, government agencies, and the Internal Revenue Service.

It is important to recognize that not all financial statements follow precisely the same format. The fact that different organizations generate income in different ways suggests that when it comes to financial statements, one size definitely does not fit all. Manufacturing firms, service providers, and nonprofit organizations each use a different set of accounting principles or rules upon which the public accounting profession has agreed. As we have already mentioned, these are sometimes referred to as *generally accepted accounting principles (GAAP)*. Each country has a different set of rules that the businesses within that country are required to use for their accounting process and financial statements. Moreover, as is the case in many other disciplines, certain concepts have more than one name. For example, *sales* and *revenues* are often interchanged, as are *profits, income,* and *earnings.* Table 14.2 lists a few common equivalent terms that should help you decipher their meaning in accounting statements.

| TABLE 14.2 | Term | Equivalent Term |
|---|---|---|
| Equivalent Terms in Accounting | Revenues | Sales |
| | | Goods or services sold |
| | Gross profit | Gross income |
| | | Gross earnings |
| | Operating income | Operating profit |
| | | Earnings before interest and taxes (EBIT) |
| | | Income before interest and taxes (IBIT) |
| | Income before taxes (IBT) | Earnings before taxes (EBT) |
| | | Profit before taxes (PBT) |
| | Net income (NI) | Earnings after taxes (EAT) |
| | | Profit after taxes (PAT) |
| | Income available to common stockholders | Earnings available to common stockholders |

## The Income Statement

The question, "What's the bottom line?" derives from the income statement, where the bottom line shows the overall profit or loss of the company after taxes. Thus, the **income statement** is a financial report that shows an organization's profitability over a period of time, be that a month, quarter, or year. By its very design, the income statement offers one of the clearest possible pictures of the company's overall revenues and the costs incurred in generating those revenues. Other names for the income statement include profit and loss (P&L) statement or operating statement. A sample income statement with line-by-line explanations is presented in Table 14.3,

**income statement**
a fianancial report that shows an organization's profitability over a period of time—month, quarter, or year

---

**TABLE I4.3**   Sample Income Statement

The following exhibit presents a sample income statement with all the terms defined and explained.

| Company Name for the Year Ended December 31 | |
|---|---|
| Revenues (sales) | Total dollar amount of products sold (includes income from other business services such as rental-lease income and interest income). |
| Less: Cost of goods sold | The cost of producing the goods and services, including the cost of labor and raw materials as well as other expenses associated with production. |
| Gross profit | The income available after paying all expenses of production. |
| Less: Selling and administrative expense | The cost of promoting, advertising, and selling products as well as the overhead costs of managing the company. This includes the cost of management and corporate staff. One non-cash expense included in this category is depreciation, which approximates the decline in the value of plant and equipment assets due to use over time. In most accounting statements, depreciation is not separated from selling and administrative expenses. However, financial analysts usually create statements that include this expense. |
| Income before interest and taxes (operating income or EBIT) | This line represents all income left over after operating expenses have been deducted. This is sometimes referred to as operating income since it represents all income after the expenses of operations have been accounted for. Occasionally, this is referred to as EBIT, or earnings before interest and taxes. |
| Less: Interest expense | Interest expense arises as a cost of borrowing money. This is a financial expense rather than an operating expense and is listed separately. As the amount of debt and the cost of debt increase, so will the interest expense. This covers the cost of both short-term and long-term borrowing. |
| Income before taxes (earnings before taxes—EBT) | The firm will pay a tax on this amount. This is what is left of revenues after subtracting all operating costs, depreciation costs, and interest costs. |
| Less: Taxes | The tax rate is specified in the federal tax code. |
| Net income | This is the amount of income left after taxes. The firm may decide to retain all or a portion of the income for reinvestment in new assets. Whatever it decides not to keep it will usually pay out in dividends to its stockholders. |
| Less: Preferred dividends | If the company has preferred stockholders, they are first in line for dividends. That is one reason why their stock is called "preferred." |
| Income to common stockholders | This is the income left for the common stockholders. If the company has a good year, there may be a lot of income available for dividends. If the company has a bad year, income could be negative. The common stockholders are the ultimate owners and risk takers. They have the potential for very high or very poor returns since they get whatever is left after all other expenses. |
| Earnings per share | Earnings per share is found by taking the income available to the common stockholders and dividing by the number of shares of common stock outstanding. This is income generated by the company for each share of common stock. |

**revenue**
the total amount of money received from the sale of goods or services, as well as from related business activities

**cost of goods sold**
the amount of money a firm spent to buy or produce the products it sold during the period to which the income statement applies

while Table 14.4 presents the income statement of Starbucks. The income statement indicates the firm's profitability or income (the bottom line), which is derived by subtracting the firm's expenses from its revenues.

**Revenue.**     **Revenue** is the total amount of money received (or promised) from the sale of goods or services, as well as from other business activities such as the rental of property and investments. Nonbusiness entities typically obtain revenues through donations from individuals and/or grants from governments and private foundations. Starbucks' income statement (see Table 14.4) shows one main source of income: sales of Starbucks' products.

For most manufacturing and retail concerns, the next major item included in the income statement is the **cost of goods sold,** the amount of money the firm

**TABLE 14.4**

Consolidated Statements of Earnings for Starbucks (in thousands, except earnings per share)

| Fiscal Year Ended | Sept 30, 2007 | Oct 1, 2006 | Oct 2, 2005 |
|---|---|---|---|
| Net revenues: | | | |
| Company-operated retail | $7,998,265 | $6,583,098 | $5,391,927 |
| Specialty: | | | |
| Licensing | 1,026,338 | 860,676 | 673,015 |
| Foodservice and other | 386,894 | 343,168 | 304,358 |
| Total specialty | 1,413,232 | 1,203,844 | 977,373 |
| Total net revenues | 9,411,497 | 7,786,942 | 6,369,300 |
| Cost of sales including occupancy costs | 3,999,124 | 3,178,791 | 2,605,212 |
| Store operating expenses | 3,215,889 | 2,687,815 | 2,165,911 |
| Other operating expenses | 294,136 | 253,724 | 192,525 |
| Depreciation and amortization expenses | 467,160 | 387,211 | 340,169 |
| General and administrative expenses | 489,249 | 479,386 | 361,613 |
| Total operating expenses | 8,465,558 | 6,986,927 | 5,665,430 |
| Income from equity investees | 108,006 | 93,937 | 76,648 |
| Operating income | 1,053,945 | 893,952 | 780,518 |
| Net interest and other income | 2,419 | 12,291 | 15,829 |
| Earnings before income taxes | 1,056,364 | 906,243 | 796,347 |
| Income taxes | 383,726 | 324,770 | 301,977 |
| Earnings before cumulative effect of change in accounting principle | 672,638 | 581,473 | 494,370 |
| Cumulative effect of accounting change for FIN 47, net of taxes | — | 17,214 | — |
| Net earnings | $ 672,638 | $ 564,259 | $ 494,370 |
| Per common share: | | | |
| Net earnings—basic | $      0.90 | $      0.74 | $      0.63 |
| Net earnings—diluted | $      0.87 | $      0.71 | $      0.61 |
| Weighted average shares outstanding: | | | |
| Basic | 749,763 | 766,114 | 789,570 |
| Diluted | 770,091 | 792,556 | 815,417 |

Source: media.corporate-ir.net/media_files/irol/99/99518/2007AR (accessed September 18, 2008).

spent (or promised to spend) to buy and/or produce the products it sold during the accounting period. This figure may be calculated as follows:

Cost of goods sold = Beginning inventory + Interim purchases − Ending inventory

Let's say that Anna's Flowers began an accounting period with an inventory of goods for which it paid $5,000. During the period, Anna bought another $4,000 worth of goods, giving the shop a total inventory available for sale of $9,000. If, at the end of the accounting period, Anna's inventory was worth $5,500, the cost of goods sold during the period would have been $3,500 ($5,000 + $4,000 − $5,500 = $3,500). If Anna had total revenues of $10,000 over the same period of time, subtracting the cost of goods sold ($3,500) from the total revenues of $10,000 yields the store's **gross income or profit** (revenues minus the cost of goods sold required to generate the revenues): $6,500. For Starbucks, cost of goods sold was just under $4 billion in 2007. Notice that Starbucks calls it cost of sales, rather than cost of goods sold. This is because Starbucks buys raw materials and supplies and produces drinks.

**gross income (or profit)**
revenues minus the cost of goods sold required to generate the revenues

**expenses**
the costs incurred in the day-to-day operations of an organization

Expenses.    **Expenses** are the costs incurred in the day-to-day operations of an organization. Three common expense accounts shown on income statements are (1) selling, general, and administrative expenses; (2) research, development, and engineering expenses; and (3) interest expenses (remember that the costs directly attributable to selling goods or services are included in the cost of goods sold). Selling expenses include advertising and sales salaries. General and administrative expenses include salaries of executives and their staff and the costs of owning and maintaining the general office. Research and development costs include scientific, engineering, and marketing personnel and the equipment and information used to design and build prototypes and samples. Interest expenses include the direct costs of borrowing money.

**depreciation**
the process of spreading the costs of long-lived assets such as buildings and equipment over the total number of accounting periods in which they are expected to be used

The number and type of expense accounts vary from organization to organization. Included in the general and administrative category is a special type of expense known as **depreciation,** the process of spreading the costs of long-lived assets such as buildings and equipment over the total number of accounting periods in which they are expected to be used. Consider a manufacturer that purchases a $100,000 machine expected to last about 10 years. Rather than showing an expense of $100,000 in the first year and no expense for that equipment over the next nine years, the manufacturer is allowed to report depreciation expenses of $10,000 per year in each of the next 10 years because that better matches the cost of the machine to the years the machine is used. Each time this depreciation is "written off" as an expense, the book value of the machine is also reduced by $10,000. The fact that the equipment has a zero value on the firm's balance sheet when it is fully depreciated (in this case, after 10 years) does not necessarily mean that it can no longer be used or is economically worthless. Indeed, in some industries, machines used every day have been reported as having no book value whatsoever for over 30 years.

**net income**
the total profit (or loss) after all expenses, including taxes, have been deducted from revenue; also called net earnings

Net Income.    **Net income** (or net earnings) is the total profit (or loss) after all expenses including taxes have been deducted from revenue. Generally,

*Firms and corporations like this lumber mill shown here depreciate, or spread out the cost, of their many assets over a certain number of accounting periods.*

# Entrepreneurship in Action

## Pursuing a Life-Long Dream, a Social Worker and Teacher Gets an A+ for His Goat's Milk Cheeses

Paul Trubey

**Business:** Beltane Farm

**Founded:** Cheese production began in 1999, Beltane Farm was formed in 2002.

**Success:** Trubey's cheeses have won awards and are popular on the farmer's market circuit.

Paul Trubey always wanted to raise goats. Trained as a social worker, he finally got his wish in 1994. After a move to Lebanon, Connecticut, Trubey decided that he needed a break from working hospice. He took a job teaching Latin for a local school, thinking that he would be able to save some money and move to Massachusetts with his partner so they could start a farm. Fate had other plans for Trubey, however. Dorothy Joba, a co-worker, had goats on the farm she had run with her partner for more than a decade, Highwater Farm. To indulge his desire to work with goats, Trubey began working for Joba on nights and weekends. With Joba's permission,

he began making cheese from the goat milk produced there, experimenting with artisanal recipes.

After a while, Joba and Trubey came to the conclusion that he should pursue cheese-making as a profession. The farm was licensed for cheese production in 1999, forming Highwater Dairy LLC. Trubey, who had little business experience, had to learn the ins and outs of finance and accounting in order to record costs and revenues, as well as detail profits for tax purposes. Trubey had to learn on the job because soon after establishing the dairy, he started selling at the region's farmer's markets and to retail stores and restaurants. In 2000, Trubey's Chevre won a blue ribbon in the American Cheese Society's national competition. In 2002, Trubey purchased the herd from Joba and moved them to Beltane Farm in Lebanon, Connecticut. Although Trubey is back to part-time hospice work, his business still brings in a profit and his cheeses remain a farmer's market favorite; people can also visit the farm to make purchases.[10]

accountants divide profits into individual sections such as operating income and earnings before interest and taxes. Starbucks, for example, lists earnings before income taxes, net earnings, and earnings per share of outstanding stock (see Table 14.4). Like most companies, Starbucks presents not only the current year's results but also the previous two years' income statements to permit comparison of performance from one period to another.

**Temporary Nature of the Income Statement Accounts.** Companies record their operational activities in the revenue and expense accounts during an accounting period. Gross profit, earnings before interest and taxes, and net income are the results of calculations made from the revenues and expenses accounts; they are not actual accounts. At the end of each accounting period, the dollar amounts in all the revenue and expense accounts are moved into an account called "Retained Earnings," one of the owners' equity accounts. Revenues increase owners' equity, while expenses decrease it. The resulting change in the owners' equity account is exactly equal to the net income. This shifting of dollar values from the revenue and expense accounts allows the firm to begin the next accounting period with zero balances in those accounts. Zeroing out the balances enables a company to count how much it has sold and how many expenses have been incurred during a period of time. The basic accounting equation (Assets = Liabilities + Owners' equity) will not balance until the revenue and expense account balances have been moved or "closed out" to the owners' equity account.

One final note about income statements: You may remember from Chapter 5 that corporations may choose to make cash payments called dividends to shareholders out of their net earnings. When a corporation elects to pay dividends, it decreases the cash account (in the assets category of the balance sheet) as well as a capital account (in the owners' equity category of the balance sheet). During any period of time, the owners' equity account may change because of the sale of stock (or contributions/withdrawals by owners), the net income or loss, or from the dividends paid.

## The Balance Sheet

The second basic financial statement is the **balance sheet,** which presents a "snapshot" of an organization's financial position at a given moment. As such, the balance sheet indicates what the organization owns or controls and the various sources of the funds used to pay for these assets, such as bank debt or owners' equity.

The balance sheet takes its name from its reliance on the accounting equation: Assets *must* equal liabilities plus owners' equity. Table 14.5 provides a sample balance sheet with line-by-line explanations. Unlike the income statement, the balance sheet does not represent the result of transactions completed over a specified accounting period. Instead, the balance sheet is, by definition, an accumulation of all financial transactions conducted by an organization since its founding. Following long-established traditions, items on the balance sheet are listed on the basis of their original cost less accumulated depreciation, rather than their present values.

Balance sheets are often presented in two different formats. The traditional balance sheet format placed the organization's assets on the left side and its liabilities and owners' equity on the right. More recently, a vertical format, with assets on top

**balance sheet**
a "snapshot" of an organization's financial position at a given moment

---

**TABLE l4.5   Sample Balance Sheet**

The following exhibit presents a balance sheet in word form with each item defined or explained.

| Typical Company December 31 | |
|---|---|
| Assets | This is the major category for all physical, monetary, or intangible goods that have some dollar value. |
| Current assets | Assets that are either cash or are expected to be turned into cash within the next 12 months. |
| Cash | Cash or checking accounts. |
| Marketable securities | Short-term investments in securities that can be converted to cash quickly (liquid assets). |
| Accounts receivable | Cash due from customers in payment for goods received. These arise from sales made on credit. |
| Inventory | Finished goods ready for sale, goods in the process of being finished, or raw materials used in the production of goods. |
| Prepaid expense | A future expense item that has already been paid, such as insurance premiums or rent. |
| Total current assets | The sum of the above accounts. |
| Fixed assets | Assets that are long term in nature and have a minimum life expectancy that exceeds one year. |
| Investments | Assets held as investments rather than assets owned for the production process. Most often the assets include small ownership interests in other companies. |
| Gross property, plant, and equipment | Land, buildings, and other fixed assets listed at original cost. |
| Less: Accumulated depreciation | The accumulated expense deductions applied to all plant and equipment over their life. Land may not be depreciated. The total amount represents in general the decline in value as equipment gets older and wears out. The maximum amount that can be deducted is set by the U.S. Federal Tax Code and varies by type of asset. |
| Net property, plant, and equipment | Gross property, plant, and equipment minus the accumulated depreciation. This amount reflects the book value of the fixed assets and not their value if sold. |
| Other assets | Any other asset that is long term and does not fit into the above categories. It could be patents or trademarks. |
| Total assets | The sum of all the asset values. |

(continued)

**TABLE 14.5** Sample Balance Sheet *(Continued)*

| | |
|---|---|
| Liabilities and Stockholders' Equity | This is the major category. Liabilities refer to all indebtedness and loans of both a long-term and short-term nature. Stockholders' equity refers to all money that has been contributed to the company over the life of the firm by the owners. |
| Current liabilities | Short-term debt expected to be paid off within the next 12 months. |
|   Accounts payable | Money owed to suppliers for goods ordered. Firms usually have between 30 and 90 days to pay this account, depending on industry norms. |
|   Wages payable | Money owned to employees for hours worked or salary. If workers receive checks every two weeks, the amount owed should be no more than two weeks' pay. |
|   Taxes payable | Firms are required to pay corporate taxes quarterly. This refers to taxes owed based on earnings estimates for the quarter. |
|   Notes payable | Short-term loans from banks or other lenders. |
|   Other current liabilities | The other short-term debts that do not fit into the above categories. |
|     Total current liabilities | The sum of the above accounts. |
| Long-term liabilities | All long-term debt that will not be paid off in the next 12 months. |
|   Long-term debt | Loans of more than one year from banks, pension funds, insurance companies, or other lenders. These loans often take the form of bonds, which are securities that may be bought and sold in bond markets. |
|   Deferred income taxes | This is a liability owed to the government but not due within one year. |
|   Other liabilities | Any other long-term debt that does not fit the above two categories. |
| Stockholders' equity | The following categories are the owners' investment in the company. |
|   Common stock | The tangible evidence of ownership is a security called common stock. The par value is stated value and does not indicate the company's worth. |
| Capital in excess of par (a.k.a. contributed capital) | When shares of stock were sold to the owners, they were recorded at the price at the time of the original sale. If the price paid was $10 per share, the extra $9 per share would show up in this account at 100,000 shares times $9 per share, or $900,000. |
|   Retained earnings | The total amount of earnings the company has made during its life and not paid out to its stockholders as dividends. This account represents the owners' reinvestment of earnings into company assets rather than payments of cash dividends. This account does not represent cash. |
| Total stockholders' equity | This is the sum of the above equity accounts representing the owner's total investment in the company. |
|   Total liabilities and stockholders' equity | The total short-term and long-term debt of the company plus the owner's total investment. This combined amount *must* equal total assets. |

**current assets**
assets that are used or converted into cash within the course of a calendar year

**accounts receivable**
money owed a company by its clients or customers who have promised to pay for the products at a later date

followed by liabilities and owners' equity, has gained wide acceptance. Starbucks' balance sheet for 2004 and 2005 is presented in Table 14.6. In the sections that follow, we'll briefly describe the basic items found on the balance sheet; we'll take a closer look at a number of these in Chapter 16.

**Assets.**    All asset accounts are listed in descending order of *liquidity*—that is, how quickly each could be turned into cash. **Current assets,** also called short-term assets, are those that are used or converted into cash within the course of a calendar year. Cash is followed by temporary investments, accounts receivable, and inventory, in that order. **Accounts receivable** refers to money owed the company by its clients or customers who have promised to pay for the products at a later date. Accounts receivable usually includes an allowance for bad debts that management does not expect to collect. The bad-debts adjustment is normally based on historical

**TABLE I4.6**   Consolidated Balance Sheets (in thousands, except share data)

| Fiscal Year Ended | Sept 30, 2007 | Oct 1, 2006 |
|---|---|---|
| Assets | | |
| Current assets: | | |
| Cash and cash equivalents | $ 281,261 | $ 312,606 |
| Short-term investments—available-for-sale securities | 83,845 | 87,542 |
| Short-term investments—trading securities | 73,588 | 53,496 |
| Accounts receivable, net | 287,925 | 224,271 |
| Inventories | 691,658 | 636,222 |
| Prepaid expenses and other current assets | 148,757 | 126,874 |
| Deferred income taxes, net | 129,453 | 88,777 |
| Total current assets | 1,696,487 | 1,529,788 |
| Long-term investments—available-for-sale securities | 21,022 | 5,811 |
| Equity and other investments | 258,846 | 219,093 |
| Property, plant and equipment, net | 2,890,433 | 2,287,899 |
| Other assets | 219,422 | 186,917 |
| Other intangible assets | 42,043 | 37,955 |
| Goodwill | 215,625 | 161,478 |
| Total Assets | $5,343,878 | $4,428,941 |
| Liabilities and Shareholders' Equity | | |
| Current liabilities: | | |
| Commercial paper and short-term borrowings | $ 710,248 | $ 700,000 |
| Accounts payable | 390,836 | 340,937 |
| Accrued compensation and related costs | 332,331 | 288,963 |
| Accrued occupancy costs | 74,591 | 54,868 |
| Accrued taxes | 92,516 | 94,010 |
| Other accrued expenses | 257,369 | 224,154 |
| Deferred revenue | 296,900 | 231,926 |
| Current portion of long-term debt | 775 | 762 |
| Total current liabilities | 2,155,566 | 1,935,620 |
| Long-term debt | 550,121 | 1,958 |
| Other long-term liabilities | 354,074 | 262,857 |
| Total liabilities | 3,059,761 | 2,200,435 |
| Shareholders' equity: | | |
| Common stock ($0.001 par value)—authorized, 1,200,000,000 shares; issued and outstanding, 738,285,285 and 756,602,701 shares, respectively, (includes 3,420,448 common stock units in both periods) | 738 | 756 |
| Other additional paid-in-capital | 39,393 | 39,393 |
| Retained earnings | 2,189,366 | 2,151,084 |
| Accumulated other comprehensive income | 54,620 | 37,273 |
| Total shareholders' equity | 2,284,117 | 2,228,506 |
| Total Liabilities and Shareholders' Equity | $5,343,878 | $4,428,941 |

Source: media.corporate-ir.net/media_files/irol/99/99518/2007AR (accessed September 18, 2008).

collections experience and is deducted from the accounts receivable balance to present a more realistic view of the payments likely to be received in the future, called net receivables. Inventory may be held in the form of raw materials, work-in-progress, or finished goods ready for delivery.

Long-term, or fixed assets represent a commitment of organizational funds of at least one year. Items classified as fixed include long-term investments, plant and equipment, and intangible assets, such as corporate "goodwill," or reputation, as well as patents and trademarks.

**Liabilities.**   As seen in the accounting equation, total assets must be financed either through borrowing (liabilities) or through owner investments (owners' equity). **Current liabilities** include a firm's financial obligations to short-term creditors, which must be repaid within one year, while long-term liabilities have longer repayment terms. **Accounts payable** represents amounts owed to suppliers for goods and services purchased with credit. For example, if you buy gas with a BP credit card, the purchase represents an account payable for you (and an account receivable for BP). Other liabilities include wages earned by employees but not yet paid and taxes owed to the government. Occasionally, these accounts are consolidated into an **accrued expenses** account, representing all unpaid financial obligations incurred by the organization.

**Owners' Equity.**   Owners' equity includes the owners' contributions to the organization along with income earned by the organization and retained to finance continued growth and development. If the organization were to sell off all of its assets and pay off all of its liabilities, any remaining funds would belong to the owners. Not surprisingly, the accounts listed as owners' equity on a balance sheet may differ dramatically from company to company. As mentioned in Chapter 5, corporations sell stock to investors, who then become the owners of the firm. Many corporations issue two, three, or even more different classes of common and preferred stock, each with different dividend payments and/or voting rights. Because each type of stock issued represents a different claim on the organization, each must be represented by a separate owners' equity account, called contributed capital.

### The Statement of Cash Flows

The third primary financial statement is called the **statement of cash flows,** which explains how the company's cash changed from the beginning of the accounting period to the end. Cash, of course, is an asset shown on the balance sheet, which provides a snapshot of the firm's financial position at one point in time. However, many investors and other users of financial statements want more information about the cash flowing into and out of the firm than is provided on the balance sheet in order to better understand the company's financial health. The statement of cash flows takes the cash balance from one year's balance sheet and compares it with the next while providing detail about how the firm used the cash. Table 14.7 presents Starbucks' statement of cash flows.

The change in cash is explained through details in three categories: cash from (used for) operating activities, cash from (used for) investing activities, and cash from (used for) financing activities. *Cash from operating activities* is calculated by combining the changes in the revenue accounts, expense accounts, current asset accounts, and current liability accounts. This category of cash flows includes all the accounts on the balance sheet that relate to computing revenues and expenses for the accounting period. If this amount is a positive number, as it is for Starbucks,

**current liabilities**
a firm's financial obligations to short-term creditors, which must be repaid within one year

**accounts payable**
the amount a company owes to suppliers for goods and services purchased with credit

**accrued expenses**
is an account representing all unpaid financial obligations incurred by the organization

**statement of cash flows**
explains how the company's cash changed from the beginning of the accounting period to the end

then the business is making extra cash that it can use to invest in increased long-term capacity or to pay off debts such as loans or bonds. A negative number may indicate a business that is in a declining position with regards to operations. Negative cash flow is not always a bad thing, however. It may indicate that a business is growing, with a very negative cash flow indicating rapid growth.

*Cash from investing activities* is calculated from changes in the long-term or fixed asset accounts. If this amount is negative, as is the case with Starbucks, the company is purchasing long-term assets for future growth. A positive figure indicates a business that is selling off existing long-term assets and reducing its capacity for the future.

**TABLE 14.7**   Starbucks Consolidated Statements of Cash Flows (in thousands)

| Fiscal Year Ended | Sept 30, 2007 | Oct 1, 2006 | Oct 2, 2005 |
|---|---|---|---|
| **Operating Activities:** | | | |
| Net earnings | $ 672,638 | $ 564,259 | $ 494,370 |
| Adjustments to reconcile net earnings to net cash provided by operating activities: | | | |
| Cumulative effect of accounting change for FIN 47, net of taxes | — | 17,214 | — |
| Depreciation and amortization | 491,238 | 412,625 | 367,207 |
| Provision for impairments and asset disposals | 26,032 | 19,622 | 19,464 |
| Deferred income taxes, net | (37,326) | (84,324) | (31,253) |
| Equity in income of investees | (65,743) | (60,570) | (49,537) |
| Distributions of income from equity investees | 65,927 | 49,238 | 30,919 |
| Stock-based compensation | 103,865 | 105,664 | — |
| Tax benefit from exercise of stock options | 7,705 | 1,318 | 109,978 |
| Excess tax benefit from exercise of stock options | (93,055) | (117,368) | — |
| Net amortization of premium on securities | 653 | 2,013 | 10,097 |
| Cash provided/(used) by changes in operating assets and liabilities: | | | |
| Inventories | (48,576) | (85,527) | (121,618) |
| Accounts payable | 36,068 | 104,966 | 9,717 |
| Accrued compensation and related costs | 38,628 | 54,424 | 22,711 |
| Accrued taxes | 86,371 | 132,725 | 14,435 |
| Deferred revenue | 63,233 | 56,547 | 53,276 |
| Other operating assets and liabilities | (16,437) | (41,193) | (6,851) |
| Net cash provided by operating activities | 1,331,221 | 1,131,633 | 922,915 |
| **Investing Activities:** | | | |
| Purchase of available-for-sale securities | (237,422) | (639,192) | (643,488) |
| Maturity of available-for-sale securities | 178,167 | 269,134 | 469,554 |
| Sale of available-for-sale securities | 47,497 | 431,181 | 626,113 |
| Acquisitions, net of cash acquired | (53,293) | (91,734) | (21,583) |
| Net purchases of equity, other investments and other assets | (56,552) | (39,199) | (7,915) |
| Net additions to property, plant and equipment | (1,080,348) | (771,230) | (643,296) |
| Net cash used by investing activities | (1,201,951) | (841,040) | (220,615) |

(continued)

**TABLE 14.7**    Starbucks Consolidated Statements of Cash Flows (in thousands) *(Continued)*

| Financing Activities: | | | |
|---|---:|---:|---:|
| Repayments of commercial paper | (16,600,841) | — | — |
| Proceeds from issuance of commercial paper | 17,311,089 | — | — |
| Repayments of short-term borrowings | (1,470,000) | (993,093) | — |
| Proceeds from short-term borrowings | 770,000 | 1,416,093 | 277,000 |
| Proceeds from issuance of common stock | 176,937 | 159,249 | 163,555 |
| Excess tax benefit from exercise of stock options | 93,055 | 117,368 | — |
| Principal payments on long-term debt | (784) | (898) | (735) |
| Proceeds from issuance of long-term debt | 548,960 | — | — |
| Repurchase of common stock | (996,798) | (854,045) | (1,113,647) |
| Other | (3,505) | — | — |
| Net cash used by financing activities | (171,887) | (155,326) | (673,827) |
| Effect of exchange rate changes on cash and cash equivalents | 11,272 | 3,530 | 283 |
| Net increase/(decrease) in cash and cash equivalents | (31,345) | 138,797 | 28,756 |
| **Cash and Cash Equivalents:** | | | |
| Beginning of period | 312,606 | 173,809 | 145,053 |
| End of the period | $ 281,261 | $ 312,606 | $ 173,809 |
| **Supplemental Disclosure of Cash Flow Information:** | | | |
| Cash paid during the period for: | | | |
| Interest, net of capitalized interest | $ 35,294 | $ 10,576 | $ 1,060 |
| Income taxes | $ 342,223 | $ 274,134 | $ 227,812 |

Source: media.corporate-ir.net/media_files/irol/99/99518/2007AR (accessed September 18, 2008).

Finally, *cash from financing activities* is calculated from changes in the long-term liability accounts and the contributed capital accounts in owners' equity. If this amount is negative, the company is likely paying off long-term debt or returning contributed capital to investors. As in the case of Starbucks, if this amount is positive, the company is either borrowing more money or raising money from investors by selling more shares of stock.

# Ratio Analysis: Analyzing Financial Statements

**ratio analysis**
calculations that measure an organization's financial health

The income statement shows a company's profit or loss, while the balance sheet itemizes the value of its assets, liabilities, and owners' equity. Together, the two statements provide the means to answer two critical questions: (1) How much did the firm make or lose? and (2) How much is the firm presently worth based on historical values found on the balance sheet? **Ratio analysis,** calculations that measure an organization's financial health, brings the complex information from the income statement and balance sheet into sharper focus so that managers, lenders, owners, and other interested parties can measure and compare the organization's productivity, profitability, and financing mix with other similar entities.

You can look on Web sites like Yahoo! Finance under a company's "key statistics" link to find many of its financial ratios, such as its return on assets, return on equity, and current ratio. Other ratios require a closer look at a company's actual financial statements.

As you know, a ratio is simply one number divided by another, with the result showing the relationship between the two numbers. Financial ratios are used to weigh and evaluate a firm's performance. An absolute value such as earnings of $70,000 or accounts receivable of $200,000 almost never provides as much useful information as a well-constructed ratio. Whether those numbers are good or bad depends on their relation to other numbers. If a company earned $70,000 on $700,000 in sales (a 10 percent return), such an earnings level might be quite satisfactory. The president of a company earning this same $70,000 on sales of $7 million (a 1 percent return), however, should probably start looking for another job!

Ratios by themselves are not very useful. It is the relationship of the calculated ratios to both prior organizational performance and the performance of the organization's "peers," as well as its stated goals, that really matters. Remember, while the profitability, asset utilization, liquidity, debt ratios, and per share data we'll look at here can be very useful, you will never see the forest by looking only at the trees.

## Profitability Ratios

**Profitability ratios** measure how much operating income or net income an organization is able to generate relative to its assets, owners' equity, and sales. The numerator (top number) used in these examples is always the net income after taxes. Common profitability ratios include profit margin, return on assets, and return on equity. The following examples are based on the 2007 income statement and balance sheet for Starbucks, as shown in Tables 14.4 and 14.6. Except where specified, all data are expressed in millions of dollars.

The **profit margin,** computed by dividing net income by sales, shows the overall percentage profits earned by the company. It is based solely upon data obtained from the income statement. The higher the profit margin, the better the cost controls within the company and the higher the return on every dollar of revenue. Starbucks' profit margin is calculated as follows:

**profitability ratios**
ratios that measure the amount of operating income or net income an organization is able to generate relative to its assets, owners' equity, and sales

**profit margin**
net income divided by sales

$$\text{Profit margin} \quad = \quad \frac{\$672{,}638}{\$9{,}411{,}487} \quad = \quad 7.15\%$$

Thus, for every $1 in sales, Starbucks generated profits of just over 7 cents.

# Consider Ethics and Social Responsibility

## Holding Companies Responsible: The Public Company Accounting Oversight Board

The Financial Accounting Standards Board (FASB) has been establishing standards for financial accounting and reporting in the private sector since 1973. Its main mission is to provide guidance for the utilization of responsible accounting methods, reporting, and policies to protect investors, lenders, and the public. By the turn of the 21st century, however, it was clear that the FASB did not provide strong enough regulatory measures. In response to public outrage surrounding corporate accounting scandals at Enron, WorldCom, and many other firms, in which many thousands of investors and employees lost much of their savings, Congress passed the Sarbanes-Oxley Act (SOX) in 2002 to restore stakeholder confidence in business financial reporting. Among its many provisions, the Sarbanes-Oxley Act established oversight of public corporate governance and financial reporting obligations and redesigned accountability and ethics standards for corporate officers, auditors, and analysts. Before SOX established an oversight mechanism for accounting, it had, to some extent, been self-regulatory.

The Sarbanes-Oxley Act established the Public Company Accounting Oversight Board (PCAOB), which oversees the audit of public companies in order to protect the interests of investors and further the public interest in the preparation of informative, accurate, and independent audit reports for companies. The duties of the PCAOB include registration of public accounting firms; establishment of standards for auditing, quality control, ethics, independence, and other issues relating to preparation of audit reports; inspection of accounting firms; investigations, disciplinary actions, and sanctions; and enforcement of compliance through the use of accounting rules of the board, professional standards and securities laws for the preparation and issuance of audit reports, and obligations and liabilities of accountants. The accounting oversight board established by SOX placed considerable government control over the accounting industry and the public firms they serve.

The oversight board files reports with the Securities and Exchange Commission (SEC) on an annual basis that include any new established rules and any final disciplinary rulings. The SEC itself is responsible for protecting investors, maintaining fair and efficient markets, and facilitating capital creation.

While the FASB has been involved in accounting standards for decades, it has butted heads with the SEC from time to time, particularly because the SEC has to approve the FASB's budget. Essentially, the SEC has a hand in every pot both in the world of private business and in government.

Since the 2002 introduction of Sarbanes-Oxley, much adjustment has occurred. Although accounting seems to be straightforward, it is not; and the standards applied to company accounting undergo nearly constant revision. Also under reconsideration are the organizations in charge of creating these standards. Accounting is critical in that it is used to create the public's perception of a company. To this end, there is a constant battle raging over whether or not accounting should be considered public or private policy. In the heat of the battle are the SEC, the FASB, the PCAOB, the American Institute of Certified Public Accountants (AICPA), public accounting firms, and the business lobby. The reason for the battle goes back to the Sarbanes-Oxley Act, which was created, as previously mentioned, to clarify and delineate the positions held by all those involved in setting the rules of accounting. After five years, the SEC has come out on top and is beginning to seriously exert its strength.

The powerful stance of the current SEC makes businesses nervous for a number of reasons. First, politicians control the SEC, a situation that can create a sense of imbalance. Second, the SEC's drive toward one set of standards throughout the global world of business may simplify things, but at the same time it may make necessary an overhaul of all accounting practices. Some worry that, although the restrictions created by Sarbanes-Oxley are objectionable to many firms, these may pale in comparison to what the SEC has in mind for the future.[11]

### Discussion Questions

1. Why do the SEC and the FASB disagree on some accounting issues?
2. Why was the Sarbanes-Oxley Act created?
3. Opponents of increased accounting and regulatory oversight have cited increased costs of complying with SOX as a reason it should be repealed—do you think this is a valid complaint?

---

**return on assets**
net income divided by assets

**Return on assets,** net income divided by assets, shows how much income the firm produces for every dollar invested in assets. A company with a low return on assets is probably not using its assets very productively—a key managerial failing. For its construction, the return on assets calculation requires data from both the income statement and the balance sheet.

$$\text{Return on assets} = \frac{\$672,638}{\$5,343,878} = 12.59\%$$

In the case of Starbucks, every $1 of assets generated a return of around 12.6 percent, or profits of around 12.6 cents per dollar.

Stockholders are always concerned with how much money they will make on their investment, and they frequently use the return on equity ratio as one of their key performance yardsticks. **Return on equity** (also called return on investment [ROI]), calculated by dividing net income by owners' equity, shows how much income is generated by each $1 the owners have invested in the firm. Obviously, a low return on equity means low stockholder returns and may indicate a need for immediate managerial attention. Because some assets may have been financed with debt not contributed by the owners, the value of the owners' equity is usually considerably lower than the total value of the firm's assets. Starbucks' return on equity is calculated as follows:

**return on equity** net income divided by owner's equity; also called return on investment (ROI)

$$\text{Return on equity} = \frac{\$672,638}{\$2,284,117} = 29.45\%$$

For every dollar invested by Starbucks stockholders, the company earned a 29.45 percent return, or 29.45 cents per dollar invested. The reason the amount is higher than the return on assets is that owners' equity only accounts for about 43 percent of Starbucks' assets, while the other 57 percent is financed by debt.

## Asset Utilization Ratios

**Asset utilization ratios** measure how well a firm uses its assets to generate each $1 of sales. Obviously, companies using their assets more productively will have higher returns on assets than their less efficient competitors. Similarly, managers can use asset utilization ratios to pinpoint areas of inefficiency in their operations. These ratios (receivables turnover, inventory turnover, and total asset turnover) relate balance sheet assets to sales, which are found on the income statement.

**asset utilization ratios** ratios that measure how well a firm uses its assets to generate each $1 of sales

The **receivables turnover,** sales divided by accounts receivable, indicates how many times a firm collects its accounts receivable in one year. It also demonstrates how quickly a firm is able to collect payments on its credit sales. Obviously, no payments means no profits. Starbucks collected its receivables 32.7 times per year. The reason the number is so high is that most of Starbucks' sales are for cash and not credit.

**receivables turnover** sales divided by accounts receivable

$$\text{Receivables turnover} = \frac{\$9,411,497}{\$287,925} = 32.69 \times$$

**inventory turnover** sales divided by total inventory

**Inventory turnover,** sales divided by total inventory, indicates how many times a firm sells and replaces its inventory over the course of a year. A high inventory turnover ratio may indicate great efficiency but may also suggest the possibility of lost sales due to insufficient stock levels. Starbucks' inventory turnover indicates that it replaced its 13.6 times lost year, or more than once a month.

$$\text{Inventory turnover} = \frac{\$9,411,497}{\$691,658} = 13.61 \times$$

**total asset turnover** sales divided by total assets

**Total asset turnover,** sales divided by total assets, measures how well an organization uses all of its assets in creating sales. It indicates whether a company is using its assets productively. Starbucks generated $1.76 in sales for every $1 in total corporate assets.

$$\text{Total asset turnover} = \frac{\$9,411,497}{\$5,343,878} = 1.76 \times$$

## Liquidity Ratios

**liquidity ratios**
ratios that measure the speed with which a company can turn its assets into cash to meet short-term debt

**Liquidity ratios** compare current (short-term) assets to current liabilities to indicate the speed with which a company can turn its assets into cash to meet debts as they fall due. High liquidity ratios may satisfy a creditor's need for safety, but ratios that are too high may indicate that the organization is not using its current assets efficiently. Liquidity ratios are generally best examined in conjunction with asset utilization ratios because high turnover ratios imply that cash is flowing through an organization very quickly—a situation that dramatically reduces the need for the type of reserves measured by liquidity ratios.

**current ratio**
current assets divided by current liabilities

The **current ratio** is calculated by dividing current assets by current liabilities. Starbucks's current ratio indicates that for every $1 of current liabilities, the firm had $0.79 of current assets on hand. This number may appear troublesome, and it should be a ratio on which the company keeps a close watch. Overall liquidity has decreased somewhat between 2006 and 2007. Additionally, accounts receivable has increased over the same time period. This shows that Starbucks' asset turnover rate is beginning to slow in addition to decreasing liquidity—all coming at a time of sales and expansion slowdowns for Starbucks.

$$\text{Current ratio} = \frac{\$1,696,487}{\$2,155,566} = 0.79 \times$$

**quick ratio (acid test)**
a stringent measure of liquidity that eliminates inventory

The **quick ratio** (also known as the **acid test**) is a far more stringent measure of liquidity because it eliminates inventory, the least liquid current asset. It measures how well an organization can meet its current obligations without resorting to the sale of its inventory. In 2007, Starbucks had just 47 cents invested in current assets (after subtracting inventory) for every $1 of current liabilities, a slight increase over 2006.

$$\text{Quick ratio} = \frac{\$1,004,829}{\$2,155,566} = 0.47 \times$$

## Debt Utilization Ratios

**debt utilization ratios**
ratios that measure how much debt an organization is using relative to other sources of capital, such as owners' equity

**Debt utilization ratios** provide information about how much debt an organization is using relative to other sources of capital, such as owners' equity. Because the use of debt carries an interest charge that must be paid regularly regardless of profitability, debt financing is much riskier than equity. Unforeseen negative events such as recessions affect heavily indebted firms to a far greater extent than those financed exclusively with owners' equity. Because of this and other factors, the managers of most firms tend to keep debt-to-asset levels below 50 percent. However, firms in very stable and/or regulated industries, such as electric utilities, often are able to carry debt ratios well in excess of 50 percent with no ill effects.

The **debt to total assets ratio** indicates how much of the firm is financed by debt and how much by owners' equity. To find the value of Starbucks' total debt, you must add current liabilities to long-term debt and other liabilities.

$$\text{Debt to total assets} = \frac{\$3,059,7617}{\$5,343,878} = 57.26\%$$

Thus, for every $1 of Starbucks' total assets, nearly 57.3 percent is financed with debt. The remaining 42.7 percent is provided by owners' equity.

The **times interest earned ratio,** operating income divided by interest expense, is a measure of the safety margin a company has with respect to the interest payments it must make to its creditors. A low times interest earned ratio indicates that even a small decrease in earnings may lead the company into financial straits. Since Starbucks has more interest income than interest expense, it would appear that their times interest earned ratio is not able to be calculated by using the income statement. However, in the statement of cash flows in Table 14-7 on the second line from the bottom, we can see that Starbucks, just under $35.3 million in interest expense, an amount that was covered nearly 29.9 times by income before interest and taxes. A lender would probably not have to worry about receiving interest payments.

$$\text{Times interest earned} = \frac{\$1,053,945}{\$35,294} = 29.86 \times$$

## Per Share Data

Investors may use **per share data** to compare the performance of one company with another on an equal, or per share, basis. Generally, the more shares of stock a company issues, the less income is available for each share.

**Earnings per share** is calculated by dividing net income or profit by the number of shares of stock outstanding. This ratio is important because yearly changes in earnings per share, in combination with other economywide factors, determine a company's overall stock price. When earnings go up, so does a company's stock price—and so does the wealth of its stockholders.

$$\text{Diluted earnings per share} = \frac{\$672,638}{\$770,091} = 0.87 \quad (2007)$$

$$= \frac{\$564,259}{\$792,556} = 0.71 \quad (2006)$$

We can see from the income statement that Starbucks' basic earnings per share increased from $0.74 in 2006 to $0.90 in 2007. Notice that Starbucks lists diluted earnings per share, calculated here, of $0.71 for 2006 and $0.87 for 2007. You can see from the income statement that diluted earnings per share include more shares than the basic calculation; this is because diluted shares include potential shares that could be issued due to the exercise of stock options or the conversion of certain types of debt into common stock. Investors generally pay more attention to diluted earnings per share than basic earnings per share.

**Dividends per share** are paid by the corporation to the stockholders for each share owned. The payment is made from earnings after taxes by the corporation but

---

**debt to total assets ratio**
a ratio indicating how much of the firm is financed by debt and how much by owners' equity

**times interest earned ratio**
operating income divided by interest expense

**per share data**
data used by investors to compare the performance of one company with another on an equal, per share basis

**earnings per share**
net income or profit divided by the number of stock shares outstanding

**dividends per share**
the actual cash received for each share owned

is taxable income to the stockholder. Thus, dividends result in double taxation: The corporation pays tax once on its earnings, and the stockholder pays tax a second time on his or her dividend income. Starbucks has never paid a dividend, so the calculation of dividends per share does not apply in this case.

$$\text{Dividends per share} = \frac{\$0}{\$770{,}091} = 0$$

## Industry Analysis

We have used McDonald's as a comparison to Starbucks because there are no real national and international coffee houses that compete with Starbucks on the same scale. While McDonald's is almost four times larger than Starbucks in terms of sales, they both have a national and international presence and to some extent compete for the consumer's dollars. Table 14.8 shows that while McDonald's earns more profit per dollar of sales, Starbucks earns more dollars per dollar of invested assets. This is because a Starbucks coffee shop is much less expensive to build and operate than a McDonald's. Both companies have very little accounts receivable relative to the size of their sales. McDonald's pushes off much of its inventory holding costs on its suppliers and so has much less inventory per sales dollar compared with Starbucks. Because McDonald's has very little inventory, its current ratio is almost the same, and its quick ratio is much higher than Starbucks. This is of little consequence to the financial analyst because both companies have high times interest earned ratios, with Starbucks significantly higher than McDonald's. Starbucks earns less per share than McDonald's, but McDonald's pays a dividend and Starbucks does not. In summary, both companies are in good financial health, and it is hard to say which company is better managed. One thing for sure, if Starbucks could earn the same profit margin as McDonald's, they would improve their other profitability ratios dramatically.

**TABLE 14.8**

Industry Analysis

|  | Starbucks | McDonald's |
|---|---|---|
| Profit margin | 7.15% | 10.51% |
| Return on assets | 12.59% | 8.15% |
| Return on equity | 29.45% | 15.67% |
| Receivable turnover | 32.69× | 21.64× |
| Inventory turnover | 13.61× | 182.30× |
| Total asset turnover | 1.76× | 0.78× |
| Current ratio | 0.79× | 0.80× |
| Quick ratio | 0.47× | 0.77× |
| Debt to total assets | 57.26% | 48.01% |
| Times interest earned | 29.86× | 9.46× |
| Earnings per share | $ 0.87 | $ 1.98 |
| Dividends per share | $ 0.00 | $ 1.50 |

By tracking and analyzing the financial data of 18 million-plus U.S. businesses, BizMiner.com is able to deliver industry analysis information to its online subscribers.

# So You Want to Be an Accountant

Do you like numbers and finances? Are you detail oriented, a perfectionist, and highly accountable for your decisions? If so, accounting may be a good field for you. If you are interested in accounting, there are always job opportunities available no matter the state of the economy. Accounting is one of the most secure job options in business. Of course, becoming an accountant is not easy. You will need at least a bachelor's degree in accounting to get a job, and many positions require additional training. Many states demand coursework beyond the 120 to 150 credit hours collegiate programs require for an accounting degree. If you are really serious about getting into the accounting field, you will probably want to consider getting your master's in accounting and taking the CPA exam. The field of accounting can be complicated, and the extra training provided through a master's in accounting program will prove invaluable when you go out looking for a good job. Accounting is a volatile discipline affected by changes in legislative initiatives.

With corporate accounting policies changing constantly and becoming more complex, accountants are needed to help keep a business running smoothly and within the bounds of the law. In fact, the number of jobs in the accounting and auditing field are expected to increase 18 percent between 2006 and 2016, with more than 1.5 million jobs in the United States alone by 2016. Jobs in accounting tend to pay quite well, with the national average salary standing at just over $57,000 annually. If you go on to get your master's degree in accounting, expect to see an even higher starting wage. In 2006, accountants with a bachelor's degree received an average opening offer of $47,618, while employees with master's degrees were offered $49,277 starting. Of course, your earnings could be higher or lower than these averages, depending on where you work, your level of experience, the firm, and your particular position.

Accountants are needed in the public and the private sectors, in large and small firms, in for-profit and not-for-profit organizations. Accountants in firms are generally in charge of preparing and filing tax forms and financial reports. Public-sector accountants are responsible for checking the veracity of corporate and personal records in order to prepare tax filings. Basically, any organization that has to deal with money and/or taxes in some way or another will be in need of an accountant, either for in-house service or occasional contract work. Requirements for audits under the Sarbanes Oxley Act and rules from the Public Company Accounting Oversight Board are creating more jobs and increased responsibility to maintain internal controls and accounting ethics. The fact that accounting rules and tax filings tend to be complex virtually assures that the demand for accountants will never decrease.[12]

# Review Your Understanding

### Define accounting, and describe the different uses of accounting information.

Accounting is the language businesses and other organizations use to record, measure, and interpret financial transactions. Financial statements are used internally to judge and control an organization's performance and to plan and direct its future activities and measure goal attainment. External organizations such as lenders, governments, customers, suppliers, and the Internal Revenue Service are major consumers of the information generated by the accounting process.

### Demonstrate the accounting process.

Assets are an organization's economic resources; liabilities, debts the organization owes to others; owners' equity, and the difference between the value of an organization's assets and liabilities. This principle can be expressed as the accounting equation: Assets = Liabilities + Owners' equity. The double-entry bookkeeping system is a system of recording and classifying business transactions in accounts that maintain the balance of the accounting equation. The accounting cycle involves examining source documents, recording transactions in a journal, posting transactions, and preparing financial statements on a continuous basis throughout the life of the organization.

### Decipher the various components of an income statement in order to evaluate a firm's "bottom line."

The income statement indicates a company's profitability over a specific period of time. It shows the "bottom line," the total profit (or loss) after all expenses (the costs incurred in the day-to-day operations of the organization) have been deducted from revenue (the total amount of money received from the sale of goods or services and other business activities). The cash flow statement details how much cash is moving through the firm and thus adds insight to a firm's "bottom line."

### Interpret a company's balance sheet to determine its current financial position.

The balance sheet, which summarizes the firm's assets, liabilities, and owners' equity since its inception, portrays its financial position as of a particular point in time. Major classifications included in the balance sheet are current assets (assets that can be converted to cash within one calendar year), fixed assets (assets of greater than one year's duration), current liabilities (bills owed by the organization within one calendar year), long-term liabilities (bills due more than one year hence), and owners' equity (the net value of the owners' investment).

### Analyze financial statements, using ratio analysis, to evaluate a company's performance.

Ratio analysis is a series of calculations that brings the complex information from the income statement and balance sheet into sharper focus so that managers, lenders, owners, and other interested parties can measure and compare the organization's productivity, profitability, and financing mix with other similar entities. Ratios may be classified in terms of profitability (measure dollars of return for each dollar of employed assets), asset utilization (measure how well the organization uses its assets to generate $1 in sales), liquidity (assess organizational risk by comparing current assets to current liabilities), debt utilization (measure how much debt the organization is using relative to other sources of capital), and per share data (compare the performance of one company with another on an equal basis).

### Assess a company's financial position using its accounting statements and ratio analysis.

Based on the information presented in the chapter, you should be able to answer the questions posed in "Solve the Dilemma" on page 454 to formulate a plan for determining BrainDrain's bottom line, current worth, and productivity.

## Revisit the World of Business

1. It is difficult to encourage competition in basic service industries, like phone service. What might Calderón suggest to Slim that could allow for increased competition?

2. What are some of the problems associated with monopoly powers?

3. How might the declining global economy affect Slim's business and his wealth?

## Learn the Terms

accounting 425
accounting cycle 431
accounting equation 431
accounts payable 442
accounts receivable 440
accrued expenses 442
annual report 429
asset utilization ratios 447
assets 430
balance sheet 439
budget 428
cash flows 428
certified management accountants (CMAs) 427
certified public accountant (CPA) 425
cost of goods sold 436

current assets 440
current liabilities 442
current ratio 448
debt to total assets ratio 449
debt utilization ratios 448
depreciation 437
dividends per share 449
double-entry bookkeeping 431
earnings per share 449
expenses 437
gross income (or profit) 437
income statement 435
inventory turnover 447
journal 432
ledger 432
liabilities 431
liquidity ratios 448

managerial accounting 428
net income 437
owners' equity 431
per share data 449
private accountants 427
profit margin 445
profitability ratios 445
quick ratio (acid test) 448
ratio analysis 444
receivables turnover 447
return on assets 446
return on equity 447
revenue 436
statement of cash flows 442
times interest earned ratio 449
total asset turnover 447

# Check Your Progress

1. Why are accountants so important to a corporation? What function do they perform?

2. Discuss the internal uses of accounting statements.

3. What is a budget?

4. Discuss the external uses of financial statements.

5. Describe the accounting process and cycle.

6. The income statements of all corporations are in the same format. True or false? Discuss.

7. Which accounts appear under "current liabilities"?

8. Together, the income statement and the balance sheet answer two basic questions. What are they?

9. What are the five basic ratio classifications? What ratios are found in each category?

10. Why are debt ratios important in assessing the risk of a firm?

# Get Involved

1. Go to the library or the Internet and get the annual report of a company with which you are familiar. Read through the financial statements, then write up an analysis of the firm's performance using ratio analysis. Look at data over several years and analyze whether the firm's performance is changing through time.

2. Form a group of three or four students to perform an industry analysis. Each student should analyze a company in the same industry, and then all of you should compare your results. The following companies would make good group projects:

Automobiles: DaimlerChrysler, Ford, General Motors
Computers: Apple, IBM, Dell
Brewing: Anheuser-Busch, Adolph Coors, G. Heileman
Chemicals: Du Pont, Dow Chemical, Monsanto
Petroleum: Chevron, ExxonMobil, Amoco
Pharmaceuticals: Merck, Lilly, UpJohn
Retail: Sears, JCPenney, Kmart, The Limited

# Build Your Skills

### FINANCIAL ANALYSIS

**Background:**
The income statement for Western Grain Company, a producer of agricultural products for industrial as well as consumer markets, is shown below. Western Grain's total assets are $4,237.1 million, and its equity is $1,713.4 million.

*Consolidated Earnings and Retained Earnings Year Ended December 31*

| (Millions) | 2002 |
|---|---|
| Net sales | $6,295.4 |
| Cost of goods sold | 2,989.0 |
| Selling and administrative expense | 2,237.5 |
| Operating profit | 1,068.9 |
| Interest expense | 33.3 |
| Other income (expense), net | (1.5) |
| Earnings before income taxes | 1,034.1 |
| Income taxes | 353.4 |
| Net earnings | 680.7 |
| (Net earnings per share) | $2.94 |
| Retained earnings, beginning of year | 3,033.9 |
| Dividends paid | (305.2) |
| Retained earnings, end of year | $3,409.4 |

**Task:**
Calculate the following profitability ratios: profit margin, return on assets, and return on equity. Assume that the industry averages for these ratios are as follows: profit margin, 12 percent; return on assets, 18 percent; and return on equity, 25 percent. Evaluate Western Grain's profitability relative to the industry averages. Why is this information useful?

# Solve the Dilemma

### EXPLORING THE SECRETS OF ACCOUNTING

You have just been promoted from vice president of marketing of BrainDrain Corporation to president and CEO! That's the good news. Unfortunately, while you know marketing like the back of your hand, you know next to nothing about finance. Worse still, the "word on the street" is that BrainDrain is in danger of failure if steps to correct large and continuing financial losses are not taken immediately. Accordingly, you have asked the vice president of finance and accounting for a complete set of accounting statements detailing the financial operations of the company over the past several years.

Recovering from the dual shocks of your promotion and feeling the weight of the firm's complete accounting report for the very first time, you decide to attack the problem systematically and learn the "hidden secrets" of the company, statement by statement. With Mary Pruitt, the firm's trusted senior financial analyst, by your side, you delve into the accounting statements as never before. You resolve to "get to the bottom" of the firm's financial problems and set a new course for the future—a course that will take the firm from insolvency and failure to financial recovery and perpetual prosperity.

### Discussion Questions

1. Describe the three basic accounting statements. What types of information does each provide that can help you evaluate the situation?

2. Which of the financial ratios are likely to prove to be of greatest value in identifying problem areas in the company? Why? Which of your company's financial ratios might you expect to be especially poor?

3. Discuss the limitations of ratio analysis.

# Build Your Business Plan

### ACCOUNTING AND FINANCIAL STATEMENTS

After you determine your initial *reasonable selling price*, you need to estimate your sales forecasts (in terms of units and dollars of sales) for the first year of operation. Remember to be conservative and set forecasts that are more modest.

While customers may initially try your business, many businesses have seasonal patterns. A good budgeting/planning system allows managers to anticipate problems, coordinate activities of the business (so that subunits within the organization are all working toward the common goal of the organization), and control operations (how do we know whether spending is "in line").

The first financial statement you need to prepare is the income statement. Beginning with your estimated sales revenue, determine what expenses will be necessary to generate that level of sales revenue. Refer to Figure 15.4 to assist you with this process.

The second financial statement you need to create is your balance sheet. Your balance sheet is a snapshot of your financial position in a moment in time. Refer to Figure 15.6 to assist you in listing your assets, liabilities and owner's equity.

The last financial statement, the cash flow statement, is the most important one to a bank. It is a measure of your ability to get and repay the loan from the bank. Referring to Figure 15.8, be as realistic as possible as you are completing it. Allow yourself enough cash on hand until the point in which the business starts to support itself.

# See for Yourself Videocase

### ENRON: QUESTIONABLE ACCOUNTING PRACTICES BRING NEW REGULATION TO THE UNITED STATES

Even someone who does not have any interest in business dealings could not have helped hearing something about Enron's scandal in the early 2000s. Enron was only one of the numerous major corporations accused of dirty dealings (some others were WorldCom, Arthur Andersen and Adelphia), but it was certainly among the most famous. Once ranked among the top *Fortune 500* companies, Enron reported revenues of $111 billion in 2000. Primarily an energy trader, Enron also had dealings in many other areas, including communications and paper. In spite of the investor confidence and fantastic financial reports, only one year after reporting stellar earnings, Enron Corporation collapsed under a mountain of debt. Enron had not experienced problems earlier because the debt had been concealed through a complex scheme of off-balance-sheet partnerships and the use of a method of accounting called *mark-to-market*. Mark-to-market accounting involves assigning a value to an asset that is yet-to-be-obtained based on current market prices. It is used most frequently in futures markets so that investors can value the current value of a future asset. The method allowed Enron to record expected future profits on the books as current revenue and to ignore large sources of debt, therefore boosting the company's revenues on paper. In fact, many of the ventures Enron claimed were profitable had never been anything but a source of increasing debt.

Forced to declare Chapter 7 bankruptcy, the energy firm promptly laid off 4,000 employees. Thousands more lost their entire retirement savings, which primarily had been invested in Enron stock. The company's shareholders also lost tens of billions of dollars after the stock price quickly plummeted from over $90 to mere pennies. More than any other scandal, the actions and events surrounding Enron's demise engendered a global loss of confidence in corporate integrity that had been heretofore unseen. The three men implicated as the chief culprits of the company's fall were founder and CEO Kenneth Lay, former CEO Jeffrey Skilling, and former CFO Andrew Fastow. After years in court, Jeffrey Skilling, was sentenced to just over 24 years in prison and required to pay $45 million in restitution for his part in the scandal. Andrew Fastow, the company's chief financial officer, is serving a six-year prison term in exchange for providing prosecutors with information. Kenneth Lay passed away before he began serving his sentence, which would have been 20 to 30 years in prison.

WorldCom was another high-profile company that was found culpable in the early 2000s. A large telecommunications company, its chief executives were also accused of using questionable accounting practices and improperly recording $3.8 billion in capital expenditures beginning in 1999 and continuing through May 2002. These false claims fraudulently covered up declining cash flows and profit. An internal auditor for the company uncovered the fraudulent accounting in June 2002, and in July the company filed for the largest Chapter 11 bankruptcy protection filing in U.S. history. WorldCom then changed its name to MCI and moved its headquarters from Mississippi to Virginia in 2003. As a result of the company's unethical actions, former CEO Bernard Ebbers was found guilty of fraud, conspiracy, and filing false documents and was sentenced to 25 years in prison in 2005.

Adelphia Communications was one of the largest cable companies in the United States before filing for bankruptcy in 2002. Founded and run by John Rigas and family, the company was widely admired at its peak, and John Rigas received numerous honors for his success as a businessman. All of this changed in the early 2000s when it was discovered that the Rigas family had fraudulently amassed $3.1 billion in off-balance-sheet loans backed by the company. John Rigas and his son Timothy Rigas were both sentenced to jail time (15 years for John, 20 years for Timothy) for bank, wire, and securities fraud.

While these examples may seem like the height of corporate greed, they are only a few of the major corporate shakedowns that occurred in the late 1990s to early 2000s. In response to this wave of serious corporate scandals, the Sarbanes-Oxley Act (SOX) was signed into law in July 2002. Among its many provisions, the Sarbanes-Oxley Act established oversight of public corporate governance and financial reporting obligations and redesigned accountability and ethics standards for corporate officers, auditors, and analysts. Before the passage of SOX, accounting oversight was perceived to be a self-regulating function. However, the examples given here made it very clear that some companies were not capable of self-regulation. The establishment of the accounting oversight board placed more government control over the accounting industry and the public firms they serve. Although most believe that SOX has helped, there are always ways to bend the rules, and new accusations of corporate scandals still pop up. For example, the government has now investigated more than 100 companies in relation to the possible manipulation of stock option prices.

SOX has made it much more expensive for companies to keep track of their accounting and therefore has not been a popular measure among many firms. Since its implementation, a number of companies have fought to have SOX removed or at least weakened. In November 2007, a collection of well-known business, legal, and academic personalities proposed that the government ease corporate governance restrictions, class-action lawsuits, and criminal prosecution related to corporate scandal. The U.S. Chamber of Commerce actually sued the Securities and Exchange Commission, citing excessive regulation. Those from many sectors of the business community began to take serious notice when Treasury Secretary Henry Paulson publicly pondered the damage such restrictions might place on U.S. financial markets. Paulson had been a strong supporter of tougher restrictions; therefore, to call them into question came as something of a shock.

The internal controls provision of the SOX antifraud law is the section that most firms oppose the most vehemently, claiming that they cannot afford to comply. In 2007, the SEC did ease up on measures assessing internal control strength. However, according to many experts, scandals tend to be cyclical and therefore the government should remain vigilant about the level of control exerted over companies—a big scandal hits, the government instates tight controls, firms complain, the government loosens controls, and scandals increase. Experts also argue that businesses are blaming SOX for problems that have their origins in methods of board governance. In spite of the added time and costs of SOX, many perceive it as important to maintain. The business community will always fight restrictive legislation, and as long as the government sees fit to enforce regulations in order to keep citizens safe, there will be conflicts.[13]

**Discussion Questions**

1. Prior to the creation of SOX, the prevailing notion was that markets, and financial and accounting

mechanisms, were most efficient when left to self-regulate. What went wrong?

2. What do you think of the argument that Sarbanes-Oxley is too expensive and should be repealed? Do you think it is necessary?

3. How does making accounting practices more transparent help investors?

**Remember to check out our Online Learning Center at www.mhhe.com/ferrell7e.**

## chapter 5

# Money and the Financial System

## CHAPTER OUTLINE

**Introduction**

**Money in the Financial System**

*Functions of Money*

*Characteristics of Money*

*Types of Money*

**The American Financial System**

*The Federal Reserve System*

*Banking Institutions*

*Nonbanking Institutions*

*Electronic Banking*

*Challenge and Change in the Commercial Banking Industry*

## OBJECTIVES

*After reading this chapter, you will be able to:*

- Define money, its functions, and its characteristics.

- Describe various types of money.

- Specify how the Federal Reserve Board manages the money supply and regulates the American banking system.

- Compare and contrast commercial banks, savings and loan associations, credit unions, and mutual savings banks.

- Distinguish among nonbanking institutions such as insurance companies, pension funds, mutual funds, and finance companies.

- Investigate the challenges ahead for the banking industry.

- Recommend the most appropriate financial institution for a hypothetical small business.

## Peer-to-Peer Lending: Seeking New Ways to Prosper

The credit crisis of 2008 has caused banks, businesses, and individuals to change the ways they handle money, including how loans are issued and acquired. Banks are becoming stricter, sometimes even locking those with good credit scores out of loans. Additionally, investors are looking for new ways to invest outside of the stock market or fixed-income investing. Given the difficulties in the banking industry and the large number of people looking for novel ways to invest, online peer-to-peer lending has become increasingly popular as a means of acquiring and investing capital. Prosper.com is one of these sites.

Founded in 2006, Prosper uses a system similar to eBay's to match borrowers with lenders. Borrowers post requests for loans and set the maximum rates they are willing to pay. Lenders set the minimum rates they are willing to receive and they bid at increments of $50, with a maximum of $25,000 on loan listings. Prosper then takes all bids with the lowest rates and combines them into one loan. The site takes on the responsibility of ongoing loan administration tasks such as collections. The loans issued are usually relatively small, between $5,000 and $10,000. Borrowers with credit scores above 760 can receive loans at 7.76 percent interest. Those with credit scores in the 600s can borrow at 14.47 to 22.67 percent. Bypassing the traditional banking system, investors often earn a greater return than they would otherwise, and the system makes it easier for people to obtain financing who would have difficulty getting a loan from a bank. Prosper itself takes a one-time 1 to 3 percent fee on loans from borrowers and a 1 percent annual servicing fee

*continued*

from lenders. The formula has clearly worked because, since opening, Prosper has amassed more than 800,000 members, and has funded over $165,000,000 in loans.

While some people might be skeptical of a lending institution that is not a bank, Prosper founder and CEO, Chris Larsen, claims that it is as secure as doing business via more traditional systems. The company does not divulge any of its users' personal information, and Prosper members are in complete control of how much information they release to other members.

Peer-to-peer lending is an offshoot of the micro-lending popular in third world countries. Institutions such as the Grameen Foundation or Kiva.org have been utilizing a similar system to disperse loans among poor, primarily female, entrepreneurs for years now. What makes this model of lending both unique and appealing is the fact that people who have little collateral or credit history can obtain a loan, and that the loans are personalized. Lenders get a back-story, recommendations from friends and family, and group affiliations for each prospective borrower. Investing money in these kinds of lending schemes allow investors to not only earn profits, but to help people. The global economic downturn and credit crunch should provide more fuel for this type of lending system, as more people will be deemed not fit to receive bank loans.[1]

# Introduction

**finance**
the study of money; how it's made, how it's lost, and how it's managed

From Wall Street to Main Street—both overseas and at home—money is the one tool used to measure personal and business income and wealth. **Finance** is the study of money: how it's made, how it's lost, and how it's managed. This chapter introduces you to the role of money and the financial system in the economy. Of course, if you have a checking account, automobile insurance, a college loan, or a credit card, you already have personal experience with some key players in the financial world.

We begin our discussion with a definition of money and then explore some of the many forms money may take. Next, we examine the roles of the Federal Reserve Board and other major institutions in the financial system. Finally, we explore the future of the finance industry and some of the changes likely to occur over the course of the next several years.

## Money in the Financial System

**money**
anything generally accepted in exchange for goods and services

Strictly defined, **money,** or *currency,* is anything generally accepted in exchange for goods and services. Materials as diverse as salt, cattle, fish, rocks, shells, cloth, as well as precious metals such as gold, silver, and copper have long been used by various cultures as money. Most of these materials were limited-supply commodities that had their own value to society (for example, salt can be used as a preservative and shells and metals as jewelry). The supply of these commodities therefore determined the supply of "money" in that society. The next step was the development of "IOUs," or slips of paper that could be exchanged for a specified supply of the underlying commodity. "Gold" notes, for instance, could be exchanged for gold, and the money supply was tied to the amount of gold available. While paper money was first used in North America in 1685 (and even earlier in Europe), the concept of *fiat money*—a paper money not readily convertible to a precious metal such as gold—did not gain full acceptance until the Great Depression in the 1930s. The U.S. abandoned its gold-backed currency standard largely in response to the Great Depression and converted to a fiduciary, or fiat, monetary system. In the United States, paper money is really a government "note" or promise, worth the value specified on the note.

## Functions of Money

No matter what a particular society uses for money, its primary purpose is to enable a person or organization to transform a desire into an action. These desires may be for entertainment actions, such as party expenses; operating actions, such as paying for rent, utilities, or employees; investing actions, such as buying property or equipment; or financing actions, such as for starting or growing a business. Money serves three important functions: as a medium of exchange, a measure of value, and a store of value.

**Medium of Exchange.**    Before fiat money, the trade of goods and services was accomplished through *bartering*—trading one good or service for another of similar value. As any school-age child knows, bartering can become quite inefficient— particularly in the case of complex, three-party transactions involving peanut butter sandwiches, baseball cards, and hair barrettes. There had to be a simpler way, and that was to decide on a single item— money—that can be freely converted to any other good upon agreement between parties.

**Measure of Value.**    As a measure of value, money serves as a common standard or yardstick of the value of goods and services. For example, $2 will buy a dozen large eggs and $25,000 will buy a nice car in the United States. In Japan, where the currency is known as the yen, these same transactions would cost about 160 yen and 2.6 million yen, respectively. Money, then, is a common denominator that allows people to compare the different

*For centuries, people on the Micronesian island of Yap have used giant round stones, like the ones shown here, for currency. The stones aren't moved, but their ownership can change.*

goods and services that can be consumed on a particular income level. While a star athlete and a "burger-flipper" are paid vastly different wages, each uses money as a measure of the value of their yearly earnings and purchases.

**Store of Value.**    As a store of value, money serves as a way to accumulate wealth (buying power) until it is needed. For example, a person making $500 per week who wants to buy a $500 computer could save $50 per week for each of the next

10 weeks. Unfortunately, the value of stored money is directly dependent on the health of the economy. If, due to rapid inflation, all prices double in one year, then the purchasing power value of the money "stuffed in the mattress" would fall by half. On the other hand, "mattress savings" buy more when prices fall as they did for more than 52 months in Hong Kong between 1999 and 2005.

## Characteristics of Money

To be used as a medium of exchange, money must be acceptable, divisible, portable, stable in value, durable, and difficult to counterfeit.

**Acceptability.**    To be effective, money must be readily acceptable for the purchase of goods and services and for the settlement of debts. Acceptability is probably the most important characteristic of money: If people do not trust the value of money, businesses will not accept it as a payment for goods and services, and consumers will have to find some other means of paying for their purchases.

**Divisibility.**    Given the widespread use of quarters, dimes, nickels, and pennies in the United States, it is no surprise that the principle of divisibility is an important one. With barter, the lack of divisibility often makes otherwise preferable trades impossible, as would be an attempt to trade a steer for a loaf of bread. For money to serve effectively as a measure of value, all items must be valued in terms of comparable units—dimes for a piece of bubble gum, quarters for laundry machines, and dollars (or dollars and coins) for everything else.

**Portability.**    Clearly, for money to function as a medium of exchange, it must be easily moved from one location to the next. Large colored rocks could be used as money, but you couldn't carry them around in your wallet. Paper currency and metal coins, on the other hand, are capable of transferring vast purchasing power into small, easily carried (and hidden!) bundles. Few Americans realize it, but more U.S. currency is in circulation outside the United States than within. Currently, about $725 billion of U.S. currency is in circulation, and the majority is held outside the United States.[2]

**Stability.**    Money must be stable and maintain its declared face value. A $10 bill should purchase the same amount of goods or services from one day to the next. The principle of stability allows people who wish to postpone purchases and save their money to do so without fear that it will decline in value. As mentioned earlier, money declines in value during periods of inflation, when economic conditions cause prices to rise. Thus, the same amount of money buys fewer and fewer goods and services. In some countries, people spend their money as fast as they can in order to keep it from losing any more of its value. Instability destroys confidence in a nation's money and its ability to store value and serve as an effective medium of exchange. Ultimately, people faced with spiraling price increases avoid the increasingly worthless paper money at all costs, storing all of their savings in the form of real assets such as gold and land.

**Durability.**    Money must be durable. The crisp new dollar bills you trade at the music store for the hottest new CD will make their way all around town for about 20 months before being replaced (see Table 15.1). Were the value of an old, faded bill to fall in line with the deterioration of its appearance, the principles of stability and universal acceptability would fail (but, no doubt, fewer bills would pass through the washer!). Although metal coins, due to their much longer useful life, would

| Denomination of Bill | Life Expectancy (Years) |
|---|---|
| $ 1 | 1.8 |
| $ 5 | 1.3 |
| $ 10 | 1.5 |
| $ 20 | 2 |
| $ 50 | 4.6 |
| $ 100 | 7.4 |

**TABLE 15.1**

The Life Expectancy of Paper Currency

Source: "How Currency Gets into Circulation," *Federal Reserve Bank of New York* (n.d.), www.newyorkfed.org/aboutthefed/fedpoint/fed01.html (accessed May 28, 2008).

appear to be an ideal form of money, paper currency is far more portable than metal because of its light weight. Today, coins are used primarily to provide divisibility.

### Difficulty to Counterfeit.

Finally, to remain stable and enjoy universal acceptance, it almost goes without saying that money must be very difficult to counterfeit—that is, to duplicate illegally. Every country takes steps to make counterfeiting difficult. Most use multicolored money, and many use specially watermarked papers that are virtually impossible to duplicate. Counterfeit bills represent less than 0.02 percent of the currency in circulation in the United States,[4] but it is becoming increasingly easier for counterfeiters to print money with just a modest inkjet printer. This illegal printing of money is fueled by hundreds of people who often circulate only small amounts of counterfeit bills. To thwart the problem of counterfeiting, the U.S. Treasury Department redesigned the U.S. currency, starting with the $20 bill in 2003, the $50 bill in 2004, the $10 bill in 2006, and the $5 bill in 2008. For the first time, U.S. money includes subtle colors in addition to the traditional green, as well as enhanced security features, such as a watermark, security thread, and color-shifting ink.[5] In 2006 the new Jefferson nickel was introduced, showing a profile of the nation's third president. Due to the increased price of metals, it costs 5.73 cents to make the 5 cent piece. President Lincoln was the first president to appear on a coin when the Lincoln penny was introduced in 1909.[6] As Figure 15.1 indicates it costs more than a penny to manufacture a penny, resulting in a call to discontinue it.

**Did You Know?**   Experts estimate that more than $130 million in counterfeit U.S. bills is circulating around the world.[3]

*Skyrocketing copper, zinc, and nickel prices have led some members of Congress to propose that steel pennies be made like they were during World War II. According to Rep. Luis Gutierrez, D–IL, whose subcommittee oversees the U.S. Mint, not changing the penny's content is "contributing to our national debt by almost as much as the coin is worth."*

### Types of Money

While paper money and coins are the most visible types of money, the combined value of all of the printed bills and all of the minted coins is actually rather insignificant when compared with the value of money kept in checking accounts, savings accounts, and other monetary forms.

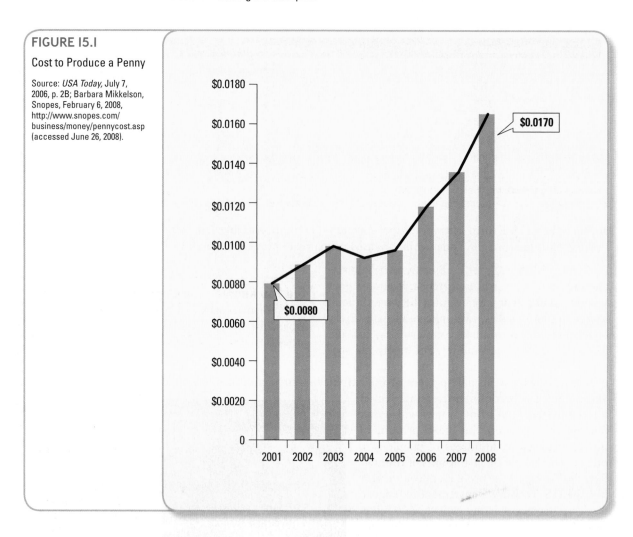

**FIGURE 15.1**

Cost to Produce a Penny

Source: *USA Today*, July 7, 2006, p. 2B; Barbara Mikkelson, Snopes, February 6, 2008, http://www.snopes.com/business/money/pennycost.asp (accessed June 26, 2008).

**checking account**
money stored in an account at a bank or other financial institution that can be withdrawn without advance notice; also called a demand deposit

You probably have a **checking account** (also called a *demand deposit*), money stored in an account at a bank or other financial institution that can be withdrawn without advance notice. One way to withdraw funds from your account is by writing a *check,* a written order to a bank to pay the indicated individual or business the amount specified on the check from money already on deposit. Figure 15.2 explains the significance of the numbers found on a typical U.S. check. As legal instruments, checks serve as a substitute for currency and coins and are preferred for many transactions due to their lower risk of loss. If you lose a $100 bill, anyone who finds or steals it can spend it. If you lose a blank check, however, the risk of catastrophic loss is quite low. Not only does your bank have a sample of your signature on file to compare with a suspected forged signature, but you can render the check immediately worthless by means of a stop-payment order at your bank.

There are several types of checking accounts, with different features available for different monthly fee levels or specific minimum account balances. Some checking accounts earn interest (a small percentage of the amount deposited in the account that the bank pays to the depositor). One such interest-bearing checking account is the *NOW (Negotiable Order of Withdrawal) account* offered by most

**FIGURE 15.2    A Check**

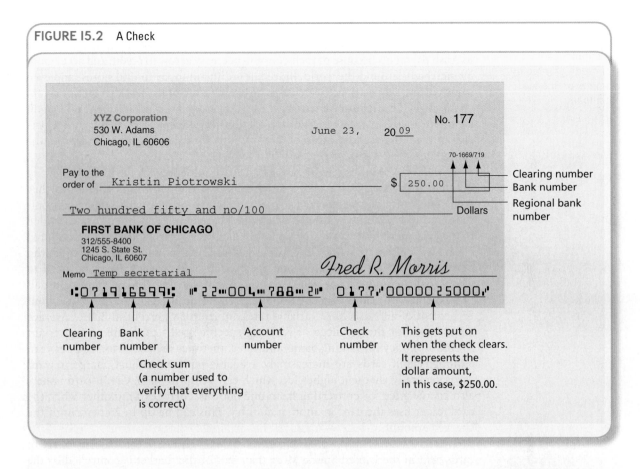

financial institutions. The interest rate paid on such accounts varies with the interest rates available in the economy but is typically quite low (ranging between 2 and 5 percent).

**Savings accounts** (also known as *time deposits*) are accounts with funds that usually cannot be withdrawn without advance notice and/or have limits on the number of withdrawals per period. While seldom enforced, the "fine print" governing most savings accounts prohibits withdrawals without two or three days' notice. Savings accounts are not generally used for transactions or as a medium of exchange, but their funds can be moved to a checking account or turned into cash.

**Money market accounts** are similar to interest-bearing checking accounts, but with more restrictions. Generally, in exchange for slightly higher interest rates, the owner of a money market account can write only a limited number of checks each month, and there may be a restriction on the minimum amount of each check.

**Certificates of deposit (CDs)** are savings accounts that guarantee a depositor a set interest rate over a specified interval of time as long as the funds are not withdrawn before the end of the interval—six months, one year, or seven years, for example. Money may be withdrawn from these accounts prematurely only after paying a substantial penalty. In general, the longer the term of the CD, the higher is the interest rate it earns. As with all interest rates, the rate offered and fixed at the time the account is opened fluctuates according to economic conditions.

**savings accounts** accounts with funds that usually cannot be withdrawn without advance notice; also known as time deposits

**money market accounts** accounts that offer higher interest rates than standard bank rates but with greater restrictions

**certificates of deposit (CDs)** savings accounts that guarantee a depositor a set interest rate over a specified interval as long as the funds are not withdrawn before the end of the period—six months or one year, for example

**credit cards**
means of access to preapproved lines of credit granted by a bank or finance company

**Credit cards** allow you to promise to pay at a later date by using preapproved lines of credit granted by a bank or finance company. They are a popular substitute for cash payments because of their convenience, easy access to credit, and acceptance by merchants around the world. Indeed, it is difficult today to find stores (and even some governmental services, such as state license plate branches) that do not accept credit cards. The institution issuing the credit card guarantees payment of a credit charge to merchants, less a small transaction fee, typically between 2 and 5 percent of the purchase, and assumes responsibility for collecting the money from the cardholder.

With few exceptions, credit cards allow cardholders great flexibility in paying off their purchases. Some people always pay off their monthly charges as they come due, but many others take advantage of the option of paying a stated minimum monthly amount with interest charges, based on yearly interest rates, added to the balance until it has been paid in full. For years, credit card companies lured clients with offers to lock in low fixed rates, sending the message for people who carry a balance on their card—and most people do—that there is no need to worry that the interest rate will rise without any warning. Today, more than half of all credit cards carry variable interest rates. According to Bankrate.com, about 55 percent of all cards have variable rates, up from 38 percent in 2003.[7] Average annual fees for the privilege of carrying specific credit cards are an important source of money for issuing banks and can sometimes reach $60 to $100 per year, although bank cards are increasingly available with no annual charge; reward cards generally charge a higher fee, which can be up to $200. Credit card issuers also charge a fee for converting from one nation's currency to another when the cardholder uses the card in another country. This can be up to 25 percent of the charged amount.

Two major credit cards—MasterCard and Visa—represent the majority of credit cards held in the United States. More than half of the market is controlled by the industry's "Big Five"—Citigroup, MBNA, First USA, American Express, and Discover.[8] Banks are not the only issuers of credit cards. American Express has long been the dominant card company in the travel and entertainment market, with millions of cards outstanding. Unlike most bank cards, the original green American Express Card requires cardholders to pay their entire balances in full each month. However, American Express has expanded its card portfolio to include traditional credit cards.

Major department stores—Sears, JCPenney, Macy's, Saks Fifth Avenue, and others—offer their own credit cards to encourage consumers to spend money in their stores. Unlike the major credit cards discussed, these "private label" cards are generally accepted only at stores associated with the issuing company.

It is estimated that banks, credit card issuers, and retailers lose more than a billion dollars annually to credit card fraud, which includes lost or stolen cards, counterfeit cards, Internet purchases made with someone else's account number, and identity theft—the most devastating of all credit card frauds. Identity theft (also known as application or true name fraud) involves the assumption of someone else's identity by a criminal who then charges in the victim's name. Another concern is the amount of debt that Americans owe to credit card issuers. In an average month, Americans owe more than $950 billion in credit card debt, while the British owe $105 billion and the Australians, $19 billion. That works out to nearly $2,900 for each U.S. man, woman, and child; $1,616 for each Briton, and $950 for each Australian.[9]

A **debit card** looks like a credit card but works like a check. The use of a debit card results in a direct, immediate, electronic payment from the cardholder's checking account to a merchant or other party. While they are convenient to carry and profitable for banks, they lack credit features, offer no purchase "grace period," and provide no hard "paper trail." Debit cards are gaining more acceptance with merchants, and consumers like debit cards because of the ease of getting cash from an increasing number of ATM machines. Financial institutions also want consumers to use debit cards because they reduce the number of teller transactions and check processing costs. Indeed, debit cards have become the most popular form of payment for grocery and gasoline purchases and at "big-box" retailers like Best Buy.[10] Some cash management accounts at retail brokers like Merrill Lynch offer deferred debit cards. These act like a credit card but debit to the cash management account once a month. During that time, the cash earns a money market return.

Traveler's checks, money orders, and cashier's checks are other common forms of "near money." Although each is slightly different from the others, they all share a common characteristic: A financial institution, bank, credit company, or neighborhood currency exchange issues them in exchange for cash and guarantees that the purchased note will be honored and exchanged for cash when it is presented to the institution making the guarantee.

# The American Financial System

The U.S. financial system fuels our economy by storing money, fostering investment opportunities, and making loans for new businesses and business expansion as well as for homes, cars, and college educations. This amazingly complex system includes banking institutions, nonbanking financial institutions such as finance companies, and systems that provide for the electronic transfer of funds throughout the world. Over the past 20 years, the rate at which money turns over, or changes hands, has increased exponentially. Different cultures place unique values on saving, spending, borrowing, and investing. The combination of this increased turnover rate and increasing interactions with people and organizations from other countries has created a complex money system. First, we need to meet the guardian of this complex system.

With just a few simple words, U.S. Federal Reserve Board Chairman Ben Bernanke has the ability to affect monetary policy across the globe. Have you ever noticed the stock market on days in which he is supposed to make an announcement? Even days before or just after?

## The Federal Reserve System

The guardian of the American financial system is the **Federal Reserve Board,** or "the Fed," as it is commonly called, an independent agency of the federal government established in 1913 to regulate the nation's banking and financial industry.

**debit card**
a card that looks like a credit card but works like a check; using it results in a direct, immediate, electronic payment from the cardholder's checking account to a merchant or third party

**Federal Reserve Board**
an independent agency of the federal government established in 1913 to regulate the nation's banking and financial industry

**FIGURE 15.3**   Federal Reserve System

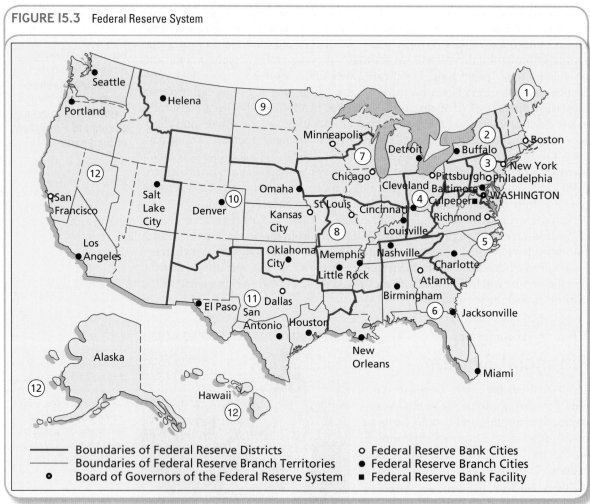

Boundaries of Federal Reserve Districts ——— Federal Reserve Bank Cities ○
Boundaries of Federal Reserve Branch Territories ——— Federal Reserve Branch Cities ●
Board of Governors of the Federal Reserve System ⊙ Federal Reserve Bank Facility ■

The Federal Reserve System is organized into 12 regions, each with a Federal Reserve Bank that serves its defined area (Figure 15.3). All the Federal Reserve banks except those in Boston and Philadelphia have regional branches. The Cleveland Federal Reserve Bank, for example, is responsible for branch offices in Pittsburgh and Cincinnati.

The Federal Reserve Board is the chief economic policy arm of the United States. Working with Congress and the president, the Fed tries to create a positive economic environment capable of sustaining low inflation, high levels of employment, a balance in international payments, and long-term economic growth. To this end, the Federal Reserve Board has four major responsibilities: (1) to control the supply of money, or monetary policy; (2) to regulate banks and other financial institutions; (3) to manage regional and national checking account procedures, or check clearing; and (4) to supervise the federal deposit insurance programs of banks belonging to the Federal Reserve System.

**monetary policy**
means by which the
Fed controls the amount
of money available in
the economy

**Monetary Policy.**   The Fed controls the amount of money available in the economy through **monetary policy.** Without this intervention, the supply

| Activity | Effect on the Money Supply and the Economy |
|---|---|
| Buy government securities | The money supply increases; economic activity increases. |
| Sell government securities | The money supply decreases; economic activity slows down. |
| Raise discount rate | Interest rates increase; the money supply decreases; economic activity slows down. |
| Lower discount rate | Interest rates decrease; the money supply increases; economic activity increases. |
| Increase reserve requirements | Banks make fewer loans; the money supply declines; economic activity slows down. |
| Decrease reserve requirements | Banks make more loans; the money supply increases; economic activity increases. |
| Relax credit controls | More people are encouraged to make major purchases, increasing economic activity. |
| Restrict credit controls | People are discouraged from making major purchases, decreasing economic activity. |

**TABLE l5.2**

Fed Tools for Regulating the Money Supply

of and demand for money might not balance. This could result in either rapid price increases (inflation) because of too little money or economic recession and a slowdown of price increases (disinflation) because of too little growth in the money supply. In very rare cases (the depression of the 1930s) the United States has suffered from deflation, where the actual purchasing power of the dollar has increased as prices declined. To effectively control the supply of money in the economy, the Fed must have a good idea of how much money is in circulation at any given time. This has become increasingly challenging because the global nature of our economy means that more and more U.S. dollars are circulating overseas. Using several different measures of the money supply, the Fed establishes specific growth targets which, presumably, ensure a close balance between money supply and money demand. The Fed fine-tunes money growth by using four basic tools: open market operations, reserve requirements, the discount rate, and credit controls (see Table 15.2). There is generally a log of 6 to 18 months before the effect of these charges shows up in economic activity.

**Open market operations** refer to decisions to buy or sell U.S. Treasury bills (short-term debt issued by the U.S. government; also called T-bills) and other investments in the open market. The actual purchase or sale of the investments is performed by the New York Federal Reserve Bank. This monetary tool, the most commonly employed of all Fed operations, is performed almost daily in an effort to control the money supply.

When the Fed buys securities, it writes a check on its own account to the seller of the investments. When the seller of the investments (usually a large bank) deposits the check, the Fed transfers the balance from the Federal Reserve account into the seller's account, thus increasing the supply of money in the economy and, hopefully, fueling economic growth. The opposite occurs when the Fed sells investments. The buyer writes a check to the Federal Reserve, and when the funds are transferred out of the purchaser's account, the amount of money in circulation falls, slowing economic growth to a desired level.

**open market operations** decisions to buy or sell U.S. Treasury bills (short-term debt issued by the U.S. government) and other investments in the open market

**reserve requirement**
the percentage of deposits that banking institutions must hold in reserve

The second major monetary policy tool is the **reserve requirement,** the percentage of deposits that banking institutions must hold in reserve ("in the vault," as it were). Funds so held are not available for lending to businesses and consumers. For example, a bank holding $10 million in deposits, with a 10 percent reserve requirement, must have reserves of $1 million. If the Fed were to reduce the reserve requirement to, say, 5 percent, the bank would need to keep only $500,000 in reserves. The bank could then lend to customers the $500,000 difference between the old reserve level and the new lower reserve level, thus increasing the supply of money. Because the reserve requirement has such a powerful effect on the money supply, the Fed does not change it very often, relying instead on open market operations most of the time.

**discount rate**
the rate of interest the Fed charges to loan money to any banking institution to meet reserve requirements

The third monetary policy tool, the **discount rate,** is the rate of interest the Fed charges to loan money to any banking institution to meet reserve requirements. The Fed is the lender of last resort for these banks. When a bank borrows from the Fed, it is said to have borrowed at the "discount window," and the interest rates charged there are often higher than those charged on loans of comparable risk elsewhere in the economy. This added interest expense, when it exists, serves to discourage banks from borrowing from the Fed.

When the Fed wants to expand the money supply, it lowers the discount rate to encourage borrowing. Conversely, when the Fed wants to decrease the money supply, it raises the discount rate. The increases in interest rates that occurred in the United States from 2003 through 2006 were the result of more than 16 quarter-point (0.25 percent) increases in the Fed discount rate. The purpose was to keep inflation under control and to raise rates to a more normal level as the economy recovered from the recession of 2001. Not surprisingly, economists watch changes in this sensitive interest rate as an indicator of the Fed's monetary policy.

**credit controls**
the authority to establish and enforce credit rules for financial institutions and some private investors

The final tool in the Fed's arsenal of weapons is **credit controls**—the authority to establish and enforce credit rules for financial institutions and some private investors. For example, the Fed can determine how large a down payment individuals and businesses must make on credit purchases of expensive items such as automobiles, and how much time they have to finish paying for the purchases. By raising and lowering minimum down payment amounts and payment periods, the Fed can stimulate or discourage credit purchases of "big ticket" items. The Fed also has the authority to set the minimum down payment investors must use for the credit purchases of stock. Buying stock with credit—"buying on margin"—is a popular investment strategy among individual speculators. By altering the margin requirement (currently set at 50 percent of the price of the purchased stocks), the Fed can effectively control the total amount of credit borrowing in the stock market.

Regulatory Functions.     The second major responsibility of the Fed is to regulate banking institutions that are members of the Federal Reserve System. Accordingly, the Fed establishes and enforces banking rules that affect monetary policy and the overall level of the competition between different banks. It determines which non-banking activities, such as brokerage services, leasing, and insurance, are appropriate for banks and which should be prohibited. The Fed also has the authority to approve or disapprove mergers between banks and the formation of bank holding companies. In an effort to ensure that all rules are enforced and that correct accounting procedures are being followed at member banks, surprise bank examinations are conducted by bank examiners each year.

Check Clearing.     The Federal Reserve provides national check processing on a huge scale. Divisions of the Fed known as check clearinghouses handle almost all

# Destination CEO
## Clarence Otis—Darden Restaurants

About 30 years ago, Clarence Otis changed the name of his restaurant from the Green Frog to the Red Lobster. Today, it is the number-one seafood chain in the country. The same parent corporation, Darden Restaurants, owns the Olive Garden chain. Darden has more than 150,000 employees and 15,000 restaurants.

At an early age, Clarence Otis had excellent guidance as his mother had very high expectations for him. His first job was a server in a full-service restaurant, where he learned the pressures associated with high expectations of customers He attended Williams College as an undergraduate. From there, he returned to northern California to attend law school at Stanford. Otis returned to the East Coast, where he practiced corporate law in New York City with a focus in mergers and acquisitions. He found that he liked the financial aspects of the business better than the legal side. Clarence Otis changed his career to that of an investment banker.

He moved to Darden in 1995 as treasurer. Eventually Otis became the CFO and advanced to the role of CEO.

Today, he sees a tremendous amount of growth potential for both the Red Lobster and Olive Garden chains. To remain relevant is the key. Both restaurants continue to evolve in concert with the guests' expectations. People who work for the Darden chains must be inspired and understand the corporate philosophy and its goals.

### Discussion Questions
1. What prepared Clarence Otis for his position as CEO of Darden?
2. How extensive is Darden Restaurants in the United States?
3. According to Otis, what is the key area for success for employees at the Darden company?

the checks written against a bank in one city and presented for deposit to a bank in a second city. Any banking institution can present the checks it has received from others around the country to its regional Federal Reserve Bank. The Fed passes the checks to the appropriate regional Federal Reserve Bank, which then sends the checks to the issuing bank for payment. With the advance of electronic payment systems and the passage of the Check Clearing for the 21st Century Act (Check 21 Act), checks can now be processed in a day. The Check 21 Act allows banks to clear checks electronically by presenting an electronic image of the check. This eliminates mail delays and time-consuming paper processing.

**Depository Insurance.** The Fed is also responsible for supervising the federal insurance funds that protect the deposits of member institutions. These insurance funds will be discussed in greater detail in the following section.

## Banking Institutions

Banking institutions accept money deposits from and make loans to individual consumers and businesses. Some of the most important banking institutions include commercial banks, savings and loan associations, credit unions, and mutual savings banks. Historically, these have all been separate institutions. However, new hybrid forms of banking institutions that perform two or more of these functions have emerged over the last two decades. The following all have one thing in common: They are businesses whose objective is to earn money by managing, safeguarding, and lending money to others. Their sales revenues come from the fees and interest that they charge for providing these financial services.

**Commercial Banks.** The largest and oldest of all financial institutions are **commercial banks,** which perform a variety of financial services. They rely mainly on checking and savings accounts as their major source of funds and use only a portion of these deposits to make loans to businesses and individuals.

**commercial banks**
the largest and oldest of all financial institutions, relying mainly on checking and savings accounts as sources of funds for loans to businesses and individuals

471

Because it is unlikely that all the depositors of any one bank will want to withdraw all of their funds at the same time, a bank can safely loan out a large percentage of its deposits.

Today, banks are quite diversified and offer a number of services. Commercial banks make loans for virtually any conceivable legal purpose, from vacations to cars, from homes to college educations. Banks in many states offer *home equity loans,* by which home owners can borrow against the appraised value of their already purchased homes. Banks also issue Visa and MasterCard credit cards and offer CDs and trusts (legal entities set up to hold and manage assets for a beneficiary). Many banks rent safe deposit boxes in bank vaults to customers who want to store jewelry, legal documents, artwork, and other valuables. In 1999 Congress passed the Financial Services Modernization Act, also known as the Gramm-Leach-Bliley Bill. This act repealed the Glass Stegal Act, which was enacted in 1929 after the stock market crash and prohibited commercial banks from being in the insurance and investment banking business. This puts U.S. commercial banks on the same competitive footing as European banks and provides a more level playing field for global banking competition. The stimulus for the Gramm-Leach-Bliley Bill was probably the merger of Citibank and Travelers Insurance. With its Salomon Smith Barney investment bank and brokerage units, Travelers Insurance, when combined with Citibank, became the largest financial services company in the United States. As commercial banks and investment banks have merged, the financial landscape has changed. Consolidation remains the norm in the U.S. banking industry. For example JPMorgan Chase completed a merger with Bank One in 2004, making it the second largest bank in the United States behind Citigroup. JPMorgan was created through a merger with Chase Manhattan Bank and JPMorgan, and Bank One acquired many Midwestern banks, with its biggest acquisition being First Chicago Corp.

**savings and loan associations (S&Ls)**
financial institutions that primarily offer savings accounts and make long-term loans for residential mortgages; also called "thrifts"

Savings and Loan Associations.   **Savings and loan associations (S&Ls),** often called "thrifts," are financial institutions that primarily offer savings accounts and make long-term loans for residential mortgages. A mortgage is a loan made so that a business or individual can purchase real estate, typically a home; the real estate itself is pledged as a guarantee (called *collateral*) that the buyer will repay the loan. If the loan is not repaid, the savings and loan has the right to repossess the property. Prior to the 1970s, S&Ls focused almost exclusively on real estate lending and accepted only savings accounts. Today, following years of regulatory changes, S&Ls compete directly with commercial banks by offering many types of services.

Savings and loans have gone through a metamorphosis since the early 1990s, after having almost collapsed in the 1980s. Congress passed legislation that allowed more competition between banks and savings and loans. The problem was the owners and managers of the savings and loans did not know how to behave like banks, and they did not have the products necessary to compete. Then, Congress passed laws in 1986 that took away many of the tax benefits of owning real estate, which caused investment in real estate to slow considerably and stimulated defaults that were spurred by a poor economy. Developers defaulted on loans, and the S&L managers who had lent the money for these high-risk ventures found themselves holding billions of dollars of virtually unsellable real estate properties.

Despite the efforts of the Federal Savings and Loan Insurance Corporation—which we discuss in more detail shortly—there were not enough funds to bail out the industry. Eventually, the insurance fund ran out of money, and Congress created the Resolution Trust Corporation (RTC) in 1989 to help the industry work its way

## Responding to Business Challenges
### Wells Fargo Uses Family Histories to Gain New Clients

Wells Fargo & Company is one of the world's largest financial services companies, with divisions dealing in banking, insurance, investment, mortgage, and consumer finance services. Founded in 1852, the company now boasts $595 billion in assets and employs 160,900 people throughout its more than 80 outlets. In 2008, Wells Fargo was the third-largest bank in the United States and *Fortune* ranked it as the 17th most profitable company in the world. One would think that, after achieving such a high level of success, clients would turn to Wells Fargo without needing much enticement. But even large and successful companies have to devise ways to lure in customers. Wells Fargo has taken a unique approach to this universal problem—it offers potential and current clients alike glimpses into their own histories via genealogical analysis. Wells Fargo keeps a corporate historian on staff, Dr. Andy Anderson, and he spearheaded this new marketing approach. He leverages high-profile clients' interest in their lineage to entice them into using Wells Fargo. According the company, the approach has netted about $1 billion in new assets thus far.

Wells Fargo's creative new approach to attracting more clients is a proactive maneuver to gear up for the future. In the next 50 years, the private banking industry is expected to expand as the fortunes of baby boomers are passed on to beneficiaries. As a result, banks participating in private banking are upping the stakes. Other companies have attempted to woo clients with trips to baseball games, parties, and social gatherings with the likes of Colin Powell and Rudolph Giuliani. Wells Fargo instead relies on Dr. Anderson and on people's innate interest in their histories. The idea came about after Anderson presented Wells Fargo's history to 200 affluent bank clients in 2003. After concluding the presentation, Anderson was inundated with numerous inquiries into how the clients could begin to research their own histories. The company seized on this demand and created "family-heritage gatherings," to which they invited both current and prospective clients. At these events, Anderson presents a brief snapshot of each client's family history. Clients may then request a more detailed history, if they so desire. As a result, Wells Fargo has won new clients and retained many others. By 2007, Anderson had created about 40 complete family histories. Most of these 40 clients have an individual net worth of more than $100 million. An added bonus to the company is that, thanks to the Internet, Dr. Anderson is able to create these histories at very little expense. Wells Fargo's private banking business currently generates about 16 percent of the company's profit, and the goal is to increase that number to 25 percent. To create this kind of growth, the company is relying, to some extent on this new tactic of roping wealthy customers in with promises of revealing their families' pasts.[11]

out of trouble. At a cost of hundreds of billions of dollars, the RTC cleaned up the industry and, with its task completed, was dissolved by 1998.

**Credit Unions.**     A **credit union** is a financial institution owned and controlled by its depositors, who usually have a common employer, profession, trade group, or religion. The Aggieland Credit Union in College Station, Texas, for example, provides banking services for faculty, employees, and current and former students of Texas A&M University. A savings account at a credit union is commonly referred to as a share account, while a checking account is termed a share draft account. Because the credit union is tied to a common organization, the members (depositors) are allowed to vote for directors and share in the credit union's profits in the form of higher interest rates on accounts and/or lower loan rates.

While credit unions were originally created to provide depositors with a short-term source of funds for low-interest consumer loans for items such as cars, home appliances, vacations, and college, today they offer a wide range of financial services. Generally, the larger the credit union, the more sophisticated its financial service offerings will be.

**Mutual Savings Banks.**     **Mutual savings banks** are similar to savings and loan associations, but, like credit unions, they are owned by their depositors. Among the oldest financial institutions in the United States, they were originally established to provide a safe place for savings of particular groups of people, such as fishermen.

**credit union**
a financial institution owned and controlled by its depositors, who usually have a common employer, profession, trade group, or religion

**mutual savings banks**
financial institutions that are similar to savings and loan associations but, like credit unions, are owned by their depositors

Found mostly in New England, they are becoming more popular in the rest of the country as some S&Ls have converted to mutual savings banks to escape the stigma created by the widespread S&L failures in the 1980s.

**Federal Deposit Insurance Corporation (FDIC)**
an insurance fund established in 1933 that insures individual bank accounts

Insurance for Banking Institutions.  The **Federal Deposit Insurance Corporation (FDIC),** which insures individual bank accounts, was established in 1933 to help stop bank failures throughout the country during the Great Depression. Today, the FDIC insures personal accounts up to a maximum of $100,000 at nearly 8,000 FDIC member institutions.[12] While most major banks are insured by the FDIC, small institutions in some states may be insured by state insurance funds or private insurance companies. Should a member bank fail, its depositors can recover all of their funds, up to $100,000. Amounts over $100,000, while not legally covered by the insurance, are in fact usually covered because the Fed understands very well the enormous damage that would result to the financial system should these large depositors withdraw their money. The *Federal Savings and Loan Insurance Corporation (FSLIC)* insured thrift deposits prior to its insolvency and failure during the S&L crisis of the 1980s. Now, the insurance functions once overseen by the FSLIC are handled directly by the FDIC through its Savings Association Insurance Fund. The **National Credit Union Association (NCUA)** regulates and charters credit unions and insures their deposits through its National Credit Union Insurance Fund.

**National Credit Union Association (NCUA)**
an agency that regulates and charters credit unions and insures their deposits through its National Credit Union Insurance Fund

When they were originally established, Congress hoped that these insurance funds would make people feel secure about their savings so that they would not panic and withdraw their money when news of a bank failure was announced. The "bank run" scene in the perennial Christmas movie *It's a Wonderful Life,* when dozens of Bailey Building and Loan depositors attempted to withdraw their money (only to have the reassuring figure of Jimmy Stewart calm their fears), was not based on mere fiction. During the Great Depression, hundreds of banks failed and their depositors lost everything. The fact that large numbers of major financial institutions failed in the 1980s and 1990s—without a single major banking panic—underscores the effectiveness of the current insurance system. While the future may yet bring unfortunate surprises, most depositors go to sleep every night without worrying about the safety of their savings.

### Nonbanking Institutions

Nonbank financial institutions offer some financial services, such as short-term loans or investment products, but do not accept deposits. These include insurance companies, pension funds, mutual funds, brokerage firms, nonfinancial firms, and finance companies. It may be a surprise to some, but General Electric Corporation's financial subsidiary, General Electric Capital Services (GECS) would rank as one of the top 10 largest U.S. banks with assets of $646 billion at the end of 2007.[13] Table 15.3 lists some other diversified financial services firms.

Diversified Firms.  Recently, a growing number of traditionally nonfinancial firms have moved onto the financial field. These firms include manufacturing organizations, such as General Motors and General Electric, that traditionally confined their financial activities to financing their customers' purchases. GE, for example, has been so successful in the financial arena that its credit subsidiary now accounts for more than 30 percent of the company's revenues and earnings. Not every nonfinancial firm has been successful with its financial ventures, however. Sears, the retail giant, once commanded an imposing financial network composed

| Company | Revenues (in millions) | Company | Revenues (in millions) |
|---|---|---|---|
| General Electric | $176,656 | SLM | $9,171 |
| American Express | 32,316 | Ameriprise Financial | 8,909 |
| GMAC | 31,490 | CITI Group | 8,605 |
| Marsh & McLennan | 12,148 | Blackstone Group | 3,050 |
| Aon | 9,973 | Annaly Capital Management | 2,417 |

Source: "Fortune 1000 Diversified Financial Companies," http://cgi.money.cnn.com/tools/fortune/custom_ranking_2008.jsp (accessed September 18, 2008).

of real estate (Coldwell Banker), credit card (Discover Card), and brokerage (Dean Witter Reynolds) companies, but losses of hundreds of millions of dollars forced Sears to dismantle its network. The very prestigious brokerage firm Morgan Stanley acquired Dean Witter Discover, thus creating one of the largest investment firms in the country—in a league with Smith Barney and Merrill Lynch. Perhaps the moral of the story for firms like Sears is "stick to what you know."

**Insurance Companies.** **Insurance companies** are businesses that protect their clients against financial losses from certain specified risks (death, injury, disability, accident, fire, theft, and natural disasters, for example) in exchange for a fee, called a premium. Because insurance premiums flow into the companies regularly, but major insurance losses cannot be timed with great accuracy (though expected risks can be assessed with considerable precision), insurance companies generally have large amounts of excess funds. They typically invest these or make long-term loans, particularly to businesses in the form of commercial real estate loans.

**insurance companies** businesses that protect their clients against financial losses from certain specified risks (death, accident, and theft, for example)

**Pension Funds.** **Pension funds** are managed investment pools set aside by individuals, corporations, unions, and some nonprofit organizations to provide retirement income for members. One type of pension fund is the *individual retirement account (IRA)*, which is established by individuals to provide for their personal retirement needs. IRAs can be invested in a variety of financial assets, from risky commodities such as oil or cocoa to low-risk financial "staples" such as U.S. Treasury securities. The choice is up to each person and is dictated solely by individual objectives and tolerance for risk. The interest earned by all of these investments may be deferred tax-free until retirement.

**pension funds** managed investment pools set aside by individuals, corporations, unions, and some nonprofit organizations to provide retirement income for members

In 1997, Congress revised the IRA laws and created a Roth IRA. Although similar to a traditional IRA in that investors may contribute $5,000 per year, the money in a Roth IRA is considered an after-tax contribution. When the money is withdrawn at retirement, no tax is paid on the distribution. The Roth IRA is beneficial to young people who can allow a long time for their money to compound and who may be able to have their parents or grandparents fund the Roth IRA with gift money.

Most major corporations provide some kind of pension plan for their employees. Many of these are established with bank trust departments or life insurance companies. Money is deposited in a separate account in the name of each individual employee, and when the employee retires, the total amount in the account can be either withdrawn in one lump sum or taken as monthly cash payments over some defined time period (usually for the remaining life of the retiree).

Social Security, the largest pension fund, is publicly financed. The federal government collects Social Security funds from payroll taxes paid by both employers and

# Going Green
## Metabolix: A Small Firm with Big Plans to Reduce Waste

For a long time it has been easier for companies to simply make new plastic than to recycle old containers or to come up with a more environmentally friendly alternative. Businesses did not have to think too much about the waste they produced; where it went; or what it did to plants, animals, and air quality. In recent decades, the fallout of this kind of thinking has begun to become clear. The hidden costs of decades of waste and pollution are turning out to be astronomically high—as global warming increases the severity of weather, global food shortages become dire, and people are sickened by pollution. A mass of trash twice the size of Texas was found floating in the Pacific Ocean in 1997, a pile that grows every day. Its discoverer, Charles Moore, estimates that in some parts of the world, pieces of plastic outnumber plankton.

Scottish-born biochemist Oliver P. Peoples has spent much of his 27-year-long career trying to build an enterprise focused on solving the problem of nonbiodegradable waste. His company, Metabolix, produces a bioplastic, called Mirel, which is a plasticlike substance produced by plant cells that then biodegrades like plant materials. Peoples has collected hundreds of patents and is set to begin large-scale production in 2009, but financing has been a problem every step of the way. The bear market and delays in manufacturing have hit share values hard. Because production has not yet paid off yet, the company is continuing to blow through cash rapidly.

However, in spite of low share values and other financing problems encountered by the company, Peoples is not concerned. As long as petroleum prices continue to rise, so does the cost of producing plastic. As production costs go up, more companies will start looking to plastic alternatives—this is where Peoples believes Metabolix comes in. Around 30 million tons of plastic is thrown away in the United States each year, only 5 percent of which is recycled. Environmentalists, and increasingly other groups, are enraged by this statistic. The sheer volume of plastic waste has become a huge problem, let alone the harm it wreaks on the environment. As plastic breaks down into smaller and smaller bits, it releases toxins into the soil, which can harm plants and animals that come in contact with it.

Metabolix is going to meet with some stiff competition as it seeks to carve out a market for itself. Multinational giants like DuPont and Cargill are already at work on their own kinds of bioplastics. The advantage of Mirel is that it is the only one that will biodegrade without the application of high temperatures. Mirel will decompose no matter where it ends up—on the ground, in the ocean, or in a compost heap. Within 180 days, Mirel bioplastic containers will turn into regular brown dirt fit for gardening. Peoples says that an additional feature of Mirel is that the manufacturer can control how fast the material will break down.

Peoples is an unlikely hero for the bioplastics movement. He grew up in poverty, one of 11 children, whose father died when he was 16. It was a high school chemistry teacher who saw potential in him and helped Peoples get into Aberdeen University, where he earned a PhD in molecular biology. He then moved to the United States to pursue postgraduate work at the Massachusetts Institute of Technology. Pulling himself out of poverty, and then attending top-level universities forged a competitive streak in Peoples, as well as a sense for how to make finances work. However, starting up and financing a little biotech firm in a fledgling industry proved more difficult than Peoples could have imagined. In the span of about a decade, the company went through 11 rounds of financing and finally went public in 2006.

In 2004, after decades of research, Metabolix hit upon the right formula to make his idea work, and company saw a light at the end of the tunnel. While demand for biomaterials grows along with environmental concerns and accumulating trash, there remains a lot of room for more growth. It is estimated that by 2010 bioplastics production will still only be 1/500 that of traditional plastic. However, with oil prices pushing ever higher, petro-based plastics are becoming an extravagance many companies cannot afford. Even the petro-giant Dow Chemical raised the price of all its plastics products by 20 percent in June of 2008, already making bioplastics an economically cheaper alternative.

To continue its growth, Metabolix has garnered some serious backing. It recently negotiated a joint venture with Archer Daniels Midland, which will supply feedstocks and a $200 million plant in Iowa for plastics production. The hope is that in the future Metabolix will develop new ways of producing Mirel that will not require food crops like corn so that the product will neither pollute nor cut into an already dwindling food supply.[14]

### Discussion Questions
1. In spite of huge financing obstacles, why is Oliver Peoples not concerned about his company's ultimate success?
2. What are different ways that Peoples has raised capital to finance his company?
3. Even though Mirel appears to be a superior product, what kinds of competition will be a problem for Metabolix?

employees. The Social Security Administration then takes these monies and makes payments to those eligible to receive Social Security benefits—the retired, the disabled, and the young children of deceased parents.

**Mutual Funds.**    A **mutual fund** pools individual investor dollars and invests them in large numbers of well-diversified securities. Individual investors buy shares in a mutual fund in the hope of earning a high rate of return and in much the same way as people buy shares of stock. Because of the large numbers of people investing in any one mutual fund, the funds can afford to invest in hundreds (if not thousands) of securities at any one time, minimizing the risks of any single security that does not do well. Mutual funds provide professional financial management for people who lack the time and/or expertise to invest in particular securities, such as government bonds. While there are no hard-and-fast rules, investments in one or more mutual funds are one way for people to plan for financial independence at the time of retirement.

A special type of mutual fund called a *money market fund* invests specifically in short-term debt securities issued by governments and large corporations. Although they offer services such as check-writing privileges and reinvestment of interest income, money market funds differ from the money market accounts offered by banks primarily in that the former represent a pool of funds, while the latter are basically specialized, individual checking accounts. Money market funds usually offer slightly higher rates of interest than bank money market accounts.

**Brokerage Firms and Investment Banks.**    **Brokerage firms** buy and sell stocks, bonds, and other securities for their customers and provide other financial services. Larger brokerage firms like Merrill Lynch, Charles Schwab, and A. G. Edwards offer financial services unavailable at their smaller competitors. Merrill Lynch, for example, offers the Merrill Lynch Cash Management Account (CMA), which pays interest on deposits and allows clients to write checks, borrow money, and withdraw cash much like a commercial bank. The largest of the brokerage firms (including Merrill Lynch) have developed so many specialized services that they may be considered financial networks—organizations capable of offering virtually all of the services traditionally associated with commercial banks.

Most brokerage firms are really part financial conglomerates that provide many different kinds of services besides buying and selling securities for clients. For example, Merrill Lynch also is an investment banker, as is Smith Barney, and Goldman Sachs. The **investment banker** underwrites new issues of securities for corporations, states, and municipalities needed to raise money in the capital markets. The new issue market is called a *primary market* because the sale of the securities is for the first time. After the first sale, the securities trade in the *secondary markets* by brokers. The investment banker advises on the price of the new

Mutual funds are considered an excellent method for investing for retirement.

**mutual fund**
an investment company that pools individual investor dollars and invests them in large numbers of well-diversified securities

**brokerage firms**
firms that buy and sell stocks, bonds, and other securities for their customers and provide other financial services

**investment banker**
underwrites new issues of securities for corporations, states, and municipalities

securities and generally guarantees the sale while overseeing the distribution of the securities through the selling brokerage houses. Investment bankers also act as dealers who make markets in securities. They do this by offering to sell the securities at an asked price (which is a higher rate) and buy the securities at a bid price (which is a lower rate)—the difference in the two prices represents the profit for the dealer.

**finance companies**
businesses that offer short-term loans at substantially higher rates of interest than banks

**Finance Companies.**     **Finance companies** are businesses that offer short-term loans at substantially higher rates of interest than banks. Commercial finance companies make loans to businesses, requiring their borrowers to pledge assets such as equipment, inventories, or unpaid accounts as collateral for the loans. Consumer finance companies make loans to individuals. Like commercial finance companies, these firms require some sort of personal collateral as security against the borrower's possible inability to repay their loans. Because of the high interest rates they charge and other factors, finance companies typically are the lender of last resort for individuals and businesses whose credit limits have been exhausted and/or those with poor credit ratings. Major consumer finance companies include Household Finance and Wells Fargo. All finance companies—commercial or consumer—obtain their funds by borrowing from other corporations and/or commercial banks.

## Electronic Banking

**electronic funds transfer (EFT)**
any movement of funds by means of an electronic terminal, telephone, computer, or magnetic tape

Since the advent of the computer age, a wide range of technological innovations has made it possible to move money all across the world electronically. Such "paperless" transactions have allowed financial institutions to reduce costs in what has been, and continues to be, a virtual competitive battlefield. **Electronic funds transfer (EFT)** is any movement of funds by means of an electronic terminal, telephone, computer, or magnetic tape. Such transactions order a particular financial institution to subtract money from one account and add it to another. The most commonly used forms of EFT are automated teller machines, automated clearinghouses, and home banking systems.

**automated teller machine (ATM)**
the most familiar form of electronic banking, which dispenses cash, accepts deposits, and allows balance inquiries and cash transfers from one account to another

**Automated Teller Machines.**     Probably the most familiar form of electronic banking is the **automated teller machine (ATM),** which dispenses cash, accepts deposits, and allows balance inquiries and cash transfers from one account to another. ATMs provide 24-hour banking services—both at home (through a local bank) and far away (via worldwide ATM networks such as Cirrus and Plus). Rapid growth, driven by both strong consumer acceptance and lower transaction costs for banks (about half the cost of teller transactions), has led to the installation of hundreds of thousands of ATMs worldwide. Table 15.4 presents some interesting statistics about ATMs.

**automated clearinghouses (ACHs)**
a system that permits payments such as deposits or withdrawals to be made to and from a bank account by magnetic computer tape

**Automated Clearinghouses.**     **Automated clearinghouses (ACHs)** permit payments such as deposits or withdrawals to be made to and from a bank account by magnetic computer tape. Most large U.S. employers, and many others worldwide, use ACHs to deposit their employees' paychecks directly to the employees' bank accounts. While direct deposit is used by only 50 percent of U.S. workers, nearly 100 percent of Japanese workers and more than 90 percent of European workers utilize it. The largest user of automated clearinghouses in the United States is the federal government, with 99 percent of federal government employees and 65 percent of the private workforce receiving their pay via direct deposit. And, more than 82 percent of all Social Security payments are made through an ACH system.

TABLE I5.4

Facts about ATM Use

- An ATM costs between $9,000 and $50,000, depending on the functions it has been designed to perform.
- The top six ATM owners are Bank of America, Cardtronics, U.S. Bancorp, JPMorgan Chase, Wells Fargo, and 7-Eleven.
- In 2005, there were 396,000 ATMs in the United States.
- Transactions at these machines totaled $10.5 billion.
- 21 percent of Americans prefer to bank via ATMs.
- The first ATM was in use in 1969 at the Chemical Bank in Long Island, NY.

Source: ATM Fact Sheet, *2006 ABA Issue Summary,* American Bankers Association, www.aba.com, http://www.aba.com/NR/rdonlyres/80468400-4225-11D4-AAE6-00508B95258D/41765/2ATMFacts1.pdf (accessed September 18, 2008).

In 2005, more than 5 million companies made payments through an automated clearinghouse network.

The advantages of direct deposits to consumers include convenience, safety, and potential interest earnings. It is estimated that more than 4 million paychecks are lost or stolen annually, and FBI studies show that 2,000 fraudulent checks are cashed every day in the United States. Checks can never be lost or stolen with direct deposit. The benefits to businesses include decreased check-processing expenses and increased employee productivity. Research shows that businesses that use direct deposit can save more than $1.25 on each payroll check processed. Productivity could increase by $3 to $5 billion annually if all employees were to use direct deposit rather than taking time away from work to deposit their payroll checks.

Some companies also use ACHs for dividend and interest payments. Consumers can also use ACHs to make periodic (usually monthly) fixed payments to specific creditors without ever having to write a check or buy stamps. The estimated number of bills paid annually by consumers is 20 billion, and the total number paid through ACHs is estimated at only 8.5 billion. The average consumer who writes 10 to 15 checks each month would save $41 to $62 annually in postage alone.[15]

**Online Banking.**   With the growth of the Internet, banking activities may now be carried out on a computer at home or at work, or through wireless devices such as cell phones and PDAs anywhere there is a wireless "hot point." Consumers and small businesses can now make a bewildering array of financial transactions at home or on the go 24 hours a day. Functioning much like a vast network of personal ATMs, computer networks such as America Online allow their subscribers to make sophisticated banking transactions, buy and sell stocks and bonds, and purchase products and airline tickets without ever leaving home or speaking to another human being. Many banks allow customers to log directly into their accounts to check balances, transfer money between accounts, view their account statements, and pay bills via home computer or other Internet-enabled devices. Computer and advanced telecommunications technology have revolutionized world commerce, with 53 percent of adult Internet users engaging in online banking activities.[16]

## Challenge and Change in the Commercial Banking Industry

In the early 1990s, several large commercial banks were forced to admit publicly that they had made some poor loan decisions. Bank failures followed, including that of the Bank of New England, the third-largest bank failure in history. The vibrant economic

# Entrepreneurship in Action
## Independent Bank Hits Gold by Staying True to Its Roots

Denny Buchanan

**Business:** Independent Bank

**Founded:** 2005

**Success:** Since the bank opened, all of its numbers have continued to climb in record time.

After working in the banking industry for years, Denny Buchanan decided to use his knowledge to open a community bank of his own. In 2001, he tried to get his idea started, but investors were not interested. In 2005 he tried again and, luckily for him, the financial tides had turned. This time he was able to acquire $7.5 million in equity capital, allowing him to launch Independent Bank of Austin. The bank officially opened on June 6, 2005, and was profitable within the first three months. At the end of its first year, the bank had amassed a $1.4 million profit. Originally, Buchanan and his team hoped to come up with $100 million in assets within the first 5 to 10 years of operation. The bank's performance exceeded their expectations and reached this goal within 18 months.

Good timing played a part in Independent Bank's rapid success; 2005 marked the start of a rise in the number of new community banks. According to analysts, the move toward smaller banks generally occurs a few years after a round of industry consolidation as a backlash against banks growing so large and impersonal. Independent Bank has continued to ride its wave of success. In 2007, it was ranked the number-one bank in return on average equity (ROE) out of all banks founded in 2005. Buchanan attributes Independent Bank's success on the company's expanding services, prompt lending decisions, and competitive rates, and, most of all, on maintaining quality customer relationships.[17]

growth in the 1990s substantially improved what had been a rather bleak picture for many financial institutions. Better management, combined with better regulation and a robust economy, saved commercial banks from the fate of the S&Ls. Indeed, low inflation rates meant low interest rates on deposits, and high employment led to very low loan default rates. Combined, these factors helped to make the 1990s one of the most profitable decades in the history of the banking industry.

The banking industry continued to change in the 2000s, and with the passage of the Gramm-Leach-Bliley Bill, banks are expected to continue their "urge to merge." Now that banks are allowed to offer insurance, brokerage, and investment banking services, there will be a hunt to find likely merger partners that will expand their customer reach and the services they are able to offer. On the other side of the coin, even as banks such as Bank of America continue to buy up competition, as it recently did with Countrywide, and to become national banks with offices in more than half the states, small community banks continue to start up to serve the customer who still wants personal service. The ability of these small banks to buy state-of-the-art technology from nonbank service providers allows them to offer Internet banking and many sophisticated services at competitive costs. They also provide a local face and service to the consumer who is more and more likely to be unwelcome at some large banks that cater to corporations and wealthy individuals.

CitiBank is one of the largest international banks in the world and has locations in Asia, Latin America, Europe, and of course North America. People living in Manila can use CitiBank's online banking services from abroad, and CitiBank customers can pay their bills on the Internet while traveling around the world in addition to having access to their money with their CitiBank ATM card. Banking will continue to become more international with large international banks continuing to acquire banking assets in the United States. For instance in Chicago, The Bank of Montreal owns The Harris Bank.

Indeed, the recent trend toward ever bigger banks and other financial institutions is not happening by chance alone. Financial services may be an example of a "natural oligopoly," meaning that the industry may be best served by a few very large firms rather than a host of smaller ones. As the largest U.S. banks merge into even larger international entities, they will erase the relative competitive advantages now enjoyed by the largest foreign banks. It is by no means implausible that the financial services industry of the year 2020 will be dominated by 10 or so internationally oriented "megabanks."

Rapid advances and innovations in technology are challenging the banking industry and requiring it to change. As we said earlier, more and more banks, both large and small, are offering electronic access to their financial services. ATM technology is rapidly changing, with machines now dispensing more than just cash. Online financial services, ATM technology, and bill presentation are just a few of the areas where rapidly changing technology is causing the banking industry to change as well.

# So You're Interested in Financial Systems or Banking

You think you might be interested in going into finance or banking, but it is so hard to tell when you are a full-time student. Classes that seem interesting when you take them might not translate in an interesting work experience after you graduate. A great way to see if you would excel at a career in finance is to get some experience in the industry. Internships, whether they are paid or unpaid, not only help you figure out what you might really want to do after you graduate but they are also a great way to build up your résumé, put your learning to use, and start generating connections within the field.

For example, for the past four years, Pennsylvania's Delaware County District Attorney's Office has been accepting business students from Villanova University for a six-month internship. The student works in the economic-crime division, analyzing documents of people under investigation for financial crimes ranging from fraud to money laundering. The students get actual experience in forensic accounting and have the chance to see whether this is the right career path. On top of that, the program has saved the county an average of $20,000 annually on consulting and accounting fees, not to mention that detectives now have more time to take on larger caseloads. Michael Busby, a student who completed the program, spent his six months investigating a case in which the owner of a sewage treatment company had embezzled a total of $1 million over the course of nine years. Busby noted that the experience helped him gain an understanding about how different companies handle their financial statements, as well as how accounting can be applied in forensics and law enforcement.

Internship opportunities are plentiful all over the country, although you may need to do some research to find them. To start, talk to your program advisor and your professors about opportunities. Also, you can check company Web sites where you think you might like to work to see if they have any opportunities available. City, state, or federal government offices often provide student internships as well. No matter where you end up interning, the real-life skills you pick up, as well as the résumé boost you get, will be helpful in finding a job after you graduate. When you graduate, commercial banks and other financial institutions offer major employment opportunities. In 2008–2009, a major downturn in the financial industry resulted in mergers, acquisitions, and financial restructuring for many companies. While the immediate result was a decrease in job opportunities, as the industry recovers, there will be many challenging job opportunities available.[18]

# Review Your Understanding

### Define money, its functions, and its characteristics.

Money is anything generally accepted as a means of payment for goods and services. Money serves as a medium of exchange, a measure of value, and a store of wealth. To serve effectively in these functions, money must be acceptable, divisible, portable, durable, stable in value, and difficult to counterfeit.

### Describe various types of money.

Money may take the form of currency, checking accounts, or other accounts. Checking accounts are funds left in an account in a financial institution that can be withdrawn (usually by writing a check) without advance notice. Other types of accounts include savings accounts (funds left in an interest-earning account that usually cannot be withdrawn without advance notice), money market accounts (an interest-bearing checking account that is invested in short-term debt instruments), certificates of deposit (deposits left in an institution for a specified period of time at a specified interest rate), credit cards (access to a pre-approved line of credit granted by a bank or company), and debit cards (means of instant cash transfers between customer and merchant accounts), as well as traveler's checks, money orders, and cashier's checks.

### Specify how the Federal Reserve Board manages the money supply and regulates the American banking system.

The Federal Reserve Board regulates the U.S. financial system. The Fed manages the money supply by buying and selling government securities, raising or lowering the discount rate (the rate of interest at which banks may borrow cash reserves from the Fed), raising or lowering bank reserve requirements (the percentage of funds on deposit at a bank that must be held to cover expected depositor withdrawals), and adjusting down payment and repayment terms for credit purchases. It also regulates banking practices, processes checks, and oversees federal depository insurance for institutions.

### Compare and contrast commercial banks, savings and loan associations, credit unions, and mutual savings banks.

Commercial banks are financial institutions that take and hold deposits in accounts for and make loans to individuals and businesses. Savings and loan associations are financial institutions that primarily specialize in offering savings accounts and mortgage loans. Credit unions are financial institutions owned and controlled by their depositors. Mutual savings banks are similar to S&Ls except that they are owned by their depositors.

### Distinguish among nonbanking institutions such as insurance companies, pension funds, mutual funds, and finance companies.

Insurance companies are businesses that protect their clients against financial losses due to certain circumstances, in exchange for a fee. Pension funds are investments set aside by organizations or individuals to meet retirement needs. Mutual funds pool investors' money and invest in large numbers of different types of securities. Brokerage firms buy and sell stocks and bonds for investors. Finance companies make short-term loans at higher interest rates than do banks.

### Investigate the challenges ahead for the banking industry.

Future changes in financial regulations are likely to result in fewer but larger banks and other financial institutions.

### Recommend the most appropriate financial institution for a hypothetical small business.

Using the information presented in this chapter, you should be able to answer the questions in "Solve the Dilemma" on page 484 and find the best institution for Hill Optometrics.

# Revisit the World of Business

1. What are the risks associated with peer-to-peer lending?
2. What are the advantages and disadvantages of not using a bank?
3. Could the peer-to-peer lending model have other applications in the business world?

# Learn the Terms

automated clearinghouses
    (ACHs)   478
automated teller machine (ATM)    478
brokerage firms   477
certificates of deposit (CDs)    465
checking account    464
commercial banks    471
credit cards    466
credit controls    470
credit union    473
debit card    467

discount rate    470
electronic funds transfer (EFT)    478
Federal Deposit Insurance
    Corporation (FDIC)    474
Federal Reserve Board    467
finance    460
finance companies    478
insurance companies    475
investment banker    477
monetary policy    468
money    460

money market accounts    465
mutual fund    477
mutual savings banks    473
National Credit Union Association
    (NCUA)    474
open market operations    469
pension funds    475
reserve requirement    470
savings accounts    465
savings and loan associations
    (S&Ls)    472

# Check Your Progress

1. What are the six characteristics of money? Explain how the U.S. dollar has those six characteristics.

2. What is the difference between a credit card and a debit card? Why are credit cards considerably more popular with U.S. consumers?

3. Discuss the four economic goals the Federal Reserve must try to achieve with its monetary policy.

4. Explain how the Federal Reserve uses open market operations to expand and contract the money supply.

5. What are the basic differences between commercial banks and savings and loans?

6. Why do credit unions charge lower rates than commercial banks?

7. Why do finance companies charge higher interest rates than commercial banks?

8. How are mutual funds, money market funds, and pension funds similar? How are they different?

9. What are some of the advantages of electronic funds transfer systems?

# Get Involved

1. Survey the banks, savings and loans, and credit unions in your area, and put together a list of interest rates paid on the various types of checking accounts. Find out what, if any, restrictions are in effect for NOW accounts and regular checking accounts. In which type of account and in what institution would you deposit your money? Why?

2. Survey the same institutions as in question one, this time inquiring as to the rates asked for each of their various loans. Where would you prefer to obtain a car loan? A home loan? Why?

# Build Your Skills

**MANAGING MONEY**

**Background:**
You have just graduated from college and have received an offer for your dream job (annual salary: $35,000). This premium salary is a reward for your hard work, perseverance, and good grades. It is also a reward for the social skills you developed in college doing service

work as a tutor for high school students and interacting with the business community as the program chairman of the college business fraternity, Delta Sigma Pi. You are engaged and plan to be married this summer. You and your spouse will have a joint income of $60,000, and the two of you are trying to decide the best way to manage your money.

**Task:**
Research available financial service institutions in your area, and answer the following questions.

1. What kinds of institutions and services can you use to help manage your money?

2. Do you want a full service financial organization that can take care of your banking, insurance, and investing needs or do you want to spread your business among individual specialists? Why have you made this choice?

3. What retirement alternatives do you have?

## Solve the Dilemma

### SEEING THE FINANCIAL SIDE OF BUSINESS

Dr. Stephen Hill, a successful optometrist in Indianapolis, Indiana, has tinkered with various inventions for years. Having finally developed what he believes is his first saleable product (a truly scratch-resistant and lightweight lens), Hill has decided to invest his life savings and open Hill Optometrics to manufacture and market his invention.

Unfortunately, despite possessing true genius in many areas, Hill is uncertain about the "finance side" of business and the various functions of different types of financial institutions in the economy. He is, however, fully aware that he will need financial services such as checking and savings accounts, various short-term investments that can easily and quickly be converted to cash as needs dictate, and sources of borrowing capacity—should the need for either short- or long-term loans arise. Despite having read mounds of brochures from various local and national financial institutions, Hill is still somewhat unclear about the merits and capabilities of each type of financial institution. He has turned to you, his 11th patient of the day for help.

#### Discussion Questions

1. List the various types of U.S. financial institutions and the primary function of each.

2. What services of each financial institution is Hill's new company likely to need?

3. Which single financial institution is likely to be best able to meet Hill's small company's needs now? Why?

## Build Your Business Plan

### MONEY AND THE FINANCIAL SYSTEM

This chapter provides you with the opportunity to think about money and the financial system and just how many new businesses fail every year. In some industries the failure rate is as high as 80 percent. One reason for such a high failure rate is the inability to manage the finances of the organization. From the start of the business, financial planning plays a key role. Try getting a loan without an accompanying budget/forecast of earnings and cash flow.

While obtaining a loan from a family member may be the easiest way to fund your business, it may cause more problems for you later on if you are unable to pay the money back as scheduled. Before heading to a lending officer at a bank, contact your local SBA center to see what assistance they might provide.

## See for Yourself Videocase

### STRATEGIC PLANNING: STATE FARM BANK

The well-known company State Farm is a conglomerate comprised of a combination of insurance and financial services companies. Founded in 1922, State Farm originally provided car insurance for farmers. The company grew quickly from there, and it has been ranked as the largest auto insurance company in the United States since 1942. The company is less known for its mutual fund and banking services, in addition to providing a variety of insurance plans for home, life, health, and business. The banking division of State Farm is relatively new, having been approved for a charter by the Office of Thrift Supervision in November 1998. A thrift charter is similar to a banking charter, but with some additional limitations such as the size of commercial loans and with which institutions a bank can do business. Additionally, under the thrift (or savings and loan) charter, the Federal Deposit Insurance Corporation (FDIC) is the bank's governing body. Because State Farm Bank deposits are insured, its members would be able to recover their savings up to $100,000, even if the bank fails. While most banks are covered by the FDIC, State Farm Bank is unconventional in its other aspects.

For one, State Farm does not have any physical branch offices. However, it is unlike other online banks as well. The bulk of State Farm Bank business is conducted via State Farm insurance agents, with additional services provided through the Internet, telephone call centers, and the mail. Because State Farm Bank has no physical banks, members must make transactions through ATMs. They are entitled to use any ATM owned by State Farm Bank, or any other full-service ATM offering deposit sharing and the NYCE® or STAR® designation. Online banking services come free with a checking account, as well as bill payer services, transaction details, and transfers between State Farm accounts.

In addition to the standard checking and savings accounts, State Farm Bank also offers certificates of deposit, which are savings accounts that guarantee a depositor a set interest rate over a specified period of time as long as the funds are not withdrawn before the end of the time period; individual retirement accounts, which are investment pools set up by corporations, nonprofits, or individuals to provide retirement income for members; money market accounts, which are similar to interest-bearing checking accounts but are more restrictive on the number of transactions that can be made; and health savings accounts, which are tax-exempt trusts in which a person can save money for future medical expenses. Also like most banks, State Farm Bank offers different types of credit cards, home mortgages, and home equity and vehicle loans.

Although it is a fairly new division of the company, State Farm Bank has experienced strong success. By the close of 2007, State Farm Bank had more than $15.9 billion in assets and had handled 807,413 financial cards, 353,563 vehicle loans, 50,817 home equity lines, 29,605 mortgages, and 1,501 business loans.[19]

### Discussion Questions

1. Given their other lines of business, did it make sense for State Farm to branch out into banking?

2. What are the advantages to customers of being able to obtain insurance, loans, and do banking all with the same institution?

3. Are there drawbacks of diversifying the company into other branches of finance?

**Remember to check out our Online Learning Center at: www.mhhe.com/ferrell7e.**

# chapter 16

## CHAPTER OUTLINE

**Introduction**

**Managing Current Assets and Liabilities**
*Managing Current Assets*
*Managing Current Liabilities*

**Managing Fixed Assets**
*Capital Budgeting and Project Selection*
*Assessing Risk*
*Pricing Long-Term Money*

**Financing with Long-Term Liabilities**
*Bonds: Corporate IOUs*
*Types of Bonds*

**Financing with Owners' Equity**

**Investment Banking**

**The Securities Markets**
*Stock Markets*
*The Over-the-Counter Market*
*Measuring Market Performance*

# Financial Management and Securities Markets

## OBJECTIVES

*After reading this chapter, you will be able to:*

- Describe some common methods of managing current assets.

- Identify some sources of short-term financing (current liabilities).

- Summarize the importance of long-term assets and capital budgeting.

- Specify how companies finance their operations and manage fixed assets with long-term liabilities, particularly bonds.

- Discuss how corporations can use equity financing by issuing stock through an investment banker.

- Describe the various securities markets in the United States.

- Critique the short-term asset and liabilities position of a small manufacturer, and recommend corrective action.

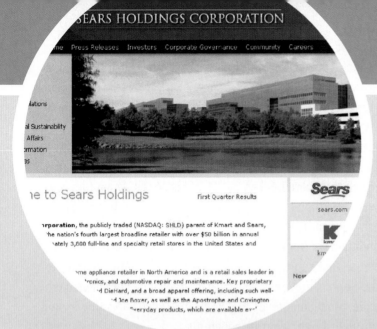

## Sears Holdings Corporation: Using Brand Names to Create Bonds

Sears Holdings Corporation (SHC) is the parent of Kmart and Sears, Roebuck and Co. SHC has more than 3,400 broad-line and specialty stores in the United States. The business segments operated by SHC are currently Kmart, Sears Domestic, and Sears Canada. While not notable for its fashionable clothing, Sears is famous for its appliances, sold under the brand Kenmore, and its home improvement products, sold under the Craftsman and DieHard labels.

In 2006, the chairman of SHC, billionaire hedge fund manager Edward Lampert, carried out the largest securitization of intellectual property in history. This means that he created nearly $2 billion worth of bonds based on the Sears brand names, effectively transferring ownership of Kenmore, Craftsman, and DieHard to an outside entity, which then must pay for the right to use the brands. Word of this monumental feat took nearly a year to get out to the press because the bonds were never sold to outside investors and were never disclosed by Sears—they are held in an insurance subsidiary in Bermuda.

Using the bonds, Lampert created a company within an existing company called Kenmore Craftsman DieHard Intellectual Property (KCD IP). The value of the securities is then backed by the intellectual property of these brands. KCD charges Sears royalties to license the brands and uses the royalty money to pay interest on the bonds, creating a profitless and debtless system. The bonds were sold to the insurance subsidiary in order to protect against future losses. In the meantime, the insurer protects Sears from financial problems—and does so at a lower cost because it is a subsidiary of SHC.

*continued*

All of these complicated maneuvers allow Sears to save money on insurance. Because it is a closed system with Sears owning every piece, no one currently makes any money on the deal. However, if SHC ever sold the bonds or licensed the brands to outside parties, the company could stand to make $1.8 billion, which is the value of the securities.

Intellectual property bonds are a relatively new idea, and come with an unlikely back-story. In 1997 David Bowie, of Ziggy Stardust fame, floated bonds worth $55 million that were backed by 300 of his songs. The future royalties from the songs were then used to pay the interest on the bonds. Since then, various industries from film to fashion to food have utilized IP bonds. The KCD arrangement differs from Bowie's in that it did not involve preexisting royalties payments—the source of cash needed to be created in order to issue the bonds. The Sears situation is also rare in that is does not have cash flows from the outside. Most companies that securitize assets like Bowie sell the bonds right away in order to generate revenues.

While Sears, Roebuck and Co. has not been performing well of late, the deal involving KCD is a novel one, and it has generated a lot of interest among other companies, as they too have become interested in intellectual property deals. IP has become an increasingly relevant topic of discussion as more companies are forced to think about how to protect their own intellectual property from forgery or theft. Some financial analysts believe that IP bonds could be the junk bonds of the future—a way for investors to earn high yields while companies make quick cash off of something they already own.[1]

# Introduction

While it's certainly true that money makes the world go around, financial management is the discipline that makes the world turn more smoothly. Indeed, without effective management of assets, liabilities, and owners' equity, all business organizations are doomed to fail—regardless of the quality and innovativeness of their products. Financial management is the field that addresses the issues of obtaining and managing the funds and resources necessary to run a business successfully. It is not limited to business organizations: All organizations, from the corner store to the local nonprofit art museum, from giant corporations to county governments, must manage their resources effectively and efficiently if they are to achieve their objectives.

In this chapter, we look at both short- and long-term financial management. First, we discuss the management of short-term assets, which companies use to generate sales and conduct ordinary day-to-day business operations. Next we turn our attention to the management of short-term liabilities, the sources of short-term funds used to finance the business. Then, we discuss the management of long-term assets such as plant and equipment and the long-term liabilities such as stocks and bonds

used to finance these important corporate assets. Finally, we look at the securities markets, where stocks and bonds are traded.

# Managing Current Assets and Liabilities

Managing short-term assets and liabilities involves managing the current assets and liabilities on the balance sheet (discussed in Chapter 14). Current assets are short-term resources such as cash, investments, accounts receivable, and inventory. Current liabilities are short-term debts such as accounts payable, accrued salaries, accrued taxes, and short-term bank loans. We use the terms *current* and *short term* interchangeably because short-term assets and liabilities are usually replaced by new assets and liabilities within three or four months, and always within a year. Managing short-term assets and liabilities is sometimes called **working capital management** because short-term assets and liabilities continually flow through an organization and are thus said to be "working."

*A firm can be profitable but still go out of business if its managers aren't able to manage its cash flow so it can meet its financial obligations on time.*

**working capital management**
the managing of short-term assets and liabilities

## Managing Current Assets

The chief goal of financial managers who focus on current assets and liabilities is to maximize the return to the business on cash, temporary investments of idle cash, accounts receivable, and inventory.

# Going Green
## Going Green, or Greenwashing?

The words "green," "environmentally friendly," "made from recycled materials," and "organic" feature on the labels of a wide assortment of products these days. They appeal to those consumers who would like to help the environment, but not at the expense of the products they are accustomed to consuming. Eco buzzwords give marketers a means of taking advantage of people's desire to feel like they are making a difference, while at the same time encouraging them to consume new products. While some companies have put their money where their mouths are is and have demonstrated a true commitment to environmentalism, others are merely using the lingo to pay lip service to the cause. The latter group of companies is concerned with increasing profits far more than encouraging conservationism. Pottery Barn, the furniture and home accessories company owned by Williams-Sonoma, may be just such a company. Its Eco Chic line of furniture and accessories has raised a lot of eyebrows as to the true motivations of the company. Is it only an attempt to increase profits, or is the company really trying to be ecofriendly?

The Eco Chic line offers products made with organic materials, but only a couple of the bedding collections are 100 percent organic and the rest only contain around 5 percent organic fibers. The line does utilize reclaimed materials in its furniture, but not in all of it. Some of the pieces advertise that they are made with Forest Stewardship Council–certified wood and recycled steel. Other sustainably harvested materials utilized in the collection are seagrass, bamboo, and jute.

While these steps are certainly demonstrating movement in the right direction, critics are accusing Pottery Barn of "greenwashing," or misleading their customers into thinking that the products are better for the environment than they really are. As you can gather from the name, TreeHugger.com is a Web site for those committed to environmental causes. The site has a "Greenwash Watch," on which one can find the Pottery Barn line. This Web site criticizes the company for not indicating that much of the Eco Chic line featured in the catalog also includes conventional cotton and fiberboard.

Apartment Therapy in Los Angeles is a forum for designers, and it has pointed out that it is best to be wary of a company that launches a green line but does nothing to change the rest of its products. This should indicate to the consumer a lack of true interest in the cause, and a lack of commitment to promoting long-term sustainability. Companies that use the trendy language of the moment tend to be interested in profits over everything else.

Environmentally concerned consumers should always ask a series of questions: What kinds of materials does this company use? Were does it get those materials? Who did the harvesting or production of the materials, and how was it done? Pottery Barn may be utilizing the current "green" buzzwords as a way of marketing itself, but it is far from the only company doing so these days. Trying to increase profits and market value through greenwashing could backfire if consumers see that the company is presenting a false image.

Like many U.S. retailers, Williams-Sonoma has had a rough time the past few years. In the letter to shareholders in the 2007 annual report, Chairman and CEO W. Howard Lester confessed that 2006 and 2007 had been difficult for the company, with Pottery Barn suffering a loss of in-store revenues in 2007. Lester attributes the sales slowdown, in part, to the volatile economy and especially the decline in the housing market. Executives made it their mission in 2007 to help revitalize the Pottery Barn name, partly through collections like the Eco Chic line. It certainly makes one wonder, with environmental awareness on the upswing, and Pottery Barn's sales down, what truly motivated the company to go green?[2]

### Discussion Questions
1. What would be the financial motivation behind starting a line that claims to be eco-friendly?
2. Why are Williams Sonoma and its brand Pottery Barn experiencing slowed growth and financial difficulties?
3. What might the company do to increase sales and improve its image?

---

**Managing Cash.** A crucial element facing any financial manager is effectively managing the firm's cash flow. Remember that cash flow is the movement of money through an organization on a daily, weekly, monthly, or yearly basis. Ensuring that sufficient (but not excessive) funds are on hand to meet the company's obligations is one of the single most important facets of financial management.

Idle cash does not make money, and corporate checking accounts typically do not earn interest. As a result, astute money managers try to keep just enough cash on hand, called **transaction balances,** to pay bills—such as employee wages, supplies, and utilities—as they fall due. To manage the firm's cash and ensure that enough cash flows through the organization quickly and efficiently, companies try to speed up cash collections from customers.

**transaction balances**
cash kept on hand by a firm to pay normal daily expenses, such as employee wages and bills for supplies and utilities

To facilitate collection, some companies have customers send their payments to a **lockbox,** which is simply an address for receiving payments, instead of directly to the company's main address. The manager of the lockbox, usually a commercial bank, collects payments directly from the lockbox several times a day and deposits them into the company's bank account. The bank can then start clearing the checks and get the money into the company's checking account much more quickly than if the payments had been submitted directly to the company. However, there is no free lunch: The costs associated with lockbox systems make them worthwhile only for those companies that receive thousands of checks from customers each business day.

Large firms with many stores or offices around the country, such as Household International (parent company of the finance company, Household Finance), frequently use electronic funds transfer to speed up collections. Household Finance's local offices deposit checks received each business day into their local banks and, at the end of the day, Household's corporate office initiates the transfer of all collected funds to its central bank for overnight investment. This technique is especially attractive for major international companies, which face slow and sometimes uncertain physical delivery of payments and/or less-than-efficient check-clearing procedures.

More and more companies are now using electronic funds transfer systems to pay and collect bills online. Companies generally want to collect cash quickly but pay out cash slowly. When companies use electronic funds transfers between buyers and suppliers, the speed of collections and disbursements increases to one day. Only with the use of checks can companies delay the payment of cash by three or four days until the check is presented to their bank and the cash leaves their account.

**Investing Idle Cash.**   As companies sell products, they generate cash on a daily basis, and sometimes cash comes in faster than it is needed to pay bills. Organizations often invest this "extra" cash, for periods as short as one day (overnight) or for as long as one year, until it is needed. Such temporary investments of cash are known as **marketable securities.** Examples include U.S. Treasury bills, certificates of deposit, commercial paper, and Eurodollar loans. Table 16.1 summarizes a number of different marketable securities used by businesses and some sample interest rates on these investments as of June 23, 2006 and May 23, 2008. The safety rankings are relative. While all of the listed securities are very low risk, the U.S. government securities are the safest. You can see from the table that interest rates have declined during the two periods presented.

**lockbox**
an address, usually a commercial bank, at which a company receives payments in order to speed collections from customers

**marketable securities**
temporary investment of "extra" cash by organizations for up to one year in U.S. Treasury bills, certificates of deposit, commercial paper, or Eurodollar loans

**TABLE 16.1**   Short-Term Investment Possibilities for Idle Cash

| Type of Security | Maturity | Seller of Security | Interest Rate 6/23/2006 | 5/23/2008 | Safety Level |
|---|---|---|---|---|---|
| U.S. Treasury bills | 90 days | U.S. government | 4.80% | 1.82% | Excellent |
| U.S. Treasury bills | 180 days | U.S. government | 5.05 | 1.89 | Excellent |
| Commercial paper | 30 days | Major corporations | 5.14 | 2.28 | Very good |
| Certificates of deposit | 90 days | U.S. commercial banks | 5.40 | 2.66 | Very good |
| Certificates of deposit | 180 days | U.S. commercial banks | 5.43 | 2.86 | Very good |
| Eurodollars | 90 days | European commerical banks | 5.48 | 2.85 | Very good |

Source: www.federalreserve.gov/releases/h15/current and http://research.stlouisfed.org/Fred2/series

**Treasury bills (T-bills)**
short-term debt
obligations the U.S.
government sells to
raise money

Many large companies invest idle cash in U.S. **Treasury bills (T-bills),** which are short-term debt obligations the U.S. government sells to raise money. Issued weekly by the U.S. Treasury, T-bills carry maturities of between one week to one year. U.S. T-bills are generally considered to be the safest of all investments and are called risk free because the U.S. government will not default on its debt.

**commercial certificates of deposit (CDs)**
certificates of deposit
issued by commercial
banks and brokerage
companies, available
in minimum amounts of
$100,000, which may be
traded prior to maturity

**Commercial certificates of deposit (CDs)** are issued by commercial banks and brokerage companies. They are available in minimum amounts of $100,000 but are typically in units of $1 million for large corporations investing excess cash. Unlike consumer CDs (discussed in Chapter 15), which must be held until maturity, commercial CDs may be traded prior to maturity. Should a cash shortage occur, the organization can simply sell the CD on the open market and obtain needed funds.

**commercial paper**
a written promise from
one company to
another to pay a
specific amount of
money

One of the most popular short-term investments for the largest business organizations is **commercial paper**—a written promise from one company to another to pay a specific amount of money. Because commercial paper is backed only by the name and reputation of the issuing company, sales of commercial paper are restricted to only the largest and most financially stable companies. As commercial paper is frequently bought and sold for durations of as short as one business day, many "players" in the market find themselves buying commercial paper with excess cash on one day and selling it to gain extra money the following day.

**eurodollar market**
a market centered in
London for trading
U.S. dollars in foreign
countries

Some companies invest idle cash in international markets such as the **eurodollar market,** a market for trading U.S. dollars in foreign countries. Because the Eurodollar market was originally developed by London banks, any dollar-denominated deposit in a non-U.S. bank is called a eurodollar deposit, regardless of whether the issuing bank is actually located in Europe, South America, or anyplace else. For example, if you travel overseas and deposit $1,000 in a German bank, you will have "created" a eurodollar deposit in the amount of $1,000. Because the U.S. dollar is accepted by most countries for international trade, these dollar deposits can be used by international companies to settle their accounts. The market created for trading such investments offers firms with extra dollars a chance to earn a slightly higher rate of return with just a little more risk than they would face by investing in U.S. Treasury bills.

*You can buy and redeem T-bills and other government securities directly from the U.S. Department of the Treasury at www.treasurydirect .gov.*

**Maximizing Accounts Receivable.**   After cash and marketable securities, the balance sheet lists accounts receivable and inventory. Remember that accounts receivable is money owed to a business by credit customers. For example, if you charge your Shell gasoline purchases, until you actually pay for them with cash or a check, they represent an account receivable to Shell. Many businesses make the vast majority of their sales on credit, so managing accounts receivable is an important task.

Each credit sale represents an account receivable for the company, the terms of which typically require customers to pay the full amount due within 30, 60, or even 90 days from the date of the sale. To encourage quick payment, some businesses offer some of their customers discounts of between 1 to 2 percent if they pay off their balance within a specified period of time (usually between 10 and 30 days). On the other hand, late payment charges of between 1 and 1.5 percent serve to discourage slow payers from sitting on their bills forever. The larger the early payment discount offered, the faster customers will tend to pay their accounts. Unfortunately, while discounts increase cash flow, they also reduce profitability. Finding the right balance between the added advantages of early cash receipt and the disadvantages of reduced profits is no simple matter. Similarly, determining the optimal balance between the higher sales likely to result from extending credit to customers with less than sterling credit ratings and the higher bad-debt losses likely to result from a more lenient credit policy is also challenging. Information on company credit ratings is provided by local credit bureaus, national credit-rating agencies such as Dun and Bradstreet, and industry trade groups.

Optimizing Inventory.   While the inventory that a firm holds is controlled by both production needs and marketing considerations, the financial manager has to coordinate inventory purchases to manage cash flows. The object is to minimize the firm's investment in inventory without experiencing production cutbacks as a result of critical materials shortfalls or lost sales due to insufficient finished goods inventories. Every dollar invested in inventory is a dollar unavailable for investment in some other area of the organization. Optimal inventory levels are determined, in large part, by the method of production. If a firm attempts to produce its goods just in time to meet sales demand, the level of inventory will be relatively low. If, on the other hand, the firm produces materials in a constant, level pattern, inventory increases when sales decrease and decreases when sales increase. One way that companies are attempting to optimize inventory is through the use of radio frequency identification (RFID) technology. Companies such as Wal-Mart are attempting to better manage their inventories by using RFID tags. An RFID tag, which contains a silicon chip and an antenna, allows a company's to use radio waves to track and identify the products to which the tags are attached—even after the products have left the store.

The automobile industry is an excellent example of an industry driven almost solely by inventory levels. Because it is inefficient to continually lay off workers in slow times and call them back in better times, Ford, General Motors, and Chrysler try to set and stick to quarterly production quotas. Automakers typically try to keep a 60-day supply of unsold cars. During particularly slow periods, however, it is not unusual for inventories to exceed 100 days of sales.

Although less publicized, inventory shortages can be as much of a drag on potential profits as too much inventory. Not having an item on hand may send the customer to a competitor—forever. Complex computer inventory models are frequently employed to determine the optimum level of inventory a firm should hold to support a given level of sales. Such models can indicate how and when parts inventories should be ordered so that they are available exactly when required—and not a day before. Developing and maintaining such an intricate production and inventory system is difficult, but it can often prove to be the difference between experiencing average profits and spectacular ones.

## Managing Current Liabilities

While having extra cash on hand is a delightful surprise, the opposite situation—a temporary cash shortfall—can be a crisis. The good news is that there are several potential sources of short-term funds. Suppliers often serve as an important source through credit sales practices. Also, banks, finance companies, and other organizations offer short-term funds through loans and other business operations.

Accounts Payable.   Remember from Chapter 14 that accounts payable is money an organization owes to suppliers for goods and services. Just as accounts receivable must be actively managed to ensure proper cash collections, so too must accounts payable be managed to make the best use of this important liability.

look stronger on paper than it is. Although the SEC first made its recommendations in 2005, no major changes to financial reporting have been made.[3] We'll take a closer look at long-term financing in a moment, but first let's address some issues associated with fixed assets, including capital budgeting, risk assessment, and the costs of financing fixed assets.

## Capital Budgeting and Project Selection

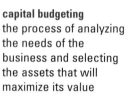

**capital budgeting**
the process of analyzing the needs of the business and selecting the assets that will maximize its value

One of the most important jobs performed by the financial manager is to decide what fixed assets, projects, and investments will earn profits for the firm beyond the costs necessary to fund them. The process of analyzing the needs of the business and selecting the assets that will maximize its value is called **capital budgeting,** and the capital budget is the amount of money budgeted for investment in such long-term assets. But capital budgeting does not end with the selection and purchase of a particular piece of land, equipment, or major investment. All assets and projects must be continually reevaluated to ensure their compatibility with the organization's needs. As Figure 16.1 indicates, financial executives believe most budgeting activities are occasionally or frequently unrealistic or irrelevant. If a particular asset does not live up to expectations, then management must determine why and take necessary corrective action. Budgeting is not an exact process, and managers must be flexible when new information is available.

## Assessing Risk

Every investment carries some risk. Figure 16.2 ranks potential investment projects according to estimated risk. When considering investments overseas, risk assessments must include the political climate and economic stability of a region. The decision to introduce a product or build a manufacturing facility in England would be much less risky than a decision to build one in the Middle East, for example.

Not apparent from Figure 16.2 are the risks associated with time. The longer a project or asset is expected to last, the greater its potential risk because it is hard to predict whether a piece of equipment will wear out or become obsolete in 5 or 10

### FIGURE 16.1

How Reliable Is Budgeting and Planning?

*How often is planning and budgeting information unrealistic or irrelevant?*

Source: Don Durfee, "By the Numbers: Alternative Budgeting," *CFO,* June 2006, p. 28.

- Frequently
- Occasionally
- Rarely

27%
28%
45%

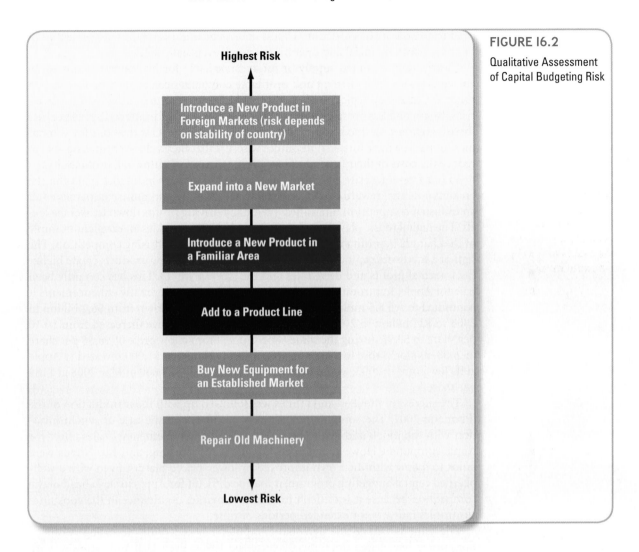

FIGURE 16.2

Qualitative Assessment of Capital Budgeting Risk

years. Predicting cash flows one year down the road is difficult, but projecting them over the span of a 10-year project is a gamble.

The level of a project's risk is also affected by the stability and competitive nature of the marketplace and the world economy as a whole. IBM's latest high-technology computer product is far more likely to become obsolete overnight than is a similar $10 million investment in a manufacturing plant. Dramatic changes in the market-place are not uncommon. Indeed, uncertainty created by the rapid devaluation of Asian currencies in the late 1990s wrecked a host of assumptions in literally hundreds of projects worldwide. Financial managers must constantly consider such issues when making long-term decisions about the purchase of fixed assets.

## Pricing Long-Term Money

The ultimate profitability of any project depends not only on accurate assumptions of how much cash it will generate, but also on its financing costs. Because a business must pay interest on money it borrows, the returns from any project must cover not only the costs of operating the project but also the interest expenses for the debt used to finance its construction. Unless an organization can effectively cover all of its costs—both financial and operating—it will eventually fail.

Clearly, only a limited supply of funds is available for investment in any given enterprise. The most efficient and profitable companies can attract the lowest-cost funds because they typically offer reasonable financial returns at very low relative risks. Newer and less prosperous firms must pay higher costs to attract capital because these companies tend to be quite risky. One of the strongest motivations for companies to manage their financial resources wisely is that they will, over time, be able to reduce the costs of their funds and in so doing increase their overall profitability.

In our free-enterprise economy, new firms tend to enter industries that offer the greatest potential rewards for success. However, as more and more companies enter an industry, competition intensifies, eventually driving profits down to average levels. The digital music player market of the early 2000s provides an excellent example of the changes in profitability that typically accompany increasing competition. The sign of a successful capital budgeting program is that the new products create higher than normal profits and drive sales and the stock price up. This has certainly been true for Apple. It introduced the first iPod in 2001, and after many enhancements it continued to sell 8.3 million iPods in 2007. Its sales have grown from $6.2 billion in 2003 to $24 billion in 2007, while its earnings per share have increased from $0.10 per share to $3.93 during the same time frame. From a low price of $6.36 per share in 2003, its stocks rose to a high of $202 in 2007. Note that $1,000 invested in Apple at its low point in 2003, would be worth approximately $29,000 in May 2008 at $184 per share.[4]

The success of the iPod and iTunes was followed up with the introduction of the iPhone in 2007. The combination of these products and the ease of synchronization with the iBook and iMac computers caused a complementary sales effect for Apple computers. However, competitors like Dell, Samsung, and Rio Nitrus were quick to follow with their own improved or lower-priced players. Even with a well-planned capital budgeting program, it may be difficult for Apple to stay ahead of the competition because it is difficult to maintain market dominance in the consumer electronics industry for extended periods of time.

The same is true in the personal computer market. With increasing competition, prices have fallen dramatically since the 1990s. Even Dell and Gateway, with their low-cost products, have moved into other markets such as servers and televisions in order to maintain growth in a maturing market. Weaker companies have failed, leaving the most efficient producers/marketers scrambling for market share. The expanded market for personal computers dramatically reduced the financial returns generated by each dollar invested in productive assets. The "glory days" of the personal computer industry—the time in which fortunes could be won and lost in the space of an average-sized garage—have long since passed into history. Personal computers have essentially become commodity items, and profit margins for companies in this industry have shrunk as the market matures. With sales falling and profits falling faster. Hewlett-Packard and Compaq merged to gain the economies of scale that saved money and created efficiencies.

## Financing with Long-Term Liabilities

As we said earlier, long-term assets do not come cheaply, and few companies have the cash on hand to open a new store across town, build a new manufacturing facility, research and develop a new life-saving drug, or launch a new product worldwide.

To develop such fixed assets, companies need to raise low-cost long-term funds to finance them. Two common choices for raising these funds are attracting new owners *(equity financing)*, which we'll look at in a moment, and taking on long-term liabilities *(debt financing)*, which we'll look at now.

**Long-term liabilities** are debts that will be repaid over a number of years, such as long-term bank loans and bond issues. These take many different forms, but in the end, the key word is *debt*. Companies may raise money by borrowing it from commercial banks or other financial institutions in

An IBM bond certificate.

the form of lines of credit, short-term loans, or long-term loans. Many corporations acquire debt by borrowing money from pension funds, mutual funds, or life-insurance funds.

Companies that rely too heavily on debt can get into serious trouble should the economy falter; during these times, they may not earn enough operating income to make the required interest payments (remember the times-interest-earned ratio in Chapter 14). In severe cases when the problem persists too long, creditors will not restructure loans but will instead sue for the interest and principal owed and force the company into bankruptcy.

## Bonds: Corporate IOUs

Much long-term debt takes the form of **bonds,** which are debt instruments that larger companies sell to raise long-term funds. In essence, the buyers of bonds (bondholders) loan the issuer of the bonds cash in exchange for regular interest payments until the loan is repaid on or before the specified maturity date. The bond itself is a certificate, much like an IOU, that represents the company's debt to the bondholder. Bonds are issued by a wide variety of entities, including corporations; national, state, and local governments; public utilities; and nonprofit corporations. Most bondholders need not hold their bonds until maturity; rather, the existence of active secondary markets of brokers and dealers allows for the quick and efficient transfer of bonds from owner to owner.

The bond contract, or *indenture,* specifies all of the terms of the agreement between the bondholders and the issuing organization. The indenture, which can run more than 100 pages, specifies the basic terms of the bond, such as its face value, maturity date, and the annual interest rate. Table 16.2 briefly explains how to determine these and more things about a bond from a bond quote, as it might appear in *The Wall Street Journal.* The face value of the bond, its initial sales price, is typically $1,000. After this, however, the price of the bond on the open market will fluctuate along with changes in the economy (particularly, changes in interest rates) and in the creditworthiness of the issuer. Bondholders receive the face value

**long-term liabilities**
debts that will be repaid over a number of years, such as long-term loans and bond issues

**bonds**
debt instruments that larger companies sell to raise long-term funds

**TABLE 16.2**

A Basic Bond Quote

| Bonds | Cur Yld | Vol | Close | Net Chg |
|---|---|---|---|---|
| ATT 8⅛ 22 | 7.9 | 121 | 102½ | .... |
| FordCr 6⅜ 08 | 6.4 | 45 | 100 | −⅞ |
| IBM 7½ 13 | 6.7 | 2 | 112 | +1½ |
| (1) (2) (3) | (4) | (5) | (6) | (7) |

(1) **Bond**—the name or abbreviation of the name of the company issuing the bond; in this case, IBM.

(2) **Annual Interest Rate**—the annual percentage rate specified on the bond certificate: IBM's is 7.5 percent so a $1,000 bond will earn $75 per year in interest.

(3) **Maturity date**—the bond's maturity date; the year in which the issuer will repay bondholders the face value of each bond; 2013.

(4) **Current yield**—percentage return from interest, based on the closing price (column 4); if you buy a bond with a $1,000 par value at today's closing price of 112.00 ($1,120) and receive $75 per year, your cash return will be 6.7 percent.

(5) **Volume**—the number of bonds trading during the day; 2.

(6) **Close**—the closing price; 112.00 = 112 percent of $1,000 per value or $1,120 per bond.

(7) **Change**—change in the price from the close of the previous trading day; IBM's went up 1½ percent of its $1,000 par value or $15.00 per bond.

**unsecured bonds**
debentures, or bonds that are not backed by specific collateral

**secured bonds**
bonds that are backed by specific collateral that must be forfeited in the event that the issuing firm defaults

**serial bonds**
a sequence of small bond issues of progressively longer maturity

**floating-rate bonds**
bonds with interest rates that change with current interest rates otherwise available in the economy

**junk bonds**
a special type of high interest-rate bond that carries higher inherent risks

of the bond along with the final interest payment on the maturity date. The annual interest rate (often called the *coupon rate*) is the guaranteed percentage of face value that the company will pay to the bond owner every year. For example, a $1,000 bond with a coupon rate of 7 percent would pay $70 per year in interest. In most cases, bond indentures specify that interest payments be made every six months. In the example above, the $70 annual payment would be divided into two semiannual payments of $35.

In addition to the terms of interest payments and maturity date, the bond indenture typically covers other important topics, such as repayment methods, interest payment dates, procedures to be followed in case the organization fails to make the interest payments, conditions for the early repayment of the bonds, and any conditions requiring the pledging of assets as collateral.

## Types of Bonds

Not surprisingly, there are a great many different types of bonds. Most are **unsecured bonds,** meaning that they are not backed by collateral; such bonds are termed *debentures*. **Secured bonds,** on the other hand, are backed by specific collateral that must be forfeited in the event that the issuing firm defaults. Whether secured or unsecured, bonds may be repaid in one lump sum or with many payments spread out over a period of time. **Serial bonds,** which are different from secured bonds, are actually a sequence of small bond issues of progressively longer maturity. The firm pays off each of the serial bonds as they mature. **Floating-rate bonds** do not have fixed interest payments; instead, the interest rate changes with current interest rates otherwise available in the economy.

In recent years, a special type of high-interest-rate bond has attracted considerable attention (usually negative) in the financial press. High-interest bonds, or **junk bonds** as they are popularly known, offer relatively high rates of interest because

# Entrepreneurship in Action
## Ready for Takeoff: RealKidz Clothing

Merrill Guerra

**Business:** RealKidz Clothing

**Founded:** 2007

**Success:** Spring line launched in April 2008, press coverage in the *Detroit Free Press, The Ann Arbor Business Journal,* and *BusinessWeek.*

Merrill Guerra, a Stanford and University of Michigan–educated housewife located in Ypsilanti, Michigan, always used to have trouble finding clothing for her plus-sized daughter, Gabi. If the clothes were big enough around, the arms and legs were too long or the styles were too grown-up. If the clothing was age-appropriate, it was not big enough around. She knew that she was not alone. With one-third of all children in the United States considered overweight or obese, plus-sized children's clothing is already a $6.2 billion industry. The overall plus-size clothing market is set to explode 41 percent by 2012. Because she knew there was such a strong need for clothes that fit today's larger kids, Guerra started RealKidz Clothing in 2007 and rolled out her first line in the spring of 2008. The startup currently only produces clothing for girls, but intends to branch out into boys' clothes in the future.

Guerra hopes to fill a niche in the clothing market that remains fairly wide open. Many companies have been reluctant to produce clothing for overweight children partly because of the extra space larger clothes take up in the store, and partly because companies do not want to be seen as condoning an epidemic of childhood obesity. In a time when more and more Americans are becoming overweight, the stigma of buying and selling plus-sized clothing remains. Guerra hopes to bypass these potentially sensitive issues by combining her clothing business with a social network for parents on how to help their families make healthy lifestyle changes. She stresses that people need to concentrate on being healthy and feeling good, but that part of that is dressing well.

Given the obvious need for fashionable clothing for plus-sized kids—especially overweight girls—Guerra thought it would be easier than it has been to finance the business. An introductory startup line costs around $90,000, with a full launch coming in at around $500,000. She started working toward this amount by using her and her husband's 401(k) funds, she drew on her parents for more money, and she has been seeking out donors in the Detroit area. Guerra also hopes to enlist personal salespeople to help spread awareness of her brand via word-of-mouth. Once production gets rolling and sales take off, Guerra has another venture up her sleeve as well—a line of clothing for skinny kids who cannot find standard sizes that fit either. To generate additional finances and to realize all of her business visions, Guerra may have to look into an initial public offering. She hired a CFO, Al Bacon, in the spring of 2008. Green had decades of experience working for ING and Mellon Bank before entering the world of small business finance, and Guerra hopes that his expertise will help her makes sound financial decisions and investments that will help the business to grow and flourish.[5]

they have higher inherent risks. Historically, junk bonds have been associated with companies in poor financial health and/or startup firms with limited track records. In the mid-1980s, however, junk bonds became a very attractive method of financing corporate mergers; they remain popular today with many investors as a result of their very high relative interest rates. But higher risks are associated with those higher returns (upward of 12 percent per year in some cases) and the average investor would be well-advised to heed those famous words: Look before you leap!

## Financing with Owners' Equity

A second means of long-term financing is through equity. Remember from Chapter 14 that owners' equity refers to the owners' investment in an organization. Sole proprietors and partners own all or a part of their businesses outright, and their equity includes the money and assets they have brought into their ventures. Corporate owners, on the other hand, own stock or shares of their companies, which they hope will provide them with a return on their investment. Stockholders' equity includes common stock, preferred stock, and retained earnings.

Common stock (introduced in Chapter 5) is the single most important source of capital for most new companies. On the balance sheet, the common stock account is separated into two basic parts—common stock at par and capital in excess of par. The *par value* of a stock is simply the dollar amount printed on the stock certificate and has no relation to actual *market value*—the price at which the common stock is currently trading. The difference between a stock's par value and its offering price is called *capital in excess of par*. Except in the case of some very low-priced stocks, the capital in excess of par account is significantly larger than the par value account. Table 16.3 briefly explains how to gather important information from a stock quote, as it might appear in *The Wall Street Journal* or on the NASDAQ Web site.

Preferred stock was defined in Chapter 5 as corporate ownership that gives the stockholder preference in the distribution of the company's profits but not the voting and control rights accorded to common stockholders. Thus, the primary advantage of owning preferred stock is that it is a safer investment than common stock.

All businesses exist to earn profits for their owners. Without the possibility of profit, there can be no incentive to risk investors' capital and succeed. When a corporation has profits left over after paying all of its expenses and taxes, it has the choice of retaining all or a portion of its earnings and/or paying them out to its shareholders in the form of dividends. **Retained earnings** are reinvested in the assets of the firm and belong to the owners in the form of equity. Retained earnings are an important source of funds and are, in fact, the only long-term funds that the company can generate internally.

**retained earnings** earnings after expenses and taxes that are reinvested in the assets of the firm and belong to the owners in the form of equity

When the board of directors distributes some of a corporation's profits to the owners, it issues them as cash dividend payments. But not all firms pay dividends.

Many fast-growing firms retain all of their earnings because they can earn high rates of return on the earnings they reinvest. Companies with fewer growth opportunities typically pay out large proportions of their earnings in the form of dividends,

**TABLE 16.3    A Basic Stock Quote**

| 1 | | 2 | 3 | 4 | 5 | 6 | 7 | 8 |
|---|---|---|---|---|---|---|---|---|
| **Stock Price 52 Week** | | | | | | | | |
| Hi | Low | Stock | Sym | Div | Yld. % | Vol | Close | Net Chg |
| 70.60 | 51.50 | Nike | NKE | 0.92 | 1.35 | 2,934,372 | 68.39 | +1.01 |
| 33.49 | 16.05 | Skechers USA | SKX | 0.00 | 0 | 1,000,241 | 24.65 | +0.79 |
| 27.76 | 12.83 | Timberland | TBL | 0.00 | 0 | 429,555 | 19.05 | +0.79 |
| 31.21 | 19.85 | Wolverine Worldwide | WWW | .44 | 1.52 | 311,697 | 28.87 | +0.27 |

1. The **52-week high and low**—the highest and lowest prices, respectively, paid for the stock in the last year; for Nike stock, the highest was $70.60 and the lowest price, $51.50.
2. **Stock**—the name of the issuing company. When followed by the letters "pf," the stock is preferred stock.
3. **Symbol**—the ticker tape symbol for the stock; NKE.
4. **Dividend**—the annual cash dividend paid to stockholders; Nike paid a dividend of $0.92 per share of stock outstanding.
5. **Dividend yield**—the dividend return on one share of common stock; 1.35%.
6. **Volume**—the number of shares traded on this day 2,934,372.
7. **Close**—Nike's last sale of the day was for $68.39.
8. **Net Change**—the difference between the previous day's close and the close on the day being reported; Nike was up $1.01.

Source: finance.yahoo.com/q?s, May 29, 2008.

*A McGraw-Hill stock certificate.*

thereby allowing their stockholders to reinvest their dividend payments in higher-growth companies. Table 16.4 presents a sample of companies and the dividend each paid on a single share of stock. As shown in the table, when the dividend is divided by the price the result is the **dividend yield.** The dividend yield is the cash return as a percentage of the price but does not reflect the total return an investor earns on the individual stock. If the dividend yield is 3.1 percent on Campbell Soup and the stock price increases by 10 percent from $28.62 to $31.48, then the total return would be 13.1 percent. It is not clear that stocks with high dividend yields will be preferred by investors to those with little or no dividends. Most large companies pay their stockholders dividends on a quarterly basis.

**dividend yield**
the dividend per share divided by the stock price

| Ticker Symbol | Company Name | Price Per Share | Dividend Per Share | Dividend Yield | Earnings Per Share | Price Earnings Ratio (P-E) |
|---|---|---|---|---|---|---|
| ANF | Abercrombie & Fitch | $74.07 | $0.70 | 0.95% | $5.20 | 14.24 |
| AXP | American Express | 46.75 | 0.72 | 1.54 | 3.33 | 14.04 |
| AAPL | Apple | 186.69 | 0.00 | 0.00 | 4.85 | 38.49 |
| CPB | Campbell Soup | 33.21 | 0.88 | 2.65 | 2.11 | 15.74 |
| DIS | Disney | 33.81 | 0.35 | 1.04 | 2.22 | 15.23 |
| F | Ford | 6.71 | 0.00 | 0.00 | −1.14 | NA |
| HOG | Harley Davidson | 40.52 | 1.32 | 3.26 | 3.80 | 10.66 |
| HD | Home Depot | 27.71 | 0.90 | 3.25 | 2.37 | 11.69 |
| MCD | McDonald's | 59.48 | 1.50 | 2.52 | 2.15 | 27.67 |
| PG | Procter & Gamble | 65.47 | 1.60 | 2.44 | 3.38 | 19.37 |
| LUV | Southwest Airlines | 13.18 | 0.02 | 0.15 | 0.78 | 16.90 |
| SBUX | Starbucks | 18.33 | 0.00 | 0.00 | 0.84 | 21.82 |

**TABLE 16.4**

Estimated Common Stock Price-Earnings Ratios and Dividends for Selected Companies

Earnings per share are for the latest 12-month period and do not necessarily match year-end numbers.
NA—not applicable because of negative earnings
Source: finance.yahoo.com/q?s, May 29, 2008.

# Investment Banking

A company that needs more money to expand or take advantage of opportunities may be able to obtain financing by issuing stock. The first-time sale of stocks and bonds directly to the public is called a *new issue.* Companies that already have stocks or bonds outstanding may offer a new issue of stock to raise additional funds for specific projects. When a company offers its stock to the public for the very first time, it is said to be "going public," and the sale is called an *initial public offering.*

New issues of stocks and bonds are sold directly to the public and to institutions in what is known as the **primary market**—the market where firms raise financial capital. The primary market differs from **secondary markets,** which are stock exchanges and over-the-counter markets where investors can trade their securities with other investors rather than the company that issued the stock or bonds. Primary market transactions actually raise cash for the issuing corporations, while secondary market transactions do not.

**primary market**
the market where firms raise financial capital

**secondary markets**
stock exchanges and over-the-counter markets where investors can trade their securities with others

**investment banking**
the sale of stocks and bonds for corporations

**Investment banking,** the sale of stocks and bonds for corporations, helps such companies raise funds by matching people and institutions who have money to invest with corporations in need of resources to exploit new opportunities. Corporations usually employ an investment banking firm to help sell their securities in the primary market. An investment banker helps firms establish appropriate offering prices for their securities. In addition, the investment banker takes care of the myriad details and securities regulations involved in any sale of securities to the public.

Just as large corporations such as IBM, General Motors, and Microsoft have a client relationship with a law firm and an accounting firm, they also have a client relationship with an investment banking firm. An investment banking firm such as Merrill Lynch, Goldman Sachs, or Morgan Stanley can provide advice about financing plans, dividend policy, or stock repurchases, as well as advice on mergers and acquisitions. Many now offer additional banking services, making them "one-stop shopping" banking centers. When Pixar merged with Disney, both companies used investment bankers to help them value the transaction. Each firm wanted an outside opinion about what it was worth to the other. Sometimes mergers fall apart because the companies cannot agree on the price each company is worth or the structure of management after the merger. The advising investment banker, working with management, often irons out these details. Of course, investment bankers do not provide these services for free. They usually charge a fee of between 1 and 1.5 percent of the transaction. A $20 billion merger can generate between $200 and $300 million in investment banking fees. The merger mania of the late 1990s allowed top investment bankers to earn huge sums. Unfortunately, this type of fee income is dependent on healthy stock markets, which seem to stimulate the merger fever among corporate executives.

# The Securities Markets

**securities markets**
the mechanism for buying and selling securities

**Securities markets** provide a mechanism for buying and selling securities. They make it possible for owners to sell their stocks and bonds to other investors. Thus, in the broadest sense, stocks and bonds markets may be thought of as providers of liquidity—the ability to turn security holdings into cash quickly and at minimal expense and effort. Without liquid securities markets, many potential investors would sit on the sidelines rather than invest their hard-earned savings in securities. Indeed, the ability to sell securities at well-established market prices is one of the very pillars of the capitalistic society that has developed over the years in the United States.

Unlike the primary market, in which corporations sell stocks directly to the public, secondary markets permit the trading of previously issued securities. There are many different secondary markets for both stocks and bonds. If you want to purchase 100 shares of Du Pont common stock, for example, you must purchase this stock from another investor or institution. It is the active buying and selling by many thousands of investors that establishes the prices of all financial securities. Secondary market trades may take place on organized exchanges or in what is known as the over-the-counter market. Many brokerage houses exist to help investors with financial decisions, and many offer their services through the Internet. One such broker is Paine Webber. Its site offers a wealth of information and provides educational material to individual investors.

## Stock Markets

Stock markets exist around the world in New York, Tokyo, London, Frankfort, Paris, and other world locations. The two biggest stock markets in the United States are the New York Stock Exchange (NYSE) and the NASDAQ market. There are other smaller markets such as the American Stock Exchange, the Chicago Stock Exchange, and exchanges in Philadelphia, Boston, Cincinnati, and Los Angeles.

Exchanges used to be divided into organized exchanges and over-the-counter markets, but during the last several years, dramatic changes have occurred in the markets. Both the NYSE and NASDAQ became publicly traded companies. They were previously not-for-profit organizations but are now for-profit companies. Additionally both exchanges bought or merged with electronic exchanges, the NYSE with Archipelago and the NASDAQ with Instinet. Electronic trading is faster and less expensive than floor trading (where brokers meet to transact business) and now accounts for most of the stock trading done worldwide.

In an attempt to expand their markets, NASDAQ acquired the OMX, a Nordic stock exchange headquartered in Sweden, and the New York Stock Exchange merged with Euronext, a large European electronic exchange that trades options and futures contracts as well as common stock. Both the NYSE and NASDAQ have expanded their reach, their product line, and their ability to trade around the world. What we are witnessing is the globalization of the world's financial markets.

Traditionally, the NASDAQ market has been an electronics market, and many of the large technology companies such as Microsoft, Oracle, and Apple Computer trade on the NASDAQ market. The NASDAQ operates through dealers who buy and sell common stock (inventory) for their own accounts. The NYSE has traditionally been a floor-traded market, where brokers meet at trading posts on the floor of the New York Stock Exchange to buy and sell common stock. The brokers act as agents for their clients and do not own their own inventory. This traditional division between the two markets is becoming less significant as the exchanges become electronic.

## The Over-the-Counter Market

Unlike the organized exchanges, the **over-the-counter (OTC) market** is a network of dealers all over the country linked by computers, telephones, and Teletype machines. It has no central location. While many very small new companies are

**over-the-counter (OTC) market**
a network of dealers all over the country linked by computers, telephones, and Teletype machines

# Consider Ethics and Social Responsibility
## Subprime Lending: What Is It, and Why Has It Caused So Much Trouble?

All of the talk of subprime lending in the news may have some students asking what it is. Simply put, subprime lending means lending money to borrowers at a rate higher than the prime rate, although how far above the prime rate depends on credit score, size of down payment (when referring to mortgages), debt-to-income ratio, and recent delinquencies. Subprime lending contains a high risk factor, and its critics view the industry with suspicion. Although subprime rates are offered for cars, and credit cards, the news has made us most familiar with subprime mortgages, which can be devastating to low-income families. Subprime mortgages fall into three categories. First is the interest-only mortgage, through which borrowers pay only interest for a set period of time. The second option allows the borrower to choose the monthly payment. Often, this means that a borrower opts for a payment lower than the amount required to reduce the loan. Third, borrowers may end up with mortgages that sport fixed rates for a certain time frame before converting to variable rates.

Typically, subprime loans are offered to high-risk individuals unable to qualify for conventional loans. The typical borrower has a credit score under 620; often this borrower is also low-income. However, a 2007 study conducted by *The Wall Street Journal* revealed that, while the majority of subprime loans do go to low-income, inner-city borrowers, between 2004 and 2006 the rate of middle-class and wealthy subprime borrowers rose dramatically. The explanation lies in the real estate price boom of the earlier 2000s. As real estate prices peaked, financially sound borrowers turned to subprime mortgages in order to afford more expensive homes.

While the subprime risk to borrowers is clear—a racking up of hidden fees, terms, and conditions and, of course, foreclosure—the risk to U.S. financial markets may require explanation. The average individual may not know that subprime loans are often sold, becoming bonds, securities, and other types of investments. These investments have been popular with banks, traders, and hedge funds throughout the United States, Europe, and Asia. This means that it is the investor that is left holding the bag if subprime lenders cannot pay up.

Late 2007 and the early months of 2008 marked the beginning of a severe subprime crisis. Foreclosure rates skyrocketed, and borrowers and investors are feeling the full ramifications of taking the subprime risk. The banks are suffering as well, a situation well documented by news outlets. In 2007, investors began to abandon their mortgage-backed securities, causing heavy hitters such as Morgan Stanley, Merrill Lynch, and Citigroup to loose large sums of money. Morgan Stanley, for example, lost $265 billion globally. Bear Stearns required government intervention to help bail it out of the subprime mess. Analysts attribute the banks' failings to poor inner-bank communication and a lack of effective risk management. Although, in many companies, the chief financial officer (CFO) is in charge of risk management, it appears that many banks viewed the CFO as merely an advisory position.

Generally speaking, those banks that survived the crisis the best had highly active and involved CFOs. As it turns out, using a CFO as merely an advisor is a risky proposition. Not only have many of these banks failed at risk management, but according to Sarbanes-Oxley, a CFO must verify a company's ability to internally control its financial reporting. Therefore, a CFO not directly in charge of a company's finances is verifying something that he or she really knows little about and is defying the rules laid out by SOX. The extent of the subprime lending fallout has made it clear that an overhaul of the system is necessary. For corporations, this means that they must improve their abilities to assess risk. Analysts believe that borrowers, lenders, and investors are going to be feeling the pain of the subprime crisis for years to come.[7]

### Discussion Questions
1. What is subprime lending, and why did the crisis get so bad?
2. What needs to be done to make sure that the economy does not suffer a similar crisis in the future?
3. What is the role of the CFO, and how can an engaged CFO help avoid financial disasters?

traded on the OTC market, many very large and well-known concerns trade there as well. Indeed, thousands of shares of the stocks of companies such as Apple Computer, Intel, and Microsoft are traded on the OTC market every day. Further, because most corporate bonds and all U.S. securities are traded over the counter, the OTC market regularly accounts for the largest total dollar value of all of the secondary markets.

## Measuring Market Performance

Investors, especially professional money managers, want to know how well their invest-ments are performing relative to the market as a whole. Financial managers also need to know how their companies' securities are performing when compared with their competitors'. Thus, performance measures—averages and indexes—are very impor-tant to many different people. They not only indicate the performance of a particular securities market but also provide a measure of the overall health of the economy.

Indexes and averages are used to measure stock prices. An *index* compares current stock prices with those in a specified base period, such as 1944, 1967, or 1977. An *average* is the average of certain stock prices. The averages used are usually not simple calculations, however. Some stock market averages (such as the Standard & Poor's Composite Index) are weighted averages, where the weights employed are the total market values of each stock in the index (in this case 500). The Dow Jones Industrial Average is a price-weighted average. Regardless of how they are constructed, all mar-ket averages of stocks move together closely over time.

Many investors follow the activity of the Dow Jones Industrial Average to see whether the stock market has gone up or down. Table 16.5 lists the 30 companies that currently make up the Dow. Although these companies are only a small fraction of the total number of companies listed on the New York Stock Exchange, because of their size they account for about 25 percent of the total value of the NYSE.

The numbers listed in an index or average that tracks the performance of a stock market are expressed not as dollars but as a number on a fixed scale. If you know, for example, that the Dow Jones Industrial Average climbed from 860 in August 1982 to a high of 11,497 at the beginning of 2000, you can see clearly that the value of the Dow Jones Average increased more than 10 times in this 19-year period, making it one of the highest rate of return periods in the history of the stock market. With U.S. interest rates at modest levels and inflation at 30-year lows, many people think that as long as U.S. companies can continue to produce growing earnings, stock prices will continue to climb. If inflation rises and interest rates go up, and if corpo-rate earnings slow down or decline, the market will most likely be in for a tumble.

A period of large increases in stock prices is known as a *bull market,* with the bull symbolizing an aggressive, charging market and rising stock prices. The bull market of the 1990s was one of the strongest on record, with the Dow Jones Indus-trial Average rising from 3,300 in April 1992 to over 11,000 in 2000. After going up

| | | | |
|---|---|---|---|
| 3M | Coca-Cola | JPMorgan Chase | **TABLE 16.5** |
| Alcoa | Du Pont | McDonald's | The 30 Stocks in the |
| American Express | ExxonMobil | Merck | Dow Jones Industrial |
| American International Group | General Electric | Microsoft | Average |
| AT&T | General Motors | Pfizer | |
| Bank of America | Hewlett-Packard | Procter & Gamble | |
| Boeing | Home Depot | United Technologies | |
| Caterpillar | IBM | Verizon | |
| Chevron | Intel | Wal-Mart | |
| Citigroup | Johnson & Johnson | Walt Disney | |

another 5 percent, the market dropped in the early 2000s, and was at about 12,600 in May 2008. A declining stock market is known as a *bear market,* with the bear symbolizing sluggish, retreating activity. When stock prices decline very rapidly, the market is said to *crash.* The worst point loss in history (684.81 points) occurred on September 17, 2001, after markets were closed for four days following the terrorist attacks on September 11 that destroyed the World Trade Center and portions of the Pentagon.[8] The stock market—and indeed all of American industry — occasionally stumbles, but it eventually returns to its long-term pattern of growth. (See Figure 16.3.)

For investors to make sound financial decisions, it is important that they stay in touch with business news, markets, and indexes. Of course, business and investment magazines, such as *BusinessWeek, Fortune,* and *Money,* offer this type of information. Many Internet sites, including the CNN/*Money, Business Wire, USA Today,* other online newspapers, and *PR Newswire,* offer this information, as well. Many sites offer searchable databases of information by topic, company, or keyword. However investors choose to receive and review business news, doing so is a necessity in today's market. Table 16.6 Provides information about total shareholder return by industry over the past 10 years.

**FIGURE 16.3**    Long-Term Performance of the Stock Market

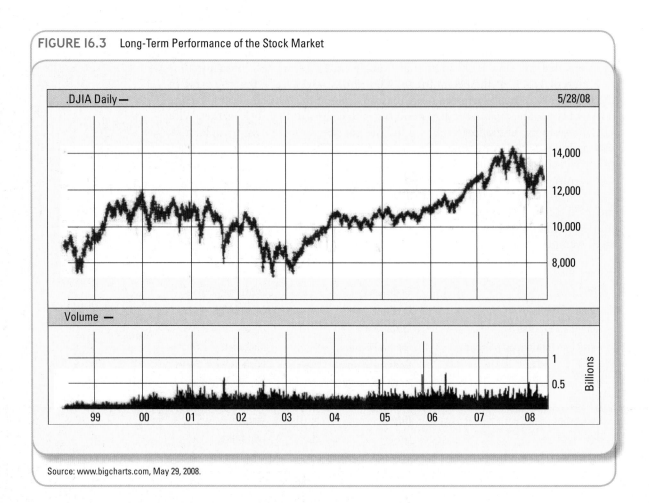

Source: www.bigcharts.com, May 29, 2008.

**TABLE I6.6**   Annual Total Return to Shareholders by Industry (2001–2006)

| 1 year | 5 years | 10 years |
|---|---|---|
| 1 Oil and gas equipment, services | Metals | Mining, crude oil production |
| 2 Mining, crude-oil production | Petroleum refining | Petroleum refining |
| 3 Engineering, construction | Mining, crude oil production | Engineering, construction |
| 4 Healthcare: pharmacy, other | Engineering, construction | Food services |
| 5 Petroleum refining | Oil and gas equipment, services | Health care: insurance, managed care |
| 6 Beverages | Health care: insurance, managed care | Wholesalers: health care |
| 7 Wholesalers: health care | Wholesalers: diversified | Wholesalers: diversified |
| 8 Aerospace and defense | Railroads | Industrial and farm equipment |
| 9 Electronics, equipment | Industrial and farm equipment | Oil and gas equipment, services |
| 10 Railroads | Electronics, electrical equipment | Metals |

Source: "Fortune 500 Top Performers: Best Investments by Industry," *Fortune* 2008, http://money.cnn.com/magazines/fortune/fortune500/2008/performers/ (accessed June 18. 2008).

# So You Want to Work in Financial Management or Securities

Taking classes in financial and securities management can provide many career options. From managing a small firm's accounts receivables to handling charitable giving for a multinational to investment banking to stock brokerage. We have entered into a less certain period for finance and securities jobs, however. In the world of investment banking, the past few years have been especially challenging. Tens of thousands of employees from Wall Street firms have lost their jobs. This phenomenon is not confined to New York City either, leaving the industry with a lot fewer jobs around the country. This type of phenomenon is not isolated to the finance sector. In the early 2000s, the tech sector experienced a similar downturn, from which it has subsequently largely recovered. Undoubtedly, markets will bounce back and job creation in finance and securities will increase again—but until that happens the atmosphere across finance and securities will be more competitive than it has been in the past. However, this does not mean that there are no jobs. All firms need financial analysts to determine whether a project should be implemented, when to issue stocks or bonds, or when to initiate loans. These and other forward-looking questions such as how to invest excess cash must be addressed by financial managers. Economic uncertainty in the financial and securities market has made for more difficulty in finding the most desirable jobs.

Why this sudden downturn in financial industry prospects? A lot of these job cuts came in response to the subprime lending fallout and subsequent bank failures such as Bear Stearns, which alone lost around 7,000 employees. All of these people will be looking for new jobs in new organizations, increasing the competitive level in a lot of different employment areas. For young jobseekers with relatively little experience, this may result in a great deal of frustration. On the other hand, by the time you graduate, the job market for finance majors could be in recovery and rebuilding with new employees. Uncertainty results in hiring freezes and layoffs, but leave firms lean and ready to grow when the cycle turns around, resulting in hiring from the bottom up.

Many different industries require people with finance skills. So do not despair if you have a difficult time finding a job in exactly the right firm. Most students switch companies a number of times over the course of their careers. Many organizations require individuals trained in forecasting, statistics, economics, and finance. Even unlikely places like museums, aquariums, and zoos need people who are good at numbers. It may require some creativity, but if you are committed to a career in finance, look to less obvious sources—not just the large financial firms.[9]

# Review Your Understanding

### Describe some common methods of managing current assets.

Current assets are short-term resources such as cash, investments, accounts receivable, and inventory, which can be converted to cash within a year. Financial managers focus on minimizing the amount of cash kept on hand and increasing the speed of collections through lockboxes and electronic funds transfer and investing in marketable securities. Marketable securities include U.S. Treasury bills, certificates of deposit, commercial paper, and money market funds. Managing accounts receivable requires judging customer creditworthiness and creating credit terms that encourage prompt payment. Inventory management focuses on determining optimum inventory levels that minimize the cost of storing and ordering inventory without sacrificing too many lost sales due to stockouts.

### Identify some sources of short-term financing (current liabilities).

Current liabilities are short-term debt obligations that must be repaid within one year, such as accounts payable, taxes payable, and notes (loans) payable. Trade credit is extended by suppliers for the purchase of their goods and services. A line of credit is an arrangement by which a bank agrees to lend a specified amount of money to a business whenever the business needs it. Secured loans are backed by collateral; unsecured loans are backed only by the borrower's good reputation.

### Summarize the importance of long-term assets and capital budgeting.

Long-term, or fixed, assets are expected to last for many years, such as production facilities (plants), offices, and equipment. Businesses need modern, up-to-date equipment to succeed in today's competitive environment. Capital budgeting is the process of analyzing company needs and selecting the assets that will maximize its value; a capital budget is the amount of money budgeted for the purchase of fixed assets. Every investment in fixed assets carries some risk.

### Specify how companies finance their operations and manage fixed assets with long-term liabilities, particularly bonds.

Two common choices for financing are equity financing (attracting new owners) and debt financing (taking on long-term liabilities). Long-term liabilities are debts that will be repaid over a number of years, such as long-term bank loans and bond issues. A bond is a long-term debt security that an organization sells to raise money. The bond indenture specifies the provisions of the bond contract—maturity date, coupon rate, repayment methods, and others.

### Discuss how corporations can use equity financing by issuing stock through an investment banker.

Owners' equity represents what owners have contributed to the company and includes common stock, preferred stock, and retained earnings (profits that have been reinvested in the assets of the firm). To finance operations, companies can issue new common and preferred stock through an investment banker that sells stocks and bonds for corporations.

### Describe the various securities markets in the United States.

Securities markets provide the mechanism for buying and selling stocks and bonds. Primary markets allow companies to raise capital by selling new stock directly to investors through investment bankers. Secondary markets allow the buyers of previously issued shares of stock to sell them to other owners. The major secondary markets are the New York Stock Exchange, the American Stock Exchange, and the over-the-counter market. Investors measure stock market performance by watching stock market averages and indexes such as the Dow Jones Industrial Average and the Standard and Poor's (S&P) Composite Index.

### Critique the short-term asset and liabilities position of a small manufacturer, and recommend corrective action.

Using the information presented in this chapter, you should be able to "Solve the Dilemma" on page 513 presented by the current bleak working capital situation of Glasspray Corporation.

# Revisit the World of Business

1. What is different about Sears's intellectual property bond arrangement that had not been done before?
2. What does the securitization of intellectual property mean for the company and for investors?
3. David Bowie was the first to use IP bonds. How did they work in his case?

# Learn the Terms

bonds   499
capital budgeting   496
commercial certificates of deposit (CDs)   492
commercial paper   492
dividend yield   503
eurodollar market   492
factor   495
floating-rate bonds   500
investment banking   504
junk bonds   500

line of credit   494
lockbox   491
long-term (fixed) assets   495
long-term liabilities   499
marketable securities   491
over-the-counter (OTC) market   505
primary market   504
prime rate   494
retained earnings   502
secondary markets   504
secured bonds   500

secured loans   494
securities markets   504
serial bonds   500
trade credit   494
transaction balances   490
Treasury bills (T-bills)   492
unsecured bonds   500
unsecured loans   494
working capital management   489

# Check Your Progress

1. Define working capital management.
2. How can a company speed up cash flow? Why should it?
3. Describe the various types of marketable securities.
4. What does it mean to have a line of credit at a bank?
5. What are fixed assets? Why is assessing risk important in capital budgeting?
6. How can a company finance fixed assets?
7. What are bonds and what do companies do with them?
8. How can companies use equity to finance their operations and long-term growth?
9. What are the functions of securities markets?
10. Define bull and bear markets.

# Get Involved

1. Using your local newspaper or *The Wall Street Journal,* find the current rates of interest on the following marketable securities. If you were a financial manager for a large corporation, which would you invest extra cash in? Which would you invest in if you worked for a small business?
   a. Three-month T-bills
   b. Six-month T-bills
   c. Commercial certificates of deposit
   d. Commercial paper
   e. Eurodollar deposits
   f. Money market deposits
2. Select five of the Dow Jones Industrials from Table 16.5. Look up their earnings, dividends, and prices for the past five years. What kind of picture is presented by this information? Which stocks would you like to have owned over this past period? Do you think the next five years will present a similar picture?

# Build Your Skills

## CHOOSING AMONG PROJECTS

### Background:

As the senior executive in charge of exploration for High Octane Oil Co., you are constantly looking for projects that will add to the company's profitability—without increasing the company's risk. High Octane Oil is an international oil company with operations in Latin America, the Middle East, Africa, the United States, and Mexico. The company is one of the world's leading experts in deep-water exploration and drilling. High Octane currently produces 50 percent of its oil in the United States, 25 percent in the Middle East, 5 percent in Africa, 10 percent in Latin America, and 10 percent in Mexico. You are considering six projects from around the world.

**Project 1**—Your deep-water drilling platform in the Gulf of Mexico is producing at maximum capacity from the Valdez oil field, and High Octane's geological engineers think there is a high probability that there is oil in the Sanchez field, which is adjacent to Valdez. They recommend drilling a new series of wells. Once commercial quantities of oil have been discovered, it will take two more years to build the collection platform and pipelines. It will be four years before the discovered oil gets to the refineries.

**Project 2**—The Brazilian government has invited you to drill on some unexplored tracts in the middle of the central jungle region. There are roads to within 50 miles of the tract and British Petroleum has found oil 500 miles away from this tract. It would take about three years to develop this property and several more years to build pipelines and pumping stations to carry the oil to the refineries. The Brazilian government wants 20 percent of all production as its fee for giving High Octane Oil Co. the drilling rights or a $500 million up-front fee and 5 percent of the output.

**Project 3**—Your fields in Saudi Arabia have been producing oil for 50 years. Several wells are old, and the pressure has diminished. Your engineers are sure that if you were to initiate high-pressure secondary recovery procedures, you would increase the output of these existing wells by 20 percent. High-pressure recovery methods pump water at high pressure into the underground limestone formations to enhance the movement of petroleum toward the surface.

**Project 4**—Your largest oil fields in Alaska have been producing from only 50 percent of the known deposits. Your geological engineers estimate that you could open up 10 percent of the remaining fields every two years and offset your current declining production from existing wells. The pipeline capacity is available and, while you can only drill during six months of the year, the fields could be producing oil in three years.

**Project 5**—Some of High Octane's west Texas oil fields produce in shallow stripper wells of 2,000- to 4,000-foot depths. Stripper wells produce anywhere from 10 to 2,000 barrels per day and can last for six months or 40 years. Generally, once you find a shallow deposit, there is an 80 percent chance that offset wells will find more oil. Because these wells are shallow, they can be drilled quickly at a low cost. High Octane's engineers estimate that in your largest tract, which is closest to the company's Houston refinery, you could increase production by 30 percent for the next 10 years by increasing the density of the wells per square mile.

**Project 6**—The government of a republic in Russia has invited you to drill for oil in Siberia. Russian geologists think that this oil field might be the largest in the world, but there have been no wells drilled and no infrastructure exists to carry oil if it should be found. The republic has no money to help you build the infrastructure but if you find oil, it will let you keep the first five years' production before taking its 25 percent share. Knowing that oil fields do not start producing at full capacity for many years after initial production, your engineers are not sure that your portion the first five years of production will pay for the infrastructure they must build to get the oil to market. The republic also has been known to have a rather unstable government, and the last international oil company that began this project left the country when a new government demanded a higher than originally agreed-upon percentage of the expected output. If this field is in fact the largest in the world, High Octane's supply of oil would be ensured well into the 21st century.

### Task:

1. Working in groups, rank the six projects from lowest risk to highest risk.

2. Given the information provided, do the best you can to rank the projects from lowest cost to highest cost.

3. What political considerations might affect your project choice?

4. If you could choose one project, which would it be and why?

5. If you could choose three projects, which ones would you choose? In making this decision, consider which projects might be highly correlated to High Octane Oil's existing production and which ones might diversify the company's production on a geographical basis.

# Solve the Dilemma

### SURVIVING RAPID GROWTH

Glasspray Corporation is a small firm that makes industrial fiberglass spray equipment. Despite its size, the company supplies to a range of firms from small mom-and-pop boatmakers to major industrial giants, both overseas and here at home. Indeed, just about every molded fiberglass resin product, from bathroom sinks and counters to portable spas and racing yachts, is constructed with the help of one or more of the company's machines.

Despite global acceptance of its products, Glasspray has repeatedly run into trouble with regard to the management of its current assets and liabilities as a result of extremely rapid and consistent increases in year-to-year sales. The firm's president and founder, Stephen T. Rose, recently lamented the sad state of his firm's working capital position: "Our current assets aren't, and our current liabilities are!" Rose shouted in a recent meeting of the firm's top officers. "We can't afford any more increases in sales! We're selling our way into bankruptcy! Frankly, our *working capital* doesn't!"

### Discussion Questions

1. Normally, rapidly increasing sales are a good thing. What seems to be the problem here?

2. List the important components of a firm's working capital. Include both current assets and current liabilities.

3. What are some management techniques applied to current liabilities that Glasspray might use to improve its working capital position?

# Build Your Business Plan

### FINANCIAL MANAGEMENT AND SECURITIES MARKET

This chapter helps you realize that once you are making money, you need to be careful in determining how to invest it. Meanwhile, your team should consider the pros and cons of establishing a line of credit at the bank.

Remember the key to building your business plan is to be realistic!!

# See for Yourself Videocase

### LEADERSHIP: THE MCFARLANE COMPANIES

Coming off a long string of rejections, Todd McFarlane got a job drawing for Marvel/Epic Comics in 1984. His first assignment was illustrating a story entitled "Scorpio Rose" that was included in the back of another comic book. He then drew for the *Incredible Hulk* series, and Batman comics *Detective* and *Batman: Year Two.* McFarlane's big break came, however, while working on Marvel Comic's *Amazing Spider-Man.* His drawings helped lift the comic from number nine to number one on the comic book best-sellers lists. Because of his success, McFarlane was put in charge of his own comic, *Spider-Man,* which was first released in September 1990. It sold 2.5 million copies and quickly became a best-seller.

Because he felt that working for a mainstream comic publisher was stifling his creativity, McFarlane and fellow artists left Marvel and launched their own Image Comics. Free to create, McFarlane crafted and published his own comic, *Spawn,* which had been a labor of love 10 years in the making. Audiences clearly responded to *Spawn,* which sold 1.7 million copies, making it the best-selling independent comic book to date. In addition to being able to call his own shots, McFarlane also has appreciated the financial security that owning his own business affords—his earnings are not limited by salary, only by how successful he can make Image Comics.

Because of *Spawn's* success, McFarlane began to be approached by companies looking to cut licensing deals for toys based on the characters. Again, control became an issue for McFarlane. Because the companies did not want to grant him complete creative control, McFarlane opened his own toy company in 1994 instead of granting licensing rights. McFarlane Toys has a reputation for producing detailed, high-quality collectible figurines at affordable prices.

In 1998, McFarlane, a former baseball player and lifetime fan, paid $3 million for Mark McGwire's 70th home run baseball. Because of his success in the comics world, combined with the publicity generated by his expensive purchase, he was able to land a licensing agreement with Major League Baseball that gave his toy company the right to produce baseball figurines. Shortly thereafter, McFarlane Toys began producing sports figures for football, basketball, and hockey as well. While for many, spending $3 million on a single baseball would be a foolish investment, for McFarlane it was a calculated business decision that allowed him to expand his comics empire into the sports world. McFarlane Toys maintains its edge over the competition by producing extremely detailed, lifelike, and high-quality toys at a price most people can afford.

While McFarlane was working out the details of his expansion into sports, he also began to venture into other media. New Line Cinema produced *Spawn* the movie, and HBO aired an animated series based upon the comic. McFarlane delved into music, directing award-winning videos for groups such as Pearl Jam and Korn.

Over the years, McFarlane has developed a reputation for being not only an exceptional artist, but also a visionary with good business sense. McFarlane is known for planning all his business moves and keeping a close watch on the management of his companies (Todd McFarlane Productions, McFarlane Toys, and Todd McFarlane Entertainment).

To maintain full control over everything, McFarlane's businesses remain private. In a private company, one is not accountable to stockholders. Because of this,

changes can be made more easily when deemed necessary. Another benefit to being private is that a company is not committed to constantly increasing profits in order to satisfy stockholders. Even through difficult financial times, McFarlane's business acumen and ability to see the big picture has carried his ventures through. According to McFarlane, himself, no matter what the arena, his greatest asset is consistently delivering an excellent product. The numbers don't lie—as of 2007, The McFarlane Companies were earning $50 million annually and had 200 employees located in three countries. Not bad for a man who started out his career illustrating secondary stories to fill the back of comic books.[10]

### Discussion Questions

1. What has helped Todd McFarlane become such a huge success in multiple media?
2. For McFarlane, what are the advantages of keeping his enterprises private?
3. What is the competitive advantage of McFarlane's products over the competition?

**Remember to check out our Online Learning Center at www.mhhe.com/ferrell7e.**

# Appendix D

# Personal Financial Planning*

## The Financial Planning Process

**Personal financial planning** is the process of managing your finances so that you can achieve your financial goals. By anticipating future needs and wants, you can take appropriate steps to prepare for them. Your needs and wants will undoubtedly change over time as you enter into various life circumstances. Although financial planning is not entirely about money management, a large part of this process is concerned with decisions related to expenditures, investments, and credit.

Although every person has unique needs, everyone can benefit from financial planning. Even if the entire financial plan is not implemented at once, the process itself will help you focus on what is important. With a little forethought and action, you may be able to achieve goals that you previously thought were unattainable. Table D.1 shows how teens handle finances.

The steps in development and implementation of an effective financial plan are:

- Evaluate your financial health.
- Set short-term and long-term financial goals.
- Create and adhere to a budget.
- Manage credit wisely.
- Develop a savings and investment plan.
- Evaluate and purchase insurance.
- Develop an estate plan.
- Adjust your financial plan to new circumstances.

## Evaluate Your Financial Health

Just as businesses make use of financial reports to track their performance, good personal financial planning requires that individuals keep track of their income and expenses and their overall financial condition. Several software packages are readily available to help track personal finances (for example, Quicken and Microsoft Money), but all that is really needed is a simple spreadsheet program. This appendix includes some simple worksheets that can be reproduced to provide a starting point for personal financial planning. Comprehensive financial planning sites are also available on the Internet. For example, **www.moneycentral.msn.com** and **www. smartmoney.com** both provide information and tools to simplify this process.

| | | TABLE D.I |
|---|---|---|
| Learned about money from their parents | 87% | Teens and Money |
| Agree that saving and investing can help you achieve the freedom to do what you want in life | 89% | |
| Feel that it's more important as a teen to save money than to spend it | 20% | |
| Know how to use a debit card/credit card | 54%/48% | |
| Get money from a job | 57% | |
| Get money from a credit card | 20% parents' card; 14% own card | |
| Are in debt either to a person or a company | 31% | |
| Would like to learn more about money management in school | 76% | |

Source: Charles Schwab Foundation, "Teens & Money 2006 Survey Findings," "Insights into Money Attitudes Behaviors and Concerns of Teens," www.aboutschwab.com/teensurvey2006.pdf (accessed May 15, 2006).

*This appendix was contributed by Dr. Vickie Bajtelsmit.

While it is possible to track all kinds of information over time, the two most critical elements of your finances are your personal net worth and your personal cash flow. The information necessary for these two measures is often required by lending institutions on loan applications, so keeping it up-to-date can save you time and effort later.

## The Personal Balance Sheet

For businesses, net worth is usually defined as *assets minus liabilities,* and this is no different for individuals. **Personal net worth** is simply the total value of all personal assets less the total value of unpaid debts or liabilities. Although a business could not survive with a negative net worth since it would be technically insolvent, many students have negative net worth. As a student, you probably are not yet earning enough to have accumulated significant assets, such as a house or stock portfolio, but you are likely to have incurred various forms of debt, including student loans, car loans, and credit card debt.

At this stage in your life, negative net worth is not necessarily an indication of poor future financial prospects. Current investment in your "human capital" (education) is usually considered to have a resulting payoff in the form of better job opportunities and higher potential lifetime income, so this "upside-down" balance sheet should not stay that way forever. Unfortunately, there are many people in the United States who have negative net worth much later in their lives. This can result from unforeseen circumstances, like divorce, illness, or disability, but the easy availability of credit in the last couple of decades has also been blamed for the heavy debt loads of many American families. No matter the immediate trigger, it is usually poor financial planning—the failure to prepare in advance for those unforeseen circumstances—that makes the difference between those who fail and those who survive. It is interesting to note that we could say the exact same thing about business failures. Most are attributable to poor financial planning. If your net worth is negative, you

---

**TABLE D.2**    Personal Net Worth

| Assets | $ | Liabilities | $ |
|---|---|---|---|
| Checking accounts | ___ | Credit cards balances (list) | ___ |
| Savings accounts | ___ | 1 _____ | ___ |
| Money market accounts | ___ | 2 _____ | ___ |
| Other short-term investment | ___ | 3 _____ | ___ |
| | ___ | Personal Loans | ___ |
| Market value of investments (stocks, bonds, mutual funds) | ___ | Student loans | ___ |
| | ___ | Car Loans | ___ |
| Value of retirement funds | ___ | Home mortgage balance | ___ |
| College savings plan | ___ | Home equity loans | ___ |
| Other savings plans | ___ | Other real estate loans | ___ |
| Market value of real estate | ___ | Alimony/child support owed | ___ |
| Cars | ___ | Taxes owed (above withholding) | ___ |
| Home furnishings | ___ | Other investment loans | ___ |
| Jewelry/art/collectibles | ___ | Other liabilities/debts | ___ |
| Clothing/personal assets | ___ | | ___ |
| Other assets | ___ | | ___ |
| TOTAL ASSETS | ___ | TOTAL LIABILITIES | ___ |

PERSONAL NET WORTH = TOTAL ASSETS MINUS TOTAL LIABILITIES = $ ___

should definitely include debt reduction on your list of short and/or long-term goals.

You can use Table D.2 to estimate your net worth. On the left-hand side of the balance sheet, you should record the value of *assets,* all the things you own that have value. These include checking and savings account balances, investments, furniture, books, clothing, vehicles, houses, and the like. As with business balance sheets, assets are usually arranged from most liquid (easily convertible to cash) to least liquid. If you are a young student, it should not be surprising to find that you have little, if anything, to put on this side of your balance sheet. You should note that balance sheets are sensitive to the point in time chosen for evaluation. For example, if you always get paid on the first day of the month, your checking balance will be greatest at that point but will quickly be depleted as you pay for rent, food, and other needs. You may want to use your average daily balance in checking and savings accounts as a more accurate reflection of your financial condition. The right-hand side of the balance sheet is for recording *liabilities,* amounts of money that you owe to others. These include bank loans, mortgages, credit card debt, and other personal loans and are usually listed in order of how soon they must be paid back to the lender.

### The Cash Flow Statement

Businesses forecast and track their regular inflows and outflows of cash with a cash budget and summarize annual cash flows on the statement of cash flows. Similarly, individuals should have a clear understanding of their flow of cash as they budget their expenditures and regularly check to be sure that they are sticking to their budget.

What is cash flow? Anytime you receive cash or pay cash (including payments with checks), the dollar amount that is moving from one person to another is a **cash flow.** For students, the most likely cash inflows will be student loans, grants, and income from part-time jobs. Cash outflows will include rent, food, gas, car payments, books, tuition, and personal care expenses. Although it may seem obvious that you need to have enough inflows to cover the outflows, it is very common for people to estimate incorrectly and overspend. This may result in hefty bank overdraft charges or increasing debt as credit lines are used to make up the difference. Accurate forecasting of cash inflows and outflows allows you to make arrangements to cover estimated shortfalls before they occur. For students, this can be particularly valuable when cash inflows primarily occur at the beginning of the semester (for example, student loans) but outflows are spread over the semester.

How should you treat credit card purchases on your cash flow worksheet? Since credit purchases do not require payment of cash *now,* your cash flow statement should not reflect the value of the purchase as an outflow until you pay the bill. Take for example the purchase of a television set on credit. The $500 purchase will increase your assets and your liabilities by $500 but will only result in a negative cash flow of a few dollars per month, since payments on credit cards are cash outflows when they are made. If you always pay your credit card balances in full each month, the purchases are really the same thing as cash, and your balance sheet will never reflect the debt. But if you purchase on credit and only pay minimum balances, you will be living beyond your means, and your balance sheet will get more and more "upside down." A further problem with using credit to purchase assets that decline in value is that the liability may still be there long after the asset you purchased has no value.

Table D.3 can be used to estimate your cash flow. The purpose of a cash flow worksheet for your financial plan is to heighten your awareness of where the cash is going. Many people are surprised to find that they are spending more than they make (by using too much credit) or that they have significant "cash leakage"—those little expenditures that add up to a lot without their even noticing. Examples include afternoon lattes or snacks, too many nights out at the local pub, eating lunch at the Student Center instead of packing a bag, and regularly paying for parking (or parking tickets) instead of biking or riding the bus to school. In many cases, plugging the little leaks can free up enough cash to make a significant contribution toward achieving long-term savings goals.

# Set Short-Term and Long-Term Financial Goals

Just as a business develops its vision and strategic plan, individuals should have a clear set of financial goals. This component of your financial plan is the road map that will lead you to achieving your short-term and long-term financial goals.

# TABLE D.3  Personal Cash Flow

| Cash Inflows | Monthly | Annual |
|---|---|---|
| Salary/wage income (gross) | $ _____ | $ _____ |
| Interest/dividend income | _____ | _____ |
| Other income (self-employment) | _____ | _____ |
| Rental income (after expenses) | _____ | _____ |
| Capital gains | _____ | _____ |
| Other income | _____ | _____ |
| Total income | _____ | _____ |

| Cash Outflows | Monthly | Annual |
|---|---|---|
| Groceries | $ _____ | $ _____ |
| Housing | _____ | _____ |
|    Mortgage or rent | _____ | _____ |
|    House repairs/expenses | _____ | _____ |
|    Property taxes | _____ | _____ |
| Utilities | _____ | _____ |
|    Heating | _____ | _____ |
|    Electric | _____ | _____ |
|    Water and sewer | _____ | _____ |
|    Cable/phone/satellite/Internet | _____ | _____ |
| Car loan payments | _____ | _____ |
| Car maintenance/gas | _____ | _____ |
| Credit card payments | _____ | _____ |
| Other loan payments | _____ | _____ |
| Income and payroll taxes | _____ | _____ |
| Other taxes | _____ | _____ |
| Insurance | _____ | _____ |
|    Life | _____ | _____ |
|    Health | _____ | _____ |
|    Auto | _____ | _____ |
|    Disability | _____ | _____ |
|    Other insurance | _____ | _____ |
| Clothing | _____ | _____ |
| Gifts | _____ | _____ |
| Other consumables (TVs,etc) | _____ | _____ |
| Child care expenses | _____ | _____ |
| Sports-related expenses | _____ | _____ |
| Health club dues | _____ | _____ |
| Uninsured medical expenses | _____ | _____ |
| Education | _____ | _____ |
| Vacations | _____ | _____ |
| Entertainment | _____ | _____ |
| Alimony/child support | _____ | _____ |
| Charitable contributions | _____ | _____ |
| Required pension contributions | _____ | _____ |
| Magazine subscriptions/books | _____ | _____ |
| Other payments/expenses | _____ | _____ |
| Total Expenses | $ _____ | $ _____ |

NET PERSONAL CASH FLOW = TOTAL INCOME − TOTAL EXPENSES = $ _____

**Short-term goals** are those that can be achieved in two years or less. They may include saving for particular short-term objectives, such as a new car, a down payment for a home, a vacation, or other major consumer purchase. For many people, short-term financial goals should include tightening up on household spending patterns and reducing outstanding credit.

**Long-term goals** are those that require substantial time to achieve. Nearly everyone should include retirement planning as a long-term objective. Those who have or anticipate having children will probably consider college savings a priority. Protection of loved ones from the financial hazards of your unexpected death, illness, or disability is also a long-term objective for many individuals. If you have a spouse or other dependents, having adequate insurance and an estate plan in place should be part of your long-term goals.

# Create and Adhere to a Budget

Whereas the cash flow table you completed in the previous section tells you what you are doing with your money currently, a **budget** shows what you plan to do with it in the future. A budget can be for any period of time, but it is common to budget in monthly and/or annual intervals.

### Developing a Budget

You can use the cash flow worksheet completed earlier to create a budget. Begin with the amount of income you have for the month. Enter your nondiscretionary expenditures (that is, bills you *must* pay, such as tuition, rent, and utilities) on the worksheet and determine the leftover amount. Next list your discretionary expenditures, such as entertainment and cable TV, in order of importance. You can then work down your discretionary list until your remaining available cash flow is zero.

An important component of your budget is the amount that you allocate to savings. If you put a high priority on saving and you do not use credit to spend beyond your income each month, you will be able to accumulate wealth that can be used to meet your short-term and long-term financial goals. In the bestseller *The Millionaire Next Door,* authors Thomas J. Stanley and William D. Danko point out that most

millionaires have achieved financial success through hard work and thriftiness as opposed to luck or inheritance. You cannot achieve your financial goals unless your budget process places a high priority on saving and investing.

### Tracking Your Budgeting Success

Businesses regularly identify budget items and track their variance from budget forecasts. People who follow a similar strategy in their personal finances are better able to meet their financial goals as well. If certain budgeted expenses routinely turn out to be under or over your previous estimates, then it is important to either revise the budget estimate or develop a strategy for reducing that expense.

College students commonly have trouble adhering to their budget for food and entertainment expenses. A strategy that works fairly well is to limit yourself to cash payments. At the beginning of the week, withdraw an amount from checking that will cover your weekly budgeted expenses. For the rest of the week, leave your checkbook, ATM card, and debit and credit cards at home. When the cash is gone, don't spend any more. While this is easier said than done, after a couple of weeks, you will learn to cut down on the cash leakage that inevitably occurs without careful cash management.

A debit card looks like a credit card but works like a check. For example, in the Netherlands almost no one writes a check, and everything is paid by debit card, which drafts directly from a checking account. You do not build up your credit rating when using a debit card. Figure D.1 indicates that the use of debit cards is growing rapidly in the United States. On the other hand, credit cards allow you to promise to pay for something at a later date by using preapproved lines of credit granted by a bank or finance company. Credit cards are easy to use and are accepted by most retailers today.

# Manage Credit Wisely

One of the cornerstones of your financial plan should be to keep credit usage to a minimum and to work at reducing outstanding debt. The use of credit for consumer and home purchases is well entrenched in our culture and has arguably fueled our economy and enabled Americans to better their standard of living as compared to earlier generations. Nevertheless, credit abuse is a serious problem in this country,

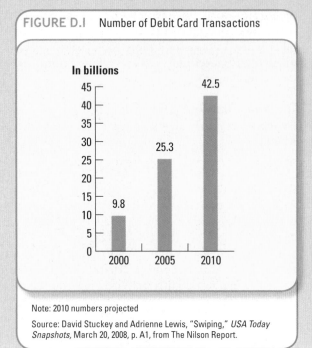

FIGURE D.I    Number of Debit Card Transactions

In billions

Note: 2010 numbers projected

Source: David Stuckey and Adrienne Lewis, "Swiping," *USA Today Snapshots,* March 20, 2008, p. A1, from The Nilson Report.

and the economic downturn of 2001 undoubtedly pushed many households over the edge into bankruptcy as a result.

To consider the pros and cons of credit usage, compare the following two scenarios. In the first case, Joel takes an 8 percent fixed-rate mortgage to purchase a house to live in while he is a college student. The mortgage payment is comparable to alternative monthly rental costs, and his house appreciates 20 percent in value over the four years he is in college. At the end of college, Joel will be able to sell his house and reap the return, having invested only a small amount of his own cash. For example, if he made an initial 5 percent down payment on a $100,000 home that is now worth $120,000 four years later, he has earned $12,800 (after a 6 percent commission to the real estate agent) on an investment of $5,000. This amounts to a sizable return on investment of more than 250 percent over four years. This example is oversimplified in that we did not take into account the principal that has been repaid over the four years, and we did not consider the mortgage payment costs or the tax deductibility of interest paid during that time. However, the point is still clear; borrowing money to buy an asset that appreciates in

value by more than the cost of the debt is a terrific way to invest.

In the second case, Nicole uses her credit card to pay for some of her college expenses. Instead of paying off the balance each month, Nicole makes only the minimum payment and incurs 16 percent interest costs. Over the course of several years of college, Nicole's credit card debt is likely to amount to several thousand dollars, typical of college graduates in the United States. The beer and pizza Nicole purchased have long ago been digested, yet the debt remains, and the payments continue. If Nicole continues making minimum payments, it will take many years to pay back that original debt, and in the meantime the interest paid will far exceed the original amount borrowed. Credit card debt in the amount of $1,000 will usually require a minimum payment of at least $15 per month. At this payment level, it will take 166 months (almost 14 years) to pay the debt in full, and the total interest paid will be more than $1,400!

So when is borrowing a good financial strategy? A rule of thumb is that you should borrow only to buy assets that will appreciate in value or when your financing charges are less than what you are earning on the cash that you would otherwise use to make the purchase. This rule generally will limit your borrowing to home purchases and investments.

## Use and Abuse of Credit Cards

Credit cards should be used only as a cash flow management tool. If you pay off your balance every month, you avoid financing charges (assuming no annual fee), you have proof of expenditures, which may be necessary for tax or business reasons, and you may be able to better match your cash inflows and outflows over the course of the month. There are several aspects of credit cards that you should be familiar with.

- *Finance charges.* Credit card companies make money by lending to you at a higher rate than it costs them to obtain financing. Since many of their customers don't pay back their debts in a timely fashion (default), they must charge enough to cover the risk of default as well. Interest is usually calculated on the average daily balance over the month, and payments are applied to old debts first. Although there are "teaser" rates that may be less than 5 percent, most credit cards regularly charge 8 to 24 percent annual interest. The low introductory rates are subject to time limitations (often six months or less), and they revert to the higher rates if you don't pay on time.

- *Annual fee.* Many credit cards assess an annual fee that may be as low as $15 or as much as $100 per year. If you regularly carry a very low balance, this amounts to the equivalent of a very high additional interest charge. For example, a $50 annual fee is the equivalent of an additional 5 percent on your annual interest rate if your balance is $1,000. Because the cards with fees do not generally provide you with different services, it is best to choose no-annual-fee credit cards.

- *Credit line.* The credit line is the maximum you are allowed to borrow. This may begin with a small amount for a new customer, perhaps as low as $300. As the customer shows the ability and intent to repay (by doing so in a timely fashion), the limit can increase to many thousands of dollars.

- *Grace period.* The grace period for most credit cards is 25 days. This may amount to twice as long a period of free credit depending on when your purchase date falls in the billing cycle. For example, if you used your card on January 1 and your billing cycle goes from the 1st to the 31st, then the bill for January purchases will arrive the first week in February and will be due on February 25. If you pay it in full on the last possible day, you will have had 55 days of free credit. Keep in mind

that the lender considers the bill paid when the check is *received,* not when it is mailed.

- *Fees and penalties.* In addition to charging interest and annual fees, credit card companies charge extra for late payments and for going over the stated limit on the card. These fees have been on the rise in the last decade and $25 or higher penalties are now fairly common.

- *ATM withdrawals.* Most credit cards can be used to obtain cash from ATMs. Although this may be convenient, it contributes to your increasing credit card balance and may result in extra expenditures that you would otherwise have avoided. In addition, these withdrawals may have hidden costs. Withdrawing cash from a machine that is not owned by your credit card lender will usually cause you to incur a fee of $1 or $1.50. The effective interest that this represents can be substantial if you are withdrawing small amounts of cash. A $1 charge on a withdrawal of $50 is the equivalent of 2 percent interest in addition to any interest you might pay to the credit card lender.

- *Perks.* Most credit cards provide a number of additional services. These may include a limitation on your potential liability in the event your card is lost or stolen or trip insurance. Some cards promise "cash back" in the form of a small rebate based on dollar volume of credit purchases. Many credit card companies offer the opportunity to participate in airline mileage programs. The general rule of thumb is that none of these perks is worth the credit card interest that is charged. If, however, you use your credit card as a cash management tool only, paying off your balance every month, then these perks are truly free to you.

## Student Loans

Student loans are fairly common in today's environment of rising college tuition and costs. These loans can be a great deal, offering lower interest rates than other loans and terms that allow deferral of repayment until graduation. Furthermore, the money is being borrowed to pay for an asset that is expected to increase in value—your human capital. Don't underestimate, however, the monthly payments that will be required upon graduation. Students today graduate with average student loan debt of more

*Credit card debt is at an all-time high. The average U.S. household carries a balance of roughly $7,500 to $8,000.*

than $19,000. Table D.4 shows the monthly payments required to repay the debt under various term and interest scenarios. For larger outstanding debt amounts, new college graduates in entry-level positions find that it is difficult to make the necessary payments without help.

# Develop a Savings and Investment Plan

The next step to achieving your financial goals is to decide on a savings plan. A common recommendation of financial planners is to "pay yourself first." What this means is that you begin the month by setting aside an amount of money for your savings and investments, as compared to waiting until the end of the month and seeing what's left to save or invest. The budget is extremely important for deciding on a reasonable dollar amount to apply to this component of your financial plan.

As students, you might think that you cannot possibly find any extra dollars in your budget for saving, but, in fact, nearly everyone can stretch their budget a little. Some strategies for students might include taking public transportation several times a week and setting aside the gas or parking dollars you would have spent, buying regular coffees instead of Starbucks lattes, or eating at home one more night per week.

## Understanding the Power of Compounded Returns

Even better, if you are a college student living on a typically small budget, you should be able to use this experience to help jump-start a viable savings program after graduation. If you currently live on $10,000 per year and your first job pays $30,000, it should be easy to "pay yourself" $2,000 or more per year. Putting the current maximum of $3,000 in an individual retirement account (IRA) will give you some tax advantages and can result in substantial

TABLE D.4   How Much Will It Take to Pay That Debt?

| Months to Pay | Interest Rate | $1,000 | $2,500 | $5,000 | $10,000 |
|---|---|---|---|---|---|
| 12 | 15% | $90.26 | $225.65 | $451.29 | $902.58 |
| | 18% | $91.68 | $229.20 | $458.40 | $916.80 |
| | 21% | $93.11 | $232.78 | $465.57 | $931.14 |
| 24 | 15% | $48.49 | $121.22 | $242.43 | $484.87 |
| | 18% | $49.92 | $124.81 | $249.62 | $499.24 |
| | 21% | $51.39 | $128.46 | $256.93 | $513.86 |
| 36 | 15% | $34.67 | $86.66 | $173.33 | $346.65 |
| | 18% | $36.15 | $90.38 | $180.76 | $361.52 |
| | 21% | $37.68 | $94.19 | $188.38 | $376.75 |
| 48 | 15% | $27.83 | $69.58 | $139.15 | $278.31 |
| | 18% | $29.37 | $73.44 | $146.87 | $293.75 |
| | 21% | $30.97 | $77.41 | $154.83 | $309.66 |
| 60 | 15% | $23.79 | $59.47 | $118.95 | $237.90 |
| | 18% | $25.39 | $63.48 | $126.97 | $253.93 |
| | 21% | $27.05 | $67.63 | $135.27 | $270.53 |
| 72 | 15% | $21.15 | $52.86 | $105.73 | $211.45 |
| | 18% | $22.81 | $57.02 | $114.04 | $228.08 |
| | 21% | $24.54 | $61.34 | $122.68 | $245.36 |

wealth accumulation over time. An investment of only $2,000 per year from age 22 to retirement at 67 at 6 percent return per year will result in $425,487 at the retirement date. An annual contribution of $5,000 for 45 years will result in retirement wealth of about $1 million, not considering any additional tax benefits you might qualify for. If you invest that $5,000 per year for only 10 years and discontinue your contributions, you will still have about half a million dollars at age 67. And that assumes only a 6 percent return on investment!

What happens if you wait 10 years to start, beginning your $5,000 annual savings at age 32? By age 67, you will have only about a half million. Thirty-five years of investing instead of 45 doesn't sound like a big difference, but it cuts your retirement wealth in half. These examples illustrate an important point about long-term savings and wealth accumulation—the earlier you start, the better off you will be.

## The Link between Investment Choice and Savings Goals

Once you have decided how much you can save, your choice of investment should be guided by your financial goals and the investment's risk and return and whether it will be long-term or short-term.

In general, investments differ in risk and return. The types of risk that you should be aware of are:

- Liquidity risk—How easy/costly is it to convert the investment to cash without loss of value?
- Default risk—How likely are you to receive the promised cash flows?
- Inflation risk—Will changes in purchasing power of the dollar over time erode the value of future cash flows your investment will generate?
- Price risk—How much might your investment fluctuate in value in the short run and the long run?

In general, the riskier an investment, the higher the return it will generate to you. Therefore, even though individuals differ in their willingness to take risk, it is important to invest in assets that expose you to at least moderate risk so that you can accumulate sufficient wealth to fund your long-term goals. To illustrate this more clearly, consider a $1 investment made in 1926. If this dollar had been invested in short-term Treasury bills, at the end of 2000 it would have grown to only $16.57. If the dollar had been invested in the S&P 500 index, which includes a diversified mix of stocks, the investment would be worth $2,586 in 2000 and about the same value in 2008, almost 200 times more than an investment in Treasury bills. But this gain was not without risk. In some of those 70 years, the stock market lost money and your investment would have actually declined in value.

## Short-Term versus Long-Term Investment

Given the differences in risk exposure across investments, your investment time horizon plays an important role in choice of investment vehicle. For example, suppose you borrow $5,000 on a student loan today but the money will be needed to pay tuition six months from now. Because you cannot afford to lose *any* of this principal in the short run, your investment should be in a low-risk security such as a bank certificate of deposit. These types of accounts promise that the original $5,000 principal plus promised interest will be available to you when your tuition is due. During the bull market of the 1990s, many students were tempted to take student loans and invest in the stock market in the hopes of doubling their money (although this undoubtedly violated their lender's rules). However, in the recent bear market, this strategy might have reduced the tuition funds by 20 percent or more.

In contrast to money that you are saving for near-term goals, your retirement is likely to be many decades away, so you can afford to take more risk for greater return. The average return on stocks over the last 25 years has been around 17 percent. In contrast, the average return on long-term corporate bonds, which offer regular payments of interest to investors, has been around 10 percent. Short-term, low-risk debt securities have averaged 7 percent but are lower in 2008. The differences in investment returns between these three categories is explainable based on the difference in risk imposed on the owners. Stock is the most risky. Corporate bonds with their regular payments of interest are less risky to you since you do not have to wait until you sell your investment to get some of your return on the investment. Because they are less risky, investors expect a lower percentage return.

## Investment Choices

There are numerous possible investments, both domestic and international. The difficulty lies in deciding which ones are most appropriate for your needs and risk tolerance.

**Savings Accounts and Certificates of Deposit.**   The easiest parking spot for your cash is in a savings account. Unfortunately, investments in these low-risk (FDIC-insured), low-return accounts will barely keep up with inflation. If you have a need for liquidity but not necessarily immediate access to cash, a certificate of deposit wherein you promise to leave the money in the bank for six months or more will give you a slightly higher rate of return.

**Bonds.**   Corporations regularly borrow money from investors and issue bonds, which are securities that contain the firm's promise to pay regular interest and to repay principal at the end of the loan period, often 20 or more years in the future. These investments provide higher return to investors than short-term, interest-bearing accounts, but they also expose investors to price volatility, liquidity, and default risk.

A second group of bonds are those offered by government entities, commonly referred to as municipal bonds. These are typically issued to finance government projects, such as roads, airports, and bridges. Like corporate bonds, municipal bonds will pay interest on a regular basis, and the principal amount will be paid back to the investor at the end of a stated period of time, often 20 or more years. This type of bond has fewer interested investors and therefore has more liquidity risk.

**Stocks.**   A share of stock represents proportionate ownership interest in a business. Stockholders are thus exposed to all the risks that impact the business environment—interest rates, competition from other firms, input and output price risk, and others. In return for being willing to bear this risk, shareholders may receive dividends and/or capital appreciation in the value of their share(s). In any given year, stocks may fare better or worse than other investments, but there is substantial evidence that for long holding periods (20-plus years) stocks tend to outperform other investment choices.

**Mutual Funds.**   For the novice investor with a small amount of money to invest, the best choice is mutual funds. A mutual fund is a pool of funds from many investors that is managed by professionals who allocate the pooled dollars among various investments that meet the requirements of the mutual fund investors. There are literally thousands of these funds from which to choose, and they differ in type of investment (bonds, stocks, real estate, etc.), management style (active versus passive), and fee structure. Although even small investors have access to the market for individual securities, professional investors spend 100 percent of their time following the market and are likely to have more information at their disposal to aid in making buy and sell decisions.

**Purchase of a Home.**   For many people, one of the best investments is the purchase of a home. With a small up-front investment (your down payment) and relatively low borrowing costs, modest appreciation in the home's value can generate a large return on investment. This return benefits from the tax deductibility of home mortgage interest and capital gains tax relief at the point of sale. And to top it off, you have a place to live and thus save any additional rental costs you would incur if you invested your money elsewhere. There are many sources of information about home ownership for investors on the Internet. How much house can you afford? What mortgage can you qualify for? How much difference does investment choice make?

Everyone needs to have a place to live, and two-thirds of Americans own their own homes. Nevertheless, owning a home is not necessarily the best choice for everyone. The decision on when and how to buy a house and how much to spend must be made based on a careful examination of your ability to pay the mortgage and to cover the time and expense of maintenance and repair. A home is probably the largest purchase you will ever make in your life. It is also one of the best investments you can make. As in the example given earlier, the ability to buy with a small down payment and to deduct the cost of interest paid from your taxable income provides financial benefits that are not available with any other investment type.

Few people could afford to buy homes at young ages if they were required to pay the full purchase price on their own. Instead, it is common for people to borrow most of the money from a financial institution and pay it back over time. The process of buying a home can begin with your search for the perfect home or it can begin with a visit to your local lender, who can give you an estimate of the amount of mortgage for which you can qualify. Mortgage companies and banks have specific guidelines that help them determine your creditworthiness. These include consideration of your ability and willingness to repay the loan in a timely fashion, as well as an estimate of the value of the house that will be the basis for the loan.

A **mortgage** is a special type of loan that commonly requires that you make a constant payment over time to repay the lender the original money you borrowed (**principal**) together with **interest,** the amount that the lender charges for your use of its money. In the event that you do not make timely payments, the lender has the right to sell your property to get its money back (a process called **foreclosure**).

Mortgage interest rates in the last decade have ranged from 5 to 10 percent per year, depending on the terms and creditworthiness of the borrower. There are many variations on mortgages, some that lock in an interest rate for the full term of the loan, often 30 years, and others that allow the rate to vary with market rates of interest. In low-interest-rate economic circumstances, it makes sense to lock in the mortgage at favorable low rates.

Several measures are commonly applied to assess your *ability to repay* the loan. In addition to requiring some work history, most lenders will apply two ratio tests. First, the ratio of your total mortgage payment (including principal, interest, property taxes, and homeowners insurance) to your gross monthly income can be no more than a prespecified percentage that varies from lender to lender but is rarely greater than 28 percent. Second, the ratio of your credit payments (including credit cards, car loan or lease payments, and mortgage payment) to your gross monthly income is limited to no more than 36 percent. More restrictive lenders will have lower limits on both of these ratios.

Lenders also consider your *willingness to repay* the loan by looking at how you have managed debt obligations in the past. The primary source of information will be a credit report provided by one of the large credit reporting agencies. Late payments and defaulted loans will appear on that report and may result in denial of the mortgage loan. Most lenders, however, will overlook previously poor credit if more recent credit management shows a change in behavior. This can be helpful to college students who had trouble paying bills before they were gainfully employed.

The value of the home is important to the lender since it is the **collateral** for the loan; that is, in the event that you default on the loan (don't pay), the lender has the right to take the home in payment of the loan. To ensure that they are adequately covered, lenders will rarely lend more than 95 percent of the appraised value of the home. If you borrow more than 80 percent of the value, you will usually be required to pay a mortgage insurance premium with your regular payments. This will effectively increase the financing costs by ½ percent per year.

To illustrate the process of buying a home and qualifying for a mortgage, consider the following example. Jennifer graduated from college two years ago and has saved $7,000. She intends to use some of her savings as a down payment on a home. Her current salary is $36,000. She has a car payment of $250 per month and credit card debt that requires a minimum monthly payment of $100 per month. Suppose that Jennifer has found her dream home, which has a price of $105,000. She intends to make a down payment of $5,000 and borrow the rest. Can she qualify for the $100,000 loan at a rate of 7 percent?

Using Table D.5, her payment of principal and interest on a loan of $100,000 at 7 percent annual interest will be $665. With an additional $150 per month for property taxes and insurance (which may

**TABLE D.5   Calcualting Monthly Mortgage Payments** (30 year loan, principal and interest only)

| Annual Interest % | Amount Borrowed | | | |
|---|---|---|---|---|
| | $75,000 | $100,000 | $125,000 | $150,000 |
| 6.0 | $450 | $600 | $749 | $899 |
| 6.5 | $474 | $632 | $790 | $948 |
| 7.0 | $499 | $665 | $832 | $998 |
| 7.5 | $524 | $699 | $874 | $1,049 |
| 8.0 | $550 | $734 | $917 | $1,101 |
| 8.5 | $577 | $769 | $961 | $1,153 |
| 9.0 | $603 | $805 | $1,006 | $1,207 |
| 9.5 | $631 | $841 | $1,051 | $1,261 |
| 10.0 | $658 | $878 | $1,097 | $1,316 |

vary substantially in different areas of the country), her total payment will be $815. Since her gross monthly income is $3,000, the ratio of her payment to her income is 27 percent. Unless her lender has fairly strict rules, this should be acceptable. Her ratio of total payments to income will be ($815 + $250 + $150)/$3,000 = 40.5 percent. Unfortunately, Jennifer will not be able to qualify for this loan in her current financial circumstances.

So what can she do? The simplest solution is to use some of her remaining savings to pay off her credit card debt. By doing this, her debt ratio will drop to 35.5 percent and she will be accomplishing another element of good financial planning—reducing credit card debt and investing in assets that increase in value.

## Planning for a Comfortable Retirement

Although it may seem like it's too early to start thinking about retirement when you are still in college, this is actually the best time to do so. In the investment section of this Appendix, you learned about the power of compound interest over long periods of time. The earlier you start saving for long-term goals, the easier it will be to achieve them.

**How Much to Save.**   There is no "magic number" that will tell you how much to save. You must determine, based on budgeted income and expenses, what amount is realistic to set aside for this important goal. Several factors should help to guide this decision:

- Contributions to qualified retirement plans can be made before tax. This allows you to defer the payment of taxes until you retire many years from now.

- Earnings on retirement plan assets are tax deferred. If you have money in nonretirement vehicles, you will have to pay state and federal taxes on your earnings, which will significantly reduce your ending accumulation.

- If you need the money at some time before you reach age 59½, you will be subject to a withdrawal penalty of 10 percent, and the distribution will also be subject to taxes at the time of withdrawal.

In planning for your retirement needs, keep in mind that inflation will erode the purchasing power of your money. You should consider your ability to replace preretirement income as a measure of your success in retirement preparation. You can use the Social Security Administration Web site (**www.ssa.gov**) to estimate your future benefits from that program. In addition, most financial Web sites provide calculators to aid you in forecasting the future accumulations of your savings.

**Employer Retirement Plans.**   Many employers offer retirement plans as part of their employee benefits package. **Defined benefit plans** promise a specific benefit at retirement (for example, 60 percent of final salary). More commonly, firms offer **defined contribution plans,** where they promise to put a certain amount of money into the plan in your name every pay period. The plan may also allow you to make additional contributions or the employer may base its contribution on your contribution (for example, by matching the first 3 percent of salary that you put in). Employers also may make it possible for their employees to contribute additional amounts toward retirement on a tax-deferred basis. Many plans now allow employees to specify the investment allocation of their plan contributions and to shift account balances between different investment choices.

Some simple rules to follow with respect to employer plans include the following:

- If your employer offers you the opportunity to participate in a retirement plan, you should do so.
- If your employer offers to match your contributions, you should contribute as much as is necessary to get the maximum match, if you can afford to. Every dollar that the employer matches is like getting a 100 percent return on your investment in the first year.
- If your plan allows you to select your investment allocation, do not be too conservative in your choices if you still have many years until retirement.

**Individual Retirement Accounts (IRAs).**   Even if you do not have an employer-sponsored plan, you can contribute to retirement through an individual retirement account (IRA). There are two types of IRAs with distinctively different characteristics (which are summarized in Table D.6). Although previously subject to a $2,000 maximum annual contribution limit, tax reform in 2001 increases that limit gradually to $5,000 by 2008. The critical difference between Roth IRAs and traditional IRAs is the taxation of contributions and withdrawals. Roth IRA contributions

**TABLE D.6**   Comparing Individual Retirement Account Options

| | Roth IRA | Traditional IRA |
|---|---|---|
| 2003–2005 allowable contribution | $3,000 | $3,000 |
| Contributions deductible from current taxable income | No | Yes |
| Current tax on annual investment earnings | No | No |
| Tax due on withdrawal in retirement | No | Yes |
| 10% penalty for withdrawal before age 59½ | Yes | Yes |
| Mandatory distribution before age 70½ | No | Yes |
| Tax-free withdrawals allowed for first-time homebuyers | Yes | No |

are taxable, but the withdrawals are tax-free. Traditional IRAs are deductible, but the withdrawals are taxable. Both types impose a penalty of 10 percent for withdrawal before the qualified retirement age of 59½, subject to a few exceptions.

**Social Security.**   Social Security is a public pension plan sponsored by the federal government and paid for by payroll taxes equally split between employers and employees. In addition to funding the retirement portion of the plan, Social Security payroll taxes pay for Medicare insurance (an old-age health program), disability insurance, and survivors benefits for the families of those who die prematurely.

The aging of the U.S. population has created a problem for funding the current Social Security system. Whereas it has traditionally been a pay-as-you-go program, with current payroll taxes going out to pay current retiree benefits, the impending retirement of baby boomers is forecast to bankrupt the system early in this century if changes are not made in a timely fashion. To understand the problem, consider that when Social Security began, there were 17 workers for each retiree receiving benefits. There are currently fewer than four workers per beneficiary. After the baby boom retirement, there will be only two workers to pay for each retiree. Obviously, that equation cannot work.

Does that mean that Social Security will not be around when you retire? Contrary to popular belief, it is unlikely that this will happen. There are simply too many voters relying on the future of Social Security for Congress to ever take such a drastic action. Instead, it is likely that the current system will be revised to help it balance. Prior to the heavy declines in the stock market in 2001, there was some general support for a plan that would divert some of the current payroll taxes to fund individual retirement accounts that could be invested in market assets. In addition, it seems likely that the retirement age will increase gradually to age 67. Other possible changes are to increase payroll taxes or to limit benefits payable to wealthier individuals. The proposed solutions are all complicated by the necessity of providing a transition program for those who are too old to save significant additional amounts toward their retirement. Figure D.2 indicates that most people are saving more because they are concerned about the future of Social Security.

# Evaluate and Purchase Insurance

The next step in personal financial planning is the evaluation and purchase of insurance. Insurance policies are contracts between you and an insurance company wherein the insurer promises to pay you money in the event that a particular event occurs. Insurance is important, not only to protect your own assets from claims but also to protect your loved ones and dependents. The most common types of insurance for individuals are identified and briefly described below.

## Automobile Insurance
In most states, drivers are required by law to carry a minimum amount of **auto liability insurance.** In the event that you are in a car accident, this coverage promises to pay claims against you for injuries to persons or property, up to a maximum per person and per accident. The basic liability policy will also cover your own medical costs. If you want to insure against damage to your own vehicle, you must purchase an additional type of coverage called **auto physical damage insurance.** If you have a car loan, the lender will require that you carry this type of insurance, since the value of the car is the collateral for that loan and the lender wants to be sure that you can afford to fix any damage to the vehicle following

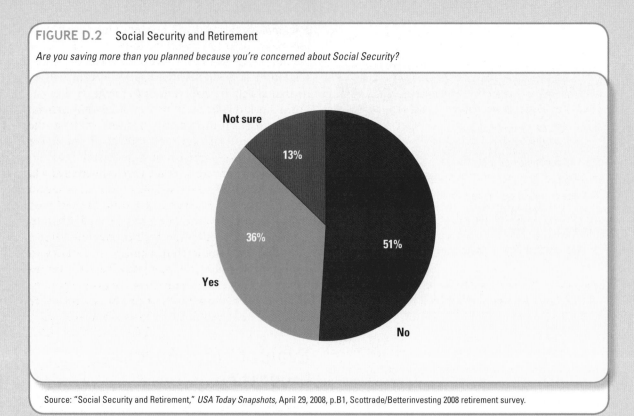

**FIGURE D.2**   Social Security and Retirement

*Are you saving more than you planned because you're concerned about Social Security?*

Not sure 13%

Yes 36%

No 51%

Source: "Social Security and Retirement," *USA Today Snapshots*, April 29, 2008, p.B1, Scottrade/Betterinvesting 2008 retirement survey.

an accident. The minimum limits in most states are too low to cover typical claim levels. Good financial planning requires that you pay for insurance coverage with much higher limits.

Auto physical damage insurance coverage is always subject to a **deductible.** A deductible is an amount that you must pay before the insurance company will pay. To illustrate this, suppose your policy has a $250 deductible. You back into your garage door and damage your bumper, which will cost $750 to fix. The insurer will only pay $500, because you are responsible for the first $250. Once you receive the check from the insurer, you are free to try to get it fixed for less than the full $750.

## Homeowners/Renters Insurance

**Homeowners insurance** provides coverage for liability and property damage in your home. For example, if someone slips and falls on your front steps and sues you for medical expenses, this insurance policy will pay the claim (or defend you against the claim if the insurer thinks it is not justified). If your house and/or property are damaged in a fire, the insurance

will pay for lost property and the costs of repair. It is a good idea to pay extra for replacement cost insurance, since otherwise the insurance company is only obligated to pay you the depreciated value, which won't be enough to replace your belongings.

**Renters insurance** is similar to homeowners in that it covers you for liability on your premises (for example, if your dog bites someone) and for damage to your personal property. Because you do not own the house, your landlord needs to carry separate insurance for his building. This insurance is very cheap and is well worth the cost, since your landlord's insurance will not pay anything to you in the event that the house burns down and you lose all your belongings.

## Life Insurance

As compared to other types of insurance, the primary purpose of life insurance is to provide protection for others. **Life insurance** pays a benefit to your designated beneficiary (usually your spouse or other family members) in the event that you die during the coverage period. Life insurance premiums will depend on the face amount of the policy, your age and health, your habits (smoker versus nonsmoker), and the type of policy (whether it includes an investment component in addition to the death benefit).

The simplest type of life insurance is **term insurance.** This policy is usually for one year and the insurer promises to pay your designated beneficiary only the face amount of the policy in the event that you die during the year of coverage. Because the probability of dying at a young age is very small, the cost of providing this promise to people in their 20s and 30s is very inexpensive, and premiums are fairly low. Term insurance becomes more expensive at older ages, since the probability of dying is much higher and insurers must charge more.

Other types of life insurance usually fall into a category often called **permanent insurance,** because they are designed to provide you with insurance protection over your lifetime. To provide lifetime coverage at a reasonable cost, premiums will include an investment component. While there are many variations, typically in the early years of the policy you are paying a lot more than the actual cost of providing the death protection. The insurer takes that extra cost and invests it so that when you are older, the company has sufficient funds to cover your death risk. The primary difference between different types of permanent insurance is the way that they treat the investment component. Some policies allow the buyer to direct the investment choice and others do not.

### Health Insurance

**Health insurance** pays the cost of covered medical expenses during the policy period, which is usually six months or one year. Most health insurance is provided under group policies through employers, but it is possible to purchase an individual policy. Because those who want to buy individual insurance are likely to be people who anticipate medical expenses, individual policies can be very expensive and are usually subject to exclusions, high coinsurance (the percentage of each dollar of expenses that you must pay out of pocket), and deductibles (the amount you must pay in full before the insurance pays).

From a financial-planning perspective, the type of health coverage that is most important is that which will protect you and your family from unexpected large medical costs. The usual checkups, shots, and prescription drugs are all budgetable expenses so

need not be insured. At a minimum, you should have a policy that covers hospitalization and care for major disease or injury. This can be accomplished at relatively low cost by contracting for a large deductible (e.g., you pay the first $1,000 of costs per year).

The two main types of health insurance plans are *fee-for-service* and *managed care.* In a fee-for-service arrangement, the insurer simply pays for whatever covered medical costs you incur, subject to the deductible and coinsurance. Blue Cross and Blue Shield plans are the best known of this type. Managed care includes health maintenance organizations (HMOs) and preferred provider organizations (PPOs). In these health insurance arrangements, your health insurer pays all your costs (subject sometimes to small co-pays for office visits), but the care you receive is determined by your physician, who has contracted with the health insurer and has incentives to control overall costs. You are often limited in your choice of physician and your ability to seek specialist care under these plans.

### Disability Insurance

One of the most overlooked types of insurance is **disability insurance,** which pays replacement income to you in the event you are disabled under the definition in your policy. One in three people will be disabled for a period of three months or more during their lifetime, so disability insurance should be a component of the financial plan for anyone without sufficient financial resources to weather a period of loss of income.

# Develop an Estate Plan

As with retirement planning, it is difficult to think about estate planning when you are young. In fact, you probably don't need to think much about it yet. If you have no dependents, there is little point in doing so. However, if you are married or have other dependents, you should include this as a necessary part of your financial plan. The essential components of an **estate plan** are

- Your will, including a plan for guardianship of your children.
- Minimization of taxes on your estate.
- Protection of estate assets.

Estate planning is a complicated subject that is mired in legal issues. As such, appropriate design and implementation of an estate plan requires the assistance of a qualified professional.

## The Importance of Having a Will

There are several circumstances that necessitate having a will. If you have a spouse and/or dependent children, if you have substantial assets, or if you have specific assets that you would like to give to certain individuals in the event of your death, you *should* have a will. On the other hand, if you are single with no assets or obligations (like many students), a will is probably not necessary—yet.

Having a valid will makes the estate settlement simpler for your spouse. If your children are left parentless, will provisions specify who will take guardianship of the children and direct funds for their support. You might also like to include a *living* *will*, which gives your family directions for whether to keep you on life support in the event that an illness or injury makes it unlikely for you to survive without extraordinary interventions. Lastly, you may want to make a will so that you can give your CD collection to your college roommate or Grandma's china to your daughter. Absent such provisions, relatives and friends have been known to take whatever they want without regard to your specific desires.

## Avoiding Estate Taxes

As students, it will likely be many years before you will have accumulated a large enough estate (all your "worldly possessions") to have to worry about estate taxes. Although recent tax law changes have effectively eliminated the estate tax through 2009, the law includes a provision that reinstates current tax laws

---

## Gender Differences Create Special Financial Planning Concerns

Although most people would agree that there are some essential differences between men and women, it is not as clear why their financial planning needs should be different. After all, people of both sexes need to invest for future financial goals like college educations for their children and retirement income for themselves. In the last few years, professionals have written articles considering this subject. The results are both controversial and eye-opening.

- Even though 75 percent of women in the United States are working, they still have greater responsibility for household chores, child care, and care of aging parents than their husbands. This leaves less time for household finances.
- Women still earn much less than men, on average.
- Women are much less likely to have a pension sponsored through their employer. Only one-third of all working women have one at their current employer.
- Women are more conservative investors than men. Although there is evidence that women are gradually getting smart about taking a little more risk in their portfolios, on average they allocate half as much as men do to stocks.
- Most women will someday be on their own, either divorced or widowed.

Because women live an average of five years longer than men, they actually need to have saved more to provide a comparable retirement income. The combined impact of these research findings makes it difficult but not impossible for women to save adequately for retirement. Much of the problem lies in education. Women need to be better informed about investing in order to make choices early in life that will pay off in the end. If they don't take the time to become informed about their finances or can't due to other obligations, in the end they will join the ranks of many women over age 65 who are living in poverty. But when women earn less, they don't have access to an employer pension, and they invest too conservatively, it is no surprise that women have so little wealth accumulation.

In her book, *The Busy Woman's Guide to Financial Freedom,* Dr. Vickie Bajtelsmit, an associate professor at Colorado State University, provides a road map for women who are interested in taking charge of their financial future. With simple-to-follow instructions for all aspects of financial planning, from investing to insurance to home buying, the book provides information for women to get on the right financial track.

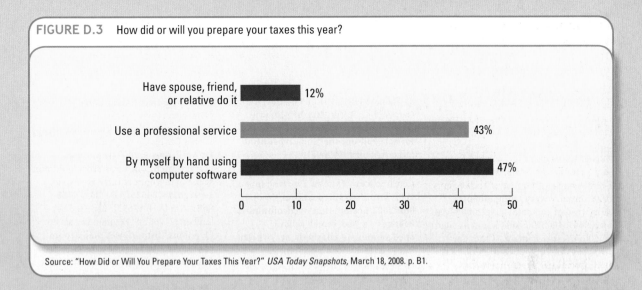

FIGURE D.3    How did or will you prepare your taxes this year?

Source: "How Did or Will You Prepare Your Taxes This Year?" *USA Today Snapshots,* March 18, 2008. p. B1.

in 2010. Because no one can predict the date of his or her death, this implies that estate tax planning should be done assuming the worst-case scenario. Current estate taxes can take a big bite (more than half) out of your family's inheritance for wealthy taxpayers. Thus, much of estate planning is actually tax-avoidance planning. Professionals can help set up trust arrangements that allow all or part of your estate to pass to your heirs without incurring taxes.

## Adjust Your Financial Plan to New Circumstances

Finally, to ensure the success of your overall financial plan, it is vital that you evaluate it on a periodic basis and adjust it to accommodate changes in your life, such as marriage, children, or the addition or deletion of a second income from your spouse. You may be preparing income tax returns now, but as your income increases you may have to make a decision about professional assistance. Figure D.3 indicates that most people prepare their own taxes, but many taxpayers use a professional service. Your plan also must be adjusted as your financial goals change (for example, desires to own a home, make a large purchase, or retire at an early age). Whatever your goals may be, the information and worksheets provided here will help with your personal financial planning.

# Notes

## CHAPTER I

1. Diane Anderson, "When Crocs Attack," *Business 2.0,* November 2006, pp. 51–53; Crocs 2006 Annual Report; Jennifer Huget, "Not Such a Croc, Might a Fad Shoe's Health Claims Stand?" *Special to The Washington Post,* August 1, 2006, pp. HE01, **http://www.washingtonpost .com/wp-dyn/content/article/2006/07/31/ AR2006073100890.html** (accessed August 17, 2007); Jessica Packard, "Crocs, Inc. Launches Unique Footwear Line for Fashion Conscious Women," *You by Crocs™ Press Release,* **http://www.youbycrocs. com** (accessed August 17, 2007); Peter Case, "Crocs, Inc. Enters Into Definitive Agreement to Acquire Bite Footwear," *Crocs Press Release,* July 30, 2007, **http://www.crocs.com/company/press** (accessed August 17, 2007).

2. "HP Recycles Nearly 250 Million Pounds of Products in 2007—50 Percent Increase Over 2006," February 5, 2008, **http://www.hp.com/hpinfo/newsroom/ press/2008/080205a.html** (accessed March 17, 2008).

3. Staff Writer, "Old TVs Bad Landfill Reception," *The Baltimore Sun,* December 24, 2007, **http://www.terradaily.com/reports/ Old_TVs_bad_landfill_reception_999 .html** (accessed April 17, 2008).

4. **www.cummins.com;** "Community Involvement Teams," Cummins Diesel, South Africa CIT, **www.cummins.com/ cmi/content.jsp?siteId=1&langId=1033 &menuId=82&overviewId=5&anchorId =393&index=2&menuIndex=0** (accessed May 31, 2006).

5. "Diversity Pipeline Alliance," **http:// www.diversitypipeline.org/public/ publicpage.asp?WCE=C=32|K=S221485** (accessed April 17, 2008).

6. "U-Haul Lends a Helping Hand to Arkansas Tornado and Flood Victims, With 30 Days of Free Storage," *News Release U-Haul International, Inc.* **http:// www.primenewswire.com/newsroom/ news.html?d=139560** (accessed April 17, 2008).

7. Liz Clarke, "While Nascar Takes Stock, Racing's Popularity Wanes," *The Washington Post,* November 4, 2007, p. D3.

8. Elaine Appleton, "Roll Out the Fine Carpet," *Inc.,* April, 2008. **http://www. inc.com/magazine/20080401/business- for-sale-roll-out-the-fine-carpet.html** (accessed April 17, 2008).

9. Elizabeth M. Whelan, "Kellogg's: A Sad Cereal Sellout," *The New York Post,* June 17, 2007. **http://www.nypost.com/seven/ 06172007/postopinion/opedcolumnists/ kelloggs__a_sad_cereal_sellout_ opedcolumnists_elizabeth_m__whelan .htm** (accessed April 17, 2008).

10. "Health and Wellness" (n.d.), **www. fritolay.com/fl/flstore/cgi-bin/health_ wellness.htm?** (accessed June 1, 2006).

11. **http://www.whymilk.com/celeb.php** (accessed March 29, 2008).

12. Toddi Guttner, "In the Venture Drought, an Oasis," *BusinessWeek,* July 16, 2001, pp. 86E2, 86E4.

13. "About Bill Daniels" **http://www. danielsfund.org/BillDaniels/index.asp** (accessed April 23, 2008).

14. James T. Areddy and Craig Karmin, "China Stocks Once Frothy, Fall By Half in Six Months," *The Wall Street Journal,* April 16, 2008, pp. 1, 7.

15. "Reforms Please Cubans, But is it Communism?" *Associated Press,* April 2, 2008, **http://www.msnbc.msn.com/ id/23925259** (accessed April 18, 2008).

16. "Survey: Gas Prices Skyrocket to All-time High," *CNN.com,* March 23, 2008. **http://www.cnn.com/2008/US/03/23/gas. prices** (accessed March 29, 2008).

17. Greg Farrell and Noelle Knox, "Record: 1 Million Homes in Foreclosure," *USA Today,* March 7, 2008, p. B1.

18. "Focused on Serving Customers," *Home Depot Annual Report 2006,* pp. A4–A7 **http://ir.homedepot.com/downloads/ HD_2006_AR.pdf** (accessed October 4, 2007); "What's Changed? Everything and Nothing," *Lowe's Annual Report 2006,* pp. b–d, 3–4, 7–8, **http://images.lowes.com/ animate/Lowes2006AnnualReport.pdf** (accessed October 4, 2007); "All About Us," "Did You Know?," **http://corporate. homedepot.com/wps/portal/!ut/p/.cmd/ cs/.ce/7_0_A/.s/7_0_113/_s.7_0_A/7_ 0_113** (accessed October 4, 2007); Mary Ellen Lloyd, "Lowe's Popularity Can't Beat Home Depot's Locations—Survey," *Dow Jones Newswires,* September 5, 2007; Jennifer Waters, "Home Depot, Lowe's Facing Up to Challenges," *MarketWatch,* July 9, 2007 **http://www. marketwatch.com/news/story/goldman- sees-buying-opportunity-rivals/story. aspx?guid={84525FAB-C31A-4368- 86B9-1254A5BA7652}** (accessed September 27, 2007); "Frequently Asked Questions," **http://lowes.mediaroom. com/index.php?s=faqs** (accessed October 4, 2007); "Battle for the Wallets of American Homeowners: The Home Depot vs. Lowe's" **http://www. retailforward.com/Marketing/ BattlefortheWallets_ReportOverview .pdf** (accessed September 27, 2007).

19. "U.S. Patent Statistics Chart Calendar Years 1963–2006," **http://www.uspto. gov/go/taf/us_stat.htm** (accessed March 17, 2008).

20. "Zimbabwe inflation hits 100,000%," *BBC.com,* February 20, 2008, **http://news. bbc.co.uk/2/hi/business/7255588.stm** (accessed March 29, 2008).

21. "Debt to the penny and who holds it," *Treasury Direct,* March 27, 2008, **http://www.treasurydirect.gov/NP/ BPDLogin?application=np** (accessed March 29, 2008).

22. Preston Lerner, "The Future is Now," *Automobilemag.com,* March 2008, pp. 46–52; Kim Reynolds, "First Drive: 2008 Tesla Roadster," *Motor Trend,* 2008, **www.motortrend.com/roadtests/ alternative/112_0803_2008_tesla_ roadster** (accessed February 22, 2008); Mike Adams, "Review: Tesla Motors Pioneers All-Electric Performance Sports Car," *Flixya.com,* March 23, 2007, **http:// www.flixya.com/post/tavatchaibt/10020/ Tesla_Motors_pioneers_all-electric_ performance** (accessed February 18, 2008); "Electric Power," Tesla Motors, **www. teslamotors.com/performance/electric_ power.php** (accessed February 22, 2008).

23. "Women in the Labor Force, 1900–2002," *InfoPlease* (n.d.), **www. infoplease.com/ipa/A0104673.html** (accessed March 9, 2004).

24. **http://tacochicsalsa.com/html/ history.htm** (accessed April 19, 2008).

25. "About the Hershey Co.," **www. thehersheycompany.com** (accessed April 19, 2008).

26. Tom McNichol, "Building a Wiki World," *Business 2.0,* March 2007, pp. 102–108; Jonathan Dee, "All the News That's Fit to Print Out," *The New York Times,* July 1, 2007, **http://www. nytimes.com/2007/07/01/magazine/ 01WIKIPEDIA-t.html?ex=1189828800 &en=b2e607ab370a06f8&ei=5070** (accessed September 13, 2007); Daniel Terdiman, "Growing Pains for Wikipedia," *News.com,* December 7, 2005, **http:// www.news.com/2102-1025_3-5981119 .html?tag=st.util.print** (accessed September 13, 2007).

27. Anthony Bianco and Wendy Zellner, "Is Wal-Mart Too Powerful?" *Business-Week,* October 6, 2003, pp. 100–10. Hoover's Guide to Business (n.d.), **www. hooverscom/wal-mart/--ID-11600--/ free-co-factsheet.xhtm/** (accessed June 2, 2006), **www.walmartfacts.com** (accessed April 9, 2008).

28. Karen Richardson, Liam Plevin and Amir Efrati, "Jury Convicts Five of Fraud in Gen Re, AIG Case," *The Wall Street Journal,* February 26, 2008, **http://online.wsj.com/article_print/ SB120396729370091225.html** (accessed April 19, 2008).

29. Dennis Schaal, "100 Best Corporate Citizens 2008," *The CRO,* http://www. thecro.com/node/615 (accessed April 4, 2008).

30. 2003 National Business Ethics Survey (n.d.), **www.ethics.org/nbes/2003/ 1003nbes_summary.html** (accessed January 6, 2004). "2007 National Business Ethics Survey: An Inside View of Private Sector Ethics," *Ethics Resources Center,* 2007.

31. Lindsey Gerdes (2008) "Where Undergrads Dream of Working," Business Week Online, May 23, **http://www. businessweek.com/managing/content/ may2008/ca20080523_988667.htm? chan=search,** (accessed June 19, 2008).

32. "New Belgium Gets 'Best Place To Work' Honors," *cbs4denver.com,* April 17, 2008, **http://cbs4denver.com/seenon/ New.Belgium.Brewing.2.702603.html** (accessed June 10, 2008); "Our Story," **www.newbelgium.com** (accessed June 20, 2008); "Ownership," **www.newbelgium .com** (accessed June 20, 2008); "Sustainability," **www.newbelgium.com**

(accessed June 20, 2008); Cari Merrill, "New Belgium Goes Aluminum," *The Fort Collins Coloradoan,* March 13, 2008, **http://www.coloradoan.com/apps/pbcs. dll/article?AID=/20080313/BUSINESS/ 803130397/1046/CUSTOMERSERVICE02** (accessed June 20, 2008).

## CHAPTER 2

1. "About Ethisphere," *Ethisphere,* **http:// ethisphere.com/about** (accessed April 21, 2008); Greg Allan, "50 Codes of Conduct Benchmarked: How Does Your Organization Stack Up?," **http://ethisphere.com/50-codes-of-conduct-benchmarked-q1-2008** (accessed March 27, 2008); Sean M. Connolly and Dorn C. McGrath, "Governmental Contractor Ethics 2008 Ratings," *Ethisphere,* Quarter 1, 2008; Staff writer, "2007 World's Most Ethical Companies," *Ethisphere,* **http://ethisphere.com/2007-worlds-most-ethical-companies** (accessed March 17, 2008); Cathy Planchard, "World's Most Ethical Companies Ranking Issued by Ethisphere Magazine," *The Corporate Social Responsibility Newswire,* May 08, 2007, **http://csrwire.com/News/ 8413.htmlis** (accessed March 26, 2008).

2. Greg Farrell, "Lay, Skilling Found Guilty," *USA Today,* May 26, 2006, pp. A1, B1; *The New York Times* coverage of the Enron trial, **www.nytimes.com/business/ businessspecial3/index.html?adxnnl=1 &adxnnlx=1147986237-z56Vd16RUkp-6eHnHTTXBHw** (accessed May 18, 2006).

3. Doreen Carvajal, "Worried for the Littlest Callers," *The New York Times,* March 8, 2008, p. B1.

4. Ronald Alsop, "Corporate Scandals Hit Home," *The Wall Street Journal,* February 18, 2004, **http://online.wsj.com.**

5. Carrie Johnson, "Jury Acquits Health-South Founder of All Charges," June 29, 2005, p. A01, **www.washingtonpost. com/wp-dyn/content/article/2005/06/28/ AR2005062800560.html** (accessed June 2, 2006).

6. O. C. Ferrell, John Fraedrich, Linda Ferrell, *Business Ethics: Ethical Decision Making and Cases,* 6th ed. (Boston: Houghton Mifflin, 2005), p. 7.

7. David Callahan, as quoted in Archie Carroll, "Carroll: Do We Live in a Cheating Culture?" *Athens Banner-Herald,* February 21, 2004, **www.onlineathens.com/ stores/022204/bus_20040222028.shtml.**

8. Mike Esterl, "In Germany, Scandals Tarnish Business Elite," *The Wall Street Journal,* March 4, 2008, p. A1.

9. Jenny Anderson, "3 Executives Under Fire on Exit Pay," *The New York Times,* March 8, 2008, pp. B1, B4.

10. John Lyman, "Who Is Scooter Libby? The Guy Behind the Guy," *Center for American Progress.* October 28, 2005; Amy Goldstein, "Bush Commutes Libby's Prison Sentence," *The Washington Post,* July 3, 2007, **http://www.washingtonpost. com/wp-dyn/content/article/2007/07/02/ AR2007070200825.html** (accessed April 15, 2008).

11. Laurie P. Cohen and Amir Efrati, "Spitzer Engulfed in Sex Scandal," *The Wall Street Journal,* March 11, 2008, p. A1.

12. "Colorado Places Barnett on Administrative Leave," *SI.com,* February 19, 2004, **http://sportsillustrated.cnn.com/.**

13. Mark Long, "Jimmy Johnson's Crew Chief Thrown Out of Daytona 500," Star-Tribune.com, February 13, 2006, **www. startribune.com/694/story/244568.html.**

14. Ferrell, Fraedrich, Ferrell, *Business Ethics.*

15. Bobby White, "The New Workplace Rules: No Video Watching," *The New York Times,* March 3, 2008, p. B1.

16. "National Business Ethics Survey 2005," "Survey Documents State of Ethics in the Workplace," and "Misconduct" Ethics Resource Center (n.d.), **www.ethics .org/nbes/2005/release.html** (accessed April 11, 2006); Staff writer, "National Business Ethics Survey 2007: An Inside View of Private Sector Ethics," *Ethics Resource Center,* http://www.ethics.org (accessed April 4, 2008).

17. Stop Workplace Bullying!, **http:// www.bullyfreeworkplace.org.**

18. Peter Lattman, "Boeing's Top Lawyer Spotlights Company's Ethical Lapses," *The Wall Street Journal,* Law Blog., January 30, 2006, **blogs.wsj.com/law/2006/01/31/ boeings-top-lawyer-rips-into-his-company** (accessed March 31, 2006).

19. Janet Guyon, "Jack Grubman Is Back. Just Ask Him," *Fortune,* May 16, 2005. pp. 119–26.

20. "Three Ex-IBM Korea Officials Are Sentenced," *The Wall Street Journal,* February 18, 2004, **http://online.wsj.com.**

21. "Transparency International 2007 Corruption Perceptions Index," Transparency International, **http:// transparency.org/policy_research/ surveys_indices/cpi/2007** (accessed April 4, 2008).

22. "Pens and Post-Its Among Most Pilfered Office Supplies, Says New Vault Survey," November 16, 2005. (**www.vault.com/nr/newsmain.jsp?nr_page=3&ch_id=420&article_id=25720773** (accessed June 2, 2006).

23. David Whelan, "Only the Paranoid Resurge," *Forbes,* April 10, 2006.

24. Yuri Kageyama, "Mitsubishi Motors Says Massive Defect Cover-ups Were Intentional," *Boston Globe,* August 22, 2000, **www.boston.com;** "Mitsubishi Cover-up May Bring Charges," *Detroit News,* August 23, 2000, **www.det-news.com/2000/autos/0008/23/b03-109584.htm.**

25. Michael Josephson. "The Biennial Report Card: The Ethics of American Youth." Josephson Institute of Ethics, press release, **www.josephsoninstitute.org/survey2004/** (accessed August 11, 2005).

26. "Teens Respect Good Business Ethics." *USA Today,* Snapshots, December 12, 2005, p. 13–1.

27. Marianne Jennings, "An Ethical Breach by Any Other Name. . .," *Financial Engineering News.* January/February 2006.

28. "The 'Skinny Pills' Do Not Make You Skinny, Says the FTC," Federal Trade Commission, press release, February 4, 2004, **www.ftc.gov/opa/2004/02/skinnypill.htm.**

29. "Campaign Warns about Drugs from Canada," *CNN,* February 5, 2004, **www.cnn.com;** Gardiner Harris and Monica Davey, "FDA Begins Push to End Drug Imports," *The New York Times,* January 23, 2004, p. C1.

30. Bruce Horovitz, Greg Farrell, and Sharon Silke Carty, "Mattel's stellar reputation tainted," *USA Today,* August 14, 2007, **http://www.usetoday.com/money/world/2007-08-14-mattel-toy-recall_N.htm** (accessed April 7, 2008); Mattel/Fischer-Price Recall Information, "Voluntary Safety Recall Facts," 2008, **http://www.mattel.com/safety/us** (accessed April 7, 2008); Parija B. Kavilanz, "China to eliminate lead paint in toy exports," *CNN Money,* September 11, 2007, **http://money.conn.com/2007/09/11/news/economy/cpsc_chinasafety/index.htm?postversion=2007091111** (accessed April 7. 2008); Staff writer, "Mattel CEO: 'Rigorous Standards' after Massive Toy Recall," *CNN,* August 14, 2007, **http://cnn.com/2007/US/08/14/recall/index.html** (accessed April 7, 2008); Mindy Fetterman, Greg Farrell, and Laura Petrecca,

"Recall of More China-Made Toys Unnerves Parents," *USA Today,* August 3, 2007, pp. 1B, 3B.

31. "Briefing: Tobacco Packaging and Labelling," Information Resource Center, **http://infolink.cancerresearchuk.org/publicpolicy/briefings/prevention/tobacco.** Accessed July 31, 2006.

32. 2005 National Business Ethics Survey (Washington D.C.: Ethics Resource Center, 2005), p. 43.

33. Susan Pullman, "Ordered to Commit Fraud, A Staffer Balked, Then Caved," *The Wall Street Journal,* June 23, 2003, **http://online.wsj.com.**

34. Blake Morrison, "Ex-USA Today Reporter Faked Major Stories," *USA Today,* March 19, 2004, **www.usatoday.com/.**

35. Thomas M. Jones, "Ethical Decision Making by Individuals in Organizations: An Issue-Contingent Model," *Academy of Management Review* 2 (April 1991), pp. 371–73.

36. Sir Adrian Cadbury, "Ethical Managers Make Their Own Rules," *Harvard Business Review* 65 (September–October 1987), p. 72.

37. Ferrell, Fraedrich, and Ferrell, pp. 174–75.

38. "The 2007 National Business Ethics Survey," **http://www.ethics.org** (accessed April 30, 2008).

39. "The 2007 National Business Ethics Survey."

40. Richard Lacavo and Amanda Ripley, "Persons of the Year 2002—Cynthia Cooper, Coleen Rowley, and Sherron Watkins," *Time,* December 22, 2002, **www.time.com/personofth-year/2002.**

41. Ferrell, Fraedrich, and Ferrell, p. 13.

42. John Galvin, "The New Business Ethics," *SmartBusinessMag.com,* June 2000, p. 99.

43. Archie B. Carroll, "The Pyramid of Corporate Social Responsibility: Toward the Moral Management of Organizational Stakeholders," *Business Horizons* 34 (July/August 1991), p. 42.

44. Bryan Walsh, "Why Green Is the New Red, White and Blue," *Time,* April 28, 2008, p. 46.

45. Walsh, p. 46.

46. Walsh, p. 54.

47. Alan Beattie, "Countries Rush to Restrict Trade in Basic Foods," *Financial Times,* April 2, 2008, p. 1.

48. Laura Petrecca, "Marketing Efforts May End up in a Green Blur," *USA Today,* April 22, 2008, 10B.

49. Alexandra Zendrian, "Workers: Employers Not Green Enough," *Inc.,* April 17, 2008, **http://www.inc.com/news/articles,2008/04/green.html.**

50. Indra Nooyi, "The Responsible Company," *The Economist, The World in 2008 Special Edition,* March 2008, p. 132.

51. Ferrell, Fraedrich, and Ferrell, pp. 13–19.

52. Rachel Emma Silverman, "On-the-Job Cursing: Obscene Talk Is Latest Target of Workplace Ban," *The Wall Street Journal,* May 8, 2001, p. B12.

53. Jennifer Alsever, "Wind Power: the Home Edition," *Business 2.0,* January/February 2007, **http://wwwindenergy.com/index_wind.htm** (accessed February 1, 2008); Skystream 3.7 product information, **http://www.skystreamenergy.com/skystream/product-info** (accessed February 1, 2008); Skystream 3.7 fact sheet, **http://www.skystreamenergy.com/documents/datasheet/skystrea_%203.7t_datasheet.pdf** (accessed February 1, 2008).

54. Wendy Zellner, "No Way to Treat a Lady?" *BusinessWeek,* March 3, 2003, pp. 63–66.

55. Chad Terhune, "Jury Says Home Depot Must Pay Customer Hurt by Falling Merchandise $1.5 Million," *The Wall Street Journal,* July 16, 2001, p. A14.

56. Laura Judy, "Green from the Ground Up," *Atlanta Home Improvement,* January 2006, **www.homeimprovementmag.com/Articles/2006/06Jan_ground_up.html** (accessed June 15, 2007); Earthcraft House, **www.earthcrafthouse.com** (accessed October 5, 2007); "Earthcraft House Program," "Green Fast Facts: Did You Know. . .," **www.atlantahomebuilders.com/education/earthcraft.cfm** (accessed October 5, 2007); Melanie Lindner, "Living Green" EarthCraft House," *Atlanta Intown Newspaper,* January 2007, **www.atlantaintownpaper.com/features/EarthCraftHouseJAN07.php** (accessed October 5, 2007).

57. Laura Judy, "Green from the Ground Up," *Atlanta Home Improvement,* January 2006, **www.homeimprovementmag.com/Articles/2006/06Jan_ground_up.html** (accessed June 15, 2007); Earthcraft House, **www.earthcrafthouse.com** (accessed October 5, 2007); "Earthcraft House Program," "Green Fast Facts: Did You Know…," **www.atlantahomebuilders.**

com/education/earthcraft.cfm (accessed October 5, 2007); "Living Green" Earth-Craft House," Melanie Lindner, Atlanta Intown Newspaper, January 2007, **www.atlantaintownpaper.com/features/EarthCraftHouseJAN07.php** (accessed October 5, 2007).

58. Lauren Etter, "Earth Day: 36 Years on, Plenty of Concerns Remain," *The Wall Street Journal,* April 22–23, 2006, p. A7.

59. Cornelia Dean, "Drugs Are in the Water, Does It Matter?," *The New York Times,* April 3, 2007, HEALTH, **http://www.nytimes.com/2007/04/03/science/earth/03water.html?_r=1&scp=55&sq=%22cornelia+dean%22&st=nyt&oref=slogin** (accessed April 30, 2008).

60. Michael Grunwald, "The Clean Energy Scam," *Time,* April 7, 2008, **http://www.time.com/time/magazine/article/0,9171,1725975,00.html** (accessed April 30, 2008).

61. Lauren Etter, "Earth Day: 36 Years on, Plenty of Concerns Remain," *The Wall Street Journal,* April 22–23, 2006, p. A7.

62. Staff writer, "Diamant Corporation Furthers National Consumer Awareness Efforts as British Prime Minister Gordon Brown Announces Tougher Measures to Drastically Reduce the Society's Dependence on Single-Use Plastic Bags," *CNN Money,* March 25, 2008, **http://money.cnn.com/news/newsfeeds/articles/marketwire/0379140.htm** (accessed March 25, 2008).

63. Matthew Knight, "Plastic Bags Fly into Environmental Storm," *CNN.com,* March 17, 2008, **http://edition.cnn.com/2007/TECH/11/14/fsummit.climate.plasticbags/index.html** (accessed March 17, 2008)

64. Staff writer, "Whole Foods to Sack Disposable Plastic Grocery Bags," January 22, 2008, **http://www.wholefoodsmarket.com/cgi-bim/print10pt.cgi?url=/pressroom/pr_01-22-08.html** (accessed March 17, 2008).

65. Alan K. Reichert, Marion S. Webb, and Edward G. Thomas, "Corporate Support for Ethical and Environmental Policies: A Financial Management Perspective," *Journal of Business Ethics* 25 (2000), pp. 53–64.

66. EPA Newsroom, "Fifty-Three Fortune 500 Corporations Surpass EPA Green Power Goals," January 28, 2008, **http://yosemite.epa.gov/opa/admpress.nsf/a883dc3da7094f97852572a00065d7d8/**

6c85f7cb2c4e0380852573de005d3732!OpenDocument** (accessed April 30, 2008).

67. "Trend Watch," *Business Ethics,* March/April 2001, p. 8.

68. David & Lynch "Corporate American Warms to Fight Against Global Warming," *USA Today,* June 1, 2006, p. B1.

69. Jim Rogers, "Point of View: A New Model for Energy Efficiency," The News & Observer, February 19. 2008, http://**www.newsobserver.com/print/tuesday/opinion/story/951188.html** (accessed March 26, 2008).

70. Daniel Fischer, "A Dirty Game," *Forbes,* March 10, 2008; *The Dictionary of Sustainable Management,* "Greenwashing," **http://www.sustainabilitydictionary.com/g/greenwashing.php** (accessed March 26, 2008).

71. "GreenChoice: The #1 Green Power Program in America," Austin Energy (n.d.), **www.austinenergy.com/Energy%20Efficiency/Programs/Green%20Choice/index.htm** (accessed February 24, 2004).

72. "Certification," Home Depot (n.d.), **www.homedepot.com/HDUS/EN_US/corporate/corp_respon/certification.shtml** (accessed April 6, 2004).

73. "Yes, We Have No Bananas: Rainforest Alliance Certifies Chiquita Bananas," *AgJournal* (n.d.), **www.agjournal.com/story.cfm?story_id_1047** (accessed April 6, 2004).

74. "Charity Holds Its Own in Tough Times (Giving USA 2003: The Annual Report on Philanthropy for the Year 2002)," American Association of Fundraising Council, press release, June 2003, **http://aafrc.org/press_releases/trustreleases/charityholds.html**.

75. Mark Calvey, "Profile: Safeway's Grants Reflect Its People," *San Francisco Business Times,* July 14, 2003, **http://sanfrancisco.bizjournals.com/sanfrancisco/stories/2003/07/14/focus9.html**.

76. "About Avon," Avon (n.d.), **www.avoncompany.com/about/** (accessed February 25, 2004; "The Avon Breast Cancer Crusade," Avon (n.d.), **www.avoncompany.com/women/avoncrusade/** (accessed February 25, 2004).

77. "Take Charge of Education," Target (n.d.), **http://target.com/common/page.jhtml;jsessionid=GWORM5AQSLBLDLARAAVWW4FMCEACU1IX?content=target_cg_take_charge_of_education** (accessed February 25, 2004).

78. Reena Jana (2007) "The Business of Going Green," Business Week Online, June 22, **http://www.businessweek.com/innovate/content/jun2007/id20070622_491833.htm?chan=search,** accessed June 19, 2008.

79. Staff writer, "Who Really Pays for CSR Initiatives," *Environmental Leader,* February 15, 2008, **http://www.environmentalleader.com/2008/02/15/who-really-pays-for-csr-initiatives/** (accessed March 17, 2008); "Global Fund," **http://www.joinred.com/globalfund** (accessed March 25, 2008).

80. Permission granted by the author of *Gray Matters,* George Sammet Jr., Vice President, Office of Corporate Ethics, Lockheed Martin Corporation, Orlando, Florida, to use these portions of *Gray Matters: The Ethics Game* © 1992. If you would like more information about the complete game, call 1-800-3ETHICS.

81. *Patagonia,* **http://www.patagonia.com** (accessed June 3, 2008); Jennifer Alsever, "Gear makers get green to meet demand," *MSNBC.com,* April 30, 2007, **www.msnbc.msn.com/id/18142220** (accessed June 3, 2008); Brooke Sapelsa, "Well Worn Works For Apparel Industry," *CNBC.com,* April 18, 2008, **www.cnbc.com/id/24112140?_source=yahoo/headline/quote/text/&par=yahoo** (accessed June 3, 2008); Staff writer, "Designers opt for green, ethical look at Montreal Fashion Week," The Canadian Press, March 27, 2008, **http://www.greenlivingonline.com/BeautyFashion/cp-5481** (accessed June 3, 2008).

82. M.P. McQueen, "Agency Misses Chance to Curb Lead in Jewelry," *The Wall Street Journal,* February 12, 2008, p. D1.

83. Avery Johnson, "Pfizer Will Pull Some Lipitor Ads in Wake of Probe." *The Wall Street Journal,* Feb. 26, 2008. p. B5, **http://online.wsj.com/article/SB120396972593291395.html;** Vanessa Aristide, "Pfizer Voluntarily Withdraws Lipitor Advertising Featuring Dr. Robert Jarvik." *Pfizer Press Release,* Feb. 25, 2008, **http://www.pfizer.com/news/press_releases/pfizer_press_releases.jsp?rssUrl=http://mediaroom.pfizer.com/portal/site/pfizer/index.jsp?ndmViewId=news_view&ndmConfigId=1010794&newsId=20080225006247&newsLang=en;** *Better Business Bureau,* **http://us.bbb.org/WWWRoot/SitePage.aspx?site=113&id=8e20ba59-acb8-4dcf-a1e2-0cc3ab9cfbb4,** p. Section 14.

84. Terry Maxon, "Frontier's Credit Card Company Has its Say," *Airline Biz Blog* April 11, 2008, **http://aviationblog.dallasnews.com/archives/2008/04/frontiers-credit-card-company.html** (accessed June 19, 2008); Jim Kelly, "Aloha Airlines Goes Out of Business," *East Bay Business Times,* Monday, March 31, 2008, **http://eastbay.bizjournals.com/eastbay/stories/2008/03/31/daily1.html** (accessed May 19, 2008).

85. Julie Jargon, "Retailers' Lawsuits Accuse Candy Makers of Fixing Prices," *The Wall Street Journal,* April 1, 2008, p. B3.

86. Peppi Kivniemi, "EU Raids Intel's Office in Germany," *The Wall Street Journal,* February 13, 2008, p. B14.

87. Maureen Dorney, "Congress Passes Federal Anti-Spam Law: Preempts Most State Anti-Spam Laws," *DLA Piper,* December 3, 2003, **http://franchiseagreements.com/global/publications/detail.aspx?pub=622** (accessed May 19, 2008).

88. Joseph Pereira, "Chains Report Stolen Card Data," *The Wall Street Journal,* March 18, 2008, p. B4.

## CHAPTER 3

1. "Fresh, But Far from Easy," *The Economist,* June 21, 2007, **www.economist.com/PrinterFriendly.cfm?story_id=9358986** (accessed September 20, 2007); Matthew Boyle, "Will Tesco Get a Rocky Mountain High?," *Fortune,* February 27, 2007, **http://money.cnn.com/2007/02/26/magazines/fortune/pluggedin_tesco.fortune/index.htm** (accessed September 20, 2007); Parija Bhatnagar, "Wal-Mart, Kroger, Safeway Better Watch Out. The British Are Coming!," *CNNMoney.com,* February 27, 2007, **http://money.cnn.com/2006/02/24/news/companies/tesco_us/index.htm** (accessed September 20, 2007); "Tesco to Enter United States," **tescocorporate.com,** September 20, 2006, **http://www.tescocorporate.com/page.aspx?pointerid=14163CB2412F41B1BD7765AC8DBE49EB** (accessed September 20, 2007); Amanda Shaffer and Robert Gottlieb, "Filling in 'Food Deserts,'" *The Los Angeles Times,* November 5, 2007, **http://www.latimes.com/news/opinion/la-oe-gottlieb5nov05,0,7040113.story?track=rss** (accessed November 6, 2007); **www.freshandeasy.com,** "About Fresh & Easy Neighborhood Market," October 2007, **http://www.freshandeasy.com/pdfs/Fresh%20%20Easy%20Quick%20Facts%2010-25-07.pdf** (accessed November 6, 2007).

2. Tim Kelly, "Squash the Caterpillar," *Forbes,* April 21, 2008, p. 136.

3. "About McDonald's," 2007–2008, **http://www.mcdonalds.com/corp/about.html** (accessed May 13, 2008).

4. **www.starbucks.com/aboutus/Company-Factsheet.pdf,** February 2008, (accessed April 30, 2008).

5. Elisabeth Sullivan, "Choose Your Words Wisely," *Marketing News,* February 15, 2008, p. 22.

6. Dexter Roberts and David Rocks, "China: Let a Thousand Brands Bloom," *BusinessWeek,* October 17, 2005, pp. 58, 60.

7. Sullivan, "Choose Your Words Wisely."

8. Ed Crooks, "Colombia Sitting On Big Oil Reserves," *Financial Times,* April 2, 2008, p.3.

9. "2007 Annual Trade Highlights, Dollar Change from Prior Year," *U.S. Census Bureau, Foreign Trade Statistics,* **http://www.census.gov/foreign-trade/statistics/highlights/annual.html** (accessed April 4, 2008).

10. Dexter Roberts and David Rocks, "China: Let a Thousand Brands Bloom," *BusinessWeek,* October 17, 2005, pp. 58, 60.

11. Joseph O'Reilly, "Global Logistics: In China, Bigger Bull's-eye Better," *Inbound Logistics,* April 2008, p. 26.

12. "2007 Annual Trade Highlights, Dollar Change from Prior Year," *U.S. Census Bureau, Foreign Trade Statistics,* **http://www.census.gov/foreign-trade/statistics/highlights/annual.html** (accessed April 4, 2008).

13. Robert E. Scott and David Ratner, "Trade Picture," *Economic Policy Institute,* February 10, 2006, **www.epinet.org/content.cfm/webfeatures_econindicators_tradepict20060210** (accessed June 5, 2006). "2007 Annual Trade Highlights, Dollar Change from Prior Year," *U.S. Census Bureau, Foreign Trade Statistics,* **http://www.census.gov/foreign-trade/statistics/highlights/annual.html** (accessed April 4, 2008).

14. Dexter Roberts and David Rocks, "China: Let a Thousand Brands Bloom," *BusinessWeek,* October 17, 2005, pp. 58, 60.

15. Neal E. Boudette, Norihiko Shirouzu, and John D. Stoll, "Detroit Sets Bold Goal: Exporting U.S. Cars," *The Wall Street Journal,* April 8, 2008, p. A1.

16. Evan Ramstad, "Samsung's Chairman May Be Gone, But His Stock Won't Let Him Be Forgotten," *The Wall Street Journal,* April 23, 2008, p. B1.

17. O'Reilly, "Global Logistics: New Tax Treaty Raises U.S. Stakes in Belgium's Lowlands," *Inbound Logistics,* April 2008, p. 24.

18. Yuri Kageyama, "Japan Imports American Culture via Calories," *Marketing News,* May 1, 2007, p. 11; Dan Hilton, "Japan's Junk-Food Obsession," *CBC News,* July 5, 2006, **www.cbc.ca/news/viewpoint/vp_hilton/20060705.html** (accessed September 20, 2007); Joanne Lutynec, "American Junk Food Big Hit in Japan," *Slashfood,* April 4, 2007, **www.slashfood.com/2007/04/04/american-junk-food-is-a-big-hit-in-japan** (accessed September 20, 2007).

19. Stan Beer, "Global Software Piracy Cost US $40 billion in 2006: BSA," *IT Wire,* May 15, 2007, **http://www.itwire.com.au/content/view/12171/53** (accessed June 7, 2007).

20. Alan Beattie, "Countries Rush to Restrict Trade in Basic Foods," *The Financial Times,* April 2, 2008, p. 1.

21. Helene Cooper, "WTO Rules Against U.S.'s Quota on Yarn from Pakistan in Latest Textiles Setback," *The Wall Street Journal,* April 27, 2001, p. A4.

22. Kitty Bean Yancey and Laura Bly, "Door May Be Inching Open for Tourism," *USA Today,* February 20, 2008, p. A5; Sue Kirchhoff and Chris Woodyard, "Cuba Trade Gets 'New Opportunity,'" *USA Today,* February 20, 2008, p. B1.

23. "WTO Panel Rules U.S. Duties on Canadian Lumber Are Illegal," *The Wall Street Journal,* March 22, 2004, **http://online.wsj.com.**

24. Michael Zhao, "60-Mile Wi-Fi," *Forbes,* April 9, 2007 **http://www.forbes.com/forbes/2007/0409/076.html** (accessed March 18, 2008); "Bio for Eric Brewer," University of California—Berkeley, **www.cs.berkeley.edu/ brewer/bio.html** (accessed March 18, 2008); Wildnet Research Overview, **http://tier.cs.berkeley.edu/wiki/Wireless** (accessed March 18, 2008).

25. Julie Bennett, "Product Pitfalls Proliferate in Global Cultural Maze," *The Wall Street Journal,* May 14, 2001, p. B11.

26. Greg Botelho, "2003 Global Influentials: Selling to the World," *CNN,* December 9, 2003, **www.cnn.com.**

27. Slogans Gone Bad, **www.joe-ks.com/archives_apr2004/slogans_gone_bad.htm** (accessed June 6, 2006).

28. Sydney B. Leavens, "Father-Daughter Ad Breaks Latino Mold," *The Wall Street Journal,* p. B7.

29. J. Bonasia, "For Web, Global Reach Is Beauty—and Challenge," *Investor's Business Daily,* June 13, 2001, p. A6.

30. Michelle Kessler, "PC Makers Look Far and Wide for Growth," *USA Today,* March 7, 2008, p. B1.

31. Jim Hopkins, "Other Nations Zip by USA in High-Speed Net Race," *USA Today,* January 19, 2004, pp. 1B, 2B.

32. "What Is the WTO," World Trade Organization (n.d.), **www.wto.org** (accessed February 25, 2004).

33. "WTO: U.S. Steel Duties Are Illegal," *USA Today,* November 10, 2003, **http://usatoday.com.**

34. "Bush Ends Steel Tariffs," *CNNMoney,* December 4, 2003, **http://cnnmoney.com.**

35. U.S. Bureau of the Census, *Statistical Abstract of the United States, 2008,* pp. 825–827, 837; "NAFTA: A Decade of Success," Office of the United States Trade Representative, July 1, 2004, **http://ustr.gov/Document_Library/Fact_Sheets/2004/NAFTA_A_Decade_of_Success.html.**

36. CIA, *The World Fact Book.* "Trade with Canada: 2006"; U.S. Bureau of the Census, **www.census.gov/foreign-trade/balance/c1220.html** (accessed January 28, 2008).

37. William C. Symonds, "Meanwhile, to the North, NAFTA Is a Smash," *BusinessWeek,* February 27, 1995, p. 66.

38. CIA, *The World Fact Book;* "Trade with Mexico: 2006," U.S. Bureau of the Census, **www.census.gov/foreign-trade/balance/c2010.html#2006** (accessed January 28, 2008); U.S. Bureau of the Census, *Statistical Abstract,* p. 802.

39. Felipe Calderón Hinojosa, "Mexico's Road," *The Economist,* November 15, 2007, p. 48.

40. Chris Hawley, "Mexico Takes on More Aircraft Construction," *USA Today,* April 7, 2008, p. A11.

41. Geri Smith and Cristina Lindblad, "Mexico: Was NAFTA Worth It?" *BusinessWeek,* December 22, 2003, pp. 66–72; Cheryl Farr Leas, "The Big Boom," *Continental,* April 2001, pp. 85–94.

42. "A Tale of Two Mexicos: North and South," *The Economist,* April 26, 2008, pp. 53–54.

43. "Antecedents of the FTAA Process," Free Trade Area of the Americas (n.d.), **www.ftaa-alca.org/View_e.asp** (accessed February 25, 2004); "FTAA Fact Sheet," Market Access and Compliance, U.S. Department of Commerce (n.d.), **www.mac.doc.gov/ftaa2005/ftaa_fact_sheet.html** (accessed November 3, 2003).

44. "U.S.-Brazil Split May Doom Americas Free-Trade Zone," *The Wall Street Journal,* November 7, 2003, **http://online.wsj.com.**

45. "Archer Daniels to File NAFTA Claim Against Mexico," *Inbound Logistics,* October 2003, p. 30.

46. Smith and Lindblad "Mexico: Was NAFTA Worth It?"

47. "Europe in 12 Lessons," **http://europa.eu/abc/12lessons/lesson_2/index_en.htm** (accessed April 4, 2008).

48. Joaquín Almunia, "The Euro Zone: Bigger and Better?" *The Economist,* November 15, 2007, p 142.

49. Stanley Reed, with Ariane Sains, David Fairlamb, and Carol Matlack, "The Euro: How Damaging a Hit?" *BusinessWeek,* September 29, 2003, p. 63; "The Single Currency," *CNN* (n.d.), **www.cnn.com/SPECIALS/2000/eurounion/story/currency/** (accessed July 3, 2001).

50. "Microsoft Hit by Record EU Fine," *CNN,* March 24, 2004, **www.cnn.com.**

51. **http://www.apec.org/content/apec/about_apec.html** (accessed May 6, 2008).

52. Smith and Lindblad, "Mexico: Was NAFTA Worth It?"

53. Clay Chandler, "China Is Too Darn Hot!" *Fortune,* November 10, 2003, pp. 39–40; Clay Chandler, "How to Play the China Boom," *Fortune,* December 22, 2003, pp. 141, 142.

54. James T. Areddy, James Hookway, John Lyons, and Marcus Walker, "U.S. Slump Takes Toll Across Globe," *The Wall Street Journal,* April 3, 2008, p. A1; Pam Woodall, "The New Champions," *The Economist,* November 15, 2008, p 55; Matt Jenkins, "A Really Inconvenient Truth," *Miller-McCune,* April/May 2008, p. 42.

55. Peter Collins, "A Special Report on Vietnam: Halfway from Rags to Riches," *The Economist,* April 26, 2008, p 3–16.

56. David J. Lynch, "The IMF is . . . Tired Fund Struggles to Reinvent Itself," *USA Today,* April 19, 2006. p. B1.

57. John Reed, "Tesla to Sell Electric Cars in Europe," *Financial Times,* April 2, 2008, p. 21.

58. Brad Fishman, "International Trade Shows: The Smartest Ticket for Overseas Research," International Franchise Association (n.d.), **www.franchise.org/news/fw/april03c.asp** (accessed July 27, 2001).

59. Ben Worthen, "The Crazy World of Outsourcing," *WSJ.com,* February 25, 2008. **http://blogs.wsj.com/biztech/2008/02/25/the-crazy-world-of-outsourcing/?mod=relevancy** (accessed May 6, 2008).

60. "Bank of America to Outsource 1,000 Jobs to India," [Albany] *Business Review,* February 18, 2004, **www.bizjournals.com/albany/stories/2004/02/16/daily18.html.**

61. Nick Easen, "Firms Get Savvy About Outsourcing," *CNNMoney,* February 18, 2004, **www.cnn.com.**

62. Walter B. Wriston, "Ever Heard of Insourcing?" commentary, *The Wall Street Journal,* March 24, 2004, p. A20.

63. "Bharti of India Will Outsource IT Needs to IBM," *The Wall Street Journal,* March 29, 2004, **http://online.wsj.com.**

64. Jason Bush, "GM: On the Road to Russia," *BusinessWeek,* January 19, 2004, p. 14.

65. "What We're About," NUMMI (n.d.), **www.nummi.com/co_info.html** (accessed February 26, 2004).

66. Sharon Silk Carty, "Ford Plans to Park Jaguar, Land Rover with Tata Motors," *USA Today,* March 26, 2008, p B1.

67. O. C. Ferrell, John Fraedrich, and Linda Ferrell, *Business Ethics,* 6th ed. (Boston: Houghton Mifflin, 2005), pp. 227–30.

68. Kim Jung Min, "Asian Company's Perfume Passes French Smell Test," *The Wall Street Journal,* March 19, 2004, **http://online.wsj.com.**

69. Vanessa O'Connell, "Exxon 'Centralizes' New Global Campaign," *The Wall Street Journal,* July 11, 2001, p. B6.

70. Conscious Management Scandinavia, "Nutriset: Hope for Undernourished," **http://www.lots.mindo.com/EN/news.aspx?id=330** (accessed October 23, 2007); Nutriset company Web site, "Plumpy-nut," **http://www.nutriset.fr/index.php?option=com_content&task=view&id=30&Itemid=28** (accessed October 23, 2007); World Hunger Education Service, "World Hunger Facts 2007," **http://www.worldhunger.org/articles/Learn/world%20hunger%20facts%202002.htm**

(accessed October 23, 2007); Anderson Cooper, "A Life Saver Called "Plumpynut" *CBS News 60 Minutes* October 21, 2007, **http://www.cbsnews.com/stories/2007/10/19/60minutes/main3386661_page3.shtml** (accessed October 23, 2007); Medicians Sans Frontieres, Doctors Without Borders, "Malnutrition, MSF Warns More Food Will Not Save Malnourished Children," October 10, 2007, **http://www.doctorswithoutborders.org/news/malnutrition/** (accessed October 23, 2007).

71. Export.gov, **www.export.gov/comm_svc/about_home.html** (accessed February 9, 2006), CIBER *Web,* **http://CIBERWEB.msu.edu** (accessed February 9, 2006).

72. Jeff Chu "Happily Ever After?" *Time,* Mar. 18, 2002, **http://www.time.com/time/magazine/article/0,9171,901020325-218398,00.html** (accessed June 20, 2008); Wendy Leung, "Disney Set to Miss Mark on Visitors," *The Standard,* September 05, 2006, **http://www.thestandard.com.hk/news_detail.asp?pp_cat=11&art_id=26614&sid=9732977&con_type=1&d_str=20060905&sear_year=2006** (accessed June 20, 2008); The Walt Disney Company 2007 Annual Report, **http://corporate.disney.go.com/investors/annual_reports/2007/pr/part5.html** (accessed June 9, 2008); Robert Mendick, "Race Against Time to Make That Disney Magic Work," *The London Independent,* February 6, 2000, **http://www.independent.co.uk/news/uk/this-britain/race-against-time-to-make-that-disney-magic-work-726623.html** (accessed June 23, 2008).

**CHAPTER 4**

1. Cheryl Lu-Lien Tan, "Haggling 2.0," *The Wall Street Journal,* June 23–24, 2007, pp. P1, P3; Nordstrom.com, "Pricing Policy," **http:about/Nordstrom.com/help/our-policies/pricing-policy.asp** (accessed September 28, 2007); The PC Guide, "Price Matching," **www.pcguide.com/buy/ven/eval/priceMatching-c.html** (accessed September 28, 2007); Haggle Point, "Haggling," **www.hagglepoint.com/about.html** (accessed September 27, 2007).

2. Dennis K. Berman, "Business.com Could Hit Jackpot on Auction Block," *The Wall Street Journal,* June 22, 2007, p. B3; "About Us," *Business.com,* **www.business.com/info/press/index.asp** (accessed September 17, 2007); Giselle

Abramovich, "R.H. Donnelley to buy Business.com," *DMNews,* July 31, 2007, **www.dmnews.com/cms/dm-news/ad-agencies/41964.html** (accessed September 17, 2007); Lisa LaMotta, "The Most Expensive Web Addresses," *Forbes.com,* June 29, 2007, **http://www.forbes.com/entrepreneurs/2007/06/28/google-news-corp-ent-tech-cx_ll_0629webaddresses.html** (accessed October 2, 2007).

3. "Apple Confirms #1 Music Retailer Status With Four Billion Songs Sold," *Gizmodo.com,* **http://gizmodo.com/375816/apple-confirms-1-music-retailer-status-with-four-billion-songs-sold** (accessed April 8, 2008).

4. "Wikipedia: About," 2008, **http://en.wikipedia.org/wiki/Wikipedia:About** (accessed May 15, 2008).

5. **www.cosmetics.com** (accessed June 6, 2006).

6. "God Save the Queen . . . On YouTube?" *Marketing News,* February 15, 2008, p. 3; **http://www.youtube.com/user/BarackObamadotcom** (accessed May 15, 2008).

7. Jane Spencer and Kevin J. Delaney, "YouTube Unplugged," *The Wall Street Journal,* March 21, 2008, p B1.

8. Roger W. Ferguson Jr., "Remarks by Vice Chairman Roger W. Ferguson Jr.," American Economic Association meeting, January 4, 2004, San Diego, California, available at **www.federalreserve.gov/boarddocs/speeches/2004/200401042/default.htm.**

9. Edward P. Lazear and Katherine Baicker, "America at Work," *The Wall Street Journal Online,* May 8, 2006, **http://online.wsj.com/article/SB114705083956846285-search html?KEYWORDS=productivity+adds+to+GDP&COLLECTION=wsjie/ 6month,** (accessed June 6, 2006).

10. Jodh Tyrangiel, "Radical Remix," *Time,* October 15, 2007, p. 60.

11. "Data," *Webopedia,* October 28, 2003, **www.webopedia.com/TERM/D/data.html.**

12. "Anheuser Busch Goes Full Tilt," August 8, 2005, **www.anheuserbusch.com/news/tilt080805.htm** (accessed June 6, 2006).

13. "What Is OnStar?" OnStar (n.d.), **www.onstar.com** (accessed March 2, 2004).

14. "About IRI," Information Resources Inc. (n.d.), **www.infores.com/public/global/about/default.htm** (accessed April 23, 2004); "On-line Purchases of Consumer Packaged Goods on the Rise,"

study by Information Resources Inc., *DSN Retailing Today,* June 4, 2001.

15. Information Resources Inc, Company Overview, **http://us.infores.com/page/about/company_overview** (accessed June 8, 2006).

16. "OECD Broadband Statistics to June 2007," Organization for Economic Cooperation and Development, June 2007, **http://www.oecd.org/document/60/0,3343,en_2649_33703_39574076_1_1_1_1,00.html** (accessed April 4, 2008); Loretta Chao, "China Internet Use Passes U.S.," *The Wall Street Journal,* March 14, 2008, p B3; "Internet World Stats, Usage and Population Statistics," Internet World Stats, November 2007, **http://www.internetworldstats.com/stats.htm** (accessed April 4, 2008).

17. "How Duke Helps Students Connect," April 5, 2004, *BusinessWeek Online,* **www.businessweek.com/bschools/content/apr2006/bs2006045_8177.htm?campaign_id=search** (accessed June 6, 2006).

18. "On Strike, Virtually," *The Economist,* March 15, 2008, p. 80; Tim Stevens, "Students Stage Virtual Protest on Facebook," *switched,* August 31, 2007, **www.switched.com/2007/08/31/students-stage-virtual-protest-on-facebook** (accessed April 3, 2008); "Designer Takes Anti-Fur Protest to Virtual World," *MSNBC.com,* June 29, 2007, **www.msnbc.msn.com/id/19506442/print/1/displaymode/1098** (accessed April 3, 2008); **www.stopglobalwarming.org** (accessed April 3, 2008).

19. "S&P500," *BusinessWeek,* April 5, 2004, p. 157.

20. Edward C. Baig, "Livescribe Pulse Digital Pen Brings Your Notes to Life," *USA Today,* May 8, 2008, p B1.

21. Adam Wright, "Mobile Phones Could Soon Rival the PC as the World's Dominant Internet Platform," April 18, 2006, **http://www.ipsos-na.com/news/pressrelease.cfm?id=3049#** (accessed June 6, 2006).

22. "Japan's Camera Phone Craze Spreads to Funerals," *msnbc.com,* February 16, 2006, **http://www.msnbc.msn.com/id/11385672/** (accessed June 6, 2006).

23. **www.epicurious.com** (accessed June 7, 2006).

24. **www.bluetooth.com/bluetooth** (accessed June 7, 2006).

25. Leslie Cauley, "Deal Shakes Up Wireless World," *USA Today,* May 7, 2008, p B1;

Leslie Cauley, "Big Investors Join Clear-wire's WiMax Plan for Wireless Nation," *USA Today,* May 8, 2008, p B3.

26. FCC Consumer Facts, "VoIP/Internet Voice," **www.fcc.gov/ cgb** (accessed June 6, 2006).

27. "Wal-Mart Leading the RFID Retail Revolution," *CNN.com,* May 22, 2006, **http://www.cnn.com/2006/TECH/05/22/ rfid.retail.ap/index.html** (accessed June 6, 2006).

28. "Shaping the Future Mobile Information Society," International Telecommunication Union (n.d.), **www.itu. int/osg/spu/ni/futuremovile** (accessed March 21, 2004).

29. Josh Quitter, "How Jeff Bezos Rules the Retail Space," *Fortune,* May 5, 2008, pp. 127–132.

30. John Gaffney, "How Do You Feel about a $44 Tooth-Bleaching Kit?" *Business 2.0,* October 2001, p. 126; Stephanie Stahl and John Soat, "Feeding the Pipeline: Procter & Gamble Uses IT to Nurture New Product Ideas," *Information Week,* February 24, 2003, **www. informationweek.com/story/show-Article.jhtml;-jsessionid=4SA2EIBSJY SZCQSNDBGCKHY?articleID=870056 8&pgno=1.**

31. Jefferson Graham, "Veoh Aims to Be One-stop Shop for Net TV Viewers," *USA Today,* February 27, 2008, p. B8.

32. Michael J. Mandel and Robert D. Hof, "Rethinking the Internet," *BusinessWeek,* March 26, 2001, p. 118.

33. Peter Passi, "Goodbye, Waiting Rooms," April 8, 2006, **http://www.duluthsuperior .com/mld/duluthsuperior/news/ 14295747.htm** (accessed June 14, 2006).

34. G. Jeffrey MacDonald, "Education of Global Reach," *USA Today,* February 27, 2008, p. D6.

35. Mandel and Hof, "Rethinking the Internet."

36. Bobby White, "The New Workplace Rules: No Video-Watching," *The Wall Street Journal,* March 4, 2008, p. B1.

37. "How It Works," *The Wall Street Journal,* May 21, 2001, p. R8.

38. Mandel and Hof, "Rethinking the Internet."

39. *BusinessWeek,* special supplement, February 28, 2000, p. 74.

40. Anjali Cordeiro, "Online Market Lets Companies Buy and Sell Ideas," *The Wall Street Journal Online,* **http://online.wsj**

.com/article/SB120882814463933399 .html (accessed May 22, 2008).

41. Quitter, "How Jeff Bezos Rules the Retail Space."

42. Travel Industry Association of America, "Leading Travel Industry Consumer Survey Reports Significantly More Travelers Plan and Book Trips Online," November 16, 2005, **www.tia.org/ pressmedia/pressrec.asp?Item=689** (accessed June 14, 2006).

43. Jayne O'Donnell, "Online Buyers Crack the Code on Deals," *USA Today,* April 4, 2008, p. B3.

44. Tessa Romita. "Sky's the Limit for Airlines Online," *Business 2.com,* January 23, 2001, p. 4.

45. Adapted from Judy Strauss and Raymond Frost, *Emarketing,* 2nd ed. (Upper Saddle River, NJ: Prentice-Hall, 2001).

46. Adapted from William M. Pride and O.C. Ferrell, *Marketing,* 13th ed. (Boston: Houghton Mifflin, 2005).

47. **www.olay.com/clubolay/intro.htm** (accessed June 15, 2006).

48. O. C. Ferrell, Michael D. Hartline, and George H. Lucas, Jr., *Marketing Strategy* (Fort Worth, TX: Dryden, 2002), p. 97.

49. **www.salesforce.com/products/sales-force-automation.jsp, www.salesforce. com/partners/** (both accessed June 15, 2006).

50. Edward Prewitt, "How to Build Customer Loyalty in an Internet World," *CIO,* January 1, 2002, **www.cio.com/ archive/010102/loyalty_content.html**.

51. Eve M. Caudill and Patrick E. Murphy, "Consumer Online Privacy: Legal and Ethical Issues," *Journal of Public Policy & Marketing,* 19 (Spring 2000), pp. 7–12.

52. Merissa Marr, "MTV Workers' Data Stolen," *The Wall Street Journal,* March 10, 2008, p. B5.

53. **www.truste.org/about/fact_sheet .php** (accessed June 16, 2006).

54. Better Business Bureau Online (n.d.), **www.bbbonline.org/** (accessed April 28, 2004).

55. Matt Asay, "Study: 95 Percent of All E-Mail Sent in 2007 Was Spam," *CNET. com,* **http://www.cnet.com/8301-13505_ 1-9831556-16.html** (accessed April 8, 2008).

56. Tim Hanrahan and Jason Fry, "Spammers, Human Mind Do Battle Over Spelling," *The Wall Street Journal,* February 9, 2004, **http://online.wsj.com.**

57. "EU Orders Anti-Spam Legislation," *CNN,* April 1, 2004, **www.cnn.com**.

58. Alan Rappeport, "Second Life's John Zdanowski," *CFO,* October 2007, pp. 46–48; June Arney, "Big Firms and Startups Seek Profit in Simulated Businesses," *baltimoresun.com,* October 25, 2007, **www.baltimoresun.com/business/bal-bz. secondlife25oct25,2146959,print.story** (accessed November 6, 2007); Mike Shields, "CNN Goes Virtual," *Mediaweek. com,* October 29, 2007, **www.mediaweek .com/mw/current/article_display.jsp? vnu_content_id=1003664347** (accessed November 6, 2007); "Economic Status," Second Life, **http:secondlife.com/ whatis/economy_stats.php** (accessed November 6, 2007); "What Is Second Life?," **secondlife.com/whatis/** (accessed January 4, 2007); Dan Zehr, "Dell Gets Virtual with Second Life Island," *Austin American-Statesman,* **www.statesman .com/business/content/business/stories/ technology/11/15/15dell.html** (accessed November 15, 2006); Richard Siklos, "A Virtual World but Real Money," *The New York Times,* October 19, 2006, **http:// select.nytimes.com/gst/abstract.html** (accessed November 16, 2006); Andrew LaVallee, "Now, Virtual Fashion," *The Wall Street Journal,* September 22, 2006, **online. wsj.com/article/SB115888412923570768 .html** (accessed November 16, 2006); Arun Sudhaman, "The Virtual World of Second Life," *Media Asia,* November 3, 2006; Jennifer Mears and Ann Bednarz, "You Know It's Cool When Vendors Want In," **www.nelworkworld.com,** October 10, 2006; "Living a Second Life," *The Economist,* September 30, 2006.

59. "FTC Releases List of Top Consumer Fraud Complaints in 2007," January 13, 2008, **http://www.ftc.gov/opa/2008/02/ fraud.shtm** (accessed April 8, 2008).

60. Andrea Chipman, "Stealing You," *The Wall Street Journal,* April 26, 2004, **http:// online.wsj.com**.

61. Christine Dugas, "Identity Theft on the Rise," USA Today, May 11, 2001, p. 3B.

62. 2007 Identity Fraud Survey Report, **http://www.javelinstrategy.com/uploads/ 701.R_2007IdentityFraudSurveyReport_ Brochure.pdf** (accessed May 22, 2008).

63. Jack McCarthy, "National Fraud Center: Internet Is Driving Identity Theft," *CNN,* March 20, 2000, **www.cnn.com**.

64. Juan Carlos Perez, "Biggest Security Threat? Insiders," *PC World,* October 2,

2002, **www.pcworld.com/news/article/ 0,aid,105528,00.asp**.

65. Fifth Annual BSA and IDC Global Software Piracy Study, **http://global.bsa .org/idcglobalstudy2007/** (accessed May 22, 2008).

66. "States Approve Effective Date for Sales Tax Simplification Agreement," **www.govtech.net/news/news .php?id=94929#** (accessed June 15, 2006).

67. Frank Ahrens, "Viacom Sues YouTube Over Copyright," *The Washington Post,* March 14, 2007, **http://www.washing-tonpost.com/wp-dyn/content/arti-cle/2007/03/13/AR2007031300595.html** (accessed June 9, 2008); "YouTube Law Fight 'Threatens Net,'" *BBC News,* May 27, 2008, **http://news.bbc.co.uk/2/hi/ technology/7420955.stm** (accessed June 9, 2008); John W. Schoen, "Media World Eyes Viacom-YouTube Slugfest," *MSNBC,* March 13, 2007, **http://www.msnbc. msn.com/id/17593962** (accessed June 9, 2008); Eric Bangeman, "Google Cites Safe Harbor, Fair Use in Viacom v. YouTube Defense," *ars technica,* May 1, 2007, **http:// arstechnica.com/news.ars/post/20070501- google-cites-safe-harbor-fair-use-in- viacom-v-youtube-defense.html** (accessed June 9, 2008); Joseph Weisen-thal, "Viacom Ups Ante In YouTube Copyright Spat: Google More Than A Mere Enabler," *The Washington Post,* May 27, 2008, **http://www.washingtonpost. com/wp-dyn/content/article/2008/05/27/ AR2008052702870.html** (accessed June 9, 2008); David A. Utter, "Google, Viacom Spar Over YouTube Again," *WebProNews,* May 27, 2008, **http://www.webpronews. com/topnews/2008/05/27/google- viacom-spar-over-youtube-again** (accessed June 9, 2008).

## CHAPTER 5

1. Hannah Clark "A New Kind of Com-pany," *Inc.,* July 2007, p. 23–24; B Corpo-ration, **www.bcorporation.net** (accessed October 1, 2007); "B Corporation," Evo, **www.evo.com/content/3152** (accessed October 1, 2007); "About Us," Give Something Back, **http://www.givesome-thingback.com/about_us.html** (accessed February 25, 2008).

2. Max Chafkin, "Gordon Segal of Crate and Barrel," *Inc.,* May 2008, **http://www. inc.com/magazine/20080501/gordon- segal-of-crate-and-barrel.html** (accessed May 8, 2008).

3. The Entrepreneurs's Help Page, **http://www.tannedfeet.com/sole_ proprietorship.htm,** accessed May 8, 2008; Kent Hoover, "Startups Down for Women Entrepreneurs, Up for Men," *San Francisco Business Times,* May 2, 2008, **http://sanfrancisco.bizjournals.com/ sanfrancisco/stories/2008/05/05/ smallb2.html** (accessed May 8, 2008).

4. Maggie Overfelt, "Start-Me-Up: The California Garage," *Fortune Small Busi-ness,* July/Aug. 2003, **www.fortune.com/ fortune/smallbusiness/articles/0,15114, 475872,00.html**.

5. Megan Kamerick, "Santa Fe Trio Builds Furniture Business on Rich Tradition," *New Mexico Business Weekly,* June 8–14, 2007, p. 13; Taos Furniture, **www. taosfurniture.com** (accessed September 1, 2007).

6. Digital Artists Agency, **http://www.d- a-a.com/clients/clientindexframe.html,** (accessed May 9, 2008).

7. Linda Tischles, "Join the Circus," *Fast Company,* July 2005, pp. 53–58.

8. "BP's Russian Oil Row Intensifies," *BBC News,* June 9, 2008, **http://news. bbc.co.uk/2/hi/business/7443380.stm** (accessed June 9, 2008).

9. "What Is Community Supported Agriculture and How Does It Work?" Local Harvest, **www.localharvest.org/ csa.jsp** (accessed 2-18-08); "Community Supported Agriculture at Indian Line Farm," Indian Line Farm, **http://www. indianlinefarm.com/csa.html** (accessed February 25, 2008).

10. Deborah Orr, "The Secret World of Mars," *Forbes,* April 28, 2008, **http://www. forbes.com/2008/04/28/billionaires- mars-wrigley-biz-billies-cz_do_ 0428marsfamily_print.html** (accessed May 9, 2008).

11. Shlomo Reifman, "America's Largest Private Companies," *Forbes,* November 8, 2007, **http://www.forbes.com/business/ 2007/11/08/largest-private-companies- biz-privates07-cx_sr_1108privateintro .html** (accessed May 9, 2008).

12. David Kiley, "Ford Family Celebrates 100 Years of Cars," *USA Today,* June 10, 2003, pp. 1B, 2B.

13. Scott DeCarlo, "The World's Biggest Companies," *Forbes,* April 2, 2008, **http:// www.forbes.com/business/2008/04/02/ worlds-largest-companies-biz-2000 global08-cx_sd_0402global_land.html** (accessed May 9, 2008).

14. Staff Writer, "Intrepid Potash," *MSN Money,* IPO Central, **http:// moneycentral.hoovers.com/global/ msn/index.xhtml?pageid=10021&PDate =M:2008:4** (accessed May 9, 2008).

15. Neal E. Boudette and Terry Kosdro-sky, "Chrysler's Unconventional Plan: Sell Fewer Models, Increase Profit," *The Wall Street Journal Online,* Feb. 11, 2008, **http:// moneycentral.hoovers.com/global/msn/ index.xhtml?pageid=10021&PDate=M :2008:4** (accessed May 9, 2008); Sholnn Freeman and Dale Russakoff "Daimler to Split with Chrysler, At a Cost," *Wash-ington Post,* May 15, 2007, **http://www. washingtonpost.com/wp-dyn/content/ article/2007/05/14/AR2007051400004_ pf.html** (accessed May 9, 2008).

16. O. C. Ferrell, John Fraedrich, and Linda Ferrell, *Business Ethics: Ethical Deci-sion Making and Cases,* 6th ed. (Boston: Houghton Mifflin, 2005), p. 84.

17. Julie Daum, "Board Talent Getting Scarcer," *BusinessWeek Online,* January 29, 2008, **http://www.businessweek.com/ print/managing/content/jan2008/ ca20080129_376288.htm** (accessed May 9, 2008).

18. Joseph McCafferty, "Building an Exceptional Board," *BusinessWeek Online,* April 17, 2008, **http://www.businessweek .com/managing/content/apr2008/ ca20080417_289218.htm?chan=search** (accessed May 9, 2008).

19. Joseph Nathan Kane, *Famous First Facts,* 4th ed. (New York: The H. W.Wilson Company, 1981), p. 202.

20. David Kiley, "Audi, VW Must Share a U.S. Factory," *BusinessWeek Online,* May 7, 2008, **http://www.businessweek .com/lifestyle/content/may2,** (accessed May 9, 2008).

21. Robert D. Hisrich and Michael P. Peters, *Entrepreneurship,* 5th ed. (Bos-ton: McGraw-Hill, 2002), pp. 315–16.

22. Dawn Barnes Karate Kids, **http:// www.karatekids.net** (accessed May 18, 2008); Dawn Barnes, **http://www. dawnbarnes.com** (accessed May 18, 2008).

23. Ariel Nelson, "Mars Acquisition of Wrigley: 3rd Biggest Deal of 2008," *CBNC.com,* April 28, 2008, **http://www. cnbc.com/id/24351497** (accessed June 9, 2008); "Hershey Shares Jumps Amid New Venture Talk," *Reuters,* May 27, 2008, **http://uk.reuters.com/article/UK_ HOTSTOCKS/idUKN2731687420080527** (accessed June 9, 2008).

24. Alex Crippen, "Busch Tapping Buffet?," *CNBC.com,* June 16, 2008, **http://www.cnbc.com/id/25190248** (accessed June 16, 2008).

25. Sources: Paul Solman, "Green Industry Hub Rises From Rust Belt Ruins," *PBS,* aired May 12, 2008, **www.pbs.org/newshour/bb/business/jan-june08/greenjobs_05-12.html** (accessed May 16, 2008); Paul Solman, "Pittsburgh Renews Itself With 'Green' Technologies," *PBS,* aired April 25, 2008, **www.pbs.org/newshour/bb/environment/jan-june08/green_04-25.html** (accessed May 16, 2008); Jerome N. Dettore, "Brownfield Development in Pittsburgh," Pittsburgh GreenStory.org, **www.pittsburghgreenstory.org/html/brownfields.html** (accessed May 16, 2008); Grow Pittsburgh, **www.growpittsburgh.org** (accessed May 16, 2008); Fossil Fuel Free, **www.fossilfreefuel.com** (accessed May 16, 2008).

## CHAPTER 6

1. Nicholas Day, "Wheeling Down the CT Cheese Trail," *The Hartford Advocate,* October 18, 2007, pp. 19–21; "Farmstead Cheese," Cato Corner Farm, **www.catocornerfarm.com** (accessed May 4, 2008); Robin Raisfeld and Rob Patronite, "The Greenmarket Effect," *New York Magazine,* July 16, 2006, **http://nymag.com/restaurants/features/17656/** (accessed May 4, 2008); "Cato Corner Farm," *Cheese by Hand,* http://cheesebyhand.com/?cat=21 (accessed May 4, 2008).

2. "U.S. Government Sees Number of Small Businesses Growing to Nearly 24 Million," *Bnet Business Network,* April 10, 2006, **http://findarticles.com/p/articles/mi_m0EIN/is_2006_April_10/ai_n16120182** (accessed May 13, 2008).

3. "Environmentalism: What We Do," Patagonia, **http://www.patagonia.com/web/us/patagonia.go?assetid=2329,** (accessed May 13, 2008).

4. "Small Business Statistics," Small Business Administration (n.d.), **www.sba.gov/aboutsba/sbastats.html** (March 16, 2004).

5. "Key Facts About Women-Owned Business," Center for Women's Business Research, **http://www.nfwbo.org/facts/index.php,** (accessed May 13, 2008).

6. Staff Writer, "Minority Business Fast Facts Profiles," Minority Business Development Agency, November 8, 2007, **http://www.mbda.gov/?bucket_id=847&content_id=6239&section_id=12,** (accessed May 13, 2008).

7. Jose M. Ledon, "A One-Stop Developer," *Fortune,* May 5, 2008, p. S14.

8. **http://app1.sba.gov/faqs/faqindexall.cfm?areaid=24** (accessed June 1, 2006).

9. "Statistics about Business Size (including Small Business)," U.S. Census Bureau, **www.census.gov/epcd/www/smallbus.html#EMpSize** (accessed May 3, 2004).

10. **www.molles.com/news** (accessed June 1, 2006); John D. Stoll, "Visions of the Future" *The Wall Street Journal,* April 17, 2006, P. R8.

11. Lindsay Blakely, "One Man Brands," *Money.CNN.com,* July 6,2007, **http://money.cnn.com/galleries/2007/biz2/0706/gallery.building_brands.biz2/5.html** (accessed May 14, 2008).

12. "How to Finance a New Business," *Consumer Reports,* April 2008, **http://www.consumerreports.org/cro/money/credit-loan/how-to-finance-a-new-business/overview/how-to-finance-a-new-business-ov.htm** (accessed May 14, 2008).

13. Peter Svensson, "U.S. Economy Grows at a Slower Pace," *Washingtonpost.com,* June 5, 2006, **www.washingtonpost.com/wp-dyn/content/article/2006/06/05/AR2006060500376.html** (accessed June 5, 2006).

14. News Release, "PRO-TEC Coating Company Wins Prestigious Malcolm Baldrige National Quality Award," ProTecCoating.com, November 21, 2007, http://www.proteccoating.com/pdf/PRO-TEC-BaldrigeAward.pdf (accessed May 15, 2008).

15. Jessie Hempel, "Finding Cracks in Facebook," *Money.CNN.com,* May 13, 2008, **http://money.cnn.com/2008/05/12/technology/cracks_facebook_hempel.fortune/index.htm** (accessed May 15, 2008).

16. "Small Business Statistics."

17. Emily Lambert, "Pesticide Prince," *Forbes,* April 9, 2007, pgs. 68-70; Staff Writer, "About Us," Albaugh, Inc., **http://www.albaughinc.com/aboutus.htm** (accessed September 14, 2007).

18. Dana Knight, "Big-Headed Guy Gets a Big Idea for Sunglasses Business," *USA Today,* March 21, 2006, p. 4B; Fatheadz, **http://wwwfatheadz.com** (accessed June 5, 2006); Jennifer Whitson, "Sunglass Firm Lands Wal-Mart Deal," Fatheadz, **http://www.fatheadz.com/IBJarticle.php** (accessed May 15, 2008).

19. "You're not the Boss of Me Now," *Weekend Today,* October 21, 2005, **msnbc.msn.com/id/9762771/** (accessed June 5, 2006).

20. "Small Business Resource," **www.2-small-business.com** (accessed June 5, 2006).

21. Kelly Crow, "The Oldest Crop," *The Wall Street Journal,* June 8, 2007, pp. W1, W10; Mark Potter, "The Dinosaurs of South Dakota," *MSNBC.com,* September 20, 2007, **http://www.msnbc.msn.com/id/20894357** (accessed February 22, 2008); Joanne Fox, "Fossil hunters really dig their hobby," *Sioux City Journal,* September 25, 2007, **http://www.siouxcityjournal.com/articles/2007/09/25/news/top/e6cd21c5655fde5886257361000d4cd8.txt** (accessed February 22, 2008).

22. "Spring 2005 Interland Business Barometer," *USA Today,* Snapshots, October 26, 2005.

23. Jennifer Martin, "From Cow Pies to Cow Pots: A Creative Way to Manage Farm Waste," Cooperative State Research, Education, and Extension Service, July 17, 2007, **http://www.csrees.usda.gov/newsroom/research/2007/cowpots.html** (accessed May 15, 2008).

24. Robert Tomsho, "Ask the Volk Family: 30 Million Turkeys Can't Be Wrong," *The Wall Street Journal,* November 22, 2005, p. A1; **www.volkenterprises.com/about_us/index.html,** "About Us," (accessed June 5, 2006).

25. Nick Hodge, "Solar Energy Venture Capital," *Wealth Daily,* January 23, 2008, **http://www.wealthdaily.com/articles/solar-venture-capital/1120** (accessed May 15, 2008).

26. Thomas W. Zimmerer and Norman M. Scarborough, *Essentials of Entrepreneurship and Small Business Management,* 4th ed. (Upper Saddle River, NJ: Pearson Prentice Hall, 2005), pp. 118–24.

27. Ibid.

28. Nitasha Tiku, "Making the Most of a Brush With Fame," *Inc.,* August 2007, p. 19; Recycline, **http://www.recycline.com/** (accessed May 4, 2008); "Recycline: Sitting on Mainstream's Doorstep," Sustainable Is Good, **http://www.sustainableisgood.com/blog/2007/03/recycline_produ.html** (accessed May 4, 2008).

29. "Make Dreams Come True. Join Score Today," *Score,* **http://www.score.org/volunteer.html** (accessed May 15, 2008).

30. Adapted from "Tomorrow's Entrepreneur," *Inc. State of Small Business,* 23, no. 7 (2001), pp. 80–104.

31. "The Boomer Stats," Baby Boomer HQ, **www.bbhq.com/bomrstat.htm** (accessed March 17, 2004).

32. Molly Smith, "Managing Generation Y as They Change the Workforce," *Reuters,* Jan. 8, 2008, **http://www.reuters.com/ article/pressRelease/idUS129795+08-Jan-2008+BW20080108** (accessed May 15, 2008).

33. Jeffrey Passal and D'Vera Cohn, "Immigration to Play Lead Role in Future U.S. Growth," Pew Research, February 11, 2008, **http://pewresearch.org/pubs/729/ united-states-population-projections** (accessed May 15, 2008).

34. Gifford Pinchott III, *Intrapreneuring* (New York: Harper & Row, 1985), p. 34.

35. Paul Brown, "How to cope with hard times," *The New York Times,* June 10, 2008, **http://www.nytimes.com/2008/06/10/ business/smallbusiness/10toolkit.html?_ r=1&ref=smallbusiness&oref=slogin** (accessed June 25, 2008).

36. Adapted from Carol Kinsey Gorman, *Creativity in Business: A Practical Guide for Creative Thinking,* Crisp Publications Inc., 1989, pp. 5–6. © Crisp Publications Inc., 1200 Hamilton Court, Menlo Park, CA 94025.

37. Sources: The Direct Selling Association, **http://www.dsa.org** (accessed June 11, 2008); Doncaster, **http://www.doncaster.com** (accessed June 11, 2008); "Back to Business Clothes from Doncaster," ABC channel 7, Chicago, May 2, 2006, http://abclocal.go.com/ wls/story?section=resources&id=4135134 (accessed June 11, 2008); Longaberger, http:// **www.longaberger.com** (accessed June 11, 2008); Pampered Chef, **http://www. pamperedchef.com** (accessed June 11, 2008).

## CHAPTER 7

1. Stanley Homes, "Higher Grounds," *BusinessWeek,* February/March 2007, pp. 66–70; Espresso Vivace, **www. espressovivace.com/intro.html** (accessed May 9, 2008); Leah Caims, Josh Levine, Sarah Silvemale, Kelsey Clinton, Margaret Anderson, Mary Patterson, "A Commodity Biography: Gourmet Coffee and Place," Faculty Website, The University of Washington, **http://faculty.washington .edu/dmercer/490coffee.htm** (accessed May 9, 2008).

2. Michael V. Copeland, "Boeing's Big Dream," *Fortune,* May 5, 2008, p 182.

3. Denese McDonald, "Partners in Success," *Fortune,* May 5, 2008, p. S12.

4. Amelia Patterson, "Fallen Forests Salvaged," *Colorado Biz Magazine,* September 2007, pgs. 34–36; "About Dennie Ibbotson and Laughing Sun Custom Handcarved Signs and Doors," *Laughing Sun,* **www. handcarveddoors.com/info.html** (accessed May 9, 2008); D. A. Leatherman, I. Aguayo and T. M. Mehall, "Mountain Pine Beetle," Colorado State University Extension—Horticulture, **www.ext. colostate.edu/pubs/insect/05528.html** (accessed May 9, 2008).

5. Alex Taylor III, "Can This Car Save Ford?," *Fortune,* May 5, 2008, p. 170–173.

6. "Our Mission," Celestial Seasonings, **www.celestialseasonings.com/whoweare/ corporatehistory/mission.php** (accessed June 12, 2006).

7. Procter & Gamble R&D Mission, **www.pg.com/science/rdmission.jhtml** (accessed June 12, 2006).

8. Points of Light Foundation, "2005 Honorees," **www.pointsoflight.org/ awards/workplace/CorpWinnerDetails .cfm?ID=88** (accessed June 12, 2006).

9. Kelly Kurt, "Tulsa Bids Zebco Fishing Reels Farewell," *Chicago Tribune,* March 11, 2001, section 5, p. 7.

10. G. Tomas, M. Hult, David W. Cravens, and Jagdish Sheth, "Competitive Advantage in the Global Marketplace: A Focus on Marketing Strategy," *Journal of Business Research* 51 (January 2001), p. 1.

11. Telis Demos, "Copter Crisis," *Fortune,* May 12, 2008, p 20.

12. Telis Demos, "Bag Revolution," *Fortune,* May 12, 2008, p 18.

13. Stanley Reed, "Media Giant or Media Muddle," *BusinessWeek,* May 12, 2008, p. 47.

14. Bryce Hoffman, "Ford Downsizing Will Cut Deeper Than Expected," *DetroitNews. com,* January 21, 2006, **www.detnews.com/ apps/pbcs.dll/article?AID=/20060121/ AUTO01/601210384** (accessed June 12, 2006).

15. John Barfield, "Staffing Up for Growth," *Fortune,* May 5, 2008, p. S10.

16. John Shepler, "Managing After Downsizing," JohnShepler.com (n.d.), **www. johnshepler.com/articles/managedown .html** (accessed May 18, 2004).

17. "The Big Picture," *BusinessWeek,* July 16, 2001, p. 12.

18. Lynette Ryals, "Directing Sales and Key Account Management," Cranfield University School of Management, **http://www.som.cranfield.ac.uk/som/ executive/course/overview.asp?id=204** (accessed May 19, 2008).

19. "ASPO-USA Response to Exxon Mobil Peak Oil Advertisement," March 3, 2006, Association for the Study of Peak Oil & Gas-USA, **www.aspo-usa.com/news. cfm?nd=1468** (accessed June 12, 2006).

20. David Kiley, "Ghosn Hits Accelerator," *BusinessWeek,* May 12, 2008, p. 46.

21. Steve Ulfelder, "Chief Privacy Officers: Hot or Not?" *Computer World,* March 15, 2004, **www.computerworld .com/securitytopics/security/story/ 0,10801,91168p3,00.html;** Steve Ulfelder, "CPOs on the Rise?" *Computer World,* March 15, 2004, **www.computerworld. com/securitytopics/security/story/0,108 01,91166,00.html.**

22. "2002 Catalyst Census of Women Corporate Officers and Top Earners," Catalyst (n.d.), **www.catalystwomen .org/press_room/factsheets/COTE%20 Factsheet%202002.pdf.** (accessed April 9, 2004).

23. Tim Hanrahan, "At Ford, Travel Remains Expensive Perk," *The Wall Street Journal,* April, 7, 2008, p. C1.

24. Pearl Meyer, "Executive Pay: What Really Makes Sense," *BusinessWeek Online,* April 24, 2008, **http://www.businessweek .com/managing/content/apr2008/ ca20080424_081309.htm?chan=search** (accessed May 15, 2008); Pearl Meyer, "The Issue: A CEO Cedes More Power to Subordinates," *BusinessWeek Online,* May 8, 2008, **http://www.businessweek.com/managing/ content/may2008/ca2008058_428759 .htm?chan=search** (accessed May 15, 2008).

25. Annie Finnigan, "Different Strokes," *Working Woman,* April 2001, p. 44.

26. W. Garrison Jackson, "Multicultural Advertising," *Fortune,* May 5, 2008, p. S23.

27. "Developing Colleagues with Passion," *Inbound Logistics,* April 2004, p. 14.

28. David Welch, "GM's Good News: A $3 Billion Loss," *Business Week,* May 12, 2008, p. O31.

29. David Welch, "GM Live Green or Die," *BusinessWeek,* May 26, 2008, pp. O40–41.

30. Eric Schmidt, "How Google Fuels its Idea Factory," *BusinessWeek,* May 12, 2008, p. O54.

31. "Corporate Information," **www. google.com/corporate/facts.html**

(accessed June 12, 2006); "The Google Culture," **www.google.com/corporate/ culture.html** (accessed June 12, 2006).

32. "Tougher to Be a Leader," *USA Today* Snapshot, March 6, 2006, p. B1.

33. Kathryn Kranhold, "His Bright Idea: Dominate Energy-Saving Light Bulbs," *The Wall Street Journal,* December 27, 2007, pp. B1–B2; Julie Scelfo, "Any Other Bright Ideas?" *The New York Times,* January 10, 2008, **http://www.nytimes .com/2008/01/10/garden/10lighting .html?ex=1357621200&en=e017408dffa b6416&ei=5088&partner=rssnyt&emc= rss** (accessed February 22, 2008); "About TCP," "FAQ," TCP School Program, **http:// schoolprograms.tcpi.com** (accessed February 22, 2008).

34. Carol J. Loomis, "Can Anyone Run Citigroup?" *Fortune,* May 5, 2008, pp. 81–84.

35. Deborah Orr, "Bulldog Blues," *Forbes,* April 21, 2008, pp. 144–46.

36. Kara Scannell, "The Few . . . The Proud. The . . . M.B.A.s (?!)," *The Wall Street Journal,* June 5, 2001, pp. C1, C18.

37. Alex Taylor III, "Gentlemen, Start Your Turnaround," *Fortune,* January 21, 2008, p. 71–78; Alex Taylor III, "Rick Wagoner's worst nightmare," *CNNMoney.com,* April 8, 2008, **http://money.cnn.com/ 2008/04/08/news/companies/taylor_gm .fortune** (accessed May 5, 2008); Michael Kanellos, "Can This CEO Paint GM Green?" *News.com,* January 15, 2008, **http://www.news.com/2102-13833_3- 6226106.html** (accessed May 5, 2008).

38. Kerrie Unsworth, "Unpacking Creativity," *Academy of Management Review,* 26 (April 2001), pp. 289–97.

39. Pallavi Gogoi, "A Bittersweet Deal for Wrigley," *BusinessWeek,* May 12, 2008, p. O34.

40. *Harvard Business Review* 60 (November–December 1982), p. 160.

41. "2007 National Employment and Wage Estimates," Bureau of Labor Statistics, **http://www.bls.gov/oes/current/oes_nat .htm#b11-0000** (accessed June 27, 2008); "Career Guide to Industries 2008-2009 Edition: Management and Business and Financial Operations Occupations," *Bureau of Labor Statistics,* **http://www.bls.gov/oco/ oco1001.htm** (accessed June 27, 2008).

42. Kris Maher, "The Jungle," *The Wall Street Journal,* May 29, 2001, p. B16.

43. **www.selfmarketing.com/about.html** (accessed June 12, 2006).

44. Panera Bread, **http://www. panerabread.com;** Christopher Tritto, "Best Places to Work, Panera Bread Co., Category 5, Second Place," *St. Louis Business Journal,* April 13, 2007, **http:// stlouis.bizjournals.com/stlouis/stories/ 2007/04/16/focus22.html?from_msn_ money=1** (accessed June 1, 2008); "Workplace Surveys: Panera Bread," *Vault,* **http://www.vault.com/companies/ company_main.jsp?co_page=13 &product_id=29685&type=workplace** (accessed June 20, 2008).

## CHAPTER 8

1. Abigail Goldman, "Bloggers Bark and Get Heard," *The Miami Herald,* May 25, 2007, pp. 1C, 6C; Elizabeth Weise, "Pet-Owning Bloggers Mobilize on Food Front," *USA Today,* June 4, 2007, **www.usatoday .com/tech/webguide/internetlife/2007- 06-04-pet-blog-centerpiece_N.htm? casp=34** (accessed May 13, 2008); "Homepage," **PetConnection.com** (accessed May 13, 2008).

2. Michael O'Neill, "From Wharton to War," *Fortune,* June 12, 2006, pp. 105–8.

3. Michelle Kessler, "Dell Reverses, Steps into Wal-Mart," *USA Today,* May 25, 2007, p. B1; Peter Svensson, "Dell to Sell Desktops at Nation's Top Retailer," *The Miami Herald,* May 25, 2007, p. 6C; Erica Ogg, "What Wal-Mart Means to Dell," *News.com,* May 25, 2007, **http:// news.com.com/What+Wal-Mart+ means+to+Dell/2100-1042_3-6186402. html** (accessed May 14, 2008); Jessica Davis, "Analyst: Dell's Wal-Mart Choice 'Creative'," *eWeek Channel Insider,* May 25, 2007, **www.channelinsider.com/ article/Analyst+Dells+WalMart+Choice +Creative/208346_1.aspx** (accessed May 14, 2008).

4. "How Google Fuels Its Idea Factory," *BusinessWeek,* April 29, 2008, **http://www. businessweek.com/magazine/content/ 08_19/b4083054277984.htm?chan =search** (accessed May 15, 2008); "The Google Culture," **http://www.google. com/corporate/culture.html** (accessed May 15, 2008).

5. Benjamin Fulford, "The Tortoise Jumps the Hare," *Forbes,* February 2, 2004, pp. 53–56.

6. Kevin Kingsbury, "Merck Agrees to Pay $58 to Settle Vioxx Advertising Claims," *The Wall Street Journal,* May 20, 2008, **http://online.wsj.com/article/ SB121130041562407333.html** (accessed May 20, 2008).

7. Ashley Petry, "Ethical, and Profitable," *Indianapolis Star Online,* May 19, 2008, **http://www.indystar.com/apps/ pbcs.dll/article?AID=/20080519/ BUSINESS05/805190323** (accessed May 19, 2008).

8. Adam Smith, *Wealth of Nations* (New York: Modern Library, 1937; originally published in 1776).

9. Chris Perttila, "Keep It Simple," *Entrepreneur,* February 2006, pp. 60–64.

10. Dennis Hays, "Kodak's Faraci Named President, Chief Operating Officer," *Photo News Today,* September 24, 2007, **www. photonewstoday.com/?p=7890** (accessed May 20, 2008).

11. Sandra Bretting, "Growing a Market for a Unique Product," *The Houston Chronicle,* March 9, 2008 p. D6; "Green Garlic," gourmetsleuth.com, **www. gourmetsleuth.com/greengarlic.htm** (accessed May 14, 2008); Gourmet Country Farm Web site, **http://www. gourmetcountryfarm.com** (accessed May 14, 2008).

12. Peter Gumbel, "Big Mac's Local Flavor," *CNN.com,* May 2, 2008, **http:// money.cnn.com/2008/04/29/news/ companies/big_macs_local.fortune/ index.htm** (accessed May 22, 2008).

13. Gary Hamel, "What Google, Whole Foods Do Best," *CNN.com,* September 26, 2007, **http://money.cnn.com/2007/ 09/26/news/companies/management_ hamel.fortune/index.htm,** (accessed May 22, 2008).

14. Alex Taylor III, "A Tale of 2 GM's," February 14, 2008, *CNN.com,* **http:// money.cnn.com/2008/02/13/magazines/ fortune/taylor_gmoverseas.fortune/ index.htm** (accessed May 22, 2008).

15. Aaron O. Patrick and Betsy McKay, "A Bittersweet Victory?" *The Wall Street Journal,* April 11, 2008, p. C1.

16. Jon R. Katzenbach and Douglas K. Smith, "The Discipline of Teams," *Harvard Business Review* 71 (March–April 1993), pp. 111–20.

17. Ibid.

18. Leah Buchanan, "When Absence Makes the Team Grow Stronger," *Inc.,* June 2008, p. 40.

19. Darryl Haralson and Adrienne Lewis, "USA Today Snapshots," *USA Today,* April 26, 2001, p. B1.

20. "Coca-Cola Task Force Named," PRNewswire, press release, July 2, 2001, via **www.prnewswire.com/cgi-bin/**

stories.pl?_ACCT=104&STORY=/www/ story/07-02-01/0001525462&EDATE=.

21. Julia Chang, "A View from the Top," *Sales & Marketing Management,* February 2004, p. 19.

22. Jerry Useem, "What's That Spell? TEAMWORK," *Fortune,* June 12, 2006, p. 66.

23. Jia Lynnyang, "The Power of Number 4.6," *Fortune,* June 12, 2006, p. 122.

24. Nicole Miller, "UW-Madison's Product Development Team Beats the Odds," College of Architecture and Life Sciences News, January 3, 2006, **http://news.cals. wisc.edu/newsDisplay.asp?id=1445** (accessed May 29, 2008).

25. Richard S. Wellins, William C. Byham, and Jeanne M. Wilson, *Empowered Teams: Creating Self-Directed Work Groups That Improve Quality, Productivity, and Participation* (San Francisco: Jossey-Bass Publishers, 1991), p. 5.

26. Josh Kyatt, "The Soul of a New Team," *Fortune,* June 12, 2006. pp. 134–150.

27. Peg Kelly, "Vampire Meetings and How to Slay Them," *WebPro News,* January 7, 2003, **www.webpronews.com/ articles/2003/0102pk.html.**

28. Fulford, "The Tortoise Jumps Over the Hare."

29. Wikipedia, "Intranet," **http://er. wikipedia.org/wiki/intranet** (accessed June 12, 2006).

30. Nielsen Norman Group Report, *Intranet Design Annual 2006: Ten Best Intranets of the Year,* **www.nngroup.com/ reports/intranet/design/** (accessed June 12, 2006).

31. "Personal Use Abuse," *Internet Works* 66 (January 2003), **www.iwks.com.**

32. "New Products Add Fun and Humor to Employee Communications and Training," PRNewswire, press release, June 5, 2001, via **www.prnewswire.com.**

33. Stacy Perman, "Concrete Decision," *BusinessWeek,* February/March 2007; Rick Hampson, "Tree Roots Can't Ravage This Sidewalk," *USA Today,* **www.usatoday. com/news/nation/2006-09-19-side- walks_x.htm** (accessed May 13, 2008); **www.rubbersidewalks.com** (accessed May 13, 2008).

34. Erika Germer, "Huddle Up," *Fast Company,* December 2000, p. 86.

35. "Privacy (Employee)," Business for Social Responsibility, **www.bsr.org/ CSRResources/IssueBriefDetail.cfm? DocumentID=538** (accessed May 20, 2004).

36. Michael D. Maginn, *Effective Teamwork,* 1994, p. 10. © 1994 Richard D. Irwin, a Times Mirror Higher Education Group, Inc., company.

37. New Belgium Brewing Company Website. **http://www.newbelgium.com/ index.php** (accessed June 22, 2006); Greg Owsley, New Belgium Brewing Marketing Director "The Necessity for Aligning Brand with Corporate Ethics," In Sheb True, Linda Ferrell, O.C. Ferrell, "Fullfilling our Obligation," Kennesaw State University, 2005. Bryan Simpson, New Belgium Brewing, "New Belgium Brewing: Brand Building Through Advertising and Public Relations."

## CHAPTER 9

1. Barbara De Lollis, "At Goya, It's All in la Familia," *USA Today,* March 24, 2008, p. 1B-2B; Pan Demetrakakes, "Hispanic Consumers Are Goya's Gold Mine," *Food & Drug Packaging,* August 2003 **http:// findarticles.com/p/articles/mi_m0UQX/ is_8_67/ai_108000120** (accessed April 20, 2008); "About Goya Foods," **www.goya .com/english/about.html** (accessed April 20, 2008)

2. Dan Reed, "Jet Blue Tries to Bounce Back from Storm of Trouble," *USA Today,* June 7, 2007, pp. B1–B2; Steve Huettel, "Jet Blue Issues Fliers' Bill of Rights," *St. Petersburg Times,* February 20, 2007, **www.sptimes.com/2007/02/20/news_pf/ Business/Jet_Blue_issues_flier.shtml** (accessed May 14, 2008); Lior Arussy, "Effective Customer Complaints Handling, Focus: Customer," *CRMXchange,* April 2007, **www.crmxchange.com/ focus_customer/april07.asp** (accessed May 14, 2008); Roger Yu, "Airlines' Performance New 20 Year Low," *USA Today,* April 8, 2008, p. B1.

3. Valerie A. Zeithaml and Mary Jo Bitner, *Services Marketing,* 3rd ed. (Boston: McGraw-Hill Irwin, 2003), p. 7.

4. Bruce Horovitz, "A whole New Ballgame in Grocery Shopping," *USA Today,* March 9, 2005, p. B1.

5. Tahl Raz, "A Recipe for Perfection," *Inc.,* July 2003, pp. 36–38.

6. Leonard L. Berry, *Discovering the Soul of Service* (New York: The Free Press, 1999), pp. 86–96.

7. Zeithaml and Bitner, *Services Marketing,* pp. 3, 22.

8. Bernard Wysocki Jr., "To Fix Health Care, Hospitals Take Tips from the Factory Floor," *The Wall Street Journal,* April 9, 2004, **http://online.wsj.com.**

9. Ibid.

10. Jean Halliday, "Nissan Delves into Truck Owner Psyche," *Advertising Age,* December 1, 2003, p. 11.

11. David Kiley, "Ghosn Hits the Accelerator," *BusinessWeek,* May 12, 2008, p. 49.

12. Faith Keenan, "Opening the Spigot," *BusinessWeek e.biz,* June 4, 2001, **www. businessweek.com/magazine/content/ 01_23/b3735616.htm.**

13. Ryan Underwood, "Dear Customer . . . Managing E-mail Campaigns," *Inc.,* March 2008, p. 59.

14. Kiri Blakeley, "Entrepreneurs: Fancy Footwork," *Forbes,* April 9, 2007; "MINK Shoes Story: Rebecca Brough Bio," **www. minkshoes.com/story** (accessed August 20, 2007).

15. "Overview of Assembly," Honda (n.d.), **www.hondacorporate.com/america/ index.html?subsection = manufacturing** (accessed May 13, 2004).

16. "Hershey's Chocolate Kisses," Hershey (n.d.), **www.hersheys.com/products/ kisses.shtml** (accessed April 21, 2004).

17. Dannis Simenaitis, "Just Puffin' Corn?" *Road & Track,* June 2008, pp. 95–96.

18. "Tesla Motors Building Car Plant in New Mexico," *Silicon Valley/San Jose Business Journal,* February 20, 2007, **http://albuquerque.bizjournals.com/ sanjose/stories/2007/02/19/daily19.html** (accessed June 3, 2008).

19. "Good Jobs First—Shopping for Subsidies," *Spokane Spokesman Review,* May 2004, **http://walmartwatch.com/pdf/ ad-nyt-042005-backup.pdf.** (accessed June 13, 2006).

20. Stacy Perman, "Automate or Die," *eCompany,* July 2001, p. 62.

21. "First Quarter 2006 Robot Sales Impacted by Downturn in Automotive Market," *Robotics Online,* May 3, 2006, **www.roboticsonline.com/public/articles/ articlesdetails.cfm?id=2377.**

22. David Noonan, "The Ultimate Remote Control," *Newsweek,* via **www. msnbc.com/news/588560.asp** (accessed July 18, 2001).

23. Robot Assisted Heart Surgery: Information from Answers.com **www.answers. com/topic/robot-assisted-heart-surgery www.answers.com/topic/robot-assisted- heart-surgery** (accessed June 13, 2006).

24. Keith Johnson, "Wal-Mart: We Are Not Green," *The Wall Street Journal,* March 13, 2008, p. A1.

25. www.wal-mart.com (accessed May 20, 2008).

26. Bryan Walsh, "Why Green Is the New Red, White and Blue," *Time,* April 28, 2008, p. 53.

27. David Welch, "GM Live Green or Die," *BusinessWeek,* May 26, 2008, p. 40.

28. Megan Kamerick, "How To Go Green," *New Mexico Business Weekly,* May 23–29, 2008, p. 3.

29. O. C. Ferrell and Michael D. Hartline, *Marketing Strategy* (Mason, OH: South-Western, 2005), p. 215.

30. John Edwards, "Orange Seeks Agent," *Inbound Logistics,* January 2006, pp. 239–242.

31. Ferrell and Hertline, *Marketing Strategy,* p. 215.

32. Robert Guy Matthews, "Fast-Rising Steel Prices Set Back Big Projects," *The Wall Street Journal,* May 15, 2008, p. B1

33. Bob Daniell, John Tracy, and Simon Kaye, "Made in China: Perspectives on the Global Manufacturing Giant," *Inbound Logistics,* March 2008, pp. 46–49.

34. Bruce Nussbaum, "Where Are the Jobs?" *BusinessWeek,* March 22, 2004, pp. 36–37.

35. Lisa H. Harington, "Balancing on the Rim," *Inbound Logistics,* January 2006, pp. 168–170.

36. "Opinion Research Corporation, Survey of 1,012 Respondents," *USA Today Snapshots,* Public Influence on Outsourcing. October 4, 2005, p. B1.

37. Alex Taylor III, "The $12K Smart Car's Wheeler Dealer," *Fortune,* October 15, 2007, http://money.cnn.com/2007/10/04/autos/smartcar_penske.fortune/index.htm (accessed May 14, 2008); Kellen Schetter, "Smart Car Offers Drivers New High MPG Option," Greencar.com, 2008, www.greencar.com/features/smart-car (accessed May 14, 2008); Michelle Krebs, "Smart Moves: Microcar Goes for Big Splash," *Auto Observer,* July 3, 2007, www.autoobserver.com/2007/07/smart-moves-mic.html (accessed May 14, 2008); "FAQ: Smart Car America", www.smartcarofamerica.com/faqs (accessed May 14, 2008); GasBuddy.com (accessed May 14, 2008).

38. Roger Yu, "Airlines' Performance Near 20-year Low," *USA Today,* April 8, 2008, p. B1.

39. Michael E. Newman, "Presidential Award for Excellence Honors Five U.S. Organizations, Two Nonprofits Recognized in First Year of Category," National Institute of Standards and Technology News Release, November 20, 2007, http://www.nist.gov/public_affairs/releases/2007baldrigerecipients.htm (accessed June 4, 2008).

40. Christopher Lawton, "The War on Product Returns," *The Wall Street Journal,* May 8, 2008, p. D1.

41. Ibid.

42. Philip B. Crosby, *Quality Is Free: The Art of Making Quality Certain* (New York: McGraw-Hill, 1979), pp. 9–10.

43. Nigel F. Piercy, *Market-Led Strategic Change* (Newton, MA: Butterworth-Heinemann, 1992), pp. 374–385.

44. Global Investment Recovery, "E-Scrap Meets Its Re-maker," *Fortune,* May 12, 2008, p S3.

45. "Hershey's Chocolate Kisses," Hershey.

46. "Employment Opportunities," Careers in Supply Chain Management, http://www.careersinsupplychain.org/career-outlook/empopp.asp (accessed June 27, 2008).

47. James Wetherbe, "Principles of Cycle Time Reduction," *Cycle Time Research,* 1995, p. iv.

48. Stan Davis and Christopher Meyer, *Blur: The Speed of Change in the Connected Economy* (Reading, MA: Addison-Wesley, 1998), p. 5.

49. Video; Michael Arndt, "McDonald's 24/7," *BusinessWeek,* February 5, 2007, http://www.businessweek.commagazine/content/07_06/b4020001.htm?campaign_id=nws_insdr_jan26&link_position=link1 (accessed June 12, 2008); Conor Cunneen, "McDonald's Turnaround Offers Crucial Lessons for All Operators," *Nation's Restaurant News,* February 18, 2008, http://www.nrn.com/article.aspx?keyword=&menu_id=1508&id=350558 (accessed June 12, 2008).

## CHAPTER 10

1. "Inc. 5000: The Fastest Growing Private Companies in America, No. 1,155: Amadeus Consulting," *Inc.com,* 2008, www.inc.com/inc5000/2007/company-profile.html?id=200711550 (accessed April 20, 2008); Lyla D. Hamilton, "Amadeus Consulting Composes Code for Growth," *ColoradoBiz,* October 2007, www.cobizmag.com/articles.asp?id=1832 (accessed April 20, 2008); "About Us," Amadeus Consulting, www.amadeusconsulting.com/AboutUs.aspx (accessed April 20, 2008); Melissa Johnson, "Lisa Calkins-'Geek Girl' Turned Business Pioneer," *Boulder Women's Magazine,* April 2008, www.boulderwomensmag.com/articles/2006/04/01/news/profile/profile.txt (accessed April 20, 2008).

2. Adam Lashinsky, "Where Does Google Go Next?" May 12, 2008, http://money.cnn.com/2008/05/09/technology/where_does_google_go.fortune/index.htm (accessed June 3, 2008).

3. "The Flip Side of Productivity," Ceredian, newsletter, Spring 2004, www.ceredian.com/myceredian/article/1,2481,11337-=3923,00.html.

4. "Jobs," Nikebiz.com, http://www.nike.com/nikebiz/jobs/usa/p_benefitdetails.jhtml;bsessionid=1XFACZ0XX0VIWCQFTC2CF4YKAWMLSIZB (accessed June 3, 2008).

5. "Why Individual Incentives?" http://marriott.com/incentives/Travel.mi (accessed June 20, 2006); "Teamwork Incentive Program," www.secstate.wa.gov/productivityboard/tip.aspx (accessed June 20, 2006).

6. Ben Rooney, "Most CEO Salaries Were Stunted in 2007," May 29, 2008, http://money.cnn.com/2008/05/29/news/economy/executive_pay/index.htm (accessed June 3, 2008).

7. Civic Ventures, "The Purpose Prize: Meet Ray Anderson," www.purposeprize.org/finalists/finalists2007/anderson.cfm (accessed April 28, 2008); Interface, Inc., "Annual Report 2006," pp. 3-4, 7-8, 13-14, http://library.corporate-ir.net/library/11/112/112931/items/242191/Interface_AR06.pdf (accessed April 28, 2008); Interface Inc., "Who We Are/Founder," www.interfaceinc.com/who/founder.html (accessed April 28, 2008); Jennifer Beck, "Business Hero: Ray Anderson," www.myhero.com/myheroaprint.asp?hero=r_anderson (accessed April 28, 2008).

8. Abraham Maslow, *Motivation and Personality* (New York: Harper & Row, 1954).

9. "Global Workforce Study Ranks Employees Low on Loyalty, Commitment to Employers," *SHRM HR News,* September 25, 2000, www.shrm.org/hrnews/articles/default.asp?page=bna0925c.htm.

10. *L.L. Bean News,* February 21, 2008, http://www.llbean.com/customerService/

aboutLLBean/newsroom/stories/ 02212008_LLBean_News.html (accessed June 3, 2008).

11. John Tschohl, "Empowerment: The Key to Customer Service," www. bizonline-content.com/BizResource Online/harris/displayarticle.asp?clientid =4&categoryid=4&id=54 (accessed June 21, 2006).

12. Douglas McGregor, *The Human Side of Enterprise* (New York: McGraw-Hill, 1960), pp. 33–34.

13. Ron Mott, "For Best Buy Workers, a 'Racial' Orientation," *NBC Nightly News with Brian Williams,* www.msnbc.msn .com/id/3032619/#23960059 (accessed May 9, 2008); Zac Bissonnette, "Best Buy Workers Make a Serious Commitment to Diversity," *BloggingStocks,* April 6, 2008, http://www.bloggingstocks.com/2008/ 04/06/best-buy-workers-makes-a-serious- commitment-to-diversity (accessed May 9, 2008); Best Buy Corporate Responsibil- ity, http://69.12.100/csr/people.asp; "Diversity," Best Buy Career Center, http://69.12.100/CareerCenter/Diversity. asp (accessed May 9, 2008); "Culture," Best Buy Career Center, http://69.12.100/ CareerCenter/Culture.asp (accessed May 9, 2008); "About the Museum," National Civil Rights Museum, www. civilrightsmuseum.org/about/about.asp (accessed May 9, 2008).

14. Ibid, pp. 47–48.

15. Jon L. Pierce, Tatiana Kostova, and Kurt T. Kirks, "Toward a Theory of Psy- chological Ownership in Organizations," *Academy of Management Review* 26, no. 2 (2001), p. 298.

16. Associated Press, "WalMart Strug- gling with Rising Loss from Shoplifting and Employee Theft," June 13, 2007, http://www.kxmb.com/News/133302.asp (accessed June 3, 2008).

17. Archie Carroll, "Carroll: Do We Live in a Cheating Culture?" *Athens Banner- Herald,* February 21, 2004, www. onlineathens.com/stories/022204/bus_ 20040222028.shtml.

18. Geoff Colvin, "How Top Companies Breed Stars," September 20, 2007, http:// money.cnn.com/magazines/fortune/ fortune_archive/2007/10/01/100351829/ index.htm (accessed June 3, 2008).

19. My Guides USA.com, "Which Jobs Offer Flexible Work Schedules?" http:// jobs.myguidesusa.com/answers-to-my- questions/which-jobs-offer-flexible- work-schedules?/ (accessed June 3, 2008).

20. Robert Preidt, "Workplace Flexibility Can Boost Healthy Behaviors," *Business- Week,* December 14, 2007, http://www. businessweek.com/lifestyle/content/ healthday/610798.html?chan=search (accessed June 3, 2008).

21. My Guides USA.com, "Which Jobs Offer Flexible Work Schedules?" http:// jobs.myguidesusa.com/answers-to-my- questions/which-jobs-offer-flexible- work-schedules?/ (accessed June 3, 2008).

22. Adam Geller, "Employers Cut 'Work/ Life' Programs," *Sun,* October 23, 2003, www.thesunlink.com/redesign/2003–10– 23/business/290909.shtml.

23. Larry Muhammad, "Help for the Helpers," *[Louisville] Courier-Journal,* April 20, 2004, www.courier-journal .com/features/2004/04/20/helpers.html.

24. "Annual Survey Shows Americans Are Working from Many Different Locations Outside Their Employer's Office," October 4, 2005, www.workingfromanywhere. org/news/pr100405.htm (accessed June 21, 2006).

25. "Telecommuting Benefits Docu- mented," www.telecommutect.com/con- tent/benifits.htm (accessed June 21, 2006).

26. "HR Executives Split on Telecommut- ing," *USA Today,* March 1, 2006, p. B1.

27. James Park, "You're Hired!," *Entrepreneur.com,* October 2007, www. entrepreneur.com/article/printthis/ 184466.html (accessed March 20, 2008); "Our Companies," Emerging Demograph- ics, Inc., www.emergingdemographics. com/our_companies.htm (accessed March 20, 2008); "Management," HireWorkers.com, www.hireworkers. com/management.php (accessed March 20, 2008); "Pricing and Information for Hiring Help," HireWorkers.com www.hireworkers.com/hire_now.php (accessed March 20, 2008); "About Us," HireWorkers.com, www.hireworkers. com/AboutUs.php (accessed March 20, 2008); "Online Service Allows Low-wage Jobseekers to Access Recruitment Service by Phone in Multiple Languages," *PRNewswire,* May 30, 2007, www.java. sys-con.com/read/382561_p.htm (accessed March 20, 2008).

28. Stephanie Armour, "Telecommuting Gets Stuck in the Slow Lane," *USA Today,* June 25, 2001, pp. 1A, 2A.

29. Ask Inc., "How Can We Keep Employ- ees Excited and Motivated When We're No Longer Seeing Skyrocketing Growth?" *Inc.,* June 2008, p 64.

30. "The Best Places for Business and Careers," *Forbes,* March 19, 2008, http:// www.forbes.com/lists/2008/1/bestplaces08 _Best-Places-For-Business-And-Careers_ Rank.html (accessed June 28, 2008).

31. Marcia Pennington Shannon, "Work- Life Balance: Promoting a Vacation- Friendly Firm," *Law Practice Magazine,* March 2008, www.abanet.org/lpm/maga- zine/articles/v34/is2/pg62.shtml (accessed June 13, 2008); Deb Perelman, "How to Improve Your Chances of Taking an Unwired Vacation," *eWeek.com,* May 29, 2008, www.eweek.com/c/a/careers/How- to-Improve-Your-Chances-of-Taking- an-Unwired-Vacation (accessed June 13, 2008); "Chicago Hotel Helps Clients Beat BlackBerry Addiction," *Foxnews.com,* June 9, 2006, www.foxnews.com/story/ 0,2933,198697,00.html (accessed June 13, 2008); "Everyone Wins with Paid Time Off," *JobsInME.com,* June 13, 2008, www.jobsinme.com/misc/page.aspx? pagenum=697 (accessed June 13, 2008).

## CHAPTER II

1. Dee Gill, "Do Your Employees Qualify for Overtime? The Answer May Surprise You," *Inc.,* January 2007, p. 37; Jayne O'Donnell, "Slow Times Mean Pay Cuts for Many," *USA Today,* June 2, 2008, pp. B1–B2; Stephanie Armour, "Fuel Prices Drive Some to Try Four-day Work- weeks," *USA Today,* June 2, 2008, p. B1; "How Can We Keep Employees Motivated When We're No Longer Seeing Skyrocket- ing Growth?," *Inc.,* June 2008, p. 64.

2. "P&G: Recruiting Processes," http://www.pg.ma/careers/index. php?option=com_content&task=view&i d=34&Itemid=49 (accessed June 4, 2008).

3. Jason Dean, "The Forbidden City of Terry Gou," *The Wall Street Journal,* August 11-12, 2007, pp. A1, A5; Luisa Kroll, "The World's Billionaires: #160 Terry Gou," *Forbes.com,* March 5, 2008, http://www.forbes.com/lists/2008/10/ billionaires08_Terry-Gou_X28Q.html (accessed May 15, 2008); "The Informa- tion Technology Top 100: #2 Hon Hai Pre- cision Ind.," *BusinessWeek,* http://www. businessweek.com/it100/2005/company/ HONHI.htm (accessed June 12, 2008).

4. Ibid.

5. "MBTI Basics," The Myers-Briggs Foundation, http://www.myersbriggs. org/my-mbti-personality-type/mbti- basics/ (accessed June 4, 2008).

6. "What Does Employee Alcohol & Drug Use Cost Your Business," DWI Resource

Center, **http://www.dwiresourcecenter. org/bizcenter/workplace/cost.shtml** (accessed June 4, 2008).

7. Associated Press, "Food Network Chef Fired After Resume Fraud," *USA Today,* March 3, 2008 **http://www.usatoday. com/news/nation/2008-03-03-chef-fired_N.htm** (accessed June 4, 2008).

8. "Charge Statistics FY 1992 through FY 2003," Equal Employment Opportunity Commission (n.d.), **www.eeoc.gov/stats/ charges.html** (accessed May 28, 2004).

9. Joseph Daniel McCool, "Diversity Picture Rings Hollow," *BusinessWeek,* February 5, 2008, **http://www. businessweek.com/managing/content/ feb2008/ca2008025_080192.htm? chan=search** (accessed June 4, 2008).

10. Stephen Bastien, "12 Benefits of Hiring Older Workers," *Entrepreneur .com,* September 20, 2006, **http://www. entrepreneur.com/humanresources/ hiring/article167500.html** (accessed June 4, 2008).

11. Ellen Wulfhorst, "U.S. Gender Pay Gap Emerges Early, Study Finds," *Reuters,* April 23, 2007, **http://www. reuters.com/article/topNews/ idUSN2029109620070423,** accessed June 5, 2008.

12. Gina Ruiz, "Cheesecake Factory Cooks Up a Rigorous Training Program," *Workforce Management,* **http://www. workforce.com/section/11/feature/ 24/35/18/index.html** (accessed June 5, 2008).

13. "FAQs," Procter & Gamble (n.d.), **www.pg.com/jobs/jobs_us/faqs/index .jhtml** (accessed May 7, 2004).

14. Patrick Thibodeau, "Best Buy Settles Age Discrimination Lawsuit with Former IT Workers," *Computerworld,* June 26, 2007, **http://www.computerworld.com/ action/article.do?command=viewArticle Basic&articleId=9025759** (accessed June 5, 2008).

15. Maury A. Peiperl, "Getting 360-Degree Feedback Right," *Harvard Business Review,* January 2001, pp. 142–48.

16. Chris Musselwhite, "Self Awareness and the Effective Leader," *Inc.com,* **http:// www.inc.com/resources/leadership/ articles/20071001/musselwhite.html** (accessed June 5, 2008).

17. Laura Lorber, "A Corporate Culture Makeover," *The Wall Street Journal,* **http://online.wsj.com/article/ SB120827656392416609.html** (accessed June 5, 2008).

18. Anne Fisher, "Workplace: Turning Clock Watchers into Stars," *Fortune,* March 8, 2004, **www.fortune.com**.

19. Associated Press, "General Motors Downsizing Plants, Cars," *Herald Net,* **http://www.heraldnet.com/article/ 20080604/BIZ/91714729** (accessed June 5, 2008).

20. "100 Best Companies to Work for: 2008," *Fortune,* February 4, 2008, **http:// money.cnn.com/magazines/fortune/ bestcompanies/2008/snapshots/7.html** (accessed April 22, 2008); Starbucks 2006 Annual Report, pp. 11–15, **http:// media.corporate-ir.net/media_files/ irol/99/99518/reports/Starbucks AnnualReport.pdf** (accessed April 22, 2008); Starbucks 2007 Annual Report, p. 7, **http://www.starbucks.com/flash/ yearinreview/Starbucks_Fiscal_2007_ Annual_Report.pdf** (accessed April 22, 2208); Sonia Narang, "Carbon With That Latte?" *Forbes,* July 3, 2007, **www.forbes. com/2007/07/02/starbucks-emissions-environment-biz-cz_sn_0703green_ carbon.html** (accessed April 22, 2008); "Starbucks: Company Fact Sheet," **www. starbucks.com/aboutus/Company_ Factsheet.pdf** (accessed April 22, 2008).

21. U.S. Department of Labor, "Minimum Wage," **http://www.dol.gov/dol/ topic/wages/minimumwage.htm** (accessed June 5, 2008).

22. David Kiley, "Crafty Basket Makers Cut Downtimes,Waste," *USA Today,* May 10, 2001, p. C1.

23. "Kele & Co: First Innovative Jewelry Company in Direct Sales," May 5, 2008, **http://www.24-7pressrelease.com/press-release/kele-co-the-first-innovative-jewelry-company-in-direct-sales-48835 .php** (accessed June 5, 2008).

24. Kemp Powers, "Happy Employees," *Fortune,* March 25, 2004, **www.fortune.com**.

25. Winston Wood, "Work Week," *The Wall Street Journal,* May 1, 2001, p. A1.

26. "Employer Costs for Employee Compensation," U.S. Bureau of Labor Statistics, March 12, 2008, **http://www.bls .gov/news.release/ecec.nr0.htm** (accessed June 5, 2008).

27. "Microsoft Reins in Benefits," *Austin American-Statesman,* May 21, 2004, **www. statesman.com**.

28. Jesse Russell, "Despite Union Percentage Declines, Union Workers Make More Money," *Workers Independent News,* January 31, 2007, **http://www.laborradio.org/ node/5182** (accessed June 6, 2008).

29. "5-Month Grocery Strike Draws to an End," *CNN,* March 1, 2004, **www.cnn.com**.

30. "Work Stoppages Involving 1,000 or More Workers, 1947-2007," U.S. Department of Labor, February 13, 2008, **http:// www.bls.gov/news.release/wkstp.t01 .htm** (accessed June 16, 2008).

31. Jerry Bowles, "Putting Supplier Diversity to Work," *BusinessWeek,* April 16, 2007, pp.68-69; "AT&T," **www.att.com** (accessed February 26, 2008); "AT&T Selected as the No. 1 Organization for Multicural Business Opportunities," **http://www.attsuppliers.com/diversity. asp** (accessed May 16, 2008); "NMSDC Announces Top Regional Minority Suppliers," National Minority Supplier Development Council, **http://www.nmsdc. org/news/2007_NMSDC_%20Regional_ %20Suppliers_of_%20the_Year.pdf** (accessed May 16, 2008).

32. "Characteristics of the Civilian Labor Force, 1990–2010," *InfoPlease* (n.d.), **www. infoplease.com/ipa/A0904534.html** (accessed May 28, 2004).

33. Annie Finnigan, "Different Strokes," *Working Woman,* April 2001, p. 42; Linda Tischler, "Where Are the Women?" *Fast Company,* February 2004, pp. 52–60.

34. Feliciano Garcia, "US West Has the Tool," *Fortune,* July 10, 2000, p. 198.

35. Taylor H. Cox, Jr., "The Multicultural Organization," *Academy of Management Executives* 5 (May 1991), pp. 34–47; Marilyn Loden and Judy B. Rosener, *Workforce America! Managing Employee Diversity as a Vital Resource* (Homewood, IL: Business One Irwin, 1991).

36. Steven Greenhouse, "Working Life (High & Low)," *The New York Times,* April 20, 2008, **http://www.nytimes. com/2008/04/20/business/20work. html?pagewanted=1&_r=2&sq=patag onia&st=nyt&scp=3&adxnnlx=12137 16680-NwDtpNW5AJGLZteoOMxTGg** (accessed June 17, 2008); **www.patagonia .com** (accessed June 17, 2008); "Patagonia Is Awarded 'Eco Brand of the Year' at the Volvo EcoDesign Forum," *The Earth Times,* February 4, 2008, **http://www.earthtimes .org/articles/show/patagonia-is-awarded-eco-brand-of-the-year-at-the,269911 .shtml** (accessed June 17, 2008); Susan Casey, "Patagonia: Blueprint for green business," *Fortune,* May 29, 2007, **http://money.cnn.com/magazines/ fortune/fortune_archive/2007/04/02/ 8403423/index.htm (accessed June 20, 2008).**

## CHAPTER 12

1. Rachel Dodes, "The Bargain Bride," *The Wall Street Journal,* June 16–17, 2007, pp. P1, P6; Michele Meyer, "Bargain Bridal Gowns," *USA Weekend,* October 26–28, 2007, p. 16; "Our World Famous Briday Event," Filene's Basement, **www. filenesbasement.com/bridal.jsp** (accessed March 20, 2008).

2. Sean Gregory, "Cool Runnings," *Time,* October 15, 2007, p. Global 9-10.

3. John D. Stoll, "GM Shifts Its Strategy into Reverse," *The Wall Street Journal,* June 4, 2008, pp. B1, B9.

4. "McDonald's Adult Happy Meal Arrives."

5. Marguerite Higgins, "McDonalds Labels Nutrition," *The Washington Times,* October 26, 2005, **washingtontimes.com/ business/20051025-102731-2213r.htm** (accessed June 16, 2006).

6. Dave Carpenter, "McDonald's Cooking Fries in Trans-Fat-Free Oil," *Yahoo news,* May 22, 2008, **http://news.yahoo .com/ap/20080522/ap_on_bi_ge/ mcdonald_s_oil** (accessed June 5, 2008).

7. Matthew Miller, "Playing Cupid to the Rich and Famous," *Forbes,* May 30, 2007, **http://www.forbes.com/entrepreneurs/ management/2007/05/30/matchmaking- small-business-ent-manage-cx_mm_ 0530match.html?feed=rss_entrepreneurs_ entremgmt** (accessed February 4, 2008); Samantha's Table, **www.samanthastable .com** (accessed February 5, 2008).

8. "Beauty Queen," *People,* May 10, 2004, p. 187.

9. Michael Treacy and Fred Wiersema, *The Discipline of Market Leaders* (Reading, MA: Addison Weslsey, 1995), p. 176.

10. Apple Annual Report 10-k, 2005.

11. "Customer Is King—Says Who," *Advertising Age,* April 15, 2006, p. 4.

12. Venky Shankar, "Multiple Touch Point Marketing," American Marketing Association Faculty Consortium on Electronic Commerce, Texas A&M University, July 14–17, 2001.

13. **www.amazon.com** (accessed June 16, 2006).

14. Stephanie Kang, "The Swoosh Finds Its Swing, Targeting Weekend Golfers," *The Wall Street Journal,* April 8, 2004, p. B1.

15. Mary Lower, "5 Tips to Help Men Target Women Authentically," *Marketing News,* April 15, 2006, p. 9.

16. Allison Marr, "Household-Level Research Gives Clearer Picture," *Marketing News,* April 15, 2006, p. 18.

17. Emily Bryson York, "Hispanic Boom Sparks Wal-Mart Turn to Tacos," *Advertising Age,* May 19, 2008, pp. 3, 45.

18. Deborah L. Vance, "Mix It Up," *Marketing News,* October 15, 2006, pp. 19–22.

19. Mya Frazier, "Staples Gains Footing in Hispanic Market," *Advertising Age,* April 3, 2006, p. 58.

20. "Dynamic Demographics," The Diversity Training Group, **http://www. diversitydtg.com/articles/demogs.html** (accessed June 12, 2008).

21. Laura Sonderup, "Keys to reaching the new American marketplace," *ColoradoBiz,* October, 2007, p. 12.

22. Courtney E. Counts, "Interactivism Allows Consumers to Co-create, Grows Loyalty," *Marketing News,* October 1, 2006, p. 6.

23. Dean Reynolds, "The Price of the Perfect Name? $350," *ABC News,* July 10, 2007, **http://abcnews.go.com/ print?id=3363739** (accessed September 17, 2007); Baby Naming Central, **http:// www.babynamingcentral.com** (accessed September 17, 2007); Name Structures, **http://namepower101.com** (accessed September 18, 2007); Alexandra Alter, "The Baby-Name Business," *The Wall Street Journal,* June 22, 2007, pp. W1, W12.

24. Charles Passy, "Your Scoop Is in the Mail," *The Wall Street Journal,* May 25, 2001, pp. W1, W6.

25. The Coca-Cola Company, **www. questions.coca-cola.com/vrep/CokeSay .htm** (accessed June 2, 2004).

26. Dan Reed, "Summer Fares Double, Triple, Quadruple," *USA Today,* June 5, 2008, p. B1.

27. Chris Woodyard, "Sales Plunge Spares Small Cars," *USA Today,* June 4, 2008, p. B1.

28. John Simons, "Don't Count Blockbuster Out," *Money.CNN.com,* March 6, 2008, **http://money.cnn.com/2008/03/06/ technology/simons_blockbuster.fortune/ index.htm** (accessed June 13, 2008).

29. Laura Petrecca, "Marketers Say 'Tanks' for Buying with Gifts of Gas," *USA Today,* June 4, 2008, p. 3B.

30. Michael J. Weiss, "To Be About to Be," *American Demographics* 25 (September 2003), pp. 29–36.

31. Matthew Heimer, "Mystery Shopper," *Smart Money,* December 2005, pp. 96–101.

32. "Focus Groups in Nebraska Help Market Tourism," *Marketing News,* January 6, 2003, p. 5.

33. "Online Research Spending Predicted to Grow to $4 Billion," GMI press, June 14, 2005, **www.gmi-mr.com/press/ release.php?p=2005–06–14** (accessed June 16, 2006).

34. Look-Look, **http://look-look.com** (accessed June 13, 2008).

35. Mountain Dew Dewmocracy, **http:// www.dewmocracy.com** (accessed June 13, 2008).

36. Iams, **http://us.iams.com/iams/ en_US/jsp/IAMS_Page.jsp?pageID=GSP** (accessed June 13, 2008).

37. Lisa McLaughlin, "Paper, Plastic or Prada?," *Time,* August 13, 2007, pp. 49–51; Megha Bahree, "Bag Lady," *Forbes,* November 26, 2007, http://members. forbes.com/forbes/2007/1126/109.html (accessed December 4, 2007).

38. Emily Nelson, "P&G Checks Out Real Life," *The Wall Street Journal,* May 17, 2001, p. B1.

39. Bryan Walsh, "Why Green Is the New Red, White and Blue," *Time,* April 28, 2008, pp. 45–58; Denis Ryan, "Taking the Green Change," *The Vancouver Sun,* May 31, 2008, pp. 136–37.

40. Ritz Carlton, **http://www.ritzcarlton .com** (accessed June 17, 2008); Four Seasons, **http://www.fourseasons .com** (accessed June 17, 2008); Mark V. Lomanno, "Luxury Hotel Segment Outperforms Industry," *Hotel & Motel Management,* April 16, 2007, **http://www. hotelmotel.com/hotelmotel/article/ articleDetail.jsp?id=418276&ref=25** (accessed June 17, 2008); Jonathan Barsky and Lenny Nash, "Are Luxury Hotels recession proof?," Center for Hospitality Research, Cornell University School of Hotel Administration, May 21, 2008, **http://www.hotelschool.cornell.edu/ research/chr/news/newsroom/detail. html?sid=32742** (accessed June 18, 2008).

## CHAPTER 13

1. Robert Levine, "Reincarnated Soul," Fortune, October 15, 2007, pp. 59-60; "About Concord Music Group," **www. concordmusicgroup.com/about.html** (accessed June 17, 2008); Ayala Ben-Yehuda, "Starbucks, Concord Music Group Form Label," Billboard.biz, March 12, 2007, **www. billboard.biz/bbbiz/content_display/ industry/e3i35ff0462bf2b53467e9a6cfee 0025b48** (accessed June 17, 2008); "Starbucks to Release CD by Hilary McRae," USA Today, October 30, 2007, **www. usatoday.com/life/music/2007-10-30- 137354059_x.htm** (accessed February 7, 2008); "Respect Yourself: The Stax Record Story," www.pbs.com, **http://www.pbs.**

org/wnet/gperf/shows/stax/index.html (accessed June 17, 2008); Katie Hasty, "Rascal Flatts Races to No. 1 In Debut-Heavy Week," **www.billboard.com, October 3, 2007, http://www.billboard.com/bbcom/news/article_display.jsp?vnu_content_id=1003650421** (accessed June 17, 2008).

2. **www.dominos.com/Public-EN/site+Content/secondary/inside+dominos/pizza+particulars/** (accessed June 17, 2008).

3. William Hupp, "The Dog Days of Dieting," *Advertising Age,* April 14, 2008, p. 14.

4. Michelle Krebs, "2007 Detroit Auto Show: Chevrolet Volt," *Edmunds,* January 7, 2007, **http://www.edmunds.com/insideline/do/Features/articleId=119088?mktcat=chevrolet-volt-pricing-ad-copy&kw=chevrolet+volt+pricing+ad+copy&mktid=gc47736448** (accessed June 17, 2008).

5. "Shuffle Master, Inc. Reports Second Quarter 2008 Results," Shuffle Master, Inc, June 9, 2008, **http://www.shufflemaster.com/01_company/news_press/news_detail.asp?newsID=146** (accessed June 17, 2008).

6. Brett Shevack, "Open Up to a New Way to Develop Better Ideas," *Point,* June 2006, p. 8.

7. Judann Pollack, "The Endurance Test, Heinz Ketchup," *Advertising Age,* November 14, 2005, p. 39.

8. Faith Keenan, "Friendly Spies on the Net," *BusinessWeek e.biz,* July 9, 2001, p. EB27.

9. Seasons 52, **www.seasons52.com** (accessed June 17, 2008).

10. Bruce Horovitz, "Scooping Out New Territory: Soft Serve," *USA Today,* May 8, 2008, p. 3B.

11. "Light Truck Sales Plummet in 2008," Green Car Congress, June 3, 2008, **http://www.greencarcongress.com/2008/06/light-truck-sal.html** (accessed June 25, 2008); "April 2008 Dashboard: Hybrids Sales Defy Recession," *HybridCars.com,* May 13, 2008, **http://www.hybridcars.com/market-dashboard/april-2008-hybrids-defy-recession.html** (accessed June 25, 2008).

12. "Tide Unveils Milestone in Fabric Care with New Tide Stainbrush," Procter & Gamble, press release, February 13, 2004, **www.pg.com/news/**.

13. Philip Elmer-DeWitt, "How to Grow the iPod as the MP3 Player Market Shrinks," *Fortune.com,* January 29, 2008, **http://apple20.blogs.fortune.cnn.com/2008/01/29/beyond-the-incredible-shrinking-ipod-market/** (accessed June 19, 2008); "iTunes Store Tops Over Five Billion Songs Sold," Apple.com, **http://www.apple.com/pr/library/2008/06/19itunes.html** (accessed June 19, 2008); Charles Gaba, "iPod Sales Quarterly and Total," *Mac Vs PC System Shootout* **http://www.systemshootouts.org/ipod_sales.html** (accessed June 19, 2008).

14. Bruce Horovitz, "Snacks: Does This Bag Make Me Look Fat?" *USA Today,* February 20, 2008, p B1.

15. T. L. Stanley, "Barbie Hits the Skids," *Advertising Age,* October 31, 2005, pp. 1, 33.

16. Michael Fielding, "Private-Label Brands Use New Tools to Compete," *Marketing News,* May 15, 2006, p. 11.

17. Alessandra Galloni, "Advertising," *The Wall Street Journal,* June 1, 2001, p. B6.

18. Mike Barris, "20-Ounce Sales Lose Fizz, Sinking Coke Enterprises," *The Wall Street Journal,* May 28, 2008, **http://online.wsj.com/article/SB121197848027325835.html** (accessed June 19, 2008).

19. "ACSI: Customer Satisfaction Halts Slide, Glimmer of Hope for the Economy?," American Customer Satisfaction Index, May 20, 2008, **http://www.theacsi.org/images/stories/images/news/0508Q1.pdf** (accessed June 25, 2008); Joe Kleinsasser, "AirTran Takes Top AQR Spot; Industry Score Falls To New Low," *This Is Wichita State,* April 16, 2008, **http://www.wichita.edu/thisis/wsunews/news/?nid=182** (accessed June 26, 2008).

20. Stephanie Miles, "Consumer Groups Want to Rate the Web," *The Wall Street Journal,* June 21, 2001, p. B13.

21. "American Demographics 2006 Consumer Perception Survey," *Advertising Age,* January 2, 2006, p. 9. Data by Synovate.

22. Rajneesh Suri and Kent B. Monroe, "The Effects of Time Constraints on Consumers' Judgments of Prices and Products," *Journal of Consumer Research* 30 (June 2003), pp. 92 + .

23. Elisabeth A. Sullivan, "Value Pricing: Smart Marketers Know Cost-Plus Can Be Costly," *Marketing News,* January 15, 2008, p.8.

24. Linda Tischler, "The Price Is Right," *Fast Company,* November 2003, pp. 83 + .

25. Andy Stone, "Drill Bits Are Forever," *Forbes,* December 10, 2007, p. 200.

26. "All Cayenne Models," Porsche, **http://www.porsche.com/usa/models/cayenne/** (accessed June 25, 2008).

27. Reena Jana, "Green Threads for the Eco Chic," *BusinessWeek,* September 27, 2006, **www.businessweek.com/print/innovate/content/sep2006/id20060927_111136.htm** (accessed June 20, 2007); Laura Petrecca and Theresa Howard, "Eco-marketing a Hot Topic for Advertisers at Cannes," *USA Today,* June 22, 2007, **www.usatoday.com/money/advertising/2007-06-22-cannes-green-usat_N.htm?csp=34** (accessed June 23, 2007); Laura McClure, "Green Jeans," *Reader's Digest,* June 2007, p. 213; "Levi's Brand Launches 100% Organic Cotton Jeans," www.levitrauss.com, July 5, 2006, **http://www.levistrauss.com/News/PressReleaseDetail.aspx?pid=784** (accessed June 20, 2007).

28. David Luhnow and Chad Terhune, "Latin Pop: A Low-Budget Cola Shakes Up Markets South of the Border," *The Wall Street Journal,* October 27, 2003, pp. A1, A18.

29. Emily Bryson York, "Taco Bell Tops Yum Portfolio After Tough Year," *Advertising Age,* May 12, 2008, p. 16.

30. Emily Bryson York, "McD's Dollar-Menu Fixation Sparks Revolt," *Advertising Age,* June 2, 2008, p. 1.

31. O. C. Ferrell and Michael D. Hartline, *Marketing Strategy* (Mason, OH: South-Western, 2005), p. 215.

32. "Top Threats to Revenue," *USA Today,* February 1, 2006, p. A1.

33. Brad Howarth, "Hear This, iPods from a Vending Machine," *The Sydney Morning Herald,* November 14, 2006, **http://www.smh.com.au/news/biztech/hear-this-ipods-from-a-vending-machine/2006/11/13/1163266481869.html** (accessed June 25, 2008).

34. Katy McLaughlin, "Kombucha Grows On You, Some Say, Like a Fungus," *The Wall Street Journal,* June 23–24, 2007, pp. A-1, A-7; Conan Milner, "Kombucha, Part 1," *The Epoch Times,* March 16, 2007, **http://en.epochtimes.com/news/7-3-16/52931.html** (accessed September 11, 2007); Conan Milner, "Kombucha, Part 2," *The Epoch Times,* March 22, 2007, **http://en.epochtimes.com/news/7-3-22/53236.html** (accessed September 11, 2007); "What Can Kombucha Do for Me?" **www.gtskombucha.com** (accessed September 11, 2007); "The Story Behind the Bottle," **www.gtskombucha.com** (accessed September 11, 2007).

35. Abbey Klaassen, "Even Google Has to Advertise," *Advertising Age,* June 2, 2008, p. 4.

36. Jonathon Ramsey, "Danica Patrick's GoDaddy.com Ad Banned from Super Bowl Because of Beavers," autoblog.com, Jan 24th 2008, **http://www.autoblog. com/2008/01/24/danica-patricks-godaddy-com-ad-banned-from-super-bowl-because-o/** (accessed June 25, 2008).

37. Stephanie Kang, "BMW Ran Risk With Silent Role in Mockumentary," *The Wall Street Journal,* June 20, 2008, p. B5.

38. Michael J. Weiss, "To Be About to Be," *American Demographics* 25 (September 2003), pp. 29–36.

39. Gerry Khermouch and Jeff Green, "Buzz Marketing," *BusinessWeek,* July 30, 2001, pp. 50– 56.

40. Olga Kharif, "An Epidemic of 'Viral Marketing,'" *BusinessWeek,* August 30, 2001, **www.businessweek.com**.

41. Donna L Montaldo, "2006 Coupon Usage and Trends,"About.com, **http:// couponing.about.com/od/localcoupons/ a/2006couponusage.htm** (accessed June 25, 2008).

42. Kate MacArthur, "Sierra Mist: Cie Nicholson," *Advertising Age,* November 17, 2003, p. S-2.

43. Michelle Maynard, "Amid the Turmoil, A Rare Success at DaimlerChrysler," *Fortune,* January 22, 2001, p. 112.

44. "Coca-Cola North America Announces the Launch of VAULT," February 17, 2006, **www2.coca-cola.com/ presscenter/newproducts_vault.html** (accessed June 16, 2006).

45. Anthony Bianco, "Wal-Mart's Midlife Crisis," *BusinessWeek,* April 30, 2007, **www.businessweek.com/magazine/con-tent/07_18/b4032001.htm** (accessed June 18, 2008); "Performance of Wal-Mart vs. Target," *Analytical Wealth,* May 20, 2008, **http://p9.hostingprod.com/analytical-wealth.com/blog/2008/05/20/walmart_vs_target.html** (accessed June 18, 2008).

## CHAPTER 14

1. Luisa Kroll, "The World's Billionaires," *Fortune,* March 5, 2008, **http://www. forbes.com/2008/03/05/richest-people-billionaires-billionaires08-cx_lk_ 0305billie_land.html** (accessed June 14, 2008); David Luhnow, "The Secrets of the World's Richest Man," *The Wall Street Journal,* August 4-5, 2007, pp. A1, A8; Tim Padgett, "Carlos Slim's Embarrassment of Riches," *Time,* July 11, 2007, **www.time. com/time/printout/06,8816,1642286,00 .html** (accessed March 20, 2008).

2. "Post-Enron Restatements Hit Record," *MSNBC,* January 21, 2003, **www.msnbc. com/news/862325.asp**.

3. "Break up the Big Four?" *CFO,* June 1, 2004, **www.cfo.com/article/ 1,5309,14007%7C%7CM%7C926,00 .html**.

4. Ken Rankin, "Silver Linings: Scandals May Create Job Security for CPAs," *Accounting Today,* May 17–June 6, 2004, **www.webcpa.com**.

5. Laura Demars, "Protectionist Measures," *CFO,* March 2006, p. 18.

6. Kris Frieswick, "How Audits Must Change," *CFO,* July 2003, p. 44.

7. "About the ACFE," The Association of Certified Fraud Examiners, **http://www. acfe.com/about/about.asp** (accessed June 23, 2008).

8. "Accounting Scandal Could Cost German FDP Millions," *Deutsche Welle- World,* June 16, 2008, **http://www. dw-world.de/dw/article/0,2144, 3414777,00.html** (accessed June 18, 2008).

9. Emily Main, "Fresh Finds: Your Eco-Radar for All Products New and Earth-Worthy: Automatic Transition," *Green Guide,* June 20, 2007, **www.thegreenguide .com/blog/freshfinds/831** (accessed April 2, 2008); John Donnelly and Matthew Spolar, "Car Rental Outfits Head in a Green Direction," *The Boston Globe,* August 9, 2007, **http://www.boston.com/ business/globe/articles/2007/08/09/car_ rental_outfits_head_in_a_green_ direction** (accessed April 2, 2008); "Hertz, Avis Plan to Boost Hybrid Fleets," *CNBC. com,* June 15, 2007, **www.cnbc.com/ id/19239398/print/1/displaymode/1098** (accessed April 2, 2008); "Hertz Green Collection," Hertz Rent-a-Car, **https:// www.hertz.com/rentacar/byr/index. jsp?targetPage=USgreencollection. jsp&leftNavUserSelection=globNav_3_ 5_1&region=United%20States** (accessed April 2, 2008).

10. Nicholas Day, "Wheeling Down the CT Cheese Trail," *The Hartford Advocate,* October 18, 2007, pp. 19–21; "About Us," Beltane Farm, **http://www.beltanefarm. com** (accessed November 1, 2007); Saxelby Cheesemongers, **http://www/ saxelbycheese.com** (accessed November 1, 2007).

11. Liza Hunn, "Significant Provisions of the Sarbanes-Oxley Act of 2002," unpublished research paper, Colorado State University, 2004; Sarbanes-Oxley Act, 2002 (H.R. 3763), text available at *Find Law,* **news.findlaw.com/hdocs/docs/gwbush/ sarbanesoxley072302.pdf** (accessed June 24, 2008); "The Investor's Advocate: How the SEC Protects Investors, Maintains Market Integrity, and Facilitates Capital Formation," The Securities and Exchange Commission, **http://www.sec.gov/about/ whatwedo.shtml** (accessed April 30, 2008); Kate O'Sullivan, "The SEC Rules," *CFO,* August 2007, pp. 46–52.

12. "Occupational Outlook Handbook 2008-2009: Accountants and Auditors," Bureau of Labor Statistics, **http://www. bls.gov/oco/ocos001.htm** (accessed June 27, 2008).

13. "Business Pushes Back on Scandal Reforms," *Associated Press,* March 11, 2007, **http://www.msnbc.msn.com/id/17568316** (accessed June 21, 2008); Adelphia Restructuring, **http://www.adelphiarestructuring .com** (accessed June 23, 2008); O. C. Ferrell, John Fraedrich, Linda Ferrell, *Business Ethics* (New York: Houghton Mifflin, 2005), pp. 62, 248, 273.

## CHAPTER 15

1. Prosper, **http://www.prosper.com/ about** (accessed June 17, 2008); Grameen Foundation, **http://www.gra-meenfoundation.org** (accessed June 17, 2008); Kiva, **http://www.kiva.org** (accessed June 17, 2008); Jane J. Kim, "Where Either a Borrower Or a Lender Be," *The Wall Street Journal,* March 12, 2008, **http://online.wsj.com/article/ SB120526439925827991.html** (accessed May 9, 2008); Jeninne Lee St. John, "Hey, Buddy, Can You Spare $10,000?" *Time,* February 29, 2008, www.time.com/time/ magazine/article/0,9171,1781569,00.html (accessed May 9, 2008); Mark Calvey, "Prosper CEO Sees Company Benefiting from Credit Crunch," *San Francisco Business Times,* February 25, 2008, **http://sanfrancisco.bizjournals.com/ sanfrancisco/stories/2008/02/25/daily9 .html** (accessed May 9, 2008).

2. "How Currency Gets into Circulation," Federal Reserve Bank of New York (n.d.), **www.newyorkfed.org/aboutthefed/ fedpoint/fed01.html** (accessed June 28, 2006).

3. Barbara Hagenbaugh, "It's Too Easy Being Green," *USA Today,* May 13, 2003, **www.usatoday.com/**.

4. Ibid.

5. "U.S. Unveils New $50 Note with Background Colors," Bureau of Engraving and

Printing, U.S. Department of the Treasury, press release, April 26, 2004, **www.moneyfactory.com/newmoney/main.cfm/media/**.

6. Barbara Hagenbaugh, "In a Mint First, Jefferson Puts His Best Face Forward," *USA Today,* January 12, 2006, **www.usatoday.com/money/economy/2006-01-12-nickel_x.htm** (accessed June 28, 2006).

7. Jane J. Kim, "The Credit-Card Catapult," *The Wall Street Journal,* March 25–26 2006, p. B1.

8. Emily Thornton, Heather Timmons, and Joseph Weber, "Who Will Hold the Cards," *BusinessWeek,* March 19, 2001, p. 90.

9. Tammi Luhby, "Barely Surviving on Credit Cards," *Money.CNN.com,* May 13, 2008, **http://money.cnn.com/2008/05/09/news/economy/creditcards/index.htm** (accessed June 17, 2008).

10. David Breitkopf, "MasterCard, Pulse Report Wider Use of Debit Cards," *American Banker,* May 17, 2004, p. 5.

11. Ann Carrns, "A Bank's Historian Shakes Money From Family Trees," *The Wall Street Journal,* May 19–20, 2007, pp. A1, A4; "Company Overview—1st Quarter 2007," http://www.wellsfargo.com/about/today1 (accessed June 24, 2008).

12. "FDIC: Statistics on Banking," FDIC, **www.fdic.gov/bank/statistical** (accessed June 10, 2004).

13. "2007 Annual Report," General Electric, p. 29.

14. Mara der Hovanesian, "I Have Just One Word For You: Bioplastics," *BusinessWeek,* June 30, 2008, pp. 44–47; Metabolix: Bio-Industrial Evolution, **http://www.metabolix.com/** (accessed June 26, 2008); Photodegradation, *Answers.com,* **http://www.answers.com/topic/photodegradation?cat=technology** (accessed June 26, 2008).

15. "NACHA Reports More Than 18 Billion ACH Payments in 2007," NACHA: The Electronic Payments Association, May 19, 2008, **http://nacha.org/News/news/pressreleases/2008/Volume_Final.pdf** (accessed June 24, 2008).

16. "Internet Activities Poll," Pew Internet, September 2007, **http://www.pewinternet.org/trends/Internet_Activities_2.15.08.htm** (accessed June 24, 2008).

17. Jeremy Quittner, "I Am My Own Banker," *BusinessWeek,* February/March 2007, p. 16; "Lakeway's Independent Bank Earns Top National Ranking," *Lake Travis Business,* April 26, 2007, **www.ibankaustin.com/3004-01-IBA/UserFiles/File/LTV%201%20Ranking.pdf** (accessed August 31, 2007); Press Release, "Independent Bank of Austin (TX), SSB, 2nd Qtr. Net Profit up 16.6%; Assets, Loans, Deposits Rise Sharply at Lakeway, Georgetown Operations; Bank Adds Employees, Announces HQ Construction Progress," *PR Newswire,* **www.prweb.com/releases/2007/7/prweb542320.htm** (accessed June 24, 2008).

18. "CSI Pennsylvania," *CFO Magazine,* March 2008, p. 92.

19. State Farm Bank, http://www.statefarm.com (accessed June 18, 2008); Simon Kwan, "Bank Charters versus Thrift Charters, Federal Reserve Bank of San Francisco, April 24, 1998, **http://www.frbsf.org/econrsrch/wklyltr/wklyltr98/el98-13.html** (accessed June 24, 2008).

## CHAPTER 16

1. Robert Berner, "The New Alchemy at Sears," *BusinessWeek,* April 16, 2007, pp. 58-60; "Sears Holdings Securitizes Primary Brands," *Seeking Alpha,* April 11, 2007, **http://seekingalpha.com/article/31960-sears-holdings-securitizes-primary-brands** (accessed March 20, 2008); "Topics: Sears Holdings Corporation," *The New York Times,* **http://topics.nytimes.com/top/news/business/companies/sears_holdings_corporation/index.html?offset=10&s=newest** (accessed June 18, 2008).

2. Collin Dunn, "Greenwash Watch: Pottery Barn's Eco Chic Collection," *Treehugger,* January 9, 2008, **www.treehugger.com/files/2008/01/greenwash-watch-pottery-barn-eco-chic.php** (accessed March 12, 2008); "Pottery Barn's Eco Chic Line: Eco Friendly?," *Apartment Therapy Los Angeles,* January 7, 2008, **http://www.apartmenttherapy.com/la/seating-sofas-armchairs/pottery-barns-eco-chic-line-ecofriendly-039690** (accessed March 13, 2008); Williams-Sonoma 2007 Annual Report, **http://www.williams-sonomainc.com/inv/anr/WS_07AR.pdf** (accessed June 25, 2008); ecoChic, Pottery Barn, **http://www.potterybarn.com/content/shop/wys_ec/index.cfm?words=eco** (accessed June 25, 2008).

3. Tim Reason, "Hidden in Plain Sight," *CFO Magazine,* August 2005, p. 59.

4. Financial information, Apple Inc., **http://finance.yahoo.com/q?s=AAPL**.

5. Aili McConnon, "Bigger Kids Want to Dress Cool, Too," *BusinessWeek,* June 30, 2008, p. 62; RealKidz, **http://www.realkidzclothing.com;** Kathrine Yung, "Funding isn't child's play," *Detroit Free Press,* June 15, 2008, **http://www.freep.com/apps/pbcs.dll/article?AID=/20080615/BUSINESS06/806150553** (accessed June 26, 2008); Special Health Issue: Our Super-Sized Kids, *Time,* June 23, 2008.

6. "Company Research," *The Wall Street Journal,* **http://online.wsj.com** (accessed June 17, 2004); Selena Maranjian, "The Math of the Dow," Motley Fool, January 29, 2004, **http://netscape.fool.com/News/mft/2004.mft04012904.htm**.

7. Vincent Ryan, "Atonement, Companies in All Industries Are Paying for the Transgressions of the Banking Sector," *CFO Magazine,* March 2008, p. 49; Avital Louria Hahn, "Missing Pieces," *CFO Magazine,* March 2008, pp. 51–58; Rick Brooks and Constance Mitchell Ford, "The United States of Subprime," *The Wall Street Journal,* **http://online.wsj.com/article/SB119205925519455321.html?mod=hps_us_whats_news** (accessed April 3, 2008); "Subprime mortgages," *Bankrate.com,* **www.bankrate.com/brm/green/mtg/basics2-4a.asp?caret=8** (accessed April 3, 2008).

8. "Dow Data, 2000–2009," Dow Jones Indexes (n.d.), **www.djindexes/jsp/avgDecades.jsp?decade=2000** (accessed June 18, 2004).

9. Vincent Ryan, "From Wall Street to Main Street," *CFO Magazine,* June 2008, pp. 85–86.

10. Spawn.com: The Todd McFarlane Web site, **http://mcfarlane.com** (accessed June 25. 2008); Adam Piore, "The Other Home Run Chase," *Condé Nast Portfolio,* August 16, 2007, **http://www.portfolio.com/executives/features/2007/08/16/The-Other-Home-Run-Chase#page1** (accessed June 20, 2008).

# Glossary

## A

**absolute advantage** a monopoly that exists when a country is the only source of an item, the only producer of an item, or the most efficient producer of an item.

**accountability** the principle that employees who accept an assignment and the authority to carry it out are answerable to a superior for the outcome.

**accounting** the recording, measurement, and interpretation of financial information.

**accounting cycle** the four-step procedure of an accounting system: examining source documents, recording transactions in an accounting journal, posting recorded transactions, and preparing financial statements.

**accounting equation** assets equal liabilities plus owners' equity.

**accounts payable** the amount a company owes to suppliers for goods and services purchased with credit.

**accounts receivable** money owed a company by its clients or customers who have promised to pay for the products at a later date.

**accrued expenses** all unpaid financial obligations incurred by an organization.

**acquisition** the purchase of one company by another, usually by buying its stock.

**administrative managers** those who manage an entire business or a major segment of a business; they are not specialists but coordinate the activities of specialized managers.

**advertising** a paid form of nonpersonal communication transmitted through a mass medium, such as television commercials or magazine advertisements.

**advertising campaign** designing a series of advertisements and placing them in various media to reach a particular target market.

**affirmative action programs** legally mandated plans that try to increase job opportunities for minority groups by analyzing the current pool of workers, identifying areas where women and minorities are underrepresented, and establishing specific hiring and promotion goals, with target dates, for addressing the discrepancy.

**agenda** a calender, containing both specific and vague items, that covers short-term goals and long-term objectives.

**analytical skills** the ability to identify relevant issues, recognize their importance, understand the relationships between them, and perceive the underlying causes of a situation.

**annual report** summary of a firm's financial information, products, and growth plans for owners and potential investors.

**arbitration** settlement of a labor/management dispute by a third party whose solution is legally binding and enforceable.

**articles of partnership** legal documents that set forth the basic agreement between partners.

**Asia-Pacific Economic Cooperation (APEC)** an international trade alliance that promotes open trade and economic and technical cooperation among member nations.

**asset utilization ratios** ratios that measure how well a firm uses its assets to generate each $1 of sales.

**assets** a firm's economic resources, or items of value that it owns, such as cash, inventory, land, equipment, buildings, and other tangible and intangible things.

**attitude** knowledge and positive or negative feelings about something.

**automated clearinghouses (ACHs)** a system that permits payments such as deposits or withdrawals to be made to and from a bank account by magnetic computer tape.

**automated teller machine (ATM)** the most familiar form of electronic banking, which dispenses cash, accepts deposits, and allows balance inquiries and cash transfers from one account to another.

## B

**balance of payments** the difference between the flow of money into and out of a country.

**balance of trade** the difference in value between a nation's exports and its imports.

**balance sheet** a "snapshot" of an organization's financial position at a given moment.

**behavior modification** changing behavior and encouraging appropriate actions by relating the consequences of behavior to the behavior itself.

**benefits** nonfinancial forms of compensation provided to employees, such as pension plans, health insurance, paid vacation and holidays, and the like.

**board of directors** a group of individuals, elected by the stockholders to oversee the general operation of the corporation, who set the corporation's long-range objectives.

**bonds** debt instruments that larger companies sell to raise long-term funds.

**bonuses** monetary rewards offered by companies for exceptional performance as incentives to further increase productivity.

**boycott**  an attempt to keep people from purchasing the products of a company.

**branding**  the process of naming and identifying products.

**bribes**  payments, gifts, or special favors intended to influence the outcome of a decision.

**brokerage firms**  firms that buy and sell stocks, bonds, and other securities for their customers and provide other financial services.

**budget**  an internal financial plan that forecasts expenses and income over a set period of time.

**budget deficit**  the condition in which a nation spends more than it takes in from taxes.

**business**  individuals or organizations who try to earn a profit by providing products that satisfy people's needs.

**business ethics**  principles and standards that determine acceptable conduct in business.

**business plan**  a precise statement of the rationale for a business and a step-by-step explanation of how it will achieve its goals.

**business products**  products that are used directly or indirectly in the operation or manufacturing processes of businesses.

**business-to-business (B2B)**  use of the Internet for transactions and communications between organizations.

**business-to-consumer (B2C)**  delivery of products and services directly to individual consumers through the Internet.

**buying behavior**  the decision processes and actions of people who purchase and use products.

## C

**capacity**  the maximum load that an organizational unit can carry or operate.

**capital budgeting**  the process of analyzing the needs of the business and selecting the assets that will maximize its value.

**capitalism, or free enterprise**  an economic system in which individuals own and operate the majority of businesses that provide goods and services.

**cartel**  a group of firms or nations that agrees to act as a monopoly and not compete with each other, in order to generate a competitive advantage in world markets.

**cash flow**  the movement of money through an organization over a daily, weekly, monthly, or yearly basis.

**centralized organization**  a structure in which authority is concentrated at the top, and very little decision-making authority is delegated to lower levels.

**certificates of deposit (CDs)**  savings accounts that guarantee a depositor a set interest rate over a specified interval as long as the funds are not withdrawn before the end of the period—six months or one year, for example.

**certified management accountants (CMAs)**  private accountants who, after rigorous examination, are certified by the National Association of Accountants and who have some managerial responsibility.

**certified public accountant (CPA)**  an individual who has been state certified to provide accounting services ranging from the preparation of financial records and the filing of tax returns to complex audits of corporate financial records.

**checking account**  money stored in an account at a bank or other financial institution that can be withdrawn without advance notice; also called a demand deposit.

**classical theory of motivation**  theory suggesting that money is the sole motivator for workers.

**codes of ethics**  formalized rules and standards that describe what a company expects of its employees.

**collective bargaining**  the negotiation process through which management and unions reach an agreement about compensation, working hours, and working conditions for the bargaining unit.

**commercial banks**  the largest and oldest of all financial institutions, relying mainly on checking and savings accounts as sources of funds for loans to businesses and individuals.

**commercial certificates of deposit (CDs)**  certificates of deposit issued by commercial banks and brokerage companies, available in minimum amounts of $100,000, which may be traded prior to maturity.

**commercial paper**  a written promise from one company to another to pay a specific amount of money.

**commercialization**  the full introduction of a complete marketing strategy and the launch of the product for commercial success.

**commission**  an incentive system that pays a fixed amount or a percentage of the employee's sales.

**committee**  a permanent, formal group that performs a specific task.

**common stock**  stock whose owners have voting rights in the corporation, yet do not receive preferential treatment regarding dividends.

**communism**  first described by Karl Marx as a society in which the people, without regard to class, own all the nation's resources.

**comparative advantage**  the basis of most international trade, when a country specializes in products that it can supply more efficiently or at a lower cost than it can produce other items.

**competition**  the rivalry among businesses for consumers' dollars.

**compressed workweek**  a four-day (or shorter) period during which an employee works 40 hours.

**computer-assisted design (CAD)** the design of components, products, and processes on computers instead of on paper.

**computer-assisted manufacturing (CAM)** manufacturing that employs specialized computer systems to actually guide and control the transformation processes.

**computer-integrated manufacturing (CIM)** a complete system that designs products, manages machines and materials, and controls the operations function.

**concentration approach** a market segmentation approach whereby a company develops one marketing strategy for a single market segment.

**conceptual skills** the ability to think in abstract terms and to see how parts fit together to form the whole.

**conciliation** a method of outside resolution of labor and management differences in which a third party is brought in to keep the two sides talking.

**consumer products** products intended for household or family use.

**consumer-to-consumer (C2C)** market in which consumers market goods and services to each other through the Internet.

**consumerism** the activities that independent individuals, groups, and organizations undertake to protect their rights as consumers.

**continuous manufacturing organizations** companies that use continuously running assembly lines, creating products with many similar characteristics.

**contract manufacturing** the hiring of a foreign company to produce a specified volume of the initiating company's product to specification; the final product carries the domestic firm's name.

**controlling** the process of evaluating and correcting activities to keep the organization on course.

**cooperative or co-op** an organization composed of individuals or small businesses that have banded together to reap the benefits of belonging to a larger organization.

**corporate charter** a legal document that the state issues to a company based on information the company provides in the articles of incorporation.

**corporate citizenship** the extent to which businesses meet the legal, ethical, economic, and voluntary responsibilities placed on them by their stakeholders.

**corporation** a legal entity, created by the state, whose assets and liabilities are separate from its owners.

**cost of goods sold** the amount of money a firm spent to buy or produce the products it sold during the period to which the income statement applies.

**countertrade agreements** foreign trade agreements that involve bartering products for other products instead of for currency.

**credit cards** means of access to preapproved lines of credit granted by a bank or finance company.

**credit controls** the authority to establish and enforce credit rules for financial institutions and some private investors.

**credit union** a financial institution owned and controlled by its depositors, who usually have a common employer, profession, trade group, or religion.

**crisis management or contingency planning** an element in planning that deals with potential disasters such as product tampering, oil spills, fire, earthquake, computer virus, or airplane crash.

**culture** the integrated, accepted pattern of human behavior, including thought, speech, beliefs, actions, and artifacts.

**current assets** assets that are used or converted into cash within the course of a calendar year.

**current liabilities** a firm's financial obligations to short-term creditors, which must be repaid within one year.

**current ratio** current assets divided by current liabilities.

**customer departmentalization** the arrangement of jobs around the needs of various types of customers.

**customer relationship management (CRM)** focuses on using information about customers to create strategies that develop and sustain desirable long-term customer relationships.

**customization** making products to meet a particular customer's needs or wants.

## D

**data** numerical or verbal descriptions related to statistics or other items that have not been analyzed or summarized.

**database** a collection of data stored in one place and accessible throughout the network.

**debit card** a card that looks like a credit card but works like a check; using it results in a direct, immediate, electronic payment from the cardholder's checking account to a merchant or third party.

**debt to total assets ratio** a ratio indicating how much of the firm is financed by debt and how much by owners' equity.

**debt utilization ratios** ratios that measure how much debt an organization is using relative to other sources of capital, such as owners' equity.

**decentralized organization** an organization in which decision-making authority is delegated as far down the chain of command as possible.

**delegation of authority** giving employees not only tasks, but also the power to make commitments, use resources, and take whatever actions are necessary to carry out those tasks.

**demand** the number of goods and services that consumers are willing to buy at different prices at a specific time.

**departmentalization** the grouping of jobs into working units usually called departments, units, groups, or divisions.

**depreciation** the process of spreading the costs of long-lived assets such as buildings and equipment over the total number of accounting periods in which they are expected to be used.

**depression** a condition of the economy in which unemployment is very high, consumer spending is low, and business output is sharply reduced.

**development** training that augments the skills and knowledge of managers and professionals.

**direct investment** the ownership of overseas facilities.

**directing** motivating and leading employees to achieve organizational objectives.

**discount rate** the rate of interest the Fed charges to loan money to any banking institution to meet reserve requirements.

**discounts** temporary price reductions, often employed to boost sales.

**distribution** making products available to customers in the quantities desired.

**diversity** the participation of different ages, genders, races, ethnicities, nationalities, and abilities in the workplace.

**dividend yield** the dividend per share divided by the stock price.

**dividends** profits of a corporation that are distributed in the form of cash payments to stockholders.

**dividends per share** the actual cash received for each share owned.

**double-entry bookkeeping** a system of recording and classifying business transactions that maintains the balance of the accounting equation.

**downsizing** the elimination of a significant number of employees from an organization.

**dumping** the act of a country or business selling products at less than what it costs to produce them.

## E

**e-business** carrying out the goals of business through utilization of the Internet.

**earnings per share** net income or profit divided by the number of stock shares outstanding.

**economic contraction** a slowdown of the economy characterized by a decline in spending and during which businesses cut back on production and lay off workers.

**economic expansion** the situation that occurs when an economy is growing and people are spending more

money; their purchases stimulate the production of goods and services, which in turn stimulates employment.

**economic order quantity (EOQ) model** a model that identifies the optimum number of items to order to minimize the costs of managing (ordering, storing, and using) them.

**economic system** a description of how a particular society distributes its resources to produce goods and services.

**economics** the study of how resources are distributed for the production of goods and services within a social system.

**electronic funds transfer (EFT)** any movement of funds by means of an electronic terminal, telephone, computer, or magnetic tape.

**embargo** a prohibition on trade in a particular product.

**entrepreneur** an individual who risks his or her wealth, time, and effort to develop for profit an innovative product or way of doing something.

**entrepreneurship** the process of creating and managing a business to achieve desired objectives.

**equilibrium price** the price at which the number of products that businesses are willing to supply equals the amount of products that consumers are willing to buy at a specific point in time.

**equity theory** an assumption that how much people are willing to contribute to an organization depends on their assessment of the fairness, or equity, of the rewards they will receive in exchange.

**esteem needs** the need for respect—both self-respect and respect from others.

**ethical issue** an identifiable problem, situation, or opportunity that requires a person to choose from among several actions that may be evaluated as right or wrong, ethical or unethical.

**eurodollar market** a market for trading U.S. dollars in foreign countries.

**European Union (EU)** a union of European nations established in 1958 to promote trade among its members; one of the largest single markets today.

**exchange** the act of giving up one thing (money, credit, labor, goods) in return for something else (goods, services, or ideas).

**exchange controls** regulations that restrict the amount of currency that can be bought or sold.

**exchange rate** the ratio at which one nation's currency can be exchanged for another nation's currency.

**exclusive distribution** the awarding by a manufacturer to an intermediary of the sole right to sell a product in a defined geographic territory.

**expectancy theory** the assumption that motivation depends not only on how much a person wants something but also on how likely he or she is to get it.

**expenses** the costs incurred in the day-to-day operations of an organization.

**exporting** the sale of goods and services to foreign markets.

**extranet** a network of computers that permits selected companies and other organizations to access the same information and may allow collaboration and communication about the information.

**extrinsic rewards** benefits and/or recognition received from someone else.

## F

**factor** a finance company to which businesses sell their accounts receivable—usually for a percentage of the total face value.

**Federal Deposit Insurance Corporation (FDIC)** an insurance fund established in 1933 that insures individual bank accounts.

**Federal Reserve Board** an independent agency of the federal government established in 1913 to regulate the nation's banking and financial industry.

**finance** the study of money; how it's made, how it's lost, and how it's managed.

**finance companies** business that offer short term loans at substantially higher rates of interest than banks.

**financial managers** those who focus on obtaining needed funds for the successful operation of an organization and using those funds to further organizational goals.

**financial resources** the funds used to acquire the natural and human resources needed to provide products; also called capital.

**first-line managers** those who supervise both workers and the daily operations of an organization.

**fixed-position layout** a layout that brings all resources required to create the product to a central location.

**flexible manufacturing** the direction of machinery by computers to adapt to different versions of similar operations.

**flextime** a program that allows employees to choose their starting and ending times, provided that they are at work during a specified core period.

**floating-rate bonds** bonds with interest rates that change with current interest rates otherwise available in the economy.

**franchise** a license to sell another's products or to use another's name in business, or both.

**franchisee** the purchaser of a franchise.

**franchiser** the company that sells a franchise.

**franchising** a form of licensing in which a company—the franchiser—agrees to provide a franchisee a name, logo, methods of operation, advertising, products, and other elements associated with a franchiser's business, in return for a financial commitment and the agreement to conduct business in accordance with the franchiser's standard of operations.

**free-market system** pure capitalism, in which all economic decisions are made without government intervention.

**functional departmentalization** the grouping of jobs that perform similar functional activities, such as finance, manufacturing, marketing, and human resources.

## G

**General Agreement on Tariffs and Trade (GATT)** a trade agreement, originally signed by 23 nations in 1947, that provided a forum for tariff negotiations and a place where international trade problems could be discussed and resolved.

**general partnership** a partnership that involves a complete sharing in both the management and the liability of the business.

**generic products** products with no brand name that often come in simple packages and carry only their generic name.

**geographical departmentalization** the grouping of jobs according to geographic location, such as state, region, country, or continent.

**global strategy (globalization)** a strategy that involves standardizing products (and, as much as possible, their promotion and distribution) for the whole world, as if it were a single entity.

**grapevine** an informal channel of communication, separate from management's formal, official communication channels.

**gross domestic product (GDP)** the sum of all goods and services produced in a country during a year.

**gross income (or profit)** revenues minus the cost of goods sold required to generate the revenues.

**group** two or more individuals who communicate with one another, share a common identity, and have a common goal.

## H

**human relations** the study of the behavior of individuals and groups in organizational settings.

**human relations skills** the ability to deal with people, both inside and outside the organization.

**human resources** the physical and mental abilities that people use to produce goods and services; also called labor.

**human resources management (HRM)** all the activities involved in determining an organization's human resources needs, as well as acquiring, training, and compensating people to fill those needs.

**human resources managers** those who handle the staffing function and deal with employees in a formalized manner.

**hygiene factors** aspects of Herzberg's theory of motivation that focus on the work setting and not the content of the work; these aspects include adequate wages, comfortable and safe working conditions, fair company policies, and job security.

**I**

**import tariff** a tax levied by a nation on goods imported into the country.

**importing** the purchase of goods and services from foreign sources.

**income statement** a financial report that shows an organization's profitability over a period of time—month, quarter, or year.

**inflation** a condition characterized by a continuing rise in prices.

**information** meaningful and useful interpretation of data and knowledge that can be used in making decisions.

**information technology (IT)** processes and applications that create new methods to solve problems, perform tasks, and manage communication.

**information technology (IT) managers** those who are responsible for implementing, maintaining, and controlling technology applications in business, such as computer networks.

**infrastructure** the physical facilities that support a country's economic activities, such as railroads, highways, ports, airfields, utilities and power plants, schools, hospitals, communication systems, and commercial distribution systems.

**initial public offering (IPO)** selling a corporation's stock on public markets for the first time.

**inputs** the resources—such as labor, money, materials, and energy—that are converted into outputs.

**insurance companies** businesses that protect their clients against financial losses from certain specified risks (death, accident, and theft, for example).

**integrated marketing communications** coordinating the promotion mix elements and synchronizing promotion as a unified effort.

**intensive distribution** a form of market coverage whereby a product is made available in as many outlets as possible.

**intermittent organizations** organizations that deal with products of a lesser magnitude than do project organizations;

their products are not necessarily unique but possess a significant number of differences.

**international business** the buying, selling, and trading of goods and services across national boundaries.

**International Monetary Fund (IMF)** organization established in 1947 to promote trade among member nations by eliminating trade barriers and fostering financial cooperation.

**Internet** global information system that links many computer networks together.

**intranet** a network of computers similar to the Internet that is available only to people inside an organization.

**intrapreneurs** individuals in large firms who take responsibility for the development of innovations within the organizations.

**intrinsic rewards** the personal satisfaction and enjoyment felt after attaining a goal.

**inventory** all raw materials, components, completed or partially completed products, and pieces of equipment a firm uses.

**inventory control** the process of determining how many supplies and goods are needed and keeping track of quantities on hand, where each item is, and who is responsible for it.

**inventory turnover** sales divided by total inventory.

**investment banking** the sale of stocks and bonds for corporations.

**ISO 9000** a series of quality assurance standards designed by the International Organization for Standardization (ISO) to ensure consistent product quality under many conditions.

**J**

**job analysis** the determination, through observation and study, of pertinent information about a job—including specific tasks and necessary abilities, knowledge, and skills.

**job description** a formal, written explanation of a specific job, usually including job title, tasks, relationship with other jobs, physical and mental skills required, duties, responsibilities, and working conditions.

**job enlargement** the addition of more tasks to a job instead of treating each task as separate.

**job enrichment** the incorporation of motivational factors, such as opportunity for achievement, recognition, responsibility, and advancement, into a job.

**job rotation** movement of employees from one job to another in an effort to relieve the boredom often associated with job specialization.

**job sharing** performance of one full-time job by two people on part-time hours.

**job specification** a description of the qualifications necessary for a specific job, in terms of education, experience, and personal and physical characteristics.

**joint venture** a partnership established for a specific project or for a limited time.

**journal** a time-ordered list of account transactions.

**junk bonds** a special type of high interest rate bond that carries higher inherent risks.

**just-in-time (JIT) inventory management** a technique using smaller quantities of materials that arrive "just in time" for use in the transformation process and therefore require less storage space and other inventory management expense.

## K

**knowledge** an understanding of data gained through study or experience.

## L

**labeling** the presentation of important information on a package.

**labor contract** the formal, written document that spells out the relationship between the union and management for a specified period of time—usually two or three years.

**labor unions** employee organizations formed to deal with employers for achieving better pay, hours, and working conditions.

**leadership** the ability to influence employees to work toward organizational goals.

**learning** changes in a person's behavior based on information and experience.

**ledger** a book or computer file with separate sections for each account.

**leveraged buyout (LBO)** a purchase in which a group of investors borrows money from banks and other institutions to acquire a company (or a division of one), using the assets of the purchased company to guarantee repayment of the loan.

**liabilities** debts that a firm owes to others.

**licensing** a trade agreement in which one company—the licensor—allows another company—the licensee—to use its company name, products, patents, brands, trademarks, raw materials, and/or production processes in exchange for a fee or royalty.

**limited liability company (LLC)** form of ownership that provides limited liability and taxation like a partnership but places fewer restrictions on members.

**limited partnership** a business organization that has at least one general partner, who assumes unlimited liability, and at least one limited partner, whose liability is limited to his or her investment in the business.

**line of credit** an arrangement by which a bank agrees to lend a specified amount of money to an organization upon request.

**line-and-staff structure** a structure having a traditional line relationship between superiors and subordinates and also specialized managers—called staff managers—who are available to assist line managers.

**line structure** the simplest organizational structure in which direct lines of authority extend from the top manager to the lowest level of the organization.

**liquidity ratios** ratios that measure the speed with which a company can turn its assets into cash to meet short-term debt.

**lockbox** an address, usually a commercial bank, at which a company receives payments in order to speed collections from customers.

**lockout** management's version of a strike, wherein a work site is closed so that employees cannot go to work.

**long-term (fixed) assets** production facilities (plants), offices, and equipment—all of which are expected to last for many years.

**long-term liabilities** debts that will be repaid over a number of years, such as long-term loans and bond issues.

## M

**management** a process designed to achieve an organization's objectives by using its resources effectively and efficiently in a changing environment.

**management information system (MIS)** used for organizing and transmitting data into information that can be used for decision making.

**managerial accounting** the internal use of accounting statements by managers in planning and directing the organization's activities.

**managers** those individuals in organizations who make decisions about the use of resources and who are concerned with planning, organizing, staffing, directing, and controlling the organization's activities to reach its objectives.

**manufacturer brands** brands initiated and owned by the manufacturer to identify products from the point of production to the point of purchase.

**manufacturing** the activities and processes used in making tangible products; also called production.

**market** a group of people who have a need, purchasing power, and the desire and authority to spend money on goods, services, and ideas.

**market segment** a collection of individuals, groups, or organizations who share one or more characteristics and thus have relatively similar product needs and desires.

**market segmentation**  a strategy whereby a firm divides the total market into groups of people who have relatively similar product needs.

**marketable securities**  temporary investment of "extra" cash by organizations for up to one year in U.S. Treasury bills, certificates of deposit, commercial paper, or Euro-dollar loans.

**marketing**  a group of activities designed to expedite transactions by creating, distributing, pricing, and promoting goods, services, and ideas.

**marketing channel**  a group of organizations that moves products from their producer to customers; also called a channel of distribution.

**marketing concept**  the idea that an organization should try to satisfy customers' needs through coordinated activities that also allow it to achieve its own goals.

**marketing managers**  those who are responsible for planning, pricing, and promoting products and making them available to customers.

**marketing mix**  the four marketing activites—product, price, promotion, and distribution—that the firm can control to achieve specific goals within a dynamic marketing environment.

**marketing orientation**  an approach requiring organizations to gather information about customer needs, share that information throughout the firm, and use that information to help build long-term relationships with customers.

**marketing research**  a systematic, objective process of getting information about potential customers to guide marketing decisions.

**marketing strategy**  a plan of action for developing, pricing, distributing, and promoting products that meet the needs of specific customers.

**Maslow's hierarchy**  a theory that arranges the five basic needs of people—physiological, security, social, esteem, and self-actualization—into the order in which people strive to satisfy them.

**material-requirements planning (MRP)**  a planning system that schedules the precise quantity of materials needed to make the product.

**materials handling**  the physical handling and movement of products in warehousing and transportation.

**matrix structure**  a structure that sets up teams from different departments, thereby creating two or more intersecting lines of authority; also called a project-management structure.

**mediation**  a method of outside resolution of labor and management differences in which the third party's role is to suggest or propose a solution to the problem.

**merger**  the combination of two companies (usually corporations) to form a new company.

**middle managers**  those members of an organization responsible for the tactical planning that implements the general guidelines established by top management.

**mission**  the statement of an organization's fundamental purpose and basic philosophy.

**mixed economies**  economies made up of elements from more than one economic system.

**modular design**  the creation of an item in self-contained units, or modules, that can be combined or interchanged to create different products.

**monetary policy**  means by which the Fed controls the amount of money available in the economy.

**money**  anything generally accepted in exchange for goods and services.

**money market accounts**  accounts that offer higher interest rates than standard bank rates but with greater restrictions.

**monopolistic competition**  the market structure that exists when there are fewer businesses than in a pure-competition environment and the differences among the goods they sell are small.

**monopoly**  the market structure that exists when there is only one business providing a product in a given market.

**morale**  an employee's attitude toward his or her job, employer, and colleagues.

**motivation**  an inner drive that directs a person's behavior toward goals.

**motivational factors**  aspects of Herzberg's theory of motivation that focus on the content of the work itself; these aspects include achievement, recognition, involvement, responsibility, and advancement.

**multidivisional structure**  a structure that organizes departments into larger groups called divisions.

**multinational corporation (MNC)**  a corporation that operates on a worldwide scale, without significant ties to any one nation or region.

**multinational strategy**  a plan, used by international companies, that involves customizing products, promotion, and distribution according to cultural, technological, regional, and national differences.

**multisegment approach**  a market segmentation approach whereby the marketer aims its efforts at two or more segments, developing a marketing strategy for each.

**mutual fund**  an investment company that pools individual investor dollars and invests them in large numbers of well-diversified securities.

**mutual savings banks**  financial institutions that are similar to savings and loan associations but, like credit unions, are owned by their depositors.

## N

**National Credit Union Association (NCUA)** an agency that regulates and charters credit unions and insures their deposits through its National Credit Union Insurance Fund.

**natural resources** land, forests, minerals, water, and other things that are not made by people.

**net income** the total profit (or loss) after all expenses, including taxes, have been deducted from revenue; also called net earnings.

**networking** the building of relationships and sharing of information with colleagues who can help managers achieve the items on their agendas.

**nonprofit corporations** corporations that focus on providing a service rather than earning a profit but are not owned by a government entity.

**nonprofit organizations** organizations that may provide goods or services but do not have the fundamental purpose of earning profits.

**North American Free Trade Agreement (NAFTA)** agreement that eliminates most tariffs and trade restrictions on agricultural and manufactured products to encourage trade among Canada, the United States, and Mexico.

## O

**oligopoly** the market structure that exists when there are very few businesses selling a product.

**open market operations** decisions to buy or sell U.S. Treasury bills (short-term debt issued by the U.S. government) and other investments in the open market.

**operational plans** very short-term plans that specify what actions individuals, work groups, or departments need to accomplish in order to achieve the tactical plan and ultimately the strategic plan.

**operations** the activities and processes used in making both tangible and intangible products.

**operations management (OM)** the development and administration of the activities involved in transforming resources into goods and services.

**organizational chart** a visual display of the organizational structure, lines of authority (chain of command), staff relationships, permanent committee arrangements, and lines of communication.

**organizational culture** a firm's shared values, beliefs, traditions, philosophies, rules, and role models for behavior.

**organizational layers** the levels of management in an organization.

**organizing** the structuring of resources and activities to accomplish objectives in an efficient and effective manner.

**orientation** familiarizing newly hired employees with fellow workers, company procedures, and the physical properties of the company.

**outputs** the goods, services, and ideas that result from the conversion of inputs.

**outsourcing** the transferring of manufacturing or other tasks—such as data processing—to countries where labor and supplies are less expensive.

**over-the-counter (OTC) market** a network of dealers all over the country linked by computers, telephones, and Teletype machines.

**owners' equity** equals assets minus liabilities and reflects historical values.

## P

**packaging** the external container that holds and describes the product.

**partnership** a form of business organization defined by the Uniform Partnership Act as "an association of two or more persons who carry on as co-owners of a business for profit."

**penetration price** a low price designed to help a product enter the market and gain market share rapidly.

**pension funds** managed investment pools set aside by individuals, corporations, unions, and some nonprofit organizations to provide retirement income for members.

**per share data** data used by investors to compare the performance of one company with another on an equal, per share basis.

**perception** the process by which a person selects, organizes, and interprets information received from his or her senses.

**personal selling** direct, two-way communication with buyers and potential buyers.

**personality** the organization of an individual's distinguishing character traits, attitudes, or habits.

**physical distribution** all the activities necessary to move products from producers to customers—inventory control, transportation, warehousing, and materials handling.

**physiological needs** the most basic human needs to be satisfied— water, food, shelter, and clothing.

**picketing** a public protest against management practices that involves union members marching and carrying anti-management signs at the employer's plant.

**plagiarism** the act of taking someone else's work and presenting it as your own without mentioning the source.

**planning** the process of determining the organization's objectives and deciding how to accomplish them; the first function of management.

**preferred stock** a special type of stock whose owners, though not generally having a say in running the company, have a claim to profits before other stockholders do.

**price** a value placed on an object exchanged between a buyer and a seller.

**price skimming** charging the highest possible price that buyers who want the product will pay.

**primary data** marketing information that is observed, recorded, or collected directly from respondents.

**primary market** the market where firms raise financial capital.

**prime rate** the interest rate that commercial banks charge their best customers (usually large corporations) for short-term loans.

**private accountants** accountants employed by large corporations, government agencies, and other organizations to prepare and analyze their financial statements.

**private corporation** a corporation owned by just one or a few people who are closely involved in managing the business.

**private distributor brands** brands, which may cost less than manufacturer brands, that are owned and controlled by a wholesaler or retailer.

**process layout** a layout that organizes the transformation process into departments that group related processes.

**product** a good or service with tangible and intangible characteristics that provide satisfaction and benefits.

**product departmentalization** the organization of jobs in relation to the products of the firm.

**product layout** a layout requiring that production be broken down into relatively simple tasks assigned to workers, who are usually positioned along an assembly line.

**product line** a group of closely related products that are treated as a unit because of similar marketing strategy, production, or end-use considerations.

**product mix** all the products offered by an organization.

**product-development teams** a specific type of project team formed to devise, design, and implement a new product.

**production** the activities and processes used in making tangible products; also called manufacturing.

**production and operations managers** those who develop and administer the activities involved in transforming resources into goods, services, and ideas ready for the marketplace.

**profit** the difference between what it costs to make and sell a product and what a customer pays for it.

**profit margin** net income divided by sales.

**profit sharing** a form of compensation whereby a percentage of company profits is distributed to the employees whose work helped to generate them.

**profitability ratios** ratios that measure the amount of operating income or net income an organization is able to generate relative to its assets, owners' equity, and sales.

**project organization** a company using a fixed-position layout because it is typically involved in large, complex projects such as construction or exploration.

**project teams** groups similar to task forces which normally run their operation and have total control of a specific work project.

**promotion** an advancement to a higher-level job with increased authority, responsibility, and pay.

**promotional positioning** the use of promotion to create and maintain an image of a product in buyers' minds.

**psychological pricing** encouraging purchases based on emotional rather than rational responses to the price.

**public corporation** a corporation whose stock anyone may buy, sell, or trade.

**publicity** nonpersonal communication transmitted through the mass media but not paid for directly by the firm.

**pull strategy** the use of promotion to create consumer demand for a product so that consumers exert pressure on marketing channel members to make it available.

**purchasing** the buying of all the materials needed by the organization; also called procurement.

**pure competition** the market structure that exists when there are many small businesses selling one standardized product.

**push strategy** an attempt to motivate intermediaries to push the product down to their customers.

## Q

**quality** the degree to which a good, service, or idea meets the demands and requirements of customers.

**quality control** the processes an organization uses to maintain its established quality standards.

**quality-assurance teams (or quality circles)** small groups of workers brought together from throughout the organization to solve specific quality, productivity, or service problems.

**quasi-public corporations** corporations owned and operated by the federal, state, or local government.

**quick ratio (acid test)** a stringent measure of liquidity that eliminates inventory.

**quota** a restriction on the number of units of a particular product that can be imported into a country.

## R

**ratio analysis** calculations that measure an organization's financial health.

**receivables turnover** sales divided by accounts receivable.

**recession** a decline in production, employment, and income.

**recruiting** forming a pool of qualified applicants from which management can select employees.

**reference groups** groups with whom buyers identify and whose values or attitudes they adopt.

**reserve requirement** the percentage of deposits that banking institutions must hold in reserve.

**responsibility** the obligation, placed on employees through delegation, to perform assigned tasks satisfactorily and be held accountable for the proper execution of work.

**retailers** intermediaries who buy products from manufacturers (or other intermediaries) and sell them to consumers for home and household use rather than for resale or for use in producing other products.

**retained earnings** earnings after expenses and taxes that are reinvested in the assets of the firm and belong to the owners in the form of equity.

**return on assets** net income divided by assets.

**return on equity** net income divided by owner's equity; also called return on investment (ROI).

**revenue** the total amount of money received from the sale of goods or services, as well as from related business activities.

**routing** the sequence of operations through which the product must pass.

## S

**S corporation** corporation taxed as though it were a partnership with restrictions on shareholders.

**salary** a financial reward calculated on a weekly, monthly, or annual basis.

**sales promotion** direct inducements offering added value or some other incentive for buyers to enter into an exchange.

**savings accounts** accounts with funds that usually cannot be withdrawn without advance notice; also known as time deposits.

**savings and loan associations (S&Ls)** financial institutions that primarily offer savings accounts and make long-term loans for residential mortgages; also called "thrifts."

**scheduling** the assignment of required tasks to departments or even specific machines, workers, or teams.

**secondary data** information that is compiled inside or outside an organization for some purpose other than changing the current situation.

**secondary markets** stock exchanges and over-the-counter markets where investors can trade their securities with others.

**secured bonds** bonds that are backed by specific collateral that must be forfeited in the event that the issuing firm defaults.

**secured loans** loans backed by collateral that the bank can claim if the borrowers do not repay them.

**securities markets** the mechanism for buying and selling securities.

**security needs** the need to protect oneself from physical and economic harm.

**selection** the process of collecting information about applicants and using that information to make hiring decisions.

**selective distribution** a form of market coverage whereby only a small number of all available outlets are used to expose products.

**self-actualization needs** the need to be the best one can be; at the top of Maslow's hierarchy.

**self-directed work team (SDWT)** a group of employees responsible for an entire work process or segment that delivers a product to an internal or external customer.

**separations** employment changes involving resignation, retirement, termination, or layoff.

**serial bonds** a sequence of small bond issues of progressively longer maturity.

**small business** any independently owned and operated business that is not dominant in its competitive area and does not employ more than 500 people.

**Small Business Administration (SBA)** an independent agency of the federal government that offers managerial and financial assistance to small businesses.

**social classes** a ranking of people into higher or lower positions of respect.

**social needs** the need for love, companionship, and friendship—the desire for acceptance by others.

**social responsibility** a business's obligation to maximize its positive impact and minimize its negative impact on society.

**social roles** a set of expectations for individuals based on some position they occupy.

**socialism** an economic system in which the government owns and operates basic industries but individuals own most businesses.

**sole proprietorships** businesses owned and operated by one individual; the most common form of business organization in the United States.

**spam** unsolicited commercial e-mail.

**span of management** the number of subordinates who report to a particular manager.

**specialization** the division of labor into small, specific tasks and the assignment of employees to do a single task.

**staffing** the hiring of people to carry out the work of the organization.

**stakeholders** groups that have a stake in the success and outcomes of a business.

**standardization** the making of identical interchangeable components or products.

**statement of cash flows** explains how the company's cash changed from the beginning of the accounting period to the end.

**statistical process control** a system in which management collects and analyzes information about the production process to pinpoint quality problems in the production system.

**stock** shares of a corporation that may be bought or sold.

**strategic alliance** a partnership formed to create competitive advantage on a worldwide basis.

**strategic plans** those plans that establish the long-range objectives and overall strategy or course of action by which a firm fulfills its mission.

**strikebreakers** people hired by management to replace striking employees; called "scabs" by striking union members.

**strikes** employee walkouts; one of the most effective weapons labor has.

**structure** the arrangement or relationship of positions within an organization.

**supply** the number of products—goods and services—that businesses are willing to sell at different prices at a specific time.

**supply chain management** connecting and integrating all parties or members of the distribution system in order to satisfy customers.

## T

**tactical plans** short-range plans designed to implement the activities and objectives specified in the strategic plan.

**target market** a specific group of consumers on whose needs and wants a company focuses its marketing efforts.

**task force** a temporary group of employees responsible for bringing about a particular change.

**team** a small group whose members have complementary skills; have a common purpose, goals, and approach; and hold themselves mutually accountable.

**technical expertise** the specialized knowledge and training needed to perform jobs that are related to particular areas of management.

**technology** the application of knowledge, including the processes and procedures to solve problems, perform tasks, and create new methods to obtain desired outcomes.

**test marketing** a trial minilaunch of a product in limited areas that represent the potential market.

**Theory X** McGregor's traditional view of management whereby it is assumed that workers generally dislike work and must be forced to do their jobs.

**Theory Y** McGregor's humanistic view of management whereby it is assumed that workers like to work and that under proper conditions employees will seek out

responsibility in an attempt to satisfy their social, esteem, and self-actualization needs.

**Theory Z** a management philosophy that stresses employee participation in all aspects of company decision making.

**times interest earned ratio** operating income divided by interest expense.

**Title VII of the Civil Rights Act** prohibits discrimination in employment and created the Equal Employment Opportunity Commission.

**top managers** the president and other top executives of a business, such as the chief executive officer (CEO), chief financial officer (CFO), and chief operations officer (COO), who have overall responsibility for the organization.

**total asset turnover** sales divided by total assets.

**total quality management (TQM)** a philosophy that uniform commitment to quality in all areas of an organization will promote a culture that meets customers' perceptions of quality.

**total-market approach** an approach whereby a firm tries to appeal to everyone and assumes that all buyers have similar needs.

**trade credit** credit extended by suppliers for the purchase of their goods and services.

**trade deficit** a nation's negative balance of trade, which exists when that country imports more products than it exports.

**trademark** a brand that is registered with the U.S. Patent and Trademark Office and is thus legally protected from use by any other firm.

**trading company** a firm that buys goods in one country and sells them to buyers in another country.

**training** teaching employees to do specific job tasks through either classroom development or on-the-job experience.

**transaction balances** cash kept on hand by a firm to pay normal daily expenses, such as employee wages and bills for supplies and utilities.

**transfer** a move to another job within the company at essentially the same level and wage.

**transportation** the shipment of products to buyers.

**Treasury bills (T-bills)** short-term debt obligations the U.S. government sells to raise money.

**turnover** occurs when employees quit or are fired and must be replaced by new employees.

## U

**undercapitalization** the lack of funds to operate a business normally.

**unemployment** the condition in which a percentage of the population wants to work but is unable to find jobs.

**unsecured bonds**  debentures, or bonds that are not backed by specific collateral.

**unsecured loans**  loans backed only by the borrowers' good reputation and previous credit rating.

## V

**venture capitalists**  persons or organizations that agree to provide some funds for a new business in exchange for an ownership interest or stock.

## W

**wage/salary survey**  a study that tells a company how much compensation comparable firms are paying for specific jobs that the firms have in common.

**wages**  financial rewards based on the number of hours the employee works or the level of output achieved.

**warehousing**  the design and operation of facilities to receive, store, and ship products.

**whistleblowing**  the act of an employee exposing an employer's wrongdoing to outsiders, such as the media or government regulatory agencies.

**wholesalers**  intermediaries who buy from producers or from other wholesalers and sell to retailers.

**working capital management**  the managing of short-term assets and liabilities.

**World Bank**  an organization established by the industrialized nations in 1946 to loan money to underdeveloped and developing countries; formally known as the International Bank for Reconstruction and Development.

**World Trade Organization (WTO)**  international organization dealing with the rules of trade between nations.

**World Wide Web**  a collection of interconnected Web sites or pages of text, graphics, audio, and video within the Internet.

# Photo Credits

## CHAPTER 16

p.487, Courtesy of Sears Holdings Corporation. SEARS ® is a registered trademark of Sears Brands, LLC.; p. 489, © Ryan McVay/Getty Images; p. 492, Courtesy of U.S. Department of the Treasury, Bureau of the Public Debt; p. 499, Courtesy of International Business Machines Corporation. Unauthorized use not permitted.; p. 503, © The McGraw-Hill Companies, Inc.; p. 521, © Image Source/PunchStock; p. 530, Courtesy of AMACOM Books. Used with permission.

# Name Index

Note: Page numbers followed by n indicate notes.

## A

Abramovich, Giselle, 538
Acres, Shelly, 30
Adams, Mike, 532
Aguayo, I., 542
Ahuja, Anita, 378
Albanese, Joe, 250
Albaugh, Dennis, 181
Allan, Greg, 533
Almunia, Joaquín, 537
Alsever, Jennifer, 534, 535
Alsop, Ronald, 533
Alter, Alexandra, 548
Amos, Daniel P., 211, 212
Anderson, Andy, 473
Anderson, Diane, 532
Anderson, George, 229
Anderson, Henry R., 428n
Anderson, Jenny, 533
Anderson, Margaret, 542
Anderson, Ray, 300
Areddy, James T., 532, 537
Aristide, Vanessa, 535
Armour, Stephanie, 546
Arndt, Michael, 545
Arney, June, 539
Arussy, Lior, 544
Asay, Matt, 539

## B

Bacon, Al, 501
Bahree, Megha, 548
Baicker, Katherine, 538
Baig, Edward C., 538
Bajtelsmit, Vickie, 513n, 530
Baker, Bill, 70
Baker, Marcia, 70
Barfield, John, 542
Barnard, Jon, 67–68
Barnes, Dawn, 163, 540
Barris, Mike, 549
Barsky, Jonathan, 548
Basso, John, 295
Bastien, Stephen, 546
Beattie, Alan, 534, 536
Beck, Jennifer, 545
Becker, Marty, 233–34
Bednarz, Ann, 539
Beer, Stan, 536
Bennett, Julie, 536
Berman, Dennis K., 538
Bernanke, Ben, 467
Berner, Robert, 551
Berry, Halle, 303
Berry, Leonard L., 544
Bezos, Jeff, 251
Bhatnagar, Parija, 536
Bianco, Anthony, 533, 550
Bissonnette, Zac, 545

Bitner, Mary Jo, 544
Blakeley, Kiri, 544
Blakely, Lindsay, 541
Blankfein, Lloyd C., 211, 217
Bly, Laura, 536
Bodett, Tom, 417, 418
Bonasia, J., 536
Bono, 68, 191
Botelho, Greg, 536
Boudette, Neal E., 536, 540
Bowie, David, 191, 488
Bowles, Jerry, 547
Boyle, Matthew, 536
Breeding, Mark, 389
Breitkopf, David, 551
Bretting, Sandra, 543
Brewer, Eric, 95
Brin, Sergey, 157, 175
Brooks, Rick, 551
Brown, Paul, 541
Brown, Susan, 178
Buchanan, Denny, 480
Buchanan, Leah, 543
Buffett, Jimmy, 191
Buffett, Warren, 165, 217, 423
Burnes, Enid, 133n
Busby, Michael, 481
Busch, August IV, 165
Bush, Ali, 169
Bush, Jason, 537
Byham, William C., 543

## C

Cadbury, Adrian, 534
Caims, Leah, 542
Calderón, Felipe, 424
Caldwell, James C., 428n
Calkins, Lisa, 295
Callahan, David, 40, 307, 533
Calvey, Mark, 535, 550
Cantalupo, Jim, 292
Carey, Mariah, 215
Carmack, Juanita, 23
Carnegie, Andrew, 23
Carpenter, Dave, 548
Carrns, Ann, 551
Carroll, A. B., 52n
Carroll, Archie, 533, 546
Carroll, Archie B., 534
Carty, Sharon Silke, 534, 537
Carvajal, Doreen, 533
Case, Peter, 532
Casey, Susan, 547
Castro, Fidel, 11
Castro, Raul, 11
Cateora, Philip R., 538
Caudill, Eve M., 539
Cauley, Leslie, 538
Cervantes, Esther, 336n
Chafkin, Max, 540

Chandler, Clay, 537
Chang, Julia, 543
Chao, Loretta, 538
Charles, Ray, 387
Chávez, Hugo, 94
Cher, 191
Chipman, Andrea, 539
Chizen, Bruce, 120
Choudhury, Bikram, 178
Chouinard, Malinda, 352
Chouinard, Yvon, 352
Clapton, Eric, 105
Clark, Hannah, 540
Clarke, Liz, 532
Clinton, Kelsey, 542
Clooney, George, 20
Cohen, Ben, 151
Cohen, Laurie P., 533
Cohen, Marshall, 69
Cohn, D'Vera, 541
Collins, Peter, 537
Colvin, Geoff, 546
Connolly, Sean M., 533
Cooper, Cynthia, 51
Cooper, Helene, 536
Coors, Adolph, 157
Copeland, Michael V., 542
Corbett, Tom, 236
Cordeiro, Anjali, 539
Corn, Andrew, 129n
Counts, Courtney E., 548
Couric, Katie, 191
Cox, Taylor H., Jr., 547
Cravens, David W., 542
Crippen, Alex, 540
Crooks, Ed, 536
Crosby, Philip B., 545
Crow, Kelly, 541
Crow, Sheryl, 8
Cunneen, Conor, 545

## D

Damon, Matt, 20
Daniell, Bob, 544
Daniels, Bill, 9
Daniels, Samantha, 366
Danko, William D., 519
Daum, Julie, 540
Dave, G. T., 408
Davey, Monica, 534
Davis, Jessica, 543
Davis, Stan, 545
Day, Nicholas, 540, 550
Dayton, Sky, 117
Dean, Cornelia, 534
Dean, Jason, 546
DeCarlo, Scott, 211n, 540
Dee, Jonathan, 533
Deere, John, 21
DeFalco, Mark, 7–8

Delaney, Kevin J., 538
Dell, Michael, 175
De Lollis, Barbara, 544
Demars, Laura, 550
Demetrakakes, Pan, 544
Demos, Telis, 542
De Noble, Alex, 180n
Derflinger, Bucky, 184
Dettore, Jerome N., 540
DeWitt, Philip Elmer, 549
Diegel, Mike, 176n
Dodes, Rachel, 547
Donnelly, John, 550
Dorney, Maureen, 536
Drake, Paula, 16
Dudley, Robert, 152
Dugas, Christine, 539
Dunn, Collin, 551
Durfee, Don, 496n
Dyson, James, 177–78

**E**

Easen, Nick, 537
Easterwood, Paul, 139
Ebbers, Bernard, 455
Eberhard, Martin, 20
Edison, Thomas, 23
Edwards, John, 544
Efrati, Amir, 533
Ellison, Lawrence J., 211, 299
Elmore, Rico, 182
Esterl, Mike, 533
Etter, Lauren, 534, 535

**F**

Fairbank, Richard D., 211
Fairlamb, David, 537
Faraci, Philip J., 242
Farrell, Greg, 532, 533, 534
Fastow, Andrew, 38, 455
Faust, Eric, 148
Faust, Kurt, 148
Ferguson, Roger W., Jr., 538
Ferrell, Linda, 83n, 533, 534, 537, 540,
     544, 550
Ferrell, O. C., 83n, 249n, 403n, 404n, 533,
     534, 537, 539, 540, 544, 549, 550
Ferrell, Will, 189
Fetterman, John, 170–71
Fetterman, Mindy, 534
Fielding, Michael, 549
Fields, Mark, 211
Finnigan, Annie, 542, 547
Fischer, Daniel, 535
Fisher, Anne, 547
Fishman, Brad, 537
Ford, Constance Mitchell, 551
Ford, Henry, 21, 23, 156
Ford, William Clay, Jr., 156
Fox, Joanne, 541
Fraedrich, John, 83n, 533, 534, 537, 540, 550
France, Brian, 7
Frazier, Mya, 548
Freeman, Sholnn, 540
Freund, Ben, 185
Freund, Matthew, 185
Frieswick, Kris, 550

Frost, Raymond, 539
Fry, Jason, 539
Fulford, Benjamin, 543

**G**

Gaba, Charles, 549
Gaba, Hal, 387
Gaffney, John, 538
Galloni, Alessandra, 549
Galvin, John, 534
Garcia, Feliciano, 547
Gareeb, Nabeel, 211
Gates, Bill, 23, 175, 423
Gatewood, Robert, 249n
Gauba, Sandeep, 344
Gauthier, Daniel, 149
Geller, Adam, 546
George, Jennifer M., 216n
Gerdes, Lindsey, 533
German, Carol Kinsey, 541
Germanakos, Bill, 8
Germer, Erika, 544
Ghosn, Carlos, 209
Gilbreth, Frank, 299
Gilbreth, Lillian, 299
Gill, Dee, 546
Giuliani, Rudolph, 473
Gogoi, Pallavi, 543
Goldman, Abigail, 543
Goldstein, Amy, 533
Gore, Bill, 236
Gore, Vieve, 236
Gorges, Keith, 148
Gottlieb, Robert, 536
Gou, Terry, 325
Graham, Jefferson, 539
Graves, Michael, 396
Gray, Jack, 196
Green, Jeff, 549
Greenfield, Jerry, 151
Greenhouse, Steven, 547
Gregory, Sean, 547
Grubman, Jack, 44
Grunwald, Michael, 535
Guerra, Merrill, 501
Gumbel, Peter, 543
Gupta, Rajat, 159
Gutierrez, Luis, 463
Guttner, Toddi, 532
Guyon, Janet, 533

**H**

Haefner, Rosemary, 318
Hagenbaugh, Barbara, 550
Hahn, Avital Louria, 551
Hakuhodo, Hikaru, 92
Halliday, Jean, 544
Hamel, Gary, 543
Hamilton, Lyla D., 545
Hampson, Rick, 544
Hannigan, Mike, 143
Hanrahan, Tim, 539, 542
Haralson, Darryl, 543
Harington, Lisa H., 544
Harris, Gardiner, 534
Hartline, Michael D., 539, 544, 549
Hasty, Katie, 548

Hawley, Chris, 537
Hayek, Nicholas, 282
Hayes, Isaac, 387
Haynes, Judie, 96n
Hays, Dennis, 543
Heathfield, Susan M., 217n, 298n
Heimer, Matthew, 548
Hempel, Jessie, 541
Henricks, Mark, 183n
Herman, Catherine, 150
Hershey, Milton, 23
Herzberg, Frederick, 303–4, 309
Higgins, Marguerite, 548
Hill, Stephen, 484
Hilton, Dan, 536
Hindmarch, Anya, 378
Hinojosa, Felipe Calderón, 537
Hisrich, Robert D., 540
Hodge, Nick, 541
Hof, Robert D., 539
Hoffman, Bryce, 542
Hoffman, Leslie, 69
Holden, Betsy, 212
Hookway, James, 537
Hoover, Kent, 540
Hopkins, Jim, 537
Horovitz, Bruce, 534, 544, 549
Hovanesian, Mara der, 551
Howard, Ron, 191
Howard, Theresa, 549
Howarth, Brad, 549
Hudson, Eric, 189
Huettel, Steve, 544
Huget, Jennifer, 532
Hult, M., 542
Humphreys, Jeffrey M., 371n
Hunn, Liza, 550
Hupp, William, 548
Hurley, Elizabeth, 8

**I**

Ibbotson, Dennie, 204
Immelt, Jeffrey, 217
Irvine, Robert, 327

**J**

Jackson, Michael, 191
Jackson, W. Garrison, 212, 542
Jana, Reena, 549
Jargon, Julie, 536
Jarvik, Robert, 74
Jenkins, Matt, 537
Jennifer Mears, 539
Jennings, Marianne, 534
Jimin Kim, 113n
Joba, Dorothy, 438
Jobs, Steve, 217
John, Jeninne Lee St., 550
Johnson, Avery, 535
Johnson, Carrie, 533
Johnson, Jimmy, 41
Johnson, Keith, 544
Johnson, Lyndon B., 346
Johnson, Melissa, 545
Johnson, Robert, 177
Jones, David, 251
Jones, Gareth R., 216n

Jones, Thomas M., 534
Jordan, Kim, 31, 260–61
Josephson, Michael, 534
Judy, Laura, 534

## K

Kageyama, Yuri, 534, 536
Kaihla, Paul, 327n
Kamerick, Megan, 540, 544
Kane, Joseph Nathan, 540
Kane, Louis, 229
Kanellos, Michael, 542
Kang, Stephanie, 548, 549
Karmin, Craig, 532
Karter, Trish, 55
Kasindorf, Martin, 75n
Katzenbach, Jon R., 543
Kavilanz, Parija B., 534
Kaye, Edita, 46
Kaye, Simon, 544
Keenan, Faith, 544, 549
Kelley, Jack, 48
Kelly, Jim, 535
Kelly, Peg, 543
Kelly, Tim, 536
Kemp, Dave, 261
Kennedy, John F., 57
Kessler, Michelle, 536, 543
Kharif, Olga, 550
Khermouch, Gerry, 549
Kiley, David, 540, 542, 544, 547
Kilmer, Val, 191
Kim, Jane J., 550
Kim Jung Min, 537
King, Larry, 134
King, Martin Luther, Jr., 305
King, Stephen, 303
Kingsbury, Kevin, 543
Kirchhoff, Sue, 536
Kirks, Kurt T., 545
Kivniemi, Peppi, 536
Klaassen, Abbey, 549
Kleinsasser, Joe, 399n, 549
Knaus, Chad, 41
Knight, Dana, 541
Knight, Matthew, 535
Knowles, Beyonce, 8
Knox, Noelle, 532
Koch, Charles, 156
Korwitts, Maryanna, 372
Kosdrosky, Terry, 540
Kostova, Tatiana, 545
Kotter, John P., 224
Kranhold, Kathryn, 542
Krebs, Michelle, 545, 548
Kroc, Ray, 177
Kroll, Luisa, 546, 550
Kurlantzick, Joshua, 180n
Kurt, Kelly, 542
Kwan, Simon, 551
Kyatt, Josh, 543

## L

Lacavo, Richard, 534
Lafley, A. G., 217
Laliberte, Guy, 149
Lambert, Emily, 541

LaMotta, Lisa, 538
LaMotta, Richard, 150
Lampert, Edward, 487
Lane, Robert, 269
Larsen, Chris, 460
Lashinsky, Adam, 545
Latley, Alow, 7
Lattman, Peter, 533
Lauder, Estée, 366
LaVallee, Andrew, 539
Lawton, Christopher, 545
Lay, Ken, 38, 51, 455
Lazear, Edward P., 538
Lear, Norman, 387
Leas, Cheryl Farr, 537
Leatherman, D. A., 542
Leavens, Sydney B., 536
Lebesch, Jeff, 31, 260–61
Ledon, Jose M., 175–76, 541
LeDoux, Chris, 148
Lee Kum-hee, 91
Lempicka, Lolita, 107
Lenzner, Robert, 333n
Lerner, Preston, 532
Lescanne, Michel, 108
Lester, W. Howard, 490
Letterman, David, 191
Levine, Josh, 542
Levine, Robert, 548
Lewis, Adrienne, 520, 543
Libby, Irv Lewis, 41
Lindblad, Cristina, 537
Lindner, Melanie, 534
Lloyd, Mary Ellen, 532
Locklear, Heather, 191
Loden, Marilyn, 343n, 547
Lomanno, Mark V., 548
Long, Mark, 533
Loomis, Carol J., 542
Lorber, Laura, 547
Lowe, Rob, 191
Lowell, Francis Cabot, 21
Lower, Mary, 548
Lucas, George H., Jr., 539
Luhby, Tammi, 551
Luhnow, David, 549, 550
Lutynec, Joanne, 536
Lyman, John, 533
Lynch, David J., 537
Lynnyang, Jia, 543
Lyons, John, 537

## M

Maathai, Wangari, 123
MacArthur, Kate, 550
MacDonald, G. Jeffrey, 539
Maginn, Michael D., 544
Maher, Kris, 543
Main, Emily, 550
Mandel, Michael J., 539
Maranjian, Selena, 551
Marr, Allison, 548
Marr, Merissa, 539
Martin, Carole, 326n
Martin, Jennifer, 541
Marx, Karl, 11
Marx, Sean, 143

Maslow, Abraham, 301–3, 545
Matlack, Carol, 537
Matthews, Robert Guy, 544
Maxon, Terry, 535
Maynard, Michelle, 550
Mayo, Elton, 300
McCafferty, Joseph, 540
McCarthy, Jack, 539
McCartney, Paul, 378, 387–88
McCartney, Stella, 123, 378
McClendon, Aubrey K., 211
McClure, Laura, 549
McConnon, Aili, 551
McCool, Joseph Daniel, 546
McDonald, Denese, 542
McDonald, Matthew, 107
McFarlane, Todd, 513–14
McGrath, Dorn C., 533
McGregor, Douglas, 304, 305, 545
McGwire, Mark, 513
McKay, Betsy, 543
McLaughlin, Katy, 549
McLaughlin, Lisa, 548
McNichol, Tom, 533
McQueen, M. P., 535
McRae, Hilary, 388
McVay, Bruce, 196
Mehall, T. M., 542
Mellon, Andrew, 23
Merrill, Cari, 533
Meyer, Christopher, 545
Meyer, Michele, 547
Meyer, Pearl, 542
Mikkelson, Barbara, 464n
Miles, Stephanie, 549
Miller, Matthew, 547
Miller, Nicole, 543
Miller, William, 50n
Milner, Conan, 549
Mitchell, Joni, 388
Mizrahi, Isaac, 361
Moelleman, Juergen, 429
Moller, Paul, 177
Monroe, Kent B., 549
Montaldo, Donna L., 550
Moore, Charles, 476
Morgan, J. P., 23
Morris, Doug, 215
Morrison, Blake, 534
Mott, Ron, 545
Mozilo, Angelo R., 40, 211
Muhammad, Larry, 546
Mulally, Alan, 212
Mulcahy, Anne, 220, 332
Murphy, Patrick E., 539
Murray, Ian, 180
Murray, Shep, 180
Musk, Elon, 20
Musselwhite, Chris, 547

## N

Naik, Dilip, 244
Nakamura, Kunio, 235, 253
Narang, Sonia, 547
Nash, Lenny, 548
Needles, Belverd E., 428n
Nelson, Ariel, 540

Nelson, Emily, 548
Newman, Michael E., 545
Newman, Paul, 143
Nierenberg, Andrea, 224–25
Noonan, David, 544
Nooyi, Indra, 54, 534
Nordstrom, Blake, 402
Nordstrom, John, 402
Nussbaum, Bruce, 544

## O

O'Connell, Vanessa, 537
O'Donnell, Jayne, 539, 546
O'Grady, Thomas, 170
O'Neal, Stanley, 40
O'Neill, Michael, 543
O'Reilly, Joseph, 536
O'Sullivan, Kate, 550
Ogg, Erica, 543
Orr, Deborah, 540, 542
Ortiz, Emeterio, 22–23
Osher, John, 183n
Otellini, Paul, 25
Otis, Clarence, 471
Ouchi, William, 306
Overfelt, Maggie, 540
Owens, William T., 40
Owsley, Greg, 544

## P

Packard, Jessica, 532
Padgett, Tim, 550
Page, Larry, 157, 175
Panner, Morris, 255
Park, James, 546
Passal, Jeffrey, 541
Passi, Peter, 539
Passy, Charles, 548
Patrick, Aaron O., 543
Patrick, Danica, 410
Patronite, Rob, 540
Patterson, Amelia, 542
Patterson, Mary, 542
Paulson, Henry, 455
Peiperl, Maury A., 547
Penske, Roger, 282
Peoples, Oliver P., 476
Pereira, Joseph, 536
Perelman, Deb, 318, 546
Perez, Juan Carlos, 539
Perman, Stacy, 544
Perttila, Chris, 543
Peters, Michael P., 540
Petrecca, Laura, 534, 548, 549
Petry, Ashley, 543
Pierce, Jon L., 545
Piercy, Nigel F., 545
Pinchot, Gifford III, 541
Piore, Adam, 551
Planchard, Cathy, 533
Plevin, Liam, 533
Pollack, Judann, 549
Portman, Natalie, 68
Portnoy, Eli, 313
Poses, Frederic M., 211
Potter, Mark, 541

Powell, Colin, 473
Preidt, Robert, 546
Press, Jim, 158
Prewitt, Edward, 539
Pride, William M., 403n, 404n, 539
Prince, Charles, 40, 218–19
Pullman, Susan, 534

## Q

Quitter, Josh, 538, 539
Quittner, Jeremy, 551

## R

Raisfeld, Robin, 540
Ramsey, Jonathon, 549
Ramstad, Evan, 536
Rankin, Ken, 550
Rappeport, Alan, 539
Ratner, David, 88n, 536
Raz, Tahl, 544
Reason, Tim, 551
Redding, Otis, 387
Reed, Dan, 544, 548
Reed, John, 537
Reed, Stanley, 537, 542
Reena Jana, 535
Reichert, Alan K., 535
Reifman, Shlomo, 540
Reynolds, Dean, 548
Reynolds, Kim, 532
Richardson, Karen, 533
Rigas, John, 455
Rigas, Timothy, 455
Ripley, Amanda, 534
Roberts, Dexter, 113n, 536
Rockefeller, John D., 23
Rocks, David, 536
Rodriguez, Juan, 212n
Rogers, Jim, 535
Romita, Tessa, 539
Rooney, Ben, 545
Rose, Stephen T., 513
Rosener, Judy B., 343n, 547
Rossisky, Bryan, 170
Rowley, Colleen, 51
Ruiz, Gina, 547
Russakoff, Dale, 540
Russell, Jesse, 547
Ryals, Lynette, 542
Ryan, Denis, 548
Ryan, Tom, 369
Ryan, Vincent, 509, 551

## S

Sains, Ariane, 537
Sammet, George, Jr., 535
Sandberg, Sheryl, 179
Sapelsa, Brooke, 535
Scannell, Kara, 542
Scarborough, Norman M., 541
Scelfo, Julie, 542
Schaal, Dennis, 533
Schetter, Kellen, 545
Schmidt, Eric, 7, 215, 217, 542
Schomer, David, 201–2
Schultz, Howard D., 211, 217

Schwab, Charles, 489
Scott, H. Lee, 419
Scott, Robert E., 88n, 536
Scrushy, Richard, 40
Segal, Carole, 145
Segal, Gordon, 145
Selden, Annette, 538
Shaffer, Amanda, 536
Shaich, Ronald M., 229, 230
Shankar, Venky, 548
Shannon, Marcia Pennington, 546
Shepler, John, 542
Sheth, Jagdish, 542
Shevack, Brett, 549
Shields, Brooke, 8
Shields, Mike, 539
Shirouzu, Norihiko, 536
Shook, Carrie, 333n
Siklos, Richard, 539
Silvemale, Sarah, 542
Silverman, Rachel Emma, 534
Silverstone, Alicia, 366, 378
Simenaitis, Dannis, 544
Simons, John, 548
Simpson, Bob R., 211
Simpson, Bryan, 544
Simpson, O.J., 191
Skilling, Jeff, 38, 455
Skinner, B. F., 309
Slater, Samuel, 21
Slim Helú, Carlos, 423
Smith, Adam, 12, 14, 238, 543
Smith, Douglas K., 543
Smith, Fred, 23, 217, 389
Smith, Geri, 537
Smith, John F., 159
Smith, Lindsay, 254
Smith, Molly, 541
Smith, Robert Ellis, 81
Soat, John, 538
Solman, Paul, 540
Somers, Suzanne, 191
Sonderup, Laura, 548
Spacey, Kevin, 191
Spadafori, Gina, 233–34
Spencer, Jane, 538
Spielburg, Steven, 191
Spitzer, Eliot, 41
Spolar, Matthew, 550
Stahl, Stephanie, 538
Stallone, Sylvester, 191
Standen, Amy, 535
Stanley, T. L., 549
Stanley, Thomas J., 519
Steiner, Ivan, 251
Stephens, Robert, 179
Stern, Howard, 191
Stevens, Tim, 538
Stewart, James, 474
Stewart, Martha, 396
Sting, 215
Stoll, John D., 536, 541, 547
Stone, Andy, 549
Stone, Oliver, 191
Strauss, Judy, 539
Stuckey, David, 520

Sudhaman, Arun, 539
Sullivan, Elisabeth, 536, 549
Suri, Rajneesh, 549
Svensson, Peter, 541, 543
Swanson, Robert, 214
Symonds, William C., 537

**T**

Tan, Cheryl Lu-Lien, 538
Tarpenning, Marc, 20
Taylor, Alex III, 542, 543, 545
Taylor, Frederick W., 299
Taylor, Robert, 249n
Terdiman, Daniel, 533
Terhune, Chad, 534, 549
Thibodeau, Patrick, 547
Thomas, Edward G., 535
Thornton, Emily, 550
Tiku, Nitasha, 541
Timmons, Heather, 550
Tischler, Linda, 547, 549
Tischles, Linda, 151n, 540
Tomas, G., 542
Tomsho, Robert, 541
Tracy, John, 544
Treacy, Michael, 548
Tritto, Christopher, 543
Trubey, Paul, 438
True, Sheb, 544
Tschohl, John, 545
Tuss, Larry, 184
Tyrangiel, Jodh, 538

**U**

Ulfelder, Steve, 542
Unanue, Bob, 263, 264
Unanue, Don Prudencio, 263

Underwood, Ryan, 544
Unsworth, Kerrie, 542
Useem, Jerry, 543

**V**

Valeriano, Richard, 254
Vance, Deborah L., 548
Vinson, Betty, 48
Volk, Tony, 186
Vroom, Victor, 308

**W**

Wagoner, Rick, 222
Wales, Jimmy, 24
Walker, Marcus, 537
Walsh, Bryan, 534, 544, 548
Walton, Sam, 23, 185
Watanabe, J., 152n
Watanabe, Katsuaki, 217
Waters, Jennifer, 532
Watkins, Sherron, 51
Watson, Mark, 539
Webb, Marion S., 535
Weber, Joseph, 550
Weill, Sanford, 44
Weise, Elizabeth, 543
Weiss, Michael J., 548, 549
Welch, David, 542, 544
Weldon, William C., 217
Wellins, Richard S., 543
Wetherbe, James, 545
Whelan, David, 534
Whelan, Elizabeth M., 532
White, Bobby, 533, 539
Whitney, Eli, 21
Whitson, Jennifer, 541
Wiersema, Fred, 548

Williams, Serena, 8
Wilson, Jeanne M., 543
Winebaum, Jake, 117
Witherspoon, Reese, 378
Wood, Winston, 547
Woodall, Pam, 537
Woodyard, Chris, 536, 548
Worthen, Ben, 537
Wright, Adam, 538
Wright, Orville, 367
Wrigley, William Jr., 223
Wriston, Walter B., 537
Wulfhorst, Ellen, 546
Wysocki, Bernard, Jr., 544

**X**

Xiong Ying, 330

**Y**

Yan, Ellis, 218
Yancey, Kitty Bean, 536
Yehuda, Ayala Ben, 548
York, Emily Bryson, 548, 549
Yu, Roger, 544, 545
Yung, Kathrine, 551

**Z**

Zedillo, Ernesto, 159
Zehr, Dan, 539
Zeithaml, Valerie A., 544
Zellner, Wendy, 533, 534
Zendrian, Alexandra, 534
Zhao, Michael, 536
Zimmerer, Thomas W., 541
Zuckerberg, Mark, 179
Zupek, Rachel, 338n

# Company Index

## A

A. G. Edwards, 477
Abercrombie & Fitch, 503
Accenture, 130, 281, 331
Accounting Systems, 162
Ace Hardware, 163
ACNielsen, 376, 390, 391
Adecco, 270
Adelphia, 454, 455
Adobe, 120, 139
Adolph Coors Inc., 157
Advanced Micro Devices, 45
AFE Cosmetics and Skincare, 117
Aflac, 211, 212
Aggieland Credit Union, 473
Agrolinz, 181
AIG, 24, 426
AirTran, 266, 283, 398, 399
Alaska Airlines, 399
Albaugh Inc., 181
Albertsons, 85, 342, 403
Alcoa, 37, 61, 507
Aloha Airlines, 78
Aluminum Company of America, 23
Amadeus Consulting, 295–96
Amazon.com, 87, 125, 128, 129, 138,
        174, 251, 288, 368, 404
America Online, 383, 479
American Airlines, 399
American Apparel, 134
American Axle, 222
American Electric Power, 62
American Express, 63, 127, 211, 345,
        466, 475, 503, 507
American Fidelity Assurance, 312
American International Group, 157, 507
American Stock Exchange, 510
AmorePacific Corporation, 107
Anheuser-Busch, 113, 119, 165
Ann Taylor, 361
AOL, 135, 164
Aon, 475
Apple, 14, 27, 45, 63, 117, 123, 127, 146, 151,
        192, 217, 234, 312, 325, 363, 367,
        383, 394, 406, 498, 503, 506
Arbitron, 376
Archer Daniels Midland, 99, 159, 476
Arthur Andersen, 24, 51, 426, 454
Ashland Oil, 206
AT&T, 44, 156, 157, 164, 219, 246, 310,
        312, 344, 409, 507
Atanor, 181
Athlete's Foot, 95
Au Bon Pain, 229
Audi, 162
Audiotech Electronics, 112
Austin Energy, 62
Automated clearinghouses, **478**–79
Avalon, 105
Aventis SA, 164

Avon, 63, 197, 246
Avtovaz, 105

## B

Babies R Us, 178
Bank of America, 104, 157, 480, 507
Bank of Montreal, 480
Bank of New England, 479
Bank One Corporation, 164, 472
Barneys New York, 68
Bartech Group, 207
BASF, 106
Baskin-Robbins, 390–91
BDO Seidman, 427
Bear Stearns, 206
Bed, Bath & Beyond, 243
BellSouth, 164
Beltane Farm, 438
Ben & Jerry's, 23
Berkshire Hathaway, 24, 157, 217
Best Buy, 113, 179, 285, 305, 330–31, 395, 467
Betty Crocker, 375
Bharti TeleVentures, 105
Big Boy, 95
BigWords.com, 126
Bikram Yoga, 178
Bird, 113
Black Entertainment Television, 177
Blockbuster, 374
Blue Cross, 529
Blue Cross and Blue Shield of Florida, 345
Blue Diamond Growers, 162
Blue Shield, 529
BMW, 20, 376, 410
The Body Shop, 59
Boeing, 159, 201, 202, 251, 507
Bonus Building Care, 188
Booz Allen Hamilton, 312
BP, 152, 442
Braddock Farm, 171
British Airways, 242
British Petroleum, 106
Buick, 430
Burger King, 164, 264, 269
Business.com, 117

## C

Cablevision, 9
Cadbury Schweppes, 106, 164, 248
California Milk Processor Board, 96
Callaway Golf, 375
Campbell's Soup, 63, 264, 503
Capgemini, 281
Capital One Financial, 211, 253
Cardinal Health, 157
CareerBuilder.com, 324
Cargill, 156, 203, 476
Carpinteros, 148
Carrefour, 85, 403
Caterpillar, 242, 507

Cato Corner Farm, 173–74
CB Richard Ellis Group, 475
Celestial Seasonings, 138, 204, 238
Centex Corp., 37
Central Market, 244
Century 21, 330
Cerebus, 158
Charles Schwab, 126, 136, 274, 477, 489
Chase Manhattan Bank, 472
Checkers Pizza, 67–68
Cheesecake Factory, 330
Chesapeake Energy, 211
Chevrolet, 374
Chevron, 61, 157, 209, 255, 507
Chiquita, 62
Chrysler, 20, 91, 156, 158, 209, 334, 375,
        412, 493
Cirque du Soleil, 149
Cirrus, 478
Cisco, 83, 128, 130, 136, 191, 205, 312
CIT Group, 475
Citibank, 127, 472, 480
Citigroup, 40, 44, 157, 211, 218, 225, 466,
        506, 507
Citizens for Humanity, 401
Clarkston Consulting, 332
CNN, 134
Coach, 225
Coca-Cola, 63, 77, 86, 95, 103, 242, 250, 345,
        374, 390, 397, 398, 400, 413, 507
Cold Stone Creamery, 92
Colgate-Palmolive, 107, 212, 302, 392, 393
Colorado Rockies, 236
Comcast, 124, 164
Commodore Builders, 250
Concord Music Group, 387–88
Conoco Phillips, 157
Conserve, 378
Continental Airlines, 399
Converse, 205
Coors, 278
Cort Musical Instruments Company, 105
Costco, 113, 335, 336, 403, 419
Countrywide Financial, 40, 211, 475, 480
CouponCabin.com, 128
Covisint, 128
CowPots, 185
Cox Communications, 345
Crate & Barrel, 145
Cray, 406
Crocs, 3–4
Cummins Inc., 6, 345
Curves, 104
CVS, 369

## D

Daewoo, 101
Daimler-Benz, 219
DaimlerChrysler, 158
Dairy Queen, 264

Dancing Deer Baking Company, 55
Darden Restaurants, 390, 471
David's Bridal, 361–62
Dawn Barnes Karate Kids LLC, 163
De Beers, 87, 400
Dean Witter, 475
Deckers Outdoor, 68–69
Dell Computer, 23, 45, 63, 97, 128, 130,
        136, 146, 174, 185, 264, 272, 275,
        366, 498
Deloitte, 130, 313, 345
Deloitte & Touche, 46, 425, 427
Delphi, 222
Delta Airlines, 127, 165, 242, 399
Delta Marine Industries, 272
Deluxe Chips, 418
Denny's, 384
Deutsche Post AG, 40
DHL, 40
Digital Artists Agency, 147–48
Discover, 466
Disney, 503, 504, 507
Disney World, 235
Disneyland, 235
Dollar General, 156
Domino's Pizza, 75, 104, 105, 388, 389
Doncaster, 197
Donna Karan, 68
Doughnut Planet, 92
Dow Chemical, 61, 476
Dr Pepper, 23
Dream Works Animation, 148
DreamMaker, 337
Du Pont, 505, 507
Duke Power, 62
Dunkin' Donuts, 92, 104, 187, 188
DuPont, 61, 476

**E**

E*Trade.com, 138
Eagle Pharmaceutical, 317
Earl Jeans, 401
Earth First Technologies, 191
EarthCraft House, 60
Eastman Kodak, 164
Eaton Corporation, 37
eBay, 129, 138, 146, 159, 191, 268, 312, 459
Eckerd Drugs, 369
Electrolux, 95, 251
Eli Lilly, 310
Elm Street Publishing Services, 176
EMI, 118
*Encyclopedia Britannica,* 117
Endangered Species Chocolate, 237
Endesa SA, 164
Enron, 24, 38–39, 51, 77, 236, 446, 454–55
E.on AG, 164
Epicurious, 124
ePredix, 327
Equifax, 494
Ernst & Young, 27, 345, 425, 427
EToys.com, 126
Eureka Ranch Technology Ltd., 128
Exo Italia, 4
Expedia, 128
Experian, 494
ExxonMobil, 106, 107, 157, 209, 507

**F**

Facebook, 179, 297
Fantasy Records, 387
Fatheadz, 181–82
Federal Express, 174, 389
FedEx, 23, 205, 217
Fidelity Investments, 269
Filene's, 362
First Chicago Corp., 472
First USA, 466
Foam Creations, 3
Food Network, 225, 327
Ford, 20, 91, 106, 128, 151, 154, 156,
        157, 192, 203–4, 207, 211,
        246, 334, 374, 378, 409,
        430, 493, 503
Fossil Free Fuel, 171
Fountain of Youth Group LLC, 46
Four Seasons, 385
Franklin Templeton Investments, 477
Freescale, 45
Fresh & Easy Neighborhood Markets,
        85–86
Frito-Lay, 208, 242
Frontier Airlines, 77–78, 399
Fury, 4

**G**

Galeries Lafayette, 366
The Gap, 63, 375
Garden.com, 126
Gateway Computer, 185, 498
Gazprom, 152
GE, 37, 218, 219, 244
Geek Squad, 179, 285, 305
General Electric, 106, 157, 192, 217, 251,
        368, 474, 475, 507
General Foods, 310
General Mills, 154, 212, 242
General Motors, 20, 88, 91, 105, 106, 120,
        128, 157, 159, 161, 203, 207, 214,
        215, 222, 247–48, 277, 280, 334,
        363, 369, 389, 409, 493, 504, 507
General Re, 24
Georgia-Pacific, 156
Gillette, 396
Give Something Back, 143
Glasspray Corporation, 510, 513
Glaxo Wellcome, 164
GlaxoSmithKline, 409
Global Investment Recovery, 286
GMC, 264
godaddy.com, 410
Gold Violin, 190
Goldman Sachs, 151, 157, 211, 217, 312,
        477, 504
Google, 7, 27, 118, 124, 146, 157, 179,
        215, 217, 235, 244, 297, 338,
        339, 395, 409
Gourmet Country Farm, 244
Goya Foods, 263–64
Graeter's, 372
Grant Thornton, 427
Greenmarket, 173
Grupo Modelo, 165
GTECH, 171
Gulf Oil, 23

**H**

H&M, 68
Hagberg Consulting Group, 327
Haier, 113
Hannaford Bros, 81
Hardware.com, 126
Harley-Davidson, 280, 503
Harris Bank, 480
Hawaiian Airlines, 78
HBO, 514
HealthSouth, 40
Hear Music, 387–88
Hebrew National, 412
Heinz, 70, 206, 390
Helena Chemical, 181
Hermès, 378
Hershey, 23, 78, 164, 223, 287
Hertz, 430
Hewlett-Packard, 5, 127, 146, 157,
        211, 219, 234, 265, 280,
        325, 373, 384, 507
Highwater Dairy LCC, 438
Hill Optometrics, 484
Hilton, 177
HiPiHi, 330
HireWorkers.com, 313
Hogan Assessment Systems, 327
Holiday Inn, 23, 104
Home Depot, 6, 16, 57, 58, 62, 218,
        503, 507
Hon Hai Precision Industry Co.,
        325
Honda, 97, 273
Honeywell, 38
Hoover, 117, 364
Hotjobs.com, 324
Household International, 491
HSBC Bank USA, 123, 345
Hyatt Hotels, 268, 310
Hyperion, 318
Hyundai, 97, 113, 430

**I**

Iams, 377
IBM, 45, 105, 106, 123, 127, 128, 134,
        157, 192, 212, 219, 244, 253,
        274, 280, 281, 310, 345, 396,
        406, 497, 499, 504, 507
IceCreamSource.com, 372
Ikea, 403
Image Comics, 513
InBev, 165
Independent Bank of Austin, 480
Indian Line Farm, 153
Industrias Añaños, 400
Infinity Computers, 229
Information Resources Inc., 121
Infosys Technologies, 281
ING, 126, 501
Inktomi Corporation, 95
Inn at Little Washington, 267–68
Instant Tax Service, 188
Intel, 25, 45, 78–80, 95, 101, 130, 219,
        270, 506, 507
Interface Inc., 300
Intrepid Potash, 156
Ivory Soap, 392

## J

J. D. Power & Associates, 284
Jackson Hewitt Tax Service, 188
Jani-King, 188
Jan-Pro, 188
JCPenney, 244, 361, 396, 403, 466
J.Crew, 361, 371
JetBlue, 266, 268, 283, 399
Jiangxi Copper, 330
Jibbitz, 4
Jiffy Lube, 187
John Deere, 37, 93, 269
John Paul Mitchell Systems, 59
Johnson & Johnson, 206, 217, 345, 409, 507
Jones Soda, 375
JPMorgan Chase, 157, 164, 206, 345, 472, 507
JVC, 113

## K

KCD IP, 487–88
Kele & Co Jewelers, 336
Kellogg's, 8, 37, 396
Kenmore Craftsman DieHard Intellectual Property, 487–88
KFC, 81, 104
Kiplingers, 37
Kleenex, 395
Kmart, 396, 487–88
Koch, 156
Kodak, 63, 241
Komatsu, 86
KPMG, 425, 427
Kraft, 122, 212, 383, 395
Krispy Kreme, 92
Kroger, 63, 85, 205, 403, 419, 420

## L

Laughing Sun, 204
LEGO, 371
Lehman Brothers, 220, 477
Lenovo, 113
Leucadia National, 475
Levi Strauss, 23, 174, 401
LG, 113
Liberty Tax Service, 188
LifeSpring, 190
Linden Labs, 134
Li-Ning, 113
Lionel, 205
Livescribe, 123
L.L. Bean, 304
Lockheed Martin, 37, 66, 164
Longaberger, 197, 336
Look-Look.com, 377
Louis Vuitton, 378
Lowe's, 16

## M

Macy's, 236, 403
Major League Baseball, 514
MapQuest, 128
March & McLennan, 475
Market Metrix, 385
Marriott, 177, 299, 345
Mars, Inc., 156, 164, 223, 368

Martin Marietta, 164
Marvel/Epic Comics, 513
MasterCard, 466
Matsushita, 106, 235, 253
Mattel, 47, 146, 395, 403
Maytag, 310
Mazda, 384
MBNA, 466
McDonald's, 23, 77, 86, 87, 92, 95, 104, 127, 174, 177, 181, 187, 235, 243, 244, 245, 269, 279, 282–83, 292, 365, 370, 395, 402, 450, 503, 507
McDonnell Douglas, 66
McFarlane Toys, 513, 514
McGladrey & Pullen, 427
MCI, 455
McKeeson, 157
McKing Corporation, 291
McKinsey, 159
Medallion Corporation, 351
Medtronic, 300–301
Mellon Bank, 501
MEMC Electronic Mats, 211
Mercedes-Benz, 20, 282, 395
Merck & Co., 74, 236, 507
Mercy Health System, 285
Merrill Lynch, 40, 126, 253, 328, 345, 467, 475, 477, 504, 506
Metabolix, 476
Metasys Technologies, 344
MGM Entertainment, 156
Microsoft, 23, 63, 100, 174, 179, 211, 296, 300, 338, 389, 423, 504, 506, 507
Millennium Products, 408
Mintel, 401
Mitsubishi, 45, 101, 106
Moen, 271
Monsanto, 181
Monster.com, 324
Montana Rugs and Furniture, 7–8
Morgan Stanley, 475, 504, 506
Motel 6, 417–18
Motorola, 63, 234, 325
Mountain Dew, 377
Movado, 270
Mrs. Acres Homemade Pies, 30
MTC, 81
My StudentBiz, 150
myemma.com, 272
MySpace, 179
MySQL, 252–53

## N

Name Structures, 372
NASCAR, 7
NASDAQ, 505
NDP Group, 69
Nestlé, 106, 242, 243
Net Zero, 124
Netflix, 374
Netscape, 139
Neutrogena, 406
New Balance, 15
New Belgium Brewing Company, 31–32, 62, 192, 260–61, 277
New Century Financial, 475
New Line Cinema, 514

New United Motor Manufacturing, 105
New York Stock Exchange, 505, 507, 510
Newman's Own, 143
Nierenberg Group Inc., 224
Nike, 15, 244, 297–98, 363, 369, 502
Nissan, 209, 271
Nokia, 270, 310
Nordstrom, 115, 402
Nortel Networks, 164
North Fork Bank, 15
Northrop Grumman, 66
Northwest Airlines, 165, 283, 399
Novo King, 330
NUMMI, 105
Nutriset, 108
Nuts About Ice Cream, 372

## O

Ocean Minded, 4
Ocean Spray, 162
Office Depot, 113
Old Navy, 375
OpenAir.com, 255
Oracle, 191, 211, 299
Outkast, 373

## P

Paine Webber, 505
Pampered Chef, 197, 198
Panasonic, 113
Panera Bread, 229–30
Paramount Pictures, 209
Patagonia, 68, 69, 174, 352
PayPal, 135
Pennzoil, 414
Penske Automotive Group, 282
Pentaverate Inc., 139
PepsiCo, 8, 54, 86, 103, 398, 400, 412
Petco, 399
PetConnection.com, 233–34
Peterbilt, 277
Pets.com, 126
Pfizer, 74, 164, 214, 389, 507
Pharmacia, 164
Phillips Petroleum, 61
Pioneer Airlines, 15
Pitney Bowes, 83, 308
Pixar, 504
Pixel Magic, 148
Pizza Hut, 86, 104
Plus Network, 478
Polaroid, 16
Pollo Campero, 370
Pontiac, 378
Porsche, 4, 270, 371, 373, 400
Pottery Barn, 178, 490
PPG Industries, 171
PricewaterhouseCoopers, 345, 425, 427
Principal Financial Group, 312
Procter & Gamble, 7, 37, 87, 117, 122, 126, 128, 129, 159, 174, 205, 217, 220, 240, 277, 324, 325, 330, 345, 379, 389, 393, 409, 503, 507
Prosper.com, 459–60
PRO-TEC Coating, 179, 285
Prudential Securities, 270
Publix Supermarkets, 156

## Q

Quaker, 395
Qualcomm, 312
Quest Star, 259

## R

R. H. Donnelley, 117
Raleigh, 371
Ralph's, 342
Ramtech Building Systems Inc., 55
Rayovac, 251
Raytheon, 61
RCA, 113
RealKidz Clothing, 501
Recycline, 189
Reebok, 15, 104
Reesycakes.com, 115
Reflect.com, 117
Regina Corporation, 251
RE/Max, 104, 188
Renault, 209
RetailMeNot.com, 128
Reuters Group, 207
Rio Nitrus, 498
Ritz-Carlton, 242, 385
Rogan, 68
Rolex, 270
Rolls Royce, 369
Royal Dutch Petroleum, 164
Royal Dutch/Shell Group, 106
Rubbersidewalks, 254

## S

S. C. Johnson & Son, 312
Saab, 130
Safeway, 62, 419, 420
Saint Louis Bread Company, 229
Saks Fifth Avenue, 466
Salesforce.com, 130
Salomon Smith Barney, 44, 472
Sam's Wholesale Club, 396, 403
Samantha's Table, 366
Samsung, 91, 101, 113, 498
Sanofi-Synthelabo SA, 164
Sanyo, 101, 318
Sara Lee, 396
Saturn, 222, 248
Scheid Vineyards, 119
Schweppes, 95
Scott Paper, 61
Sears, 113, 403, 466, 474–75, 487–88
Sears Holdings Corporation, 487–88
Sears World Trade, 103
Segway, 162
Selective distribution, **406**–7
Service Merchandise, 403
Seven for All Mankind, 401
7-Eleven, 188, 279
Shared Technologies, 312
Sharp HealthCare, 285
Shell, 102, 164, 492
Shopstyle.com, 115
Shuffle Master, 389
Siemens, 106
Sigma Assessment Systems, 327
Singer, 187

Sirius, 164
Skechers USA, 502
Skyf, 146
Skype, 124
SLM, 475
Smart Car of America, 282
Smith Barney, 475, 477
SmithKline Beecham, 164
Sodexo, 345
Sodhexo, 281
Solar Attic, 192
Sonic Drive In, 104
Sony, 45, 86, 87, 101, 113, 214, 396, 406
Sony Pictures Imageworks, 148
Southern Companies, 62
Southwest Airlines, 192, 220, 268, 283, 383, 399, 503
Southwest Windpower, 56, 191
Spalding, 104
Spectrum Brands, 251
Sprint, 124, 127, 424
Standard & Poor's, 206
Standard Oil, 23
Staples, 253, 371
Starbucks, 87, 105, 174, 201, 203, 211, 217, 285, 335, 339, 364, 383, 387, 388, 399, 436, 437, 438, 441, 442, 443–44, 445, 447, 448, 449, 503
Starwood Hotels & Resorts Worldwide, 345
State Farm, 484–85
Stax, 387
Steel City Biofuels, 171
Stella McCartney, 68
Sterling Drug, 164
Stonyfield Farm, 189
Stop & Shop, 189
Subway, 4, 104, 188, 370
Sub-Zero, 399
Sun Microsystems, 191
Sunny Delight, 277–78
Sunrocket, 124
Superior Health, 126
Suzuki, 101
SVA, 113
Sweetbay, 81
Sylvania, 218

## T

Taco Bell, 81, 402
Taco Chic Salsa, 23
Taco Maker, 370
Taos Furniture of Santa Fe, 148
Target, 63, 68, 113, 125, 189, 361, 395, 396, 403, 419, 420
Tata Motors, 106
TCL, 113
Technical Consumer Products, 218
Telarc Records, 387
Teléfonos de México, 423–24
Telmex, 423–24
Tesco, 85–86
Tesla Motors, 20, 102, 274
Texaco, 106, 396
Theladders.com, 324
Thermal Scan, 251
THK-BP, 152
Thompson, 207

Thompson Hayward, 181
3M, 192, 507
TIAA-CREF, 225
Ticketcity.com, 337
Tierra Concepts Inc., 148
Tiffany, 225
Timberland, 502
Time, Inc., 225
Time Warner, 124, 164, 409
TiVo, 395
TJX Cos, 131
T-Mobile, 319
TNS Intersearch, 229
TNS Media Intelligence, 401
Todd McFarlane Entertainment, 514
Todd McFarlane Productions, 514
Tom's of Maine, 138
Toshiba, 86, 101
Toyota, 64, 101, 105, 106, 134, 217, 268, 271, 375, 412, 430
Toys 'R' Us, 403
Trane, 211
TransUnion, 494
Travelers Insurance, 312, 472
Travelocity, 128
True Religion, 401
TsingTao, 113
Tupperware, 197
Tyco, 24, 77

## U

U-Haul, 6
Unilever, 106, 409
Union Pacific, 203
United Airlines, 78, 399
U.S. Postal Service, 158, 211, 243, 268, 371
United States Steel Corporation, 23
United Technologies, 507
Universal Music, 215
UOneNet, 330
UPS, 136, 205, 219, 264, 278
UPS Store/Mail Boxes Etc., 104
US West, 345
USAA Insurance, 304

## V

Valero Energy, 157
Ventura Motors, 384
Verichip Corporation, 124
Verizon Communications, 157, 159, 207, 345, 409, 507
Verizon Wireless, 37
VF Corporation, 107
Viacom, 177
Vineyard Vines, 180
Visa, 466
Vivace Espresso, 201–2
Volkswagen, 162, 414
Volvo, 219, 378, 414
Vonage, 124
Von's, 342

## W

W. Atlee Burpee and Co., 182
W. L. Gore & Associates, 236
Wachavia, 345
Wahaha, 113

Walgreens, 369
Wal-Mart, 23, 56, 85, 101, 113, 122, 124–25, 157, 178, 182, 185, 192, 205, 218, 274, 276–77, 307, 335, 336, 370, 389, 395, 396, 403, 419–20, 507
Walt Disney, 27, 61, 146, 304, 409
Warner Music, 215
Warner-Lambert, 396
Waste Management, 219
WD-40, 383, 395
Wells Fargo, 473, 478
Wendy's, 104
Western Electric Company, 300
Western Grain Company, 453
Westin Hotels and Resorts, 242

Westinghouse, 159, 330
Whole Foods, 61, 164, 189, 205, 244, 245, 267, 378, 420
Wikipedia, 24
Wild Oats, 164
Wildnet, 95
Williams-Sonoma, 490
Winn-Dixie, 403
Wm. Wrigley Jr. Company, 156, 164, 223, 368
Wolverine Worldwide, 502
WorldCom, 24, 48, 51, 77, 236, 446, 454, 455
Wrigley, 223
Wyndham Hotels and Resorts, 265

**X**
Xerox, 16, 63, 113, 192, 220, 332, 395
XM Satellite Radio, 164
XTO Energy, 211

**Y**
Yahoo!, 95, 179, 312, 445
Yonghe-King, 113
Yoplait, 103
Young American Bank, 9

**Z**
Zebco, 205
Zoom Systems, 406

# Subject Index

Note: **Boldface** entries indicate key terms.

## A

Ability to repay, 525
**Absolute advantage, 87**
Abusive behavior, 43–44
Acceptability of money, 462
Accessory equipment, 392
**Accountability, 242**–243
Accountants, 425–427
**Accounting**
  balance sheets, 439–442
  cash flow statements, 442–444
  elements of, 430–434
  importance to business, **425**–430
  income statements, 435–438
  ratio analysis, 444–450
  terminology, 434
**Accounting cycle, 431**–434
**Accounting equation, 430**–**431**
Accounting scandals; *see also* **Sarbanes-Oxley Act**
  environmental factors in, 48
  in German political party, 429
  impact on financial reporting, 446, 454–456
  social responsibility and, 39
  whistleblowers in, 51
Accounting systems, 82–83
**Accounts payable, 442,** 493–494
**Accounts receivable**
  defined, **440**
  maximizing, 492–493
  selling, 495
  turnover, 447
**Accrued expenses, 442**
Acid rain, 59
**Acid test, 448**
Acquired immune deficiency syndrome (AIDS), 63, 328
**Acquisitions, 163**–166, 472; *see also* **Mergers**
Active Corps of Executives, 189
Ad valorem tariffs, 93
Administrative law, 70
**Administrative managers, 215**–216
**Advertising**
  career opportunities, 415
  false claims, 46, 73, 74
  puffery, 74
  strategies, **409**–410, 412, 414
**Advertising campaigns, 409**
Advil, 15
**Affirmative action programs, 346**
Age Discrimination in Employment Act, 328
**Agency, 76**–77
**Agendas, 224**
**Agents, 76**
Agriculture
  artisan cheese-making, 173–174
  cooperatives in, 162–163
  economies based on, 20
  organic, 153, 171

AIDS, 63, 328
Air pollution, 59–60, 101
Air transport, 407
Airlines
  bankruptcies, 77–78
  customer service, 266, 283, 284
  quality rankings, 398, 399
Alien corporations, 156
Alternative energy sources, 52–53, 56, 62, 171, 277
Aluminum cans, 31, 277
American Lung Association, 158
American management style, 306
American Red Cross, 158
Americans with Disabilities Act, 328
Analysis of options, 223
**Analytical skills, 219**
Animal rights, 58–59
Annual fees, 521
**Annual reports, 161, 429**
Anti-trust laws, 78–80, 91, 100
Antidiscrimination laws, 328–329
Antiglobalization activists, 106
Antitrust Improvements Act, 79
Apartment Therapy, 490
**Appellate courts, 71**
Application forms, 325
**Arbitration, 71, 342**
Article II (UCC), 74
Articles of incorporation, 155
**Articles of partnership, 149,** 150, 153
Artisan cheeses, 173–174
**Asia-Pacific Economic Cooperation, 100**–101
Assembly lines, 275
Assessing performance, 330–331
**Asset utilization ratios, 447**–448
**Assets**
  on balance sheets, 439, 440–442
  defined, **430**–431
  personal, 186, 517
  return on, 446–447
Association of Certified Fraud Examiners, 426
**ATMs, 478,** 479, 485, 521
Attestation, 432
**Attitude, 377**
Audited financial statements, 429
Authority, delegating, 242–243, 244, 248
**Auto liability insurance, 527**
**Auto physical damage insurance, 527**–528
Autocratic leaders, 217–218
**Automated teller machines, 478,** 479, 485, 521
Automobile manufacturing
  inventory management, 493
  product development, 271
  Smart car, 282
  workforce reductions, 334

Automobiles
  emission standards, 219
  fuel economy standards, 60
  U.S. exports, 88, 91
Avatars, 134
Average stock prices, 507

## B

B Corporations, 143–144
B Labs, 144
Baby boomers, 190, 191
Background checking, 327
Bad-debts adjustment, 440–442
**Balance of payments, 90**
**Balance of trade, 88**
**Balance sheets, 439**–442, 516–517
Baldrige Award, 285
Bankruptcies, 71, 160
Bankruptcy law, 77–78
Banks
  challenges to, 479–481
  decision-making authority in, 243
  electronic transactions, 478–479
  lending activities, 187, 471–472, 479–480, 494–495
  lockbox services, 491
  outsourcing by, 104–105
  regulation, 470
  U.S. system, 471–474
  use of financial statements, 429
Barbie dolls, 395
Bargaining online, 115–116
Barter, 102, 187, 461
Battery-powered cars, 20
BBBOnline, 398
Bear markets, 508
**Behavior modification, 309**
Behavioristic segmentation, 373
Belgium, tax benefits, 91
Benchmarking, 38, 285
**Benefits, 297**–299, **337**–339
Better Banana Project, 62
Better Business Bureau Online, 131
Big Five, 466
Big Four accounting firms, 425, 427
Big Tasty, 244
Billion Dollar Roundtable, 344
Biofuels, 171, 273
Bioplastics, 476
Bluetooth technology, 124
**Boards of directors, 158,** 159, 211
Body language, 95–96
Bond quotes, 499, 500
**Bonds**
  corporate financing with, **499**–501
  intellectual property, 487–488
  as personal investments, 523, 524
**Bonuses, 337**
Bookkeeping, 427, 431, 432
Boppy pillow, 178

Boredom, 309, 310
Bottles, 398
**Boycotts, 342**
Braddock, PA, 170–171
Brand marks, 395
**Branding, 395**–396
Brands
  from China, 113
  development approaches, 395–396
  securitization of, 487
  strategies based on, 107
Bratz dolls, 395
**Breach of contract, 76**
Breast Cancer Awareness Crusade, 63
**Bribes, 44**
Bridal gowns, 361–362
Broadband Internet access, 97
Broadway Avenue Chamber of Commerce,
  201
**Brokerage firms, 477**
Brokers, online, 126
**Budget deficits, 18**–19
**Budgets, 428**–429, 496, 519
BudNet, 119–120
Bull markets, 507–508
Bullying, 43–44, 45
Bureau of Consumer Protection, 57
**Business**
  basic elements, **4**–8
  economic principles, 9–10, 13–19
  economic systems, 10–13
  reasons to study, 9
Business analysis, 390
Business descriptions, 33
**Business ethics, 38;** *see also* Ethics
**Business law, 70,** 73–78
Business magazines, 508
Business ownership
  alternative forms, 162–163
  corporations, 154–161
  mergers and acquisitions, 163–166
  overview, 144, 145
  partnerships, 149–154
  sole proprietorships, 145–149
**Business plans,** 30–31, 33–34, **185**
**Business products, 392,** 406
Business relationships, 48
**Business-to-business e-business, 127–128**
**Business-to-consumer e-business, 128–129**
Business.com Network, 117
*Busy Woman's Guide to Financial*
    *Freedom,* 530
Buyers, 415
**Buying behavior, 377**–379
Buzz marketing, 412
Bylaws, corporate, 155

**C**

CAFE standards, 60
Cafeteria benefit plans, 339
Call centers, 88, 130
Camera phones, 124
CAN-SPAM Act, 81, 132, 133
Canada, U.S. trade with, 98
**Capacity, 272**–273
**Capital budgeting, 496**
Capital in excess of par, 440, 502

**Capitalism,** 10, **11**–12
Carbon emissions
  air pollution and, 59
  in China, 101
  corporate citizenship and, 52
  impact of concerns on marketing, 380
  trading, 64
Care, duty of, 77
Careers
  accounting, 451
  in ethics and social responsibility, 64
  finance, 481, 509
  globalization, 109
  human relations, 314
  human resources, 347
  information technology, 136
  in management, 225
  marketing, 381, 415
  ongoing changes in, 27
  operations management, 288
  organizational culture and structure, 256
  personal planning outline, 353–358
  in various business forms, 166
**Cartels, 94**
**Cash flow, 428,** 517
Cash flow management, 490–493
Cash flow statements, 442–444, 517
Cash flow worksheet, 518
Catalog showrooms, 403
Cease-and-desist orders, 73
Cell phones, 123–124
Celler-Kefauver Act, 79
Censorship, 118
Centers for International Business
    Education and Research, 108
Central planning, 11
Centralization, 243–244
**Centralized organizations, 243**
Certificates of deposit
  from commercial banks, **492**
  defined, **465**
  as personal investments, 523, 524
  from State Farm Bank, 485
Certification (ISO), 286
Certified fraud examiners, 426
**Certified management accountants, 427**
**Certified public accountants, 425**–426
Chapter 7 bankruptcy, 78
Chapter 11 bankruptcy, 78
Chapter 13 bankruptcy, 78
Charitable donations, 62–63
Cheap-chic, 419
Check clearinghouses, 470–471
Check 21 Act, 471
**Checking accounts, 464,** 491
Cheese-making, 173–174, 438
Chevrolet Volt, 277, 389
Chief executive officers, 158
Chief financial officers, 506
Chief privacy officers, 211
Child care, 352
Children
  marketing to, 8, 39
  naming, 372
  online protections, 80, 81, 132
Children's Online Privacy Protection Act,
  80, 81, 132

Children's Television Workshop, 158
China
  brands originating in, 113
  capitalism in, 11
  dangerous toys from, 47, 73, 281
  exports to, 88
  Internet use, 118, 121
  manufacturing growth, 101
  U.S. trade deficit with, 89
Chocolate industry, 78
Cholesterol medications, 74
Cigarette labeling, 46–47
Cities' green initiatives, 277
City of Coral Springs, 285
Civil law, 70
Civil Rights Act of 1964, 328
**Classical theory of motivation, 299**
Classifying products, 391–392
Classroom training, 329–330
**Clayton Act,** 79, **80**
Cleantech, 186
Climate change, 380
Closing sales, 411
Clothing, 68–69, 107
**Codes of ethics, 50**
Collaborative commerce, 127–128
**Collateral,** 187, 472, **525**
**Collective bargaining, 340**–341
College courses online, 126–127
College loans, 521–522
Colorado Enterprise Fund, 178
Columbian oil reserves, 87
Comic books, 513
**Commercial banks, 471**–472, 479–481
**Commercial certificates of deposit, 492**
**Commercial paper, 492**
Commercial Service, 108
**Commercialization, 390**–391
**Commissions, 336**
**Committees, 250**
Common law, 70
Common mistakes of startups, 183
**Common stock, 159,** 501–502; *see also* **Stock**
Common Threads Garment Recycling
    program, 69
Communications
  channel types, 253–256
  ethical, 46–48
  as trade barriers, 95–96
**Communism,** 10, **11**
Communities, 6–7
Community banking, 480
Community relations, 7, 62–63
Community-supported agriculture, 153
Compact fluorescent lights, 218
**Comparative advantage, 87**–88
Compensation
  averages for management, 225
  impact of economic conditions on,
    321–322
  motivation and, 297–299
  planning, 334–339
  top management, 211–212, 299
Compensation committees, 250
**Competition**
  forms of, **14**–16
  harmful practices, 45

impact on marketing, 379
in retailing, 403–404
self-esteem and, 303
Competitive advantage, 204, 281
Competitive analyses, 33
Complaints, 283, 284
Component parts, 392
Compounding, 522–523
**Compressed workweeks, 311**
Compulsory arbitration, 342
**Computer-assisted design, 275**
**Computer-assisted manufacturing, 275**
**Computer-integrated manufacturing, 276**
Computer Matching and Privacy Protection
    Act, 132
Computer Security Act, 132
Computers; *see also* **Information
    technology; Technology**
global market, 97
impact on manufacturing, 275–276
mainframe distribution, 406
market maturation, 498
**Concentration approach, 371**
**Conceptual skills, 219**
**Conciliation, 342**
Conflicts, ethical, 49–50
Conflicts of interest, 44
Conglomerate mergers, 164
Connectivity, 290
Consideration, 76
Consolidations; *see* **Mergers**
Constitutional law, 70
Construction industry, 340
Consumer Goods Pricing Act, 79
Consumer Price Index, 19
Consumer Product Safety Commission,
    72, 73
**Consumer products, 391**, 405–406
**Consumer-to-consumer e-business, 129**
**Consumerism, 57**
ConsumerReports.org, 398
Consumers, responsibilities to, 57
**Contingency planning, 206**
Continuous improvement, 285
**Continuous manufacturing organizations,
    275**
**Contract manufacturing, 104**
Contractions, economic, **17**
**Contracts, 75**–76, 340
Contractual capacity, 76
Contributed capital, 442
**Controlling, 208–209**
Controlling the Assault of Non-Solicited
    Pornography and Marketing
    law, 133
Convenience products, 391
Cookies, 80, 131
**Cooperatives, 162**–163
Copyrights, 77, 81, 92, 135
**Corporate charters, 155**, 161
**Corporate citizenship, 52**–53; *see also* **Social
    responsibility**
Corporate cultures, 215, 234–236
Corporate raiders, 164
*Corporate Responsibility Officer* magazine, 53
Corporate scandals; *see* **Sarbanes-Oxley Act;
    Scandals**

**Corporations**
advantages and disadvantages, 159–161
basic features, 145, **154**–155, 158–159,
    166
types, 155–158
Corpus Christi organizational chart, 241
Corruption Perceptions Index, 44, 45
Cosmetics.com, 117
**Cost of goods sold, 436–437**
Cost-of-living adjustments, 340
Costs, small business advantages, 181
Cotton, organic, 401
Cotton gin, 21
Council of Better Business Bureaus, 131
Counterfeit products, 77, 92
Counterfeiting, money's resistance, 463
**Countertrade agreements, 102**
Coupon rate, 500
Coupons, 412
Court systems, 70–71
Crashes, 508
Creative salespersons, 410–411
Creativity, 219, 223
**Credit cards, 466**, 517, 520–521
**Credit controls, 470**
Credit lines, 187, 494, 521
Credit-rating services, 494
Credit reports, 525
**Credit unions, 473**
Credit usage, 519–522
Credits, in accounting, 431
Creditworthiness, 525
Criminal law, 70
**Crisis management, 206**
Critical path, 283
Crocs footwear, 3–4
Cruiser bikes, 261
CSAs, 153
Cuba, embargo against, 93–94
**Culture;** *see also* **Organizational cultures**
impact on buying behavior, **379**
impact on ethics, 42, 43
impact on incentives, 314
as trade barrier, 95–97
Currencies; *see also* **Money**
common, 100
defined, 460
exchange controls, 93
exchange rates, 90–91
**Current assets, 439, 440**, 489–493
**Current liabilities, 440, 442**, 493–495
**Current ratio, 448**
**Customer departmentalization, 242**
**Customer relationship management,
    129–130**, 368, 381
Customer service, 402
Customer support, 130
**Customization**
in manufacturing, **272**
mass, 128, 272
of services, 269
Cybersquatters, 81
Cycle time reduction, 290–291

**D**

Damage awards, 75
Daniels College of Business, 9

**Data**
collection, 120–121
defined, **118**
types, 376
**Databases, 120**–121
Day care, 56
**Debit cards, 467**, 519
Debits in accounting, 431
Debt financing, 186–187, 498–501
**Debt to total assets ratio, 449**
**Debt utilization ratios, 448**–449
**Decentralized organizations, 244**
Deceptive advertising, 73, 74
Decision making
employee involvement, 217, 218
ethical, 48–49
as management function, 216, 221–224
partnership advantages, 151
sole proprietorship advantages, 146
Decisional role of managers, 216
Decline stage (product life cycle), 395
**Deductibles, 528**, 529
Default risk, 523
Defective products, 75
Deficits, 18–19
**Defined benefit plans, 526**
**Defined contribution plans, 526**
Deflation, 17, 469
Deforestation, 61
Delaware County District Attorney's
    Office, 481
**Delegation of authority, 242**–243, 244, 248
**Demand, 13**, 273, 412–413
Demand curves, 13–14
Demand deposits, 464
Democratic leaders, 217–218
Demographic segmentation, 372
Demographic trends, 190
Department stores, 403
**Departmentalization, 239**–242
Depository insurance, 471, 474, 485
**Depreciation, 437**
**Depressions, 17**
Deregulation, 191–192
Design, 272, 275
Devaluation of currency, 91
**Development, 330**
Diagonal communication, 255
Diamond trade, 87, 400
Digital Millennium Copyright Act, 80, 135
Digital music players, 498
Diligence, duty of, 77
Dinosaur fossils, 184
Direct deposit, 478–479
**Direct investment, 105**–106
Direct marketing, 381
Direct selling, 197–198
**Directing, 208**
Directors (corporate), 158, 159
**Disability insurance, 529**
Discharging employees, 333–334
Disciplinary procedures, 333–334
Disclosures, 161
**Discount rate, 470**
Discount stores, 403
**Discounts, 401**–402, 492–493, 494
Discretionary expenses, 519

Discrimination in employment, 328–329, 346
Dishonesty, 45–46
Disinflation, 469
Dispute resolution, 70–72, 341–342
**Distribution**
  career opportunities, 415
  channels and strategies, 402–408
  in marketing mix, **374**
Diversified firms, 474–475
**Diversity**
  achieving, 346
  benefits of, 344–346
  creativity and, 212
  elements of, **343**
  market segmentation and, 370–371
  training, 305
Diversity Accountability Tool, 345
Diversity Pipeline Alliance, 6
**Dividend yield, 503**
**Dividends**
  accounting for, 438
  decision to pay, 502–503
  defined, **155**
  preferred versus common stock, 159
  taxes on, 161
**Dividends per share, 449**–450
Divisibility of money, 462
Divisions, 247–248
Do Not Call Implementation Act, 80, 132
Doctor visits, online, 126
Doctors Without Borders, 108
Domain names, 81
Domestic corporations, 155
Domestic system, 21
**Double-entry bookkeeping, 431,** 432
Double taxation, 161
Dow Jones Industrial Average, 507
Down payments, 470
**Downsizing,** 192, **207**–208, 334
Downward communication, 253–255
Dreamliner jet, 202
Driver Privacy Protection Act, 132
Drug testing, 327
Duke University intranet, 121–122
**Dumping,** 94
Durability of money, 462–463
Duties of agents, 77

**E**

**E-business, 125**–130
E-commerce; *see also* **Information**
    **technology; Internet**
  advertising, 410
  current U.S. volume, 22, 403
  elements of, 125–126
  price negotiations in, 115–116
  trends, 191
e-HUB, 128
E-mail, 131–133, 253, 255
E-services, 128–129
e-Visit, 126
Early payment discounts, 492–493, 494
**Earnings per share,** 435, **449**
Earth Pledge, 68, 69
Echo boomers, 190
Eco Chic line, 490

Economic conditions
  expansions and contractions, 16–17
  impact on marketing, 379
  workforce effects, 314, 321–322
**Economic contractions, 17**
**Economic expansions, 16**–17
**Economic order quantity model, 280**
**Economic systems, 10**–13, 20–25
**Economics, 9**
Education, 63
E85 fuels, 273
Efficiency, 204
Egalitarianism, 11
8 Wings, 8
Electric cars, 20, 277, 389
**Electronic funds transfer, 478,** 491
Electronic trading, 505
Electronic waste, 5–6
Elements of contracts, 76
Elks Clubs, 158
**Embargoes, 93**–94
Emission standards, 219
Employee assistance programs, 338
Employee stock ownership plans, 161, 337
Employees; *see also* **Motivation**
  attracting to sole proprietorships, 148–149
  firms' responsibilities to, 55–57
  involvement in decision making, 217, 218
  misuse of company resources, 42, 44–45
  motivating, 208
  owners versus, 161
  as resources, 203
  theft by, 44–45, 46, 307
  time wasting, 127
  unionized, 340–342
Employer retirement plans, 526
Encyclopedias, 117
Energy alternatives, 52–53, 56, 62, 171, 277
Energy-efficient building, 59, 60; *see also*
    Environmental concerns; Green
    business strategies
ENERGY STAR appliances, 59
**Entrepreneurs, 22**
**Entrepreneurship;** *see also* **Small businesses**
  defined, **174**
  economic role, 22–24
  firms promoting, 150
  in large corporations, 193
  in various business forms, 166
  well-known examples, 174–175
Entry-level salaries, 338
Environmental concerns; *see also* Green
    business strategies
  in auto manufacturing, 282
  CFL bulbs, 218
  of electronics firms, 5–6
  employee motivation and, 300
  greenwashing and, 490
  impact on employment opportunities, 64
  impact on pricing, 401
  major areas, 58–62
  New Belgium Brewery, 31–32
  in operations planning, 276–277
  as part of corporate citizenship, 52
  of Patagonia, 352
  plastic alternatives, 476

  reusable bags, 378
  of Starbucks, 335
  vehicle pollution standards, 219
Environmental Protection Agency, 72, 73, 219, 430
EPA SmartWay rating system, 430
Equal employment opportunity, 56
Equal Employment Opportunity
    Commission, 72, 328
Equal Pay Act, 329
**Equilibrium prices, 14**
Equipment, 437, 495
Equity
  in accounting equation, 431
  on balance sheets, 440, 442
  managing, 501–503
  return on, 447
Equity financing, 186, 501–503
**Equity theory, 307**
Espresso, 201–202
**Estate plans, 529**–531
**Esteem needs, 303**
**Ethical issues, 41**
Ethics
  cultural influences, 42, 43
  defined, 38
  fossil hunting case, 184
  growing importance to business, 24–25, 40–41
  impact on employment opportunities, 64
  improving, 49–51
  legal requirements, 81–83
  major types of abuse, 43–48
  recognizing issues, 41–42, 48–49
Ethics committees, 250
Ethics officers, 64
Ethisphere Institute, 37, 38
*Ethisphere* magazine, 37
Ethnic minorities; *see* Minorities
Ethnographic research, 376
**Eurodollar market, 492**
Euronext, 505
**European Union, 100**
Euros, 100
Evaluating performance, 330–331
Even/odd pricing, 401
**Exchange controls, 93**
**Exchange rates, 90**–91, 100
**Exchanges, 363**–364
**Exclusive distribution, 407**
Executive compensation, 211–212, 299
Executive employment agencies, 220, 324
Executive misconduct; *see also* Ethics;
    Scandals
  Enron case, 38–39, 51
  impact on business environment, 24–25, 40
  legal environment for, 81–83
  organizational cultures and, 236
  reporting, 50–51
Executive summaries, 33
Exito Empressarial, 371
Expansions, economic, 16–17
**Expectancy theory, 308**–309
**Expenses, 437,** 519
Expertise, 219
Export agents, 103

Export managers, 109
**Exporting, 88,** 102–103
**Express warranties, 74**
External job candidates, 324
**Extranets, 122–123**
**Extrinsic rewards, 297**

## F
Facilities planning, 273–276
**Factors, 495**
Failure risk, 182–183, 193
Fair Credit Reporting Act, 132
Fair Labor Standards Act, 322
Fair Packaging and Labeling Act, 79
Fairness, 44–46, 307, 333–334
Fake Web sites, 134–135
False advertising, 73, 74
Family roles, 96
Farm cooperatives, 162–163
Fast-food restaurants in Japan, 92
Fat Tire beer, 31
Federal Aviation Administration, 72
Federal Bankruptcy Court, 71
Federal Communications Commission, 72, 424
Federal courts, 71
Federal Deposit Insurance Corporation, 135, 474, 485
Federal Energy Regulatory Commission, 72
Federal Highway Administration, 72
**Federal Reserve Board, 467,** 468
Federal Reserve system, 467–471
Federal Savings and Loan Insurance Corporation, 472, 474
Federal Sentencing Guidelines for Organizations, 81–82
Federal Trade Commission
    major functions, 12, 72, 73
    privacy regulation, 131
Federal Trade Commission Act, 79
Federal Trademark Dilution Act, 79, 81
Fee-for-service plans, 529
Fees, 466, 504, 521
Fiat money, 461
Fiduciary duties, 76–77
Figurehead role, 216
**Finance,** 8, **460**
Finance charges, 520–521
Finance committees, 250
Finance companies, 478
Financial Accounting Standards Board, 425, 446
Financial health, 515–517
Financial management
    current assets, 489–493
    current liabilities, 493–495
    fixed assets, 495–498
    investment banking, 504
    long-term liabilities, 498–501
    owners' equity, 501–503
    securities markets, 504–508
**Financial managers, 213–214,** 225
Financial planning; see **Personal financial planning**
Financial projections, 34
**Financial resources, 9–10,** 186–187
Financial Services Modernization Act, 472

Financial statements
    basic uses, 427–430
    legal environment for, 82
    preparing balance sheets, 439–442
    preparing cash flow statements, 442–444
    preparing income statements, 435–438
    ratio analysis, 444–450
    terminology, 434
    when prepared, 432–434
Financial system
    banking institutions, 471–474
    challenges to, 479–481
    electronic banking, 478–479
    Federal Reserve role, 467–471
    money in, 460–467
    nonbanking institutions, 474–478
    subprime loan risk, 506
Financing activities, cash from, 444
Finished-goods inventory, 279
Firing employees, 333–334
**First-line managers, 213**
**Fixed assets,** 439, 442, **495**–498
Fixed interest rates, 494
**Fixed-position layouts, 274**
Fixed tariffs, 93
Flash technology, 120
Flat organizations, 246
Flex fuels, 273
Flexibility of operations, 181
**Flexible manufacturing, 276**
Flexible scheduling strategies, 310–313
Flexible work schedules, 56–57
**Flextime, 311**
Flier's Bill of Rights, 266
**Floating-rate bonds, 500**
Floating-rate loans, 494–495
Flying cars, 177
Focus groups, 376
Focus of small firms, 181–182
Food and Drug Administration, 72, 73
Food price increases, 53
Footwear, 3–4, 15
Forecasting demand, 273
**Foreclosure, 525**
Foreign corporations, 155
Forensic accounting, 426, 481
Forest Stewardship Council, 62
Formal communication channels, 253–255
Fossil hunting, 184
**Franchisees, 187**
**Franchises, 187**
**Franchising, 104,** 187–188
**Franchisors, 187**
**Fraud, 75,** 426, 466; see also Accounting scandals; Identity theft; Legal environment
Free enterprise, **11**–13, 23
**Free-market systems, 12**
Free-rein leaders, 217–218
Free trade agreements, 97–101
Free Trade Area of the Americas, 99
Freeware development, 139
Freie Demokratische Partei, 429
Fringe benefits, 297–299, 337–339
Fuel economy
    cars designed for, 282
    measurement, 284

    of rental cars, 430
    standards for, 60
Fuel surcharges, 205
**Functional departmentalization, 239**–240
Funding; see also **Financial management**
    of corporations, 160
    of partnerships, 151, 154
    small business challenges, 183–184
    for small business startups, 186–187
    of sole proprietorships, 147

## G
Gender differences in financial planning, 530
Genealogical analysis, 473
**General Agreement on Tariffs and Trade, 97**
General and administrative expenses, 437
General ledgers, 433
General merchandise retailers, 403
**General partnerships, 149,** 152, 166
Generally accepted accounting principles (GAAP), 425, 432, 434
Generation Y, 190, 375
**Generic products, 396**
Geographic segmentation, 372–373
**Geographical departmentalization, 242**
Germany, FDP accounting scandal, 429
Gifts, 42
Givebacks, 340–341
Glass ceiling, 329
Glass Stegal Act, 472
Global Employee Relationship Report, 303
The Global Fund, 63
Global positioning systems, 124–125
**Global strategies, 107**
Global warming, 52, 59–60, 380
**Globalization, 106, 107,** 109; see also **International business**
Glyphosate, 181
Goal setting, 296, 517–519
Gold notes, 461
Goods, 373
Government; see also Regulation; **Sarbanes-Oxley Act**
    budget deficits, 18–19
    economic role, 11, 12, 24
    ethical violations in, 41
    ethics regulations, 39–40
    monopolies permitted by, 15
Grace periods, 521
Grading of products, 365
Gramm-Leach-Bliley Bill, 472
**Grapevine, 255**
*Gray Matters,* 66
Green business strategies; see also Environmental concerns
    career opportunities, 64
    employee involvement, 261
    employee motivation and, 300
    misrepresentation as, 490
    in operations planning, 276–277
    plastic alternatives, 479
    public expectations, 380
    recycled products, 189
    by rental car companies, 430
    of Starbucks, 335
    urban renewal via, 171
    of Wal-Mart, 420

Green Collection cars, 430
Green garlic, 244
Green home building, 59, 60
Green Power Market Development
        Group, 335
GreenChoice program, 62
Greenhouse gases; *see* Carbon emissions
Greenwashing, 62, 490
**Gross domestic product, 18**
**Gross income, 437**
**Gross profit,** 434, 435, **437**
**Groups, 249**–253
Growth, 184–185, 204, 237
Growth stage, product life cycle,
        394–395

## H

Haggling online, 115–116
Handheld computers, 118
Handicotti, 252
Handshake deals, 76
Hawthorne studies, 300–301
Headhunters, 220, 324
Health care, 276, 308
**Health insurance,** 338, **529**
Health maintenance organizations, 529
Health savings accounts, 485
Healthy fast-food products, 365
Healthy sTarts, 252
Helicopters, 205
Herzberg's two-factor theory, 303–304
High-interest bonds, 500–501
High-speed Internet, 97
High technology, 179–180; *see also*
        **Information technology;**
        **Technology**
Hiring, 220–221, 323–329; *see also*
        **Human resources management**
Hispanic customers, 370
Holidays, 96
Home buying, 524–526
Home equity loans, 472
Home improvement stores, 16
**Homeowners insurance, 528**
Honesty, 44–46
Horizontal communication, 255
Horizontal hierarchies, 31
Horizontal mergers, 164
Hospital service quality, 268–269
Hostile takeovers, 165
Hot-desking, 312
Hoteling, 312
**Human relations, 296**–299
**Human relations skills, 219**–**220**
**Human resources, 9,** 323
**Human resources management**
        compensation planning, 334–339
        employee development, 329–331
        overview, **322**–323
        recruiting and selection, 323–329
        turnover and separations, 331–334
        union relations, 340–342
**Human resources managers, 214**
Hybrid vehicles, 392, 394
Hydroponics, 244
**Hygiene factors, 303**–304
Hypermarkets, 403

## I

Ibuprofen, 15
Ice cream, 390–391
Ideas
        for business plans, 30–31
        development and screening, 389–390
        marketing of, 373
Identity theft, 81, 131, 134–135, 466
Idle cash, investing, 491–492
Illegal immigration, 424
Immigration trends, 190, 424
Implementation, 223
**Implied warranties, 74**
Import quotas, 93
**Import tariffs, 93**
**Importing, 88,** 102–103
Income before interest and taxes, 435
Income before taxes, 434, 435
Income disparities in Mexico, 99
**Income statements, 435**–438
Income to common stockholders, 434, 435
Incompetence, 184
Incorporators, 155
Indentures, 499, 500
Independence of small firms, 180
Independent distributors, 197
Indexes, 507
Individual retirement accounts, 475, 485,
        522–523, 526–527
Industrial-grade diamonds, 400
Industrial Revolution, 21
Industrial services, 392
Industrialized nations, 90
Industry analyses, 33, 450
Industry returns to shareholders, 509
Inexperience, 184
**Inflation, 17,** 19, 469
Inflation risk, 523
Infomercials, 410
Informal communication channels, 255
**Information, 118**
Information management, 118–121, 225
**Information technology;** *see also*
        E-commerce
        defined, **116**
        e-business, 125–130
        everyday influences, 116–118
        historic milestones, 122
        impact on entrepreneurship, 175
        information management, 118–121, 225
        Internet services, 121–123
        legal and social issues, 130–136
        marketing information systems, 375–377
        trends, 191
**Information technology (IT) managers, 215**
Informational advertising, 414
Informational role of managers, 216
**Infrastructure, 90**
**Initial public offerings, 156,** 504
Innovation
        cultures promoting, 215, 235, 236
        by small businesses, 176–178
**Inputs, 265,** 269, 272–273
Inside directors, 158
Insourcing, 105
Inspection, 286–287

Institute of Management Accountants, 427
Insurance, 527–529
**Insurance companies, 475**
Intangible property, 77
**Integrated marketing communications, 409**
**Intellectual property**
        defined, **77**
        foreign laws, 92
        Internet's impact on, 81, 135
        securitization of, 487–488
**Intensive distribution, 406**
**Interest, 525**
Interest expenses, 437, 497–498
Interest-only mortgages, 506
Interest rates
        on commercial loans, 494–495
        on credit cards, 466, 520–521
**Intermittent organizations, 275**
Internal job candidates, 324
**International business**
        barriers to, 90–97
        basic principles, 86–90
        defined, **86**
        forms of involvement, 102–106
        organizations promoting, 101–102
        strategy development, 106–108
        trade agreements, 97–101
International Development Association, 101
International Finance Corporation, 101
International Franchise Association, 187
**International Monetary Fund, 101**–**102**
International Organization for
        Standardization, 286
**Internet;** *see also* E-commerce
        access in less-developed countries, 95
        banking via, 479, 480
        broadband access, 97
        defined, **121**
        employee abuse, 255–256
        financial planning resources, 508, 515
        overview of technology, 121–123
        price negotiations via, 115–116
        privacy concerns, 80–81
        trends, 191, 403
        wireless technologies, 95, 123–125
Internet Voice, 124
Interpersonal role of managers, 216
Interstate Commerce Commission, 72
Interviews, 325, 326, 327
Intimidating behavior, 43–44
**Intranets, 121**–**122,** 127, 253
**Intrepreneurs, 193**
**Intrinsic rewards, 297**
Introductory stage, product life cycle,
        393–394
Inventories
        accounting for, 431, 442
        managing, 278–280
        optimizing, 493
        RFID tagging, 124–125, 493
**Inventory control, 279**
**Inventory turnover, 447**
Investing activities; *see also* Financial
        management; Financial system
        cash from, 443
        by Federal Reserve, 469
        for idle cash, 491–492

major types, 475–478
performance measurement, 506–508
personal, 523–526
**Investment banking,** 477–478, **504,** 509
Investment trading, 126
Investors, 186, 429
IOUs, 461
IOWatch, 139
iPhones, 123, 498
iPods, 363, 394, 498
IRAs, 475, 485, 522–523, 526–527
**ISO 9000, 286**
iTunes, 117, 127, 394–395

**J**

Japanese fast-food restaurants, 92
Japanese management style, 306
Jefferson nickel, 463
**Job analysis, 323**
Job creation, 176
**Job descriptions, 323**
**Job enlargement, 310**
**Job enrichment, 310**
**Job rotation, 309**–310
**Job sharing, 311**–312
**Job specifications, 323**
Job Web sites, 136
Jobs; *see* Careers
**Joint ventures, 105, 162**
**Journals, 432,** 433
**Junk bonds, 500**–501
**Jurisdiction, 71**
**Just-in-time inventory management, 280**

**K**

Karate schools, 163
**Knowledge, 118**
Kola Real, 400–401
Kombucha tea, 408

**L**

**Labeling, 398**
Labor, manufacturing versus service, 270
**Labor contracts, 340**
**Labor unions, 340**–342
Laissez-faire capitalism, 12
Land pollution, 61
Lanham Act, 79
Late payment fees, 521
Laws; *see* Legal environment
**Lawsuits, 70**–72, 75
Layoffs, 334, 351
Layout of facilities, 274–275
Lead paint, 47, 73, 281
**Leadership, 216**–219
**Learning, 377**
Leasing equipment, 495
Lectures online, 127
**Ledgers, 432,** 433
Legal environment
business practices laws, 78–80
forms of business law, 73–78
impact on marketing, 379
for information technology, 130–136
for international business, 91–92
for misconduct, 81–83
online privacy, 80–81

in recruiting and selection, 328–329
sources of law, 70
Legality of contracts, 76
Lenders, 429; *see also* Loans
Less-developed countries, 90, 95
**Leveraged buyouts, 165**
**Liabilities**
on balance sheets, 440, 442
defined, **431**
managing, 493–495, 498–501
personal, 517
Liability (legal), 147, 152, 160
Liability insurance, 527
**Licensing, 103,** 104
**Life insurance, 528**–529
Lifetime value of customer, 130
**Limited liability companies, 145, 162**
Limited liability in corporations, 160
**Limited partnerships, 149,** 152, 166
**Line-and-staff structures, 246**–247
**Line structures, 246**
Lipitor, 74
Liquidity, 440, 504–505
**Liquidity ratios, 448**
Liquidity risk, 523
Lithium ion batteries, 20
Living wills, 530
Loans
from banks, 472, 479–480, 494–495
for education, 521–522
peer-to-peer, 459–460
for small business startups, 186–187
to sole proprietorships, 147
Location, 16, 274
**Lockboxes, 491**
**Lockouts, 342**
Logistics, 277–283; *see also* **Operations management**
**Long-term assets, 495**
Long-term financial goals, 517–**519**
Long-term investment, 523
**Long-term liabilities, 440, 498**–501
Lorraine Motel, 305
Losses, 221–222
Low-wage jobs, 313
Loyalty, 77
Luxury hotels, 385

**M**

Magnuson-Moss Warranty Act, 79
Mainframe computers, 406
Major equipment, 392
Make Your Mark volunteer program, 335
Malcolm Baldrige National Quality Award, 179, 285
Malnutrition, 108
Managed care plans, 529
Management
conflicts of interest in, 44
decision-making in, 216, 221–224
elements of, 7–8, **202**–203, 224–225
legal environment for, 81–83
levels of, 209–213
major areas, 213–216
major functions, 203–209
skill requirements, 216–220

as small business challenge, 184
span of, 244–245
training, 220–221
**Management information systems, 119**–120
**Managerial accounting, 428**
**Managers, 202,** 220–221, 246–247
Mandatory retirement, 158–159
**Manufacturer brands, 395**–396
**Manufacturing;** *see also* **Operations management**
capacity and facilities planning, 272–276
contract, 104
defined, **265**
e-business role, 127
growth in China, 101
outsourced, 15, 47, 107
services versus, 268–270
small business opportunities, 179
standardization and customization, 271–272
U.S. evolution, 21–22
Manufacturing economies, 21
*Maquiladoras,* 98–99
Margin requirements, 470
Marine Corps, 234
Mark-to-market accounting, 455
Market analyses, 33
**Market segmentation, 370**–373
**Market segments, 370**
Market value of stock, 502
**Marketable securities, 491**–492
**Marketing**
elements of, 8, **362**–368
false claims, 46, 74
online, 125–126
puffery, 74
**Marketing channels, 402**–406
**Marketing concept, 365**–368
Marketing economies, 21–22
Marketing environment, 379–380
Marketing information systems, 375–377
**Marketing managers, 214**
**Marketing mix**
in business plans, 33
competitive advantage from, 388–389
elements of, **373**–375
exercise, 383–384
pricing in, 400
**Marketing orientation, 367**–368
Marketing plans, 33
**Marketing research**
on buying behavior, 377–379
elements of, **375**–377, 381
online, 126
in product planning, 270–271
**Marketing strategies**
developing, **369**–375
distribution in, 402–408
marketing mix, 33, 373–375, 388–389
pricing in, 399–402
product strategies, 389–399
promotion in, 408–414
**Markets, 369**
*Masa trigo,* 379
**Maslow's hierarchy, 301**–303
Mass customization, 128, 272
Master budgets, 428

Matchmaking, 366
**Material-requirements planning, 280**
**Materials handling, 408**
**Matrix structures, 248**–249
Maturity stage, product life cycle, 395
McGregor's Theory X and Theory Y, 304–306
McKinsey Global Institute, 277
Media, advertising, 410
**Mediation, 71, 342**
Medicare, 527
**Mergers**
  in banking industry, 472, 480–481
  common approaches, **163**–166
  investment banking role, 504
Metric system, 96–97
Mexico, 98–99, 423–424
Micro-lending, 460
**Middle managers, 213**
Middlemen, 403
Milk moustache campaign, 8
Millennials, 190
Millionaires, 519
**Mini-trials, 71**–72
Minimum wages, 335
Minorities; *see also* **Diversity**
  employment opportunities, 56–57
  in executive ranks, 328
  market segmentation and, 370–371
  U.S. businesses owned by, 175, 344
Mirel, 476
**Mission, 204**
Mission Zero, 300
Mistakes of startup firms, 183
**Mixed economies, 12**
Mobile phones, 123–124
Model Business Corporation Act, 155
Modified capitalism, 12
**Modular design, 272**
**Monetary policy, 468**–470
**Money**
  basic functions, **460**–463
  long-term pricing, 497–498
  regulation of supply, 468–470
  types, 463–467
Money market accounts, **465,** 485
Money market funds, 477
Monitoring communications, 255–256
Monitoring outcomes, 224
**Monopolies**
  absolute advantage from, 87
  basic features, **15**–16
  for international trade, 91
  laws against, 78–80
  Mexican telephone industry, 423–424
**Monopolistic competition, 14**–15, 16
**Morale, 208, 297,** 332; *see also* **Motivation**
Mortgage-backed securities, 506
Mortgage lenders, 25, 506
Mortgage loans, 187, 472, 494–495, 525
Most admired companies, 217
**Motivation**
  defined, **296, 377**
  early research, 299–301
  human relations concepts and, 296–299
  as management function, 208

strategies, 309–314
  theories, 301–309
**Motivational factors, 304**
MoveOn.org, 123
**Multidivisional structures, 247**–248
Multimedia messaging services, 125
**Multinational corporations, 106**
**Multinational strategies, 106**–107
**Multisegment approach, 371**
Municipal bonds, 524
Musicians, services to, 147–148
**Mutual funds, 477,** 524
**Mutual savings banks, 473**–474
Myers-Briggs Type Indicator, 326

# N

**NAFTA, 98**–99
Names of businesses, 155
Naming children, 372
Narrow span of management, 245
NASDAQ, 505
National Aeronautics and Space Administration, 158
National Alliance of Businessmen, 63
National Association of Home Builders, 59
National Business Ethics Survey, 42
National Civil Rights Museum, 305
National Credit Union Association, 474
National debt, 18–19
National Fluid Milk Processor Promotion Board, 8
National Quality Research Center, 398
**Natural resources, 9**
Needs
  marketing to, 366
  Maslow's hierarchy, 301–303
  motivation and, 296–297
Negative cash flow, 443
Negative net worth, 516–517
Negotiable Order of Withdrawal accounts, 464–465
Negotiation
  collective bargaining, 340–341
  in dispute resolution, 71–72
  as management function, 216
  online bargaining, 115–116
**Net income, 434,** 435, **437**–438
Net receivables, 442
Net worth, 516–517
**Networking, 190, 224**–225
New issues, 504
New product development, 389–391
New product pricing, 400–401
New York Stock Exchange, 505, 507
Niche marketing, 371–372
Niche players, 138
Nike Plus iPod kit, 363
92nd Street Y nursery school, 44
Nonbank liabilities, 495
Nonbanking institutions, 474–478
Nondiscretionary expenses, 519
**Nonprofit corporations, 158**
**Nonprofit organizations, 5**
Nonverbal communication, 95–96
**North American Free Trade Agreement, 98**–99
Notebook computers, 229

NOW accounts, 464–465
Nutella, 108
Nutrition Labeling and Education Act, 79

# O

Objective assessments, 330
Objectives
  advertising, 409–410
  of firms, 204–205, 366
  pricing, 400
  promotional, 413–414
Obscene language, 55
Observational research, 376
Occupational Safety and Health Administration, 72
Office supply theft, 44–45, 46
Oil reserves, 87
**Oligopolies, 15**
OMX, 505
On-the-job training, 329
Online advertising, 410
Online banking, 479, 480
Online bargaining, 115–116
Online college courses, 126–127
Online marketing research, 377
Online privacy, 80–81, 131
Online protests, 123
OnStar Telematics, 120
**Open market operations, 469**
Operating activities, cash from, 442–443
Operating income, 434
**Operational plans, 206**
**Operations, 265**
**Operations management**
  overview, **264**–270
  quality management, 283–287
  supply chain management, 277–283
  systems planning, 270–277
Optimizing inventories, 493
Options, considering, 222–223
Order takers, 410
Organic Exchange, 68
Organic farming, 153, 171
Organic products, 68–69, 401, 490
Organization of Petroleum Exporting Countries, 94
**Organizational charts, 237**
**Organizational cultures, 215, 234**–236, 352, 402
**Organizational layers, 245**–246
Organizational structures
  assigning responsibilities, 242–246
  communication channels, 253–256
  creating, 236–238
  groups and teams in, 249–253
  major forms, 246–249
  specialization and departmentalization, 238–242
**Organizing, 207**
**Orientation, 329**
**Outputs, 265,** 268–270, 272–273
Outside directors, 158
Outside hires, 220, 324
**Outsourcing**
  by clothing manufacturers, 107
  defined, **88**
  by shoe manufacturers, 15

in supply chain management, 280–281
technology's role, 127
by toy manufacturers, 47
varieties of, 104–105
**Over-the-counter market, 505**–506
Overcentralization, 243
Overspecialization, 239
Overtime pay, 322
**Owners' equity**
on balance sheets, 440, 442
defined, **431**
managing, 501–503
return on, 447
Owners, firms' responsibilities to, 54–55
Ownership forms; *see* Business ownership

**P**

**Packaging, 396**–398
Par value, 502
Part-time work, 312
Participative management, 307
Partido Revolucionario Institucional (PRI),
424
Partnership capital, 149
**Partnerships**
basic features, 145, 149–154, 166
defined, **149**
joint ventures, 162
Patents, 15–16, 77, 92
Pay for performance, 299
Payables; *see* **Accounts payable**
Payment schedules, 193
Payment terms, 494
Peaceful separations, 333
Peer-to-peer lending, 459–460
Penalties (credit card), 521
**Penetration pricing, 400**–401
Pennies, 463, 464
**Pension funds, 475**–477
People for the Ethical Treatment of Animals,
59, 123
**Per share data, 449**–450
**Perception, 377**
Performance appraisals, 330–331
Perishability of services, 268
Perks (credit card), 521
**Permanent insurance, 529**
Perpetual life of corporations, 160
Personal assets, 186, 517
Personal computers, 97, 498; *see also*
Computers; **Technology**
Personal digital assistants, 123
**Personal financial planning**
budgeting and credit management,
519–522
defined, **515**
estate planning, 529–531
evaluating financial health, 515–517
goal setting, 517–519
insurance, 527–529
savings and investments, 522–527
**Personal net worth, 516**–517
Personal privacy protections, 80–81
**Personal property, 77**
**Personal selling, 410**–411
Personal space, 96
**Personality, 377**–378

PERT diagrams, 282–283
Pesticides, 181
Pet care information, 233–234
Phishing, 134–135
**Physical distribution, 407**–408
**Physiological needs, 302**
**Picketing, 341**–342
Piece-rate systems, 299, 336
Piece wages, 336
Pine beetles, 204
Pipelines, 407
Pirated software, 48, 92
Pittsburgh, 170–171
**Plagiarism, 48**
**Planning**
controlling and, 209
human resources, 323
as management function, **203**–204,
205–206
operations systems, 270–277
Plastic alternatives, 476
Plastic bags, 61, 378
Plumpy'nut, 108
Plus-size clothing, 501
Poison pills, 165
Policies, 50–51, 61
Political barriers to trade, 94
Pollution, 59–62, 219; *see also* Environmental
concerns
Polygraph tests, 327
Pop-up turkey timers, 186
Portability of money, 462
Positioning, 414
Posting transactions, 432, 433
Potash, 156
Power of attorney, 76
Preemptive rights, 159
Preferred provider organizations, 529
**Preferred stock, 159**, 502
Prescription drug benefits, 338
Preserve product line, 189
Price risk, 523
**Price skimming, 400**
**Prices**
equilibrium, 14
fixing, 78
in marketing mix, **374**
online bargaining, 115–116
strategies for, 399–402
Primary characteristics of diversity, 343
**Primary data, 376**
**Primary markets, 477, 504**, 505
**Prime rate, 494**, 506
Principal of loan, 494, 525
**Principals in agency law, 76**
Print media, 410
Privacy Act, 132
Privacy online, 80–81, 131
**Private accountants, 427**
**Private corporations, 156**, 157–158, 514
**Private court systems, 72**
**Private distributor brands, 396**
Private label cards, 466
**Process layouts, 275**
Processed materials, 392
**Product departmentalization, 240**–242
Product development, 389–391

**Product-development teams, 251**–252
Product labeling, 46–47
**Product layouts, 275**
**Product liability, 75**
Product life cycle, 392–395
**Product lines, 392**, 393
Product managers, 415
**Product mix, 392**, 393
Product planning, 270–271
Product safety, 47, 57, 73
Product strategies
classification, 391–392
development, 389–391
identification, 395–399
life cycle, 392–395
lines, 392
Product testing, 126
**Production, 264**–**265**
**Production and operations managers, 214**
Production orientation, 367
Productivity; *see also* **Motivation**
Hawthorne studies, 300
manufacturing versus service, 270
of teams, 251
technology's role, 118
of telecommuting, 312
Product(Red) campaign, 63
**Products**
counterfeit, 77, 92
defined, **4**–5
in marketing mix, 373–374
Profanity, 43, 55
**Profit margins, 445**
**Profit sharing, 337**
**Profitability ratios, 445**–447
**Profits**
as company objective, 204
defined, **5**
distribution in partnerships, 154
gross, 434
impact of discounts, 493
on income statements, 435, 437–438
social responsibility and, 54
Program Evaluation and Review Technique,
282–283
**Project organizations, 274**
**Project teams, 248**–249, **251**
**Promotion**
basic tools, 409–412
in marketing mix, **374**–375, 408
objectives, 413–414
push and pull strategies, 412–413
Promotion mix, 409–412
Promotional discounts, 402
**Promotional positioning, 414**
**Promotions (job), 220, 332**
Property law, 77
Proposals, 33
Prospecting, 411
Protective tariffs, 93
Protests, 123
Prototypes, 390
Proxy voting, 159
Psychographic segmentation, 373
Psychological factors in buying behavior,
377–378
**Psychological pricing, 401**

Psychological tests, 326, 327
Public accountants, **425**–426
Public Company Accounting Oversight
    Board, 425, 446
**Public corporations, 156**
Public relations, 411
**Publicity, 411**–412
Puffery, 74
**Pull strategies, 412**–413
Pulse smart pen, 123
Punishments, 309
**Purchasing, 278**
Pure capitalism, 12
**Pure competition, 14**
**Push strategies, 412,** 413
Pyramid of Social Responsibility, 52

**Q**

**Quality, 398**–399
**Quality-assurance teams, 252**
**Quality circles, 252,** 306
**Quality control, 285**
Quality management, 283–287
Quality of life concerns, 6
Quantico course, 220–221
Quantity discounts, 401
**Quasi-public corporations, 158**
**Quick ratio, 448**
**Quotas, 93**

**R**

Racial diversity; *see* **Diversity**
Racial groups in U.S. population, 344, 345
Radio frequency identification, 124–125, 493
Radiohead, 118
Railroads, 407
Rain forest destruction, 61
Ranking systems, 330
**Ratio analysis, 444**–450
Raw materials, 279, 392
**Real property, 77**
Rebates, 521
Recalls, 47, 73
Receivables; *see* **Accounts receivable**
**Receivables turnover, 447**
**Recessions, 17**
**Recruiting, 324**
Recycling, 62, 277, 476
Reference checking, 327–328
**Reference groups, 378**–379
Regional managers (retail), 415
Regional trade agreements, 97–101
Regulation; *see also* Legal environment;
    **Sarbanes-Oxley Act**
    business practices laws, 78–80
    Federal Reserve role, 470
    impact on marketing, 379
    major federal agencies, 72, 73
    of partnerships, 151
    of sole proprietorships, 147
Reinforcement promotion, 414
Relationships, ethical, 48
Religious practices, 96
Renewable energy, 56, 186; *see also* Energy
    alternatives; Green business
    strategies
Rental cars, 430

**Renters insurance, 528**
Reputation, 182
Research and development costs, 437
**Reserve requirements, 470**
Resolution Trust Corporation, 472–473
Resource allocation, 216
**Responsibility, 242**
Résumés, 327
**Retailers, 403**–404
Retailing, 178, 403–404, 415
**Retained earnings, 438, 440, 502**
Retention, 298
Retirement savings, 526–527
**Return on assets, 446**–447
**Return on equity, 447**
Reusable bags, 378
Revaluation of currency, 91
**Revenues, 434, 435, 436**–437
Reverse discrimination, 346
Rewards, 297, 309; *see also* **Motivation**
RFID chips, 124–125
Right-sizing, 192
Right to Financial Privacy Act, 132
Rights of consumers, 57
Rights under free enterprise, 12–13
Risk assessment, 496–497
Risk in marketing, 365
Risk management, 506
Risk types, 523
Robinson-Patman Act, 79
Robots, 276
Roth IRAs, 475, 526–527
**Routing, 281**–282
Royal Channel, 117

**S**

**S corporations, 145, 162**
Safe deposit boxes, 472
Safety, 57
Safety regulations, 56
**Salaries, 136, 336**–337, 338; *see also*
    Compensation
Sales, stabilizing, 414
Sales agreements, 74
Sales of businesses, 148, 153–154
Sales of partnership interests, 153–154
Sales orientation, 367
**Sales promotion, 412**
Sales Tax Simplification Agreement, 135
Sales taxes, 135
Salesforce motivation, 317
Salespersons, 410–411
Salsa, 23
Samples of products, 412, 413
Sampling for inspection, 287
**Sarbanes-Oxley Act**
    financial reporting requirements, 446,
        455, 506
    impact on business environment, **82**–83,
        455–456
    impact on corporate boards, 158
    purposes, 39, 80
**Savings accounts, 465,** 524
**Savings and loan associations, 472**–473
Savings plans, 519, 522–523
Scandals; *see also* Ethics
    Enron case, 38–39

    impact on business environment,
        24–25
    organizational cultures and, 236
    preventing with competent directors,
        158
    regulations in response to, 39–40
**Scheduling, 282**–283
Screening ideas, 389–390
Seasonal discounts, 401–402
Seasons 52, 390
Second Life, 123, 134, 330
Secondary characteristics of diversity, 343
**Secondary data, 376**
**Secondary markets, 477, 504,** 505
Secrecy, 146
Section managers, 415
**Secured bonds, 500**
**Secured loans, 494**
Securities
    bonds, 487–488, 499–501
    Fed transactions, 469
    for idle cash, 491–492
    issuance, 477–478, 504
    major markets, 504–508
    in mutual funds, 477
Securities and Exchange Commission
    accounting standards criticisms, 446,
        495–496
    corporate reports to, 161
    regulatory role, 72, 425
**Securities markets, 504**–508
**Security needs, 302**
Security of personal data, 131
Segmentation, 370–373
**Selection, 324**–328
Selection of options, 223
**Self-actualization needs, 303**
**Self-directed work teams, 252**–253, 307
Selling expenses, 437
Selling process, 365
Seniority, 332
Sentencing guidelines, 81–82
**Separations, 333**–334
September 11 attacks, 508
**Serial bonds, 500**
Service Corps of Retired Executives
    (SCORE), 189–190
Service economies, 22
Services
    defined, 373
    online, 128–129
    operations management, 267–270
    quality measurement, 285, 398–399
    small business opportunities, 179
Sexual harassment, 43
Share accounts, 473
Shark repellant, 165
**Sherman Antitrust Act, 78**–80
Shipping, 124–125
Shoes, 3–4, 15
Shoplifting, 307, 404
Shopping bags, 61
Shopping products, 391
Short-term financial goals, 517–**519**
Short-term funding, 493–495
Short-term investment, 523
Silly Squirts, 390

Slentrol, 389
**Small Business Administration, 175,** 186, 189–190
Small Business Development Centers, 189
Small Business Institutes, 190
**Small businesses;** *see also* **Entrepreneurship**
 advantages and disadvantages, 180–185, 193
 approaches to starting, 185–190
 defined, **175**
 industries attracting, 178–180
 role in U.S. economy, 27, 175–178
 trends for, 190–192
Smart car, 282
Smart pens, 123
SmartWay rating system, 430
Social barriers to trade, 95–97
**Social classes, 379**
Social factors in buying behavior, 378–379
**Social needs, 303**
**Social responsibility**
 arguments for and against, 54
 community relations, 7, 62–63
 to company stakeholders, 54–57, 58
 defined, **39**
 environmental concerns, 6–7, 52, 58–62
 growing importance to business, 24–25
 impact on employment opportunities, 64
 major elements, 51–53
 in marketing, 8
 New Belgium Brewery, 31–32
**Social roles, 378**
Social Security, 475–477, 527, 528
**Socialism,** 10, **11**
Soft benefits, 339
Soft drinks, 380, 398, 400–401
Soft-serve ice cream, 390–391
Software pirating, 48, 92
**Sole proprietorships, 145**–149, 166
Source documents, 432
SOX; *see* **Sarbanes-Oxley Act**
Spam, 131–133
**Span of management,** 244–**245**
*Spawn* comics, 513
**Specialization, 238**–239, 299, 309
Specialty products, 391
*Spider-Man* comics, 513
Sports, 41
Stability of money, 462
Stabilizing sales, 414
Staff managers, 246–247
**Staffing function, 207**–208
**Stakeholders, 5,** 52, 54–57
Standard & Poor's Composite Index, 507
**Standardization, 271**–272
Standards for quality, 286
State courts, 71
**Statements of cash flow, 442**–444, 517
**Statistical process control, 286**
Statutory law, 70
Steel industry decline, 170
Steel prices, 279
Steel tariffs, 98
**Stock;** *see also* **Dividends**
 accounting for, 442
 buying on margin, 470

defined, **154**
employee ownership, 161, 337
financing with, 501–502
per share data, 449–450
as personal investment, 523, 524
of private corporations, 156
sales of, 160
types, 159
Stock markets, 504–508
Stock quotes, 502
Stockholders
 defined, **154**–155
 firms' responsibilities to, 54–55
 use of financial statements, 429
Stockholders' equity, 440
Stop-payment orders, 464
Stopglobalwarming.org, 123
Storage, 365
*Stranger Than Fiction,* 189
**Strategic alliances, 105**
**Strategic plans, 205**
Strategies, 106–108, 369–375
Stress, 182, 183
**Strikebreakers, 342**
**Strikes, 342**
**Structure, 236;** *see also* Organizational structures
Student loans, 521–522
Subjective assessments, 330–331
Subprime lending, 506
Subprime mortgage crisis, 78, 506
Substance abuse, 327, 338
Supermarkets, 403
Superstores, 403, 419
Supplier Diversity Programs, 344
Suppliers, credit from, 187, 494
Supplies, 392
**Supply, 13**
Supply and demand, 13–14
**Supply chain management, 277**–283, 288, 405
Supply curves, 13–14
Support salespersons, 411
Supreme Court (U.S.), 70
Surgical robots, 276
Sustainability; *see* Environmental concerns; Green business strategies
Sweet Home Project, 55
Symbolic/prestige pricing, 401

## T

**T-bills,** 469, **492**
**Tactical plans, 205**–206
Take Charge of Education program, 63
Tall organizations, 245–246
Tangible property, 77
**Target markets, 369**–371
Tariffs, 93, 98
**Task forces, 250**
Taxes
 on corporations, 161
 estate, 530–531
 managing, 495
 on online purchases, 135
 on partnerships, 154
 on retirement funds, 526–527
 on sole proprietorships, 147, 149

**Teams**
 benefits of, 250–251
 defined, **249**
 in matrix structures, 248–249
 types, 251–253, 306–307
 work groups versus, 249–250
**Technical expertise, 219**
Technological barriers to trade, 97
**Technology;** *see also* **Information technology**
 defined, **116**
 everyday influences, 116–118
 impact on banking, 478–479, 480
 impact on entrepreneurship, 175
 impact on marketing, 379
 information management, 118–121
 in manufacturing, 275–276
 small business opportunities, 179–180
 trends, 191–192
Teenagers and money, 515
Teenagers' views on cheating, 46
Telecommuting, 57, 312, 313
Telephone Consumer Protection Act, 79, 132
Television sets, 6
Tender offers, 164–165
Tennessee Valley Authority, 12
**Term insurance, 529**
**Test marketing, 390**
Testing
 job applicants, 324, 326, 328
 as sales promotions, 412
 virtual, 376
Theft
 credit card, 466
 identity, 81, 131, 134–135, 466
 of office supplies, 44–45, 46
 shoplifting, 307, 404
**Theory X, 304**–306
**Theory Y, 305**–306
**Theory Z, 306**
360-degree feedback, 331
Thrift charters, 485
Tide Stainbrush, 393–394
Time and motion studies, 299
Time perceptions, 96
Time wages, 335–336
**Times interest earned ratio, 449**
**Title VII of the Civil Rights Act, 328**
Toothbrushes, 189
**Top managers, 209**–212
**Torts, 75**
Total asset turnover, 447–448
Total-market approach, 369–370
**Total quality management, 285**–286, 288
Toy making, 513–514
Toy recalls, 47, 73
Trade; *see* **International business**
Trade agreements, 97–101
Trade balance, 19
Trade barriers, 90–97
**Trade credit,** 187, **494**
**Trade deficits, 88**–90
Trade surpluses, 89–90
Trademark Counterfeiting Act, 79
Trademark Law Revision Act, 79
**Trademarks,** 77, 81, **395**
**Trading companies, 103**
Traditional IRAs, 526–527

Training
in diversity, 305
major types, **329**–330
for management, 220–221
**Transaction balances, 490**
**Transfers, 332**
Transformation process, 265–267
Translations, 95
**Transportation, 407**
Transporting process, 365
Travel, impact on morale, 332
Travel services, 128
**Treasury bills,** 469, **492**
TreeHugger.com, 490
Trial balances, 432
**Trial courts, 71**
Truck transport, 407
Trust, 40–41
TRUSTe, 131
Turkey timers, 186
**Turnover,** 298, **331**–334
Two-factor theory, 303–304

**U**

**Undercapitalization, 183**–184
**Unemployment, 17,** 19
Uniform Commercial Code, 73–**74**
Uniform Partnership Act, 149
Uniformity of inputs and outputs, 269–270
Unions, 340–342, 429
United Auto Workers, 222
United Food and Commercial Workers, 342
U.S. Army Armament Research,
Development and Engineering
Center, 285
**U.S. Treasury bills,** 469, **492**
University of Michigan Business School, 398
Unlimited liability, 147, 152
**Unsecured bonds, 500**
**Unsecured loans, 494**
Upward communication, 253
Uruguay Round, 97

USA National Innovations Marketplace, 128
Usury, 76
UWeb, 127

**V**

Vacations, 318–319
Variable interest rates, 466, 494–495
VAULT soda, 413
Vehicle pollution standards, 219
**Venture capitalists, 186**
Veoh, 126
Vertical mergers, 164
Video online, 126
Video Privacy Protection Act, 132
Vietnam, 101
Vioxx, 236
Viral marketing, 412
Virtual protests, 123
Virtual teams, 250
Virtual testing, 376
Virtual worlds, 134, 330
Voice over Internet Protocol, 124, 146
Voluntary agreement, 76
Volunteerism, 205

**W**

**Wage/salary surveys, 335**
**Wages, 335;** *see also* Compensation
Warehouse clubs, 403
Warehouse managers, 288
Warehouse showrooms, 403
**Warehousing, 407**
Warning labels, 46–47
Warranties, 74
Wars, 17
Waste disposal, 61
Water pollution, 59
*The Wealth of Nations,* 238
Web Credibility Project, 398
Web sites, 138, 324; *see also* **Internet**
Webb-Pomerene Export Trade Act, 91
Wedding gowns, 361–362

Weighted averages, 507
Wellness programs, 308
Wheeler-Lea Act, 79
**Whistleblowing, 50**–51
White knights, 165
**Wholesalers, 404**–405
Wholesaling opportunities, 178–179
Wi-Fi, 95, 124
Wide span of management, 245
Wikipedia, 117
Willingness to repay, 525
Wills, 530
WiMax, 124
Wind power, 56, 192, 277
Windows operating system, 100
Wines, 364
Wireless technologies, 95, 123–125
Women
employment opportunities, 56–57, 313
financial planning, 530
as market segment, 370
U.S. businesses owned by, 175
in U.S. workforce, 345
Women's Leadership Forum, 305
Work-in-process inventory, 279
Work/life balance, 301, 352
Work.com, 117
Workforce development, 329–331
**Working capital management, 489**
Workplace safety, 56
**World Bank, 101**
World Research Institute, 335
**World Trade Organization, 98**
**World Wide Web, 121;** *see also* **Internet**

**Y**

Yale University online courses, 126–127
YouTube, 117, 118

**Z**

Zocor, 74